Artist's rendition of Canada as seen from far
above Central America. Projection courtesy
M. Feuchtwanger and S.L. Pattison,
Department of Geography, Simon Fraser
University. Artwork by Michael J. Lee.

THE CANADIAN ENCYCLOPEDIA

SECOND EDITION

VOLUME IV
Sta – Z

Hurtig Publishers
Edmonton

Hurtig Publishers Ltd.
10560 – 105 Street
Edmonton, Alberta
Canada T5H 2W7

Every attempt has been made to identify and credit sources for
photographs. The publisher would appreciate receiving
information as to any inaccuracies in the credits for
subsequent editions.

Canadian Cataloguing in Publication Data

Main entry under title:
The Canadian Encyclopedia

Editor in Chief: James H. Marsh.

ISBN 0-88830-326-2 (set) –ISBN 0-88830-327-0
(v. 1). –ISBN 0-88830-328-9 (v. 2). –ISBN
0-88830-329-7 (v. 3). –ISBN 0-88830-330-0 (v.4)

1. Canada–Dictionaries and encyclopedias.
I. Marsh, James H.
FCwe.C36 1985   971'.003'21   C84-091250-1
F1006.C36 1985

Designed, typeset and manufactured
in Canada

Stairs, William Grant, explorer, soldier (b at Halifax 28 Feb 1863; d at Chinde, Mozambique 9 June 1892). He was discoverer of one source of the Nile, the Semliki R, and the first non-African to climb Mt Ruwenzori. Stairs was educated in Halifax, Edinburgh and RMC and was a civil engineer in New Zealand 1882-85. He was then commissioned captain of the Royal Engineers, and achieved distinction as a military commander in the Emin Pasha Rescue Expedition, 1886-89. He became a fellow of the Royal Scottish Geographical Soc in 1890. After accepting a commission in the Royal Welsh Regiment, he was appointed by King Leopold to command the force that seized the Katanga (Shaba) copper lands for Belgium. Shortly afterward he died of fever. *See also* SOLDIERS OF FORTUNE.   ALLAN LEVINE

Stamp Collecting Almost immediately after their issue in 1840, POSTAGE STAMPS became a collectible item. The first stamp catalogues were published in Europe as early as 1861 (Potiquet, Paris). The first magazine devoted to stamp collecting in N America was published in 1864 in Montréal (*Stamp Collectors Record*, S. Allan Taylor). Stamp collecting, or philately, is a truly international hobby with its own local, national and international organizations. At the local level clubs exist where collectors may meet to exchange or exhibit stamps, and there are national

"50-cent Bluenose" stamp of 1929 (top) was considered the world's most beautifully engraved stamp. The Twelve-Pence Black of 1851 (upper left) was one of the first 3 stamps issued in Canada; next to it is the David Thompson commemorative, issued 1957. The Expo 67 was issued 5 June 1967 (left); the Totem Pole pictorial was issued 2 Feb 1953. The modern stamp commemorating "Tall Ships" (lower left) was issued 1984; the Garden Stamp (lower right), was issued in 1980 (*all stamps courtesy Canada Post Corporation*).

and international conventions held each year. Canada's national society is the Royal Philatelic Society of Canada, based in Ottawa. The Canadian Post Office (now CANADA POST CORPORATION) has also had a special philatelic service since 1932.

The variety of themes and colours of stamps is endless and stamps often give a miniature pictorial history of a country, its culture and development, and even its flora and fauna. Collectors may form basic collections by country, by series, by period or by specialty, such as airmail stamps, first-day covers, postmarks or plate numbers. Some people collect stamps because they are rare; others collect a particular subject such as Canadian ships. The "50-cent Bluenose" of 1929 is said to be the world's most beautifully engraved stamp. A 1933 stamp commemorated the ROYAL WILLIAM, the first ship to cross the Atlantic almost entirely under steam. One of the scarcest Canadian stamps is the 1851 Twelve-Pence Black, showing Queen Victoria at the age of 19. It was, along with the Three-Pence Beaver (designed by Sandford FLEMING) and the Six-Pence Prince Consort, which carried a portrait of Prince Albert, Canada's first issue. Canada's first stamp following Confederation was a profile of Queen Victoria issued in 1868.

Canada issues 2 kinds of stamps. Definitive or regular stamp issues are printed from the same plates for 3 to 5 years. Commemoratives, or special issues, recognize specific subjects or events each year; when the issue is run off the plates are destroyed.   K. ROWE AND H. GRIFFIN

Reading: Cimon Morin, *Canadian Philately, Bibliography and Index* (1979); *Supplement* (1983).

Standard of Living, a measure of economic welfare. It generally refers to the availability of scarce goods and services, usually measured by per capita income or per capita consumption, calculated in constant dollars, to satisfy wants rather than needs. Because the well-being that living standards are supposed to measure is an individual matter, per capita availability of goods and services in a country is a measure of general welfare only if the goods and services are distributed fairly evenly among people. If income distribution is very uneven, then despite high per capita availability of commodities, large numbers of persons may have a very low standard of living and others a very high standard – valid comparisons can be made only among reasonably homogeneous groups. Improvement in standard of living can result from improvements in economic factors such as productivity or per capita real economic growth, income distribution and availability of public services, and noneconomic factors, eg, protection against unsafe working conditions, clean environment, low crime rate, etc.

GDP per capita is a commonly used measure of the standard of living but not necessarily an accurate one because, among other reasons, it does not distinguish between consumer and capital goods; it does not take income distribution into account; it does not take account of differences in the economic goods and services that are not measured in GDP at all; it is subject to the vagaries of translating income measures into a common currency (*see* NATIONAL INCOME) and it fails to take into account differences of tastes among nations. According to the OECD, Canada's 1985 GDP per capita (measured in $US) was about $13 600, compared with about $16 500 for the US, $12 000 for Sweden and $8000 for the UK.

Stanfield, Robert Lorne, lawyer, politician, premier of NS (b at Truro, NS 11 Apr 1914). Member of a family that had long contributed to the industrial and political life of NS and Canada,

Robert Stanfield (right). As premier of NS, he sought to make the province more self-reliant. He was national Conservative leader 1967-76 but failed in 3 elections to become PM (*courtesy Canapress Photo Service*).

Stanfield began the rehabilitation of the provincial Conservative Party in 1946 during the only period in which it held no assembly seats. Becoming its leader 2 years later, he improved its position in the next 2 elections and became premier in 1956, the first of his party since Confederation to do so under noncrisis conditions. In the 3 subsequent elections he became the undisputed political master of the province. A man of moderation, common sense and genuine humility, he sought to create a self-reliant NS.

On becoming national Conservative leader in 1967, he tried to build a party with national appeal. He sought to have official bilingualism fully accepted by his party and was prepared, at least in moderation, to grant special arrangements to Québec. But he found it difficult to project across Canada the image that had led to his success in NS or to win seats in Québec against PM Pierre TRUDEAU. After 3 successive defeats he gave up the leadership in 1976. Eschewing highly doctrinaire politics, his conservatism, which caused him to be called a "pink" if not a RED TORY, was above all a compassionate conservatism with a genuine concern for the disadvantaged. He ranks as one of the outstanding premiers of NS since Confederation. From 1983 to 1987 he was chairman of the Institute for Research on Public Policy and in Dec 1986 he was appointed the first Canadian chairman of the Commonwealth Foundation.

J. MURRAY BECK

Stanier, Roger Yate, microbiologist, professor (b at Victoria 22 Oct 1916; d at Paris, France 29 Jan 1982). Stanier was a major influence in the development of modern microbiology and correlated biochemical, physiological, ecological, and taxonomic studies to provide a remarkably coherent view of the bacteria. He studied at UBC, U of Calif (Los Angeles) and Stanford. His research included oxidative degradation and the adaptation of enzyme pathways, bacterial carotenoids and photosynthesis, and the biology and taxonomy of many groups including photosynthetic bacteria, pseudomonads, cytophagas and cyanobacteria, among other studies. Stanier was professor of microbiology at U of Calif, Berkeley 1947-71. An accomplished interpreter of the biology and taxonomy of bacteria, he expressed his understanding in major essays and reviews (1941-79) and in a remarkable textbook, *The Microbial World* (1975). The last decade of his life was spent as a professor at the Institut Pasteur, Paris, initiating a study of pure cultures of cyanobacteria (BLUE-GREEN ALGAE). His accomplishments were recognized by awards such as the Légion d'Honneur (France) and by election as a foreign member of the Royal Soc, the French Academy of Sciences and of the National Academy of Sciences (US), and as honorary member of the American Soc for Microbiology. He worked abroad for most of his life but retained Canadian citizenship.   R.G.E. MURRAY

The Stanley Cup is the oldest trophy in professional sports in N America (*photo by Bob Mummery*).

Stanley Cup Champions 1892-1987

Season	Club	Season	Club	Season	Club
1892-93	Montreal AAA	1924-25	Victoria Cougars	1956-57	Montreal Canadiens
1984-95	Montreal Victorias	1925-26	Montreal Maroons	1957-58	Montreal Canadiens
1895-96	Winnipeg Victorias	1926-27	Ottawa Senators	1958-59	Montreal Canadiens
1896-97	Montreal Victorias	1927-28	New York Rangers	1959-60	Montreal Canadiens
1897-98	Montreal Victorias	1928-29	Boston Bruins	1960-61	Chicago Black Hawks
1898-99	Montreal Shamrocks	1929-30	Montreal Canadiens	1961-62	Toronto Maple Leafs
1899-1900	Montreal Shamrocks	1930-31	Montreal Canadiens	1962-63	Toronto Maple Leafs
1900-01	Winnipeg Victorias	1931-32	Toronto Maple Leafs	1963-64	Toronto Maple Leafs
1901-02	Montreal AAA	1932-33	New York Rangers	1964-65	Montreal Canadiens
1902-03	Ottawa Silver Seven	1933-34	Chicago Black Hawks	1965-66	Montreal Canadiens
1903-04	Ottawa Silver Seven	1934-35	Montreal Maroons	1966-67	Toronto Maple Leafs
1904-05	Ottawa Silver Seven	1935-36	Detroit Red Wings	1967-68	Montreal Canadiens
1905-06	Montreal Wanderers	1936-37	Detroit Red Wings	1968-69	Montreal Canadiens
1906-07	Kenora Thistles (Jan)[1]	1937-38	Chicago Black Hawks	1969-70	Boston Bruins
1906-07	Montreal Wanderers (Mar)[1]	1938-39	Boston Bruins	1970-71	Montreal Canadiens
1907-08	Montreal Wanderers	1939-40	New York Rangers	1971-72	Boston Bruins
1908-09	Ottawa Senators	1940-41	Boston Bruins	1972-73	Montreal Canadiens
1909-10	Montreal Wanderers	1941-42	Toronto Maple Leafs	1973-74	Philadelphia Flyers
1910-11	Ottawa Senators	1942-43	Detroit Red Wings	1974-75	Philadelphia Flyers
1911-12	Quebec Bulldogs	1943-44	Montreal Canadiens	1975-76	Montreal Canadiens
1912-13	Quebec Bulldogs[2]	1944-45	Toronto Maple Leafs	1976-77	Montreal Canadiens
1913-14	Toronto Blue Shirts	1945-46	Montreal Canadiens	1977-78	Montreal Canadiens
1914-15	Vancouver Millionaires	1946-47	Toronto Maple Leafs	1978-79	Montreal Canadiens
1915-16	Montreal Canadiens	1947-48	Toronto Maple Leafs	1979-80	New York Islanders
1916-17	Seattle Metropolitans	1948-49	Toronto Maple Leafs	1980-81	New York Islanders
1917-18	Toronto Arenas	1949-50	Detroit Red Wings	1981-82	New York Islanders
1918-19	No champion[3]	1950-51	Toronto Maple Leafs	1982-83	New York Islanders
1919-20	Ottawa Senators	1951-52	Detroit Red Wings	1983-84	Edmonton Oilers
1920-21	Ottawa Senators	1952-53	Montreal Canadiens	1984-85	Edmonton Oilers
1921-22	Toronto St Pats	1953-54	Detroit Red Wings	1985-86	Montreal Canadiens
1922-23	Ottawa Senators	1954-55	Detroit Red Wings	1986-87	Edmonton Oilers
1923-24	Montreal Canadiens	1955-56	Montreal Canadiens		

[1] split season   [2] Victoria defeated Quebec in challenge series. No official recognition
[3] series called off by the local department of health because of influenza epidemic

Stanley, Frederick Arthur, Baron Stanley of Preston, 16th Earl of Derby, governor general of Canada 1888-93 (b at London, Eng 15 Jan 1841; d at Holwood, Eng 14 June 1908). His father was 3 times British PM, and Stanley himself was an MP 1865-86, and then sat in the House of Lords. He was a member of the government 1874-80 and 1885-88, including a short stint as secretary of state for the colonies. Although a strong advocate of closer ties between Great Britain and dominions such as Canada, he was a publicly shy and politically careful governor general. He is primarily remembered for his donation in 1893 of the STANLEY CUP, designed to determine a Canadian hockey champion in a fair and uniform manner.   NORMAN HILLMER

Stanley, George Francis Gillman, historian, educator, lt-gov of NB (b at Calgary 6 July 1907). Educated at U of A and Oxford, Stanley was a professor and administrator at Mount Allison 1936-40 and 1969-75, UBC 1947-49 and RMC 1949-69. He served in WWII, becoming an invaluable aide to C.P. STACEY and retiring in 1946 as deputy director of the army's historical section. His first book, *The Birth of Western Canada* (1936), combined his passion for the West with an appreciation of the importance of military factors; later he wrote a biography of Louis RIEL (1963). Other major works are *Canada's Soldiers* (1954), *New France: The Last Phase* (1968), *Canada Invaded 1775-1776* (1973) and *The War of 1812: Land Operations* (1983). He proposed the basic design of Canada's flag in 1965. He was lt-gov of New Brunswick 1982-87.   NORMAN HILLMER

Stanley, Robert Crooks, mine executive, metallurgist, (b at Little Falls, NY 1 Aug 1876; d at Dongan Hills, Staten Island, NY 12 Feb 1951). Stanley joined International Nickel in 1902 and was president 1922-49. He was responsible for the development of monel metal, a nickel-copper alloy, and promoted peacetime commercial applications for Inco's NICKEL, which prior to 1919 had been used primarily in armament production. In the late 1920s he played a major role in the merger of Inco and the Mond Nickel Company.   J. LINDSEY

Stanley Cup, the oldest trophy competed for by professional athletes in N America. Donated by Gov Gen Lord STANLEY in 1893 for presentation to the amateur HOCKEY champions of Canada, it was first awarded to Montreal AAA (1892-93) and except for 1918-19 (owing to an influenza epidemic) it has been presented every year since. Before professional hockey concentrated the sport in a few large urban centres, the cup was contested under a variety of formats and was captured by such far-flung teams as Winnipeg Victorias (1895-96, 1900-01), Ottawa Silver Seven (1902-03, 1903-04, 1904-05), Kenora Thistles (1906-07), the Vancouver Millionaires (1914-15), Seattle Metropolitans (1916-17) and Victoria Cougars (1924-25). A professional team (Ottawa Senators) first won the cup in 1909 and in 1926 it came under the exclusive control of the NATIONAL HOCKEY LEAGUE. The MONTREAL CANADIENS, with 23 victories (including 5 straight 1956-60), have been by far the most successful team in Stanley Cup history, followed by TORONTO MAPLE LEAFS with 11 wins. The New York Islanders' string of 4 consecutive victories was ended by the EDMONTON OILERS in 1984.

The cup itself has had a colourful history. It has been lost, misplaced and stolen (once from its home in the HOCKEY HALL OF FAME and Museum). The original silver bowl is now on permanent display at the Hockey Hall of Fame and a replica sits on top of the existing structure. The names of all the players on winning teams since 1930 are engraved on the base.   JAMES MARSH

Staple Thesis, a theory asserting that the export of natural resources, or staples, from Canada to more advanced economies has a pervasive impact on the economy as well as on the social and political systems. Furthermore, different staples (fur, fish, timber, grain, oil, etc) have differing impacts on rates of settlement, federal-provincial conflicts, etc. The thesis was formulated in the 1920s by economic historians Harold A. INNIS and W.A. MACKINTOSH. Agreeing that Canada had been born with a staple economy, they differed insofar as Mackintosh saw a continuing evolution toward a mature industrialized economy based on staple production, whereas Innis saw a tendency for Canada to become permanently locked into dependency as a resource hinterland. Contemporary proponents of the thesis argue that Innis's version more accurately describes the Canadian situation to the present. The thesis may be the most important single contribution to scholarship by Canadian social scientists and historians; it has also had some influence internationally, notably in the analysis of a comparable country such as Australia.   MEL WATKINS

Reading: W.T. Easterbrook and Mel H. Watkins, eds, *Approaches to Canadian Economic History* (1967).

Star, Alta, UP, pop 26 (1986c), 24 (1981c), is located 60 km NE of Edmonton. It is the oldest Ukrainian Catholic parish in Canada, founded 1897 by UKRAINIAN immigrants who settled in the area 1892-94. The impressive parish church – the third – was built in 1926-27.   ERIC J. HOLMGREN

Star, large, self-luminous sphere of hot gas held together by its own gravitational force. There are over a billion stars in each of the more than one billion GALAXIES in the universe; yet the SUN (at a distance of 150 million km) is the only star close enough to show directly the details of its surface. Stellar SPECTROSCOPY in Canada was pioneered at the Dominion Astrophysical Observatory near

Victoria (est 1918). Canadian astronomers have made important contributions to knowledge about the physical and chemical nature of stars.

The masses of stars range from 0.1 x 10^{30} kg to 100 x 10^{30} kg. The sun's mass is 2 x 10^{30} kg. A star's mass controls its basic structure, the most massive stars being the hottest, brightest and largest. Most stars, including our sun, are called main sequence or dwarf stars. A star is held together by gravity. Heat liberated by the conversion of hydrogen to helium inside the star results in high central pressure that prevents gravity from further compressing it. Four hydrogen atoms produce one helium atom. During this nuclear fusion reaction, 0.7% of the mass of the hydrogen atoms is converted to energy. A small amount of helium is converted to heavier elements. Since a star's mass is finite, eventually all available nuclear fuel will be expended. Larger stars radiate vast amounts of energy; consequently, their nuclear fuel is used rapidly, resulting in a shorter lifetime. The reverse is true for low-mass stars. As the fuel burns low, gravity can no longer be resisted and dramatic changes result. The radius of the star increases ten- to a hundredfold (depending on mass) and its surface temperature decreases: the star becomes a giant or supergiant. The brightest supergiants are about 2 million times brighter than the sun. Sometimes an explosive event (nova or supernova) occurs, such as Supernova Shelton 1987A, the first to be sighted near Earth's galaxy, discovered by Ian Shelton of U of T. Further rapid changes follow in which gravity dominates: the star shrinks, becoming a white dwarf, a neutron star (pulsar) or a BLACK HOLE.

Stars and gaseous nebulae can be chemically analysed on the basis of the spectral lines present in their light. In most cases, hydrogen is overwhelmingly dominant (up to 99% of a star's mass). The chemical composition of the universe at its origin is unknown; however, since stars produce heavier elements out of hydrogen and as some of the stellar material is sent back into interstellar space by stellar winds, novae and supernovae, succeeding generations of stars have more heavy elements. The earliest-formed stars have as little as 1% of the heavy elements present in the sun.

Stars form from clouds of interstellar gas and dust, which are pulled together by gravity until collisions between the molecules generate enough pressure to slow the contraction. Internal nuclear reactions have not yet started. The time required for contraction is a small fraction of the star's total lifetime; for example, our sun would have a contraction time of about 100 000 years, compared to a main sequence lifetime of about 10 billion years. The contracting star begins to shine during this relatively short stage. Contraction ceases and the star joins the main sequence when internal nuclear reactions start. Rotation of a star arises from the spin-up of the clouds from which it formed. Larger stars rotate rapidly, some near the point of "break-up" (ie, material spinning off their equators). Smaller stars rotate much more slowly because escaping mass gets caught in the magnetic field of the star. The "magnetic brake" reduces the rotation of main sequence stars by about 2 each billion years.

The photosphere is the atmosphere from which light leaves the star. Convection columns are clearly visible in the solar photosphere. Other stars are too far away for the surface markings to be seen and, instead, convection is detected from the shapes of spectral lines using D.F. Gray's technique (U of Western Ontario). When convection is present, it generates magnetic and sound waves which heat the upper layers of the atmosphere (chromosphere and corona). K.O. Wright of DAO measured chromospheres in supergiants by observing eclipsing binary stars. In the outermost atmosphere (corona), temperatures of several million degrees are found and X rays are emitted.

Beyond the corona, a small amount of mass streams away. J.B. Hutchings (DAO) measured the rates of mass loss in many hot stars. Mass loss from our sun is responsible for auroras and radio fade-outs on Earth (*see* NORTHERN LIGHTS).

Cool dark spots are detected on stars. Dark spots on the sun were seen in 1611 when Johannes Fabricius and Galileo Galilei turned the first telescopes on it. The number and sizes of spots, along with explosions (flares) and enhanced emission from the upper atmosphere, are referred to as "activity." Many stars, including the sun, show cyclic changes (about 10 years) in the amount of activity. Activity is produced by the star's magnetic field, which itself is generated by the interaction of the star's rotation with convection, in a process call a dynamo.

Binaries and Multiple Stars

A binary star is a system of 2 stars that travel in periodic orbits around a common centre of gravity. Multiple systems of 3 or more stars are called binaries or multiple systems. The orbital motions of the stars are determined by the law of gravity. Binaries composed of components so widely separated that they can be seen separately through a telescope are called visual binaries. The orbital periods of visual binaries may be only 2 years; however, the average is several centuries. A spectroscopic binary is a system with components too close together to be seen separately and with an orbital plane tilted toward Earth. The orbital motion produces a periodic change in the apparent motions of the stars toward and away from Earth. This change is detected as a periodic Doppler shift of the spectral lines. The orbital periods of spectroscopic binaries are usually a few days or weeks, but some are less than 20 minutes and others longer than 20 years.

Many spectroscopic binaries and a few visual binaries have orbital planes which are seen edge on. During each orbit, first one star and then the other passes in front of (ie, eclipses) its companion. Eclipsing binaries are studied by observing their periodic variations in brightness. Many of the brightest stars in the sky are binaries. Algol (Persei) is an eclipsing system in which the brightness decreases to one-third its normal value every 69 hours, a change visible to the unaided eye. Algol is a triple system; its third component has been detected spectroscopically. Albireo (Cygni) is a visual binary with red and blue components which can be resolved in a small telescope; its orbital period is at least 30 000 years.

The study of binary stars provides the only way of measuring stellar masses and yields information about the sizes and surface temperatures of stars. Many spectroscopic and eclipsing binaries have so small a separation that one is tidally distorted into an ellipsoid by its companion's gravitational field. This physical distortion may produce additional periodic variations in brightness. As stars evolve they expand. In a binary, expansion may result in the transfer of matter from the atmosphere of one star to its companion. This mass exchange is a common phenomenon that can alter the future evolution of both stars, may give rise to radio and X-ray emission, probably accounts for nova explosions and has led to the detection of possible black holes. The DAO, Victoria, and the David Dunlap Observatory, U of T, have been leading centres of research on binary stars for many years.

DOUGLAS P. HUBE

Variable Stars

Strictly, the term variable star refers to a star that appears to vary in any sense (eg, light, velocity, spectrum); in practice the term is generally reserved for a star that varies because of some internal cause (usually pulsation) and excludes variations arising externally (eg, eclipses by an orbiting companion). There are about 35 000 variable stars designated in the 88 constellations.

Whether or not a star pulsates is determined mainly by its mass, radius and surface temperature. Stars that have combinations of these near any one of several critical combinations will pulsate in varying degrees. Variable stars thus tend to form families, all members of which have similar properties. Variable stars are very important in astronomy. The period of pulsation, measured by the cycle of light variation, is related to the star's intrinsic brightness. Once this relation is calibrated, observations of light changes in a distant variable will reveal how bright it really is. When this information is combined with data about how bright it appears to be, the star's distance can be calculated. Thus, by observing variable stars in distant galaxies we can establish the scale of the universe. Furthermore the pulsation period is a sensitive diagnostic of a variable star's internal conditions and so serves as an important check on theories of stellar constitution and evolution.

J.D. FERNIE

White Dwarfs

A white dwarf is a star containing approximately the same amount of matter as the sun, compressed into a sphere about the size of Earth. It is therefore extraordinarily dense, approximately a million times denser than water. Because a white dwarf is both small and massive, its gravitational pull is extremely strong; an object at its surface would weigh roughly 100 000 times more than at the Earth's surface. The star supports its own outer layers against the pull of gravity through electron degeneracy pressure, ie, pressure provided by the electrons stripped from the atoms of its interior, which are forced to move very rapidly when compressed to such extremes of density. The interior of the white dwarf is a bizarre kind of solid, somewhat like a very dense metal; it is also extremely hot, typically 10 million °C. However, electron degeneracy pressure would provide support against gravity even if the white dwarf were quite cold inside. The outermost, visible surface of a white dwarf is covered by a thin atmosphere usually composed of almost pure hydrogen or almost pure helium. In various white dwarfs the temperature of this atmosphere may be anywhere from 60 000°C to about 5000°C. The atmosphere emits visible radiation. A few white dwarfs contain extraordinarily strong magnetic fields, ranging from 200 million to 500 million times that of Earth.

A white dwarf is the remnant of a star like the sun that has exhausted its nuclear fuel. The star thus loses its ability to support itself against gravity and collapses. If at the time of collapse the star is less than 1.4 times as massive as the sun, it becomes a white dwarf; if it is more massive the white dwarf structure is not strong enough to support the star and it collapses still farther to become a neutron star or even a black hole. Once formed, a white dwarf changes little in structure but simply cools until after more than 10 billion years it becomes too cool to be visible. The hottest observed white dwarfs were formed only millions of years ago; very cool ones have been white dwarfs for billions of years. Because 80-90% of all stars become white dwarfs, white dwarfs are very common in space: about 10% of all stars near the sun are white dwarfs. The nearest white dwarfs are the faint companions of the bright stars Sirius and Procyon.

JOHN D. LANDSTREET

Star Cluster

Many stars in our galaxy are found, not isolated in space, but in clusters of stars bound together

Supernova Shelton 1987A, discovered 24 Feb 1987 by Ian Shelton at University of Toronto's southern observatory in north-central Chile (*courtesy Ian Shelton, U of T, Southern Observatory, Chile*).

by their mutual gravity. Clusters are of 2 types, open and globular.

Open Clusters may contain only a few dozen or as many as several thousand stars and are mainly found in the galactic plane or disc (ie, our Milky Way). Hundreds of open clusters have been identified within about 3000 parsecs of the sun. Their location near the obscuring gas and dust of the galactic plane makes more distant clusters difficult to find, but there are undoubtedly thousands more in the entire Galaxy. Although not all stars are found in clusters, it is possible that most (or all) of the stars in the Galaxy were born in such groups. However, with time, clusters gradually move away from their formation regions, and many "dissolve" into the general field-star population. Only the most populous clusters are likely to have survived disruption over the galactic disk's 10-billion-year history. The youngest open clusters can still be found near the gas and dust from which they formed and make valuable tracers of the spiral structure typical of galaxies such as ours.

Open clusters range in age from those still forming to those more than 5 billion years old. An individual cluster will contain stars of various masses, but the most massive stars generate energy at a rapid rate and evolve through their various stages in "life" much more quickly than do stars of lower mass. Thus, any single cluster provides a "snapshot" of a gradually changing family of stars in which all have the same age but in which individual stars are at different stages of evolution, depending on their mass. Observations of many different clusters permit astrophysicists to test their theoretical models of stellar evolution and thus build up a general picture of the life histories of stars.

Globular Clusters Our own galaxy is believed to contain perhaps 200 globular star clusters, of which about 130 have been directly observed. Each may hold anywhere from a few thousand to a million or more stars. The greatest visible concentrations of mass in the Galaxy are in its nucleus, disc and spiral arms. By contrast, globular clusters lie scattered throughout the vastly larger and more tenuous spherical surrounding region called the halo. Their stars are older than any other known objects in the Galaxy; current measurements set their ages at roughly 15 billion years. Globular cluster stars also have simpler, more primitive compositions than do stars in the galactic disc or nucleus; they contain much lower amounts of "heavier" atoms (ie, elements more complex than hydrogen and helium) built up by NUCLEAR FUSION processes inside stars. These characteristics suggest that globular clusters were formed when the Milky Way was still in its "protogalaxy" state as a large, primordial gas cloud, not long after the universal Big Bang (*see* COSMOLOGY).

Globular clusters are known in many large galaxies beyond ours. Even among widely different parent galaxies, these clusters bear many similarities (eg, age, size, composition) which seem to represent a unifying thread in the histories of the galaxies in general.

Canadian astronomers have made significant contributions to globular cluster studies. Among many who should be cited are H.B. Sawyer HOGG-PRIESTLEY and her later associates, C. Coutts Clement and A. Wehlau (for surveys of the RR Lyrae stars, a type of pulsating variable star typically found in globular clusters); F.D.A. Hartwick, W.E. Harris and J.E. Hesser (analysis of HR diagrams); and D.A. Hanes, W.E. Harris, R. Racine and S. VAN DEN BERGH (clusters in external galaxies).

GRETCHEN L. H. HARRIS AND WILLIAM E. HARRIS

Reading: G.O. Abell, et al, *Exploration of the Universe* (1987); T. Ferris, *The Red Limit* (1977); J.R. Gribben, *In Search of the Big Bang: Quantum Physics and Cosmology* (1986); W. Kaufmann III, *Universe* (1988).

Star Weekly began publication in Apr 1910 in Toronto. Founded by J.E. Atkinson, the publisher of the TORONTO STAR, *Toronto Star Weekly* was an attempt to create a Canadian counterpart to the popular British type of Sunday newspapers. Initially the *Weekly* was a grab-bag of features, articles by the daily paper's reporters, ADVERTISING and pieces purchased cheaply from syndicates. Before long, however, the *Weekly* had comic strips, good illustrations and cartoons, and by 1920 it was lavishly using colour. Eventually, able writers were recruited as free lances or put on staff, a list that included at various times Morley CALLAGHAN, Ernest Hemingway and Gregory Clark; artists found in the *Star Weekly*'s pages included Arthur LISMER, Fred VARLEY, C.W. JEFFERYS, and in the cartoons, Jimmy Frise's "Birdseye Centre." The *Weekly* had a national audience, and after 1938 the "Toronto" identification was dropped from the masthead. Like the MONTREAL STANDARD, the *Star Weekly* fell victim to television and the NEWSPAPERS' weekend supplements, and it ceased publication in 1973. *See also* MAGAZINES.

J.L. GRANATSTEIN

Reading: R. Harkness, *J.E. Atkinson of the Star* (1963).

Stare Decisis [Lat, "let the decision stand"] refers to the doctrine of precedent, according to which the rules formulated by judges in earlier decisions are to be similarly applied in later cases. The reason for the doctrine is that similar cases should be treated alike so as to ensure consistency and certainty in the law. It evolved in the primarily "judge-made" COMMON LAW system of the law and attained its most formal expression in late 19th-century England.

In practice today the doctrine means only that prior decisions of higher courts are binding on lower courts of the same jurisdiction, for neither the Supreme Court of Canada nor many of the provincial courts of appeal consider themselves bound by their own previous decisions. Lower courts are also free to analyse the reasons (*ratio decidendi*) given by the higher court and to decide, in light of the facts of the actual dispute before them, whether to apply the precedent or to distinguish the rule contained on the basis of factual differences in the 2 cases. The doctrine, within these same limits, also applies in the interpretation of statutes. Its role in Quebec civil law is of less importance and is a matter of debate.

JOHN E.C. BRIERLEY

Starfish, or sea star, common marine animal found from seashore to ocean depths; 1600 species are known worldwide. They belong to the INVERTEBRATE phylum ECHINODERMATA. Starfish are usually radially symmetrical, often with 5 radiating arms joined to a central disc. The mouth is located on the underside and anus on the upper surface of the disc. Another important characteristic is the water-vascular system, an arrangement of canals and tubes that operates the starfish's tube feet by hydraulic pressure. Tube feet occur on undersurface of arms and are the principal means of locomotion and attachment.

Although feeding habits are varied, starfish are often formidable predators which generate frantic escape behaviour in snails and bivalve prey. There are many species on Canada's coasts, ranging in size from tiny (50 mm) *Leptasterias hexactis* to giant *Pycnopodia helianthoides*, up to 1 m in diameter and with as many as 24 arms.

R.D. BURKE

Starling, common name for Old World family (Sturnidae) of birds, comprising 111 principally tropical species. Two introduced species occur in Canada: European starling (*Sturnus vulgaris*) and crested myna (*Acridotheres cristatellus*). In fall the European starling has buff-coloured spots resembling stars at tips of fresh feathers, hence its name. These disappear as feathers wear, leaving a glossy, iridescent plumage in spring. This bird, introduced worldwide, seems to owe its colonizing success to its omnivorous diet and ability to live with man. The European starlings in N America are derived from 2 introductions in New York City: 60 birds, 1890; 40 birds, 1891. They have spread to the US Pacific coast and up into central Canada. The crested myna, introduced to Vancouver from SE Asia about 1900, has not spread successfully.

A.J. BAKER

Starnes, John Kennett, public servant (b at Montréal 5 Feb 1918). A WWII veteran, Starnes was with the Dept of External Affairs 1944-70. He was ambassador to Germany 1962-66 and to the United Arab Republic and Sudan 1966-67, when he oversaw the withdrawal of the Canadian contingent of the UN Emergency Force set up after the SUEZ CRISIS. The first civilian director general of the RCMP Security Service in the eventful years 1970-73, Starnes was criticized by the McDonald Commission (INQUIRY INTO CERTAIN ACTIVITIES OF THE ROYAL CANADIAN MOUNTED POLICE) for his acquiescence in unlawful undercover operations. He has written *Deep Sleepers* (1981), *Scarab* (1982), *Orion's Belt* (1983), and *The Cornish Hug* (1985).

ANNE HILLMER

Starowicz, Mark, radio and TV producer (b at Worksop, Eng 8 Sept 1946). The son of Polish émigrés, he lived in England and Argentina before coming to Montréal at age 7. He was educated at McGill where he edited the *McGill Daily* and he worked for the Montréal *Gazette*. He covered Québec politics for the *Toronto Star* and in 1969 moved to that city. In 1970 he began to produce national programs for CBC Radio. After improving "As It Happens" (1973-76), he created the popular 3-hour "Sunday Morning" current-affairs show, serving as its executive producer 1976-80 and winning a number of ACTRA awards. After a study of CBC-TV programming, he conceived "The Journal" to follow the CBC evening news (1982). His 3 programs have been the most influential and innovative news programs in Canada since 1970. In 1985 he was Atkinson Lecturer at Ryerson.

ALLAN M. GOULD

Staryk, Steven, violinist, teacher (b at Toronto 28 Apr 1932). He is widely considered to be the leading Canadian-born virtuoso of his generation. Beginning as a Toronto orchestral violinist in 1950, also competing successfully in international competitions, Staryk soon became concertmaster of 3 prestigious orchestras: London Philharmonic (1956), Amsterdam Concertgebouw (1960) and Chicago Symphony (1963-67). In

1969 he formed a duo with pianist John Perry, which performed extensively in major Canadian and US cities. He became concertmaster of the Toronto Symphony in 1982. In 1987 he became professor of violin at U of Washington in Seattle. Staryk's gifted teaching at institutions in Canada and abroad has helped launch many successful violinists. Several Canadian composers have dedicated compositions to him. Performances of some of these are included among Staryk's many recordings of solo and orchestral works.

BARCLAY MCMILLAN

State, a broad concept that includes government as the seat of legitimate authority in a territory but also includes bureaucracy, judiciary, the ARMED FORCES and internal POLICE, structures of legislative assemblies and administration, public corporations, regulatory boards, and ideological apparatuses such as the education establishment and publicly owned media. The distinguishing characteristic of the state is its monopoly over the use of force in a given territory.

The state as a concept in political research was for a long time unfashionable in Western SOCIAL SCIENCE, largely because of the pluralist notion, dominant for some 2 decades after WWII, that the key questions traditionally asked about it – especially those concerning the state as an apparatus of power over society – were resolved in Western democracies. It was assumed that power in society was now competitive, fragmented, and diffused among virtually all social groups and that the "political system" represented a neutral and evenhanded mechanism for fulfilling or harmonizing conflicting demands.

The state has now re-emerged as a central concept of social science in Canada and elsewhere. The increasing size and scope of the state in advanced capitalist countries, the failure of elected social democratic parties to effect fundamental changes in society, and the emergence of many new Third World states which have all the formal attributes of sovereignty but preside over economies dependent on foreign capital (a subject particularly relevant to Canada) have helped revive the question of the state in social science.

In medieval Europe, the term "state" was associated with the rank and status of royalty and nobility. The state was seen as embodying power and sovereignty, but not in a way that was distinctive from the hierarchical ordering of feudal society itself. As capitalism developed, "state" took on a more distinctly political meaning. The class relations in society between owners and non-owners were no longer formally codified in the state, which instead presented itself as the sole political community and the guarantor of the legal equality of individuals. Sovereignty and power now became exclusively political notions, and a generalized and formal disjuncture developed between the public and the private.

In the growing awareness of this disjuncture from the 17th to the 19th centuries modern social science sunk its roots, turning the old question of political philosophy, "What is the art of politics?" into "What is the nature of the state in relation to society?" Different philosophical traditions continued to provide different answers. The conservative tradition (particularly strong in Canada) maintained the medieval notion of the state as embodying the mutual rights and obligations of hierarchically arranged social orders. The liberal tradition oscillated between characterizing the state as a necessary evil designed for defence against external enemies and for the internal expression of unbridled individual self-interest, and seeing it as the foremost human community designed to develop the potential of the individual in market society. In the socialist tradition (and

particularly in its intellectual bedrock, MARXISM) the state was perceived as the product of class division in society, playing the role of reproducing class relations and moderating or repressing class conflict (*see* SOCIAL CLASS). In the anarchist view, the state was the prime source of human inequality and alienation.

Recent work on the theory of the state has attempted to uncover the development and dynamics of particular types of state in relation to particular types of society. The most progress has been made in work dealing with the liberal democratic states of advanced capitalist societies. The growth of the state in the 20th century is seen not in some vague sense as "creeping socialism" but as an ineluctable aspect of the development of capitalism. By absorbing many of the private risks and social costs of production, the state facilitated capital accumulation and regulated class conflict. The connections between state and class structure have also been examined, in an attempt to understand the link between the formal political equality of liberal democracy and the socioeconomic inequality of capitalist society. In this respect, the concept of the "relative autonomy of the state" has been used to amend the classical Marxist notion of the state as "the executive committee of the bourgeoisie," so as to invite investigation of the full range of social forces represented in the state as well as of the political compromises that dominant classes undertake to maintain their hegemonic position.

One of the virtues of Canadian social science is that it has long recognized that the large role of the state in the Canadian economy has not been antithetical to Canadian society; it has been part of the nature of that society. The Canadian POLITICAL ECONOMY tradition has emphasized that in a dependent, staples-oriented economy such as Canada's, the state has provided, partly out of economic necessity, partly out of close ties with the capitalist class, much of the technical infrastructure and economic regulation necessary to keep capitalism viable. The state has attempted to provide a favourable fiscal and monetary climate for economic growth; it has underwritten the private risks of production at public expense through grants, subsidies and depreciation allowances; it has played a crucial role, via land and immigration policies, in developing the labour market and, more recently, in absorbing the social costs of production through sanitation services, medicare, unemployment insurance, educational facilities, etc; and it has often directly provided the infrastructures for economic development (canals, railways, airports, utilities) when this was too risky or costly for private capital. Research that has uncovered the close ties between state personnel and private capitalists in Canada has also demonstrated that while these ties at times may have inhibited innovative WELFARE STATE activities, they hardly preclude active state involvement in sustaining the capitalist economy. The Canadian state is distinctive, however, because it tends to be equally active in this role at the provincial and federal levels, reflecting the binational character of Canadian society and the geographic and cultural diversity as well as the unevenly developed economies of the various regions. It also reflects the limited relative autonomy of the state from the capitalist class, in that regional fractions of this class have been able to use the provincial state to represent their interests to the federal government and to other regional capitalists (*see* PRESSURE GROUP; ELITES).

To speak of a liberal democratic state such as Canada's as also a capitalist state does not mean that the institutions of parliamentary government, regular elections among competing political parties, freedom of association, speech, press

and assembly are merely ephemeral in the representation of a very broad array of social forces. It rather means that in the context of the hierarchical mature state decision making wherein executive and bureaucratic dominance is enshrined, the state's role entails not only reflecting the balance of social forces but at the same time maintaining the social conditions for economic growth and the reproduction of classes in a way consistent with a hegemonic capitalist social order. The degree to which a state is relatively autonomous from immediate domestic or international capitalist pressures cannot be judged abstractly; it can only be assessed through concrete analyses of the balance of forces at each particular juncture. In this respect, an important restructuring of state activity has become increasingly visible over the past decade. Although "neo-conservative" trends have not been as prevalent in Canada as in the US or Britain in the context of the re-emergence of severe crisis tendencies in the economy and the domestic and international restructuring of capital and labour that has resulted therefrom, there has nevertheless been a shift away from welfarist and regulatory criteria and towards more explicit free-market criteria in the making of Canadian state policy. FREE TRADE with the US is an important aspect of this development insofar as it removes some of the historical and material basis for a large role for the state in providing the infrastructure for and co-ordinating a specifically Canadian, albeit dependent, economic space north of the 49th parallel.

These developments do not necessarily mean there will be "less state" rather than "more state," as the popular language of political discourse often suggests. The greater "free market" orientation of Western states in the 1980s has been accompanied by an expansion of the state's military and "law and order" expenditures, establishments and concerns. This expansion of the more explicitly coercive apparatus of the state has in turn brought forth renewed concern about a "strong state" which limits liberal democratic freedoms even as it promotes market freedoms. The explicitly coercive dimension of Canadian state behaviour has indeed been one of its traditional aspects. Often identified in this respect are the historical role of the RCMP in suppressing strikes and radical political protest; violations of fundamental rights and freedoms during wartime (eg, the internment of Japanese Canadians during WWII); the discrimination against Communists during the Cold War and the suspension of civil liberties during the FLQ crisis in 1970. Added to this has been the exposure through the 1970s and 1980s of illegal activities undertaken by the RCMP and more recently by the CANADIAN SECURITY INTELLIGENCE SERVICE in the course of routine state surveillance or infiltration of radical political parties, peace groups and trade unions. Some of these activities, moreover, pertain to the requirements of Canada's close military and intelligence relationship with the American state in the global political order. Despite the entrenchment of the CANADIAN CHARTER OF RIGHTS AND FREEDOMS in Canada's Constitution Act, 1982, it is by no means clear, given the provisions of the Charter itself or the inclinations of the judiciary, that the new constitution effectively inhibits the growth of the "strong state" in the context of domestic and international pressures toward the "free market." Notably, the Supreme Court of Canada, in an important judgement in April 1987, endorsed growing legislative restrictions on the right to strike and bargain collectively by ruling that these were not covered by the guarantee of freedom of association in the Charter.

As Canada approaches the end of the 20th century, the classical questions regarding the nature of the state first raised with the rise of capitalism take on growing rather than diminishing relevance. More than ever, Canadians are faced with the task of determining not only the meaning and scope of Canadian state sovereignty vis-à-vis the American state and economy, but also the meaning and scope of individual and societal freedoms Canadians can assert vis-à-vis the Canadian state.

LEO PANITCH

Reading: H.A. Innis, *Political Economy in the Modern State* (1946); Leo Panitch, *The Canadian State: Political Economy and Political Power* (1977); K. Banting, *State and Society: Canada in Comparative Perspective* (1986); A. Cairns and C. Williams, *Constitutionalism, Citizenship and Society in Canada* (1986); James Littleton, *Target Nation: Canada and the Western Intelligence Network* (1986).

Station PAPA Ocean Weather Station "P" is commonly called Station PAPA after the code word for the letter P in the phonetic alphabet used by radio operators. Station PAPA is located in the N Pacific Ocean (50° N, 145° W) and has a water depth of 4200 m. Weather ships, stationed there from 1949 through 1981, were intended primarily to support aviation by providing surface and upper air weather observations and navigational assistance as well as potential rescue for downed aircraft. They also provided search-and-rescue services for mariners and were used to collect a wide variety of scientific data for oceanographic and meteorological research and for WEATHER FORECASTING. Several international scientific experiments were conducted near Station PAPA to take advantage of the presence of the weather ships and the large base of existing information from the site.

Initially the ships stationed at OWS "P" were provided by the US Coast Guard. Canadian occupation of the station began in 1950 using converted frigates (CCGS *St. Catharines* and CCGS *Stonetown*) operated by the Canadian Coast Guard. These ships were replaced in 1967 by the CCGS *Quadra* and CCGS *Vancouver*, built and equipped specially for the task. OWS "P" was continuously occupied; each weather ship spent 6 weeks on station and one travelling to and from its home port of Esquimalt, BC. Required to remain within 100 km of the station position, the ships normally drifted while on station, occasionally steaming upwind to remain within the grid. The ships were withdrawn in 1981 as an economy measure.

JOHN GARRETT

Statistics, the SCIENCE concerned with the collection and analysis of numerical information in order to answer questions wisely. The term also refers to the numerical information that has been collected. Humourist Stephen LEACOCK wrote: "In earlier times, they had no statistics, and so they had to fall back on lies. Hence the huge exaggerations of primitive literature – giants or miracles or wonders! They did it with lies and we do it with statistics; but it is all the same." Thomas Chandler HALIBURTON's picaresque character, Sam Slick, stated: "Figures are the representatives of numbers, and not things." It is usual to think of statistics as collections of numbers, ie, data or facts in numerical form (eg, birth rates, death rates, amounts of rainfall, oil reserves, hockey records). However, numbers alone have little significance; to be meaningful, they must be placed in context. Statisticians work with numbers, but their goals are ambitious: insight, discovery, exploitation, confirmation, explanation, prediction, control and decision.

Statistics is the technology of science, the tool of commerce and industry, and an instrument of government. Science is characterized by the scientific method, which involves formulation of theories, deduction of consequences and verification of predictions. Analysis of data leads to formulation of theories. Verification involves checking facts against predictions. These stages correspond to important subfields of statistics, ie, exploratory data analysis and hypothesis testing. Commerce and industry are concerned with efficient use of resources and with decision making in the face of uncertainty. Statisticians have developed methods for the efficient design of investigations, be they surveys, observational studies or experiments. The subfield of decision theory is concerned with the making of effective choices in uncertain situations. Finally, government has a responsibility to know the status and protect the well-being of its people. This responsibility may be realized, in part, through censuses, continuing surveys, data banks and forecasts, each of which has major statistical components.

Statistical Concepts

Statistics depends on certain basic concepts, including sample, stratification, randomization, replication and stochastic modelling. By the use of these concepts, statisticans and scientists have often been able to provide wise answers to important questions. These are all major contributions to human knowledge.

Sample is a collection of objects or individuals meant to represent a larger collection (eg, the population). The innovation of statisticians was the recognition that, if objects were selected randomly from a population of interest, then those selected (the sample) would be representative of that population and that measures of the error resulting from the use of the sample (ie, rather than the population) might be computed.

Stratification is the operation of grouping objects into collections of similar objects, before selecting a sample or experimenting on the objects. For example, students at school might be grouped by grade and then separate samples selected for each grade.

Randomization is the scientific breakthrough of 20th-century British statistician R.A. Fisher. For example, to discover which of 2 methods of language instruction is better, an educator might use a randomized experiment, involving obtaining a group of similar students and randomly choosing half to experience the first method of instruction. Those remaining experience the second method. At the end of the experiment, test scores for those experiencing methods one and 2 would be compared. The random division of the students would make it most unlikely that the brighter students would all be taught by just one method, thereby biasing the results.

Replication is the act of repeating a measurement of interest, eg, in the instructional experiment just referred to, repeating the study for a number of groups of students. Replication allows improved estimation of quantities of interest, and facilitates computation of the error of the estimates.

Stochastic Model is a simplified description of a circumstance in mathematical language (eg, equations) that includes some element of randomness. Stochastic models lead to effective summarization and analysis of complex circumstances.

The statistical history of Canada began many years ago. The first systematic census (ie, complete enumeration of a population) was carried out in NEW FRANCE in 1666 for Louis XIV by Intendant Jean TALON. The documents he prepared are in the National Archives, Ottawa. The first nationwide census took place in 1871. The census is now the responsibility of STATISTICS CANADA, formerly the Dominion Bureau of Statistics (est 1918). Some Canadian universities have separate statistics departments (eg, Alberta, British Columbia, Manitoba, Toronto, Waterloo, Western Ontario); others have joint departments or have kept statistics within mathematics departments. Statistics often forms part of the curriculum of the subjects that make use of quantitative techniques (eg, economics departments, schools of business and commerce, various physical, social and biological sciences). The Canadian statistics profession is represented by the Statistical Society of Canada (est 1978), which publishes *The Canadian Journal of Statistics.*

DAVID R. BRILLINGER

Reading: D. Freedman, R. Pisani and R. Purves, *Statistics* (1978); R.J. Wonnacott and T.H. Wonnacott, *Statistics, Discovering its Power* (1982).

Statistics Canada, est in 1918 as the Dominion Bureau of Statistics, is the nation's central statistical agency. It adopted its present name in 1971. Under the Statistics Act of that year, it has the responsibility to "collect, compile, analyse, abstract and publish statistical information relating to the commercial, industrial, financial, social, economic and general activities and condition of the people of Canada." The agency collaborates with government departments in the development of integrated social and economic statistics for Canada and the provinces. In addition, Statistics Canada is a scientific research organization responsible for leadership in the development of statistical methodologies and techniques. The agency, which is subject to the budgetary control of Parliament, is committed to meeting the statistical needs of all levels of government and the private sector for research, policy formulation, decision making and general information purposes. Some of its major programs are the Census of Population, the Labour Force Survey, the Consumer Price Index, the Gross Domestic Product and the International Balance of Payments.

Statistics Canada issues about 700 titles a year. The *Canada Handbook*, the monthly *Canadian Statistical Review*, the *Statistics Canada Daily*, vehicle of first release for agency data, and *Infomat*, a weekly summary of statistical highlights, are among the agency's most widely used publications. Statistics Canada also makes its information available on microfiche, microfilm, computer tape, and through the agency's extensive machine-readable data base CANSIM. Regional offices in St John's, Halifax, Montréal, Sturgeon Falls (Ont), Toronto, Winnipeg, Regina, Edmonton, Calgary and Vancouver conduct survey and census operations and also offer reference and consultative services to statistical users.

Status of Women The first European expeditions that came to Canada to explore and trade for furs did not include women. Early records of fur-trading companies suggest it was common for both French and English traders to enter into marriage with Indian women *à la façon du pays* – by a mix of European and Indian customs.

The Indian women who married fur traders provided an important link between the 2 cultures: the trader secured the trade of his wife's band or tribe and he learned from her survival skills, native customs and languages. Some Indian women acted as unpaid interpreters for fur-trading companies and achieved a good deal of importance. Such marital arrangements continued until missionaries and fur-trading companies actively discouraged them in the 19th century. In the early days of the FUR TRADE an Indian woman whose husband had left her would return to the tribe, but as the economic base of Indian life deteriorated, it became difficult for tribes to reabsorb women and their children. Their vulnerability was confirmed with the passage of the INDIAN ACT in 1876. Indian women who married non-Indian men immediately lost their status and relinquished the right to live on reserves. Such discrimination, since native men marrying whites were not affected, was the source of great distress and ultimately political protest for native women.

French Colonization A few French women arrived in NEW FRANCE beginning in the early 1600s. Their numbers remained small until 1663 when young women of marriageable age, known as FILLES DU ROI, were given free passage to New France and provided with a dowry. The majority of women in the colony, including widows, were quickly married. They were expected to bear and raise children for the colony, to care for their homes, cook, sew and garden. Early French Canadian records also indicate that it was not unusual for women to own property, run inns, keep books and generally manage the family business (*see* COMMUNAUTÉ DES BIENS). The resourcefulness and fortitude of these pioneers was exemplified by Agathe de Saint-Père, who took over the raising of 10 brothers and sisters when she was only 15 and continued her own business career after marrying at age 28. She had weaving looms installed in houses throughout Montréal and ran the cloth industry for 8 years until she retired and devoted herself to work at a Québec hospital.

Women in religious orders played a significant role in developing the early institutions of New France. Marguerite BOURGEOYS founded the Congrégation de Notre-Dame, which opened its first school in 1658, and was active in the establishment of many more schools, including La Providence, an industrial school for girls. In 1753 Marie d'YOUVILLE was granted a Royal Charter for the Grey Nuns, Sisters of Charity. The Grey Nuns ran the Hôpital Général in Québec and became the most active order of nursing sisters in the hospital field (*see* CHRISTIAN RELIGIOUS COMMUNITIES).

The British Period, 1713-1914 The predominantly rural nature of BNA before 1850 had implications for the position of women in society. Settlement was characterized by small independent landholdings and the labour of women was crucial to the survival of the economic unit (*see* HOMESTEADING). Census figures for the 19th century indicate that more than 90% of female children born in any decade between 1810 and 1870 eventually married. Married women and their children worked as a production unit on the farm in the area immediately surrounding the house and outbuildings. Women produced a great deal of the goods that their families required: they tended livestock, managed the garden, preserved fruit and vegetables, spun yarn, wove cloth and sewed clothing. Accounts of 19th-century writers like Susanna MOODIE and Catharine Parr TRAILL describe some of the work of women during this century (*see* PIONEER LIFE).

As the century progressed a number of trends converged to alter the traditional position of women in society. The agricultural unit was increasingly drawn into the money economy as demand increased for cash crops and as agricultural technology improved. Many necessities that had been produced on the farm were replaced by purchased goods. The mixed production characteristic of early landholdings gave way to more specialized agricultural production. As there was less for children to do on farms and as urbanization progressed, children spent less time in productive work and more time at school. The tendency of these changes was also to diminish the involvement of women in agricultural and domestic production and to emphasize their role as one of service towards family members as they related to the larger society. More than city women, however, rural women found themselves still bound, albeit in fewer ways, to the pace and needs of production.

The rapid growth of WOMEN'S ORGANIZATIONS by the end of the 19th century reflected the increasing politicization of women. Women's missionary societies were formed in most Canadian churches in the 1870s and 1880s; the first Canadian YOUNG WOMEN'S CHRISTIAN ASSOCIATION was founded in 1870; the WOMAN'S CHRISTIAN TEMPERANCE UNION in 1874 (*see* TEMPERANCE MOVEMENT); the Dominion Order of King's Daughters in 1886; and women's organizations in Ontario and Manitoba formed the first suffrage associations in the 1880s and 1890s (*see* WOMEN'S SUFFRAGE). By the end of the century a number of women's associations had achieved national stature and a federation of women's groups, the NATIONAL COUNCIL OF WOMEN OF CANADA, was formed in 1893. The women who agitated for the vote were often those who had gone through a period of "apprenticeship" for political action in organizations that preceded the suffrage movement.

Despite vigorous debate on the advisability of educating female children, the percentage of girls attending school rose from 23.1% in 1842 to 75.6% in 1881 (*see* WOMEN AND EDUCATION). Female students who went on for training in normal schools could enter the paid labour force as teachers, the first of the so-called "female professions." By the final quarter of the century, women occupied the majority of teaching positions in Canada. Religious orders had provided nursing care for centuries, as they had played a significant role in teaching. Women had acted in a voluntary capacity as midwives in rural communities (*see* BIRTHING PRACTICES), and the establishment of training schools for lay nurses after 1874 permitted graduates to find work as paid nurses. In 1875 Grace Annie LOCKHART became the first woman to earn a university degree in Canada, at Mt Allison U. Emily STOWE, Canada's pioneering woman doctor, began to practise in 1867, although she had been obliged to take her medical training in the US. Clara Brett Martin became the first Canadian woman lawyer in 1897.

Industrialization was given a boost in Canada after Sir John A. MACDONALD introduced his NATIONAL POLICY of protective tariffs in 1879. Girls and women moved to the towns and cities looking for work, and many found jobs in sweatshops and factories. Garment and textile industries, in particular, hired large numbers to labour in factories or to do piecework in small shops or at home (*see* WOMEN IN THE LABOUR FORCE). Though poorly paid, factory work did provide women with more freedom than traditional work in DOMESTIC SERVICE and on farms.

The demand for household servants continued throughout the 19th century and IMMIGRATION policies encouraged women to come to Canada in domestic service. By 1891 census figures reflected the entrance of women into the economy as paid workers. Almost 196 000 women had jobs and they represented 11.07% of the labour force. The jobs they held were predominantly in low-paying "female" occupations: domestic service (41%), dressmaking, teaching, sewing, tailoring, housekeeping, laundering, millinery and salesclerking.

Canada remained a predominantly rural nation until after WWI, but the manufacturing sector was growing in importance, and with it the service-producing sector whose operation required large numbers of office workers. Between 1901 and 1911 the female labour force increased by 50%, particularly in occupations such as clerk, typist and salesclerk. Female pay was regularly 50-60% of male pay and in 1907 the National Council of Women adopted a resolution calling for "equal pay for equal work." Owing to the prevailing ideology of separate spheres for men and women, of the male breadwinner and of woman's place in the home, it was mostly single women who held jobs in the prewar years; other women who took paid work were considered

"unfortunates" – widows, divorcées, deserted or separated women, or wives of the unemployed.

1914 to 1945 During WWI women were brought into the labour force as new jobs were created and as men left their jobs to join the armed forces. Most found familiar jobs as secretaries, clerks, typists and factory workers. For the first time, however, many women worked in heavy industry, particularly the munitions industry where by 1917 there were 35 000 women employed in munitions factories in Ontario and Montréal. Most of the women who worked during the war were unmarried. Although their wages increased during the war years, they never equalled men's; in the munitions factories women's wages were 50-80% of those paid men. Despite the movement of women into a few new areas of the economy, domestic service remained the most common female occupation.

The war effort increased women's political visibility. Women's organizations had supported the war effort by recruiting women to replace men in the domestic labour force and by collecting massive amounts of comforts for Canadian troops. A Women's War Conference was called by the federal government in 1918 to discuss the continuing role of women, who took the opportunity to raise a number of political issues, including suffrage. Suffrage movements had been gaining strength since the turn of the century, particularly in the West, and in 1916 Manitoba, Saskatchewan and Alberta had given women the provincial vote; Ontario and BC followed in 1917. On 24 May 1918 the Parliament of Canada bestowed the federal franchise on women, and by 1922 women had the provincial vote in all provinces except Québec. In the early 1920s the WOMEN'S INTERNATIONAL LEAGUE FOR PEACE AND FREEDOM was formed in Canada in order to work for peace and disarmament.

In 1919 women were granted the right to hold political office in Parliament, and in 1921 Agnes MACPHAIL was the first woman to be elected as a federal member. In 1929, 5 Alberta women led by Judge Emily MURPHY successfully brought the PERSONS CASE before the Judicial Committee of the Privy Council in England with the result that women in Canada became eligible for senatorial appointment.

Cutbacks and layoffs of women took place in the years immediately following the war, but by the 1920s women had re-established their wartime levels of labour-force involvement. Some new "female" professions, such as library work, social work (*see* Charlotte WHITTON) and physiotherapy were emerging, but the most rapidly growing occupations were clerical. Domestic service remained the most common paid occupation of women, but for the first time in the century the percentage of women working as domestics fell below 20%. Women were entering universities in large numbers and, by 1930, 23% of all undergraduates and 35% of all graduate students were female. The GREAT DEPRESSION reversed this trend and in the 1930s many women were forced back into domestic service. Federal employment figures show that even in the garment industry, a longtime employer of women, they were being laid off at a higher rate than men.

Canada entered WWII with a high level of unemployment, but by 1942 the government was facing a labour shortage. With the help of 21 national women's organizations, a federal National Selective Service program was launched to recruit women into the industrial labour force. The program first sought to register only single women for employment, but continuing labour shortages forced it to recruit childless married women and finally married women with children. As an enabling measure, federal-provincial child-care agreements were drawn up, eventually leading to the establishment of 28 day nurseries in Ontario and 5 in Québec. Large numbers of married women joined the paid work force for the first time, and by 1945, 33.2% of all women were employed (*see* CANADIAN WOMEN'S ARMY CORPS).

1945 to the Present After WWII women were expected and, in the case of federal government employees, required to relinquish their jobs to returning servicemen. The day nurseries were closed, many women returned to the home, often to have children, and by 1946 the rate of women's participation in the labour force had dropped to Depression levels. The patterns of married employment had been established, however, and married women began entering the labour force in such numbers that by the 1960s they made up one-third of the labour force and represented 55% of the labour-force growth. Despite their numbers, the earnings of working women continued to be significantly lower than those of men: in 1961 earnings of women employed full-time, year-round, were 59% of the earnings of men in the same categories; when part-time workers were added, women's wages dropped to 54% of men's.

This phenomenon could be partially attributed to limitations in federal legislation governing equal pay and to a lack of enforcement of its provisions because women were paid less than men on the average even when they did the same work. Full-time female clerical workers earned 74% of the wage of male clerical workers in 1961. The situation was more clearly attributable to the different occupational structures for men and women: men were more likely to work in unionized occupations, to be employed in highly paid professions, and they held 89.7% of all proprietorial and managerial positions. Women remained locked into "female" occupations, predominantly clerical. Over 20% of the female labour force still worked in personal service jobs as maids and baby-sitters, and those women in professions tended to be dieticians and librarians rather than doctors and lawyers.

Women in the 1960s remained underrepresented in political institutions, faced the quota system in some universities, and were generally subject to a range of discriminatory policies and legislation in both the public and private sectors. By the end of the decade the burgeoning WOMEN'S MOVEMENT voiced protest in the form of women's centres, consciousness-raising groups and rape crisis centres.

As a response to the issue of equality for women, a Royal Commission on the STATUS OF WOMEN IN CANADA was established in 1967. In 1970 the commission presented its report, making 167 recommendations on such matters as employment, educational opportunities and family law. The publication of the report, the continued proliferation of women's organizations, and the establishment of the NATIONAL ACTION COMMITTEE ON THE STATUS OF WOMEN as a lobby group ensured that the political visibility of women's issues continued into the 1970s.

The federal government responded by creating new offices and procedures to deal with women's rights: a portfolio for the status of women in the federal Cabinet (1971); an Office of the Co-ordinator of the Status of Women to monitor the progress of all federal ministries in implementing the RCSW's recommendations (1971); an Office of Equal Opportunities in the Public Service Commission (1972); and an Advisory Council on the Status of Women (1973). Certain federal statutes were amended to remove sections that were discriminatory to women, in particular the Canada Labour Code (1971); sections of the Criminal Code pertaining to jury duty (1972); the Public

Service Superannuation Act (1975); a Federal Omnibus Bill on the Status of Women containing amendments to 11 statutes (1975); the Citizenship Act (1975); and an Omnibus Bill to amend the Labour Code (1978).

In 1978 the Canadian Human Rights Act came into effect prohibiting discrimination on the basis of sex (among other things) in the case of employees under federal jurisdiction. The Act contains provisions to ensure "equal pay for work of equal value," specifying that "value" should be determined with reference to skill, effort, responsibility and working conditions. A Woman's Program was established within the Secretary of State and began to make money available for special projects of women's centres, rape crisis centres, women's research programs and professional associations, and transition houses for physically abused women.

By the mid-1980s women in Canada still did not have equality. Full-time female employees earned 60% of that earned by men, two-thirds of all minimum-wage earners were women, and only 10% of women were employed in managerial or administrative positions. Only 26% of working women were unionized and 70% of all part-time workers were women – a situation which allowed women to be excluded from employee and pension benefits. Since work-related pensions are based on earnings, women on average receive significantly lower amounts; Ontario is the last province to sign an agreement with the federal government on the "child-care drop-out provision" to protect pension entitlements of mothers who leave the labour market to raise children. In the 1970s most provinces passed FAMILY LAW reform Acts which ensured that assets accumulated during marriage, including pensions, would be split on divorce. Equity pay laws began to be passed in the 1980s federally and in 3 provinces (Qué, Ont and Man). Still, 3 out of 4 women over the age of 65 who live alone live below the poverty level. In 1987, an estimated 1 in 8 Canadian women were battered by the men they lived with and, in 1986, 22 623 sexual assaults were reported to the police; an additional 4731 sexual offences were reported that year. Women's groups fought hard to ensure that the Charter of Rights and Freedoms in the Canadian Constitution (1982) enshrined equality for both sexes, but many controversial issues affecting the status of women – ABORTION, PORNOGRAPHY, equal pay, PENSIONS – remain unresolved. *See also* CHILDHOOD, HISTORY OF; FAMILY; HOUSEWORK; SOCIAL HISTORY.   DORIS ANDERSON

Reading: J. Acton and B. Shepard, eds, *Women at Work* (1974); P. and H. Armstrong, *The Double Ghetto* (1978); P. Connelly, *Last Hired, First Fired: Women and the Canadian Work Force* (1978); G. Matheson, ed, *Women in the Canadian Mosaic* (1976); *Report of the Royal Commission on the Status of Women in Canada* (1970); Status of Women, Canada, *Towards Equality for Women* (1979); M. Stephenson, ed, *Women in Canada* (1977); S.M. Trofimenkoff and A. Prentice, eds, *The Neglected Majority* (1977); S. Van Kirk, *Many Tender Ties: Women in Fur Trade Society 1670-1870* (1980).

Status of Women in Canada, Royal Commission on the, instituted by PM Lester B. PEARSON on 16 Feb 1967 in response to a campaign mounted by a coalition of 32 women's voluntary groups. The campaign lasted 6 months and was led by Ontario activist Laura Sabia. It was a direct response to the WOMEN'S MOVEMENT and similar initiatives by other governments in the 1960s. Florence BIRD, an Ottawa journalist and broadcaster, was appointed as chairwoman. The other commissioners were Jacques Henripin, professor of demography, Montréal; John HUMPHREY, professor of law, Montréal; Lola Lange, farmer and community activist, Claresholm, Alta; Jeanne

Lapointe, professor of literature, Québec City; Elsie Gregory MACGILL, aeronautical engineer, Toronto; and Doris Ogilvie, judge, Fredericton, NB. The RCSW, the first Canadian commission headed by a woman, was given a mandate to investigate and report on all matters pertaining to the status of women and to make specific recommendations for improving the condition of women in those areas which fell within the jurisdiction of the federal government.

The commission's public investigation began in the spring of 1968, and for 6 months public hearings were held across Canada, including the Far North. This commission attracted extensive public interest, hearing 468 briefs and additional testimony, all of which attested to widespread problems experienced by women in all walks of Canadian society.

The RCSW produced a 488-page report containing 167 recommendations on such matters as equal pay for work of equal value, maternity leave, DAY CARE, BIRTH CONTROL, FAMILY LAW, the INDIAN ACT, educational opportunities, access of women to managerial positions, part-time work and PENSIONS. The recommendations were based on fundamental principles which assumed that equality of opportunity for Canadian men and women was possible, desirable and ethically necessary. The *Report of the Royal Commission on the Status of Women in Canada* was tabled in the House of Commons on 7 Dec 1970. The RCSW played a major role in defining the STATUS OF WOMEN as a legitimate social problem. It focused attention on women's grievances, recommended changes to eliminate sexual inequality by means of social policy, and mobilized a constituency of women's groups to press for implementation of the commission's recommendations.

By the 1980s most of the 167 recommendations in the RCSW report had been partially implemented and many had been fully implemented. Several controversial recommendations, however, had not been acted upon by the federal government.   CERISE MORRIS

Reading: Advisory Council on the Status of Women, *Ten Years Later* (1979); N. Griffiths, *Penelope's Web* (1976); *Report of the Royal Commission on the Status of Women in Canada* (1970).

Statute of Westminster, 11 Dec 1931, a British law clarifying the powers of Canada's Parliament and those of the other Dominions, and granting the former colonies full legal freedom except in those areas where they chose to remain subordinate. Until this time the British government had certain ill-defined powers, and ultimately overriding authority, over Dominion legislation. The Imperial Conference of 1926 began to give legal substance to the BALFOUR REPORT declaration that Britain and the Dominions were constitutionally "equal in status." The 1929 Conference on the Operation of Dominion Legislation and the Imperial Conference of 1930 continued to work towards agreement on fundamental changes in the COMMONWEALTH's complex legal system. Finally, at the request and with the consent of the Dominions, the Statute of Westminster was passed by the British Parliament. After consultation between Canada's federal and provincial governments, the repeal, amendment or alteration of BRITISH NORTH AMERICA ACTS, 1867-1930, was specifically excepted from the terms of the statute: the amendment of the Canadian Constitution remained exclusively the preserve of the British Parliament until passage of the CONSTITUTION ACT, 1982. Nor did Canada immediately take up all of its new powers under the statute. Not until 1949, for instance, did the JUDICIAL COMMITTEE OF THE PRIVY COUNCIL cease to be a final court of appeal for Canadians.   NORMAN HILLMER

Stavert, Reuben Ewart, mine executive (b at Kingston, Jamaica 3 Oct 1893; d at Montréal 19 Nov 1981). Stavert graduated from McGill in 1914 and served in the CEF in WWI. He worked at Canadian General Electric 1919-22; then he joined the British Metal Corp of Canada, of which he was president 1931-34. He then became assistant to the president of Consolidated Mining and Smelting. Appointed VP in 1941 and president in 1945, Stavert played a major role in Cominco's postwar expansion, which included the development of Pine Point Mines at Great Slave Lk, the construction of an ammonium-phosphate plant in Kimberley, BC, and the formation of Cominco Products Inc. He retired as president in 1959 and as chairman in 1964. He was a governor of U de M and a director of several large corporations.

J. LINDSEY

Steacie, Edgar William Richard, physical chemist, scientist-statesman (b at Westmount, Qué 25 Dec 1900; d at Ottawa 28 Aug 1962). Steacie was an internationally acclaimed research authority in free radical kinetics and, as a senior administrator at the NATIONAL RESEARCH COUNCIL, was influential in increasing Canada's capabilities in scientific research in both government and the universities. Steacie followed the military tradition of his father, Capt Richard Steacie, by enrolling in RMC in 1919. Not finding this life to his liking, he transferred to Chemical Engineering at McGill in 1920. There he was strongly influenced by the distinguished physical chemist, Dr Otto MAASS. As a result, after completing his engineering degree in 1923, he began graduate work in physical chemistry. Steacie took his PhD in 1926 at McGill, remaining there as a research fellow in physical chemistry. In 1930 he became assistant professor and began his pioneering research studies in free radical kinetics, the measurement of the rates of chemical reactions and the determination of the mechanisms of such processes. In 1939 he was appointed director of the Chemistry Division of NRC, which under his leadership became an international centre for chemical research. By 1944 Steacie was an obvious choice for deputy director under Sir John Cockcroft of the joint British-Canadian Atomic Energy Project. Steacie's major treatise, *Atomic and Free Radical Reactions* (1946), rapidly became the essential reference in its field.

He was appointed vice-president (scientific) of NRC in 1950 and became president in 1952. Through his efforts, many distinguished scientists were appointed to the NRC staff, including Gerhard HERZBERG. Steacie also persuaded the federal government to provide more support to universities for scientific research. Instrumental in upgrading industrial research as well, he obtained special tax concessions to assist companies in financing research, and through his efforts a new program of federal research grants was initiated to support innovative industrial research. For his outstanding contributions to both science and scientific administration, Steacie received numerous honours and recognitions from the national and international scientific communities, culminating in 1961 with his election as the first Canadian president of the International Council of Scientific Unions. Steacie not only laid the foundation for the development of Canadian science but also pioneered the government support structure necessary to promote those research industries that represent the growth points of modern industrial technology.

HARRY EMMET GUNNING

Stead, Robert James Campbell, writer, civil servant (b at Middleville, Ont 4 Sept 1880; d at Ottawa 26 June 1959). Raised in Manitoba, Stead began his writing career as a journalist and poet but he is best known for his novels. In his early poetry, such as *The Empire Builders and Other Poems* (1908), Stead mixed with styles of Service and Kipling to produce a virulently nationalist concept of Canada and Canadians. This strain was continued when he turned to novels in 1914, and wartime tensions seemed to exacerbate his prejudices. His postwar novels are calmer, more tolerant and less romantic than his first work, as his style shifted from Ralph CONNOR's romanticism towards F.P. GROVE's realism, this being most apparent in his seventh novel, *Grain* (1926). Although it retained some romantic elements, his fiction exemplified the tendency towards "prairie realism" in Canadian literature. TERRENCE CRAIG

Steamboats and Paddle Wheelers Steamboat refers to the flat-bottomed, shallow-draft, steam-powered vessels, generally associated with inland navigation, as opposed to deep-keeled, oceangoing steamships. As invented in 1685 by French physicist Denis Papin, the paddle wheel (driven by compressed steam from wood- or coal-fired boilers) was affixed to the boat hull either laterally (side-wheeler) or at the rear of the boat (stern-wheeler) and provided forward and reverse propulsion.

Demonstrated in France on the Saône R in 1783, the paddle-wheel steamboat first appeared in N America for use on the Delaware R in 1787. After inauguration at New Orleans in 1811 by Robert Fulton, hundreds of boats worked the Mississippi R system between 1830 and 1870. The first paddle steamer in Canadian waters, the ACCOMMODATION, was a side-wheeler launched for a 36-hour maiden voyage from Montréal to Québec in 1809. Other paddle-wheel steamboat firsts in Canada include the *Frontenac* on Lk Ontario (1816); the *General Stacey Smyth* on the Saint John R (1816); the *Union* on the lower reaches of the Ottawa R (1819); the *Richard Smith* visiting PEI (1830); the ROYAL WILLIAM steaming from Québec to Halifax (1831); the seagoing BEAVER, which first plied waters off BC (1836); the *Spitfire*, first steamboat into St John's harbour (1840); and the ANSON NORTHUP, first paddle wheeler to cross the international boundary on the Red R (1859).

Paddle steamers figure significantly in Canadian history. The *Swiftsure* moved troops on the St Lawrence during the War of 1812. The *Royal William*, built at Québec, was the first vessel to cross the Atlantic almost entirely under the power of steam in 1833. BC steamers ferried thousands of gold seekers into the Fraser (1858), Cariboo (1862) and Yukon (1898) river valleys (300 steamboats worked BC and Yukon waterways between 1836 and 1957). The Red R steamer *In-*

Stern-wheelers at Whitehorse, YT, c1900 (*courtesy National Archives of Canada/PA-122784*).

ternational was commandeered by the forces of Louis Riel at Fort Garry in 1870; and the Saskatchewan R stern-wheeler *Northcote* engaged Gabriel Dumont's Métis at the Battle of BATOCHE.

Paddle steamers carried the first wheat exported from Manitoba, precipitated a sophisticated inland canal and lock system in Ontario, freighted the first locomotive to Winnipeg for the CPR, brought the first mail to the Klondike and ferried the first fresh fruits and missionaries into the Far North. The utilitarian steamboat was also a social force. Staterooms, grand pianos and fine wines came with first-class passage aboard even the frontier steamers, and cabin and boiler decks below had fiddle playing, folk dances and card games. After 1900, when railways replaced steamboats as the major means of freight transport, hunting and picnic excursions and moonlight cruises were commonplace aboard steamboats. The last fully operational stern-wheeler, the *Samson V* (built in 1936 for use on the Fraser R), was taken out of service in 1981. TED BARRIS

Reading: Ted Barris, *Fire Canoe: Prairie Steamboat Days Revisited* (1977); Peter Charlebois, *Sternwheelers & Sidewheelers, The Romance of Steamdriven Paddleboats in Canada* (1978); Art Downs, *Paddlewheels on the Frontier; The Story of British Columbia and Yukon Sternwheel Steamers* (1972).

Stedman, Donald Frank, scientist (b at Tunbridge Wells, Eng 4 Apr 1900; d at Ottawa 2 May 1967). Primarily a chemist, he was one of the earliest staffers of the NATIONAL RESEARCH COUNCIL (1930). As a youngster in BC, Donald began his higher education by correspondence courses, gained a BSc from UBC and a doctorate in physical chemistry from U of London. Returning to Canada in 1924, he was engaged in industry and academia before joining the NRC. There he was soon involved in the exploitation of the Turner Valley, Alta, gas deposits. One outcome was his invention of the Stedman fractionating column, which was to become widely used by industry. His work in Ottawa diversified, as he studied, among other things, windshield rain repellents, forest-fire hazard indicators, the physics of time and the classification of the chemical elements. He also invented a wondrous "sea-walker suit" to facilitate lifesaving in marine accidents. An eccentric loner, not all Stedman's ideas fulfilled their early promise, and he had to abandon a search for "new heavy inert gases" on account, he believed, of sabotage by supernatural forces.

N.T. GRIDGEMAN

Stedman, Ernest Walter, aircraft engineer (b at Malling, Eng 21 July 1888; d at Ottawa 27 Mar 1957). Stedman trained as an engineer and ended his WWI service as a lt-col in the RAF. He then joined the Handley-Page aircraft company and came to N America with the firm's (unsuccessful) entry in the 1919 race to fly the Atlantic (won by J.N.W. Alcock and A.W. Brown). He liked Canada and immigrated in 1920, planning to manufacture aircraft parts, but took the post of director of the technical branch of the newly appointed Canadian Air Board. Thus, he was from 30 Oct 1920 the government's chief aeronautical engineer, under various titles, until his retirement in 1946 as an air vice-marshal, director general of air research of the RCAF. His work involved every aspect of aviation in Canada, including the W.R. TURNBULL propellor, J.H. PARKIN's research at U of T and the NATIONAL RESEARCH COUNCIL, the R-100 airship flight to Canada in 1930, practical work on winter flying (eg, starting cold engines and landing on snow), the foundation of TRANS-CANADA AIRLINES, buying and building aircraft for WWII, and jet-engine design in 1944. After retirement he was a Canadian witness at the Bikini atomic bomb test of 1946 and founded the engineering faculty of Carleton. His *From Boxkite to Jet: the Memoirs of an Aeronautical Engineer* was published posthumously in 1963.

DONALD J.C. PHILLIPSON

Steel, *see* IRON AND STEEL INDUSTRY.

Steel, William Arthur, radio pioneer (b 3 Nov 1890; d at Ottawa 28 Nov 1968). Steel was chief wireless officer in the Canadian Corps in France at the end of WWI and chief radio engineer of the Canadian Army Signals Corps throughout the 1920s, when he organized the Northwest Territories radio system and, together with A.G.L. MCNAUGHTON, invented the Cathode Ray Direction Finder, an early form of RADAR. He organized the NATIONAL RESEARCH COUNCIL's radio laboratory 1931-32 and was commissioner in charge of engineering operations of the Canadian Radio Broadcasting Commission 1933-36. He retired from the army with the rank of lt-col in 1936 and had a brief excursion in politics, in W.D. HERRIDGE's New Democracy Party. He thereafter worked in Ottawa as a consulting engineer in radio and radar, notably aircraft navigation aids and the construction of the DEW Line radar system.

DONALD J.C. PHILLIPSON

Steele, Mount, elev 5073 m, is located among Canada's highest mountains in the St Elias Range of the YT. It is joined to Mt LUCANIA by a high snow saddle; their summits are 13 km apart. Together, they form a huge snow and ice massif covering over 90 km² and spawning many glaciers, the 2 largest being Walsh and Chitina. Mt Steele's triangular, ice-covered NE face helps feed Steele Glacier, which flows NE. The mountain was named after Sam STEELE, former NWMP commander stationed in the Yukon during the gold rush. Its first ascent was made Aug 1935 by W. Wood, H. Wood, J. Fobes and H. Fuhrer via the E ridge.

GLEN BOLES

Steele, Sir Samuel Benfield, mounted policeman, soldier (b at Purbrook, Canada W 5 Jan 1849; d at London, Eng 30 Jan 1919). Steele joined the militia in 1866 during the FENIAN troubles, was a private in the Red River Expedition (1870), joined the Permanent Force Artillery in 1871 and, in 1873, became a sergeant major in the newly created NWMP. A man of enormous physical strength and endurance, Steele managed to be where the action was hottest. He achieved commissioned rank in 1878, acquired his first command at Ft Qu'Appelle in 1879, where he was in charge of police detachments supervising

Sam Steele, a man of enormous strength and endurance, managed throughout his eventful career to be where the action was hottest (*courtesy National Archives of Canada/PA-28146*).

the building of the CPR, and was promoted superintendent in 1885. In 1898 he helped establish the authority of the Canadian government during the KLONDIKE GOLD RUSH. Steele was given command of Lord Strathcona's Horse in the SOUTH AFRICAN WAR, and in 1915 he commanded the second Canadian contingent to be sent overseas. In 1916 he was appointed general officer commanding the Shorncliffe area in England, a post he held until the end of the war and his retirement in 1918.

R.C. MACLEOD

Reading: S. Garrod, *Sam Steele* (1979); S.B. Steele, *Forty Years in Canada* (1915); R. Stewart, *Sam Steele* (1979).

Steele Narrows Battle, at Loon Lake, 95 km NE of Lloydminster, scene of the last shots fired in the NORTH-WEST REBELLION on 3 June 1885. Often called the Battle of Loon Lake, it was a minor skirmish between about 65 men under North-West Mounted Police Superintendent Sam STEELE and Woods and Plains Cree retreating after the Battle of Frenchman's Butte. None of Steele's men died but Cree losses were heavy. Four were killed, including prominent Woods Cree chief Cut Arm. The battlefield is a provincial historic site, marked with interpretive plaques.

BOB BEAL

Stefansson, Baldur Rosmund, plant breeder (b at Vestfold, Man 26 Apr 1917). Stefansson has been a leader in development of rapeseed from an unadapted crop producing modest amounts of industrial oil to an adapted food and feed crop (CANOLA) rivalling wheat in acreage and value. He is an internationally acclaimed plant breeder, best known for suggesting elimination of erucic from rapeseed oil and for production of the oil's first low erucic, low glucosinolate varieties. He is also recognized for subsequent significant genetic alterations to the food value of the oil, industrial quality of the oil, and feed value of meal produced from the seed. Stefansson was active in studies relating to production of hybrid rape. In recognition of his achievements he has earned many awards, including the Royal Bank Award, the Manitoba Institute of Agrologists' Distinguished Agrolo-

gist Award (1981); he is an Officer of the Order of Canada (1985). Although retired from active leadership of the Canola project, he has been appointed senior scholar in the department of plant science at U Man, where he has been since 1952.

ANNA K. STORGAARD

Stefansson, Vilhjalmur, arctic explorer, ethnologist, lecturer, writer (b at Arnes, Man 3 Nov 1879; d at Hanover, NH 26 Aug 1962). One of Canada's most renowned arctic explorers and winner of a host of international awards, Stefansson was no stranger to controversy and created more interest in the Arctic among Canadians than any other individual of his time.

The son of ICELANDERS who moved to the Dakotas in 1880, educated at the universities of Iowa, N Dakota and Harvard, Stefansson made 3 forays into the Arctic between 1906 and 1918, travelling more than 32 000 km² of arctic territory. In 1910 he "discovered" a little-known group of Victoria Land natives whom he called the "Blond Eskimos" (ie, COPPER INUIT) and sparked a controversy, which would impugn his scientific expertise by suggesting that their lighter and European features could be the result of generations of intermingling with a Scandinavian colony of Greenlanders that had vanished in the 15th or 16th century; subsequent scientific investigations have since discounted this theory and did nothing to enhance Stefansson's reputation. As commander of the CANADIAN ARCTIC EXPEDITION (1913-18), which was fraught with internal dissension, he discovered some of the world's last major landmasses – Lougheed, Borden, Meighen and Brock islands – while drifting dangerously, but deliberately, on ice floes.

A prolific writer, his most famous book being *The Friendly Arctic* (1921), Stefansson had a simple message regarding Canada's NORTH: the Arctic was not a bleak, frozen waste but a habitable region that must be developed. The over-the-pole routes of today's airlines, nuclear submarines surfacing at the N Pole, and the possibility of using gigantic submarine tankers all had their origin in Stefansson's vision of a strategic and commercial polar Mediterranean which, if controlled and exploited by Canada (and the British Empire), could make the Dominion one of the great powers of the 20th century. To some he was the "prophet of the North"; to others he was an arrogant charlatan. He left Canada under a cloud, partly because he had made enemies during the Canadian Arctic Expedition but also because the projects he later undertook to prove his theories failed. His poorly planned scheme for the domestication of reindeer in northern Canada (1921-25) ended in chaos; his unauthorized claiming of WRANGEL I, N of Siberia, for Canada generated an international incident (1921-24) that upset the USSR and the US and embarrassed Great Britain. The Canadian government was infuriated, seeing his action as high-handed and undercutting Canada's claims to its ARCTIC ARCHIPELAGO. Also, all 4 members of the Wrangel I expedition, including a young Canadian student, died tragically and, some say, unnecessarily. Stefansson, who had not gone on this expedition, was now perceived as a troublemaker whose ideas and presence in Canada were unwelcome. From the mid-1920s on, most of his time was spent in the US, where he was regarded as one of the world's foremost arctic experts. *See also* ARCTIC EXPLORATION.

RICHARD J. DIUBALDO

Reading: W.R. Hunt, *STEF: A Biography of Vilhjalmur Stefansson, Canadian Arctic Explorer* (1986).

Stefansson Island, 4463 km², elev 256 m, in the ARCTIC ARCHIPELAGO, is a low, gently rolling, lake-strewn plain. Being largely barren, with continuous vegetation only in wet lowlands, it supports few muskoxen and Peary caribou. It was discovered in 1917 by some members of V. STEFANSSON's expedition.   S.C. ZOLTAI

Steinbach, Man, Town, pop 7473 (1986c), 6676 (1981c), inc 1946, is located 48 km SE of Winnipeg. Eighteen Kleine Gemeinde families developed a traditional MENNONITE agricultural village at the Steinbach site in 1874. They were among several thousand Mennonites who emigrated from southern Russia in the 1870s to 2 reserves established for them in Manitoba. Despite the absence of rail links, Steinbach developed as an agricultural centre and later as a commercial, industrial and administrative centre. Located in a mixed-farming region, the town serves a trade-area population of 30 000.

Steinbach's economic activities include farm-products processing, concrete products, trucking, millworking, boat manufacturing and automobile retailing. Steinbach also has a Bible institute. Its heritage is celebrated during annual Pioneer Days in Aug and by the Mennonite Village Museum, a reconstruction of the original settlement.   D.M. LYON

Steinberg, Samuel, grocer (b in Hungary 1905; d at Montréal 24 May 1978). In 1909 the Steinberg family immigrated to Canada and established a small grocery store in Montréal. Samuel and his 4 brothers began working in it in 1917 and turned it into one of Canada's largest supermarket chains. In 1934, under Samuel's management, Steinberg's opened Québec's first self-service store in Montréal. Five years later Samuel opened a branch at Arvida, Qué. In 1959 Steinberg's bought the 38 Ontario stores of Grand Union Ltd. When Steinberg died, the company was grossing over $1 billion a year from its Steinberg and Miracle Mart stores and other enterprises. At that time it was the largest supermarket chain in Québec and was owned completely by the family. Steinberg was also a director of Petrofina, Ivanhoe and Pharmaprix.   JORGE NIOSI

Steinberg Inc is a diversified Canadian retailing organization with head offices in Montréal. It was incorporated in 1930 as Steinberg's Limited, and adopted its present name in 1978. Between 1958 and 1981 the company expanded by acquiring other enterprises, including the entire chain of Grand Union stores in Ontario. Today, it has several wholly owned subsidiaries, including Steinberg Foods Limited. It is engaged in food retailing and manufacturing, general merchandise retailing and real estate. Among other enterprises, it or its subsidiaries operate 334 supermarkets and grocery stores, 24 department stores, 154 restaurants and 35 shopping centres. In 1987, it had sales or operating revenue of $4.5 billion, assets of $1.5 billion and more than 36 000 employees. In early 1988, despite a well publicized family feud, the company was still 88% owned by Steinberg family trusts.   DEBORAH C. SAWYER

Steinhauer, Henry Bird, Shahwahnegezhik (Ojibwa) or Sowengisik (Cree), meaning "Southern Skies," Methodist minister, native leader (b at Rama Indian settlement, Lk Simcoe, UC *c*1818; d at Whitefish Lake, Alta 29 Dec 1884). After an American benefactor named Steinhauer in Philadelphia provided his foster name and funds, he attended Cazenovia College, NY, and Upper Canada Academy, Cobourg, UC. He accompanied James EVANS to the Hudson's Bay Company territories in 1840. Appointed to Oxford House in 1850, he was ordained by the Canada Conference (Methodist) in 1855 and sent to Lac La Biche, Alta. In 1858 Steinhauer moved to Whitefish Lake, Alta, to found a native Christian community.   GERALD M. HUTCHINSON

Steinhauer, Ralph Garvin, farmer, Indian leader, lt-gov of Alberta (b at Morley, Alta 8 June 1905; d at Edmonton 19 Sept 1987). The first native person to serve as lieutenant-governor, he was educated at Brandon Indian Residential School and farmed at Saddle Lk, Alta. He founded the Indian Assn of Alta and was president of the Alberta Indian Development Corp. In 1963 he ran as a Liberal candidate in the federal election. On 2 July 1974 he was sworn in as lt-gov of Alberta and served until 1979. He was made a Companion of the Order of Canada.   ERIC J. HOLMGREN

Steinhouse, Tobie Thelma, née Davis, printmaker, painter (b at Montréal 1 Apr 1925). Her intricate abstractions gleam through effects of prism-coloured glass, fish nets or cobwebs, reflecting the soft haze of Paris, where she lived 1948-57, and revealing her continuing search for light. She was strongly influenced by Montréal painter and teacher Anne SAVAGE. Steinhouse studied graphics and painting at Montréal, New York and Paris, where she had a solo exhibition in 1957. Returning to Montréal she has worked at the Atelier libre de recherches graphiques since 1965. Frosted glass and snow storms are Canadian motifs now forming part of her muted, restrained style.   ANNE MCDOUGALL

Stelco Inc, with headquarters in Toronto, is Canada's largest steel producer. Incorporated in 1910 as The Steel Company of Canada, Ltd, the company consolidated existing companies engaged in the production of iron, steel and related products: Montreal Rolling Mills Co, The Hamilton Steel and Iron Co, Canada Screw Co, Canada Bolt & Nut Co, and Dominion Wire Manufacturing Company. The company grew steadily through acquisitions, and in 1969 amalgamated with Page-Hersey Tubes Ltd, Premier Steel Mills Ltd and The Canadian Drawn Steel Co Ltd. The present name was adopted in 1980. Stelco produces a wide range of flat-rolled and coated steels, bars, rods, wire and wire products as well as pipe and tubing, fasteners and forgings. Its annual raw steel capacity is over 16 million t and it operates 18 plants in Ont, Qué and Alta. It annually produces almost 35% of Canada's steel. Stelco also has interests in coal, iron-ore and limestone properties in Canada and the US, either directly or through its subsidiaries. Since 1971 it has been involved in a joint venture with the T. EATON COMPANY LTD and TRW Inc of Cleveland, Ohio, in the Canada Systems Group (EST) Ltd, which applies computer technology, data processing and systems technology to environmental problems. In 1986 it had revenues of $2.4 billion (39th in Canada), assets of $2.9 billion (28th) and 17 768 employees. Its shares are widely held and foreign ownership stands at 2%.   DEBORAH C. SAWYER

Stellarton, NS, Town, pop 5259 (1986c), inc 1889, bordering the East R, 18 km SW of Pictou, was settled (1774) by 5 HECTOR families. Coal enticed English colliers in 1827, who built the community of Albion Mines. Their foundry built the SAMSON, Nova Scotia's first steam engine (1827) and steamboat (1830), and cast rails for the first locomotive run on iron rails in Canada (1839). The town became an important railway hub. In 1870 Albion Mines was renamed Stellarton, after its Stellar Coal. Mining flourished, attracting British and European immigrants. Stellarton coal fueled Pictou County's industrial boom (1870-1920): by 1910 the Acadian Co employed 1350 miners. Mining gradually declined, except during WWII, finishing in 1957 for economic and safety reasons. 650 men perished in these dangerous pits, including 88 in the 1918 Allan Explosion. The Acadia Rescue Corps was famous for mine rescue exploits.   JUDITH HOEGG RYAN

Stephansson, Stephán Gudmundsson, Stefán Gudmundur Gudmundsson, poet, pioneer farmer (b at Kirkjuhóll, Skagafjördur, Iceland 3 Oct 1853; d at Markerville, Alta 10 Aug 1927). Known as "the poet of the Rocky Mountains," Stephansson became the foremost west-Icelandic poet in Canada and one of Iceland's major poets. Although he wrote in Icelandic, his poetry reflects his love for Alberta, his concern with contemporary political issues and awareness of 20th-century thought as well as his Icelandic heritage. He lived at Kirkjuhóll until 1862, at Vídimýrarsel until 1870 and at Mýri in Bárdardalur until he was 20. In 1873 he immigrated with his parents to Wisconsin and worked as a day labourer. Later he claimed land in Shawano County and worked as a farmer and logger. He moved to N Dakota in 1880 and to Canada in 1889, homesteading and farming near Markerville, Alta, until his death. Largely self-educated, Stephansson took an active part in the social and cultural life of Icelandic Canadians, as well as writing prolifically and carrying on a large correspondence. He was a romantic realist and satirist, known for his pacifism and interest in women's rights. His poems were published in west-Icelandic magazines after 1890. His published books are *Úti a Vídavangi* (poems, 1894); *Á Ferd og Flugi* (poems, 1900); his collected poems *Andvökur* I-VI (1909-38); *Kolbeinslag* (poetry, 1914); *Heimleidis* (poems from his 1917 visit to Iceland); *Vígslódi* (antiwar poem, 1920) and his collected letters and essays, *Bréf og Ritgerdir* I-IV (1938-48). His own essays are an excellent source of information on his life and writing.   KRISTJANA GUNNARS

Stephen, George, 1st Baron Mount Stephen, banker, railway president (b at Dufftown, Scot 5 June 1829; d at Hatfield, Eng 29 Nov 1921). Stephen has been described as the person most responsible for the success of the CANADIAN PACIFIC RY. He immigrated to Montréal at 21 to join a relative's draper establishment and by 1860 was the sole proprietor. His energy and capital, however, were increasingly directed to banking and railways. He became a director of the Bank of Montreal in 1873 and was president 1876-81. In 1873-74 he participated along with his cousin Donald SMITH and J.J. HILL in the syndicate which bought the ailing St Paul, Minneapolis and Manitoba Ry. It became a favoured route for settlers and made its owners wealthy. In a reorganization of the revived railway in 1879, Stephen was named president. A much larger project, the Pacific railway, engaged his attention after 1880. One of its original promoters, Stephen was the first president of the CPR, 1880-88. His wealth and standing in the Montréal business community were of inestimable benefit in gaining the investors' confidence, but his personal contribution to the line was enormous. Resourceful and cool, he never lost faith in the project nor in the future of the West. Stephen moved to England in 1888. Created a baronet in 1886, he was raised to the peerage as Baron Mount Stephen in 1891. He was a generous philanthropist in Montréal and England and is said to have given away over $1 million during his life. The Royal Victoria Hospital, Montréal, and hospitals in England benefited from his wealth.   D.M.L. FARR

Reading: Heather Gilbert, *Awakening Continent* (1965), and *The End of the Road* (1977).

Stephen Leacock Medal for Humour is a silver medal awarded each year to the Canadian writer of the best book of humour. Since 1946 it has been offered by the Stephen Leacock Associates, based in Orillia, Ont. After Stephen LEACOCK died in Mar 1944 in Montréal, the association was formed by people who wanted to remember their kinship with him and his unique talent as a writer of humour. Sculptor Emanuel Hahn was commissioned to design the medal. Books entered in the contest each year are read by 5 judges from across Canada. They report to a committee of the association. At a media reception the winner is announced. At an award dinner, the winner receives the medal and a cash award. A series of corporations since the mid-1970s have donated cash awards to accompany the medal. Among award recipients are Harry J. BOYLE (*Luck of the Irish* and *Homebrew and Patches*), Robertson DAVIES (*Leaven of Malice*), Pierre BERTON (*Just Add Water and Stir*), W.O. MITCHELL (*Jake and the Kid*) and Farley MOWAT (*The Boat Who Wouldn't Float*). Eric NICOL has won the award 3 times. The most recent winners are Joey Slinger in 1986 (*No Axe Too Small to Grind*) and W.P. Kinsella in 1987 (*The Fencepost Chronicles*). JIM HARRIS

Stephenson, Sir William Samuel, inventor, businessman, master spy (b at Winnipeg 11 Jan 1896). Stephenson flew as a fighter pilot in WWI, winning several medals for bravery. While a student at U Man he invented the wirephoto and then a radio facsimile method of transmitting pictures without need of telephone or telegraph wires. He moved to Britain in 1921 to develop and market this invention to newspapers and rapidly earned a fortune and an entrée to influential political circles in London. Thus, for example, he served on a royal commission in the 1930s to plan the development of India's natural resources.

At the beginning of WWII, Stephenson was placed in charge of British Security Co-ordination (counterespionage) in the Western Hemisphere, with headquarters in New York C (where the telegraphic address was INTREPID — later popularized as Stephenson's code name). His organization's activities ranged from censoring transatlantic mail, breaking letter codes (which exposed at least one German spy in the US) and forging diplomatic documents, to obtaining Vichy French and Italian military codes, protection against sabotage of American factories producing munitions for Britain, and training (at CAMP X, near Oshawa, Ont) allied agents for surreptitious entry into Nazi-occupied Europe.

Although Stephenson was knighted by King George VI and awarded the US Medal for Merit, not much was known about his war services until the publication of H. Montgomery Hyde's *The Quiet Canadian* (1962). William Stevenson (no relative to Stephenson) later published 2 books about him, *A Man Called Intrepid* (1977) and *Intrepid's Last Case* (1983). The claims made regarding Stephenson's career have been treated with reserve by professional historians and experts on intelligence. Stephenson lived in the W Indies after WWII, becoming chairman of the Caribbean Development Corp, and eventually retired to Bermuda. DONALD J.C. PHILLIPSON

Stephenville, Nfld, Town, pop 7994 (1986c), 8876 (1981c), inc 1952, is located on the N shore of St George's Bay in southwestern Newfoundland. Named for Acadian pioneer Stephen Le Blanc, it was settled as a fishing/farming site around 1845. On the great circle air route between the US and Europe, it was chosen as the site for the American-built Ernest Harmon Air Force Base, which opened in 1941, causing the small town to grow rapidly. The base closed in 1966 with severe economic consequences for the region, but the Harmon Field airport was converted to a commercial air facility run by the Canadian Dept of Transport; the base passed to the provincial government and was administered by the Crown's Harmon Corp, formed in 1967 to attract new industry. In 1972 a $140-million linerboard mill went into production, but it closed 1977. In

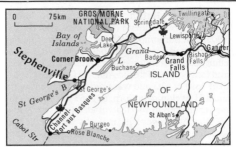

1979 the world's largest producer of newsprint, Abitibi-Price, purchased the mill and converted it for newsprint. It opened 1981, providing significant employment for the town.

JANET E.M. PITT AND ROBERT D. PITT

Steppenwolf, Los Angeles-based blues-rock band (fl 1967-72), had its genesis in the Toronto quintet Sparrow (fl 1964-67). Popular for its blustery recordings "Born to be Wild" and "Magic Carpet Ride," the group initially included 3 musicians from Sparrow: singer John Kay, drummer Jerry Edmonton and organist Goldy McJohn. Kay's attempts to revive Steppenwolf after 1972 had mixed success. MARK MILLER

Sternberg, Charles Mortram, paleontologist (b at Lawrence, Kansas 18 Sept 1885; d at Ottawa 8 Sept 1981). From a family of famous American fossil collectors, Sternberg worked for some years in the western US before the family came to Canada to exploit the rich fossil fields of the Red Deer R valley in Alberta for the GEOLOGICAL SURVEY OF CANADA. Charles stayed in Canada and after 1919 progressively took over the scientific description of fossil vertebrates for the Geological Survey. But his field collecting continued, mainly in Alberta, but also in Saskatchewan, northeastern BC and NS. He published 47 papers on fossil vertebrates, mostly dinosaurs, many based on his own remarkable discoveries. He retired as assistant biologist, National Museum of Canada, in 1950. Later he helped set up DINOSAUR PROVINCIAL PARK in Alberta. He was elected a fellow of the Royal Soc of Canada in 1949 and was granted honorary degrees by U of Calgary and Carleton. L.S. RUSSELL

Reading: C.H. Sternberg, *Hunting Dinosaurs in the Bad Lands of the Red Deer River, Alberta, Canada* (1917).

Stettler, Alta, Town, pop 5147 (1986c), inc 1906, county seat for County of Stettler, is located on the rolling prairie of south-central Alberta 203 km SE of Edmonton on a creek flowing N to the Battle R. In an area first settled by homesteaders brought by Swiss-born Carl Stettler in 1903, the largely Swiss hamlet of Blumenau was established in 1905 but deserted that same fall for the new CPR townsite of Stettler. The new town flourished until WWI, but levelled off from then until after WWII. Stimulated by new petroleum and natural gas development, Stettler again grew steadily after WWII. It remains the chief service centre for a diversified regional economy featuring grain and livestock agriculture as well as oil and gas production. CARL BETKE

Steven, Donald Anstey, composer, professor (b at Montréal 26 May 1945). A composer whose influences include jazz, serialism and Asian music, Steven's music is a highly colouristic synthesis of these and other elements. Following a period of involvement in popular music, Steven entered McGill where his music instructors included Bruce Mather. He then continued his music studies at Princeton under Milton Babbitt. Returning to Canada in 1974, Steven began a career as a university instructor, first at the U of Western Ontario, and then at McGill. His works include *Illusions - An Elegy for Solo Cello* which makes use of serial structures, *Images - Refractions of Time and Space* which combines electronic and acoustic sounds, and *Breath of Many Flowers* which is strongly influenced by the music of the Far East.

COLIN EATOCK

Stevens, Dorothy, portrait and figure painter (b at Toronto 2 Sept 1888; d there 5 June 1966). Entering the Slade School of Art, London, at age 15, she studied under Wilson Steer and Henry Tonks. She subsequently studied in Paris and travelled on the continent before returning to Canada. Her early etchings were highly regarded; she was elected a member of the Chicago Soc of Etchers 1912 and awarded the silver medal for etching at the 1915 Panama Pacific Exposition at San Francisco. In later years she was highly regarded as a painter of oil and pastel portraits of women and children in Toronto, Mexico and the West Indies. She taught children's art classes for 15 years at the Women's Art Assn in Toronto and later served as that organization's president. Described as "loud, raucous, profane [and] amusing," with a "voice like Tallulah Bankhead," she is reputed to have thrown the best parties in the city. Unfortunately, her sensitive etchings and figure paintings have not yet benefited from the revival of interest in women Canadian painters. CHRISTOPHER VARLEY

Stevens, Henry Herbert, politician, businessman (b at Bristol, Eng 8 Dec 1878; d at Vancouver 14 June 1973). An MP for nearly 30 years, he was one of the most controversial figures in Canadian politics in the 1930s. First elected to Parliament in 1911 as the Conservative member for Vancouver City, he was a minister in the MEIGHEN governments (1921, 1926) and minister of trade and commerce (1930-34) in R.B. BENNETT's government (as member for E Kootenay). In 1934 he was made chairman of a royal commission on price spreads after an inquiry he had headed exposed serious abuses by big business. Stevens embarrassed Bennett by attacking large-business interests and calling for drastic reform, and later resigned from Cabinet and the commission chairmanship. Stevens formed the Reconstruction Party in 1935, hoping to protect the "little man" against economic abuse and the GREAT DEPRESSION. Though his party took nearly 10% of the popular vote in the 1935 election, Stevens was its only successful candidate. He returned to the Conservative caucus in 1939. After 3 election defeats and an unsuccessful bid to become the Tory leader in 1942, Stevens turned to full-time business interests in Vancouver. BILL CAMERON

Stevens, Sinclair McKnight, politician (b at Esquesing Twp, near Milton, Ont 11 Feb 1927). A graduate of Western and Osgoode Law School, Stevens was called to the Ontario Bar in 1955. He practised law and established his own business before being elected a Conservative MP in the 1972 election. He ran for the leadership of the PC Party in 1976, finishing seventh on the first ballot and throwing his support to the eventual winner, Joe CLARK. Stevens was a highly visible and somewhat controversial (in part because of his advocacy of big cuts in the public service) president of the Treasury Board in the Clark government 1979-80. A believer in free enterprise, a strong defence and closer ties with the US, he was a prominent supporter of Brian MULRONEY for the Conservative leadership in 1983. Stevens was appointed minister of regional industrial expansion and chairman of the committee on economic and regional development in the Mulroney government in 1984. Stevens resigned from Cabinet in 1986 over alleged conflict-of-interest violations, which were investigated by a commission of enquiry. In Dec 1987 the commission ruled that Stevens had violated conflict-of-interest guidelines on 14 occasions. NORMAN HILLMER

Stewart, BC, District Municipality, pop 858 (1986c), 1456 (1981c) located next to the Alaska Panhandle at the end of the Portland Canal on the BC coast. Lying at the foot of the Coast Mts, Stewart has been the access to a region rich in mineral resources. The town is named after 2 prospecting brothers John W. and Robert M. Stewart who settled there in 1902. Before long Stewart became a boom town with a population of 10 000. During WWI the population dropped to its all-time low of 17 people. After 1919 other rich gold and silver mines opened in the area and since then the town and the economy have expanded and contracted with the ups and downs of the various mineral markets. Stewart was revitalized with development of the large Granduc Copper mine in 1964 but had problems with a decline in world markets in the 1980s. The region is full of old mines and has a colourful history. JOHN R. STEWART

Stewart, Charles, farmer, politician, premier of Alberta 1917-21 (b at Strabane, Ont 26 Aug 1868; d at Ottawa 6 Dec 1946). Stewart brought his family to the Killam area of central Alberta in 1906. He represented Sedgewick in the Legislative Assembly 1909-21 and entered the Executive Council in 1912, holding first the municipal affairs and later the public works portfolios. On the resignation of Premier A.L. SIFTON, Stewart was sworn in as premier and minister of railways and telephones on 13 Oct 1917, but his effectiveness as government leader at the head of a party divided by railway scandals and the federal CONSCRIPTION crisis was constantly in question. The entry of the UNITED FARMERS OF ALBERTA into politics in the 1921 election ended the Liberal administration. Stewart accepted PM KING's invitation to enter the federal Cabinet and served as minister of the interior, minister of mines and superintendent general of Indian affairs 1921-30, except for a brief interlude in 1926. CARL BETKE

Stewart, Charles James, second Anglican bishop of Québec (b at London, Eng 13 Apr 1775; d there 13 July 1837). A man of independent means, a former fellow of All Souls, Oxford, closely related to men and women prominent in social and political life and in the British army and navy, Charles Stewart was an unusual recruit for pioneer missionary service in the diocese of Québec. But from 1807, when he came to Canada as a missionary under the Soc for the Propagation of the Gospel and began working in mission stations in the Eastern Townships, through his 7 years as travelling missionary in Lower and Upper Canada, and in his 11-year episcopate from 1826 to 1837, he created a record for unremitting toil and devotion to duty. He raised money for the building of 40 churches and was instrumental in the opening of 25 missions, in creating a body of lay catechists, in maintaining clergy stipends at a critical time, and in raising the level of education from Sunday school and elementary school to university. Though he was said to have been somewhat ungainly and at times lacking in political and business sense, his deep religious faith, asceticism, generosity of spirit and purse, and his genuine care for the spiritual interests of pioneer immigrants and native Indians earned the bachelor bishop the affection of his clergy and people, and a secure place among the builders of the church in Canada. T.R. MILLMAN

Stewart, Frances, née Browne, diarist, letter writer (b at Dublin, Ire 24 May 1794; d near Peterborough, Ont 24 Feb 1872). One of the first white settlers in Douro Township, Upper Canada, Stewart's lively letters and journals describe pioneer life and nearby friends – the Stricklands, Traills and Langtons – providing the earliest account of settlement around Peterborough. Frances was raised and educated by her cousin, author Harriet Beaufort. Married to Thomas Alexander Stewart, 17 Dec 1816, she immigrated with him and 3 infant daughters to unsurveyed bush in 1822, overcoming isolation and initial privations to become an established settler. For 50 years Frances wrote regularly to Irish relatives describing her experiences. A proposal by Maria Edgeworth to publish some of these letters was withdrawn, but after Frances's death her daughter, E.S. Dunlop, published a heavily edited collection entitled *Our Forest Home* (1889). A second edition was published in 1902. JOYCE C. LEWIS

Stewart, George Lawrence, business executive (b at Winnipeg 2 Dec 1890; d at Toronto 21 Mar 1985). Graduating in engineering from McGill in 1914, he served on McGill's engineering faculty for 2 years before joining Imperial Oil at its Sarnia, Ont, refinery as a draughtsman. Four months later he rejoined McGill for another year, then returned to Imperial. In 1918 he was in charge of constructing its refinery at Dartmouth, NS, and after working at Regina and Toronto, returned to Sarnia to become superintendent of the company's largest refinery in 1931. In 1934 he was appointed general manager of overall refining operations. Appointed a director of the company in 1944, he was chairman of the board 1947-49, president 1949-53 and again chairman 1953-55. EARLE GRAY

Stewart, Herbert Leslie, philosopher (b in County Antrim, Ire 31 Mar 1882; d at Halifax 19 Sept 1953). He arrived in Halifax to teach philosophy in 1913, having written his first book, *Questions of the Day in Philosophy and Psychology* (1912). In Canada his commitment shifted from realism to idealism. Realist causal explanations for WWI seemed insufficient, and Stewart looked to the history and continuity (or fragmentation) of ideas common to all people. In his later years he made national CBC broadcasts on public affairs, commenting on the evils of communism and supporting militarism and capital punishment in his campaign against the incursion of destructive ideas. His books on religion, *Modernism Past and Present* (1932) and *A Century of Anglo-Catholicism* (1929), rounded out his successful career. He founded the DALHOUSIE REVIEW in 1921 and served as editor for 26 years. ELIZABETH A. TROTT

Stewart, James David, lawyer, politician, premier of PEI (b at Lower Montague, PEI 15 Jan 1874; d at Charlottetown 10 Oct 1933). Stewart was premier of PEI 1923-27 and from 1931 until his death. The defeat of his Conservative government in 1927 resulted primarily from his promise to end PROHIBITION in the province. H.T. HOLMAN

Stewart, Nelson Robert, Nels, "Old Poison," hockey player (b at Montréal 29 Dec 1902; d at Toronto 21 Aug 1957). He was the first player to score 300 goals and his record of 324 goals held until broken by Maurice RICHARD. A big, rugged player with a deadly shot, he performed many of his scoring feats on a line with Hooley Smith and Babe Siebert. He played for Montreal Maroons (1925-32), Boston Bruins (1932-35), New York Americans (1935-36), the Bruins again in 1936-37 and New York again from 1937 to 1940. He won the HART TROPHY in 1926 and 1930 and still holds the record for the fastest 2 goals – 4 seconds. The story that he spat tobacco juice in the eyes of opposing goalies may be apocryphal but apparently is in keeping with his temperament on the ice. JAMES MARSH

Stewart, Robert Meldrum, astronomer (b at Gladstone, Man 15 Dec 1878; d at Ottawa 2 Sept 1954). Astronomer at the Dominion Observatory, Ottawa, 1902-24 and director 1924-46, Stewart supervised the scientifically complex installation of the Meridian Circle telescope at the observatory between 1907 and 1911, using it to improve the catalogue positions of stars used in the survey of western Canada. Subsequently, he added thousands of observations to improve the international star catalogue, established a time service within the government offices in Ottawa which ultimately became the source of correct time for Canada, used wireless time signals for longitude determination, approved Canada's participation in 2 world longitude campaigns (1926, 1933), using international wireless time signals, and devised an ingenious mechanical method for producing mean time from a sidereal primary standard. MALCOLM THOMSON

Stewart, Robert William, scientist (b at Smoky Lk, Alta 21 Aug 1923). Stewart is known internationally for original work in turbulence, oceanography and meteorology and is a recognized authority on exchange processes between ocean and atmosphere. He has held visiting professorships at universities in N America, the UK and at the Institute of Atmospheric Physics, USSR. Stewart was one of the first to recognize the importance of studying the oceans and atmosphere as a combined system. During his career, he has been a scientist with the Defence Research Board 1950-61; professor of physics and oceanography at UBC 1960-70; director general, Institute of Ocean Sciences, Sidney, BC, 1970-79; BC's deputy minister of universities, science and communications 1979-84; and was president of Alberta Research Council (1984-87). He then became founding director of the Centre for Earth and Ocean Research, affiliated with U Vic. He received the Patterson Medal of the Canadian Meteorological Soc and the Sverdrup Medal of the American Meteorological Soc. C.R. MANN

Stewart, Ron, football player (b at Toronto 25 Sept 1934). The diminutive running back starred for the OTTAWA ROUGH RIDERS for 13 seasons (1958-70). He recorded his best season in 1960, rushing for 1020 yards on 139 carries (including a CFL record 287 yards in one game) and scoring 15 touchdowns. He was awarded the Jeff Russell Memorial Trophy and was named the SCHENLEY most outstanding Canadian player that year. Stewart went on to lead the Eastern Football Conference in rushing in 1964, with 867 yards, and was again awarded the Russell Trophy in 1967. His career totals of 983 carries for 5690 yards and 42 touchdowns rushing and 25 more receiving earned Stewart induction into the Canadian Football Ball of Fame in 1977. PETER WONS

Stewart, Wilson Nichols, paleobotanist, educator (b at Madison, Wis 7 Dec 1917). An imaginative and creative scientist, Stewart strongly influenced the field of BOTANY during his tenure at U of Alberta. Following completion of a PhD at U of Wisconsin (1947), Stewart established a sound reputation at U of Illinois, Urbana, for work with Isoetales and their fossil relatives and with pteridosperms. He became a professor at U of A in 1966 and was chairman of its botany department until 1971. Following retirement in 1978, Stewart undertook the writing of a comprehensive and finely illustrated textbook, *Paleobotany and the Evolution of Plants* (1983), a lasting contribution. JAMES BASINGER

Stickleback (Gasterosteidae), family of fishes found in freshwater lakes, streams and along northern coastlines of the Northern Hemisphere. There are 5 genera and about 8 species worldwide; 4 genera and 5 species in Canada. Canadian sticklebacks are most common in the Maritimes but occur in all provinces and much of the NWT. Brook and nine-spine sticklebacks are common from the prairies to Québec. Three-spine stickle-backs, well known in Europe, occur along the Pacific and Atlantic coasts; some populations enter the ocean, while others live only in fresh water a short distance inland. The other 2 species are confined to the East Coast. Sticklebacks derive their common name from a row of spines along the back and their scientific name from a bony plate beneath the stomach area which supports 2 pelvic spines. In a few areas of their range (particularly in western Canada), some sticklebacks fail to develop pelvic spines. Three-spine sticklebacks show a wide diversity of forms. In some lakes and streams of BC different forms occur in the same or adjacent areas, which suggests that there is actually more than one species. Sticklebacks rarely exceed 8 cm in length and range in colour from green to black, with a silver underbelly. Most males of three-spine sticklebacks at mating time are distinguished by bright red underparts. Stickleback males are territorial when mating. They build nests of aquatic material in which females lay eggs. Males fertilize eggs, fan them and guard the nest. Despite their spines, which in some situations function to deter predators, sticklebacks can be important in the diet of other fish and birds. They feed on small crustaceans and insects. Well known as subjects of studies on behaviour, physiology and EVOLUTION, they can be used to test for WATER POLLUTION.   JOSEPH S. NELSON

Stikine River, 539 km long, rises in Spatsizi Wilderness Park in northwest BC, and flows in a wide arc N and W out of the Stikine Plateau uplands, then S through the spectacular COAST MTS Range to meet the Pacific Ocean near Wrangell, Alaska. It drains about 50 000 km², its largest tributary being the Iskut R. Separating the upper and lower sections of the river is the 90 km unnavigable Grand Canyon, where a precipitous narrow gorge has been cut through volcanic rock to a depth of 450 m. Stikine, meaning "the (great) river," is the name given by the powerful TLINGIT, who came upriver regularly to collect berries and catch and dry salmon in the arid climate E of the Coast Mts, and also to trade with the Tahltan of the upper Stikine watershed.

In 1824 Samuel Black of the HBC crossed the headwater drainage of the Stikine. In 1838 Robert Campbell was sent by the HBC to open communication with its posts and shipping on the coast from the Mackenzie R, and was led by Indian guides to their great trading rendezvous at the Stikine-Tahltan confluence. Shortly afterwards the HBC acquired the Russian Fort Dionysius (now Wrangell) near the mouth of the Stikine. The discovery of gold near present-day Telegraph Creek in 1861 led to a minor gold rush and the establishment of a river steamer service. For the next 100 years the Stikine was an important transportation route for penetration of the interior by non-Indians. Traffic reached its peak in 1898, when thousands used the Stikine to reach the Klondike goldfields. Along with Dease Lake and river, the Stikine was an important water highway for transporting materials used in the construction of the Watson Lake airport (1941-43) of the NORTHWEST STAGING ROUTE.

Since the advent of airplane and highway access to the North, the Stikine is no longer a major route. The people of Telegraph Creek, the only town on the river, who are mostly Tahltans, and the people of Wrangell rely heavily on the salmon that ascend up the Grand Canyon to the Tahltan R. Although development of minerals and timber resources around the river and a potential massive hydroelectric scheme in the canyon could at any time change the river drastically, it remains essentially a scenic wilderness waterway increasingly used for recreation.   ROSEMARY J. FOX

Stikine Territory Between 1839 and the 1867 American purchase of Alaska, the HUDSON'S BAY COMPANY leased the continental portion of the Alaska Panhandle from the Russian American Fur Co. In 1861 gold was found on the Stikine R in British territory contiguous to the leased area; the region was removed from HBC authority and organized as Stikine (or Stickeen) Territory on 19 July 1862. The boundaries were, on the west, Alaska; on the south, the colony of BRITISH COLUMBIA; on the east, 125° W long; and on the north, 62° N lat. BC's governor was territorial administrator, with the power to appoint officials; the BC Supreme Court was responsible for civil and criminal matters, and English law was in force. Thus, Britain ensured British authority in a region with a potential GOLD RUSH. Stikine Territory had a short existence: in July 1863 most of it was absorbed into an enlarged BC. *See also* TERRITORIAL EVOLUTION.   J.W. SHELEST

Stirling, David, architect (b at Galashiels, Scot 6 Dec 1822; d at Charlottetown 13 Apr 1887). Stirling immigrated to St John's in 1847 and worked on the rebuilding of the town after the fire of 1846. He established practices in Charlottetown and Halifax, designing and supervising the construction of all kinds of buildings in a career spanning 35 years. In 1872 Stirling was appointed Dominion architect for federal works in NS and in 1880 was made an associate architect of the Royal Canadian Academy of Arts. His buildings include the Pictou County Court House (1855), the Halifax Club, and, with W.C. HARRIS in 1877, Hensley Chapel, King's College, Windsor, NS, and the Kirk of St James, Charlottetown.
                GRANT WANZEL AND KAREN KALLWEIT

Stock and Bond Markets are created by associations of brokers and dealers to trade company shares. Shares represent ownership of companies and their prices depend largely on the companies' expected profits. They represent only the right, under certain conditions, to receive payments in the future. Ultimately, no security is worth more than it will fetch in the marketplace. Companies can issue new shares to raise funds. Firms of investment dealers underwrite these new issues, buying them from the companies directly and re-selling them to the public through sales offices across the country and abroad. Although issues are usually marketed through groups of dealers, occasionally a single dealer may place an entire issue.

After shares are issued they may be listed on various stock exchanges and bought or sold through brokerage firms. Shares may be listed on a stock exchange if the companies have the size, stability and financial strength and are willing to report publicly on their operations. Not all shares are listed on stock exchanges; some are traded in the over-the-counter (OTC) market, which is a securities market made up of dealers who may or may not be members of a stock exchange, and the types of securities traded are ones not listed on any recognized stock exchange, as well as bonds and debentures. The OTC market is also called the "unlisted market," the "street market" or the "between-dealer market."

While shares represent ownership, bonds represent only a borrower's promise to make certain payments of interest and repayment of principal. Companies and governments are major issuers of bonds. Probably the best-known bonds in Canada are CANADA SAVINGS BONDS, issued by the federal government; they can be redeemed for their face value at any time. Most other bonds fluctuate daily in price because each one entitles its owner to receive a specific series of interest payments – a rise in interest rates is equivalent to a fall in bond prices, as the given series of payments will represent a higher rate of interest only if the cost of purchasing the bonds falls. Bond holders may be protected if the issuer mortgages specific assets against bankruptcy or other default. Shares and bonds are underwritten by investment dealers and can be bought and sold through brokerage firms. Government of Canada bonds can also be purchased through banks or other financial institutions and, in the case of savings bonds, through popular employer payroll-deduction plans.

Shares are either "preferred" or "common." When a company cannot pay regular dividends on all its shares, holders of preferred shares are ranked ahead of those holding common shares in receiving whatever dividends are available (these provisions may be overridden in the case of bankruptcy).

Shares may or may not carry the right to vote at shareholders' meetings and to elect the company's board of directors. An investor wanting to buy or sell bonds or shares contacts a brokerage firm and opens an account. The sales representative ("broker") of a firm advises on the relative merits of available investments and might permit an investor (with sufficient collateral) to buy or sell "on margin" – eg, the firm would lend the investor a considerable percentage of the funds required (against the investor's collateral security in case the price went to his disadvantage), charging interest on the borrowed funds. If they expect the price to drop quickly, investors can even "sell short" bonds or shares they do not own, so that they can buy them back cheaply and make a speculative profit. In such cases the firm would borrow the shares and sell them for the investor's account.

Brokers can provide a wide range of specialized services, such as the "stop order," an order to buy or sell shares only if the price touches a certain level. Investors can place a "stop sell" order at a price slightly below the current price so that if prices decline the shares would automatically be sold out at a small loss. Brokers can also sell "options," which give the right to buy or sell certain shares at preset prices at any time up to a pre-specified future date, but the value of these options can fluctuate dramatically, creating a risk for the investor.

The Board of Stock and Produce Brokers was set up in Montréal in 1842 and the Montreal Stock Exchange (MSE) in 1874. The MSE listed 63 securities, including stock in banks, gas utilities, railways and mining companies and government debentures. The Toronto Stock Exchange (TSE) was established in 1852 by a group of Toronto businessmen who formed an association of brokers to create a market in industrial securities. At first they met informally in each other's offices but by 1871 they had a common meeting place and formal rules and regulations.

Expansive mining activity led to the establishment of the Standard Stock and Mining Exchange (SSME) in 1899. After the discovery of important silver and gold deposits in northern Ontario in the first decade of the 20th century, transactions on the SSME expanded dramatically and in 1934 the TSE merged with the SSME, keeping the name Toronto Stock Exchange. The Montreal Curb Market, which started on the curb outside the MSE as a place to trade shares in ventures too small or risky to meet listing requirements of the latter exchange, became the Canadian Stock Exchange but then joined the MSE in a merger in 1974. Canada's 3 western stock exchanges are in Vancouver, Winnipeg and Calgary. They have provided local trading facilities primarily for shares in small, new ventures. By 1986 the dollar value of shares traded on the Toronto, Montréal, Vancouver, Alberta and Winnipeg stock exchanges was $84.6 billion, of which 75.3% was

New Toronto Stock Exchange, Toronto (*photo by John deVisser/Masterfile*).

transacted on the TSE. The quoted market value of all Canadian-based firms' shares listed on the TSE at the end of 1986 was $255.7 billion. Share values typically fluctuate considerably through time. The year 1987 was particularly turbulent, with the TSE 300 index high at 4118.9 and low at 2783.3; one of the most dramatic declines occurred on "Black Monday," 19 Oct 1987.

Although the exchanges are regulated by provincial securities commissions, they are essentially self-regulating. The public's risk is minimized because brokers and dealers must be adequately capitalized against default. Public issues of new corporate bonds or shares must be cleared for distribution by the securities commissions of the provinces in which they are offered, and printed prospectuses outlining and updating important facts on the new securities must be provided to potential buyers. Because public information about the economy or companies' prospects is quickly reflected in the prices of the securities, it is difficult even for professional investors (such as managers of pension funds) to earn consistently higher rates of return than those provided by the market as a whole. However, because "insiders" with privileged information about company affairs have been able to trade profitably on such information, the law requires public disclosure of, or may even outlaw, their trading. There have been many instances of promotional fraud and manipulation of the prices of shares, but such abuses are now illegal and severely penalized. No security is worth more than it will fetch in the marketplace. Security prices are ultimately dependent on expectations, since they represent only the right, under certain conditions, to receive payments in the future. Securities markets uniquely blend risk, uncertainty, potential profit and potential loss; by doing so, they provide a cornerstone of the modern capitalist economy.   JOHN GRANT

Stoicheff, Boris Peter, physics professor (b at Bitola, Yugoslavia 1 June 1924). A specialist in SPECTROSCOPY, LASER physics and nonlinear optics, he is known for his innovative use of lasers. After receiving a PhD from U of T in 1950 he joined the National Research Council of Canada in 1951. In 1964 he joined the physics department at U of T and was chairman of engineering science 1972-77. He was president of the Optical Society of America in 1976, a member of the council of the NRC 1977-80 and 1981-83, and president of the Canadian Association of Physicists 1983-84. Fellow of the Royal Society of Canada, honorary fellow of the Indian Academy of Sciences and fellow of the Royal Society, London, he has received the Ives Medal of the Optical Society of America, the Gold Medal of the Canadian Association of Physicists and the Order of Canada. His 150 articles in scientific journals discuss light, spectroscopy, molecular structures and lasers in relation to physics.   J. KNELMAN

Stone Angel, The, by Margaret LAURENCE (Toronto, London and New York, 1964), is the first of Laurence's "Manawaka" novels. Hagar Shipley relives her life by narrating memories as she battles to come to terms with herself before she dies. Hagar at 90 is a proud, powerful, tyrannical woman suffering the indignities of old age. *The Stone Angel* is shaped by the alternating rhythms of Hagar's voice, searching through her past and returning to her present condition; her widely ranging tones reveal the labyrinths of her pride. Hagar's character and voice are justly praised as Laurence's most inspired creations. As she tells her story, Hagar also looks back to Manawaka (a fictionalized small town that Laurence has placed in Manitoba), recalling and recreating the effects of the town's constricting mores and her own family's position in the rigid hierarchy of Manawaka's deeply puritan society. Many readers find Hagar to be a rich fictional composite of actual women's lives in small towns on the Prairies. *The Stone Angel* has been translated into French, as *L'Ange de pierre* (Montréal, 1976), and into German.   NEIL BESNER

Stonefly, common name for small to medium-sized, usually brown, aquatic insects of order Plecoptera [Gk, "folded wings"]. About 2000 species are known worldwide, almost 300 in Canada. Because the aquatic larvae normally cannot live in warm or polluted water, stoneflies are more common in mountainous areas of Canada. Eggs are deposited in cool, clean, running water. The larval stage lasts 1-3 years, depending on species. Larvae are generally elongate, with a pair of long antennae at the front of the body, and a pair of thin appendages (cerci) at the rear. Most feed on plant material; others are predators, feeding on MAYFLY or midge larvae. Larvae crawl out of the water before transformation to the adult stage. Although most adults have wings, they tend to walk rather than fly. Some do not feed as adults; others feed on algae and lichens and may live 3-4 weeks. Before mating, adults often communicate by drumming with the end of their abdomen.   G. PRITCHARD

Stonewall, Man, Town, inc 1908, pop 2349 (1986c), is located 24 km NW of Winnipeg on a limestone outcrop in the southern Interlake. The townsite was established by S.J. Stonewall Jackson who acquired the land in 1875. Jackson, a provincial MLA and Winnipeg alderman, named the town and supported several of its early industries. Limestone quarries became the town's greatest asset after the railway reached Stonewall in 1880. Quarrying activity peaked early in the century when 150 people were employed, first in the production of construction stone, then lime. The abandoned quarries have now been converted into a recreation centre and an important historic park. The town, containing some impressive buildings reflecting its early prosperity, is now a service and retirement centre for the local farming community, and a dormitory town for Winnipeg.   JOHN SELWOOD

Stoney (stone) or *îyârhe Nakodabi*, "Rocky Mountain Sioux," are culturally and linguistically allied to the Plains ASSINIBOINE, but in Saskatchewan and Montana are characterized by differences in language and culture. They speak the N dialect of the Dakota language. Stoney oral tradition asserts that their forefathers resided along the Rocky Mt foothills from time immemorial. The first recorded story (cited in the JESUIT RELATIONS) was that the Stoney-Assiniboine separated from the Sioux nation sometime before 1640 and then migrated westward with the CREE as the FUR TRADE moved W along the Saskatchewan R trade routes. HUDSON'S BAY COMPANY trader Anthony HENDAY

met Stoney-Assiniboine camps on his journey to Alberta in 1754; Father de Smet reported in 1840 that the Rocky Mt Stoney separated from the Plains Assiniboine about 1790, though he might have been referring to groups such as the Bearspaw band who have by oral accounts had a tradition of fleeing westward to escape devastating smallpox epidemics.

The Stoney bands, commonly composed of extended families, lived along Alberta's Rocky Mt foothills from the headwaters of the Athabasca R south to Chief Mt in Montana. These forest and foothill people hunted bison and other big game animals. With the establishment of Edmonton House (1795) and ROCKY MOUNTAIN HOUSE (1799), they traded furs, hides and fresh meat, and were invaluable guides to traders, explorers (Lord Southesk, John PALLISER, James HECTOR), surveyors (CANADIAN PACIFIC RAILWAY; GEOLOGICAL SURVEY OF CANADA) and missionaries. They were introduced to Christianity by Methodist missionaries after 1840. The Stoney, led by Chiefs Jacob Bearspaw, John Chiniki (also Chiniquay) and Jacob Goodstoney, signed Treaty No 7 at Blackfoot Crossing in Sept 1877. The original reserve of 109 square miles was surveyed at Morleyville mission in 1879. The Bearspaw and Wesley bands later claimed additional reserve land to the south and north. After years of petitions and negotiations, both the Bighorn reserve (west of Nordegg) and the Eden Valley reserve (west of Longview) were established in 1948. Stoney people also live on the Alexis and Paul reserves west of Edmonton, which were set aside under the provisions of Treaty No 6 (1876).

The economic base of the Stoney includes trapping, big-game hunting, guiding, ranching, lumbering, handicrafts, labouring and various professions. The bands at Morley enjoy a high standard of living based on natural gas royalties and operate several commercial enterprises (such as stores, restaurants, service stations and tourist facilities). Their social life centres on family and cultural activities – the POWWOWS, TREATY DAYS, RODEO, stampede and camp meeting. Band members live at Morley, Bighorn, Eden Valley, at Alexis reserve and Paul band; in 1986 there were 2643 Stoney.   IAN A.L. GETTY

Reading: H.A. Dempsey, *Indian Tribes of Alberta* (1978); J.G. MacEwan, *Tatanga Mani-Walking Buffalo of the Stonies* (1969); Chief John Snow, *These Mountains are our Sacred Places* (1977).

Stoney Creek, Ont, City, pop 43 554 (1986c), inc 1974, is situated in the Niagara Peninsula immediately E of Hamilton; it was formed from the towns of Stoney Creek and Saltfleet. The first European settlers, primarily Loyalists, arrived from the US in 1786. The area was cleared for mixed farming and Stoney Creek attracted many grain and sawmills and other agricultural service activities. After the 1880s the area between Lake Ontario and the Niagara Escarpment became a tender-fruit and grape growing area, attracting packing and canning plants and a winery. Good communications with Hamilton, first by inter-urban railway and then by road, have resulted in extensive residential, commercial and industrial development; the western part of the city is now physically linked to Hamilton. A park incorporates the site of the Battle of STONEY CREEK in the War of 1812 and the now worldwide Women's Institutes originated here in 1897.   H.J. GAYLER

Stoney Creek, Battle of During the night of 5-6 June 1813, Lt-Col John Harvey led 700 British regulars and Canadian militia in a surprise attack on 3500 invading American troops encamped near Stoney Creek, UC. After a confused and bloody battle with high losses on both sides, each army feared that it had suffered a setback. In fact, the Americans, having had their 2 brigadier-generals taken prisoner, withdrew to Fort George on the Niagara R. Along with the battle at BEAVER DAMS 2 weeks later, the engagement at Stoney Creek returned the Niagara Peninsula to British and Canadian control and ended the US attempt to conquer the western part of the province.

CARL A. CHRISTIE

Stony Plain, Alta, Town, pop 5802 (1986c), located about 25 km W of Edmonton, incorporated as a village in 1907 and as a town in 1908. Settlement began in 1881 about 3 km S of the present town. This settlement was called Dogrump Creek but in 1892 was renamed Stony Plain. In 1891 German-Russian settlers arrived and settled several km N of the present town. In 1905 the Canadian Northern Ry passed N of the original settlement and Stony Plain's few buildings were moved N to meet the rail line. The area's economy was based on mixed farming. Population numbers have shown great variation (eg, from 1000 in 1908 to 489 in 1930). Postwar economic development in Alberta has contributed to Stony Plain's growth. It remains a service centre but more importantly its location allows residents to commute to work in nearby Edmonton.

D.G. WETHERELL

Storey, Frederick Lewis, curler (b at Empress, Alta 3 Mar 1932). He won Canadian and world curling championships in 1966, 1968 and 1969, playing lead for Ron NORTHCOTT, and was selected all-star lead at several briers. He participated in 10 Alberta provincial curling championships and 7 Canadian curling championships (briers). He has won numerous provincial and national titles, including the Canadian curling championship Edmonton Carspiel in 1965, Evergreen Tournament of Champions (Vancouver) in 1971 and 1973, Edmonton Tournament of Champions in 1961, CBC Cross Canada in 1964 and Ontario Invitational in 1968.

PAULINE McGREGOR

Storm-petrel (order Procellariiformes, family Hydrobatidae), small SEABIRD (14-25 cm long) related to albatrosses and like them having nostrils encased in a tube. Storm-petrels are usually blackish with a white rump. The name petrel derives from the habit of fluttering low over the waves and seeming to "walk on water," like St Peter. Superstitious seamen, believing they warned of coming storms, called them Mother Carey's chickens, the birds which Mater Cara (Virgin Mary) sent to protect them. Petrels nest in burrows on offshore islands, visiting these only at night. Introduced cats and rats have caused havoc in many colonies. The fork-tailed storm-petrel (*Oceanodroma furcata*) and Leach's storm-petrel (*O. leucorhoa*) breed in BC. Leach's also breeds in Atlantic Canada; its huge colonies in SE Newfoundland contain most of the N Atlantic population. Large numbers of Wilson's storm-petrel (*Oceanites oceanicus*) from Antarctica and Tierra del Fuego occur off NS in summer.

R.G.B. BROWN

Stornoway, located at 541 Acadia Ave in the Village of Rockcliffe Park, near Ottawa, is the official residence of the LEADER OF THE OPPOSITION. A simple and commodious 2-storey, stucco-sheathed house located in spacious grounds, it was one of the earliest permanent buildings in this prestigious neighbourhood. Designed by local architect Allan Keefer, who was responsible for many luxurious homes in Rockcliffe Park, it was built in 1913-14 for a prosperous Ottawa merchant, Ascanio J. Major. During WWII it was the residence of Crown Princess Juliana of the Netherlands and her family. Purchased in 1950 by a private trust, Stornoway has been owned by the Government of Canada since 1970. It has served as the residence of every leader of the Opposition since George Drew.

ROBERT HUNTER

Stowe, Emily Howard, née Jennings, physician (b at Norwich, UC 1 May 1831; d at Toronto 30 Apr 1903). A lifelong champion of women's rights, Emily Stowe taught school in Brantford and Mount Pleasant, Canada W, and in 1856 married John Stowe, whose illness from tuberculosis inspired her to seek a career in medicine. No Canadian college would accept a woman student, so she enrolled at the New York Medical College for Women and on her graduation in 1867 set up a practice in Toronto. She was the first Canadian woman to practise medicine in Canada, although she was not licensed until 1880. Emily Stowe's struggle to enter the medical profession caused her to organize the Woman's Medical College, Toronto, in 1883. In 1876 she had founded the Toronto Women's Literary Club, Canada's first suffrage group, and she was principal founder and first president of the Dominion Women's Enfranchisement Assn (1889).

CARLOTTA HACKER

Reading: Carlotta Hacker, *The Indomitable Lady Doctors* (1974).

Emily Stowe was the first Canadian woman to practise medicine in Canada (*courtesy National Archives of Canada/C-9480*).

Stowe-Gullen, Ann Augusta, née Stowe, physician (b at Mount Pleasant, Canada W 27 July 1857; d at Toronto 25 Sept 1943), daughter of Emily STOWE. She was the first woman to gain a medical degree in Canada, graduating from Victoria Coll, Cobourg, Ont, in 1883, having studied at Toronto School of Medicine. On graduation she married Dr John B. Gullen, who was a founder in 1896 of Toronto Western Hospital, with which she was associated for many years. Meanwhile, she taught at the Ontario Medical Coll for Women (known 1883-94 as the Woman's Medical Coll, Toronto) and was on U of T Senate 1910-22. A leading figure in the suffrage movement, she succeeded her mother as president of the Dominion Women's Enfranchisement Assn in 1903.

CARLOTTA HACKER

Reading: Carlotta Hacker, *The Indomitable Lady Doctors* (1974).

Strachan, John, Anglican bishop, educator (b at Aberdeen, Scot 12 Apr 1778; d at Toronto 1 Nov 1867). One of 6 children of a quarryman, Strachan was sent to grammar school to fulfil his mother's hope that one son would become a minister, but his father's early accidental death forced him into teaching. He studied divinity part-time at St Andrews U and in 1799 came to Kingston,

The patriarchal Bishop John Strachan, who was convinced that it was his destiny to keep Upper Canada British and free of American "democratic" influences (*courtesy National Archives of Canada/C-7432*).

UC, to tutor the children of Loyalist Richard Cartwright. Strachan was ordained by Bishop Jacob MOUNTAIN in 1803 and became a government-paid missionary in Cornwall, UC. There he opened a school and in 1807 married Ann Wood, widow of fur trader Andrew McGill. In 1812 Strachan accepted the rectorship of York [Toronto] after Sir Isaac BROCK added to it the garrison and legislative council chaplaincies.

For Strachan the WAR OF 1812 proved another turning point. When the Americans occupied York in Apr 1813, he assumed leadership of the town to protect lives and property. Convinced that his destiny was to keep Upper Canada British, he tried after the war to exclude democratic and American influences. Many former pupils now had senior posts in government, and Strachan himself was made executive councillor in 1817 and legislative councillor in 1820. To promote loyalty he began a school system, capped with the charter of King's College (U of T) in 1827. He sought special status for the Church of England and became the centre of politico-religious controversy as he defended Anglican monopoly of the CLERGY RESERVES and Anglican dominance in politics and education. Strachan was removed from the Executive Council in 1835 by Lt-Gov Sir John COLBORNE, and his political decline was completed when the 1841 union of Upper Canada and Lower Canada destroyed the conservative FAMILY COMPACT that had dominated Upper Canada for a quarter century.

Strachan's religious influence, however, was rising. In 1839 he became bishop of Toronto, ruling the Anglican Church in Upper Canada. The Reformers secularized King's College in 1849 and the Clergy Reserves in 1854, but Strachan responded by opening Trinity College (Anglican) in 1852 and by including laymen in church government as early as 1851. In 1857 he formed a self-governing synod of clergy and laity and began dividing his large diocese by holding synodic elections for new bishops. Strachan proposed a convention of all Anglican bishops, which took shape as the Lambeth Conference in 1867, but he was too frail to attend.

JOHN S. MOIR

Strait of Anian, part of the legendary NORTH-WEST PASSAGE linking the Atlantic and Pacific oceans, likely Bering Strait. The name probably originated with Ania, a Chinese province mentioned in a 1559 edition of Marco Polo's book; it first appears on a map issued by Italian cartographer Giacomo Gastaldi about 1562. Five years later Bolognini Zaltieri issued a map showing a narrow and crooked Strait of Anian separating Asia from America. The strait grew in European imagination as an easy sea-lane linking Europe with the residence of the Great Khan in Cathay (northern China).

Voyages by John CABOT, CORTE-REAL, Jacques CARTIER and Sir Humphrey GILBERT were motivated by its supposed existence, and cartographers and seamen tried to demonstrate its reality. Sir Francis DRAKE sought the western entrance in 1579. The Greek pilot Juan de FUCA claimed he had sailed the strait from the Pacific to the North Sea and back in 1592. The Spaniard Bartholomew de Fonte (who, some scholars have stated, was fictitious) claimed to have sailed from Hudson Bay to the Pacific via the strait in 1640. James COOK dispelled rumours of its existence in 1778 during his third Pacific voyage. The myth was finally destroyed by George VANCOUVER 1792-94, and by Alexander MACKENZIE in his journeys to the Arctic and Pacific oceans in 1789 and 1793, respectively.   BARRY M. GOUGH

Strange, Thomas Bland, army officer (b at Meerut, India 15 Sept 1831; d at Camberley, Eng 9 July 1925). After active service with the artillery in India, including service during the Indian Mutiny (1857), Strange became inspector of artillery and warlike stores in the Canadian Militia, where he laid the essential groundwork for the development of the Canadian artillery and commanded one of its founding permanent units, 1871-82. Too eccentric and controversial for more senior command, he retired to ranch in Alberta, but on the outbreak of the NORTH-WEST REBELLION, he commanded the improvised Alberta Field Force and led it in action at Frenchman's Butte. He published his lively memoirs, *Gunner Jingo's Jubilee,* in 1894.   ROGER SARTY

Stratas, Teresa, née Anastasia Stratakis, soprano (b at Toronto 26 May 1938). Daughter of Greek immigrant restaurateurs, Stratas began as a singer of Greek pop songs and had ambitions of becoming a nightclub singer. She made her operatic debut as Mimi in *La Bohème* at the Toronto Opera Festival (1958) and was co-winner of the Metropolitan Opera auditions in Mar 1959. Since her debut at the Met in 1959 Stratas has sung more than 25 roles there. She appeared at Vancouver's International Festival in 1960 and sang Desdemona in *Otello* at EXPO 67. She has sung at La Scala, the Bolshoi Opera, Vienna State Opera, Covent Garden, the Deutsche Oper Berlin, Bavarian State Opera, San Francisco Opera and the Salzburg Festival. At the Paris Opera, May 1979, she sang the title role in the first performance of the complete version of Alban Berg's *Lulu.* Stratas has appeared in Norman CAMPBELL'S CBC television production of *La Rondine* (1972) and in numerous opera films, including Franco Zeffirelli's *La Traviata* (1983) and in a NY musical, *Rags* (1986), for which she received a nomination for a Tony Award for best actress in a musical. Her recordings include Berg's *Lulu,* Mozart's *Così fan tutte,* Verdi's *Otello* and the widely acclaimed *The Unknown Kurt Weill.* Her performances combine a strong stage personality with an instinctive sense of drama and, despite an earthy sense of comedy, her interpretations are profoundly emotional and rich in subtlety and intelligence. She was named artist of the year by the Canadian Music Council in 1980.   MABEL H. LAINE

Strate, Grant, dancer, choreographer, educator (b at Cardston, Alta 7 Dec 1927). A graduate of U of A, Strate was a charter member of the NATIONAL BALLET OF CANADA as dancer in 1951 and was resident choreographer 1964-70. Among his more than 50 ballets for many companies are *Ballad*

and *The House of Atreus* (music by Harry SOMERS), *Bird Life* and *Cyclus.* Strate has continued to foster artistic experimentation and the development of DANCE EDUCATION as founder of York's dance dept (1970) and of Dance in Canada Assn (1973), organizer of National Choreographic Seminars (1978, 1980) and director, Centre for the Arts, Simon Fraser (since 1980).   PENELOPE DOOB

Stratford, Ont, City, pop 26 451 (1986c), 26 262 (1981c), inc 1886, the highest city in Ontario (elev 364 m), is located 143 km W of Toronto and 52 km NE of London. Settlement began in the 1830s after the townsite, beside the Avon R, had been selected and named by the CANADA CO as a focal point for peopling the million-acre Huron Tract. The ethnic mix of immigrants to the Stratford area was about 40% Irish, 30% German, 20% Scottish and 10% English. The blend has changed little, except for Dutch and German immigration since 1945. Urban growth was slow until the railway-building boom of the 1850s. Stratford businessmen lobbied for the forming in 1853 of the County of Perth, with Stratford as the county seat, and the county at once voted bonuses to railway companies. Stratford became the intersection point of 3 railways, which successively became bankrupt and were merged with the CNR. For 80 years railways were the principal employer in divisional offices and motive-power shops for repair of steam engines. When diesels replaced steam and Stratford ceased to be a divisional point in the 1950s, the city lost 2000 jobs, which have since been replaced by diversified industry. Thirty-two manufacturing firms employ 25 or more people each; 11 employ 100 or more. Civic policy has kept industry on the perimeter and prevented encroachment on the 70 ha park in the city's middle, adjacent to the commercial core. World-class theatre is provided by the STRATFORD FESTIVAL, founded in 1953.

STAFFORD JOHNSTON

Stratford Festival (fd 1953). In 1951 Stratford businessman Tom Patterson formed a local committee to explore the prospects for an annual drama festival. The following year Tyrone GUTHRIE, a leading British director, agreed to be artistic director and to present a Shakespeare festival in a tent theatre. The festival opened in July 1953 for a 6-week season, and presented *Richard III,* with Alec Guinness playing the lead, and *All's Well That Ends Well.* The 1954 season ran for 9 weeks and contained a non-Shakespearean play, *Oedipus Rex.*

Musical programs, including jazz and pop concerts, symphony concerts, opera, comic opera and solo performances, were introduced in 1955, and in 1957 the tent theatre was replaced by the Festival Theatre, designed by Canadian architect Robert Fairfield, at a cost of over $2 million. Guthrie was succeeded by Michael LANGHAM (1956-67 seasons), followed by Jean GASCON (1968-74), Robin PHILLIPS (1975-80), John HIRSCH (1981-85) and John NEVILLE (1985-89). In 35 years, the Stratford Festival has developed such actors as William HUTT, Tony Van Bridge,

Stratford Festival Theatre. The main theatre was revolutionary for its time, seating over 2000 on 3 sides of the stage (*courtesy Stratford Festival*).

Douglas Campbell, Richard Monette, Martha HENRY, Frances Hyland, Douglas Raine, Kate REID, John COLICOS and Christopher PLUMMER, and has made a great contribution to the training of Canadian actors, designers, technicians and directors (*see* STAGE AND COSTUME DESIGN).

The stage of the main theatre, designed by Tanya Moiseiwitsch with Guthrie, was revolutionary for its time. Guthrie wanted a return to the open stage of the Elizabethans, but not an antiquarian copy. The amphitheatre is steeply sloped, with a 220-degree sweep around the stage. Although the auditorium seats 2262, on 3 sides of the stage, no spectator is more than 19.8 m from the stage. The festival later acquired 2 more stages. The Avon Theatre (seating 1102) in downtown Stratford was purchased in 1963 and redesigned by Moiseiwitsch. It has a conventional proscenium stage. Since 1971 the festival has also presented drama and music at the Third Stage, a small, modestly equipped theatre suited for workshops, experimental work and the training of young actors.

The Stratford Festival is an internationally acclaimed drama festival. It offers a program of classical and modern plays, and musical productions. Including school previews, the season ran for 6 months and included 500 performances in 1988. The festival has a permanent administration and requires an acting corps of around 100. Though the festival is supported by the CANADA COUNCIL and the Ontario provincial government, most income is generated from box-office receipts and private contributions. The theatre possesses a major archive, which maintains records of all productions. Foreign tours to the US, Australia and Europe have consolidated its reputation as the leading classical theatre in N America. *See also* THEATRE, ENGLISH-LANGUAGE.   RALPH BERRY

Reading: R. Davies et al, *Renown at Stratford* (1953), *Twice Have the Trumpets Sounded* (1954) and *Thrice the Brinded Cat Hath Mew'd* (1955); P. Raby, *The Stratford Scene* (1968) and *Stratford Festival Story 1953-1982* (1982); T. Patterson, *First Stage: The Making of the Stratford Festival* (1987); G. Shaw, *Stratford under Cover* (1977); R. Stuart, "The Stratford Festival and Canadian Theatre," in L.W. Conolly, ed, *Theatrical Touring and Founding in North America* (1982).

Strathcona Provincial Park, est 1911, includes some 2310 km² of mountain wilderness in central VANCOUVER ISLAND, 9 km E of Gold R and 26 km W of CAMPBELL RIVER. The park includes numerous peaks, valleys and lakes; elevations range from sea level at Herbert Inlet to 2200 m at GOLDEN HINDE, the island's highest peak. Small GLACIERS, remnants of an ice sheet that sculptured the area thousands of years ago, cling to a few peaks in the S. Small, swift streams and waterfalls in the centre of the park drain into Buttle Lk. Vegetation and wildlife distribution reflect the marked variations in altitude, aspect and climate. Vegetation at lower elevations is dominated by western red cedar, various firs and western hemlock; subalpine fir, mountain hemlock and creeping juniper are found higher up. Between the TREELINE and the glaciers are extensive alpine meadows offering spectacular displays of WILDFLOWERS (eg, paintbrush) in the short summer. The island's isolation has limited the area's fauna, but wildlife includes deer (common), Roosevelt elk, wolves and cougars. Birdlife includes kinglets, gray jays, grouse and white-tailed ptarmigan. Trout are common in such areas as Buttle Lk. The area was explored in the mid-1800s. When designated BC's first provincial park in 1911, it was named after Donald SMITH, 1st Baron Strathcona and Mount Royal. Logging, mining and reservoir development have influenced the park and aroused debate and opposition by CONSERVATION groups. The Forbidden Plateau, on the park's E side, was added to the park later. Recently, 3 roadless tracts, comprising 122 500 ha, have been designated Nature Conservancy Areas to protect the environment. Facilities include campgrounds, backpacking and cross-country skiing trails, and downhill ski resorts. Strathcona Park Lodge, on Campbell Lk, is a popular centre for wilderness courses and outdoor education. JOHN S. MARSH

Strawberry, *see* BERRIES, CULTIVATED; BERRIES, WILD.

Street Railways (also known as streetcars or trams) began operation in Canada during the era of horse-powered local TRANSPORTATION, expanded rapidly with electrification, shrank with a public policy switch in favour of rubber-tired vehicles, and recently re-emerged as light rail transit. With a simple, robust technology, street railways have had a profound impact on our society, not only as a transportation mode but also in the development of the electric-power industry and on the shaping of our cities.

Technology The low rolling resistance of steel wheels on steel rails, plus the simple guidance mechanism offered by flanges, has made railbound transport attractive for a variety of applications. Montréal and Toronto were the first cities with horse-drawn tramcars in Canada, using systems incorporated in 1861 by Alexander Easton of Philadelphia. In spite of the need to substitute sleighs for the cars in winter, both operations did well. Toronto had 109 km of track, 361 trams and 100 sleighs at its peak. The Montréal network extended over 40 km, using 150 trams, 104 sleighs and 49 horse omnibuses. Other cities to establish such services included Hamilton, Winnipeg, Halifax and Saint John.

Railway lines between cities developed rapidly, moving to steam power and long trains. As cities grew, so did urban railways, which were characterized by smaller vehicles more appropriate for mingling with pedestrians and other street traffic. Steam and later cable traction systems were applied in some US cities but never caught on in Canada. The major breakthrough came with electric power in the 1880s, and here Canada was a leader. In 1884 the Toronto Industrial Exhibition (now CANADIAN NATIONAL EXHIBITION) offered railway service at the initiative of a local citizen, J.J. Wright. In 1885 this service was converted to trolley-pole operation, using the technique of Belgian inventor Charles J. Van Depoele. As the technology matured, the typical system had tracks mounted flush with the pavement, current collection by trolley, and overhead wire supported by poles, often also used for lighting. Costs for both installation and operation were low, and streetcar services spread rapidly. Windsor, Ont, installed the first Canadian electric tram system in 1886. Vancouver followed in 1890, Winnipeg in 1891, Montréal, Hamilton and Toronto in 1892, Edmonton in 1908, Calgary in 1909 and Regina

Yonge Street north from King, 1910. With a simple, robust technology, street railways have had a profound effect on urban society. The first electric tram system in Canada was installed at Windsor, Ont, in 1886 (*courtesy Toronto Transit Commission*).

in 1911. By WWI, 48 Canadian cities and towns boasted streetcar systems.

The first intercity application of electric street railway technology was at St Catharines in 1887, with a line to Thorold, Ont, followed by construction of a 13-mile (20 km) interurban system between New Westminster and Vancouver in 1891. Some of these interurban lines were later overtaken by urban expansion and became part of city streetcar lines (eg, the Long Branch line in Toronto); others provided a right-of-way for eventual rapid transit construction (eg, Vancouver to New Westminster). In the 1930s the street railway industry responded to increased competition from automotive transport by developing lightweight, high-performance cars, best typified by the (US) Street Railway Presidents' Conference Car. Licensed for manufacture in Canada, these popular, comfortable machines were used in Vancouver, Montréal and Toronto. Toronto still uses them, but in other cities they gave way to the motorbus and trolleybus, which can operate on roads built at public expense, rather than requiring track provided by the transit system itself.

Technological changes came into play again during the 1970s and 1980s, with the use of trains of modern articulated cars (having several body sectors joined together by flexible joints) to provide transit service that has many of the characteristics of conventional "heavy" rapid transit with lower costs. Capable of running on city streets, Light Rail Transit services are reinstating the street railway. Edmonton opened the first all-new LRT service in N America in 1978, using a combination of subway and freight railway alignments. In 1981 Calgary followed, combining a new streetcar operation downtown, with short tunnel sections, roadside alignments and a freight railway line. A second line, opened in 1985, made extensive use of central medians of major roadways. The success of these installations has inspired plans for LRT lines in Toronto and Vancouver and in a number of western US cities.

Social and Economic Impact Transit systems were the first major consumer of electricity and promoted the use of electricity for other purposes, such as lighting. Many electric-power companies began life as streetcar companies, eg, those of Winnipeg, Montréal, Québec City, Saint John,

Halifax, Victoria and Vancouver. Some power companies operated transit systems into the 1970s: Nova Scotia Light and Power ran motorbuses and trolleybuses until 1969, and BC Hydro in Vancouver and Victoria until 1978.

Electric street railways produced a revolution in social and political life. The low price and widespread availability of streetcar service meant that for the first time people could gather en masse from all over a city and, in an era preceding radio or widespread telephones, have a major impact on political responsiveness and institutions. Streetcars also had a major impact on the shape of cities. "Streetcar suburbs" offered an entirely new way of life for Canadians, providing access to urban amenities while at the same time permitting relatively low-density housing, yet avoiding the major sprawl often associated with later auto-dominated suburbs.

The "streetcar strip," a linear development of retail and professional service establishments, remains to this day even where streetcars have disappeared, in Vancouver's Broadway, Calgary's 17th Ave, Edmonton's 124th St, Ottawa's Bank St, Toronto's Eglinton Ave and Montréal's St Laurent St. Wherever 2 or more lines met or crossed, surrounding land became particularly attractive for retail, office or apartment construction. *See also* URBAN TRANSPORTATION; SUBWAYS AND LIGHT RAPID TRANSIT. BRIAN E. SULLIVAN

Streit, Marlene Stewart, golfer (b at Cereal, Alta 9 Mar 1934). Streit played junior golf in Fonthill, Ont. She was a powerful competitor, her game marked by fierce pride and will to win. She won the Canadian Ladies' Open Amateur title 11 times between 1951 and 1973, the Ontario Ladies' Amateur Championship 11 times, the Ladies' British Open Amateur in 1953, the US Women's Amateur in 1956 and the Australian Women's Amateur in 1963. Streit was voted Canada's athlete of the year in 1951 and 1956. She continued to compete into the mid-1980s. She is a Member of the Order of Canada, of the Canadian Golf Hall of Fame and of the Canadian Sports Hall of Fame. LORNE RUBENSTEIN

Stress was originally viewed as an overpowering external force acting upon individuals or objects. The mechanical engineer still uses the word in this sense, but human biologists have been less consistent in their terminology. Some retain classical usage, whereas others regard stress as the physiological and psychological reaction to adverse circumstances, or as a subjective response to any situation that the individual regards as unfavourable. Any factor threatening the constancy of the stable internal environment which the body's mechanisms are designed to preserve may be viewed as a "stressor," whether self-imposed (eg, by excessive physical or mental work) or external (eg, a hot and humid environment).

Much of the early investigation of stress was undertaken by Dr Hans SELYE, of the Institute of Experimental Medicine and Surgery at Université de Montréal, who defined stress as the state manifested by a specific syndrome that consists of all nonspecifically induced changes within a biological system. He postulated a general 3-phase reaction of the body to any stressor. First, an acute alarm reaction was associated with the discharge of hormones from the adrenal glands, a decrease in the size of the thymus, a decrease in one type of white blood cell (eosinophils) and a propensity to gastric ulcers. In the second phase, resistance or adaptation to the stressor was manifested by a hypertrophy (exaggerated growth) of the adrenal glands. If the exposure continued, exhaustion resulted; in animals, damage to the outer part (cortex) of the adrenal glands might result, and in humans there was indirect evidence of parallel changes. Based on this research, Selye postulated a condition of "eustress," an ideal amount of stress that maintains individuals in the phase of adaptation.

In popular thought stress is defined mainly in psychological terms (although hard physical work or a hot and noisy environment also increase the stress imposed by a mental task). Stress usually results if the pace of work is too fast, if the consequences of error are grave or if there is inadequate definition of the task to be performed. However, researcher David Coburn (then working at U of Victoria) suggested that boring, monotonous and repetitive work also imposes stress on a worker. It may be that in such circumstances much effort must be devoted to sustaining the necessary vigilance to avoid accidents and maintain quality production. Psychologists describe an inverted U-shaped relationship between task difficulty and performance – moderately demanding work ensures the best performance and imposes the least stress upon the employee.

Attempts to relate poor health to stress exposure have been unsatisfactory because "stressful" work is often associated with adverse habits such as inadequate physical exercise and heavy cigarette smoking. However, occasional reports have linked stressful employment, eg, air-traffic control, with an increased incidence of heart attacks and gastric ulcers. It has been hard to prove, through research, that exercise helps to counter either psychological stress or the resultant strain. If a task is boring, exercise can certainly act as a countermeasure, increasing the total stress on the body to the "eustress" level. Exercise also offers a pleasant relaxation to the overstressed individual, although exercise may be no more effective than some other type of respite from an overdemanding task.

According to observers, humans have always encountered stress, but modern automation of the workplace has both increased the proportion of "mindless" tasks and provided supervisors with the tools to monitor employee performance ever more closely. Moderate amounts of stress may be essential to both worthwhile effort and a resultant sense of achievement, but happiness and health depend upon a careful matching of the demands of work with the skills of the employee.
R.J. SHEPHARD

Reading: H. Selye, *The Stress of Life* (1976); R.J. Shephard, *Fitness and Health in Industry* (1986).

Strickland, Edgar Harold, entomologist, soldier (b at Erith, Eng 29 May 1889; d at Victoria 31 May 1962). After studies in England 1909-11,

Strickland attended Harvard 1911-13. In 1913 he was "loaned" to Canada to obtain field experience for proposed research on sleeping sickness in Africa. He was entomology officer for Alberta 1913-21, operating an entomological field station at Lethbridge. He founded and headed U of A's entomology dept 1922-54 (the sole member for 24 years). Strickland's 60 entomological papers range through history, ecology, life cycles, taxonomy and adverse effects of DDT, with pest control a major concern of his careeer. His academic endeavours were paralleled by military activity, in the Canadian Machine Gun Corps during WWI, as CO of U of Alta COTC 1935-40 and the Canadian Army Base at Wetaskiwin, Alta, 1942-44, and as aide-de-camp to the lieutenant-governor of Alberta 1936-39. Honours included the King's Jubilee Medal (1935) and the Coronation Medal (1937).   MARTIN K. MCNICHOLL

Strickland, John Douglas Hipwell, biological oceanographer (b at London, Eng 3 Aug 1920; d at La Jolla, Calif 12 Nov 1970; naturalized Canadian). Strickland was a senior scientist with the Pacific Oceanographic Group of the Fisheries Research Board, Nanaimo. BC, 1956-66 and head of the Marine Food Chain Group at the Institute of Marine Resources, La Jolla, after 1966. He initiated biological oceanographic studies as part of the West Coast research effort of the FRB. A scientist of international acclaim, Strickland started many new studies on the ecology of the oceans, which later gave rise to a new generation of biological oceanographers. He is best remembered for his analytical work on micronutrients and his initiation of marine mesocosm experiments in Departure Bay, BC, during the early 1960s. A research vessel of U of Victoria and part of the Marine Ecology Laboratory at Bedford Institute of Oceanography, Dartmouth, NS, are named after him.
T.R. PARSONS

Strikes and Lockouts A strike is the withholding of labour by workers in order to obtain better working conditions; such withholding of labour is generally accompanied by demonstrations, such as picketing, parades, meetings. A lockout is the opposite, a temporary shutdown by an employer of his business to compel his employees to accept certain conditions.

Strikes are as old as subordinate work itself, and they occurred before the workers were organized in trade unions. For instance, the Irish canal builders in the 1840s were backed in their violent actions for better living and working conditions by their clannish secret societies. Their protest was crushed no less violently, as were most major strikes until the 1930s.

More often than not, strikes erupted when labour organizations tried to form themselves and be recognized. Information on strikes is sporadic in the 19th century. Strike action is mentioned, for instance, in 1836 by Toronto printers in favour of the 10-hour day, in 1855 by Montréal railway workers and in the 1860s by shoemakers in different cities. Strikes were generally unsuccessful; workers did make some inroads when economic activity happened to be booming and labour was scarce.

The most famous strike of the 19th century is that of the Toronto printers in 1872. It was part of a wider campaign for the 9-hour day (*see* NINE-HOUR MOVEMENT). It lasted from Mar 25 to mid-May 1872, and involved more than 100 members of the International Typographical Union. The striking workers won the 54-hour work week and better wages, but the general campaign for the 9-hour day suffered a setback from the negative publicity around the strike and from the arrests that were made following a mass demonstration in Queen's Park on Apr 15. A political

Parade in Hamilton during the 1946 steel strike (*courtesy National Archives of Canada/PA-120506/United Steelworkers of America Coll*).

debate ensued, and its outcome was the adoption by the Parliament of Canada of the Trade Union Act, assented to 14 June 1872. The Act declared the unions not to be considered as associations in restraint of trade. The right to strike was thus implicitly recognized, but picketing remained a criminal offence until the Criminal Code was amended in 1934 in order to allow for information picketing.

During the latter part of the 19th century, strikes occurred in railways, construction, cigar-making and mining. Coal mining on Vancouver I experienced labour unrest since its beginnings around 1850. It reached its peak in 1903 with a 5-month strike involving 700 employees. Other strikes, also in coal mining and in 1903, were staged in southeastern British Columbia and in Alberta. A royal commission was established to look into the situation.

The early 1900s saw other major strikes, especially in railways. The most important was that of the CPR track maintenance workers from June to late Aug 1901, involving 5000 men from the Atlantic to the Pacific. In 1903, another major strike in BC opposed the non-running tradesmen to the CPR from Feb to June.

These strikes prompted the federal government to adopt its first compulsory investigation and conciliation measures regarding industrial disputes. The Railway Disputes Act of 1903 inspired a more general and permanent legislation 4 years later in 1907, the Industrial Disputes Investigation Act. This Act remained the dominant piece of labour legislation in Canada until the 1930s.

The publication of the *Labour Gazette*, beginning in 1901, gave the public better information on industrial disputes. Throughout the 20th century, 3 waves of work stoppages, of different duration, were identified. The first 2 coincide rough-

	Work stoppages	Workers involved	Person-days lost	% of estimated working time
Strikes and Lockouts in Canada: Selected years 1901-1986				
1901	99	24 089	737 808	—
1911	100	29 285	1 821 084	—
1919	336	148 915	3 400 942	0.60
1921	168	28 257	1 048 914	0.22
1931	88	10 738	204 238	0.04
1941	231	87 091	433 914	0.06
1946	226	135 914	4 515 030	0.54
1951	258	102 793	901 620	0.09
1961	287	97 959	1 335 080	0.11
1966	617	411 459	5 178 170	0.34
1971	539	211 493	2 714 560	0.16
1972	567	686 129	7 423 140	0.41
1976	1 039	1 570 940	11 609 890	0.55
1981	1 048	338 548	8 878 490	0.37
1986	(900)*	429 401	5 651 700	0.22

* estimate

ly with the 2 world wars, 1911 to 1919 and 1943 to 1948. In the 1950s a higher plateau was established. The third wave went from 1965 to 1981, with a year of relative labour peace in 1977. It might be worth noting that time lost through work stoppages, even at their peaks, hardly surpassed one-half of 1% of total estimated working time, much less than time lost because of accidents or unemployment.

The first wave of strike activity shows 2 peaks. The 1.8 million days lost in 1911 were mainly lost in the same industries as before: coal mining in western Canada and the Maritimes, textile and shoemaking in Québec, construction and railway throughout Canada. By far the most notable strike of this period was the WINNIPEG GENERAL STRIKE of 1919. The June 21 confrontation with the Mounties and soldiers, following earlier arrests and confiscation of documents, resulted in 30 casualties, including 1 death. The reasons for the strike were never clear, except that it was influenced by the general climate and some similar action in Vancouver and the US. The ONE BIG UNION, established at the Western Labour Conference in Calgary in the same year, benefited from the interest arising from the Winnipeg events; but after a few years of a spectacular rise, the OBU quickly disappeared: that part of organized labour which made up radical unionism lost it faith in it and turned its efforts resolutely to business unionism.

Such disappointment and the GREAT DEPRESSION of the early 1930s might explain the low level of strike activity until the late 1930s. The textile industry in Québec had been so troublesome that Justice Turgeon had been appointed to conduct a public inquiry into its difficulties. This inquiry revealed so many sore spots that, instead of solving the problems, it contributed to a province-wide strike in all of Québec textile mills in 1937. It was the first major fight carried on by the Québec-based Canadian and Catholic Confederation of Labour (now CONFEDERATION OF NATIONAL TRADE UNIONS). Its second and best known strike is the ASBESTOS STRIKE of 1949.

Despite the government's severe restrictions on the right to strike in the war industries and the freezing of prices and wages, there were major strikes during and after WWII; restrictions were lifted only on 1 Dec 1946, to allow for readjustment of the industry to civil production. Strikes causing the greater loss of working days in the war period occurred in the aircraft industry in Montréal (1943) and in the auto industry in Ontario (1944 and 1945). In the latter case, the award by arbitrator Ivan C. RAND included a compulsory union dues checkoff which applied even to nonunion workers; this has been known ever since as the RAND FORMULA.

In the recess period of 1950 to 1965, there were still a half-dozen highly significant strikes, with a million days lost in most of them. The railways were beginning their long decline, and their employees were then fighting for their jobs, threatened by a technological change in the form of diesel engines. BC logging and the Ontario automotive industry were still in the race. That period also saw the first strike by first-line managers for union recognition (the CBC producers' strike in 1959) and the first of many desperate strikes against the introduction of computers in the newspaper industry. The workers belonging to one of the oldest unions in the printing trades were not struggling to obtain better conditions any more, but to keep their jobs.

The third wave was a mixture of recurring old conflicts (primary metal workers, building trades, autoworkers) and new ones stemming from public-sector unionization. The postal strike of 1965 forced the federal legislator to include the possi-

31 Most Significant Strikes in Canadian History[1]
(Source: Labour Canada, *Strikes and Lockouts in Canada*)

Town or Area	Group Involved	Starting date / Termination date	Person-days lost	Outcome - Impact
Toronto	Printers – ITU	25 Mar 1872 / 15 May 1872	5000	Setback for 9-hour campaign Adoption of Trade Union Act
Ladysmith, BC	Dominion Coal Mines – Western Fed of Miners	11 Feb 1903 / 4 July 1903	88 200	Royal Commission and federal legislation
Winnipeg	General Strike – One Big Union	15 May 1919 / 25 June 1919	594 000	Vanishing of radical union at a later date
Montréal and Québec prov	Dominion Textile – Can Cath Conf of L	2 Aug 1937 / 30 Aug 1937	200 000	For better working conditions Recognition of CCCL
Montréal	Fairchild Aircraft – IAM	3 Aug 1943 / 16 Aug 1943	200 000	Full indexation of wages
Windsor, Ont	Motor vehicle (Ford) – UAW	20 Apr 1944 / 11 May 1944	228 000	On an interpretation of grievance procedure
Windsor, Ont	Motor vehicle (Ford) – UAW	12 Sept 1945 / 29 Dec 1945	915 000	Arbitration (I.C.Rand): the Rand formula
BC Coast	Logging and Sawmills – IWW	15 May 1946 / 26 June 1946	1 100 000	Federal inquiry commission BC Ind Conc Arbitr Act
Canada-wide	CNR CPR – Non-operating Ry U	22 Aug 1950 / 30 Aug 1950	1 000 000	Beginning of 16 years of turmoil in railways
BC Coast	Logging and Sawmills – IWW	16 June 1952 / 30 July 1952	1 035 000	Change of political party and new LRA 1954
Ontario	General Motors – UAW	19 Sept 1955 / 20 Feb 1956	1 500 000	Introduction of SUB in collective agreements
Montréal	CBC – Producers' Union	29 Dec 1958 / 9 Mar 1959	70 010	Recognition of a managers union ("cadres")
BC Coast	Logging and Sawmills – IWW	6 July 1959 / 14 Sept 1959	1 240 000	Wage increase
Toronto	Newspapers – ITU 01	9 July 1964 / 31 Dec 1967	473 190	Lasted $3\frac{1}{2}$ years. Computers entered the composing room
Canada-wide	Post Office – Letter Carriers & Postal W	22 July 1965 / 8 Aug 1965	89 830	Right to strike will be part of 1967 PSSR Act
Canada-wide	CNR CPR – Several Railway Unions	26 Aug 1966 / 5 Sept 1966	766 090	Back-to-work legislation Task Force on IR established
Sudbury, Ont	Inco – USWA (6500)	10 July 1969 / 14 Nov 1969	1 449 500	Wage dispute
BC	Construction LRA – Several Bldg TU	14 Apr 1970 / 27 July 1970	1 080 000	Back-to-work legislation Future revision of Labour Code
Ontario	General Motors – UAW	14 Sept 1970 / 18 Dec 1970	1 598 600	Wage dispute
Québec prov	Government of Québec – Common Front	11 Apr 1972 / 22 Apr 1972	1 636 960	Loss of public support (hospitals, schools, etc)
BC	Construction LRA – Several Bldg TU	28 Apr 1972 / 31 July 1972	1 079 980	Wage increase
BC	Construction LRA – 10 Bldg TU	6 May 1974 / 29 June 1974	1 420 680	Package of $2.90, an increase of 35% to 50% in 2 years
Québec prov	Alcan - Federation of Alum Synd (Indep)	3 June 1976 / 15 Nov 1976	1 021 710	Average general increase of 22% over 3 years
Canada-wide	"Day of Protest" (CLC)	14 Oct 1976	830 000	To mark 1st anniversary of AIB
Québec prov	Qué Constr Emplrs Assn – Qué Fed of Labour	19 Aug 1976 / 18 Oct 1976	1 837 000	First bargaining round following Cliche Comm Report
Sudbury, Ont	Inco Metals – USWA (6500)	15 Sept 1978 / 6 June 1979	1 156 980	Average of 20% increase after a 9-month strike
Hamilton, Ont	Stelco – USWA (1005)	1 Aug 1981 / 31 Dec 1981	1 159 170	A wage dispute in early recession
Québec prov	Gov of Qué Reg Educat Various Unions	26 Jan 1983 / 2 Feb 1983	1 238 280	In protest of a wage rollback imposed by law
Québec prov	A Constr Emplrs Assn – Qué Fed of Labour	2 May 1986 / 16 June 1986	1 152 000	Back-to-work legislation and modification to CILR Act
BC	Forest and Forest Prod IWW	Aug 1986 / Dec 1986	2 000 000	IWW to leave International Union
BC	General 1-day strike ($\frac{1}{4}$ of labour force)	1 June 1987	300 000	To protest proposed change to Labour C (Bills 19-20)

1. Significant because of size or special impact

bility of strike action in the 1967 Public Service Staff Relations Act. The biggest-ever work stoppage occurred in 1972 in Québec, when a COM-MON FRONT of unions struck the provincial government, the hospitals and the schools at the same time. The public-sector unions won big gains in money and various benefits, but this was the beginning of their loss of public support.

There were at least 2 cases of political strikes, the Day of Protest called by the CANADIAN LABOUR CONGRESS on 14 Oct 1976, to mark the anniversary of the implementing of the Anti-Inflation law and regulations, and the 1-day general strike in British Columbia on 1 June 1987, to protest against the proposed changes to British Columbia labour laws in bills 19 and 20.

There is no accurate provincial distribution of strike statistics, mainly because there have been several interprovincial strikes. But a general estimate reveals that BC has had the most strikes, accounting in certain cases for up to 50% of all person-days lost in Canada. In the 1970s, Québec took the lead with its all-encompassing public-sector bargaining structures. The other provinces have led the platoon, proportionally to their labour force, in successive periods. Until recently statistics did not separate lockouts from strikes. Both were counted as work stoppages, partly because some stoppages are both a strike and a lockout at the same time. In fact, lockouts were very uncommon until the 1960s, and they are still much less frequent than strikes.

Employers have always been inclined to use strikebreakers as their most efficient weapon. In the 19th and early 20th centuries some employers arranged to have an immigrant work force come from overseas to fill the jobs of the strikers. This often led to violence. There seems to be a renewed interest in strikebreaking tactics; it might be related to the high level of unemployment experienced since 1975, for an immigrant labour force in now less easily available. Some contend that freedom to operate a plant is part of our basic freedoms and even necessary as part of the mechanism that will eventually bring the parties to agree. The Canada Labour Code and most provincial legislation explicitly state that strikers keep their employee status, and thus implicitly give a priority of rights to the striking employees. Two provinces have gone further and have taken a position on strikebreaking. Since the 1970s, BC has forbidden the use of professional strikebreakers and Québec has forbidden subcontracting of strike operations as well as the use of any employee (except local management personnel) to continue production during a legal strike.

Until certification became open to unions in 1944, most strikes were waged for union recognition. With the certification system set up by law, recognition strikes have become theoretically unnecessary and certainly illegal. Since then, strikes were initiated primarily for better working conditions. In the late 1970s, strikes were increasingly directed at levels of governments as employers or as legislators. Public-sector strikes hit the public harder than the employers.

The causes of greater strike activity in certain periods of time have never been definitely established, although workers are less likely to strike when unemployment is high and more likely to strike in periods of increasing or high economic activity. The long crest of the third wave has taken place in a period of relative prosperity and rising inflation; the recession of the early 1980s has brought a decline in the number of days lost.

The growth of public-sector unions is another factor. Each negotiation in this sector tends to involve more employees than in most private- sector cases, causing more time to be lost and greatly influencing the general picture of work stoppages. Conflicts in the 1970s were more violent and involved more illegal activities than before. The practice of wiping out disciplinary measures and calling off any court action taken during a strike as a condition for returning to work has condoned violence and illegal actions, and made

any type of conduct during a strike almost sanctionless. Wildcat strikes and political strikes have also become more important. *See also* COLLECTIVE BARGAINING; LABOUR RELATIONS; LABOUR ORGANIZATIONS; WORKING-CLASS HISTORY.   GÉRARD HÉBERT

Reading: Labour Canada, *Strikes and Lockouts in Canada* (published annually until 1985, afterwards in *Collective Bargaining Review*); Jean Hamelin et al, *Répertoire des grèves dans les province de Québec au XIXe siècle* (1970); S.M. Jamieson, *Times of Trouble: Labour Unrest and Industrial Conflict in Canada, 1900-1966* (1971).

Stringer, Arthur John Arbuthnott, popular novelist and expatriate bohemian (b at Chatham, Ont 26 Feb 1874; d at Mountain Lakes, NJ 14 Sept 1950). Despite his trilogy of novels about the Canadian Prairies – *Prairie Wife* (1915), *Prairie Mother* (1920) and *Prairie Child* (1922) – Stringer was not in any recognizable stream of Canadian writing but rather was a prolific American hack-fiction writer of the David Graham Phillips strain, able to satisfy, by his facile and compromising pen, the demands of the popular magazine press for sentimental tales. The fact that he lived most of his life in the US, however, did not prevent him from frequently inventing Canadian characters and sometimes, starting with *Empty Hands* (1924), setting them in the Far North, a region he misunderstood lavishly, thereby contributing to foreign stereotyping of Canada.   D. FETHERLING

Strom, Harry Edwin, farmer, politician, premier of Alberta (b at Burdett, Alta 7 July 1914; d at Edmonton 2 Oct 1984). Strom's parents were both born in Sweden. He served as municipal councillor, school trustee and chairman of the local Rural Electrification Assn and was also interested in water conservation. First elected to the Alberta legislature in 1955, he was re-elected in 1959, 1963, 1967 and 1971 as a Social Credit member. He served as minister of agriculture 1962-68 and minister of municipal affairs July-Dec 1968 in the administration of E.C. MANNING. In Dec 1968 he became premier on the retirement of Manning but in Sept 1971 the Social Credit government was defeated by the Progressive Conservatives under Peter LOUGHEED. From 1971 to 1973 he was leader of the Opposition, and following the provincial election of 1975 he retired from politics. He was the first Alberta-born premier. He was active in the Evangelical Free Church.   ERIC J. HOLMGREN

Strong, Maurice Frederick, business administrator, environmentalist, statesman (b at Oak Lk, Man 29 Apr 1929). Strong began a business career as a trading-post employee for the HUDSON'S BAY CO in the Arctic in 1944. His business talents developed as he quickly moved from being accountant for a mining group in Toronto (1945) through a series of management and investment positions with various energy and financial corporations (1948-66). In 1966 he shifted to international and later environmental affairs. He headed Canada International Development Assistance Programme and its successor, the CANADIAN INTERNATIONAL DEVELOPMENT AGENCY until 1970, defining its long-term strategies. He then was secretary-general of the UN Conference on the Human Environment and undersecretary-general of the UN Switzerland office (1970-72), then executive director of the UN Environment Programme in Nairobi, Kenya (1973-75). Strong returned to business as head of PETRO-CANADA (1976-78), after which he became chairman of the International Energy Development Corp (1980-83), chairman of the Canada Development Investment Corp (1982-84), and again undersecretary-general of the UN (1985-). Numerous volunteer activities have included positions with the International Union for the Conservation of Nature and Natural

Resources; the World Wildlife Fund; the World Council of Churches; the Soc for Development, Justice, and Peace (the Vatican); the North-South Inst; and the World Commission on Environment and Development. His numerous conservation and humanity awards include the Freedom Festival Award (1975) and the first Pahlavi Environment Prize (1976). He became an Officer of the Order of Canada (1976) and by 1986 was the recipient of no less than 25 honorary degrees.   MARTIN K. MCNICHOLL

Stuart, Kenneth, army officer (b at Trois-Rivières, Qué 9 Sept 1891; d at Ottawa 3 Nov 1945). Stuart graduated from RMC in 1911 and served with the Royal Canadian Engineers overseas 1915-18. Editor of the *Canadian Defence Quarterly* while at headquarters in the 1930s, he was appointed chief of the general staff in Dec 1941 and chief of staff, Canadian Military Headquarters, London, from Dec 1943 to Nov 1944. Instrumental in removing Gen A.G.L. MCNAUGHTON as commander, 1st Canadian Army, Stuart was sacked by McNaughton when the latter became defence minister in Nov 1944. Stuart's miscalculations in forecasting infantry casualties helped force the government to impose CONSCRIPTION in Nov 1944.   STEPHEN HARRIS

Student Rights Basically 2 sorts of rights apply to students: substantive rights, ie, the actual rights that students should enjoy, and procedural rights, ie, methods by which students claim their rights. This article is concerned with students in public institutions, although those in private schools can claim rights under the common law and provincial education Acts.

Provincial governments affirm the basic right to an education when they approve financing for primary and secondary schools. Governments also extend the right to an education by underwriting part of the expenses for colleges and universities. When education budgets are debated, arguments occasionally surface to augment this principle, eg, to make small class sizes a moral right or to guarantee that all qualified high-school graduates may have access to post-secondary education. Courts are usually reluctant to enter this debate, not wishing to define "good" teaching or to rule on government spending.

A second substantive right, particularly important for minority groups, guarantees equal EDUCATIONAL OPPORTUNITY. In the spirit of this provision, which mirrors the value that governments should treat persons equally, provincial policymakers have attempted to reduce imbalances between schools and regions. To some extent, equity has been guaranteed by sections such as 15 and 23 of the CANADIAN CHARTER OF RIGHTS AND FREEDOMS. Provinces are moving unevenly, however, toward achieving sex-based equity in vocational training, sports, curricular materials and financial aid.

Legislatures also require boards to institute special education programs for students limited by handicaps and learning disabilities. Generally these students have a right to a free appropriate public education in the least restrictive environment. Parents and child advocates try to ensure that students' rights are not abridged through malpractice, improper diagnosis or inaccurate placements in remedial groupings. Separate or demonstrably substandard education for handicapped children may be challenged in courts under the Charter.

Administrators have the legal power to punish students for disruptions in schools. Offences may include persistent opposition to authority, habitual neglect of duty, use of profane or improper language, and conduct "injurious" to a moral tone. A number of schools and post-secondary institutions now extend to students the right of due process, according to which administrators must (in detail) state the reasons for suspensions or expulsions; within days, students and their parents can appeal these administrative actions, and authorities thereafter can reverse or modify punishments that cannot be justified or supported by the evidence. In post-secondary schools, students may turn to ombudsmen or directors of student services for help in redressing such problems for them as sexual harassment, undeclared grading practices and too-restricted access to records about themselves. These students may also expect that their academic, counselling, and medical records will remain confidential.

In varying degrees, institutions are refining their codes of conduct so that students may confront accusers, engage council, contest the evidence, cross-examine witnesses, appeal beyond immediate supervisors, participate in hearings where each side makes cases in the presence of the other, and have controversies settled by rules that are known to all in advance. The formality of the disciplinary hearing can increase with the severity of the potential penalties.

Elementary Schools In academic and political matters, students in primary and junior high schools enjoy the least latitude. Teachers in these institutions are empowered to exercise the discipline of a kind, firm and judicious parent. This empowerment, *in loco parentis* ("in place of the parent"), stems from the European practice of wealthy parents voluntarily and individually contracting with tutors for their children's training. The idea of teacher as substitute parent has been so absorbed into the compulsory and mass education systems of N America that school boards and governing bodies for private schools are slow to question constraints that elementary educators may impose on learners' expression, association, opinion and assembly.

Deriving their authority from the COMMON LAW, teachers in the past have administered corporal punishment. In recent years, officials in ministries of education have disapproved of the strap, but its use has not been forbidden in all provinces. In restraining a child, teachers have to stay within limits set by their boards. Educators charged with assault have used the Criminal Code of Canada as a defence for their actions although what is reasonable in the circumstances may well be the test.

Secondary Schools Adolescents are more likely to use the provocative language of "demanding" their rights. During the activist 1960s, some students wore armbands, picketed and clashed with officials, seeking the unqualified exercise of speech, press and assembly for which university students were clamouring. In the process, Canada's secondary students did gain some influence over cigarette smoking (within designated areas) and appearance (if hair length and dress do not cause disruptions of orderly procedure). In Canada, as elsewhere throughout the industrialized world, subsequent conflicts over students' academic and political freedoms have not been as widespread or as intense.

Regulation of student life has increased in the 1980s, however. High schools have adopted codes of behaviour that spell out requirements for attendance, preparedness for class, academic honesty, access to school areas, punctuality, and respect for others. A few boards of education have forbidden students to gather signatures on political petitions within their communities.

Secondary-school educators generally believe that students should have little or no involvement in determining curricular activities, but critics of this point of view argue that students should have a greater share in this aspect of policymaking, noting that such involvement would provide

training in democracy. In response, many educators claim that the student body has such unequal standing in relation to themselves that an equal voice in school governance would be inappropriate. Although guaranteed by the Charter of Rights, a student's privilege to be secure from unreasonable search and seizure must be balanced with the educators' long-standing responsibilities to protect pupils from enticement into illegal behaviour and to insure safety of persons and property. Accordingly, if an educator has a reasonable suspicion that stolen goods or contraband materials, such as drugs or weapons, may be secreted in a student's desk or locker, that teacher or administrator may have the right to search the desk or locker without a warrant and without prior consent from the student. Educators are expected to proceed, however, only after weighing the suspect's age, history, record in school, and the immediate seriousness of the situation.

Post-secondary Institutions Students in colleges and universities have made the greatest strides in acquiring privacy rights. Typically, searches (of lockers, rooms, attendees at social events, etc) are sanctioned (and conducted warily) only in cases of emergency or with high-level authorization and in circumstances which indicate a serious threat to security. University students have also won the right of freedom of association. As a result of the protests of the 1960s and early 1970s, post-secondary students are relatively free from regulations that guide their lives outside class. On some campuses, undergraduates can operate their own pubs. University students sit on department committees and at intermediate levels of their institutions' governing councils but few students actually participate in such governing. In some provinces graduate students, employed as part-time teaching assistants, have won the right to bargain collectively for better wages and improved working conditions.

RICHARD G. TOWNSEND

Students, Financial Aid to Some form of financial support to needy post-secondary students has always been available in Canada. Until 1939 this primarily took the form of privately funded assistance from universities and colleges to students with high scholastic achievement.

The foundation of a national co-ordinated policy for student assistance began in a modest way with the federal government's passage of the Dominion-Provincial Student Aid Program (DSAP) in 1939. All provinces had joined the plan by 1944. The CONSTITUTION ACT, 1867, granted the provincial legislatures the exclusive right to "make laws in and for each province" in relation to education, but the federal initiation of a national aid program was legitimized on the grounds that it related to activities in areas under federal jurisdiction, eg, economic growth, labour training and labour mobility. Thus, DSAP formed a part of the Youth Training Act, which was part of a national economic policy.

Under DSAP the federal government contributed funds to each participating province and the province was expected to provide an equal amount of assistance. Some provinces provided only loans, others only grants. It has been estimated that overall the federal government contributed less than $5 million to DSAP, and that fewer than an average of 3000 students a year received support under the program.

The implementation of the DSAP affected financial aid to students in 3 major ways. First, provincial responsibility for administrating aid regardless of source of funding stimulated a diversity in provincial programs. Second, merit alone became less than a criterion for determining eligibility for aid than need, ie, aid shifted from schol-

arships to bursaries. Third, the role of the federal government in financing and co-ordinating aid increased in importance. Québec opted out of the joint arrangement in 1954, citing constitutional reasons of provincial primacy and autonomy in higher education.

The 1960s witnessed rapid growth in post-secondary education and a consequent need for reformed student aid plans. The Canada Student Loans Plan (CSLP) established in 1964, superseded the DSAP, which was discontinued in 1967. Under the CSLP, the federal government guarantees loans to all full-time students who demonstrate financial need to a provincial or territorial government on the understanding that the money will be repaid over a period not exceeding 9.5 years at a rate of interest set annually beginning 6 months after studies are terminated. The federal government guarantees the loan with a designated lender, such as a chartered bank or credit union, and pays the annual interest before repayment is made.

In seeking assistance, students first apply to a province or territory for aid, providing information about their financial resources and needs. The province or territory then determines the amount of aid for which the student is eligible, either in the form of a nonrepayable grant or bursary, or as an authorization for a guaranteed loan, or a mix of both. The student negotiates the loan at a bank or other commercial lending institution.

In Feb 1980 the Federal-Provincial Task Force on Student Assistance was created. Its report was tabled Dec 1980, and in 1983 the CSL Act was amended according to the task force's recommendations. The maximum loan was increased from $56.25 to $105 a week for full-time students. The amendments also permitted loans for part-time students (up to $2500 at any one time), interest relief for unemployed borrowers, and cancellation of debt for certain borrowers. Neither these amendments nor the provincial systems of aid are intended to supplement the student's available resources. Each province administers the program under jointly agreed-upon administrative criteria. Under the CSLP, each province must establish an appeals process for students who are denied loans.

In all provinces except Québec, student assistance programs include a mix of aid provided from the CSLP and from supplementary provincial funds for loans, bursaries and special grants (money granted to students as a result of a special government policy or program, often to encourage students to follow specified careers after graduation). Students cannot apply directly to the federal government for a CSLP loan. Québec elected to remain outside the formal joint financing and administrative arrangements, choosing to make its own financial arrangements with Ottawa.

Provincial systems of aid under the CSLP differ. While all provinces use administrative criteria developed annually for CSLP by federal, provincial and territorial officials and approved by their respective governments, differences occur because national criteria set only maximum allowances. Individual provinces can set tighter criteria and offer less than the maximum loans and have established methods of calculating the total amount of assistance to each student. Loans and bursaries are issued by the province where the student resides and not where he or she studies. Each province designates the post-secondary institutions, inside or outside the province, to which students may take their loans and grants. As part of general fiscal restraint, in the 1980s most provinces adopted much more stringent criteria for loan eligibility.

CSLP has been criticized on a number of counts, including the following.

Loan-Bursary Balance The Canadian Federation of Students, which represents 500 000 postsecondary students, contends that the debt load held by students after graduation represents a heavy burden. Although a few provinces are introducing a loan rebate program to ease this burden, the trend seems to be towards giving more loans than grants. Several provinces have also raised loan requirements.

Neglected Groups Critics maintain that many of the disadvantaged, eg, native people, single parents, children of lower-income families, are not served well by the existing student aid programs. They argue that financial pressures, the reluctance of low-income families to assume loan commitments, and inadequate information combine to restrict aid accessibility for certain groups of Canadians.

Loose Criteria Critics have also charged that financial aid is more readily available for some student applicants than others, eg, that the test used by provinces to decide the amount each student receives favours members of groups such as the self-employed.

Since CSLP's inception, the federal government has authorized $4.3 billion in bank loans to 3.2 million students. In 1986-87 alone, 235 000 students received $621 million. In the late 1980s about 46% Canadian post-secondary students received some form of government aid.

One of the difficulties behind financial assistance programs is that they seek to meet diverse goals, ie, to ensure access to post-secondary education to students in financial need and to provide indirect support to post-secondary institutions which are under the financial control of the provinces.

Supplementary aid schemes are available in most provinces for groups such as the handicapped, native people and single parents on welfare. New Brunswick and Alberta offer different kinds of loan remissions to graduates. In Québec, interest-free loans are available for study at certain post-secondary institutions. A work-study program is available for exceptionally needy students in Ontario. Loans are available in Saskatchewan for applicants studying in some courses where the entrance requirements do not meet CSLP criteria.

Education of registered Indians and Inuit is the constitutional responsibility of the federal government. Eligible Indian and Inuit people may attend provincial universities and colleges; the Department of Indian Affairs and Northern Development provides financial and other assistance. Certain provinces also provide special programs of assistance.

Various priorities deemed in the national interest have prompted the implementation of other significant federal programs. The Veterans Rehabilitation Act, 1945, provided financial aid to returning veterans. An extensive scholarship program in the arts, humanities and social sciences was supported by the Canada Council, 1957-67, and 10 years later the Social Sciences and Humanities Research Council and the Engineering Research Council became responsible for the grant and scholarship programs of the Canada Council.

The National Training Act, 1982, authorizes the Canada Employment and Immigration Commission to operate adult vocational programs that support the training and upgrading of workers needed in a wide variety of occupations. Student youth-employment programs encourage summer employment as well as co-operative programs that enable students to alternate university study with periods of employment. These programs overshadow early federal initiatives (1919) in providing loans to disabled veterans

and grants and fellowships (est 1916) from the National Research Council. LIONEL ORLIKOW

Reading: Council of Ministers of Education, *Report of the Federal-Provincial Task Force on Student Assistance* (1981); Secretary of State, *Support to Education By The Government of Canada* (1983).

Studholme, Allan, stovemounter, labour leader and politician (b at Drake's Cross, Worcestershire, Eng 8 Dec 1846; d at Hamilton, Ont 20 July 1919). After immigrating to Canada in 1870 and taking up work as a stovemounter, Studholme was drawn into labour organizing in Hamilton, Ont, first in the KNIGHTS OF LABOR and later in the Stovemounters' International Union, whose president he became in 1901-02. In 1906, in the wake of a violent street railway strike in Hamilton, Studholme won a by-election for the East Hamilton seat in the Ontario Legislature, where he served until his death. As the only independent labour member in the house, he fought for many reforms, notably the 8-hour day, a minimum wage and women's suffrage. CRAIG HERON

Studhorse Man, The, novel by Robert KROETSCH (Toronto, London and New York, 1969). The story of Hazard Lepage, Kroetsch's studhorse man, is told by Demeter Proudfoot, a madman in a bathtub. Lepage undertakes an Albertan odyssey in quest of a mare for his virgin stallion, the noble Poseidon; the stallion and Lepage's adventures acquire mythological dimensions in a text that comments on the nature of sexuality, history, time and the western Canadian character. *The Studhorse Man* exemplifies Kroetsch's powers as an explorer of western Canadian mythology and demonstrates his exuberant use of language. NEIL BESNER

Stump, Sarain, native name Sock-a-jaw-wu, meaning "the one who pulls the boat," painter, poet (b at Fremont, Wyo 1945; d by drowning near Mexico City, Mexico 20 Dec 1974). He had little formal education and was encouraged to learn from his Shoshone-Cree elders. Moving to an Alberta ranch in 1964, he began the poems and drawings for *There Is My People Sleeping* (1969). Stump promoted traditional Indian values and sought to help young Indians gain pride in their heritage while coping with the modern world. He was the Indian art program co-ordinator at the Saskatchewan Indian Cultural College 1972-74. As a painter he was influenced by the traditional art of the Plains Indian; as well he was interested in searching for what he called his Aztecan roots, since the Shoshone tribe is related by language to the Uto-Aztecan family. His paintings dealt with social-realist themes of Indian religion and history and their modern urban struggles. GERALD R. MCMASTER

Stupart, Sir Robert Frederic, meteorologist (b at Aurora, Canada W 24 Oct 1857; d at Toronto 27 Sept 1940). A pioneer in METEOROLOGY, Stupart's career spanned 6 decades. He was first Canadian-born director of the national meteorological service 1894-1929 and led the expansion of the service throughout the West and into the North as telegraph and radio communication became available for transmitting weather data and forecasts. Employed by the service when he was 15, Stupart learned meteorology on the job and prepared the first public weather forecasts in 1876. As director, he was the first Canadian to participate in the activities of the International Meteorological Organization. A fellow of the RSC, he was knighted in 1916. MORLEY THOMAS

Sturgeon, large, primitive, bony fish of class Osteichthyes, family Acipenseridae. The 4 genera and 23 species live in fresh and coastal waters of the Northern Hemisphere. In Canada, 5 species, all of genus *Acipenser,* occur: white and green sturgeons in Pacific coastal waters and rivers; lake sturgeon in fresh waters E of the Rockies; and Atlantic and shortnose sturgeons in Atlantic coastal waters and rivers. At least some populations of each Canadian species venture, at times, into brackish or salt water. Sturgeons are characterized by a long snout with 4 barbels (hairlike appendages) underneath, a toothless mouth, and 5 rows of shieldlike, bony plates on the body. The upper lobe of the tail fin is longer and more slender than the lower lobe. Sturgeons are an ancient group; fossils are known that date back to the Upper Cretaceous, about 65 million years ago.

Sturgeons typically grow slowly, but they may attain a great size. A white sturgeon weighing 629 kg was caught in the Fraser R at New Westminster in 1897, and an Atlantic sturgeon caught in the St Lawrence weighed 160 kg and was 267 cm long and 60 years old. Female Atlantic sturgeon must be at least 10 years old before spawning, and they usually spawn in rivers where the current is rapid. They grow to 22 cm in one year, 49 cm in 5 years and 90 cm in 10 years. Sturgeon usually feed on bottom invertebrates (eg, insect larvae, amphipods, molluscs, marine worms), but some also eat fishes. They feed on the bottom, using their protruding, sucking lips. They probably locate food with their barbels.

Sturgeons are valuable commercial fish; perhaps 150 000 t are caught annually. The flesh, delicious fresh or smoked, fetches a high price; the caviar is worth several dollars per kilogram. Each year, 9000-14 000 kg of white sturgeon is taken by anglers in the Fraser R. Anglers also seek lake sturgeon. Populations have declined drastically. In 1845, 800 000 kg of lake sturgeon were caught in Lake of the Woods, Ont. By 1957 the catch was only 0.005% of the maximum catch. Pollution, impassable dams and overfishing, combined with late maturity, have all taken their toll. The shortnose sturgeon is classified as rare by the Committee on the Status of Endangered Wildlife in Canada and is an endangered species in the US. Other sturgeons in Canada, eg, lake sturgeon, are declining in parts of their ranges. D.E. MCALLISTER

Sturgeon Falls, Ont, Town, pop 5895 (1986c), 6045 (1981c), inc 1895, located 5 km up the Sturgeon R from Lk Nipissing. Long a site of Indian activity, and known to European fur traders since the 17th century, town growth awaited the arrival of the CPR in 1881. Earliest to arrive were English Canadians from Simcoe and Muskoka; their numbers were engulfed by lumber and pulp-and-paper workers, the latter industry beginning 1884. Closure of the Abitibi Power & Paper, Ltd, plant in 1912 caused a considerable English exodus; the town became 75-80% French speaking, an early voice for French-language rights and culture in Ontario. Paper, tourism, outdoor recreation and local agricultural supply provide economic sustenance in the still largely francophone and Roman Catholic community. PETER KRATS

Submersible, small vehicle designed to operate under water, to carry out such tasks as research, equipment recovery and seabed surveys. A submersible must be supported by a surface vessel or platform; hence, it differs from a submarine, which is an independent, self-supporting vessel.

Manned submersibles are used worldwide. Several classes have been designed and manufactured in Canada, eg, Pisces, a one-atmosphere vehicle, and SDL, a lock-out vehicle, both operated by branches of the Canadian government. Manned submersibles have depth capabilities exceeding 6000 m, but generally operate at depths less than 2200 m. Remotely operated vehicles (ROVs) are operational worldwide and are manufactured by several nations, Canada being a major contributor. ROVs designed and manufactured in Canada include the Dart, Trec and Trov classes of free-swimming vehicles.

The Canadian government took delivery of a HYSUB 5000 ROV in 1987. This submersible was designed and manufactured by International Submarine Engineering of Port Moody, BC, and will be the deepest diving unmanned submersible in the world. The HYSUB 5000 and the Pisces IV Submersible (manned) will both be operated from the Institute of Ocean Sciences, Sidney, BC, and will give Canada the leading edge in underwater operations.   F.J. CHAMBERS

Substantive Law, body of law concerned with rights and obligations, as opposed to PROCEDURAL LAW which concerns how to enforce and defend such rights and obligations. For example, murder is a criminal offence (substantive law) while the rules to be followed in prosecuting an offender of that law are referred to as procedural law.
                                          K.G. MCSHANE

Subways and Light Rapid Transit Subways, sometimes referred to as heavy rail transit, are urban, electric, rapid-transit lines capable of carrying large numbers of people: between 20 000 and 40 000 passengers per hour in each direction. No other traffic is permitted to interfere with the separate rights-of-way of subway trains. Most subways are underground, hence the name, but portions can be at grade (ground level) with suitable fences or barriers, depressed in a cut without covering, or even elevated. Power is supplied to the trains by means of a "third rail," although overhead wire is sometimes also used. Station platforms are built at the same level as the floor of the subway car, eliminating steps for entry and exit. Fare collection occurs in stations rather than on vehicles, and a full signal system is used for operation to ensure safety. Light rail transit is simpler and less costly than a subway but also has less capacity, between 8000 and 20 000 passengers per hour in each direction. The vehicles are lighter than subway cars and are essentially streetcars. The right-of-way may be only partially separated, with grade crossings and portions of a line operating in mixed traffic on the street. Power collection is from overhead wires; passenger loading may use platforms or steps or both, and fare collection can be either on board or at the stations. Light rail systems are usually, but not always, signalized (*see* STREET RAILWAYS).

Canada has 2 subway systems, in Toronto and Montréal. Toronto had the first system, with the Yonge St line (7.4 km in length) opening in Mar 1954. The Toronto system was expanded in stages; by 1988 it was 54.4 km long and had 65 stations on 3 major lines. The Montréal system opened its initial portion in 1966, with 3 lines, 26 stations and a total length of 22 km. By June 1986, it was 55.0 km long and had 61 stations. A further 9 km expansion of the Montréal Metro opened in 1988, with a total of 4 new stations. The Toronto subway cars are 3.15 m in width, with steel wheels running on rails. The Montréal cars are 2.5 m in width, and use rubber tires.

There were 2 light rapid transit (or light rail transit) systems in Canada by 1981. The Edmonton LRT line, 10.3 km in length, was opened in 1978 and extensions were opened in 1981 and 1983. It has 8 stations, 4 of them underground. The capacity is 6800 passengers per hour per direction on a fully separate right-of-way. The Calgary LRT line, opened in 1981, is 22 km in length, and has 25 stations. This LRT facility has both at-grade and below-grade crossings at road intersections and uses railway-type signals and lights giving the LRT vehicles priority. Line capacity is 9400 passengers in the peak direction per hour.

The design capacity of the Edmonton and Calgary lines is much higher than present usage. Both the Edmonton and Calgary systems use 2-section, 23 m articulated LRT vehicles designed and built in West Germany. Ontario's Urban Transportation Development Corporation has designed an advanced LRT technology using automated train control, lightweight cars and linear-induction motors with steerable trucks to reduce noise levels. Apart from the vehicle technology and totally grade separated right-of-way, the major difference of this system is its capacity, which is between those of LRT and subway. A 21.4 km line using the ALRT technology opened in 1986 in Vancouver, and a similar line of some 6.5 km in length opened in Toronto in March 1985.
                                          JURI PILL

Such Is My Beloved, novel by Morley CALLAGHAN (Toronto and New York, 1934) is, on the surface, the story of an idealistic young Catholic priest's failure to help 2 prostitutes he befriends. Stephen Dowling's relationship with the prostitutes is condemned by his rich, sanctimonious parishioners and his bishop; Dowling's anguish over the girls' fate drives him mad, and the novel closes on his realization of the purely Christian love he bears for them and for humanity. But the novel's apparent simplicity becomes the means to a symbolic exploration of Dowling's faith, as set against the various secular, socioeconomic and political creeds of the time. *Such Is My Beloved* has been translated into French as *Telle est ma bien-aimée* (Montréal, 1974).   NEIL BESNER

Sucker, freshwater fish of the family Catostomidae, closely related to MINNOWS. There are about 65 species of suckers; most occur in N America but one extends into eastern Siberia and another occurs in China. There are 7 genera and 17 species in Canada; none are found in Newfoundland or Vancouver I. Longnose and white suckers have the largest distribution, in lakes and rivers from the Maritimes to BC. The longnose sucker even extends N to near the arctic coastline. The family also includes quillbacks (carplike fish) and redhorses (which can have reddish fins). Very few suckers exceed 40 cm in length. Most species have a ventral mouth (located on lower body surface) with large lips covered with papillae (small, nipple-shaped protuberances). Most species feed primarily on small, bottom-dwelling organisms which are sucked up (giving rise to the common name). Spawning usually occurs in spring or early summer. Breeding males, especially, may have nuptial tubercles (small, white, horny projections) on parts of the body and certain fins. Suckers are usually drably coloured, but a spawning male longnose sucker can have a bright red stripe along its side. Suckers, usually regarded as coarse fish, are rarely fished commercially or recreationally in Canada, although they occur in large numbers and can be readily taken. Although bony, they are eaten occasionally (sometimes marketed as "mullet") and are used for dog food. Suckers are important in the diets of many other fish. They may compete with salmonids, but the extent is not well known and is probably exaggerated.
                                          JOSEPH S. NELSON

Sudbury, Ont, City, judicial seat for Dist of Sudbury in NE Ontario, is located on Lk Ramsey near the Sudbury Basin, a geological structure likely formed by meteorite impact. Situated 390 km N of Toronto on the TRANS-CANADA HWY, it serves as a gateway to northern Ontario. From 1981 to 1986, its population declined from 91 829 to 88 717.

Settlement and Development The area was originally inhabited by Ojibwa belonging to the Algonquian group of Indians. Though HBC trading posts had operated in the area earlier in the centu-

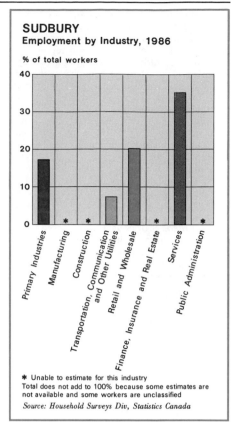

SUDBURY
Employment by Industry, 1986

% of total workers

* Unable to estimate for this industry
Total does not add to 100% because some estimates are not available and some workers are unclassified
Source: Household Surveys Div, Statistics Canada

ry, the construction of the CPR main line in 1883, which included a station at this location, marked Sudbury's beginning. James Worthington, superintendent of construction, gave the site the name of his wife's birthplace in England. The discovery of NICKEL and COPPER during digging for the railway provided the impetus for growth. The Canadian Copper Co was formed 1886 and smelting operations were started 1888. In 1902 Canadian Copper merged with Orford Refining Co to later form International Nickel (INCO LTD). Falconbridge Nickel Mines was formed in 1928. After 1960 the significance of the mining sector declined in relation to employment in health care (4 major hospitals), telecommunications (Bell Canada), government (Revenue Canada), tourism (Science North) and education (LAURENTIAN U and Cambrian College).

Cityscape Sudbury's development was constrained by railway lines and the topography. The community was also hindered by the lack of a solid property-tax base, receiving no taxes from the mining industry. It gradually expanded outwards along the major roads divided by rocky ridges into the adjoining townships and the "valley" within the Sudbury Basin, the centre of which forms an extensive plain. Planning in the 1950s led to numerous projects, including one of Canada's most successful urban renewal schemes and an outstanding civic centre. The mining industry created some barren landscapes, but the area has been the site of one of the world's largest urban land-reclamation schemes.

Population: 88 717 (1986c), 91 829 (1981c); 148 877 (1986 CMA), 156 121 (1981 ACMA)
Rate of Increase (1981-86): (City) -3.4%; (CMA) -4.6%
Rank in Canada: Twenty-first (by CMA)
Date of Incorporation: Town 1893; City 1930
Land Area: City 262.73 km²; 2612.11 km² (CMA)
Elevation: 347 m
Climate: Average daily temp, July 18.7°C, Jan -13.7°C; Yearly precip 860.6 mm; Hours of sunshine 2059.8 per year

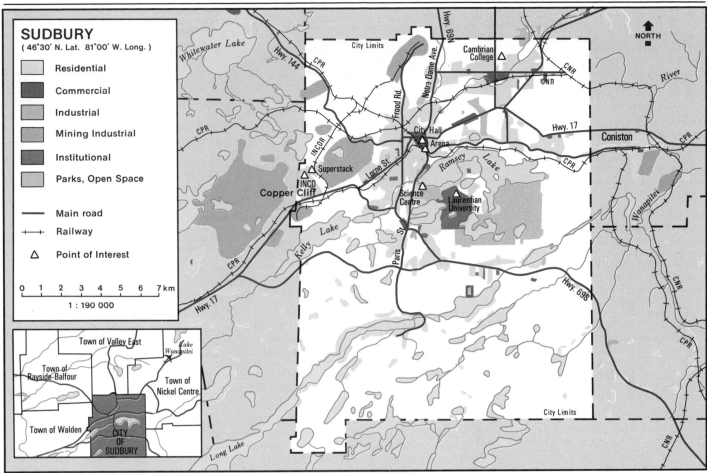

SUDBURY
(46°30′ N. Lat. 81°00′ W. Long.)

Residential

Commercial

Industrial

Mining Industrial

Institutional

Parks, Open Space

Main road

Railway

△ Point of Interest

0 1 2 3 4 5 6 7 km

1 : 190 000

Population Sudbury's population was 2027 in 1901 and doubled in each census decade up to 1931; as a result of a major amalgamation and annexation (1960) it rose to 80 120 by 1961. In 1971 city and metropolitan area totalled 90 535 and 155 424, respectively. With another expansion in 1973, the city reached 91 829 by 1981. Massive layoffs, a long strike and low metal prices combined to reduce the population to 88 717 by 1986. The ethnic makeup is bicultural, with the British and French each constituting at least 30% of the population. More than 60% is Roman Catholic.

Economy and Labour Force Sudbury is Canada's most important mining community. In 1951 more than 40% of the population was engaged in mining, though by 1985 that sector employed less than 15% of the community. The area remains the largest single source of nickel in the world and is Canada's largest copper producer. IRON-ORE pellets, acid and precious metals are also produced. Employment in services and public administration has grown considerably, along with wholesaling and distribution operations. With uncertain long-term prospects for mining, Sudbury will capitalize on its location and political importance for new employment opportunities. The labour force has contributed significantly to Canada's union movement.

Transportation After 1883 rail connections were established with Sault Ste Marie (1887) and Toronto (1908). Highway links with North Bay and Sault Ste Marie were initiated in 1912. In 1956 Hwy 69 S to Gravenhurst was opened. The first connection with Timmins, via Hwy 144, began in 1970. Air service has been provided by the Sudbury Municipal Airport from 1954. Since 1971, Norontair, a provincially owned airline, has offered an important connective service.

Government and Politics Town and city status

were acquired in 1893 and 1930, respectively. In 1973 the city became part of the Regional Municipality of Sudbury, which includes the towns Capreol, Nickel Centre, Onaping Falls, Rayside-Balfour, Valley East and Walden. A major political issue is the need to diversify the economy.

Cultural Life The cultural scene has been enhanced by the establishment of Laurentian U (1960) and Cambrian College (1966). An increasing francophone influence is evidenced by the organization La Slague and the opening of Place St Joseph. Sudbury has 3 main museums: Laurentian Museum and Arts Centre, Flour Mill Museum and Copper Cliff Museum. Professional theatre is performed by the Sudbury Theatre Centre and Le Théâtre du Nouvel-Ontario. The Philharmonic Society (1957) was reconstituted in 1975 as the Sudbury Symphony Orchestra. Other musical groups include the Karl Pukara Accordian Orchestra, the singing group CANO and several ethnic choirs. The Northern Lights Folk Festival is a popular event. Local newspapers include the Sudbury *Daily Star*, *Northern Life*, *Le Voyageur* and *Northern Ontario Business*. The Sudbury Wolves is a major Junior A hockey team.

O.W. SAARINEN

Reading: Laurentian University, *Centennial History of Sudbury* (1983).

Suez Crisis On 26 July 1956 Egyptian President Nasser seized the predominantly Anglo-French Suez Canal Co, which had operated the canal since 1869. Nasser's takeover of the canal, connecting the Mediterranean and Red seas, was a blow to Western pride and commerce. Diplomacy failed, and Britain, France and Israel secretly agreed to move against Egypt. Israel attacked Oct 29, advancing in a single day to within 42 km of the canal. As planned with Israel beforehand, Britain and France ordered Israel and Egypt to withdraw from the immediate area of the canal.

Nasser refused. On Oct 31 Britain and France intervened directly, bombing the Canal Zone.

Privately the Canadian government was angry at an action which split the COMMONWEALTH and alienated the US. Publicly the Canadian role was that of conciliator. L.B. PEARSON, secretary of state for external affairs, and his colleagues at the UNITED NATIONS won overwhelming General Assembly support Nov 4 for an international force "to secure and supervise the cessation of hostilities." Canadian Gen E.L.M. BURNS was immediately named commander of the UN Emergency Force (UNEF). The British and French, however, ignored the UN resolution and landed paratroopers in the Canal Zone late on Nov 4. Under pressure, largely American, placed on British PM Sir Anthony Eden, a cease-fire was achieved Nov 6. Pearson fought successfully to have Canadian soldiers included in UNEF; advance units of the force arrived in mid-Nov. Although Pearson was awarded the 1957 Nobel Peace Prize for his peacemaking efforts at the UN, there were many in Britain and Canada who were dismayed by Ottawa's apparent lack of support for Britain. Such sentiment was probably a factor in the Liberal government's defeat in the general election of 1957. *See also* PEACEKEEPING. NORMAN HILLMER

Sugar Industry, a sector of Canada's FOOD AND BEVERAGE INDUSTRIES composed of companies that make cane, beet and invert sugars, sucrose syrup, molasses and beet pulp. The Canadian sugar-refining industry (excluding the MAPLE-SUGAR segment) began in the early 1850s with the establishment of a cane sugar-refining company in Montréal. By the early 1900s there were refining operations in Halifax, NS; Saint John, NB; Toronto, Ont; and Vancouver, BC. All of these operations produced refined sugar from imported raw sugar, extracted from tropical sugarcane plants. Another important source of Canadian sugar has been domestically grown sugar beets. The first refinery in Canada designed to extract sugar from beets, La Compagnie de sucre de betterave de Québec, was established in Farnham, Qué, in 1881. Two more Québec-based beet refineries started in the same year. By 1902 there were 4 sugar-beet manufacturing plants in operation in Ontario; in 1903 the Knight Sugar Company was established in Alberta. At present, no beet sugar is produced in Ontario; all Canadian production comes from plants situated in Québec, Manitoba and Alberta.

The latest sweetening agent, high-fructose corn syrup or sweetener (HFCS), is increasingly important. This product is already used in SOFT-DRINK production and some CONFECTIONERY products, and many more food products will use it in future. Two large HFCS production facilities were in operation in Ontario in 1982; a third began production in 1983. At present, only 5% of the sweetener demand in Canada is supplied by HFCS.

The traditional profile of the sweetener industry was also changed in 1982 when the Health Protection Branch of Health and Welfare Canada approved the use of "aspartame" in Canadian foods. This artificial sweetener, which adds no calories, was immediately used for diet soft drinks and, within a year, appeared in at least 8% of the industry's total beverage output. Industry executives feel that aspartame will eventually be used in some 20% of Canadian soft-drink production and, increasingly, in diet or low-calorie food products (eg, processed fruits, fruit fillings, etc).

Most countries that produce or use sugar, including Canada, are signatories to the International Sugar Agreement (ISA), which aims to prevent extremes in world sugar prices, and thus aims to protect the interests of both cane-producing countries and consumers of raw sugar. In Canada the industry is regulated by several federal agencies, including Agriculture Canada and Consumer and Corporate Affairs. The industry is represented by the Canadian Sugar Institute in Toronto; members include all Canadian refining companies.

In recent years, annual production of refined sugar from raw sugarcane has averaged about 0.9-1.0 billion kg and production of refined sugar from Canadian-grown sugar beets has fluctuated between 90-135 million kg. Nine sugar-refining establishments now operate in Canada (excluding HFCS facilities): NB has 1; Qué, 3; Ont, 2; Man, 1; Alta, 1; and BC, 1. This number has decreased since 1980.

The sugar-refining industry employed 1500 in 1985, down from 1800 in 1980; and spent $249 million in 1985, down from $641 million in 1980, for materials and supplies. The extremely volatile nature of international raw-sugar prices accounts for the radical cost fluctuation. The international situation also drastically influences the annual value of the refining industry's shipments, which from 1975 to 1985 ranged from $437 million to $859 million. In 1985 the value of shipments was $454 million.   ROBERT F. BARRATT

Suicide is the act of voluntary and intentional self-destruction. Many Western philosophers have employed the concept of suicide as a starting point for reflection on human existence. Suicide was decriminalized in Canada in 1972; someone who now attempts suicide is not liable to sanction under the Criminal Code. However, anyone found guilty of counselling another to take his or her own life or of aiding a suicide is liable to imprisonment of up to 14 years, whether or not the suicide is successful. A peace officer or a physician may order involuntary detention of any person judged a danger to himself or herself.

Suicide statistics are described in Statistics Canada records as "deaths reported by coroners and medical examiners of official death registrations as having been due or 'probably due' to suicide, following the usual postmortem inquiry, investigation, or inquest as required by law." Official statistics on suicide in most countries are inadequate because of poor record keeping, insufficient information, and tendencies on the part of medical personnel and other officials to mislabel or hide suicides, or to refrain from investigations of suspicious deaths to protect the survivors of the victim. However, suicide statistics from many nations do indicate trends over time, differences among countries, and differences among specific groups within a country. Canada's 1986 rate of 14.5 suicides per year per 100 000 people places it between nations with rates of over 20 suicides per 100 000, eg, Hungary, Czechoslovakia and Sweden, and those with rates of approximately 5 or under, eg, Mexico, Ireland and Israel. Émile Durkheim's observation in *Suicide* (1897) on the suicide rates of nations is still true: a given nation has a characteristic suicide rate which fluctuates very little from year to year and which generally remains relative to the rates of other nations. In 1986, 3670 suicides were recorded in Canada, 2850 by males, 820 by females. Suicide is among the top 10 causes of death in Canada and is second to accidents as the leading cause of death for people under 35. Males are more likely to employ more violent and certain methods, eg, firearms, explosives, hanging, while females are more likely to use drugs.

There is substantial provincial variation across Canada, ie, suicide rates rise from east to west. Prince Edward Island has the lowest rate of all the provinces and the territories; the Yukon has the highest rate. Generally, in Canada the incidence of suicide is low among youth, increases until the middle years and declines after the age of 55 except among single males, for whom it increases until approximately 75 years of age. However, there has been a recent increase in rates among younger people, especially younger males. Married people are less likely to commit suicide than single, widowed or divorced people, the exception being widowed women over 75, who have a

low rate of suicide. Proportionately, native people and prison inmates also have a far higher incidence of suicide than that of the general Canadian population.

While it has been established that climate and heredity bear no relationship to the incidence of suicide, a considerable array of social and psychological characteristics have been linked with self-destruction. Students of suicide agree that some personality types seem to be more vulnerable to suicidal behaviour. The major psychological theory of suicide, deriving from Freud, links suicide with hostile impulses turned back upon the self. Karl Menninger has suggested that every suicide reflects the wish to kill, the wish to be killed, and the wish to die. Immediate difficulties (eg, loss of a loved one, a career), despair, loneliness or an unhappy home life may also precipitate self-destruction.

Programs aimed at preventing suicide range from those that attempt to identify potential suicides to those that provide effective first-aid and follow-up for suicide attempters. Restricting the availability of firearms, erecting barriers on bridges and other "attractive hazards," and reducing the toxicity of gas have reduced suicide rates in some locations. Recently, the growth of

	Total number of suicides		Per 100 000 of population	
	Male	*Female*	*Male*	*Female*
Canada	2850	820	22.8	6.4
Nfld	17	6	59.9	2.1
PEI	10	4	15.9	6.3
NS	78	16	18.1	3.6
NB	79	17	22.5	4.7
Qué	885	263	27.6	7.9
Ont	854	276	19.1	6.0
Man	120	33	22.9	6.1
Sask	107	31	21.2	6.1
Alta	342	82	28.7	7.0
BC	337	88	23.6	6.0
Yukon	8	2	65.1	17.9
NWT	13	2	47.4	8.1

Suicide (Male-Female Ratios): Totals and per 100 000 for Canada and Provinces and Territories, 1986 (Source: Statistics Canada)

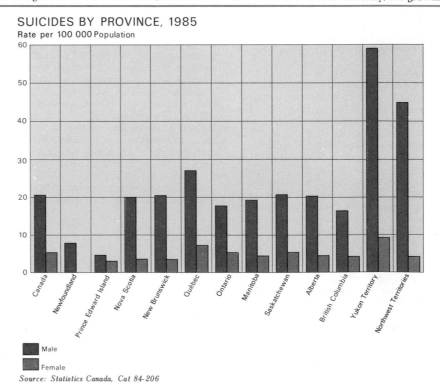

SUICIDES BY PROVINCE, 1985
Rate per 100 000 Population

■ Male
■ Female

Source: Statistics Canada, Cat 84-206

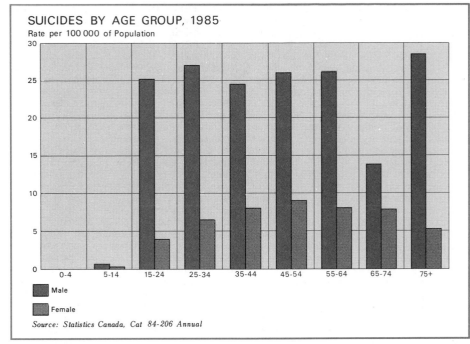

SUICIDES BY AGE GROUP, 1985
Rate per 100 000 of Population

Male

Female

Source: Statistics Canada, Cat 84-206 Annual

crisis or distress centres, which provide the opportunity for people to telephone trained volunteers and discuss problems anonymously, have been regarded as hopeful developments in suicide prevention.   F.K. ANDREWS

Suknaski, Andrew, poet (b at Wood Mountain, Sask 30 July 1942). Suknaski's 1976 volume, *Wood Mountain Poems*, is one of the most important and influential books in contemporary western Canadian poetry. Born of Ukrainian and Polish parents, Suknaski bears witness to the ethnic history and heritage of the West. He writes of Wood Mountain's people, both past and present, of the various nationalities and generations of settlers, and of the native peoples whose land it first was. His poems recreate the vividness of oral narration; they celebrate the lives and struggles of his literal and symbolic ancestors. Suknaski's narrative style has been the dominant influence on Prairie poetry of the late 1970s and 1980s; his own recent work has been in search of a form to contain the vast reach of his historical vision. A representative sampling of Suknaski's poetry may be found in *The Land They Gave Away: New and Selected Poems* (1982). *Silk Trail* was published in 1985.   STEPHEN SCOBIE

Sullivan, Francis Conroy, architect (b at Kingston, Ont 2 July 1882; d at Phoenix, Ariz 4 Apr 1929). The only Canadian pupil of Frank Lloyd Wright, Sullivan designed a remarkable group of buildings, in the Prairie School style, 1911-1916, including the Connors house and the Lansdowne Park Horticulture Building, Ottawa; Sainte-Claire de Goulbourne, near Dwyer Hill, Ont; public library, Pembroke, Ont; and post offices at Stonewall, Man, and Shawville, Qué. Wright's influence was crucial for Sullivan's mature style, but there are important differences. Horizontals predominate in Wright's designs; Sullivan's strong verticals create tension within the masses. This feature has been attributed to Ontario Victorian Gothic. But it may instead stem from the classical buildings of George BROWNE in Kingston, where Sullivan grew up in an Irish family which had long been active in the building trade.   J. DOUGLAS STEWART

Sullivan, Sir William Wilfred, journalist, lawyer, politician, premier of PEI 1879-89, judge (b at Hope River, PEI 6 Dec 1843; d at Memram-

cook, NB 30 Sept 1920). Appointed assistant editor of the *Charlottetown Herald* 1864, Sullivan was elected, initially as a Liberal, to the PEI Legislative Assembly in 1872 and thereafter until he resigned in 1889. Elected leader of the Opposition in 1877, Sullivan, a Catholic, formed a Conservative government in 1879. Premier for over 10 years, a strong advocate of the Island's rights, Sullivan was appointed chief justice in 1889 and created a knight bachelor in 1914, 3 years before he retired from the bench.   NICOLAS J. DE JONG

Sulphur (S), bright yellow to yellowish brown, brittle, nonmetallic element which melts at 119°C. Sulphur is widely distributed: in elemental form, especially associated with gypsum and limestone in SEDIMENTARY ROCKS of Tertiary age; and in combined form, in most rock types of all ages. Sulphur has been used since antiquity; today it is employed in the production of almost everything we eat, wear or use. In Canada sulphur is obtained mainly from hydrocarbons, but also from metallic sulphides. The processing of metallic sulphides for their sulphur content began in 1866. Early operations involved roasting pyrite (an iron ore, FeS_2) for the production of sulphuric acid (H_2SO_4). In the 1920s use of base-metal smelter gases for the manufacture of by-product sulphuric acid began near Sudbury, Ont, and at Trail, BC. Effluent gas from smelting sulphide ores contains 1-12% sulphur dioxide (SO_2). Recovered SO_2 is used directly to manufacture sulphuric acid. The largest smelter H_2SO_4 plant in Canada is that of INCO Metals Company at Copper Cliff, Ont. Pyrite and pyrrhotite concentrates produced as a by-product of base-metal mining operations are sometimes marketed for their sulphur content.

Although major efforts have been made by some smelting companies to reduce their emissions of sulpher dioxide, much remains to be done to resolve the acid rain problem in eastern Canada. This will require large capital expenditures for the construction of sulphur recovery equipment by industry and is likely to require assistance from governments in some form or another to alleviate the negative impact on the economic viability of the companies involved, at least initially.

Before the first sour-gas recovery plant was built in 1951, almost all Canadian sulphur pro-

duction was from metallic sulphides. Highly toxic and corrosive hydrogen sulphide (H_2S), the dominant sulphur compound in sour natural gas, is at present the most important source of sulphur. There are plants in Alberta, BC and Saskatchewan. Most producing sour-gas fields contain 1-20% sulphur by weight; however, some Canadian companies are currently pursuing research on the recovery of high H_2S (60% or higher) gases for their sulphur value. Currently sulphur is recovered by the modified Claus Process. In the process H_2S is extracted by means of a chemical reaction and fed to a furnace. Gas from the furnace is then passed through a condenser-converter series and liquid sulphur is removed until 95% or more of the original sulphur has been drawn off. The liquid sulphur is either pumped to outside blocks where it solidifies, to storage tanks for direct shipping in liquid form, or to slating or prilling plants. Declining production has led to the development of sulphur melters to reclaim base pad sulphur from block storage. A minor amount of sulphur is recovered from domestic and imported crude oils and tar sands. Some crude oils contain as much as 5% sulphur; domestic crudes generally have less sulphur than imported ones. Recovery techniques are similar to those used in sour gas. As yet almost no sulphur is recovered from COAL.

World production of all forms of sulphur was 54.8 million t in 1985 and about 55 million t in 1986. Shipments by Canadian producers were 8.9 million t in 1985 and 7.6 million t in 1986. Production value was $1.1 billion and $1.0 billion respectively, which represents about 8% of the total value of Canadian nonfuel mineral production. Canada ranks third in world production (after the US and the USSR) and is the world's largest exporter of elemental sulphur. The principal export markets in recent years were Africa and Asia, with 27% each, and the US, accounting for about 14% of exports. Canadian consumption of sulphur in all forms was 1.4 million t in 1985. The principal users are the fertilizer (55%), pulp and paper (20%) and metal-refining (10%) industries. *See also* ACID RAIN; CHEMICAL INDUSTRIES.
              J.Y. TREMBLAY and M.A. BOUCHER

Sulpicians, society of diocesan priests founded in Paris in 1641 by Jean-Jacques Olier de Verneuil to put into practice the decisions of the Council of Trent (1545-1563) concerning the formation of diocesan clergy. The first foundation was the Seminary of St Sulpice, Paris; hence their official name, the Company of Priests of St Sulpice. Olier can also be considered to be one of the founders of the city of Montréal; along with the Servant of God Jérôme le Royer de la Dauversière he founded the Society of Our Lady of Montréal, in whose name Paul de Chomedey, sieur de MAISONNEUVE, led the expedition which founded VILLE-MARIE [Montréal] in 1642. In 1657 the Sulpicians arrived. Seigneurs of Montréal until the English Conquest, they were missionaries and educators, and trained some of the clergy, a role which they still carry out today, as well as parish ministry and other pastoral duties. In 1986 there were 130 Canadian members (26.7% of the world total).
              MICHEL THÉRIAULT

Sumac, shrub of genus *Rhus* of family Anacardiaceae. Family includes cashew, smoke tree, mango, pistachio, POISON IVY and several cultivated tropical ornamentals. In eastern Canada, the most familiar variation is staghorn sumac (named because hairy twigs resemble stags' horns), a large, nonpoisonous, clone-forming shrub bearing scarlet leaves in autumn, used as an ORNAMENTAL. Red, hairy fruits can be made into pink "lemonade" by bruising them, straining the acid water and adding sugar. Fragrant sumac (*R. aromatica*) is a small, nonpoisonous, thicket-forming

Staghorn sumac (*Rhus typhina*), the most familiar sumac in eastern Canada (*artwork by Claire Tremblay*).

shrub about 1 m tall. Poison sumac (*R. vernix*), a 5 m tall shrub, is extremely poisonous; contact results in the dermatitis associated with poison ivy. Smooth sumac (*R. glabra*) is most common in BC and extends to Ontario. It resembles staghorn sumac but has smooth twigs. *See also* POISONOUS PLANTS.   J.M. GILLETT

Summerland, BC, District Municipality, inc 1906, pop 7775 (1986c), 7473 (1981c), located on the W bank of Okanagan Lk in the southern interior of BC between Kelowna and Penticton. The area was originally inhabited by the Okanagan Indians and became grazing land for them and white settlers in the 1880s. Fruit orchards, particularly for peaches, began in the 1890s and a townsite was laid out in 1902 by developer John M. Robinson. He named the townsite Summerland in reference to the warm, dry climate of the OKANAGAN VALLEY. The original townsite was a harbour for steamboats on the lake but after 1905 "West Summerland," away from the lake, became the town centre. The federal government established the Summerland Research Station, serving the tree fruit and grape industries, in 1914. The Kettle Valley Railway opened a station in the community in 1915 which closed in 1964. Since the early 1960s the population of Summerland has doubled with many of the orchards being subdivided. Today close to 40% of the population are retirees. The economy is based on tourism, agriculture, fruit packing, a winery and a sawmill.   JOHN R. STEWART

Summerside, PEI, Town, pop 8020 (1986c), 7828 (1981c), inc 1877, is located near the head of Bedeque Bay on the province's southern shore, 60 km W of Charlottetown. Until the Loyalist arrival in Prince County, the first settlers in the area

A View of Summerside, PEI, c 1880, watercolour on paper, by George Ackerman (*courtesy Confederation Centre Art Gallery, Charlottetown*).

had been MICMAC and then ACADIANS. Around 1800 the tiny village was known as Green's Shore, after Daniel Green, the tract's former owner. It was likely named after Summerside House, a licensed inn (est 1840). The village was launched as a shipbuilding centre when inadequate draught at his shipyard in Bedeque compelled Joseph Pope to rebuild his company in deeper water across the bay. After the late 19th-century collapse of shipbuilding, trade with the county's farming community sustained Summerside's economy. Beginning around 1910, the town experienced renewed prosperity as a fur-trading centre, stimulated by Sir Charles Dalton and Robert T. Oulton's successful breeding of silver foxes in captivity. In 1920 Summerside was established as the headquarters of the Canadian National Silver Fox Breeders' Assn. Owing to overproduction, changing women's fashions and innovative dyeing techniques, this highly profitable enterprise collapsed around 1945. However, economic decline was offset by the 1941 construction of an air force base in nearby St Eleanors. As the Island's principal port for potato shipments, and with the development of a number of small manufacturing businesses, as well as the trade with CFB Summerside and the county's farmers and fishermen, Summerside is today a thriving community.   W.S. KEIZER

Sun, a typical star, is an incandescent gaseous globe, 1.39 million km in diameter, with a mass of 2×10^{30} kg, an effective temperature of approximately 5800 K and surface radiant power of 4×10^{20} megawatts (MW). Earth intercepts only 17×10^{10} MW, mostly as visible light and infrared radiation; for comparison, the total generating capacity of Canadian electrical plants is under 10^5 MW. The current theory, called solar nucleosynthesis, states that the sun's power originates in nuclear reactions occurring in a hot (15 million K) core which contains half the solar mass in only 1.5% of its volume. Geological and astronomical evidence suggests that the reactions were triggered 5 billion years ago when the temperature and density at the centre of a condensing cloud of primordial interstellar gas rose to levels where hydrogen atoms fused into helium atoms. The heat released by this NUCLEAR FUSION creates enough internal pressure to counterbalance gravitational contraction. This equilibrium will last for billions of years before the sun's outflow of energy is drastically altered. The theory of solar nucleosynthesis is being challenged because observational tests have failed, so far, to detect the predicted flux of neutrinos, ie, highly penetrating particles which should be emitted from the sun's nuclear furnace.

Because the sun's visible surface (photosphere) is opaque, the nature of its interior must be deduced by applying fundamental laws of PHYSICS to the measured surface properties. The application of seismic methods to "sunquakes" (ie, vibrations of the entire sun) can fix the location and motions of internal disturbances and reveals that convective turbulence extends to a depth of 200 000 km. Such knowledge is vital to explain sunspot formation. The cool (about 3700 K), strongly magnetic spots are believed to emerge from below the photosphere. They range in size from pores of 1000 km to elongated, irregular clusters of spots spanning 200 000 km. A typical spot, 30 000 km across, emerges in a day or 2, accompanied by smaller companions of opposite magnetic polarity; the group disintegrates in under 2 weeks. Intense

magnetic fields exist outside of sunspots as clusters of elements, each element being no more than 300 km across. An active region consists of a sunspot group embedded in irregular, dense aggregates of magnetic elements. The sun does not rotate as a rigid body about its axis: the solar equator rotates in 25 days, a solar parallel of latitude at 60°, in 29 days. This differential rotation organizes the churning gaseous fluid in the sun's shell in a dynamo action which creates the magnetic patterns characteristic of sunspot activity. The average number of spots grows and fades in an 11-year cycle. Successive cycles can vary greatly in amplitude; however, extremely low activity can last for almost a century (eg, the "Maunder Minimum," 1645-1715 AD). Solar activity may influence CLIMATE CHANGE on Earth but no direct, physical link has been identified.

The sun's rarefied outer atmosphere (chromosphere and corona) is too faint to be visible to the unaided eye, except when the moon blocks the photosphere during a total solar eclipse. The chromosphere then appears as a highly irregular, pink-red band, a few thousand kilometres thick, which is surrounded by the pearly corona that extends in jagged streamers for millions of kilometres. Magnetic fields shape both regions. A temperature inversion begins 300 km above the photosphere: the top of the chromosphere is 15 000 K hotter than its base; the corona is at 1.5 million K. The explanation of the high temperatures is disputed. The corona is too hot to be restrained by the sun's gravity; it expands as a supersonic solar wind consisting chiefly of electrons, protons and helium atoms and having a speed, near Earth, of 300-800 km/s. The rate of mass loss, in millions of tonnes per second, is only 3×10^{-14} solar masses annually.

Explosions called solar flares erupt when magnetic stresses stored in active regions are suddenly released. Terrestrial side effects of large flares include geomagnetic storms, enhanced NORTHERN LIGHTS and ionospheric disturbances. In addition, high-speed streams in the solar wind, unrelated to flares or sunspots, strongly agitate the Earth's magnetosphere. These streams originate in "coronal holes," vast spaces of reduced temperature and density, where coronal magnetic field lines are open to interplanetary space.

Canadian research in solar physics dates from the construction in 1905 of spectrographic apparatus at the Dominion Observatory, Ottawa, for application to solar eclipses and to the measurement of the sun's differential rotation. Solar radio ASTRONOMY in Canada began in 1946 at the Radio and Electrical Engineering Division of the NATIONAL RESEARCH COUNCIL, Ottawa. Since then, NRC laboratories have daily monitored the flux of microwaves emitted by the sun at 2800 MHz, a measurement used worldwide as an index of solar activity. NRC's Ottawa River Solar Observatory (est 1970) records and analyzes fine chromospheric structures related to sunspot activity and flares. Observations of the sun's far infrared spectrum are made by U of C from BALLOONS and high-altitude aircraft.

                    V. GAIZAUSKAS

Sun, Vancouver's largest daily newspaper (1986 average paid circulation Mon-Thur: 229 692), first appeared as the *Vancouver Sun,* 12 Feb 1912, "to consistently advocate the principles of Liberalism." Under publisher Robert Cromie and his sons, notably Donald Cromie, the *Sun* tended to support the Liberals but was often critical of them. The *Sun* expanded by buying out other NEWSPAPERS. With its 1917 purchase of the *Daily News-Advertiser* (est 1886), it claimed to be the city's oldest newspaper; with its 1924 acquisition of the *Evening World* (est 1888), it became undisputedly the city's second most important newspaper. Not until its chief rival, the *Vancouver Daily Province,* suffered a prolonged labour dispute (1946-49) did the *Sun* emerge as the leading journal of the province. The majority of Cromie family holdings in Sun Publishing Co were sold to FP Publications Ltd in 1963 and in 1980 SOUTHAM INC bought the newspaper. The *Sun* has been politically independent for many years.   PATRICIA E. ROY

Sun Dance, an annual Plains Indian culture ceremony given at midsummer when bands and tribes congregated at a predetermined location. The Sun Dance was forbidden under the Indian Act of 1885, but this ban was generally ignored and dropped from the Indian Act of 1951. The ceremony was arranged by an individual either as a request for supernatural aid or in response to a vision. Among the BLACKFOOT and SARCEE, women took the initiative. Following 4 days of preliminary ritual, the Sun Dance lasted another 4 days and focused on erecting the sacred dance pole and sacred lodge. On the final day several dances took place. The Sun-Gaze Dances symbolized capture, torture, captivity and escape, and involved self-torture. Dancers enjoyed prestige from that time on. The Sun Dance was an emotional experience and an opportunity to renew kinship ties, arrange marriages and exchange property.
RENÉ R. GADACZ

Sun Newspapers The Toronto Sun Publishing Corporation (Sun Publishing), Canada's largest publisher of English language tabloid newspapers, was formed on 4 Feb 1978, through the amalgamation of Toronto Sun Holdings Ltd and Toronto Sun Publishing Ltd. In 1971, Toronto Sun Publishing Ltd purchased syndication operations and newspaper vending boxes from the *Toronto Telegram*, which had ceased publication. With the aid of staff also recruited from the *Telegram*, on 1 Nov 1971, it published its first edition of the *Toronto Sun*. On 16 Sept 1973, it introduced the *Sunday Sun*. Unlike traditional Canadian newspaper publishers, Toronto Sun, except for its Sunday edition, did away with home delivery and concentrated its effort primarily on street sales to early morning commuters.

On 14 Feb 1978, the company entered into a partnership agreement with Edmonton Sun Publishing Ltd to publish its second tabloid, the *Edmonton Sun* – first edition 2 Apr 1978. In 1981 the *Edmonton Sun* became a wholly owned operation with the acquisition of all outstanding shares of Edmonton Sun Publishing Ltd. The *Calgary Albertan*, acquired on 31 July 1980 for $1.3 million, was subsequently transformed into the company's third daily tabloid, the *Calgary Sun* – first edition 3 Aug 1980. The fiscal year of 1983 was significant for the company. In May 1982, control passed from Sun Publishing's founding shareholders to MACLEAN HUNTER LIMITED (MH), one of Canada's largest cross-media owners. Maclean Hunter acquired approximately 50% of the Toronto Sun Publishing Corp for $55 million. For MH, although already a major publisher, this acquisition marked its only venture into Canadian daily newspaper publishing. MH currently holds 51% interest. Sun Publishing expanded its operations into the US in 1983 with its acquisition, for approximately $100 million US, of the *Houston Post*, largest morning paper in the American Southwest. The paper was sold for $150 million US in Nov 1987. In Oct 1987 Sun Publishing acquired the Financial Post Division of Maclean Hunter Ltd for $46 million. It became Canada's first daily financial paper 2 Feb 1988; it still retains its weekly issue. In 1986 Sun Publishing Corp employed 2500 full-time and its 4 newspapers sold over 750 000 copies daily and over one million each Sunday. Net income for its 1986 operations was $15 million, based on total revenues of $334 million and total assets of $8.2 billion.   PETER S. ANDERSON

John Sunday as a young man. Painting by W. Gush (*courtesy Methodist Archives and Research Centre, Manchester, England*).

Sunday, John, or Shah-wun-dais, meaning "sultry heat," Mississauga (Ojibwa) chief, Methodist missionary (b at New York C 1795; d at Alderville, Ont 14 Dec 1875). This hardened warrior, a veteran of the WAR OF 1812, only knew 3 words of English before his conversion to Christianity: "pint," "quart" and "whisky." After he joined the Methodists in 1826 he immediately stopped drinking and won back his self-respect and the respect of his tribe. An eloquent speaker in Ojibwa, he was a travelling missionary in the Lk Superior region and later in 1836 was ordained a regular minister. Elected chief of his band, the Ojibwa of the Belleville and Kingston area, he presented their LAND CLAIMS to the government of Upper Canada. After his return from a missionary tour of Britain in 1837 he served for 20 years at missions at Alderville, Rice Lk and Muncey. Among his Methodist brethren Shah-wun-dais was in constant demand as a speaker at church gatherings.   DONALD B. SMITH

Sunday Schools, fd 1780 in Gloucester, Eng, by newspaper publisher Robert Raikes to take labouring children off the streets on Sundays. Religious instruction, later the main curriculum, was at first secondary to teaching reading and writing. Religious education has been an element in the Roman Catholic Church for some 2000 years, primarily through catechism classes. However, Sunday schools have been limited almost exclusively to the Reformed or Protestant traditions, largely as a legacy of Swiss theologian John Calvin's stress on rational learning. Raikes's innovation, quickly copied in Britain, was brought to Canada mainly by the PRESBYTERIAN and CONGREGATIONAL churches.

The date and location of Canada's first Sunday school are unclear. The Church of England (*see* ANGLICANS) had one in Halifax in 1783. A Congregational minister, Rev Francis Dick, may have organized the first Sunday school in the Canadas, in Québec in 1801. The first documented inauguration was by Secessionist Presbyterian minister Rev William Smart, who arrived in Brockville, Ont, 7 Oct 1811 and opened a Sunday school the following Sunday. The movement grew rapidly. The Montréal-based Sunday School Union of Canada was founded probably in 1822, and in

1836 its apparent successor, the Canada Sunday School Union, was formed to promote development in new regions. In 1865 a convention of teachers and leaders resulted in the new Sunday Schools Association of Canada.

Initially the Bible was the sole curriculum, with much emphasis placed on memorization of scripture. Gradually supplementary curricula were developed locally, and in 1874 the International Uniform Lessons series was introduced, based on current pedagogical methods. In 1908 a graded curriculum became available and refinements followed. The first curriculum developed entirely in Canada was the UNITED CHURCH's "New Curriculum" of 1963. It was attacked in the media by conservative denominations for being too "liberal" in its theology and ended several decades of curriculum co-operation between the United and BAPTIST churches. Though widely praised by educators and theologians and copied in varying degrees by other denominations, the New Curriculum had the misfortune to be introduced just when Sunday school populations began to plummet in all denominations. United Church registration declined from 757 338 in 1961 to 231 535 in 1981; during the same period some 1400 Sunday schools were closed.

Other denominations experienced similar losses. Sociologist Reginald Bibby notes that 2 out of 3 Canadian adults claim to have attended religious services regularly as children, but only one in 3 now exposes children to religious education in the churches. Since the Protestant churches have traditionally depended on Sunday schools as the source of adult memberships, Bibby forecasts church attendance declining to one in 6 by the turn of the century.

It is of interest to note that some Roman Catholic and Eastern Orthodox churches have recently adopted the use of Sunday schools to augment the traditional religious formation provided by the Divine Liturgy. A number of Jewish, Moslem, Hindu, Buddhist and Sikh communities have also adapted this Christian institution to provide their children with an intentional religious education deemed necessary to combat the Christian culture and secular society of N America. Curriculum style has been taken from the Christian models. For example, Jodo Shinshu Buddhist churches have incorporated the singing of Sunday school choruses such as, "Yes Jesus loves me," by simply replacing the key word so it goes, "Yes Buddha loves me."   JAMES TAYLOR

Sunday Shopping On 24 Apr 1985 the Supreme Court of Canada in the BIG M DRUG MART case struck down the Lord's Day Act on the grounds that it contravened the freedom of religion and conscience provision in the CANADIAN CHARTER OF RIGHTS AND FREEDOMS. Mr Justice Dickson concluded that the purpose of the Lord's Day Act was sabbatical observance and held that "To the extent that it binds all to a sectarian Christian ideal, the Lord's Day Act works a form of coercion inimical to the spirit of the Charter and the dignity of all non-Christians. ...It takes religious values rooted in Christian morality and, using the force of the state, translates them into a positive law binding on believers and non-believers alike."

The federal Lord's Day Act made it an offence to transact business on Sunday. It was part of a legislative tradition which started in the 17th century in England. An "Act for punishing divers Abuses committed on the Lord's Day," called Sunday, was passed during the reign of Charles I.

While the *Big M* case was a landmark decision, it did not end the Sunday closing controversy. In fact it was probably just the first case of what will likely become known as the Supreme Court Sunday closing trilogy. The *Big M* decision stands for the proposition that legislation which has as its purpose the promotion of religious values is constitutionally suspect. It did not address the constitutional validity of provincial Sunday closing legislation designed to accomplish other than religious purposes, such as the promotion of family activities, or the impact the equal protection section of the Charter will have on Sunday closing legislation.

The Supreme Court of Canada tackled the former issue in the *Edwards Books* case in 1986. At stake was the constitutionality of Ontario's Retail Business Holiday Act, a law which made it an offence to carry on retail business on Sunday and other holidays. The court was satisfied that the purpose of the impugned law was the provision of uniform holidays for retail workers and dismissed claims that the statute was a colourable attempt to promote the religious observance of Sunday. Consideration was also given to the effect the Retail Business Holiday Act had on business, consumers and others in society. The Court appreciated that those with a religious obligation to rest on a day other than Sunday paid a higher price for religious fidelity than those who observed Sunday or no day. This was true for retailers and consumers who observed Saturday as the Sabbath. The latter would be open for business one less day a week than the Sunday observer and the former would find few stores open for business on Sunday. However, as significant as these burdens were on Saturday observers, they did not deter the court from adjudging that the state interest in a common pause day was of overriding importance and that the Act was valid. Of vital importance was the fact that the Act provided an exemption for those businesses which closed on Saturday.

In spite of the clarity and scholarship of the Supreme Court of Canada's *Big M* and *Edwards Books* decisions, Canadians still do not know whether Sunday closing laws are free of all Charter defects. As noted above, one important question remains outstanding. What effect will the equal protection provision of the Charter have on provincial and municipal Sunday closing laws? That question was not before the Supreme Court in the *Edwards Books* case, as the equal protection section of the Charter did not come into effect until 17 Apr 1985, a date later than that on which Edwards Books was charged with contravening Ontario's Retail Business Holiday Act.

The significance of equal protection values is likely to be considerable. It will force provinces and municipalities which are intent on enforcing Sunday closing laws to treat those who are similarly situated alike. Laws which impose burdens on retailers or classes of retailers, as opposed to wholesalers, manufacturers, contractors and other forms of economic activity, may well miss the constitutional mark. Challenges to legislative schemes which display these features are currently before lower courts. They will likely be decided by the Supreme Court of Canada sometime in 1989. Until then, the constitutionality of Sunday closing laws which single out retailers for adverse treatment must be regarded as doubtful.
                                    THOMAS W. WAKELING

Sunflower (genus *Helianthus*), common name for annual or perennial herbaceous plants native to the Western Hemisphere and belonging to the family Compositae. Some N American Indians grew a species of sunflower, later brought to Europe by Spanish explorers. It evolved into an important crop (*H. annuus* var. *macrocarpa*) in Russia in the 18th century and was introduced to Canada in 1875. Modern cultivars (commercial varieties) are mainly single cross or three-way hybrids. Sunflowers grow 1.25-1.75 m tall and ma-

Balsam root sunflower. The sunflower was introduced to Canada in 1875 (*photo by Tim Fitzharris*).

ture in 90-120 days. The more important or OIL-SEED type has dark, thin-hulled seeds, with 40-50% oil content. The confectionery type has larger, lighter-coloured seeds, with thicker hulls and lower oil content. Sunflowers grow in soils ranging from sand to clay, but prefer well-drained soils. Intertillage and herbicides control weeds. PLANT DISEASE is controlled by resistant cultivars and rotations with crops not attacked by the several pathogens of sunflowers. Natural parasites, insecticides and cultural practices combat INSECT PESTS. The highly polyunsaturated oil, popular for cooking, is also used in margarine and mayonnaise. The high-protein meal remaining after the oil is extracted is formulated into livestock feeds. Confectionery seed is sold whole, roasted and salted, or dehulled. Significant Canadian seed production started with 2000 ha in 1943. Most plantings are of the oilseed type; over 90% of the sunflower seed crop comes from Manitoba, while Saskatchewan produces much of the balance. Plantings vary from year to year, eg, from 89 000 t (1984) to 70 000 t (1985).   ERIC D. PUTT

Sung, Alfred, aka Sung Wang Moon, fashion designer (b at Shanghai, Hong Kong 26 Apr 1948). The son of a Hong Kong textile importer, Sung studied at Chambre syndicale de la couture parisienne and New York's Parsons School of Design. Moving to Toronto in 1972, he designed sportswear and in 1976 opened his own boutique, Moon. In 1981, with partners Saul and Joseph Mimran, he formed The Monaco Group in Toronto, which with Alfred Sung and Club Monaco shops in Canada and the US grossed $50 million-plus annually by 1986. Sung's work includes women's and men's wear, sportswear, fashion accessories, luggage, home fashions, watches and perfume. Known primarily for his uncomplicated and uncluttered design sense focusing on classic, clean lines, Sung is Canada's highest-profile designer.   GORDON MORASH

Sunken Ships/Shipwrecks As long as man has gone to sea, there have been shipwrecks. A frequent cause in earlier times was simply losing one's way and running aground; but failure of man's technology when pitted against the unforgiving sea also accounts for some of history's most infamous shipwrecks. The best-known example

of this was the sinking, on its maiden voyage, of the SS TITANIC, the greatest technological achievement of its day. It went to the bottom after a brief encounter with an iceberg on a foggy April night in 1912, 320 nautical miles off Newfoundland, with a loss of over 1500 lives.

Canada has also had its share of spectacular shipwrecks including, most notably, the Canadian Pacific passenger liner SS EMPRESS OF IRELAND which sank in the Gulf of St Lawrence after a collision off Rimouski 29 May 1914. Of the 1477 passengers and crew, 1014 perished, a death toll exceeded to that point only by the *Titanic* incident. However, both the passenger list and the ship itself lacked the glamour of the SS *Titanic*, and the incident was soon forgotten in a world about to be engulfed in war. SABLE ISLAND, a crescent shaped sandbar 300 km ESE (160 nautical miles) of Halifax, is also infamous for its shipwrecks, and is known as "The Graveyard of the Atlantic" as its shifting sands have been the site of over 100 such incidents.

The sudden loss in 1975 of the modern bulk carrier *Edmund Fitzgerald*, which went down in Lake Superior with all 29 hands during a Nov storm, was a more recent Canadian tragedy, reminding us that modern ships are not infallible. Fortunately, shipwrecks are now infrequent, though, as the size and complexity of ships increases, a single wreck (and the resulting pollution clean-up) can be very costly. Just over 300 ships were reported lost from all causes in 1985, but this was out of a world fleet of over 76 000 merchant ships over 100 tons.

Shipwrecks have long held a special fascination for many, including a new breed of marine archaeologists. The easy availability of SCUBA diving apparatus has caused an enormous resurgence of interest in shipwrecks over the past 2 decades but serious archaeologists worry about the damage which amateur explorers and treasure hunters can cause to older fragile wrecks. Nonetheless, archaeologists and hobby divers are now finding many wrecks of historic interest in Canadian waters. The remains of the sunken vessels of Admiral Walker's British fleet, which supported General Wolfe's capture of Québec, have been found off of Scatari I, NS, and near English Pt in the St Lawrence R. In Lk Ontario, the British warships *Hamilton* and *Scourge*, which sank in a fierce storm during the War of 1812, have been found and are now being protected. And in arctic waters are the remains of the BREADALBANE, sunk during the FRANKLIN SEARCH.

In addition to a complete vessel which has sunk, run aground or burned usually being referred to as a "shipwreck," the terms "flotsam," "jetsam" and "derelict" are still used on occasion. "Flotsam" refers to the material or goods left floating on the sea as a result of a wreck, while "jetsam" is material intentionally jettisoned in an attempt to lighten the load of a sinking vessel, and "derelict" refers to any property, whether vessel or cargo, abandoned at sea without hope or intention of recovery. The term "wreck" also includes any part of a ship or boat, its equipment or cargo. In Canada, the laws governing the treatment of shipwrecks and marine salvage are embodied in the Canada Shipping Act, administered by the CANADIAN COAST GUARD. *See also* DISASTERS.
                                    MICHAEL A.H. TURNER

Sunny's Halo, racehorse (b at Oshawa, Ont 11 Feb 1980). Sired by Halo out of Mostly Sunny, he was only the second Canadian-owned and -bred thoroughbred to win the Kentucky Derby (after NORTHERN DANCER). Owned by D.J. "Pud" Foster of Toronto and trained by David Cross of Mississauga, Ont, the handsome chestnut colt was the 1982 Canadian 2-year-old champion, winning 7 of 11 races, including the Coronation Futurity. After winning the Arkansas Derby in 1983, he was one of the favourites for the 109th Kentucky Derby which, on 7 May 1983, he won by 2 lengths. A mysterious rash and a sore ankle may have contributed to his poor performances at the Preakness and Arlington Classic. He was last raced on 16 Oct 1983 and then was retired to stud for a syndicated $7.5 million. In all he won 9 of his 20 races and over $1 million in purses.

J. THOMAS WEST

Sunshine Sketches of a Little Town, by Stephen LEACOCK (Toronto, New York, London, 1912), is a series of vignettes dramatizing the comedy of day-to-day life in Mariposa, a bustling and big-time small town on the shores of the magnificent Lake Wissanotti. Thrumming with self-importance, endowed with a solemnly quirky populace, Mariposa is modelled on ORILLIA, Ont; for generations of readers, it has also been the centre of Leacock's fondest and most amusing portrait of small-town life. Leacock's humour depends on his gift for creating a straight-faced storyteller, an earnestly deadpan narrator who cannot imagine what his readers are laughing about. Nowhere is this gift more apparent than in Leacock's warm but gently mocking scrutiny of both the foibles and pretensions of his Mariposan Canadians.

NEIL BESNER

Superior, Lake, area 82 100 km², of which 28 749 km² lies in Canada; elev 183 m. It is 563 km long, 257 km wide and 406 m at its greatest depth. The lake is fed by some 200 rivers, including the Nipigon, St Louis, Pigeon, Pic, White, Michipicoten and Kaministikquia, and it discharges via the St Mary's R into Lk Huron. Being the most northwesterly of the GREAT LAKES, it was called Lac Supérieur by the French, a name that is appropriate in English as well – Superior is the largest freshwater lake in the world. It has 2 large islands: Isle Royale, which is a US national park, and Michipicoten in Canadian waters.

Vast, remote, deep and cold, with sheer rock cliffs rising on the N shore, the lake's austere beauty has become part of the Canadian imagination. The tale of billions of years of GEOLOGICAL HISTORY is exposed in its rocks. Stromatolites, the oldest fossils found anywhere, have been found in the rocks along Whitefish R – evidence of life 1.8 billion years ago. At AGAWA BAY, volcanic action has created one of the finest pebble beaches in the world. The rocks around Superior also contain valuable mineral deposits, especially IRON ORE in the great Mesabi Range in Minnesota. Silver was taken from beneath the lake at SILVER ISLET and copper was mined by the Indians long before the arrival of Europeans. Gold has been discovered at Hemlo, some 30 km E of Marathon.

Étienne BRÛLÉ was likely the first European to see the lake (1622). Hugues Randin was in the SAULT STE MARIE area around 1670, and Sieur DULHUT laid formal claim to the area around the lake in 1679. For 100 years the voyageurs braved the storms of Superior and carried furs along the N shore to GRAND PORTAGE and later FORT WILLIAM. Ft Michipicoten, at the eastern end of the lake, was established in 1725 and operated until 1904. After 1855 a ship canal was operated at Sault Ste Marie, and steamers passed in increasing numbers as huge quantities of grain and iron ore were carried to the lower lakes. Today, THUNDER BAY is one of the largest ports by volume in Canada. LAKE SUPERIOR PROVINCIAL PARK fronts on the lake between the Montréal and Michipicoten rivers and PUKASKWA NATIONAL PARK between the Pukaskwa and White rivers. The parks preserve a rugged environment of ancient mountains scoured in the last ICE AGE.

JAMES MARSH

Supply and Services, Department of, is the purchasing and accounting arm of the federal government. It was established in 1969 through the merger of the departments of defence production and public printing and stationery (Queen's Printer), the shipbuilding branch of the transport department, the office of the comptroller of the treasury, the central data-processing service bureau of the Treasury Board and the bureau of management consulting services from the Public Service Commission. The 2 branches (*Supply* and *Services*) operate under their own deputy ministers. The supply administration is responsible for purchasing, printing, publishing, traffic management, security, equipment maintenance and repair for the federal public service. It offers its services to customers on a cost-recovery basis. The services administration provides payment or cheque-issuing services for all federal departments and accounting, auditing and computer services for federal departments and agencies. The department is also responsible for the redistribution of tax dollars to the provinces. The minister of supply and services acts as the receiver general for Canada and reports to Parliament for Crown Assets Disposal Corporation, the Royal Canadian Mint and STATISTICS CANADA. The department's 1986-87 budget was $546 million.

Supreme Court of Canada has been the highest court for all legal issues of federal and provincial jurisdiction since 1949, when appeals to the JUDICIAL COMMITTEE OF THE PRIVY COUNCIL of the UK were abolished. In 1875 Parliament passed a statute of the CONSTITUTION ACT, 1867 (s101), establishing a General Court of Appeal for Canada and an Exchequer Court (now FEDERAL COURT OF CANADA). The creation of the Supreme Court had caused sharp debate among the FATHERS OF CONFEDERATION. In 1865 John A. MACDONALD argued that the Constitution did not anticipate the creation of such a court, and attempts by his Conservative government in 1867 and 1870 to set up a general court of appeal suffered overwhelming defeat. Many Liberal and Conservative MPs opposed the project, fearing the possible consequences for provincial rights. By establishing a supreme court, Parliament would be providing itself with a constitutional interpreter, and some MPs questioned the impartiality of such an arbiter because the federal government would appoint its members and determine the court's field of competency. The Liberal government of Alexander MACKENZIE finally persuaded Parliament to vote for a supreme court, arguing that it was needed to standardize Canadian law and to provide constitutional interpretations on issues that would affect the evolution of the new federation.

A chief justice and 8 puisne (junior) justices, ap-

pointed by the governor-in-council, comprise the Supreme Court. Members may be selected from among provincial superior court judges, or from among those barristers and advocates who have belonged to a provincial bar for at least 10 years (*see* JUDICIARY). The Supreme Court Act stipulates that at least 3 of the judges be appointed from Québec; they can be judges of the Court of Queen's Bench (appeal court), the Superior Court or lawyers. Traditionally, 3 other judges from Ontario, one from the Maritimes and 2 from the western provinces are appointed. The judges may not hold any other salaried position while sitting on the Supreme Court Bench. The Supreme Court meets in Jan, Apr and Oct. Five justices constitute a quorum, but for constitutional cases the justices normally sit as a full court. Under the Supreme Court Act (s55), the court not only pronounces judgement but also advises the federal and provincial governments on important questions of law or fact concerning the interpretation of the Constitution, or the constitutionality or interpretation of federal or provincial legislation, or the powers of Parliament and the provincial legislatures. The most famous and perhaps most important of these opinions is that of 28 Sept 1981 on the constitutionality of the patriation of the Constitution.

The Supreme Court is also a general court of appeal for criminal cases. In theory any citizen may come before the Supreme Court to plead his own case, but such instances are rare. In criminal cases the court will hear appeals if an acquittal has been set aside or if there has been a dissenting judgement in a provincial Court of Appeal on a question of law. A guilty verdict in a case of first-degree murder may automatically be appealed to the Supreme Court. If it first grants leave to appeal, the court may also hear appeals on questions of law arising from summary convictions or indictable offences. In civil cases appeals may only be presented with the prior permission of the court; such permission is granted when the court believes that the case raises a question of public importance or an important issue of law or of mixed law and fact that ought to be decided by the court in the national interest. The DRYBONES and MURDOCH cases are 2 famous examples. The limitation on appeals was included in the 1975 modifications to the Supreme Court Act. However, the number of appeals on constitutional or administrative issues has increased.

In about 75% of its cases, the court explains its reasoning along with its decision. In about 56% of these cases, it has upheld the decision of the lower court. Normally the justices go into conference immediately after the argument of a case, review its elements and compare their opinions. One of

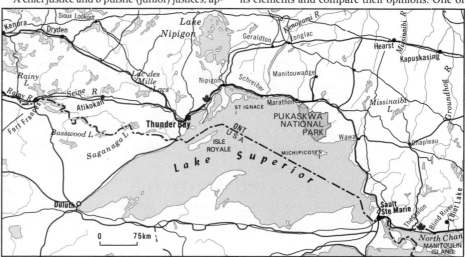

the justices drafts the court's judgement. If, after receiving and reading this judgement, his colleagues disagree with it, there may be further work sessions. In principle, the court tries to hand down unanimous verdicts, but frequently this cannot be done, and the justices who disagree with the majority opinion write a dissenting judgement which is published along with the other. These dissensions are very important because they permit jurists to see the tendencies at work within the court. The rules of procedure ensure that the parties provide the court with a dossier of everything that happened in the court of first instance and in appeal, including all transcripts and main procedural documents. As well, parties must present a factum containing a summary of the case facts, the points in dispute, the reasons the case is being pursued and their conclusions.

After Confederation the Judicial Committee of the Privy Council was the major interpreter of the Constitution Act. With difficulty the Judicial Committee established a certain balance between federal and provincial legislative responsibilities. The committee had to interpret texts which in a number of ways were more appropriate to a unitary state than to a federated one. In 1949 the important question arose of whether the Supreme Court was bound by the decisions of the Judicial Committee. It is essential for the functioning of Canada's judicial system – which is based primarily on common law, on precedent as an authority and on respect for the rule of STARE DECISIS – that courts of appeal ensure uniform application of law. This principle of upholding judgements, which means that the decision of a superior court is binding on lower courts, is the very heart of the judicial system. The principle also means that the courts are to some extent bound by their own judgements. Although the Judicial Committee of the Privy Council did not respect this rule rigorously, generally it took its own previous decisions into account. Until 1949 the Supreme Court had to respect the judgement of the Judicial Committee on appeals of its decisions. Even though it now seems the court is no longer legally bound to follow decisions of the Judicial Committee and reserves for itself the right to examine and review those decisions, as well as its own, it frequently refers to Judicial Committee judgements and always feels the need to explain carefully any decision it may take which appears to run contrary to them. This is a fortunate development because it allows the court greater creativity, but it can be dangerous in constitutional matters, given the problems that may arise from disregard for the federalist principles that were firmly established by the Judicial Committee.

The few Supreme Court decisions overturned by the Judicial Committee were not in fact significant. The Supreme Court had tended to interpret the Constitution Act very literally, whereas the Judicial Committee had taken sociopolitical considerations into account in its decision making. It is usually said that the Judicial Committee favoured the provinces but that the Supreme Court was and still is centralist in nature, an oversimplified view of Canada's JURISPRUDENCE. In fact, the difference between these 2 great interpreters is essentially one of approach. The Judicial Committee was frequently more political than juridical, whereas the Supreme Court, until recently, stuck to strictly legal interpretations. It is also true that some of the Judicial Committee judgements that most favoured the provinces seemed to amount to legal sleight-of-hand. The English high court had managed to give a federalist character to the Canadian Constitution that had not necessarily been implied in the Constitution Act. Moreover, all Judicial Committee judgements are publicly unanimous, precluding more balanced thought

Supreme Court judges, 1987. The red robes are worn only at special ceremonies. Back row, l to rt: The Hon Gérard La Forest, The Hon Bertha Wilson, The Hon Gerald Le Dain, The Hon Claire L'Heureux-Dubé; front row, l to rt: The Hon William McIntyre, The Hon Jean Beetz, The Rt Hon Brian Dickson, PC (Chief Justice of Canada), The Hon Willard Estey, The Hon Antonio Lamer (*courtesy SSC Photocentre, photo by Bedford Studio*).

within the committee and encouraging the domination of some committee members by others. It would probably be more accurate to arrive at the history of the Judicial Committee's constitutional interpretation by studying the lords who have sat on its bench than by studying their decisions. The controversial question of whether courts must interpret the law and the constitution in a literal, textual sense or whether they must consider as well the social, political and economic context is now more important than ever, because of the patriation of the Constitution with its CANADIAN CHARTER OF RIGHTS AND FREEDOMS. The Charter will be whatever the Supreme Court chooses to make it, because only a constitutional amendment approved by Parliament and 7 provinces totalling at least 50% of the population of all the provinces may alter a Supreme Court decision. The Supreme Court's momentous decision in early 1988 to strike down the ABORTION law illustrates the power of the court to abolish laws which are inconsistent with the Charter.

The new role of the court, with its social and political dimensions, will significantly alter the way Canadians think of it. Reform of the method of appointing justices and of the composition and methodology of the court has also become important. The court must try to reflect the dominant characteristics of Canadian society, such as regionalism, dualism and multiculturalism. The constitutional agreement reached on 3 June 1987 completes and improves the work begun by the Constitution Act, 1982. The existence and jurisdiction of the Supreme Court will be clearly entrenched in the Constitution. The provinces will now have a say in appointing judges to the Supreme Court. The Constitution will also guarantee that at least 3 Supreme Court judges will come from Québec. However, this constitutional agreement must be ratified by the Parliament of Canada and the provincial legislatures before it can be enforced (*see* MEECH LAKE ACCORD).

GIL RÉMILLARD

Reading: G.A. Beaudoin, ed, *The Supreme Court of Canada: Proceedings of the October 1985 Conference* (1985); J. Shell and F. Vaughan, *The Supreme Court of Canada* (1985); P. Weiler, *In the Last Resort* (1974); Articles commemorating the 100th anniversary of the Supreme Court of Canada appear in special editions of the *Alberta Law Review* 14 (1976) and *Canadian Bar Review* 53 (1975).

Surfacing, novel by Margaret ATWOOD (Toronto, 1972; New York and London, 1973). *Surfacing* takes its title from its central metaphor, dramatizing a woman's passage from a precarious sense of self through madness towards a fuller identity. The novel is a powerfully poetic and political exploration of Canadian consciousness, personal

and social, defined against a metaphorically "American" state of mind. To be "American" is to be violently depersonalized, disembodied, without a language, a past or a relation with nature. The woman and 3 friends go to her father's isolated cottage in northern Québec where, after a few days, relationships deteriorate and sexuality becomes a currency to bargain with. The woman's search for her missing father ends with the discovery of his drowned body, precipitating her descent into temporary, healing madness before she surfaces with a less "American," saner vision. The novel has been translated into French as *Faire Surface* (Montréal, 1978). NEIL BESNER

Surrey, BC, District Municipality, pop 181 447 (1986c), 147 138 (1981c), area 36 039 ha, inc 1879, is the second-largest municipality in BC, after Vancouver. Part of the Greater Vancouver Regional Dist, it is bounded by the FRASER R on the N and the State of Washington on the S. The municipalities of Langley and Delta lie to the E and W. The residential development of Surrey is spread along 3 upland areas of glacial till extending into N Delta, Langley and White Rock. Intervening lowland areas of peat and other deltaic materials are primarily agricultural, and the floodplains of the Fraser R are used for industry.

Surrey grew slowly in the beginning, with lumbering and agriculture as the main industries. A double-span bridge across the Fraser (1904) provided Surrey's only access to New Westminster and Vancouver until the Pattullo Bridge was built 1937. Railways and roads brought steady industrial and commercial growth, which was furthered by an influx of people from the drought-stricken Prairies in the 1930s. Political unrest led to the secession in 1957 of Ward 7, which became the municipality of White Rock. In 1960 the opening of the Port Mann Bridge and subsequent freeway development brought further growth and change. A 5-town concept emerged, with Whalley, Guildford, Newton, Cloverdale, and South Surrey developing around shopping malls, recreation facilities, housing, green belts, industrial lands and farms.

Key features of the economy are manufacturing (sawmilling and metal fabrication), wholesaling, agriculture and commerce (especially in Guildford Town Centre and Surrey Place Mall). ALAN F.J. ARTIBISE

Surrey, Philip Henry, painter (b at Calgary 8 Oct 1910). He studied at the Winnipeg School of Art (1926-27), with Fred VARLEY in Vancouver, and at the Art Students League, New York (1936). Surrey was a member of the Eastern Group of Painters and a founding member of the Contemporary Arts Soc (1939). The surrealistic tendencies in his work melded well with the society's goal of promoting modern art movements in a Canadian context. His cityscapes have dreamlike groupings of figures taking part in familiar activities, often in juxtaposition, conveying more than one level of reality (eg, *La procession* 1940). The aim of Surrey's illusion is to caution the viewer to question perceptions of reality and to address the problems of city life. KATHLEEN LAVERTY

Survenant, Le (1945), a novel by Germaine GUÈVREMONT – the first in a projected trilogy – depicts the life of the HABITANT with a blend of sympathy and sophistication new to French Canadian fiction. Set in Le Chenal du Moine, near Sorel, Qué, it employs local speech and folklore to portray the daily and seasonal rhythms of a passing era. A figure of mythical proportions, the "survenant" (mysterious stranger) doubles as the heroic son whom Didace Beauchemin has failed to produce and the romantic suitor whom Angélina Desmarais has secretly desired. For a year,

Venant unsuccessfully fights the wanderlust setting him apart from his neighbours. Revisiting the romantic myth of MARIA CHAPDELAINE and the naturalistic tragedy of TRENTE ARPENTS, Guèvremont's novel survived as a popular radio and television serial. *The Outlander* (1950; published in England as *Monk's Reach*), Eric Sutton's translation of the novel and its sequel, *Marie-Didace* (1947), won the Governor General's Award.

MICHÈLE LACOMBE

Surveying is the scientific measurement of natural or man-made features of the Earth's surface. On any area of land to be measured, it is always possible to choose 2 points and measure the distance between them, thus creating a line which can be drawn to scale on a map, plan or section (*see* CARTOGRAPHY). Other points can be located, relative to the line, by taking 2 other measurements, which can also be drawn to scale. These measurements may be 2 angles, one measured line and one angle, or 2 measured lines. From these measurements, a map can be built up with the features accurately located with reference to each other. Surveying is used to make maps of all kinds, to locate buildings and engineering works (eg, dams, bridges, tunnels) accurately, to establish property lines, to chart waterways, and to position such devices as SATELLITES and oceangoing oil-drilling platforms.

Location of points is made through operations which deal with the 2 dimensions of the horizontal plane and those which locate the vertical or levelling plane. Plane surveys of small areas treat the surveyed area as a horizontal plane, perpendicular to the direction of gravity as defined by a plumb bob (ie, a suspended weight which, when hanging freely, points to the Earth's centre). Plane surveys are limited to an area of about 250 km^2. In larger areas, the discrepancy between the horizontal plane and the curvature of the Earth's surface becomes too great. Geodetic surveys correct for the curvature by establishing a network of precisely located "control points" on the surface. They are used to locate the position of parallels of latitude and meridians of longitude and to build up a grid to serve as a control for other types of survey work. Cadastral or land surveying determines property lines and other legal boundaries. Hydrographic surveys chart the features of waterways, determining the shape of the coastlines, currents and underwater terrain, and the position of shoals and other hazards to navigation (*see* HYDROGRAPHY).

Until very recently, manually controlled instruments were used to take distance and angular measurements. The surveyor's chain, introduced in 1620, was 66 feet (about 20 m) long, composed of 100 links. The chain was used as a standard measurement in many Canadian surveys, eg, the Dominion Lands Survey, until replaced by steel tapes. Distance could also be determined through the use of telescopic sighting devices (eg, transit) and optical devices (eg, range finder). Angular measurements were made with the theodolite and the transit, telescopic measuring devices that permitted precise determination of angles between 2 sighted targets. Astronomical observations and magnetic compass readings were used to determine location and magnetic bearings, while levels and barometers were used for vertical measurement.

On larger projects electronic instruments, which use radio, RADAR or LASER frequencies to determine distance very precisely, are employed. Signals may be bounced off a reflector target and received by the instrument again; or signals may be sent out to a repeating transmitter which rebroadcasts them immediately back to the transmitter. In both cases, the elapsed time is mea-

English surveyor's sextant *c*1820-30 (*courtesy Royal Ontario Museum*).

sured, allowing precise determination of distance. Many of these electronic distance meters provide a simultaneous printout of measurements being made.

Location through the satellite method involves triangulation from a point on Earth to the position of 2 satellites and is exact to millionths of a metre. Calculations can be made and co-ordinated through computers, which can also be used as an aid in plotting maps and sections.

Photogrammetry, the method of determining the shapes and sizes of objects and their relative positions using photographs, has been in use since the 1860s. Aerial photogrammetric techniques (ie, aerial surveys) have been developing in Canada since about 1920. REMOTE SENSING is a more recent technology which uses information or images from orbiting satellites, such as the Landsat satellite, to build up comprehensive data on features of Earth's surface.

Canada has a land area of nearly 10 million km^2; hence, survey work has developed as a major public enterprise. After Confederation, 1867, a vigorous period of BOUNDARIES surveying began, with the determination of the FORTY-NINTH PARALLEL between the Rocky Mts and Lake of the Woods completed in 1874. By 1925 the joint Canadian-American INTERNATIONAL BOUNDARY COMMISSION had completed work on about 8000 km of border between the YT and Alaska, western Canada and the US and through the Great Lakes and eastern Canada to the Bay of FUNDY.

The Dominion Lands Survey of the Dominion Lands Branch was established in 1871 to survey the western territories of the HUDSON'S BAY COMPANY, which had become part of Canada (*see* RUPERT'S LAND; DOMINION LANDS POLICY). Under J.S. DENNIS from the office of the surveyor general, work began to divide the newly acquired lands into 6 mile square (10 km by 10 km) townships, containing 36 sections of 640 acres (about 259 ha) and, thus, to open the lands for settlement. The areas surveyed were record breaking. In 1883 about 11 million ha were surveyed in connection with land grants to the CANADIAN PACIFIC RY, along its western route.

The GEOLOGICAL SURVEY OF CANADA was founded in 1842 under Sir William LOGAN. Throughout the 19th and early 20th century, exploratory and geological surveys were performed in remote regions of the country by adventurous surveyors such as A.P. LOW, G.M. DAWSON, D.B. Dowling, R.G. MCCONNELL and J.L. Charles. In the same period, hydrographic and topographic surveying intensified. Edouard DEVILLE introduced photogrammetric techniques into surveying, while the work of Otto Klotz and W.F. KING in extending longitude meridians to the Pacific led to the founding of the Dominion Observatory for ASTRONOMY in Ottawa.

Canadian surveying techniques have undergone continual refinement in the 20th century, and precise maps have now been made for all parts of the country. The accuracy of present-day surveying is an important factor in sophisticated transportation networks, major hydroelectric installations, communications networks and other facilities where safety and success depend upon exact location. Surveying is an important field within CIVIL ENGINEERING and students can receive training at schools or faculties of engineering or other educational establishments (eg, RYERSON POLYTECHNICAL INSTITUTE). Graduates may complete articling programs to become eligible to take the Canada Land Surveyor examinations.

CLAUDE LAJEUNESSE

Reading: D.W. Thomson, *Men and Meridians*, 3 vols (1966, 1967, 1969).

Survival: A Thematic Guide to Canadian Literature, by Margaret ATWOOD (Toronto, 1972), has enjoyed a controversial, sometimes heated reception. Readers who disagree with Atwood find her thesis – that most Canadian literature deals with victims of various types and that "grim survival" is its central theme – forced, and argue that she has selected works which will support her argument. But those who see more merit in Atwood's thesis find the book challenging and exciting. In either case, *Survival* is written with intelligence, candour and wit and has had a powerful influence on readers of Canadian literature.

NEIL BESNER

Sussex, NB, Town, inc 1904, pop 4114 (1986c), located in south-central NB in a rich agricultural area, 73 km from Saint John on the Kennebecasis R. The area, originally known as Pleasant Valley, was renamed Sussex Vale in 1811 in honour of a son of George III, the duke of Sussex. The current name was adopted in 1900. Although the area was part of an Acadian seigneury and the first permanent settlers were the LOYALISTS who arrived in 1786, it did not become a village until the construction of the railway in 1859. Sussex Vale was a training area for the militia throughout the latter half of the 19th century and it became a military town in 1890 with the establishment of Camp Sussex. It retained a major military presence until after WWII. The town remains an agricultural centre with the processing of dairy products a major industry. Three potash mines are in operation within 32 km of the town. The *King's County Record* has been published there since 1887.

BURTON GLENDENNING

Sutherland, Donald, actor (b at Saint John 17 July 1935). His tall, earnest and diffident image is a familiar one throughout the world: he is now probably Canada's best-known film actor. After studying at U of T, he trained in the UK and appeared on the London stage before beginning his prolific movie career. Although most of his work has been for Hollywood, he has been seen in some Canadian movies, such as *The Act of the Heart* (1970), *Murder by Decree* (1978) and *Threshold* (1981), where, apart from his gifts as an actor, his

Actor Donald Sutherland.

high visibility has attracted investment dollars and his nationality has satisfied Canadian-content requirements. He has made notable appearances in *The Dirty Dozen* (1967), *M*A*S*H* (1970), *Klute* (1971), *Don't Look Now* (1973), *Day of the Locust* (1975), *Invasion of the Body Snatchers* (1978), *Ordinary People* (1980) and *Eye of the Needle* (1981) and also in the CBC television drama *Bethune* (1977). In 1987 Sutherland was on location in China for the production of *Bethune: The Making of a Hero*, in which he portrayed the doctor. His reputation for seriousness, his evident distaste for the Hollywood glitz-parade, and his unique physical appearance prompted Bertolucci to cast him in *1900* (1976) and Fellini to give him the title role in *Casanova* (1976): together the epitome of his "gargoyle phase." Unlike many internationally successful Canadians, he is affectionately regarded in his own country. He is John SUTHERLAND's half-brother. WILLIAM BEARD

Sutherland, John, writer, editor (b at Liverpool, NS 21 Feb 1919; d at Toronto 1 Sept 1956). Sutherland's formal studies (Queen's 1936-37 and McGill 1941-42) were interrupted by ill health which dogged him all his life. He brought critical insight and energy to his editorship of the important literary journal, *First Statement* (1942-45). This journal eventually merged with another, *Preview*, to become NORTHERN REVIEW, first appearing in 1946. Through his fervent, Marxist-slanted criticism and editing, he championed the emergence of modern Canadian literature. Poetry became his dominant interest at the end of his life, at which time he was a convert to Catholicism. This religious conversion informed his book on the poetry of E.J. PRATT. A collection of his writing is *John Sutherland: Essays, Controversies and Poems*, ed by Miriam Waddington (1972).

PETER STEVENS

Sutil and Mexicana In 1792, after exploratory voyages by Spaniards Manuel Quimper (1790) and Francisco de Eliza (1791), the extent of JUAN DE FUCA STR remained a mystery. Some still believed the strait held the entry to the fabled NORTHWEST PASSAGE. Moreover, pressures caused by the NOOTKA SOUND CONTROVERSY suggested the strait as a possible boundary between Spanish and British territories. Alejandro Malaspina, who had completed his own voyage to the NORTHWEST COAST in 1791 (*see* MALASPINA EXPEDITION), recommended Dionisio Alcalá-Galiano and Cayetano Valdés to command the small schooners *Sutil* and *Mexicana*. They were to survey the strait and the coast S to San Francisco. In early June 1792 they visited the Spanish post of Nuñez Gaona [Neah Bay, Wash] and, guided by Indian chief Tetacu, they

crossed to Vancouver I. After charting many of the Gulf Is, on June 21 the Spaniards sighted George VANCOUVER's *Discovery* and *Chatham* near present-day Vancouver. Each side was mortified to discover its major competitor, but relations were amicable. The 2 groups shared provisions and information before continuing separately to circumnavigate Vancouver I. The 4-month Spanish expedition produced a wealth of geographical and ethnological information but no evidence of usable resources. The voyage became better known than other Spanish expeditions since the government permitted publication of the journal recording the voyages in 1802. *See also* SPANISH EXPLORATION. CHRISTON I. ARCHER

Suttles, Duncan, chess grandmaster (b at San Francisco, Calif 21 Dec 1945). He moved to Vancouver as a child and became Canada's second grandmaster in 1972. He played on 6 Canadian national teams in the World Olympiads beginning at Tel Aviv (1964), and represented Canada in the Interzonal tournaments of 1967 and 1970. He won the Canadian Closed Championship in 1969 and the Canadian Open in Ottawa in 1973. In 1975 he retired from tournaments to concentrate on stock analysis and correspondence chess. In 1981 he received the title of correspondence grandmaster and returned to over-the-board play to share first place in international competition in Vancouver. Suttles is also a pioneer of modern chess strategy, particularly the King's Fianchetto Defence. LAWRENCE DAY

Sutton, Catherine, née Sonego, or Nahnebahwequay or "upright woman," Mississauga (Ojibwa) spokesperson (b on the Credit R flats, UC 1824; d in Sarawak Township, Canada W 26 Sept 1865), niece of Peter JONES. She grew up on the Credit R Mission, but because of her marriage to Englishman William Sutton she eventually lost the Indian annuity money owing her and her children. Annoyed by the Indian Dept's treatment of both her family and Indians in general, the determined Mrs Sutton went to England in 1860, even obtaining a private audience with Queen Victoria. Little changed, however, and 2 years later she wrote bitterly that the whites' "ideas of justice [were] that might is right."

DONALD B. SMITH

Sutton, Francis Arthur, "One-Arm," engineer, inventor, adventurer (b at Hylands, Eng 14 Feb 1884; d at Hong Kong 22 Oct 1944). As a young engineer Sutton built railways in Argentina and in Mexico prior to WWI. He lost his right hand at Gallipoli, becoming overnight a hero, "One-Arm Sutton," and more famous later as an inventor and designer of weapons. After searching for gold in Siberia (1919-20) he became adviser to Chinese warlords and was given the rank of general in the Chinese army. In 1927 he arrived in Canada and proposed the opening of the Peace River Country through a railway linking it with Vancouver and Edmonton. The scheme set off a period of speculation of which Sutton became the centre of publicity. His plans failed to materialize and his own heavy investment in Vancouver real estate was lost in the fallout from the Great Crash in 1929. He returned to China in 1931 as a war correspondent, moving later to Korea to engage in mining. He was expelled by the Japanese in 1941 and moved to Hong Kong where he died a prisoner of war. A champion golfer, he took his clubs everywhere – even to Gallipoli – marked as "Theodolite, Legs of." BRIAN L. EVANS

Reading: Charles Drage, *General of Fortune* (1954).

Suzor-Coté, Marc-Aurèle de Foy, painter, sculptor, church decorator (b at Arthabaska, Qué

5 Apr 1869; d at Daytona Beach, Fla 27 Jan 1937). Suzor-Coté's highly successful career was the result of his sure talent, his extroverted personality and favourable circumstances. In secondary school, his talent for drawing attracted attention and in 1887 he became involved in the church decoration projects of the Joseph Rousseau company of St-Hyacinthe. Through family connections he met Wilfrid LAURIER, from whom he secured numerous commissions. He led a cosmopolitan existence between 1891 and 1912, travelling constantly between Canada, the US and Europe. He studied in France (1891-94, 1897-1901) where he acquired sound training from Bonnat at the École des beaux-arts, and later from Harpignies, and in the open studios of Julian and Colarossi. From 1892 on, he attracted attention at exhibitions of the Art Assn of Montreal (he won the Jessie Dow award for *Les fumées, por de Montréal* in 1912), at the salons of the Société des artistes français in Paris as early as 1894, and at Royal Canadian Academy of Arts exhibitions. In 1901, William Scott and Son of Montréal became his dealer, spreading his popularity. Further travels 1904-07 and 1911-12 firmly established his reputation. As his fame grew, however, so did his desire for a more private life. After 1912 he worked in the Arthabaska studio he had built in 1895 and in his Montréal studio. He mastered pastels as well as oils, and in 1911 began developing his talent for sculpting, in which he excelled after 1918. In this medium he returned to the rural subjects of his canvases and, inspired by his surroundings or by literary works such as *Maria Chapdelaine*, he gave them new life. He was able to capture famous historical events as well as winter scenes with subtle use of colour and disciplined execution. A master artist, he had to abandon all his activity after becoming paralysed in 1927. LAURIER LACROIX

Suzuki, Aiko, fibre artist (b at Vancouver 1937). Although not a weaver or tapestry designer in the traditional sense, she is one of a growing number of Canadian artists who use fibres and textile techniques as a medium for expressing abstract concepts. She began her artistic career as a painter, but her involvement with the TORONTO DANCE THEATRE in the late 1960s as a free-form set designer opened unexpected possibilities for her creativity. She worked with strands of fibre to explore 3-dimensional spatial forms of dramatic, emotional impact. Her suspended fibre sculpture, *Lyra*, was installed in the Toronto Public Library in 1981. In 1985 she designed the set for the National Ballet's production of David EARLE's *Realm*.

REBECCA SISLER

Suzuki, David Takayoshi, geneticist, broadcaster (b at Vancouver 24 Mar 1936). Of Japanese parentage (he was interned with his family in WWII), Suzuki joined UBC after study at the universities of Amherst and Chicago (PhD 1961) and in 1969 won a Steacie Memorial Fellowship as the best young Canadian scientist. He specialized in meiosis, the early division of living cells where differentiation begins (eg, between reproductive and other cells), and the study of mutations caused by changes in temperature. The TV series "Suzuki on Science" began to make him a public figure in 1971. While continuing his university teaching and research in GENETICS (his work on the fruit fly gained him worldwide recognition), he wrote widely on science and SCIENCE POLICY, created the radio series "Quirks and Quarks" in 1976, and served on the SCIENCE COUNCIL. Some academic colleagues criticized Suzuki's broadcasting as a waste of his talents, but Suzuki was convinced that public awareness of science would contribute to both better science policies and an enriched culture. His rare combination of personal charm and scientific ability, as displayed for 10 years in the CBC-TV series "The Nature of Things," have made Suzuki a unique figure in English-speaking Canada. He has received the Royal Bank Award and in 1986 he was awarded the UNESCO Kalinga prize for science writing. Recent work includes *Metamorphosis* (1987), an autobiography, and *Looking at Insects/Looking at Plants* (2 vols, 1987), for children.

DONALD J.C. PHILLIPSON

Sverdrup, Otto Neumann, arctic explorer (b at Bindal, Norway 31 Oct 1854; d at Oslo 26 Nov 1930). An experienced sailor and outdoorsman, he was introduced to arctic travel by Fridtjof Nansen, who invited him in 1888 to ski across Greenland's interior. From 1893 to 1896 Sverdrup was captain of Nansen's ship *Fram* when it made its celebrated drift across the top of the world. Sverdrup is known chiefly for his expedition to the ELLESMERE I area between 1898 and 1902. During 4 winters in the ice he discovered several islands W of Ellesmere and mapped large portions of the High Arctic. Eventually Canada claimed this territory and purchased Sverdrup's maps.

DANIEL FRANCIS

Sverdrup Islands, located in the High Arctic, comprise a large island, AXEL HEIBERG, and 2 smaller ones, ELLEF RINGNES and AMUND RINGNES. Their geological history began as an area of subsidence and sedimentation on a landmass margin. Deformation occurred, followed by a second episode of uplift. In the early Tertiary, after a long period of sedimentation, the basin sediments were folded and faulted and the present land surface was uplifted and mountains formed. Today, glaciers occupy a large proportion of the mountainous area – some reaching the sea. A narrow coastal strip of thin sediments was laid down in the early Pleistocene along the arctic shore. The discovery of these islands by the Second Norwegian Polar Expedition (1898-1902), under the command of Otto SVERDRUP, led to a sovereignty dispute, settled in Canada's favour only in 1931.

DOUG FINLAYSON

Swallow (Hirundinidae), small family of birds including 80 species worldwide, of which 7 breed in Canada, including the PURPLE MARTIN. All feed mainly on flying insects, spending much time in flight. Their long wings give the impression of a larger bird, but they are actually small. Many are colonial, build nests in enclosed situations, and lay 4-6 eggs. In Canada most swallows rear one brood annually; in the West, barn swallows raise 2. Several species nest around settlements. Native swallows fall into 3 groups. The brown-backed species – bank swallow (*Riparia riparia*) and northern rough-winged swallow (*Stelgidopteryx serripennis*) – nest in burrows in sea cliffs or riverbanks and in crevices in rock cliffs, respectively. Both range across the continent. Bank swallows are found far into the North and in Europe. Northern rough-winged swallows enter Canada only in the south, ranging down to S America. Tree swallows (*Tachycineta bicolor*) and violet-green swallows (*T. thalassina*) are early migrants, harbingers of spring. Both are iridescent blue-green above and white below. They nest in tree-holes or nest boxes. Tree swallows range across Canada, N to TREELINE; violet-green swallows are strictly western. Cliff swallows (*Hirundo pyrrhonota*) and barn swallows (*H. rustica*) are metallic blue above and rusty brown below. Both construct nests from clay pellets in situations sheltered from rain and runoff water. The enclosed, gourd-shaped nests of cliff swallows are under cliff overhangs or eaves. Originally, barn swallows nested in caves or under cliff overhangs; now, they almost always nest under eaves of or inside buildings. Ca-

Seven species of swallow breed in Canada, including the tree swallow (*Tachycineta bicolor*), an early migrant and harbinger of spring (*photo by Tim Fitzharris*).

nadian swallows do not sing but all have distinctive call notes. They are accomplished, graceful fliers. In late summer, they mass in flocks on roadside wires, often several species together. Within a few weeks they have gone S, not returning to Canada for 7-8 months.

A.J. ERSKINE

Swamp, Marsh and Bog, the most common wetland habitats, are similar in having the water table at, near or above the soil surface or root layer of plants. The most important factors influencing development and maintenance of these wetlands are climate, mineral nutrient availability, water levels and water flow. Their most obvious distinguishing features are the plant species characteristically found in each and the amount of standing water present.

Swamp, wetland characterized by the presence of trees growing on silty to organic muck soils, usually occurring along river floodplains and in poorly drained basins. Swamps are often inundated seasonally, or remain continually flooded. Most swamps in N America are found in the southeastern US and in the Great Lakes region. Representative of the swamps of this region is Ontario's Minesing Swamp, a 6000 ha wetland in the Nottawasaga River drainage basin west of Lake Simcoe. It is rich in herbaceous flowering plants, and is forested by such common deciduous swamp trees as red maple, black ash, white elm and silver maple. Eastern white cedar, a conifer, is also common in many swamp forests and tends to form dense associations on shallow, wet soils where limestone is near the surface.

Marsh, treeless wetland where lush growths of herbaceous plants (eg, GRASSES, SEDGES, reeds and CATTAILS) predominate. Marshes usually form in quiet shallows of ponds, lakes and rivers, and along sheltered coastlines where mineral nutrients are available. Freshwater marshes are abundant and widely scattered across N America. In Canada, the better known freshwater marshes border Lake St Clair, Lake Erie, Lake Ontario and the shores of the upper St Lawrence R. Freshwater marshes are also common and extensive in the Red R deltas of Manitoba and in the Peace-Atha-

Spring bog, Québec-Labrador (*photo by J.A. Kraulis*).

basca R delta of N Alberta. The prairie pothole region of central N America is a vast area dotted with countless sloughs, ponds, and lakes and with abundant marsh vegetation, that serves as the most important WATERFOWL nesting area on the continent. About 750 000 square km of this region occurs in Canada across southern Manitoba, Saskatchewan and Alberta. Saltwater marshes are restricted to temperate regions. In N America, they are found mainly along the southern and eastern coastlines from the Gulf of Mexico states to the Maritime provinces. TANTRAMAR MARSH, near Amherst, NB, is a historically famous and important saltwater marsh. Others of particular importance in Canada are found at Kamouraska, in Québec, along the broad low coastline of Hudson Bay and James Bay, and at the Fraser R estuary in British Columbia. In western N America, numerous inland saltwater marshes fringe the shores of saltwater lakes (the remnants of ancient seas) and alkali ponds. Marshes are highly productive ecosystems, teeming with life.

Bog, poorly drained, peat-filled depression dominated by sphagnum mosses, evergreen shrubs of the heather family and conifers such as black spruce and larch. The water table, at or near the surface of the living moss layer, may be visible as open pools of water. The extensive cover of sphagnum mosses makes bog waters acidic, preventing the growth of many micro-organisms. Because of lack of adequate water movement for aeration, water is low in oxygen, and because of the insulating effect of the surface blanket of moss, it is also relatively cold. As a result, little decay occurs in the accumulating layers of organic debris which build up as peat. Bogs are only one of several kinds of wetlands, called "peatlands," that develop in cool, moist, previously glaciated regions of the Northern Hemisphere. Bogs are particularly common features of poorly drained regions of the boreal forest on the Precambrian SHIELD of northern Canada. Bogs south of the boreal forest such as the Mer Bleue near Ottawa are remnants of the boreal forest formed after the retreat of the Wisconsinian ice sheets. Such bogs have remained restricted to the poorly drained sites in which they were formed. Bogs are also common features in most of the Maritimes. They are abundant in Newfoundland, and in NS are found from near sea level on Briar I at the western tip of the province to the heights of the Cape Breton Highlands. In countries such as Ireland, dried peat has traditionally been used as fuel. Peat moss is also used extensively as a soil conditioner; peat harvesting for this purpose is readily evident along the Trans-Canada Highway in parts of the Gaspé peninsula of Québec. *See also* BIOMASS ENERGY; GROUNDWATER.

ERICH HABER

Reading: C.W. Johnson, *Bogs of the Northeast* (1985); B. Thomas, *The Swamp* (1976); P.D. Moore and D.J. Bellamy, *Peatlands* (1974); W.A. Niering, *The Life of the Marsh* (1966).

Swamp Angel, Ethel Wilson's finest novel (Toronto, 1954), follows Maggie Vardoe's movement from an unhappy marriage toward the vision she gains by re-establishing her own identity. Maggie's flight from Vancouver into the BC interior symbolizes her return to the natural world of time, change and mortality. Through serene passages of natural description and quiet evocations of Maggie's strength, Wilson makes her character's transformation seem to arise naturally but also dramatically out of her circumstances; like its protagonist, *Swamp Angel* moves quietly but with assurance toward its realization.

NEIL BESNER

Swan, large WATERFOWL with elongated neck and narrow patch of naked skin in front of the eye.

Only 2 species of swan are native to Canada, the whistling swan (*Cygnus columbianus)* and the trumpeter swan (*C. buccinator*). The latter, shown here, breeds in the YT, the Grande Prairie region of Alberta and the Cypress Hills (*photo by Tim Fitzharris*).

Swans (genus *Cygnus*), the largest members of family Anatidae, are found in N and S temperate and arctic zones, including Australia and S America. Swans have longer necks with more vertebrae (23-25), shorter legs and larger feet than geese, which they superficially resemble (*see* GOOSE). There is some dispute as to the number of genera. Five species of true swans are recognized. The 3 Northern Hemisphere species are pure white; the S American, white with black neck; the Australian, black with white primaries. All young swans (cygnets) are unpatterned, white, grey or black. Whistling and trumpeter swans (*Cygnus columbianus* and *C. buccinator*) are native to Canada; the mute swan (*C. olor*), native to Eurasia, has become established as a breeding bird in Canada. The whistling swan breeds in the lower arctic islands, Mackenzie Delta, northern Hudson Bay and northeastern Manitoba. The trumpeter swan breeds in the Yukon, the Grande Prairie region of Alberta and the CYPRESS HILLS. It has been reintroduced at Swan Lake, near Vernon, BC, and winters in western British Columbia. The whistling swan, the most numerous species in N America, has a population of 200 000; the trumpeter swan, now greatly reduced, fewer than 15 000; the mute swan, perhaps 5000 feral (wild) individuals in N America.   F.G. COOCH

Swan, Anna Haining, giantess (b at Mill Brook, NS 7 Aug 1846; d at Seville, Ohio 5 Aug 1888). In 1862 she joined P.T. Barnum's American Museum in New York, attracted by the monthly salary of $1000 and by the opportunity to further her education through private tutoring. She became one of Barnum's star attractions. Promoted as being 246 cm (8'1") tall, Anna was in reality 228 cm (7'6"), and at age 22 weighed 160 kg (352 lbs). When the museum burned in 1865, it took 18 men with a block and tackle to rescue her. In 1871, during an overseas tour, Anna met and married Martin Van Buren Bates, a Kentucky giant. They were presented to Queen Victoria, travelled throughout Europe, and then settled on an Ohio farm; summers were spent touring with the W.W. Cole circus. Before her death from tuberculosis, Anna had 2 children; both were abnormally large and died within hours of birth.
                                        LOIS KERNAGHAN

Swan River, Man, Town, pop 3946 (1986c), 3782 (1981c), inc 1908, is a regional trade centre and transportation hub to northern Manitoba, located on the Swan R 525 km NW of Winnipeg. Agriculture, logging, forest products, services, tourism and transportation have been the mainstays of Swan River's economy since its founding in 1899. The region has a rich heritage of aboriginal culture, fur trade rivalry (1790s to mid-1800s) and missionary work. A wide diversity of Europeans were among the settlers to rush to the area beginning in 1897-98, after earlier settlement was delayed when a more southerly route was chosen for the transcontinental railway. From 1926 to 1958, Swan River was the headquarters of the missionary and philanthropic work of Bishop's Messengers of St Faith's established by Margeurita D. Fowler for the Church of England.   D. M. LYON

Sweat Lodge, used by most N American Indian tribes, was significant in certain purification rites. There were 2 sweating techniques, reflected in lodge construction. The system of direct exposure to fire within the confines of a small, often semisubterranean, structure was prevalent in northern Alaska, California and parts of Mesoamerica. The common system was to heat stones in a fire, place them inside a small domed structure and pour water on them to produce steam. Direct fire sweathouses doubled as men's houses, but steam lodges were often used by a single person.   RENÉ R. GADACZ

Swedes Three Swedish names appeared among Lord Selkirk's group of settlers in the Red River Valley of Manitoba, the first evidence of Swedish settlers in Canada. From 1868 to 1914, more than one million Swedes moved to the United States and Canada. Land opportunities in the United States attracted them, but as farmland became scarce and costly in the American West, they began to migrate to the Canadian West. By 1971 there were 101 870 people of Swedish Canadian origin and by 1981 their number had decreased to 78 360.

Origins In the early years of the 19th century, Sweden experienced a rapid growth in population. A very large segment of the agrarian population became landless and social divisions between the propertied and unpropertied classes hardened. Many Swedish farmers sought new opportunities elsewhere. A series of crop failures (1866-68) brought starvation and economic hardship to many parts of Sweden and provided an added impetus to emigration.

Migration and Settlement The greatest proportion of the more than 1 million Swedish emigrants were landless labourers and the sons and daughters of small landholders and crofters. The state Lutheran Church in Sweden actively encouraged destitutes to emigrate. Labour organizers blacklisted by their employers in Sweden also left, and as women became more economically emancipated, many found their way overseas. Emigration promoters from the US and Canada worked actively in Sweden to attract settlers.

Until 1914, most Swedish immigrants arrived in Canada primarily from Minnesota and North Dakota. Between 1921 and 1930, over 20 000 Swedes (many of them industrial workers) migrated directly to Canada. By 1930 Sweden had developed a large industrial base, and since 1945 Swedish migration to Canada has been primarily on an individual basis.

In the early 1870s, some Swedes travelled by boat along the Red River to Winnipeg. With the completion of the CPR, many Swedes took advantage of the Canadian government policy offering inexpensive Prairie farmland (*see also* IMMIGRATION POLICY). Winnipeg attracted many Swedish immigrants and for years it was the main centre for most nationwide Swedish organizations. Swedes in Manitoba settled as well in Scandinavia, Erickson, Teulon, Mulvihill and Eriksdale. Saskatchewan also attracted Swedish settlers; one of every 4 Swedes listed in the 1931 census lived in that province, particularly in the Qu'Appelle Valley communities of Stockholm and Dubuc. Swedes settled in Alberta before it became a province, and Swedish communities still exist in Edmonton and Calgary. During WWII many Swedes moved to the Pacific because of the milder climate and the job opportunities. Today, BC has the largest number of Swedish Canadians.

Many early Swedish immigrants settled in northwestern Ontario as farmers and lumber workers, particularly around Kenora; after WWII a large number of Swedish immigrants settled in Toronto.

Economic Life The great majority of the early Swedish immigrants to Canada were attracted by the opportunity of owning farmland. Around the turn of the century, skilled and unskilled workers immigrated to the urban-industrial areas of Canada. After 1945 Swedish immigrants included engineers, businessmen and representatives of Swedish export industries. Over the years, large numbers of Swedish Canadians moved from farms into industry, business and the professions.

Social Life and Community Swedish settlers, especially in western Canada, established a number of social clubs and organizations. Temperance societies established in a number of communities were among the first Swedish-language clubs. In 1901 the Norden Society was organized as a benefit society.

The Vasa Order of America, now a social and cultural organization, was founded in 1896 in the US and in 1913 in Canada as a mutual-benefit society; it maintains lodges throughout the US and Canada.

Religion and Cultural Life Much of the religious and cultural life of the early Swedish communities in Canada centered around churches, which became bastions of the Swedish language and provided a cultural link between Swedish immigrants and their Canadian-born children. For many immigrants, religious dissension in the homeland had been a major factor for leaving Sweden and it affected their choice of religious denomination in N America.

The Lutheran Church has been the strongest church organization in N America among Swedes. In 1860 the Swedish Lutheran congregations in the US established the Augustana Synod which, for over a century, guided Swedish Lutheran activities throughout Canada and the US before becoming the Lutheran Church in America. The Canada Conference of the Augustana Evangelical Lutheran Church was located in Winnipeg.

Canada-Tidningen (est in Winnipeg in 1892), was the longest-running and most influential Swedish-language newspaper in Canada. In 1970 it amalgamated with the *Swedish-American Tribune* of Chicago. A number of other Swedish-language periodicals have been published, in Winnipeg, Vancouver and Toronto.

Education The children of the early Swedish settlers adapted readily to the Canadian educational system and to the English language. Preliminary estimates from the 1986 census record 11 970 Canadians whose mother tongue was Swedish.

Politics Many Swedish Canadians actively participated in community activities, eg, co-operatives, credit unions and wheat pools of the Prairie provinces, and in the early BC trade-union movement. Many Swedes supported populist movements such as the CO-OPERATIVE COMMONWEALTH FEDERATION in Saskatchewan and SOCIAL CREDIT in Alberta. Harry STROM, former Social Credit premier of Alberta (1968-71), was of Swedish origin.
                                        LENNARD SILLANPAA

Sweezey, Robert Oliver, engineer, promoter (b at Trois-Rivières, Qué 8 Dec 1883; d at Montréal 13 May 1968). Sweezey was the promoter and president of the massive Beauharnois Light, Heat and Power Corp and of other hydroelectric, forestry and transportation endeavours. The Beauharnois project was designed not only to divert and harness the flow of the St Lawrence R, but also as part of the ST LAWRENCE SEAWAY. As an engineering project it was a great success, but Sweezey and other company officials became implicated in a monumental political scandal. As a result the Sweezey interests were removed and control passed to the rival Montreal Light, Heat and Power Consolidated. Thereafter, Sweezey was involved in several mining and power schemes, mainly in western Canada. A graduate of Queen's, Sweezey was an important benefactor, fund raiser and trustee of that institution for many years.   T.D. REGEHR

Swift, common name for about 80 species of birds in 2 closely related families (Apodidae, Hemiprocnidae), sometimes grouped with HUMMINGBIRDS. Swifts occur almost worldwide, wherever their flying-insect prey is sufficiently abundant. Four species breed in Canada. Long, slender, pointed wings and cylindrical bodies make possible the rapid, acrobatic flight for which these most aerial of birds are named. Family name, Apodidae [Gk, "footless"], is derived from the tiny feet, with strong claws on 4 toes showing specialized grasping abilities ideal for clinging to cliff faces. Swifts are mostly dull coloured. Most species nest colonially in caves or hollow trees; others under waterfalls, in sandbanks, in old swallow nests and even on palm leaves. The saliva that glues together most nests is the sole component of nests of some oriental species – which are used for bird's-nest soup! Chimney swifts (*Chaetura pelagica*), which breed across southern Canada from E Saskatchewan to the Maritimes, and sometimes Vaux's swift (*C. vauxi*) of southern BC may attach nests inside chimneys and building walls. Two cliff-dwelling species nest in western Canada, the large black swift (*Cypseloides niger*) through much of BC and locally in Alberta, and the white-throated swift (*Aeronautes saxatalis*) generally restricted to the Okanagan, but occasionally wandering to coastal sites.
                                    MARTIN K. McNICHOLL

Swift Current, Sask, City, pop 15 606 (1986c), 14 747 (1981c), inc 1914, is situated in southwestern Saskatchewan, 245 km W of Regina. The city took its name from a creek that flows through it and eventually empties into the S SASKATCHEWAN R. Since this particular creek bore the same name as the S Saskatchewan in the 1860s, fur traders avoided confusion by referring to it as Swift Current, the English derivative of the word "Saskatchewan." In 1882 the CPR bridged the creek and established a depot at the present site. Swift Current began to adopt the persona of a community in 1883 with the appearance of a dam, water tank, freight sheds, roadhouse and dining room. For many years it has served a large ranching, mixed-farming and grain-farming area. Oil, natural-gas, sodium-sulphate and helium production have diversified the expanding economy of the city.   DON HERPERGER

Swimming, Speed Competition is recognized for 4 swimming styles – freestyle (usually the crawl), breaststroke, backstroke and butterfly – over various distances up to 1500 m. In medley events, the swimmer uses all 4 strokes, in a prescribed order. Freestyle and medley relay races are also staged, usually with 4 swimmers per relay team. Most top-level competitions are held in 50 m pools, but some are raced over 25 m lengths, and records are maintained for both distances. Long-distance, or MARATHON, swimming is organized separately from speed swimming.

Swimming was considered to be an important survival skill by the ancient Egyptians, Greeks and Romans but was not contested as a sport. The first country to organize swimming on a national scale was Japan; an imperial decree of 1603 ordered swimming to be included in the country's educational program. Swimming meets were held in Japan for over 300 years; however, no impact was made on other countries because Japan was closed to the outside world until 1867. Competitive swimming in Great Britain started in the 1830s, and the first international competition was held in Melbourne, Australia, in 1858. The first European championships were held in 1889, and swimming for men was included in the 1896 Olympic Games. Women began participating in Olympic events in 1912. The governing body for international competition, the Fédération Internationale de Natation Amateur (FINA), was formed in 1908 and is responsible for all amateur aquatic sports: speed swimming, diving, synchronized swimming and water polo. Its first world championships were held in 1973.

In Canada, speed swimming is controlled by the Canadian Amateur Swimming Assn (CASA), formed in 1909. Prior to then, swimming had been organized by a committee of what became the Amateur Athletic Union of Canada. The CASA remained the dominant aquatic-sports organization in Canada, and assumed control of diving, water polo and synchronized swimming. By 1969, this arrangement was no longer satisfactory to diving and water polo (synchronized swimming had withdrawn in 1950), and the Aquatic Federation of Canada was created as an umbrella organization. All 4 aquatic sports are members of the federation, which in turn serves as the Canadian affiliate to FINA.

Swimming clubs in Canada began to organize meets in the 1870s. The Dolphin Club of Toronto, formed in 1875, and the Montreal Swimming Club, established one year later, were influential in the development of competition, and the 1876 meet of the Montréal club was the first such event in Canada. But lack of facilities hampered the spread of the sport in most parts of the country. Races were often held in open waters, over courses marked by floats and booms. Long-distance swimming was very popular. The outstanding Canadian swimmer in the early days of competition was George HODGSON, who swam with the Montreal Amateur Athletic Assn. In 1911, he won the mile race at the Festival of Empire Games in London, and the next year thrilled Canadians by winning the 400 m and 1500 m events at the Olympics. He set world records at these distances that stood until 1924. At the 1920 Olympics, George Vernot, also of Montréal, was 2nd in the 1500 m race and 3rd at the 400 m distance.

With the inauguration of the British Empire Games in 1930, Canadian swimmers began to excel at shorter distances. The outstanding swimmer of the pre-WWII era was Phyllis DEWAR, of Moose Jaw and Vancouver. At the 1934 Games she won 4 events; her 5th win in 1938 set a record for gold medals won by a Canadian that stood until 1978. After the war, BC swimmers coached by Percy Norman of the Vancouver Amateur Swim Club and George Gate of the Ocean Falls Swim Club began to dominate Canadian speed swimming. It was during the 1950s and early 1960s that swimmers such as Lenora Fisher, Jack Kelso,

Anne Ottenbrite in action at the 1984 Los Angeles Olympics, at which she won gold and silver medals (*courtesy Athlete Information Bureau/Service Information-Athlètes*).

Dick Pound, Peter Salmon, Helen Stewart, Mary Stewart and Beth Whittall among others started to establish Canada's status as a world power in speed swimming.

In 1966, Elaine TANNER, coached by Howard Firby of Vancouver's Dolphin Swim Club, set world records and won a number of British Commonwealth and Pan-American Games events, as well as 2 silver medals and one bronze in the 1968 Olympic Games. Other outstanding swimmers emerged at this time, and during the 1960s and 1970s Canada gradually rose to a position close to 3rd in the world, 2nd in the Pan-American Games and 1st in the Commonwealth. Bruce Robertson of Vancouver won the 100 m butterfly at the 1973 world championships, the first world title for Canada since George Hodgson's 1912 achievements. Leslie Cliff (Vancouver), Nancy GARAPICK (Halifax) and Donna-Marie Gurr (Vancouver) were the leaders of a remarkably strong group of women swimmers; and Graham SMITH, of Edmonton, with 6 gold medals, led the 1978 team that completely dominated the Commonwealth Games. Later that year, Smith won the 200 m individual medley race at the World Aquatic Championships. Other outstanding swimmers during this period were Wendy Cook, Angela Coughlin, Cheryl Gibson, Ralph Hutton, Ron Jacks, Marion Lay, Becky Smith, Shannon Smith, Patti Stenhouse and Judith Wright. The postwar improvement of Canadian swimmers can be measured by the achievements of its Commonwealth Games teams: 1 gold and 2 silver medals in 1950; 2 gold, 3 silver and 6 bronze in 1962; and 15 gold, 7 silver and 9 bronze in 1978.

At the 1984 Los Angeles Olympics Canadian swimmers won 4 gold medals, 3 silver and 3 bronze, contributing greatly to Canada's most successful Olympic competition. The medal winners were as follows: Alex BAUMANN (gold in the 200 m IM, world record, and the 400 m IM, world record); Victor DAVIS (gold in the 200 m breaststroke, world record, and silver in the 100 m breaststroke); Anne OTTENBRITE (gold in the 200 m breaststroke and silver in the 100 m breaststroke); Davis, Sandy Goss, Tom Ponting and Mike West (silver in the 400 m medley relay); West (bronze in the 100 m backstroke); Cam Henning (bronze in the 200 m backstroke); Ottenbrite, Reema Abdo, Michelle MacPherson and Pamela Rai (bronze in the 400 m medley relay). In the 1987 Pan-Am Games Canada won 19 medals: 1 gold (Keltie Duggan of Edmonton in the 100 m breaststroke), 5 silver and 13 bronze.

Competitive swimming in Canada has traditionally been organized through swimming clubs. The Toronto Dolphin Club was one of the leading clubs during the 1930s, and the Vancouver Amateur Swim Club dominated Canadian swimming during the 1940s and 1950s. The

Ocean Falls, BC, club produced outstanding swimmers far out of proportion to the size of that small, isolated coastal community; its swimmers were featured in Canadian meets, record books and teams during the 1950s and 1960s. The Montreal Amateur Athletic Assn team re-emerged as a strong club during the 1950s, with coaches Ed Healey and George Gate. The successor to the Vancouver Club has been that city's Dolphin Swim Club, coached by Howard Firby and then Derek Snelling. In 1964 George Gate moved to the Pointe Claire Club near Montréal, and the strength of that club was demonstrated through the 1970s. Other important clubs of the 1970s and early 1980s were the Thunder Bay Thunderbolts, under Don Talbot; the Etobicoke Club of Toronto, coached by Derek Snelling; the New Westminster Hyack Swim Club, with Ron Jacks; and the Keyano Club of Edmonton, coached by Tom and Dave Johnson. At the start of the 1980s, efforts to build Canada's university swim teams began to bear fruit, and the trend of Canadian swimmers training at universities and colleges in the US was reversed as Canadian programs became more attractive.

Competitive swimming is one of the most popular and successful sports in Canada, with age-group and summer swim meets supplementing the regular program of regional, national and international championships. BARBARA SCHRODT

Swiss In 1604 reference was made to the military quarters of Swiss soldiers at St Croix I in Acadia, soldiers who were followed in 1643 by 5 young Swiss who served under the lieutenant-governor of Acadia and by (1721-45) a small contingent of the Karrer Regiment, which reinforced the LOUIS-BOURG garrison for the French king. By 1881, 4588 people of Swiss origin had settled in Canada. Preliminary results from the 1986 census estimate 19 130 Canadians of Swiss descent.

One of the first Swiss to settle in what is now Canada was Pierre Miville (1602-69). He and his son were granted lands on the seigneury of Lauzon on the S shore of the St Lawrence R across from the Plains of Abraham. Records also show the Miville family were granted lands in 1665 by de Tracy, who named the land "Canton des Suisses fribourgeois." Jacques Bizard (1642-92), who accompanied Count Frontenac to New France, became seigneur of Île de Bonaventure, now known as Île Bizard. Lawrence Ermatinger (1736-89) was one of the founders of the NORTH WEST COMPANY; Sir Frederick HALDIMAND became governor general of Québec in 1778 and Sir George PREVOST (born in the US but of Swiss origin) was governor-in chief of Canada between 1812 and 1815. Prevost's armies, which helped defend Canada during the WAR OF 1812, included the Swiss de Watteville and DE MEURON regiments.

Many of the approximately 2000 German-speaking Mennonites who immigrated to Upper Canada from Pennsylvania (1786-1820) were of Swiss origin. After the War of 1812 and the disbanding of the de Watteville and de Meuron regiments, a small number of Swiss officers and civilians established themselves in Perth (Ont), and near Drummondville in Lower Canada. Another 30 or so Swiss from these regiments joined expeditionary forces with Lord SELKIRK, who was organizing relief for the RED RIVER COLONY.

Swiss-born Sebastian Fryfogel (1791-1873) was credited with opening the Huron Tract E of Lk Huron. Later in the 19th century and early in the 20th century other Swiss communities were founded in Blumenau, Alta, and Zurich, Ont. A small group of Swiss alpinists helped open the Rockies to tourism and the first western painter, Peter RINDISBACHER, was Swiss.

Despite their small numbers in Canada, the

Swiss support several associations and clubs, eg, the Swiss National Society, est 1874; the Swiss Club, est 1918; the Matterhorn Young Swiss Club; and various periodicals. Nevertheless, Swiss settlers never felt the need to unite as a group. They became immersed in the well-organized German and French community groups and associations. Swiss-born Canadians have made outstanding contributions in many fields, eg, hotel and restaurant business, dairy farming, music, arts, education and sports. ROXROY WEST

Sydenham, Charles Edward Poulett Thomson, 1st Baron, politician, colonial administrator (b at Wimbledon, London, Eng 13 Sept 1799; d at Kingston, Canada W 19 Sept 1841). Son of a prominent merchant, he entered the family firm at age 16. An outspoken free trader, he was first elected to the House of Commons in 1826 and became vice-president (1830) then president (1834) of the Board of Trade. Appointed governor general of British N America in 1839, he persuaded the legislature of Upper Canada to consent to a union with Lower Canada and framed the constitution of the united province. Although he opposed the principle of RESPONSIBLE GOVERNMENT and acted as his own prime minister, he turned the Executive Council into a Cabinet composed of heads of departments who sat in the legislature. He also established a variant of this system in NS in 1840. It could work only so long as the proponents of complete responsible government did not control the Assembly, and in Canada he interfered flagrantly in the 1841 election to prevent a Reform victory. His policy of anglicization won him the support of the anglophone majority in the colony but the hatred of the French Canadians. His system was already beginning to collapse when he died in 1841. P.A. BUCKNER

Reading: Adam Shortt, *Lord Sydenham* (1926); J.M.S. Careless, *The Union of the Canadas* (1967).

Sydney, NS, City, pop 27 754 (1986c), 29 444 (1981c), inc 1900, is located near the eastern ex-

tremity of CAPE BRETON ISLAND. It is the principal city of Cape Breton and centre of the second-largest urban complex in NOVA SCOTIA. Its fine harbour, known as Spanish Bay in colonial times, is ringed by the richest coalfield in eastern Canada. Since 1900 it has been noted for its huge steel mill, the largest and most modern in Canada at its construction. The industrial core around the mill has been in decline since the end of WWII as the coal mines of the surrounding communities became less productive and the obsolete steel mill less competitive with central Canadian producers.

History When Cape Breton was separated from Nova Scotia in 1784 as a refuge for LOYALISTS, Sydney was chosen as its capital. A townsite was developed under the direction of Governor J.F.W. DESBARRES and named for Lord Sydney, then colonial secretary. Less successful as a separate colony than New Brunswick, Cape Breton was rejoined to Nova Scotia in 1820 after nearly 4 decades of maladministration, political intrigue and general underdevelopment. Sydney, still a tiny outpost of a few hundred residents, but with the pretensions of a colonial capital, was reduced to being shire town to Cape Breton County, which then included the entire island. It was generally underdeveloped throughout the 19th century, but remained the administrative centre of the island.

Economy Sydney's fate has been inextricably linked to the mining of coal. Sea coal had been taken by the French during the occupation of LOUISBOURG in the 18th century, but it only came under intensive development towards the middle of the 19th century, responding to increased demand first in the US and later in central Canada. Sydney provided services and shipping facilities for surrounding coal towns. The location of steel-making there in 1899 transformed Sydney. The Dominion Iron and Steel Co (later Dominion Steel Corp) occupied prime waterfront property and invested several hundred million dollars in plant and land. The town's population doubled

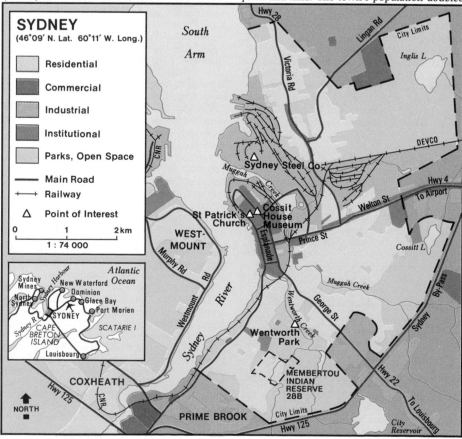

Sydney, NS, on the eastern extremity of Cape Breton Island, is ringed by the richest coalfield in eastern Canada (*courtesy City of Sydney*).

and redoubled several times over the next decade, drawing migrants from the exhausted farms of the island and large numbers of Europeans as well, giving the city the most polyglot population in the region. Thereafter the steel mill, based on local coal resources, limestone from nearby quarries and iron ore from BELL ISLAND, Nfld, formed the city's core. Hospitals, government services, cultural and educational institutions all centered here. The island's commercial life radiated from the core of merchants along Sydney's waterfront. Connection to central Canada by rail in the 1880s solidified its commercial dominance. Yet, like most similar communities in Canada, it has risen and fallen with the development of its hinterland region. Sydney's has been in decline for some time.

Townscape Sydney's oldest portions were established along the waterfront, much like all seaport towns in the Atlantic provinces. Bisected by the steel mill, which occupies most of the S side of the outer harbour, it spread out to encroach on a series of hills behind. The mill is surrounded by rings of drab company-built frame houses in which reside one of the most militant work forces in Canada. The steelworkers of Sydney struggled from the beginning to establish their right to collective bargaining. They did not succeed until WWII when the United Steelworkers of America finally gained recognition as bargainers for the steelworkers. Sydney has a fine central park and several large institutional buildings, including UNIVERSITY COLLEGE OF CAPE BRETON, located on the outskirts of the city.   D.A. MUISE

Reading: P. MacEwan, *Miners and Steelworkers* (1976).

Sydney Mines, NS, Town, pop 8063 (1986c), 8501 (1981c), inc 1889, is located on the N side of Sydney Harbour, 19 km from SYDNEY. The presence of coal was noted by Nicolas DENYS in 1672 and strip-mined coal was shipped out as early as 1724. Large-scale operations began in 1826 when the General Mining Assn took over the mines. Shafts were sunk, ironworks established and railway tracks laid. The NS Steel and Coal Co succeeded the GMA in 1900, later expanding operations and building blast furnaces. The town enjoyed a period of prosperity and expansion until 1920 when the blast furnaces shut down. The last mine, Princess Colliery, closed in 1975. There is no other industry, and unemployment is high. The "Princess" was once a museum where visitors could descend in a mine that at one time operated as far as 8 km out below the ocean floor.   HEATHER MACDONALD

Sydney Steel Corporation (Sysco) Steel has been produced in SYDNEY, NS, since 1899, when the Dominion Iron and Steel Co established a steelworks to exploit Cape Breton COAL and Newfoundland IRON ORE. Production of railway rails began in 1905. Several changes in ownership took place until Hawker-Siddeley took over and ran the plant in the 1960s. The steelworks has been operated by the NS government since 1967. The government, faced with a socially unacceptable shutdown, formed a CROWN CORPORATION to keep the industry alive. The plant consists of 2 small blast furnaces and several basic open-hearth furnaces, with an annual raw-steel capacity of about 910 000 tonnes. The low productivity of the plant and the poor demand and prices for its products (mainly rails and semifinished steel) made Sysco's future as a steel producer uncertain until 1987 when the federal government approved financing for Sysco's $275 million mill modernization which includes the installation of a modern electric-arc furnace.   JOHN G. PEACEY

Sylvestre, Joseph Jean Guy, essayist, literary critic and librarian (b at Sorel, Qué 17 May 1918). After studies at Collège Sainte-Marie de Montréal and the U of Ottawa, he became literary critic for *Le Droit* (1940-1948), private secretary to the Hon Louis ST. LAURENT (1945-50), then director of the National Library of Canada (1968-85). A member of the Académie canadienne-française (1954), president of the Royal Society (1973-74), an honorary doctor of several universities, he was founder and director of the magazine *Gants du ciel* (1943-56) and author of several books: *Situation de la poésie canadienne* (1941), *Poètes catholiques de la France contemporaine* (1943), *Sondages* (1957) and *Amours Délices et Orgues* (1953, under the pseudonym Jean Bruneau). He is best known for his *Anthologie de la poésie canadienne-française,* which went through 7 editions between 1942 and 1974.   PAUL WYCZYNSKI

Symbols of Authority One of the earliest signs of authority (the right to enforce obedience) was probably a wooden club, in which symbolism grew directly out of practical application: the humble club became both an instrument by which power was exercised and (consequently) a symbol of authority. Today, long dignified by the name "mace," the caveman's club, which evolved into the steely weapon of medieval knightly combat and then into a symbol of kingly power, still serves as the symbol of authority in Canada's Parliament and in the provincial legislative assemblies. It is part of Canada's British heritage. Until the mace has been placed on the table before the Speaker's chair, the legislators have no authority under which to make or repeal laws. They are, in effect, without power, for they have no authority to wield it: although Parliament has the power to govern, it has that power only under the authority of the CROWN.

Within the COMMONWEALTH, the Crown is the supreme symbol of unity and authority; and all laws are enacted and carried out in the name of the Crown. Its supremacy in Canada is evident from the representation of this symbol of authority at the upper end of the mace, substituting for the deadly bulge of the caveman's club and the spiked ball of the medieval warrior's mace. Here is evidence of the fine line that developed between authority and power. Centuries ago the Crown appeared in small replica, capping what was then the handle of the king's mace. Grasped by the hand of authority, the power was in the hitting end. But the need for brute force receded and the royal mace ceased to be an instrument for exercising power directly on the battlefield. It became a symbol of authority under which legislation could take place. Today the configuration of the mace is reversed, a large crown, the symbol of authority, now dominating the mace's onetime hitting end.

The Crown, an ancient symbol of monarchy, is easily recognized, appearing as it does ensigning the coat of arms of Canada (*see* EMBLEMS OF CANADA) and displayed in many other ways to indicate governmental, judicial and military authority. We also speak of the Crown as the prosecutor in courts of law, as the possessor of government-owned lands, and with respect to governmental agencies such as crown assets and various CROWN CORPORATIONS. In fact, "Crown" is used as the general term expressing the legal personality of the executive of government. Executive power, originally in the monarch's own hands, has come, through constitutional evolution, to be entrusted to bodies of legislators – who still exercise it in the sovereign's name. One place where the authority of the Crown is still in evidence is the giving of royal assent. No bill can become law until it has been read the appropriate number of times and passed in both Houses of Parliament. This having been done, it automatically receives royal assent, the symbolic agreement of the supreme authority, and becomes law.

The symbolism of the Crown is deeply entrenched in the entire process of British democracy, to which Canada has fallen heir. Authority is vested in the Crown, but in practice the Crown acts only on the advice of those members of the PRIVY COUNCIL who make up the Cabinet of the day. Since Cabinet ministers are also members of Parliament, they are, as members, responsible to the electorate, so that the people are in fact sovereign. The Crown therefore becomes the symbol of the sovereignty (or authority) of the people. The Crown is also a symbol of political unity, for the government and Her Majesty's Loyal Opposition are still united under the Crown for the betterment of the country, although pursuing different policies in an effort to achieve that betterment.

Coats of arms were developed during the Crusades as aids to the identification of warriors on the battlefield. These soon became symbols of authority when the designs on the warriors' surcoats, banners and shields were transferred to the wax seals which served as signatures in those days, when even the most authoritative in the land was likely to be illiterate. The first recorded use of a coat of arms to proclaim supreme authority in Canada was on 24 July 1534, when French explorer Jacques CARTIER erected a cross at the entrance to the Baie de Gaspé. "Under the cross-piece we put a coat of arms with 3 fleurs de lys in relief and over this was a wooden placard engraved with large letters that read *Vive Le Roi de France.*" Three conventionalized golden lilies on a blue shield were the armorial bearings of François Ier; his arms, raised by Cartier, identified him as the possessor of the new land and were the symbol of his authority over it.

Since armorial bearings are found not only upon shields but also upon banners, it is not surprising that the symbol of authority which John CABOT set up on Newfoundland soil in 1497, when he claimed that territory for Henry VII of England, was "the royal banner." A banner is either a square or an oblong flag. In the age of imperialism no greater symbol of authority existed than the flag of any nation establishing or claiming authority over some distant undeveloped territory. Numerous imperial flags – notably British, French and Spanish – have flown over what is now Canadian soil. In addition, flags such as those of the HUDSON'S BAY COMPANY and the NORTH WEST COMPANY have been used to indicate claims of territory by corporate interests.

Authority, no matter what its source, becomes embodied in either a person or an office. In Canada each of these embodiments has its own seal, by means of which every conferment of authority is marked. The Great Seal of Canada is the official seal. It gives formal expression to the traditional and legal authority of the state to make provisions for the well-being of the nation. The seal depicts Elizabeth II on the Coronation throne, wearing St Edward's Crown and holding other symbols of royal authority in her hands. Before the queen are the armorial bearings of Canada. This seal is used to sanction the commissions issued to persons appointed to the most important offices of state. It is also used to confer approval upon various kinds of documents, such as letters patent constituting the office of governor general, proclamations, land grants by the Crown and election writs.

The Governor General's Privy Seal, which is a personal seal, depicts the personal arms of the incumbent. Among the commissions issued under the Privy Seal are those of the officers of the ARMED FORCES, of which the governor general is commander in chief. This particular application of the Privy Seal testifies to an important feature of our Constitution: that the legal use of military force in Canada is ultimately dependent on the personal authority of the monarch's representative. It is not dependent on the power of the leader of the government, even though, since the beginning of RESPONSIBLE GOVERNMENT, he has had access to the official seal.

When a party leader takes the oath of office and receives the commission as PRIME MINISTER, power, coming from the people, and authority, coming from the Crown, are joined. Thus the party leader who forms the government becomes, while in office, the most powerful person in the country. Yet no one, according to the German sociologist Max Weber, has greater authority than the monarch, for his or her authority rests on all 3 of the bases of authority that we have accepted as legitimate: charisma, tradition and law.

Not only nations, but religious communities, public and secret societies and countless other organizations around the world possess symbols of authority under which their citizens, adherents or members respond to the laws and regulations that govern and sustain them. Symbols of authority come in many forms. Crowns, maces, coats of arms, seals, flags – even the "tin star" worn by gun-slinging US lawmen of fact and fiction – are symbols of authority under which people are governed. In Canada's history perhaps no symbol of authority has been more quickly and universally recognized than the scarlet jacket of the NORTHWEST MOUNTED POLICE and their successors, the ROYAL CANADIAN MOUNTED POLICE. STROME GALLOWAY

Reading: A.B. Beddoe, *Beddoe's Canadian Heraldry* (ed Strome Galloway, 1981); C. Swan, *Symbols of Sovereignty* (1977).

Symington, Herbert James, lawyer, executive (b at Sarnia, Ont 22 Nov 1881; d at Montréal 28 Sept 1965). Symington, admitted to the Manitoba Bar in 1905, became a prominent corporation lawyer and a notable figure in Winnipeg public affairs. A Liberal, he was a member of the informal "Sanhedrin" around J.W. DAFOE and T.A. CRERAR, and he was put on the board of the CNR in 1936. During WWII he controlled the allocation of supplies of electrical power, and from 1941 to 1947 he was president of TRANS-CANADA AIRLINES. He helped found the International Civil Aviation Organization and later became chairman of the board of Price Brothers.
ROBERT BOTHWELL

Symonds, Norman, composer (b near Nelson, BC 23 Dec 1920). Symonds came to the forefront of the Canadian third-stream movement under Gordon Delamont in Toronto. His major compositions, combining elements of jazz (improvisation, colour) and classical music (structure, orchestration), include *Concerto Grosso* for jazz quintet and symphony orchestra (1957), *Autumn Nocturne* (1960), *The Nameless Hour* (1966) and *The Democratic Concerto* (1967). Symonds has composed works for TV (*Black Hallelujah*) and stage (*Lady in the Night*), as well as such expressionist pieces as *Big Lonely* (1975) and *The Gift of Thanksgiving* (1980), both inspired by Canada's natural beauty. Later works explore electronic and choral idioms; Symonds has also composed works for student audiences. Some of his concert pieces have been recorded by the CBC and National Youth orchestras and by Ron COLLIER; some of his stage works have been produced by the CBC and by the CANADIAN OPERA CO.
MARK MILLER

Symons, Thomas Henry Bull, teacher, historian, university president, author (b at Toronto 30 May 1929). He was educated at U of T, Oxford and the Sorbonne. As an academic and administrator he has played many roles. He was founding president of TRENT UNIVERSITY (1961-72), and founding vice-president of the SOCIAL SCIENCES AND HUMANITIES RESEARCH COUNCIL OF CANADA (1978-84). He is perhaps best known as chairman of the Commission on Canadian Studies (1972-84). As author of *To Know Ourselves: The Report of the Commission on Canadian Studies* (1975), he alerted Canadians and Canadian universities to the importance of teaching and research about Canada, its prospects, problems and circumstances. That report, and the challenges contained in it, are balanced by Symons's concern that Canadians participate in the wider scholarly world, both through contributions about Canada and by a willingness to learn about, and be open to, the perspectives of others. His view of the importance of a Canadian presence on the wider international academic stage is demonstrated by international service, which has included work with the Commonwealth Standing Committee on Student Mobility (1982-), chairmanship of the Int Board of United World Colleges (1980-), and chairmanship of the Assn of Commonwealth Universities (1971-72).

Not only a theoretician but a practitioner, Symons has advised the provincial government of Ontario as the chairman of the Ontario Human Rights Commission (1975-78), for example, and the federal government as a member of the Federal Cultural Policy Review Committee (1979-82). He was also chairman of the Policy Advisory Committee to R.L. STANFIELD (1968-75). His publications, articles, reviews and monographs on a host of topics include *Life Together: A Report on Human Rights in Ontario* (1977), with Rosalie Abella et al, and *Some Questions of Balance: Human Resources, Higher Education and Canadian Studies* (1984), with James E. Page. As well, he contributed to *Ontario Universities: Access, Operations and Funding* (ed D.W. Conklin and T.J. Courchene, 1985). Symons is a fellow of the Royal Soc of Canada, Officer of the Order of Canada (1976), holder of the Queen's Silver Jubilee Medal and of the Canadian Centennial medal, as well as many other honours. *See also* CANADIAN STUDIES.
JAMES E. PAGE

Synagogues Jewish law defines any place where 10 men can gather for worship to be a synagogue. The most common belief as to the exact origin of the synagogue is that there was a need to establish a supplementary institution to the Temple for those who could not travel to Jerusalem. The absence of sacrificial rites, the rise of Rabbinic teachings and the ceremony for reading the Torah gave the synagogue its unique character and, soon after the destruction of the Second Temple in 70 AD, it was this institution that became the focus of Jewish communal worship.

The first congregation in Canada was established in Montréal. Founded in 1768, the Shearith Israel Congregation built their first building at the intersection of Notre Dame and St James streets in 1777 and this building remained the only formal place for Jewish worship until 1846 when, in that same city, the Sha'ar Hashomayim was established. Little is known about the architecture of these buildings.

By the late 1870s there were established congregations in Victoria, Winnipeg, Toronto, Hamilton, Montréal, Trois-Rivières and Québec City. Of the synagogues of that era, the Temple Emanu-el of Victoria is the lone remaining building and it has been in continuous use by the Jewish community since 1863, the year of its completion. The building is a 2-storey clay brick structure in the Romanesque style with fine corbelling under the eaves and gables. The windows were paned with stained glass in simple geometric patterns. Prominent on the main façade is a circular "rose" window – a motif common to synagogues in the first half of the 20th century. The interior is almost entirely occupied by the sanctuary; the main floor seating men around a central Bimah (platform for Torah reading) and focused towards the east wall. It is in this east wall that the Holy Ark is housed in a niche which protrudes outside the perimeter of the square (in plan) building. The second storey is a women's gallery – U-shaped in plan and creating a double height central space between the east wall and Bimah. This central space is further accentuated by a dome in the ceiling above.

In many ways this building typifies the architecture of those buildings built as synagogues in Canada from the mid-19th century to the onset of WWII. Common to these buildings are façades which combine elements of local vernacular with styles then perceived as best fitting the image of a synagogue. The traditional plan of the sanctuary is typified by the description of the Temple Emanu-el of Victoria. In 1887 the Shearith Israel of Montréal built their new synagogue on Stanley St in what was referred to as the Judeo-Egyptian style – a templelike building with a pediment resting on a collonade of Egyptian pillars which sits on a solid base one-half storey high. This sort of romantic and mystical styling was also exhibited in the Holy Blossom Temple of Toronto, built in 1897, which combined the local tradition of intri-

Interior of Holy Blossom Temple, Toronto (*photo by Leonard Sandler*).

cately detailed stone craftsmanship with Byzantine influences expressed by the onion-shaped domes of the 2 side towers on the main façade.

Although the synagogue in Canada remained principally a place of worship until the beginning of WWII, other community activities began to exert their influence on these institutions and reshape the form of the building itself. The Temple Emanu-el of Montréal, built in 1911 and enlarged in 1922, was one of the first congregations in Canada to be based on the Reform service. The founding members planned their building to include facilities for education, social gatherings and auxiliary groups. Thus while the façades of the building rigorously adhered to the accepted Byzantine style, the sanctuary was auditorium-like – men and women sat together and the building sprawled on a spacious site, unlike the traditional urban lots that most synagogues were fit into. In 1921 the Sha'ar Hashomayim of Montréal purchased land at Côte St-Antoine Road and Kensington Ave and built their new building, which was described as being "cathedral-like." The façades were constructed of grey vitrified brick and sandstone and there were small Moorish cupolas that alluded to "mystic orientalism." The sanctuary, with its coffered ceiling and combined Bimah and Holy Ark, accomplished separate seating by 2 sides flanking women's galleries rather than a balcony. With the building of the Holy Blossom Temple of Toronto on Bathurst St in 1938 came the last major innovations in synagogue architecture before the modern (post-WWII) period; these innovations include a campuslike planning of the institution, the inclusion of a parking lot and the use of modern building materials. Although the new Holy Blossom's sanctuary borrows significantly from the Temple Emanu-el in New York City, built 10 years earlier and of stone, this structure is formed and finished in reinforced concrete.

In the period beginning soon after the end of WWII, Jews in the major urban centres began to move from inner-city neighbourhoods to the burgeoning suburbs. Along with this move came the formation of many new congregations and the relocation of older congregations whose former buildings were often abandoned. The new, suburban buildings also abandoned the search for the "appropriate style" and, for the duration of the 1950s and 1960s, the new buildings reflected a more adventurous and expressive spirit. As with the Holy Blossom Temple, the sanctuary was often a visibly distinct element in the overall composition of the building. Common forms and motifs include open courtyards (Beth El, St John's, Nfld, built in 1959); colourful mosaic murals on the façade (Young Israel of Montréal, built 1953); and interesting methods of bringing natural light indirectly into the sanctuary through clerestory or imposing vertical windows (Shaarey Tzedec, Calgary, and Beth Tzedec, Toronto).

Often, the modern synagogue is built in stages, the first stage being a hall followed by a permanent sanctuary which is joined to the multipurpose hall by a movable partition. This allows for increased seating on holidays and festivals.

Modern sanctuary motifs include stained glass with pictorial images (Beth Sholom, Toronto); abstract yet nongeometrical images in stained glass (Rosh Pina, Winnipeg); stained glass ark doors (Beth Israel, Calgary); bronze ark doors (Shaarey Zedec, Winnipeg); and relief murals (Beth Emeth, Toronto).

During the 1970s, synagogue building was greatly curtailed owing to the increased cost of building and the cost of maintaining existing congregations' programs. Smaller Jewish communities continued to sell off their buildings as the Jewish population continued to migrate to and concentrate in the major urban centres, principally Toronto and Montréal. However, renewed appreciation for the older "downtown" synagogues has promoted rehabilitation programs for several of the buildings that remained. This, along with the embellishing and refurbishing of existing structures with new artistic interpretations and the building of, generally, smaller synagogues to serve new suburban Jewish communities, are the main areas of synagogue-building activity in the mid-1980s. SHELDON LEVITT

Reading: Sheldon Levitt, Lynn Milstone and Sidney Tenenbaum, *Treasures of a People: The Synagogues of Canada* (1985).

Synchronized Swimming is the performance in water of a series of movements in time to music. It is a popular activity for many in N America and increasingly so around the world. Canada has developed an excellent recreational program for all ages and skill levels called the "Star" program, and has a highly developed competitive program as well as programs for training both officials and coaches.

The basic skills of synchronized swimming are strokes and figures, which were originally part of the Royal Life Saving Society program. In 1924, the first competition in strokes and figures in Canada was held at the YWCA in Montréal. In the following 2 years, swimmers in Ontario and Québec became more interested in this kind of competition, and the first Dominion championship in strokes and figures was held at the Montreal Amateur Athletic Assn in 1926. Margaret Shearer (Mrs Peg Seller) became the first Canadian champion, winning the Frances C. Gale Trophy. The rules for this competition changed slightly over the years, but the trophy has continually been in competition to the present time. By 1954, Canadian synchronized-swimming championships included competitions in solo, duet and team, and Canadian synchronized swimmers have competed around the world. The 1979 Canadian Female Athlete of the Year, Helen Vanderburg, won gold medals in Canadian, Pan-American, Pan-Pacific, FINA Cup and World Aquatic championships in 1978 and 1979. Synchronized swimming was in the Olympics for the first time at the 1984 Los Angeles Games; Canada's duet and solo entries placed 2nd behind the US. In 1985 Carolyn Waldo of Alberta won an unprecedented 4-gold sweep of the prestigious FINA World Cup. Canada won international gold at the 1986 Commonwealth Games and at the World Aquatic Championships. At the 1987 Pan-Am Games, Canada won 3 silver medals. GLADYS BEAN

Reading: Gladys Bean, *History of Synchronized Swimming in Canada* (1975).

Szilasi, Gabor, photographer, teacher (b at Budapest, Hungary 3 Feb 1928). He immigrated to Canada in 1957. Both as a teacher (Collège du Vieux Montréal 1970-79 and Concordia 1979-) and as a photographer he has influenced a generation with his carefully considered approach to photographing people. He has recorded people within their environments, particularly in Québec regions such as Charlevoix County (Île-aux-COUDRES), Beauce County, Abitibi, Lac SAINT-JEAN and Lotbinière. His large format and panoramic photographs of Québec architecture demonstrate his interest in the built environment. He was associated with the Groupe d'action photographique in Montréal 1970-72 and, as a participant in "A Photographic Project: Alberta 1980," documented Falher, a small town in northwestern Alberta. ANN W. THOMAS

Taber, Alta, Town, pop 6382 (1986c), 5988 (1981c), inc 1907, is located 50 km E of Lethbridge. Taber was settled by MORMONS in the first decade of the 20th century, and the name is said to come from the first part of the word "tabernacle," although the first post office (1904) was called "Tabor," presumably after Mt Tabor, Palestine. The local economy at first depended upon beef cattle and wheat but, with the development of irrigation, the cultivation of sugar beets became important and a processing plant was built in the town. ERIC J. HOLMGREN

Taber Child In 1961 fragments of skull from a human infant were recovered from the banks of the Oldman R near TABER, Alta. The find sparked an archaeological controversy, as the bones were said to have come from geological deposits which dated between 20 000-40 000 years old. If correct, this would make the Taber Child site far older than the conventionally accepted date for the arrival of the first people in the New World – about 12 000 years ago. Subsequent excavations at the site failed to recover any additional human bone. However, 2 recent analyses – measurement of bone protein, and dating by the new accelerator radiocarbon technique – have indicated that the bone specimens are in fact only some 4000 years old, and thus from a time period when prehistoric peoples were well established on the Canadian Plains. JACK BRINK

Table Tennis is played by 2 (singles) or 4 (doubles) players, normally indoors. Opponents face each other and hit the ball with a racquet, alternately, over a 6-inch (15.25 cm) net stretched midway across an 9 x 5 ft (274 cm x 152.5 cm) table. The celluloid ball makes a hollow sound that led to "ping-pong" as a common name for the game, although it could not be used officially for some time since it was a registered trademark. It first appeared in the late 19th century as an attempt to miniaturize tennis for play indoors. The pimpled-rubber racquet covering was developed in 1903, allowing for the development of spin on strokes. World championships have been held since 1926. The sponge racquet was introduced by the Japanese in 1952 and since 1954 the championships have been dominated by players from Japan and China.

The Canadian Table Tennis Assn was formed in 1929, with Québec as the founding provincial member and Ontario joining 5 years later. A long association with the Canadian National Exhibition began in 1936, when the first Canadian Table Tennis Championships were staged there. The CTTA operates a computerized rating system that allows any competitive player to be ranked, both provincially and nationally. Canada's table-tennis stars of the 1930s were Paul Chapdelaine and J.J. Desjardins of Montréal. In the 1970s, Violette Nesukaitis, of Toronto, emerged as a strong international player. Winner of 4 N American open championships, she travelled to China in 1971 on a Canadian team, the first table-tennis team to be invited to that country. In 1973 she was ranked 3rd among Commonwealth women players. She retired in 1976. At the 1979 Pan-American Games, Ed Lo won the men's singles event. In the 1987 Pan-Am Games, Canada's team won 2 gold, 2 silver and 3 bronze. That year Joe Ng was the winner of golds in singles and doubles and bronzes in mixed doubles and the team event. Mariana Domontos of Larrimac, Qué, is now the queen of table tennis, winning 9 consecutive national singles titles 1976-85 as well as many international titles. Table tennis will be included in the Olympics for the first time in 1988. BARBARA SCHRODT

Taché, Alexandre-Antonin, missionary, Roman Catholic priest, archbishop (b at Rivière-du-

Loup, Qué 23 July 1823; d at St-Boniface, Man 22 June 1894). He entered the Oblates of Mary Immaculate in 1844, went to the RED RIVER COLONY in 1845 and was ordained priest on 12 Oct 1845 by Bishop Norbert PROVENCHER. After studying the Saulteaux language in St-Boniface, he left for the immense territory of the Île-à-la-Crosse [Sask] mission in 1846. He was named coadjutor to Provencher in 1850. He founded many new missions and helped the large number of settlers who flooded into the region. The bishop was at a Vatican Council when the RED RIVER REBELLION began, and he was called back to Canada by government authorities and helped restore order. His promises to the Métis in so doing, however, were controversial. He fought just as vigorously for French and Catholic schools (*see* MANITOBA SCHOOLS QUESTION). The bishop left behind him important accomplishments in the country. A devoted missionary and enlightened patriot, he was one of the great Catholic bishops of Canada.

GASTON CARRIÈRE, OMI, CR

Taché, Sir Étienne-Paschal, doctor, politician (b at St-Thomas [Montmagny], Qué 5 Sept 1795; d there 30 July 1865). He began studying medicine while serving as an officer in the WAR OF 1812. After completing his studies in Philadelphia, he practised medicine in Montmagny for 22 years, 1819-41. Though he did not participate in the REBELLIONS OF 1837, he was an ardent PATRIOTE. After the union of the Canadas, along with his compatriots A.N. MORIN, L.H. LAFONTAINE, and G.É. CARTIER, Taché became more willing to compromise. He was first elected to the new Assembly in 1841. In 1846 he resigned to become deputy adjutant general of the Canada East militia, and was responsible for its reorganization. In 1848 he became an executive councillor, commissioner of public works and then legislative councillor, and was a member of every government until 1857. He replaced Morin as leader of Canada E and formed a ministry with A.N. MACNAB 27 Jan 1855. After MacNab resigned in May 1856, Taché joined John A. MACDONALD in a ministry that sealed the alliance of Upper Canadian Conservatives and Canadien Liberals in a unified party. The Taché-Macdonald government manoeuvred well under difficult circumstances, but Taché resigned in 1857, though he remained a legislative councillor. He returned to active politics in 1864 amidst yet another political crisis. At Governor MONCK's request, he formed a coalition government with J.A. Macdonald, an entirely Conservative administration which lasted only one month – the third government to fall in 2 years. On 22 June 1864 Taché subsequently formed the coalition ministry that was to give birth to the CONFEDERATION he so passionately promoted. Before his death, he presided over the QUEBEC CONFERENCE

and defended the 72 Resolutions determining the shape of Confederation. ANDRÉE DÉSILETS

Taconis, Kryn, photographer (b at Rotterdam, Holland 7 May 1918; d at Toronto 12 July 1979). In the 1960s and 1970s, he became one of Canada's leading photojournalists, known for his integrity and compassion. The outbreak of WWII shaped his career in still photography. He joined the Dutch resistance movement and clandestinely recorded the appalling suffering resulting from acute food shortages. In 1950 he became a member of the free-lance photo agency Magnum. He travelled throughout Europe, the Middle East, Africa and Australia, and his work appeared in the great picture magazines of the day, including *Life* and *Paris-Match*. In 1959 Taconis and his wife moved to Toronto, where he began to free-lance for publications such as the *Star Weekly*. He also worked for the National Film Board for 3 years. Among his best-known Canadian work is a photo-essay of HUTTERITE communities in the West. LOUISE ABBOTT

Tadoussac, Qué, Village, pop 838 (1986c), 900 (1981c), inc 1899, is located at the confluence of the SAGUENAY and ST LAWRENCE rivers, 210 km NE of Québec City. In the Montagnais language, its name means "nipples" or "breasts," from the rounded hills found here. When Europeans arrived, Tadoussac was already an important trading centre for tribes of the N and S shores of the St Lawrence. This activity drew European traffickers by the mid-16th century. Pierre Chauvin tried in vain to establish a colony here in 1600, and it was here that Samuel de CHAMPLAIN concluded a first treaty between Europeans and Indians (1603). Tadoussac was captured by Sir David KIRKE in 1628 but was returned to France later. A major fur-trading centre from the 17th century on, Tadoussac gained a new and lasting role in the 19th century – forestry and tourism. Chauvin's habitation has been reconstructed. One of the oldest wooden chapels in N America (1647) is found here as well. MARC ST-HILAIRE

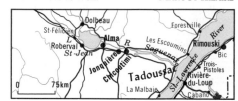

Tagish, numbering 175 (1986), live in northern BC and the southern Yukon Territory around a series of lakes that are part of the Yukon R headwaters. The high Coast Mts prevent the nearby Pacific Ocean from ameliorating the harsh climate of the plateau. Until the 20th century the Tagish camped at the junction of Tagish and Marsh lakes, but they did not stay year round because of their seminomadic subsistence cycle. After 1900, most Tagish began to live permanently in Carcross.

The traditional subsistence economy was that of boreal forest hunters, fishers and trappers, later augmented by fur trading with surrounding Athapaskans. The near extinction of the coastal sea otter by about 1800 led to a demand for fine land-animal furs from the subarctic Cordillera. The Tagish acted as middlemen between Indians farther inland and the Coast TLINGIT, for until shortly before the KLONDIKE GOLD RUSH of 1898-99 the Tlingit prevented the Tagish from crossing the passes to trade directly with white fur traders. The gold discovery was made by George Carmack, a white man prospecting in HAN country with a party of Tagish.

The Tagish originally spoke a dialect of Tagish-Tahltan-Kaska, but they became Tlingit speakers and adapted Tlingit social organization because of extensive trade and intermarriage with Coast Tlingit. The 2 Tagish matrilineal clans belong to the Wolf (Eagle) and Crow (Raven) moieties, respectively, and each clan built a coast-style HOUSE embellished with clan crests. Concepts of rank associated with a fixed pool of personal names, renewed each generation through reincarnation, and elaborate memorial potlatches were incorporated into Tagish life (*see* NATIVE PEOPLE: NORTHWEST COAST; POTLATCH). A rich repertoire of oral literature, singing and dancing reflected concerns with living harmoniously with powerful spirits of the natural world, and with social etiquette and morals. There were rigorous puberty observances for both boys and girls.

In the 20th century, Tagish have become successful big-game guides. Some Tagish leaders have taken the initiative in efforts to settle native LAND CLAIMS and to ensure adequate social services for both status and nonstatus Indians (*see* INDIAN). Since the 1970s they have actively promoted many earlier Tagish traditions. *See also* NATIVE PEOPLE: SUBARCTIC and general articles under NATIVE PEOPLE. CATHARINE McCLELLAN

Tahltan inhabit the STIKINE R drainage, a dry, rugged plateau between the Coast Mts and the Rocky Mts in northern BC. They number 976 (1986). The Tahltan, TAGISH and neighbouring KASKA speak dialects of an Athapaskan language. The Tahltan frequently visited, traded and intermarried with the Kaska and the Stikine TLINGIT. Relations were often hostile with the Taku R Basin Tlingit and Athapaskan speakers to the N and the Nass R TSIMSHIAN.

The Tahltan ancestors infiltrated the Stikine Valley from the E about 300 years ago. The large, dependable salmon runs and excellent drying conditions on the Stikine R provided a year-round food supply larger and more reliable than that E of the Rockies. A more settled and prosperous life developed, enhanced by elements derived from the Tlingit at the Stikine R mouth. Such characteristics as mortuary houses and posts, wooden boxes, matrilineal clans and moieties, POTLATCH ceremonies, inherited titles and RAVEN myths were incorporated into Tahltan culture (*see* NATIVE PEOPLE: NORTHWEST COAST). While the earliest records report that the Tahltan organized into bands, each with a territory, gradually the BAND organization was superseded in social importance by matrilineal clans, some bearing Tlingit names. One clan chief, holding the title Nan-nok, was regarded as chief of the Tahltan.

In the early 1800s the Tahltan monopolized trade along the Stikine "grease trail" (so-called because of the importance of fish oil in the trade) between the Tlingit and groups farther into the interior. Eulachon (candlefish) oil, dentalium shells, and Tlingit and European artifacts were exchanged for furs, tanned hides and other interior products. The monopoly and the relative isolation of the Tahltan were ended by the GOLD RUSHES to the Cassiar (1872-80) and the Yukon (1898-99). With the onslaught of new diseases, the Tahltan dwindled and concentrated at a single site, Tahltan Village, which was subsequently abandoned in favour of Telegraph Creek, the head of navigation on the Stikine R and the local seat of Canadian government and commerce. In the 1920s the Tahltan were joined at Telegraph Creek by a group of SEKANI, who were incorporated into the officially recognized Tahltan Band. The Sekani left Telegraph Creek 40 years later and were officially called the Iskut Band. The 2 bands remain closely affiliated as constituents of the Tahltan Tribal Council. Many modern Tahltan work in government jobs, sport hunting, prospecting and mining, though hunting, fishing

and gardening are also important. *See also* NATIVE PEOPLE: SUBARCTIC and general articles under NATIVE PEOPLE. BRUCE B. MacLACHLAN

Tahsis, BC, UP, village, pop 1445 (1986c), 1739 (1981c), located on west coast of Vancouver I at the end of Tahsis Inlet. The inlet leads N from NOOTKA SOUND, which was discovered by Capt COOK in 1778. "Tahsis" is a Nootka word meaning passage or crossing. A remote logging and sawmill village accessible by water and a gravel road, Tahsis was founded in 1949 when the first sawmill was opened. A second sawmill was added in 1970. Most of the lumber from the mills is shipped directly overseas from the village's own deep-sea docks. JOHN STEWART

Taiga, *see* VEGETATION REGIONS.

Sundance Scene, Blood Reserve, 1906 (1956), watercolour by Gerald Tailfeathers, typical of the artist's nostalgic vision of his people in the 19th century (*courtesy Glenbow Museum, Calgary*).

Tailfeathers, Gerald, artist (b at Stand Off, Alta 13 or 14 Feb 1925; d at Blood IR, Alta 3 Apr 1975). One of the first native Canadians to become a professional artist, he came to prominence in the 1950s. His art had several influences: study in the Summer Art School in Glacier National Park (Montana) with New York portrait painters Winold Reiss and Carl Linck, the cowboy school of painting led by Charles Russell, the Oklahoma school of Indian painting; the Banff Centre School of Fine Arts, and the Provincial School of Technology and Art in Calgary. In the main, his work exhibits a romantic and nostalgic vision of his BLOOD people's life in the late 19th century. Thus, it features warriors in their traditional activities of warfare, hunting and ceremonial life. Tailfeathers later began experimenting with cast-bronze sculpture that depicted themes inspired by cowboy art, which he had studied on a 1969 visit to the Arizona studio of George Phippin. JOHN ANSON WARNER

Taillon, Sir Louis-Olivier, lawyer, premier of Québec 1887, 1892-96 (b at Terrebonne, Qué 26 Sept 1840; d at Montréal 25 Apr 1923). Known for his ultraconservative stance, especially on educational issues, he was first elected Conservative MNA in Montréal-Est (1875). He resigned in 1884, only to return a few months later. Premier for 4 days in Jan 1887, he had to yield to Honoré-MERCIER, who then attacked him for his support of the federal Conservative government in its actions towards Louis RIEL. Again premier from Dec 1892 to Apr 1896, he headed an extremely conservative administration. After his resignation he briefly served as federal postmaster general. DANIEL LATOUCHE

Takakkaw Falls, situated just W of the Continental Divide in YOHO NATIONAL PARK, is Canada's highest WATERFALL and the sixteenth highest in the world. Not as panoramic or as extensive as Niagara Falls, but having a spectacular total vertical drop of 503 m, the falls cascade into the Yoho R below. Measured by its vertical drop, Takak-

kaw is the highest waterfall in N America. One of the park's most prominent attractions, the falls are fed by snow and ice melt that originate in Daly Glacier in the Rocky Mts and then course through a U-shaped hanging valley. DAVID EVANS

Takijuq Lake, 1080 km², elev 381 m, max length 60 km, is located in the NWT almost on the Arctic Circle, 173 km S of Coppermine, NWT. The lake is fed by a tributary of the COPPERMINE R and drains NE to Bathurst Inlet via the Hood R. It was discovered by Samuel HEARNE (May 1771) and appears on his map as *Thaye Chuckgyed* Lake and in his narrative as *Thoy-noy-kyed* Lake. Mackenzie called it *Theye Check* Lake, which appears to have evolved into the present name. DAVID EVANS

Talbot, Thomas, soldier, settlement promoter, colonial official (b at Malahide, Ire 19 July 1771; d at London, Canada W 5 Feb 1853). A member of the Anglo-Irish aristocracy, Talbot spent 50 years developing the Talbot Settlement in Upper Canada. He was educated in Malahide and Manchester, Eng, and at age 11 received his first commission in the British army. During the turbulent period of Anglo-French conflict in the late 18th century, Talbot saw duty in Europe and N America. He was private secretary to Gov SIMCOE of Upper Canada 1791-94. Not only did he visit many parts of the Great Lks area but he cultivated the friendship of Simcoe, which later proved invaluable. In 1801 Talbot sold his commission and immigrated to UPPER CANADA. There he became an official promoter of settlement in the London Dist and within 10 years had developed 3 principal routes — the Talbot streets — as well as a dozen separate townships. His ability to acquire personal property as well as successfully settle extensive tracts of land made Talbot unique. By 1836 he had settled portions of 29 townships extending over a huge area of present-day southwestern Ontario along the N shore of Lk Erie, with a population of over 30 000. Success resulted, in large part, from Talbot's insistence on actual settlement on the land, including clearance and house construction. Full, legal possession was withheld until these conditions were met.

After 1825, Talbot's power began to decline for reasons that included a popular spirit of reform, increasing bureaucracy and Talbot's eccentricity. Socially intolerant and exclusive, he lived alone and isolated in his Pt Talbot "castle." On his death he bequeathed his considerable estate largely to his personal servants. A.G. BRUNGER

The eccentric Thomas Talbot successfully settled large tracts of land extending over present-day SW Ontario (*courtesy McIntosh Art Gallery/U of Western Ontario*).

Talirunili, Joe, artist (b near Kuujjuaraapik [Great Whale R], Qué *c*1899; d at Povungnituk, Qué 11 Sept 1976). He is best known for carving a theme erroneously entitled "Migration," but which usually describes returning from his own baptism, his party stranded on a melting ice floe, fashioning a boat of sealskins and sled parts; and his own heroic sea rescues. Three other subjects dominate his repertoire and have designated him "the chronicler": heavily accoutered stone figures signifying wealth and status; stone-cut prints depicting summer or winter hunting scenes often simultaneously; and enormous, overpowering owls, which are a regular feature of his work. His carvings and prints, nonconformist and crudely executed, command an emotional response and have a wide international representation in public and private collections.   MARY M. CRAIG

Talon, Jean, INTENDANT of New France (bap at Châlons-sur-Marne, France 8 Jan 1625/26; d in France 24 Nov 1694). As "Intendant of Justice, Public order and Finances in ... Canada, Acadia and Newfoundland" 1665-68 and 1669-72, Talon was a determined, energetic and imaginative servant of the king and his minister, Jean-Baptiste Colbert.

This first intendant of NEW FRANCE was to convert a small, weak, fur-trading and missionary outpost under company rule into a profitable, well-populated royal province, capable of defending itself. To diversify the economy, Talon had the mineral and timber resources evaluated; encouraged commercial farming, domestic crafts, shipbuilding and the fishery; and established a brewery and fostered trade with the French West Indies. Almost 2000 immigrants and disbanded soldiers were settled on the land. It was assumed that the population would increase through intermarriage with Indians instructed in the religion and ways of the French, but few natives abandoned their culture. Talon relied on penalties against bachelors and rewards for early marriage and large families among the French for population growth.

When his dream of a territorial empire conflicted with Colbert's desire for a compact, defensible colony, Talon obediently encouraged continuous settlement in the St Lawrence Valley and founded 3 villages. Talon had accepted the post in Canada as a route to promotion, and in 1671 asked the king's permission to return to France in view of

Jean Talon, imaginative and energetic intendant of New France (1665-68 and 1669-72), who sought to develop New France into a viable, profitable royal province (*courtesy National Archives of Canada/C-7100*).

"my obedience in leaving Europe for America, exposing my life to the different perils of sea and sickness ... and my labours in a land as rough as this was in its beginnings." He returned in 1672 and was appointed secretary to the king, member of the royal household and was named Count d'Orsainville. In New France, Talon's industries, commercial agriculture and trade with the West Indies failed; for 3 years there was no intendant and the Crown would no longer invest large sums of money in colonial development. Talon is remembered as an industrial entrepreneur and originator of the family allowance, but his enduring legacy was the centralized, royal administrative and legal framework.   PETER N. MOOGK

Tamarack, *see* LARCH.

Tamarack Review (1956-82), a literary magazine founded at an especially bleak time for Canadian literary reviews. John SUTHERLAND'S NORTHERN REVIEW had ceased publication, and for some years *Tamarack Review* had the field virtually to itself. It filled the space with distinction until it ceased publication. Robert Weaver was the leading spirit in the founding of *Tamarack* and remained its most active editor to the end, although Anne WILKINSON, William Toye and John Robert COLOMBO also played considerable roles. *Tamarack Review* covered all literary genres, publishing fiction, poetry, travel memoirs, autobiography, criticism and even drama. The early work of many distinguished Canadian writers, including Timothy FINDLEY, Jay MACPHERSON, Hugh HOOD, Alice MUNRO and Mordecai RICHLER, appeared in its pages. It set the standard by which later Canadian LITERARY MAGAZINES have been judged.   GEORGE WOODCOCK

Tanabe, Takao, artist, painter (b at Prince Rupert, BC 16 Sept 1926). His art studies included the Winnipeg School of Art (1946-49), Hans Hofmann (1951), Central School of Arts and Crafts, London, Eng (1954), and Tokyo U of Fine Arts (1959-61), where he combined painting and calligraphy with travel in Japan. He worked in Vancouver as a graphic designer (1956-59) and established Periwinkle Press (1963). He began teaching at the Vancouver School of Art in 1962. He regularly exhibited his paintings throughout Canada and did murals on commission. In 1968 he left for Philadelphia and he painted in New York 1969-73. He was head of the art department at the BANFF CENTRE 1973-80. His mature paintings, from this period, reveal a gradual synthesis of earlier influences, including Japanese art and the hard-edge style of New York. Dominated by a strong horizontal sweep, his progressively more simple and dramatic compositions examine the nature of space and light. Series such as *The Land*, influenced by his experience of the Prairies, and the seascapes, which have become the artist's principal subject since his return to BC in 1980, allude to a larger and metaphysical experience of space. A 1985 show, *Takao Tanabe: The West Coast*, was a collection of new seascapes.   JOYCE ZEMANS

Tanager (Thraupinae), subfamily comprising about 240 species of small songbirds of the family Emberizidae. The subfamily is sometimes given family rank. Tanagers are found only in the Americas, largely in tropical regions. They are not noted as singers. Many are brightly coloured, often in boldly contrasting, solid patches. Bills are typically short and conical with a notch or "tooth" on the upper jaw. Tanagers are mainly nonmigratory, arboreal birds which eat insects, fruit and flowers. Only 2 migratory species (genus *Piranga*) breed in southern Canada (a third, summer tanager, *P. rubra*, occurs occasionally in southern Ontario and as an accidental in Manito-

ba). The bright red, yellow and black western tanagers (*P. ludoviciana*) breed in coniferous woods from British Columbia to Saskatchewan; the red and black scarlet tanagers (*P. olivacea*) prefer deciduous forests from Manitoba to New Brunswick. Females of both species are olive green. Nests are loosely constructed of small twigs and are placed 3-30 m high in trees. The pale blue, brown-spotted eggs are incubated by the female for about 2 weeks. Males assist with rearing young. Tanagers' songs are robinlike, but hoarser. Scarlet tanagers, the most migratory of the family, are the only species known to undergo pronounced seasonal molt, with males also becoming olive green in winter.   R.D. JAMES

Tandy, Jessica, actress (b at London, Eng 7 June 1909). Tandy has had a long and distinguished career on the major stages of England, the US and Canada. Educated at the Ben Greet Academy of Acting in London, 1924-27, she established herself as an immensely versatile actress, equally successful in the classics and in contemporary drama. She played Ophelia to John Gielgud's Hamlet in 1934 and Cordelia to his King Lear in 1940. She married Canadian actor Hume CRONYN in 1942 and they have acted together in numerous memorable productions. The much-honoured actress has received Tony Awards for her historic performance as Blanche DuBois in Tennessee Williams's *A Streetcar Named Desire* (1948); and in *The Gin Game* (1978) and *Foxfire* (1982); as well she has received Obie and Drama Desk Awards for her performances in Samuel Beckett's *Happy Days* and *Not I* (1972). She has played important roles in Canada, including Hesione Hushabye in *Heartbreak House* at the Shaw Festival in 1968, Hippolyta/Titania in *A Midsummer Night's Dream* and Lady Wishfort in *The Way of the World* at Stratford in 1976, and Annie Nations in *Foxfire* in 1980. At Theatre London in 1977, Robin Phillips directed her in *Long Day's Journey Into Night*. She has also appeared in numerous movies, including *Batteries Not Included* (1987). She received an honorary LLD from the U of Western Ontario in 1974.   JAMES DEFELICE

Tanner, Elaine, "Mighty Mouse," swimmer (b at Vancouver 22 Feb 1951). Tanner's career in international competition was brief but outstanding, and she is considered Canada's best female swimmer. Her specialties were the backstroke, butterfly and individual medley; she also swam on winning freestyle relay teams. In 1966 she set world records in the 220-yard individual medley and 220-yard butterfly and, at the Commonwealth Games, won 4 gold and 3 silver medals — the most successful woman swimmer at the Games. She received the LOU MARSH TROPHY as Canada's outstanding athlete that year at age 15 — the youngest ever to receive the award. She won 2 gold and 2 silver medals at the 1967 Pan-American Games, and 2 silver and 1 bronze at the 1968 Mexico City Olympics. In 1969 she received the Order of Canada.   BARBARA SCHRODT

Tanner, John, "The Falcon," scout, interpreter, amateur ethnologist (b in Virginia *c*1780; d at Sault Ste Marie, Ont 1846?). Son of a clergyman who migrated to Kentucky, Tanner was captured by Shawnee about 1789 and sold to the OTTAWA. He grew up as an Indian in the area W of Lk Superior, participating in wars against the Sioux. Later he showed up at the settlement founded by Lord SELKIRK, remembering little English and hardly his name. Here he was employed as a guide and scout, while Selkirk helped him contact his relatives in Kentucky. A marginal man who drifted between white and Indian societies, Tanner settled at Sault Ste Marie. In 1830, with the aid of Dr Edwin James, Tanner wrote his *Narrative*, an account of 30 years with Indians together with the first detailed descriptions of the Saulteaux and Cree. He spent his remaining years in trying circumstances and disappeared under suspicion, charged with murder. GEORGE A. SCHULTZ

Tantalum (Ta), grey, heavy, very hard metal with a high melting point (2996°C). When pure, it is ductile and can be easily fabricated. Tantalum has good rectifying properties (ie, converts alternating to direct current) and dielectric properties (ie, does not conduct direct current). Alloyed with other metals it imparts strength, ductility and a high melting point. The principal industrial use is in electric capacitors and cemented carbide cutting tools. Because of its high resistance to corrosion by most acids, tantalum is used increasingly by petroleum and chemical plants. It occurs principally in the mineral columbite-tantalite. Tantalum ores are found in Canada, Australia, Brazil, Zaire and China. In Thailand and Malaysia, it is recovered mainly from tin slags. Tantalum Mining Co of Canada, Ltd (TANCO), Canada's only producer, is located in Bernic Lake, Man. In 1986 Canada produced 39 t ($2.1 million) of tantalum. D.G. FONG

Tantramar Marsh is one of 4 saltwater tidal marshes covering 20 230 ha on the narrow Chignecto Isthmus that connects New Brunswick and Nova Scotia. Its complex system of bogs, rivers, lakes and marshes once provided a habitat for thousands of waterfowl. However, the building of dikes to reclaim the land for farming, which the ACADIANS began in the 1670s, drained more than 90% of the Chignecto marshes by the early 1900s. At that time the nutrient-rich silt deposited by Bay of FUNDY tides supported a lucrative haying industry and the region came to be called "the world's largest hayfield." The hay market declined with the subsequent growth of the automobile industry, however, and the dikeland gradually fell into disrepair. In recent years, hundreds of hectares of marshland are being reclaimed for waterfowl by federal, provincial and private concerns. The largest project, conducted by the CANADIAN WILDLIFE SERVICE, involves restoration of a suitable wildlife habitat on 1740 ha in the Tintamarre National Wildlife Reserve on the upper reaches of the Tantramar R. The present-day marshes are among the densest breeding grounds in the world for some species, such as the marsh hawk, and support small industries in muskrat and wild rice. The name derives from the French *tintamarre* ("din"), referring to the noise of the rushing tide in the river or of flocks of wild geese in the marshes. *See* SWAMP, MARSH AND BOG. P.C. SMITH

Tardif, Jean-Paul, financier (b at Québec City 15 May 1923). After graduating from Laval, Tardif began work in 1947 with his father's investment company, Savings and Investment Corp, first as treasurer and then as managing director. In 1951 he became chief executive officer and in 1959, president. In the 1960s and 1970s several subsidiaries were created and the company became a conglomerate. The companies within the group include Savings and Investment Trust, Aeterna-Life and La St-Maurice (assurance company), Savings and Investment Fund, and Savings and Investment American Fund Ltd. The Savings and Investment Group is one of the major conglomerates under francophone control. Tardif is also a member of the board of the Donohue Co Ltd. JORGE NIOSI

Tardivel, Jules-Paul, journalist, novelist (b at Covington, Ky 2 Sept 1851; d at Québec C 24 Apr 1905). Tardivel came to Québec in 1868 to study French. After working for *Le Courrier* in St-Hyacinthe in 1873, *La Minerve* in Montréal 1873-74

and *Le Canadien* in Québec 1874-81, he founded his own weekly paper, *La Vérité*, in Québec in 1881. Until his death he devoted himself to this newspaper, concentrating on 2 lifelong obsessions: ULTRAMONTANISM and nationalism. Tardivel was a strong proponent of the ultramontane, conservative doctrine that dominated Québec in the second half of the 19th century. A ferocious adversary of liberalism, socialism, democracy and freemasonry, he relentlessly promoted his plan for a rural, agricultural, hierarchical society controlled by the Roman Catholic Church. After CONFEDERATION Tardivel was the first Québecois to envision Québec's separation from Canada and to recommend creation of an independent French Canadian republic. In 1895 he published *Pour la patrie*, a futuristic novel in which he synthesized separatist thinking, a position that he first outlined in 1885 but received little support during his lifetime. RÉAL BÉLANGER

Tarragon Theatre in Toronto was founded in 1971 by Bill GLASSCO as a showcase for new Canadian plays interpreted by Canadian theatre artists. Glassco remained artistic director until 1982, when he was succeeded by Urjo Kareda. From its first production, *Creeps,* by David Freeman, the Tarragon established itself as a primary source for the Canadian dramatic repertoire. Works premiered at the Tarragon (and subsequently presented elsewhere) include plays by David French (*Leaving Home; Of the Fields, Lately; Jitters; Salt-Water Moon*); James REANEY (*The Donnellys* trilogy); Joanna M. Glass (*Artichoke*); Carol BOLT (*One Night Stand*); Tom WALMSLEY (*White Boys*); Steve Petch (*Sight Unseen; Cousins*); Mavis GALLANT (*What Is To Be Done?*); Judith Thompson (*White Biting Dog*); Don Hannah (*The Wedding Script*); and the first productions in English by Québec playwrights Michel TREMBLAY (*Hosanna; Forever Yours, Marie-Lou; Bonjour, là, bonjour; Albertine, in Five Times*); Roland Lepage (*Le Temps d'une vie*); and René-Daniel Dubois (*Being At Home With Claude*). The 230-seat theatre occupies a former warehouse. In 1980 the Tarragon opened the Maggie Bassett Studio as an additional space for professional training classes, workshops and rehearsals; in 1983 the Extra Space – a second performing facility, seating 100 – was added to the complex; and in 1987 the Tarragon purchased the building that it had occupied since its founding in 1971. The Tarragon maintains extensive ongoing programs for script analysis and development. The company has also taken its productions on tour to the Edinburgh Festival, to London and Birmingham, and to theatres across Canada. *See also* THEATRE, ENGLISH-LANGUAGE. URJO KAREDA

Tarte, Joseph-Israël, journalist, politician (b at Lanoraie, Canada E 11 Jan 1848; d at Montréal 18 Dec 1907). A brilliant, caustic and often impulsive polemicist, Tarte owned and edited several newspapers in the course of his career, including *Le Canadien, L'Événement, La Patrie* and the *Quebec Daily Mercury*. He used these newspapers to serve a variety of causes and political factions.

As a Liberal-Conservative in the early 1870s, Tarte opposed the *Programme catholique;* in 1876, however, he shifted to ULTRAMONTANISM and for 7 years was one of its chief exponents. (He sat in the Québec Assembly 1877-81.) When Rome resolved the issue of clerical interference in politics, Tarte returned to a more moderate position. Undoubtedly his greatest moment came in 1890-91 when, first in the pages of *Le Canadien*, then on the floor of the House of Commons to which he was elected in 1891, he exposed the McGreevy-Langevin scandal. This affair discredited the Conservative Party, forced Sir Hector LANGEVIN's resignation from the Cabinet and eventually brought

Tarte into the Liberal fold. The MANITOBA SCHOOLS QUESTION cemented this alliance, and Tarte contributed greatly to LAURIER's triumph in Québec in the 1896 election.

As minister of public works in the Laurier Cabinet, Tarte distributed patronage, strengthened Liberal links with the Montréal business community and oversaw the development of the Port of Montréal. He was most notorious, however, for his outspoken and often contradictory views on controversial issues. In 1899 he vigorously opposed sending Canadian troops to South Africa; in 1900 his speeches on Canadian independence drew bitter condemnation from the Conservative press in Ontario; and finally, in 1902, his campaign in favour of imperial economic unity and a higher level of tariff protection led to his dismissal by Laurier and the end of his political career. RICHARD JONES

Taschereau, Elzéar-Alexandre, Roman Catholic archbishop of Québec C and first Canadian cardinal (b at Sainte-Marie-de-la-Beauce, LC 17 Feb 1820; d at Québec C 12 Apr 1898). His father Jean-Thomas, a descendant of the leading seigneurial family of the Beauce, distinguished himself as a politician and through his articles for *Le Canadien* opposing Gov James CRAIG. His mother, Marie Panet, was niece of Bishop Bernard-Claude Panet of Québec. After precocious and brilliant studies at the SÉMINAIRE DE QUÉBEC (1826-36, 1837-42), which he capped with a doctorate in canon law obtained in Rome (1856), Taschereau had a dual career in teaching and the episcopacy. At the Séminaire de Québec, he was a teacher, director, prefect of studies and superior; he helped found Laval U in 1852 and served as its second rector (1860-66, 1869-71); he made several trips to Rome to defend the institution.

Adviser to archbishops Pierre-Flavien Turgeon and Charles-François Baillargeon, theologian for the latter to the First Vatican Council and vicar general from 1862, Taschereau became archbishop of Québec in Dec 1870 and was consecrated 19 Mar 1871. He quickly showed his intention to reaffirm the prerogatives of his position and his willingness to oppose the determined ULTRAMONTANES. As leader of a diverse group of suffragan bishops, he brought a moderate approach to the resolution of the great debates on Catholic liberalism, excessive clerical influence in politics, reform of the civil code, and church-state relations. At the same time he unswervingly defended Québec C's university monopoly against Montréal's claims and the efforts of Laval U's opponents, notably bishops Ignace BOURGET and Louis-François LAFLÈCHE. Because of his energy and a network of friends in Rome created by the archbishopric's representative, Benjamin Pâquet, the Holy See backed him unconditionally, despite contrary opinions of 2 apostolic delegates, George Conroy (1877-78) and Dom Henri Smeulders (1883-84). At the urging of, among others, the Canadian government, on 7 June 1886 Pope Leo XIII created Taschereau cardinal, an honour that gave him unequalled prestige throughout the country. He could not long enjoy it, for illness soon forced him first to reduce and then abandon his workload to a coadjutor, Louis-Mazaire Bégin, named in 1891. A man of great culture and ability, though taciturn, Cardinal Taschereau strongly influenced the Catholic Church (*see* CATHOLICISM) in Québec and helped it avoid confrontation with the state, even as he strengthened its religious vitality and political power. NIVE VOISINE

Taschereau, Louis-Alexandre, lawyer, liberal politician, premier of Québec July 1920-June 1936 (b at Québec C 5 Mar 1867; d there 6 July 1952), son and father of Supreme Court justices. The *bête noire* of Québec nationalists, he welcomed the surge of American investment in the 1920s and resisted calls for social and economic reform in the 1930s.

Destined to continue his family's brilliant legal tradition, Taschereau rose slowly and somewhat unexpectedly to the premiership. He believed that industrial development in Québec was critical and that it could be achieved only with the help of outside capital and expertise. In his early years as premier, he was accused of anticlericalism for attempting reforms in education and social service, and of sacrificing agriculture to industry for rapid development of Québec's natural resources. As premier, Taschereau championed provincial autonomy but defended Sir Wilfrid LAURIER's moderate approach to the problem of Canadian unity, condemning both the tactics of Henri BOURASSA and the intolerance of English Canadian nationalists.

His downfall came with the Depression. Though he worked to protect major industries and municipalities from bankruptcy, his refusal to establish permanent social-security measures or nationalize hydroelectric power created the impression that he was "a tool of the Trusts," an image reinforced by his links with major financial institutions. In 1934 young rebels in his own party formed the ACTION LIBÉRALE NATIONALE and, in alliance with the Conservatives, nearly defeated him in 1935. The next year Taschereau was further humiliated and driven from office by scandalous revelations about his brother and several high government officials. *See also* QUÉBEC HISTORY SINCE CONFEDERATION. BERNARD L. VIGOD

Reading: Bernard L. Vigod, *Québec Before Duplessis: The Political Career of Louis-Alexandre Taschereau* (1986).

Taschereau Legal Dynasty Spanning 3 centuries and 2 legal cultures, the Taschereau family perpetuated itself, along with several other groups, as a core constituent in Québec's law-making institutions.

The patriarch of the family, Gabriel-Elzéar Taschereau, member of the Legislative Council of Lower Canada, seigneur and judge (b at Québec C 27 Mar 1745; d at Sainte-Marie-de-la-Beauce, LC 18 Sept 1809), was twice married, and a distinct and distinguished legal lineage arose from each marriage.

As a result of his marriage to Marie-Louise-Élisabeth Bazin in 1773 he became the father of Jean-Thomas, MLA, judge, and publisher (b at Sainte-Marie-de-la-Beauce 26 Nov 1778; d at Québec C 14 June 1832), and the grandfather of Jean-Thomas, puisne justice of the Supreme Court of Canada (b at Québec C 12 Dec 1814; d there 9 Nov 1893). The younger Jean-Thomas was the father of Sir Henri-Thomas, chief justice of the Court of King's Bench of Québec (b in Québec C 6 Oct 1841; d at Montmorency, France 11 Oct 1909) and of Louis-Alexandre TASCHEREAU, lawyer and premier of Québec, and the grandfather of Robert, chief justice of the Supreme Court of Canada (b at Québec C 10 Sept 1896; d at Montréal 26 July 1970).

Through his second marriage to Louise-Françoise Juchereau Duchesnay (d 1841) in 1789, Gabriel-Elzéar was also grandfather of Joseph-André, solicitor general of Lower Canada (b at Sainte-Marie-de-la-Beauce, 30 Nov 1806; d at Kamouraska, Canada E 30 Mar 1867); and great-grandfather of Sir Henri-Elzéar, chief justice of the Supreme Court of Canada (b at Sainte-Marie-de-la-Beauce, 7 Oct 1836; d at Ottawa 14 Apr 1911). This powerful seigneurial family was also related through marriage to members of other prominent Québec legal families. Although many Canadian families constituted legal dynasties, one family's continuing presence on the bench is rare. G. BLAINE BAKER

Task Force, established, like a ROYAL COMMISSION, under the Inquiries Act. Members are appointed by the governor-in-council. The subject matter of a task force is generally less important than that of a royal commission. Investigation is less formal and extensive, and with smaller budgets the reports are not as lengthy. Less impartial and authoritative, the reports are usually more closely identified with the government and need not be made public.

The government is not bound to follow the advice of a task force or even to comment on its report. Like the Task Force on CANADIAN UNITY, which was established in 1977 and reported in 1979, a task force is often one voice in a debate. The weakness of interest groups and their inability to represent adequately all members of society means that, unlike their Swedish counterparts, Canadian task forces cannot be used to gain the consent of the general public through that of their spokesmen. The House of Commons has established some small special COMMITTEES to investigate topics such as North-South relations. These are not to be confused with task forces established under the Inquiries Act, nor with the interdepartmental project committees of civil servants, also called task forces, which are dependent, internal tools of the government. C.E.S. FRANKS

Tata, Sam Bejan, photojournalist, portrait photographer (b at Shanghai, China 30 Sept 1911). He immigrated to Canada in 1956. An unobtrusive but lively personality permitted him to witness discreetly the events surrounding the 1949 Chinese Revolution. His extraordinary work recorded life on the streets and in the courts of Shanghai in 1948; in India, he had seen the photographs of Henri Cartier-Bresson and found his approach to photography radically altered. Tata's portraits of Canadian artists, writers, poets and photographers are an important contribution to Canadian history and photography.

ANN W. THOMAS

Tatamagouche, NS, UP, located on NORTHUMBERLAND STR, 50 km NW of NEW GLASGOW, takes its name from the MICMAC *Takamegoochk* ("barred across the entrance with sand"). ACADIANS may have settled here as early as 1710, mining a deposit of copper ore. In the Expulsion of 1755 the village of 12 buildings was burned by the English. In 1770 Joseph Frederick DESBARRES settled 18 Lunenburg families on a grant of 8100 ha in a futile attempt to manage a manor estate like an English landlord. In 1790 a shipbuilding industry began, enduring until 1917. In 1958 the Atlantic Christian Training Centre, owned and operated by the United Church, was built. Today, agriculture is the chief industry, with fishing, farming, lumbering and service industries also important. Recreational facilities and a 19 ha park along the scenic Northumberland shore draw tourists and campers. JANICE MILTON

Taube, Henry, chemist, Nobel laureate (b at Neudorf, Sask 30 Nov 1915) was educated at U Sask where he studied with J.W.T. SPINKS and took classes in physics from Gerhard HERZBERG, receiving the degrees of BSc (1935), MSc (1937) and honorary LLD (1973). He earned a PhD from U of California and remained in the US to teach at the universities of California (Berkeley 1940-41), Cornell (1941-46) and Stanford (1961-present). His fundamental research into the mechanism of chemical reactions, particularly those involving inorganic materials, has been recognized by many honours and awards including the Nobel Prize for chemistry in 1983. ROBERT J. WOODS

Taverner, Percy Algernon, ornithologist (b at Guelph, Ont 10 June 1875; d at Ottawa 9 May 1947). Taverner first earned a living as an architectural draughtsman while studying birds in his spare time. In 1911 he was appointed ornithologist at the National Museum of Canada, where he developed a unique system of distributional maps linked to card indexes on individual species containing up-to-date information on bird distribution in Canada. Taverner played an important part in Canadian ornithology and in wildlife conservation, such as the designation of POINT PELÉE as a national park (1918) and the protection of Bonaventure I and Percé Rock in the Gulf of ST LAWRENCE as bird sanctuaries (1919). His ornithological writings culminated in *Birds of Canada* (1934). Comprehensive and readable, with coloured illustrations by Allan Brooks, it did much to develop a better understanding of ornithology and make birdwatching a popular recreation. J.L. CRANMER-BYNG

Tax Court of Canada, est 1983, is an independent body under the federal minister of justice. Its objective is to provide an easily accessible tribunal for the disposition of disputes between taxpayers and the minister of national revenue. Known previously as the Tax Review Board (1958-83) and the Tax Appeal Board (1946-58), it has the powers, rights and privileges of a superior court of Canada. The board consists of up to 12 judges and 5 deputy judges who must be former judges or barristers of not less than 10 years standing at a provincial bar. At any time, either the chief judge or associate chief judge must have been a judge of the Superior Court of Québec or a member of the bar of that province.

Taxation Taxes are compulsory payments by individuals and corporations to government, levied to finance government services, to redistribute income and to influence the behaviour of consumers and investors. Of the various methods available for financing government activities, only taxation payments are compulsory. Taxes are imposed on individuals, business firms and property to finance public services or enable governments to redistribute resources, allowing governments to increase expenditures without causing inflation of prices, because private spending is reduced by an equivalent amount.

The CONSTITUTION ACT, 1867 (formerly BNA Act), gave Parliament unlimited taxing powers and limited those of the provinces to direct taxation (*see* DISTRIBUTION OF POWERS). The federal government was responsible for national defence and economic development, the provinces for education, health, social welfare and local matters which then involved only modest expenditures. The provinces needed access to direct taxation mainly to enable their municipalities to levy property taxes. For more than 50 years customs and excise duties provided the bulk of Dominion revenues; by 1913 they constituted over 90% of the total. Provincial revenue derived primarily from licences and permits, public domain and sales of commodities and services; in addition, the provinces received substantial federal subsidies. They hesitated to impose direct taxes but by the late 1800s were taxing business profits and successions. Taxes on real and personal property were the bulwark of local government finance, and by 1930 municipal revenues surpassed those of the Dominion.

The GREAT DEPRESSION bankrupted some municipalities and severely damaged provincial credit. Customs and excise duties declined by 65% 1929-34. Parliament resorted more to personal and corporate taxation and raised sales taxes dramatically. To finance WWI, Parliament had introduced personal income tax (1917), corporate taxes and, in 1920, manufacturers' sales tax and other sales taxes. Before the Depression was over, all provinces were taxing corporate income; all but 2 levied personal income taxes, and 2 had retail sales taxes.

The Canadian tax structure changed profoundly during WWII. To distribute the enormous financial burden of the war equitably, to raise funds efficiently and to minimize the impact of inflation, the major tax sources were gathered under a central fiscal authority. In 1941 the provinces agreed to surrender the personal and corporate income-tax fields to the federal government for the duration of the war and for one year thereafter; in exchange they received fixed annual payments. In 1941 the federal government introduced succession duties; an excess-profits tax was imposed, and other federal taxes increased drastically. By 1946 direct taxes accounted for more than 56% of federal revenue. The provinces received grants, and the yields from gasoline and sales taxes increased substantially. The financial position of the municipalities improved with higher property-tax yields. In 1947, contrary to the 1942 plan, federal control was extended to include succession duties as well, but Ontario and Québec opted out, choosing to operate their own corporate income-tax procedures. There was public pressure for federal action in many areas, and the White Paper on EMPLOYMENT AND INCOME advocated federal responsibility for employment and income. As a result, direct taxes became a permanent feature of federal finance. But the provinces also have a constitutional right to these taxes and there is a growing demand for services under provincial jurisdiction, such as health, education and social welfare. The difficulties of reconciling the legitimate claims of both levels of government to income taxation have since dominated federal-provincial negotiations (*see* INTERGOVERNMENTAL FINANCE).

From 1947 to 1962 the provinces, with mounting reluctance, accepted federal grants as a substitute for levying their own direct taxes. In 1962, however, the federal government reduced its own personal and corporate income-tax rates to make tax room available to the provinces. Because taxpayers would pay the same total amount, provincial tax rates would not be risky politically. Further federal concessions between 1962 and 1977 have raised the provincial share of income-tax revenues significantly. To taxpayers' advantage, provincial income taxes are integrated with federal taxes; all provinces except Québec use the federal definition of taxable income (Québec has operated its own income tax since 1954), while provincial tax rates, which now differ considerably among the provinces, are simply applied to basic federal tax. For all provinces except Québec the federal government collects personal income taxes; it also collects and administers the corporate income tax for all provinces except Ontario and Québec, which administer their own, and Alberta. In 1986, provincial personal income-tax rates, as a percentage of basic federal tax, ranged from 43.5% (Alberta) to 60% (Newfoundland). The federal government allows an abatement equal to 10% of corporate taxable income earned in the province; lower provincial tax rates apply to small businesses rather than to large ones in all provinces.

Principles of Taxation The criteria by which a tax system is judged include equity, efficiency, economic growth, stabilization and ease of administration and compliance. According to one view, taxes, to be fair, should be paid in accordance with the benefits received, but the difficulty of assigning the benefits of certain government expenditures, eg, defence, restricts the application of this principle. Provincial motor-fuel taxes are one instance of the benefit principle. According to another view, individuals should be taxed on the basis of their ability to pay (typically indi-

Tax Revenues of all Levels of Government by Major Source, 1985-86

	Millions$	% distribution
Income taxation:		
Personal	57 650	36.4
Corporate	13 459	8.5
Sales tax	21 113	13.3
Excise taxes & duties	4 535	2.9
Natural resource taxes	10 979	6.9
Property taxes	14 925	9.4
Subtotal	122 661	
Other taxes	35 557	22.5
Total tax revenue	158 218	100.0

cated by income). The personal income tax is in part a reflection of this principle. Horizontal equity (individuals with equal taxpaying ability should be treated equally) is not easily achieved because income alone is an imperfect measure of an individual's ability to pay. Vertical equity (higher incomes should be taxed accordingly) has been opposed by business and those with higher incomes, who claim that progressive tax rates discourage initiative and investment, although with the progressive tax, tax deductions benefit those with high taxable incomes. Taxes can affect the rate of economic growth as well. Income taxes limit capital accumulation, and corporate taxes, it is claimed, reduce capital investment. Business so strongly opposed the royal commission's recommendations for full inclusion of corporate gains as taxable income that only 50% of capital gains in Canada are taxable – the lowest rate of any Western industrialized country. The cost of taxpayer compliance increased in 1971, although the broadened and complicated income-tax base did introduce more equity.

Tax Shifting and Incidence Taxes levied on some persons but paid ultimately by others are "shifted" forward to consumers wholly or partly by higher prices or are "shifted" backward on workers if wages are lowered to compensate for the tax. Some part of corporate income taxes, federal sales and excise taxes and local property taxes is shifted, altering and obscuring the final distribution of the tax burden.

Revenue Elasticity The more elasticity (the percentage change in tax revenue resulting from a change in national income) a tax has, the greater its contribution to economic-stabilization policy. Income taxes with fixed monetary exemptions and rate brackets have an automatic stabilization effect because tax collections will grow faster than income in times of economic growth and will fall more sharply than income in recession. In Canada, the revenue elasticity of personal income tax is attenuated by indexing; since 1974 both personal exemptions and tax brackets have been adjusted according to changes in the CONSUMER PRICE

Federal Tax Revenues, 1985-86

(Source: Statistics Canada, CANSIM, supplied by Canadian Tax Foundation, Apr 1987)

	Millions$	% distribution
Income taxation:		
Personal	35 458	39.5
Corporate	9 497	10.6
Nonresident	1 050	1.2
Sales tax	9 385	10.4
Customs duties	3 975	4.4
Excise taxes and duties	4 535	5.0
Natural resource taxes	3 445	3.8
Unemployment insurance contributions	8 653	9.6
Pension plan contributions	4 967	5.5
Total taxes	80 965	90.2
Nontax revenue	8 724	9.7
Total gross general revenue	89 869	100.0

INDEX. But sales taxes have less revenue elasticity because consumption changes less rapidly in response to changes in income, and these taxes are not progressive in relation to consumption. While property-tax yields do not grow automatically with rising NATIONAL INCOME, they exhibit some revenue elasticity.

Current Tax System

Taxes levied by all governments in Canada represented 82.5% ($158.2 billion) of total government revenues in the 1985-86 fiscal year. The remaining percentage was derived from a wide variety of charges and profits of public enterprises, and for provinces and municipalities from intergovernmental transfers. Personal income taxes alone raised over 36% of total tax revenues, followed by sales taxes (13.3%), property taxes (9.4%) and corporate income taxes (8.5%). The remaining percentage was derived from sources ranging from federal customs duties and excise taxes, provincial health-insurance premiums and motor-fuel taxes to the relatively minor municipal business taxes.

Federal Tax Revenues

Tax receipts, particularly from income taxation, including the withholding tax on interest and dividends earned by nonresidents, accounted for about 90% of total federal revenues in fiscal year 1985-86; personal, corporation and nonresident tax collections combined comprised 51% of federal budgetary revenues. Compared with the manufacturers' sales tax (10.4% of total revenue), and unemployment insurance contributions (9.6%) the other federal sources of revenue are modest. Personal income tax applies to all sources of income of residents in Canada, with the exception of gifts and inheritance and some other specific exemptions (*see* UNDERGROUND ECONOMY). Tax reforms (1972) significantly broadened the tax base, especially by the inclusion of 50% of capital gains realized after that date. Single taxpayers are allowed a basic personal exemption; larger exemptions apply to married persons and to taxpayers over the age of 65. Deductions are also permitted for certain expenses, eg, child-care expenses, unemployment-insurance premiums, Canada or Québec Pension Plan contributions and the employment-expense deduction. Since 1974 personal exemptions and tax brackets have been increased annually to take account of INFLATION. In 1986 a minimum tax of 24% on incomes greater than $50 000 was introduced.

The manufacturers' sales tax applies to all goods produced in Canada or imported into the country unless specifically exempted, eg, foodstuffs, electricity and fuels, drugs, clothing and footwear, materials incorporated into manufactured goods, farming and mining machinery, pollution-control equipment and construction equipment. The tax on goods manufactured in Canada is applied to the manufacturer's selling price, exclusive of all other excise taxes, but inclusive of import duties; for imported goods, the tax is levied on the duty-paid value. The sales tax is difficult to administer and is widely criticized for several reasons, including the unequal burden it places on different consumer purchases. In 1966 the Royal Commission on Taxation recommended its replacement by a retail sales tax; in 1984 the federal Liberal government withdrew its intention to shift the sales tax to the wholesale level.

Federal Tax Reform

In 1986 the Conservative government announced plans to proceed with comprehensive reform of the federal tax system. Extensive tax reform under way in the US prompted Ottawa's initiative in order to keep the tax system competitive with that of the US. Intentions are to broaden the income tax base to enable a reduction in personal and corporate rates; the sales tax would be replaced by a "business transfer" tax which is expected to be a broadly based value added tax (the value added to a product would be taxed at each stage in the productive process). Besides lower tax rates, a key objective is to reduce reliance on the personal income tax by improving the revenue balance between personal income and other taxes; a simplified tax system is also expected to promote economic growth.

Provincial Tax Revenues

In 1985-86, taxation constituted 61% of provincial revenues, 20% of which were attributable to federal transfers and 18% of which were classified as nontax revenues, including motor-vehicle user charges, natural-resource levies and liquor-store profits. Sixty-one percent of provincial tax revenues derive from personal and corporate income taxes and general sales taxes. Succession duties have disappeared in every province except Québec following the introduction of the capital-gains tax. Retail sales taxes are imposed by all provinces except Alberta. All provinces exempt certain categories of consumer goods from these taxes (usually food, fuel, prescription drugs and medical appliances, most books, and children's clothing), but the treatment of others varies widely. Most provinces tax hotel rooms and restaurant meals above a specified minimum, but typically at differential rates. These exemptions are designed to reduce the regressivity of these taxes, which bear more heavily on lower-income families.

Municipal Tax Revenues

The municipalities derive the smallest proportion of their revenues from taxation. Over 48% of total municipal revenues were transfers from the other levels of government, particularly the provinces. The property tax provided nearly 99.6% of municipal tax revenue, but only 37% of gross municipal revenue. The property tax in all provinces is levied on real property (land and buildings). Personal property tax still applies in several provinces to machinery and fixtures that provide services to buildings. In the 1960s, property-tax laws were extensively reviewed in all provinces except Newfoundland and BC, and further studies were conducted in several provinces and municipalities in the 1970s. The property tax has been criticized for, among other things, imposing regressive burdens on low-income families, for its indifference towards people's financial status and because it is unfairly administered. Ontario and Manitoba introduced reforms allowing a property-tax credit against provincial income tax, and BC allows rental tax credits to reduce the tax burden for low-income persons. Centralization of assessment administration ranges from complete provincial responsibility in PEI, NS, NB, Ontario, Sask and BC, to local responsibility in Québec. General reforms have included broadening the tax base by reducing or eliminating a number of exemptions and implementing equalized assessment.

Federal-Provincial Fiscal Arrangements

Income-tax sharing, federal financing of specific provincial programs, EQUALIZATION PAYMENTS and special tax abatements to Québec characterize federal-provincial fiscal arrangements. In time, the revenues of one level of government will no longer meet expenditure needs, while the opposite situation will develop at the other level. As it is, public policies now often require joint

Provincial Tax Revenues, 1985-86
(Source: Statistics Canada, CANSIM, supplied by Canadian Tax Foundation, Apr 1987)

	Millions$	% distribution
Income taxation:		
Personal	22 192	21.9
Corporate	3 962	3.9
General sales tax	11 728	11.6
Motor fuel taxes	3 285	3.2
Health insurance premiums	3 824	3.8
Natural resource revenue	7 534	7.4
Social insurance levies	4 074	4.0
Alcoholic beverages and tobacco taxes	1 865	1.8
Other	3 800	3.7
Total taxes	62 264	61.4
Nontax revenue	18 581	18.3
Federal transfers:		
General purpose	6 279	6.2
Specific purpose	14 275	14.1
Total gross general revenue	101 399	100.0

federal-provincial action. Technological change in transportation, communications and methods of production, population growth and urbanization have increased interdependence and population mobility. Consequently, government programs legitimately combining national and provincial interests have greatly expanded.

Federal conditional grants and shared-cost programs have enabled the provinces to expand the provision or improve the quality of a remarkable number of provincial services, but the grants are now politically unpopular. Québec in particular regards them as federal intrusions into areas of provincial jurisdiction. Since 1965 Québec has been allowed to opt out of the important programs, receiving compensatory assistance in the form of federal abatements of the personal income tax. In 1977 hospital insurance, medical care and post-secondary education were consolidated under the Established Programs Financing (EPF) arrangement. The provinces have gained flexibility over the use of the funds. Federal EPF cash transfers and remaining conditional grants, eg, the Canada Assistance Plan and the program for promoting bilingualism in education amounted to almost $14 billion in 1986-87.

Equalization grants, which originated in 1957, enable provincial governments in poorer provinces to provide services at levels comparable to those of other provinces. Since 1982-83 federal grants have gone to each province whose per capita yields from specified provincial and local revenue sources would fall below the weighted per capita average of 5 "representative" provinces. In 1986-87 all provinces except Ontario, Alberta and BC will receive equalization grants, reaching about $5.4 billion. GEORGE E. CARTER

Municipal Tax Revenues, 1985
(Source: Statistics Canada, CANSIM, supplied by Canadian Tax Foundation, Apr 1987)

	Millions$	% distribution
Property and related taxes	14 925	37.1
Other taxes	64	0.1
Total taxes	14 989	37.2
Revenues from sales & service	4 153	10.3
Other nontax revenue	1 970	4.9
Transfer from other governments		
General purpose	2 299	5.7
Specific purpose	16 852	41.9
Total gross general revenue	40 262	100.0

Taxation, Royal Commission on, under Kenneth Carter, appointed (1962) by PM John Diefenbaker to examine and to recommend improvements to the entire federal TAXATION system. In 1966 the 6-volume report declared that fairness should be the foremost objective of the taxation system; the existing system was not only too complicated and inefficient, but under it the poor paid more than their fair share while the wealthy avoided taxes through various loopholes. The commissioners proposed that the same tax be levied on increases in economic power of the same amount however acquired, for as Carter reputedly said, "a buck is a buck." If its recommendations were implemented, the commission estimated, nearly 50% of taxpayers would have their taxes reduced by more than 15%; 10% would face increased tax liabilities of more than 15%, and the remaining taxpayers would notice little change. The wealthy, paying more taxes, would nevertheless share in the benefits of an efficient taxation system. A White Paper was released (1969) proposing implementation of some recommendations. Opposition, however, especially from several provincial governments and from oil and mining companies and small business groups, was so vociferous, as it had been to the report, that the Trudeau government retreated from any major reform. The new Income Tax Act contained many special exemptions and incentives which the commission had found objectionable and removed the federal Estate Tax Act, which had been a significant obstacle to the increasing concentration of wealth. Nevertheless, while the post-1972 federal taxation system bears little resemblance to that advocated in the Carter report, the report's influence is reflected in the partial taxation of capital gains and changes in tax administration. LES MACDONALD

Taylor, Sir Andrew Thomas, architect (b at Edinburgh, Scot Oct 1850; d at London, Eng 5 Dec 1937). He immigrated to Montréal in 1883 and during the next 20 years established 2 partnerships – Taylor, Gordon and Bousfield, and Taylor and Gordon. The latter firm was at the forefront of the architectural trends imported into late Victorian Montréal. Taylor and William Gordon were responsible for many MCGILL UNIVERSITY buildings during the decade of its greatest expansion and they did much to define the character of the campus as it is today. As architect to the Bank of Montreal, Taylor brought the New York firm of McKim, Mead and White to Montréal to renovate the bank on Place d'Armes (1900). He retired to London in 1904 and pursued a political career, for which he was knighted. JULIA GERSOVITZ

Taylor, Charles, philosopher, political theorist (b at Montréal 5 Nov 1931). He was educated at McGill and Oxford. In *Explanation of Behaviour* (1964), Taylor maintained that explanations of human actions involve reference to purposes and an element of interpretation. As a result he saw the SOCIAL SCIENCES as different in method from the physical sciences. After teaching philosophy and political science at McGill, he became Chichele Professor of political and social theory at Oxford (1976); he returned to the political science department at McGill in 1982, was VP of the federal NEW DEMOCRATIC PARTY and president of the Québec NDP. In addition to his well-known *Pattern of Politics* (1970), he produced a noteworthy philosophical commentary, *Hegel* (1975), and in 1979 published *Hegel and Modern Society*. His shorter pieces are collected in *Philosophical Papers* (2 vols, 1985). THOMAS MATHIEN

Taylor, Edward Plunkett, "E.P.," businessman (b at Ottawa 29 Jan 1901). Educated at McGill, Taylor joined the stockbroking firm

By 1935 industrialist E.P. Taylor was rich enough to indulge in his hobby of horse breeding. He is shown here with the famed Northern Dancer in the 1960s (*courtesy Canada's Sports Hall of Fame*).

MCLEOD, YOUNG, WEIR AND CO in Ottawa in 1923, moving to Toronto in 1928 and becoming a director in 1929. In 1930, through a series of mergers, Taylor formed the Brewing Corp of Canada Ltd (later Canadian Breweries) and, by 1935, could indulge in his hobby of horses and horse racing. In 1940 C.D. HOWE placed Taylor on the executive committee of the Dept of Munitions and Supply. In 1941 he was moved to the US to handle the exchange of supplies between Canada and the US. He was appointed president and vice-chairman of the British Supply Council in N America and in Jan 1942 became head of the British Purchasing Commission as well. Exhaustion forced his resignation from the latter in Sept 1942, but he continued as Howe's deputy on the Anglo-American-Canadian Combined Production and Resources Board. After the war Taylor formed an "investment company," ARGUS CORPORATION, with Wallace McCutcheon and Eric PHILLIPS. Taylor was president until 1969 and chairman 1969-71. In later years he concentrated on land development in the Bahamas and on his racing interests. He helped expand the Ontario Jockey Club in the 1950s and was president of the club (1956-63), chairman of the board (1962-73) and honorary chairman of the board (since 1973). His thoroughbred operation, Windfields Farms, grew to be among the most successful in N America, NORTHERN DANCER and NIJINSKY II being 2 of its famous horses. His son Charles is now president of the operation.   ROBERT BOTHWELL

Taylor, Frederick Wellington, "Cyclone," hockey's first great star (b at Tara, Ont 23 June 1883; d at Vancouver 9 June 1979). He played in Listowel, Ont, and Portage la Prairie, Man, and joined hockey's first professional team in Houghton, Mich (1906). A swift, agile skater, Taylor attracted crowds and commanded high salaries. He played for Ottawa in 1908, Renfrew Millionaires 1910-11 and Vancouver Millionaires 1913-21, scoring 194 goals in 186 games. His fame as the outstanding player of hockey's formative years spread even to the Soviet Union, which he visited twice.   JAMES MARSH

Taylor, George William, clergyman, entomologist, conchologist (b at Derby, Eng 1854; d 22 Aug 1912, buried at Nanaimo, BC). After immigrating to Victoria, BC, in 1882, he studied theology and was ordained an Anglican priest in 1886. With the exception of 2 years in Ottawa (1888-90), he served his entire ministry in BC. Always an avid insect collector, he compiled the first list of insects, mainly moths and butterflies, native to the province. He was appointed the first provincial entomologist (honorary) of BC in 1887 in

recognition of his expertise. Many new species of Lepidoptera were described by him in the *Canadian Entomologist* and the *Ottawa Naturalist*. He had, in addition to his collection of insects, the most comprehensive collection of marine shells in Canada, was a recognized authority on conchology, and published often on the molluscs of BC in *Nautilus*. In 1907 he was appointed curator of the Marine Biological Station on Departure Bay, a station that would be built under his direction.
                    P.W. RIEGERT

Taylor, Kenneth Douglas, diplomat, businessman (b at Calgary, Alta 5 Oct 1934). Joining the Trade Commissioner Service in 1959, Taylor became ambassador to Iran in 1977 and was catapulted to prominence by engineering the "Canadian Caper"; for over 2 months, he and immigration officer John Sheardown and their wives hid 6 Americans after the US Embassy had been seized by Iranian revolutionaries and 66 hostages taken; on 28 Jan 1980 the 6 Americans, with Taylor not far behind, escaped the country using Canadian passports. Coming at a low point in America's self-esteem, the news was sensational, and the stylish, gregarious, unorthodox Taylor became an instant celebrity. He received the US Congressional Gold Medal and thousands of other gifts in a 10-month orgy of gratitude. He was Canadian consul general in New York, 1981-84, and then left the public service, remaining in the US as a senior executive with Nabisco Brands; in 1987 Taylor was appointed senior VP of RJR Nabisco Inc.   NORMAN HILLMER

Taylor, Roy Lewis, botanist (b at Olds, Alta 12 Apr 1932). A taxonomist and cytologist, Taylor was involved in the first major study of the QUEEN CHARLOTTE IS flora (1957-65), culminating in *Flora of the Queen Charlotte Islands* (1968). From 1965 to 1968 he was head of the taxonomy and economic botany section of the Dept of Agriculture, Ottawa. From 1968 to 1985 he was director of the botanical garden and professor of botany and plant science at UBC. In 1985 he became president of the Chicago Horticultural Society and director of the Chicago Botanic Garden. Taylor's major research interest is development of BC's cytological flora. Author, coauthor or editor of over 120 publications (1963-), he has received many awards and honours, such as the Queen's Silver Jubilee Medal and membership honoris causa in the Linnean Soc of London.   SYLVIA TAYLOR

Taylor, Thomas Griffith, geographer, educator, explorer (b at Walthamstow, Eng 1 Dec 1880; d at Sydney, Australia 4 Nov 1963). A dynamic personality who did research on every continent, Taylor founded the first Canadian department of geography at U of T (1935). He was educated as a geologist at U of Sydney, Australia, and at Emmanuel College, Cambridge. He was chosen chief geologist for the 1910-12 Scott Antarctic Expedition and did the first mapping of that continent. A glacier and a dry valley are named for him. Taylor also founded the first department of geography in Australia in 1920 at U of Sydney, then moved to U of Chicago's dept of geography (1927). It was on the initiative of economist Harold INNIS that Taylor was invited to U of T in 1935. He remained there until 1951 during which time the department achieved an international reputation. An outstanding teacher, Taylor was the author of some 20 books and 200 scientific articles.
                    MARIE SANDERSON

Reading: T.G. Taylor, *Journeyman Taylor* (1958).

Teacher's Cove is one of the largest of nearly 100 prehistoric sites discovered in southern NB's PASSAMAQUODDY BAY region. An extensive shell-midden deposit represents over 2000 years of hu-

man habitation. The site was inhabited, at different times, both on a year-round basis and as a seasonal camp. A distinctive feature first found at this site was the use of semi-subterranean house dwellings of about 2000 years ago. In later times, the WIGWAM became the major house type. The site was most intensively occupied about 1000 years ago. Shellfish, deer, moose, bear and beaver provided the major food sources as well as raw materials for clothing and tools. These ancient people were probably ancestors of MICMAC-MALISEET natives now living in the Maritimes.
                    DAVID L. KEENLYSIDE

Teaching Profession, broadly defined, includes all those offering instruction in public or private institutions or independently. As defined here, the teaching profession includes only those who are licensed by the provincial and territorial authorities to provide instruction to elementary and secondary students in publicly supported schools.

The gradual development of publicly supported SCHOOL SYSTEMS in the early 1800s was the critical factor in the creation of Canada's teaching profession. The ideals of free and universal education accorded well with the aspirations of many pioneers who had immigrated to Canada to seek a better life (*see* EDUCATION, HISTORY OF). Initially, communities hired almost anyone who was willing to teach. By the mid-1800s, however, the colonial governments had begun to express more interest in public education and to provide more financial support; at the same time, various superintendents of education were fighting to establish schools for the training of teachers (NORMAL SCHOOL) and a certification system that would ensure minimal teacher qualifications.

Formation of Teachers' Associations The advances in education in the 1800s were accompanied by repeated attempts by teachers to form local associations. In the early days teachers' organizations were dominated by Department of Education officials, inspectors, clergymen and influential laymen. As a result, association meetings tended to be devoted principally to inspirational addresses or discussions of teaching methods and rarely to teachers' concerns about their living and working conditions, which in the early 1900s were very poor. In 1910 annual salaries for women elementary-school teachers in urban schools were in the $300-$1000 range, while those for men ranged from $600 to $1400. In the secondary schools, salaries ranged from $800 to $1800 for women and $1000 to $2100 for men. Job security was virtually nonexistent. Conditions were particularly harsh in rural areas, where poorly paid teachers were assigned to spartan, ill-equipped, one-room schools and were often obliged to function as janitors and to accept primitive and isolated accommodation.

Teacher dissatisfaction finally came to a head in the years during and immediately after WWI. Teachers' salaries had remained static, but the cost of living had nearly doubled. In one area after another, teachers formed provincial associations to fight for improvements in salary, tenure and pensions. A national body, the Canadian Teachers' Federation (CTF), was founded in 1920, by which date there was at least one association in every province. Much of this organizational activity took place in secret because of the general hostility towards labour unions at that time. Although a majority of the modern teacher associations existed by 1920, the profession was not in fact completely organized in the provinces and territories until 1955. In 1986 the 14 provincial and territorial associations which are members of the CTF represented more than 220 000 teachers.

In Québec the first provincial organization of French-speaking teachers was a federation of rural female teachers formed in 1937. In 1946 this group and 2 others, representing rural male teachers and urban teachers, became federated as Corporation générale des instituteurs et institutrices catholiques du Québec. In 1967 the name was changed to Corporation des enseignants du Québec. A fundamental organizational change occurred in 1974 when CEQ abandoned corporation status and became instead a UNION CENTRAL. Renamed Centrale de l'enseignement du Québec, CEQ represents not only teachers but various other groups employed in the education sector. Neither CEQ nor any of its predecessors have ever been members of the CTF.

The fledgling teacher associations sought, first of all, to improve salaries and procure TENURE protection and pensions, and to attain professional status and advances in education. In 1919 a group of 178 teachers in Victoria, BC, staged a 2-day strike over salaries – the first teacher strike in the British Empire. The BC Department of Education succeeded in mediating an amicable settlement. The government subsequently took the first step toward establishing an arbitration procedure for salary disputes. Further strikes and resignations occurred in the western provinces during the 1920s. A particularly bitter incident occurred in Brandon, Man, in 1922, when 80 teachers resigned in protest against the board's request that they accept a 25% reduction in salary.

The early economic goals of the teacher associations were not met quickly. Although the delegates to the 1920 CTF convention adopted the slogan "Double the 1914 basis" as part of a Canada-wide campaign, the average annual salary ($1600) to which they aspired was not achieved until after WWII. On the other hand, pension protection was more easily achieved. In 1920 only Québec (since 1856), NB, Newfoundland and Ontario had pension plans for teachers. In the next 20 years plans were established in Man (1925), NS (1928), BC (1929), Sask (1930), PEI (1931) and Alta (1939).

During the GREAT DEPRESSION, teaching salaries were cut and competition for employment increased. Although economic conditions improved generally, the federal government's order-in-council of 1942-43 froze teachers in their jobs and severely limited their salary increases. The postwar period of prosperity and rapidly expanding population brought a critical shortage of teachers that continued until the early 1970s. The number of teachers rose from 38 000 in 1910, to 76 000 in 1940, to 249 000 in 1970 and to a peak of 270 000 in 1978. Although the number of full-time teachers has dropped to 256 000 (1986), the size of the teaching force has continued to grow as a result of the increasing employment of part-time teachers. The percentage of teachers employed part-time rose from 2% in 1973 to more than 8% in 1985.

Collective Bargaining Rights The Alberta Teachers' Association was, in 1941, the first association to acquire full bargaining rights, including the right to strike. The Manitoba Teachers' Society acquired similar rights in 1948. However, in 1956, negotiation procedures substituting binding arbitration for strike rights were written into the Manitoba Public Schools Act. Saskatchewan teachers also gained the right to bargain in the 1940s.

Teachers in the other provinces continued to bargain informally and to obtain improvements in salaries and benefits without resorting to sanctions. There were only 5 or 6 minor strikes in the 1950s, but in the 1960s there were 6 mass resignations and 42 strikes in 5 provinces. The majority of the strikes occurred in Québec. Strike action by teacher associations that still had no formal bargaining rights continued in the 1970s.

Professional Concerns Founders of the various teachers' associations sought not only economic security but the establishment of teaching as a profession that was equal in status to LAW and MEDICINE. In particular, teachers fought for compulsory membership in their association, a code of ethics, the power to discipline members who did not abide by the code, and for control over standards of entrance to the profession.

The legislatures of Saskatchewan (1935) and Alberta (1936) enacted teaching profession Acts making membership in teachers' professional organizations mandatory for all teachers employed in the publicly supported schools. By 1960 membership in all provincial associations was automatic or compulsory and most associations had acquired some disciplinary powers. All of the teacher associations outside Québec have adopted professional codes of ethics that serve as guides to teacher conduct.

Teacher Education and Certification Although the provincial departments of education reserve the power to issue teaching certificates, teachers have nevertheless campaigned for higher standards of certification. Initially the goal was to ensure that all teachers completed high school before entering normal school, a goal that had not been achieved by 1939. After WWII it was agreed that all teachers should hold degrees and that all teacher preparation should take place under university auspices. In 1950, 10% of teachers held degrees and most were still trained in teachers' colleges; by 1986, 81% held degrees. Eight provinces currently require all or most new teachers to hold a degree. The transfer of teacher training to the universities was not completed until the late 1970s.

Self-Regulatory Powers Teachers' associations have not yet assumed complete responsibility for the certification, decertification, competence and continuing education of their members. In the early 1980s, however, Ontario and Alberta proposed to the teachers' associations that they adopt a full self-governing role on the condition that the teachers agree to split their organizations into 2 groups – a professional college in which membership would be compulsory, and a voluntary-membership association responsible for collective bargaining. Teachers rejected the proposal, preferring to maintain single united associations. In 1987 the BC government, over the objections of the BC Teachers' Federation, introduced legislation creating a College of Teachers, with power to certify, discipline and otherwise regulate teachers.

Educational and Social Concerns Canadian teachers have long argued for the reorganization of the school system into larger units of administration in order to ensure the availability of schools with better facilities and broader course offerings. They have also consistently pressed for adequate financing for the school system.

Evaluation of students has been a source of persistent concern among teachers. For example, the need for external examinations for secondary-school students has been debated within educational circles for decades. Teachers have generally maintained that evaluation of student progress should be the responsibility of the school in which the student is enrolled. Teachers have also participated actively in revisions of provincial curriculum guidelines (*see* CURRICULUM DEVELOPMENT) and in developing local modifications of curriculum and units of work in CANADIAN STUDIES. The maintenance of discipline in the classroom and school appears to be an increasing problem. Studies reveal that, although violence is rare in Canadian schools, verbal abuse of teachers is fairly common.

Teachers have consistently supported equal

rights and opportunities for women (who now comprise only 54% of the full-time teaching force, compared to 81% in 1910). Nevertheless, although sex discrimination in salary schedules has disappeared and no overt barriers to promotion exist, the proportion of principalships held by women has declined dramatically, from 34% in 1960 to 14% in 1985.

International Development In 1962 CTF initiated a program of assistance through which Canadian teachers devote their vacation periods to providing in-service programs for teachers in various countries. Since 1962 over 900 volunteer Canadian teachers have provided academic and professional upgrading for over 22 000 overseas teachers.   GERALDINE GILLISS

Reading: S. McCurdy, The Legal Status of the Canadian Teacher (1968).

Team Handball is also known as European or Olympic handball. The object is to score goals by passing and throwing a ball (slightly smaller than a soccer ball) into the opponents' goal. It is played indoors on a court similar in size to that for basketball, with teams of 7 players. The game was introduced in Germany in the 1890s but did not become popular until after WWI, when it adopted many rules from SOCCER. At first played outdoors with teams of 11 players, the indoor version became the standard form in 1952. It has been an Olympic Games event since 1972. Team handball is widely played in Europe, where its popularity is second only to that of soccer. In Canada, the game was originally called "Borden Ball" because a simplified version was introduced during WWII by European prisoners of war detained at Camp Borden, Ont. During the 1950s, team handball became an organized competitive sport, and the Canadian Team Handball Federation was formed in 1962.   BARBARA SCHRODT

Technical University of Nova Scotia, Halifax, was founded in 1907 by Act of the Nova Scotia Legislature (as Nova Scotia Technical College) and was the result of collaboration by Acadia, Dalhousie, King's College and Mount Allison universities, with the Halifax Board of Trade and the Mining Society of Nova Scotia. It was established to afford facilities for scientific research and instruction and professional training in engineering and any other departments that might be added. Today programs are offered in most branches of modern engineering and in such other technical professional subjects as architecture, planning, construction administration, food science, computer science and naval architecture. The university concentrates upon the later, specialized years of professional and technical programs so that undergraduate students are required to first complete 2 successful years in an associated university. The university has major research centres in such fields as fisheries technology, energy studies, water resources, applied microelectronics, CAD/CAM (*see* ROBOTICS), materials science and biomedical engineering. TUNS furthers technical and economical development through the work of the academic departments, the research centres, the Atlantic Region Management Training Centre and the Division of Continuing Education. International educational and research projects, conducted in such regions as Africa, S America, the Caribbean and India, are administered through an International Programs Office. In 1985-86 there were 898 full-time undergraduate and 155 graduate students enrolled at the university.

Technology Definitions of technology have ranged from "everything we learn" to "the application of science to the solution of industrial problems." A more useful definition might be "technology is the skills, tools and machines used by members of a society to convert material objects [eg, natural RESOURCES] into products useful to themselves." Technologies affect and are affected by the society that uses them, and the importance of a technological development can only be evaluated after consideration of a variety of social and technical factors. Technological developments depend upon necessary pre-existing technology as well as a favourable political or economic climate.

The technologies by which the native people adapted to the regions of Canada, from the Great Lakes to the Far North, depended greatly on geographical conditions and local resources. Notable achievements include the birchbark CANOE, the SNOWSHOE, the TIPI, the IGLOO and the KAYAK. Long after European settlement began, Canada still had a relatively sparse population, and because of its colonial status was primarily a source of raw materials and an importer of manufactured goods and technology (*see* MERCANTILISM). MANUFACTURING remained proportionally smaller in Canada than in Europe or the US until WWI, and most ENGINEERING achievements to that time involved the solution of special problems associated with settlement in a cold climate, TRANSPORTATION over long distances and to remote areas, or extraction of natural resources.

The Pioneer Period (1600-1850)

The first period, extending from the arrival of the first Europeans to the beginning of the RAILWAY age, covers the settlement of Canada as a European colony. Generally the technologies practised were transplanted directly from Europe and with minor changes were those in use since the medieval period. Houses were built using timber frames; canal locks had mitre gates and cut-stone chambers; and mines were developed with brute force and black powder. Such modifications as were made reflected the efforts of settlers to adjust to Canadian GEOGRAPHY, climate and natural resources, and to native technologies. They paralleled political and social adjustments experienced by the young colony.

Fisheries The earliest significant technology was associated with the FISHERIES. The international rivalry for the GRAND BANKS cod resource resulted in the first English and French settlements in Newfoundland and NS. These settlements were directly affected by existing fishing technology. The French and Portuguese salted their catch immediately and sailed for home without much contact with land (ie, the "green" fishery). English fishermen, on the other hand, did not have cheap supplies of salt and were forced to establish shore stations to dry their catch to preserve it for transportation to market (ie, the "dry" fishery). During the period, this basic technology changed very little, but it undoubtedly shaped the character of the people and led to establishment of the SHIPBUILDING industry for which Maritimers became world famous in the 1860s and 1870s.

Construction The major technical problem facing all settlers was shelter. In the first urban areas, construction directly copied European methods; in rural areas it illustrated adaptations to local materials and conditions. Western European timber-frame construction, familiar to most colonists, was first used and adapted by the HABITANTS and ACADIANS. Wood, rather than masonry, was used to fill in walls. LOYALISTS, settling in the Maritimes and in Upper Canada, built houses of logs fastened together at the corners, an excellent way of using the abundant timber resource (*see* LOG HOUSES). Settlers on the treeless prairies near the Red R used heavy prairie sod (*see* SOD HOUSES) for their first shelters.

Philemon Wright's mill at the Chaudière Falls on the Ottawa R in 1823. Early industrial development depended largely on wind, water or animal power (*courtesy National Archives of Canada/C-608*).

Agriculture All pioneers practised some form of AGRICULTURE, which involved probably the most universal technology. Often Canadian agriculture was quite different from that practised in Europe. Agricultural technology, more than any other, is profoundly affected by local conditions of weather, soil, water and pests, and by land-tenure systems.

The Canadian farmer did not inherit a farm, he created one: Acadian farmers had to build dikes to protect their fields in the Fundy marshes; habitants or Loyalists in the St Lawrence Valley had to clear thick stands of huge trees with primitive tools and inadequate labour. Each group of 5 Loyalist families received a set of tools. Every 2 families received a crosscut saw and a whipsaw. The axes that were issued to the settlers were short-handled ship axes, rather than felling axes, and were almost useless because they would not hold an edge (*see* TOOLS, CARPENTRY). It often took many years for these pioneer farmers to clear a few hectares, while building shelters, cultivating crops and looking after animals.

Early farmers were fortunate in being able to learn from the Indians how to use indigenous animals, birds, fish and plants (*see* PLANTS, NATIVE USES). The culture of corn, beans and squash, a legacy of the Huron, was invaluable. Gradually, subsistence mixed farming was established. Heavy plows, called "French" plows, similar to the medieval 2-wheeled plow drawn by oxen, were first used by the Acadians and habitants. A smaller, rugged implement called the bull plow, with no wheels or coulter, was developed for maneuvering around stumps and rocks. Gradually, iron was substituted for wood, and frequently an all-iron "Scotch" plow was imported to Canada. Plows continued to be refined in shape and size until the steel-bladed plow was designed for the heavy sod of the prairies in the 1880s. Wherever farmers had access to markets, they sold surpluses and improved their farms with the proceeds. In the early 19th century, horse-drawn mowers were brought in from the US; local blacksmiths adopted the design and the Canadian AGRICULTURAL IMPLEMENTS INDUSTRY was born.

Mills The 2 greatest chores facing settlers were grinding grain and sawing lumber. Champlain built a gristmill in 1607, probably the first mill of any kind in N America, at PORT-ROYAL on the Bay of Fundy. It was the right and responsibility of the seigneur in NEW FRANCE to build gristmills and sawmills, although they were seldom built as often as they were needed. Many early mills had simple saws and a run of stones using the same waterwheel. The arrival of the Loyalists in Upper Canada brought an immediate need for additional mills. Gristmills and sawmills were established in Kingston Mills on the Cataraqui R in 1783-84 and at Napanee in 1797. Both operations, which

had been mechanized during the Middle Ages in Europe, could be fairly easily adapted to Canadian conditions. Most areas of eastern Canada had waterpower to drive mills; some relied on wind or tide. Eventually, mills were established to produce TEXTILES and to work iron. Mills were the nuclei of many small villages and introduced mechanical engineering to Canada.

Transportation has been the greatest challenge facing Canadian engineers. The rough country, scattered settlements and difficult climate posed problems seldom encountered in western Europe. The first solutions involved the importation from Europe of various forms of water transport which varied from full-rigged ships to smaller boats (oar and sail) that were normally carried on the larger ships. The French were quick to adopt the Indian birchbark canoe for travel on the inland waterways of the Canadian Shield. The Hudson's Bay Co developed the YORK BOAT for the journey inland from Hudson Bay. Early settlement was restricted to water routes and, as it spread westward along the St Lawrence past the Lachine rapids, these routes were improved by construction of CANALS, varying from tiny ditches transporting bateaux, to complex waterways, eg, the RIDEAU CANAL.

Shipbuilding began in the 17th century but was generally retarded by colonial restrictions until the mid-19th century, when shipyards in the Atlantic provinces and Québec City began to turn out larger and larger ships. Steamship technology, developed by Robert Fulton in the US, was quickly borrowed by engineers and businessmen on the St Lawrence and Great Lakes. John MOLSON financed the construction of the ACCOMMODATION in Montréal in 1809 to service the busy route to Québec City, using a locally made steam engine. On 7 Sept 1816 the *Frontenac*, a comparatively large ship with a Boulton and Watt engine imported from England, was launched and became the first steamship to operate on the Great Lakes. These simple, low-pressure steam engines were not very powerful and used large quantities of fuel wood. In the second period of development the compound engine, which burned coal, increased the efficiency of these vessels so much that they virtually eliminated sailing ships.

Early land-vehicle transportation was limited almost exclusively to urban areas. Initially, construction of roads over the long distances between settlements was prohibitively expensive, even for dirt trails.

By the end of the pioneer period some arterial roads were completed. Cedar logs were used to build "corduroy" sections in swampy locations and gravel surfaces were laid where traffic was heaviest. In the 1840s Canadians even experimented with plank roads, using cheap forest products, but the winter ice and spring thaw left most of these roads a shambles. Only urban roads were paved, usually with crude cobblestones. The RED RIVER CART, drawn by oxen or horses, was used in the reasonably level and treeless prairies.

Lumbering The TIMBER TRADE began along the major rivers of NB and spread to the St Lawrence and Ottawa rivers in the early 19th century. The single-bitted axes for felling, broad axes for squaring, and sleighs for hauling to water were borrowed almost unchanged from similar operations in eastern Baltic countries.

Mining The first loads of ore hauled back to Europe by CARTIER and FROBISHER proved worthless and it was not until the discovery of gold in BC and the Klondike, and of silver and gold in the Canadian Shield in the late 19th century, that the great MINERAL RESOURCES of Canada were successfully exploited. COAL was mined sporadically in Cape Breton from the early 18th century. Bog IRON ORE was mined, smelted and processed at

FORGES SAINT-MAURICE near Trois-Rivières (mining construction had begun in 1733 and the first iron was not poured until 1738) and at Normandale in Upper Canada. The GEOLOGICAL SURVEY OF CANADA (est 1842) played an enormous part in developing Canada's MINERAL wealth as field parties meticulously examined the country's rock outcroppings, interpreted their significance and plotted their results on maps, which led many prospectors to new deposits of economic minerals.

Summary The pioneer period is characterized by the struggle to survive in a new and often hostile climate. Pioneers brought familiar technologies from Europe and the US, and skilfully adapted them to local conditions. Examples of such adaptations include the infilling of timber-frame houses by logs, rather than masonry; the use of local woods such as tamarack for shipbuilding; and the positioning of waterwheels inside mills to protect them from snow and ice. During this period, Canada was a water-oriented society, dependent on water for agriculture, fish, transportation and power. Many of the engineers who were to play a vital role in Canada's development received their first training on transportation projects. Although they were practical people with little theoretical education, they successfully undertook very large construction projects. Thomas KEEFER started his career on the Erie Canal and the WELLAND CANAL and went on to build railways, bridges and aqueducts. Sandford FLEMING worked as an engineer on the INTERCOLONIAL RY and later developed Standard TIME.

Developmental Period (1850-1900)

Sweeping changes in machines, materials and power moved engineering from the Middle Ages to the Machine Age in these 50 years. In the 1850s, political as well as economic forces promoted the growth of railways, while steam engines and new MACHINERY began to transform mill and farm. Confederation, 1867, brought about the Intercolonial Ry, and eventually the NATIONAL POLICY, the Patent Act, the CANADIAN PACIFIC RY and the opening of the PRAIRIE WEST. The Atlantic provinces saw the end of the sailing ship, and the fishing industry was expanded by refrigeration and use of the steamship. Domestic manufacturing became established on a modest scale, encouraged by the National Policy.

Transportation The advantages of railways for Canada were obvious: they were far more flexible than canals and did not freeze up in winter. When the GUARANTEE ACT (1849) offered financial help, many local railways were started in Upper and Lower Canada and the Atlantic provinces. While most of the expertise and rolling stock came originally from England, Canadian engineers did much of the construction. Canadian shops, which began by making spikes and rolling rails, moved on to building locomotives. By 1860 most major communities in the Canadas were connected by the GRAND TRUNK RY, while the ST LAWRENCE AND ATLANTIC RAILROAD joined Montréal with Portland, Maine. Completion of the Intercolonial Ry in 1876 fulfilled a condition of Confederation by joining central Canada and NS and NB. Construction of the CPR (through the incredibly difficult rock and muskeg of the Precambrian Shield, across the prairies and through the Rockies) became one of Canada's greatest engineering feats. This task brought the highest levels of railway technology to Canada from the US (Canadian innovations were negligible), opened the vast grainfields of the prairies, encouraged immigration and literally tied the country together. Railway technology also had an effect on BRIDGE building. The tubular construction of the Victoria Bridge at Montréal (completed Dec 1859) was an

Grand Trunk Railway locomotive No 162 (*c* 1860). Development of steam technology had a profound influence on transportation and industrial development (*courtesy National Gallery of Canada*).

engineering marvel of the day. Some of the world's first cantilever bridges were constructed over the Niagara and Fraser rivers in 1883 and over the Saint John R in 1884.

Canals were recognized as efficient carriers of bulk cargo, and as shipping increased on the Great Lakes improvements were needed. The Welland Canal was rerouted and deepened, from 2.7 m to 3.7 m, in 1883; by 1887 it was deepened again, to 4.3 m. A canal was opened at Sault Ste Marie in 1895; the Soulange Canal was opened in 1899. In NS the long-awaited Shubenacadie Canal, connecting the Bay of Fundy and Dartmouth, was opened in 1861. More construction was undertaken on the TRENT CANAL to provide another route to the upper Great Lakes.

In Atlantic Canada, the shipbuilding industry began to mature, and, as Canadian sailing ships, such as the MARCO POLO, began to acquire a world reputation, dozens of yards in Québec, NS, NB and PEI entered a period of great activity. Ships built in Canada for Britain traded all over the empire. Meanwhile, steamboat technology matured and wooden hulls with crude engines were replaced by high-pressure compound engines, contained in iron and steel hulls. The changing technology had a devastating effect on the Maritime shipbuilding industry.

In the 1880s, Canadian cities began to grow beyond the size where everyone could walk to work and public transportation was needed. Horse-drawn omnibuses were followed by horse-drawn streetcars on rails, and when the electric street car was developed, Toronto (1885) and Windsor, Ont (1886), had some of the earliest lines in North America. The safety bicycle appeared in the 1890s, radically transforming the common person's transportation.

Agriculture Eastern Canada lost its preferential markets in Britain for wheat and gradually adopted DAIRY FARMING. The concept of CHEESE factories was brought to Upper and Lower Canada from New York in the early 1860s; factories produced a more uniform cheese of higher quality suitable for sale in the cities. Farm machinery took over many tasks. Massey, Harris, Hamilton, Shantz, Frost and Wood, and other companies developed a full line of farm machinery for most operations. Various kinds of food processing, meat packing and, eventually, refrigeration greatly extended produce markets. In western Canada, the initial problems of adjusting to the climate, and adapting new techniques and marketing procedures, had been solved by 1900. Steam tractors, steel plows, efficient binders and threshing machines

transformed the grasslands into a granary. Although many traction engines and implements were imported from the US and Britain, the Massey and Harris mowers and binders were world famous for efficiency and reliability.

Fishing By the 1860s Atlantic fishing technology had been changed by the introduction of the longline or "bultow." Refrigeration and railways increased the fresh-fish market. The growth of the live lobster trade and the rapid spread of the lobster-canning industry occurred towards the end of the period, as the New England lobster beds were depleted.

Lumbering continued in eastern Canada as huge sawmills were built to supply the growing cities of New England. By the late 1860s, wood pulp was being incorporated into the papermaking process in Canada, and pulpwood cutters began to harvest bush areas that had previously been thought valueless. The railways brought large-scale lumbering to BC, where some of the greatest stands of trees began to fall for lumber and PULP AND PAPER. Technology differed somewhat in eastern and western Canada: western mountains did not have convenient river systems to float out the huge logs; more mechanization was needed and sawmills were therefore on a larger scale.

Mining started dramatically in BC with the Fraser R gold rush of the late 1850s. Of more lasting technical implication was the discovery of base-metal deposits in southeastern BC. These deposits, such as Sullivan Mine (COMINCO), which are still being worked, launched one of Canada's first large-scale mining camps. The huge nickel-copper deposits in the Sudbury Basin were originally uncovered in a CPR rock cut. Metallurgical techniques were often the final key to unlocking the wealth of these mines. The Orford process was used to separate the copper-nickel ores of the Sudbury Basin; differential flotation was used to extract the complex ores, containing mostly lead and zinc, at the Trail smelter in BC. Pools of tar and PETROLEUM had been known and used by the Indians for medicine for generations, but the first commercial development did not occur until after 1857 when a small well was dug with ordinary water-well equipment at Oil Springs [Ont]. A refinery was built at nearby Sarnia where the oil was taken by a pipeline. Although the field was depleted in a few decades, the tremendously important OIL AND NATURAL GAS industries started in Canada. The ASBESTOS mines in the Eastern Townships of Québec went into production in this period. The KLONDIKE GOLD RUSH (1898) attracted world attention and forced the establishment of new transportation routes. One of the main routes was forged through the WHITE PASS to Whitehorse by the narrow-gauge WHITE PASS AND YUKON RAILWAY. The Canadian engineer's first confrontation with PERMA-

FROST occurred in the gold diggings, where it was penetrated by wood fires and then steam thawing hoses. The real challenge for engineers came later when they had to redesign dredges in order to withstand the increased wear caused by the rock-hard permafrost.

Power Steam engines transformed transportation and, when applied to INDUSTRY and agriculture, gave a much more flexible power source. Steam power was only gradually applied to industry. Mills or factories would often add steam as a backup or would use steam if expanding. Steam power permitted new plants to locate near suppliers or markets because they were not tied to waterpower sites. Finally, ELECTRIC POWER made its Canadian debut in the 1880s. Many waterpower sites were developed to exploit this new and adaptable ENERGY source. Some of the earliest sites were developed to provide electric lighting for big commercial mills (where open flames were a fire hazard), such as at Young's sawmill, Ottawa, in 1882, and at the Canada Cotton Co in Cornwall, Ont, in 1883. The harnessing of the awesome power of NIAGARA FALLS in the next decade heralded a new age.

Manufacturing The farm machinery industry grew dramatically, employing new sources of power, manufacture and assembly; the railway made possible wider distribution and greater concentration. Engine and tool companies were established to provide machinery to the railway and forestry industries, eg, the Victoria Foundry and Machine Shops (1854), Ottawa, which manufactured steam engines, boilers and sawmill machinery; the Canadian Locomotive Co started as Tutton and Duncans Foundry in Kingston (1854); and Goldie-McCulloch (1859), Galt, which manufactured boilers, engines, pumps and flour-mill equipment. Flour milling was radically changed by the introduction of rolling mills, which processed hard western wheat more quickly. One of the first to try the new roller mills was the E.W.B. Snider mill at St Jacobs, Ont, in the 1870s. The Ogilvie Flour Milling Co, founded in 1801, built a huge new plant in Montréal in 1886, incorporating the latest reduction roller mills. Bessemer patented his method of producing steel in 1856, but it was nearly the end of the century before steel was available in large quantities for bridge and building construction in Canada. Most of the early steel imported to Canada was used by the railways for rails. The changeover from iron rails to steel started in the early 1870s. However, it took many years for metallurgists to improve the quality of steel so that it could withstand the varied strains of a structure such as a bridge. One of the first all-steel bridges in Canada was the cantilever railway bridge built at Saint John, NB, in 1884. Like steel, CEMENT had been used for centuries, but reliable, cheap, hydraulic cement was not available in Canada until the 1890s. The first plant to manufacture true hydraulic or "Portland" cement was likely in 1889 at the plant in Hull, Qué, owned by C.B. Wright and Sons.

Wood continued to be a basic material in construction, as commercial sawmills made standard-sized lumber available. The balloon frame, built up from the common "two-by-four" (about 5 cm by 10 cm), began to replace timber-frame construction. Wire nails became cheap and universally available. In composite buildings, cast-iron columns and wrought-iron beams gradually gave way to steel by 1900. The federal PARLIAMENT BUILDINGS in Ottawa, constructed in the 1860s, were among the first buildings in N America to have an interior iron frame. Brick construction became much more common as beehive and downdraft kilns and brick-forming machines were introduced. Concrete began to be used more frequently in floors and foundations and, when

reinforced with steel, eventually took over, transforming the CONSTRUCTION INDUSTRY. By the end of the period, multistoreyed urban buildings and factories had central heating, electric light, elevators, and water and sewer services.

Communication technology advanced rapidly with the electric TELEGRAPH, ushered in as a companion to the railways in the 1850s. Bell's TELEPHONE appeared in the 1870s and, by the 1880s and 1890s, exchanges were common in most larger cities. The first telephone exchange in Canada was installed in 1878 in Hamilton and by the end of the year it had 40 telephones.

Water and Sanitation Urban areas require large supplies of water for domestic and industrial use and fire protection and a corresponding system to handle WASTE DISPOSAL. By the 1870s the water supplies of most large cities were pumped by steam, and by 1900 some were using sand filters or hypochlorite of lime for WATER TREATMENT. Toronto and Kingston had pumping stations by 1841 and 1850, respectively. Halifax and Saint John had gravity systems even earlier (1848 and 1838, respectively). Many cities had drainage systems designed to handle surface water from heavy rain and snow, but not sewage.

Technical Education began in this period in the workshops of railways, factories and schools. Formal engineering education began slowly with CIVIL ENGINEERING at King's College, Fredericton (1854); McGill (1871); School of Practical Science, Toronto (1873); École Polytechnique, Montréal (1873); Royal Military College, Kingston, Ont (1876); and the School of Mining and Agriculture, Queen's University, Kingston (1893). Most of these universities offered courses in civil, MINING and MECHANICAL ENGINEERING, and quickly added ELECTRICAL and CHEMICAL ENGINEERING programs. The engineering profession had grown rapidly since the great canal and railway building days. Engineers of the time included Thomas Keefer and his brother Samuel, Sir Casimir GZOWSKI, Sir John KENNEDY and the SHANLY brothers.

Early Modern Period (1900-40)

The first decade of the century brought unparalleled agricultural development and prosperity, and appeared to mark the maturation of the national economy. The harnessing of Niagara (1895) began a new industrial revolution based largely on electricity and related CHEMICAL INDUSTRIES. WWI was a proving ground for the internal combustion engine in vehicles and aircraft. WWI developments, applied to BUSH FLYING, helped open the Canadian North. The gasoline engine found many uses after the war, and the diesel engine became popular in public transportation. Finally, RADIO, TELEVISION and aircraft allowed Canadians to communicate more effectively.

Agriculture Mechanization of the prairie farm continued through the boom of 1901 to 1911. The gasoline tractor replaced the steam tractor during WWI and power takeoff, pneumatic tires and hydraulic-lifting equipment were developed in the 1920s. Many cultivating and harvesting machines were developed, eg, row cultivators for tobacco and corn crops and the Sylvester auto-thresher that appeared in western Canada. New strains of early maturing wheat (eg, MARQUIS, Garnet, Reward) permitted farming farther N on the prairies. The new technologies of pasteurization, refrigeration and the commercial canning of meat, vegetables and fruit, as well as condensed milk and processed cheese, helped provide food to growing urban areas after the war. In 1900 farming was still mainly traditional, but by the end of WWII it was becoming a highly mechanized industry.

Fishing in the Maritime provinces underwent great changes. Corporate amalgamations provided more capital for technological development and, by 1908, many steamships were converted to trawlers, as were naval minesweepers after WWI. The traditional schooner began to disappear. Improved refrigeration, transportation and communication provided better facilities for handling fresh fish. Freezing of bait fish had been introduced in the 1890s, but the freezing of fresh fish was developed in the Great Lakes fisheries at the turn of the century. The practice was adopted on both the Atlantic and Pacific coasts, although the process gave only short-term preservation. In 1929 the American Clarence Birdseye demonstrated that quick-freezing produced a better product, and the greater use of freezers by retailers greatly changed marketing procedures. Finally the introduction of the internal combustion engine to small craft gave fishermen increased mobility.

Transportation The success of the CPR encouraged 2 competitors, the GRAND TRUNK PACIFIC and the CANADIAN NORTHERN, to build transcontinental lines. The Temiskaming and Northern Ontario Railway (ONTARIO NORTHLAND) was constructed from North Bay, Ont, to James Bay (1903-31). The HUDSON BAY RY (1909-29) was built to open another saltwater port, at Churchill, Man, to prairie grain. Many branch lines were started into the PEACE RIVER LOWLAND.

Canals on the St Lawrence at Cornwall and Williamsburg, Ont, and Beauharnois, Qué, were enlarged (1900-03). A final effort was made to complete the Trent Canal between 1895 and 1920, when the various sections were linked together. The PETERBOROUGH lift lock, designed by R.B. Rogers, was the largest of its kind in the world and an outstanding engineering achievement. In 1910 Manitoba's only canal lock was completed on the Red R at St Andrews. The increased size and number of ships on the Great Lakes made the New Welland Canal obsolete and a larger, more direct canal, called the Welland Ship Canal, was started in 1913, interrupted by the war and officially opened in 1932.

Cars and trucks passed from being curiosities to necessities. In the 1920s, provincial departments of highways were given authority to take over major trunk roads and to plan and supervise road planning and construction at all levels within the province.

The building of highways was facilitated by a new generation of trucks and trawler tractors, adapted for road construction. Public transport was vital to the growing cities: horse-drawn buses had been replaced by electric STREET RAILWAYS in 46 Canadian cities by the 1920s. The first motor buses were also appearing; a diesel bus was used in Montréal as early as 1932.

The flight of the SILVER DART (at Baddeck, NS, in 1909) was the first in the British Empire. Canadian pilots made major contributions to the war effort in WWI and returned home eager to fly. Surplus military aircraft were quickly adapted to peacetime tasks, often associated with lumbering and mining in northern areas. In 1919 a federal government agency, the Associate Air Research Committee, was established to foster aeronautical research in Canada. In 1927 W.R. TURNBULL perfected the electrically operated variable-pitch propeller, which was adopted around the world. The most famous of a new generation of bush planes was the NOORDUYN NORSEMAN, which was designed by Robert Noorduyn after he consulted with a large number of active pilots in 1935. During the GREAT DEPRESSION, one of the government's most successful, innovative, make-work programs involved building a string of AIRPORTS across the country (*see* AVIATION).

Mining The building of the Ontario Northland Ry led prospectors to the huge deposits of silver at Cobalt, then gold at Timmins and Kirkland Lk. These mines financed and encouraged other ventures, eg, the mines at Rouyn, Qué, and Flin Flon, Man. They also pioneered many of the underground hard-rock mining practices used throughout the rest of Canada. The Precambrian Shield was thoroughly examined by geologists and prospectors, who discovered many other precious- and base-metal deposits. The BC coalfields expanded with the railways and deposits of natural gas were tapped in southern Alberta.

Metallurgists were forced to keep up with this expansion. New processes, varying from mine to mine, were needed for the extraction and refinement of ore. In 1903 Bett's electrolytic process was installed at the refinery in Trail, BC, to refine the lead content of the ore. In 1911 the first basic lined converters in Canada were used to smelt copper matte at Copper Cliff. International Nickel built a new electrolytic refining plant at Port Colborne, Ont, in 1916 to take advantage of the cheap electrical power available. Part of the solution to the problem in the Flin Flon smelter was the introduction of a suspended magnesite furnace arc in 1930. Electricity was fundamental to many of these processes. For example, in 1901, the manufacture of ALUMINUM and aluminum products began at Shawinigan, Qué. This valuable industry advanced rapidly almost from coast to coast because, although the ore was imported and many of the finished products were exported, the processing required huge amounts of electricity, available at several locations in Canada.

Power In Québec many rivers were tapped primarily to serve new mines and pulp and paper mills, eg, at Grand Falls, NB (1928), pulp and paper; Shawinigan (1902 on), pulp and paper, aluminum, industry; Saguenay Power at Isle-Maligne, Qué (1925), pulp and paper, aluminum; Quinze R, western Qué (1923), mining; Abitibi Canyon, northern Ont (1929-33), mining, pulp and paper; Island Falls, Churchill R, Sask (1930), mining; West Kootenay Power, Bonnington Falls, BC (1897 on), mining. Industries which had used steam or waterpower converted to electricity whenever feasible, especially when the technology of transmission over long distances developed. The first long-distance transmission of electricity in Canada, and perhaps the British Empire, was carried out between the Batiscan R and Trois-Rivières, Qué, in 1897. The line was about 29 km long and carried 11 000 volts. Another new source of power, the internal-combustion engine, found many uses as a stationary power source for running pumps, saws, etc.

Manufacturing The AUTOMOTIVE INDUSTRY was added to the established and expanding industries related to railways and resource extraction. While dozens of cars were designed and built across Canada, only the McLaughlin really achieved success. Gordon McGregor, manager of the Walkerville Wagons Works, in Windsor, Ont, established the FORD MOTOR COMPANY OF CANADA in 1904. Production began almost immediately using Ford's famous assembly-line process, probably the first use in Canada. TEXTILE production, primarily woolens, continued in eastern Ontario and southern Québec, mostly using imported technology and raw material. Most new factories began employing the latest machine tools and electrical equipment, particularly during the serious labour shortages of the war.

US investment in Canada increased steadily after the American Civil War and by WWI had eclipsed British investment. As American investment was mostly equity investment, American ownership of Canadian companies rose from approximately 100 companies in 1900 to 1350

Robotic welding, General Motors of Canada (*photo by Mike Dobel/Masterfile*).

companies in 1934. Most advanced technology was imported directly from the US and many large manufacturers were subsidiaries of US companies (*see* FOREIGN INVESTMENT).

Forestry Starting in the early 20th century, steam "donkey" engines powered winches that dragged the huge logs out of the BC forests in a system called "ground leading." Eventually, "high leading" replaced the process because of greater efficiency. The first power saws appeared in 1939 but were so heavy and unreliable that they had to be operated by 2 men. The one-man light chain saw appeared after WWII.

Construction The skyscraper was pioneered in Chicago and New York, but tall buildings with steel skeletons soon appeared in Winnipeg (1904) and Toronto (1914), and when the federal Parliament Buildings were rebuilt (1916) a structural steel frame was used. Longer-span bridges were built, culminating in the QUÉBEC BRIDGE (1917). Toronto's Governor's Bridge (1923) is said to be the world's first welded-steel bridge. In the 1920s reinforced concrete was used extensively in bridges in Peterborough, Calgary and Saskatoon. These bridges are among the most beautiful in Canada.

Industrial Chemistry The rapid expansion of electrochemistry in the 20th century permitted the economical production of many chemicals. A Canadian, Thomas WILLSON, developed the first successful commercial process for manufacturing calcium carbide. The first plant was established at Merritton, Ont, in 1896. The Shawinigan Carbide Co was formed in 1901 but actual production of carbide did not start until 1904. The first contract sulphuric acid plant was established at Sulphide, Ont, in 1908.

The SALT deposits at Windsor, Ont, were used to produce a number of sodium and chlorine compounds, such as the electrolytic production of sodium carbonate in 1919. Liquid and gaseous chlorine was produced at Sandwich, Ont, in 1911 for water purification, bleaching of pulp and many other purposes. The electrolytic cell, used for many of these processes, was patented in Canada in 1908 by A.E. Gibbs. Another important technology was the manufacture of artificial fibres. The production of viscose rayon in Canada was started by the British firm Courtaulds in Cornwall, Ont, in 1925. The process used cellulose from wood pulp. In 1928 Canadian Celanese Ltd started to manufacture cellulose acetate rayon at Drummondville, Qué. Canadian Industries Ltd (CIL) began to manufacture transparent cellulose film at Shawinigan Falls in 1931.

Sanitation services improved as better sand filters cleansed city drinking water, but sewage treatment advanced slowly. Methods of decomposing sewage in tanks were adopted after 1910, and by 1916 the activated sludge process had been adopted by many cities. Some large cities disposed of garbage by incineration in high-temperature furnaces.

Communications The early telephone was improved with better cable sheathing and instruments; the improved loading coil appeared in 1916. Vacuum-tube telephone repeaters (installed in 1917) improved long-distance telephony, making possible the TRANSCANADA TELEPHONE SYSTEM (formally opened in 1932). Dial telephones were first installed in Edmonton (1905), and during the 1920s and 1930s most urban areas of Ontario and Québec were converted.

Marconi established long-range, wireless telegraphy across the Atlantic in 1901, and in the 1920s the development of shortwave transmission vastly improved the signal. The first "wireless" (radio) broadcast was sent by a Canadian, Reginald FESSENDEN, in 1906 from a station in the US. In 1920 Marconi followed with the first broadcast in Canada, from Montréal. Commercial broadcasting progressed slowly as receiving sets became available, first in kit form, then preassembled. By 1927 Canadians could telephone Europe via the US, and by 1931 direct connections were possible. In 1925 a rudimentary form of telephotography (television) was established.

Technical Education Engineering colleges were established at the western universities (1906-13). The engineering profession increased in numbers and prestige, and separate provincially chartered professional organizations were established in all provinces, except PEI, by 1923. Provincial associations were given the right to control entry into the profession, thus ensuring that only legally qualified engineers could practise in the provinces. This period witnessed the foundation of most of Canada's modern primary and secondary industries. A basic network of transportation existed across the country and the conquest of the Canadian Shield was almost complete. The interdependence of technologies became more apparent as mining, electrical power, machine-tool factories, metallurgical and chemical industries were interconnected. Much of the impetus built up during and after WWI was lost during the Great Depression but revived after.

Modern Period (1940-present)

The modern period of technology was ushered in by WWII. Canada's participation placed enormous demands on primary and secondary industries, transport and manpower. By 1945 farms, mines, shipyards and factories were highly mechanized and as efficient as any in the world. The war accelerated the development of young industries (eg, aluminum products) and brought about entirely new industries (eg, those centered around uranium).

Manufacturing During WWII Canadian industry expanded rapidly to produce munitions. This expansion stimulated the manufacture of tools, electrical apparatus, and chemicals and materials (eg, synthetic rubber). Heavy industries, eg, ship and aircraft manufacture, were vital to the war effort. The creation of atomic weapons by the US ushered in the field of NUCLEAR POWER, which stimulated Canada's uranium mining. By the end of the war, Canada had truly become industrialized: more people worked in secondary (ie, manufacturing) industry than on the farms or in the forests, and the output of secondary industry exceeded that of primary industry by any system of measurement. The postwar challenge was to convert this manufacturing potential to consumer goods, eg, in the Canadian automotive industry (mainly as a subsidiary of giant US corporations), and the rapid expansion of mining and agricultural equipment manufacture.

Power A further challenge was to provide the energy necessary to sustain industry and to fuel public and private transportation. More hydroelectric sites were developed in BC, Ontario,

Québec and Manitoba. Thermoelectric stations were built in the Maritimes and the Prairie provinces. Ontario opened the first nuclear-powered thermal station, at Rolphton in 1962. Natural-gas exploration continued in Alberta and Saskatchewan; the huge LEDUC oil field was discovered in 1947. The oil industry became very complex, producing gasoline, diesel and heating fuels, heavy oils for lubrication, and developing the huge PETROCHEMICAL INDUSTRY with its hundreds of by-products. Sarnia and Montréal became centres of the petrochemical industries, although gradually some industry shifted closer to the oil fields.

Mining and Metallurgy Chemical technology helped solve the metallurgical problems of the expanding mining industry. Plants producing war explosives were altered to produce mining and construction explosives. Mining technology was also in great demand after the war. Oil exploration revealed one of the world's largest deposits of POTASH in Saskatchewan. The extraction of this deep-lying mineral was a great challenge. The need to develop new sources of iron became urgent as US mines began to be depleted. Huge projects at Steep Rock, Ont, and in Labrador required the most modern, large-scale, earth-moving equipment, as well as hydroelectric power to bring the ore to steel mills in Hamilton and the US. The gold-mining industry that had supported Canada through 2 world wars was waning and the major postwar effort was directed to base metals and coal.

Transportation One of the largest engineering projects in Canada was the construction of the ST LAWRENCE SEAWAY, undertaken in conjunction with the US. This enterprise not only opened the upper Great Lakes to foreign and domestic saltwater ships, but also facilitated shipment of iron ore from Labrador to steel mills on the shores of Lks Ontario and Erie, as well as providing additional hydroelectric supplies.

Canada's wartime aircraft industry would have disappeared in competition with industries in other nations. Its demise was almost assured when the federal government cancelled the AVRO ARROW project. The cancellation of the most advanced military aircraft of its kind has been considered a great setback to the development of technology in Canada, although the Canadian aircraft industry continued to develop innovative STOL (*short-take-off-and-landing*) aircraft, such as the DE HAVILLAND OTTER and DE HAVILLAND DASH-7.

Postwar shipbuilding dwindled until only a few LAKE CARRIERS and saltwater fishing boats were produced. Canadian shipyards have already produced some of the most advanced ICEBREAKERS and, with increased exploration for oil, gas and minerals in the Arctic, this technology has great potential.

Agriculture and Forestry Powerful and sophisticated machinery and new chemicals have made Canadian farmers among the most productive in the world. New, large-scale technologies of cutting and hauling were introduced into forestry, particularly in BC, as loggers pushed farther into the mountains. Canadian paper mills now possess new, high-speed machinery that supplies much of the world's newsprint.

Canada has long depended on imported technology to fuel its economic development and Canadian INVENTORS AND INNOVATIONS have seldom received the kind of support necessary for long-term developments. Canada's widely dispersed population, its dependence on foreign investment and resource exploitation and its tradition of regional political independence have made the task of formulating a coherent industrial strategy very difficult. Although Canadian engineers lead the world in the use of computers for communi-

The Avro Arrow was one of the most advanced aircraft designs in the world. Its abrupt cancellation and replacement by American weapons was to many a symbol of Canada's unwillingness to develop its technology (*courtesy The Arrow Heads/Boston Mill Press, Erin, Ont*).

cation, and although dramatic advances in COMMUNICATIONS IN THE NORTH have taken place, Canada cannot compete with foreign producers of ELECTRONIC and domestic electrical equipment. Without reliable access to HIGH TECHNOLOGY there is the danger that secondary industries will not be competitive and that Canada may revert to its traditional role as supplier of raw materials. *See also* ENGINEERING, HISTORY OF.   W.G. RICHARDSON

Tecumseh, Shawnee war chief (b in the Ohio Valley *c*1768; d at what is now Thamesville, Ont 5 Oct 1813). Tecumseh attempted, like other native leaders including Joseph BRANT, to form an alliance of tribes to combat US territorial ambitions more effectively.

Tecumseh participated in the futile Indian struggle to preserve the Ohio Valley and was present at the battle of Fallen Timbers in Aug 1794. Along with his half-brother, The Prophet, who preached a return to native religion and traditional values, he tried to rally the tribes in a common defence against the Americans, and visited the southern nations in 1811 to try to induce them to join. He allied his forces with those of the British and Canadians during the WAR OF 1812, and his active participation was crucial during the critical summer months of 1812. He was present at Detroit (16 Aug 1812) and won a decisive victory against the Americans in the woods at Ft Meigs (May 1813). Following the defeat of the British fleet at the battle of PUT-IN-BAY, the British retreated from the Detroit front, and at the follow-up battle of Moraviantown (5 Oct 1813), Tecumseh was killed fighting with his people after the British had broken and fled. Tecumseh's death virtually marked the end of Indian resistance S of the Great Lakes. Tecumseh, as a heroic and tragic figure, has captured the imagination of writers over the years, including John RICHARDSON and Charles MAIR.   ROBERT S. ALLEN

Teit, James Alexander, ethnographer (b in Shetland Is, Scot 1864; d at Spences Bridge, BC 30 Oct 1922). Much of our knowledge of traditional Salish cultures of Interior BC is based on Teit's meticulous descriptions and artifact collections for major museums in Ottawa, New York and Chicago (*see* SALISH, INTERIOR). Teit's wife was from a Thompson Indian village near his home at Spences Bridge, and he became conversant with Thompson language and culture, as well as the Shuswap and Lillooet languages. His enthnographic work was stimulated in 1895 when he met anthropologist Franz BOAS, who was on a field trip to BC; they collaborated periodically for the rest of Teit's life. Teit published not only on Interior Salish culture and mythology but also on the traditions of several DENE groups farther N. With his deep interest in native affairs, Teit helped form and served as secretary for the Allied Tribes of BC organization, working

until his death for the protection of Indian land and other rights.   KATHLEEN MOONEY

Tekakwitha, Kateri (Catherine), known as the Lily of the Mohawks, first N American Indian candidate for sainthood (b at Ossernenon [near Auriesville, NY] 1656; d at the St-François-Xavier Mission [Caughnawaga], New France 17 Apr 1680). Her rejection of several marriage offers and desire for a life of virginity put her at odds with Mohawk life even before she became a Christian. Her baptism in 1676 led to persecution, and a year later she left home for the Christian Indian village at Caughnawaga. There she became known for her sanctity and was given permission by the Jesuits in 1679 to make a private vow of chastity. Her death the next year from a prolonged illness was perhaps partly brought on by her penitential life-style. Her relics are preserved in a shrine at Caughnawaga, and numerous miracles have since been reported there. A portrait of her was painted in 1681 by Jesuit Father Claude Chauchetière, who also wrote a biography of her. She was beatified 22 June 1980.
          JOHN RASMUSSEN

Telecommunications is the transmission of signals over long distances. The earliest form was visual signalling with smoke, flags or lamps. Today, electronic telecommunication systems transmit messages to many locations throughout Canada and the world. The first method used to send messages by electricity was the TELEGRAPH. On 24 May 1844 Samuel Morse sent the first telegraph message, "What hath God wrought!" between Washington, DC, and Baltimore, Md. Over the next 50 years systems of wires were constructed across the US, Canada and other countries, bringing a revolution in the speed of communication over distance.

On 10 Mar 1876 Alexander Graham BELL spoke the first words over a telephone, "Mr Watson, come here. I want you," at his laboratory in Boston. In Aug 1876 he received the first one-way long-distance call over a 13 km line he had built between Brantford and Paris, Ont. Construction soon began on systems of telephone wires and cables within cities and towns, and switchboards to provide interconnections of TELEPHONES in a network organization.

Early telephone systems could only carry intelligible voice signals for several miles, but continuing research and development led to technical improvements that kept extending the distance over which calls could be made. Hard-drawn copper wire was stronger than ordinary copper wire and a better conductor of electricity than steel wire. Dry-core cables and 2-wire circuits improved transmission so that by 1900 long-distance circuits had been extended as far as 1900 km (1200 miles). The loading coil doubled this distance by reducing signal distortion and the repeater provided a means of amplifying the signal. By 1920 coast-to-coast transmission was possible, and thereafter most local telephone systems were upgraded to long-distance standards, which in turn have been continually improved over time.

Sending signals across the ocean proved more difficult. The working lives of repeaters were short and in a submarine cable they could not be replaced. Shortwave radio was used beginning in 1926, but an undersea cable awaited the development of the higher capacity coaxial cable and the vacuum-tube amplifier with an expected working life of 20 years. The first ocean cables were laid in 1956 between Scotland and Newfoundland with a capacity of 60 telephone circuits. This has been followed with many additional cables of substantially increased capacity connecting many locations throughout the world. Satellites became available for international service in 1964 and domestically in Canada in 1973. Distance has been conquered.

System Characteristics The basic functional components of the telecommunication system are (1) the communication terminal, which today could be a telephone, a teletypewriter, a facsimile machine, a personal computer or a large computer central processor; (2) the local loop, ie, the network of wires, cable, poles and related equipment that connects terminals to a local central office; (3) switching equipment in the central office that provides the necessary connections when calls are made; (4) larger capacity trunk cables that connect central offices, eg, a local end office with a long-distance toll office; (5) transmission equipment that sends and receives signals over long distances, including higher capacity cable, microwave radio and satellites. For signals to be communicated effectively over this system, there must be technical compatibility among all functional components, and each component must be capable of handling the signals of the highest quality service that will be provided over it. When the system was upgraded to meet the requirements of national and international long distance, it involved not only the transmission function but others as well, including the telephone instrument.

The telecommunication system is used to provide a variety of different communication services. Each service provides connections within a network of potential users, employing a particular type or quality of communication signal. Local telephone service provides public access to telephones in the local area at voice-grade technical standards. The local telecommunication facilities also provide private connections for voice, telegraph, video and data signals that are separate from the local public telephone network, such as private communication lines connecting only a few locations, or local data networks. Some services require 4-wire loop connections for higher quality service rather than the 2-wire loop required for voice telephone. The local facilities also provide access to the public long-distance network and, if the particular facilities have been upgraded, to national networks for video or data signals, eg, airline reservation systems.

The telecommunication system has been designed to meet the standards of voice communication. It employs the analogue transmission method which uses signals that are exact reproductions of the pattern of sound waves being transmitted. But this restricts the speed with which digital data signals can be transmitted. In addition, signal distortions which do not significantly affect the quality of voice communication create errors in data transmission. A major thrust of research and development is a search for new techniques that will improve error performance in data communications.

Telephone companies now are converting their signal standards from analogue to digital and are upgrading the system to the standards of digital computers. Progress has been most rapid for the transmission function, and digital terminals are widely available. The conversions of local switching and loops are more costly and are being implemented more slowly. POTS (the plain old telephone system) is being converted to an ISDN (integrated services digital network), a sophisticated multipurpose network used to provide a wide variety of communication and information services (*see* COMMUNICATIONS TECHNOLOGY).

The Canadian Industry and its Regulation The installation of telephone wires and cables required use of city streets and public rights-of-way. Thus the approval of government authorities was required. Although there was some experience

with competitive telephone companies in some cities, generally it was concluded that the public interest would be served better by a single local company, and competitive companies were not licensed. For most of its history, the telecommunication system has been operated as a monopoly subject to government regulation or government ownership, or both.

Telephone companies in Canada range in size from BELL CANADA ENTERPRISES INC (BCE), the largest (a transnational corporation serving two-thirds of Canadian telephones in Ontario, Québec and the eastern NWT), to small-town private companies and municipal operators. The Maritime provinces are served primarily by private companies in which BCE has major ownership interests, subject to provincial regulation. In the Prairie provinces the systems are publicly owned. The British Columbia Telephone Co (a subsidiary of the US General Telephone Co) and Bell Canada are regulated by the federal CANADIAN RADIO-TELEVISION AND TELECOMMUNICATIONS COMMISSION, as is Telesat Canada (a quasi-public/private corporation), the monopoly supplier of domestic satellite service. Telesat and the larger companies that provide long-distance services in their respective provinces are members of Telecom Canada, through which they provide nationwide services. Teleglobe Canada is a crown corporation that provides international satellite and cable services in conjunction with other countries and international agencies.

CNCP Telecommunications (est 1967) provides an alternative long-distance network. It grew from telecommunication facilities initially established by the CANADIAN NATIONAL RAILWAYS and CANADIAN PACIFIC RAILWAY to control their rail operations. Now it competes with Telecom Canada for a small portion of business long-distance private-line and data services. Subsidiaries of CN serve the Yukon and the western NWT and part of Newfoundland. Within this larger framework, many small companies, of which Edmonton Telephones is the largest, provide only local facilities and services.

Telecommunication services have traditionally been supplied under the concept of end-to-end service by a monopoly supplier. The telephone companies owned all the equipment, including

The CN Tower, Toronto, is topped by a sophisticated communications antenna (*photo by J.A. Kraulis*).

the terminals, purchasing the great majority of it from affiliated manufacturing companies. The attachment of other equipment, or the interconnection of other systems, has been prohibited. Services to the public have been provided at rates approved by government regulatory agencies. The agencies have attempted to limit the profit of the telephone companies to a reasonable level, although great flexibility has been allowed in setting individual rates.

Since the early 1970s this end-to-end service concept has come under increasing criticism, stemming primarily from the growing use of the telecommunication system by the computer industry. Other manufacturers of equipment and other potential suppliers of service have claimed that they could provide improvements to the system that would benefit consumers. As of 1984, the CRTC and some provincial regulatory agencies have ordered the telephone companies under their respective jurisdictions to unbundle their services, separating the terminal and network components of service so that subscribers can choose to purchase their own terminals from any supplier and plug them in like electrical appliances. Businesses such as hotels may purchase their entire internal communications systems from alternative suppliers if they choose.

In 1984 the CRTC held hearings on a 1983 application by CNCP to provide long-distance telephone service to the public in competition with Telecom Canada. To supply this service, CNCP must be able to obtain, at a reasonable price, the necessary interconnections to the local facilities of the telephone companies, which resist this potential new competition.

The telephone companies claim that competition for long-distance service will mean that they no longer will be able to subsidize local service, that local rates will have to increase dramatically, and that the near-universal telephone service in Canada will be threatened. By the term "subsidy," they mean revenue contributions from long-distance services to cover a share of the local facility costs used in common for both local and long-distance services. Telephone companies that supply only local service claim that this contribution is not enough and that local service subsidizes long-distance services. In 1985 the CRTC rejected the CNCP application. In 1986 a federal-provincial task force was established to examine telecommunication pricing and the universal availability of affordable telephone service. However, its extensive report did not address the issue of competition policy in long distance services. In 1987 BCE proposed to the CRTC a major change in its rate structure that would reduce long distance rates and increase local service rates. Whether this change in rate structure is "rebalancing" to reduce a subsidy of local by long distance services, or "unbalancing" by increasing the subsidy of long distance by local services in order to thwart potential future competition, can only be determined by a detailed examination of telephone company costs. This is a matter that Canadian regulatory agencies have been hesitant to pursue to date. CRTC regulatory policies will be instrumental in determining whether Canada will follow the US in permitting competition in public long-distance services, or whether it will attempt to retain the monopoly approach.

Of even greater significance for the future is determining which services will be assigned the massive costs of the system upgrading to computer standards. Under current industry accounting and regulatory practices, the great majority of these costs will be allocated to local telephone service and could require dramatic local rate increases, thereby threatening universal

Control room of Telesat Canada, Ottawa. Telesat, a quasi-public/private corporation, is the monopoly supplier of domestic satellite service (*photo by Jim Merrithew*).

telephone service. More detailed accounting and rate regulatory standards will have to be adopted by the regulatory authorities if these costs are to be assigned to the services responsible for the system upgrading. The CRTC (and its predecessor, the Canadian Transport Commission) have been engaged in a telecommunication cost inquiry since 1972, attempting to address these issues, but little progress has been made.

One possible scenario for future telecommunication service pricing is a flat monthly charge for the right of access to the system and usage charges for all services actually used, including local telephone service. This approach is favoured by industry, but consumer groups feel that high access charges and local measured service may force low-income people to disconnect from the system, losing basic telephone service. These issues will be actively debated for some time. The task of the CRTC and the provincial regulatory agencies of fashioning effective policy, in an environment of rapid technological change and increasing competitive market forces, will be formidable. *See also* COMMUNICATIONS; INFORMATION SOCIETY; SATELLITE COMMUNICATIONS.   WILLIAM H. MELODY

Reading: R.J. Buchan et al, *Telecommunications Regulation and the Constitution* (1982); Canada, Telecommunications and Canada, *Report of the Consultive Committee on the Implications of Telecommunications for Canadian Sovereignty* (1979); CRTC, *Interchange Competition and Related Issues*, Telecom Decision CRTC 85-19, 29 Aug 1985; Dept of Communications, *Instant World: A Report on Telecommunications in Canada* (1971); Dept of Consumer and Corporate Affairs, *Telecommunications in Canada*, 3 vols (1981-83); *Federal/Provincial Examination of Telecommunications Pricing and the Universal Availability of Affordable Telephone Service: Working Papers* (1986); P.S. Grant, ed, *Telephone Operation and Development in Canada, 1921-1971* (1974).

Telefilm Canada, *see* CANADIAN FILM DEVELOPMENT CORPORATION.

Telegraph, conceived in N America by Samuel Morse, in 1837 and in Europe by the English partnership of William Cooke and Charles Wheatstore. It is a means of electrically transmitting encoded messages through the systematic opening and closing of electric circuits. In Canada, the first telegraph company, the Toronto, Hamilton and Niagara Electro-Magnetic Telegraph Co, was formed in 1846. The company in Canada during the early years of the industry, however, was the Montreal Telegraph Co, controlled by Hugh ALLAN (founded in 1847); it connected such centres as Sackville (NB), Detroit, Montréal, Ottawa, Buffalo and Portland. In 1868 the Montreal Telegraph Co began facing direct competition from the newly established Dominion Telegraph Co and price wars broke out. In 1880 the Great North Western Telegraph Co was established to connect Ontario and Manitoba but by 1881 it had been taken over by Western Union Co of the US

and was used by Western Union to consolidate the Canadian industry, attaining leases on the lines of both the Montreal and Dominion telegraph companies. As a result, for a brief time Western Union controlled virtually all telegraphy in Canada.

Canadian Pacific Railway Telegraphs commenced service in a commercial telegraph service between Lake Superior and the Rockies in 1885, extended soon to Ontario and thereafter to Atlantic Canada, breaking Western Union's monopoly. Perhaps attributable to this new competition, the Great North Western Telegraph Co faced bankruptcy and was taken over by the telegraph subsidiary of Canadian Northern Railway Co on 1 Jan 1915. The railway itself was in financial difficulty, however, and was soon purchased by the federal government, subsequently forming a component of Canadian National Railways Co. In this way Great North Western Telegraph Co became Canadian National Telegraph Co.

By the 1930s CN and CP railway companies had established themselves as the principal providers of telegraph service in Canada, the latter interchanging traffic with Postal Telegraph and the former with Western Union. They continued to operate competitively until 1967, when agreement was reached for reciprocal office abandonment. Today, CNCP Telecommunications is jointly owned by Canadian National (owned by the federal government) and Canadian Pacific (a private enterprise). CNCP Telecommunications offers a wide range of business-telecommunications services in competition with members of the Telecom Canada (previously known as Trans-Canada Telephone System). In 1979, by order of the CANADIAN RADIO-TELEVISION AND TELECOMMUNICATIONS COMMISSION, CNCP Telecommunications was authorized nondiscriminatory access to Bell Canada's switched telephone network for the purpose of offering competitive data-transmission services. In 1985 the CRTC denied CNCP permission to compete for long-distance public voice communications, however.

A major principle of provisioning TELECOMMUNICATIONS facilities, namely the separation of control of the content of messages from control over transmission, was established in 1910 by the Board of Railway Commissioners for Canada. Almost since the inception of the Canadian telegraph, news gathering had been controlled by the major telegraph companies. In 1894 Canadian Pacific Telegraphs contracted with Associated Press, the major news agency in the US, and itself condensed and selected AP news items for distribution to Canadian newspapers. Canadian telegraph operators remained the principal collectors of Canadian news. In 1907, Canadian Pacific Telegraphs attempted to quadruple prices charged for its news service to 3 Winnipeg newspapers which, in opposition, joined to form an independent news service, the Western Associated Press (WAP). Subsequently, Canadian Pacific cut off its news service to the Nelson, BC, *News*, an action attributable to publication of articles critical of CP. Upon appeal from WAP, the Board of Railway Commissioners in 1910 ruled CP rates to be unlawful and hence the company abandoned the field of news gathering and selection. Today, there is general recognition that telecommunications companies should operate as common carriers only, by accepting for transmission all messages without interference, upon payment of lawful rates.   ROBERT E. BABE

Telephones The invention of the TELEGRAPH (1837) by Samuel Morse and the telephone (1876) by Alexander Graham BELL were milestones in the quest to communicate over great dis-

tances with reliability, accuracy and speed. Previously, communication over distance necessarily entailed encoding human thought through such means as drum and smoke signals, semaphores and trumpets or physically transporting written messages by carrier pigeons and human travel.

Telegraph and telephone both encode messages electrically at their origin; consequently, they may be transmitted literally at the speed of light over various types of transmission facilities such as copper wire, coaxial cable, fibre optics and through space to their destinations, where they are decoded into original form. The telegraph [Gk, *tele graphos*, meaning "writing at a distance"] encodes each letter of the alphabet into a combination of long and short bursts of electric current through a circuit by the systematic depression of a key which thereby completes an electric circuit. The telephone [Gk, *tele phone*, meaning "distant voice"] encodes variations in sound waves (that is, changes in the density of air which we perceive as sound) into variations of electrical waves through vibrations of a diaphragm in the mouthpiece of the telephone instrument.

The telephone, as compared to the telegraph, encodes messages directly for transmission, thereby permitting greater individual autonomy in sending messages. Moreover the telephone allows instantaneous routing of messages to the receiver through complex switching devices, whereas the public telegraph service routes messages to a central terminal and thereafter requires delivery of the message to the addressee. The telephone permits simultaneity in message exchanges, whereas the telegraph transmits complete messages unidirectionally.

The basic configuration of the telephone network comprises the terminal device (which may be, but is no longer limited to, the telephone instrument); a "local loop," a pair of copper wires or fibre-optic cables connecting the terminal to a local switching centre; trunk cables connecting switching centres or exchanges within a community; toll switching centres, which route long-distance messages; and long-line facilities (cables, fibre optics, microwave towers, communications satellites), which provide electrical interconnection between communities.

In 1876 the world's first definitive tests of the telephone occurred in Brantford, Ont. These were one-way transmissions. The era of the telephone in Canada was inaugurated in 1877 when its inventor transferred, for 1 dollar, 75% interest in the telephone patent for Canada to his father, Alexander Melville Bell. A.M. Bell hired agents to solicit subscribers for "private lines" (that is, unswitched or point-to-point service), and in 1880 the Dominion Telegraph Co secured a licence to operate the Bell patent for Canada for 5 years. Subsequently, however, the Dominion Telegraph Co was unable to raise $100 000 asked by Bell for outright purchase of the patent, and Canadian patent rights were sold in 1880 to the National Bell Telephone Co of Boston (today, American Telephone and Telegraph Co). Rival service was offered until 1880 by the Montreal Telegraph Co, using disputed patents of Elisha Gray, Thomas A. Edison and others.

In 1880 the National Bell Telephone Co had incorporated, through an Act of Parliament, the Bell Telephone Company of Canada (today also known as BELL CANADA), which was thereby authorized to construct telephone lines over and along all public property and rights-of-way. In Nov 1880 agreement was reached with rival companies (principally Western Union Telegraph Co and its Canadian affiliates) to surrender their patents, and by 1881 the Bell Telephone Co of Canada had acquired all other existing telephone interests in Canada. In 1885, however, the Bell patents were voided by the Government of Canada, and independent telephone companies were now entitled to offer service, even in direct competition with Bell. Several hundred independent companies later came into existence.

The rise of competing companies in Nova Scotia and New Brunswick may have been instrumental in causing Bell Telephone to withdraw from these provinces, thereby enabling Bell to pursue consolidation of its operations in its remaining territory. In 1885 Bell abandoned Prince Edward Island to the newly formed Telephone Company of Prince Edward Island. In 1888 Bell sold its facilities in NB and NS to the newly formed Nova Scotia Telephone Co, although at the time the latter was still controlled by Bell. Later in 1888 the New Brunswick Telephone Co was incorporated by legislative Act and was given an exclusive franchise to provide long-distance service in much of the province; in the following year it acquired the provincial facilities of the NS Telephone Co. In 1910 Maritime Telegraph and Telephone Co (MT and T) was incorporated, and in 1911 it acquired both the Telephone Co of PEI and the NS Telephone Co. In 1966 Bell Canada procured a majority interest in both MT and T and NB Telephone.

Newfoundland's principal telephone company was incorporated in 1919 as the Avalon Telephone Co, which was operated on a private basis by the Murphy family. The company's controlling interest was acquired by a group of Newfoundland and Montréal businessmen in 1954. In 1962 Bell Canada became the major shareholder. On 1 Jan 1970 the Avalon Telephone Co became Newfoundland Telephone Co Ltd, and in 1976 public shares were issued, making Newfoundland Telephone a widely held company with Bell Canada holding majority ownership. Today, Newfoundland Telephone is regulated provincially and provides a wide range of telecommunications services to approximately 75% of the 550 000 people of Newfoundland and Labrador.

In other regions of the country, however, Bell Telephone met the emerging competition more aggressively. Two policies that were developed at the turn of the century – pricing and interconnection practices – are of particular interest, since they have remained controversial to the present. Bell's pricing was alleged to be noncompensatory and hence detrimental to competition in instances where direct or potential competition existed; indeed, telephone service was for a time offered free in some communities (Peterborough, Ft William, Pt Arthur). Moreover, Bell Telephone did not interconnect rivals to its local or long-distance network, thereby disadvantaging subscribers to independent companies. Nonetheless the independent telephone industry in Ontario and Québec continued to grow, especially through the period 1906-19. By 1915 independent telephone companies in Ontario accounted for 79 000 telephones, or one-third of the provincial total. However, during the 1950s and 1960s Bell acquired most of these independents, with the result that in Ontario at present non-Bell telephone companies account for under 5% of the province's telephones.

In the years before 1906 there was much dissatisfaction with rates and with the reluctance of Bell to extend service to less lucrative rural areas. Consequently, PM Sir Wilfrid Laurier formed a select committee of the House of Commons in 1905, chaired by Postmaster Gen William MULOCK, to investigate the telephone industry in Canada and make recommendations. The committee published verbatim proceedings which provide a valuable history.

In 1906, through revisions to the Railway Act, certain aspects of the operations of the Bell Tele-

"Dr Bell and Party at the Home of the Telephone," 1906, Brantford, Ont (*by permission of the British Library*).

phone Co of Canada were brought within the jurisdiction of the Board of Railway Commissioners for Canada. Henceforth, all telephone tolls charged to the public by the company were subject to the prior approval of the board; the board was also empowered to order interconnection between Bell and other telephone companies. Regulatory jurisdiction over Bell Telephone was transferred to the CANADIAN TRANSPORT COMMISSION in 1967 and to the CANADIAN RADIO-TELEVISION AND TELECOMMUNICATIONS COMMISSION in 1976, the major responsibilities of these regulatory tribunals being to ensure that the tolls charged are reasonable and just, and not unduly preferential or discriminatory; furthermore, terms and conditions of interconnection with other companies must be authorized by the regulator. Long, complex public hearings are frequently held to ascertain the ramifications of applications put forth by Bell.

The retention of Bell Canada under private ownership after 1906 was in opposition to policies advocated by certain municipal and provincial governments and led to further dramatic changes in the structure of the Canadian telephone industry. In 1908 and 1909 Bell Telephone operations in Manitoba, Alberta and Saskatchewan were purchased by the provincial governments and are operated today as provincially owned utilities.

The Canadian telephone industry in 1985 consisted of 106 companies, comprising 16.0 million telephones and employing more than 94 000 workers. Canadians placed 34.7 billion telephone calls in 1985, representing 1361 calls per capita. The Canadian telephone industry in 1985 received revenues of $10 billion, had net fixed assets of $18.6 billion and paid wages and salaries of $3.2 billion.

Next to Bell Canada the largest telephone company in Canada is the British Columbia Telephone Co (BC Tel), serving all of BC apart from the city of Prince Rupert, which is served by a municipally owned system. BC Tel is controlled by General Telephone and Electronics Corporation of the US. BC Tel in turn controls AEL Microtel, an unregulated manufacturer of TELECOMMUNICATIONS equipment from which BC Tel procures the

largest portion of its equipment. BC Tel is about 20% the size of Bell and, like the latter company, is regulated by the CRTC.

Manitoba Telephone System (MTS), owned by the provincial government and regulated by the Public Utilities Board, is the sole provider of telephone service in Manitoba. It is about 40% as large as BC Tel. Saskatchewan Telecommunications (Sask Tel) is a provincially owned telephone utility which, together with numerous co-operatively owned systems, serves Saskatchewan. The Public Utilities Review Commission supervises Sask Tel. Sask Tel is about the same size as MTS. The third provincially owned telephone system in Canada is Alberta Government Telephones (AGT). AGT and a municipally owned system in Edmonton (Edmonton Telephones) are the exclusive suppliers of telephone service in Alberta. AGT, which is about 75% the size of BC Tel, is regulated by the Alberta Public Utilities Board, and Edmonton Telephones is supervised by the city council. Other municipally owned systems in Canada are located in Thunder Bay and Kenora.

Telesat Canada and 9 major telephone companies in Canada participate in an association, Telecom Canada (previously the TRANS-CANADA TELEPHONE SYSTEM), for national co-ordination of telephone service. Though telephone service is provided primarily on the basis of monopoly in each area, federal regulatory initiatives in recent years have reopened competition for selective services. In 1979, for example, the CRTC ordered Bell Canada to grant CNCP Telecommunications access to Bell's local switching network for purposes of offering business-communications services in competition with Bell Canada. In 1977 the CRTC ruled that Bell Canada must afford cable TV companies access to its poles and ducts, without restriction to the services sold by such companies. In 1979 the CRTC required Bell Canada to afford access to its switching facilities to a mobile-telephone company. These new pockets of competition again bring into question the issue of compensatory pricing. Following a 1982 CRTC decision, changes have been effected regarding subscriber ownership of terminal equipment. Single-line residence and business subscribers, with or without extension telephones, are now able to own or lease their telephones. However, the inside wiring remains the property of the telephone company.

Western societies are entering the information age, or post-industrial society, and telecommunications companies are of great significance in this transition. It has been estimated that up to 50% of the labour force is now engaged in information production or distribution. At the same time, technology is transforming hitherto distinct information industries into a highly complex, interrelated system. Microelectronic circuitry, communications satellites, broadband cable and fibre optics brought into the home appear to be eradicating previously distinct industry boundaries. Also, online word processors allow office-to-office transfer of messages. Virtually all forms of information that were defined by their singular mode of material encapsulation (film, newsprint, books, computer printouts) can now be encoded and diffused electrically over vast geographic areas at low cost. There is increased interdependence between telephone companies and newspapers, banks and financial institutions, computer companies, etc. The future may bring increased competition for telephone companies from cable TV systems and SATELLITE COMMUNICATIONS firms.   ROBERT E. BABE

Television is one thing most Canadians have in common. Almost all of Canada's 9 million or so households have a TV set – over 98%. This is more than households that own an FM radio (93%) or an automobile (77%), and far outnumbers specialized amenities like microwave ovens (about 33%) and home computers (about 10%). The ownership of colour TV sets grew dramatically through the 1970s and 1980s, and they are now in about 93% of Canadian homes.

The popularity of set ownership is reflected in the time devoted to watching television, which continues to be our major leisure activity. In 1986 Canadians spent on average some 24.2 hours a week, over 3 hours a day, in front of their sets, up from 22.1 hours per week in 1977. Thirty-three percent of viewing time is spent on "drama," 19% on news and public affairs, 14.5% on comedy, 9.8% on variety and game shows, and 6.5% on sports. Not all of this time is spent concentrating on the screen. As much as one-third of reported "viewing" time actually goes to other activities while the set is on – homework, laundry, phoning friends. Radio broadcasts get fewer overall hours of consumer time. Other leisure activities such as reading, hobbies and attendance at concerts and sports events are also much less popular.

Television watching is not a mass experience, like going to a football game or even to the local movie-house. It is essentially private, taking place alone or in small groups, and is often an adjunct to other domestic activities. And even though highly rated shows – a Stanley Cup final or "Anne of Green Gables" – may reach a huge national audience, they are still highly visible exceptions to the rule. On a day-to-day basis, television's millions of regular viewers are usually not all looking at – or for – the same thing. The national audience is therefore less a homogenous mass than a collection of dozens or hundreds of sub-audiences. Advertisers put enormous efforts into defining these audiences, as well as into trying to predict their "tuning behaviour" – what viewers tune into, when and for how long, and why they make the choices they do. A lot of advertising dollars ride on the broadcaster's ability to find the right target audience for programs.

Although over-the-air local television is "free," the majority of Canadians – 2 out of 3 households – subscribe to CABLE TELEVISION. Subscribing to cable is not expensive, but it remains beyond the reach of many families on low incomes. Even so-called free television means an outlay of several hundred dollars for a set, not to mention options or peripheral devices such as a videocassette recorder.

Geography has a major influence on what is available to Canadian audiences. The average Canadian can receive some 7.5 English-language channels, including the American networks. Like all averages, this figure conceals great disparities. Residents of Ontario, eg, have 2.5 times more channels available to them than residents of Newfoundland. Those who live in remote communities enjoy nothing like the choices available to residents of major cities, who with cable may receive as many as 30 channels.

Whatever their tastes or options, most viewers regard television as an escapist activity, even if they occasionally tune in to one of Canada's EDUCATIONAL BROADCASTERS – TVOntario, Radio-Québec, ACCESS Alberta, BC's Knowledge Network. But television has other roles to play. For one thing, it's a big business. Advertising revenue in Canadian television amounts to over a billion dollars a year, more than one-seventh of combined media revenues. Viewers tend not to see television programs as commodities, since no direct payment is involved (PAY-TELEVISION still being somewhat exceptional). What the viewers may also not see is that they themselves are the commodity. Commercial broadcasters make programs not to sell to audiences, but to attract audiences so they will be exposed to advertising messages. These audiences are sold to the manufacturers of cars and soap flakes according to formulas based on the type of program, the time of day it will run, the number of exposures, the "demographics" of the typical viewer and so on. But the key factor is sheer tonnage – the more viewers, the more revenue.

In Canada, television has been given yet another role to play by politicians and policymakers – it is an instrument of social policy and nation-building. This role is spelled out in the Broadcasting Act, which requires broadcasters to contribute to goals such as the use of predominantly Canadian creative resources and the promotion of national identity (see BROADCASTING). The policy issues surrounding television hinge on the controversial nature of Canadian content quotas. These quotas effectively set limits on the amount of American programming broadcast by Canadian stations. Nevertheless, English-language viewers spend three-quarters of their viewing time watching American programs. Viewers to French-language television show a similar tendency. Some observers find the control over programming entrusted to the federal regulator, the CRTC, ineffectual, since it has failed to produce the desired results – better Canadian programs and larger audiences for them. The search for consensus on these issues continues to dominate public debate on the uses of television.

In the meantime television itself has been changing. Technically and legally, broadcasting is the propagation of an electromagnetic signal over the airwaves for reception by the general public; ie, anyone within the broadcaster's coverage area equipped with a TV set. At the same time, its "broad" appeal, being able to reach large audiences by programming to mass tastes, has been made possible by affiliation agreements between local stations and national or regional networks: TVA in Québec, CBC and CTV nationally, along with looser arrangements among independent stations. This gives the networks and their advertisers wide exposure, while allowing local stations to pull in audiences with glossy programs like soap operas that would be too expensive for them to produce on their own.

Both the local nature of television and the dominance of the established networks began to diminish with the advent of cable. Cable began as a purely technical solution to a technical problem: how to improve reception of a few local or regional stations. Like many communications technologies in which Canadians have taken the lead, however, cable has had wide-ranging effects, especially since the period of rapid growth in cable penetration through the 1970s. The 2 out of 3 Canadians who now subscribe to cable have a different viewing profile from those who do not. They watch more television in general and more American television in particular. Such tendencies are more pronounced in the larger urban markets where cable penetration tends to run far above the national average, as high as 80% or 90% of households. This means that few Canadians living in large centres now receive even local television signals over the air, but rather pay their cable operator to have local and other stations brought into their homes through a coaxial drop wire. Television delivered in this manner is thus neither broadcast nor free. This evolution has produced even more noticeable changes in the quantity and nature of program services. Beginning in the early 1980s, Canadian cable subscribers could for the first time purchase pay-television and specialty services like the sports or movie channels. At first, the sheer number of signals available caused audiences and revenues to fragment. Secondly, suppliers of programming that concentrates on one subject area, such as sports, or one ethnic group, such as Hispanics, are not in the business of appealing to viewers who dislike sports or do not speak Spanish. Although few such services have become profitable, they are part of a trend to sell consumer goods by targeting small but carefully defined demographic groups.

Broadcasting is fiercely competitive and these developments are not without casualties. The many signals made newly available over cable, whether conventional stations or satellite services, have taken their toll on the major American networks, whose viewing shares declined from 76% to 64% over the first half of the 1980s. The proliferation of signals available to Canadians prompted an even more dramatic decline in the viewing hours devoted to CBC's English television network, which fell from almost 35% in 1967 to under 20% by the mid-1970s.

Although few observers are predicting the ultimate demise of network television, competition and fragmentation continue unabated, even at the level of the TV set itself. Not only do viewers have a lot more channels to choose from, but they are also able to roam through these choices with the greatest of ease, thanks to the remote control channel changer. In combination with the videocassette recorder (VCR), which is in more than half of all television households, viewers can indulge in changing channels or advancing a recorded program to avoid commercials. This phenomenon has prompted advertisers to adopt radically new commercial strategies.

Just as there is likely to be a continuing role for the conventional networks, so too local television continues to serve viewer needs. But the introduction of communications satellites gave birth to the "superstation," a local off-air signal which is fed to cable operators far beyond the station's natural coverage area. This enables small-town Saskatchewan to watch its favourite entertainment programs, and even the supper-hour news, on the "local" Detroit stations. Opinions are divided as to whether satellite television's insensitivity to distance will reduce barriers between social groups or instead will promote the collapse of a sense of community and, ultimately, of a sense of nationhood.

The ability of American television to reach beyond its own borders has taken on global proportions. The stories told on American television have a seductive appeal; they also have production values and budgets that sweep away foreign competition, since more than $1 million is typically spent on producing a single, hour-long series episode. Canadians have long been familiar with the lure of American television and the dilemmas this poses for nurturing our own national culture. The same problem has extended to some of the other Western democracies, where worried public broadcasters and policymakers have dubbed the American cultural invasion via television the "Canadian" problem. In 1986, Canadians spent 64.1% of their viewing time watching foreign programs.

Because of escalating costs, even indigenous program production in Canada and elsewhere is often forced to assume the look and values of its Hollywood counterparts in order to sell successfully on the international market, let alone in the US. From one perspective, increased production activity means more jobs, more talent development, a wider window on the world. To the viewers, such issues may be largely irrelevant, as long as content quotas and other public policies do not constrain freedom of choice. Nevertheless, the very conditions that have allowed unprecedented access to American and world television may in the long run mean that Canadian viewers will see their television choices diminished rather than enhanced.   DAVID ELLIS

Reading: Minister of Supply and Services Canada, *Report of the Task Force on Broadcasting Policy* (1986); M. Wolfe, *Jolts: The TV Wasteland and the Canadian Oasis* (1985); J. Meyrowitz, *No Sense of Place: The Impact of Electronic Media on Social Behavior* (1985).

Television Drama, English-Language, is fictional narrative material ranging from short illustrative sketches to original, full-length scripts. The term covers various forms, though situation comedies, mysteries, soap operas, serials, miniseries, family adventures, revues, docudramas and topical dramas are most popular. Throughout the history of Canadian television drama, the anthology has survived. Under titles such as "Folio," "Festival," "First Performance," "Q for Quest," "To See Ourselves" and "For the Record," self-contained teleplays revealed a mixture of experiment, sentiment, history, comedy, tragedy and adaptations of the best of foreign and domestic, classic and contemporary storytelling. Since 1952 Toronto and Montréal have been the major national production centres for drama, with Vancouver, Winnipeg, Halifax and St John's producing fine regional drama during some periods.

Kinescopes (8 mm films made from the image on a monitor) were made of early live productions and shipped to remote locations for transmission. When recordings on reusable videotape replaced kinescopes, fewer copies were made and those were sometimes erased for reuse. Nevertheless, scattered collections of drama scripts, kinescopes and tapes from the CANADIAN BROADCASTING CORPORATION's first 4 decades of television have survived.

The CTV network, established in 1961, has bought from independent Canadian producers only a handful of situation comedies and police and animal shows. These programs were indistinguishable from their American prototypes despite the conditions attached to the licence by the Board of Broadcast Governors and its successor, the CANADIAN RADIO-TELEVISION AND TELECOMMUNICATIONS COMMISSION. Up to 1988 the history of Canadian TV drama has been primarily a history of CBC drama or CBC collaborations with independent producers.

During the past 35 years, many of the forms of

TV drama have become more complex while others, like the Western, simply disappeared. The CBC has both created distinctive variants on many familiar forms and pioneered others: eg, from 1959 to 1967 "Cariboo Country" was a completely distinctive contemporary Western; "Wojeck," 1967-69, was innovative in both visual style and content. Over the years a daily ration of TV drama has become a habit for most people. Yet in 1982 only 3% of TV drama shown in Canada was Canadian in origin. However, well over one million Canadians will watch a particular CBC drama special.

A variety of broadcasting Acts have evolved a mandate for the CBC to meet the changing needs of the country and the rapidly changing technology. In the 1980s the CBC was expected to educate, inform and entertain people of different ages, interests and tastes; to present a balance of views on controversial issues over the whole range of TELEVISION PROGRAMMING; to serve as a patron of the arts; and to promote Canadian unity, provide for continuing expression of regional diversity, and reflect the Canadian identity. CBC drama has responded with fictional characters as diverse as Charlie Farquharson, Bob and Doug McKenzie, Ada, Nick Adonidas and Relic, "The King" of Kensington, Wojeck, Maria, Louie Ciccone, Ol' Antoine and others in "Cariboo Country," Katie, and real-life folk heroes such as Sir John A. MACDONALD, Norman BETHUNE, Louis RIEL, Emily CARR, Stephen LEACOCK and Emily MURPHY.

At its worst, Canadian TV drama is derivative, bland, sometimes incoherent, and self-indulgent – ranging from "Radisson" (an inept riposte to the Davy Crockett phenomenon of the 1950s) to plays which reinforce society's unthinking stereotypes. The CBC has never developed a consistent focus on unions, small towns or the political process at the municipal or provincial levels. However, TV is a 2-way mirror reflecting its audience, and audience attitudes have changed in 4 decades. As always, TV drama can stimulate discussion about controversial issues or it can widen an audience's perceptions through innovative and imaginative scripts in the hands of talented producers, directors and actors. "Flight into Danger" thrilled its audience; "The Open Grave," a "direct cinema" version of the Resurrection, raised questions in Parliament; and the musical "Anne of Green Gables" went on to become a stage hit then returned to television in a new independently produced version with the largest audience for drama ever recorded. "Tar Sands" provoked Prem LOUGHEED of Alberta into a successful lawsuit.

In the mid-1950s and 1960s there were few Canadian playwrights and fewer stage companies. CBC TV drama took over from CBC radio as our national theatre, providing training and work for actors, designers, producers, directors, technicians and composers. Zoom lenses, more mobile cameras and sound equipment, videotape and the introduction of colour freed some kinds of drama from the confines of studios. Live television drama disappeared. Yet from the very beginning, the limitations of the technology and the dramatic conventions were transformed into art, a very few examples being "Ward Number Six" (1959), "Kim" (1963), "Pale Horse, Pale Rider" (1964), "The Freedom of the City" (1975) and "Blind Faith" (1980). When taste shifted from anthology drama to series drama which focuses on one set of characters, the CBC produced "Wojeck," the forerunner of topical series drama; "Quentin Durgens MP"; and later, when teams of characters or families became popular, "The Manipulators," "The Beachcombers," "The Collaborators," "Sidestreet," "A Gift to Last" and "Home Fires." In the 1980s "Seeing Things" and

"Hangin' In" continued the pattern of blurring television genres with swiftly changing tones and a wide variety of topical issues.

Characteristics which have distinguished the best of Canadian TV drama are a tolerance of moral ambivalence, open-ended narrative structures, a willingness to experiment with the medium itself and an ironic vision of authoritarian values. When Canadian series function well they retain many of the characteristics of anthology drama. From the early days, distinctively Canadian TV dramas have been sold in large numbers all over the world. The CBC has also shown some of the best of contemporary Canadian theatre, adapted with varying success for television: "Ten Lost Years," "The Farm Show," "On the Job," "Paper Wheat," "Leaving Home," "Les Belles Soeurs," "La Sagouine," "Billy Bishop Goes to War," as well as adaptations of the finest international and classical drama.

Television drama performs many functions. We stay in touch with one another by caring about the PLOUFFES or the Sturgesses, by arguing about Riel or laughing at "The King." We tell our children stories about themselves through an excellent children's TV service. We educate ourselves about issues, recapture history, debunk old myths and create new ones.   MARY JANE MILLER

Reading: Canadian Drama 9 (Spring 1983), an issue directed to articles on Canadian radio and TV drama; M.J. Miller, "Canadian Television Drama, 1952-1970," *Theatre History Journal* 5 (Spring 1984) and *Turn Up the Contrast: CBC Television Drama Since 1952* (1987).

Television Drama, French-Language Television has greatly enriched Québec drama. Since 1952, writers and actors originally drawn to RADIO DRAMA have helped produce a body of television drama which, after 30 years, has reached impressive proportions: more than 800 television plays, 80 televised novels, 100 works of children's drama and, since 1980, a growing number of miniseries. The most prestigious form of televison drama is televised theatre, most of it produced by Radio-Canada (more precisely, by CBFT in Montréal). The first evening that Radio-Canada was on the air, 6 Sept 1952, the station broadcast Cocteau's *Oedipe-Roi*. Between 1952 and 1958 television theatre had pride of place in Radio-Canada's programming. In those days of live broadcasting, and despite the difficulties and costs involved, CBFT offered one or even 2 plays a week, peaking in 1958 with almost 100 hours of televised theatre. Production then declined and from 1965 to 1983 averaged about 20 hours a year, or one play each month.

At first both classic and contemporary plays were selected, running 30-120 minutes. Novels and short stories were then adapted, followed by texts written specifically for the small screen. Be-

Members of the cast of the television series "La Famille Plouffe" (1953-59). Standing: Pierre Valcourt, Jean-Louis Roux, Denise Pelletier, Émile Genest; seated: Amanda Alarie, Paul Guèvremont (*courtesy National Archives of Canada/MISA/CBC Coll/#6949*).

tween 1952 and 1977, 80% of the theatrical works televised were the original work of, or were translated or adapted by, Canadian (especially Québecois) authors. Although foreign plays left their mark on viewers' memories, Québec playwrights made the strongest impression. Marcel DUBÉ, Hubert AQUIN, Françoise Loranger, Pierre Dagenais, Jacques Languirand and Michel TREMBLAY, in particular, provided high-quality television drama and innovated in ways that expanded the televisual vocabulary. Since 1952, plays by more than 150 Québec writers have been produced on television.

Most of Radio-Canada's theatrical presentations have been part of series such as "Théâtre d'été" (1954, 1955, 1958 and 1961), "En Première" (1958-60), "Théâtre du dimanche" (1960-61), "Jeudi Théâtre" (1961-62) and "Théâtre d'une heure" (1963-66). The 2 most important series were "Le Téléthéâtre de Radio-Canada" (which, 1953-66, offered more than 160 works) and "Théâtre populaire" (which, 1956-58, presented more than 100). However, since 1966, television theatre has only appeared as an increasingly rare offering on the program "Les Beaux Dimanches."

Critics have generally applauded the televised plays, but the greatest public acclaim has gone to televised novels. Ever since the 1953 debut of the first Québec serial ("La Famille Plouffe" by Roger LEMELIN), these weekly instalments have known immediate and lasting success. Televised serials, broadcast in 30-minute episodes in peak hours, usually from September to May, generally run 2-3 years. Two, however, have lasted much longer: "Les Belles Histoires des pays d'en haut" (14 years) by Claude-Henri GRIGNON and "Rue des Pignons" (11 years) by Louis Morisset and Mia Riddez.

The first televised serials were usually adapted from novels or radio serials, their success being guaranteed by previous popular acclaim and their quality by the calibre of their authors. In the 1960s original serials were more contemporary in topic and structure, and the majority were serious in tone and in subject.

Until 1965, public television broadcast the most popular series, among them "Quatorze, rue de Galais" (1954-57) by André GIROUX, "Le Survenant" (1954-57, 1959-60) by Germaine GUÈVREMONT, "Cap-aux-sorciers" (1955-58) by Guy Dufresne, "La Pension Velder" (1957-61) by Robert Choquette, "La Côte de sable" and "De 9 à 5" (1960-62, 1963-66) by Marcel Dubé, "Sous le signe du lion" (1961) by Françoise Loranger, and "Septième nord" (1963-67) by Guy Dufresne. Although Télé-Métropole produced a daily serial from 13 Mar to 19 May 1961 ("Ma femme et moi" by Pierre Dagenais), private television only began competing with Radio-Canada with the 1965-70 production of "Cré Basile" (written by Marcel Gamache, starring comedian Olivier Guimond).

The comic nature of "Cré Basile" was a turning point for television drama, and Télé-Métropole went on to schedule burlesques ("Lecoq et fils," "Symphorien," "Les Brillant") and situation comedies ("Chère Isabelle," "Dominique," "Peau de banane"). Radio-Canada (through CBFT) met the competition after 1966 with comedy series ("Moi et l'autre," "La P'tite Semaine," "Du tac au tac," "Jamais deux sans toi," "Poivre et sel") or, at least, with lighter productions than those of the early 1960s. Thereafter, Radio-Canada and Télé-Métropole competed fiercely for audience favour. When the private network produced its celebrated "Berger" series in 1970, competition moved to the level of family "sagas" as well. The public could enjoy "Rue des Pignons," "Grand-papa," "Terre humaine" or

"Le Temps d'une paix" on Radio-Canada, and "Les Berger," "Le Clan Beaulieu," "Marisol" or "Les Moineaux et les pinsons" on Télé-Métropole. Finally, after 1980, Radio-Québec produced the occasional serial.

Television serials, whether humorous or dramatic, historical or contemporary, are strongly and specifically Québecois, despite the inevitable influence of American and European series. Their success has not been limited to French Canada: several series ("Quelle famille!," "La P'tite Semaine," "Le Temps d'une paix") have been sold abroad.

Since 1952, children's drama has kept a young public glued to the screen. Also, in the early 1980s several miniseries, "Les Plouffes," "Duplessis" and "Bonheur d'occasion," proved very popular.

CHRISTINE EDDIE

Television Programming Television must provide information and entertainment suited to the tastes and needs of a very large public. This cultural fact dictates that television programming will come in many different forms: newscasts and news magazines or documentaries, talk shows, sports broadcasts, games and quizzes, variety shows, children's programs, as well as a range of dramatic entertainment. The same fact helps to explain why this programming appears repetitive, even hackneyed, for familiarity breeds popularity; why it is expensive, since success requires stars and high production values; and why it commonly employs the format of storytelling, because no other mode of explanation or diversion is so universally accepted.

What has been called the golden age of Canadian programming occurred during the first decade of television (1952-62), when the publicly owned CANADIAN BROADCASTING CORPORATION enjoyed a monopoly of network broadcasting. The CBC organized separate French- and English-language networks (which reached over 85% of Canadian homes by 1962), beginning its schedule at first in the evening for family viewing but slowly extending into the afternoon for women, children and teenagers. Producers created a mix of programming, representative of all the major forms of television and derived from their past experience with radio, as well as from lessons learned from British and American initiatives. It proved to be a time of excitement and experiment.

The CBC was determined to inform the public about life and affairs. Regular newscasts commenced in the spring of 1954 on both networks. Much air time was devoted to major, and sometimes controversial, public affairs shows, notably "Point de mire" (1956-59) hosted by René LÉVESQUE and "Close-Up" (1957-63) produced by Ross McLean. There were talk shows, interview series such as Toronto's popular "Tabloid," specializing in personalities, and sports roundups such as the "Jim Coleman Show."

Even greater effort went into entertainment, reflecting the special importance of television as the main source of mass diversion. Highbrows could enjoy the quiz show "Fighting Words," regular concert hours and, more infrequently, ballets, operas and sophisticated drama. Sports fans were better served with weekend broadcasts of hockey and football – the telecast of National Hockey League games began in 1952. Montréal producers developed a host of games and quizzes with titles like "Le nez de Cléopâtre" and "La clé de champs," although it was their Toronto counterparts who fashioned the long-lasting FRONT PAGE CHALLENGE in the summer of 1957. The English-language service worked hard to foster variety favourites: the comedy team of Johnny Wayne and Frank Shuster (see WAYNE AND SHUSTER), that enduring singing star JULIETTE (Sysak),

and assorted country-music groups such as those led by Gordie Tapp, King Ganam, Tommy Common, Tommy HUNTER and Don MESSER. Both networks boasted a number of dramatic anthologies – "Téléthéâtre," "General Motors Presents," "En Première" and "Festival" – which specialized in original plays. Only Radio-Canada, the French-language network, succeeded in the realm of popular drama with a series of téléromans such as "La Famille Plouffe," "La Pension Velder" and "Marie Didace," each drawing upon the history and culture of Québec (see TELEVISION DRAMA, FRENCH-LANGUAGE).

Many of these programs proved successful. French Canadian television, in particular, won enormous audiences, earning the title of a tribal medium because it seemed to reflect the "soul" of old and new Québec. Yet there were signs of trouble ahead. In the 1950s the CBC was unable to manufacture an appealing brand of popular English Canadian drama, although it tried with "The Plouffe Family" (1954-59), with a prime-time historical adventure series for children called "Radisson" (1957-58), and with a big-budget crime drama entitled "RCMP" (1959-60). To its evening schedule, the network added American situation comedies and action/adventure series such as "I Love Lucy" and "Have Gun, Will Travel." Even Radio-Canada began to air translations of American shows like "The Naked City" (a crime drama) and "The Donna Reed Show" (a situation comedy). Furthermore the CBC soon discovered that imported variety, such as "The Ed Sullivan Show" or "The Perry Como Show," was usually judged more pleasing by English Canadian audiences than the homegrown equivalent. In competitive markets such as Toronto and Vancouver, where viewers could easily pick up American stations, the CBC lost large chunks of its audience at peak times when Canadian shows were aired. Indeed, across the country, public pressure had increased for greater choice, an end to the CBC monopoly, and a more popular style of television entertainment modelled on the American experience.

One myth of the times was that commercial interests would somehow fashion a television service which could act as an agency for made-in-Canada popular culture. Moreover, in 1959, the Board of Broadcast Governors had issued a series of Canadian-content regulations which were supposed to ensure the persistence of indigenous programming. These served to justify the introduction of a new era of competition, which had changed the shape of Canadian television by the mid-1970s. Acting first through the BBG and later through the CANADIAN RADIO-TELEVISION AND TELECOMMUNICATIONS COMMISSION, the state licensed competing stations across the land, authorized the operations of private networks (the English-language Canadian Television Network, or CTV, in 1961, Télé-Diffuseurs Associés or TVA in Québec in 1971 and Global in Ontario in 1974), and allowed the extension of CABLE TELEVISION to over 40% of Canadian households by 1975.

The language and culture of French Canada ensured the survival of local programming in Québec. Yet there were changes. The dramatic anthologies of the 1950s virtually disappeared, because French-language programmers, especially those on the independent station CFTM-Montréal, turned to movies to win peak-time audiences. The amount of American programming did rise, particularly on the non-CBC stations. Yet from the beginning CFTM-Montréal originated variety programs to showcase Québec's comedians and singers. Nor did popular drama suffer. The homegrown situation comedy, Radio-Canada's "Moi et l'autre," running 9:00-9:30 PM on Tuesdays (1966-71), purportedly attracted around 2 million viewers a week in the early 1970s. The private challenger, TVA, had to respond with its own series. And Radio-Canada strove to improve the quality of its information programming by moving the newscast "Télé-journal" to 10:30 PM (1971-72), by adding a popular late-night talk show on Fridays with Lise Payette, entitled "Appelez-moi Lise," and by broadening the scope of its public-affairs and feature programming. A survey of programming 1974-75 showed that Radio-Canada offered a more balanced schedule of quality performances in the realm of drama, music and dance (5%), information (32%) and light entertainment (63%), while TVA was emphatically popular, emphasizing light entertainment (82%) and a limited quantity of information (18%). The rival networks shared almost equally the French Canadian audience.

Events took a very different course in English Canada. The only route to quick popularity open to the newcomers was to schedule as many Hollywood-produced shows during prime-time as could be allowed under what proved to be the very loose regulations about Canadian content. So CTV's evening schedule 1966-67 offered the American favourites "The FBI," "Bewitched," "Dean Martin," "Mission Impossible," "Run for your Life" and "The Jackie Gleason Show." Global's schedule was similarly peppered with imports a decade later. What might seem more puzzling was that the same could be said of the CBC. One explanation was financial: a typical 1974-75 import cost $2000 a half- hour (the actual production cost being roughly $125 000) and yet it could generate a profit of between $20 000 and $24 000 in advertising revenue on the CBC or CTV. Contrast this with domestic production: a half-hour show cost about $30 000 (meaning its production values were inferior to American shows) and realized a profit of $55 on CTV and a loss of $2050 on the CBC. The scheduling of a Canadian show, moreover, usually meant a loss of audiences and revenues in that time slot, since viewers could change channels to find an import that was more appealing. True, the networks did offer variety and game shows where the costs could be kept down. On the CBC, "Front Page Challenge" continued, Tommy Hunter became a regular with his own show and "The Irish Rovers" rose to fame; CTV boasted such imitations as "Headline Hunters," "The Ian Tyson Show" and "Pig & Whistle." CTV actually had a Canadian situation comedy, "Excuse My French" (1974-75), on which it was losing about $14 000 an episode. Both networks offered wide sports coverage. In effect, however, the networks had given up the notion of competing effectively with Hollywood for mass audiences.

Where the CBC and eventually CTV did work hard was in the fields of news and public affairs, genres which capitalized on viewers' interest in their collective or public life. Early on, the CBC aired one smash hit in the field of public affairs, THIS HOUR HAS SEVEN DAYS (1964-66), a news magazine which boasted an eclectic mix of showbiz techniques, hard reporting and interviewing, and much editorializing to win a huge audience of excited viewers. "Seven Days" was a highly dramatic show, a collection of sensational stories, which sparked too much controversy to survive on an increasingly cautious network. This said, the network did carry excellent documentaries, did offer a range of features and public-affairs shows like "Telescope," "Man Alive," "Take 30," and "the fifth estate," and did improve "The National," its nightly newscast. Though less active, CTV aired an equivalent national newscast, a major news magazine called "W5," and a news documentary series entitled "Maclear." Indeed the record of

The cast of "Front Page Challenge," CBC, 1962. The show first aired in 1957 and continues. Shown left to right: Gordon Sinclair, Betty Kennedy, Fred Davis and Pierre Berton (*courtesy National Archives of Canada/MISA/CBC Coll/#7692*).

English Canadian television was better than that of its American counterpart.

Competition had brought English Canadians a breathtaking range of choice. The CBC remained the most balanced network, giving viewers a diversity of program types, while CTV and Global were clearly more restricted and popular in their offerings. Cable brought in several American channels. Ratings data showed that the CBC had lost heavily in the competition for viewers amongst English-language channels. By 1984 US stations had captured a third of the audience, CTV slightly under 30% (falling from a higher total in the mid-1970s), the CBC nearly 24%, and other independent Canadian stations 15%. Put another way, some 65% of the programs people viewed on English-language television were foreign (and overwhelmingly American) in origin. This figure has remained constant.

This situation has provoked a series of agonizing reappraisals of the whole television scene. Even so, the situation has not changed dramatically since the mid-1970s, except perhaps to worsen. News, public affairs, sports and, in Québec, the téléromans remain the best and most popular forms of Canadian television. In English Canada, the CBC attempted to bring about a renaissance, increasing the amount of Canadian content in prime time and returning to the field of light entertainment. This resulted in the highly successful family program "The Beachcombers," a hit situation comedy "The King of Kensington," an assortment of variety specials, the serial "Home Fires," and above all "The National/Journal," a combination of news and views on weekdays from 10:00 to 11:00 PM. The private networks did not follow the CBC's lead, perhaps because competition raised the costs of acquiring foreign programs and threatened their profit margins. The CRTC's efforts to coerce more Canadian drama out of the CTV, and by implication out of all private stations, have been fiercely resisted. The government's plans to foster more Canadian production through the licensing of PAY TELEVISION, a willingness to subsidize independent producers, and the revamping of Canadian content regulations have not yet borne fruit.

Everywhere in Canada, American imports and stations have retained their importance. The audience share of the most Canadian network, the CBC and Radio-Canada, has fallen from roughly a half of the national audience in 1967 to stabilize just above a quarter in the 1980s. Statistics show that even the viewers of French-language television watch a lot of dubbed Hollywood drama (up to 80% of all drama viewed in 1984 was foreign produced), which has raised fears that

Québec will fall victim to the same ills that afflict English Canada. Hollywood movies, prime-time soap operas such as "Dallas," children's shows such as "The Wonderful World of Disney" and situation comedies such as "The Cosby Show," typically dominate the rankings. Although Canada has built one of the most sophisticated television systems in the world, the irony still remains that it has not been able to fill that system with the products of its own culture. *See also* BROADCASTING, RADIO AND TELEVISION; COMMUNICATIONS IN THE NORTH; COMMUNICATIONS IN QUÉBEC; MUSIC BROADCASTING.   PAUL RUTHERFORD

Reading: A. Barris, *Front Page Challenge* (1981) and *The Pierce-Arrow Showroom Is Leaking: An Insider's View of the CBC* (1969); H. Hardin, *Closed Circuit: The Sellout of Canadian Television* (1985); P. Hindley, G. Martin and J. McNulty, *The Tangled Net: Basic Issues in Canadian Communications* (1977); *Report of the Task Force on Broadcasting Policy* (1986); P. Trueman, *Smoke & Mirrors: The Inside Story of Television News in Canada* (1980); M. Wolfe, *Jolts: The TV Wasteland and the Canadian Oasis* (1985).

Telidon, a combination of the Greek words meaning "to know at a distance," is a relatively new form of technology, developed by researchers in the federal Department of COMMUNICATIONS in Ottawa in the mid-1970s. This technology combines aspects of television, the TELEPHONE and the computer to produce a new medium of communication and information processing. From television comes the ability to display letters and images on a screen; from the telephone, the ability to communicate over a distance; from the computer, the ability to manipulate, store and retrieve information quickly and inexpensively. The federal government hoped that this combination of capabilities into a new medium of communication would stimulate the development of high-technology industries and help Canada take a position of leadership in the developing field of information technology.

There are 3 major ways to implement Telidon systems: videotex, teletext and as stand-alone systems; and there are significant differences in the capabilities of the resultant systems.

Videotex systems allow the user to receive information from and send information back to a computer located in a different place. These systems may use telephone lines, coaxial cable, optical fibre, laser or radio-communication links to connect the user to the computer. The 2-way capability enables users to exchange messages and perform such interactive tasks as information retrieval, banking and shopping. The Grassroots system, for example, provides agricultural information and services to farmers and ranchers in Manitoba.

Teletext systems are not interactive in the same way as videotex systems. The information is broadcast in the unused portion of a regular television signal called the "vertical blanking interval" and is decoded by a device attached to the television set. Teletext is a one-way system that neither requires nor permits communication from the user back to the computer. The information to be displayed is simply cycled again and again. Most teletext systems display a menu or index page on the screen when the decoder is first turned on. The user decides which topic is of interest and enters the number on a keypad attached to the unit. When the page the user wants comes around, the "frame grabber" on top of the TV set "grabs" it, stores it in its memory, decodes and displays it on the screen until the user requests the next frame. A major limitation is the amount of information – the number of "pages" or "frames" – that can be kept cycling around.

Stand-alone systems differ from videotex and teletext systems mostly in the way they connect the computer with the user. Because these units may have everything combined into a single box, they are sometimes called "electronic slide projectors." They can be programmed to run a fixed cycle, or may be connected to keypads or other kinds of input devices that allow the user to select the desired pages or to use various "action pages" that have a wide range of response possibilities.

The Telidon Coding System In addition to the hardware items already mentioned – the television set, the telecommunications link, the computer – a decoder is required to accept the coded instruction from the computer and generate an electronic signal that creates the display on the screen. The heart of any Telidon system is the Picture Description Instruction – the special code that instructs the decoder what to draw on the display screen. The coding scheme, known as the North American Presentation Level Protocol Syntax (NAPLPS), is now the N American standard. It uses a system whereby different kinds of geometric shapes – lines, points, arcs, polygons – are specified in concise form. In this "alpha-geometric method," images may be created and manipulated with comparative ease; only a small amount of information is required to specify an image; and the quality of the final image is dependent mainly on the ability of the display device to resolve fine detail.

Telidon/NAPLPS was designed to be resistant to technological change. The success of the designers in this respect is becoming increasingly evident.

Service Development Initially, it was believed that videotex and teletext systems would find consumer acceptance in Canada and the US. However, this has not proven to be the case and all the applications of Telidon/NAPLPS now in place are for business or educational purposes. Some examples of services available in Canada are Marketfax – a stock market information service; Grassroots, an agricultural information service; and TABS, an information system for pilots. In Canada, Infomart of Toronto, among many others, was prominent in attempting to develop videotex services. While Infomart achieved some success with services such as Grassroots, they did not achieve success in penetrating the consumer market and have now turned their attention to other aspects of electronic publishing.

Despite the difficulties experienced with videotex start-ups, many companies still remain interested in this topic. This includes such well-known companies as IBM, Sears, AT & T and J.C. Penney, all of whom are rumoured to be planning the introduction of videotex services or products over the next few years. The latest entry into the Telidon/NAPLPS videotex market in Canada is Bell Canada, which is hoping to emulate the success of the French Minitel service.

Industry Development When Telidon was first announced in 1978, videotex activity in Europe was already gaining momentum and predictions about videotex services becoming almost a necessity in every home within a few years were rampant. France and the UK were particularly active and were marketing their brands. In response, a Canadian Videotex Consultative Committee (CVCC) was established to advise the government on actions to be taken. By March 1985 the government had spent approximately $55 million and industry had invested approximately $200 million in the development of videotex products and services. Canada, therefore, has developed a small videotex industry which is capable of responding to the demand for videotex products and services in Canada and is capable of supplying a small export market. While this industry faces increasing competition from abroad, there is hope that it will strengthen its position if

videotex and teletext services show strong development in Canada.

The inventors of Telidon received several awards for the important contribution they made to the development of information technology in Canada. Herb Bown received the Order of Canada and the gold medal for engineering excellence from the Assn of Professional Engineers of Ontario. The Touche Ross New Perspectives Award was awarded to Herb Bown and Doug O'Brien. *See also* COMPUTER COMMUNICATIONS; INFORMATION SOCIETY; OFFICE AUTOMATION.

WILLIAM RICHARDS AND ROY MARSH

Reading: D. Godfrey and D. Parkhill, eds, *Gutenberg Two* (1979); Godfrey and E. Chang, eds, *The Telidon Book* (1983).

Temagami, Ont, Town, pop 1137 (1986c), 1224 (1981c), inc 1968, located on NE arm of Lk Temagami, 100 km N of North Bay. Temagami originated in the 1890s as a tourist centre, when campers from southern Ontario first discovered the natural beauty of the area, celebrated in a well-known poem by Archibald LAMPMAN. It had previously been an Indian settlement dependent on fur trading. With building of the Temiskaming and Northern Ontario Ry, 1903-09 (later ONTARIO NORTHLAND), a trickle of summer visitors became a flood. One of them was Archie BELANEY, better known as "Grey Owl," who lived in Temagami 1906-10. For most of this century tourism has been the town's raison d'être, with periodic developments in lumbering and iron mining since the 1920s.

MATT BRAY

Témiscaming, Qué, Town, pop 2071 (1986c), 2097 (1981c), is located at the southern end of Lac Témiscamingue (spelled TIMISKAMING in Ont) near the rapids that link the lake with the Ottawa R. It was established in 1917 by the Riordon Pulp and Paper Co, which built it to house the employees of its Kipawa Mills paper mill. Since 1896, the hamlet of South Témiscaming had been the CPR terminal for the area and the steamship port for goods destined for the new communities to the N of Lac Témiscamingue. The name is derived from an Algonquin expression meaning "deep water," a reference to the lake. Témiscaming was for many years a COMPANY TOWN. Originally owned by the Riordan Co (1917-25), it was then directly administered by the Canadian International Paper Co until the end of the 1960s. CIP had bought the town as well as the Kipawa Mills plant. Témiscaming's economy is still based on its paper mill, which is now owned by Tembec, a Québec crown corporation.

BENOÎT-BEAUDRY GOURD

Temperance Movement, a movement to control alcohol consumption, arising early in the 19th century, when social aid was negligible and when a majority of Canadians were self-employed as farmers, fishermen or small businessmen. From the belief that self-discipline was essential to economic success and that alcohol was an obstacle to self-discipline followed the decision to be temperate in the use of alcohol or to abstain entirely. Many concluded that the urban poverty developing with the growth of cities in the mid-19th century was caused by drink. Accordingly, there was a shift of emphasis from temperance as an individual decision to legal PROHIBITION as a social one. Religious belief and concern about crime were secondary incentives, though

disorders arising from drinking among railway construction workers in the Prairie West provided a powerful motive.

By 1900 prohibitionists also argued that prohibition would force European immigrants to conform to what the prohibitionists perceived to be Canadian standards of behaviour.

The first temperance societies in Canada appeared about 1827 in Pictou County, NS, and Montréal. These tolerated moderate use of beer and wine, an attitude which was to persist in Québec but soon gave way elsewhere to abstinence or prohibition of all alcoholic beverages. Despite the shift from temperance to prohibition, temperance, abstinence and prohibition groups were all commonly called temperance groups. About 1848 the Sons of Temperance lodge, a fraternal and prohibitionist society modelled on the Odd Fellows, reached Canada from the US. Other such lodges were the Royal Templars of Temperance and the International Order of Good Templars. Though popular for many years, the temperance lodges declined sharply after 1890. The most important temperance society for women was the WOMAN'S CHRISTIAN TEMPERANCE UNION, an American movement whose Canadian counterpart was founded 1874 by Letitia YOUMANS of Picton, Ont, as one of the few organizations through which women could play a political role. In 1875 the hundreds of societies, lodges and church groups committed to prohibition convened at Montréal to form a federation named the Dominion Prohibitory Council. Renamed in 1876 the Dominion Alliance for the Total Suppression of the Liquor Traffic, it became the major organizing force for prohibition campaigns. A decisive figure for much of its history was its secretary, Francis Stephens Spence of Toronto. The predominantly English and Protestant Dominion Alliance discouraged francophone and Catholic participation. Furthermore, Catholics, particularly francophone Catholics, regarded prohibition as an extreme measure. When La Ligue anti-alcoolique was formed 1906 as a counterpart of the Dominion Alliance, it supported legal restriction of the liquor trade, but not full prohibition.

Jurisdiction over the trade was shared by governments, since the provinces could prohibit retail sale, whereas the federal government could prohibit the manufacture of alcohol and retail, wholesale and interprovincial trade. However, neither level was enthusiastic about prohibition, since it would cause losses of tax revenue and party support. Both often put forward compromise legislation known as local option, eg, the Canada Temperance Act of 1878, which gave local governments the right to prohibit by popular vote the retail sale of alcohol (*see* RUSSELL CASE). The referendum was also frequently used as a delaying tactic or to shift responsibility for legislation from governments to voters. A side effect was to give prohibitionists political experience, through organizing local-option and referendum campaigns, which led to a major success when in 1900 the PEI government prohibited the retail sale of alcohol.

When WWI broke out, the movement was close to its peak. Alcohol consumption, though beginning to rise after a half century of decline, was relatively low; organization and funding for the movement were substantial; and local option was widely accepted. Finally the Dominion Alliance campaigned for prohibition as a patriotic measure. Such an appeal made further opposition almost impossible; in 1915 and 1916 all provinces but Québec prohibited retail sale of alcohol. Québec prohibited retail sale of distilled liquor in 1919, but only briefly. Prohibition was short-lived. Though the federal government prohibited the manufacture, importation and sale of alcohol by orders-in-council in 1918, these expired shortly after the war. Most provincial legislation was abandoned during the 1920s in favour of government sale. PEI followed in 1948. Meanwhile, Canadian liquor interests found a large, illegal market in the US, which was under prohibition until 1933. There has been a substantial Canadian presence in that market ever since. The assertion that prohibition was ended because it failed is unconvincing. The laws were in effect so briefly and were so inconsistently enforced that their effectiveness must remain a question. As to the claim that prohibition encouraged drinking, the steady rise of alcohol consumption under conditions of legal sale must raise further questions. More likely, changes in Canadian society and within the movement doomed prohibition.

Those self-employed Canadians who saw temperance as an aid to economic success were a diminishing proportion of the population, displaced by urban workers to whom self-betterment seemed a remote possibility. Hence the decline of the prohibition vote in the 1920s. Within the movement, prohibitionism had provided an opportunity for close study of urban problems, leading many to conclude that those problems had more to do with the political and economic system than with alcohol. Many left the movement for other forms of activism. It had been thought that the extension of the franchise to women would sustain prohibition, since it was commonly believed that women were sympathetic to it. However, referenda of the 1920s, in which women had the vote, showed a consistent decline of support. The temperance movement was the creature of a society that was already fading when its prohibition victories were won. However, as a means by which Canadians came to grips with social problems and formulated responses, the movement was valuable.

GRAEME DECARIE

Reading: M.G. Decarie, "Something Old, Something New," in Donald Swainson, ed, *Oliver Mowat's Ontario* (1972); *The Facts of the Case: a summary of the most important evidence and argument presented in the Report of the Royal Commission on the Liquor Traffic* (1973); James H. Gray, *Booze* (1972); R.E. Spence, *Prohibition in Canada* (1919).

Temple, Sir Thomas, governor of Nova Scotia (b at Stowe, Eng Jan 1615; d at Ealing, Eng 27 Mar 1674). One of 3 partners obtaining rights of trade and government in NS following the English conquest of 1654, Temple emerged as sole governor by 1662 but was forced to restore the colony to France in 1670. JOHN G. REID

Templeton, Charles Bradley, evangelist, journalist, broadcaster, editor, author (b at Toronto 7 Oct 1915). Templeton began a career in journalism as a sports cartoonist. In 1936 he turned to religion but, although he became a renowned evangelist, introducing the "Youth for Christ" movement to Canada in 1945 and then to Europe and Japan, he later became an agnostic. He achieved new prominence as senior editor of the *Toronto Star* and *Maclean's* and news public-affairs director of CTV, and contender for leadership of the Ontario Liberal Party in 1964. His nonfictional *Jesus* (1971) and 2 thrillers, *The Kidnapping of the President* (1974) and *Act of God* (1977) were best-sellers. Two later novels, *The Third Temptation* (1980) which foreshadows the American TV-evangelist scandals of 1987 and *The Queen's Secret* (1986) which speculates on the implications of the actual break-in of an intruder in Buckingham Palace, were less successful but equally fascinating. His autobiography, *Charles Templeton: An Anecdotal Memoir* (1983), is a self-portrait of a multifaceted personality.

GERALD J. RUBIO

Tenant League, popular name for the Tenant Union of Prince Edward Island, a militant agrarian movement fd 19 May 1864 in Charlottetown, PEI. The organization opposed payment of rent by tenant farmers and advocated sale of lands by estate owners to the farmers in actual occupation (*see* LAND QUESTION, PEI). Members who were tenants were pledged to pay no further rent, and all members were expected to support tenants who refused payment, even in open defiance of law officers. Crowds of members and supporters numbering as many as 200, alerted by the blowing of tin trumpets, would surround and harass a sheriff and his assistants, with the result that by mid-1865 the authorities found it impossible to enforce the law between landlord and tenant by ordinary means, particularly in Queens County. The Conservative government of James Colledge POPE summoned troops from Halifax in August, and in the autumn used them to assist the sheriff in 2 lengthy forays into the countryside. The tenant organization seemed to collapse in the face of this pressure, and by mid-1866 it was apparently defunct. Nonetheless, pro-Tenant Union sentiment remained alive, and several Liberals openly sympathetic to the movement were elected to the legislature in 1866 and 1867. The disorders of 1865 marked a crucial turning point in undermining the leasehold system of land tenure in PEI, and the use of troops against the tenantry was a major factor in the defeat of the Conservative government on 26 Feb 1867.

IAN ROSS ROBERTSON

Tennant, Veronica, ballet dancer (b at London, Eng 15 Jan 1947). As ballerina with the NATIONAL BALLET OF CANADA, she has achieved international recognition for her dramatic intensity and superb technique. Trained at the NATIONAL BALLET SCHOOL, she made her debut with the company as principal in 1965, dancing Juliet in John Cranko's *Romeo and Juliet*. Leading roles in *The Nutcracker* and *Swan Lake* during her second season marked an unusually rapid establishment in the top rank of the company. Since then she has performed in a wide range of ballets and has been partnered by most of the world's great male dancers, including Nureyev, Baryshnikov, Dowell and Schaufuss. She has also appeared internationally as a guest artist and in the Emmy-award-winning CBC productions of "Cinderella" (1968) and "Sleeping Beauty" (1972). Tennant is the author of a children's book, *On Stage, Please* (1977). In 1987 she

Veronica Tennant in the National Ballet of Canada production of *Onegin* (*courtesy National Ballet of Canada/photo by Barry Gray*).

The 1892 Port Sandfield lawn tennis champions, Muskoka Lakes, Ont (*courtesy National Archives of Canada/PA-68320/F.W. Micklethwaite*).

played lead role of Hanna in the National Ballet's production of *Merry Widow*. In Sept 1987 she received the Toronto Arts Award (performing arts). She is an Officer of the Order of Canada.

JILLIAN M. OFFICER

Tennis Lawn tennis is a game played on a rectangular court (23.7 m long and 8.2 m wide for singles play, divided into equal halves by a net 0.914 m high at the centre and 1.07 m high at the posts) by 2 players (or 4 in doubles) whose objective is to hit the cloth-covered rubber ball with their racquets into their opponent's side of the court so that it cannot be returned. Top-class players demonstrate superb fitness and psychomotor skills; the action may be rapid and heated or fluidly graceful. Matches usually last one to 2 hours but often continue for longer; one Canadian Davis Cup match was contested for more than 6 hours. Emotions are intense in such contests, and successful players must demonstrate exceptional concentration and mental control.

Modern tennis almost certainly originated in France in the 11th century as a form of handball called *le jeu de paume*. The game, also called "court tennis" or "real tennis," was played on an indoor court – originally in a monastery – with a ball, and by 1500 a racquet was introduced. The word "tennis" likely derived from the French *tenez* – "hold" or "take heed," perhaps called before service. The unusual scoring came from the medieval use of 60 as a base number (as we use 100 today), and the term "love" for zero perhaps came from French *l'oeuf* ("egg," implying "zero") or from English usage, in which love is the equal of nothing ("love or money"). Lawn tennis developed as an outdoor game in England during the mid-19th century. An early popularizer was Major W.C. Wingfield, who devised a set of rules and a court in the shape of an hourglass, with a net 1.5 m high. Wingfield conducted the first game at a garden party in Wales in 1873. In the next few years, the game was improved as the court was made rectangular and the server was moved to the baseline. When the first Wimbledon championship was held in 1877, the game was basically in the form it is played today.

Lawn tennis began to develop and spread in Canada soon after its popularization in England. J.F. Helmuth formed a club in Toronto that is believed to be the forerunner of the Toronto Lawn Tennis Club (fd 1875). The first Canadian tournament was held at the Montreal Cricket Club in 1878 and the first indoor tournament took place in Ottawa in 1881. The 1880s saw clubs formed in

Winnipeg; London, Ottawa, Niagara and Kingston, Ont; Fredericton and Saint John, NB; Halifax, NS; Victoria and Vancouver, BC; Regina, Sask; Lethbridge and Edmonton, Alta (1891). In 1890 the Canadian Lawn Tennis Assn was formed and the first Canadian championships were held in Toronto. Today, in addition to the national governing body (called Tennis Canada since 1977), each province has an autonomous association. Co-operatively the associations organize extensive programs, championships and team competitions for juniors, elite players and seniors. It is estimated that over 2 million people play tennis in Canada, making it the third most popular sport activity after swimming and ice skating.

Since 1968 the annual national championships have been divided into open and closed competitions. The commercially sponsored Canadian Open Men's Championships now have prize money of $525 000 (1987) and the tournament results count towards a larger, year-long international grand prix circuit. Similarly the Women's Open Championships are a segment of the major women's commercially sponsored annual international tour. The revamped Canadian Nationals (closed) also receive commercial sponsorship. Among the lead-up tournaments to the national championships are a variety of commercially sponsored regional tournaments and circuits as well as the various provincial championships.

The Davis Cup international competition for men was first held in 1900; the Federation Cup for women was inaugurated in 1963. The International Lawn Tennis Federation (ILTF, now ITF) was founded in 1913; open competition between amateurs and professionals received ILTF sanction in 1968. Canada entered the worldwide Davis Cup competition for the first time in 1913, losing to the US in the final played at Wimbledon. The team was led by R.B. Powell and included B.P. Schwengers, H.G. Mayers and J.F. Foulkes, with G.H. Meldrum acting as nonplaying team captain. In the years since, Canada has continued to participate in international competitions but has had no major successes; however, the Canadian Women's team reached the quarter finals in 1987. The most successful Canadian player since 1981 has been Carling BASSETT, who was placed 8th in the 1985 Women's Tennis Assn computer ranking. Helen KELESI, who in 1986 ranked 25th, in 1987 became the Canadian Women's Champion. The highest ranking achieved by a Canadian male was 48th, by Glen Michibata in 1986. In 1987, Michibata, Stephane Bonneau, Doug Burke, Martin Wostenholme, Andrew Sznajder, Martin Laurendeau, Grant Connell and Chris Pridham were all ranked in the top 250. The group won or reached the finals of 8 professional tournaments in 1987. The harsh winter climate is often blamed for Canada's lack of success in tennis competition, but fine indoor facilities, good

Davis Cup tennis match between the Canadian and Ecuadorian teams, Edmonton, Aug 1987 (*photo by J.H. Marsh*).

coaching programs and tennis scholarships in the US have brought a promising start.

JOHN J. JACKSON

Tenure, generally, is the holding of a secure position within an educational institution or system, although it can also refer to an individual's length of service in a particular position or system. Usually associated with appointments of university or college faculty members, the granting of tenure by the institution signifies that the individual so classified has an ongoing appointment that may be terminated only through resignation, retirement, or dismissal for good reasons as established by a proper hearing.

University and college professors consider tenure essential because it enables the holder to exercise free but responsible criticism of his institution and all aspects of society without fear of dismissal. Among the more widely publicized tenure cases in Canada has been that of Frank UNDERHILL, a history professor at University of Toronto, whose resignation was demanded by the university's board of governors in 1941 because of his "ill-considered" statements about Canada's changing relationships with Britain and the US. Despite considerable controversy, Underhill remained, signalling to the Canadian academic community and the public that academic tenure continued to be in effect, even in wartime. Despite the strong arguments set forth by academics in defence of a system of tenure, however, it has on occasion offered refuge to those who have ceased to meet the high standards of scholarship expected of them by colleagues and by the public. The effects of such a tenure policy are not likely to be as deleterious in a period when universities and colleges are expanding in number and size (eg, in the 1960s in Canada) as in a period of limited growth or retrenchment (1970s and 1980s). To counter these effects, some people have supported the elimination of tenured positions and the introduction of 3- or 5-year contracts open for free competition, charging that because of the scarcity of academic jobs and the overabundance of qualified candidates, the standards required of new academics have steadily escalated and tenure is denying them the right to compete for jobs on the basis of equality. It should be noted that in times of financial crises in universities and colleges, even tenured academic positions may disappear. *See also* ACADEMIC FREEDOM.   W. BREHAUT

Tepee, *see* TIPI.

Termite, term referring to nearly 2000 species of mostly tropical and subtropical insects generally placed in order Isoptera, but closely related to COCKROACHES (Dictuoptera). Often called "white ants," termites are unrelated to true ANTS. In Canada, 3 native species are known (from BC and western Alberta); another dubiously native species occurs in southern Ontario. The latter and other introduced species may establish themselves indoors. The earliest known termite was discovered recently in 120-million-year-old deposits in England; previously the 100-million-year-old *Cretatermes carpenteri*, from Labrador, held this distinction. Living species resemble these forms. Termites, typically, are pale, and about 5-15 mm long; swollen, egg-laying queens may be much larger. They have short legs and antennae. Reproductive forms have 4 long wings, of similar shape, shed after the nuptial flight. Eyes are reduced or absent. Like other fully social insects, colony members are divisible into castes: reproductive males and females, and sterile workers and soldiers. Unlike ants, wasps and BEES, sterile termites are of either sex, not females alone, and the reproductive female (queen) retains the services of the king. Complexity of social

organization and size of colonies vary among species. Termites are sophisticated architects, having invented effective air conditioning and concrete. Sanitation is perfect; the dead are consumed and excrement recycled for building materials. Some exotic species are excellent fungus gardeners. Their habitations are often shared by other animals, mostly arthropods. Termites feed on cellulosic substances (especially in wood or vegetable fibre products), digested by intestinal micro-organisms – usually bacteria, but protozoa in 2 species. Termites may be divided into categories: drywood termites living in seasoned wood; damp-wood termites living in decaying wood in contact with the ground; mound-building termites, plant-feeders that construct conspicuous "termitaria" on the ground or on trees but are most active beneath soil surface; and "subterranean" termites, humus-feeders, nesting entirely underground. Termites frequently destroy structural and other timber and may damage crops. Canadian species may do significant structural damage.   D.K. McE. KEVAN

Tern, medium-sized bird of the GULL family. Terns are usually grey and white; in spring and summer most species have a black cap. Similar to gulls in appearance, terns differ in having more pointed wings and usually a noticeably forked tail. Terns are more streamlined than gulls and fly more buoyantly. When feeding, most species dive into the water, which gulls rarely do. Approximately 40 tern species occur worldwide, most in the Pacific Ocean. In Canada 12 species occur, 6 as breeders. Of the latter, Caspian, common, roseate and usually arctic terns (*Sterna caspia, S. hirundo, S. dougallii, S. paradisaea*, respectively) nest on grass, sand or small pebble substrates, usually on low-lying islands or peninsulas. Nests usually consist of a small scrape or depression in the ground. Black and Forster's terns (*Chlidonias niger, S. forsteri*) sometimes build their nests over water, attached to emergent vegetation or a structure in the water. Terns usually lay 2-3 eggs. Their breeding cycle is shorter and their young develop more quickly than those of gulls. In Canada, arctic terns generally nest above TREELINE. They migrate down the eastern N American coast, over to southern Europe, partway down the African coast, and over to southern S America, a round trip of over 16 000 km and one of the longest bird MIGRATIONS.   D.V. WESELOH

The arctic tern (*Sterna paradisaea*) nests above the treeline and migrates to southern S America via Europe and Africa (*photo by G.J. Harris*).

Terra Nova National Park (est 1957, 396 km²), Canada's most easterly national park, is located on BONAVISTA BAY, Nfld. The park's rocky headlands, drumlins, till deposits and numerous ponds show the influence of glacial activity on the landscape. Island-sprinkled bays and deep fjords indent the coastline. Inland, the boreal forest, composed mainly of black spruce and balsam fir, is home for native species, including beaver, meadow vole, black bear, otter and lynx, and introduced species such as common shrew, snowshoe hare, mink and moose. Numerous PEAT bogs provide an ideal environment for orchids and pitcher plants, while the rocky shoreline supports colonies of arctic tern, herring gulls and crevice-nesting black guillemots. The park shows evidence of Paleo-Eskimo, DORSET, Maritime Archaic and BEOTHUK cultures; all are now extinct. Lumbering and fishing began in the park area in the late 1700s, after colonization, and evidence of these activities still can be found. LILLIAN STEWART

Terrace, BC, District Municipality, pop 10 532 (1986c), 10 914 (1981c), area 2143 ha, inc 1927, is located at the junction of the SKEENA R and Kalum R, 60 km by road N of Kitimat and 140 km E of Prince Rupert. Because of the protection of the mountains and proximity to the ocean, Terrace enjoys less than half the rainfall of the coast. Its name describes the terraces formed during the ice age as part of the old river banks of the Skeena. It is the largest community in the Regional Dist of Kitimat-Stikine and is governed by a mayor and 6 aldermen. The site was originally the location of a TSIMSHIAN village. The present townsite was laid out by the Grand Trunk Pacific Ry in 1910. Terrace grew from a sawmill town to serve as a distribution and commercial centre during construction of the new town of Kitimat in the 1950s. Its economy today is based on forest industries, although it has diversified as the regional centre of commerce, service and government. Terrace is also an important transshipment point for rail, air and truck freight. Tourism growth has resulted from traffic using the highways to the Yukon, Alaska, Queen Charlotte Is and the "Inside Passage." Local attractions include fishing, hot springs, lava beds, fossil beds and five provincial parks at Kleanza Creek, Lakelse Lake, Red Sand Lake and Exchamsiks River. The local Kermodei bear, a white variety of the North America black bear, is protected by law. ALAN F.J. ARTIBISE

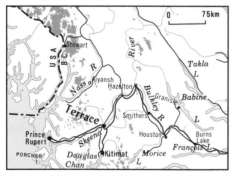

Territorial Evolution The evolution of CANADA as a political entity began with the arrival of French and English colonists at the beginning of the 17th century, and the establishment of the HUDSON'S BAY COMPANY in 1670. By the Treaty of PARIS (1763) all of eastern N America except Saint-Pierre and Miquelon became British. Britain established governments for NOVA SCOTIA (including the present NB and PEI), NEWFOUNDLAND (which included Labrador, Île d'Anticosti, Îles de la Madeleine) and the PROVINCE OF QUEBEC (lower St Lawrence watershed). All other territory was assigned to the Crown or to the HBC. In 1769 St John's Island (PRINCE EDWARD ISLAND) was administratively separated from Nova Scotia, and in 1774 Québec was enlarged to include Île d'Anticosti, Îles de la Madeleine and the land SW between the Ohio and Mississippi rivers. After the US became independent, Québec was confined to the area N of the Great Lakes, and in 1784 NEW

BRUNSWICK was created as a home for LOYALISTS. From 1784 to 1820 CAPE BRETON was also administered as a separate colony. After the US acquired LOUISIANA from France in 1803, it became necessary to determine its boundary with British territory W of the Great Lakes. This was established as essentially the FORTY-NINTH PARALLEL to the Rocky Mts by the CONVENTION OF 1818; the area W of the Rockies was occupied by both Britain and the US. The limits between British territory and Russian Alaska were described in 1825. The area under joint British-American occupation was divided by the OREGON TREATY of 1846. The 1842 ASHBURTON-WEBSTER TREATY settled the NB-Maine boundary, and described the boundary between BNA and the US from Lk Huron to Lake of the Woods. In the far West, the British colonies, Vancouver's I, est 1849, and British Columbia, est 1858, were united in 1866. In 1867, 3 provinces of BRITISH NORTH AMERICA, Canada, Nova Scotia and New Brunswick, were united in CONFEDERATION, the former PROVINCE OF CANADA being divided into Ontario and Québec. In 1870 RUPERT'S LAND and the North-West Territory, purchased 1869-70 by the federal government from the HBC, were officially transferred to Canada, and from them a small province of Manitoba was created to accommodate agricultural colonies established after 1812 (*see* RED RIVER COLONY). In 1871 BC joined the federation, and PEI followed in 1873. In 1876 the District of Keewatin was created from part of the North-West Territories to deal with the administrative problems arising from settlement N of Manitoba. The Territories were enlarged in 1880, when British rights to the arctic islands passed to Canada, but were reduced again when Manitoba, Ontario and Québec were enlarged in 1881, 1889 and 1898. The remainder of the North-West Territories was divided into provisional districts for administrative and postal purposes, beginning with Athabaska, Alberta, Saskatchewan and Assiniboia in 1882, and then Yukon, Mackenzie, Franklin and Ungava in 1895 (in 1898 Yukon District became a separate territory in order to provide proper government for gold seekers moving into the region; *see* KLONDIKE GOLD RUSH). In 1905, as agricultural settlement spread into the Prairies, the provinces of Alberta and Saskatchewan were created. Their expansion north to the 60th parallel gave rise to requests from Manitoba, Ontario and Québec for northern extensions. In 1912 these provinces attained their present limits, and the NWT districts disappeared except for Mackenzie, Keewatin (which had been a disputed territory first governed by Manitoba then in 1912 awarded to Ontario) and Franklin. The final addition of territory came when Newfoundland joined Confederation in 1949 with the area determined by the Imperial Privy Council in 1927. A maritime area of Canada only recently delineated consists of the waters of its arctic archipelago, around which straight baselines were established Sept 1985. Canada claims full sovereignty over all those waters, including the straits of the NORTHWEST PASSAGE. *See* map on page 2133. N.L. NICHOLSON

Reading: Energy, Mines and Resources Canada, *Canada Then and Now* (1982); N.L. Nicholson, *The Boundaries of the Canadian Confederation* (1979).

Territorial Government Canada's 2 territories, the NORTHWEST TERRITORIES and the YUKON TERRITORY, are governed by the federal government and by territorial governments which may legislate where the former has delegated the necessary authority. The government of the NWT holds its legislative powers under the NWT Act; the powers of the Yukon Territory's government are set out in the Yukon Act. The government of each territory is headed by a federally appointed com-

missioner and an elected body, known in both the NWT and in Yukon as the Legislative Assembly. The commissioner reports directly to the federal minister of Indian affairs and northern development. In the NWT the government leader chairs the Executive Council which comprises 8 members of the Legislative Assembly. The commissioner is not required to act on the advice of the executive council or that of the legislative assembly, but does so by tradition. In 1979 the federal Conservative government transferred executive power in the Yukon from the commissioner to an Executive Council, or Cabinet, comprising members from the 16-member Legislative Assembly. The commissioner does not sit on the Executive Council and has been specifically instructed by the federal minister to follow its decisions, except in matters of special concern to Ottawa. In contrast to the NWT, candidates for seats in the Yukon Territorial Legislative Assembly are affiliated with political parties. In both territories the legislative responsibilities of the commissioners-in-council are roughly analogous to those allocated to the provinces under the Constitution Act, 1867. The federal government retains control over lands, natural resources, taxation and claims of native rights. In April 1982, 56% of voters in a NWT plebiscite endorsed the division of the NWT. The then minister of Indian affairs and northern development indicated the territories would be divided when residents agreed on a boundary between the eastern and western territories and when outstanding native LAND CLAIMS were settled. Since 1984 the federal government has pursued a policy of devolving policy and program responsibilities to the territorial governments. KATHERINE A. GRAHAM

Terrorism, refers to the strategy of achieving a political objective by means of a campaign of seemingly random violence. Acts of terrorism such as bombings, assassinations and kidnappings, may be carried out either by those seeking to challenge the political status quo (insurgent terrorism) or preserve it (repressive terrorism). What distinguishes terrorism from justifiable acts of force is a matter of controversy and is exemplified by the phrase, "one man's terrorist is another man's freedom fighter." For liberal democratic societies, coping with the threat posed by insurgent terrorism without succumbing to repression to defeat it has become an enduring challenge.

Although the use of terrorism in pursuit of various causes can be traced to Biblical times, the term was first used to refer to a specific phase of the French Revolution, known as the "Reign of Terror" (1793-94). For more than a year, thousands of French citizens suspected of disloyalty to the Revolution were guillotined, imprisoned or tortured. The "Reign of Terror" is considered a forerunner of the large-scale repressive terrorism practised by some 20th-century totalitarian regimes. Many of the tactics commonly used by insurgent terrorist groups today were developed and refined by the Russian Anarchist movement of the latter part of the 19th century, which sought to overthrow the Tsarist autocracy through dramatic acts of violence (*see* ANARCHISM). The popular conception in plays and novels of the terrorist as bomb-throwing fanatic dates from this period.

The size, motivation and technical ability of contemporary insurgent terrorist organizations varies considerably. While it is impossible to isolate a single cause of terrorism, it is possible to evaluate at least in general terms how the strategy of terrorism operates to achieve certain political ends. Its central appeal to those who wish to challenge the status quo is, of course, its economy. A terrorist campaign requires only a handful of ac-

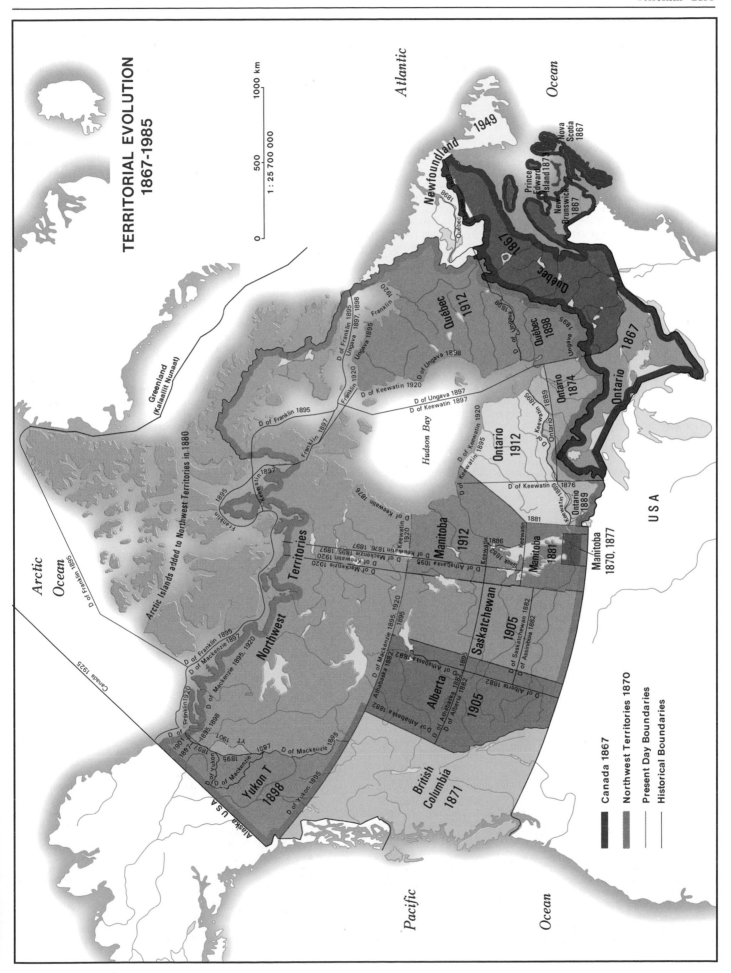

TERRITORIAL EVOLUTION 1867-1985

1 : 25 700 000

0   500   1000 km

Arctic Ocean

Pacific Ocean

Atlantic Ocean

Greenland (Kalaallit Nunaat)

Hudson Bay

Northwest Territories

Canada 1925

Alaska USA

Yukon T 1898

British Columbia 1871

Alberta 1905

Saskatchewan 1905

Manitoba 1912

Manitoba 1881

Manitoba 1870, 1877

Ontario 1912

Ontario 1889

Ontario 1876

Ontario 1874

Ontario 1867

Québec 1912

Québec 1898

Québec 1867

Newfoundland 1949

Nova Scotia 1867

Prince Edward Island 1873

New Brunswick 1867

USA

Arctic Islands added to Northwest Territories in 1880

D of Franklin 1895
D of Franklin 1897
D of Franklin 1895
D of Franklin 1895
D of Mackenzie 1897
D of Mackenzie 1895, 1920
D of Mackenzie 1895, 1920
D of Mackenzie 1920
D of Mackenzie 1895
D of Yukon 1895
D of Yukon 1895
YT 1901
D of Keewatin 1876
D of Keewatin 1895, 1897
D of Keewatin 1876, 1897
D of Keewatin 1920
D of Keewatin 1895
D of Keewatin 1920
D of Keewatin 1897
D of Ungava 1897
D of Ungava 1898
D of Ungava 1895
Franklin 1920
Franklin 1897
Ungava 1897, 1898
Ungava 1895
Keewatin 1897
Keewatin 1920
Keewatin 1886
Sask 1882
D of Athabaska 1895
D of Athabaska 1882
D of Athabaska 1882
D of Alberta 1882
D of Alberta 1882
D of Alberta 1882
D of Saskatchewan 1882
D of Assiniboia 1882
1881
1886

Canada 1867
Northwest Territories 1870
Present Day Boundaries
Historical Boundaries

tivists and a minimum of resources. Although the extent of damage or injury which the terrorist organization causes may in some instances be minimal, if an incident is skilfully executed its psychological impact can be enormous. Fear can have a corrosive and destabilizing effect on society. Acts of terrorism may stiffen the resolve of some to resist such intimidation; however, for many it has the opposite effect. An escalating campaign of terrorism can convince the citizenry that the issue or grievance which motivates it is so deeply and fervently held that some way must be found to accommodate it.

Despite the appeal of terrorism as a possible shortcut for the achievement of specific political goals, it is in fact a very difficult strategy to pursue. While almost any group can carry out an incident of terrorism, few have sufficient imagination and public relations skill to translate such acts into popular support. Most terrorist organizations can expect to fulfil certain short-term objectives, such as the acquisition of publicity. Long-term objectives, such as the attainment of political power or a change in the political status quo, are much more difficult to realize. Terrorist organizations which, miscalculate in their choice of tactics or targets can rapidly alienate potential supporters.

Compared with many countries in western Europe and the Middle East, Canada has had a limited experience with terrorism. This is primarily owing to the capacity of Canadian society to accommodate ethnic and linguistic diversity through a process of peaceful change and reform. Given its largely positive image as a peacekeeper and mediator in international disputes, Canadian diplomats and citizens abroad have rarely been the target of international terrorists. The acts of terrorism that have occurred within Canada have been limited and sporadic and can be classified as either domestic or foreign-based.

Only 2 significant domestic terrorist organizations have operated in Canada in recent years: the Front de Libération du Québec (FLQ), which is discussed below, and Direct Action. Direct Action was a small BC-based Anarchist group motivated primarily by concern over pollution and the danger posed by nuclear weapons. It made a sudden appearance in 1982 by bombing a hydroelectric facility on Vancouver I and later the Litton Systems Canada Ltd factory in Toronto. The group was preparing to undertake several other operations when its entire membership was taken into custody by police in Jan 1983 at a fake highway construction roadblock. Although its operations were amateurish and clumsy, Direct Action focused public attention on its issues of concern.

Foreign-based terrorists, while not targetting Canadian interests per se, have carried out attacks in Canada against diplomats and citizens of countries with which they have a grievance. ARMENIAN terrorists were responsible for the shooting of 2 Turkish diplomats in Ottawa in separate incidents in 1982, and the seizure of the Turkish embassy compound in Mar 1985, in which a Canadian security guard was killed. SIKH terrorists, motivated by a desire for an independent homeland, are believed to have been responsible for placing bombs on 2 India-bound airliners in Canada in June 1985, resulting in 331 fatalities. In May 1986, a visiting Indian Cabinet minister was shot by Sikh extremists in an assassination attempt in BC.

An international legal framework has begun to evolve to combat terrorism. Progress is most notable in measures to protect air travellers and diplomats. At the United Nations and in regional forums, Canada has played a role in developing a number of conventions, declarations and treaties. Canada is a signatory of 3 international conventions prohibiting air piracy: the Tokyo Convention of 1963, the Hague Convention of 1970 and the Montréal Convention of 1971. As a member of the Summit Seven, Canada was a participant in the Bonn Declaration of 1978, designed to isolate any nation guilty of supporting or harbouring aircraft hijackers. Canada was also a party to UN initiatives such as the 1973 Convention protecting diplomats and the 1979 Convention against the taking of hostages. In addition, Canada is a signatory of 44 bilateral extradition treaties, which could be invoked to return alleged terrorists to Canada for trial. THOMAS H. MITCHELL

The FLQ The waves of violence that occurred in Québec between 1963 and 1971, for which the FRONT DE LIBÉRATION DU QUÉBEC claimed responsibility, were the most important outbreak of terrorism in Canada. As in other countries, this type of terrorism was justified and rationalized with various arguments. The FLQ defended its actions by claiming that Francophones in Canada suffered economic discrimination; that the constitutional system was unjust; and that democratic channels to change were blocked.

The terrorist acts of the FLQ increased in intensity from 1963 to 1971. Bombs became increasingly sophisticated and powerful, and selective kidnappings forced the governments of the day to enter into negotiations. Although its activists generally attempted to issue a warning by telephone before each explosion, the FLQ caused 7 violent deaths, including that of Québec Cabinet minister Pierre LAPORTE.

Terrorism is generally not the term used to describe the violence on the part of public authorities because of the legal monopoly the state enjoys over certain forms of power. However, implementation of the WAR MEASURES ACT in 1970, the army's occupation of Québec, and above all the arrest, without formal proceedings, of more than 450 persons, have been challenged as a disproportionate response to FLQ actions. MARC LAURENDEAU

Teslin, YT, UP, pop 181 (1986c), located on Teslin Lake at the mouth of the Nisutlin R, and on the ALASKA HIGHWAY, 183 km by road SE of Whitehorse. The first whites to see the lake arrived in the 1870s and its tributaries were prospected in the following decade. During the great GOLD RUSH of 1898, the lake was part of an all-Canadian route to the Klondike and a few temporary settlements were established at its southern end in BC. Tom Smith opened a trading post at the mouth of the Nisutlin in 1903 but sold it soon afterward. The Whitehorse firm of Taylor and Drury operated it until 1955. The village has a landing strip and is a service centre for travellers on the Alaska Highway. Its name is derived from the Indian expression for "long narrow water." H. GUEST

Tessier, François-Xavier, doctor, politician (b at Québec C 15 Sept 1799; d there 1835). Tessier studied in Québec City and New York and was admitted to the practice of medicine in 1823. He is known primarily for founding the first medical newspaper in Canada, *Le Journal de médecine de Québec* (Jan 1826-Oct 1827). Despite his short life, his exceptional qualities brought him several important positions in the Québec region. He was named apothecary of the Emigrant Hospital in 1823; health officer for the port of Québec and administrator of the Pointe-Lévy Fever Hospital in 1830; and doctor of the Marine and Emigrant Hospital in 1834. He represented Saguenay in the Assembly of Lower Canada from 1833 until his death. JACQUES BERNIER

Texaco Canada Inc is one of Canada's largest integrated petroleum companies, with world-scale conventional oil and natural gas production in Alberta; active exploration programs in Canada's Western Basin and Beaufort Sea; and significant exploration prospects in Canada's offshore as well as in Brazil and West Africa. Incorporated in 1927 as McColl-Frontenac Oil Co Ltd, the company became Texaco Canada Ltd in 1959. It adopted its present name in 1978 as a result of its merger with Texaco Explorations Canada Ltd. With head offices in Toronto, Texaco Canada refines and distributes a full range of quality petroleum products through wholesale marketers and more than 2000 retail outlets coast to coast. In 1986, the company had revenues of $2.7 billion (ranking 33rd in Canada), assets of $3.7 billion (ranking 27th in Canada), and 3326 employees. Foreign ownership stands at 80%.

Texada Island, 28 700 ha, lies in the Str of GEORGIA near POWELL RIVER, BC. The island was named for Felix de Texada, a spanish rear-admiral, by Spanish explorer Jose Maria Narvaez (1791). In 1883 American capital started the first of several iron and copper-gold mines around Vananda. Mining was a mainstay until the 1920s and from WWII to 1976. A local smelter (1898) concentrated copper by-products; both ore and concentrates were shipped from deep-sea berths. Since about 1895 limestone quarries and lime kilns on the island have furnished material for cement, stucco, Kraft pulp and other off-island manufactures. Texada I now produces most of BC's limestone. The island's timber has been intensively logged since the 1940s. PETER GRANT

Textile Industry includes establishments that convert man-made and natural fibres into yarn, cloth, felt, etc, for use in MANUFACTURING clothing, upholstery, household linens, etc. The textile and CLOTHING INDUSTRIES together are among Canada's largest manufacturing-sector employers. Total employment averages about 170 700, broken down as follows: textiles, 60 000 and clothing factories, 110 600. Textile-mill shipments average about $6 billion annually.

History Records show that as long ago as 1671 pioneer settlers were making wool materials for clothing and furnishings. Eventually, there were hundreds of custom carding and cloth-fulling mills scattered in communities throughout Upper and Lower Canada and the Maritimes. The first complete factory system of woollen cloth manufacture started in 1826 when Mahlon Willett established a mill at l'Acadie in Lower Canada. Some evidence exists that a small cotton mill operated at Chambly (or St Athanase), Lower Canada, from 1844 to at least 1846. However, more evidence exists that a cotton mill was built in Sherbrooke, LC, in 1844. It operated until it burned in 1854 and, as it had some knitting machines in use, may have a claim to being the first knitting mill as well. In 1853 a small cotton mill was established at the St-Gabriel lock on the Lachine canal; it operated until at least 1871. Other early records include a knitting factory with powered knitting machines established in a mill at Ancaster [Ont] in 1859 and the Lybster Mills, established in Merritton [Ont] in 1860. The first silk-manufacturing concern was established in Montréal by Belding Paul & Co in 1876.

The age of synthetics began in 1925 when Courtaulds (Canada) Ltd built a plant in Cornwall, Ont, to make the then new viscose rayon, often called artificial silk. Courtaulds was quickly followed in 1926 by Celanese Canada, which erected a plant in Drummondville, Qué, to make acetate yarn. In 1942 the first nylon yarn was produced in Canada by DuPont. At the time, the height of WWII, nylon remained a well-kept secret; the first production was 45 denier yarn for weaving into parachute cloth. The first product made after the war was nylon hosiery yarn.

Polyester was introduced to Canada in the 1950s by ICI Ltd. Later, DuPont and Celanese became important manufacturers of this synthetic fibre, with the trade name "Dacron" used by DuPont and "Fortrel" by Celanese. Another major producer of nylon fibre in Canada is Badische Canada, of Arnprior, Ont. Its product is used mainly in carpets. Polypropylene, a most versatile synthetic fibre made by Celanese, is widely used for indoor-outdoor carpeting and for types of nonwoven textiles.

There are about 1085 textile-manufacturing plants in Canada, most of them located in Québec and Ontario. The Canadian clothing or apparel industry, with 2465 plants, is the largest single consumer of textiles, using about 40% of the industry's output (fibre-weight equivalent). The ability of the textile industry to supply its home furnishings and industrial customers depends, in large part, on the continued existence of the clothing industry. Without the economies of scale made possible by the total market, almost every subsector of the textile industry would be threatened. Thus, textiles and clothing, while separate industries, are indivisible from the standpoint of industrial survival. They are also only 2 links in a long chain that starts with the consumer, goes back through retailers to apparel manufacturers, dyers and finishers, weavers and knitters, fibre producers, the PETROCHEMICAL INDUSTRY (from which the raw materials for synthetic fibres come), and finally to the oil and gas wells. The disappearance of any link would weaken, perhaps fatally, the rest of the chain.

The employment links are also important. The weighted average employment multiplier for the textile and clothing industries has been estimated to be 1.65; ie, each job in textiles and clothing supports 1.65 jobs elsewhere in the economy. By this measure, the industries' 170 700 jobs support 281 650 additional jobs in other sectors.

Canada remains a relatively open market for textile and clothing imports from developed and developing nations. Canada's consumption of textiles and clothing by volume is about 2% of the world's total, and Canadian mills now supply less than 50% of this amount. The largest proportion of textile imports comes from developed countries (although in recent years this proportion has decreased somewhat as more come from developing countries); the largest proportion of clothing imports from developing countries. Despite substantial import-restraint legislation, Canada accepts 9 times more per capita in textiles from developed countries than the US and 3 times as much as the European Economic Community. Steps by the Canadian government, assuring the textile industry of the continuation of special protection measures, have created a fairly stable climate of confidence and have stimulated investment. The proposed FREE TRADE agreement with the US has caused some uncertainty about the future in the industry; however, it would favour free trade with the US if "the adjustment and transition conditions are adequate" to retain this level of confidence.

The Canadian textile industry is internationally competitive with other developed countries in price, quality and product variety. The primary industry is as technologically efficient and productive as any in the world. Major technological advances have been introduced to accompany the shift from natural to man-made fibres and blends, including the adoption of advanced spinning, weaving, knitting, nonwoven and finishing machinery, electronic and computerized control equipment and methods of reducing energy consumption. Canada was a pioneer in introducing a new open-end type of yarn spinning and is a leader in the use of shuttleless weaving machines. Canada rates with the leaders in the production and technical development of nonwoven fabrics,

Cotton mill, St Stephen, NB, in 1900 (*courtesy Provincial Archives of New Brunswick*).

particularly in their use in geotextiles (eg, ASBESTOS fibres). Computers and microprocessors are widely used in manufacturing operations.

Today the industry consists of the survivors of an extended and rigorous period of rationalization. The remaining firms are efficient, cost conscious and adaptable to the changing marketplace. Dominion Textile Inc, headquartered in Montréal, is by far the largest textile manufacturer in Canada, with annual sales of about $927 million in 1986. The company has 40 manufacturing facilities, 26 located in Canada, 7 in the US, 6 in Europe and one in Hong Kong. Of the Canadian plants, 17 are in Québec, 8 in Ontario and one in NS. Total employment is 10 500. Thirteen percent of the shares are owned by the Caisse de dépôt.

The textile industry continues to spend large sums on new machinery and modernization of facilities. For example, spending on capital equipment and repairs during the 1970s amounted to $1.8 billion, and it will be more than $3.0 billion in the 1980s. The industry has improved its export performance without imposing sacrifices on its domestic customers. To be successful in the export of commodities, such as textiles, a secure domestic base must underpin the higher risks, costs and lower net returns inherent in export marketing. The industry has recently operated in a more confident climate, which has encouraged a strong flow of investment into efficient, highly productive textile processes.   W.A.B. DAVIDSON

Textiles, Woven Canada has a rich history of weaving stretching back to the precontact native peoples and enriched by each succeeding wave of immigrants. The working together of lengths of fibre (threads) to make a fabric can be done in simple and universal forms by the fingers alone to produce braiding and basketry constructions. Netted and knitted fabrics can be made with very simple tools. To produce a woven textile, 2 sets of threads must be interlaced: one set, the warp, is held by some kind of support; the other, the weft, is worked over and under the warp threads to hold them together in a firm but flexible form. With simple weaving equipment every movement is done by hand; however, over a long period of time, technological advances meant that more work was done by the loom and less by the weaver. The key development that turned the weaving frame into a true loom was the heddle which, in its simplest form, is made up of a pair of rods with attached string loops through which the warp threads pass. These rods can be manipulated to make an opening (a shed) through the warp threads for an easy passage of the weft. From these simple beginnings looms have become more and more complex with increasingly automatic action.

The native peoples produced beautiful weaving without benefit of a shed-making device. Therefore, although their weaving was skilful and of high quality, it was very time consuming. Skins were used for utilitarian purposes; woven

textiles were reserved for prestige items such as the magnificent ceremonial blankets used on the West Coast (see CHILKAT BLANKET), bands and exquisite ornaments woven with porcupine quills. The weave used was a special technique (weft-twined weave), which developed from the making of baskets.

In weft twining, 2 weft threads enclose each warp or group of warps in turn and then twist around each other before moving on to the next warp. From early times, this technique was used in many parts of the country with wide variations of texture, material and design. As trade goods became available, they supplanted the native weaving, but for some purposes the skills were maintained and are still practised.

The first migrants to come from Europe were the French, who settled along the St Lawrence and in parts of the Atlantic region in the early 17th century. At that time France was famous for tapestry weaving, but the settlers brought with them the simple country skills, home spinning of yarn and weaving of cloth for utilitarian clothing and bed coverings. At first, few textiles were produced but, as time went on, home production of textiles became important; girls were taught to spin, and farmhouses contained looms on which household goods and some material for barter were produced. The loom used in New France was very simple; the cloth woven, very plain. For bed coverings, 2 simple hand-patterning techniques were used: *à la planche*, in which a narrow board was used to open a pattern shed for a coloured weft to form simple block designs; and *boutonné*, in which multicoloured wefts were pulled up in loops to make motifs (eg, stars, pine trees). There was also a considerable production of heavy lengths of material with a weft of old cloth torn into rag strips. In the early days these *catalogne* lengths were used for bed coverings; in more recent times, for floor coverings.

LOYALISTS who moved N to the Atlantic region and to what was to become the provinces of Québec and Ontario were from a variety of ethnic backgrounds, many of them British. Most of the women could spin and some could weave. As soon as possible, flax was grown to provide fibre for linen and sheep were raised for wool. Household linens and blankets and warm lengths for clothing were made in many homes, but among the settlers there were a number of trained professional handweavers, usually men, who could operate complex pattern looms. These craftsmen wove fancy linens and ornamental bed coverings, often the pride of a bride's trousseau. The coverlets were usually in either summer and winter weave or double cloth, both of which produced striking geometric patterns and were usually of dark blue wool and white linen or cotton.

Of the many European immigrants who followed the Loyalists, those who had the most impact on Canadian weaving traditions were the SCOTS, IRISH and GERMANS. Trained craftsmen had been thrown out of work during the Industrial Revolution by the mechanization of the weaving industry in Scotland and Germany, and many of the out-of-work weavers came to Canada. They expected to farm but found they could again practise their profession profitably. One or more of these experienced weavers could be found in most areas in the older parts of English-speaking Canada. Housewives usually prepared the yarns, but much of the weaving was done by the professionals. Imported materials could be purchased in settled areas of Canada from the early 19th century on, but many of the blankets, carpets, linens and clothing materials were locally produced by handweavers, until quite late in the century, when it ceased to be profitable.

Ornamental bed coverings, or coverlets, were an especially popular production of the local professional weavers. In the Scottish-Irish areas the usual weave was one called overshot, ie, an extra weft shoots over and under a plain ground, forming complex and striking geometric patterns and making a very warm covering. The patterns were usually in wool, dark blue or plain, bright red, sometimes banded. The ground was almost always white cotton. In German areas the weaves used for ornamental coverlets and decorative horse blankets required very complex handlooms for elaborate twill interlacings and a patterning that had rows of stars alternating with diamonds.

The complex Jacquard loom, in which the opening of the pattern sheds is controlled by a series of punched cards, was introduced in the 1830s. The loom was used by a comparatively small number of local professional handweavers in Ontario. The patterns that were possible with this new loom were semirealistic with flowers and birds and other motifs that were beyond the capabilities of earlier looms. A Jacquard coverlet was a much-treasured possession and often survives from a wedding trousseau.

Spinning and weaving are crafts that go with pioneering and, just as the skills were falling into disuse in eastern Canada (around 1900), the West was opening up. Store-bought goods were available by mail-order catalogue, but many textiles were produced locally. Pioneers from eastern Canada or Britain had, for the most part, lost their textile-making skills a generation or 2 before. Those from Scandinavia, Germany or eastern Europe were accustomed to spinning yarn from their own home-grown wool, flax and hemp. Many spinning wheels used on the prairies have survived, but the hand-spun yarn was knitted into warm garments that have worn out. Fewer looms have survived; most of the weaving was for perishable things like rag RUGS, few of which still exist. UKRAINIANS and DOUKHOBORS did more ornamental weaving, some of which has been preserved. Ukrainians furnished their homes with handsome, woven bench covers of linen, hemp and wool banded in colour, and gave their rooms a warm brightness with tapestry-woven woollen wall hangings in bright geometric patterns. The Doukhobors produced coarse tapestry weave in very bright colours and rugs with a thick woollen pile knotted into a plain firm ground (in the same way that oriental carpets are made). These 2 patterning techniques, typical of their earlier homes in the Caucasus, have been quite widely used since the Doukhobors settled in Saskatchewan and BC. Canada's weaving traditions reflect the nation's fascinating cultural diversity. Some of the older traditions have blended together; those that came later still stand uniquely on their own.
DOROTHY K. BURNHAM

Reading: Harold B. Burnham and Dorothy K. Burnham, *'Keep me warm one night': Early Handweaving in Eastern Canada* (1972); Dorothy K. Burnham, *The Comfortable Arts; Traditional Spinning and Weaving in Canada* (1981).

Thacker, Herbert Cyril, army officer (b at Poona, India 16 Sept 1870; d at Victoria 2 June 1953). Thacker, briefly chief of the general staff in 1927-28, was commissioned in the Royal Canadian Artillery in 1891. He fought in the SOUTH AFRICAN WAR and accompanied the Japanese army as military attaché during the Russo-Japanese War 1904-05, the first appointment of its kind for a Canadian officer. Thacker commanded divisional artilleries of the CANADIAN EXPEDITIONARY FORCE, 1915-19. He took the position of chief of the general staff reluctantly and despite ill health.
NORMAN HILLMER

Thanksgiving Day Proclaimed as "a day of General Thanksgiving to Almighty God for the bountiful harvest with which Canada has been blessed," Thanksgiving draws upon 3 traditions: harvest celebrations in European peasant societies for which the symbol was the cornucopia (horn of plenty); formal observances, such as that celebrated by Martin FROBISHER in the eastern Arctic in 1578 — the first North American Thanksgiving; and the Pilgrims' celebration of their first harvest in Massachusetts (1621) involving the uniquely American turkey, squash and pumpkin. The celebration was brought to Nova Scotia in the 1750s and the citizens of Halifax commemorated the end of the SEVEN YEARS' WAR (1763) with a day of Thanksgiving. Loyalists brought the celebration to other parts of the country. In 1879 Parliament declared Nov 6 as a day of Thanksgiving; it was celebrated as a national rather than a religious holiday. Later and earlier dates were observed, the most popular being the third Monday in Oct. After WWI, Thanksgiving and Armistice (later Remembrance) Day were celebrated in the same week. It was not until 31 Jan 1957 that Parliament proclaimed the observance of Thanksgiving on the second Monday in Oct. E.C. DRURY, the former "Farmer-Premier" of Ontario lamented later that " the farmers' own holiday has been stolen by the towns" to give them a long weekend when the weather was better.
DAVID MILLS

Thatcher, Wilbert Colin, rancher, politician (b at Toronto, Ont 25 Aug 1938). The only son of Liberal premier Ross THATCHER, Colin Thatcher entered Saskatchewan politics in 1975 as Liberal MLA for Thunder Creek. In 1977 he switched to the Conservatives, acting as finance critic and house leader until that party's victory in 1982, after which he was named minister of energy and mines. Although regarded by some as the best minister in the government, his overbearing personality and erratic behaviour made him unpopular in the Cabinet and in 1983 he was forced to resign. His arrest and conviction in 1984 for the brutal murder of his ex-wife, with whom he had for several years been locked in bitter dispute, marked the first time in Canadian history that a former government minister had been convicted of such a crime.
STANLEY GORDON

Reading: H. Bird, *Not Above the Law* (1985); G. Wilson and L. Wilson, *Deny, Deny, Deny* (1986); M. Siggins, *A Canadian Tragedy* (1986).

Thatcher, Wilbert Ross, premier of Saskatchewan (b at Neville, Sask 24 May 1917; d at Regina 23 July 1971). Educated locally and at Queen's U, Thatcher was a businessman. After holding aldermanic office, he was elected CCF member of Parliament in 1945, 1949 and 1953, but left his party in 1955, sitting first as an Independent and then as a Liberal. He ran unsuccessfully in the 1957 and 1958 federal elections. Critical of CCF administration, he termed Saskatchewan's crown corporations a dismal failure, a charge which led to the Mossbank debate (May 1957) with CCF premier T.C. DOUGLAS and established him as the anti-CCF standard bearer. In Sept 1959 Thatcher defeated 3 other challengers for the provincial Liberal leadership. Under him Saskatchewan Liberals became identified with free-enterprise rhetoric but pragmatic policies and won the provincial election in 1964 – the first time in 20 years a provincial Liberal government had ruled west of Québec. His devotion to economic development led to friction with federal Liberals, whose priorities differed: social welfare under Lester PEARSON and constitutional reform under Pierre TRUDEAU. Party organizational disputes so fractured Saskatchewan Liberals that Thatcher entered the 1971 provincial election beleaguered by partisan allies and partisan foes alike, losing 20 of 35 seats to the NDP under Allan BLAKENEY. He died one month later.
DAVID E. SMITH

Reading: D. Eisler, *Rumours of Glory: Saskatchewan and the Thatcher Years* (1987); David E. Smith, *Prairie Liberalism* (1975); J. Wearing, *The L-Shaped Party* (1981).

The Pas, Man, Town, pop 6283 (1986c), 6390 (1981c), inc 1912, is located on the S bank of the SASKATCHEWAN R, about 50 km N of where the river enters CEDAR LK. At first an Indian encampment, The Pas site was visited by early explorers Henry KELSEY, the LA VÉRENDRYE sons and Sir John FRANKLIN. It became a FUR-TRADE centre, beginning with the French Ft Paskoyac (also spelled Pasquia and Paskoya) in the mid-1700s. Members of a rescue expedition sent to search for the missing Franklin helped create a new Anglican mission while wintering at The Pas in 1847. A Roman Catholic mission established in 1887 played a significant role in the development of various institutions, including the hospital. The origin of the name is uncertain but may derive from a Cree word meaning "a narrow place" (in the river). The townsite was obtained in 1906 from the Cree, who subsequently moved to the N bank of the Saskatchewan.

In the early 1900s mining and commercial fishing in the N, lumbering and development of a railway divisional point enhanced the town's importance as an economic and administrative centre. Mixed farming became more viable W of the town following completion of a major drainage project in 1960. The Pas is an important link between the mining, fishing and trapping areas of the Canadian SHIELD and the mainly agricultural lands of southern Manitoba. Its principal employer is Manitoba Forestry Resources Ltd, an integrated sawmill and pulp and paper complex owned by the Manitoba government. Among facilities at The Pas is Keewatin Community College.
D.M. LYON

Reading: S. Wilton, *The Pas ... A History: Adventure and Romance* (1970).

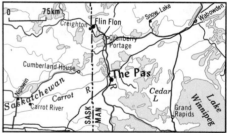

Theatre, English-Language It is a common misconception that theatre on the N American continent began with the arrival of Spanish and French explorers and settlers.

Indian and Inuit ceremonials and rituals evidenced a highly sophisticated sense of mimetic art, and occupied a central place in the social and religious activities of their peoples (*see* NATIVE PEOPLE, RELIGION). Masks, costumes and properties were used to enhance dialogue, song and chants in performances designed to benefit the community by influencing such crucial matters as the weather, the hunt, or spiritual and physical well-being. Great ritual dramas (such as those of the British Columbia Kwakiutl Indians) sometimes took the form of a long cycle, encompassing some 4 to 5 months of performance. Subsequent development of drama in Canada, however, was shaped by European rather than by indigenous traditions.

When Sir Humphrey GILBERT took his expedition to Newfoundland in 1583, he was equipped with "toyes ... Hobby horse, and Maylike conceits to delight the Savage people," which suggests some kind of rudimentary theatrics. The first significant theatrical events, however, were created by French military and religious visitors and settlers. The Jesuits sponsored productions of original and classical plays throughout the 17th century, until the controversial suppression of Molières *Tartuffe* in 1694 brought theatrical activity in New France to a virtual halt (*see* THEATRE, FRENCH-LANGUAGE). Québec enjoyed little public theatrical entertainment again until after the 1763 CONQUEST. Subsequently the British garrison in Montréal revived theatre with, ironically, productions of Molière, and was soon emulated by local francophone groups. Popular English plays were also performed by the garrisons of Montréal and Québec City; amateur thespian societies were formed, and Jesuit students once more began staging plays in their colleges.

This new theatrical impetus in late 18th-century Québec was matched by developments in Atlantic Canada. Performing in makeshift theatres in taverns and other public buildings, at first with all-male casts, the officers and men of the British garrisons promoted theatre. The Halifax garrison built the New Grand Theatre, fitted with boxes and 2 pits, which opened on 26 Feb 1789 with a production of *The Merchant of Venice*. Charlottetown built its first theatre in 1800, and by 1809 Saint John had its own Drury Lane Theatre. Thus a lively garrison and amateur theatrical tradition emerged in the Maritimes, hampered sometimes by puritanical attacks ("a Christian cannot with a safer Conscience enter into the Play-House than into a Brothel," declared a writer in the *Nova Scotia Chronicle* in Jan 1770), but confident enough to mount full-length productions from the classical and contemporary English repertoire, as well as new Canadian works. Among these was a romantic comedy called *Acadius; or, Love in a Calm*, the first recorded English Canadian play, performed in Halifax in 1774.

Theatrical activity in Québec and the Maritimes in the 18th century was predominantly amateur, but the growing population in both regions began to attract professional companies from the US. The first resident professional company in Canada was the American Company of Comedians, believed to have performed at the Pontac Inn, Halifax, in the summer and fall of 1768. Another group of actors, headed by an Englishman, Edward Allen, arrived in Montréal from Albany, NY, in March 1786 for a 4-month season, then moved on to Québec City. Other professional entertainment was provided by the American circus of John B. Ricketts, whose company performed in Montréal and Québec City in 1797 and 1798.

By the end of the 18th century Canadian theatre was poised for rapid growth, and the 19th century provided a rich mosaic of theatrical development in all regions of the country. Elaborate theatres were constructed in the Maritimes and Québec. Montréal's THEATRE ROYAL, built by a group of investors headed by John MOLSON, Sr, in 1825 to seat an audience of 1000, cost $30 000, and featured a Doric portico, 2 tiers of boxes, a pit and a gallery, comfortable backstage facilities and lavish decorations. The Theatre Royal at Spring Gardens, Halifax, opened in 1846 and had boxes to accommodate over 160 patrons. By this time theatre had also firmly established itself in Upper Canada, again encouraged by amateur groups and enthusiastic garrisons in settlements on the sites of such present-day cities as Toronto, Ottawa, London and Kingston. As early as 1809 there was a performance at York [Toronto] by New York actors of *The School for Scandal*, but it was not until 1834 that Toronto had its first real theatre, a converted Wesleyan church. Others followed, including the Royal Lyceum (1848) and the Grand Opera House, which opened in 1874 and burned down

in a spectacular fire 5 years later. London's Grand Opera House (1881) was also destroyed by fire, but, like its Toronto counterpart, was replaced (*see* GRAND THEATRE). Numerous smaller towns across the country boasted opera houses of various sizes and longevity.

When the West began to be accessible to touring companies, theatres were among the first priorities of new communities. The Royal Engineers built a rudimentary theatre in New Westminster in 1858, and Victoria's Colonial Theatre opened in Feb 1860, following some years of theatrical productions performed by sailors on British ships anchored in Esquimalt Harbour. By 1891 Vancouver had a 1200-seat Opera House, and adequate theatres also existed in prairie cities. Winnipeg's Walker Theatre (1907) was especially impressive, with seating for close to 2000 and a liberal supply of ivory and marble in its fittings.

Audiences that regularly filled Canadian theatres in the 19th century were, with some notorious exceptions, mostly polite, attentive and self-disciplined. Ontario audiences were more inhibited than their Québec counterparts, whether the latter were Anglo-Canadians vigorously assaulting American visitors with sticks and canes for not removing their hats during the playing of the national anthem in a Montréal theatre in 1811, or French Canadian students rapturously welcoming Sarah Bernhardt to Montréal in 1880. Torontonians gave Adelaide Neilson a standing ovation after her Canadian farewell performance in 1880, but the most volatile audiences in 19th-century Canada were to be found in the West. A serious race riot occurred in the Colonial Theatre, Victoria, in Nov 1860, when black members of the audience forced their way into areas reserved for whites; Winnipeg audiences in the 1880s were enlivened by the presence of boisterous youths and uninhibited prostitutes; Klondike theatres were often uproarious; and a performance of *The Cowboy's Romance* in High River [Alta] in May 1902 ended with the director of the Great Bostock Theatrical Company wielding a club against the egg-flinging audience.

The social, cultural and educational benefits of theatre were stressed by many apologists, but the Catholic Church and some Protestants (especially Methodists) continued their strong moral opposition, holding theatrical entertainment responsible for debauchery, dissipation and sundry other ungodly habits. Bishop BOURGET of Montréal issued condemnations of the theatre in pastoral letters in 1859 and again in 1872, and in 1880 Bishop Fabre forbade his parishioners to attend performances by the visiting French actress Sarah Bernhardt. In Winnipeg the Reverend J.B. Silcox delivered a sermon in Feb 1883 that condemned theatre for sinning against morality and decency; in Toronto, he claimed, "Within the last few years, there were scenes on the boards that would cause even the Sodomites to blush, and stop their ears for shame." And when Winnipeg playwright and critic C.W. Handscomb saw Ibsen's *Ghosts* in March 1904 he voiced his worry that this "unwholesome, degrading [and] disgusting" play might pollute the "wholesome prairie atmosphere."

Despite these handicaps, and the necessity of competing with foreign plays and players, Canadian playwrights, actors and managers began to achieve some prominence. In English Canada the turgid poetic dramas of Charles HEAVYSEGE, Charles MAIR and Wilfred CAMPBELL received little attention, but lively farces and political satires by Nicholas Flood DAVIN, J.N. McIlwraith and W.H. Fuller found audiences, as did the comic fantasies and masques of Frederick Augustus DIXON, conventional melodramas by McKee Rankin and

the historical romances of W.A. Tremayne. Rankin also achieved recognition as an actor, both in Canada and abroad; and Tremayne wrote for American actor Robert Mantell, a popular star in Canada. Many Canadian actors spent much of their time performing in the US and Britain: Julia Arthur worked with Henry Irving in London, and later founded an American touring company; Margaret ANGLIN, who, it was said, could wring emotion from a keg of nails, was renowned for her productions of Greek plays in Berkeley, Calif; Franklin McLeay spent 5 years of his brief career with Wilson Barrett's company in London; Marie Dressler made her name in American vaudeville; and Henry Miller, who began his career in Toronto in 1878, became well-known as an actor-manager in New York. There were, however, Canadian actors who made their livelihood primarily in Canada. John Nickinson managed Toronto's Royal Lyceum Theatre from 1853 to 1859, and his daughter, Charlotte Morrison, ran a successful stock company in Toronto in the 1870s. Ida Van Cortland (with her husband, Albert Tavernier) toured her company from Winnipeg to St John's in the 1880s. The 7 companies of the famous Marks Brothers toured melodramas to small-town Canada regularly from 1879 to 1922, making a great deal of money in the process. Melodramas were also the staple fare of actor-manager H. Price Webber, whose company travelled throughout the Maritimes, Québec and New England until 1915. At the turn of the century Harold Nelson, one of the country's first acting teachers, began a remarkable career producing Shakespeare, melodrama and comedy across the western provinces.

Throughout the 19th century, and well into the 20th, Canadian producers, actors and playwrights faced overwhelming competition from foreign touring stars and companies. This competition seriously retarded the development of indigenous professional theatre. In 1911 critic Bernard K. SANDWELL bemoaned the annexation of the Canadian stage by US theatre magnates such as Charles Frohman, the Shubert Brothers and the powerful New York Theatrical Syndicate formed in 1896. The British Canadian Theatrical Organization Society (1912) attempted to balance American influence by organizing tours of British actors. The result was that British and US managements, by acquiring controlling interests in Canadian theatres, held a commercial and cultural stranglehold on the country's theatrical growth. The Trans-Canada Theatre Society (1915) was Canadian owned, but its purpose was to organize tours by foreign companies.

The process had begun, haphazardly, a century before, first with the arrival of minor actors from the US, then with major stars from America and Europe. Virtually every leading actor from Edmund Kean onwards performed in Canada. Kean acted in Montréal and Québec City in 1826, and scores of actors followed: W.C. Macready, the Kembles, E.A. Sothern, Charles and Ellen Kean, Charles Fechter, Edwin Booth, Joseph Jefferson, Sarah Bernhardt, Coquelin, Helena Modjeska, Tommaso Salvini, Laurence Barrett, Julia Marlowe, Henry Irving, Ellen Terry, John Martin-Harvey, Mrs Fiske, Mrs Campbell, Robert Mantell, the Kendals, Ben Greet and Johnston Forbes-Robertson, as well as distinguished companies from Dublin's Abbey Theatre and England's Stratford. As dedicated professionals, these performers brought good acting and, sometimes, good plays, but most saw Canada as a theatrical appendage to the US, with some commercial potential. WWI interrupted the touring circuits. Escalating costs, competition from film and radio and the Depression then combined to end touring companies. Foreign touring stars and companies helped create and sustain a tradition of theatregoing, and they gave impetus to the building of many excellent theatres. But when the touring era ended, Canada, having failed to nurture its own professionals, was left with negligible professional theatre.

Visiting companies still appeared in Canadian theatres, and resident foreign repertory companies performing popular Broadway and London plays sometimes established themselves. One example is Vaughan Glaser's company in Toronto (1921-27). There were also intermittently successful Canadian professional and semiprofessional companies working throughout Canada. At the beginning of the century the Winnipeg-based Permanent Players ran for 21 consecutive seasons at the Winnipeg Theatre, and Ontario-born Mae Edwards toured her company in Ontario and the Maritimes until 1935. The John Holden Players performed in Bala, Ont, and Winnipeg in the late 1930s. Sidney Risk's Everyman Theatre Co, which originated in Saskatchewan as a student touring company, opened in Vancouver in 1946 and performed a classical repertoire throughout the West for many years. Toronto's Jupiter Theatre started in 1951, and in Ottawa the Canadian Repertory Theatre, with actress and director Amelia Hall, was prominent in the early 1950s.

Toronto's New Play Society, though benefiting throughout its history from volunteer help, operated for some years on a professional basis. Founded by Dora Mavor MOORE (1946), the NPS succeeded in developing Canadian talent in all areas of theatre. Plays by Morley CALLAGHAN, Harry BOYLE, John COULTER, Mavor MOORE, Lister Sinclair and Andrew ALLAN were produced in the theatre of the ROYAL ONTARIO MUSEUM. NPS also originated the famous annual touring revue *Spring Thaw*. Dora Mavor Moore contributed to the creation of the STRATFORD FESTIVAL and many NPS actors appeared there.

Nevertheless, Canadian theatrical activity in the first half of the 20th century was predominantly amateur. Having relied heavily on imported theatre for a century or more, Canada had no established professional base on which to build when the imports declined. When a growing national self-consciousness demanded theatrical expression, it was largely amateurs who were available to provide it. The need for theatrical self-expression was enunciated by Gov Gen Earl Grey in 1907 when he created the Earl Grey Musical and Dramatic Competition for the encouragement of dramatic arts throughout the Dominion. The competition was held annually until 1911, and was by invitation. Unlike the later Dominion Drama Festival, there was no regional screening process, and Canadian judges were used. The Earl Grey Competition was short-lived and had only a minimal effect on Canadian theatre, but vice-regal approval of theatrical endeavour was a welcome change from puritanical opposition by church authorities.

Grey's initiative coincided with important developments elsewhere in amateur theatre. In 1908 the Arts and Letters Players of Toronto was formed. Dedicated to serious noncommercial theatre, and performing in cramped quarters in the Old Court House of Adelaide St, the company was at the forefront of the LITTLE THEATRE MOVEMENT. Led by Roy Mitchell, the Arts and Letters Players demonstrated the value of innovative and experimental theatre with productions of plays by Maeterlinck, Yeats, Tagore, Synge and Lady Gregory.

When U of Toronto's Hart House Theatre opened in 1919, it absorbed the ideals and energies of the Arts and Letters Players, and Mitchell became the new theatre's first director. Hart House Theatre fostered the distinguished careers of many directors, actors and playwrights, among them Bertram Forsyth, Raymond MASSEY, Carroll Aikins, Dora Mavor Moore, Edgar Stone, Merrill DENISON, Herman VOADEN, Jane Mallet, Andrew Allan, Robert GILL, Kate REID, Barbara Chilcott, Elizabeth Sterling Haynes, William HUTT, Donald SUTHERLAND, Charmion King and Donald and Murray Davis. Other Little Theatres emerged and sometimes flourished — the Ottawa Drama League (1913), the Vancouver Little Theatre (1921), the Community Players of Winnipeg (1921), the Montreal Repertory Theatre (1930) and the Halifax Theatre Arts Guild (1931), for example. At the Sarnia Drama League (1927), Voaden experimented with "symphonic expressionism" and generally challenged theatrical norms. By the 1930s all major cities, as well as many smaller communities, had an established amateur theatre.

In an attempt to co-ordinate and give some focus to amateur theatre activity in the country, the DOMINION DRAMA FESTIVAL was formed in 1932. Initiated by Gov Gen Lord Bessborough, and relying heavily on the influence and expertise of Vincent MASSEY, the DDF organized bilingual competitions and regional drama festivals from which the best productions were selected to compete in the annual final, held in a different city each year. In 1970 the DDF was succeeded by Theatre Canada, which survived until 1978. The DDF outlived its purpose, as amateur enthusiasm, however skilled, was overtaken by professional expertise. Yet the DDF can justifiably claim a major contribution to 20th-century theatre. By providing incentives and opportunities for actors, playwrights, designers, directors and technicians, and by building and maintaining audiences across the country, the DDF helped create the circumstances that made possible a fully professional theatre.

Other early 20th-century amateur activity of note occurred in the universities. The lead was taken by western Canada, particularly at U of Saskatchewan, where the first chair of drama in the British Commonwealth was founded in 1945; U of Alberta established a department of fine arts in 1946 and the BANFF CENTRE School of Fine Arts produced the early works of Gwen Pharis RINGWOOD and other Canadian playwrights. Drama and theatre programs, the majority of them established in the 1960s, are now found at universities and colleges in every province. In many instances the universities, unfettered by commercial considerations or social convention, have premiered deserving plays by Canadian and foreign playwrights. The universities have also provided a vital educational and training service in all aspects of theatre production, history and criticism (*see* THEATRE EDUCATION). Another form of amateur drama emerged and briefly flourished in the Depression years. The Progressive Arts Club was formed in Toronto in 1932 for the development of a militant working-class art and literature. From PAC developed the Workers' Experimental Theatre, consisting largely of groups of unemployed workers who performed short plays and political skits on topical issues wherever they could find a space, which was frequently outdoors and often on picket lines. The most celebrated production of the Workers' Theatre was *Eight Men Speak* (1933), a full-length play based on the trial and imprisonment of 8 Canadian communists. The play was later banned in Toronto and Winnipeg. The Workers' Theatre, with its international political and cultural links, had a unique excitement and inventiveness, but faded after the Depression and left no lasting mark on subsequent developments in Canadian theatre.

A vital impetus to continued progress of professional theatre came from the 1951 Report of the Royal Commission on NATIONAL DEVELOPMENT IN THE ARTS, LETTERS AND SCIENCES. Chaired by Vincent Massey, the commission made recommendations that led to the formation of the CANADA COUNCIL in 1957.

The transition from a predominantly amateur to a predominantly professional theatre began with the founding of the Stratford Festival in 1953. Thereafter, professional theatre rapidly began to consolidate itself. The Crest Theatre opened in Toronto in 1954, and the Canadian Players, an offshoot of the Stratford company, undertook tours throughout the US and Canada. The founding of major regional theatres and government acceptance of a responsibility to fund the arts revitalized professional theatre. Unlike the professional theatre of the 19th century, however, the new professionalism had national as well as international interests, and the early 1960s opened a phase of advancement in Canadian theatrical arts of greater scope and intensity than anything previously witnessed in its 350-year history. L.W. CONOLLY

Contemporary

One serious attempt at a bilingual theatre was Gratien GELINAS's Comédie-Canadienne (fl 1958-69) in Montréal, which set out to produce original plays in both French and English. Gélinas had been part of Michael LANGHAM's 1956 Stratford production of *Henry V* with its co-operative and symbolic juxtaposition of anglophone and francophone actors. The last gasp of this kind of nationalism was the founding of the colingual National Theatre School in 1960, which serves both languages and was located originally in Stratford as well as Montréal. However, in the early 1960s Québecois theatre was destined to go its own way, and soon BC and the Atlantic and Prairie provinces would free themselves from any hint of Toronto domination. This decentralization (or "democratization" as it was called in Canada) was championed by the newly formed Canada Council (1957) and its arts supervisor, Peter Dwyer. The "Regional Theatre Movement" was defined and became the first major phase of Canada's postwar professional development. Non-profit stock companies were created to serve the principal municipalities and, wherever possible, tour their particular region.

Toronto's Crest Theatre (1954-66) under Donald and Murray Davis, had evolved out of Hart House Theatre and the Straw Hat Players, but did not become the regional model. This honour went to Winnipeg and the MANITOBA THEATRE CENTRE, one of the earliest recipients of a Canada Council grant. Founded by John HIRSCH and Tom HENDRY in 1958 out of a merger of 2 amateur groups, MTC attained full professionalism within 4 years, thereby demonstrating the value of government support for the arts.

Summer festivals and winter stock companies sprouted across the country. In 1962, the SHAW FESTIVAL was added to the Vancouver International Festival (1958-68), and in 1963 the VANCOUVER PLAYHOUSE and Halifax's NEPTUNE THEATRE anchored the national chain. Others followed in rapid succession: the CHARLOTTETOWN FESTIVAL, home of the Canadian musical (1964-); the CITADEL in Edmonton (1965-); the Globe in Regina (1966-); the Saidye Bronfman Centre in Montréal (1967-82); Theatre New Brunswick in Fredericton and Theatre Calgary (1968-); Ottawa's NATIONAL ARTS CENTRE and Montréal's CENTAUR THEATRE (1969-); and Toronto Arts Productions (later CentreStage) at the St Lawrence Centre (1970-). Theatre London (now the

Grand Theatre Co), Sudbury Theatre and Victoria's Bastion Theatre all went professional in 1971, leaving Newfoundland as the only province without a regional theatre.

Provincial and civic arts councils mushroomed to broaden the base of private and governmental support, until Canada's nonprofit theatre was subsidized sometimes to the extent of 50%. Concurrent with the nationwide establishment of professional acting companies was a 1960s rash of theatre construction, the first such in 40 years. Civic centres, opera houses and huge multipurpose auditoriums were erected, usually to help celebrate various provincial anniversaries or Canada's impending 100th birthday as a nation in 1967. Regrettably, most of these large playing-spaces were unsuitable for the new Canadian troupes burgeoning around them. However, the era of ballet and opera in hockey arenas was over, and the new buildings reopened the touring circuits for American musicals and palladium-type entertainments that had not flourished since the 1920s. There was even a Canadian musical comedy triumph: the cross-country tour of *My Fur Lady* in 1957-58, a delightful spoof that originated at McGill U and helped launch the careers of Brian MACDONALD and Galt MacDermot. Smaller pocket theatres (*théâtres de poche*) also began to appear in the late 1950s, primarily in Montréal and Toronto, and produced some of the first cabaret revues and original plays of the postwar period. *Up Tempo* (1956-65) ran for over 8 years in Montréal and Toronto's *Clap Hands* revue even proved to be a rare successful export to London (1961-63). Among the dramas, Len PETERSON's *The Great Hunger* (1960, publ 1967) stood out, as did *Hey, Rube!* (1961), one of the initial "collective creations" produced by George Luscombe's Toronto Workshop Productions (1959-).

Tom Patterson's dream of a Yukon festival flickered only briefly in Dawson City during the summer of 1962, but the idea would have its day again in the 1980s with Dawson's annual "Discovery Days" and the Gold Rush Theatre of Barkerville, BC. Montréal lost a beloved roadhouse in 1963, Her Majestys, while in Toronto Ed MIRVISH rescued the Royal Alexandra from the wreckers, just as he would buy and refurbish England's famed Old Vic Theatre 20 years later. Stratford successfully toured Tyrone GUTHRIE's Gilbert and Sullivan productions to London in the early 1960s, and took Shakespeare and Molière to Chichester in 1964 (Chichester had copied the Stratford stage). Canadian input to New York was less happily received. Robertson DAVIES's *Love and Libel* (1960) and Eric NICOL's *Like Father, Like Fun* (retitled *A Minor Adjustment*, 1966-67) were unfortunate failures. But in 1967 John Herbert's *Fortune and Men's Eyes* cracked the off-Broadway jinx. CENTENNIAL YEAR marked a watershed for Canadian nationalism. The Canadian Theatre Centre hosted an international theatre Colloquium '67 in Montréal and there were important new plays: George RYGA's *The Ecstasy of Rita Joe*, Ann Henry's *Lulu Street*, James REANEY's *Colours in the Dark* and a cross-Canada tour of the 1965 musical version of Lucy Maud MONTGOMERY's enduring hit *Anne of Green Gables*. In 1966 the pioneering Crest Theatre and touring Canadian Players (1954-66) were allowed to collapse, causing shock waves in Toronto, the nominal English-language centre. A new organization, Theatre Toronto, made a bid for world-class status in 1968-69. Its production of Rolf Hochhuth's *Soldiers* caused a stir in New York and London, but the company itself lasted only 2 seasons. Although Canada had produced a first generation of postwar dramatists, writers such as Davies, Herbert, Nicol, Peterson and Ryga, as well as John COULTER, Patricia JOUDRY, W.O. MITCHELL, Arthur Murphy, Lister SINCLAIR, Wilfred WATSON and Bernard Slade, Canadian plays were seldom seen on regional stages. The winter stock companies and summer festivals were labelled "dinosaurs," producing only imported of "museum" theatre, and they became targets for a jingoistic fervor.

A flurry of small groups rose to provide an alternative to the established regional companies, ensembles like Vancouver's Savage God (1966-80), Toronto's Passe Muraille (1968-) and Canadian Place Theatre at Stratford (1969). They were the spearhead of the second phase of Canada's postwar development. At first, the alternate theatre produced American Vietnam or "hippie" dramas that utilized the newfound freedoms of nudity and explicit language to make political protest. Passe Muraille's *Futz* (1969) and the year-long run of *Hair* at the ROYAL ALEXANDRA (1970) were symbols of the times. A 1970 Canadian Festival of Underground Theatre (FUT) in Toronto was also important. But it took Ken Gass's Factory Theatre Lab (1970-) and Bill Glassco's TARRAGON THEATRE (1971-), both in Toronto, to dramatically shift the emphasis to original plays and provide the "alternates" with a Canadian cause.

Clashes over indigenous works occurred at several regional theatres between artistic directors and their boards of governors. In the summer of 1971 the Canada Council, at the instigation of theatre officer David Gardner, convened a historic think tank in the Gaspé on "The Dilemma of Canadian Playwrighting." It produced the catalytic recommendation that a 50% subsidy should entail at least 50% Canadian content. This conference was followed quickly by a larger and more public gathering at Niagara-on-the-Lake, which led to the formation of Playwrights Co-op (now Playwrights Union of Canada) to foster the publishing of original dramatic works, a field already opened up on the West Coast by Talonbooks in 1969. The 1970s saw hundreds of new plays produced and printed, an exciting turnaround as Canada's professional theatre became more truly Canadian and accessible. Noteworthy among the second wave of writers were Carol BOLT, Peter Colley, Michael COOK, Rex DEVERELL, David FENNARIO, David Freeman, David FRENCH, Joanna Glass, John GRAY, Cam Hubert (also known as B.A. Cameron), Ken MITCHELL, John MURRELL, Sharon POLLOCK, James Reaney, Erika RITTER, Rick SALUTIN, George F. Walker and Tom WALMSLEY. Eventually, even the regional theatres clambered on the bandwagon, picking up the new hits produced by the "alternates" and giving them major mainstage productions.

Between 1971 and 1974, 2 federal make-work schemes, Local Intiatives Programs and Opportunities for Youth, provided funds for another spate of instant theatre companies. Many of these survived to swell the alternate ranks: groups such as Edmonton's Theatre 3 (1970-81); BC's horse-drawn puppet theatre, Little People's Caravan (1970-), which became the Caravan Stage Co in 1976; Vancouver's experimental Tamahnous (Chilcotin for "magic," 1971-); Magnus Theatre Co North-west in Thunder Bay (1972-); Winnipeg's Manitoba Theatre Workshop (1973-), in 1981 renamed the Prairie Theatre Exchange; Theatre Aquarius from Ottawa which relocated in Hamilton (1973-); Toronto Free Theatre (1972-); Toronto's Actor's Lab Theatre (1973-) and Famous People Players (1974-), a blacklight puppet troupe employing young mentally handicapped adults. Another yardstick of the times was the isolated English summer festival at Lennoxville, Qué (1972-82), devoted to repeat showings of lesser-known Canadian plays. However, unlike Ontario's BLYTH FESTIVAL, FESTIVAL LENNOXVILLE originated no drama of its own.

In 1972 a statistical survey of leisure activities revealed that over 2 million Canadians, or about 10% of the population, attended live theatre at least once annually, if not regularly, and that participation in arts activities exceeded that of sports, a radical reversal of traditional patterns. New companies continued to multiply. Some of the most interesting were Vancouver's New Play Centre (1970-) which now shares the Waterfront Theatre on Granville I with the Carousel Theatre for young audiences (1974-); Calgary's Alberta Theatre Projects (1972-); Saskatoon's 25th Street House Theatre (1972-) and Persephone (1974-); Thunder Bay's Kam Theatre Lab (1974-); Edmonton's Northern Light (1975-) and Theatre Network (1975-); Victoria's Belfrey Theatre (1975-); Vancouver's Green Thumb Theatre for Young People (1975-); The Mulgrave Road Co-op (1977-) in Guysborough Town, NS; and in Toronto, Open Circle (1972-82), Toronto Truck (1971-), THEATRE PLUS (1973-), and N America's 2 renowned satiric ensembles, the Second City Comedy Cabaret (1973-) and Yuk Yuk's Komedy Kabaret (1975-). With over 90 nonprofit theatre and dance companies, and a host of independent commercial enterprises, Toronto has emerged as the world's third-largest centre for English-language theatre, behind only London and New York. Inevitably, with such a large metropolitan population, groups with special identities have emerged; eg, companies devoted to women's interests (Nightwood, 1978-); senior citizens (the Smile Company, 1972-); young people (Young People's Theatre, 1966- , Theatre Direct Canada, 1976- , Erewhon, 1979-); gays (Buddies in Bad Times, 1979-); female impersonation (La Cage, 1986-); medieval drama (Poculi Ludique Societas at U of T since 1964); musical theatre (Comus, 1975-87); and technological experiments (Videocabaret, 1975-). Since 1975 Toronto has sponsored an annual multicultural festival and its ethnic diversity is served by 2 professional French-language troupes, Théâtre française de Toronto (1967- , formerly Le Théâtre de p'tit bonheur) and the bilingual Theatre Ensemble (1987-); 2 companies for blacks, Black Theatre Canada (1973-) and Theatre Fountainhead (1973-); and 2 Jewish organizations, the Leah Posluns Theatre (1977-) and Nephesh Theatre Co (1978-), among many others catering to specific language interests.

Of great satisfaction was the establishment of Native Earth Performing Arts in 1983, a Toronto theatre venue for the Indian peoples. It was not the first such enterprise in Canada by any means, but it signalled a new professionalism. The Forest Theatre at the Six Nations Reserve near Brantford, Ont, has produced an annual dramatic pageant since 1948. Vancouver's Chief Dan George brought focus to native peoples' problems with his performance in *The Ecstasy of Rita Joe* and subsequent fame to Canada with his Hollywood films. Between 1973 and 1975 the Tillicum Theatre of Nanaimo, BC performed plays with Indian themes, as has the Atchemowin (meaning "storytelling"), an all-native Edmonton group since 1976, remembered for their CBC-TV soap opera series *Muskeg Flats* (1978). George Kenny's play *October Stranger*, about a young Indian in white society, toured Ontario and was taken to the Monaco festival of amateur theatre in 1977. Indigenous Theatre Festivals were hosted at York U (1980) and at the Curve Lake Reserve near Peterborough (1982), attracting first peoples' troupes from around the world. There were tours of N Ontario in 1984 and 1985 by the Northern Delights Theatre Co and Sudbury's N'Swakamok Native Players (Ojibwa for "where three roads meet"). In 1986 the CBC produced a 6-part TV drama series called *Spirit Bay* using native performers and, in the same year, Linda Griffith's adaptation of Maria Campbell's story of a Métis woman, *Jessica: A Transformation*, won "best Canadian play" at the Quinzaine internationale festival at Québec City. In 1987, Tomson Highway's *Rez Sisters* captured a Dora Mavor Moore Award for the outstanding new play of 1986 in the Toronto area and was runner-up for a Chalmers Award. The native peoples had found their modern dramatic voice and entered the mainstream.

Newfoundland reversed the pattern and had its alternate theatre first. Chris Brookes's highly political Mummers Troupe (1972-82) not only revived the 19th-century Christmas tradition of MUMMING plays but with dramas like *Gros Mourn* (1974) and *They Club Seals Don't They?* (1978) brought collective creation techniques to bear on injustices in the outports. They also established the 200-seat LSPU Hall (Longshoreman's Protective Union) as the creative home for original drama in St John's, and it survives as the Resource Centre for the Arts (RCA), shared by many groups. After the Mummers came the zany Codco Company (1973-79), also disguised as WNOBS (White Niggers of Bond Street), whose irreverent influence can still be felt, although the company per se is supposedly dissolved. Codco performers such as Tommy Sexton and Greg Malone polished a comedy duo with the Wonderful Grand Band and then scored on CBC-TV in 1986-88 with their satiric *S and M Comic Book*. Cathy Jones had a great hit with her one-person show *Wedding in Texas and Other Stories* (1986-87) as did Andy Jones earlier in *Out of the Bin* (1984) and Mary Walsh with *Bloomsdays* (1982), her evocation of James Joyce. In 1986 the RCA staged a retrospective of past shows in a special "Decade of Performance" season and, in the summer of 1986, *The Best of Codco* toured successfully. The CBC sponsored an outrageous 1987-88 late-night Codco TV series that attracted a cult following. Rising Tide Theatre (1978-) evolved as a splinter group from the Mummers Troupe and performed early collectives like *Daddy...What's a Train?* (1978). Then, under Donna Butt and David Ross, they moved into the 1100-seat, government-operated Arts and Culture (Centennial) Centre and changed their format to larger, well-made plays in a determined bid to become Newfoundland's eastern regional theatre. Other St John's companies include Sheila's Brush (1979-) bringing folklore to schools, the overambitious Newfoundland Shakespeare Co (1983-), and Elysian Theatre (1986-) which has taken an anticollective and antinationalist stance. On the W coast at Stephenville, a training project under Maxim Mazumdar spawned the Stephenville (summer) Festival of the Arts (1979-), while Theatre Newfoundland and Labrador (1981-) makes its base at Corner Brook. In Labrador itself a Creative Arts Festival involving thousands of students from over 20 communities has been celebrated annually since 1976. One Inuit drama group from the tiny village of Nain, Labrador, the Nanuksuamiut (People of the Country), have committed themselves to original work and have begun to broadcast radio plays in both Inuktitut and English. Their 1983 stage production of *Sinnatomanguik REM (Dream Sleep)* represented Canada and Newfoundland in the International Multicultural Theatre Festival in Calgary.

An undoubted peak of the 1970s was Tarragon's epic presentation of James Reaney's Donnelly's trilogy (1973-75) and its autumn 1975 national tour under the banner of the NDWT (Ne'er do well thespians, 1975-82). (Reaney described his Canadian application of Kabuki techniques as "Canuki theatre.") There were further forays into New York and London, though to little acclaim. Broadway

saw Tarragon's *Hosanna* in 1974 and, in 1976, Charlottetown's *Kronborg: 1582* (renamed *Rockabye Hamlet*), a pop-rock muscial treatment of Shakespeare's masterpiece. Canadian productions exported to Britain in the mid-1970s rarely saw the West End but toured the more obscure provincial circuits or turned up on the fringes of the Edinburgh Festival. However, Canadian plays such as *Rita Joe* and John Murrell's *Waiting for the Parade* were given London presentations in 1975 and 1979 respectively, and were dismissed as "melodrama" or "deadening worthiness." But success or failure abroad seemed to matter less as Canadians recognized themselves in the mirror of their freshly minted dramas and found pride in the differences they saw.

By 1975 the first flush of excitement was over and a slump set in. Many of the "alternative theatres" were well on the way to becoming the new establishment and the spotlight swung back to the larger theatres. Vancouver's Playhouse added a theatre school in 1974 and the Robin PHILLIPS era began at Stratford (1975-80). The importation of British directors such as Phillips and the late Peter Coe at the Citadel 1978-80, provoked controversy and the imposition of protectionist policies. In 1980 a crisis over leadership at Stratford rocked the nation's cultural community and threatened the very existence of the renowned festival. Ironically, the succeeding artistic directors, John Hirsch and John NEVILLE, although Canadian citizens, were not born in Canada. Since the inception of Stratford only one Canadian-born leader, Jean GASCON, has emerged. Robin Phillips's later application of a repertory/ensemble system at London's Grand Theatre (1983-84) proved too radical an approach for the entrenched regional subscribers; however, his return to Stratford in 1986 as the director of *Cymbeline* and subsequent appointment as head of the Young Company (1987-) proved propitious. On 13 Nov 1976 the Citadel in Edmonton opened the first phase of its new theatre complex and in 1984 unveiled Citadel Phase II, ending with 5 theatres linked by an indoor tropical garden complete with waterfall, undoubtedly the country's finest facility. This was answered 14 Sept 1985 by Calgary's $80-million Arts Centre, a 6-level home to Alberta Theatre Projects, Theatre Calgary and the Calgary Philharmonic Orchestra. In Vancouver the ever-popular Arts Theatre Club (1964-) also did some empire-building, adding 2 extra theatre-spaces on the Granville I restoration project, first in 1979 and then in 1983. In Toronto on 29 Jan 1987, CentreStage and Toronto Free Theatre completed an historic merger destined to provide Toronto with a supercompany on a heightened scale. But all was not growth. In Halifax, Neptune had to close its doors for 8 months during 1976, owing to financial losses. It survived, but pointed to the hard times that have contributed to Halifax's continuing failure to root a sturdy alternative or second theatre. The year 1976 was also the occasion of the Olympics in Montréal and the poorly organized performing arts festival (or "cultural Olympics") that accompanied it. Calgary's Winter Olympics in 1988 were better planned. The 1976 Games provided theme material for several collective creations, although some critics were finding that since the hey-day of Passe Muraille's *Farm Show* (1972), this distinctive Canadian style and mainstay of the alternate movement was beginning to wear thin. In response to the crucial election of the Parti Québécois in Nov 1976, federal monies were made available for 1977-78 "unity" tours of Canada by the National Arts Centre companies in both languages. More from the heart were Rick Salutin's *Les Canadiens* (1977, publ 1977) and David Fennario's bilingual *Balconville* (1979, publ 1980), both at Centaur.

Also significant in 1977 were the first signs of an extended economic recession that would change the tone and direction of the youthful Canadian professional theatre until the mid-1980s. Cutbacks in arts funding necessitated smaller-cast plays and a more commercial and less historical approach in the new writing of the late 1970s and early 1980s. Comedies, musicals and thrillers began to dominate the playbills; works such as *Same Time, Next Year* (1975, publ 1975), *18 Wheels* (1977, publ 1987), *One Night Stand* (1977, publ 1977), *Eight to the Bar* (1978, publ 1979), *Jitters* (1979, publ 1980), *I'll Be Back for You Before Midnight* (1979, publ 1985), *Automatic Pilot* (1980, publ 1980), *Nurse Jane Goes to Hawaii* (1980, publ 1982), *Rock 'n Roll* (1981, CTR, 1982), *Talking Dirty* (1981, publ 1983), *Broue* (1979, in English as *Brew*, 1983) and *B-Movie, the Play* (1986). The carefully balanced subscription seasons of the regional and larger alternate theatres started to give way to more open-ended runs and a scramble for transfer-houses.

Corporate sponsorship of individual productions became a pattern and for the first time some independent entrepreneurs eschewed subsidy and mounted shows for private profit. Ed and David Mirvish picked up Stratford's 1982 production of *The Mikado*, one of the company's Gilbert and Sullivan revivals of the early 1980s, and toured it to resounding kudos in Britain, the US and across Canada, earning its director/choreographer Brian Macdonald 2 Broadway "Tony" nominations in 1987. There were also more co-productions and co-operative exchanges between companies so that costs could be shared and seasons not shortened. A stunning, Bunraku-inspired puppet production of Strindberg's *A Dream Play* in 1977, for instance, was sponsored by 4 different theatres, as was Paul Ledoux's and David Young's original evangelical rock musical *Fire* (1985-86).

Cross-country touring also extended the life of productions. There were several triumphs: *Ten Lost Years* from the East (1974-75); *Cruel Tears* (1975, publ 1977) and *Paper Wheat* (1977-78, publ 1982) from the West. Of course, since *Hair*, extended runs of a year or more were no longer a surprise. *The Mousetrap*, London's perpetual tourist attraction, has continued unbroken at Toronto Truck since 19 Aug 1977; Regina's *The Trial of Louis Riel* has played every summer since 1967 and Charlottetown's *Anne of Green Gables* since 1965. The professional record, however, still belongs to *Spring Thaw* (1948-71), the New Play Society's comedy revue which appeared annually for 24 years and was reincarnated in 1980 and 1986. On the amateur level, *The Vic Bob* has been an annual party/revue at Toronto's Victoria U since 1874 and the Arts and Letters Club of Toronto has produced a spring revue fairly continually since 1930. Sherman Snukal's *Talking Dirty* (1981-84) at the Vancouver Arts Club, and on tour, makes claim to be the longest run, to date, for a straight Canadian play.

In the search for new solutions to the economic problems, the medieval idea of combining spiritual and bodily refreshment was re-examined. Late-night cabarets and revues were a relatively new twist in Canada. Lunchtime theatre had been tried by Montréal's Instantheatre between 1965 and 1971. In the 1970s and 1980s the chief exponents were Citystage in Vancouver (1972-86), Lunchbox Theatre in Calgary (1975-), Northern Light (1975-) and Nexus (1982-) in Edmonton, and Solar Stage in Toronto (1978-). One of the most ambitious and prosperous dinner theatres was Stage West, an eventual sextet of supper clubs in Edmonton (1975-), Regina (1977-82), Winnipeg (1980-85) until the land was expropriated, Calgary (1982-), Palm Springs, Calif

(1983-84), and Mississauga, Ont (1986-), with prospects of a future outlet in Vancouver. All-nude revues were money-makers in the 1980s. In Toronto *O! Calcutta* ran for over a year and *Let My People Come* has thrived since Feb 1981. But Passe Muraille's *I Love You Baby Blue* had provided far more erotic sparks in 1975, before the police interrupted (but did not close) its 12-week run with charges of "an immoral stage performance." Vancouver's Touchstone Theatre (1976-) collective *Sex Tips for Modern Girls* (1985) and CentreStage's explicit Toronto production of Wedekind's *Spring Awakening* (1986) also created controversy, but few piqued national curiosity as much as the surprising f-word furor accompanying Charlottetown's 1987 summer production of the Elvis Presley musical play *Are You Lonesome Tonight?*

The other money-saving phenomenon of the late 1970s and 1980s was the one-person show. It had been essayed as early as 1965 by John Drainie (*Laugh With Leacock*) and, in 1970, by both Paddy Crean (*The Sun Never Sets*) and Tony Van Bridge as G.K. Chesterton. In the years that followed, they were joined by literally scores of others. One wonders if the prevalence of the soliloquy in 1980s playwrighting was influenced by this embracement of the solo performer. Eric Peterson's *Billy Bishop Goes to War* (1978-81, publ 1981), Linda Griffith's *Maggie and Pierre* (1979-81, publ 1981) and Viola Léger as *La Sagouine* (1974 in French, 1979 in English) were probably the most noteworthy early exponents, while Alan Williams's Cockroach and Texas trilogies (1981-87), Kenneth Brown's *Life After Hockey* (1985), Peter Boretski as *Einstein* (1985), Wayne Best (1986), Robert Haley (1987) and Stephen Black (1987-88) as *McClure*, are representative of the latter half of the decade.

The quest for better marketing techniques resulted in computerized ticket sales at most of the major theatres and, in 1983, Toronto borrowed the NYC idea of special downtown kiosks to sell tickets at half price on the day of the performance. Also, the pay-what-you-can Sunday matinee has become standard. To reduce their overhead many of the smaller theatrical organizations in the large urban areas banded together to co-operatively rent a single playing-space. The resident Tamahnous Theatre Society shares the Vancouver East Cultural Centre with other companies and the peripatetic Theatre Centre in Toronto has housed up to 30 groups. Theatres such as Tarragon and Toronto Free also make money renting their extra performance spaces. These spatial circumstances have contributed to the creation of several nomadic troupes like Toronto's Necessary Angel (1978-) who are not identified with any specific theatre but take their personality and the quality of their work from their director. Established companies such as Stratford, Shaw and London's Grand Theatre, as well as Edmonton's social-action Catalyst Theatre (1978-), have sweetened their budgets by turning 1980s productions into films and videotapes for the lucrative TV market.

Supper theatre was given a new wrinkle in the mid-1980s when Live Murder Mystery Games were introduced in Ottawa, Toronto, Montréal and Québec City. These staged "murders" (dinner included) occur in real dining rooms or resorts rather than in playhouses; even on board weekend train trips or boat cruises. After the body falls, the audience participates in tracking down the murderer and the motives, while the anonymous actors (amateur and professional) blend in with the paying guests and cleverly improvise their characters in response to the would-be sleuths.

However, for all the advantages wrung from the tight money situation, there were a disturbing number of small and middle-range companies that went bankrupt or closed shop in the 1980s: the Mummers Troupe in Newfoundland; Citystage and Westcoast Actors in Vancouver; Theatre 3 in Edmonton (succeeded immediately by Phoenix Theatre in 1981); Stage West in Regina; Festival Lennoxville; the Saidye Bronfman Centre in Montréal (although it revived briefly in the spring of 1987); and the Stephen Leacock Festival of Humour (1974-83) in Orillia, Ont. Toronto was hit badly with the loss of Open Circle, NDWT, the Phoenix, Adelaide Court, the Pauline McGibbon Centre, Theatre in the Dell, the Variety and Teller's Cage dinner theatres, and the magazine *Scene Changes* (1973-81), while in Ottawa, Penguin (1976-82), Theatre 2000 (1978-83), and the bulk of the National Art's Centre's indigenous theatre program, were some of the nearly 30 casualties. Ironically, the curtailment of inhouse production at the NAC was one of the very few theatre recommendations made by the disappointing Applebaum-Hébert Report in Nov 1982. However, where the NAC lost an artistic director it gained a producer, and the centre reverted to its original mandate to provide a showcase for the finest regional companies. It also presents a sterling example of the new spirit of co-operation. For example, for their 1987-88 season, the NAC entered into coproductions with Citadel, the Manitoba Theatre Centre, the Blyth Festival, CentreStage, and even south of the border with the Kennedy Centre in Washington, DC.

Alongside the waning influence of the regionals and the regrettable losses and inevitable ossifications within the alternate ranks, a new third generation of fringe theatre companies has emerged in the 1980s. Often these are not permanent companies but occasional productions brought together under various festival umbrellas across the country. The most famous umbrella is Edmonton's annual August Fringe Theatre Event held in the Old Strathcona district. First organized in 1982 by Brian Paisley, then artistic director of the Chinook Theatre (1978-), the 9-day, Edinburgh-inspired, Fringe festival has increased its audience every year since its inception, and attracts over 150 nonjuried entertainments often from as far away as England, France, Sweden, New Zealand, Australia, Florida and California. The first-come-first-served companies pay their own production and transportation expenses in return for 100% of the box office sales. Edmonton's mask and clown troupe, Small Change Theatre (1982-), was one of the companies born out of the festival. Vancouver picked up on the concept in 1985 with its "On the Fringe" September festival, often extending the run of some of the Edmonton attractions. While Toronto has not organized its events into a major fringe festival, nor called them by that name, fringe productions have existed as a primary means of showcasing new writing. Some of the various guises include Factory Lab's week-long "Brave New Works" series; the Theatre Centre's research and development workshops; Buddies in Bad Times' "Rhubarb!" and 4-play festivals; Tarragon's Spring Performing Arts Fair; Nightwood's "Groundswell"; and an annual feminist cabaret consisting of original 5-minute selections. Toronto has also welcomed a third wave of new, smaller, performing arts groups: the Acting Company, Act IV, Crow's Theatre, Theatre Columbus, DNA, Eclectic Theatre, 45.3, Mercury Theatre, Mixed Company and Ground Zero, among others, as well as a Harbourfront outlet for "Theatresports." This distinctive game, in which improvisational teams compete like a sporting match, originated with Calgary's Loose Moose Theatre (1977-) and national theatresports tournaments are held regularly with entrants from Calgary, Toronto, Halifax and Vancouver participating. Theatresports teams from Canada also compete internationally and one Toronto trio, The Out of the Way Players (1982-), won the 1983-84 International Improv Olympix and Ripley's *Believe It Or Not* recognition for the world's longest improvisational performance (48 nonstop hours). Late-night improvised soap operas and sitcoms have also become quite popular; Vancouver's is labelled under the generic title "Scared Scriptless."

Other innovative fringe companies doing original work have emerged in Winnipeg, Vancouver and Atlantic Canada. The mandate for Agassiz Productions (1979) is to produce only Manitoba playwrights using Manitoba talent. Vancouver's Headlines collective (1981-) has presented revues that were critical of disarmament and the housing crisis, while Fredericton's Comedy Asylum (1982-) created the *Maritime Mixed Grill* (1984), a revue which toured nationally in 1987-88. *Lucien*, a one-man show about an Acadian millworker, was developed from a character in this revue for Contact Theatre, a second stage for Theatre New Brunswick. Another young playwright's haven in Fredericton is Enterprise Theatre (1983-), producing pertinent, small-cast shows reflecting the Maritimes. In PEI the Island Community Theatre (ICT) Performance Group was founded in 1981 to provide winter fare to balance the busy summer season. They hold an annual "New Voices" playwrighting competition and have produced intriguing dramas like Michael Hennessey's *The Trial of Minnie McGee* (1983), a true story reminiscent of Lizzie Borden, concerning a downtrodden Island woman who poisoned her 6 children. This play had its premiere at the King's Playhouse, a summer theatre in Georgetown, PEI, housed in a heritage building that dated from 1897. Destroyed by fire in 1983, King's Playhouse was faithfully restored in time for the 1984 season and is contemplating year-round operation. Additional PEI companies include Charlottetown's Theatre Bandwagon (1982-) a political collective; Theatre After All, a 2-person alternative; and the Victoria Playhouse (1981-), a summer theatre in Victoria-by-the-sea, which went year-round in 1984-85. Another enterprising summer venture is Nova Scotia's Ship's Company which performs homemade drama on the decks of the resuscitated Kipawo Showboat docked at Parrsboro. A former Salvation Army building on Cunard St in Halifax has been established since 1985 as the home of Neptune North, Neptune's second stage. It is hoped that the Cunard St playhouse will survive as a home for alternate theatre to offset the more than 6 Halifax fringe troupes that have failed since the early 1970s. Two Calgary groups with intriguing names are Trickster, dedicated to clowning, and the One Yellow Rabbit Performance Troupe which has embraced the mid-1980s international phenomenon of "performance art" or "image theatre," with its stress on visual, physical and metaphoric values rather than literary or narrative plotting. The expressionistic tools of film, video, slide projections, mime, dance, music, circus, etc, were utilized by the mixed-media experimentalists of the late 1980s to move the parameters of the Canadian theatre towards new extremes of fantasy and dream-state. In direct contrast to performance art were the occasional plays that embraced hyper-realism. We think of the Shaw Festival's 1984 Winter Project production of *Delicatessen*, for example, at Toronto Free Theatre.

One of the great Canadian experimental successes of the 1980s was John Krizanc's play *Tamara*, produced by Necessary Angel and directed by Richard Rose for Toronto's Onstage '81 (the first international festival that Canada had sponsored since 1967). *Tamara* was set in the 1920s mansion of Italian poet Gabriel D'Annunzio. The various plots unfold simultaneously in different rooms and the audience members choose how they move through the house to reconstruct the storyline. The play has gone on to become an elitist cult-event. It was seen in Hamilton's Dundurn Castle in Nov 1981, has played in Los Angeles since 1984 (winning 6 LA Drama Critics Circle Awards in 1985), in Mexico City since 1986 and in New York since Dec 1987. Further productions are contemplated in Chicago, London, Paris, Budapest and Australia, making *Tamara* Canada's most successful theatrical export. In 1986 Vancouver's Tamahnous Theatre borrowed the concept to reconstruct and amend Shakespeare's classic into *The Haunted House Hamlet*. The idea for this kind of simultaneous, fragmented theatre may have originated from experiments undertaken by Prof Donald Soule at UBC 1970-72.

Behind the fringe movement lies a revolution against the generalist, something-for-everybody programming popularized by the regional theatres. However, the fringe thrives only in those large centres where the size of the population warrants experimentation and special-interest activity. Much of the new writing is dreadfully unfinished and the innovation unsustained. The work of helping authors to develop better-crafted plays has been taken on by Vancouver's New Play Centre, Edmonton's Workshop West and Montreal's Playwrights Theatre Workshop, with hope for an Atlantic playwrights colony at some future date. The Banff Playwrights Colony, founded in 1974, is a 6-week summer program modelled on the O'Neill Playwrights Conference in Connecticut. Works-in-progress are read/performed by professional actors and the playwright consults with other playwrights to polish and refine a finished text for actual, arranged production in a Canadian theatre. This "finishing school" approach is a new and welcome thrust. Over the years the Stratford Festival, too, has quietly workshopped new Canadian plays, unfortunately for production by companies other than Stratford. In 1987, Calgary's Alberta Theatre Projects inaugurated their Play Rites Festival while Centaur Theatre hosted a first Canadian Young Playwrights Festival, attracting 83 entries from writers under the age of 18. These fresh catalysts remind us that the Ottawa Little Theatre has sponsored an annual National One-act Play Competition since 1939. Another exciting breakthrough of the mid-decade was the new openness and exchange between Le Centre d'essai des auteurs dramatiques (the French Tryout Centre) and Playwrights Workshop in Montréal. In 1985-86 they coproduced and toured *Transmissions*, a joint translation of plays by Marie Laberge and George F. Walker. Both francophone and anglophone playwrights, with the assistance of the federal government, have taken a stronger stance on international marketing. Through various Canadian embassies, playwrights have been sent overseas to give readings from their plays. Canada House in London regularly stages such events, and there have been reports of an upswing in Canadian drama studies in Britain, France, Germany, Hungary and the US. The increasing recognition of Canadian plays abroad became a fact in the 1980s. *Billy Bishop Goes to War* was our first theatrical "hatrick," scoring raves in Canada, New York and London. *Tamara* seems destined for even wider acceptance. In the UK, Tarragon's 1986 tour of Michel Tremblay's *Albertine, in Five Times*, Nightwood's collective *This Is For You, Anna* and Dennis Foon's *New Canadian Kid* were received triumphantly. In more exotic locales Necessary Angel's *Mein* won the Audience Choice Award at the Bel-

grade, Yugoslavia, International Theatre Festival in 1986, and in 1987 Ken MITCHELL's one-person study of Norman Bethune, *Gone the Burning Sun*, was taken to China. Canadian plays were reported in Japan, Australia, New Zealand, Belgium, the Netherlands, Poland, Puerto Rico, as well as France, the UK and the US. Somehow it seemed to compensate for all the Citadel Theatre's ambitious attempts to storm either the West End or Broadway with musical tryouts such as *Flowers for Algernon* (1979) and *Duddy* (1984). In Canada itself, a survey by the Playwrights Union revealed that of 324 plays produced by 65 companies in 1986, 30% were new Canadian plays and 29% were Canadian revivals, for a cheering total of 59% Canadian content. David French was the most-produced Canadian playwright. The third generation of contemporary dramatists putting their stamp on the 1980s includes Jim Betts, Kenneth Brown, Anne Chislett, James Defelice, Dennis Foon, Norm Foster, Ted Galay, Sky Gilbert, Linda Griffith, Paul Gross, Don Hannah, Christopher Heide, Tomson Highway, David King, John Krizanc, Lawrence Jeffery, John Lazarus, Paul Ledoux, Michael Mercer, Frank Moher, Steve Petch, Kelly Rebar, Rick Shiomi, Sherman Snukel, Raymond Storey, Allan Stratton, Eugene Strickland, Judith Thompson, Charles Tidler and Peter Eliot Weiss, among others.

But playwrights without publishers don't travel. Canada has developed its play publishing industry over recent years and, at least in Toronto and Montréal, has created a climate for bookstores that cater exclusively to theatre and film publications. After Samuel French of Canada, Talonbooks (1967-) in Vancouver was the first to publish drama on a regular basis, to be followed by the Playwrights Union of Canada, Simon and Pierre, Coach House and Ms Fit in Toronto, as well as NeWest Press (Edmonton), Breakwater Books (St John's), Turnstone (Winnipeg) and Harbour Publishing (Vancouver). Playtexts are also printed in such scholarly and critical journals as *The Canadian Theatre Review* (1974-) and *Canadian Drama* (1975-), and first anthologies of Canadian plays have been put out by Penguin (1984), Irwin (1984) and UBC Press (1985). *The Brock Bibliography of Published Canadian Plays in English 1766-1978* (1980) is already out of date.

History and research have also been served. Canada's oldest theatre magazine, *Performing Arts in Canada* (1961-), was joined in 1980 by *Theatre History in Canada* (the organ of the Association for Canadian Theatre History founded in 1976), and *Theatrum* (1985-) which reflects the alternative theatre scene. Another sign of the times was the appearance of histories of theatre for Saint John, Edmonton, the Prairies, BC and Québec, all in the 1980s, with a 2-volume survey of Ontario in the works. An interesting collection of 35 essays entitled *Contemporary Canadian Theatre: New World Visions* (1985) attempted to put the first 3 decades of postwar theatre into critical perspective for an international audience. *A World Encyclopedia of Contemporary Theatre*, due in the 1990s, is being edited and published in Canada, and an updated *Bibliography of Canadian Theatre History* and an *Oxford Companion to the Canadian Theatre* were eagerly awaited. In 1986 there was even talk of a series of theatre museums, in the same year that Toronto's renowned Metropolitan Library Theatre Section celebrated 25 years of excellence.

As the population of Canada reached 25 million, the preservation and restoration of landmark theatres such as the Imperial-Capitol in Saint John and the unique Winter Garden/Elgin complex in Toronto proved important. New architecture was also in the wind. The Sudbury Theatre Centre opened in Sept 1982, the Arts and

Culture Centre in Yellowknife, NWT, in May 1984, and the 1500-seat Thunder Bay Community Auditorium in Oct 1985. Plans were announced for a 1200-seat playhouse in the forthcoming Prince George, BC, convention centre and arts complex, and Hamilton's Theatre Aquarius is hoping for a new 500-750 seat facility to open in 1990. A former ice-house at Toronto's Harbourfront became the Du Maurier Theatrespace in 1986 and, in addition to proposals for a new ballet/opera house scheduled to open in 1993, there was talk of an additional 800-seat auditorium for the Toronto Free Theatre. Another welcome trend of the 1970s and 1980s has been the naming of Canadian theatres after revered practitioners: Denise Pelletier, Fred Barry and Paul Hébert in Québec; Nathan Cohen, Jane Mallett and Robert Gill in Toronto; Joseph SHOCTOR in Edmonton; Dorothy Somerset in Vancouver; and Gwen Ringwood in Williams Lake, BC.

Increasingly, Canada has 2 distinct seasons of theatre. The winter season lasts from September to May ending in a flurry of awards to honour achievement onstage such as the Dora Mavor Moore Awards in Toronto (1981-), the Jessie Richardson Theatre Awards in Vancouver (1983-) and welcome additions to the Clifford E. Lee (1971-81), Floyd S. Chalmers (1973-) and Governor General's Awards (1981-) for playwrighting. The summer season took on greater significance in the 1980s as Canada experienced a vogue for populist entertainment. Of course, there is a network of summer stock theatres, some dating back as early as the 1940s. They extend from the Atlantic Ocean as we have seen, to BC's White Rock Theatre (1976-) and the Sunshine Theatre in Kelowna (1977-). There is a particularly heavy concentration in Ontario's cottage country, with several moving away from the familiar pattern of American, or British, comedies and mysteries to embrace and develop their own popular Canadian material. Taking their cue, perhaps, from the all-Canadian Blyth Festival, the Kawartha Festival (Lindsay), the Gryphon Theatre (Barrie) and the Muskoka Festival (Gravenhurst and Port Carling) have become leaders in this Canadianization process.

In the tradition of London's Regent Park and New York's Shakespeare Festival in Central Park, the mid-1980s saw a rash of outdoor Shakespeare in Toronto and the suburb of North York. There were 3 productions of the *Tempest* in 1987: Toronto Free Theatre's "Dream in High Park" (1983-) version; an intriguing colonial interpretation with Haida spirits at North York's Skylight Theatre (1979-) in Earl Bales Park; and the Toronto Studio Players theatre school adaptation called *Tempest in a Teapot* at Withrow Park. Even Toronto's Theatresports got into the act, staging improvisational "Shakespeare in a Pond," at Harbourfront, with the actors wading knee-deep in water. The innovative and tented "Shakespeare on the Saskatchewan" Festival (1985-) began with *A Midsummer Night's Dream* on a golf course, graduated to a futuristic *Tempest* featuring a swimming pool, and then on to a guerrilla warfare *Macbeth* set in Central America. Vancouver's Shakespeare Festival (1983-) in Vanier Park was also under canvas probably mindful of Vancouver's well-remembered Theatre Under the Stars (1940-63), which eventually was rained out of existence. Toronto Free suffered in 1986 because of rain. While Skylight Theatre's new 1500-seat outdoor amphitheatre was ready for the 1988 season, one wished it had had the resources of Winnipeg's thriving Rainbow Stage (1954-), which has survived by covering its musical comedies with a triodetic dome. Shakespeare Plus (1984-) in Nanaimo, BC, houses its summer festival in the 300-seat Malaspina College Theatre, and has evolved an interesting formula combining a Shakespearean work, a musical and an original Canadian play. Before leaving Shakespeare, we should mention the all-female *Julius Caesar* produced by the Future Shakespeare Co in 1986 at Toronto Workshop Productions Theatre.

Summer is festival time, and in addition to the western fringe events in Edmonton and Vancouver, and the major eastern festivals at Stratford, Niagara-on-the-Lake, and Charlottetown, mention must be made of a veritable 1980s explosion of open-air activities, ranging from Hot Air Balloon Contests (St-Jean-sur-Richelieu, Qué, and Barrie, Ont), to International Fireworks Competitions (Toronto), Town Crier's Matches (Halifax) and the bronco-busting Calgary and Medicine Hat stampedes. In addition to festivals of jazz (Montréal), folklore (Drummondville) and dance (Ottawa), there were another 25 or so theatrical festivals devoted to comedy, mime and drama. Montréal's Juste pour rire/Just for Laughs, which began in 1983 as a small French celebration, has mushroomed since 1985 into a large, 10-day, international and bilingual comedy extravaganza with 115 acts from 9 countries. In 1985 it launched the N American career of Québec impressionist André-Philippe Gagnon, and in 1987 saw Toronto's madcap Frantics (1979-) perform in French, a symbol of the new give and take. Another festival of comedy and music was organized in 1987 on La Ronde's floating stage at the former site of Montréal's Expo 67, while Toronto's O'Keefe Centre (1960-) presented a summer parade of Broadway musicals. Vancouver launched an International Festival of Comedy in 1987 on Granville I making use of many of the same street entertainers that delighted the visitors to Expo 86. And on the East Coast, Halifax held Buskers 87, its first annual international competition for street performers. This 10-day carnival offered a People's Choice Award of $10 000, and was a logical successor to the 1982 Dartmouth Festival of Clowning. Cape Breton's Festival Bras D'Or in 1985 featured 3 weeks of plays, including the revue *The Rise and Follies of Cape Breton Island*. Saint John's now annual, 2-week Festival by the Sea was launched in co-ordination with the 1985 Canada Summer Games. Sports and culture have been allied since the time of the Greeks. *Rendez-Vous '87* in Québec City made a profit, unlike the ambitious *Tall Ships* festival in 1984 that lost $5 million. Calgary's Winter Olympics Arts Festival in 1988 was budgeted at $10 million, and invited the Shaw Festival, the Royal Canadian Air Farce (1973-), and Peter Brook's *Tragedy of Carmen* in addition to its local theatre companies.

The accent of the 1980s was definitely international and Toronto, Vancouver and Montréal opened their arms to artists from around the world for festivals of mime, "Le festival qui fait du bruit," in 1978, 1980, 1983 and 1986, with Canada represented by more than 25 troupes. Beginning in 1981 in Thunder Bay, the Winnipeg-based Canadian Popular Theatre Alliance sponsored a biannual international festival of left-of-centre theatre for social activists and the working classes, attracting contributions from the unions and groups from more than a dozen nations. The 5-day festival in Winnipeg in 1985 was called "Bread and Dreams"; the 10-day event in Sydney, NS, in 1987, was titled "Standin' the Gaff." Toronto's Mayworks (1986-) is another multimedia festival in which labour and the arts unite. It kicks off annually with a traditional May Day rally. In response to the 1983 publication of a study on the Status of Women in the Arts, a Women in Canadian Theatre Conference was convened at York U in Aug 1985, followed by the First International Conference on Women in the

Performing Arts at Vancouver, Sept 1986. Young people, too, have not been forgotten. Since 1978, the remarkable Vancouver Children's Festival has spawned a string of similar international spring festivals in Calgary, Edmonton, Toronto and Montréal and, in 1983, Calgary played host to World Theatre Mosaic, a congress of the best in amateur theatre from around the globe. Montréal has even introduced a marketing festival called CINARS (1984-), a biannual promotional exhibit which showcases Canadian and foreign performing artists for agents, producers and talent scouts who gather from America, Asia, Europe, Scandanavia and New Zealand. Specifically national festivals also have occurred in this extraordinary decade of multicultural internationalism. Many guest countries have brought their theatrical treasures to Canada often in reciprocal response to similar Canadian cultural exchanges abroad. Vancouver laid out the welcome mat for an Asia-Pacific Festival featuring groups from India, Korea, Malaysia, China and the Soviet Union. However, where it succeeded admirably at Vanier Park in 1985, it suffered organizational problems and financial losses in 1987 when transferred to the site of Expo 86. Toronto was the other city with a significant multicultural profile. Since the inauguration of its annual Caravan festival (1967-), with its United Nations microcosm of ethnic pavilions and exotic culinary delicacies, Toronto has partaken of the *Brecht: 30 Years After* conference (1986), which saw the N American debut of the Berliner Ensemble; Holland's *Boulevard of Broken Dreams* (1987), which also toured to Montréal and Ottawa; *Italy On Stage* (1987), a multidisiplinary arts festival including theatre, opera, ballet, music and the visual arts, catering to the more than 500 000 Italians who live in the city; and *China '87*, a summer twinning of Toronto and Chongqing, China's largest city, displaying acrobatics, dance and art.

However, out of all this proliferation of international festival activity, 3 major dramatic festivals have emerged. Starting with Toronto's *Onstage '81*, which metamorphosed into Harbourfront's *Du Maurier World Stage Showcase* in 1986, the spotlight shifted to Québec City in 1984 with its first *Quinzaine internationale du Théâtre* (International Theatre Fortnight) and Montréal's *Theatre Festival of the Americas*, which had its premiere in 1985 in association with the International Theatre Institute's World Congress held in Montréal and Toronto. These 3 festivals are held biannually (with the Québec and Montréal festivals functioning in alternate years to avoid duplication). This festival fever has provided Canada with a new window on the world, allowing Canadian plays and performers to stand alongside such international productions as Ingmar Bergman's *Miss Julie*. It has also opened doors to Europe and the US. *Tamara*'s and *Billy Bishop*'s successes were echoed in NYC in 1986 and 1987 by the Famous People Players and Judith Thompson's *Crackwalker*. In California, audiences were delighted by Québec's unique one-ring *Cirque du Soleil* (Sun Circus, 1984-) with its absence of animal acts and stress on clowning, acrobatics and inventive theatricality. And in 1987 in London, Théâtre Repère's trilingual *Dragon Trilogy* (English, French and Chinese) was hailed a triumph. Performers such as Len Cariou, Hume CRONYN, Roberta Maxwell, Kate NELLIGAN, Christopher PLUMMER and Kate REID were stars either on Broadway or in the West End, while Hollywood recognized such former stage actors as Geneviève BUJOLD, Michael J. Fox, Helen Shaver and Donald Sutherland. Saskatchewan's Joanna Glass received a 1984 Tony Award nomination for her important tragedy *Play Memory* (originally seen at MTC as *The Last Chalice*), and Toronto's Teresa

Stratas was named best actress in a musical (*Rags*) by the 1986-87 NY Drama Desk. The work of Canadian set and costume designers was also exhibited abroad, and won special recognition at the Prague Quadrenniale of Scenic Design in 1975, 1979 and 1983.

The worst of the recession was over by the end of 1984, a black year in which Stratford recorded a record deficit and the CBC was hit by drastic governmental cutbacks. In 1985 there was a turnaround. Canadian theatre entered a new phase of confidence and strength. The musical *Cats* was given a lavish Canadian production in Toronto's partially renovated Elgin Theatre, a production favourably compared to its London and New York antecedents. Its exact 2-year run in Toronto (13 Mar 1985-13 Mar 1987) grossed $40 million and it went on tour in Canada for a further, sold-out, 7 months. As well as matching world standards of excellence, *Cats* signalled a new era for the entrepreneur. The search began for Toronto theatres that could be set aside for long commercial runs. It meant that the abandoned Crest Theatre was reopened and the Danforth's 1200-seat Music Hall (1916-) was converted to the New Century Theatre. But most interesting was the change of policy for the Royal Alexandra Theatre (1907-). The venerable Shubert Brothers roadhouse may never have been intended originally for local fare but the Royal Alex has now become a major Canadian producer. Over the years there have been occasional Canadian shows and short seasons by the National Ballet and the Canadian Opera Co, but it was rare to have 3 months of consecutive Canadian production. That occurred from Oct 1984 to Feb 1985 with Stratford's *Separate Tables*, *Cinderella* (an Anglo-Canadian pantomime) and Shaw's *Cyrano de Bergerac*, starring Heath Lamberts. In mid-1985 Ed Mirvish gave over the management of the Royal Alex and London's Old Vic to his son, David, and in 1985 David turned down the American road tour of Tom Stoppard's *The Real Thing* and substituted a Canadian coproduction of the same play, mounted by Schwarz/Sewell Productions and the Manitoba Theatre Centre. This was followed in the summer of 1986 by *Kismet*, done in collaboration with the Canadian Opera Co. In 1986-87 and 1987-88 the Royal Alex presented entire seasons of Canadian productions and co-productions including, in 1987, *Henry IV, Parts 1 and 2* and *Henry V* imported from the Old Vic, a new plank in the international bridge. There were even negotiations in 1987 to export the John Hirsch production of *Three Men on a Horse* to Broadway! And that's a switch. With the 1989 plans to mount a Canadian version of the blockbuster musical hit *Les Miserables*, it seemed clear that Canada was capable now of producing international commercial properties on a par with the best in the English-speaking world. By bypassing New York's overpriced and dwindling supply of touring shows, the Canadian theatre moved a large step away from its centuries-old colonial dependence on imported productions. However, *Cats* also pointed up the danger of Canada's theatre going the way of its film and television industries, and becoming merely a franchise theatre, a Broadway North. However, the commercial experimentation also meant that the potential was there for the Royal Alex, the National Arts Centre and other theatres to become transfer houses for original Canadian hits and then Canadian play "commissions" as well, the next and final stage in reclaiming the Canadian theatre for Canada.

The mid- to late 1980s watershed was also recognized on governmental levels. There were task forces on the status of the artist, the status of women in Canadian theatre, funding of the arts, the National Arts Centre, the care and feeding of

Toronto's artistic assets, films, broadcasting, copyright and the Canadian cultural industries. But parallel to these positive studies were concerns about betraying our cultural sovereignty in the free trade negotiations with the US, the dismantling of the CBC and NFB, and the strictures of censorship in new legislation on PORNOGRAPHY. Overriding all, was the shadow of the AIDS epidemic as it made its inroads into the arts community and beyond. Statistics provided by the Dept of Communications in 1986 told us that the cultural industries were our ninth largest; earning $8.5 billion and contributing approximately $16 billion to the economy. They were also the country's fourth-largest employer, providing jobs for 236 000 people. As J. David McLaren expressed it in the *Globe and Mail*, the arts industry was stitching the country together in the same way that the CPR did 100 years ago.

The battle for recognition of Canadian talent at home and abroad was being won. Finally, there was some ongoing dialogue between the French and English theatre, to say nothing of the emergence of native peoples' plays and a multicultural rainbow of ethnic groups. As the decade ended, the regions seemed less regional; more familiar, more accessible. And apparently a fresher and more light-hearted national identity was being forged. As Robert Wallace commented in *Contemporary Canadian Theatre*, "Canada is still in the process of creating itself as a character in the play of world events" but Canadian playwrights begin "to write the land alive."

The regional theatres and major festivals survived through co-productions, new blood and a growing scale of achievement that presages the viability of a Canadian commercial theatre. The mainstream alternates had come of age, although some of their dedication to Canadian originals had softened and their artistic directors were moving on to assume control of the larger regional playhouses. From below, a sprawling, feisty, innovative fringe theatre carried the revolutionary banner, writing "brave new works" and constantly redefining the nature of the theatre itself. Mention must be made, too, of new organizations such as PACT (Professional Association of Canadian Theatres), PAND (Performing Artists for Nuclear Disarmament), the Association of Canadian Designers, the Canadian Theatre Critics Association, the Guild of Canadian Musical Theatre Writers (who hope to publish an all-Canadian songbook), and even a Council for Business and the Arts. The Canadian theatre was alive and healthy and still growing, as the 1980s came to an end. The Canada Council celebrated its 30th anniversary in 1987 by helping to fund 188 established and 20 new professional theatre companies in Canada, to which at least another 50 to 100 independent or smaller and unrecognized organizations could be added. From its minimal postwar beginnings Canada's professional theatre had been transfigured within a "second Elizabethan age." DAVID GARDNER

Reading: J. Ball and R. Plant, comps, *A Bibliography of Canadian Theatre History 1583-1975* (1976; *Supplement*, 1979; rev 1988); E. Benson and L.W. Conolly, *English Canadian Theatre* (1987) and E. Benson and L.W. Conolly, eds, *Oxford Companion to Canadian Theatre* (1988); L.W. Conolly, ed, *Theatrical Touring and Founding in North America* (1982); L. Doucette, *Theatre in French Canada: Laying the Foundations 1606-1867* (1984); M. Edwards, *A Stage in Our Past: English-language Theatre in Eastern Canada from the 1790s to 1914* (1968); C. Evans, *Frontier Theatre* (1983); F. Graham, *Histrionic Montreal* (1902); B. Lee, *Love and Whisky: The Story of the Dominion Drama Festival* (1973); H. McCallum, comp, *Research Collections in Canadian Libraries: Theatre Resources* (1973); E. Nardocchio, *Theatre and Politics in Modern Québec* (1986); J. Orrell, *Fallen Empires: The Lost Theatres of Edmonton* (1981); J. Pettigrew and J. Portman, *Stratford: The First* *Thirty Years* (2 vols, 1985); D. Rubin, ed, *Canada on Stage: Canadian Theatre Review Yearbook* (8 vols, 1974-82); T. Ryan, *Stage Left: Canadian Theatre in the Thirties* (1981); M.E. Smith, *Too Soon the Curtain Fell: A History of Theatre in Saint John 1789-1900* (1981); E.R. Stuart, *The History of Prairie Theatre: The Development of Theatre in Alberta, Manitoba and Saskatchewan* (1984); R. Usmiani, *Second Stage: The Alternative Theatre Movement in Canada* (1983); A. Wagner, ed, *Canada's Lost Plays* (4 vols, 1978), *The Brock Bibliography of Published Canadian Plays in English 1766-1978* (1980) and *Contemporary Canadian Theatre: New World Visions* (1985).

Theatre, French-Language Only 3 dramatic texts composed in Canada during the French regime survive, all belonging to a genre called *réceptions*, written and performed in celebration of the visit or return of an important religious or civil dignitary: Marc LESCARBOT's *Le* THÉÂTRE DE NEPTUNE EN LA NOUVELLE FRANCE, enacted at Port-Royal in 1606; the anonymous *Réception de monseigneur le vicomte d'Argenson* (1658); and the untitled work composed by the Jesuit Pierre de La Chasse and performed by female students in 1727 for Bishop Saint-Vallier of Québec. Despite its tiny, scattered population, NEW FRANCE seems to have known periods of regular theatrical activity, particularly during the middle years of the 17th century. Most plays were imported, however, for demography and the increasingly overt opposition of the church militated against the development of a native tradition. This opposition was crystallized in the famous *Affaire Tartuffe* 1693-94, provoked by Gov Frontenac's announced intention to stage Molière's controversial play. The affair ended with Bishop Saint-Vallier bribing Frontenac not to have the play performed, but the severe public condemnation of *Tartuffe* by the bishop and his subsequent interdiction of all public theatre would have long-lasting effects. It was only after the Treaty of PARIS (1763), when printing presses were established and true urban communities began to form, that an indigenous theatre began to take root, a process that would take more than a century to mature.

Initially, there was a continuing reliance upon imported plays, especially those of Molière, but the beginnings of a true native dramaturgy were soon perceptible, particularly in newspapers and in institutions of secondary education. Theatre composed in French Canada before WWII was of 4 kinds: religious, pedagogic, political and "social," the latter being theatre intended for the entertainment, as opposed to the edification, instruction or politicization, of its audience. Religious/pedagogic theatre, predominant in New France, reappeared soon after 1763 and was cultivated in the expanding system of collèges classiques during the 19th century, exemplified by Antoine GÉRIN-LAJOIE's *Le Jeune Latour* (1844), Hospice-Anselme Verreau's *Stanislas de Kostka* (1855) and Jean-Baptiste Proulx's *Le Mal du jour de l'an ou scènes de la vie écolière* (1870). Inspired and often composed by clergy, drama of this kind could develop without economic stress or fear of church intervention. Political theatre is the most original genre to develop in French Canada. Dramatized dialogues in early newspapers in the 1760s soon evolved into full-length satirical plays directed against political opponents, eg, the 5 *Status Quo Comedies* published in 1834. Every major political confrontation during the remaining years elicited a fresh spate of playlets, the years 1848 to 1868 being particularly active. These political dramas ranged from the sober prose of the first 18th-century examples to rollicking song and verse, and from "paratheatre" (plays not intended for performance) to works enacted with considerable public success. Elzéar Labelle's delightful operetta *La Conversion d'un pêcheur de la Nouvelle-Écosse*, a satire of both sides in the CON-

FEDERATION debate, was performed frequently in Montréal between 1868 and 1899. These plays are clear predecessors of the satirical revues (fleshed out with song and dance and stuffed with references to current events) that dominated Montréal repertory in the 1890s and continued well into the 20th century.

"Social" theatre, which elsewhere constituted the mainstream of theatrical activity, remained a backwater in Québec. French-born Joseph QUESNEL composed a successful operetta, *Colas et Colinette*, which was first performed in Montréal in 1790 and was revived occasionally thereafter, most recently in 1968. Pierre Petitclair was the first native-born author of this type of drama, for though his 1837 publication *Griphon, ou la vengeance d'un valet* was apparently never performed, 2 later plays were staged in Québec City with considerable success, *La Donation* from 1842 and *Une Partie de campagne* from 1857. Louis-Honoré FRÉCHETTE adapted *Félix Poutré* from the memoirs of a self-proclaimed Patriote hero. First performed in 1862, it became a great success, particularly with amateur groups; its strong nationalistic fervour emerged as the most salient characteristic of Québec drama for the rest of the century. A good selection of such plays is included in Étienne F. Duval's *Anthologie thématique du théâtre québécois au XIXe siècle* (1978).

By the middle of the 19th century, Montréal had become the dominant centre of theatrical and economic activity. It thus also became a regular stop for professional touring companies from the US, Britain and France. The years after 1880 in particular saw glittering tours of Parisian troupes, the most spectacular of them being those of Sarah Bernhardt. The style and repertory of touring French companies were soon emulated by local troupes and playwrights, evidenced in the theatre of Félix-Gabriel MARCHAND, Régis Roy and Fréchette. In the 1890s the first local, professional French-language companies were established, performing in professionally appointed theatres and, in conjunction with the many English-language troupes then active, creating what has been called the first Golden Age of theatre in Montréal, described by J.M. Larrue in his *Le Théâtre à Montréal à la fin du XIXe siècle* (1981).

Unfortunately, these foundations were laid at a precarious time for live theatre – just as its most serious competitor, cinema, began to make its appearance. After a decade of struggle, exacerbated by the economic effects of WWI, stage arts in Québec underwent a long period of decline, the clearest symptom of which is visible in repertory which dominated the 1920s and 1930s. Satirical revues, monologues and burlesque prevailed, interspersed with populist melodramas of little aesthetic quality, such as *Aurore l'enfant martyre* by L. Petitjean and H. Rollin, which would continue to attract huge audiences for 30 years. It was the advent of radio that led indirectly to a rekindled interest in theatre, for the new medium made it possible for authors and actors to ensure their immediate livelihood, allowing them to channel remaining energies back into the more precarious live stage (*see* RADIO DRAMA, FRENCH-LANGUAGE).

Although opposition by the Roman Catholic Church to the public performance of theatre had been one of the principal obstacles to its development in French Canada, it was generally the clergy who, by their encouragement of drama as a pedagogic tool, had also inculcated the knowledge and appreciation of dramatic forms which are prerequisite to the success of a public stage. The birth of contemporary drama in Québec can thus be traced in large part to the clergy, for it was the dedication of dynamic priests such as Émile LEGAULT, Georges-Henri d'Auteuil and Gustave LAMARCHE that helped rescue theatre from stagnation in the 1930s; the first 2 as catalysts and impresarios for student troupes in the colleges of Saint-Laurent and Sainte-Marie, and the third as author/director of some 50 religious and pedagogic plays that caught the attention of students and eventually of Québec's population at large, despite intense continuing competition from radio and cinema. Legault's contribution is more visible, because of his formation 1937-38 of a small company of dedicated amateurs, the Compagnons de Saint-Laurent, and his aim of restoring to drama its freshness and magic. He and his group set out to free the stage, to poetize, refine and Christianize it. In this he was directly influenced by attempts at revitalizing theatre then current in Europe, where he went to study 1938-39, and in particular by the work of Henri Ghéon and by the new theories of stagecraft espoused in France by Jacques Copeau and the famous "Cartel" which shared his aims. The most important role of Legault and d'Auteuil was that of inspiring and training the future leaders in the renewal of stage arts in French Canada, Jean GASCON, Jean-Louis ROUX, Pierre Dagenais, Guy Hoffman and many others. Some went on to found their own professional companies such as Dagenais's l'Équipe (1943) and Roux and Gascon's THÉÂTRE DU NOUVEAU MONDE (1951). The TNM succeeded l'Équipe on the stage of le Gésu and set professional standards in acting and in stage, set and costume design for a generation, remaining the most stable theatrical company in Québec.

By the time they disbanded in 1952, the Compagnons had succeeded in forming a large, sensitive and demanding audience, capable of appreciating genuine professional skills and talent. In conjunction with the emergence of Montréal as a true metropolis and with the burgeoning self-awareness of the province of Québec, this enthusiasm would lead to the vigorous theatrical activity which characterized the 1960s and 1970s. The influence of d'Auteuil and Legault had done much to elevate and modernize repertory, staging and interpretation, but had achieved little for native dramaturgy. Playwrights felt more secure writing for radio, and some of them, such as Robert Choquette, constructed highly successful careers writing mainly or exclusively for that medium. An important milestone in the evolution of contemporary theatre was the 1948 premiere of Gratien GÉLINAS's full-length play *Tit-Coq*, which was performed at least 200 times in Montréal alone over the next few years. Gélinas too had written for radio and was well known for his humorous monologues, collectively entitled *Fridolinades* from their fictive author, Fridolin. Gélinas would add 2 more plays to Canadian repertory, *Bousille et les justes* (1959) and *Hier, les enfants dansaient* (1966) – all 3 translated into English and frequently performed. *Tit-Coq*'s success was soon emulated by other Québec writers, just as television, a formidable competitor to live theatre, was inaugurated by Radio-Canada in 1952. Television's influence has been pervasive, and sometimes nefarious, but in enabling playwrights to earn a living writing through the performing arts, it encouraged Canada's first professional dramatists (*see* TELEVISION DRAMA, FRENCH-LANGUAGE; TELEVISION PROGRAMMING).

The playwright most successful in adapting his craft to the new medium was Marcel DUBÉ, whose prolific career has spanned 25 years and produced more than 2 dozen plays, many of them now considered classics, such as *Zone* (1953), *Un Simple Soldat* (1958) and *Au Retour des oies blanches* (1966). It was partially to counterbalance television's perceived threat to live theatre that the first 2 public agencies financing cultural activity, the CANADA COUNCIL and Montréal's Regional Arts Council, were created in 1957, followed in 1961 by Québec's provincial Ministry of Cultural Affairs. Their conjoined influence has profoundly affected the development of dramatic arts, through their diverse strategies of subsidizing theatrical companies. While there has been an impressive increase in the number of companies, sometimes at the expense of quality, a theatre "establishment" has tended to receive most of the subsidies. This imbalance has encouraged a "counter establishment" that has proven exceptionally rich and productive.

By 1960 there were enough traditional playwrights of considerable merit (Éloi de GRAMMONT, Yves THÉRIAULT, Paul Toupin, Pierre PERRAULT) to represent, along with Gélinas and Dubé, an establishment in dramaturgy as well, which in turn has fostered successive waves of "new" (antiestablishment) theatre. The first wave of *nouveau théâtre* had been prefigured in the works of Jacques FERRON (*Les Grands Soleils* 1958) and Jacques LANGUIRAND (*Les Insolites* 1956), the latter strongly influenced by European Theatre of the Absurd. By the mid-1960s, "new" theatre rapidly became identified with political commitment. Politics is the primary focus of works such as Claude Levac and Françoise LORANGER's *Le Chemin du roy*, an incisive parody, in the guise of a hockey game between Québec and Ottawa, of the confrontation caused by France's President de Gaulle's eventful visit in centennial year. Robert GURIK's *Hamlet, prince du Québec* (1968) is a savage satire of the individuals and institutions embroiled in the ongoing federal-provincial struggle, while Loranger's *Médium saignant* (1970) is more intense but more local, focusing on the exacerbated problem of language rights in the embattled Montréal suburb of Saint-Léonard. The most blatantly political theatre has been written, or rather improvised, by Le Théâtre Euh!, created in the heady atmosphere following Europe's "Student Spring" of 1968 and ending with the group's deliberate self-destruction 10 years later. Euh!'s first performance was in Apr 1970. It was not only antiestablishment and antitheatre: it soon became deeply committed to populist causes and Marxist ideology, performing throughout the province and improvising its "nontexts," such as its version of Léandre Bergeron's *Histoire du Québec* (1972) and *A bas le plan Trudeau!* (1978).

For the general evolution of theatre in Québec in the 1960s, the most important event was the performance in 1968 of Michel TREMBLAY's *Les Belles-Soeurs*. Blending stark realism with an almost lyrical compassion, this play portrays the frustration of a whole generation of women in working-class Montréal. Here, for the first time, the diction and the unalloyed accent of popular Québecois speech are faithfully reproduced, the language itself becoming a symbol of the characters' frustrations and a powerful tool for the author's purposes. Tremblay's excursion into JOUAL, the language of the semiliterate working class, has been followed by many others, most notably Jean BARBEAU (*Ben-Ur*, 1971, *and Manon Lastcall and Joualez-moi d'amour*, 1970 and publ 1972), Jean-Claude GERMAIN (*Diguidi, diguidi, ha! ha! ha!* 1969), Victor-Lévy BEAULIEU (*En attendant Trudot*, 1974) and Michel Garneau (*La Chanson d'amour du cul*, 1974). This linguistic democratization has not escaped strenuous protest from French Canada's intellectual and cultural elite, a protest sometimes evidenced in the decisions of municipal and provincial funding agencies not to allocate funds for such works (eg, for the performance of *Les Belles-Soeurs* in France).

Les Belles-Soeurs is important also for its innovations in structure and staging, its stylized chorus and chants, its imaginative use of spotlighted monologues, all within the classical unities of time, place and action. The play itself had first been read and approved in 1965 by an antiestablishment group, the Centre d'essai des auteurs dramatiques, created to fill the gap left by the discontinuation of the Dominion Drama Festival and followed a few years later by the more durable Assn Québecoise du jeune théâtre (AQJT), increasingly committed to experimentalism on stage. Best known in this area is Jean-Claude Germain, one of the founders in 1969 of Montréal's Théâtre du même nom (TMN), a mocking anagram of that most established of theatrical companies, the Théâtre du nouveau monde (TNM). The TMN has specialized in mordant social satire, such as *Un Pays dont la devise est je m'oublie* (1976), and its healthy iconoclasm has been much abetted by the Théâtre expérimental de Montréal and the Ligue nationale d'improvisation, founded in the mid-1970s. But perhaps the most influential of the experimentalist-collectivist troupes was Le Grand Cirque ordinaire (1969), whose early successes such as *T'es pas tannée, Jeanne d'Arc?* (1969) encouraged other such undertakings in Montréal (Théâtre de l'Eskable) and elsewhere (Le Théâtre Parminou in Victoriaville, Les Gens d'en bas in Rimouski).

These organizations have catalysed and channelled the most dynamic forces at work in Québec's theatre, from Tremblay's polished, masterful innovations (*À toi pour toujours, ta Marie-Lou* 1971; *Hosanna* 1973; *Sainte Carmen de la main* 1976) to the improvised "happenings" of experimental troupes, all those forces who reject identification with what they perceive as the "corporate" stage. In a natural, ironic progression, Tremblay soon became identified with the corporate "haves" as well, and was therefore a target for the next wave of "have-nots." As these groups increased in number in the 1970s, the allocation of public subsidies became a more and more critical problem, exacerbated by the deteriorating economic conditions of the province and of the nation. By 1980 a clear demarcation had appeared between the 11 "established" companies (8 in Montréal, 2 in Québec, with one semiofficial touring company, the Théâtre populaire du Québec) and the 100 or so "new" amateur or experimental troupes, most of which operated in the Montréal area and many of which were condemned to a brief and difficult existence. By 1983 there were more theatrical troupes in Québec than in all other provinces combined. The heady years of the 1960s, when Québec's dramatists, directors and actors seemed to take the lead in expressing their society's cultural and political aspirations, have given way to sober reassessment and a certain retrenchment in the 1980s.

After the Parti Québécois victory in 1976 there was also considerable movement away from narrow propagandistic works, which sometimes did disservice to the stage, and towards a healthy preoccupation with broader issues. More distance has been particularly beneficial for comedy, as demonstrated in the later works of Tremblay (*L'Impromptu d'Outremont*, 1980) and the brilliant collaborations of Louis Saia and Claude Meunier (*Broue*, 1983). But it is the feminist awakening that has brought perhaps the most promising new direction for Québec's playwrights since the late 1970s, following the creation of women's troupes such as Montréal's Théâtre expérimental des femmes. A few of their early productions appear to have been too narrowly committed to endure, but feminist concerns have been strikingly portrayed by Jovette Marchessault (*Le Saga des poules mouillées*, 1981), Marie Laberge (*C'était avant la guerre à l'Anse à Gilles*, 1981), Louisette Dussault (*Moman*, 1981), and especially by Denise Boucher, the performance of whose *Les Fées ont soif* in the spring of

1978 led to the play's temporary censorship and to a resonant legal battle that was decided by the Supreme Court only in 1980. To the names mentioned in this paragraph must be added those of Jean-Pierre Ronfard, Maryse Pelletier, Normand Chaurette and René-Daniel Dubois. Ronfard is the author of some 15 plays to date, the most notable being his monumental *Vie et mort du roi boiteux* (1981), while Pelletier is best known for her psychodrama *Duo pour voix obstinées* (1985). Chaurette's *Provincetown Playhouse, juillet 1919, j'avais 19 ans* (1982) was an outstanding success in its revival in 1985, and Dubois, one of the finest actors of his generation, has been critically acclaimed for several recent works, notably *Ne blâmez jamais les Bédouins* (1984), *Being at home with Claude* (1986), also well received in their English translations.

In the course of 2 generations, theatre has progressed from being the "weak sister" among the arts to its current status as an inseparable part of the rich fabric of French Canadian culture. Not surprisingly, in the past decade the stage arts have attracted more, and generally more competent, attention from critics and historians than in their entire previous history.

The Maritimes After the performance of Lescarbot's *Théâtre de Neptune* in 1606, some 260 years passed before dramatic activity in French returned to ACADIA. Soon after the foundation in 1864 of the Collège St-Joseph in Memramcook, NB, a literary and dramatic society was established and theatre became a regular occurrence. From their foundation in the 1890s, the Collège Ste-Anne in NS and the Collège du Sacré-Coeur in NB also introduced plays performed by students as a central part of the academic year's activities. Choice of plays ranged from "expurgated" classics to plays written by clerics in France for college theatre, but there are references as well to works written specifically for these occasions by members of the faculty.

First of these to survive is the verse drama *Subercase*, by French-born Father Alexandre Braud, performed at Ste-Anne in 1902. Acadian patriotism and loyalty to French origins are the inspiration of this play (Daniel d'Auger de Subercase was the last French governor of Acadia), as they were to be for Father Jean-Baptiste Jégo, also a native of Brittany and an instructor at Ste-Anne. Jégo's *Le Drame du peuple acadien* was performed at the college with great success in 1930, awarded a prize by the Académie Française and published in Paris (1932). Less didactic but equally patriotic were the works of another priest, James Branch, the first native Acadian dramatist whose works have survived. His 3 best-known plays were written and performed before his ordination, while he was still a student at Bathurst's Collège du Sacré-Coeur: *L'Émigrant acadien* (1929), *Jusqu'à la mort!. . . pour nos écoles* (1929) and *Vivent nos écoles catholiques! ou la Résistance de Caraquet* (1932). All 3 are intensely nationalistic, with a degree of political commitment rare in his time.

Theatre continued to thrive in Acadian colleges throughout the 1940s and 1950s, frequently enriched by touring companies from Québec. In the 1950s, formal courses in drama were instituted, and Acadian troupes began to compete regularly in the Dominion Drama Festival. But the further development of native dramaturgy had to await Antonine MAILLET, the region's outstanding writer in French, whose first play, *Entr'acte* (unpublished), was performed in 1957. With the founding in 1963 of U de Moncton, amalgamating NB's francophone colleges, a second Acadian Renaissance began, its dynamism reflected in poetry, fiction, history and theatre. Its highwater mark was probably Maillet's *La Sagouine* (1971), a dramatic monologue by an illiterate but philosophic Acadian charwoman, first written for a Moncton radio station, performed with great success in Montréal, and highly popular with television viewers across Canada in its French and English versions. Maillet has added half a dozen other plays, notably *Evangéline deusse* (1975), in which an 80-year-old Acadian exile in Montréal expresses eloquently the sorrows and aspirations of her nation. The preoccupation with past sorrows and their distillation into present struggles is the central theme of Maillet's theatre, as it has become for Laval Goupil, the only other Acadian playwright to have attracted attention outside the Maritimes. His *Tête d'eau* (1974) was followed by the more committed *Le Djibou* (1975), dealing with regional concerns. Huguette Légaré (*Les Criquets sous la neige* 1974) and Germaine Comeau (*Les Pêcheurs déportés* 1974) continue this preoccupation, the latter work depicting the forced emigration, for economic reasons, of so many contemporary young Acadians.

Ontario Ottawa-Hull was the birthplace of French-language theatre in Ontario, whose genesis has been well documented by Edgar Boutet in his *85 Ans de théâtre à Hull* (1969). The first theatre was constructed under the auspices of the Oblate order in 1884, and theatrical activity has continued with little interruption. Encouraged by the clergy and by U of Ottawa, amateur activity has been constant, its repertory generally modelled on that of Québec, with little attempt at creating any regional tradition of composition. Dedicated directors and managers of local troupes (Wilfrid Sanche, Léonard Beaulne, Ernest Saint-Jean, René Provost) assured the survival of a theatrical tradition through the worst years of the 1920s and 1930s until, with the foundation of Provost's School of Dramatic Arts in Hull in 1945, a nucleus was provided for rekindled interest in the stage. The organization, by Guy Beaulne, of the Assn canadienne du théâtre d'amateurs in 1958 was significant for regional French-language troupes across the country, and the opening in 1969 of the NATIONAL ARTS CENTRE in Ottawa has provided a stable centrepiece as well as glittering inspiration for local theatrical activity.

But if the National Capital Region has long been the principal focus of Franco-Ontarian theatre, it has not been the only one: there were (in 1980) some 25 French-language troupes active in the province, including the Troupe oxygène in Cornwall, Pourquoi pas? in Rockland, Les Franco-Fous in Sudbury, and the Théâtre du p'tit bonheur in Toronto. This strong and relatively long tradition of theatrical performance has not, however, been accompanied by a tradition of dramatic composition. The 1960s saw the publication of Jacqueline Martin's *Trois Pièces en un acte* (1966), but it is only in the next decade that sustained writing is observed: Claude Belcourt's *Les Communords* (1974); the collective text *La Parole et la loi* by Vanier's troupe, La Corvée, performed several times with great success before its publication in 1980; and in particular the collected plays of Ontario's most significant French-language dramatist to date, André Paiment (1978). Paiment's theatre, like that of the others mentioned, focuses heavily on the explication and defence of Franco-Ontarian causes. *La Vie et les temps de Médéric Boileau*, written in 1974, explores the harsh life of forest workers with great sensitivity, but his best-known work, first performed in 1975, is *Lavalléville*, a description of violence and greed in a small, fictional Ontario village governed by a dictatorial family.

Manitoba Unlike French-language theatre elsewhere outside Québec, Manitoba theatre has had a detailed, scholarly monograph devoted to it, Annette St-Pierre's *Le Rideau se lève au Manitoba* (1980). The history of stage arts began in the 1870s, again under the auspices and supervision of the teaching clergy, in this case the Grey Nuns in their boarding school at St-Boniface. Many of the plays performed in educational institutions were written by members of the local clergy, in particular by Sister Malvina Collette, one of whose plays, *Un Souvenir de la patrie*, performed in 1870, has been published in *Chapeau bas: Réminiscences de la vie théâtrale et musicale du Manitoba français* (1980), edited by the Société historique de St-Boniface. As the population grew and the school system with it, amateur theatre became a central part of local cultural activity. When, after 1885, the Jesuits were entrusted with the Collège de St-Boniface, their predilection for college theatre came to the fore, with well-advertised programs that attracted spectators from all the little settlements along the Red R. The formation of amateur theatrical societies independent of schools was the next step, as enthusiastic local troupes sprang up in nearly every settlement during the Golden Age, 1914-39. There were parish groups, organizations based on national origin (le Club belge, les Dames auxiliaires des vétérans français, les Canadiens de naissance), troupes founded by religious societies (les Enfants de Marie, la Ligue des institutrices catholiques de l'ouest) and politico-social groups (le Cercle ouvrier, les Amis de Riel, l'Union nationale métisse). But perhaps the most significant, certainly the most enduring, was the Cercle Molière, founded in 1925 and still vigorous 60 years later. Under the leadership of André Castelein de la Lande, Arthur and Pauline Boutal and their talented successors, this organization has attracted to it virtually all those interested in the performing arts in Manitoba. Despite its title, its repertory has covered everything from the French classics to light, modern theatre from Paris and Montréal.

An impressive number of plays have been composed in Manitoba as well, although relatively few have as yet been published. Auguste-Henri de Trémaudan, a Québécois by birth, but educated in France, was the author of 5 published plays, such as the melodrama *De fil en aiguille* (1925) and the historical drama *Quand même* (1928) which played with considerable local success. André Castelein de la Lande, a Belgian immigrant, composed some 50 popular plays, 4 of them published in Montréal, nearly all dealing with general, noncontroversial topics. Roger Auger, a native Franco-Manitoban, is the author of *Les Éléphants de tante Louise* (1972) and *Je m'en vais à Régina* (1976), portraying the problems encountered by a family of Francophones. *Les Manigances d'une bru* (1980) by Roger Legal and Paul Ruest deals with this theme also, whereas Rosemarie Bissonnette's *La Bagarre* (1977) portrays Manitoba's painful history for those of French origin. Other works by provincial playwrights have been performed, sometimes with great success, such as Claude Dorge's *Le Roitelet*, concerning the execution of Louis Riel, performed by the Cercle Molière in 1976. Theatre is the most visible and most vigorous of Manitoba's cultural manifestations in French. *See also* DRAMA IN FRENCH.

LEONARD E. DOUCETTE

Reading: Archives des lettres canadiennes, vol 5: *Le Théâtre canadien-français* (1976); E. Boutet, *85 Ans de théâtre à Hull* (1969); B. Burger, *L'Activité théâtrale au Québec, 1765-1825* (1974); *Dictionnaire des oeuvres littéraires du Québec* (1978-); Leonard E. Doucette, *Theatre in French Canada 1606-1867* (1984); P. Gobin, *Le Fou et ses doubles* (1978); J.C. Godin and L. Mailhot, *Théâtre québécois*, 2 vols (1970, 1980); A. Gruslin, *Le Théâtre et l'état au Québec* (1981); J. Laflamme and R. Tourangeau, *L'Église et le théâtre au Québec* (1979); E.G. Rinfret, *Théâtre canadien d'expression française* (4 vols, 1975-78); A. Saint-Pierre, *Le Rideau se lève au Manitoba* (1980).

Theatre, Multicultural, may be defined in Canada as mainly European-style theatre by groups other than that of English or French origin. Performance may be in either official language or in the native tongue of the particular ethnic group. Although examples of multicultural theatre can be found in the 19th century, it was not until the years following WWII that ethnic theatre was firmly established. Two major factors contributed to this growth: the concentration in a single area of a minority group large enough to support theatre; and the arrival of a substantial number of immigrants who had been artists in their own countries but could not practise professionally on English stages because of language difficulties. At the same time, children of immigrants, who were well educated and more financially secure than their parents, sought creative outlets to preserve their culture.

Many of the ethnic theatre companies formed prior to and in the 1950s are still thriving today. Toronto's Hungarian Art Theatre, whose dynamic founder, Sándor Kertész, emigrated in 1957 after 30 years of acting and directing in Budapest theatre companies, produces impressive large-scale musicals as well as comedies and dramas. The Ukrainian Dramatic Ensemble, "Zahrava," founded in 1956, and the Finnish Social Club, founded in 1932, both among the strongest and oldest ethnic theatres in the country, have earned faithful audiences for their consistently high-calibre work. Other noteworthy Toronto groups are the New Czech Theatre (founded in 1970) which has a regular subscription season of 6 productions yearly, the Canadian Ukrainian Opera Association (founded in 1974) which brings spectacular and authentic Ukrainian opera to the Canadian stage every 2 years, the Latvian D.V. Theatre Company which uses theatre as a teaching vehicle for the language, and the Lithuanian drama group Aitvaras (founded in 1972 with its sister group Aukuras in Hamilton founded in 1950), the longest existing Lithuanian theatre company in N America. Yiddish theatre flourished in Toronto in the late 1920s and early 1930s, with artists from both Canada and the US performing. Although there have been earnest attempts to revive Yiddish theatre, the Yiddish Drama Group of the Saidye Bronfman Centre in Montréal has the honour of being the oldest continuing theatre of its type in the country. Founded in 1956 by Dora Wasserman, a graduate of the famed Moscow Yiddish Art Theatre, the company performs many plays from the classic Yiddish repertoire including those of I.L. Peretz, Sholem Asch, Sholem Aleichem and Isaac Baashevis Singer as well as original musicals and dramas. Other contemporary Jewish theatres which present English-language productions that reflect a Jewish consciousness, sensitivity and flavour are the Jewish Heritage Theatre founded in 1972 in Vancouver and the Leah Posluns Theatre, founded in 1972 in North York, Ont. Montréal's Deutsches Theatre (formerly the German Academy Theatre, founded in 1952) has the distinction of being one of the original theatre groups that occupied the Montréal International Theatre, La Poudrière, in 1958, which was specifically set up to present multicultural theatre productions. When funding for La Poudrière collapsed in 1976, the group took the name of Deutsches Theatre and has since presented 2 productions yearly at the Centaur Theatre from the classical and contemporary German repertoire. Other established German groups in the country are Winnipeg's Deutsche Buehne (founded in 1959) and the Winnipeg Mennonite Theatre (founded in 1972), known for its outstanding opera productions in German, and the German Theatre of Vancouver (founded in 1971).

Although most ethnic or multicultural theatre companies remain amateur in status, many of the companies mentioned have subscription series, go on tour, and represent their regions in national and international festivals.

Ukrainian theatre is well represented in the West with 3 notable groups: Edmonton's Story Theatre for children, which performs throughout the school system with adaptations of Ukrainian legends; the Ukrainian Children's Theatre in Winnipeg; and the spectacular Ukrainian Shumka Dancers, a 30-year-old amateur troupe that has performed for heads of state and at professional theatres across the country. Montréal's excellent Italian theatre company, Le Maschere, founded in 1974, presents only one production a year but has represented Québec in national multicultural festivals.

While Irish drama is no stranger to professional stages, several community English-language Irish theatre groups in the country have as their goal the preservation of Gaelic heritage, among them Edmonton's Shamrock Players, Winnipeg's Tara Players, British Columbia's Stage Erieann Dramatic Society, the Toronto Irish Players and the Irish Newfoundland Association. Of the few Spanish theatre groups in the country, Montréal's 2 Hispanic companies warrant a special mention: the Teatro Valle Inclán founded in 1974 and the Teatro Experimental Horizontes founded in 1977. The latter group, dedicated to performing S American plays of a political nature, has represented Canada in Latin American theatre festivals in Nicaragua and Cuba and has also organized the Montréal Festival Latino 86, an extension of Joseph Papp's Festival Latino in New York. Newer groups which stand out because of their youth and single-mindedness are Winnipeg's Gujuarti East Indian theatre group, Toronto's Canasian Artists Group and the Philippine Carlos Bulosan Cultural Workshop.

Black theatre has been enriching our multicultural theatre scene since 1942 when the Montréal Negro Theatre Guild in a monumental breakthrough transferred it's production of Marc Connolly's *The Green Pastures* to Her Majesty's Theatre. Through the years the group continued to win awards at festivals as well as develop performers of considerable note. Also formed in the early 1970s were Toronto's Theatre Fountainhead founded by Jeff Henry and Black Theatre Canada founded by Vera Cudjoe. Both companies have concentrated on developing and producing the works of black playwrights. Cudjoe and BTC have introduced many new works in their seasons' line-up and have also brought productions into the schools as well as run successful workshops. Two other interesting black theatre companies are Winnipeg's Caribbean Theatre Workshop, which presents the plays of West Indian writers, and the only black theatre company in the Atlantic Provinces, "Kwacha" (meaning "dawn of a new day") incorporated in 1984 by artistic director Walter Borden.

While the majority of multicultural theatre companies in the country perform Western-style drama, the Chinese United Dramatic Society of Toronto has been performing Cantonese opera in the city since 1933. The elaborate productions, which are presented twice yearly, feature lavish costumes designed and made in Hong Kong and professional actors brought in from the US and Hong Kong to augment the mainly amateur but highly skilled cast. The society's 800 members and the Chinese community support the Cantonese operas, many of which are over 1000 years old. Other Chinese opera societies exist in Toronto, Montréal and Vancouver.

Native theatre, historically ceremonial dance and ritual, has undergone some dramatic changes over the last decade as native Indian groups have begun to write and perform Western-style drama. In the past, productions such as George RYGA's *The Ecstasy of Rita Joe* and Michael Cook's *On the Rim of the Curve* used native themes and performers. However, Winnipeg's Manitou Theatre, Vancouver's Tillicum Theatre and the 1977 production of George Kenney's *October Stranger* by the Assn for Native Development in the Performing and Visual Arts have introduced native playwrights as well. ANDPVA has been instrumental in promoting training in the performing arts. In 1974 it founded a native theatre school, now situated in Owen Sound, Ont, where young people are given intensive training by professional teachers. ANDPVA's founder, the late James Buller, also helped to initiate the first annual Indigenous Theatre Celebration, held in Toronto in 1980, which brought together artists from all over the world demonstrating native people's non-European concept of theatre.

Other native Canadian theatre groups of note are KSAN in BC, which presents colourful ritual potlatches; Native Theatre Productions from Winnipeg; Manitoulin I's Young De Ba Jeh Mu Jig Theatre Co which produces new works such as Roy Morris's *Ayash* and also tours; and the annual Six Nations Pageant held on the Six Nations Reserve in Brantford, Ont. In Toronto, the well-earned success of the energetic Native Earth Performing Arts company and its artistic director/playwright, Tomson Highway, has given the local theatre scene a shot in the arm. Highway's drama *The Rez Sisters*, won a coveted Chalmers Award as well as a Dora Mavor Moore Award for the Outstanding New Play of 1986 produced in the Toronto area.

The rapidly growing multicultural theatre movement in the 1970s, enhanced by the multiculturalism policy of the federal government, prompted the formation of the National Multicultural Theatre Assn (NMTA) in 1975, to foster a better understanding and a mutual appreciation of the multitude of cultures that form Canada's diverse lingual and racial theatrical mosaic. The NMTA serves as a liaison between the provincial associations and stages the National Multicultural Theatre Festival, which is held each year in a different province and city. In 1983 the NMTA organized the "World Theatre Mosaic" in Calgary, the first international community theatre festival ever held in the country. Total membership in the NMTA approximates 350 theatre groups, of which only half perform exclusively in minority languages. In 1979 the NMTA was appointed by the International Amateur Theatre Assn as the national centre for Canada's community theatres.

JENIVA BERGER

Reading: Jeniva Berger, "A Coat of Many Colours: The Multicultural Theatre Movement in Canada," *Contemporary Canadian Theatre: New World Visions,* A. Wagner, ed (1985); M. Kovacs, ed, *Ethnic Canadians Culture and Education* (1978); S.A. Reddoch, *Our Cultural Heritage* (1979); S. Kertész, *Curtain at Eight* (1981).

Theatre Ballet of Canada is a chamber troupe based in Ottawa. Much of its repertoire consists of works by artistic director Lawrence Gradus, who favours a neoclassical style of choreography. Modern dance choreographers, such as Danny GROSSMAN, also contribute works to its repertoire. The company was established in 1980 from 2 separate companies, Ballet Ys (Toronto, fd by Gloria Grant) and Entre-Six Dance Company (Montréal, fd by Gradus and Jacqueline Lemieux in 1974). The new company made its debut at the National Arts Centre 13 Feb 1981, and has since toured Canada and abroad. The troupe co-founded the biannual Canada Dance Festival/Danse Canada in 1987.

MICHAEL CRABB

Théâtre de Neptune en la Nouvelle-France, Le, drama prepared by Marc LESCARBOT and performed Nov 1606. It was written in the tradition of a *réception*, composed to celebrate the return of an important personage, in this case of Poutrincourt to PORT ROYAL. The play depicts the god Neptune bidding the travellers welcome; he is surrounded by a court of Tritons and Indians who recite the praises of the colonial leaders and sing in chorus the glory of the king. As befits the first play written in French in N America, it contains a serious attempt to depict a New World setting with "Indian" roles and a smattering of native words. Lescarbot published it as part of his collection of poems, *Les muses de la Nouvelle-France* (1609).   JAMES MARSH

Théâtre du nouveau monde (TNM), based in Montréal, was founded by Georges GROULX, Jean GASCON, Jean-Louis ROUX and Guy Hoffmann in 1951 as a repertory theatre with emphasis on Molière. A period of experimentation (1956-66) with eclectic programming proved to be a difficult time for the theatre: artistic director Roux left in 1963 and Gascon in 1966. After Roux returned in 1966, the TNM became a theatre for the Québec public. In the 1972-73 season the TNM was established in the former home of the COMÉDIE-CANADIENNE. Under the current direction of Olivier Reichenbach, the TNM is a successful "establishment theatre" with a repertory drawn from popular international and Québec playwrights.
                                    MARILYN BASZCZYNSKI

Reading: *Les Vingt-cinq ans du TNM* (1976).

Théâtre du rideau vert, founded in 1949 by Yvette Brind'Amour (still artistic director in 1988) at the Théâtre des compagnons, ceased activity shortly thereafter and resumed in the 1955-56 season. The Rideau vert preferred "boulevard" theatre and light comedies; its repertory was popular Parisian classics as well as modern authors such as Lorca, Sartre, Montherlant and Bernanos. In the mid-1960s an effort was made to create and present Québecois theatre, including Michel TREMBLAY's *Les Belles Soeurs* and Antonine MAILLET's *La Sagouine*. Between 1968 and 1979 André Cailloux ran a successful program for young children. Since 1968 the Rideau vert has been housed in the Stella in Montréal and has presented a repertory of classic and modern authors (Shakespeare, Molière, Ibsen, Giraudoux), some boulevard theatre (Feydeau, Labiche) and Québecois works (Françoise LORANGER, Antonine Maillet, Marcel DUBÉ and Michel Tremblay).
                                    MARILYN BASZCZYNSKI

Theatre Education All theatre activity connected with schools and teaching could be termed educational theatre; however, the accepted designation is confined to universities and private theatre schools. Theatre education has expanded rapidly since WWII. Statistics in the Black Report on Theatre Training in Canada (1977) suggest that educational theatre in colleges and universities is now the largest single theatre enterprise in Canada. This does not take into account the immense growth recorded in secondary-school and recreational theatre.

In Québec, a 1694 ban of the proposed production of Molière's *Tartuffe* loosed a deluge of church disapproval, and French-speaking theatre languished for almost 150 years (*see* THEATRE). However, the Jesuit practice of presenting intramural productions of the classics and morality plays in their colleges continued into the 20th century. Formal training in theatre arts in Québec began only in the 1950s, and people wishing to work in theatre before that time took courses at the Lasalle Conservatory (1907-) or from private teachers, joined existing theatre companies, or

studied in France. The dynamic priest, Father Émile LEGAULT, who founded the influential Compagnons de Saint-Laurent in 1937, added a short-lived theatre school of good reputation 10 years later. The THÉÂTRE DU NOUVEAU MONDE opened an acting school in 1951, and in 1954 the Conservatoire d'art dramatique was established in Montréal, followed by a sister conservatory in Québec City in 1958. The National Theatre School of Montréal was founded in 1960 on the artistic principles of adviser Michel Saint-Denis. Still regarded as a major acting and design school, it offered separate training in French and English. By the end of the 1960s, 2 schools at the CEGEPs of Ste-Thérèse and St-Hyacinthe were offering training to actors, technicians and designers. In the 1970s the French-speaking universities began drama divisions, most notably Ottawa, UQAM and Sherbrooke.

In the 19th century, universities in English Canada included almost no formal theatre courses. Students wishing to enter the minuscule professional theatre learned their art as apprentices in the existing professional or semi-professional companies. Their training was often supplemented by tutoring in private academies, almost all of which were short-lived. The birth of a vital Canadian professional theatre in the second half of the 20th century was greatly aided by the amateur theatre (educational and community) that preceded it (*see* LITTLE THEATRE MOVEMENT). Actors, directors and designers had their training in amateur productions.

Until the early 1960s there was no thorough training in the theatre arts at the college level. Most universities followed the English tradition of offering credit courses in dramatic literature and criticism, while regarding practical work as an extracurricular activity best left to student drama societies, departments of extension, and intercollegiate festivals. There were early signs of campus drama activity. The University Dramatic Club of Montréal, using mainly McGill personnel and alumni, staged Shaw's *Arms and the Man* for the first Earl Grey Musical and Dramatic Competition (Ottawa, 1907). During the winter of 1914-15 the dept of extension at U of Alberta distributed plays and dispensed production advice to Alberta communities. The UBC Players Club (1915-58) was the first all-student drama society. Hart House, at U of T, was established in 1919 with a mandate to encourage and develop amateur drama activities on the campus. Within a decade almost all universities had a student drama society. By 1930 McGill's dept of English was presenting plays for children. In central and eastern Canada it was often the English department that first offered academic respectability to courses in drama. However, it was not until 1941 that a few theatre courses were tentatively offered by the McGill department. In 1957 Canada's most successful college musical, *My Fur Lady*, was presented by McGill students.

Growth was much faster in the western universities. Following the American pattern of offering degree programs that included some practical courses, U of Saskatchewan founded Canada's first dept of drama in 1945, offering a BA in drama. U of Alberta followed with a drama division in 1947. The BANFF CENTRE for Continuing Education began as the Banff School of Fine Arts in 1933, and has since offered a wide spectrum of practical theatre courses. The U of Alberta was the first to offer professional training programs: the BFA in acting and in design (1966), and the MFA in design and in directing (1968). In 1966 the Graduate Centre for the Study of Drama was founded at U of T, offering the first PhD in drama. The Black Report notes only 2 private schools that have minimum requirements for acting

training; the National Theatre School of Montréal and the VANCOUVER PLAYHOUSE Acting School (1975-). While several regional professional theatres, such as Edmonton's CITADEL THEATRE and the MANITOBA THEATRE CENTRE, have teaching programs, the majority cater to hobbyists. The STRATFORD FESTIVAL and the SHAW FESTIVAL offer classical acting training programs for young actors.

By the 1980s Canadian-trained drama faculty fill six-tenths of the university and college teaching positions, compared to one-tenth in the 1960s. Graduates of university drama training programs are found in all professional theatre companies, and many others make their mark in London and New York.

Campus drama organizations have traditionally offered opportunities to the beginning playwright when none were available from the profession. Campus support for young playwrights began with the Hart House production of Merrill DENISON's first play, *Brothers in Arms* (1921). The Banff School began instruction in playwriting in 1935. Gwendolyn Pharis RINGWOOD was a student in the first classes and is the program's most famous graduate. University of British Columbia's department of English and the Alberta and Saskatchewan drama departments now have strongly supported playwriting programs.

In 1955 there were 8 full-time instructors teaching in fledgling drama programs at 4 universities. In 1987, 22 institutions offered professional or preprofessional training, and another 15 offered programs with some form of drama specialization. There are now more than 300 faculty, 50 programs and over 10 000 enrolments making up the educational theatre establishment in Canada.
                                    GORDON PEACOCK

Reading: E. Crampton, comp, *Drama Canada: Trends in Drama in Education during the Past 25 Years* (1972); *Directory of Canadian Theatre Schools* (1982); *Report of the Committee of Inquiry into Theatre Training in Canada* (Black Report) (1977).

Theatre for Young Audiences is a 20th-century phenomenon, invented in Russia shortly before the revolution by actress Natalia Sats. In 1953 Joy Coghill and Myra Benson founded Holiday Theatre, making Vancouver the first Canadian city to enjoy specialized theatre for children. Other early companies were Theatre Hour in Toronto and Jeunes Comédiens in Montréal. Repertoire performed by these pioneer troupes was dominated initially by influences from the US, England and France. Holiday Theatre produced many American adaptations of fairy tales, and Theatre Hour and Jeunes Comédiens chose English and French theatre classics for their high-school audiences. As they matured, these companies commissioned Canadian works.

Three companies formed in the 1960s eventually encouraged local writers, though they began with foreign fare. Nouvelle Compagnie théâtrale (Montréal) began performing classics for adolescents in 1964 and after 1968 added recent Québec plays and winners of an annual playwriting contest. In the late 1960s Regina's GLOBE THEATRE toured Saskatchewan schools with plays of British playwright Brian Way. His technique of participation – asking audiences to advance the plot and help the hero by contributing noises, ideas and imaginary objects – became popular and influential throughout Canada. In the 1970s the Globe hired Rex Deverell, Canada's first playwright-in-residence assigned to write children's plays. Young People's Theatre in Toronto has an eclectic approach to repertoire but always includes some new Canadian works. In 1977 it became the first Canadian company to have its own building devoted exclusively to entertainment for young audiences. Alberta Theatre Projects, established in 1972 "to bring history to life" for schoolchildren, also brought its audience to a special theatre, the historic Canmore Opera House in Calgary's Heritage Park. Despite an excellent record of success with adventurous scripts, the company has shifted its energies and priorities to its adult season.

In the 1970s Simon and Pierre, Talonbooks and the Playwrights Co-op (later Playwrights Canada) began to publish plays for young people. From 1971 to 1988, the number of groups producing theatre for young audiences increased from under 20 to over 70, and included Mermaid Theatre in Nova Scotia; Theatre New Brunswick's Young Co; Theatre Five, Carousel Players, Hexagone and l'Hexagone, Jabberwock and Sons Full Theatre Co and The Great Canadian Theatre Co in Ontario; Théâtre des pissenlits, Marmaille, Théâtre soleil, Cannerie, Bebelle, Théâtre de carton, Théâtre de l'oeil, Grosse Valise, Théâtre des confettis, Amis de chiffon, and Youtheatre in Québec; Peresphone Youth Theatre in Sask; Manitoba Theatre Workshop; Citadel-on-Wheels and Theatre Calgary's Stage-Coach Players and Calgary's Quest Theatre in Alberta; and Green Thumb, Axis Mime, Carousel Theatre and Kaleidoscope in BC. Since 1978 an International Festival of Children's Theatre has played each spring in Vancouver, Edmonton, Calgary, Toronto and Montréal.

Most companies consider school tours a vital part of their mandate and bring live theatre to a cross-section of young Canadians. The economy of means imposed by touring sometimes leads to ingenious solutions to problems of small casts, 45-minute plays, and rudimentary technical resources. Long runs in original plays encourage neophyte actors to develop skills in creating and then sustaining characterizations for dozens, sometimes hundreds, of repeat performances. Close connections with schools also present problems: educational content is implied, if not dictated; budgets often strike first at live theatre; artists feel isolated and miss media and peer feedback; and touring one-act plays for months of one-day stands is gruelling and exhausting.

Innovative influences sometimes enter the mainstream of Canadian drama through work developed for children. Because many young professionals find their first work in theatre for the young, they often bring fresh thinking to old problems. In particular, collaboration between playwrights, directors and designers produces striking and memorable effects. Improvisation, mime, mask work, collective creation and puppetry enrich our theatrical vocabulary and expand the boundaries of style. James REANEY, poet, playwright and teacher, has often conducted workshops with children to allow their energy, grace and open attitude toward myth and metaphor to contribute to his plays. Other authors and companies have followed his example and, in this way, contemporary concerns have taken their place beside archetypes, history and legend in the repertoire. Distinctive Canadian styles of writing and production have developed and there has been an increase in support for live performances that speak directly to the dreams of Canada's young people in compelling theatrical forms. JOYCE DOOLITTLE

Reading: Joyce Doolittle and Z. Burniegh, *A Mirror of Our Dreams...* (1979).

Theatre Plus, a Toronto company founded in 1973 by Polish refugee Marion André [Czerniecki] and dedicated to political and socially significant theatre. Located in the 500-seat Town Hall of the St Lawrence Centre (now the Jane Mallett Theatre), it presents a summer season of 4 plays and since 1981 an additional January pro-

duction. Under playwright/director André the plays were selected primarily from the postwar European repertoire (Anouilh, Durrenmatt, Orton, Griffiths) with some pertinent American choices (Williams, Miller, Guare, Rabe). The company has had less success with its few Canadian originals. In July 1985 Malcolm Black became artistic director, introducing a more marked British flavour. DAVID GARDNER

Theatre Royal When in the early 1800s Montréal failed to attract talented artists for lack of a decent hall, John MOLSON built the 1500-seat Theatre Royal on a vacant lot owned by him on the corner of St Paul and Victor streets. The 71-member company opened in 1825 and presented a varied but repetitive repertory of Shakespeare, and comedies and farces by Knowles, Cowley and Sheridan. Until 1840 the theatrical seasons were irregular, and during the winter the playhouse was often used for concerts and sometimes circuses. The theatre contributed greatly to the cultural development of the city: it attracted touring British and American celebrities (such as tragedian Edmund Kean, comedian John Reeve and author Charles Dickens) and many amateur groups, including the Garrison Amateurs. Under the mismanagement of Frederick Brown, the company went bankrupt in 1826. After a succession of unsuccessful managers the playhouse was sold and demolished in 1844 to make way for the Bonsecours Market. MARILYN BASZCZYNSKI

Thelon River, 904 km long, issues from Lynx Lk, E of Great Slave Lk, NWT. It has a DRAINAGE BASIN of 142 000 km² – third among rivers flowing into Hudson Bay – and a mean discharge of 804 m³/s. It flows N and then E across the Barren Lands through Beverly, ABERDEEN, Schultz and Baker lakes and empties into CHESTERFIELD INLET, on Hudson Bay. Its main tributaries are the DUBAWNT R, flowing N from DUBAWNT LK, and the KAZAN R, draining numerous lakes to the SW. The area was the haunt of the CARIBOU INUIT until the herds were depleted. J.W. and J.B. TYRRELL examined the river in 1893-94. The Thelon Game Sanctuary (38 850 km²) was established in 1927 to protect the endangered MUSKOX. JAMES MARSH

Theosophy, philosophical system based on a belief in a universal, eternal principle fundamental to all life. The mystical overtones of its proposition of the fundamental identity of all "Souls with the Universal Soul" are similar to the doctrines of Buddhism and Hinduism. The Theosophical Society was founded in New York in 1875 by Helena Petrova Blavatsky and others, "to form the nucleus of a universal brotherhood of humanity, without distinction of race, creed, sex, caste or colour." The society has also sought to encourage study of comparative religion, philosophy and science. The first Canadian branch of the society was formed in Toronto in 1891 by Algernon Blackwood, Dr Emily STOWE, Dr Augusta STOWE-GULLEN and newspaper editor Albert Smythe (father of Conn SMYTHE, who was also a lifelong member). In 1919, an autonomous Canadian section, The Theosophical Society in Canada, was formed. Albert Smythe was its head and first editor of its journal, *The Canadian Theosophist,* which has published continuously ever since. The society was closely associated with the GROUP OF SEVEN, notably Lawren HARRIS. Among other prominent members were critic William Arthur DEACON and Roy Mitchell, first director of Hart House Theatre. Related organizations in Canada include the Canadian Federation of the Theosophical Society, La Société théosophique du Québec and the United Lodge of Theosophists. Active lodges are in Montréal, Toronto, Hamilton, Edmonton, Calgary, Vancouver and Victoria.

Thériault, Gérard-Charles-Édouard, military officer (b at Gaspé, Qué 5 June 1932). The son of an RCMP officer who left the force to begin a small aviation company, Thériault's youthful ambition was to fly; after the unlikely preparation of an economics degree at Sir George Williams U [Concordia], he joined the RCAF in 1951. He was a squadron commander by 1966 and moved to the Collège militaire royal, St-Jean, Qué, as vice-commandant 1967-70 and commandant 1970-71. He was commander of 1 Canadian Air Group in Germany 1973-75, and he was promoted deputy chief of defence staff in 1978, vice chief in 1980, and chief in 1983. Outward looking, systematic, a strong believer in a unified armed forces, he was the third airman and third Francophone to hold the top job in the Canadian Forces. NORMAN HILLMER

Thériault, Yves, writer (b at Québec C 27 Nov 1915; d at Joliette, Qué 20 Oct 1983). The originality, diversity and importance of his work made Thériault one of Québec's most popular writers, both in Canada and abroad. Son of a carpenter, he tried various occupations before earning his living from writing. The 1944 publication of his first book, *Contes pour un homme seul,* attracted great public attention, but it was his novel *Agaguk,* published in 1958 and translated into 7 languages, which made him famous. He wrote in many different genres for many different audiences. The expression of insistent sexuality, of an often savage and unconquerable nature, of characters seeking the absolute, torn between their desire for power and their need for tenderness, and the effectiveness of his writing style, which alternates between the oral and the written, testify to his evocative imaginative power. MAURICE EMOND

Thesen, Sharon, poet, editor (b at Tisdale, Sask 1946). Thesen's family moved to BC in 1952, and she has lived and worked in Vancouver since 1965. She took her BA and MA at Simon Fraser U and now teaches at Capilano College, where she has been poetry editor of *The Capilano Review* since 1976. Her poetry is marked by its wit, purity of line, and command of a variety of idioms; it is capable of moments of stark emotional awareness. As a younger poet who shared Phyllis Webb's poetics, she was a fine choice to edit Webb's *The Vision Tree: Selected Poems* (1982). Her own first book, *Artemis Hates Romance* (1980), was hailed as a stunning debut. *Holding the Pose* (1983), *Confabulations: Poems for Malcolm Lowry* (1984) and *The Beginning of the Long Dash* (1987) confirmed her as one of the finest poets to emerge in the 1980s. DOUGLAS BARBOUR

Thetford-Mines, Qué, the largest asbestos production centre in the Western world. The streets of the town are built between the mines and the asbestos tailings (*photo by John deVisser*).

Thetford-Mines, Qué, City, inc 1892, pop 18 561 (1986c), 19 965 (1981c), is located on the Rivière Bécancour in the Appalachians, 107

km S of Québec City. It was named in 1905 after the town of Thetford in Norfolk, Eng. In 1876 Joseph Fecteau scraped some fibres from a greenish rock with his fingernail; without realizing it, he discovered ASBESTOS. The first mining rights were bought in 1877, production began in 1878 and in 1879 the arrival of the railway made it possible to transport the mineral in larger quantities and more quickly to LÉVIS, Qué. The town grew rapidly as the mines attracted people from other areas. Today, both underground and open-face mines are in operation, and the streets of the town are built between the mines and the asbestos tailings. Called the "Asbestos Capital" and the "City of White Gold," it is the largest production centre for this fibre in the Western world. The town has also developed other sectors such as trailer, snowmobile and mining-equipment factories. It has a famous mineralogy and mining museum.

JEAN-MARIE DUBOIS AND PIERRE MAILHOT

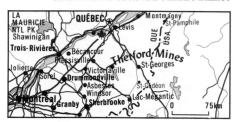

Third Option, a 1972 pronouncement by Mitchell SHARP, secretary of state for external affairs, calling for a lessening of US economic and cultural influence on Canada. It appeared in a paper by Sharp, "Canada-U.S. Relations: Options for the Future" (*International Perspectives*, 1972). Noting an increasing nationalism on both sides of the border, Sharp addressed the question of how to live "distinct from, but in harmony with" the US. He rejected 2 options, status quo and a deliberate policy of "closer integration with the United States." Instead, he argued for a "third option" which would "develop and strengthen the Canadian economy and other aspects of its national life and in the process reduce the present Canadian vulnerability." This was to be achieved through trade diversification abroad and an industrial strategy at home which emphasized specialization and Canadian ownership and, as a consequence, increased self-sufficiency.

In the cultural sphere, Sharp believed policies involving government subsidies and Canadian content regulations should be extended. The third option, Sharp insisted, was not anti-American; a stronger, more self-confident Canada would be a better neighbour.

Although the third option was easier to applaud than to implement, official Ottawa regarded it very seriously, particularly in the period 1972-76, when the FOREIGN INVESTMENT REVIEW AGENCY and PETRO-CANADA were established and Canadian businesses were discouraged from advertising on American radio and television stations. A "contractual link" was signed with the European Economic Community in 1976, but this and other efforts at trade diversification have not been notably successful. By 1986 exports to the US remained over 77% of Canada's total, while the percentage of US imports had actually increased. *See also* CANADIAN-AMERICAN RELATIONS; FREE TRADE.   NORMAN HILLMER

This Hour Has Seven Days, a weekly television program which ran from 4 Oct 1964 to 8 May 1966. Produced by CBC public affairs, the show achieved unprecedented popularity through its combination of serious topical and satirical elements, fast-moving pace and occasionally unorthodox and innovative subject matter. Its success was also due to the strong appeal of hosts

Hosts Laurier LaPierre (left) and Patrick Watson (right) of "This Hour Has Seven Days" (*courtesy National Archives of Canada/MISA/CBC Coll/14596*).

Laurier LAPIERRE, Patrick WATSON, John DRAINIE and Dinah Christie. Conceived and produced by Douglas Leiterman and Patrick Watson, it was directed deliberately at a mass audience and borrowed many of its techniques from light entertainment. At the same time, the program earned the respect of the audience by presenting 9 hour-long documentary films of considerable depth and substance, such as Beryl Fox's *The Mills of Gods* about Vietnam (Dec 1965). From the beginning, CBC management raised questions about journalistic procedures which were judged to be crusading and sensationalist. The tensions came to a climax in Apr 1966 and led to a major crisis which was defused on May 1 when PM Pearson appointed Stuart Keate, publisher of the Vancouver *Sun*, to study the conflict and make recommendations. Negotiations for the continuation of the program for the next season collapsed in July 1966 when Reeves Haggan, head of CBC public affairs, resigned.   ERIC KOCH

Thistle (Carduaceae tribe, family Compositae or Asteraceae), spiny herbaceous plant with white or purple flowers. There are 800 species worldwide, 46 in Canada (15 native). Native species (none serious WEEDS) are mainly "true" or "plumed" thistles of genus *Cirsium*. The remainder are nonspiny arctic or alpine herbs of genus *Saussurea*. Naturalized species are mainly common weeds. Common burdock (*Arctium minus*) has burs which attach themselves to clothing or skin. A chemical irritant in the bur can cause a rash similar to that caused by poison ivy. Canada thistle (*Cirsium arvense*) is not native but is found in agricultural areas of all provinces. It is variable in appearance and spreads in pastures and grasslands by root fragments. Bull thistle (*C. vulgare*), a common weed of Québec, Ontario and southern BC, is biennial and spreads by seeds only. Several species of knapweed are regarded as pernicious weeds in the BC Interior. Diffuse knapweed (*Centaurea diffusa*) and spotted knapweed (*C. maculosa*) are subjects of major efforts in biological weed control.   PAUL B. CAVERS

Thode, Henry George, scientist, university administrator (b at Dundurn, Sask 10 Sept 1910). He graduated from U of Sask, earned his doctorate from Chicago in 1934 and was appointed to McMaster in 1939. His WWII research in atomic energy was sponsored by the NRC. He served as McMaster's vice-president 1957-61 and president 1961-72. He was the moving force behind the university's developing science, engineering and health-sciences faculties and its research and graduate programs. A brilliant nuclear scientist, Thode's work led to the construction at McMaster in 1957 of the first nuclear-research reactor at a Commonwealth university. A fellow of the RSC (and its president 1959-60), the Chemical Institute of Canada and the Royal Society of London, he was named an MBE in 1946 and was the first scientist appointed Companion of the Order of Canada in 1967. Author of over 150 articles and

professor emeritus at McMaster since 1979, his current research focuses on isotopes and fission products, including isotopic abundances in terrestrial, meteoritic and lunar materials.

MANUEL ZACK

Thom, Linda, shooter (b at Hamilton, Ont 30 Dec 1943). She won the ladies match national pistol championship in 1982 and 1983 and the national ladies air pistol championships in 1983. She finished first in the Swiss International pistol tournament and third in the West German International in 1984, and then won a gold medal in the ladies sport pistol at the 1984 Los Angeles Olympics. She became a Member of the Order of Canada in 1985 and retired from the sport in 1987.

Thom, Ronald James, architect (b at Penticton, BC 15 May 1923; d at Toronto 29 Oct 1986). He first became known nationally as the designer of MASSEY COLLEGE, Toronto (1963) while still a partner of Thompson, Berwick and Pratt, Vancouver. His own Toronto-based practice, the Thom Partnership, was established in 1963. Earlier, he had designed a distinguished series of private houses and many other BC buildings. From Toronto he planned the campus and designed colleges and the main library for TRENT UNIVERSITY, Peterborough, Ont (1963-79), as well as thoughtful alterations and additions to existing buildings in town for the university's use. The SHAW FESTIVAL Theatre in Niagara-on-the-Lake, Ont (1973), was also a sensitive addition to an historic environment. A more utilitarian project was the Atria North office complex (Toronto, 1980), an energy-efficient commercial office development. An example of the unusual and highly specialized projects undertaken is the planning of the Metropolitan Toronto Zoo (1974) and the design of its major pavilions including the African and Indo-Malaysian pavilions (in association with Craig & Boake and Clifford & Laurie).

Thom was trained as a painter at the Vancouver School of Art, and his interest in architecture was awakened there by painter B.E. BINNING. His work has been notable for his ability to include richness of colour and detail within projects that encompass many buildings on large sites. His buildings manifest a clear sense of coherence without geometric rigidity. He was made an Officer of the Order of Canada in 1980.   MICHAEL McMORDIE

Thomas, Alexander, writer, native leader (b at Port Alberni, BC 25 Dec 1891; d there 28 July 1971). Chief Alex Thomas, while living by traditional hunting and fishing, was the first NOOTKA to write down and translate texts on the culture and history of his people. Working as translator for his grandfather, a field consultant of Edward SAPIR 1910-14, Alex learned to write the standard alphabet developed by Sapir and his teacher Franz BOAS. From 1914 on he gave his people a literature of thousands of pages, still today only partly published, as in E. Sapir and M. Swadesh, *Nootka Texts* (1939) and *Native Accounts of Nootka Ethnography* (1955) and in A. Thomas and E. Arima, *t'a:t'a:qsapa. A Practical Orthography for Nootka* (1970).   ROY WRIGHT

Thomas, Audrey Grace, née Callahan, writer (b at Binghampton, NY 17 Nov 1935). Thomas is a novelist and short story writer whose forte is analysis of the minutiae of women's lives. She was educated at Smith College, Mass, and St Andrews U, Scot, and then taught in England for a year. In 1959 she moved to Canada and in 1963 earned an MA at UBC. From 1964 to 1966 she lived in Ghana, and much of her subsequent fiction concerns her African experience. Thomas's novels include *Mrs Blood* (1970), *Munchmeyer and Prospero on the Island* (1971), *Songs My Mother*

Taught Me (1973), Blown Figures (1974) and Latakia (1979). As well, she has written several collections of short stories: Ten Green Bottles (1967), Ladies and Escorts (1977), Real Mothers (1981) and Goodbye Harold Good Luck (1986). Also in 1986, Room of One's Own published a special issue devoted to Thomas's work.   JEAN WILSON

Thomas, Morley Keith, climatologist (b near St Thomas, Ont 19 Aug 1918). He spent 39 years with the Canadian government's meteorological service, beginning as a weather forecaster at several RCAF stations during WWII and rising to the position of director general of the Canadian Climate Centre (1979-83). He was Canada's foremost authority on both the practical and scientific aspects of climatology, publishing over 70 books and articles including the *Climatological Atlas of Canada*, the *Bibliography of Canadian Climate* (3 eds, 1961, 1973 and 1979), and, with F.K. HARE, *Climate Canada* (2 eds, 1974 and 1979). Thomas served as president of the UN World Meteorological Organization's Commission for Climatology 1978-82, helping launch the World Climate Programme, and was the principal architect of the Canadian Climate Program. The recipient of several awards from the Canadian Meteorological and Oceanographic Society, Thomas was presented with the Massey Medal of the Royal Canadian Geographical Society in 1985. In retirement, Thomas is writing the history of meteorology in Canada.   DAVID PHILLIPS

Thomas, William, architect, engineer, surveyor (b in Suffolk, Eng 1799; d at Toronto 26 Dec 1860). Thomas is considered a founder of the Canadian architectural profession both for his contribution to ARCHITECTURAL DEVELOPMENT and for the quality and scope of his work. The elder brother of sculptor John Thomas, he established an extensive practice in Birmingham and Leamington Spa, Warwickshire, before immigrating to Toronto in 1843. Eventually with offices also in Hamilton and Halifax, his firm was one of the largest in British N America, and his works included at least 15 substantial public buildings and 15 churches, as well as numerous residences, commercial buildings and schools. Undoubtedly the best-known of his works is ST LAWRENCE HALL, Toronto. His most ambitious religious building was St Michael's Cathedral – the largest church in Toronto at the time.   NEIL EINARSON

Thomas, William Tutin, architect (b at Toronto 1828; d at Montréal 26 June 1892). A member of a distinguished family of architects (son of William THOMAS and nephew of English architect and sculptor John Thomas), he served his apprenticeship under his father and came to Montréal in 1864. He began in partnership with his brother, Cyrus Pole Thomas, then continued to practise architecture alone in Montréal when Cyrus immigrated to Chicago, Ill, in the 1870s. Stylistically eclectic, his work was characterized by a masterly proportioning.   JULIA GERSOVITZ

Thompson, Man, City, pop 14 701 (1986c), 14 288 (1981c), inc 1970, is located on the S side of the Burntwood R, 740 km N of Winnipeg. In 1956 significant NICKEL deposits were found 32 km SW of Moak Lk. INCO and the provincial government reached agreement on development of Thompson, and by winter 1957 construction was underway. A rail link with the CNR's Hudson Bay line and a fully serviced new town, named for John F. Thompson, Inco's chairman, had to be built. Production began in 1961 at what was the first integrated nickel-mining, smelting, concentrating and refining complex in the Western world. Copper, cobalt and precious metal by-products were produced as well. During the 1960s new mines were opened and the popula-

tion topped 20 000, even though the townsite was designed for 8000 to 12 000.

Thompson's economy is highly dependent on the export demand for nickel. Inco's world position has been challenged in recent years by mines in developing countries and the prospect of deep-sea mining. Unfavourable markets led to reduced operations and decline in Thompson's population in the 1970s. Despite being a retail and service centre, the city has had a limited ability to attract secondary industry.

To avoid the unplanned growth seen in many other new RESOURCE TOWNS, Thompson was created in an orderly manner, with full health, education, water and protection services.   D.M. LYON

Thompson, Berwick, Pratt and Partners, architects, Vancouver, BC. Founded in 1908 as Sharp and Thompson by Englishmen G.L.T. Sharp and Charles J. Thompson, this firm has played a major role in Vancouver and Canadian architecture through the century. Its founders first designed medieval and classically inspired commercial, institutional and residential buildings in BC, especially on UNIVERSITY OF BRITISH COLUMBIA campus whose plan they produced in 1913. In 1937 they were joined by recent U of T graduates Robert A.D. Berwick and Charles Edward Pratt, committed to developing a regional architecture inspired by the principles of European modernism. Through the 1950s and 1960s the firm received international attention for such projects as the BC Electric Building (1957). Through to the late 1980s a succession of major Canadian architects worked within the firm before pursuing independent careers, including Barry DOWNS, Arthur ERICKSON and Ron THOM.   MICHAEL MCMORDIE

Thompson, David, fur trader, explorer, surveyor, mapmaker (b at London, Eng 30 Apr 1770; d at Longueuil, Canada E 10 Feb 1857). Apprenticed to the HUDSON'S BAY CO in 1784, Thompson devoted most of his life to the study of geography and the practice of mapmaking. The maps, based primarily on his own explorations and observa-

tions, were the first to provide a comprehensive view of the vast western territories that became part of Canada in 1870 (*see* CARTOGRAPHY).

As an apprentice to the HBC, Thompson rapidly acquired the knowledge needed to be a successful trader. While recovering from a broken leg in 1790, he studied surveying and mapmaking with Philip Turnor, the HBC's official surveyor. His new skills were recognized in 1792 when he was assigned to seek a more direct route from Hudson Bay to Lk Athabasca. Frustrated by faltering support for his surveys, he left to join the NORTH WEST CO in 1797 to locate and map their posts and the waterways connecting them. Within 2 years he had completed most of this assignment, including the first accurate delineation of those parts of the West most affected by the expansion of American authority under the terms of JAY'S TREATY – the upper Red River valley, the Mandan villages on the Missouri R, the sources of the Mississippi R, and the Fond du Lac and Rainy R regions W of Lk Superior. In 1799 Thompson was given additional duty as a trader and for the next 7 years he pursued his surveys whenever his other responsibilities permitted, as he rose from clerk to partner. During these years he completed mapping the fur-trading territories E of the Rocky Mts.

In 1806 Thompson set out to open a trade with the Indians W of the Rockies. Over the next 5 years he explored the passes W from the Saskatchewan and Athabasca rivers, building posts and mapping the hitherto uncharted COLUMBIA R basin from its source to the Pacific, which he reached on 15 July 1811, a few weeks after the American PACIFIC FUR CO arrived there. His failure to reach the mouth of the river before the Americans could establish a claim to it has resulted in some debate among historians about his instructions. Most now agree that Thompson was not aware that an agreement between the NWC and Jacob Astor to support jointly the proposed voyage to the mouth of the Columbia had fallen through, and that he had not been ordered to reach the mouth first in order to forestall them.

In 1812 Thompson retired to Canada with his wife and family. After settling at Williamstown, UC, Thompson pursued his career as a surveyor and mapmaker, his most notable achievement being the completion of maps of his western explorations and the charting of the official boundary between the US and Canada from the St Lawrence R to Lake of the Woods. Business failures left him penniless, and in later life he turned to writing the narrative of his explorations in western Canada, regarded by many as his greatest legacy. *See also* EXPLORATION.   JOHN S. NICKS

Reading: J.B. Tyrrell, ed, *David Thompson's Narrative* (1916; repr 1968).

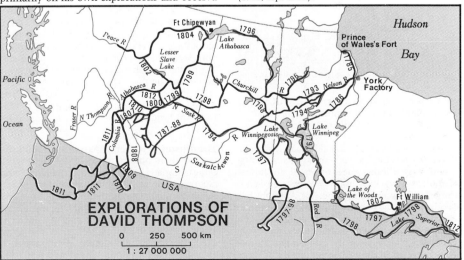

EXPLORATIONS OF DAVID THOMPSON

0   250   500 km

1 : 27 000 000

Thompson, Ian Maclaren, anatomist (b at Harbour Grace, Nfld 13 Sept 1896; d at Winnipeg 26 Dec 1981). His education at Edinburgh was interrupted by service in WWI, during which he was wounded and mentioned in dispatches. He taught anatomy at McGill 1920-27, U of Calif (Berkeley) 1927-36 and U Man, where he was head of the department 1937-65. He is remembered for his emphasis on the study of the living body and the importance of anatomical clinics and for his neuroanatomical research. A fellow of the Royal Soc of Canada (1947) and the Royal Soc of Edinburgh (1952), he was founding president of the Canadian Assn of Anatomists.

T.V.N. PERSAUD

**Sir John Sparrow David Thompson
Fourth Prime Minister of Canada**

Birth: 10 Nov 1845, Halifax, NS
Father/Mother: John/Charlotte Pottinger
Father's Occupation: Printer
Education: Free Church Academy, Halifax
Religious Affiliation: Methodist/Roman Catholic
First Occupation: Lawyer
Last Private Occupation: Justice
Political Party: Conservative
Period as PM: 5 Dec 1892 - 12 Dec 1894
Ridings: Antigonish, NS, 1885-94
Other Ministries: Justice 1885
Marriage: 5 July 1870 to Annie Affleck (1845-1913)
Children: 2 boys, 3 girls
Died: 12 Dec 1894 at Windsor Castle, Eng
Cause of Death at Age: Heart failure at 49
Burial Place: Halifax
Other Information: First Roman Catholic PM. Second to die in office. First provincial premier to become PM. KCMG, 1888.

(*photo courtesy National Archives of Canada/C-698*)

Thompson, Sir John Sparrow David, lawyer, judge, politician, prime minister (b at Halifax 10 Nov 1845 [not 1844 as often cited]; d at Windsor Castle, Eng 12 Dec 1894). He was admitted to the NS Bar in 1865 and elected alderman for Halifax in 1871, a position he held for 6 years. Although raised a Methodist, he converted to Roman Catholicism in 1871. In 1877 he was elected to the NS Assembly as member for Antigonish, a Scottish Catholic constituency, and was attorney general in the Conservative regime of Simon Holmes, 1878-82. On Holmes's retirement, he was briefly premier, but he and his government were defeated in the 1882 election. He was then appointed judge of the Supreme Court of NS.

In 1885 Thompson was persuaded to return to political life, this time at Ottawa. He was sworn in as minister of justice in Sir John A. MACDONALD's government in Sept 1885 and was elected MP for Antigonish, positions he held for the rest of his life. Confident, courteous and always master of his subject, Thompson soon became important in Cabinet. When Macdonald died in June 1891, he was the logical successor, but J.J.C. ABBOTT reluctantly took office to avoid the acrimony that would have been caused by Thompson's religion. Nevertheless, Thompson acted as House Leader and, when Abbott retired, became prime minister 24 Nov 1892, when he was 48 years old. He was a capable leader, though without Macdonald's ability to soothe his party's divisions. His main contribution was the Canadian CRIMINAL CODE of 1892. Thompson died only an hour or so after being sworn in as a member of the Imperial Privy Council by Queen Victoria at Windsor Castle. His funeral took place in Halifax 3 Jan 1895. His estate, which amounted to $20 000, was a measure of his probity in public office, but it left his family, which included a crippled daughter, hard up. A public subscription was launched. Thompson's death left the Conservative Party bereft of moral courage and force.

P.B. WAITE

Thompson, Margaret Anne Wilson, geneticist (b at Northwich, Eng 7 Jan 1920). She obtained a BA in 1943 from U Sask and a PhD in 1948 from U of Toronto where she studied under the pioneering human geneticist Norma Ford Walker. She contributed to human genetics through research on a variety of genetic disorders, particularly muscular dystrophy. She also taught at Western (1948-50), U of A (1950-63) and U of T (1963-85), where she supervised many graduate students and taught genetics to medical students. In addition to numerous scientific articles, she has written a widely used text, *Genetics in Medicine* (1966, 4th ed 1986) coauthored with her husband James Scott Thompson (1919-82). She founded a genetic counselling service at U of Alberta Hospital in 1956 and joined the staff of Toronto's Hospital for Sick Children in 1963. President of the Genetics Society of Canada in 1972, she was awarded its Presidential Citation in 1986 for outstanding contributions to genetics.

DIANE WILSON COX

Thompson, Paul, director, producer, playwright (b at Charlottetown 4 May 1940). Influenced by his work with Roger Planchon's socially and politically committed theatre in France (1965-67), he emerged as an important figure in the Canadian alternative theatre movement as artistic director of Toronto's Theatre Passe Muraille (1971-82). Thompson pioneered the development of the "collective creation" process in which actors, a director and writer develop a script through acting improvisations. His productions were characterized by their Canadian subject matter and the exploration and creation of Canadian myths. They include *Doukhobors* (1971), *The Farm Show* (1972), *1837: The Farmers' Revolt* (1972), *I Love You, Baby Blue* (1975), *Far As the Eye Can See* (1977) and *Maggie and Pierre* (1980).

ANTON WAGNER

Thompson, Robert Norman, politician, teacher (b at Duluth, Minn 17 May 1914). He came to Canada in 1918, was educated in Alberta, taught school, practised chiropractic and served in the RCAF (1941-43). His prominence in Canadian politics began in 1950 when he was elected president of the SOCIAL CREDIT Assn of Canada. In 1961 he became national leader of the Social Credit Party. He was elected to Parliament in 1962 for Red Deer, Alta, and returned in 1963

and 1965. In these elections the Social Credit Party, with Réal CAOUETTE as deputy leader, had enough success to help prevent the Conservatives or Liberals from winning a majority. Thompson resigned as Social Credit leader in Mar 1967, citing lack of support from provincial party organizations. In 1960 he joined the Progressive Conservative Party and retained his Red Deer seat in Parliament. He left politics in 1982 to teach political science at Trinity Western Coll, Langley, BC. In 1984 he was chairman of the board, Fraser Academy, Langley, a school for students with dyslexia; chairman of a foundation set up by his family to raise and distribute funds for charity; and president of Vanguard Institute, which researches political aspects of Canadian economics.

BILL CAMERON

Thompson, Thomas Phillips, journalist, socialist intellectual (b at Newcastle-upon-Tyne, Eng 25 Nov 1843; d at Oakville, Ont 20 May 1933). Under the pseudonym "Jimuel Briggs," Thompson wrote political satire for the St Catharines and Toronto press, and in 1874 he launched *The National,* a weekly paper of political commentary. After some years in the US, he returned in 1879 to editorial work on Toronto newspapers, notably the lively *News*. During the 1880s, he promoted radical challenges to the emergent industrial capitalist society and became a spokesman for the KNIGHTS OF LABOR. In 1887 he produced the labour movement's most articulate critique, *The Politics of Labor* (repr 1975). The short life of his new radical weekly, *Labor Advocate* (1890-91), did not discourage this pioneering voice of Canadian socialism; he continued to speak and write for the new socialist movement until the 1920s.

CRAIG HERON

Thompson, Walter Palmer, plant geneticist, university administrator (b near Decewsville, Ont 3 Apr 1889; d at Saskatoon 30 Mar 1970). Raised on a farm in Haldimand County, Ont, Thompson graduated from U of T in 1910 and received his PhD from Harvard in 1914. He began his career at U Sask as head of biology in 1913, became dean of arts and science in 1939 and was president 1949-59. He became famous for his work on the genetics of cereal grains, studying chromosome numbers and breeding the first new strains of rust-resistant wheat. President of the RSC in 1947, he received their Flavelle Medal in 1949, was president of the International Botanical Congress in 1959 and received honorary doctorates from 7 Canadian universities. He was chairman of Saskatchewan's Advisory Planning Committee on Medical Care; its recommendations in 1962 formed the basis for medicare in Saskatchewan.

C. STUART HOUSTON

Thompson River, 489 km long, rises in the Cariboo district of the Rocky Mts and flows S as the North Thompson R. It is joined at KAMLOOPS by the South Thompson R from Shuswap Lk, and the 2 flow united, carrying their blue-green waters into the FRASER R at LYTTON. The banks of the lower course are hilly and almost barren, except for sagebrush, and many of the spectacular terraces are used for cattle grazing and fodder crops. Both the CPR and CNR transcontinental lines follow the river from Kamloops to Lytton. Simon FRASER mistakenly believed that David THOMPSON had found the river, and named it for him.

JAMES MARSH

Thomson, Andrew, meteorologist (b at Dobbinton, Ont 18 May 1893; d at Toronto 17 Oct 1974). Following graduation from U of T in 1916, Thomson studied and worked in the US, Samoa, New Zealand and Europe before returning in 1932 to the national meteorological service. He planned Canada's participation in the 1932-33

International Polar Year and was instrumental in establishing the first graduate program in meteorology at U of T. Thomson assisted John PATTERSON in planning for and administering a program of meteorological services for continental and transatlantic civil aviation in the 1930s and for military aviation during WWII. He led the postwar expansion and development of METEOROLOGY in Canada and was one of a small group who reconstructed international meteorology after 1945. As director of the national meteorological service 1946-59 he reorganized and expanded the service for peacetime. He travelled the world as a member of the executive committee of the World Meteorological Organization. A fellow of the RSC, he was created OBE in 1946 and awarded the Patterson Medal in 1965.

MORLEY THOMAS

Thomson, Kenneth, businessman, financier (b at Toronto 1 Sept 1923). Although in 1976 he succeeded his father, Roy THOMSON, as Baron Thomson of Fleet (a title he uses only outside Canada), he waited several more years before becoming – reluctantly, one senses – a figure familiar to the Canadian public. In 1979 he purchased the HUDSON'S BAY CO and in 1980 the FP Publications newspaper chain, both after protracted takeover battles. By the time of his decision in 1981 to sell *The Times* of London, he was already one of Canada's wealthiest citizens, through newspaper properties in Canada, Britain and the US and through North Sea oil. In other circles he is renowned as an enthusiastic collector of art. In 1987 he was chairman of the board, president and CEO of Thomson Newspapers Ltd (*see* THOMSON GROUP), owners of numerous daily newspapers, including the GLOBE AND MAIL and the WINNIPEG FREE PRESS.

Thomson, Roy Herbert, Baron Thomson of Fleet, newspaper tycoon (b at Toronto 5 June 1894; d at London, Eng 4 Aug 1976). The son of a Toronto barber, Thomson showed little potential to become wealthy and notable until middle age, when he emerged as the owner of small radio stations and newspapers in northern Ontario. He went on to control hundreds of newspapers in the US, Canada and the Commonwealth, including the *Scotsman* of Edinburgh (his first large prize) and *The Times* and *Sunday Times* of London. He seemed to care little for the romance, tradition and democratic importance of newspapers, running them with the same tightfistedness and quality control he applied to his other businesses (magazines, travel agencies, TV) and for which he was notorious. Quite unburnished in manner and deportment, he was a child of the British Empire in outlook, coveting influence in Britain; at the same time he limited his Canadian holdings to smaller newspapers free of both competition and prestige. By international standards, he was already very wealthy when, late in his career, he diversified into oil exploration. He was created a peer in 1963.

Reading: R. Braddon, *Roy Thomson of Fleet Street* (1965); R.H. Thomson, *After I Was Sixty* (1975).

Thomson, Thomas John, painter (b at Claremont, Ont 4 Aug 1877; d at Canoe Lk, Ont 8 July 1917). Tom Thomson grew up on a farm near Leith, Ont, sixth of 10 children in a family much concerned with music and literature, a background that balanced his passion for hunting and fishing. During his twenties, Thomson apprenticed as a machinist, enrolled in business college and then spent a few years in Seattle, working as an engraver. He returned to Canada in 1904 and worked for several photoengraving houses in Toronto, including Grip Ltd. Within 5 years Thomson had acquired a reputation as a designer-illus-

The West Wind (1917) by Tom Thomson, oil on canvas, is one of his best-known works (*courtesy Art Gallery of Ontario/gift of the Canadian Club, Toronto, 1926*).

trator. In 1906 he took art lessons and first used oil paint. His work of this period is tentative, unpromising and rough. After joining Grip in 1907 he came alive to his own creative possibilities and was influenced by fellow artists J.E.H. MACDONALD, Albert Robson, William Broadhead and Rowley Murphy, and later by Fred VARLEY, Arthur LISMER, Franz JOHNSTON, and Franklin CARMICHAEL. This group worked past the restrictions of their commercial lives by sketching on the Don and Humber rivers and Lk Scugog. The subdued and tidy landscape these trips offered encouraged an appetite for rougher terrain.

The year 1912 was pivotal in Thomson's career. That spring he sketched in ALGONQUIN PARK for 2 weeks and from late July to Sept he made a long trip with Broadhead along the Spanish R to the Mississagi Forest Reserve. On his return, Robson and others inspired Thomson to scale *Northern Lake* into a full-sized canvas, which was purchased by Ontario for $250. At the time this was a huge sum (Thomson was then earning 75 cents an hour), and he spent the next summer and fall sketching in Algonquin.

In Toronto in Oct 1913 Thomson met his future patron Dr James MacCallum and his creative mentor, A.Y. JACKSON. MacCallum offered them a

year's expenses if they would devote themselves to painting. Jackson and Thomson moved in Jan 1914 into a studio and made another trip to Algonquin Park in late Feb. During that spring and fall Thomson painted with Varley, Lismer and Jackson in the park and in the early spring of 1915 returned to Canoe Lk. Bolstered by the $500 sale of *Northern River* to the National Gallery, his work now had the smash and stab of passion flying before thought.

The Arts and Letters Club in Toronto gave Thomson an exhibition in 1915 and he passed the winter productively in his studio. Employed as a fire ranger in Algonquin Park in the summer of 1916, Thomson managed to complete many sketches in the bravura style of his late period, his loaded brush producing images of surprising plasticity. In Apr 1917, determined to spend more time painting, he bought a guide's licence and returned to the park, where it is said he completed 62 sketches depicting the daily unfolding spring.

Near noon on 8 July 1917, Tom Thomson paddled past Wapomeo Island ostensibly to fish. His upturned canoe was discovered later that day and his body was recovered on July 16. The mystery surrounding Thomson's tragic death separated the man from the passion of his work, and his accomplishments have been obscured by endless conjecture over his death. Though middle-aged, Thomson burst free from an ordinary past, painting with heat that went to the edge separating the figurative from the abstract. The small sketch panels and even the larger canvasses could no longer contain his joy and power and needed a larger format to subsume his vision of rock, tree and sky. In the last years he had complete control of the picture plane and seemed to know instinctively which colours recede. His colour arrangements were closing in on simultaneous vibration within hue. With his instinctive technical command of the medium, fueled by an intense love of the North, Thomson, at the time of his death, had all the elements necessary to become a great

Tom Thomson's *Autumn Foliage,* oil on panel, is one of the brilliant sketches made on his trips to Algonquin Park (*courtesy Art Gallery of Ontario/gift from The Reuben and Kate Leonard Canadian Fund, 1927*).

painter. Time will dull the mystery of his death and can only enhance the lovely intense work of his last years. HAROLD TOWN

Reading: Harold Town and David B. Silcox, *Tom Thomson* (1977).

Thomson Group, one of the largest publishing empires in the world, is owned and controlled by the Thomson family. In 1987 the family, headed by Kenneth THOMSON, controlled 101 newspapers in the US, over 70 in Britain and 53 daily and weekly NEWSPAPERS in Canada, including the *Globe and Mail.* The Canadian chain is Canada's largest in number of newspapers sold and is second to SOUTHAM INC in daily circulation (1 124 200 in 1986). Other international interests include magazines and book publishing, wholesaling and retailing, real estate, oil and gas, travel, financial and management services, trucking and fur trading. Holdings in Canada include the HUDSON'S BAY CO, Zeller's and SIMPSON'S. The Thomson Group's total sales in 1986 exceeded $3.5 billion, with a net profit of $204 million. In June 1987 the group gained control of Associated Book Publishers, one of the largest publishing houses in Great Britain, with operations on 3 continents. PETER S. ANDERSON

Thorburn, Clifford Charles Devlin, snooker player (b at Victoria 16 Jan 1948). Since leaving school after grade 10, Cliff Thorburn has played snooker and pool virtually full-time. In 1971 he won the N American Snooker championship and since 1973 has played in nearly all snooker-playing countries in the world. In 1980 he became the first player from outside the UK to win the world professional championship. He has been N American champion twice, Canadian champion 5 times, Australian Masters, Canadian professional and world mixed pairs champion each once. In addition he holds the world's record of 19 perfect games (147 runs) at snooker. In 1986 he became the first person to win the Master's championship 3 times. GRAHAM DUNCAN

Thorburn, Robert, merchant, politician, premier of Newfoundland 1885-89 (b at Juniper Banks, Scot 28 Mar 1836; d at St John's 12 Apr 1906). Thorburn went to Newfoundland in 1852. For most of his political life (1870-85, 1893-1906) he was an Upper House member who championed the cause of governing the colony along "strict commercial" lines. Economic, social and political conditions had combined by 1882 to install in office a Liberal Party based on government-sponsored diversification and industrialization. When sectarian riots precipitated a political crisis in 1884, Thorburn's class exploited the resulting denominational bitterness by forming a "Protestant Rights" Party and attracted sufficient Protestant support to defeat the Liberals in 1885. The resulting Thorburn-led administration unsuccessfully tried to develop the colony along "fishery" lines. Thorburn was forced by circumstance to fall back on a belated program of public works, but then was swept from power in 1889. JOHN GREENE

Thorlakson, Paul H.T., surgeon (b at Park River, N Dak 5 Oct 1895). In 1900 the Thorlakson family moved to Selkirk, Man, and in 1919 Thorlakson graduated in medicine from Manitoba Medical College. After postgraduate study in Europe, he and Dr Neil John Maclean formed the Maclean-Thorlakson Surgical Clinic in 1926, and in 1938 he founded the Winnipeg Clinic. A pioneer in encouraging the development of medical research, Thorlakson was responsible for the formation of the Winnipeg Clinic Research Institute to advance medical education and research. Thorlakson served on innumerable committees and as chancellor of U of Winnipeg 1969-78. He

has been honoured by U Man and the universities of Winnipeg, Brandon and Iceland. On the medical faculty for many years, in 1957 he was appointed professor emeritus of surgery at U Man. He was appointed a Companion of the Order of Canada in 1970 and was first president of the Canadian Association of Medical Clinics 1969-70. In his honour, his friends and colleagues established the Paul H.T. Thorlakson Research Foundation in 1978. His biography, *The Saga of Dr Thor* (1986) was written by T.A.J. Cummings. HARRY MEDOVY

Thornton, Sir Henry Worth, railway official (b at Logansport, Ind 6 Nov 1871; d at New York C 14 March 1933). After graduating from U of Pennsylvania in 1894, Thornton joined the engineering department of the Pennsylvania Railroad. In 1914 he went to Britain as general manager of the Great Eastern Ry. He was knighted in 1919 for his wartime service as director general of railways behind the battle lines in France. In 1922 he was appointed by the Liberals as president of CANADIAN NATIONAL RYS, and under him the varied railways under government control were unified. During the 1920s there was intense rivalry between the CNR and the CANADIAN PACIFIC RY. When the Conservatives came to power in 1930, Thornton was attacked as a Liberal partisan, and feeling that he had lost the support of the government, he resigned in 1932. JOHN A. EAGLE

Thorold, Ont, City, pop 16 131 (1986c), 15 412 (1981c), inc 1975 (city), situated in the Niagara Peninsula. Though physically linked to ST CATHARINES, its large neighbour directly to the N, Thorold is independent. The area was settled in the 1780s, and was incorporated as a village in 1850 and a town in 1875. It was named after British MP Sir John Thorold (1816-66). Its growth is linked with the development of the 4 courses of the WELLAND CANAL. At the canal's commencement (1829) a townsite was laid out, and Thorold attracted various marine services and industries, such as limestone quarrying, flour milling, wood products and one of Canada's first cotton mills, many using the canal for transportation or water power. The advent of cheap hydroelectric power from nearby NIAGARA FALLS around the turn of the century led many heavy industries such as pulp and paper, abrasives and metal goods to locate here. Since 1945 the long-standing Anglo-Saxon and Irish flavour of this industrial community has been changed by sizable Italian immigration. A monument at Battle of BEAVER DAMS Park recalls the famous encounter of the War of 1812. H.J. GAYLER

Thoroughbred Racing is the racing of a special breed of horse over courses which, in N America, range from less than 1 mile to $1\frac{1}{2}$ miles in length (1.6-2.4 km). In Canada and the US, flat races on grass or dirt are the rule. In Europe, both flat and steeplechase races (in which the horse and rider are also required to clear a number of obstacles, such as hedges) are carried out. All thoroughbred horses are descended from the Arabian, Turkish and Barbary horses imported into England in the 1600s. In fact, most thoroughbreds trace their lineage to one of 3 horses – Byerly Turk, the Godolphin Arabian and the Darley Arabian.

On the one hand, horse racing is viewed as a sport of the wealthy, based on the traditions of a long and valued history. At the same time, it also has its shady side, associated with gambling and complemented by the rich subculture of its citizens on the back stretch. From its earliest days in Canada, it has reflected this dichotomy. There is ample evidence that it has always been a popular sport, particularly in a pioneer society where the horse was a vital means of transportation. Still, in

1771 horse racing was banned by Halifax authorities because they believed it turned the local citizenry into idle, immoral gamblers. Nevertheless, in 1825 the Halifax Turf Club was formed and held its first meeting. Ownership of a horse – even at the expense of economic hardship – was a potent status symbol among French Canadians, and horse racing enjoyed great popularity in Lower Canada [Québec] in the late 18th and 19th centuries – to the extent that sporting reports in newspapers of the time show a concentration on racing equal to that of almost all other sports combined. The Québec Turf Club was formed in 1789, and in 1836 the King's Plate, a race for a purse of 100 guineas, was first held in Trois-Rivières. Initially, it was restricted to horses bred in LC, but in 1859 horses from Upper Canada were admitted. The next year the QUEEN'S PLATE was held in Toronto for the first time; it has been run every year since then, making it the oldest continuing stakes race in N America – 15 years older than the Kentucky Derby. The winner of that 1860 race was a horse named Don Juan, owned by the James White Stable of Bronte and Milton, Ont. Small breeders with limited means could hope to win the race at that time. This was also a period when the quality of the horses was questionable and the practices of many owners suspect. In 1865 the judges disqualified 3 horses before declaring a winner of the Queen's Plate. Ten years later, the winner of Canada's most prestigious race was a previously unsuccessful 8 year old named Trumpeter. In August 1881, Colonel Casimir GZOWSKI held a meeting in Toronto with some of that city's most respected citizens to form the Ontario Jockey Club in order "to lift horse racing out of the mire." As the club's first chairman, Gzowski sought to bring the sport to respectability by ridding it of its bad reputation and improving the quality of Canadian thoroughbreds. A major step towards these aims occurred 2 years later when the club was successful in getting the governor general, the marquis of Lorne, and his wife, Princess Louise, 4th daughter of Queen Victoria, to attend the Queen's Plate. Not only did this result in the race being held permanently in Toronto, it also helped attract the interest of the richer classes of Canadian society. In 1891 a horse named Terror Colt, owned by Joseph Seagram, a wealthy distiller from Waterloo, Ont, won the first of 20 Plate victories for the Seagram Stables. The era of the wealthy owner was established.

The sport has also been sustained by the 2-dollar bettor, whose interest over the years helped ensure that racing would continue to draw a large share of space in the print media. At the turn of the century, the activities of bookmakers were enough to scare away even the most courageous of patrons. Odds were shortened in their favour; they ran their horses under others' names and fixed races. Finally, in 1910, the Canadian Parliament, by one vote, banned bookmakers. Next year, the establishment of pari-mutuel betting at tracks in Toronto, Winnipeg and Calgary brought more honesty to betting and helped save the sport.

It got an important boost in Canada's West from R.L. "Jim" Speers, a feed and grain entrepreneur who had moved from Toronto to Winnipeg and ultimately became the dean of the sport there. In 1922 he bought his first racetrack, and by 1925 owned 3 more. He eventually came to control tracks or meetings in Winnipeg, Regina, Saskatoon, Calgary and Edmonton. Realizing the difficulty in obtaining quality horses that would provide attractive racing meetings, he set up his own breeding farm in Winnipeg, which by the mid-1930s had become the country's largest.

The great economic difficulties experienced throughout Canada in the 1930s affected race-

Driving home from the 1980 running of the Queen's Plate (*photo courtesy Michael Burns Photography Ltd*).

track operations, heightening many of the abuses associated with the sport. Through the efforts of governments and racing operators, however, a clean up was accomplished by the late 1940s. The sport was evolving into a business, and one of the main forces behind this transformation was E.P. TAYLOR. Taylor was responsible for making horse racing more efficient by closing down several old, unprofitable tracks and using their charters to organize racing days at the rebuilt Fort Erie track and Woodbine, a large new facility in NW Toronto. The longer racing seasons that resulted saw greater attendance, higher purses and better horses. Taylor had also, in 1949, bought Parkwood Stables from R.S. MCLAUGHLIN, the Canadian automobile pioneer and one of the top racehorse breeders in the 1930s and 1940s. Renamed the National Stud Farm, it produced 15 Queen's Plate winners, including the legendary NORTHERN DANCER. The result of a long-term breeding plan instituted by Taylor, this chunky little horse displayed a tremendous will to win, and in 1964 became the first Canadian-bred horse to win the Kentucky Derby. He also won the Preakness, thus taking 2 jewels in the American triple crown. Retired to stud by a leg injury that same year, his winnings in purses totalled $580 000. In his second year at stud, he sired the magnificent NIJINSKY, which had a brilliant career in Europe, winning the Epsom Derby, Irish Derby and other major-stakes races. Another of his progeny, The Minstrel, won $2 million in prizes in 1977. It has been said that Northern Dancer influenced the bloodlines of all top N American thoroughbreds.

Other Canadians fared well in 1973. New Brunswick's Ron TURCOTTE rode Secretariat to victory in the American triple crown. Turcotte's career ended 5 years later in a spill that left him paralyzed from the waist down, but not before he had established himself as one of N America's best jockeys. The year 1973 also saw Sandy HAWLEY, of Mississauga, Ont, ride 515 winners, becoming the first jockey to surpass the 500 mark in one year. Ten years later Sunny's Halo won the Kentucky Derby. By September 1980, Hawley, at the age of 31, had ridden his 4000th career winner, becoming one of only 10 men to reach that goal. Jeffery Fell, with over 2600 career wins, was another distinguished rider until he retired in 1986. Earlier, Johnny LONGDEN rode 6032 winners between 1927 and 1966. His contemporary, George Woolf, was known as "the Iceman" because of his coolness in the saddle. He rode many major-stakes winners, including Seabiscuit during his great victory over War Admiral in a 1938 match race. Woolf was killed in 1946 in a racing accident. Another top jockey of that era was Newfoundland's Nick Wall, who rode Stagehand to win the 1938 Santa Anita Derby. Avelino Gomez, rider of 4078 winners, led all N American jockeys in victories in 1966. He was killed in an accident at Woodbine during the Canadian Oaks race in June 1980. Woolf, Longden and Gomez have been honoured by the US Racing Hall of Fame. The Canadian Horse Racing Hall of Fame, located in Toronto, honours jockeys, horses and those who have made significant contributions to Canadian horse racing.   J. THOMAS WEST

Reading: J. Coleman, *Hoofprints on My Heart* (1971); T. Frayne, *The Queen's Plate: The First 100 Years* (1959).

Thorpe, Robert, judge and political theorist (b at Dublin, Ire *c*1764; d in London, Eng 11 May 1836). Appointed puisne judge of the Court of King's Bench, Thorpe arrived in Upper Canada in 1805. He became associated with a faction of officials who, having fallen out of favour with the administration of the late lieutenant-governor Hunter, hoped to win the ear of the newly appointed Francis GORE who had yet to arrive in the colony. To this end Thorpe agitated to discredit Hunter and his favourites, denouncing their activities as contrary to the constitution. The Executive Council, he contended, was in reality not responsible to the lieutenant-governor, but was a cabinet which, after the model of the English Parliament, should be appointed from, and be responsible to, the Assembly. This, he asserted, would be the view of the new governor. It was not; and he was suspended from office.
    GRAEME PATTERSON

Thorson, Joseph Thorarinn, lawyer, educator, politician, jurist (b at Winnipeg 15 Mar 1889; d at Ottawa 6 July 1978). At age 24, already a Rhodes scholar, graduate of Manitoba College and Oxford, and barrister of the Middle Temple (London, Eng) and Manitoba, Thorson became a jurist of international repute. After serving in the army throughout WWI, he was appointed dean of the law school, U of Manitoba (1921). A Liberal, he was elected MP for Winnipeg South Centre (1926-30) and Selkirk (1935-42); Canadian delegate to the League of Nations, 1938; minister of national service, 1941. President of the Exchequer Court, 1942-64, he was also made judge of the Court Martial Appeal Court of Canada in 1959 and its president in 1964. A delegate to the founding meeting of the International Commission of Jurists, Berlin, 1952, he was elected president and served until 1959.   D.H. BROWN

Thorvaldson, Thorbergur, "TT," cement chemist (b in Iceland 24 Aug 1883; d at Saskatoon 4 Oct 1965). Settling with his parents near Gimli, Man, he went on to attend U Man and Harvard (MSc, PhD). In 1919 he became head of the dept of chemistry at U Sask, and in 1945 the first dean of graduate studies. He was made a Knight in the Icelandic Order of the Falcon in 1939 and was president of the Canadian Inst of Chemistry in 1941. His research on the chemistry of cement and the development of cements resistant to deterioration through chemical attack won him international recognition and many honours. Thorvaldson Lake in northeastern Saskatchewan was named after him in 1966 – a rare honour for a chemist.   GORDON R. FREEMAN

Thousand Islands (Ontario part), an 80 km long section of the ST LAWRENCE R, extending downstream from Lk Ontario between KINGSTON and BROCKVILLE and containing over 1000 rocky, wooded islands which range from several square kilometres to barely emergent rocks and shoals. An official count recorded 1149 islands and islets, 665 of which were on the Canadian side (241 officially named) and 484 on the American side (126 named).

This scenic landscape of varied islands and labyrinth passages owes its origin to a projection of Canada's Precambrian SHIELD extending from eastern Ontario across the St Lawrence, where it underlies the Adirondack Mts in New York state. This old (over 900 million years), complex rock, composed largely of hard granites and gneisses, was scoured and sculpted by glacial erosion into a "knob and hollow" surface. In the altered landscape after continental glaciation, the GREAT LAKES system found a new drainage route E from Lk Ontario, forming the present St Lawrence R. The hollows flooded and the rocky knobs became islands. This section of the great St Lawrence corridor is rich in flora and fauna, beauty and history. Waterfowl are abundant. As this area is on the southern limit of the Great Lakes-St Lawrence forest region, southern species such as shagbark hickory, American basswood and pitch pine mingle with the familiar southern Ontario deciduous and coniferous species. The varied bottom contours of the St Lawrence offer diverse fish habitats – some 38 species have been identified, of which northern pike, muskellunge, large and smallmouth bass, and yellow perch have long attracted fishermen.

A favourite camping ground of the IROQUOIS before European exploration, this part of the great river highway to the interior was traversed by explorers, missionaries, fur traders and soldiers. Colonial military conflict between Britain and France (SEVEN YEARS' WAR), and later between Britain and the US (WAR OF 1812), was responsible for many place-names, such as the Navy, Admiralty and Lake Fleet islands. Endymion, Camelot and Mermaid islands are named after gunboats; others such as Gordon and Stovin were named after military commanders.

Immigrants travelling to Upper Canada in the late 1700s and early 1800s and romantic writers of that period spread knowledge of the area's beauty. Accessibility to a prospering urban society in both Canada and the adjacent US also led to early recreational use. Hotels, often palatial, were built primarily for fishermen from the 1850s to 1870s. Church camping grounds proliferated on the islands and frequently evolved to cottage communities. Increased railway access on both sides of the river helped attract affluent tourists. Luxury hotels and steamboat excursions became popular, and elaborate summer homes began to appear, even before Confederation, 1867. In 1904 ST LAWRENCE ISLANDS NATIONAL PARK was established through acquisition of several dispersed islands from the Mississauga Indians.

From the early 1800s, TOURISM has been an important economic contributor. Apart from some national and provincial campsites, the islands and shoreline today are largely privately owned. The Thousand Islands International Bridge (1938) crosses the St Lawrence at Hill I, linking Ontario and New York state highways. Ontario's Macdonald-Cartier Freeway (Hwy 401) greatly increased metropolitan access after WWII, and the scenic Thousand Island Parkway skirts the wooded coves and bays of the St Lawrence shore from GANANOQUE to Brockville. Tourist services also serve an important economic function for the adjacent communities of Kingston, Brockville, Rockport, Ivy Lea and Gananoque. The Thousand Islands landscape and its history have preserved what FRONTENAC described in 1673 as "the most delightful country in the world."
    D.M. ANDERSON

Thrasher (Mimidae), small family of slender, long-tailed, medium-sized, insectivorous and frugivorous birds with loud, musical, repetitive songs. Some species mimic songs of other birds. The family comprises 32 species. Four breed in Canada, including thrashers, brownish above with whitish, brown-spotted or plain breasts; MOCKINGBIRDS, blue or grey above and whitish below; and catbirds, grey or black overall. This family, which is restricted to the New World, apparently evolved in the American tropics and is most closely related to DIPPERS and WRENS. The widespread but rare northern mockingbird is a permanent resident in Canada. The migratory gray catbird (*Dumetella carolinensis*) summers from southern BC to Cape Breton I. The brown thrasher (*Toxostoma rufum*), also migratory, occurs from southeastern Alberta to southwestern Québec. Both species frequent scrub and woodland edges. The migratory sage thrasher (*Oreoscoptes montanus*) is a local summer resident in sagebrush grassland in southern BC and, rarely, SE Saskatchewan. Mimids breed May-July, building bulky nests of twigs and grasses placed low (under 6 m) in shrubs or trees or on the ground (eg, sage thrasher). They lay 4-5 eggs per clutch. Mimids are territorially aggressive. They are parasitized, rarely, by the brown-headed cowbirds (*Molothrus ater*).   J.C. BARLOW

Thrips, order Thysanoptera, are among the smallest insects, being slender and usually less than 2 mm long. About 4500 species have been described, but only 104 of a probable 250 species are known from Canada. Thrips are most closely related to BUGS (order Hemiptera) and are adapted to life in confined spaces (eg, in flowers, under bark or in leaf litter). They are widely distributed across southern Canada but few species occur in the Arctic and Subarctic. They have asymmetric, "punch and suck" mouthparts (right mandible is absent) and feed on fungi, pollen, leaves or small animals. Adults generally have 4 long, straplike wings fringed with long hairs, but some are wingless or vary in wing length. Metamorphosis is intermediate between complete and incomplete. Two active, feeding, larval stages are followed by 2-3 sluggish, nonfeeding, "pupal" stages. Males usually develop from unfertilized eggs and females from fertilized eggs, but only females are known in some species. Thirty species are crop pests; 11 occur in Canada, including onion thrips (*Thrips tabaci*), which transmit tomato spotted wilt virus and are of major importance.
                                                    B.S. HEMING

Thrush (Muscicapidae), very large family comprising about 1400 species of small passerines (perching birds) ranging from 11 to 33 cm in length. Because of its diversity, the family has been divided into 13 subfamilies, including the Turdinae (309 species), which is devoted to thrushes alone. Thrushes have almost worldwide distribution. Twelve species regularly occur in Canada: northern wheatear (*Oenanthe oenanthe*), eastern, western and mountain BLUEBIRDS (*Sialia sialis, S. mexicana, S. currucoides*, respectively), Townsend's SOLITAIRE (*Myadestes townsendi*), veery (*Catharus fuscescens*), gray-cheeked, Swainson's, hermit, wood, and varied thrushes (*C. minima, C. ustulata, C. guttata, Hylocichla mustelina, Ixoreus naevius*) and American ROBIN. All of the above are largely migratory. Plumage can be very glossy in some species. Combinations of browns, greys, olives, black, white, chestnut and blue are often blended or contrasted in adults. Males are often more brightly coloured than females. Plumage of immature birds is almost always spotted. Bill varies in length but is usually short, straight and slender; it may curve downward at the tip and have a small notch on the mandible. The short tail can be square or slightly rounded. Wings are long and pointed, with 10 primary feathers. In most species, the feet are strong and stout and the front of the leg is covered with an undivided sheath. Thrushes, with their extremely varied voices and highly developed songs, are considered by many to be the best singers among birds. The hermit thrush is judged by some to have the most melodious song of all Canadian birds. Thrushes can be arboreal or terrestrial. They are usually solitary or in pairs, although

they flock readily during the nonbreeding season and during MIGRATIONS. Insects and other small invertebrates are main food, but small fruits and berries are eaten in season. For nesting, thrushes construct an open cup, often reinforced with a rim of mud, lined with grass or leaves. It is placed on the ground or in a bush or tree. Thrushes lay 2-6 eggs, which may be white, greenish to bluish white or olive green. Eggs may be speckled. Both parents incubate eggs and take care of young until they leave the nest.   HENRI OUELLET

Thule Culture, 1000-1600 AD, represents the expansion of Alaskan Eskimos across arctic Canada about 1000 AD and the gradual displacement of the DORSET Paleoeskimos who occupied the area previously. Thule people brought with them a sophisticated sea-hunting technology that had been developed in the Bering Sea area. They hunted animals as large as bowhead whales and were able to store sufficient food to allow winter occupation of permanent villages composed of houses built from stone, whalebones and turf. Most Thule artifacts were made from bone, antler, ivory and wood; they used few stone tools, preferring cutting edges of metal obtained either from natural deposits or from Greenlandic Norse. Thule economy declined with deteriorating climatic conditions after about 1600 AD, but the people continued to occupy arctic Canada and are directly ancestral to the historic INUIT.
                                                    ROBERT MCGHEE

Reading: Robert McGhee, *Canadian Arctic Prehistory* (1978).

Thunder Bay, Ont, pop 112 272 (1986c), 112 468 (1981c), created in 1970 by the amalgamation of the cities of Fort William and Port Arthur and the adjacent townships of Neebing and McIntyre, is located in the NW part of the province on the W shore of the LAKE SUPERIOR bay of the same name. The Port of Thunder Bay is the western terminus in Canada of the Great Lakes – ST LAWRENCE SEAWAY. The community's physical and economic hinterland is dominated by the rocks, lakes and forests of the Canadian SHIELD.

Population: 112 272 (1986c), 112 486 (1981c); 122 217 (1986 CMA), 121 948 (1981 ACMA)

Rate of Increase (1981-86): (City) 0.2%; (CMA) 4.2%

Rank in Canada: Twenty-fifth (by CMA)

Date of Incorporation: Thunder Bay, 1970; Port Arthur, 1907; Fort William, 1907

Land Area: 322.86 km² (City); 2202.55 km² (CMA)

Elevation: 183 m (harbour); 488 m (Mt McKay)

Climate: Average daily temp, July 17.6°C, Jan -15.4°C; Yearly precip 711.8 mm; Hours of sunshine 2202.8 per year

Settlement The area has been inhabited for 10 000 years, originally by Paleo-Indian hunters, and at the time of the first European contact, by OJIBWA. The bay's name refers to the thunderbird of Indian folklore. DULHUT built Ft Caministigoyan beside the Kaministikwia R in 1679, and the fort was used by French traders until the route was abandoned in favour of the GRAND PORTAGE. Permanent settlement on Thunder Bay was established only in 1803 with the construction of the North West Co's FORT WILLIAM.

Development Between 1805 and 1821, Ft William was the most important settlement in the interior of N America as the centre of the NWC fur-trading empire. Its importance declined, but settlement persisted until in 1870 it was joined by Prince Arthur's Landing some km NE, at the E end of the DAWSON ROAD. Better docking facilities and the discovery of silver allowed the landing to outpace its older neighbour, but in 1875 new life was injected into the latter when the construction of

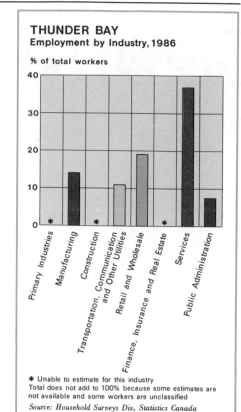

THUNDER BAY
Employment by Industry, 1986

% of total workers

* Unable to estimate for this industry
Total does not add to 100% because some estimates are not available and some workers are unclassified
Source: Household Surveys Div, Statistics Canada

the transcontinental railway commenced at Fort William. The mutual hostility and suspicion engendered by that event continued for nearly a century. The landing was incorporated as the town of Port Arthur in 1884, Ft William in 1892, and both settlements were granted civic charters in 1907. The 2 cities developed similarly but separately until 1970 when under pressure from the provincial government they were incorporated as the city of Thunder Bay.

Cityscape Thunder Bay occupies the floodplains of the lower Kaministikwia, Neebing and McIntyre rivers, the former shorelines of Lk Superior to the NE and the higher ground of the Port Arthur Hills. To the S rises Mt McKay, and E, across the bay about 25 km, stands the impressive rock formation of Nanibijou, the Sleeping Giant. The vertical rock face rises some over 300 m and is about 33 km long, forming the Sibley Peninsula. Amalgamation produced a city with 2 downtown core areas, each with its adjacent older residential districts, but both continue to suffer economically in competition with suburban malls. Since the 1960s, the city has spread W into the 2 incorporated rural townships. Industrial land is concentrated along the waterfront and the Westfort and Intercity areas, with Balmoral Industrial Park created in the mid-1970s to encourage the establishment of new light industries.

Population In keeping with the frontier nature of the economy, the late 19th-century pioneer population of the Lakehead communities fluctuated wildly in response to changing employment opportunities in railway construction, shipping and silver mining. From about 3000 inhabitants each in the late 1890s, the 2 cities grew rapidly up to 1914, with Ft William in the lead. At amalgamation, each had close to 50 000 inhabitants and since then growth has been slow. Early settlement was essentially Anglo-Saxon and that group controlled the city's economic and political establishment until WWII. Major concentrations of Ukrainians and Italians occur in Ft William, whereas in Port Arthur and adjacent McIntyre the main immigrant group is Finnish. Polish, Scandi-

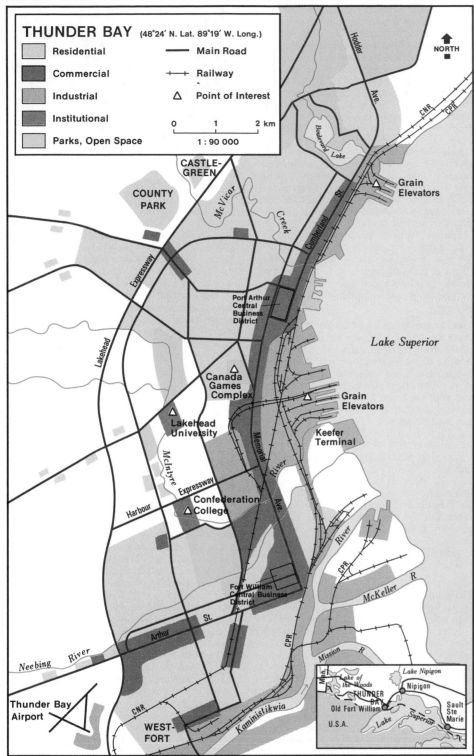

THUNDER BAY (48°24' N. Lat. 89°19' W. Long.)

Residential — Main Road

Commercial +—+ Railway

Industrial △ Point of Interest

Institutional

Parks, Open Space

0   1   2 km

1 : 90 000

ment E. With the completion of Manitoba to Port Arthur section of the CANADIAN NORTHERN RY (1902), Thunder Bay became one of the world's largest grain ports. Lakehead harbour benefited from the opening of the St Lawrence Seaway (1959) and the Keefer Terminal, a lake and ocean freight-handling dock (1962); despite the disruption of the freeze-up and periodic strikes, it remains one of the busiest ports in Canada. CP, CN and VIA Rail link Thunder Bay to the national rail network, and the Trans-Canada Hwy offers first-class road communication. Air Canada, Nordair, Norontair and Canadian Airlines International provide national and regional air services.

Government and Politics The present municipal government is headed by a city council elected every 3 years, consisting of a mayor (elected at large) and 12 aldermen (5 elected at large, 1 from each of the 7 wards). Council policies are administered by 27 departments, including the second-largest independent telephone system in Canada. The city also participates in the Lakehead Region Conservation Authority. The public and separate school boards have their administrative offices in the city with jurisdiction extending into the adjacent rural municipalities.

Cultural Life Post-secondary education is provided by Confederation College of Applied Arts and Technology and LAKEHEAD UNIVERSITY. Various ethnic groups promote an annual multicultural festival and support a variety of cultural organizations. The Thunder Bay Symphony Orchestra and Chorus and the Fort William Male Choir, along with local amateur and professional theatre groups, provide regular music and drama. Local history is kept alive at the Thunder Bay Historical Museum and at Old Fort William. There are 2 daily and 2 weekly newspapers (one in Finnish).

City teams have won national titles in hockey and curling, and the city has hosted the Ontario Winter Games (1976), the Canadian Figure Skating Championships (1980), several World Cup ski-jumping meets and, in 1981, the Canada Summer Games, which left the city a $7.5-million multi-sport complex.   DAVID D. KEMP

Reading: E. Arthur, *Thunder Bay District, 1821-1902: A Collection of Documents* (1973); G. Campbell, *Thunder Bay, Ontario* (1982); J.M. Mauro, *A History of Thunder Bay* (1981).

Thunderbird, a supernatural creature prominent in Northwest Coast Indian myths. Thunder and lightning are attributed to the thunderbird, which produces thunder by flapping its wings and lightning by opening and closing its eyes. The thunderbird is said to hunt whales, using its wings to shoot arrows. Among some Plains Indians, thunderstorms are a contest between the thunderbird and a huge rattlesnake. Individuals who had been struck by lightning and survived often became SHAMANS, for they had received the power of the monster bird.   RENÉ R. GADACZ

Thunderstorm, a towering CLOUD system that moves across the countryside accompanied by LIGHTNING, thunder activity and usually RAIN showers, together with gusty WINDS near the Earth's surface. Other possible components of the storm system are HAIL, occasionally, and TORNADOES, rarely.

Thunderstorms usually occur on summer afternoons. While a thunderstorm typically affects a given locality for only an hour or so during its passage overhead, the entire lifetime may be as long as 6-10 hours, along a pathway of several hundred kilometres. Thunderstorms generally begin with localized heating of the Earth's surface by the sun during the course of a relatively warm day. The air near the ground begins to rise here and there in a nonuniform manner, cooling

navian, Slovakian, Greek, German and Dutch groups also have strong cultural identities. Since the 1960s, there has been little direct immigration from Europe, but Chinese and East Indians moved into the community in increasing numbers in the 1970s.

Economy and Labour Force The economy of Thunder Bay continues to be based on natural-resource extraction, processing and transportation. The forest industry, with woodlands operations, pulp-and-paper mills, and wood-processing plants, is the largest industrial employer. Forest products, coal, iron ore, potash and sulphur are exported through Thunder Bay harbour, but grain predominates in one of the world's largest grain-handling facilities, with its 15 terminal elevators capable of cleaning and storing 2.2 mil-

lion t of grain. Secondary industries include railcar construction, ship repair and specialized equipment assembly and modification, brewing and the manufacture of bricks and clothing. Administrative and service functions employ a large proportion of the labour force, and the tourist industry caters to as many as 250 000 summer visitors, with others drawn in winter to the 7 ski areas around the city. This diversity and the city's dominant position in the grain trade maintain a certain buoyancy during periodic fluctuations in the resource industries.

Transportation Ft William was the very hub of the fur-trade route to the NW. It gained new importance in 1885 when the CANADIAN PACIFIC RY was completed, and a steadily increasing flow of western grain came into the Lakehead for ship-as it ascends. At some level, this convective process leads to the rising air becoming saturated with water vapour as it cools. Condensation of the excess water vapour occurs, producing myriads of tiny water droplets and a small, white structure known as a cumulus cloud results.

Further convection may cause a few of these cumulus clouds to continue growing as their updrafts remain strong and the cloud top continues to move upward. The droplets within them slowly become larger through further condensation until, at some level where the cloud is colder than 0°C, a very small fraction may freeze. These ICE CRYSTALS grow rapidly at the expense of the unfrozen, supercooled, neighbouring droplets, to form snowflakes or ice pellets. Updrafts continue to carry them towards the top of the cloud until they become too large and heavy and begin to fall out. A mature cumulonimbus or thunderstorm cloud is now in existence. At this stage lightning may occur, the cumulonimbus cloud having become electrically charged during its growth. Meanwhile, the falling frozen raindrops and hail pellets within the cloud begin to melt, once they pass back through the freezing level. Should melting be complete, rain showers will result, taking the form of intermittently light and heavy rainfall, frequently accompanied by gusty winds and intense lightning activity. Should melting be incomplete, a feature confined to the larger and more intense thunderstorms, hail will occur with the rain.

While single thunderstorms may be produced on any reasonably warm, sunny day, the more intense ones frequently occur as a line of such storms (squall line) associated with the passage of a cold front (*see* METEOROLOGY). When particularly intense, one or more tornadoes may be formed along the thunderstorm squall line. Thunderstorms occur most frequently in late afternoon but they have been observed at all hours of the day and night. They are most prevalent from late May to early Sept, peaking in July, and are very rare in Dec to Mar. The settled parts of southern Canada have some 10-25 thunderstorm days per year, with the greatest frequency averaging 30-35 in southwestern Ontario. Thunderstorms are rare on the West Coast and in Newfoundland, under 5 per year; their frequency also falls off rapidly north of 55°N to only 2-3 per year over most of the NWT.   J. MAYBANK

Thurston, Frank Russel, aircraft engineer (b at Chicago, Ill 5 Dec 1914). Thurston's British parents took him at age one to England, where he worked from 1937 at the National Physical Laboratory. He was recruited by the NATIONAL RESEARCH COUNCIL in 1947, one of hundreds of British engineers brought to Canada to develop the postwar aircraft industry. He became head of the NRC's Structures Laboratory and in 1959 director of the National Aeronautical Establishment, charged with finding a new industrial role for the NAE, after the cancellation of the AVRO ARROW project. This was done by developing new installations for low-speed aerodynamics, useful in fields from short-takeoff-and-landing aircraft to urban planning. Before retirement in 1979, Thurston was chairman of the NATO Advisory Group for Aerospace Research and Development and organized development of the CANADARM used by US space shuttles. He became an Officer of the Order of Canada in 1982.   DONALD J.C. PHILLIPSON

Tibetans Following a Chinese invasion in 1959, the Dalai Lama and 100 000 of his followers fled Tibet. In 1962 the Tibetan Refugee Aid Society (TRAS) was founded in Vancouver. Devoted first to relief and then to rehabilitation, TRAS (with the aid of CIDA from 1970 onwards) collaborated with European agencies in the resettlement of

thousands of Tibetans in craft communities in the Himalayas and large agricultural settlements in Mysore. In 1971-72, 228 Tibetan refugees immigrated to Canada under a special arrangement between the Canadian government and the Dalai Lama. Since 1973 very few Tibetans have immigrated (only 1, for example, in 1984). Tibetans settled across Canada, but primarily in Ontario, Québec and BC. In Toronto they have joined forces with the Asian community, but have also established their own societies in Toronto and Montréal, and published a newsletter. While largely assimilated into Canadian society, they retain their language and pledge their religious adherence to the Dalai Lama, who paid a pastoral visit to Canada in 1980. In a less direct way, Tibetan influence has spread in Canada through the establishment of meditation centres and other institutions in various centres, from Victoria to Montréal, devoted to spreading Mahayanist Buddhist doctrines as taught by Tibetan lamas. Two of the most important of these leaders, Karmapa (head of the Kargyupa sect) and Sakya Trizin (head of the Sakya sect) have visited Canada to further the spread of Buddhist *dharma* in this country.   GEORGE WOODCOCK

Tick, common name for bloodsucking parasites of vertebrates (mainly of terrestrial mammals and birds) belonging to class ARACHNIDA, order Acari. About 800 species are known worldwide; the 35 species in Canada are found in all areas S of TREELINE. Among the largest of Acari, ticks are 1-5 mm long when unfed, up to 30 mm when fully gorged. Ticks are distinguished by their highly modified mouthparts, used in piercing and attaching to hosts, and by a specialized sensory structure (Haller's organ) near the tip of each first leg, used in locating hosts. In Canada, ticks are important pests of humans, livestock and game animals. Members of genus *Dermacentor* sometimes cause serious loss of cattle from tick paralysis, a condition the ticks cause by feeding on the cattle, not by transmitting disease. Ticks may transmit Rocky Mountain spotted fever, tularemia, Lyme disease and several viruses, but fortunately the strains in Canada are usually not of serious medical or veterinary importance.
                                    EVERT E. LINDQUIST

Tidal Energy is a largely untapped, renewable ENERGY source based on lunar gravitation rather than solar radiation. The potential of tidal HYDROELECTRICITY has long been recognized. However, compared to river dams, tidal-power projects are very expensive, since massive structures must be built in a difficult saltwater environment. The relatively low head of water above the turbines restricts the capacity of individual generators to about 25-50 megawatts (MW = 10^6 watts); therefore, many machines are needed to produce a significant block of power. The machinery also has to withstand the rigours of saltwater operation. For all this investment, the average electric power output is severely limited by the twice-daily ebb and flow of tides: average output of tidal electricity is less than 40% of the installed generating capacity; production of power from river dams typically averages 70-100% of installed capacity. Finally, the lunar cycle of 24 hours 50 minutes means the raw production of tidal energy moves in and out of phase with the normal, solar-oriented daily pattern of electrical consumption. Unlike the energy from river dams, the daily, monthly and annual availability of tidal energy is fully predictable, but it must be either stored or integrated with other sources of generation that can be adjusted to accommodate the fluctuations of tidal generation.

There are relatively few coastal locations in the world where the tidal range (ie, the difference

Annapolis tidal power plant, officially opened Aug 1984, is the first in the Western Hemisphere to transform tidal energy into electrical energy; photo taken at the completion of construction, with dredge and erection crane still in position (*courtesy Tidal Power Corp*).

between high and low tides) is large enough to justify exploitation of the available tidal energy. Not only must there exist a sufficiently high tidal range (at least 5 m) for construction of an economically feasible plant, but the site should also include a natural bay which can store a large volume of seawater at high tide and be so situated within the estuary that the operation of the plant will not significantly change the tidal resonant system (*see* TIDE).

The world's most powerful tides occur in the upper reaches of the Bay of FUNDY, where tidal ranges up to 17 m are not uncommon. UNGAVA BAY and estuaries along the coast of BC also exhibit fairly high tides. The coasts of Argentina, NW Australia, Brazil, France, India, Korea, the UK, the USSR and the American states of California, Maine and Alaska possess coastal configurations and sufficiently large tidal ranges to provide sites at which potentially large sources of tidal energy may be exploited. The aggregate total capacity of all potential tidal-power sites in the world is currently estimated at about one billion kilowatts, with an expected electrical-energy output of 2-3 trillion kilowatt-hours annually, ie, 10 times Canada's present combined electrical output.

The idea of exploiting the energy of the tides is not new. Tidal mills were built in Britain, France and Spain as early as the 12th century. A mill powered partially by tidal energy was built at PORT-ROYAL, NS, in 1607. These early mills extracted only the equivalent of 20-75 kW, or less than the power available in modern compact cars. A few of the early mills are now preserved as historic sites.

Canadian Installations Detailed studies of the Bay of Fundy tidal-power resource concluded that the most efficient scheme of development would be one that would generate power for a period of about 5 hours, twice daily, on the ebb tide. The most cost-effective project was found to be a site in MINAS BASIN, at the mouth of Cobequid Bay in the upper reaches of the Bay of Fundy. This development would have a capacity in excess of 5300 MW, an amount equal to the entire 1980 installed generating capacity of the Maritime power systems. The development has been estimated to cost about $7 billion. A more modest alternative project, at a site in Cumberland Basin through which the NB-NS border passes, has been projected at approximately 1400 MW, about one-quarter the capacity of the larger site, but one-third the capital cost. While it is forecast that the local Maritime power systems would be able to absorb its output, the huge capital investment required for even this smaller project makes the financial considerations discouraging. However, a small, 20 MW, single-unit power station was constructed and commissioned in Aug 1984 by the NS Tidal Power Corp on a tidal reach of the Annapolis R, near ANNAPOLIS ROYAL, NS. This project was undertaken primarily to demonstrate the application of a particular type of turbine generator (trade-name Straflo) for tidal and other low-head hydro applications. The Straflo machine differs from the conventional hydroelectric turbine-generator installation in that the turbine and generator are integral rather than separate units. The average tidal range in Annapolis Basin is only about 6.4 m, but the plant, in which only one large turbine (7.6 m diameter) is installed, will produce about 50 million kW-hours annually for the electrical-utility system of NS.

Technology The most practical scheme for harnessing tidal energy is still the old tidal-mill concept, closing off an estuary or tidal basin from the sea with a structure composed of a powerhouse, a sluiceway section and a solid embankment section. The sluiceways are closed at high tide and the ebbing sea level causes a head differential between the basin level and the sea. When this differential becomes large enough, flow is permitted through the turbo-generators until the difference in levels becomes too low to drive the turbines. When the tide begins to turn and the sea level to rise, the sluiceways are then opened once more, so that the tidal basin can be filled for the next cycle of electrical generation. These cycles take place about twice a day (2 flood tides and 2 ebb tides during each lunar day). Using new technology, turbines can be built to generate electricity in both directions and also to operate as pumps in both directions.

Modern large power systems can readily absorb the intermittent output of a tidal plant. The output from conventional fossil-fueled generating stations can be reduced when the tidal plant begins generation and it can be brought back into the system during the few hours that a tidal plant must remain idle. In this way, large savings in coal and oil can result, and pollutants from such fuels can be substantially reduced.

The NS government expects that tidal power will, in the long run, provide useful energy for the province and for export. However, because of uncertainties about the costs and the export markets for this power, only the Annapolis Royal pilot project is included in the NS electrical generation expansion program of the foreseeable future. Tidal power has also been considered by the NB and BC governments, but is not included in either province's planning. The National Energy Board did not include tidal power in its 1981 estimates of Canadian energy supply and demand for the years 1980-2000 because it considered that the case for early development of tidal power in Canada has not yet been established. R.H. CLARK

Reading: R.H. Charlier, *Tidal Energy* (1982).

Tide Although tides exist in the atmosphere and the solid earth as well as in the OCEAN, only the ocean tide reveals itself in everyday experience. It is seen as a regular oscillation in WATER levels and in speed and direction of ocean currents. Tides originate with the gravitational forces of the MOON and SUN (*see* ASTRONOMY).

The Earth is actually not in orbit around the sun but around the centre of mass of the Earth-sun system. Since all parts of the Earth move in the same orbit, they experience the same acceleration, but only at the Earth's centre is this acceleration exactly balanced by the sun's gravitation. On the side near the sun, gravitation is greater; thus things (eg, water) tend to move toward the sun and away from the Earth's centre. On the side away from the sun, gravitation is less and things tend to move away from the sun and away from the Earth's centre. The unbalanced portion of the gravitation causes level surfaces to bulge outward on the sides of the Earth toward and away from the sun, and these 2 bulges pass around the Earth

once each day as the Earth rotates on its axis. Earth is also in orbit around the centre of mass of the Earth-moon system; consequently, tidal bulges also occur on the sides of the Earth toward and away from the moon. Because the sun is farther away, its tidal effect is only 0.46 that of the moon. When the sun or moon are off the equator, one bulge will be N and one S of the equator, and the 2 will not be experienced equally, except on the equator. This imbalance causes the diurnal inequality in the semidiurnal tides. At new and full moons, the lunar and solar bulges nearly coincide, causing tides of large range, called spring tides. At the moon's first and last quarters, the lunar bulges fall near the solar hollows, causing tides of small range, called neap tides. Tides also tend to have greater range when the moon is closest to Earth (perigean tides).

The range of a tide is the vertical distance between high water and the succeeding low water. Flood is horizontal flow in the landward (upstream) direction; ebb is flow in the seaward (downstream) direction. Slack water is the short period of rest as the flow reverses from flood to ebb, or vice versa. The interval between slack water and high water or low water may vary from place to place, but in most coastal regions slack waters occur near the times of high water and low water. A tide is semidiurnal when it exhibits 2 high waters and 2 low waters in a lunar day (about 25 solar hours), diurnal when it exhibits only one of each. Most tides are intermediate, with 2 daily tides differing from each other in height and range, the difference being called the diurnal inequality. A tidal bore, a tumbling wall of water moving upriver with the advancing tide, is sometimes formed when the tide rises rapidly at the entrance to a shallow, gently sloping river. Bores occur in several rivers off the Bay of FUNDY, the best known being that in the Petitcodiac R, NB. A tide race is a rapid flow of water through a narrow passage, driven by the rising or falling tide at one end. The Reversing Falls at Saint John, NB, is a tide race, flowing in on the rising and out on the falling tide (*see* WATERFALL). A tide rip is a patch of rough water formed when wind-generated ocean waves run up against a tidal flow in the opposite direction. The waves pile up on each other, steepen and break in what can be violent turmoil.

While tidal forces originate in the gravitational influences of heavenly bodies, the tides themselves propagate as long waves, experiencing reflection and amplification or attenuation along their paths. Thus, the character of the tide may differ from that of the tidal forces at the same location. The large ranges in the eastern Arctic result from tidal energy propagated in from the Atlantic Ocean, and the large Bay of Fundy tide is the result of resonance in the Bay of Fundy-Gulf of Maine system. The latter tidal range, at times reaching over 17 m, is the most remarkable in Canada and probably the world. The tide at Victoria, BC, is seen to have more diurnal inequality than that at Halifax, NS, although both locations have nearly the same latitude and thus experience almost the same tidal forces. Because of these differences, tides can be predicted for a site only after sufficient observations have been obtained to define the local tidal character in astronomical terms. Small tides (about 5 cm) occur in the Great Lakes, and a tidal flow of up to one knot has been observed in Little Current Channel, Lk Huron. The study of tides in Canada began in 1893, when the Canadian Tidal Survey was established. Its first director, W.B. DAWSON, was responsible for setting up a network of tidal stations on the Atlantic Coast and in the Gulf of ST LAWRENCE, and for prompting tidal studies on the East and West coasts. The tidal-station network

has continued to expand and is now maintained by the Department of Fisheries and Oceans. *See also* TIDAL ENERGY. W.D. FORRESTER

Reading: W.D. Forrester, *The Canadian Tidal Manual* (1983); G. Godin, *The Analysis of Tides* (1972).

Tidnish, NS, UP, is located on Northumberland Str about 25 km NE of AMHERST, near the NB border. The name, derived from a Micmac word, probably means "a paddle." The community was to have been the eastern terminus of the Chignecto ship railway begun in the 1890s. The railway was never completed, and Tidnish missed out on the population and economic boost it would have experienced. The picturesque stone bridge of the ship railway still stands, a landmark of Cumberland County. Tidnish once supported a flourishing if relatively small fishery, a small shipyard on the NB side of the community at Tidnish Bridge and several sawmills. All of these industries have since failed and today Tidnish is principally a cottage area. JANICE MILTON

Tignish, PEI, Village, pop 960 (1986c), situated 153 km NW of Charlottetown. In 1799, 8 Acadian families left Malpeque Bay and settled in the bush of northwestern PEI. Twelve years later, Irish immigrants began arriving in the area via Chaleur Bay, NB. With the potato famine in the 1840s, a more substantial wave of Irish immigrants arrived. Today, Tignish is 99% Roman Catholic and 35% of the population is French speaking. The co-operative movement has been one of the community's most distinctive features. Beginning with a 1923 union to increase fish prices, Tignishites now own co-operatively many of the community's businesses. W.S. KEIZER

Tiktak, John, sculptor (b at Kareak, a small camp between Eskimo Point and Whale Cove, NWT 1916; d at Rankin Inlet, NWT 9 June 1981). At first a hunter, he moved to Rankin Inlet in 1958 to work at the nickel mine. The mine closed in 1962, and he took up carving "professionally" in 1963, having previously carved "small sculptures representing Eskimo faces" that he sold as souvenirs. His work, dating back to 1961, is in every museum and major private collection of INUIT ART. His personal style, with its rounded shapes and hollows, has definite affinity with Henry Moore, who admired Tiktak's work greatly. Like Moore, he was an icon maker, producing form and symbols rather than subject matter. He was elected to the Royal Canadian Academy of Arts in 1973. GEORGE SWINTON

Tilley, Leonard Percy de Wolfe, lawyer, Conservative premier of NB (b at Ottawa 21 May 1870; d at Saint John 28 Dec 1947). Tilley, son of Sir Samuel Leonard TILLEY, began his career as a lawyer in Saint John and served as an MLA for 9 years before being appointed minister without portfolio in 1925 and president of the Executive Council under J.B.M. BAXTER. In 1931 he was appointed minister of lands and mines and 2 years later became premier. His government was defeated in 1935 and he was appointed exchequer court judge and judge of the county court, a position he held for 10 years. Unlike his esteemed father, Tilley is remembered for little more than holding office during the Depression and leading his party to defeat in 1935. ARTHUR T. DOYLE

Tilley, Sir Samuel Leonard, politician (b at Gagetown, NB 8 May 1818; d at Saint John 25 June 1896). Tilley got his start in a Saint John drugstore, and eventually went into partnership with his mother's relations in that business. He sat in the NB Assembly in 1850-51, 1854-56, 1857-65, 1866-67. A lifelong temperance advocate, he was provincial secretary in the Charles FISHER regime. Its members were called the "Smashers" after having tried unsuccessfully to bring prohibition to NB in 1851-52 and 1855-56. Tilley actively promoted railway development and CONFEDERATION. A delegate to the Charlottetown and Québec conferences, he and his Liberal government (elected 1861) were defeated on Confederation in NB in 1865, but were returned to power in 1866 after what amounted to a coup d'état by the lieutenant-governor, Arthur Gordon. In 1867 Tilley resigned from the NB Cabinet and became minister of customs in Sir John A. MACDONALD's first government. With the fall of Macdonald, 5 Nov 1873, Tilley was appointed, that same day, lieutenant-governor of NB. With Macdonald's return to office in 1878, Tilley became minister of finance, and as such brought in the NATIONAL POLICY tariff in 1879. In 1885, unwell, he retired to Government House, Fredericton, staying on as lieutenant-governor until 1893. Clever and adroit, he was always a sensitive political barometer, and he advised Macdonald in 1868 to pacify NS. Tilley was uneasy about the government's commitments to the CPR in the 1880s, and doubtless would have pulled the plug had he been allowed to do so. Almost the last letter he wrote (sent to Sir Charles TUPPER) was a remarkably shrewd assessment of the 1896 election.

P.B. WAITE

Tillsonburg, Ont, Town, pop 10 745 (1986c), is located in Oxford County, 40 km E of St Thomas. Founder George Tillson arrived in 1822 and opened a forge using bog iron. First known as Dereham Forge, the community became Tillsonburg in 1836. It was a POLICE VILLAGE in 1865 and a town in 1869. An agriculture servicing centre, it now produces automotive and aerospace products, tubing and gas tanks. K.L. MORRISON

Timber Axe Two basic types of axe were used in the early 19th-century eastern forest industry. The more common poll axe had a single, fan-shaped cutting edge, a narrow head weighing 1.5-2.5 kg, and a hickory or maple handle. It was used for felling, scoring and lopping branches off fallen trees. The large, distinctive broadaxe was used for hewing masts and square timber. Its 5 kg, 25 cm wide bevelled blade resembled a large chisel. The hewer cut down diagonally across the grain of the roughly squared baulk to leave a smooth, even surface. On the West Coast, larger double-bitted axes were used, their narrow 25 cm blades and long handles designed to fell the enormous trees of the Pacific slope. Smaller double-bitted axes were used in eastern pulpwood operations; they were also common in the square timber trade: one bit was used for felling and the other for clearing out stumps and roots on skid roads. By the late 19th century the crosscut saw had largely replaced the axe for felling trees.

GRAEME WYNN

Timber Duties First imposed in the 18th century to provide revenue, Britain's tariffs on imported wood were an integral component of the 19th-century British North American TIMBER TRADE. As duties increased 1803-11, in order to replenish depleted treasury coffers and in response to Napoleon's Continental Blockade, Britain established a protected market for colonial producers. With Napoleon's defeat in 1815, colonial preference was attacked by Baltic timber interests and a growing free-trade lobby. Committees in 1820 and 1821 reduced the foreign-colonial differentials without removing the after-freight advantage they gave colonial wood. During the 1830s economic uncertainty increased the instability of the colonial trade. After Britain moved toward free trade in 1842, the colonial timber preference was halved within 2 years. Imports of wood from BNA lost ground to Baltic shipments after 1850,

but despite the gloomy forebodings of colonial timber interests, the transatlantic trade was not eliminated by these changes. By 1860 foreign and colonial wood paid the same low rate and in 1866 Britain abolished the duties. Although the preference may have been essential to the establishment of N American trade, its continued high level through the 1830s probably inflated the price of wood in Britain. GRAEME WYNN

Timber Slide, water-filled chute or runway built to carry RAFTS of timber around rapids and falls; similar devices for individual pieces of wood were called "flumes." Ruggles Wright of Hull claimed to have built the first Canadian slide in 1829. Built of wood and designed to spread the river's fall over a kilometre or more, slides quickened the drive, lessened chances of a jam and reduced damage. Most common in the Ottawa Valley, slides were originally private toll-levying facilities. By 1846 public slides were operating as far up the Ottawa as Lac Coulonge, and by 1870 the Canadian government maintained many public slides to facilitate the Ottawa valley TIMBER TRADE. In 1860 the Prince of Wales (later Edward VII) rode down a timber slide during his visit to British North America. GRAEME WYNN

Timber Trade History Wood was the great staple of Canadian trade for much of the 19th century. Founded upon European demand, the timber trade brought investment and immigration to eastern Canada; it fostered economic development; and it transformed the regional environment far more radically than the earlier exploitation of fish and fur. It encouraged the building of towns and villages, the opening of roads, and EXPLORATION. It also contributed at times to economic instability. BUSINESS-CYCLE swings produced wide fluctuations in the demand for, and the price of, wood; and weather conditions, commercial uncertainties and imperfect market intelligence magnified these difficulties.

Wood entered 19th-century trade in many forms. Large masts, cut for the Royal Navy from the finest trees of the mixed forest that swept through the Maritimes and the St Lawrence Valley, were the most valuable commercial product of British North American forests, which also produced shingles, barrel staves, box shooks and, later, spoolwood for textile factories. But sawn lumber and square timber were the major wood staples. Lumber, the product of SAWMILLS, was prepared mostly as "deals" (rough pieces of wood at least 12' long, 7" wide and 2½" thick, or about 366 x 18 x 6 cm), planks and boards. Square timber, known in the Maritimes as "ton timber," were baulks or "sticks" of wood hewn square with axes and shipped to England, where they were often resawn. Strict specifications governed the market; a "wane" (bevel) and slight taper were allowed, but they varied according to the stick's dimensions and changed with time. Waste was quite considerable: 25-30% of each tree was discarded.

The naval mast trade, always limited by its specialized and high quality requirements, shifted from the Saint John to the St Lawrence Valley early in the 19th century when contractors sought oak, as well as pine, from the deciduous forests of the southern Great Lakes area. The square timber industry developed rapidly to meet the enormous demand from Britain, which was at war with Napoleonic France and was also undergoing industrialization. The transatlantic timber trade, fostered by economic and strategic imperatives, was quickly sheltered by TIMBER DUTIES when Napoleon's 1806 Continental Blockade of Britain's traditional supply areas in northern Europe drove domestic prices up some 300% in 2 years. On average, 9000 loads (almost 1.5 m³

Lumbermen's shanty, Upper Ottawa River, in 1871 (*courtesy Notman Photographic Archives*).

each) of colonial timber entered Britain annually between 1802 and 1805; in 1807 the total was 27 000, 2 years later 90 000, over 500 000 in 1840 and 750 000 in 1846. Thereafter imports fluctuated for 20 years around 600 000 loads and then declined until WWI.

The pattern of the lumber trade is less easily summarized, since international markets were widely separated. Beginning in the 1830s, increasing quantities of lumber were shipped to Britain; there was a growing trade between the Canadas and the US, and many mixed cargoes of lumber and small wood products left the Maritimes for the West Indies. During the period of RECIPROCITY with the US and the construction of railways and canals, the importance of the American market grew; 400 million board feet of BNA lumber passed through Oswego, NY, 1864-66, and wood exports to the US from the PROVINCE OF CANADA were worth almost $7 million in 1866-67. But until the 1880s combined lumber and timber sales to Britain were more valuable than those to the US. Not until 1905, with imports of some $18 million, did the US account for more than half of Canadian forest-product exports.

Although small quantities of birch, white oak, rock elm, ash, basswood and butternut were squared, although some cedar was cut, and although spruce and hemlock lumber increased in importance after mid-century, PINE was the industry's major species. Its exploitation rapidly encompassed a wide area. By 1810 only the fringes of New Brunswick's pine forests had been cut, and the Ottawa-Gatineau confluence marked the inland limit of lumbering in BNA. By 1835 barely a tributary of the Miramichi, Saint John and Ottawa rivers remained unexploited. By 1850 much of the pine had been harvested from the more accessible reaches of these river systems, and trade from many small ports and coastal inlets had ceased. Railways broke the industry's dependence on water courses for the movement of wood to markets and opened the back-country of lakes Ontario and Erie to the trade. Exports from the Peterborough area increased fivefold when the railway arrived in 1854; between 1851 and 1861, Simcoe County rose from insignificance to pre-eminence among lumber producers in Canada West. Mills proliferated along railways pushing northward into the Canadian SHIELD.

This onslaught on the forest only slowly came under government control. Initially BNA forests were ineffectively protected by the imperial "broad arrow" system, implemented in N America early in the 18th century to reserve valuable trees for the Royal Navy. As demand rose after 1806, crown reserves were violated; surveyors appointed to protect them profited from the administrative confusion. In 1824 in New Brunswick and 1826 in Upper and Lower Canada, a coherent regulatory system was established. In BNA provinces except Nova Scotia, the sale of licences conferred a temporary right to cut trees and returned revenue to the government. Periodic amendments attempted to limit the illegal cutting and trespassing which vexed administrators intent on maximizing revenues, but the basic principles of crown ownership and leasehold tenure of the resource were upheld. In marked contrast to the American pattern, present-day Canadian (with the exception of NS) forest law – shaped by the interplay of tradition, self-interest, and the limitations of a vast and hostile environment – has preserved something of the 18th-century conservative idea of how the state should serve the common good.

Logging was essentially a winter occupation, beginning with the first snowfall. In the fall, loggers would build camps (*see* SHANTY) and clear rough roads for hauling hay and provisions and for moving logs or timber to the streams. The industry depended heavily on the muscles of men and beasts. Trees were normally felled with various types of TIMBER AXES (until the 1870s, when the crosscut saw became more common), and "bucked" to stick length with a crosscut saw. Timber was squared by axemen: the log was "lined" along 2 sides to mark the dimensions of the desired square; "scorers" then removed the unwanted outside wood in rough slabs, and the sides of the log were rough-hewn and then smooth-hewn with broadaxes. The log was rolled through 90° and lined, scored and hewn on the remaining 2 sides of the square. Before transportation, the ends of the stick were trimmed to a pyramid shape. A snow road eased the hauling of logs and baulks to riverbanks by oxen, and later by horses. With the coming of the thaw, the timber drive began. Men equipped with "jam dogs" (iron hooks), canthooks or PEAVEYS, and often immersed in chilly water, engaged in the hectic and dangerous task of floating the cut out on the freshet. When more open water was reached, or where falls and rapids could be bypassed by TIMBER SLIDES, logs and timber were assembled into RAFTS to continue downstream to mills or to river-mouth booms (especially at Québec, Saint John and the mouth of the Miramichi R), where they were shipped abroad. As steampower replaced water power in sawmills, it increased mill capacity and extended the season of mill operation but did not break the pattern of winter logging. Although railways reduced the industry's dependence on rivers to transport timber to the mills, their initial importance was in carrying lumber from mill to market; by the end of the century, specialized logging railways still made only a slight impact on eastern Canadian operations.

Before 1825 most BNA timber was produced by small-scale independent operators, many of them farmers who were attracted to the work in their off-season. Good timber was readily available and little capital was required to enter the trade. By 1850, however, as lumbering moved into more remote areas, expenditure on the clearing of boulder-strewn streams became necessary, regulation of the crown domain tightened, more capital was invested and the declining trade intensified competition among operators, and entrepreneurs were seeking to make their positions secure. Large, diversifed, integrated operations emerged, although smaller enterprises persisted on the settlement frontiers. Generally the skilled, the well capitalized and the well connected dominated the trade by acquiring licences, employing lumbering gangs under contract, building large, efficient sawmills and operating their own vessels or railways. For example, in the 1840s Joseph CUNARD and 3 branch houses of the great Scottish firm of Pollok, Gilmour and Co virtually controlled the trade of northeastern New Brunswick by these means. Subsidiaries of the latter concern

Sinclair's Mill, Newcastle, NB *c*1900. The timber trade was of enormous importance to NE New Brunswick in the second half of the 19th century (*courtesy Provincial Archives of New Brunswick*).

were also important in the St Lawrence Valley. William PRICE, "le père du Saguenay," was said to employ 1000 men in the 1830s; by 1842 he had sawmills at Chicoutimi and a steam tug to take ships up from the St Lawrence. In the Ottawa country, J.R. BOOTH's firm produced over 30 million board feet of pine lumber in the 1870s; in the next decade it built the Canada Atlantic Ry to bring out the cut from its Parry Sound licences. In Canada West the firms of Mossom Boyd and D.D. Calvin experienced similarly spectacular successes. The early diffuse and informal trade gave way to an industry dominated by relatively few well-capitalized family firms and partnerships. Thus, the chronic instability of the early trade was somewhat reduced. In the 20th century, as pulp and paper production grew, capital requirements increased further. Many firms amalgamated, and joint-stock financing began to shape the patterns of corporate dominance that mark the forest industry today. Technological changes accompanied developments; long-persistent patterns and practices of forest exploitation yielded to mechanization after 1875, but generally innovations gained acceptance more slowly in the forests of eastern Canada than in the rugged, newly opened areas of BC. Working and living conditions improved as city industries and West Coast logging camps competed for labour. But for all these changes and even as the locus of Canadian wood production shifted westward with the opening of the Panama Canal, and the exhaustion of eastern forests, the eastern lumber industry retained much of its traditional and seasonal character into the 1930s.

Although James COOK's men had cut logs for masts on Vancouver I in 1778, lumbering in BC did not begin seriously until the 1850s. The early industry exploited the huge trees close to the tidewater (mainly DOUGLAS FIR and red cedar) and served markets scattered around the Pacific and as distant as S Africa. With the completion of the CPR in the 1880s, this "cargo trade" was supplemented by trade to the east. Soon, BC wood was popular worldwide. Lumbering on the rugged West Coast required considerable adaptation of eastern techniques: 3 times as many oxen were required; snowroads were impossible in the milder coastal climate, so skid roads had to be built of logs; cuts were made higher on the huge trunks, and a springboard was required for each of the 2 axemen to stand on; and heavy, double-bitted axes were developed. Manual logging techniques were used until about 1912; horses had replaced bulls by the 1890s and were used until the 1920s. By far the most important innovation was the steam-powered donkey engine, introduced about 1897 from the US, which could drag logs up to 150 m. Another innovation was the "high lead system," in which a line high over the

skids pulled or lifted the log over obstacles. In 1910 BC production surpassed Québec's; in 1917 it surpassed the production of every other province; and by the late 1920s BC was producing half of Canada's annual cut of timber. As in the East, railways as well as waterways brought timber to mills or ports; now both use primarily trucks. FORESTRY is still a vital part of Canada's export base. *See also* FOREST ECONOMICS.

GRAEME WYNN

Reading: E. Gould, *Logging* (1976); M. Allerdale Grainger, *Woodsmen of the West* (1964); A.R.M. Lower, *The North American Assault on the Canadian Forest* (1938); D. MacKay, *The Lumberjacks* (1978); Graeme Wynn, *Timber Colony* (1981).

Time Precise timekeeping in Canada began in the middle of the 19th century as an aid to navigation on the high seas, as a control for the railways and as a vital assistance to WEATHER reporting. OBSERVATORIES were commissioned in Québec City, Saint John, Montréal, Toronto and Victoria. The Meteorological Service in Toronto ultimately became responsible for co-ordinating correct time. CONFEDERATION and the survey of western Canada saw the development of a new time service centered in Ottawa and the inauguration in 1905 of the Dominion Observatory. By order-in-council in 1941, the observatory was named the source of time for official purposes. In 1970 the standards of time and frequency were amalgamated under the NATIONAL RESEARCH COUNCIL OF CANADA (NRC), which then became the custodian of official time in Canada.

Enormous strides have been made in the art of timekeeping during the past few decades. Today, as a result of exploiting the properties of atoms (particularly those of cesium and hydrogen) the second can be represented with an accuracy of 5 parts in 10^{14}, or less than four-billionths of a second per day. By contrast, the most precise pendulum CLOCKS, used until the middle of this century, could be relied upon to only about 0.01 of a second per day. Time was determined by measuring the Earth's rotation, as indicated by transit observations of the stars. The primary pendulum therefore indicated sidereal or star time, which was readily translated into mean solar time for the general public. After observations with a transit telescope, the error of the clock was known with an accuracy of about 0.05 of a second. Several nights' work was required to determine the behaviour of the primary clock to within a few milliseconds (0.001 sec). Mean solar time was the best available and was assumed to be entirely uniform. Hence, the second was defined as 1/86 400 of the mean solar day.

Developments in electronics and PHYSICS during the 1920s and 1930s led to the use of the piezo-electric properties of the quartz crystal to develop the quartz clock, which in 1951 replaced the pendulum at the Dominion Observatory. Concurrently, the visual transit telescope gave way to the photographic zenith tube (PZT). Timed by the quartz clock, the PZT was programmed to photograph certain time stars each clear night. This new method proved to be 10 times more exact and the quartz clock ultimately became about 1000 times more precise than the pendulum. The star images produced in the PZT also yield a very precise measure of the instrument's latitude, which provides valuable information to the geophysicist as well as the time keeper. Two Canadian PZTs are in operation, in Ottawa and Calgary.

Solar Time Apparent solar time, as indicated by a sundial, has long been known to lack uniformity. The orbit of the Earth is an ellipse, not a circle, and it is tilted at $23\frac{1}{2}$ degrees to the plane of the equator. Mean solar time is based on an artificial sun which moves uniformly in the plane of the equator. Even so it displays small irregularities from 4 causes: a shift in the Earth's crust with respect to the direction of the axis of rotation, resulting in polar wander which is measured as a variation in latitude; seasonal variation, a slight slowing down in late spring and a speeding up in fall; a gradual slowing, about a millisecond per century, in the Earth's rotation; random changes in the rate of the Earth's rotation. The first 2 causes are small, measurable and can be accounted for; the third is too small to be of concern; the fourth is quite unpredictable.

By the 1960s Earth's rotation had slowed so that the mean solar day was 3 milliseconds longer than the average during the previous 2 hundred years. Hence, the second, the unit of time, was not uniform.

Ephemeris time (ET) was the average solar time during the 18th and 19th centuries. Observations accumulated then formed the basis of equations of motion for members of the solar system. ET can be determined by observing the position of the MOON against the background of stars, but many observations must be combined to achieve a precision of a millisecond. In 1956 the International Committee on Weights and Measures defined the second as 1/31 556 925.9747 of the tropical year 1900, Jan 0, 12 hours ET (ie, 12 midnight between 31/12/1899 and 1/1/1900). By this definition the second is a constant.

Cesium Clock By 1955 the first cesium frequency standard had been built at the National Physical Laboratory (NPL) in England. Such a standard is similar to a clock except that it is intended to run for brief intervals only, during which the performance of a continuously running ensemble of quartz clocks can be precisely determined and their rates adjusted. A 3-year experiment between NPL and the US Naval Observatory demonstrated that the second of ET was equal to the duration of 9 192 631 770 periods of the radiation corresponding to the transition between the 2 levels of the ground state of the cesium-133 atom.

The second cesium standard, called CsI, was built at NRC in 1957, and in 1958 became the frequency reference for the quartz clocks at NRC and in the time laboratory at the Dominion Observatory. The passage of years vindicated the evaluation of the atomic second, which in 1967 was adopted by the General Committee on Weights and Measures as the official unit of time in the international system (SI) of units (*see* WEIGHTS AND MEASURES).

Further NRC research into the properties of cesium frequency standards resulted in the development of CsIII (1965), CsV (1970) and 3 CsVI clocks (1976). CsI and CsIII were frequency standards; the others are real clocks operating continuously with an accuracy of about 1×10^{-13} and a stability of few parts in 10^{14}. CsV, which in 1975 started operating as the world's first primary clock, is the official basis for time in Canada and an important contributor to the exact determination of international atomic time. Research into a more compact design resulted in CsVI, half the size of CsV. The only similar primary clock in operation is at the Physikalisch-Technischen Bundesanstalt in W Germany.

Two atomic hydrogen masers have also been built at NRC. They have very good short-term stability of a few parts in 10^{15} for periods of up to an hour, although they deteriorate to several parts in 10^{14} over several days, and to parts in 10^{13} over a year. They are not used as clocks but are valuable short-term frequency references. Hydrogen maser research is also done at U Laval; and at UBC the first tests of a promising new land of cryogenic hydrogen maser have been made.

Time Zones Across Canada

Nfld	12:30	1:30	2:30	3:30	4:30	5:30	6:30	7:30	8:30	9:30	10:30	11:30
Maritimes	12:00	1:00	2:00	3:00	4:00	5:00	6:00	7:00	8:00	9:00	10:00	11:00
Ont & Qué	11:00	12:00	1:00	2:00	3:00	4:00	5:00	6:00	7:00	8:00	9:00	10:00
Man & Sask	10:00	11:00	12:00	1:00	2:00	3:00	4:00	5:00	6:00	7:00	8:00	9:00
Alta (& Sask)*	9:00	10:00	11:00	12:00	1:00	2:00	3:00	4:00	5:00	6:00	7:00	8:00
BC & YT	8:00	9:00	10:00	11:00	12:00	1:00	2:00	3:00	4:00	5:00	6:00	7:00

*During daylight saving time, most Saskatchewan clocks do not change. Hence Saskatchewan time is the same as Alberta time during the summer daylight saving period.

Use of table: The vertical columns indicate the times that exist simultaneously. Suppose it is 4:00 PM in Ontario, then it is 5:30 PM in Newfoundland and 2:00 PM in Alberta. If it is 2:00 AM in the Maritimes, it is 11:00 PM the previous day in Alberta.

Leap Second With the adoption of the atomic second as the unit of time, a co-ordinated system of timekeeping, UTC, was established under the authority of the Bureau international de l'heure (BIH) in Paris, France. It was known that a clock operating on atomic time would not keep mean solar time. Mean solar time would run slow because of slower Earth rotation. The first solution to this problem was to use a secondary quartz clock which could be accurately offset from atomic time to represent mean solar time. Based on PZT observations, the BIH would revise the value of the offset when necessary. For the man on the street, this was entirely satisfactory. But the scientific community had to apply this offset to the time as broadcast to determine the value of the cesium second for any particular date. It was not a satisfactory arrangement, so in Jan 1972 it was changed. Atomic time was broadcast directly. When mean solar time showed a lag of about half a second with respect to atomic time, a whole second was added at midnight, UTC, on December 31 or June 30, effectively putting atomic time back. As a result, mean solar time and atomic time are permitted to differ by no more than about 0.8 second. Due notice is given when the leap second is inserted. Provision has also been made that should the Earth increase its rate of rotation so that mean solar time commences to advance on atomic time, a second may be deleted from atomic time as needed. The SI second is thus always available to everyone.

Time Distribution The distribution of precise time in Canada is performed by NRC radio station CHU at frequencies of 3330, 7335 and 14670 kHz. Seconds pulses (0.3 sec long) are accompanied by a bilingual announcement of Eastern Standard Time each minute. Every 10 seconds, the time is available by telephone: (613) 745-1576, English; (613) 745-9426, French. A highly accurate digital time signal, giving the date, hour, minute and second to 0.1 millisecond accuracy, is also available by telephone and via CHU. Decoding is by specially designed synchronizable clocks, or a computer with a standard 300 baud modem. The most familiar time signal is the one sent each weekday at 1:00 PM Ottawa time over the CBC network. Radio time signals, via WWV and WWVH of the National Bureau of Standards, US, can also be received at many places throughout Canada.

Canadian time and frequency are compared with those of other national time laboratories by the reception of Loran-C radio signals, the monitoring of transmissions and the direct exchange of time signals via satellite. The records are co-ordinated by the BIH which is responsible for establishing the international atomic time scale and the derived scale, Universal Co-ordinated Time, which is, by international agreement, the basis for civil time around the world. For legal purposes in Canada, references to Greenwich Mean Time are now interpreted as references to UTC.

Standard Time The development in the 19th century of rapid railway and telegraph communication was followed by the establishment of standard time zones. The American, Charles Ferdinand Dowd, encouraged the US railways to recognize uniform zones and the Canadian, Sir Sandford FLEMING, advocated using the principle on the international scale. The Washington Conference in 1884 recommended that the world be divided into 24 zones, each 15° wide, the first centered on the Greenwich meridian. Within each zone, time would be the same and the boundary would mark the place where time would change abruptly by one hour. Canada and the US had adopted standard time on 18 Nov 1883. In practice, time-zone boundaries now tend to conform to more convenient national or geographical divisions so that zones differ in size, shape and amount of change (eg, the Newfoundland time zone differs by only half an hour).

International Date Line Greenwich time zones are later, hour by hour, until, at the 180th meridian, the time is 12 hours later. It takes 12 hours for the sun to travel from the antimeridian to the Greenwich meridian. Similarly, to the W, the time is earlier, hour by hour, until again at the 180th meridian the time is 12 hours earlier. Thus, there is a difference of a whole day at the point directly opposite Greenwich, the International Date Line. Fortunately, the date line is located, for the most part, in the Pacific Ocean. In order that it may not pass through settled lands, the date line is deflected eastward through the Bering Str, westward to include the Aleutian Is, then eastward again to include Chatham I and the Tonga Is. The practical consequence of the date line is that, when crossing it going westward, a day is dropped from the calendar (eg, one leaps ahead from Monday into Tuesday). In the opposite direction, eg, from Hong Kong to Honolulu, a day is added (eg, one goes from Tuesday back into Monday).

Time Zones in Canada Canada extends E and W almost 90°. Originally there were 7 time zones, but with the Yukon Territory electing to use Pacific time, there are now only 6. *Newfoundland Standard Time (NST)*, centered on $52\frac{1}{2}$° W, near St John's Nfld, $-3\frac{1}{2}$ hours from Greenwich, is used throughout the island. *Atlantic Standard Time (ATS)*, centered on 60° W, near Sydney NS, -4 hours from Greenwich, is used through NS, PEI, NB, the coast of Labrador, those parts of Québec E of the 63rd meridian and the NWT E of the 68th meridian. *Eastern Standard Time (EST)*, centered on 75° W, near Cornwall, Ont, -5 hours from Greenwich, is used in Québec W of the 63rd meridian, in Ontario E of the 90th meridian and in the NWT between the 68th and 85th meridian including all of Southampton I. *Central Standard Time (CST)*, centered on 90° W, near Thunder Bay, Ont, -6 hours from Greenwich, is used in Ontario W of the 90th meridian, Manitoba, eastern and most of southern Saskatchewan, and the NWT between the 85th and 102nd meridians. *Mountain Standard Time (MTS)*, centered on 105°

W near Regina, Sask, -7 hours from Greenwich, is used parts of in western and northwestern Saskatchewan (including Lloydminster), Alberta, parts of eastern BC, and in that part of the NWT west of the 102nd meridian. *Pacific Standard Time (PST)*, centered on 120° W near Kamloops, BC, -8 hours from Greenwich, is used throughout most of BC and the YT. *Yukon Standard Time (YST)*, centered on 135° W near Whitehorse, YT, is used only in a portion of the Alaska Panhandle.

Daylight Saving Time The use of daylight saving time, in which clocks are advanced by one hour during summer, has been encouraged since early in the century. Federal legislation establishing it was limited to a portion of both world wars. Each province now has legislation controlling its adoption or rejection. Saskatchewan is the only province to legislate the use of standard time year round. All the others are expected to adopt the extended period of daylight time from the first Sunday in April to the last Sunday in October. The well-known saying, "spring forward and fall back," serves as a reminder that in spring the clocks are advanced for daylight saving and in the fall they are turned back for standard time.

The E-W expanse of Canada, and the time difference of 4½ hours from St John's to Vancouver, can result in a 9 AM call from Montréal rousing a sleepyhead at 6 AM in Victoria BC.

MALCOLM M. THOMSON

Reading: Derek Howse, *Greenwich Time and the Discovery of Longitude* (1980); Malcolm M. Thomson, *The Beginning of the Long Dash, A History of Timekeeping in Canada* (1978).

Timiskaming, Lake, 313 km², 128 km long, elev 180 m, located on the Ontario/Québec border in the SW corner of Québec; in Québec the name is spelled Témiscamingue. Varying from a few hundred metres to 8 km in width, Lk Timiskaming straddles the boundary, half in Ontario and half in Québec. Its physical character is well summarized in its name, an Algonquin word meaning "at the place of the deep water." The lake is deep – the mean depth is 122 m – except for the clay flats in the NE corner, which are dry at low water. Along its E and SE shores are steep cliffs, a part of the LAURENTIAN HIGHLANDS, which until the 19th century were covered by pine forests. On the SW shore this same topography prevails, but N of the Montréal R, where the lake widens, the hills give way to gentler slopes. Geologically, Lk Timiskaming is a remnant of Lk Barlow, a glacial lake dating back about 10 000 years.

Before European intrusion into the area, Algonquian Indians occupied lands to the NE of the lake, OJIBWA to the S and CREE to the NW. All were drawn into the FUR TRADE in the early 1670s, and from then until the beginning of the 19th century, when the trade shifted northwestward, Lk Timiskaming was mainly a transportation route for a succession of fur companies and their traders. In the 1830s and 1840s, however, missionary fervour brought first Oblates and then the Sulpicians into the area. In these same years, lumbermen acquired cutting rights along the eastern shore of the lake in the Kipawa region. By the 1870s, lumbermen had fanned northward and crossed the lake to the western shore. In the 1880s, permanent settlement began around Lk Timiskaming, on the Québec side, thanks to the efforts of missionary colonizers such as Father Paradis at VILLE-MARIE, and in Ontario through the work of such men as C.C. Farr, founder of HAILEYBURY. The first commercial steamer appeared on the lake in 1882; 14 were in operation in 1900. By then, however, railways had begun to take over the lake's transportation role. The CPR branch line, the Temiskaming Colonization Railway, running northward in Québec from Mattawa,

reached TÉMISCAMING in 1894 and Ville-Marie in 1925. The Ontario government began construction of its own colonization railway, the Temiskaming and Northern Ontario, in 1902. By 1905 the T & NO had reached NEW LISKEARD, the farming village at the mouth of Wabi Creek on Lk Timiskaming, and 3 years later it connected with the National Transcontinental Ry at COCHRANE in the Great Clay Belt. As a developmental instrument the T & NO proved to be immensely successful, making possible the establishment of a host of silver (COBALT) and gold (TIMMINS, KIRKLAND LAKE) mining towns to the W and NW of the lake. Because of these railways and the highways constructed into the area from NORTH BAY and Mattawa in the 1920s, Lk Timiskaming declined as a commercial transportation route after WWI, but became important for tourism and recreational purposes.

MATT BRAY

Timlin, Mabel Frances, "Timmie," economist, professor (b at Wisconsin Rapids, Wis 6 Dec 1891; d at Saskatoon 19 Oct 1976). In 1917 Mabel Timlin immigrated to Saskatchewan and in 1921 joined U Sask as a secretary, at the same time taking classes. She graduated in 1929 and continued her studies, completing her PhD at U Wash in 1940, and in 1950 was appointed full professor at U Sask. She applied her considerable analytical talents to theoretical and policy issues, in particular a critique of postwar monetary policy. Best known for her *Keynesian Economics* (1942, repr 1976) – a pioneering interpretation of Keynes's *General Theory* – she also published *Does Canada Need More People?* (1951) and, with Albert Faucher, *The Social Sciences in Canada: Two Studies* (1968). She was elected to the Royal Soc of Canada in 1951 and made a member of the Order of Canada in 1976.

PAUL PHILLIPS

Timmins, Ont, City, pop 46 657 (1986c), 46 114 (1981c), located 298 km NW of Sudbury. Prospecting in the region began in 1906, with the first large GOLD discoveries made in 1909 by Benjamin Hollinger, Sandy McIntyre and others. The main population centre was SOUTH PORCUPINE until 1911, when it was destroyed by fire. Noah TIMMINS, a Mattawa merchant who first made a fortune in the COBALT silver rush and then moved north, gave his name to a new town that was officially incorporated on 1 Jan 1912. For the first half-century of its existence, the town's population and prosperity fluctuated with the fortunes of the various gold mines – Hollinger, McIntyre and Dome. Since the 1960s its economic base has been diversified, with the addition of copper mining (Kidd Creek Mines) and waferboard production. Through regional amalgamation in 1971, Timmins achieved city status and claims the distinction of being, geographically (3212 km²), the second-largest city in N America.

MATT BRAY

Timmins, Noah Anthony, mining executive (b at Mattawa, Canada W 31 Mar 1867; d at Palm Beach, Fla 23 Jan 1936). In association with his brother Henry, David DUNLAP and John and Duncan McMartin, Timmins acquired the LaRose silver mine at COBALT and, in 1909, properties in the Porcupine district which formed the basis of Hollinger Consolidated Gold Mines, of which he was president. During the 1920s and 1930s he

continued to play a major role in Canadian mining development, most notably by bringing together the principals of the Hollinger and Noranda mining companies to finance the start-up costs of Noranda's copper operations in northern Québec. The town of TIMMINS, Ont, is named after him.

JOSEPH LINDSEY

Reading: D.M. LeBourdais, *Metals and Men: The Story of Canadian Mining* (1957).

Timms, Philip Thomas, commercial photographer, printer, amateur archaeologist, musician (b at Toronto 16 Sept 1874; d at Vancouver 8 Aug 1973). Perhaps Vancouver's best early photographer, Timms concentrated on postcards, prints and lantern slides which he processed and printed himself. He set out to record "everything in sight" – buildings, streets and parks – between 1900 and 1910, often carrying his large glass-plate camera by bicycle. A devout Christian, antivivisectionist and vegetarian, Timms showed a sensitive and unstudied approach in his photographs. His collection of negatives is in the Vancouver Public Library.

DANIEL O'NEILL

Tinsley, Robert Porter, Jr, football player (b at Damon, Tex 16 Aug 1924). "Buddy" Tinsley played 11 seasons for the WINNIPEG BLUE BOMBERS (1950-60) as a full-time 2-way player, an offensive and defensive tackle. His great agility inspired his coaches to use him occasionally as a ball carrier. Tinsley led by example and was named captain of the team from 1951 to 1960. His play earned him 8 Western All-Star selections, 5 on offence and 3 on defence and All-Canadian honours 4 times. Tinsley's team went to 5 GREY CUP games, winning in 1958 and 1959. He was elected to the Canadian Football Hall of Fame in 1982.

PETER WONS

Tipi, a conical skin-and-frame dwelling, was an easily moved yet substantial structure used by the nomadic Plains Indians. Used historically and perhaps prehistorically, the tipi was 4-6 m in diameter at the base, tapered upward to form a smokehole at the top, and was draped with a sewn cover of 8-12 buffalo skins arranged over as many as 20 poles. The tipi averaged 7-8 m in height, with the entrance commonly facing east. Tipis in the 19th century were often large enough to house several nuclear families, and were embroidered with QUILLWORK and painted. Women erected and dismantled these dwellings, and they specialized in cutting and sewing the buffalo robes so that they would fit the conical frame. Outside the Plains area and around the western Great Lakes, a similar dwelling was called WIGWAM in the Algonquian languages.

RENÉ R. GADACZ

Tisdale, Sask, Town, pop 3184 (1986c), 3107 (1981c), inc 1920, is located at a CNR-CPR junction, 135 km ESE of Prince Albert. Originally called Doghide after nearby Doghide Creek (1902), it was renamed to honour F.W. Tisdale, a railway civil engineer, when the CANADIAN NORTHERN RY reached the community (1904). Situated on the dark soils of the mixed wood forest, it grew gradually as a retail service centre for what became one of Saskatchewan's better mixed farming districts. It has also always possessed some agriculturally related industries: first, a flour mill and creamery; later, Saskatchewan's first honey processing co-operative, and today, an alfalfa dehydrator and fabricators of grain bins and egg trays.

MARGARET BAERWALDT

Titanic, named for mythological giants, was the largest (269 m), most luxurious ocean liner to its time. It was touted to be unsinkable, but it struck an iceberg on 14 Apr 1912, on the fifth day of its maiden voyage, and sank in 2 hrs, 40 mins, with the loss of 1522 lives, including the captain and Canadian railway tycoon Charles Melville HAYS. Lack of adequate lifeboat space, poor evacuation procedures and slowness of response to distress signals resulted in new mandatory safety rules and the formation of the International Ice Patrol. Many novels, including one from the viewpoint of the iceberg by Canadian oceanographer-ornithologist R.G.B. Brown, and the musical, *Unsinkable Molly Brown*, were both inspired by the tragedy.

After numerous attempts to find *Titanic*, a US-French expedition culminated in the discovery of the wreck on 1 Sept 1985, 73 years after its sinking, 590 km SE of Newfoundland at 3810 m depth in an undersea canyon. Four days of unmanned dives with sophisticated camera and diving equipment then and 11 manned dives a year later showed extensive rust in stalactite-like "rusticles," deterioration of wood by shipworms and colonization by sea life, but many artifacts intact. Research showed that an alleged 91 m gash did not exist, but the ship had split in two and hull and stern were 549 m apart. *Titanic* exploration allowed scientists to test sophisticated submersible, sonar and camera equipment developed by numerous researchers, including Canadian Joseph MACINNIS, who also took part in the expedition in 1987 in which a container was salvaged from the wreck. MARTIN K. MCNICHOLL

Titanium (Ti), metallic element estimated to form about 0.5% of the rocks of the Canadian SHIELD. Titanium minerals of commercial importance include rutile (TiO_2), anatase (TiO_2) and ilmenite ($FeTiO_3$). About 90% of titanium mineral production is used to make titanium dioxide pigments, some 60% of which are used in the PAINT INDUSTRY. All facets of the industry are carried out in Québec. QIT-Fer et Titane Inc mines ilmenite at Havre St-Pierre and smelts it in electric furnaces at Sorel. The smelted product, sorelslag, contained 80% TiO_2; some 900 000 t are produced annually, of which 800 000 t are exported, mainly to the US and Europe. The remainder is sold to Canadian producers of titanium pigments. Most titanium pigments are obtained through the sulphate process, in which finely crushed and concentrated ilmenite is dissolved by sulphuric acid. The product is then clarified, filtered and dried before bagging. Another process involves reacting rutile with gaseous chlorine, then reacting the product with oxygen. Most new plants use this chlorine process. Titanium metal and its alloys are light and have very high tensile strength, even at high temperatures. Utilized in aircraft and spacecraft construction, titanium is not yet produced in Canada, though both the titanium minerals and the inexpensive electricity required are readily available. M.A. BOUCHER

Tlingit, Inland, centered in Atlin in northernmost BC and Teslin in the adjacent Yukon Territory, exploit the boreal forest around the large lakes forming the headwaters of the YUKON R. In the 19th century their ancestors lived on the upper reaches of the Taku R that flows into the Pacific near Juneau, Alaska. The move across the height of land to the Yukon was prompted first by its rich fur resources, then by the KLONDIKE GOLD RUSH of 1897-99. In each homeland the Inland Tlingit intermarried with Athapaskans. While in the Taku basin, some Tlingit had married TAHLTAN, but they also feuded with them over rights to control the flow of fine furs from the interior to the coast. Both groups coveted the fur of the Liard R KASKA, but were themselves dominated by Coast Tlingit who monopolized access to white fur traders.

Nineteenth-century Inland Tlingit depended on annual salmon runs in the Taku drainage but also hunted caribou, moose, sheep and goats, as well as small game, birds and freshwater fish. This seminomadic subsistence pattern was equally adapted to the Yukon, where fur bearers were more numerous but salmon resources were poorer. Tlingit technology was like that of neighbouring Athapaskans (*see* TUTCHONE), well suited to the hard conditions of the subarctic Cordillera. Social organization, however, was modelled on that of the Coast Tlingit. Their 6 matrilineal clans, grouped into the exogamous Wolf (or Eagle) and Crow (Raven) moieties, structured rank, marriage and naming practices. Because a headman's authority was limited to his own clan segment, there were no BAND chiefs until after WWII when the Dept of Indian Affairs instituted elected band chiefs and councils. Social relations rested on reciprocal obligations between members of clans in opposite moieties, the most important being associated with death and the memorial feasts or potlatches that followed a year or so afterwards (*see* POTLATCH.)

Although increasingly acculturated to white society following the gold rushes and the building of the ALASKA HIGHWAY in 1942, the present population of 527 (1986) Inland Tlingit has renewed its interest in traditional arts. Teslin have also set up commercial enterprises such as CANOE and SNOWSHOE manufacturing. Since they have signed NO INDIAN TREATIES, the Inland Tlingit are pursuing LAND CLAIMS settlements in both the US and Canada. *See also* NATIVE PEOPLE: SUBARCTIC and general articles under NATIVE PEOPLE.
CATHARINE MCCLELLAN

Reading: J. Helm, ed, *Handbook of North American Indians,* vol 6: *Subarctic* (1981).

Toad, common name for certain members of the amphibian order Anura, the FROGS. The distinction is not firm, but the word toad is generally applied to frogs with relatively short legs and thick bodies, dry skin and reduced webbing between the toes. Toads live in drier habitats than other frogs. Most toads belong to the family Bufonidae (17 genera), which occurs worldwide, except in Antarctica. In Canada 4 species of genus *Bufo* are known: western toad (*B. boreas*), Great Plains toad (*B. cognatus*), American toad (*B. americanus*) and Fowler's toad (*B. fowleri*). Two so-called "spadefoot toads," belonging to family Pelobatidae, are known in Canada. These are the Plains spadefoot (*Scaphiopus bombifrons*) and the Great Basin spadefoot (*S. intermontanus*).
G.M. SANDERS

American toad (*B. americanus*), one of 4 species of genus *Bufo* found in Canada (*photo by Mary W. Ferguson*).

Tobacco (*Nicotiana tabacum*), annual (potentially perennial) herbaceous plant of the NIGHTSHADE family. It evolved in Central America from a natural crossing between *N. sylvestris* and *N. tomentosiformis*. The plant has a fibrous root system and a cylindrical stem which terminates in a cluster of over 150 funnel-shaped, pink flowers with 5 petals. The fruit is a capsule with 2 or 4 compartments; each capsule may produce 4000-8000 seeds. The commercially important part of the plant, the leaves, are arranged in a spiral on the stalk and are oval with a pointed apex. Leaves average 23-30 cm wide and 55-60 cm long. Canada ranks among the top 12 tobacco-producing countries and produces 5 major types: flue cured, ie, heat cured; and burley, cigar, dark and pipe, which are air cured. Tobacco is primarily smoked as cigarettes or cigars; chewing and snuff products constitute a small proportion of the consumer market.

Tobacco was cultivated by the PETUN, NEUTRAL and HURON of southwestern Ontario and was an important item of trade. Commercial tobacco cultivation in Canada began in the early 1800s and, until 1920, was mainly restricted to the burley type. Flue-cured tobacco was introduced to Ontario around 1900 and it is now the major tobacco type (95-98%) grown in Canada; 90% is produced in southwestern Ontario. Flue-cured tobacco was introduced to Québec, NS, PEI and NB in 1930, 1958, 1959 and 1963, respectively. Tobacco seeds are sown in sterile muck in greenhouses during the first week of Apr, and seedlings are transplanted into the field in late May and early June. Plants require approximately 220-250 mm of rainfall, 115-120 frost-free days, and mean monthly temperatures of 19-23°C. Pests and other problems include cutworms, hornworms, aphids, damping-off, black root rot, blue mold, NEMATODES and WEEDS. Plants are topped at a height of 16-19 marketable leaves, generally in late July. Leaves start maturing from the bottom and are harvested in batches of 2-3 leaves per harvesting or priming, a week apart. Harvested leaves are cured in a curing barn or kiln. High-temperature drying arrests the natural chemical processes and turns the leaves a golden colour. Air-cured tobaccos are usually stalk cut, hung on sticks and allowed to dry naturally in a barn. The final product is brown. *See also* SMOKING.
P.W. JOHNSON

Tobacco-Products Industry Although Canada's TOBACCO industry has developed largely during this century, tobacco growing goes back to early colonial days, when settlers around the St Lawrence R adopted the SMOKING customs of native peoples. French settlers began by copying the agricultural model set by the Indians. Some years later, a French colonial ordinance forbade retail sale of tobacco in New France, leaving the settlers without an incentive to improve crop quality or yields. Consequently, they grew only enough for their own use, curing it naturally in the open air. This simple method of preparation produced a unique tobacco, *tabac canadien*. The French colonists began trading tobacco in 1652, but the French government did not encourage tobacco growing in Canada until 1735, after which the crop was cultivated regularly. Two varieties were native, *petit canadien* and *Rose Quesnel*. In Upper Canada the tobacco-growing industry was founded around Kent and Essex counties by LOYALISTS who came from the southern US during the American Revolution and brought tobacco seeds with them.

When tobacco growing expanded commercially in the late 19th century, the principal type cultivated in Québec and Ontario was burley (with some additional varieties of pipe tobacco in Québec). At this time, Québec led production: the yield in Canada in 1870-71 was 723 589 kg, of which 181 381 kg were produced in Ontario and 542 208 kg in Québec. Production in the 2 provinces expanded rapidly, reaching 7 938 000 kg by 1910, with Québec still the leader.

At the start of the 20th century, important changes took place in the industry. During WWI the popularity of chewing and pipe tobaccos declined and the demand for cigarettes grew rapidly. At the same time, a new curing method, flue curing, produced a type of tobacco (Virginia) better suited for cigarettes. This development revolutionized the Canadian tobacco industry. William T. Gregory and his brother Francis were primarily responsible for developing flue-cured tobacco in Canada. William came to Canada from N Carolina in 1900 to work for the Empire Tobacco Co (then a subsidiary of the American Tobacco Co, later taken over by the Imperial Tobacco Co of Canada). He arrived in Leamington, Ont, where only burley tobacco was being grown, and decided to plant Virginia tobacco. Francis came to Canada in 1901 to supervise these experiments. The company encouraged the brothers, hoping to replace expensive US imports with Canadian-grown, flue-cured tobacco.

William chose the Leamington district as the initial growing area because of its desirable soil type and its claim to a longer frost-free period than any other area in Ontario. The results were encouraging, and skilled US growers were brought to Canada to teach farmers growing and curing methods. By 1920, 3.6 million kg of flue-cured tobacco were being produced around Leamington. In 1922 further experimentation with flue-cured tobacco was done in the Lk Erie area, which had large tracts of sandy soil suited for the plant. The first successful crop was grown in 1925, beginning a new era in the history of Canadian tobacco.

With the development of this new growing belt, the industry eventually spread to 12 other areas in the province. Ontario is now the major tobacco producer in Canada. The major growing areas in Québec are N of Montréal, in Montcalm and Joliette counties. Production of flue-cured tobacco in the province started in 1930 and, by 1933, 2 curing kilns had been built, one in each county. Today a flue-cured tobacco industry exists in the Maritime provinces; major production is in PEI, followed by NS and NB.

The Modern Industry Today, Canada ranks in the top 10 of the 100 tobacco-growing countries, producing over 100 million kg annually. Most of the crop is sold locally for use in domestic products, but in 1986 some 24.8 million kg, worth over $114 million, were exported, mainly to European Economic Community countries, the US and Egypt. The tobacco industry permanently employs some 6000 Canadians and creates another 51 000 seasonal jobs.

Six plants (5 in Ontario and 1 in Québec) process all tobacco for domestic manufacture and for export. More than 550 people are employed in this sector. Five cigarette-manufacturing plants (3 in Québec, 2 in Ontario) produced 55.6 billion units in 1986. Four cigar factories produced 283 million cigars (1986). In addition, tobacco-products-manufacturing plants produced 7.86 million kg of fine-cut tobacco and 37 709 kg of pipe tobacco. In 1985 the 3 major manufacturers employed 6100 workers. Sales of domestically produced cigarettes totalled $56.4 billion. In addition, nearly 500 million cigarettes were imported in 1986, mostly from the US. This was down from some 752 million in 1983. Domestic cigar sales totalled 283 million units and 18.5 million were imported. Domestic sales of fine-cut tobacco totalled 7.4 million kg in 1986, up over 20% from the 1983 total. Sales of domestic pipe tobacco were 36 526 kg; imported pipe tobacco was some 624 100 kg. Sales of chewing, plug and twist tobacco and snuff (none of which is produced domestically) were 1797 kg in 1986 down from 134 700 kg in 1983.

Sales were made through a network of 137 (1985) wholesalers and some 90 000 retailers and 23 000 vending machines. Employment in this sector is estimated at 22 000. Federal and provincial governments now receive almost 67% of the retail price of a package of cigarettes. In 1986 the federal government alone received an estimated $1.8 billion from the sale of tobacco products. The provinces collected more than $1.8 billion in taxes. In addition, major tobacco companies paid more than $83 million in corporate income tax (1984). Of the 3 major manufacturers, one is 100% American owned and 2 are publicly held companies in Canada. In the mid- to late 1980s the industry has been hard hit by the public's growing antismoking attitudes, by massive tax increases and by legislative attempts to restrict tobacco advertising.   C.M. SEYMOUR

Toboggan, historically among subarctic native groups a common means of hauling small loads or people over snow. Typically, toboggans were constructed of 2 or more thin boards of larch or birch wood, secured to one another by crossbars, with the boards turned up at the front. The wood was bent while still green or wet, then held in position by lashing until the wood dried. The Inland TLINGIT steamed the planks. Well adapted to light powder snow but useless in wet snow, toboggans were replaced by canoe-sleds during spring thaw. They were pulled by dogs or by people. Among the CHIPEWYAN toboggans were pulled by women. In addition to its recreational use, the toboggan may still serve the same purpose but has generally been replaced by the skidoo or other motorized sleds. *See also* BOBSLEDDING.   RENÉ R. GADACZ

Todd, Robert Clow, artist, decorative painter (b at Berwick-upon-Tweed, Eng *c*1809; d at Toronto 7 May 1866). Todd left a lively record of Québec winter life in a series of horse-and-sleigh paintings reminiscent of British artist Stubbs, whose work Todd may have admired while decorating carriages in Edinburgh and London before coming to Québec C in 1834. In Québec, sportsmen and officers commissioned him to paint pictures of their favourite horses; he also did summer views of MONTMORENCY FALLS and the Québec docks. He moved to Toronto in 1853, advertising as "banner, herald, sign and ornamental painter," but business was poor. He is best remembered for the crisp linear finesse and feeling for the local scene in paintings such as *The Ice Cone, Montmorency Falls* (*c*1845). He taught at both the SÉMINAIRE DE QUÉBEC and Loretto Abbey, Toronto.   ANNE McDOUGALL

Tolmie, Simon Fraser, veterinarian, farmer, politician, premier of BC (b at Victoria 25 Jan 1867; d there 13 Oct 1937), son of William Fraser TOLMIE. After graduating from the Ontario Veterinary College in 1891 and working in a professional capacity in both the provincial and federal agricultural departments, he became chief inspector of livestock for the Dominion. He also operated a successful farm in suburban Victoria. Elected as the Unionist (Conservative) MP for Victoria in 1917, he served as minister of agriculture, 1919-21 and in 1926. Although elected provincial Conservative leader in 1926 he remained an MP until 1928 when he resigned to contest the provincial election. Elected in Saanich, he became premier and minister of railways on 21 Aug 1928. His lacklustre administration gradually disintegrated under the pressure of the Depression and internal squabbles, and was soundly defeated by the Liberals under T.D. PATTULLO in 1933. Tolmie won the Victoria federal by-election in June 1936 and died in office.
          PATRICIA E. ROY

Tolmie, William Fraser, surgeon, fur trader, politician (b at Inverness, Scot 3 Feb 1812; d at Victoria 8 Dec 1886). Tolmie came to the North-West in 1833 in the service of the HBC. After serving at posts on the northern coast, he was given charge of trading and farming operations at Ft Nisqually on Puget Sound, 1843-57. His fair dealing won the Indians' respect but aroused the suspicions of American immigrants. In 1859 he moved to Victoria and was on the board of management of the HBC 1861-70. He was a member of the House of Assembly of Vancouver I 1860-66 and of the Legislative Assembly of BC 1874-78. His works include *Comparative Vocabularies of the Indian Tribes of British Columbia* (1884). For his diaries 1830-43, see *The Journals of William Fraser Tolmie* (1963).   W. KAYE LAMB

Tomahawk is a name commonly given to axes used by Indians. Soon after European contact, aboriginal stone axes were replaced by trade tomahawks with metal heads made of iron or steel, and sometimes of brass, bronze or copper. While used as a woodworking tool, the tomahawk was also a weapon of war. The handles were decorated with carvings and sometimes with feathers, fur, beads and ribbons, and heads were often elaborate, often incorporating a pipe bowl. Many tomahawks saw no use in either the woods or war, but served only as symbols of status. Highly ornate and decorated pieces were presented to noted warriors by the French and British.   RENÉ R. GADACZ

Reading: H.L. Peterson, *American Indian Tomahawks* (1971).

Tomato (*Lycopersicon esculentum*), herbaceous perennial which, in Canada, is grown as an annual because of early frost. Fruits range from a few grams to over 450 gm. Tomatoes are usually red or orange but may be pink (colourless skin) or yellow. Tomatoes contain vitamin A, thiamine, riboflavin, niacin and ascorbic acid. Worldwide, 2 species are cultivated, *L. esculentum* (including common, cherry, pear, upright and large-leaf varieties) and *L. pimpinellifolium*. The tomato originated in Peru and was used by the Indians of South and Central America in precontact times. Introduced into Europe in the 16th century, the tomato was viewed with suspicion as a member of the NIGHTSHADE family. There was no known commercial production before the early 1800s.

Outdoor production is limited in Canada by the coolness and shortness of the summer season. Tomatoes must be started by seeding and transplanting in a greenhouse. When frost danger is over, they can be transplanted to the field, where cloches or other forms of shelter can bring on an earlier start. If night temperatures fall below 14°C, many tomato varieties fail to set fruit. For good production about 70-90 days of temperatures in the mid- to high 20s °C are required. Crowding of tomato plants results in earlier maturity. Most Canadian soils must be irrigated to supplement rainfall. Tomatoes are subject to blossom-end rot (in erratic water regimes), all forms of PLANT DISEASE and insect damage. Warm-season plants, tomatoes are grown commercially, predominantly in southern Ontario. In 1985, 14 869 ha of tomatoes were grown, producing 545 410 t, valued at $87 353 000. Ontario was the largest producer. 15 510 t of tomatoes were produced in greenhouses, with a value of $22 397 000. Again, Ontario was the largest grower, although greenhouse production occurs across Canada. Tomatoes are also grown in Canadian home gardens, season permitting.   I.L. NONNECKE

Tombstones, upright markers or monuments placed at gravesites, are of 2 general types – the stele, an upright slab or pillar; and the 3-dimensional sculptural type, sometimes referred to as Victorian. The Victorian monuments were most common in Canada in the 19th and early 20th centuries. Materials for the stele are commonly stone, slate or marble; for the Victorian the range includes marble, granite in a variety of colours and finishes, stone and cast iron. The stele tombstone pattern consists, generally, of an upper panel of bas relief sculpture – angel's or death's head with wings, hourglass, willow tree or other symbols suggesting death or grief. Lettering takes up the space below and includes factual records of birth, death, marriage and usually an epitaph. The best examples of this delicate sculpture are seen in the Maritimes, but this work is very vulnerable to harsh winter weather and the growth of lichens.

The visitor to Canadian cemeteries will find, in addition to the stele, such sculpture as a grieving woman resting against a structure or the "Old Rugged Cross." Carrara marble from Italy was a favourite material.

Unfortunately, alternate freezings and thawings have caused angels to lose their wing tips and noses, and male cherubs have suffered their particular indignities. Many cemeteries started as parks to which the public was invited for picnicking. The specimen trees that have grown up now form a cool and leafy forest for the historian or the tombstone enthusiast. *See also* CEMETERIES.

ERIC ARTHUR

Tompkins, James John, Jimmy, priest, university administrator, pioneer in ADULT EDUCATION (b at Margaree, NS 7 Sept 1870; d at Antigonish, NS 5 May 1953). A visionary, communicator and propagandist, Tompkins's most lasting contribution was his transformation of a university from an elitist institution to one open to all. After studying at St Francis Xavier in Halifax and Urban College, Rome, Tompkins was ordained in 1902 and returned to St Francis Xavier as an administrator at a time of great social change. Determined to help the "common man," in 1920 Tompkins published *Knowledge for the People* (1920), a blueprint for adult education, and in 1921 founded the People's School at the university. Banished to Canso, NS, in 1922 for supporting a plan to federate Maritime universities, Tompkins began his pastoral career. He publicized the plight of Maritime fishermen so effectively that a royal commission was established to investigate their situation. Later, in Reserve Mines, NS, he introduced a credit union, inspired the first co-operative housing project (Tompkinsville) and established one of the first regional libraries. He may justly be called the father of the ANTIGONISH MOVEMENT of adult education. Both Dalhousie (1919) and Harvard (1941) conferred honorary degrees on him.

DOUGLAS F. CAMPBELL

Tonge, William Cottnam, colonial official and politician (b at Windsor, NS 29 Apr 1764; d at Georgetown, Demerara [Guyana] 6 Aug 1832). From 1799 to 1806, Tonge played a dominant role in the struggle between the legislative assembly and Lt-Gov Sir John Wentworth over control of provincial expenditures. Tonge was a spokesman for rural assemblymen distrustful of the domination of Nova Scotia's economic and political life by the Halifax merchant clique allied with Wentworth. In 1806, Wentworth disallowed Tonge's election as Speaker of the assembly, a rare use of executive power, and a year later dismissed Tonge from his position as the commercial naval officer for Nova Scotia. Tonge went to the West Indies with a British military expedition late in 1808. He never returned to Nova Scotia, holding a number of government appointments in the Caribbean until his death. Remembered as a charming bon vivant, Tonge earned a lasting place in Nova Scotia's political history for his skilful use of parliamentary tactics and his tenacious support of the rights of the assembly.

JUDITH TULLOCH

Tonnancour, Jacques Godefroy de, painter, photographer (b at Montréal 1917). His early influences ranged from the GROUP OF SEVEN and Goodridge ROBERTS in his landscapes to Picasso in figure painting. Seventeen months (1945-46) in Brazil produced a formal brilliance and truthfulness in his landscapes. Back in Canada he temporarily abandoned landscapes 1946-50, and, influenced by Picasso and Matisse, created his most accomplished still life and figurative paintings. He was a member of the 1948-49 Prisme d'yeux group which opposed the AUTOMATISTES. By 1960, Tonnancour had produced his best-known simplified landscapes, as in *Paysage de juin*. The early 1960s saw a further simplification and abstraction of his landscapes, and his subsequent experimentation with collage and foreign material, resulting in work which approaches pure abstraction. He has taught at the Musée des beaux-arts de Montréal and the École des beaux-arts de Montréal. Tonnancour's *L'Invisible dans le visible* (1986) illustrates his interest in tropical and semitropical forests.

ERIK J. PETERS

Tonquin, a ship of 269 tons built in New York in 1807 and purchased 23 Aug 1810 by New York fur merchant and entrepreneur John Jacob Astor. She sailed from New York on 6 Sept 1810, bound for the mouth of the COLUMBIA R, where Astor's PACIFIC FUR COMPANY intended to found a post and develop trade in opposition to the NORTH WEST COMPANY. The *Tonquin*'s captain, Jonathan Thorn, was a brutal disciplinarian and had little use for Astor's traders. Clerk Gabriel Franchère's journal describes the captain's tyranny and disregard for human life, especially evident when the ship arrived on 22 Mar 1811 at the Columbia R mouth, where 8 sailors drowned attempting to take soundings.

On June 5 the *Tonquin* sailed on a trading cruise from the new fort, Astoria. About June 15, evidently near Echatchet village, Templar Channel, Clayoquot Sound, Vancouver I, she was seized by local Nootka Indians and most of those on board were slain. The next day, the ship either blew or was blown up, perhaps by surviving crew to prevent her from falling into the hands of Indians, who had returned to attack the ship. The tremendous explosion sank the *Tonquin*, and with her went Thorn and Astor's hopes for dominance in the NORTHWEST COAST trade.

BARRY M. GOUGH

Tonty, Henri de, explorer, VOYAGEUR (b 1649 or 1650; d at Ft Louis-de-la-Louisiane Sept 1704). He was the son of Lorenzo de Tonty, inventor of the "tontine" system of life annuity. He served in the French army and navy and had his right hand blown away by a grenade. In 1678 he travelled to New France as lieutenant to LA SALLE and supervised construction of Ft Conti and the bark GRIFFON (1679) on the Niagara R. He led a party to the Illinois R, helping to build Ft Miami and then Ft Crèvecoeur (1680), but while he was absent from Crèvecoeur, his men mutinied, destroying the buildings. Tonty also survived an Iroquois attack, a canoe wreck near Green Bay and near starvation. In 1681 he led an advance party to Chicago portage and was rejoined by his commander La Salle; the expedition reached the Gulf of Mexico 7 Apr 1682. In 1686 Tonty and LaSalle claimed the territory for the French and helped DENONVILLE in his campaign against the Iroquois by organizing the Illinois in a rearguard action, and in 1690 he was granted the fur-trading concession after La Salle's murder. In 1698 Tonty returned to the Mississippi, under Pierre Le Moyne d'IBERVILLE's command, working to expand trade, but he died of yellow fever. The Indians called him *bras de fer* as much for his tenacity and courage as for his hook-shaped artificial arm.

JAMES MARSH

Tookoolito, "Hannah" (b near Cumberland Sound, NWT 1838; d at Groton, Conn 1876), and **Ebierbing,** "Joe" (b near Cumberland Sound, NWT; d on Baffin I, NWT *fl* 1851-79), Inuit guides. In 1851 Tookoolito (sister of EENOOLOOAPIK) and her husband Ebierbing were taken to England for 2 years by a whaling captain. There they caused a sensation and were received by Queen Victoria. After their return to Baffin I they met explorer Charles Francis HALL, who was amazed to find Tookoolito, fluent in English, knitting woollen socks and drinking tea. Ebierbing enabled him to confirm the site of Sir Martin FROBISHER's historic landfall in Frobisher Bay. They accompanied Hall back to the US and on his second expedition to Repulse Bay, searching for clues to the fate of Sir John FRANKLIN and his lost expedition. In 1872 they joined Hall's attempt to reach the North Pole and that fall they and a group of seamen were marooned on an ice floe in Smith Sound. The castaways drifted 2080 km S and, having survived the 6-month ordeal thanks to the hunting skill of Ebierbing and another Inuk, were eventually rescued off Labrador by a sealer. After Tookoolito's death, Ebierbing accompanied the British *Pandora* expedition as Frederick Schwatka's interpreter on his 1878 expedition.

JOHN BENNETT

Tools, Carpentry The craft of carpentry involves the shaping of wood for architectural, utilitarian or ornamental purposes. European colonists who settled what is now Canada brought with them a rich heritage of CRAFTS and craft tools. In N America the highly trained and experienced craftsmen worked mainly in the cities and towns; settlers and farmers, in urgent need of dwellings and furnishings, often had to be their own carpenters. Government immigration pamphlets encouraged settlers to bring a "good box with tools." These implements were used to fell trees, to build shelters, FURNITURE and vehicles, and to make a range of objects for the home and farm (ie, WOODENWARE). Industrialization, accompanied by machine TECHNOLOGY, made such craftsmanship redundant and the older tools are collected today as reminders of our pioneer past. The following is a short list of selected woodworking tools.

Axe Of all the woodworking tools brought from Europe, the axe was the most widely used and most urgently needed, for it was the tool that cleared the land and provided wood for construction and fuel. The European axe was not well suited to pioneer conditions, and in the course of settlement British colonists developed the American axe. The blade of this implement is moderately flared and the socket for the handle is long; the head is extended above the socket as a narrow, hammerlike poll. The handle (helve) is also distinctive, having an S-curve, which allows for a more natural sliding movement of the right hand during the stroke.

The pioneer dwelling, the LOG HOUSE, was constructed by placing logs one above the other to form 4 walls, the corners being secured by some form of joint. The logs were usually squared, ie, the convexities on all 4 sides were chopped away to form a roughly squared cross section. Squaring was done with a broadaxe, in which the cutting edge was long and the blade flat on one side, concave on the other. In use, the hewer stood near the log and swung the axe in a vertical arc, working his way along the log and leaving a neatly defined flat side.

A variety of small axes (hatchets) were developed for special applications. In the adze, used for fine trimming of timbers, the blade is at right angles to the socket and handle, and slopes or curves slightly toward the user.

Saw, next to the axe the most basic woodworking tool, is a flat metal blade, with one serrated edge. In most saws the teeth are "set," ie, bent a little, alternately, to one side or the other, to produce a cut (kerf) wider than the blade, thus avoiding binding. The saw was used primarily to produce boards. A pit saw, ie, a long blade with large teeth and a handle at each end, was employed. It was operated by 2 men; the log was propped up at one end or extended over a pit. When boards were available, the handsaw was the most important tool for cutting. There are 2 kinds of handsaw: the crosscut saw, a smaller saw, with finer, pointed teeth, intended for cutting across the grain of the wood; and the ripsaw, which has larger teeth with chisellike points, for cutting with the grain.

The keyhole saw, used for cutting circular openings or curved edges, has a very narrow tapering blade. The tenon saw, a short wide blade with the upper edge reinforced with a metal bar, is used for making fine cuts at various angles. Framed saws have narrow flexible blades, kept rigid by a springy bow (bucksaw) or a twisted rope stretched between extensions of the handle (bow saw). Fine carpentry requires a variety of small saws, mostly miniature framed saws (eg, coping saw, fretsaw). Fitted to a foot-powered mechanism, the flexible blade became a jigsaw.

Chisel Various carpentry tools employ a cutting edge: in the drawknife, the blade is mounted between 2 handles and pulled by the operator to shave off slices of wood; in the chisel, the long narrow blade with the cutting edge at the far end is pushed or hammered to cut grooves or holes. The gouge is a chisel with a trough-shaped blade and a curved edge, used for cutting depressions and rounded grooves.

Plane The most variable slicing tool is the plane, in which a chisellike blade is mounted at an angle in a wooden block or metal frame, the cutting edge protruding forward through an opening in the base of the tool. The plane is pushed along the wood and the cutting edge peels off a layer (ie, shaving). Planing smooths an edge or a surface. Specially shaped cutting edges and blocks enable the plane to cut grooves, channels, steps (rabbets) and moldings. Planes vary in size from the long jack plane for smoothing to tiny cabinetmaker's planes for delicate trimming.

Boring Tools The awl has a narrow blade with pointed or chisel-shaped end and is pushed or hammered into wood to make a hole. The auger is like a miniature gouge and is used with a twisting motion. The spiral drill is screwlike, with cutting edges at the lower end. It is used in a mount, usually a brace, which is a sort of hand crank, permitting rotation and application of pressure at the same time.

File is a steel blade with transverse grooves on one or both sides. When pushed across a surface, the sharp edges of the grooves cut into and remove material. The rasp has small projections instead of grooves and cuts more quickly but more roughly than the file. Both are used for minor smoothing and shaping.

Nail Pieces of wood can be held together by joints, pegs or glue, but the usual device for this purpose is the nail, a slender piece of metal (usually IRON) pointed at one end and expanded into a head at the other. Nails were originally shaped individually in a small forge on a miniature anvil. Later they were made by cutting oblique strips from a sheet of metal. Modern nails are formed from extruded, wirelike steel rods.

Hammer The carpenter's hammer or claw hammer, used to drive nails, has a head with the upper end drawn into a pair of curved claws. The tapered slot between the claws is used to grasp a protruding nail, which can then be extracted by

pulling on the handle. The mallet has a wooden head and is used to drive chisels.

A special kind of woodworking is the manufacture of barrels (cooperage), which employs modified forms of hatchet, adze, drawknife and plane to form the curved, tapered staves and the circular bottom and lid. The importance of barrels, kegs, tubs and pails at one time made cooperage a widely practised craft. Some simple tools were made, and tools and utensils were repaired by the local BLACKSMITH.   LORIS S. RUSSELL

Topley, William James, photographer (b at Montréal 13 Feb 1845; d at Vancouver 16 Nov 1930). He learned photography from his mother. In 1864 he joined the studio of William NOTMAN in Montréal. Three years later he opened Notman's new Ottawa studio and purchased the business in 1872. For the next 50 years the studio produced views from across the country and portraits of all Canadian political leaders, providing an invaluable source for Canadian social history. In 1924 Topley retired and his studio closed 2 years later.   ANDREW BIRRELL

Topographic Painters Topographic studies grew out of 16th-century Europe's interest in specific views of places and their details. Precision was important, either for reasons of pride and record taking, for strategic purposes, or for evocation of poetic views which opened new vistas to the viewer's imagination. In Canada topographic views in paintings can be seen in some rare examples of church paintings and portraits from as early as late 17th-century New France, or from the recent 20th century, when portions of the St Lawrence R were recorded before they became the Seaway. However, the richest period was the late 18th and 19th centuries, a period when the art of draftsmanship and painting in watercolour flourished, particularly in Great Britain, and was pursued by professionals and amateurs alike. Among the British soldiers and civilians stationed in Canada during this period, many were topographic painters who left a rich heritage of early views of the country and its people.

Topography was a subject taught at the Woolwich Royal Military Academy by artists such as Paul Sandby, who achieved his fame with ornamental landscapes that combined the precision of topography with a flexible and poetic visual technique. Among those influenced by such teachers were soldier-topographers such as Hervey Smyth, who depicted the size of the English military force which captured France's strongholds; Richard Short, whose drawings of Québec City after the siege show the strength of the British fleet as well as the architectural richness of the town and its good-natured inhabitants; Thomas Davies, who preferred watercolours which show scenes in which man and nature live in harmony; George HERIOT, whose illustrated *Travels Through the Canadas* enjoyed a large readership in Europe and N America; and James Patterson COCKBURN, who produced a large collection of watercolours of Québec City and its environs.

Topographic artists portrayed an idealized and often spectacular landscape. MONTMORENCY FALLS was a favourite subject with many of them. As others of their age, Davies and Heriot believed that all of nature could be drawn for man's pleasure like a large parkland in the British style, far removed from the more serious concerns of living; in their landscapes, habitants and American Indians tended to be exotic and picturesque, and colonial administrators genteel and well dressed. There were also less idealistic views, as for example those of John Webber, a crew member on the ship of James Cook when he explored the Pacific Ocean. Since such paintings or drawings were sometimes produced as engravings in Europe or

Thomas Davies's watercolours, such as *A View of Montreal in Canada* (1762), showed scenes in which both man and nature live in harmony (*courtesy National Gallery of Canada*).

the US, topographical painters helped to spread interest elsewhere in British N America.

The techniques and approaches continued to be used by others, by explorers such as George BACK, adventurers such as William HIND, wives of administrators, such as Lady Dufferin and Elizabeth SIMCOE, wives of churchmen, such as Henrietta Cartwright, or engineers such as William ARMSTRONG. Topographic painters helped, through their records, to enliven aspects of Canadian history not visually accessible otherwise, and also allowed some scope for the imagination.   PIERRE DOYON

Reading: M. Bell, *Painters in a New Land* (1973); J. Russell Harper, *Painting in Canada* (1977) and *Early Painters and Engravers in Canada* (1970); G. Heriot, *Travels Through the Canadas* (1807, repr 1971); D. Reid, *A Concise History of Canadian Painting* (1973).

Toquaht ("people of the narrow beach"), a Nootka Indian tribe of Barkley Sound on the W coast of Vancouver I, BC. Formerly a prominent tribe with extensive territories, the Toquaht were severely reduced by disease and prolonged warfare in the early historic period. Their territory in the mid-19th century consisted of the western shore of Barkley Sound, Toquart Bay, Mayne Bay and Pipestem Inlet. Today the Toquaht live at their traditional villages of Macoah and Chequis.   JOHN DEWHIRST

Torgov, Morley, author, lawyer (b at Sault Ste Marie 1927). He received a BA from U of Toronto (1950) and a LLB from Osgoode Hall, and was called to the bar in June 1954; he has practised law in Toronto since. Torgov began writing in the 1960s. He has written 2 plays, *The Builders* and *When We Go A Courting* (both produced by the CBC). He has published one collection of short stories, *A Good Place to Come From* (1974, Stephen Leacock Medal for Humour, 1975). He has written 2 novels: *The Abramsky Variations* (1977) and *The Outside Chance of Maximilian Glick* (1982) which also won a Leacock Medal for Humour (1983). Torgov writes about Jewish life in small Canadian towns. His gentle humour makes a strong statement about roots and their hold on individuals.   SHARON DRACHE

Tornado, an intense rotary storm of small diameter (tens or hundreds of metres), characterized by at least one vortex reaching the Earth's surface. The vortex is usually visible as a funnel cloud associated with a THUNDERSTORM, although on occasions it is invisible. In either case, damage results at ground level. A tornado may be composed of a single funnel, several funnels occurring simultaneously, one or more funnels re-forming one after the other, or various combinations of these states.

A tornado's life cycle typically consists of 3 stages. It starts when a funnel-shaped protuberance (tuba) develops beneath a rotating section of the SW flank of a thunderstorm. The tuba elon-

The tornado that brought havoc to Edmonton, 31 July 1987 (*photo by Steve Simon*/Edmonton Journal).

gates downwards from the cloud and is enveloped by a rotating sleeve (annulus) which develops upwards from the ground. The full merging of the 2 constitutes the mature tornado vortex. This stage is followed by the third or degenerating phase, when the tuba rises back towards the cloud base and disappears. Cases where the tuba alone develops are called "funnels aloft" and are not tornadoes. The rotation of tornadoes is almost always cyclonic (clockwise in the Northern Hemisphere, anticlockwise in the Southern Hemisphere, when the circling clouds are viewed from below).

Tornadoes occur in all parts of Canada except those with an arctic CLIMATE. They are relatively frequent in the interior, from NB to the Rocky Mts, and are most common in southern Ontario (which experiences an average of 21 per season), followed by southern Manitoba. In Canada, the tornado season begins as early as Mar and ends as late as Oct, generally lasting 107 days in the interior and about 60 days elsewhere. Activity peaks in late June and early July. The average tornado causes a damage swath with median values of 6.2 km in length, 83 m in width and 0.6 km² in area. A tornado is most likely to occur in the afternoon, 3-7 PM local standard time, and to approach from the W or SW.

Tornadoes range in intensity from very weak (winds from 64 km/h) to devastating (winds up to 509 km/h), on a scale of zero to 5 devised by T.T. Fujita. Over 90% of Canadian tornadoes can be categorized as weak, FO to F1 on the Fujita scale. The most severe so far known, the Regina tornado of 30 June 1912, which killed 28, injured hundreds and demolished much of the downtown area, is rated as F4 (winds of 330-416 km/h). This was rivalled by the Edmonton tornado of 31 July 1987, which took 27 lives, injured over 200, left over 400 homeless, and caused damage along a 40 km track estimated at over $250 million, "the greatest single storm loss in Canadian history." The severity of this tornado is unprecedented in Alberta.

Another example of an F4 tornado occurred as part of a major tornado outbreak (in this case a family of tornadoes moving along 8 well-defined tracks) which swept across southern Ontario 31 May 1985, causing an estimated $100 million in property damage. This particular tornado devastated the southern section of Barrie and was responsible for 8 of the 12 deaths that occurred during the outbreak. Fortunately less than 1% of all tornadoes fall into the F4 category; none of F5 intensity are known to have occurred in Canada.
MICHAEL J. NEWARK

Torngat Mountains extend 200 km S from Cape Chidley, Labrador, to Hebron Fjord. The Torngat (Inuktitut, "home of spirits") rise to 1652 m at Mt Caubvick (known as Mt Iberville in Qué),

crown of the Selamiut ("Aurora") Range and highest peak in Newfoundland and Québec. Other high summits such as Torngarsuak ("great spirit"), Cirque Mt, Razorback and Mt Tetragona lie entirely within Newfoundland, E of the UNGAVA BAY-LABRADOR SEA drainage divide. The mountains are part of the Precambrian SHIELD; Archean gneissic rocks at Saglek are the oldest known in N America (3.6 billion years). Proterozoic structures which govern much of the N to S trend in relief were forged around 2 billion years ago. Proterozoic sedimentary rocks in the Sorviluk Range contain chalcedony, much used in prehistoric northeastern America.

Deep FJORDS and finger lakes, bound by spectacular rock walls, cut sharply across the high ranges; they are the legacy of glaciation. The Laurentide Ice Sheet, centered far to the W, covered all but the highest summits at least once, although during the last glaciation ice cover was limited and many NUNATAKS provided refuge for arctic and alpine flora and fauna. Over 70 small, active glaciers survive in the Torngat, shaded in deep cirques and sustained by the southernmost extension of arctic climate. Vegetation is sparse TUNDRA, with willow thickets in low, sheltered valleys, and rock desert above 300 m. Wildlife is arctic, with caribou numerous.

Tent rings and stone structures remain from over 6000 years of Maritime Archaic, Dorset, Thule and more recent Inuit settlement. In 1763 over 500 Inuit inhabited the fjords; in 1935 fewer than 50; now none. Trading posts at Saglek and Nachvak and Moravian missions at Hebron and Ramah are abandoned. The closest settlements are NAIN, 200 km S, and Port-Nouveau-Québec, 100 km W. Inuit from Nain visit the fjords for the summer char fishery. An airstrip at Saglek is used in offshore oil and gas exploration.
R.J. ROGERSON

The Torngat Mountains of Labrador have deep fjords which attract Inuit from Nain for summer char fishing (*photo by John Foster*/Masterfile).

Toronto, capital city of Ontario, is situated on the southern margin of the province, fronting LAKE ONTARIO. Metropolitan Toronto, Canada's largest municipality, comprises the cities of Toronto, North York, Scarborough, York and Etobicoke, and the borough of East York. Its economic hinterland lies basically in Ontario, but in financial terms it extends across Canada. The city is

Population: 612 289 (1986c), 599 217 (1981c); 3 427 168 (1986 CMA), 3 130 392 (1981 ACMA)

Rate of Increase (1981-86): City 2.2%; CMA 9.5%

Rank in Canada: First (by CMA)

Date of Incorporation: City 1834; Metro 1953

Land Area: City 97.15 km²; CMA 5613.71 km²

Elevation: 194 m

Climate: Average daily temp, July 22°C, Jan -4.6°C; Yearly precip 800.5 mm; Hours of sunshine 2045.4 per year

Part of York, Upper Canada, on Toronto Bay in Lake Ontario (*courtesy National Archives of Canada*/C-34334).

well placed to control the populous industrial and agricultural region of southern Ontario and, being located on the neck of the Ontario peninsula which juts into the Great Lakes system, has ready access both to the Upper Lakes basin and to American territory S of the Lower Lakes. The city has been able to spread its influence through the Canadian Great Lakes area and far beyond. Toronto's physical features include a natural harbour sheltered by sandy islands (originally one long peninsula), backed by gently rolling, well-watered, fertile country. The area has a fairly mild and humid average climate, by Canadian standards, though with some changeable extremes.

Settlement Toronto, from the Huron language, has several possible meanings. Of these, "place of meeting" seems most apt, since long before settlement, native peoples went there to follow a trail and canoe route that gave a shortcut overland between Lakes Ontario and HURON. The Toronto Passage, used as early as 1615 by Étienne BRÛLÉ, became well known to French fur traders. They set a small store by its entry (1720-30) and a larger, fortified post in 1750-51. This Ft Rouillé, whose remains have been excavated in Toronto's present Exhibition Grounds, was burned in 1759 by its French garrison retreating from British forces. Following the British Conquest, the Toronto site again saw only minor traders and Mississauga Indian encampments. The American Revolution sent LOYALISTS northward to remaining British territory. Their settlements along the Upper St Lawrence and Lower Lakes led to the creation of the province of UPPER CANADA (1791), and to plans for a town at centrally located Toronto, which were effected by UC's first governor, John Graves SIMCOE. He mainly viewed the site as a commanding position for a naval and garrison base to guard a troubled American boundary. In 1794 he made it capital of UC, although in 1793 he had had a little town laid out by the harbour, naming it York; by 1796 he was using it as a capital of UC, erecting parliament buildings and cutting roads inland. York's officialdom and garrison attracted merchants, craftsmen and labourers, while the spreading rural settlement beyond made it a local market centre. By 1812 this frontier village still had only 700 residents, yet its governing role, its harbour and the rough roads inward gave it initial advantage in the Lk Ontario area.

Development During the WAR OF 1812, York was twice raided and pillaged by US forces (1813), leaving a British-minded populace with keen anti-American memories. Afterwards, it felt the rising wave of British immigration to UC. Its hinterland trade mounted with expanding farm frontiers as its merchants supplied country dealers as wholesalers, and it became the province's banking centre. By 1834 the fast-growing town of over 9000 inhabitants was incorporated as the city of Toronto, with an elected civic government led by William Lyon MACKENZIE as first mayor. This prominent Reform journalist and politician tried to seize the city by force in the UC Rebellion

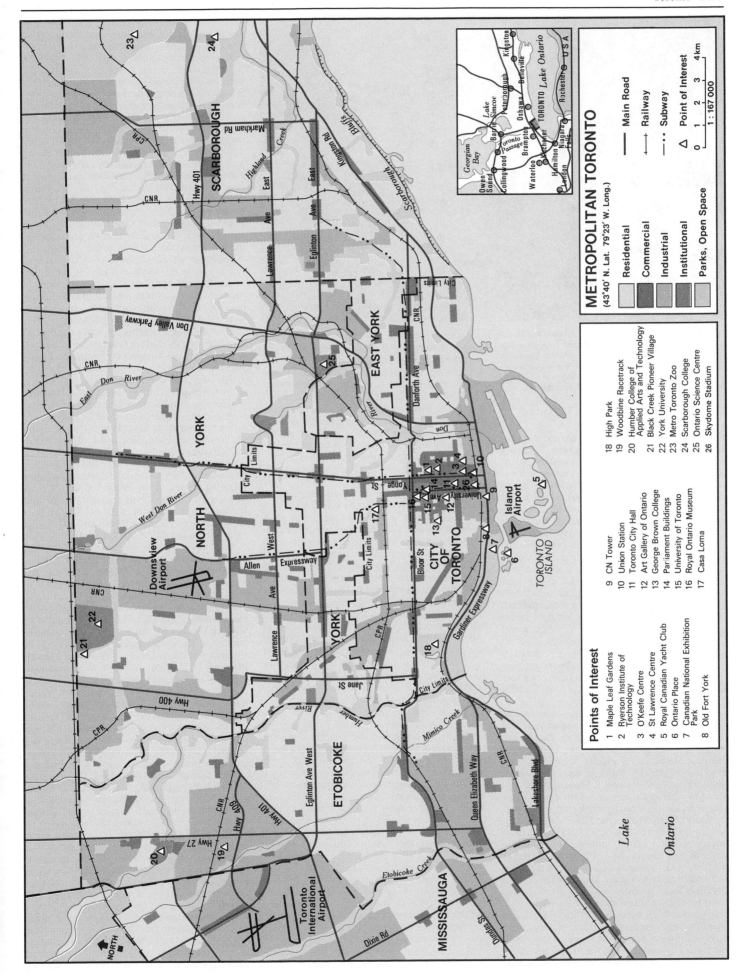

METROPOLITAN TORONTO
(43°40' N. Lat. 79°23' W. Long.)

	Residential
	Commercial
	Industrial
	Institutional
	Parks, Open Space

Main Road
Railway
Subway
△ Point of Interest

0 1 2 3 4km
1 : 167 000

Points of Interest

1 Maple Leaf Gardens
2 Ryerson Institute of Technology
3 O'Keefe Centre
4 St Lawrence Centre
5 Royal Canadian Yacht Club
6 Ontario Place
7 Canadian National Exhibition Park
8 Old Fort York
9 CN Tower
10 Union Station
11 Toronto City Hall
12 Art Gallery of Ontario
13 George Brown College
14 Parliament Buildings
15 University of Toronto
16 Royal Ontario Museum
17 Casa Loma
18 High Park
19 Woodbine Racetrack
20 Humber College of Applied Arts and Technology
21 Black Creek Pioneer Village
22 York University
23 Metro Toronto Zoo
24 Scarborough College
25 Ontario Science Centre
26 Skydome Stadium

Toronto, Ont, as seen from the CN Tower. The Royal York Hotel is seen lower right, with the dark towers of the Toronto Dominion Centre to its left, the triangular Royal Bank complex to its right and the taller Canadian Imperial Bank of Commerce and Bank of Montreal buildings beyond. Roy Thomson Hall is at the lower left (*photo by Tibor Bognàr*).

of 1837; but his attempt collapsed more in confusion than bloodshed, strengthening Toronto's conservative tendencies. In the 1840s Toronto increased its commercial lead, as busy steamboat port activity and gaslit, sewered main streets marked its urban rise. In the 1850s railway building brought the city a radiating web of tracks connecting it to New York and Montréal, the Upper Lakes at Georgian Bay, and across western UC to Detroit and Chicago. Hence its own regional grasp was widely extended; wholesaling, banking and railway entrepreneurship grew accordingly. The city was made capital of the new province of Ontario at Confederation in 1867, and by the 1870s it was becoming industrialized. Hart MASSEY's agricultural machinery firm, clothing factories, publishing plants, and metal foundries grew large in the 1880s. A city of 30 000 in 1851 was over 5 times bigger by 1891, aided by industrial tariff protection after 1879 and the promotional drive of leaders such as railway builder Casimir GZOWSKI and department-store builder Timothy EATON.

From the later 1890s into a booming early 20th century, the settlement of the Canadian West and the tapping of northern Ontario's forests and mines opened further markets and resources to Toronto. Commerce with the North and West flowed into the city, while it dealt with either Montréal or New York as outlets or suppliers. Major firms such as Eaton's spread their mail-order business into the West. Hydroelectric power provided by the Hydro-Electric Power Commission of Ontario from NIAGARA FALLS (1911) gave cheap energy for more factory growth. Above all, the city's banks, investment and insurance companies invaded regions well beyond Ontario. By 1914, although older and larger Montréal still held the lead, Toronto's financial head offices, factories and stores had made it a second national metropolis. WWI expanded its investment and manufacturing scope, the latter ranging from large-scale meat processing to munitions, both forwarded by businessman Sir Joseph FLAVELLE.

In the prosperous 1920s development contin-

ued, as new suburban municipalities rose around an overflowing city of some half million. It was checked by the GREAT DEPRESSION of the 1930s, yet Toronto was proportionately less hard hit than many other Canadian centres. Its well-developed, more varied hinterland sustained business better than regions heavily dependent on staples such as wheat or lumber. WWII revived growth, shaping electronic, aircraft and precision-machine industries. And in the postwar era Toronto boomed, as a ravaged Europe renewed its material stock. Population swelled further, to over a million in Greater Toronto by 1951.

The service needs of this urban complex and the inadequate revenue in its suburbs led to a metropolitan-area government. Set up in 1953 under a vigorous first chairman, Frederick GARDINER, the Metropolitan Toronto Authority handled area-wide requirements. The subway system begun by the city in 1949 was built up, parks and drainage projects were effected and arterial through roads constructed. In 1967 small suburbs were amalgamated, leaving a Metro structure of the city of Toronto and 5 boroughs, of which all but East York had also become cities by 1988, as their numbers soared. In recent years, Toronto has gained priority over Montréal as a national (and international) financial focus; it leads Canada in its concentration of specialized services, including professional facilities and advertising, and has a major hold on information media.

Cityscape Toronto emerged on the shore plain beside its harbour, beyond which, some 4 km inland, is a fairly abrupt rise, the shoreline of prehistoric Lake Iroquois. This rise led to higher plains, then to rounded lines of hills. The courses of rivers and creek ravines offered ways up from the plain even for fur canoes, and practicable grades for later roads and railways. Though the low-lying waterside area gave early York dank marshes and mud-filled streets, and the rise impeded road lines, these were not long-term barriers to the steady spread of the cityscape. Today, Toronto extends far E and W of the harbour stretch and to Metro limits well inland (5613.71 km²). The present Toronto-region conurbation of around 3.4 million reaches to near-suburban Richmond Hill on the N, E to Oshawa, and W approximately to Oakville – from where the urbanized "Golden Horseshoe" still runs on through Hamilton to the Niagara Peninsula.

The shore plain by the harbour has remained Toronto's downtown core, first shaped by its

waterfront relationship. Governor Simcoe's layout of 1793 was a small-town plot with a plain grid of straight streets along the eastern end of the harbour and with a military reserve for a garrison post westward to its entry. As the town grew, the basic straight-line grid pattern was essentially extended; but under municipal self-government from 1834, planning was replaced by unco-ordinated private developments. Nevertheless, the cityscape began to sort itself out. King St was a main commercial E-W artery by the 1840s, Yonge St a N-S axis, leading to the northern highway into the hinterland. As railways arrived on the waterfront in the 1850s, they built up a transport zone between the city and the lake. Thereafter, industrial areas emerged at either end of the harbour along rail lines, and to the N, close-built, working-class districts. Larger residences spread more above the central downtown, and homes of the wealthy on the rise behind the shore plain.

Streetcars advanced the sorting out. Horse-drawn cars in the 1860s and electric cars in the 1890s fostered the middle-class movement to roomier suburban fringes and promoted annexations of suburban communities, beginning with Yorkville 1883 and ending with N Toronto 1912. In another fashion, electric elevators, larger iron-framed buildings, and telephones from the 1880s facilitated greater business concentration on expensive downtown property. During the early 1900s steel skyscrapers climbed in this central district, which had further sorted out in land use: wholesaling around Yonge below King, major retailing along Yonge near Queen, and finance down Bay and along King. From WWI the massing inward and spreading outward continued, aided by the automobile, until the Depression and a second war intervened. Since the late 1940s it has surged on, with only short downturns. Public planning revived in the 1940s, but its fuller impact grew from the 1950s and with Metro; still further with the onset of environmental reformers (or conservers) in the 1960s and 1970s. The balance between the "move traffic" and "save life quality" kinds of planning remains a shifting one. The highrise now dominates Toronto – in the central business district, in residential apartment masses, and in office towers around main intersections and subway stations.

Despite its modest natural setting and largely plain street layout, Toronto has an interesting building stock and some noteworthy heritage structures. These include the original Fort York complex (rebuilt 1813-15), the GRANGE, a gentry mansion built about 1817, ST LAWRENCE HALL (1850), Osgoode Hall (rebuilt 1857), UNIVERSITY COLLEGE (1859), the Ontario Parliament Buildings (1892), the City Hall (designed 1890, completed 1899), the Royal Alexandra Theatre (1907) and UNION STATION (opened 1927) – a prime N American survivor of classical railway grandeur. Later eras have largely produced more and bigger office buildings, hotels and shopping centres, though the new City Hall (1965) is striking in design and setting. Boldly original, too, is ROY THOMSON HALL (1982). The central city skyline soars in mass and height, topped by the 72-floor Bank of Montreal (1978) and still taller CN TOWER (1976), and a 553 m telecommunications spire. In 1989 the new Skydome stadium, which will house the Toronto Blue Jays, will be completed. While the building systems have chiefly been imported throughout, Toronto designers have set their stamps on them. The lines of high-peaked Victorian brick homes in the older city have a unique Toronto character only lately appreciated.

Population From its start as a seat of colonial officialdom, Toronto had a markedly British population compared to the far more American rural society of early Upper Canada. British immigrants

Population Growth in Toronto and Suburbs 1951-86				
	1951	*1971*	*1981*	*1986*
City of Toronto	675 754	712 785	599 217	612 289
East York	64 616	101 963	101 974	101 085
Etobicoke	53 779	282 690	298 713	302 973
North York	85 897	504 150	559 521	556 297
Scarborough	56 292	334 310	443 353	484 676
York	101 582	147 305	134 617	135 401
Totals	1 037 920*	2 083 203	2 137 395	2 192 721

* Excludes Long Branch, New Toronto, Mimico, Swansea, Weston, Forest Hill and Leaside, totaling 79 550.

after the 1820s increased this predominance, also bringing a large strain of Protestant Ulster Irish. Late in the 1840s the exodus from famine-stricken Ireland added a sizable Catholic Irish minority as well, leading to religious discord in the city. The Ulstermen's ORANGE ORDER became guardians of British Protestant ascendancy, wielding power in civic politics. In the later 19th century, British immigrants, largely English, continued arriving, though Canadian-born (of British stock) were a majority by 1871. Toronto stayed remarkably homogenous, strong on church life, Sunday observance and morality.

Movement from the countryside to an expanding industrial city became a mounting factor from the 1870s, as did natural increase, especially as public-health measures improved. Immigration rose again by the 1900s and increasingly brought continental Europeans as well, including Jews, Italians and Ukrainians. Clustering first in poor inner-city areas, the new ethnic elements were a small (13%) but compact segment in an Anglo-Celtic, mainly Protestant, community by 1920. Their influx continued over the next decade. After depression and war, another far bigger inflow developed, to continue on with minor fluctuations to the 1980s. British newcomers still led at first, but Italians became a chief component by the 1960s, while Germans, Poles, Hungarians, Balkan Slavs, Greeks and Portuguese steadily widened the non-Anglo-Celtic segment. In the 1970s and 1980s W Indian, S Asian and E Asian migrants added "visible minorities" to Toronto increasingly. Preliminary figures from the 1986c show 39% of British origin, 9% Italian, 3% South Asian and 6% East Asian (including Chinese). Older "Anglo" elements continued sizably in Metro's suburban units, and they still dominate its business elite and chief social institutions. Yet in the original city, a powerful ethnic press and politics, expanded Catholicism, many languages and cultures, racial concerns and, above all, a much livelier, multifaceted community indicate how greatly Toronto's population patterns have changed.

Economy and Labour Force Toronto grew through the stages of commercial lake port, railway and industrial focus, financial nexus and high-level service and information centre. At present, its port and commercial functions remain important, though relatively less so, apart from heavy retail activity; its railway role persists, modified by air and automotive transport; its industry has lost ground to foreign competition and Canadian decentralization, but remains high in value; and its financial power continues to increase and its office-service sector stays pre-eminent in Canada. Advanced technology will likely reinforce its service and industrial sectors, while Toronto's money market keeps a national role and the city becomes more reliant on its regional Ontario domain.

Banking head offices in Toronto include the CANADIAN IMPERIAL BANK OF COMMERCE and the TORONTO DOMINION BANK. Principal Canadian insurance and investment companies centre in the city. The Toronto Stock Exchange is one of the leaders in N America outside New York. Toronto is also headquarters for national newspaper chains such as SOUTHAM and the THOMSON GROUP; the latter's Toronto *Globe and Mail* maintains national editions across the country. The MACLEAN HUNTER communications empire and English-language TV and radio similarly have main Toronto bases, as do English-Canadian book publishing and film. There is a close concentration of Canadian head offices of industrial, resource and retail corporations and of American or multinational giants – from Abitibi through Eaton's to Xerox.

The city's labour force by now is chiefly massed in office, manufacturing and retail work, in that order (1986). It is widely unionized in public sectors, large private enterprises and skilled trades. From the York printer's union of 1832, Toronto has been a centre of labour organization, though this did not become broadly based until the growth of industrialism from the 1870s. By the close of WWI union movement was firmly emplaced, and though its fortunes have varied, as in the grim 1930s, from WWII organized labour has been an influential economic and political factor in the city. To the present, Toronto labour has been largely stable and fairly conservative in character compared with other cities.

Transportation Water traffic, once Toronto's vital link outward, still brings bulk goods by lake and direct overseas shipments. From 1911, under the Toronto Harbour Commission, port facilities have been repeatedly improved, notably after the ST LAWRENCE SEAWAY (1959) opened it to ocean shipping. Docks for ocean vessels, new harbour areas behind man-made islands and large recreational and residential waterside developments (especially that called the "Harbourfront") mark the port today. Though ice closes navigation each winter, Toronto benefits by having both water and land transportation systems. On land, the railway net supplies the city and distributes its products by both CN and CP Rail, while Government of Ontario "GO" trains provide essential

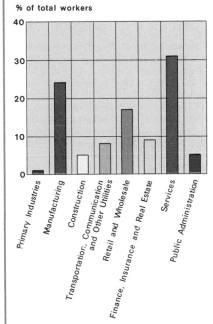

TORONTO
Employment by Industry, 1986

% of total workers

Total does not add to 100% because some estimates are not available and some workers are unclassified
Source: Household Surveys Div, Statistics Canada

commuter services. Bus, truck and car traffic use a similar main road net, especially Highway 401, a many-laned crosstown throughway, and Highway 400, now the prime route N. By air, Toronto's Lester B. Pearson International Airport (Canada's busiest), though congested, offers national and world communications, while the small Island Airport by the harbour is being redeveloped for short-leg business airflights.

This substantial external transport is complemented by good internal transit. Though automobile routes such as the Gardiner Expressway along the southern edge of the downtown, or the Don Valley Parkway running northward, bear heavy loads, the city has successfully maintained its public streetcar, bus and subway systems. Amid all the metropolitan intensity, there are bicycle paths and quiet walking routes through wooded ravine parklands.

Government and Politics At civic incorporation (1834), Toronto had a mayor and a city council elected by wards. The mayor, originally chosen from and by council, became directly elected by the voters in the 1870s; a board of control was added in the 1890s, arising from an URBAN REFORM wave for "clean," efficient government, but was abolished in the 1960s. Sizable civic departments grew for services such as roads, water, police and health, while the separately elected board of education became a powerful municipal body in its own right. Canada's first METROPOLITAN GOVERNMENT was formed in Toronto in 1953, when 13 municipalities, including the city of Toronto, were reorganized to form the Municipality of Metropolitan Toronto. The Metro Council, under a chairman, had prime responsibility for overall concerns such as finance, education, transport, welfare and water supply, to which police and housing were later added. The city proper and member boroughs kept more local service tasks. Yet clearly, the bigger duties and expenditures now lay with Metro. As the populations of the surrounding boroughs mounted, the Metro chairman elected by his council came to replace Toronto's mayor as the chief figure in municipal operations.

Civic politics have ostensibly not operated on party lines, though Conservative partisans have usually been dominant (backed through the 19th century by the then-influential Orange Order). The radical first mayor, William Lyon MACKENZIE, was a scarce exception, as was the moral reformer, Mayor William Howland, in the 1880s. Far more typical were respectably cautious guardians who gave fairly competent government but took few chances. Some pragmatic mayors also lasted as sympathetically popular, like Tommy Church through WWI and after, or Nathan Phillips from the 1950s into the 1960s, who led in promoting the new City Hall. Still, some others more associated with change, such as Horatio Hocken, who faced the needs of expanding city services before WWI, or David CROMBIE and John Sewell in the 1970s, who worked with a newer breed of civic reformers to save the quality of city life from uncontrolled development. Now, however, Metro chairmen have top political significance. Moreover, the Metro entity, so populous and financially demanding, inevitably bulks large for the Ontario government also, while federally, Toronto's major "clout" certainly affects national election and cabinet-making strategies.

Cultural Life Toronto is the main urban cultural focus in English Canada. It is the home of the big UNIVERSITY OF TORONTO (1827), more recent YORK U and RYERSON POLYTECHNICAL INSTITUTE; the ART GALLERY OF ONTARIO and Ontario College of Art, the world-renowned ROYAL ONTARIO MUSEUM and the innovative ONTARIO SCIENCE CENTRE; the

Finnish architect Viljo Revell's bold design for Toronto City Hall was chosen through an international competition (*photo by Tibor Bognàr*).

TORONTO SYMPHONY and the NATIONAL BALLET OF CANADA. Other nationally eminent artistic, musical and library institutions are found here along with top Canadian centres of medical and scientific research, and the world-class Metro Zoo. Toronto is English Canada's leading theatre town; and now its rich multicultural variety is reflected in the performing arts, as well as in ethnic journals and restaurants. The city has long been a potent factor in Anglo-Canadian literature as a national base for literary periodicals, publishing houses, and successions of noted authors from Goldwin SMITH and Sir Charles G.D. ROBERTS to E.J. PRATT, Morley CALLAGHAN, Marshall MCLUHAN, Northrop FRYE, Margaret ATWOOD and Robertson DAVIES. Similarly in art, it has been the base for Paul KANE, the GROUP OF SEVEN and Tom THOMSON and numerous contemporary painters such as Harold TOWN, as well as musicians such as Glenn GOULD.

In popular culture, the city's top-circulation TORONTO STAR, tabloid *Sun* and *Globe and Mail* have a massive combined readership. In TV, the CBC, private stations and readily available transborder American ones provide a wide choice. Popular concerts attract large crowds, notably at Ontario Place, a lakeside recreational area, or the CANADIAN NATIONAL EXHIBITION, Canada's largest annual exposition. Other leading public draws include hilly High Park, Fort York (restored to 1812 days), Casa Loma (the grandiose castle home of a 1900s financial magnate), the CN Tower and Toronto Island, a harbour park preserve. In professional sports, Toronto displays the TORONTO MAPLE LEAFS (hockey), TORONTO BLUE JAYS (baseball) and TORONTO ARGONAUTS (football). Amateur sports range from yachting to curling, Olympic-level skating, swimming and rowing. Soccer is keenly popular among the immigrant community. Facilities from Maple Leaf Gardens to local rinks, the O'Keefe Centre and Roy Thomson Hall to community dramatic and music stages, public swimming pools to park athletic fields, serve a recreation-minded citizenry year-round.

J.M.S. CARELESS

Reading: E. Arthur, *No Mean City* (1964; rev, S. Otto ed, 1986); J.M.S. Careless, *Toronto to 1918* (1984); G.P. Glazebrook, *The Story of Toronto* (1971); W. Kilbourn and R. Christl, *Toronto in Words and Pictures* (1977); J.T. Lemon, *Toronto, The English-Speaking Metropolis since 1918* (1984); H. Scadding, *Toronto of Old* (F.H. Armstrong, ed, 1966); J. Spelt, *Toronto* (1973).

Toronto Argonauts, football team. In 1873 members of Toronto's Argonaut Rowing Club formed a rugby team, choosing as their colours the double blue of the English universities of Oxford and Cambridge. They lost to U of T in their first of 17 GREY CUP appearances (1911), winning their first of 11 Grey Cups against the same club in 1914. Led by the great all-round athlete Lionel CONACHER, they defeated the EDMONTON ESKIMOS in the first East-West Grey Cup (1921) and won 8 more national championships in the ensuing 31 years (1933, 1937, 1938, 1945, 1946, 1947, 1950 and 1952), with such distinguished Canadian players as Joe KROL. Quarterback Joe Theismann took them to a 1971 championship loss to Calgary, and under coach Bob O'Billovich they lost to the Edmonton Eskimos in the 1982 Grey Cup game. The team ended 31 years of frustration with a victory in 1983 over the BC LIONS; it lost in the Grey Cup game in 1984 and in a classic contest in 1987. In 1959 they moved from Varsity Stadium to Canadian National Exhibition Stadium, which now seats 54 533. DEREK DRAGER

Toronto Blue Jays The first Canadian team admitted to baseball's American League, the franchise was awarded to a group consisting of Imperial Trust Ltd, Labatt's Breweries, and the Canadian Imperial Bank of Commerce after a bid in 1976 to purchase and move the National League Giants to Toronto was thwarted by a San Francisco court. Peter Bavasi was appointed to oversee BASEBALL operations and the Blue Jays began play in 1977 at Exhibition Stadium on Toronto's Lakeshore Blvd. They achieved their first winning season in 1983 with a record of 89-73 for a fourth-place finish. Memorable moments in the team's history include their first-place standing at the All-Star break in 1983, Dave Stieb's winning pitching assignment in the 1983 All-Star game, and Alfredo Griffin's consecutive playing streak of 391 games in 1984. In 1983 Lloyd Moseby became the first Jay to score 100 runs and Willie Upshaw the first to drive in 100 runs in a single season. In 1987, George Bell became the first team member to be named the American League's most valuable player. WILLIAM HUMBER

Toronto City Hall (architects Viljo Revell and John B. PARKIN Associates, 1965) is the product of a highly successful international competition (1957-58) which attracted 532 entries from around the world and was won by Finnish architect Revell. A minority report suggested that the 2-tower arrangement was functionally impractical, but the building has been a great popular success. The curved towers and circular council chamber created instantly recognizable shapes, unlikely to be lost among the rectangular commercial office buildings of the downtown. The elevated walkway around Phillips Square in front of the building clearly defines this space, at the expense of interrupted views inward and outward. As picturesque in its way as E.J. Lennox's sandstone and terracotta old City Hall (1886-99), Revell's building is a fitting neighbour and successor. MICHAEL MCMORDIE

Toronto Dance Theatre is a modern-dance company. In recent years it has numbered about 10 in membership. It was founded in 1968 when Patricia BEATTY, who already had her own school and company, the New Dance Group of Canada, joined forces with the young dancer-choreographers David EARLE and Peter RANDAZZO. The 3, who had all been trained in the technique of the American modern-dance pioneer Martha Graham, continued to direct the company co-operatively until 1983, when Kenny Pearl became sole artistic director. He was succeeded in 1987 by David Earle. The company is distinguished for its commitment to originality and creativity. Beatty, Earle and Randazzo have together choreographed more than 60 works for the company, half of which have used commissioned scores by Canadian composers. Since 1980, the works of resident choreographer Christopher House have also occupied an important place in the company's repertoire. The company has toured across Canada as well as in the US and Europe and, in 1987, Venezuela and Mexico. During the early 1980s the company was plagued with financial problems, in part the result of its ambitious move into a new home – a large renovated church building with accommodation for both the company and its associated school. A number of dancers developed within the company have joined some of the world's leading modern-dance groups; one dancer, Lucie Boissinot, was awarded the Canada Council's Jacqueline Lemieux Prize (1985). MICHAEL CRABB

Pitcher Jim Clancy of the Toronto Blue Jays (*courtesy Toronto Blue Jays*).

Toronto Dominion Bank, with head offices in Toronto, is a Canadian bank chartered in 1955 upon the amalgamation of the Bank of Toronto (incorporated 1855) and the Dominion Bank (incorporated 1869). The Toronto Dominion Bank has grown steadily. In 1960 it formed TD Realty Co Ltd, and in 1968, in partnership with the ROYAL BANK OF CANADA, the CANADIAN IMPERIAL BANK OF COMMERCE and the Banque canadienne nationale, formed Chargex Ltd (now VISA). Other ventures undertaken by the TD Bank, as it is popularly called, include Tordom Investments Ltd, formed in partnership with Leamor Holdings Ltd, a registered loan corporation, which subsequently became Tordom Corporation International. In 1973, in partnership with the BANK OF NOVA SCOTIA, the bank formed Scotia-Toronto Dominion Leasing Limited, which leases equipment to Canadian industry. In 1985, it acquired Euro-Pacific Finance Corp, an Australian merchant bank. With 983 branches located throughout Canada and around the world (1987), the Toronto Dominion Bank offers a full range of banking services including a stock hotline for investors. As of Oct 1986, it had revenues of $5.2 billion (ranking 5th among financial institutions in Canada), assets of $51.4 billion (ranking 5th) and 20 211 employees. Foreign ownership stood at 5%.

DEBORAH C. SAWYER

Toronto Islands, 332 ha, are an archipelago of 15 islands in Lk Ontario about 1.6 km S of downtown TORONTO. They were known to the Mississauga as "the place of trees standing out of the water." This car-free area was originally a peninsula, popularly described as an island in defiance of geography. It was made up of eroded sand and gravel carried W from the Scarborough Bluffs. Separation from the mainland occurred in 1858 during a violent storm. From an area of about 145 ha in 1870, they have more than doubled in size. Winds, currents, dredging and landfill operations have helped shape the islands, curving them into an 8 km hook broken on the inside into tiny lagoons and islets. The 8 largest islands are Centre, Muggs, Donut, Forestry, Olympic, South, Snake and Algonquin. Centre I, with its amusement park, beaches and gardens, attracts one million visitors a year. Toronto Island Airport, forming the NW area of Hanlan's Point, is one of Canada's busiest, with an average 184 000 takeoffs and landings per year (1981-85).

Lt-Gov SIMCOE, who picnicked, hiked and went horseback riding on the islands in 1793, decided to make York [Toronto] the naval and military centre of Upper Canada, with Gibraltar Point (now Hanlan's Pt) guarding Toronto harbour. In 1813, however, American soldiers landed and destroyed fortifications on the islands. A residential community for over 150 years, Ward's I, at the eastern edge of the archipelago, was named after fisherman David Ward who settled there with his family in 1834. The Ward's I community is linked by bridge to that on Algonquin I, and together their residential population occupies 250 homes, owned by islanders on land leased from Metro Toronto. In the early 1950s, 8000 people lived on Centre I, but its elegant summer resort hotels, theatres and stores were demolished in the late 1950s and 1960s to make room for parkland. Since 1956 the remaining residents have struggled to save their homes. In 1981 the Government of Ontario passed legislation ensuring that the community will continue to exist at least until 2005.

ROBERT SWARD

Reading: Robert Sward, The Toronto Islands (1983).

Toronto Maple Leafs, hockey team, was formed in 1927 when Conn SMYTHE purchased and renamed the Toronto St Pats. A veteran of

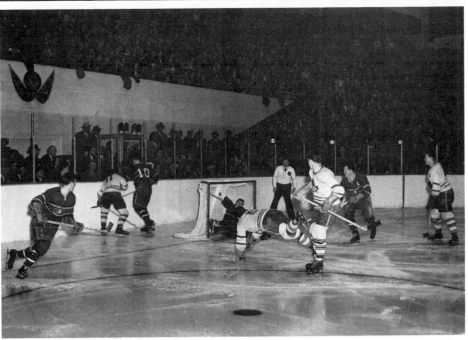

Bill Barilko of the Toronto Maple Leafs scores the winning goal in overtime of the final Stanley Cup hockey game of the 1951 season (*courtesy Hockey Hall of Fame/ Imperial Oil Turofsky Coll*).

WWI and an outspoken patriot, Smythe chose the maple leaf symbol in the hope of giving his team broader appeal. In the depths of the Depression he was able to arrange financing for a new arena, and Maple Leaf Gardens was built in 5 months in 1931. Meanwhile, the flamboyant owner purchased "King" CLANCY from Ottawa Senators for the unprecedented sum of $35 000 and 2 players, and the team won its first STANLEY CUP in 1931-32. In their most successful years the Maple Leafs were known as a gutsy, hardworking team, exemplifying Smythe's (perhaps apocryphal) dictum," If you can't beat them in the alley, you can't beat them on the ice." Members of the team have won few individual awards: the last Maple Leaf to win the scoring title was Gord Drillon in 1938, and only 2 Leafs have won the HART TROPHY – Babe Pratt (1944) and Ted KENNEDY (1955). Nevertheless, the team has won the Stanley Cup 11 times and has enjoyed 2 eras of dominance, winning in 1944-45 and, after a dramatic trade of 5 players for Max BENTLEY, again in 1946-47, 1947-48, 1948-49 and 1950-51. "Punch" Imlach rebuilt the team with a blend of aging veterans such as Bert Olmstead, Johnny Bower and Red KELLY, along with brilliant young players such as Dave Keon, Carl Brewer and Frank MAHOVLICH. The team won the Cup in 1961-62, 1962-63, 1963-64 and 1966-67. Smythe relinquished control in 1961 to his son Stafford, Harold Ballard and John Bassett, and Ballard gained complete control after Stafford's death in 1971. The team deteriorated after its unexpected triumph in 1967 and has failed to reach the Stanley Cup finals since then.

JAMES MARSH

Toronto Mendelssohn Choir, fd 1894 by Augustus Stephen VOGT as an extension of his Jarvis St Baptist Church choir, presented its first concert in MASSEY HALL 15 Jan 1895. After 3 successful years Vogt disbanded the choir, only to resume again with 200 voices in 1900. Succeeding conductors have been Herbert Austin Fricker, 1917-42, who collaborated with various US orchestras; Sir Ernest MACMILLAN, 1942-57, who merged the Toronto Conservatory of Music Choir with the

TMC and established annual performances of Handel's *Messiah* at Christmas and Bach's *St Matthew Passion* at Easter; Frederick Silvester, 1957-60; Walter Susskind, 1960-63; and Elmer ISELER, 1964- , who brought in his FESTIVAL SINGERS OF CANADA as the professional nucleus of the choir, 1968-79, when that group was succeeded by the Elmer Iseler Singers. Each conductor has introduced new repertoire, including Canadian compositions and the Canadian premiere of major European works. The choir has made frequent appearances in the US and toured Europe in 1972 and 1980. It has performed at many major festivals in Europe including the Edinburgh Festival, the Lucerne International Festival, the Festival Estival in Paris, the Flanders Festival and the Henry Wood Promenade Concerts in London's Royal Albert Hall. In 1977 a Toronto Mendelssohn Youth Choir was formed. This choir of high-school-aged singers, at present under the leadership of Robert Cooper, participates in educational workshops and presents annual Christmas and spring concerts.

ISABELLE MILLS

Toronto Star, Canada's largest newspaper, was established in 1892. In 1899 its Liberal proprietors hired Joseph E. Atkinson to run the paper; by 1913 he had become the majority shareholder. Until Atkinson's death in 1948, the *Star* reflected the highly personal style of JOURNALISM he preferred. Stressing human interest and local issues over broader coverage, Atkinson made his paper dominant in the Toronto area, and then across the S-central portion of Ontario. At the same time, he maintained a liberal attitude to public affairs, and used his newspaper to advocate a left-of-centre point of view. In 1910 he established the *Toronto STAR WEEKLY*, which plugged the gap left by the absence of Sunday newspapers from the Canadian scene.

Writing at the *Star* was determinedly lively. In the 1920s and 1930s writers included Morley CALLAGHAN, Ernest Hemingway, Gordon SINCLAIR and Gregory CLARK. The *Star*'s political stand earned it the enmity of Ontario's Conservative government during the 1940s, and after Atkinson's death there was a spectacular battle between the Government of Ontario and the Atkinson Foundation. Under Harry Hindmarsh, Atkinson's son-in-law, the *Star* became more partisan and was closely identified with the federal Liberal Party. After Hindmarsh's death in 1956 the paper recovered some of its independence, although it continued to favour the nationalist wing of the Liberal Party and particularly its spokesman, Walter GORDON. The 1960s and 1970s brought expansion and prosperity to the *Star*, which dominated the Toronto evening newspaper field after the demise of its longtime rival, the *Toronto Telegram*, in 1971. A Sunday edition and finally a morning edition appeared. The circulation of the *Star* (1986) was 525 669 (Mon-Fri), 802 397 (Sat) and 531 341 (Sun). For the 6 months preceding 31 Mar 1987 the figures were 523 458, 799 407 and 526 975, respectively. It is published by TORSTAR CORPORATION. *See also* NEWSPAPERS. ROBERT BOTHWELL

Toronto Symphony In 1922 a group of Toronto theatre pit musicians sought an outlet to perform symphonic music apart from their regular jobs. They formed the New Symphony Orchestra and persuaded Luigi von Kunits to conduct. During the 1926-27 season the orchestra's name was changed to the Toronto Symphony Orchestra, becoming the Toronto Symphony in 1964. (The Toronto orchestra that was founded in 1906 as the Toronto Conservatory Orchestra was not, technically, the precursor of the Toronto Symphony. In 1918, after regular performances, it was obliged to discontinue.)

Under conductor Luigi von Kunits, 1922-31, the New Symphony Orchestra gave its first concert in MASSEY HALL on 23 Apr 1923. Sir Ernest MACMILLAN was music director, 1931-56, and was succeeded by Walter Susskind, 1956-65, who led the orchestra in its successful Carnegie Hall debut on 3 Dec 1963. Seiji Ozawa, 1965-69, introduced new repertoire and attracted public enthusiasm and he took the orchestra on tour to Britain, France and Japan. The experienced European conductor Karel Ančerl led the orchestra, 1969-73, to artistic and financial success and began the popular summer concerts at Ontario Place Forum. Victor FELDBRILL filled in as resident conductor until a new music director was appointed: Andrew Davis, who held the post from 1975 to 1988. Under Davis the orchestra expanded its repertoire, toured China, Japan, Europe and the US, and performed annually at Carnegie Hall in New York. In Sept 1982 the orchestra moved to Roy Thomson Hall where, in its first season, it performed over 150 concerts for nearly half a million people. Davis remains associated with the symphony as conductor laureate. The current conductor is Nurhan Raman.

One of Canada's most experienced arts administrators, Walter Homburger, was succeeded by Wray Armstrong as the orchestra's managing director. The orchestra began recording under MacMillan and has since recorded extensively for RCA, CBC and CBS Masterworks. In 1974 the Toronto Symphony (the word Orchestra was dropped from the name in 1964) organized the Toronto Symphony Youth Orchestra with Victor Feldbrill as its first conductor. BARBARA NOVAK

Torstar Corporation, a broadly based information and entertainment communications company, publishes the TORONTO STAR, Canada's largest newspaper (1986 Mon-Fri circulation 525 669). Other newspaper publishing interests include Metroland Printing and Publishing, commercial printers and publishers of 40 regular weekly editions, 2 monthly and 2 biweekly tabloids reaching over 1.3 million readers in the Toronto area. Torstar's subsidiary, HARLEQUIN ENTERPRISES, the world's largest publisher of romance fiction, sold 206 million books and published 4000 different editions in 17 languages in 1986. Torstar's assets in 1986 totalled $783 million, and revenues amounted to $780 million; 95% of the company's voting shares and 31% of the total shares are controlled by a voting trust representing the Atkinson estate and the families of Beland H. Honderich, Ruth A. Hindmarsh, Burnett M. Tall and William J. Campbell. In Aug 1985 Torstar and Southam Inc exchanged shares as Southam acquired 30% of Torstar's shares and Torstar obtained 20% of Southam's, later increasing this to 22.4%. PETER S. ANDERSON

Torts [Med Latin, *tortum*, "wrong," "injustice"], a large area of private law concerned with compensating those who have been injured by the wrongdoing of others. Unlike criminal law, tort law involves only 2 parties, one of whom, the plaintiff, claims damages from the other, the defendant. Unlike contract law, where 2 parties agree to their respective rights and obligations, in tort law it is the society, through its judicial and legislative systems, that imposes obligations on everyone to act in consideration of the rights of others. The law of torts is mainly judge-made law; courts over the centuries have defined people's rights and obligations with respect to their fellows. These are constantly in flux and change to meet new technological and social concerns. Some tort law, however, originates in statutes, which vary from province to province.

The purpose of tort law is not to punish wrongdoers but to provide damages to victims as compensation for their losses. For example, monetary settlements are used, as best as possible, to restore the lives of accident victims to their condition before the accident. Intentional torts are the most serious, as they involve acts undertaken with the deliberate intention of injuring others. A battery is the intentional application of force to another; an assault is to place another in fear for his safety; a false imprisonment is to prevent unjustifiably another from going where he pleases. For these torts, not only may compensatory damages be awarded but a court may award extra or punitive damages to punish the wrongdoer, although this rarely happens. Instead, recovery is often through victim compensation funds established by statute in 8 provinces and the territories and maintained under cost-sharing agreements with the federal government. People who commit an intentional tort may plead that they had a valid defence, such as the victim's consent, self-defence, defence of property, necessity or lawful authority. If any of these defences are accepted by the court, the action will be dismissed. Intentional torts may also occur against property. To enter a person's house or land without permission is to commit a trespass; to interfere with another's goods is a conversion; to refuse to return something which belongs to another is a detinue.

People are usually injured because of the carelessness rather than the deliberate acts of others. This is the tort of negligence, the most important of the modern torts. The famous English case of *Donoghue v Stevenson*, in which a manufacturer of a soft drink carelessly allowed a snail to crawl into a bottle of drink, established the principle that everyone is under a legal obligation to take reasonable care to ensure that others will not be injured because of careless conduct. Everyone must live up to the standards of the "reasonable man," an important concept of the negligence tort. Based on objective guidelines and built on precedence, the standard allows the court to adapt to the changing circumstances of what might be considered "reasonable." Similarly, if persons by their own fault cause or contribute to their own injuries, they will be held at least partly responsible for their damages. If found liable, wrongdoers must compensate victims in full for losses. Compensation will not only include medical bills, lost income and the costs of future care, but also an award for pain and suffering and the loss of the enjoyment of life, because if a tort causes death, the estate and dependants are entitled to seek compensation from the tortfeasor (person guilty of tort) for their losses. Certain activities are so fraught with risk that compensation to those injured is awarded without the need to establish the defendant's fault. These are strict liability torts. According to the English case of *Rylands* v *Fletcher*, anyone who brings something onto his land which is not naturally there is strictly liable if the thing escapes and injures someone. People are strictly liable for injuries caused by wild animals they keep or by fires they have started.

There are other, less familiar, torts. A person who unreasonably interferes with another's use and enjoyment of his land will be liable to him for a private nuisance. Under the law of occupier's liability, everyone who occupies a building owes a duty of care to those who visit and who are injured on the premises. Manufacturers are responsible under the law of products' liability to those who are injured by defective products. Under the rules of vicarious liability, employers are responsible for the torts committed by their employees in the course of their employment. By virtue of the economic torts, persons will be held liable if they wrongfully prevent others from earning a living or making expected profits. It is tortious to encourage someone to break a contract which the latter has entered into with someone else. It is also wrongful to intimidate someone by threats of unlawful acts to force him to do something which is to his economic disadvantage.

Of course, many injuries result from pure accident, and if the victim cannot prove that the person who caused the accident acted wrongfully, he will not be entitled to any compensation, despite his own innocence. This has been strongly condemned by critics of negligence law, who consider it unfair that persons who cannot prove that their injuries resulted from someone else's negligence are left to bear their losses on their own. Many accidents occur either at work or on the road. Because of their frequency and tort law's inability to compensate adequately all those injured at work, every province has WORKERS' COMPENSATION legislation, allowing workers to receive compensation without the need to establish fault. Many Canadian provinces have enacted similar legislation for highway traffic accidents and have replaced tort law by "no fault" compensation schemes. There is a lively debate about the extent to which these schemes ought to be enlarged at the expense of the traditional tort-law process.

Recently new torts have emerged. Invasion of privacy has gained in importance. Older torts, such as negligence, are applied increasingly to professional groups, such as doctors and lawyers, to force them to live up to higher standards of competence when serving the public. People are held accountable not only for their negligent acts but for misleading advice which may cause loss to others. Even government officials and agencies are being held liable in tort for damages they cause the public in carrying out their functions. Those who support tort law have applauded these developments, arguing that the civil remedy in tort has been and can continue to be valuable to citizens fighting against more powerful elements of our society. LEWIS N. KLAR

Tory [Irish *tóraidhe*, "pursuer"], name applied to members of the CONSERVATIVE PARTY and its antecedents. The name originated as an epithet for dispossessed Irish "papists" who plundered English settlers and soldiers in Ireland. It was applied 1679-80 to supporters of the succession of the duke of York (later James II, a Roman Catholic) to the English throne. From 1689 it was the name of the political party associated with conservative beliefs and later closely identified with the Church of England. The term survived as a nickname for the British Conservative Party and was applied by analogy to the Conservative Party that emerged in Canada in the 19th century. "Tory" is still the American term for supporters of Britain during the American Revolution; those who are called LOYALISTS in Canadian parlance.

JAMES MARSH

Tory, Henry Marshall, educator (b at Port Shoreham, NS 11 Jan 1864; d at Ottawa 6 Feb 1947). Awarded one of McGill's earliest doctoral degrees in science, Tory did not himself become a researcher but was the principal founder of several universities – UBC, U of A and Carleton – and of the ALBERTA RESEARCH COUNCIL and the National Research Council Laboratories.

Son of a Methodist minister, Tory trained for the ministry but was offered a teaching post at McGill after graduation. In 1905, when professor of mathematics, he was sent to BC to advise on the future of McGill's affiliated Vancouver and Victoria colleges, leading to the 1908 UBC Act. His tour of the West led to his appointment in 1908 as founding president of U of A, which he built into a lively institution, with both services (eg, a travelling rural library and radio station) and high standards of teaching and research. In 1917 he organized the KHAKI UNIVERSITY for Canadian soldiers in England, and in 1919 was instrumental, with J.L. CÔTÉ, in creating the organization that in 1921 became the Alberta Research Council. Appointed in 1923 to the NATIONAL RESEARCH COUNCIL, Tory became its chairman within 6 months, apparently because no other member had faith in its political future. His first priority was persuading the government to build the national laboratories planned in 1919 but vetoed in 1921 through procedural confusion in Parliament. He succeeded in 1927 and the following year moved to Ottawa as the NRC's first full-time president. Tory was then 64 years old.

Depression conditions frustrated Tory's ambition of making the NRC as vigorous an influence in Canada as the university had been in Alberta, but the laboratories were completed and staffed between 1928 and 1932 with about 50 scientists, the essential nucleus for the NRC's expansion in WWII. Though embittered by the manner of his 1935 retirement, Tory regarded the NRC Laboratories as his supreme achievement. At age 77 he headed the committee that opened Carleton College in 1942, serving as unpaid president and lecturer until his death. Throughout his life, Tory's main characteristic was enthusiasm. The promotion of science was his central theme, but his interests ranged from the League of Nations to the settlement of the Canadian Prairies. The most famous educator of his day, he was a controversial and proud man: but he had much to be proud of.

DONALD J.C. PHILLIPSON

Totem Pole, the signboard, genealogical record and memorial of Northwest Coast Indian tribes. Crests carved on poles, usually erected at POTLATCHES, were lineage property and reflected the history of the lineage. Animals represented on the crests included the beaver, bear, wolf, shark, whale, raven, eagle, frog and mosquito; they were visual statements about group membership and identity. There were 6 principal types of poles: memorial or heraldic poles, grave figures, house posts, house-front or portal poles, welcoming poles and mortuary poles. Poles were skilfully carved of red cedar and were painted black, red, blue and sometimes white and yellow. They varied in size, but house-front poles could be over 1 m in width at the base, reaching heights of over 15 m and generally facing the shores of rivers or the ocean. While totem poles may have been an

Beaver figures in totem, Kitamaat Village, BC, Haisla tribe, Kwakiutl (*photo by Tom W. Parkin/Pathfinder*).

established feature of pre-contact native culture, most of the well-known poles found in parks and museums were carved after 1860. New poles have been commissioned since the 1950s for museums, parks and international exhibits, and since the late 1960s totem poles are once again being raised at potlatches. Older generation carvers such as Charlie James (d 1938), Ellen Neel (d 1966) and Mungo Martin (d 1962) have inspired artists such as Norman Tait and Douglas Cranmer to continue the tradition. *See also* NORTHWEST COAST INDIAN ART.   RENÉ R. GADACZ

Touch-me-not, or Jewelweed, common names for family of herbaceous plants (Balsaminaceae)

Totem pole "Hole in the ice," Kitwancool, BC (*photo by Karl Sommerer*).

of which *Impatiens* is the principal genus. Genus name derives from the fact that a ripe seed capsule, when touched, explodes violently, projecting seed some distance. Between 600 and 700 species occur worldwide, primarily in Eurasia and Africa. There are 4 native species in Canada (*I. ecalcarata*, southeastern BC; *I. capensis*, southern BC and Alberta; *I. noli-tangere*, the YT and BC to Manitoba; *I. pallida*, Ontario to Atlantic provinces) and 2 introduced. Flowers vary from bright orange to reddish or pale yellow. Native plants are annuals, prefer moist environments, have delicate appearance and vary in height (up to 1.5 m). The introduced perennial *I. glandulifera* is much taller, has more flowers and tends to become a WEED. The introduced perennial *I. sultani* (patience plant or busy Lizzie) is a common houseplant or bedding plant. Multicoloured introduced annual *I. balsamina* (garden balsam) is a useful bedding plant. Recently, many new species have been introduced to cultivation and hybridized, producing new strains. *I. capensis* and *I. pallida* were used medicinally by Indians and settlers, especially for poison ivy and as dye.

PATRICK SEYMOUR

Toupin, Paul, dramatist, essayist, educator (b at Montréal 7 Dec 1918). His plays, classical in language and structure and universal in theme, have been more appreciated by critics than by audiences in Québec. *Brutus* (1952) is one of the few tragedies ever composed in French Canada and was televised in 1953. *Le Mensonge* (1960) and *Chacun son amour* (1961) were performed for television only, and Toupin turned thereafter to essays, such as *L'Écrivain et son théâtre* (1964), and autobiographical memoirs. His *Souvenirs pour demain* (1960) was awarded the prize for best foreign publication in French from the Académie française in 1960. Since 1970 Toupin has lived in Spain.   L.E. DOUCETTE

Tourism, a complete and naturally related collection of services with a single unifying purpose: to provide TRANSPORTATION, accommodation, food and beverage services, recreation and entertainment to Canadians or foreigners travelling in Canada for any purpose. It is an important and fast-growing industry. At the close of 1986 Canada's tourism industry earned over $17.2 billion, contributing over 4% to the GDP and representing, directly or indirectly, more than 10% of the labour force. By the year 2000 it could be one of the most important single economic activities in Canada. Money spent on tourism products has a great impact on employment, both directly and indirectly, that is at least equal to, and in many cases more than, spending in the nation's leading 40 industries.

Visitors from outside Canada spent $6.3 billion in 1986, making tourism Canada's fifth-largest earner of foreign exchange after motor vehicles, auto parts, crude petroleum and newsprint. The bulk of Canada's tourism comes from Canadians travelling in and exploring their own country; the $10.8 billion spent on domestic tourism in 1986 far exceeded the $4.2 billion contributed by US visitors and the $2.25 billion from offshore visitors. On the international travel account, Canada has a falling share of the international market and a $1.2-billion deficit: Canadians spent $7.5 billion outside Canada. Catering to tourists in Canada involves many large companies and about 100 000 small and medium-sized businesses, including almost 300 000 hotel and motel rooms, more than 45 000 eating places and 4000 travel agencies. These businesses serve over 34 million visitors a year. Every 100 000 visitors to a community can mean $9 million in revenue throughout the local economy.

At the federal level tourism is the responsibility

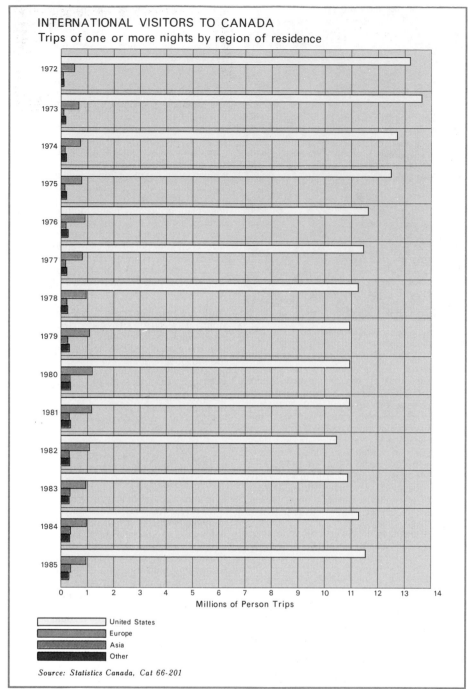

INTERNATIONAL VISITORS TO CANADA
Trips of one or more nights by region of residence

1972
1973
1974
1975
1976
1977
1978
1979
1980
1981
1982
1983
1984
1985

0 1 2 3 4 5 6 7 8 9 10 11 12 13 14
Millions of Person Trips

☐ United States
▨ Europe
▨ Asia
■ Other

Source: Statistics Canada, Cat 66-201

of the minister of state for small business and tourism through Tourism Canada in the Dept of Regional Industrial Expansion. The promotion and development of tourism through a designated federal agency dates from 1934. The recognized national industry association is the Ottawa-based Tourism Industry Assn of Canada (TIAC). It is an umbrella organization representing private sector companies, organizations, institutions and individuals engaged in tourism in Canada and working in partnership with provincial and territorial tourism-industry associations. TIAC has represented the Canadian tourism industry for 56 years and exists to lobby government, to communicate with industry, and to increase public awareness of the importance of tourism and the need for public support.

Tourism dates back to the early history of Canada. Writings by the early explorers and traders contributed to the growing knowledge of the Canadian landscape, still the primary attraction of Canada's tourism industry (*see* EXPLORATION AND TRAVEL LITERATURE). From the mid-18th to the early 19th century TOPOGRAPHIC PAINTERS recorded an idealized landscape, scenes that were often reproduced as engravings in travel books published in Europe. The CANADIAN PACIFIC RAILWAY, through its rail and steamship services, its hotels and publicity campaigns, attracted affluent European and American tourists to Canada. Modern travel and the opportunity for mass travel came with the jet airplane. Business travel illustrates the degree of change: travel and related expenses are the third-largest expenditure of Canadian business, after payroll and data-processing expenditures. Canadian companies spent $3 billion in 1986.

The Canadian tourism industry requires sophisticated marketing, delivering value and service. Beginning in 1984 Canada experienced a turnaround following 10 years of decline during which its balance of payments deficit on the international travel account grew from $300 million to $2.2 billion. 1986 was an exceptional year: foreign visitors increased 18%. The primary reasons

for this growth was EXPO 86 in Vancouver, a favourable exchange rate with the US, an aggressive federal government advertising campaign in the US and negative incidents in other parts of the world which discouraged N Americans from travelling overseas. The best potential new source for travellers to Canada is likely in the Pacific Rim countries. Arrivals from Japan and Hong Kong are expected to show an increase, continuing an upward trend that started in 1979. Australia remains stable. The US continues to be Canada's primary source of visitors; they comprise over 85% of our tourism market. Traditional European markets, including the UK, France, W Germany and the Netherlands, are expected to produce moderate growth over the next few years.

Contemporary Canadian tourist attractions are often the same as those extolled by early travel writers – the fjorded coast of BC, the majestic grandeur of the Canadian Rockies, the wide open spaces of the Prairies, the lakes, forests and rivers of central Canada, the Atlantic coast in its infinite variety of bays, coves, beaches and scenic vistas, the arctic environment and people, and, of course, such old favourites as NIAGARA FALLS. The works of man have been added to these natural assets through the development of modern and sophisticated cities, and through galleries and museums, performing arts, historic sites, FESTIVALS, and events such as Expo 86, the CALGARY STAMPEDE and winter OLYMPIC GAMES. To most of the world Canada is known as a tourist destination through its scenery, space and environment.

F.G. BRANDER and JOHN LAWSON

Tousignant, Claude, painter (b at Montréal 23 Dec 1932). Tousignant studied at the School of Design, Montreal Museum of Fine Arts, with Jacques de TONNANCOUR and Gordon Webber (1948-52). From his earliest works his intention was to make purely abstract paintings in which nothing interfered with the viewer's sensation of colour. He chose a circular format in which sequences of colour produce a dynamic optical effect. Recent works, still nonobjective, are composed of a single colour and are built to stand away from the wall on which they are hung. Tousignant was a member of the Association des artistes non-figuratifs de Montréal and, with MOLINARI and LEDUC, was a major force in the continuing development of abstraction in Montréal. His exhibition, "Polychromes," appeared at Chez Graff in Montréal in 1985.   MARILYN BURNETT

Tousignant, Serge, camera artist (b at Montréal 28 May 1942). His early work, after study at the École des beaux-arts, Montréal (1950-62), was as a painter and sculptor. His concern was the relationship between abstract structures and illusion, later broadened to include direct images of the natural world. He stopped painting after 1967 and by the early 1970s was working exclusively with photographic images. In 1978 he began the photographic series *Geometrisation solaire,* based on arrangements of sticks and the shadows they cast. The apparently arbitrary placement of the sticks is resolved by the consistent geometric figures formed by their shadows. Recent shows include photographs produced between 1982 and 1985 at the Galerie des arts visuels in Québec City in 1986.   DAVID BURNETT

Reading: David Burnett, *Serge Tousignant, geometrisations* (1981).

Towers, Graham Ford, banker, public servant (b at Montréal 29 Sept 1897; d at Ottawa 4 Dec 1975). Towers served in WWI and graduated from McGill in 1919. Although originally intending to study law, he entered the service of the ROYAL BANK OF CANADA. Towers rose rapidly, becoming assistant general manager in 1933. In 1934

PM BENNETT summoned Towers to Ottawa, making him first governor of the BANK OF CANADA, a post he occupied until 1954. Under the governments of Mackenzie KING and Louis ST. LAURENT, Towers had immense influence over economic policy and was instrumental in, for example, the appointment of the Rowell-Sirois commission in 1937. After his retirement, Towers held a number of directorships. ROBERT BOTHWELL

Spengler Writing "The Decline of the West" at his Desk on top of the Kitchen Table (1980), oil on canvas, by Harold Town (*courtesy Harold Town*).

Town, Harold Barling, artist (b at Toronto 13 June 1924). Educated in art at Western Technical School and at the Ontario College of Art, Town was first recognized as a skilful illustrator for such magazines as MACLEAN's and *Mayfair*. His reputation in the art galleries began with a 1954 exhibition at the Picture Loan Society in Toronto of his "single autographic prints." He was a central figure in PAINTERS ELEVEN, a radical group which exhibited from 1954 to 1960. Town at certain moments has shown the influence of other artists (Picasso in his early drawings, New York abstractionists in his nonobjective paintings of the 1950s and 1960s), but quite early in his career he emerged as a unique figure, the most diversely talented artist of his time and perhaps in Canadian history. He has painted murals and portraits, made drawings and sculpture, produced *collages* and prints, illustrated books and articles – all on a high level of accomplishment. He has written books on Tom THOMSON (with David P. Silcox) and Albert FRANCK, as well as many contentious articles and catalogue notes. From the late 1950s to the late 1960s, he was the most widely publicized visual artist in English Canada, a symbol of the then-dominant abstractionists. But certain elements in his work – for example, his devotion to ancient mythology and his continuing commitment to portraiture – have set him outside the mainstream of Canadian art. During 3 decades as a professional artist, he has created a body of work remarkable for its demonstration of protean talent and its consistent visual energy. From May through July 1986 the Art Gallery of Ontario mounted the largest retrospective of Town's career, 233 works over 40 years. In 1987 "Harold Town: Works on Paper" was held at the Canada House Gallery in London, Eng. ROBERT FULFORD

Townsend, William, painter (b at London, Eng 23 Feb 1909; d at Banff, Alta 4 July 1973). He studied at the Slade School of Fine Art, London (1926-30) and then worked in England as a painter and book illustrator. He came to Canada in 1951 to teach at the Banff Centre and returned regularly to teach there and at U of A until his death. He set up the Leverhulme Scholarship for Canadian artists to study abroad and edited *Canadian Art Today*. Of his many paintings produced in Alberta, his *Cascade* series (1966-68), based on one of the mountains that overlooks Banff, is considered the most accomplished of his career. The paintings and related drawings utilize abstract shapes indicating proportion, light and a sense of the atmosphere. These highly refined paintings connote a response to a vast scale. He transferred what he knew from the British tradition to this new environment, addressing the daunting nature of the landscape. He kept detailed diaries throughout his life, which he donated to University Coll, London, and *The Townsend Journals*, edited by Andrew Forge (1976), cover the period 1928-51. KARYN ELIZABETH ALLEN

Townshend, George, 1st Marquess, soldier (b in Eng 28 Feb 1724; d at Rainham, Kent, Eng 14 Sept 1807). One of James WOLFE's brigadiers at the siege of Québec in 1759, Townshend assumed temporary command of the army when Wolfe was killed and the senior officer, Robert MONCKTON, was wounded during the battle on Sept 13; on Sept 18 he accepted the surrender of the city. A skilled caricaturist, he had amused himself during the siege by circulating cartoons ridiculing Wolfe, whom he held in contempt; and when he returned to England in Oct he was sharply and publicly criticized for his disrespectful behaviour toward the country's dead hero. The controversy, though bitter, was brief and did not impede his advancement. Ultimately Townshend achieved the rank of field marshal, climaxing a career as full of public honours as it was empty of significant accomplishment. STANLEY GORDON

Township, introduced into Canada in the late 1700s, is the basic land-survey division of land. Townships of varying sizes were laid out in Nova Scotia and New Brunswick, but they were essentially superseded by the COUNTY structure. In large parts of Québec and Ontario the township was laid out in a general checkerboard pattern; a typical township has about 16 km on each side and is divided into lots and concessions. The basic unit of the township in Québec is a farm of 105 acres (42 ha), whereas the sizes in Ontario vary from 10 acres (4 ha) to 200 acres (81 ha).

The municipal township in Québec is the first order of administration. Each of the EASTERN TOWNSHIPS (now called Estrie) forms the principal network of LOCAL GOVERNMENT of one of the 14 regional county municipalities (MRCs) in the Sherbrooke area of Québec. The township in Ontario is also the first tier of government administration; groups of townships are united with villages and towns to form a county. Populations of the municipal townships in Ontario vary widely, from less than 200 for Brougham in Renfrew County to over 24 000 for Flamborough in Hamilton-Wentworth regional municipality. Hundreds of named townships in both Ontario and Québec are unpopulated and are not municipally organized.

In western Canada, the township describes a square land unit with 10 km a side. Each township has 36 sections, with the basic unit, a quarter section, being 160 acres (64 ha). Townships are numbered north from the 49th parallel. An example of a full land description is Northwest Quarter Section 15, Township 5, Range 6, West of the Third Meridian (NW1/4 Sec 15, Tp 5, R 6, W3). Each township in the western provinces does not itself have municipal or administrative structure. ALAN RAYBURN

Reading: C.R. Tindal, *Local Government in Canada* (1979).

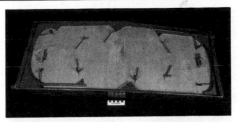

The Munro company was the biggest manufacturer of table-top hockey games in the world in the 1950s. Its games are easily recognized by the sloped wooden rink and bent wire players (*courtesy Museum and Archives of Games, U of Waterloo*).

Toys and Games In the 19th century, Canadians shared current Victorian ideas on child-raising, which saw children as a special group needing play and recreation, along with a firm and religious upbringing. This view coincided with the introduction of mass-production methods. Toy manufacturers in England, France, Germany and, after 1850, the US, supplied their own markets and also exported to Canada. Between 1860 and 1915 some 20 Canadian manufacturers also made toys for Canadian children.

Canadian toys were made almost entirely of wood, a plentiful and cheap material. Then, as now, part of play was preparation for the adult world, and toys reflected that world in miniature. Toy furniture, vehicles and horses were the basic wooden toys made by early manufacturers. In addition, cabinetmakers might, on special order, make toy tables, chairs, beds, cradles, chests of drawers, dish cupboards and sideboards. In the 1860s, makers of chairs, carriages, wagons and sleighs began to advertise child-sized versions of their products; some also offered toys. From 1880 to 1890 the C.T. Brandon Co, Toronto, included Indian clubs, toy wagons, carts and washboards in their list of WOODENWARES. In 1890, the Gendron manufacturing Co, Toronto, one of the longest-lived Canadian toy producers (1890-1970s), began making children's carriages, wooden toys, carts and wheelbarrows. Children's carriages followed the latest fashion, as did toy carriages. By the 1890s they were produced in rattan as well as wood. Two potteries advertised toys. In 1851 James Bailey, Bowmanville, Ont, offered molded toys. By the 1880s, the St Johns Stone Chinaware Co, St-Jean, Qué, made doll sets in blue or white clay.

In this early period, only 2 craftsmen made toys as their sole product. In 1876 Édouard Alfred Martineau, Montréal, began making wooden toys; he continued until 1914, supplementing his toymaking with a retail business. By 1881, Mositz Lindner, Berlin [Kitchener], Ont, was making rocking horses and toys. Cosgrove and Co (1890-91) and the Berlin Novelty Works (1899), both in Berlin, made hobby or rocking horses, perhaps as a sideline. These toymakers probably also made other popular horse toys, eg, stationary-platform rocking horses, small horse-on-platform pull toys, and, for very young children, the shoofly, 2 boards cut in the shape of a horse, mounted on rockers and joined by a flat seat.

GAMES played in the late 19th century included CHESS, checkers, cribbage, backgammon, dominoes, Parcheesi and dissected maps and pictures (jigsaw puzzles). In Québec, where checkers were particularly popular, many boards were homemade. Croquet, an American fad of the 1860s, was much played in Canada. In 1871, 2 Toronto woodturning firms, Hastings and Peterkin, and Leslie and Garden, made croquet sets for the lawn or parlour.

Although many toys were available, it is unlikely that any one child would have had many

Rocking horse of butternut and maple, from Québec, late 19th century (*courtesy Royal Ontario Museum*).

toys. For some children economic necessity meant that play was a rare luxury. Farm children were expected to help with lighter chores and, until 1880 when provincial legislation began to prevent it, children as young as 10 were allowed to work 9-hour days in some city factories. For them, toys would be improvised or homemade from available materials.

WWI curtailed German and English toy production and spurred the Canadian industry. Crokinole boards, toy battleships and building blocks were added to the staple wooden toys. Between 1915 and 1920, 80 individuals or companies made toys: some lasted only one year; others failed as a result of renewed postwar competition. A wider range of companies making more general lines of wares also made toy lines, using brass, tin, iron, lead and rubber. Some, like the Dominion Toy Manufacturing Co, Toronto (1911-34), made dolls and stuffed animals. A flourishing cottage industry produced many varieties of rag doll. Some firms, like the Toy Soldier Novelty Co, Kitchener, Ont, and the Beaver Toy Manufacturing Co, Toronto, made toy soldiers; the Incandescent Light Co, Toronto, made toy bugles and trumpets. The Consolidated Rubber Co, Toronto, made rubber balls, hockey pucks, rattles and animals. The Ideal Bedding Co, Toronto, made a line of toy brass furniture. Thomas Davidson Manufacturing Co, Montréal, made enamelware dishes and toy trunks. The Macdonald Manufacturing Co, Toronto, which made a line of decorated tinware from 1917 to 1942, also made tin toy pails, shovels, cups, plates and banks. The Coleman Fare Box Co, Toronto, made banks; the Belleville Hardware and Lock Manufacturing Co made cast-iron toys. In Toronto, the Manual Construction Co and Reliance Toy Co made steel construction sets. Canadian Toys Ltd, Hamilton, Ont, from 1920 to 1929, made metal humming and dancing tops, and steel construction toys.

However, the Canadian toy industry was not a large one. By 1928 only 10 firms specialized in toy production. The industry, concentrated in Ontario and Québec, employed 129 people. Value of toys made (excluding toy vehicles and dolls) was $465 424 ($320 986 for wooden toys). Toy vehicle production was worth $394 754; doll production, $281 393.

In the 1940s PLASTIC was introduced for rattles and later for beach toys, tractors, wagons, trucks and construction sets. Cheerio Toys and Games, Toronto, made plastic miniature furniture and gym sets. Aluminum and fibreglass were used to make flying saucers. Toy sets for all purposes made their appearance: tools (garden, carpenter, mechanic), archery, printing, construction and road racing sets, embroidery, sewing, tea, coffee and cooking sets, brushes and cleaning sets, ironing boards and irons, table and chair sets. By 1942, 17 firms (4 in Montréal, 13 in Toronto), employing 604 people, were exclusively devoted to toy making. In 1960, although 126 firms were making toys in Canada, only about 20 specialized in toy making. In the 1960s and 1970s several multinational firms began making toys in Canada (Louis Marx, Mattel, Tonka, Coleco). In 1987 there were 85 firms in the industry. In 1986 retail sales amounted to $1.2 billion, of which $372 million was from imports. In that same year, Canada exported $56 million. While the industry remained concentrated in central Canada – over one-third of the production is in Ontario and one-quarter in Québec – the period from 1970 to the 1980s saw the renewal of a CRAFT industry, in NB, PEI and BC, making perennial favourites in wood.

JANET HOLMES

Tracadie, NB, Town, pop 2444 (1986c), 2452 (1981c), inc 1966, is situated on the Gulf of ST LAWRENCE, 83 km SE of BATHURST. Known by the Indians as *Telakadik,* meaning "a place to camp," the area was used by them for temporary camping while fishing the Little and Big Tracadie rivers. There is evidence of Indian occupation here around 1000 years ago. The location was first settled in 1784 by ACADIANS who had either avoided the deportation or who had since returned, followed shortly thereafter by English settlers. In 1849 the provincial government established a lazaretto (hospital for contagious disease) at Tracadie, the first such institution in Canada. During the 19th century, economic activity in the area centered primarily on the wood industry. Both the Big and Little Tracadie rivers were used to carry timber to Tracadie mill sites or to the shipyards of the Miramichi. The present-day economy is based chiefly on tourism, farming and fishing. Tracadie also serves as a commercial centre for the many neighbouring villages.

ALLEN DOIRON

Track and Field, or athletics as it is sometimes called, is a composite sport encompassing discrete competitions in walking, running, hurdling, jumping (high jump, pole vault, long jump, triple jump), throwing (javelin, discus, shot, hammer) and multiple events (eg, decathalon, heptathalon). At the OLYMPIC GAMES, the sport's best-known competition, there are 41 events, 24 for men and 17 for women. More national communities compete at the Olympics in track and field than in any other sport.

A major goal of participation is the achievement of measurable improvement, the "*citius, altius, fortius*" of the Olympic motto. Competitors train and compete not only to surpass each other but to attain personal and group best-ever performances, or "records," which are given special status by the governing bodies in the sport, the International Amateur Athletic Federation and its Canadian affiliate, the Canadian Track and Field Assn. Organizers, athletes and followers have thus imbued track and field with a purpose significantly different from that of its classical antecedent, the athletics of the ancient Olympics. Although the ancient Greeks had the technology to measure times and distances, these results were unimportant to them – they were preoccupied by the contest – and they did not record them. It is felt by many that the heady pursuit of records in activities common to most of the world's cultures is what gives track and field its widespread fascination, for it dramatizes the modern quest for scientific progress.

While Canadians have long known about classical athletics – in 1844 a group of Montréalers staged a 2-day event they called "the Olympics" – the origins of Canadian track and field are to be found much closer to home, in the running and throwing competitions of the native peoples, the colonial athletics of British officers and civil servants, the Caledonian Games of Scottish immigrants, and the tests of strength at rural "bees" and fairs. By Confederation, 1867, highly competitive meets and match races were a regular part of the sporting scene. Perhaps the most popular event was the professional pedestrian or "go-as-you-please" race, in which competitors ran or walked to achieve a maximum distance within a fixed time, often 6 days. In 1884, to bring some order to these various competitions, the Montreal Amateur Athletic Assn worked to create a national governing body, the Amateur Athletic Union. Although briefly challenged by the more liberal Amateur Athletic Federation and a professional running circuit early in the 20th century, the AAU and the CTFA, formed in 1969, have controlled the most competitive levels of the sport ever since.

With AAU control came strict amateurism – the belief in the moral superiority of participation for its own sake, without any material reward, enforced through a list of prohibitions governing eligibility – which effectively limited participation to those individuals who enjoyed the leisure and the financial means to pursue the sport on their own and those educational and social institutions (the universities, YMCAs and police athletic associations) that accepted the accompanying ideology of self-improvement. The sport's social base was restricted by gender as well. Until the 1920s, the men who controlled the sport, aided by the physicians and moralists who sought to guard female health and virtue in a patriarchal society, were successful in keeping women out on the dubious grounds that vigorous physical activity would damage their reproductive organs and was "unseemly." In the 1920s pressure from women forced the AAU to create a women's committee and the IAAF to include women's events in the Olympic Games, but the new opportunities were never equal to those enjoyed by men.

Canadians have competed in every aspect of the sport with flair and distinction. Almost every generation has produced its fine sprinters. Early in the century, Hamilton's Robert KERR used his blazing start to dominate Canadian, American and British Empire competitions. He won gold and bronze medals at the 1908 Olympics in London. Perhaps the greatest era of Canadian sprinting began at the 1928 Olympics at Amsterdam, when Vancouver's diminutive Percy WILLIAMS won both the 100 and 200 metre sprints with his spectacular leaping finish, and Fanny ROSENFELD, Florence Bell, Ethel Smith and Myrtle Cook combined to capture the first-ever 4 x 100 metre women's relay. In the next decade, Canadian sprinters won another 6 Olympic medals and 22 in the British Empire Games. These feats were not equalled until the 1960s when Vancouver's Harry JEROME tied the world record for 100 metres and won Commonwealth and Pan-American championships and an Olympic bronze medal.

Canadian middle-distance runners have also excelled. Before he won Canada's first Olympic gold medal in the 2500 metre steeplechase at the Paris Games of 1900, Toronto miler George ORTON had compiled a long string of championships and records; in the interwar period, Montréal's Phil Edwards and Toronto's Alex Wilson brought back 7 medals from 3 Olympics; Toronto's Bill Crothers, one of the most graceful runners of all time, continued this tradition during the 1960s, winning a silver medal at the 1964 Olympics in Tokyo and dominating the 1000-yard event on the N American indoor track circuit for many years. Canadian distance runners have generally fared better on the road than on the track. They have won Olympic (Bill Sherring in the now unrecognized 1906 Athens Games), British Empire (Harold Webster in London in 1934) and Pan-American (Andy Boychuk in Winnipeg in 1967) marathon titles and the prestigious Boston Marathon 16 times. Some of these Boston champions, such as Onondaga Tom LONGBOAT (1907), Sydney's John Miles (1926 and 1929), St-Hyacinthe's Gerard Côté (1940, 1943, 1944 and

1948), Toronto's Jerome Drayton (1977) and Montréal's Jacqueline Gareau (1980) have become legendary figures in the sport. Toronto's Rich Ferguson placed third in the famous confrontation between Britain's Roger Bannister and Australia's John Landy at the 1954 COMMONWEALTH GAMES at Vancouver – won by Bannister in a time of 3:58.8.

More than half the medals Canadians have won in international competition have come in the less popular field events. The strongest tradition has been in the high jump, where Ethel CATHERWOOD (1928), Duncan MCNAUGHTON and Eva Dawes (1932) and Greg Joy (1976) have won Olympic medals; and Debbie BRILL (1970 and 1982), one of the pioneers of the now almost-universal back-layout technique, Claude Ferrange (1978) and Milt Ottey (1982) have won Commonwealth titles. Other outstanding Canadian champions include Montréal's Étienne DESMARTEAU, who won Canada's first field event Olympic gold medal at the 1904 St Louis Games in the 56-pound weight toss, throwers Ed Coy, Dave Steen, George Puce, Jane Haist and Boris Chambul; vaulters Ed Archibald, William Happeny and Bruce Simpson; and horizontal jumpers Garfield McDonald, Cliff Bricker and Hal and Wally Brown.

In the last 20 years, the structure of Canadian track and field has been radically changed, as the rapid growth of federal and provincial programs initiated by the Fitness and Amateur Sport Act of 1961 has brought about the professionalization of coaching and administration and the recruitment of the medical and scientific communities to the goals of high performance. Previously the sport was conducted almost entirely by volunteers, who often combined the roles of coaching, officiating and administration, using their homes as offices and financing much of the activity out of their own pockets. Now the sport exhibits a formal division of labour among coaching, officiating and administration. The heavily subsidized CTFA and its provincial affiliates enjoy permanent offices, full-time staffs and a network of paid coaches who direct and monitor athletes' training. The top athletes are no longer "amateur," as most receive state grants for living and training expenses (permitted by IAAF rules since 1974) and are eligible for money prizes and endorsement fees (permitted since 1982). Many pursue the sport full-time. These changes have meant significantly improved training and competitive opportunities and longer careers. As a result, the overall quality of Canadian performances is higher than ever before. In 1964 only 14 Canadians met the IAAF Olympic qualifying standard; in 1984, 71 did so.

Canada's poor medal showing at the 1968 Mexico City Olympics (no medals in track and field) gave rise to demands for further action. In 1972 the Canadian Olympic Assn (COA) and Sport Canada initiated "Game Plan," a funding partnership of the federal and provincial governments and the national sports-governing bodies, with the objective of lifting Canada into the top 10 nations by the 1976 Montréal Olympics. Game Plan would fund competition tours (such as the first Canada-US dual track meet for women in 1972) and training camps (eg, at Toronto's Fitness Institute and the National Athletic Training Camp, a converted Canadair hangar in Montréal). At the same time others, including former middle-distance runner Abigail HOFFMAN, lobbied Canada's Olympic committee to allow amateurs to train more than the prescribed 60 days every 4 years, and to be legally compensated for training expenses. Athlete assistance programs under a "carding" system, based on performance and world ranking, were initiated and

Diane Jones Konihowski at the Edmonton Commonwealth Games, Aug 1978 (*courtesy National Archives of Canada/PA-130367/D. Paterson*).

between May 1975 and the 1976 Olympics, some $2.3 million was distributed to about 600 Canadian athletes for training and living expenses. This kind of investment demanded a high return, and a dispute between the COA and the CTFA over standards (distances, heights and times required to earn positions on the national team) came to a head at the Olympic track and field trials prior to the 1972 Munich Games. Consequently, 9 of Canada's best track and field athletes were cut from the team. Pole vaulter Bruce Simpson's fifth-place finish was the best by a Canadian track and field athlete at Munich.

As work got underway in Montréal for 1976, the CTFA invited Polish sprint specialist Gerard Mach to conduct clinics in 1973; soon after, he became Canada's first professional track and field coach. The CTFA then organized its own "game plan" around a technical director, Lynn Davies, and 4 national coaches: Derek Boosey (jumps and multiple events), Jean-Paul Baert (throws), Paul Poce (distance running) and Mach (sprints, hurdles and relays). Of 56 track and field athletes at the Montréal Olympics for Canada, 9 women and 5 men achieved Olympic qualifying standard, and 4 individuals, plus 3 of the 4 relay teams, achieved personal bests and Canadian records during the games. Greg Joy's high-jump silver was the only medal in track and field, and Canada placed eleventh in overall team standings. The fruits of Game Plan '76 were harvested at the 1978 Commonwealth Games in Edmonton, as Canadian athletes placed first overall. In athletics, gold medals were won by Boris Chambul (discus), Claude Ferrange (high jump), Carmen Ionesco (discus), Diane JONES KONIHOWSKI (pentathlon), Phil Olsen (javelin) and Bruce Simpson (pole vault); the track and field team also won 8 silver medals and 9 bronze. The harvest continued at the Pan-American Games in San Juan, Puerto Rico, where Canada placed third in team standings overall, with track and field athletes bringing home 18 medals.

In spite of the setback of the boycott of the 1980 Moscow Games, the CTFA's philosophy of separating athletic events, begun with Game Plan, continued in the form of "event training centres" where recognized coaches could work with emerging talent: a Toronto sprint centre under

coach Charlie Francis; distance-running centres under coaches Ron Bowker in Victoria and Alphonse Bernard in Winnipeg; and multiple-event centres in Saskatoon under coach-athlete Diane Jones Konihowski and in Toronto under coach Andy Higgins. Trust funds, pioneered in athletics by the CTFA and approved by the IAAF at its 1982 congress, cleared the way for amateur track and field competitors to earn and spend money legally (from corporate sponsorship, commercial endorsement or government grant) for living and training expenses, without losing amateur status.

By staging the first-ever World Track and Field Championships in 1983 at Helsinki, Finland, the IAAF signalled the return of athletics to their ancient Olympic Games prominence; for the first time since the 1972 Munich Olympics (because of the African boycott at Montréal and the American boycott at Moscow), the world's track and field best competed in 41 events. Canadians won no medals at the IAAF championships but placed seventh in the world (setting one Commonwealth and 3 Canadian records) – Canada's best-ever track and field team showing to that date. In the 1984 Los Angeles Olympics Ben JOHNSON won a bronze in the 100 m and Lynn Williams a bronze in the 3000 m. The men's relay team won a silver in the 4 x 100 m and the women's a silver in the 4 x 400 m. In the 1986 Pan-Am Games, Canadians took 7 silver medals and 3 bronze. Johnson has since become the premier sprinter in the world, setting the record in the 100 m and winning the world championship in 1987, as well as breaking 2 world indoor records in the 60 m (6.41 sec) and the 50 m (5.55 sec). Angella ISSAJENKO holds the women's world indoor record for the 50 m dash (6.06 sec).

Canadians will no doubt continue to pursue and take pleasure from track and field for many years to come, but future opportunities for world-class performance are now contingent upon state support. The cost of training and competition – which includes facility rentals, coaching fees, scientific consulting, specialized medical treatment, travel and living expenses – are well beyond the resources of all but a few. Other public agencies, notably schools and the universities, bear some of these costs. The CTFA and a few clubs have been able to generate some revenue by fund raising and marketing – selling the goodwill outstanding athletes enjoy for use in advertisements. But these contributions have not proved sufficient in themselves. As much as the leaders of the sport would like to regain the autonomy of the old AAU, they remain dependent upon state funds and services and subject to government direction and control. To date, there has been a widespread consensus that the provision of high-performance opportunities in the Olympic sports such as track and field should be a public undertaking. This is the most significant measure of the transformation of the sport in Canada.   BRUCE KIDD AND TED BARRIS

Tracy, Qué, City, pop 12 546 (1986c), inc 1875, located 75 km NE of Montréal on the S shore of the St Lawrence R at the junction of the Richelieu R. The iron and steel and titanium industries are the major forms of economic activity and the largest single employers in the city. Tracy's development is linked closely with the shipbuilding economy of nearby Sorel. Formerly known as the municipal parish of St-Joseph-de-Sorel, the name Tracy was adopted in 1954 to honour Alexandre de Prouville, marquis de Tracy, the successful military governor of New France (1663-67) who built a fort near the present site. The Tracy region was part of a seigneury granted in 1672 to Pierre de Saurel, although some small-scale European settlement existed prior to this date. Following the American Revolution, some United Empire Loyalists settled here. In the late 19th century, increasing industrialization – including some shipbuilding – was accompanied by rapid population growth. A brief but severe economic recession set in after WWII – for which Tracy's industries churned out large quantities of military matériel – but in the 1950s a construction boom and spreading urbanization swelled the population base. A major archaeological discovery in 1961 produced fine examples of Iroquois pottery, tools and weapons which pre-date European colonization. In the 1980s, Tracy was plagued by high unemployment. SERGE DURFLINGER

Trade Mark, a manufacturer's or merchant's registered name, emblem or design used to identify the business or its goods or services. Some successful trade marks, eg, "Coke," are known worldwide. In the common law, trade marks were introduced to prevent goods or services being "passed off" in a way that confused the public about the source or quality of the product. A trader could complain that a mark similar to his own was being used and that the goodwill in his mark was being prejudiced.

Special remedies are provided in Canada for the breach of trade marks or names that are registered under the federal Trade Marks Act. Such marks, if registered after examination by the Trade Marks Office and passed without objection after advertising for public comment, give the trade-mark owner exclusive right to the use of the mark throughout Canada. Certain marks are prohibited, including any that suggest sanction by the Crown or association with the International Red Cross. Other marks may be disallowed if they are the name of a living or recently dead person, if they describe the goods or services in connection with the way in which they are used, or if they might be confused with already existing marks.

The use of the mark must be such that at all times there is one controlling entity for the product or services identified by the mark. However, other persons may be allowed to use the trade mark if they become registered users with the permission of the owner and with the recording of the registered user (entry of a notice) in the Register of Trade Marks. If a mark is not actively used it may be considered to have been abandoned. It may also be so commonly used that it ceases to describe the owner's products and becomes part of the general language to describe the product (eg, "Thermos," to describe a vacuum bottle). Certification marks are owned by associations not actually involved in trade and are used to indicate that products have met certain standards. Thus, "CSA" is used on all electrical goods to show that the goods have met the minimum standards prescribed by the Canadian Standards Association. PETER J.M. LOWN

Trade Unions, *see* WORKING-CLASS HISTORY; UNION CENTRALS; and entries under LABOUR.

Trades and Labor Congress of Canada, the second Canadian central labour organization, was founded in 1883 on the initiative of the Toronto Trades and Labor Council. A successor to the Canadian Labor Union (1873-77), it first met in Toronto as the Canadian Labor Congress but changed its name to TLC at its second convention in 1886. Largely controlled by the KNIGHTS OF LABOR, the TLC initially brought together trade unionists from Ontario, but by 1900 the organization had become national in character. In 1902 at the Berlin [Kitchener], Ont, convention, however, its expulsion of all unions which were also American Federation of Labor chartered bodies ended its near hegemony of the Canadian labour movement. Thereafter the movement was splintered by national unions, by overtly socialist and

syndicalist bodies, and by the rise of INDUSTRIAL UNIONISM.

In 1919 political tensions within the TLC reached crisis level, and socialist and industrial unionists bolted to form the ONE BIG UNION. After the defeats suffered by industrial unionists during the massive 1919 strike wave, the TLC re-emerged as the major central body. Its next challenge came with the renewed drive for industrial unionism led by the WORKERS UNITY LEAGUE and later by the Committee for Industrial Organization (fd 1935; became Congress of Industrial Organizations in 1938). Again splits in the US between AFL and CIO supporters led to a reluctant 1939 expulsion of Canadian industrial unionists from the TLC. The renegades founded the CANADIAN CONGRESS OF LABOUR in 1940. Rapid growth of industrial unionism during and immediately after WWII left the CCL as the major labour power.

After a hysterical witch-hunt against communists in both labour centrals in the late 1940s and early 1950s and the merger of the AFL and the CIO in the US in 1955 (*see* AFL-CIO), the CCL and the TLC united in 1956 to create the CANADIAN LABOUR CONGRESS. GREGORY S. KEALEY

Trading Post The trading post can be viewed as a large household whose size and social organization reflected the cultural heritage of its members and the post's role in the FUR TRADE. While all posts traded manufactured goods from Europe and Canada for furs and "country produce" harvested by Indians, larger posts had additional functions in the trading system. Some were major entrepôts warehousing and transshipping goods. Others manufactured trade goods such as axe heads, ice chisels and chief's coats for the trade. Auxiliary to the trade was the manufacture of nails and metal braces for construction, rundlets for containing liquor, and canoes and YORK BOATS for transportation. Unskilled servants spent long hours cutting, gathering and sawing timber for lumber and fuel. At other times they cleared the post of debris, stable refuse and snow. Where applicable crops were planted and harvested or fish were netted.

To carry out these tasks as an integrated system the trading post was structured as a social hierarchy. At a post commanding a district was a chief factor. At a principal post was a chief trader. Both were styled as "bourgeois" and both shared in the profits of the trade. Much of the bookkeeping and correspondence of the trade was conducted through clerks. Below this officer class were skilled and unskilled servants. Among the skilled servants were blacksmiths, boatwrights, carpenters and coopers, as well as hunters, steersmen, guides and interpreters. At small or temporary posts the postmaster could be a clerk but frequently was an interpreter or other senior skilled servant. Below them were the youthful unskilled servants who in later years were often sons of older servants and their native wives.

In the early years of the fur trade only the commanding officer, in the image of the head of a household, had an Indian woman as a "country wife" living in the post. Other officers and senior servants had to maintain their families in surrounding Indian bands. In time, as Indian women demonstrated their value in the fur trade, servants were given permission to have their families reside within the post, although officers and servants continued to require their bourgeois's permission to take a wife. In addition to their family domestic duties, native wives were important in preparing provisions, caring for furs and tending crops. Several served as interpreters and occasionally as skilled negotiators with Indian bands. As Indians emphasized social relations in their economic behaviour, native women were an essential component of every trading post. JOHN E. FOSTER

At the Hudson's Bay Company post, Lake Timiskaming, Ont, *c*1896 (*courtesy National Archives of Canada/PA-127 397*).

Traffic Law The regulation of traffic on highways and roads is one of the greatest legal challenges of the 20th century. Not only do 3 levels of government – federal, provincial and municipal – make traffic laws, but common-law rules still play an important role in this area as well. The federal involvement derives primarily from criminal law. The Canadian Criminal Code provides for numerous serious offences, including dangerous driving, criminal negligence in the operation of a motor vehicle, criminal negligence causing death, and impaired driving. Each province is responsible for maintaining the highways which run through it and for governing the conduct of drivers. The provincial highway-traffic Acts control all matters pertaining to the use of the roads, including licensing of drivers, registration of vehicles, safety and condition of motor vehicles and rules of the road, which in turn include speed limits, the observation of traffic signals, and rights of way at intersections. Failure to obey these rules may lead to fines, the suspension of the right to drive and even imprisonment. Municipalities also have jurisdiction, delegated to them by their provincial governments, to control highway traffic and maintain the roads within their control. Traffic rules of municipalities are created by bylaws. Municipalities are also responsible for the safe condition of their roads and can be held civilly liable to persons who are injured while on a dangerous road.

In addition to the control and regulation of traffic and roads, traffic law includes the huge area of civil liability arising from the thousands of annual traffic accidents. In most provinces, this area of law is still governed by normal negligence principles, modified somewhat by highway-traffic Acts (*see* TORTS). In some provinces civil actions have been replaced by compulsory no-fault schemes which compensate victims of motor-vehicle accidents without litigation and without regard to fault. The most extensive scheme, which has abolished civil action in all motor-vehicle cases, is in Québec. All provinces, even those that maintain fault law, have compulsory liability-insurance laws which provide for at least some compensation to motor-vehicle accident victims without the need for costly litigation. *See also* IMPAIRED DRIVING. LEWIS N. KLAR

Trail, BC, City, pop 7948 (1986c), 9599 (1981c), inc 1901, is located on the COLUMBIA R at the mouth of Trail Cr, just N of the international boundary, 630 km by road E of Vancouver. Settlement in the area began at ROSSLAND, with its proximity to the rich ore of Red Mt. Development at Trail (after the DEWDNEY TRAIL) came with the realization that shipping ore to American smelters was too costly. American F.A. Heinze built the original foundry 1895, then a narrow-gauge railway to Rossland 1896. With the CPR's decision to build lines through CROWSNEST PASS

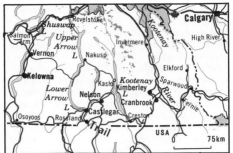

and the Kettle Valley, Heinze's smelter and railway interests were purchased by the CPR in 1898. In 1906 the mines came under CPR ownership through its subsidiary, Consolidated Mining and Smelting Co of Canada (Cominco). A move to electricity brought extensive hydro development on the Kootenay R. Trail's smelter rapidly expanded (by 1910, 40-50% of BC's output came from the Kootenays) and in time it grew to be the largest smelter in the British Empire. Long-term development was ensured by the ready access to cheap, bountiful hydroelectric power on both the Kootenay and Pend-d'Oreille rivers and the rich lead-zinc ore deposits of the Sullivan mine at Kimberley, BC.

Trail continues to be dominated by Cominco's activities, although CP sold the majority of its shares in 1986. Silver, lead and zinc ores from the Kootenay, Alberta, the NWT and the US are smelted and refined here, yielding refined metals, chemicals and fertilizers. A new smelter is scheduled to open in 1989. Trail also acts as a commercial centre for the adjoining towns of Fruitvale, Montrose, Warfield and Rossland. The Trail Smoke Eaters were, in 1961, the last Canadian hockey team to win the world championship.

WILLIAM A. SLOAN

Trail of '98, a reference to the CHILKOOT TRAIL and other northern trails scaled by prospectors during the KLONDIKE GOLD RUSH, which was at its height in 1898. Robert W. SERVICE tells the story of these prospectors in his first novel, *The Trail of '98* (1910). JOHN ROBERT COLOMBO

Traill, Catharine Parr, née Strickland, pioneer writer, botanist (b at London, Eng 9 Jan 1802; d at Lakefield, Ont 29 Aug 1899). In 1832 Catharine immigrated to Canada with her husband, half-pay Lt Thomas Traill, and settled on the Otonabee R near Peterborough, next door to her sister Susanna MOODIE. There Mrs Traill wrote her most famous book, *The Backwoods of Canada* (1836), a factual and scientific account of her first 3 years in the bush, a pragmatic and optimistic work stressing the kind of realistic detail that has become a tradition in Canadian literature in such writers as Farley MOWAT and Pierre BERTON. Her published works include juvenile fiction, a housekeeping manual, *The Female Emigrant's Guide* (1854), and treatises on Canadian botany, *Canadian Wildflowers* (1868) and *Studies of Plant Life in Canada* (1885). MARIAN FOWLER

Reading: Marian Fowler, *The Embroidered Tent* (1982).

Trakas, George, sculptor (b at Québec C 11 May 1944). After a year at Sir George Williams, Trakas continued his studies in New York, and he has remained in the US. His work belongs in the context of environmental art in that his quasi-architectural structures are inextricably integrated into the gallery interiors or landscape settings that he uses as sites. He strives for multilevelled inclusiveness, and his work is potent with symbolic and metaphoric meaning. Central to his sculpture is the idea that our perspective on the world is not only a function of vision but of the whole body. To experience a sculpture by Trakas in its entirety re-

quires that we walk, climb and otherwise physically negotiate it. Most of his work has been commissioned for specific projects or exhibitions, such as *Rock River Union* (for the Artpark, Lewiston, NY, 1976), *Union Pass* (Documenta 6, Germany, 1977) and *Extruded Routes* (Structures for Behavior, Art Gallery of Ontario, 1978). He has permanent installations of his sculptures in the Fattoria di Celli near Pistoia, Italy (1982) and at the Louisiana Museum, Humlebaer, Denmark (1986). Since 1972 Trakas has been working on a large landscape project on Cap Trinité, Baie d'Eternité, Qué. ROALD NASGAARD

Trans-Canada Airlines was created 10 Apr 1937 by Act of Paliament as a subsidiary of CANADIAN NATIONAL RAILWAYS to provide air service to all regions of Canada. TCA began with 2 passenger aircraft and a small bi-plane, which was used to survey new routes. Passenger service began between Vancouver and Montréal 1 Apr 1939, and 2 years later TCA provided scheduled flights across the Atlantic Ocean. By 1947 the line linked major centres in Canada and operated services to the US; in 1948 service began to Bermuda, the Caribbean, Florida, Shannon (Ire), London, Paris and Düsseldorf. Although it rejected the Canadian designed AVRO JETLINER, the line converted to turbines in the 1950s, with Super Constellations and Vickers Viscounts. Polar flights to Europe were introduced and TCA was the first N American airline to have direct service to Moscow. The name was changed to AIR CANADA in 1965.

JAMES MARSH

Reading: Philip Smith, *It Seems Like Only Yesterday* (1986).

Trans-Canada Highway Public agitation for a national road began as early as 1910, but more than half a century elapsed before it was completed. The 7821 km Trans-Canada Hwy was formally opened at ROGERS PASS on 30 July 1962. Canadians could now drive, using ferry services on both coasts, from St John's, Nfld, to Victoria, BC, but more than 3000 km were still unpaved. Work started in the summer of 1950 with an infusion of $150 million of federal funds (half the estimated cost) provided for in the Trans-Canada Highway Act (1949). Cost-sharing plans, revised twice, increased the federal contribution to $825 million. Standards called for pavement widths of 6.7 m and 7.3 m; ample shoulder width, bridge clear-

The Trans-Canada Highway, shown winding its way through Rogers Pass, BC (*photo by Doug Leighton*).

ances and sight distances; low gradients and curvature; elimination of railway grade crossings wherever possible; and a maximum load-bearing capacity of 9.1 t per axle. Construction was supervised by the provinces. The target date for completion was Dec 1956, but the job was more difficult and more expensive than anticipated. For example, the route between Golden and Revelstoke, BC, passes through Rogers Pass, where snowfall reaches 15.2 m per year and presents tremendous avalanche hazards. Snowsheds, earth mounds and other devices for avalanche control had to be provided. In Québec, the tunnel under the St Lawrence R at Boucherville Islands, which is part of the entranceway to Montréal, was a difficult project costing approximately $75 million and covering little more than 1 km of the highway. Finished in 1970, the highway had cost over $1 billion. It is the longest national highway in the world. C.W. GILCHRIST

TransCanada PipeLines Limited, a natural gas transmission company with executive offices in Toronto. First incorporated by Act of Parliament on 21 Mar 1951, TransCanada owns and operates a high pressure natural gas PIPELINE system extending from Alberta into parts of Québec and into the US. The company is also engaged in the search for, and production of, crude oil and natural gas, and sells natural gas to Canadian and US customers. With the federal government's deregulation of gas prices, the company expanded its marketing operations with its subsidiary Western Gas Marketing Ltd. In late 1987 it made a bid for Encor Energy Corp Inc, the largest shareholder of which was debt-plagued DOME PETROLEUM. If successful, the takeover could be the largest in Canadian history. In 1986 it had sales or operating revenue of $4.1 billion (ranking 15th in Canada), assets of $5.9 billion (ranking 14th) and 2026 employees. Bell Canada Enterprises Inc owned 49% of the shares. *See also* PIPELINE DEBATE.

DEBORAH C. SAWYER

TransCanada Telephone System (TCTS; Telecom Canada since 1983) is a voluntary association of 9 telephone companies and Telesat Canada. Formed in 1931 (opened 1932) to integrate national telephone service, the Association even in the late 1980s lacked employees and assets of its own, its requirements being met by its members. Prior to its formation, Canada had relied on transmission facilities in the US for most of its cross-Canada requirements. In 1972 the Computer Communications group was formed within TCTS to improve the service for data transmission by computer communications. Membership of TCTS comprises British Columbia Telephone Co, Alberta Government Telephones, Saskatchewan Telecommunications, Manitoba Telephone System, Bell Canada, New Brunswick Telephone Co, The Island Telephone Co, Maritime Telegraph and Telephone Co, Newfoundland Telephone Co and Telesat Canada. The system is directed by a board of management composed of directors from all member companies; unanimous agreement among the directors is required before policies are implemented. The board is supported by inter-member operational and administrative committees.

In addition to integrating and co-ordinating technical factors, TCTS also arranges the apportionment of revenues among members that may be attributed to that portion of interprovincial telephone traffic using the facilities of 3 or more members. Its members negotiate separately on other interprovincial traffic. Until recently there was little regulatory supervision of interprovincial toll rates but, since assuming jurisdiction over BC Tel, Bell Canada, Telesat Canada and CNCP Telecommunications in 1976, the CANADIAN RA-

DIO-TELEVISION AND TELECOMMUNICATIONS COMMIS-SION has been reviewing the policies of TCTS with greater thoroughness.   ROBERT E. BABE

Reading: E.B. Ogle, *Long Distance Please: The Story of the TransCanada Telephone System* (1979).

Transfer Payments, direct payments from governments to other governments or to individuals, a mechanism for providing social security, income support and for alleviating regional disparities. Federal transfer payments to individuals include family allowances, old-age pensions and unemployment insurance; in 1985-86, they represented about $24.9 billion. Federal transfer payments to provinces, including equalization payments ($5.4 billion in 1985-86), cash payments for medicare and post-secondary education under the Established Programs Financing Act ($9.0 billion in 1985-86) and other, smaller programs, represent about 20% of federal spending and a large proportion of provincial revenue. Transfer payments from provincial governments to local governments, school boards, universities and hospitals are part of provincial PUBLIC FINANCE.   RICHARD SIMEON

Translation is "the interpretation of verbal signs by some other language," according to Russian linguist Roman Jakobson. It is most often thought of as the presentation of works written in one language to a public that speaks other languages, but its original use seems to have been to facilitate administration within the ancient multilingual empires. The first known religious translation, that of the Hebrew Old Testament into Greek (the Septuagint version), occurred in the first 2 centuries BC, at about the time that the Roman authors Plautus, Caecilius and Terence were pioneering literary translation with Latin versions of Greek drama. Another major field that has long relied heavily on translation is that of trade and commerce.

For centuries translation was considered part of the art of rhetoric, and rightly so, for it is a language art that draws on sciences such as contrastive grammar and lexicology (the study of word derivations and meanings). Although theories of translation techniques were proposed as early as Roman times, it was only in the late 18th century that the issues were fully articulated. Still central to the debate is the question of whether to attempt to translate word for word (ie, literal translation) or "sense for sense" (free translation). A number of factors influence the choice of method, such as the degree of similarity between the languages and cultures involved, the genre of the text (eg, poetry, literary or technical prose) and the medium (oral, written or sign language). In Canada translation between French and English (both oral and written) predominates, although considerably more works written in French have been translated into English than the reverse. There is also a good deal of translation of other languages spoken and written here, such as Italian, German and Ukrainian. Since the QUIET REVOLUTION of the 1960s and the work of the Royal Commission on BILINGUALISM AND BICULTURALISM, changes in the political balance between French and English have caused work from French to English to increase.

The first translators in Canada were Indians. In 1534 Jacques CARTIER took 2 Indians, Taignoagny and Domagaya (sons of DONNACONA), back to France, had them taught French, and in 1535 used them as interpreters in negotiations with natives at STADACONA. Until the SEVEN YEARS' WAR most translation and interpretation work was in the hands of missionaries, who produced many glossaries, dictionaries and grammars of Indian languages. After the defeat of the French 1759-60

the major weight of translation moved to French-English and the predominant mode from oral to written. The arrival of immigrants speaking other languages necessitated translation to and from those languages, most of it unofficial.

Despite the need for translation in government, from 1760 until the late 19th century its occurence was only ad hoc. It was finally given official status by the language provisions of the BNA Act of 1867, which required that both languages be official in Parliament and in Québec; in 1870 this provision was extended to Manitoba. Early in the 20th century the translation offices of individual government departments were absorbed into the federal Bureau of Translations, which came under the control of the secretary of state. In the early 1980s both Québec and New Brunswick had translation bureaus, that of Québec also having close links with l'OFFICE DE LA LANGUE FRANÇAISE, which has a terminology bank. Canadian commercial life has also depended on translation, and commercial and technical translation firms have existed in Canada since the early 20th century.

Beginning in 1764 when the *Quebec Gazette* published in both French and English, newspapers played an important role in commissioning and publishing literary works (not necessarily Canadian) which had made their mark in their original language. As well as Toronto and Montréal, New York was an important publication centre for English versions of French work. As elsewhere, literary translators usually belonged to other professions such as journalism or had reputations as creative writers in their own language. Among the important 19th-century translators of French works into English was Rosanna LEPROHON. At this stage there seems to have been more translation from English into French. French-language newspapers feature translations from English and American originals as well as Canadian. Longfellow's EVANGELINE, for instance, was translated in 1865 by Léon-Pamphile Le May who is best known for his French version of William KIRBY'S GOLDEN DOG published in a book edition after being serialized in 1884-85 by the Montréal newspaper, *L'Étendard*. Another important 19th-century figure was Louis FRÉCHETTE, who was both translator and translated.

The cultural and political problems of the mid-20th century drew attention to the role of translation as mediator between French and English cultures. Publishers took over from newspapers in commissioning translators and important "little magazines" such as *Ellipse* (Université de Sherbrooke) specialize in translation. Since the early 1960s the CANADA COUNCIL began encouraging translation as an art form, and in 1972 the secretary of state made subsidies available to finance translation of literary and scholarly works considered important. A comprehensive list of translators and translated can be found in Newman and Stratford's *Bibliography of Canadian Books in Translation* (2nd ed, 1981). Philip Stratford himself is one of Canada's finest translators, whose range goes from the political essays of André LAURENDEAU to the drama of Antonine MAILLET. Other notable translators from French to English are Sheila Fischman, John Glassco, Joyce Marshall and the late Frank SCOTT. On the French side Jean Simard has translated Northrop FRYE and Hugh MACLENNAN, and Michelle Tisseyre has translated Morley CALLAGHAN.

The major translation association in Canada is the Council of Translators and Interpreters of Canada. Only PEI, Newfoundland and Nova Scotia do not have professional associations affiliated with CTIC. Entry to the provincial associations is by examination. Other associations are the Literary Translators' Assn and the Assn of Legal Court

Interpreters and Translators. The major professional journal is *Meta,* published by U de Montréal. Several universities have translation components in their language degrees, but the major translation schools are at U de M, U of Ottawa, Laurentian U, Laval and U de Moncton. Canadian work on the linguistic aspects of translation theory is internationally recognized, one of the most important source books being *Stylistique comparée du français et de l'anglais* (1960; rev 1968) by Jean-Paul Vinay and Jean Darbelnet. The study of literary translation is not as well organized, being normally the responsibility of university departments of French, English or comparative literature. Translators into Indian and Inuit languages draw on work done at the Summer Institute of Linguistics (Dallas, Tex), which specializes in descriptions of, and translation from and into, languages so far unknown outside their own area.

A recent development in translation is the use of computers. Extensive research in ARTIFICIAL INTELLIGENCE is taking place in Canada and elsewhere in the hope that fast, high-quality machine translation will one day be possible. At the present time, however, computers play a limited role in translation. *See also* BILINGUALISM; DICTIONARY.

LOUIS G. KELLY

Reading: "Histoire de la traduction au Canada," *Meta* 22,1 (1977; special issue); C. La Bossière, ed, *Translation in Canadian Literature* (1983); M. Newman and P. Stratford, *Bibliography of Canadian Books in Translation: French to English and English to French* (1975, 2nd ed 1981).

Transplantation is a branch of medicine which is unique in one respect: treatment depends on using a nonrenewable part of one individual to treat another. Blood transfusion and bone-marrow transplantation are renewable sources of human tissue; they are not included in this account.

The human body was not designed to receive grafts from others. Organs and tissues of others differ from our own because of certain cell wall markers, or tissue "groups," known as the HLA antigens. These factors are inherited, half from the mother, half from the father. Each person has 8 such factors (out of about 90 known possible factors, in the population); these give us our HLA profile. We can each be identified by HLA profile because the likelihood of another unrelated person having the same 8 factors is very small.

The human immune system is designed to recognise foreign proteins – or antigens – and to form an immune response against them. Immune responses also protect us from abnormal cancer cells which might arise within us from time to time. These cells, too, are recognized as foreign and attacked, provided they retain these recognition markers. The secret of successful transplantation is to control the immune system by immunosuppression in such a way that the body will not reject the graft, but will still be able to resist infection and recognise cancer cells. It would be highly advantageous if this could be done selectively, ie, dampening immunity only to the antigens of the graft, leaving other components of immunity intact. This cannot be achieved in humans yet, but it is an ultimate research goal.

Some immunosuppressive agents are "chemical," such as cyclosporin and azathioprine. Others, such as anti-lymphocyte globulin (ALG) or antibodies to T3 lymphocytes (OKT3), are highly selected antibodies of animal origin and are designed to block the immune response in very precise and selective ways. Immunosuppression is a changing field of medical therapy, though cyclosporin is justly famous as its use has markedly improved survival in a number of areas of organ transplantation.

Transplantation of Specific Organs

Kidney Transplantation Over 60 000 kidney transplants have been done in N America since 1964, the year the first successful cadaveric kidney graft in humans was reported. The procedure has evolved from being experimental or "last ditch" to being the preferred treatment for most patients with chronic kidney failure. In the early days, many live donors (family members) were used, but the main emphasis in the last 2 decades has been in using cadaveric kidneys. This has led to special criteria for the diagnosis and certification of death from acute cerebral causes (or brain death), as well as means of explaining this to the public and to recently bereaved families in seeking their permission to use the organs after death. All transplant centres now have special persons for this work and its co-ordination.

Kidney transplants developed first because the organ has an abundant blood flow (required for urine formation), has a single artery and vein (usually), is less prone to postoperative infections (maximal with the lung), and has an effective "back-up" system, the artificial dialysis machine, to provide kidney function while awaiting subsidence of a wave of rejection activity.

Cadaveric renal transplants now enjoy a graft survival of about 80% at 1 year, 73% at 3 years, 66% at 5 years and it is expected that the 10-year graft survival figure will be about 50%. Those who lose their graft go back onto dialysis and can receive another transplant. The required dose of immunosuppressive drugs falls off remarkably by about 3 months post-transplant, but the reduced intake then has to be continued indefinitely. The incidence of cancer is considerably increased and vigilance is needed to detect this complication as early as possible.

Those who obtain good function, the majority, enjoy vigorous health and have very few restrictions. Those who receive kidneys from family members have even better results than cadaveric kidney recipients, with a 10-year graft-survival of 75-80%, and more than 90% long-term patient survival.

Those who do best are those whose original disease was confined to the kidneys. Those with renal failure on the basis of DIABETES MELLITUS, for example, still suffer the other complications of that disease, even when the kidney problem has been successfully treated by a transplant.

Heart Transplantation On 3 Dec 1967, the world's attention was focused on the Groote Shure Hospital, Cape Town, by the announcement of the first successful human-to-human cardiac transplantation, though prior animal work in the USA had painstakingly established the technique. Stimulated by this success, nearly 50 centres performed over 100 similar transplantations in 1968 (the number rising to 250 by the end of 1970), but most patients died from rejection or infection. In 1968-69, of 20 such procedures in Canada (Montréal and Toronto), most patients succumbed within 1 year, though each centre had a lone long survivor of over 4 years. No further cardiac transplantations were done in Canada until 1980.

During the 1970s, a group at Stanford in the US continued working out the diagnostic and management strategies and also first introduced cyclosporin to the regimen. Their success led to a renaissance of cardiac transplantation activity around the world. In Apr 1981, the procedure was reintroduced into Canada at University Hospital, London. By Sept 1987, 150 cardiac transplantations had been performed in Canada. Worldwide, there are now more than 120 centres where more than 5000 transplantations have been performed.

Currently, the 1- and 5-year patient survival rates are 80% and 75%, respectively, and most patients are able to return to an active and productive life. Special problems are the high incidence of immunologically induced coronary artery disease in the grafted organ as well as the need for more heart donors and the support of would-be recipients during the waiting period.

Heart-Lung Transplantation Combined heart and lung transplantation was first performed in 1969; 2 more were done by the end of 1971. The longest survivor was 23 days. No further attempts were made until 1981 when the Stanford group, having obtained successful heart/lung survivals in primates, decided that it was time to try it again in humans. The first recipient was a 45-year-old woman who was still alive and well in 1987.

In May 1983, Canada's first combined heart and lung procedure was performed at University Hospital, London. By the end of 1986, over 150 similar procedures had been performed in 15-20 centres in the world. The current survival rate is only 60% at 1 year and 50% at 5. Because of the unique exposure of the lung to the external environment via the airways, infection is a major problem. In addition, the lung is also prone to severe rejections.

Liver Transplantation Liver transplantation has special problems: the organ deteriorates quickly in the donor; the surgeon must match the replacement organ for size; there is need for careful maintenance of the gall bladder and biliary drainage system; there are specially complicated disturbances of the blood clotting – coagulation – which may lead to severe postoperative bleeding; and there is no substitute or artifical back-up system to tide over periods of liver rejection.

It is not surprising that programs for liver replacement have been established more slowly, with only 4 centres doing them in Canada. The largest Canadian series is in London where 120 such transplants have been done, with results comparable to those from Pittsburgh. Since 1980, using cyclosporin, the Pittsburgh group have made such intensive and successful efforts that the procedure has been moved from the "experimental" to that of "established medical treatment." As care for such patients is very expensive, this medical achievement will have considerable repercussions in health-care economics in the next decade.

Pancreas Transplantation Pancreas transplants are undertaken because of their content of insulin-secreting islands of tissue, known as the Islets of Langerhans (see below) but the digestive secretions of the organ have to be drained somewhere and that has proved to be the principal problem. Efforts have been made to drain these secretions into the bladder, the bowel and to the skin. In all but a few centres, results have been disappointing and pancreas transplantation is not widely practised.

Transplantation of the Islets of Langerhans in Diabetes There are 200 000 Islets of Langerhans in an adult pancreas. The problems with transplantation of these islets, to cure diabetes mellitus, are separation of islets from a cadaveric pancreas without exposure to the digestive juices of the main body of pancreatic tissue; preservation of islets; and reduction of their susceptibility to rejection. Several centres in Canada are on the point of clinical trials in this area, having resolved these problems at the animal level.

Transplantation of Specific Tissues

Corneal Grafting Grafting the cornea is a well-established procedure. Immunologic rejection is not a problem for most patients, as the proteins of the cornea usually do not elicit a "foreign antigen" reaction and, in any event, the antibodies and educated lymphocytes have difficulty in mounting an attack in such a bloodless tissue.

Corneas are not in such a short supply as some other organs as they can be removed up to 6 hours after death, and from those who are older than donors of internal vital organs. Immunosuppressive drugs are not required for the uncomplicated corneal transplant.

Skin Grafting Most skin grafting involves the use of the patient's own skin to repair defects. These are known as skin autografts and present no immunological problem. In treatment of extensive and severe burns, skin allografts (obtained from skin banks of cadaveric skin) are used as burn dressings. No immunosuppression is used as it is expected that the allografts will be lost, though they may last for several vital weeks, and can then be replaced if needed. Skin banks are becoming more common and several exist in Canada.

Bone Grafting Bone is used as a graft to bridge gaps in bone resulting from the effects of trauma or cancer surgery. The bone is not used as a living graft and no immunosuppression is used. Rather, the pores of the bone become permeated with bone cells of the recipient, replacing the bone cells of the donor. Thus the recipient uses the graft as a scaffold onto which cells later grow to turn it eventually into autologous bone.

Organ Procurement and Storage

The whole of transplantation medicine depends on public acceptance and understanding. It takes time to accept new concepts of death; there is much need for open discussion. Over 2 decades, however, the Canadian public has accepted the practices of clinical transplantation as shown by willingness to give organs from the bodies of their loved ones, after death. No one appreciates this more than the community of those who wait for these gifts for "restored life." Despite this, there is a marked shortage of vital internal organs for transplantation. This is largely because only 1-2% of those who die in hospitals do so under conditions which render their dead bodies suitable for organ procurement.

Unexpected death is tragic and emotionally shocking. Yet, in this atmosphere of grief, fear, bewilderment and uncertainty, it is necessary to ask the family to give their dead relative's organs for those in need. This can be a searing experience; suffice it here to note that it is easy to understand why only about 10-20% of that 1-2% become organ donors. However, if the figure was raised to 80% of 1-2%, shortage of organs would largely cease to be a problem. For those reasons, organ procurement is becoming an increasing responsibility for hospital administrators and the health-care professions.

Organ storage is a very difficult area of research in which there has not been much progress. The ideal would be long-term preservation of organs in the ultra-low temperatures of liquid nitrogen (around -170°C), but the science of cryobiology is not able to do this for complex highly differentiated organs, except for very small portions. At present, kidneys can be preserved at 4° C for 48-72 hours, but heart, heart-lung and liver transplants must be carried out as soon as possible, within only a few hours after the donor's death.

Ethical Issues in Organ Transplantation

Ethical problems abound in transplantation. They fall into 3 areas: those which surround the diagnosis of death from cerebral causes, those which relate to organ procurement, and those which deal with organ allocation and program funding. In short, when may organs be taken?

Who owns them, after procurement? How should they be equitably distributed? Are there limitations to the rights of donor families? What are the rights of waiting potential recepients? Can we afford these costly programs from which relatively few persons derive benefit?

Decisions on these matters involve members of our society outside those in medicine or health care. Resolutions evolve differently in different communities and cultures. Special problems are encountered when organs are transported between cultures or "moral communities."

The Future of Transplantation Medicine

Speculation on medical advances is fascinating, but unreliable. Nevertheless, contemporary predictions include the following: that organ grafts will be accepted from other species, xenografts; that certain species, probably primates, will be bred for this purpose; that brain tissue will be used for treatment of certain neurological diseases (this, in fact, has already started), though restoration of cerebral cognition by grafting will not be achieved; that organ transplants will vie with gene therapy in treating enzymatic and other genetic disorders, as the control over the immune system will become highly selective and safe; that grafts of ovarian and testicular tissue will be available for treatment of sterility and associated endocrine deficiency, though this raises very serious ethical issues which must be carefully regulated by society. Indeed, ethical regulation of the field will become increasingly important if science and technology are to confer increasing benefit upon us.

JOHN B. DOSSETOR AND DENNIS L. MODRY

Transport Canada is the federal government department responsible for the regulation and administration of transportation policy in Canada. It was established in 1936 as a consolidation of the Department of Railways and Canals, the Department of Marine, and the Civil Aviation Branch of the Department of National Defence. It is now a corporate structure that includes CROWN CORPORATIONS with varying degrees of autonomy and groups responsible for various departmental activities.

The Aviation Group provides and maintains AIR TRAFFIC CONTROL and air navigational services, and carries out licencing and certification of aviation personnel, aircraft and commercial operators. The Airports Authority Group owns 139 land airports and operates 108; there are more than 1200 licenced airports in Canada including land, water and heliports.

The Marine Group is responsible for the CANADIAN COAST GUARD, 4 Crown corporations engaged in marine pilotage work and the Canarctic Shipping Company Ltd, in which the federal government has a majority holding. It also provides operational liaison advice to the minister on the activities of the St Lawrence Seaway Authority and the Canada Ports Corp.

The Surface Group is responsible for motor vehicle safety, railway safety, safe transportation of dangerous goods and the planning of emergency measures. The Policy and Coordination Group carries out policy and funding activities related to rail (passenger and freight), highways, motor carriers and ferries, and looks after air and marine policy matters. AIR CANADA, CANADIAN NATIONAL RAILWAYS, Marine Atlantic and VIA RAIL report to Parliament through the minister of transport. The Canadian Transport Commission, Aircraft Accident Review Board and Canadian Aviation Safety Board are autonomous agencies reporting to Parliament through the minister. The department's budgetary expenditures for 1985-86 amounted to $2.7 billion.

Illustration from a travel book published in 1799, showing stagecoach travel in the early Canadas (*courtesy National Library of Canada/Rare Book Div*).

Transportation Since the earliest days of recorded history, transportation has been important to mankind. Transportation vehicles and transport systems facilitate the movement of people and goods from one place to another. Transportation is of particular importance to Canada because of the country's vast size and because there are great distances between its mines, farms, forests and population centres.

Efficient transport systems are also of particular significance to trading nations such as Canada. This country exports about one-third of all that it produces, and earnings from these exports are exceedingly important to the Canadian ECONOMY. Many of Canada's exports, such as grain, coal, minerals and timber, must compete with similar products from other exporting nations. Since some of these competitors are much closer to major export markets in Japan, Europe and Asia, Canada's transport system must be efficient. Managers of Canada's transport systems seek to make them more efficient through improvements in transport technology and organization. In recent years larger, faster and more efficient transport vehicles have improved transport productivity. In future years, transport productivity may be increased by making better use of computers, by communications systems which provide more timely information, and by various devices, such as radar, which can improve transport technology.

History of Transportation Canada's history is a history of transportation and its development. In the early days, European settlers ventured only into those areas that were accessible by water and boats, and canoes were the primary mode of transportation. The first settlers made use of the nation's lakes and rivers; later they constructed CANALS. After the steam engine was invented, railways were built. Settlement in much of Canada followed the construction of railway lines. As ROADS AND HIGHWAYS were built and cars and trucks became available, regions of Canada that

Hudson's Bay Co ox train at Fort Smith, NWT, in 1875 (*courtesy Provincial Archives of Alberta/E. Brown Coll*).

had not been served by railways were developed. Today, transport by air makes it possible for Canadians to live, work and vacation in any area of the nation, regardless of how remote it may be (*see* TRANSPORTATION IN THE NORTH).

Railways have always played an important role in Canada. They were built to open new areas to settlement, to make profits for the railway builders, and for defence and political reasons. Canadians have an enormous investment in their railways. A century ago Canadian taxpayers helped finance railway construction, and since that time they have paid taxes to support passenger trains and uneconomic branch lines. When privately owned railways faced bankruptcy and were taken over by the government, their debts were assumed by the taxpayers. Since that time citizens' groups, politicians and local communities have been concerned with the costs of the nation's railways and the services they provide. Each time a railway has sought to abandon an uneconomic branch line, local groups have protested. When VIA RAIL CANADA reduced passenger services on which it was losing money, many people protested. The most contentious issue of all was the CROW'S NEST PASS AGREEMENT grain rates. For years the railways contended that these statutory rates were so low that they caused enormous losses, but it was not until 1983, after much bitter debate, that the rates were changed.

The first railway line in Canada was built in 1836, some 10 years after England built its first steam railway line. In the 1850s railway construction began in earnest with the GRAND TRUNK RAILWAY from Sarnia through Toronto and Montréal to Portland, Maine. In 1854 the GREAT WESTERN RAILWAY built a line between the Niagara and the Detroit rivers via Hamilton. It connected with US railways in New York and Michigan. Much of this early railway construction resulted from a speculative boom in which some promoters sought to make quick profits. As a result many railways were poorly planned and constructed. Much early construction was financed by British capitalists, Canadian merchants and landowners, and by municipalities. Some construction was financed by bonds. The INTERCOLONIAL RAILWAY was the largest system of all. Completed in the 1870s, it was built for national defence and unity, in fulfilment of the terms of CONFEDERATION, and was never expected to make a profit. Many of Canada's rail lines had financial problems. When it appeared that a number of them might collapse, they were amalgamated into the CANADIAN NATIONAL RAILWAYS system and taken over by the federal government after WWI. Many financial problems were thus inherited by that government-owned corporation.

The railways have been responsible, in part, for some of the provinces joining the Canadian confederation. It was not until the central government agreed to build a railway to the Pacific Ocean that BC agreed to join, an agreement that led eventually to construction of the western sections of the CANADIAN PACIFIC RAILWAY. Transportation also played an essential role in the history of PEI, which was at first unenthusiastic about Confederation; the severe financial problems of its railway played a large part in the decision to join Canada in 1873. Part of the confederation arrangement provided that the federal government would assume the railway's enormous debt. Newfoundland, the last of the provinces to join Canada, also received guarantees from the central government that it would be provided with various transport services.

Contemporary Transportation Canada has an excellent system of transportation, with each mode serving particular needs. But the system has interrelated parts, some of which serve certain areas of the country or a particular segment of the economy. As a service industry, the quality of transportation depends in large measure on the calibre of its employees and management. Since about half of every revenue dollar received by a transportation company is used for employee salaries, wages and benefits, transportation is labour intensive. Transportation provides more jobs for Canadians than any other activity. It uses more energy than any other industry, and is one of the largest purchasers of cement, steel, aluminum and other commodities. It enables Canadians to enjoy an enormous variety of world products and to sell great quantities of grain, coal, lumber, automotive products and other goods to customers on every continent.

In most areas of transportation there is competition and in some areas that competition is intense. Large shippers often have several transport alternatives available to them: rail, water or truck. Air transportation is available to most Canadians, and the shippers of petroleum, chemicals and other products in liquid or gaseous form may sometimes ship by pipeline. Passengers usually have available several transport alternatives. Because of competition between modes and companies, there is a continuing need for research to improve transport technology.

There are 5 modes of transportation: water, rail, motor carrier, air and pipeline. In Canada water transportation is generally used for the movement of bulk commodities of relatively low value per tonne, such as coal, ore, grain, gravel and salt. Rail transportation is used principally for the movement of such bulk commodities as grain, coal, ore, lumber and chemicals, for the movement of containers, and for other types of merchandise freight. Trucks are used in a variety of ways. Small trucks are used as delivery vehicles in cities and towns. In the North, trucks transport logs, petroleum, consumer goods and a great variety of industrial products. Air transportation is used to move both large and small items when speed is important. PIPELINES are used for the transportation of petroleum, petroleum products, gas and certain chemicals.

Water Transportation may be separated into 3 general categories: ocean transportation, inland water transportation and coastal transportation. Ocean transportation is important to Canada, because about one-third of all that Canada produces is exported. Much of this export traffic moves by ship to customers overseas, carried by large, oceangoing vessels which serve Canada's major ports. About one-third of all of the exports which go by sea move through Vancouver, the largest port (in tonnage) on the west coast of the Americas. Substantial export tonnages also move through the ports of Churchill, Montréal, Québec City, Halifax and Saint John.

The GREAT LAKES and the St Lawrence R system provide inland water transportation to the heartland of Canada. Great quantities of grain, coal, iron ore and other commodities are moved by vessels called lakers (*see* LAKE CARRIERS). About half of these commodities are moved by US carriers, and about half by Canadian companies. Most of the Canadian operators are represented by the Dominion Marine Assn. In recent years, more tonnes have been moved by vessels operating on the Great Lakes than have been moved by either of Canada's transcontinental railways. Much of Canada's iron ore moves via the Great Lakes-ST LAWRENCE SEAWAY system to steel mills in the US. On the return journey, many of these vessels carry coal from US mines.

Coastal water transportation is also important. Great quantities of logs, wood chips, lumber, chemicals and other bulk commodities are moved by barge in BC's coastal waters. Sometimes logs are gathered together to form a log boom, then pulled by tug from northern coastal areas to Vancouver for processing into lumber, plywood, wood pulp and paper. Other logs are moved by large self-loading barges that are able to dump themselves when they reach their destination. Barge movements on Canada's East Coast are on a much smaller scale, but are nonetheless significant. Canada's barge operators have been responsible for many improvements in barge technology. Barge transportation is slow but relatively cheap (*see* PORTS AND HARBOURS; SHIPPING INDUSTRY).

Rail Transportation Canada has 2 major railways and several smaller ones. The major railways are approximately equal in size. In 1986 the CPR operated some 34 000 km of railway, utilizing about 1200 LOCOMOTIVES. Its 1986 revenues were about $2.5 billion and it is owned by stockholders. The CNR is a federal crown corporation. The railway operates under legislation passed by Parliament which relates specifically to the CNR, and it reports to the government through the minister of transport. In 1986 the CNR operated some 51 000 km of track, using over 2000 locomotives. The BRITISH COLUMBIA RAILWAY, third largest, is owned by the BC government. In 1986 it had revenues of $313 million. Approximately 60% of the revenues of the BCR came from forest products. The BCR operates over 2300 km, largely in mountainous terrain, using 101 locomotives.

Each year Canada's railways move millions of tonnes of bulk commodities, such as coal, potash, grain and sulphur. Much coal is moved by "unit trains." These trains often consist of 100 cars or more, which can carry as much as 100 tonnes each. Railways are able to transport large quantities of bulk materials over long distances and at relatively low cost, thus enabling the products of Canada's mines, fields and forests to compete effectively in world markets.

For many years passenger trains represented an important part of the railway business. In major cities the railway station was a hub of activity. Today, railway passenger trains face intense competition from other forms of transport. The resultant loss of patronage, coupled with rising costs, has caused them to lose millions of dollars each year. For a time direct subsidies were given to the railways to compensate them for part of these losses. The government then decided to handle the matter in a different way and created a new CROWN CORPORATION, VIA Rail Canada, which is now responsible for most of the passenger train operations. It contracts with the 2 major railways for the operation and maintenance of trains. Although it has tried to make passenger trains more attractive and to increase their patronage, VIA Rail Canada's losses amounted to about $500 million in 1986. In order to reduce those losses, VIA discontinued service on several unprofitable lines.

Motor Carrier Transportation Possibly the greatest virtue of motor carrier transportation is its flexibility. Trucks do not require an airport, a waterway or a track on which to operate. They can move wherever there is a highway, a road, a street — or even a relatively flat, hard surface. They are flexible also in size. Giant trucks may move logs, coal, construction machinery or other bulky items. Tiny delivery vehicles are available that are highly fuel efficient and can maneuver in crowded city areas. In the North, enormous off-road vehicles transport tremendous tonnages of coal, logs and minerals for short distances. Throughout Canada trucks transport fruit, vegetables and manufactured products over long distances. Within our cities trucks transport mail, parcels and thousands of other items. Virtually everything that we eat or wear has made at least some of its journey to us by truck (*see* TRUCKING INDUSTRY). A number of large companies operate trucks. Both of Canada's major railways have trucking divisions. There are several other large trucking companies, owned by a single individual or family, or by a group of stockholders. There are thousands of small truck operations, some consisting of a single truck driven by its owner.

Air Transportation Canada has 2 major transcontinental airlines, several carriers, one large charter operator, and some 600 smaller operators, including specialized air services and HELICOPTER operators. Most communities have some type of air transportation service available, whether by floatplane, helicopter or conventional aircraft. For long-distance travel, far more Canadians use air transportation than train or bus (*see* AIRPORTS and AVIATION).

Canada's largest airline, AIR CANADA, is a crown corporation. In 1987 Air Canada had an operational fleet of 108 planes and had about 22 200 employees. Air Canada's overseas routes extend to Europe and the Caribbean. Within Canada the airline serves every major population centre, every provincial capital and many smaller communities. Canadian Airlines International was formed in 1987, a merger of Pacific Western Airlines and CP Air. It operates international routes to Europe, Asia, Australia and S America, in addition to serving all of the major cities and many smaller communities in Canada. It also serves Los Angeles, San Francisco and Honolulu. In 1987 Canadian Airlines International operated 84 planes and had some 2725 employees. Other Canadian airlines include QUEBECAIR, Eastern Provincial Airways, Nordair, all owned by, or affiliated with, one of the 2 major carriers. WARDAIR was an all-charter operator until 1986 when it was granted permission to schedule regular domestic and international flights. Okanagan Helicopters, one of the world's largest helicopter companies, operated about 126 helicopters in 1987. Smaller operators served many small, remote communities, providing them with milk, fresh fruits and vegetables, and also carrying mail.

STOL airport, Ottawa. The development of short-take-off-and-landing technology has been an important contribution to Canadian transportation (*photo by Roland Weber/Masterfile*).

View of Québec in the early 19th century by Lt-Col Benjamin Beaufoy showing various means of transportation (*courtesy National Archives of Canada/C-41388*).

Pipeline Transportation Pipelines, the unseen carrier, transport enormous quantities of petroleum, gasoline, chemicals and other products – sometimes for long distances. As pipeline transportation requires little labour and is relatively trouble free, it is able to provide reliable, low-cost transportation. However, pipeline transportation has 2 principal drawbacks: pipelines require an enormous amount of capital, and they are seldom efficient unless large quantities are moved from a single point of origin to a single destination over a long period of time. Pipelines have also been used for the transportation of coal (in slurry form) in the US and elsewhere, but their potential as transporters of coal and other bulk commodities has not yet been fully exploited in Canada.

Intermodal Transportation Except for items moved by truck, virtually all other movements utilize 2 or more transport modes. "Piggyback" transportation is an example. Goods may be loaded into trucks or trailers and hauled to some point on a railway where the truck or trailer is loaded on a railroad flatcar. The goods then move by rail, sometimes over a relatively long distance. At the end of their rail journey, the trailers or containers are again moved by truck to their final destination. There are other ways in which the various transport modes can co-operate to provide more efficient intermodal transportation. Trucks can be carried on ferries or ships. This is sometimes called "fishyback" transportation or Ro/Ro (roll on/roll off) transportation. In recent years, Canada Steamship Lines has experimented with the transfer of coal directly from self-unloading bulk carriers to oceangoing ships without the use of a port or other terminal facilities.

Canada's "land bridge" is also based on intermodal operations. Shipments from Japan and Hong Kong destined for Europe can move by ship via the Panama Canal. Or, by using Canada as a land bridge, they can move by water to Vancouver or other western ports, then by rail to one of Canada's eastern ports, and again by water to their European destinations, saving a significant amount of time.

Types of Carriers In legal terms there are 3 types of carriers: common carriers, contract carriers and private carriers. A common carrier transports the goods of any shipper wishing to make use of its services. Most shippers in Canada have available the services of some common carrier, and sometimes many of them.

A contract carrier makes agreements with one or more shippers to haul goods, sometimes over specific routes, and usually for a given period of time. The possible variations in such contractual arrangements are limited only by the needs of the respective parties and their ingenuity in drawing up a contract. Many large shippers in Canada use contract carriers.

A private carrier is one that transports its own goods. Many farmers transport their own grain and other products to a local elevator or to market. Logging companies ordinarily transport their own logs, at least for a short distance. Many manufacturing companies transport some of their raw materials and semifinished products. Many retail stores, including the large grocery chains, have private carrier operations. The large forest-products companies and steel, oil and chemical companies often have private carrier operations. Some operate their own trucks, barges and ships as private carriers, and they may also operate their own railway.

General Carriers and Specialized Carriers A carrier's rate schedule gives the prices charged for hauling various types of freight between various points, and its tariff describes in detail the services which the carrier undertakes to provide and the extent of its liability. For instance, the tariff may stipulate that the carrier will deliver shipments but that the consignee must unload them. It may state that the carrier is not responsible for damage to perishable commodities, for delays in shipment, or for any damage resulting from strikes, floods or so-called "acts of God." The tariff of a general freight carrier may state that it carries all types of package freight up to a given maximum size and weight, but that it does not carry liquids, explosives or live animals. Specialized carriers provide service to particular types of shippers, or for particular types of shipments. Some specialized carriers haul only bulk petroleum. Others carry only shipments of pharmaceuticals from wholesalers or retail drugstores. Some carry only live animals; others handle only refrigerated cargo. In recent years there has been a substantial growth in the number and variety of specialized carriers. For instance, some carriers specialize in carrying money, cheques, bonds and other high-value items for banks and other financial institutions. Others carry small parcels between Canada and the US and between communities in Ontario, and various other Canadian cities. Such carriers as UPS-Canada, Loomis and Purolator provide next-day delivery between much of the US and many large Canadian cities. There are hundreds of messenger and courier services in Canada, and their number appears to be growing.

Facilitators, Consolidators and Expeditors There are many organizations that provide services that are ancillary to transportation. Some deal with customs formalities and other paperwork. Some select carriers and monitor shipments, relieving industrial firms of much paperwork and detail. Some expedite shipments or take advantage of volume rates.

Many facilitators and expeditors are called freight forwarders. Domestic freight forwarders normally have trucks which pick up shipments from their customers and consolidate them with the shipments of other customers into full loads (either truck or rail). Once the full carloads reach their destination, the freight forwarder then "breaks bulk," ie, unloads the car and delivers the various shipments to the respective consignees. A foreign freight forwarder arranges for ocean shipping and for inland transportation at the foreign destination. He may also arrange for insurance, and may handle customs formalities. Sometimes the work of a freight forwarder is performed by a shippers' co-operative. Canada has several shippers' co-operatives. Canada's leading department stores operate their own freight-forwarding organization. This enables them to pool their shipments and use the lower freight rates given to volume shippers.

Transport Infrastructure Every mode of transportation has 2 essential parts: the transport vehicle itself and the road, track or way on which it operates. When 2 modes of transportation are co-ordinated, there may be a junction or terminal at which the transfer is made. Some of the transport infrastructure is natural, but much of it is manmade. A canoe, for instance, may operate quite well on a natural lake or stream, but a large, oceangoing vessel needs some man-made facilities if it is to operate well, as does a train, a plane or a truck.

Most of the man-made infrastructure for water transportation in Canada has been provided by the federal government. Hundreds of millions of dollars have been spent for ports, docks and other devices designed to facilitate water transportation. The St Lawrence Seaway system was paid for by both Canadian and US taxpayers. The rail infrastructure consists of the bridges, tunnels, tracks, roadbed and other structures necessary for the operation of a railway. Although much of the early railway infrastructure was financed by the federal government through direct grants, the gift of land and other means, in more recent years infrastructure has been financed by the transcontinental railways themselves through retained earnings.

Virtually all of the infrastructure for aviation has been financed by the federal goverment. The federal Dept of Transport (now called TRANSPORT CANADA) has built most of Canada's airports, as well as the airways and the radio and navigation systems. Most of these facilities are maintained and operated by Transport Canada.

Roads, highways and streets are the infrastructure for motor carrier transportation. Most of Canada's roads and highways have been built by provincial governments – the major exceptions being highways in national parks and INDIAN RESERVES, the ALASKA HIGHWAY and the TRANS-CANADA HIGHWAY. Most streets have been built by cities and have been financed in a variety of ways.

In recent years the federal goverment has announced a "user pay" philosophy (those using the transport infrastructure should bear the cost of such facilities). Users of airports, seaway locks and port facilities, for instance, pay landing fees, lockage fees and port duties to compensate in part for the taxpayers' investment.

Passenger Transportation includes many modes of travel, including planes, trains, boats and BUSES. Millions travel by AUTOMOBILE, taxi or limousine, others by bicycle, horse or dogsled. The automobile accounts for the greatest percentage of passenger travel in Canada today.

Urban Transportation Most of Canada's urban areas have some form of public transportation. Both Montréal and Toronto are served by com-

Where stagecoach, train and steamship meet: Canadian Pacific station, Vancouver, BC, *c*1890-1900 (*courtesy National Archives of Canada/C-85046*).

muter railway systems. Some cities have subways; others are served by buses, streetcars, electric trolley cars, or a mixture of vehicle types. Some URBAN TRANSPORTATION systems are operated by the cities themselves, some by regional districts and some by special transit authorities. Cities can minimize the downtown congestion caused by automobile traffic by providing comfortable, convenient and relatively inexpensive urban transportation. Some cities provide special transport services for handicapped persons, and others utilize "dial-a-bus" services for that purpose. Under this system a patron may telephone to have a bus stop for a pickup; the route the bus follows on any particular trip will depend on the locations of the persons who have telephoned.

Most Canadian cities have taxi service. In some cities a licence is required to operate a taxi, and a limited number of licences are issued. Some taxi companies enjoy a monopoly. One or more companies may be given the exclusive right to pick up passengers at airports, RAILWAY STATIONS or other areas where passengers originate.

Ferry Transportation The largest ferry system in Canada is operated by the BC Ferry Corp, providing service between the Vancouver area and the cities of Victoria and Nanaimo on Vancouver I. The BC Ferry Corp also provides service to many of the GULF IS and to some remote, northern communities. Other ferry service in BC is provided by the provincial Highways Dept. There are FERRIES on Canada's East Coast and on some of its lakes and inland waterways. Ferry service is provided from NB to PEI. CN Marine operates ferry services between Newfoundland and the Canadian mainland and between NS and Portland, Maine.

Some ferries carry passengers only; others carry passengers, trucks and automobiles. Some ferries carry only railcars; others sometimes carry dangerous commodities (such as dynamite). Most ferries operate at a loss, and a subsidy is often paid by federal or provincial taxpayers. Some ferries make no charge for transporting cars and passengers and are fully subsidized.

Other Transport Devices Many other devices are used for transportation. Bicycles are used for personal transportation and for the movement of letters and some small parcels. Dogsleds, motorized sleds and SNOWMOBILES are used in northern areas in the winter. Wheelchairs (motorized or human powered) are used to transport many handicapped persons. Moving sidewalks and "endless belts" transport persons in airport terminal buildings, shopping centres and elsewhere. Ski lifts and similar devices transport people in mountainous areas, and particularly in scenic areas or ski resorts. Elevators provide vertical transportation, literally moving hundreds of millions of passengers and millions of tonnes of freight each year. Horse-drawn vehicles are still used for transportation in some areas, although their numbers have decreased in the last century.

Technological Change New inventions, technological change and human ingenuity have resulted in many changes in Canada's transport. Most changes have meant greater speed, lower cost or increased productivity. Some have made possible the development of entirely new industries.

Recent advances in water transportation have resulted in greatly increased productivity. Some improvements have come through the development of larger ships. Today a large oceangoing vessel can haul 2 or 3 times more oil, coal or other commodity than a vessel could carry a decade ago. As large ships seldom require more crew members than smaller ships, crew productivity has increased, and shipping costs have been reduced. There have been advances in navigation, ship design and ship propulsion. Research has been done on the use in ships of powdered coal

and other petroleum extenders and substitutes for fueling ships. Still other increases in productivity have resulted from the use of containers. Today, enormous cranes at a modern port may load a large oceangoing liner with containerized freight in half a day. It would have taken 3 or 4 days to load that freight before the shift from manual loading of freight to the mechanical loading of containers. Much of the savings stems from ships spending less time in port. This makes it possible for them to move more cargo each year, since they can spend a greater portion of their time at sea.

Railway productivity has also increased in recent years through the use of more efficient railway cars, some of which were specially designed to carry a particular product (such as grain or coal). Other increases in productivity have come from the use of longer trains, robot locomotives and better train scheduling. Robot locomotives, placed near the middle of trains, make it possible to use longer trains. The train engineer can effectively handle 5 or 6 diesel locomotives and control a train more than a kilometre long, even in mountainous areas. Better communications and electronic signals systems make it possible to operate far more trains over a track than was possible with more primitive manual signals. Less space is required between trains, and especially between trains going in opposite directions on a single railway track. With a modern control system the railway dispatcher can determine the location and speed of every train quickly and electronically. He is able to plan train movements carefully and to shunt approaching trains onto railway sidings so that other trains may pass. This makes it possible for more trains to use the track and thus increases railway productivity. Other improvements have come from more efficient use of railway cars, locomotives and other expensive equipment. Much research has focused on the linear induction motor which is highly efficient and enables trains to accelerate and decelerate more rapidly. It was used in the demonstration train in Vancouver at Expo 86. These motors will be used in the LRC (light, rapid and convenient) trains being developed by the Urban Transport Development Corporation for urban transit. In some cities the cost of urban transit has been reduced by the introduction of articulated buses (2 passenger units pulled by a single engine). Such buses have been used in European cities for some time.

Aviation technology has changed radically in recent decades. Today's planes are much larger than the planes they replaced. Modern jets are twice as fast as propeller-driven planes, and engines are quieter and more fuel efficient. Aviation technology is changing in other areas too. Modern conveyor belts handle passengers' baggage faster and more efficiently. Photoelectric cells and other devices "read" baggage labels, and robots direct baggage and freight to specific bins and carts so that they can be quickly loaded on aircraft. Better radar and other electronic devices have been developed to enable planes to operate in bad weather with a high degree of reliability. These advances make for more efficient use of aircraft and personnel and promise lower operating costs. Aviation technology is also changing on the ground. Airlines are experimenting with better systems for reservations and ticketing. One day Canadians may be able to order their tickets by telephone and have them issued by their own personal computer and charged to their credit card, all of this being done electronically and within minutes.

There have been significant increases in productivity in the motor carrier industry. Some increases have resulted from the use of trucks and

trailers which are longer, wider and higher. Other productivity increases have come from utilizing more of the available space and in scheduling vehicles more efficiently. Some provinces permit a truck (or tractor) to pull more than one trailer. As a truck requires little more fuel to pull 2 trailers than one (and only one driver is required), trucks which pull 2 trailers can be more efficient. Motor carrier productivity has also increased because of the development of more fuel-efficient engines and because of experimentation with the use of lower grade fuel.

In pipeline transportation, productivity increases have come through the use of larger pipes and faster speeds. This has been made possible because of technological improvements in valves, compressors and friction-reducing agents.

As much of transportation is labour intensive, increases in productivity in the next decade will depend to a large degree on the effective utilization of personnel. While there have been enormous increases in transport productivity in recent years because of improvements in vehicle technology, fewer such increases can be expected in the next decade. Take for instance the productivity increases in aviation. In the 1940s when the airlines flew the DC-3, one plane could produce about 5200 passenger/kms per hour. In the 1980s one Boeing 747 could produce about 300 000 passenger/kms per hour – an increase of some 5700%. Unless the airlines use supersonic planes, they cannot increase their speed. At the present time Canadian markets cannot efficiently utilize even larger planes, so there is little prospect for improved productivity from the new planes themselves.

Interrelationship with Communications The transportation and communications industries have always been related. When good COMMUNICATIONS are established with another country, trade will often follow. Certainly, there cannot be much trade without good communications. Some system has to be available for the transmission of orders and the movement of shipping documents and other shipping details. In these areas transportation and communication are complementary. In other areas they may compete. A salesman may fly or drive to meet with a customer; on the other hand, he may simply call the customer by telephone. Thousands of dollars in cash may be shipped by armoured car; or a banking transfer may be made by telex. Valuable documents may be sent by air courier, or a facsimile may be transmitted via SATELLITE.

As transport costs increase and better communications systems are developed, transportation and communications will compete increasingly in certain areas (*see* COMPUTER COMMUNICATIONS; TELECOMMUNICATIONS). Should COMMUNICATIONS TECHNOLOGY develop in ways that some experts envisage, much that the postal service handles at present could be transmitted electronically, perhaps using satellites for transmission and cathode ray tubes (TV screens) or home teletype printers for reception. The handwritten letter could become obsolete.

Transportation and Travel About 80% of all air travel is for business reasons, although each year more Canadians travel for pleasure. The availability of comfortable, convenient and relatively low-cost transportation (by air, train and bus or automobile) has encouraged the development of the travel industry – one of the fastest-growing segments of the Canadian economy (*see* TOURISM). Much of this growth results from cooperative arrangements between transportation companies, travel agents and the operators of hotels, car rental agencies and other such facilities. Tour packages that include hotels, meals, guides and other items are frequently arranged by a tour operator (sometimes called a wholesaler) and marketed by travel agents. A number of these operators are subsidiaries of airlines.

Government Role in Transportation Since the first Europeans set foot in N America, governments have played some role in transportation. That role has taken several forms: promotion, regulation, subsidization and operation. The government began the promotion of transportation more than a century ago when it encouraged the construction of railways. It promoted railway development through loans, grants and guarantees. After the railways were built, they had enormous power over users of their services. Governments then began to regulate the rates charged by the railways to ensure the fair treatment of all shippers and a fair return to the transportation companies (*see* TRANSPORTATION REGULATION).

Governments have subsidized every form of transportation in Canada at one time or another. Transportation subsidies may be divided into 2 general categories: direct subsidies and indirect subsidies. As mentioned, enormous construction subsidies were given to the railways. Substantial operating subsidies have been given to VIA Rail Canada and to other carriers. Most urban transportation systems are subsidized. Governments have also given indirect subsidies of many kinds. Sometimes a government has permitted the use of government-constructed facilities at less than the cost of providing these facilities, thus providing an indirect subsidy to the users of the facilities. For many years the railways have carried export grain at far less than it cost them to haul it. Additional indirect subsidies result when a government agency provides transport infrastructures (such as an airport, a highway or port facilities) and does not charge sufficient user fees (*see* TRANSPORTATION AGENCIES).

Governments also operate transportation companies, usually in the form of crown corporations. Today the federal government owns railways, airlines, steamship companies and ferries, and has a financial interest in pipeline operations. Provincial governments have had interests in airlines, trucking companies, ferries, bus companies and railways. Sometimes these operations compete with stockholder-owned companies.

In Canada the federal government has generally assumed responsibility for water transportation. Through Transport Canada and Ports Canada Corp (formerly the National Harbours Board) the federal government builds, maintains and operates ports. Through the St Lawrence Seaway Authority (in co-operation with the US) it promotes, maintains and operates the St Lawrence Seaway. During WWII the government operated a large fleet of oceangoing vessels, but these were disposed of during the late 1940s.

The federal government, through Transport Canada, regulates and promotes air transportation, and builds, maintains and operates all of Canada's major airports, and most smaller airports too. In 1984 a new air transport policy was announced which de facto deregulated civil aviation; in 1985 the federal government announced far-reaching changes in the "Freedom to Move" paper, and in 1987 legislation was passed completing the program of transport deregulation and replacing the Canadian Transport Commission with the National Transportation Agency. Roads and highways generally fall within the purview of provincial governments. Large provincial departments build and maintain most of the other roads and highways. The provinces regulate truck and bus operations, and they regulate motor vehicle safety.

Transportation Research Because of the importance of transportation to Canada, transportation research is uncommonly important. The federal government sponsors transportation research in several ways. The SCIENCE COUNCIL encourages research dealing with transportation devices and engineering. Transport Canada encourages research dealing with the management of transportation enterprises and the ways in which their operation can be made more efficient. Many of the major transport companies have research departments. Some of these work with vehicle and equipment manufacturers in the development and adaptation of new technology; some engage in market research, and some make contributions to more basic research. But since much of this research is of a proprietary nature, there are no good statistics concerning its extent.

Employment Opportunities Since transportation is vital to so many sectors of the economy, it provides many good job opportunities. These vary from entry-level jobs such as a clerk, a truck driver or a maintenance apprentice to high-level jobs as the manager of an airport, a steamship company or a transportation conglomerate. Some transportation jobs require personnel who are interested in accounting, finance or marketing; others require personnel skilled in labour relations, production management or computer systems. As transportation technology changes and as greater demands are made on Canada's transport systems, job opportunities will increase, particularly for trained, hardworking and innovative personnel. KARL M. RUPPENTHAL

Reading: N.C. Bonsor, *Transportation Economics; Theory and Canadian Policy* (1984); H.L. Purdy, *Transport Competition and Public Policy in Canada* (1975); Karl M. Ruppenthal, *Canada's Ports and Waterborne Trade* (1983).

Transportation, Royal Commission on

(MacPherson Commission), appointed by the federal government (1959) to investigate transportation policy, particularly freight-rate inequities. In their 3-volume report (1961) the commissioners, under chairman M. MacPherson, recommended that railways be allowed more freedom to eliminate uneconomic passenger service and branch lines and that they receive extra subsidies for grain-handling responsibilities imposed by Parliament. A new National Transportation Act was consequently passed. Its principles, eg, the value of competition between different forms of transportation, the need to reduce regulatory control (which led to the establishment of the CANADIAN TRANSPORT COMMISSION as the one overseeing agency), and payment of reasonable charges by transportation operators for facilities provided by government, reflected the commission's influence. JOHN R. BALDWIN

Transportation Agencies The 2 major categories of government activities in transportation are administration and development of public policies, which includes the regulation of transport activities and the investment and operation of transport services and facilities. These responsibilities are allocated directly to the Department of Transport as well as to specialized government agencies and autonomous bodies.

Federal Agencies The Department of Transport (TRANSPORT CANADA) was created (1936) by amalgamation of the Department of Railways and Canals, the Department of Marine and the Civil Aviation Branch of the Department of National Defence. The department advises the federal government on transportation policy and provides and operates specific elements of the national transportation system. Furthermore, the department has technical and safety regulation functions. In addition the minister of transport has responsibility for the following crown corporations, which may enjoy different degrees of corporate autonomy: AIR CANADA, CANADIAN NATIONAL RAILWAYS, VIA RAIL, ST LAWRENCE SEAWAY AUTHORITY, 4

Pilotage Authorities and the Ports Canada Corporation (est 1983 to replace the National Harbours Board).

The twin roles of the department – development and administration of transport policies and the administration of facilities and operational programs – are reflected in the departmental structure, even if the department had been reorganized a number of times during the last few decades (the changes in names of major administrative elements are given in brackets). The policy advice and policy administration functions are now assigned to the Policy and Coordination Group (previously ADM Policy; Ministry Executive, Planning, Programming and Major Projects; Strategic Planning); aviation programs are entrusted to Aviation Group and Airports Authority Group (previously to ADM Air; Air Administration); marine transport programs, including Canadian Coast Guard and ports, are a responsibility of the Marine Group (previously ADM Marine; Marine Administration), the Surface Transport Group (previously Surface Administration) is in charge of motor vehicle and railways safety, transportation of DANGEROUS GOODS and emergency planning programs. The scale of departmental operations is indicated by the following figures: the Airports Authority Group owns 139 airports; the air traffic control system includes 61 control towers, 8 terminal control units, 7 area control centres and over 100 flight service centres; Ports Canada is responsible for the direct supervision of 15 major harbours while 9 other major harbours are operated semi-autonomously by Harbour Commissions under the supervision of Transport Canada and more than 300 public harbours are administered by the Canadian Coast Guard; the marine operations utilize 22 ICEBREAKERS with 18 icebreakers employed by the Canadian Coast Guard, which also operate 55 dedicated search-and-rescue vessels. The departmental budget in 1985-86 included $1.8 billion of operating expenses, $2.6 billion of capital expenditures and $0.8 billion of subsidies and deficit payments to the crown corporations.

Provincial Agencies With the exception of BC and Ontario, which have operated provincial railways, provincial involvement in transportation was initially restricted to the construction and maintenance of highways and highway-traffic regulation. Subsequently the range of provincial interests and activities has expanded and the highway departments have been reorganized as transport departments or ministries (often with added responsibilities for communications). At present, provincial transport departments have both the policy administration and co-ordination role as well as direct-investment, operating and regulatory functions. They are also involved in the planning and financing of urban transport. Economic regulations of transport activities under provincial jurisdiction (road transport) are administered by quasi-judicial regulatory commissions or boards. The comprehensiveness of regulations varies greatly between the provinces.

Special intergovernmental committees have been created that operate both at the ministerial and the official (ie, civil-service) levels to deal with provincial and federal transport policies and activities. They perform consultative and information-exchange roles. In general, such committees are organized regionally, and at present no national structure exists. K. STUDNICKI-GIZBERT

Transportation in the North

If Canada as a whole represents the triumph of TRANSPORTATION over geography, the same is doubly true of the Canadian NORTH. Organized settlement in the North depends to an extraordinary degree on the development of transportation systems.

Water transport was the first means of penetrating the North. Explorers came from the E, by sea, fur traders from the S, via the MACKENZIE R, and, much later, whalers from the W, around Alaska. The first organized transport in the North was connected with the FUR TRADE, either in HUDSON'S BAY COMPANY ships in the eastern Arctic or in canoes and other small craft in the West (see CANOE, BIRCHBARK). The line of settlement was so far to the S that road transport was prohibitively expensive and, while it was occasionally proposed to link the North with the S by railway, the schemes for doing so verged on the fatuous. Population and economic development N of the 60th parallel did not justify the expense, and so the North continued to be served by water, which meant that for between 7 and 9 months of the year transportation was blocked by ice. Along the Mackenzie, virtually continual water transport was possible from the railhead at Waterways (now FT MCMURRAY, Alta), in northern Alberta, all the way to the Arctic Ocean. There was one major portage, on the Slave R near Ft Smith, and shipments depended to a high degree on water levels in the southerly parts of the system. The HBC dominated the traffic, and maintained a small fleet of steamships to carry it.

Transportation was revolutionized by the appearance of the airplane. Bush pilots, often airforce veterans from WWI, could take their small craft where no boat could go (see BUSH FLYING). Better still, an airplane was virtually an all-season craft. The North's winter isolation was finally broken. Using airplanes, prospectors could work more efficiently. A PROSPECTING boom was followed by mining development, particularly at YELLOWKNIFE and at GREAT BEAR LK. Mining development raised traffic volume along the Mackenzie, and created a demand for competition to lower the rates charged by the HBC. Several companies arose, of which the most enduring was Northern Transportation Co Ltd, which became a subsidiary of Eldorado Gold Mines Ltd (now Eldorado Nuclear Ltd), a uranium- and radium-producing company. Meanwhile the bush pilots' operations were being amalgamated into larger entities, particularly Canadian Pacific Airlines, a CPR subsidiary.

WWII brought further changes. The ALASKA HIGHWAY was built from northern BC through the southern Yukon, opening the North to road traffic for the first time, as well as demonstrating that an all-weather road was possible. The US army developed airfields and an oil PIPELINE in the Mackenzie Valley, again augmenting traffic volumes in that area. Wartime saw the appearance of new and bigger airplanes, especially the DC-3 and DC-4, making air cargo something more than a luxury for the first time. Just after the war, the HBC abandoned its riverboat business, leaving the field to Northern Transportation Co Ltd, which by then had become a federal crown corporation. Northern Transportation greatly expanded its operations, particularly after the construction of the DEW Line in the mid-1950s. It operated as a common carrier down the Mackenzie and into the Arctic Ocean – W to Alaska and E to the Arctic Archipelago. In 1975 NTCL set up a branch at Churchill, Man, to service the Keewatin coastal settlements on the western side of Hudson Bay. In 1985 NTCL was sold to an Inuit corporation and thus ceased to be a crown corporation.

Airports were improved to handle the larger aircraft of the postwar period. The WHITE PASS AND YUKON RAILWAY had been built between Whitehorse and Skagway, Alaska, at the turn of the century; in 1960 another was completed linking Alberta with Great Slave Lk. A regular highway was built linking Yellowknife with northern Alberta. The DEMPSTER HWY, from Dawson to Inuvik, is Canada's northernmost highway. Ice roads, connecting such places as Great Bear Lk with Yellowknife, could also be established and kept open during the long winter. Air service increased, as did expenditure on airports. In 1987 the CANADIAN COAST GUARD operated 6 icebreakers in northern waters, and 98 vessels were recorded in Canada's Arctic waters. At the same time Maritime traffic northbound to Eastern Arctic destinations was showing little or no growth. In the west a dramatic drop in traffic of nearly 50% was a result of the almost complete cessation of oil and gas exploration in the Beaufort Sea.

Bulk cargoes have been despatched annually from Churchill (grain) since 1931; from Nanisivik (ore) since 1977; from Little Cornwallis Island (ore) since 1982; and from Cameron Island (oil) since 1986. Oil in bulk was despatched by sea from the Beaufort Sea in 1986 and is to be repeated in 1988 after which all products from that area will be transported south by pipeline.

ROBERT BOTHWELL

Reading: Dept of Indian and Northern Affairs, *Government Activities in the North, 1981.*

Transportation Regulation is administered by all levels of government (federal, provincial, municipal) and covers prices, conditions and levels of service, and the operating authority of transport units. The purpose of regulation is to assure that transportation services are provided adequately and that users of these services are protected from excessive prices or unfair practices. Regulation can also be used to assist certain regions, industries or user groups.

Canadian transport regulation began with the establishment of a Railway Committee of the Privy Council in 1868. In 1903 the regulatory powers of the committee were transferred to the Board of Railway Commissioners, an independent, quasi-judiciary regulatory agency. Subsequently the board was given jurisdiction over express, telegraph and telephone companies (1908); government-owned railways (1923); international bridges and tunnels (1929); abandonment of railway lines (1933); Hudson Bay Railway (1948); and Newfoundland Railways. The Transport Act of 1938 changed the name of the board to the Board of Transport Commissioners for Canada and gave it regulatory powers over transportation by air and water. In 1944 the regulation of civil aviation was transferred to the Air Transport Board. The National Transportation Act (1967) created the CANADIAN TRANSPORT COMMISSION (CTC).

Railway Rates Regulation The railways have occupied a prominent position in Canadian transportation. Basic geographical considerations of distance and population density, combined with economical and political disparities, have created a complex transport situation for regulation policy. Establishing fair and reasonable rate levels that are nondiscriminatory has been difficult because of variations in financial structure and resources among railways, the degree of direct or indirect competition, the commodities being transported, alternative routings and the permissible rates of return. These variations have been further complicated by political and regional policy considerations.

An important class of railway rates, grain export, was outside regulatory jurisdiction until 1983. These rates were originally established by the CROW'S NEST PASS AGREEMENT (1897) between the Dominion government and Canadian Pacific, and were redefined by legislation in 1922.

Following WWII and the growth of road transport, railway regulators were faced with additional problems. A continual increase in costs led to periodic demands by the railways to increase rates, and the growth of competition led to competitive rate applications and to special contract rates. But the increase in road transport meant that the general rate increases applied to a diminishing part of the transport market. Furthermore, competition had uneven effects in different regions of the country. The political implications resulted in intervention by the Diefenbaker government which imposed a rollback of railway freight rates and their subsequent freeze (Freight Rates Reduction Act, 1960). At the same time a ROYAL COMMISSION on transportation was appointed. The recommendations of the MacPherson Royal Commission (1961) were based on recognition of competition and the benefits of such competition in transport. The commission proposed that railways be compensated for providing uneconomic services that were imposed by government in the public interest, and that they be free to compete in the transport market. It also proposed reliance on market forces to the fullest extent possible, protection of captive shippers (shippers with no practical alternative means of transport), and prevention of predatory pricing through the requirement that rates be compensatory, ie, that they cover the variable costs of transport.

Air Transport The main concerns of air-transport regulation have been the structure of the industry and of the route network. The problems of price regulation, which at first were largely restricted to the maintenance of price stability, became more complex and important in the 1970s with the growth of charter carriers and the advent of "seat sales" and other marketing devices by scheduled airlines. In the immediate postwar period air-transport regulations had been based on the principle of route monopolies; major intercity routes were allocated to TRANS-CANADA AIRLINES (TCA, later renamed AIR CANADA), and regional and local routes were assigned to Canadian Pacific Airlines (CPA, later renamed CP Air) and to independent airlines. An increased degree of competition was gradually introduced, starting with a deregulation experiment in the small aircraft charter field and with the granting to CPA of limited access to the transcontinental market in 1958. The regulation of air transport was administered initially by the Board of Transport Commissioners (1938-44). In 1944, when the Aeronautics Act transferred regulatory powers to the Air Transport Board, the government was given considerable powers of policy intervention. Following de facto deregulation of air transport in the mid-1980s the structure of the industry has changed drastically: a near duopoly of Air Canada and Canadian Airlines International emerged through a series of acquisitions of regional carriers by CP Air and of CP Air by Pacific Western Airlines. This development paralleled a trend towards concentration of the industry in the US which followed deregulation in that country.

Canadian Transport Commission Federal transport regulations entered a new phase with the passing of the National Transportation Act in 1967. This legislation concentrated transport regulation in a new agency, Canadian Transport Commission (CTC), replacing the Board of Transport Commissioners, the Air Transport Board and Canadian Maritime Commission. The CTC has also been granted regulatory powers over commodity pipelines, and the sectors of highway transport placed under federal control. Initially the CTC also had regulatory powers over TELE-COMMUNICATIONS, but these were transferred to the CANADIAN RADIO-TELEVISION AND TELECOMMUNICATIONS COMMISSION in 1976.

Under the National Transportation Act, 1967, the structure of railway regulations followed the principles proposed by the MacPherson Commission: overall reliance on market forces except for regulatory interventions related to the protection of "captive shipper" and prohibition of noncompensatory rates: CTC also dealt with specific cases where the rates imposed a burden on shippers or regions not justified by the existence of specific cost conditions. In air transport the regulatory activities of CTC largely reflected government policies. In the 1970s the degree of competition had been gradually increased through granting competing airlines operating authorities over major scheduled routes and by permitting a substantial increase of competition by nonscheduled (charter) airlines in the discretionary travel market. Regulatory restrictions were greatly relaxed under the Clark government (1979-80) and the subsequent Liberal administration: the industry has become virtually deregulated under the Mulroney government. In addition to its strictly regulatory functions, CTC also administered transport subsidies and railway branch lines abandonment programs; it also had responsibilities in the area of railway safety and some aspects of road transport regulations.

Highway Transport Regulation is divided between the federal and provincial governments; the provinces have the right to regulate transport undertakings operating within the provinces, but interprovincial undertakings are subject to federal jurisdiction. However, federal regulatory authority has been delegated to the provincial boards (Motor Vehicle Transport Act, 1954). The National Transportation Act provides for the reassumption of federal regulatory powers over interprovincial road-transport undertakings, and provides certain authorities over some aspects of road-transport operations (mergers, Sunday operations). For all practical purposes the highway transport industry is provincially regulated. The scope of licensing and rate regulation of the TRUCKING industry varies from province to province, from virtually no regulation in Alberta to comprehensive regulation in Québec. BUS routes are regulated by exclusive franchises, or route monopolies. Municipalities regulate courier and taxicab services.

Deregulation Debate and Regulatory Reform Until the 1970s the existence and the advisability of "public utility" type regulation had been unquestioned in N America. Although US experience on transport regulation has always affected Canadian thinking on transport regulation, the policies and practices in Canada and the US have been quite distinct. Canadian railways had enjoyed a wide degree of pricing freedom (which became almost complete after 1967) while US railway rates were strictly controlled by the Interstate Commerce Commission (ICC). ICC also exercised a considerable measure of control over interstate highway transport, a situation which had no parallel in Canada. Air transport regulations were also different, which largely reflected different industrial and network structures. The 1970s witnessed serious questioning of the concept of regulation which resulted in virtual transport deregulation in the US. These events had a profound impact on Canadian policies. In 1985 the minister of transport, Don Mazankowski, issued a policy paper called "Freedom to Move" outlining far-reaching regulatory reform which formed the basis for the new legislation introduced in 1986. The main features of the new legislation are that the Canadian Transport Commission ceases to exist; that it be replaced by the National Transportation Agency with much-reduced autonomy and regulatory powers; that the National Transportation Agency has powers of "final arbitration" in cases where carrier-shipper negotiations prove unsuccessful; that the agency, however, will preserve some decision-making authority in cases where the "public interest" is affected; that the agency will

have no power to prescribe railway costing systems; and that the obligation to publish tariffs ("market transparency") disappears and confidential contracts are allowed. Also the legislation includes a number of provisions aimed at increasing intra-modal competition within the railway industry. De facto deregulation of the air transport industry is confirmed by legislation.

K. STUDNICKI-GIZBERT

Traquair, Ramsay, architect (b at Edinburgh, Scot 29 Mar 1874; d at Guysborough, NS 26 Aug 1952). Traquair's pioneer studies in the history of French Canadian building styles, culminating in *The Old Architecture of Quebec* (1947), helped awaken interest in the province's distinctive architectural heritage. Traquair studied in Edinburgh under architects S.H. CAPPER and Robert Lorimer and conducted important research on Byzantine architecture before succeeding Percy NOBBS as third Macdonald Professor of Architecture at McGill, 1914-38. He published papers on Québec's old houses, churches and woodcarvings; he also wrote *The Old Silver of Quebec* (1940).

SUSAN WAGG

Travel Literature, *see* EXPLORATION AND TRAVEL LITERATURE; FOREIGN WRITERS ON CANADA; CANADIAN TRAVELLERS ABROAD.

Travels and Adventures in Canada and the Indian Territories between the Years 1760 and 1776 (New York, 1809; Toronto, 1901), was written by Alexander HENRY (the elder), one of the first Britons to venture into western Indian territory after the defeat of the French at Québec. Henry describes his experiences among the Indians and Canadiens in sharp, clean prose. Particularly memorable is his eyewitness account of the capture of Fort Michilimackinac; the Ojibwa slaughtered the British garrison after entering the fort on the pretext of chasing a lacrosse ball, and Henry narrowly escaped with his life. Henry's comprehensive, detailed and occasionally blood-chilling narrative is among the most engaging and best written of the fur traders' records. NEIL BESNER

Travois, a device for transportation among Plains Indians, consisted of 2 long poles, each lashed to the sides of the dog (and later horse) pulling it. The poles dragged behind and a framework at the rear carried household baggage, including the TIPI cover. The webbed willow frame attached to the ASSINIBOINE travois was circular, and the BLACKFOOT constructed both round and rectangular frames. The dog travois of pre-European times was small, capable of pulling not more than 20 to 30 kg. When dogs were replaced by horses, the greater pulling power allowed tipis to increase in size and household goods to multiply. RENÉ R. GADACZ

Treason is probably the oldest and most serious offence in political society, with the possible exception of murder. The earliest English treason legislation, which dates from 1351, is the basis of all treason legislation in the English-speaking world. Originally, treason meant an attack upon the person or life of the monarch, but as the state became more important than its sovereign, treason came to indicate any act directed at the overthrow of the government or against the security of the state. Anyone participating in a rebellion or an unsuccessful revolution is technically guilty of treason, although only the leaders tend to be prosecuted. Conversely, it is not uncommon for the leaders of a successful revolution to try former politicians for treason. In Canada, it would be treason for a province to break away from the confederation without the consent of the federal government, expressed in an Act of Parliament.

For individual offenders, treason is defined in

the Canadian Criminal Code (s46) as the wounding, imprisoning, restraining or killing of the sovereign. It is treason for anyone in Canada and therefore under the protection of Canadian law (although treason can be committed outside the country as well) to raise a rebellion – in legal terminology, to wage or levy war against Canada – or to assist any enemy of Canada or to participate in a conflict with Canadian forces, even if no war (in the strict sense of the term) is being waged. The Code condemns as traitors those who use force or violence to overthrow the government, or who provide information prejudicial to Canadian security to any agent of a foreign state, or who form a CONSPIRACY, that is to say, an agreement to commit any treasonable act. It is also treasonous to intend to commit any act of treason, provided intention is manifested by some overt act. Life imprisonment has replaced CAPITAL PUNISHMENT as the penalty for treason. L.C. GREEN

Treasury Board, the only statutory committee of CABINET (thus formally a PRIVY COUNCIL committee), was created in 1867. The president of Treasury Board (ministerial portfolio), who in 1987 was Robert de Cotret, chairs a board which comprises the finance minister and 4 other ministers appointed by the governor-in-council. Its extensive staff is called the Secretariat. The board is responsible for recommendations to Cabinet on the selection of programs and appropriate allocation of funds; administrative policy for financial management in the public administration and for matters related to personnel, office space, supply and contracts for service; and government negotiations in COLLECTIVE BARGAINING arrangements with PUBLIC SERVICE unions and associations. In 1978 the addition of the office of comptroller general, with special responsibility for upgrading the quality of financial administration and program evaluation, enlarged the board's role as controller of the expenditure budget. J.E. HODGETTS

Treaties, *see* ASHBURTON-WEBSTER TREATY; BREDA; CANADA-US AUTOMOTIVE PRODUCTS AGREEMENT; COLUMBIA RIVER TREATY; GHENT; HALIBUT TREATY; INDIAN TREATIES; JAY'S TREATY; OREGON TREATY; OTTAWA AGREEMENTS; PARIS (1763); PARIS (1783); RUSH-BAGOT AGREEMENT; RYSWICK; ST GERMAIN; UTRECHT; VERSAILLES; WASHINGTON.

Treaty Day, the annual meeting at which treaty annuities were distributed by representatives of the Dept of Indian Affairs to members of particular bands under the numbered INDIAN TREATIES. These meetings were often attended by hundreds of Indians and their families. Along with the distribution of treaty monies, food, ammunition and hunting or fishing equipment were also given out. Government officials were often accompanied by doctors and officers of the law to help Indians in any way they could. Although treaty money is now often paid by cheque, treaty-day meetings still occur in many areas, particularly in the western provinces. RENÉ R. GADACZ

Reading: R. Fumoleau, *As Long as This Land Shall Last* (1973).

Treaty-Making Power describes any and all types of international agreements governed by international law which are concluded between and among states and international organizations. Terms such as "convention," "protocol" and "declaration" are sometimes used to describe such agreements. Treaties may be either bilateral, ie, between 2 parties, or multilateral, ie, between more than 2 parties. Informal agreements or understandings between states that are not intended to create legal obligations are not regarded as treaties. Most treaties that have entered into force for Canada are published in the Canada Treaty Series and the UN Treaty Series.

Only states and international organizations possessing an international personality, such as the UNITED NATIONS, have the capacity to conclude treaties. Before Canada became an independent sovereign state, a process that occurred over a number of years, Canada's EXTERNAL RELATIONS were controlled by Britain, which negotiated, signed and ratified treaties on behalf of the British Empire, which included Canada. The first multilateral treaty to be signed by Canada in its own right was the Treaty of VERSAILLES (1919). The first bilateral treaty negotiated and signed by Canada was the Halibut Fisheries Convention of 1923 with the US (*see* HALIBUT TREATY). In Canada treaty-making power remains part of the royal prerogative, the residue of authority left in the CROWN. The delegation of the prerogative powers to Canada was an evolutionary process completed with the issuance of the Letters Patent of 1947, by which the governor general was authorized to exercise all the powers of the sovereign in respect of Canada. In practice the treaty-making power is exercised on the basis of policy approval from Cabinet or the ministers most directly concerned, coupled with an executive authority in the form of an ORDER-IN-COUNCIL issued by the governor-in-council. The secretary of state for external affairs, as the minister responsible for foreign relations, advises and recommends on treaty action to be taken by Canada.

Canada is bound by the terms of treaties that it enters into and breach thereof may give rise to international claims. However, in Canada treaties are not self-executing; they do not constitute part of the law of the land merely by virtue of their conclusion. If domestic law must be changed in order to carry out treaty obligations, implementing legislation is required. It follows that if the existing laws of Canada do not give the Government of Canada the capacity to discharge treaty obligations, then it will be necessary for the appropriate legislative body, federal or provincial, or a combination of both, to enact implementing legislation. This is the effect of the Labour Conventions Case of 1937.

Although competent to conclude treaties, the federal government can only enact legislation in relation to those treaties whose subject matter falls within the federal field of competence. If the treaty concerns matters within provincial legislative competence, the provincial legislatures must adopt the necessary implementing legislation. As a general practice, the federal government carries out prior consultation with those provinces that may be called upon to implement a treaty. The modern form of the federal state clause enables Canada to become a party to international conventions, such as the 1980 Hague Convention on International Child Abduction, and to designate the provinces to which the convention applies; in practice this means the provinces that have adopted the required implementing legislation. The wording of the clause enables Canada to file subsequent declarations extending the application of the convention to other provinces as soon as they pass implementing legislation.

A general rule of international law is that only a central government can bind a state in a treaty. Thus the Canadian government alone can bind Canada internationally, but its legislative limitations restrict its implementation powers. On the other hand, the provinces cannot bind Canada internationally even in those subject matters in which they enjoy legislative competence. In recent years the provinces have entered into a variety of arrangements or understandings with foreign governments that are not considered binding in international law. For example, Ontario and Québec have signed a number of educational and cultural arrangements with foreign governments.

In spite of what is regarded by some as an unsatisfactory system of treaty making and treaty implementation, Canada is among the most active treaty-making nations in the world. Much of the INTERNATIONAL LAW governing treaties is incorporated in the Vienna Convention on the Law of Treaties to which Canada acceded in 1970.

EMILY F. CARASCO

Treeline marks the limit of trees latitudinally on continental plains and altitudinally on highlands and mountains (where it is sometimes called timberline). Tree species still occur beyond this limit, but in shrub form, extending to the "tree-species line." The treeline is controlled by climate in interaction with soil. In the North, it is correlated generally with the modal (most common) position of the southern edge of the arctic front in summer, and with such temperature indices as the July 10°C isotherm. But wherever soils are deeper and warmer than normal, as in river valleys (eg, the THELON) or on upland, sandy ESKERS, ribbons of trees extend the treeline far into the tundra. Characteristic treeline species are alpine fir, whitebark pine and alpine larch in the Rocky Mts; in Alaska and northern Canada, co-existing black spruce, white spruce and tamarack (larch). Similar species of spruce and larch, with pine and birch, continue the circumpolar treeline across Eurasia.

The pollen record (*see* PALYNOLOGY) and preserved wood show that treelines on this continent have fluctuated greatly in the past, advancing hundreds of kilometres during warm phases and retreating southward when the climate has deteriorated. Such movements take hundreds of years. Slight climatic changes can cause major shifts in the treeline, because seed production and survival of seedlings is precarious near the limit of trees. The conifers are also susceptible to fire during dry cycles, and this and cutting by man make today's treeline a diffuse and unstable boundary. The dotted lines and the label "Approximate Limit of Trees" that indicate the treeline on northern National Topographic Survey maps are appropriately vague.

J. STAN ROWE

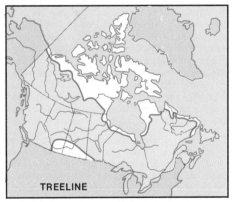

Trees are single-stemmed, perennial, woody plants taller than 3 m and exceeding 8 cm in diameter at breast height; shrubs are multistemmed and smaller. These definitions are somewhat arbitrary, since many species (eg, willow, alder, cherry, maple) can grow as trees or shrubs, depending on environment. Counting the 30-odd shrubs that assume tree form under favourable conditions, there are about 140 native Canadian trees. The largest and oldest grow in the Pacific temperate rain FOREST. Douglas fir is an imposing example and, although it does not reach the size of redwoods or the age of bristlecone pines, specimens 90 m tall, 5 m in basal diameter and older than 1000 years have been reported.

People have always been impressed by trees, by their massiveness and majesty, by the sound of

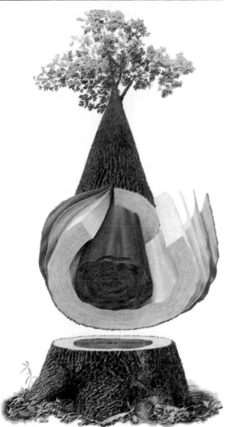

Exploded view of trunk of white ash (*Fraxinus americana*), showing heartwood, sapwood, cambial zone, the inner bark and the outer bark (*courtesy National Museums of Canada/National Museum of Natural Sciences/artwork by Bruce Bezaire*).

wind in their branches, and by their visual beauty. Legend and folklore suggest attitudes of awe and reverence: yews, symbols of eternity; birches, holy trees; larches, guardians against enchantment. The Greeks gave trees spirits (dryads), attributing religious significance to them, as did the druids, who conferred on forest groves and oak woods a sacred, precommercial value now, unfortunately, lost. Today, trees are valued for their products: pulpwood, sawtimber, poles, plywood, particle board, paper, cork, rubber, gums, tannin, pharmaceuticals, fruits, nuts, syrups. Indirect benefits include soil stabilization and prevention of erosion, windbreaks, sound barriers and air purification.

Apart from a few large, single-stemmed FERNS, trees are classified as gymnosperms (with naked seeds in cones) and angiosperms (with seeds enclosed in ovaries of flowers). Gymnosperms (CONIFERS), with scalelike or needlelike leaves, appear first in the FOSSIL record (Carboniferous period, 360-286 million years ago) and, by early Mesozoic times (Triassic, 245-208 million years ago), dominated the earth's vegetation. Later in the Mesozoic, during the Cretaceous period (144-66.4 million years ago), broadleaf angiosperms evolved to become the more important group, perhaps profiting from their close relationships with insect pollinators and with larger animals which spread their fruits. Angiosperms also developed the ability to reproduce vegetatively by sprouting, an advantage which is shared by few conifers.

Softwoods, the conifers, tend to concentrate growth in a central trunk from which many small branches are offset, producing a conical crown. They are usually evergreen, an adaptation fitting them for difficult environments by allowing internal recycling of nutrients from old to new foliage. Hardwoods, the broadleaf trees, tend to have rounded crowns because side branches grow just as well as main stems, which may fork repeatedly. They are typically deciduous, and grow on more fertile soils and in more moderate climates. There are numerous exceptions: some conifers (eg, larches, cypresses, dawn redwood) are deciduous; some pines have relatively hard wood; some broadleaf trees (eg, poplars) have soft wood; others are evergreen, especially in subtropical and tropical Canadian climates. The only native Canadian broadleaf evergreen is the red-barked arbutus of southwestern BC.

Tree roots perform both anchoring and absorbing functions. Like the tops, they are distinctive according to species and environment. They may penetrate deeply (taproots of pine) or spread horizontally just below the surface (platelike system of spruce). Buttress roots, thickened vertically, characterize wet sites, particularly in the tropics, although they are sometimes seen on elm. Adventitious roots, sprouting from the lower trunk (as on spruce and poplar), are a response to burial by accumulations of peat, silt on river floodplains, or windblown sand.

In climates that vary seasonally, the "growth ring" is a characteristic anatomical feature of trees. Regenerative, meristematic cells (cambium and cork cambium) sheathe the living trunk, branches and roots just under the bark, annually forming layers of phloem and corky cells to the outside (bark) and xylem cells to the inside (wood). Both bark and wood thicken with age. Products of photosynthesis and various other biochemicals are transported by phloem; water is transported chiefly by active xylem in sapwood surrounding older, darker, nonfunctional heartwood. The water-conducting efficiency of xylem cells is a function of their size, controlled by growth regulators released from the tree's growing tips. When shoot growth begins in spring, cambium produces large-diameter cells. Later, in summer, as growth slows and stops, wood-cell diameters decrease. Therefore a cross section of trunk, root or branch shows concentric "growth rings" outlined by the contrast between small, dense, latewood cells of one year and larger, lighter earlywood cells of the next. An uncritical count of a tree's growth rings may overestimate its true age, since extra flushes of growth in a year can be triggered by weather changes or defoliation, forming false annual rings. Ring size reflects growing conditions. Where precipitation is the limiting factor, sensitive trees record wet and dry years in wide and narrow rings. Where heat is limiting, ring sizes mirror sequences of warm and cold summers.

Trees were eliminated by ice-age GLACIERS which covered most of Canada. Deglaciation began about 17 000 years ago, allowing immigration of plants to newly exposed soils. Species with small, winged seeds travelled fastest and farthest, and the boreal zone was filled by spruce, pine, larch, fir, poplar and birch. Trees that migrated more slowly or were less stress tolerant came later, and they now characterize more favourable environments: southern BC, with numerous conifers; and southern Ontario, with an even greater variety of broadleaf deciduous trees. Altitudinal and latitudinal distributions are in part related to wood anatomy: small-diameter xylem cells of boreal species (spruce, fir, aspen, alder, willow, birch) are less prone to freezing damage than larger cells of "ring porous" southern hardwoods (oak, hickory, walnut). Each wide-ranging tree species includes locally adapted varieties. Although they seem similar, white spruces from the territories, Newfoundland and southern Manitoba are genetically different and respond differently when planted together. Successful planting is best accomplished, therefore, by using seed from trees native to the area. This variation within species means that the preservation of native trees, as well as that of other plants and animals, in all their genetic diversity, requires the protection of many large, widely distributed, natural areas as ecological preserves. *See also* individual tree entries. J. STANLEY ROWE

Reading: R.C. Hosie, *Native Trees of Canada* (1979).

Tremblant, Mont, Qué, 968 m, located 140 km N of Montréal, is the highest peak in the LAURENTIAN HIGHLANDS. The Indians called it *manitonga soutana,* meaning "mountains of the spirits." The present name echoes the Indian legend that climbers feel the mountain tremble beneath their feet. In 1894 the Québec government established the Parc de la Montagne-Tremblante, today MONT TREMBLANT PROVINCIAL PARK.
CLAUDINE PIERRE-DESCHÊNES

Tremblay, Arthur Julien, professor, educational reformer, senior public servant, senator (b at St-Bruno, Qué 18 June 1917). Educated at the Séminaire de Chicoutimi, Laval (MA in social sciences, 1942) and Harvard (MEd, 1945), he joined Laval's École de Pédagogie et d'Orientation as assistant-director in 1945. Throughout the 1950s, he pursued the reform of Québec's Catholic education system at all levels. Indeed, he was the architect of most of the reforms that would later be implemented. When the QUIET REVOLUTION was ushered in with the victory of Jean Lesage's Liberal party in June, 1960, Tremblay became executive assistant to the minister of youth, Paul GERIN-LAJOIE, and was responsible for preparing recommendations for the reforms of agricultural, technical and professional education. He was also a member of the Commission royale d'enquête sur l'enseignement, 1961-64, which recommended sweeping reforms beginning with the reestablishment of the Ministry of Education that had been abolished in 1875. The Lesage government created the ministry in 1964 and named Tremblay its first deputy minister. Before the decade was out, the ministry had restructured all the school boards, created a comprehensive public secondary system topped off by the COLLÈGE D'ENSEIGNEMENT GÉNÉRAL ET PROFESSIONNEL system, while secularizing and expanding the francophone Catholic universities. In 1971 he succeeded Claude Morin as deputy minister of Intergovernmental Affairs. He was named to the Senate in Sept 1979 and in 1984 PM Brian Mulroney made him special adviser on constitutional affairs and federal-provincial relations. MICHAEL D. BEHIELS

Tremblay, Gilles, composer, pianist, sound specialist (b at Arvida [Jonquière], Qué 6 Sept 1932). His research into the field of sound is reflected in all his work by the use of instruments at the limits of their sound possibilities. He studied with Jean PAPINEAU-COUTURE, Claude CHAMPAGNE, Germaine Malépart and Jean VALLERAND in Canada; with Yvonne Loriod, Olivier Messiaen, Maurice Martenot and Andrée Vaurabourg-Honegger in Paris, where he also studied with the Groupe de recherches musicales de l'ORTF; and with Karlheinz Stockhausen, Pierre Boulez and Henri Pousseur in Darmstadt. His magnificent *Sonorisation du Pavillon du Québec,* electroacoustic music written for EXPO 67, won him the 1968 Prix de musique Calixa-Lavallée. His commissions include one from the Société de musique contemporaine du Québec for *Souffles (Champs II),* 1968, and one from the Montréal Symphony Orchestra for *Fleuves,* 1976. His major works also include *Kékoba, Oralléluiants* and *Envoi.* In 1973 he received the medal of the Canadian Music Council, which also proclaimed him "composer of the year" for 1977. Tremblay teaches at the Montreal Conservatory of Music and is chairman of the Société de musique contemporaine du Québec. He has also taught at the Conservatoire de musique du Québec. HÉLÈNE PLOUFFE

Tremblay, Marc-Adélard, professor of anthropology (b at Les Éboulements, Qué 24 Apr 1922). After completing his PhD at Cornell U (1954), he held leading academic and administrative positions at Laval, in professional and research organizations and in national academies. For his contributions to the study of Québec society and cultural life, he earned the Québec Literary Competition (1965), Innis-Gérin Medal (1979), Centenary Medal of the Royal Society of Canada (1982) and Molson Prize (1987). His well over 150 articles and books include *Famille et parenté en Acadie* (1971), *Communities and Culture in French Canada* (1973) and *L'Identité québecoise en péril* (1983). RENÉ R. GADACZ

Tremblay, Michel, writer (b at Montréal 25 June 1942). In 1959 Tremblay entered the Institut des arts graphiques and wrote his first play, *Le Train.* He worked as a linotype operator 1963-66. In 1964 *Le Train* won first prize in the Concours des jeunes auteurs sponsored by Radio-Canada; it was broadcast on 7 June 1964. This was the beginning of a long career devoted primarily to theatrical works. The novelist side of Michel Tremblay first appeared with his *Contes pour buveurs attardés* (1966).

Le Train was produced again, at the Théâtre de la Place Ville-Marie between 1965 and 1968. The Mouvement contemporain presented excerpts from *Contes pour buveurs attardés* and the Patriote mounted *Cinq* (original version of *En pièces détachées*) in Dec 1966. In 1968 Tremblay went to Mexico on a Canada Council grant and wrote *La Cité dans l'oeuf,* a fantasy novel, and *La Duchesse de Langeais,* a one-character play about the loves and disillusionments of an old transvestite. After a public reading of *Les Belles-Soeurs* on 4 Mar 1968 by the Centre d'essai des auteurs dramatiques, the play was produced on 28 Aug 1968 by André Brassard, who has continued to stage virtually all productions and revivals of Tremblay's work. *Les Belles-Soeurs,* written in the street language JOUAL, offered a transformed vision of the working-class neighbourhood where the author was born. In 1987 his latest play, *Le Vrai Monde,* his 19th in as many years, premiered and was hailed as his greatest work. Critics have included him in the theatre of realism, but his frequent use of antirealistic devices (chorus, flashback) and of fringe characters show he is not following predecessors Gratien GÉLINAS, Marcel DUBÉ, Françoise LORANGER and Jacques LANGUIRAND.

Tremblay has also written musical comedies, has translated and adapted many American and other authors, and is a scriptwriter and songwriter. His many outstanding plays include *À toi, pour toujours, ta Marie-Lou* (1971), 1972 winner of the Chalmers Award. He is now concentrating on fiction. The first 3 novels have appeared in his Plateau Mont-Royal series, which brings to life the same world as his plays. In 1986 his sixth novel, *Le Coeur decouvert* was published. Tremblay has won many prizes and distinctions, including the Prix Victor-Morin in 1974. In Aug 1978 he was named the most remarkable Montréaler of the last 2 decades in theatre. PIERRE LAVOIE

Trent Affair, the most serious diplomatic crisis between Britain and the US federal government during the AMERICAN CIVIL WAR. On 8 Nov 1861 Capt Charles Wilkes of the Northern navy stopped the *Trent,* a British merchantman and mail packet, in neutral waters between Havana, Cuba, and London, to take captive 2 Confederate

emissaries to London and Paris. In both Britain and British North America news of the seizure (and violation of British neutrality) was greeted by demands for apologies from the US and for its surrender of the diplomats. War appeared possible between Britain and the North, with Canada bound to be a battleground, and colonial and provincial officials conferred about how best to defend Canada. When British troops, sent to reinforce the meagre border garrisons, had to cross through Maine to reach Canada, Canadian leaders recognized Canada's vulnerability. The crisis passed. The North returned the Confederate commissioners, but without apology, on Dec 26.
ROBIN W. WINKS

Trent Canal system links Lk Ontario (at Trenton) with Lk Huron (at Port Severn on Georgian Bay). The water route (388 km long) utilizes the Trent R to Rice Lk, the Otonabee R, the Kawartha Lks, man-made channels to Lk Simcoe and Lk Couchiching and the Severn R to Georgian Bay, as well as 2 marine railways (at Big Chute). Locks overcome a rise of 181 m to the summit at Balsam Lk and then a drop of 79 m to Lk Huron. Two of the locks, at Peterborough and Kirkfield, are hydraulic-lift locks, unique in N America. Early settlers constructed simple connections between some lakes to facilitate the floating of timber cut from nearby forests. Logging, milling, steamboating, grain handling and recreation were all linked to the development of the waterway. Work was sporadic and covered 87 years from 1833-1920. Under the control of Ontario until 1892, the system was taken over and completed for the federal government by the Dept of Railways and Canals. Now under Environment Canada, Parks, the waterway is used every summer for boating. It also plays a role in providing water for municipal supplies, hydroelectric-power generation, wildlife-habitat protection and flood control.
ROBERT F. LEGGET

Trent University, Peterborough, Ont. Although the university was established by statute in April 1963, it opened its doors to its first students in the 1964-65 academic year. They were accommodated in 2 downtown Peterborough locations: Peter Robinson College for men and Catharine Parr Traill College for women. Both colleges are now coeducational. The university's first administrative centre, now no longer in use, was a renovated normal school called Rubidge Hall. These downtown locations were renovated by the university's master-planning architect, Ron THOM, who also designed the first permanent buildings on the university's main campus: Champlain College (1966), the Thomas J. Bata Library (1968) and Lady Eaton College (1968). All were award-winning designs; construction ended in 1971. Trent embodies the academic objectives of its founding president, Prof Thomas H.B. SYMONS. The 5 residential colleges provide excellent small-group teaching in the traditional arts and science disciplines and in a number of interdisciplinary programs, including administrative and policy studies, Canadian studies, com-

Enrolment: Trent University, 1985-86
(*Source*: Statistics Canada)

Full-time Undergrad	Full-time Graduate	Part-time Undergrad	Part-time Graduate
3 125	47	1 096	3

puter science, cultural studies, environmental and resource studies, comparative development studies and native studies. Teacher education is carried out in co-operation with QUEEN'S UNIVERSITY. Graduate programs in specialized areas include anthropology, freshwater science, Canadian heritage and development, and watershed ecosystems. The university also provides a home for the *Journal of Canadian Studies* which has been published there since 1966. ROBERT D. CHAMBERS

Trente Arpents (1938), a novel that breaks with the tradition of the regional idyll by portraying the Canadien farmer as a tragic rather than a romantic figure, presents Québec rural life as subject at once to the vagaries of climate and the impact of URBANIZATION. Under the pseudonym "Ringuet," author Philippe PANNETON dramatizes Euchariste Moisan's fall from youthful prosperity, married to his farm, to impoverished old age, trapped in an American factory town. Conflicts between generations are equally pervasive in the country and the city; rural life before WWI is only marginally better than city life. Claiming to write realism rather than naturalism, Panneton employs the seasons as a symbolic and structuring device in order to reveal the frailty of human hopes compared to the indifferent but powerful forces of nature and time. The novel was awarded prizes in both France and Québec; Felix and Dorothea Walter's translation, *Thirty Acres*, won the Governor General's Award in 1940. It has also been translated into German. MICHÈLE LACOMBE

Trenton, Ont, City, pop 15 311 (1986c), Hastings County, 18 km W of Belleville. It was incorporated as a village in 1853, a town 1 July 1880 and a city 1 July 1980. The first settlers arrived at the mouth of the Trent R in the 1790s. Known as the gateway to the Trent-Severn Waterway, the site was called first Trent Port, then Trentown, and finally Trenton. The beneficiary of canal development, the area had a prominent lumber industry. The largest sawmill was owned by the Gilmour Co. This plant, after many years of prosperity, burned to the ground in 1910. During WWI the major industry was the munitions plant of the British Chemical Co, which was levelled by explosions in 1918. An attempt was made to turn the town into a film production centre in the 1920s but only a handful of films were ever produced. Trenton was chosen as the centre for the Royal Canadian Air Force and functioned in WWII as a training base for Commonwealth pilots; TRENTON, CANADIAN FORCES BASE remains an integral part of the economy. Industrial products include textiles, electronic components, steel and wooden items. GERALD STORTZ

Trenton, NS, Town, pop 3083 (1986c), 3155 (1981c), inc 1911, is located on the East R, immediately adjacent to New Glasgow. It is one of several Pictou County towns that played vital roles in Canada's 19th-century industrial revolution. Named after Trenton, New Jersey, by Harvey Graham, an official of the Nova Scotia Steel Co, it was the site of the first Canadian steel mill (1882-83). A forerunner of this company had established a forge here in 1878, and the town itself was laid out in 1882. Scotia Steel in time added rolling mills, railway axle, marine forging, nut and bolt plants, and a large railway car manufacturing division. Several steel-hulled ships were constructed during WWI. But during the 1920s, following a takeover by central Canadian and foreign interests, the town suffered serious decline as many of Scotia Steel's operations were dismantled.
L.D. McCANN

Trenton, Canadian Forces Base, is 167 km E of Toronto on Lk Ontario's Bay of Quinte. Begun in 1929 on 384 ha of flat farmland adjacent to the town of TRENTON, it replaced Camp BORDEN's inadequate airforce facilities. Constructed during the Great Depression as a relief project, it became the centre for the RCAF's sea and land operations and training in the 1930s. During WWII it was the hub of the BRITISH COMMONWEALTH AIR TRAINING PLAN. Renamed CFB Trenton upon unification (1968), the base at various times has housed units of air operations, training and support, their activities including air-traffic control and communications, transport and air movement, civil and military search and rescue, weather forecasting and air maintenance, and training systems for the Canadian Forces and the UN. Trenton is Canada's primary air base. With its 3738 (1987) military and civilian employees, 2300 dependants and modern urban facilities, it has an operating budget of $267 million (1986). As such, it is a prime economic influence on the nearby cities of BELLEVILLE and Trenton and the surrounding district.
R.G. HAYCOCK

Triathlon, an extremely demanding 3-part test of athletic ability: swimming, cycling and running. It consists of 4 km swimming, 182 km on the bicycle and a marathon. Two Canadian women, Sylviane and Patricia Puntous, are among the world specialists in this discipline which demands both physical endurance and sheer courage. The 2 sisters have twice dominated the famous Hawaii triathlon. The event is becoming increasingly popular in Canada. YVON DORE

Trigger, Bruce Graham, anthropologist, archaeologist (b at Preston, Ont 18 June 1937). He has received the Queen's Silver Jubilee Medal and the Cornplanter Medal for Iroquois Research. Staff archaeologist at the Oriental Institute, Trigger conducted research in the Sudan and Egypt before joining McGill in 1964. Author of articles on Egyptian and Sudanese archaeology, ethnohistory of eastern Canada and archaeological theory, Trigger is best known for *History and Settlement in Lower Nubia* (1965) and his outstanding 2-volume history of the HURON, *The Children of Aataentsic* (1976). His book, *Natives and Newcomers* (1985), begins a reinterpretation of the early history of New France. A fellow of the RSC, he was awarded the Innis-Gérin Medal in 1985.
RENÉ R. GADACZ

Trillium, common and generic name of a perennial plant of the Trilliaceae family (sometimes classified as a subfamily of the LILY family). The name derives from the arrangement of leaves, petals and sepals in groups of 3. The plant grows in clusters. It has a short, tuberlike rootstock and

Five species of trillium are native to Canada, including the white trillium (*Trillium grandiflorum*), the floral emblem of Ontario (*photo by Mary W. Ferguson*).

a fleshy stalk bearing a whorl of 3 leaves near the top. A single flower is produced in spring. The fruit is a red berry. Of the 40 species known worldwide, about 30 are American, the remainder Asiatic. Five species are native to Canada. *Trillium grandiflorum* (white trillium, white lily, wakerobin) flowers Apr-May in the hardwood forests of western and central Québec and in the lower Ottawa Valley, Ont. It has been the PROVINCIAL FLORAL EMBLEM in Ontario since 1937. The roots were valued for their astringent and antiseptic properties.   CÉLINE ARSENEAULT

Trilobite, extinct marine arthropod of the Paleozoic era (570-245 million years ago). Its closest modern relative is the horseshoe crab. Trilobites had 2 eyes on top of the head, antennae projecting from beneath the head and, in some, from under the tail, and 2 rows of paired limbs. Each paired limb consisted of 2 branches joined near the base: a comblike gill branch (exite) for breathing and swimming, and a jointed walking leg (endite). After hatching, each trilobite secreted a shell, composed of calcite, calcium phosphate and organic material. The shell consisted of head and tail pieces (cephalon and pygidium, respectively) separated by several articulated segments (thorax). Adults ranged from less than 1 cm long (eg, genus *Scharyia*) to over 60 cm (eg, *Terataspis* of Ontario).

Some trilobites were pelagic, floating near the surface of ancient oceans. Most were benthic, crawling on or plowing through seafloor mud, extracting organic particles from mud or filtering them from seawater through their comblike exites. Predatory trilobites apparently used sharp spikes on the undersides of their walking legs to clasp prey. Some could swim by using their exites as oars. Trilobites of genus *Illaenus* had smooth, hemispherical heads and lived in burrows, their heads acting as caps to the burrows if predators threatened. Seafloor dwellers left characteristic, grooved trails, or trilobite-shaped resting burrows. Trilobites appeared early in the Cambrian period. They increased in numbers and diversity and are used to date Cambrian rocks (570-505 million years old). A second period of adaptive radiation, early in the Ordovician (505-438 million years ago), produced all major post-Cambrian groups. Their number and variety dwindled until extinction at the end of the Paleozoic era. They probably died out because they were unable to compete with or escape from active, aggressive FISH. Trilobites were also preyed on by starfish, cephalopods, coelenterates, etc.

Trilobite FOSSILS are abundant from western Newfoundland to the Rocky Mts, and from the 49th parallel to the High Arctic. Their most spectacular occurrence is probably the BURGESS SHALE near Field, BC (a World Heritage Site). Here, the soft parts of trilobites and related arthropods are preserved: hence, the site has provided information on the relationships of trilobites to other arthropod groups. Specimens from the Canadian Shield are often beautifully preserved. Complete skeletons of *Triarthrus eatoni* and *Pseudogygites latimarginatus* from Collingwood, and of *Phacops rana* from southern Ontario, are particularly well known and are prized by collectors. Specimens of giant *Terataspis grandis* and *Isotelus maximus* are also known from Ontario. The Mackenzie Mts, NWT, contain a unique sequence of trilobite faunas, in which quartz has replaced the skeletons. These fossils, which range from 350 to 520 million years of age, are used to study trilobite evolution, ecology and geographic distributions.
                      BRIAN CHATTERTON

Trinity, Nfld, Community, pop 357 (1986c), 375 (1981c), inc 1969, is located on TRINITY BAY in NE Newfoundland. The first recorded English reference to the sizable, 3-armed harbour was in 1580 by Richard Whitbourne who, in 1615, held there the first court of admiralty in the New World. Though the nascent fishing outport was periodically raided by the French 1696-1713, Trinity grew as a major fortified fishing and trading centre. In the 1720s local magistrates were appointed, and in 1730 a small church was erected, among the first such events in Newfoundland. In 1762 inhabitants yielded the town and fortifications to French Admiral de Ternay in exchange for a guarantee of safety. A strong, resident merchant class, mainly from Poole, Eng, a prosperous fishery, and extensive trade ensured Trinity's growth, and by the late 1700s it was one of the few settlements with benefit of clergy, magistrates and a surgeon. In 1800 John Clinch, resident surgeon-clergyman, became the first in N America to inoculate against smallpox, using vaccine sent him by his boyhood friend, Edward Jenner. Clinch also compiled a BEOTHUK vocabulary, the only linguistic record of Newfoundland's now extinct indigenous people. In 1833 the Roman Catholic Church of St John the Baptist was built; it remains one of the oldest standing buildings and the oldest Roman Catholic church in Newfoundland. The withdrawal of the great merchant firms after 1850 led to Trinity's decline as a major fishing centre. Because of its considerable past, the preservation of many of its historic buildings and records, and the restoration of some merchant premises, Trinity retains much of the look and flavour of a 19th-century town.   JANET E.M. PITT

Reading: E. Hunt, *Aspects of the History of Trinity* (1981).

Trinity Bay, reputedly named by Gaspar CORTE-REAL on Trinity Sunday, in 1500, is entered between Grates Pt on the N side of Newfoundland's AVALON PENINSULA and the N tip of the Bonavista Pen, 60 km NW, which forms the bay's western shore. The bay stretches S nearly 110 km to Chapel Arm and has steep headlands to the NE and NW that rise over 85 m. The bay shelters superb fishing grounds and is indented with numerous coves and harbours, the largest being at TRINITY on the NW shore. English West Country mer-

Trinity, Nfld, preserves the look and flavour of a 19th-century town through its historic buildings (*photo by Freeman Patterson/Masterfile*).

chants began settlement at Trinity in the 1600s and settlers spread across the bay to the SE and SW to RANDOM I, a large island occupying a deep pocket in the bay's W coast. At HEART'S CONTENT, a fish-processing centre on the SE coast, the first successful transatlantic cable was landed in 1866. Clarenville, W of Random I, has become a major transportation and commercial centre as the importance of Trinity has declined. Communities such as Catalina and Old Perlican, near the mouth of the bay, are today principal fishing centres.
                      JANET E.M. PITT

Triticale (*Triticosecale Wittmack*), the first manmade CROP species, is initially produced by crossing wheat (genus *Triticum*) with rye (*Secale*), and resembles wheat. Treatment with the chemical, colchicine, restores fertility to the otherwise sterile hybrid. The development of triticale as a CEREAL CROP in Canada first began in 1954 at University of Manitoba, Winnipeg. Triticale is still a minor crop in Canada. Triticale grain is used either as a human food (bread and pastry products and in the BREWING INDUSTRY) or as a livestock feed. Relative to wheat, triticale grain is high in lysine, a component of protein required by humans and most other animals for normal growth and development. Hence, triticale is expected to assume an increasingly important role as a food grain in regions in which cereal crops already constitute the main dietary source of protein.   E.N. LARTER

Trois-Pistoles, Qué, Town, pop 4290 (1986c), 4445 (1981c), inc 1916, is located 250 km NE of Québec City on the S shore of the ST LAWRENCE R, between Rivière-du-Loup and Rimouski. According to legend, the name was given to the river at whose mouth the town is located because sailors once lost a silver goblet worth 3 gold *pistoles* in the river. BASQUES were among the fishermen and whale hunters who sailed to the river's estuary before John Cabot's explorations in N America. The remains of several ovens used to melt whale oil have been found on the island opposite the town, appropriately named Île-aux-Basques. The seigneury of Trois-Pistoles was granted to Denis de Vitré in 1687. The mission was served by priests from Kamouraska until 1783 and by missionaries 1783-1806, at which time the first resident priest arrived. The municipality's major economic activities were agriculture and forest resources. Trois-Pistoles is now a small service-industry town where tourism (whale observation) is growing in importance as a result of the summer ferry link with the N shore.
                      ANTONIO LECHASSEUR

Trois-Rivières, Qué, City, pop 50 122 (1986c), 50 466 (1981c), inc 1857, the regional capital of Québec's Mauricie region, is located on the E shore of the mouth of the ST-MAURICE R, midway between Québec C and Montréal. Its name derives from the 3-armed delta formed by the river's islands at its mouth.

Settlement The fortified settlement built at CHAMPLAIN's request in 1634 replaced the stockade abandoned earlier by the Algonquin, who had likely fled the hostile IROQUOIS. The former lived for a long time in or near the small French village, whose major function was to organize the FUR TRADE in the interior. After 1663 Trois-

Population: 50 122 (1986c), 50 466 (1981c); 128 888 (1986 CMA), 125 343 (1981 ACMA)
Rate of Increase (1981-86): City -.7%; CMA 2.8%
Rank in Canada: Twenty-third (by CMA)
Date of Incorporation: City 1857
Land Area: City 77.86 km²; CMA 871.91 km²
Elevation: 53 m
Climate: Average daily temp, July 19.7°C, Jan -12.1°C; Yearly precip rain 763 mm, snow 261.4 cm; Hours of sunshine 1922 per year

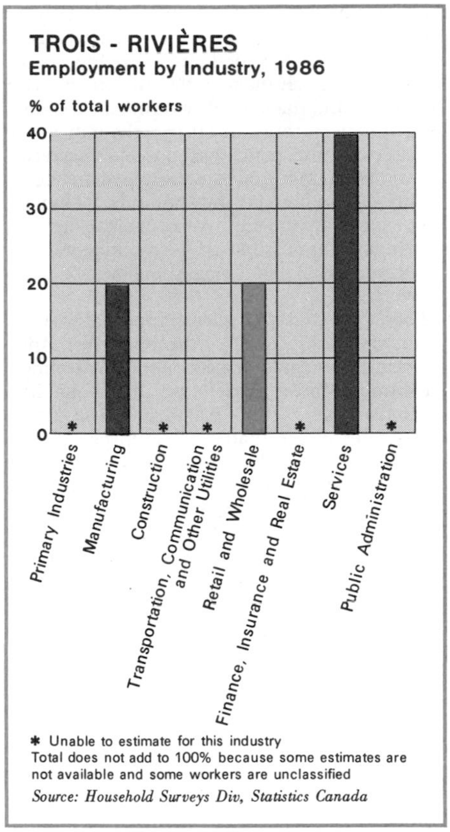
TROIS - RIVIÈRES
Employment by Industry, 1986
% of total workers
40
30
20
10
0
Primary Industries
Manufacturing
Construction
Transportation, Communication and Other Utilities
Retail and Wholesale
Finance, Insurance and Real Estate
Services
Public Administration
* Unable to estimate for this industry
Total does not add to 100% because some estimates are not available and some workers are unclassified
Source: Household Surveys Div, Statistics Canada

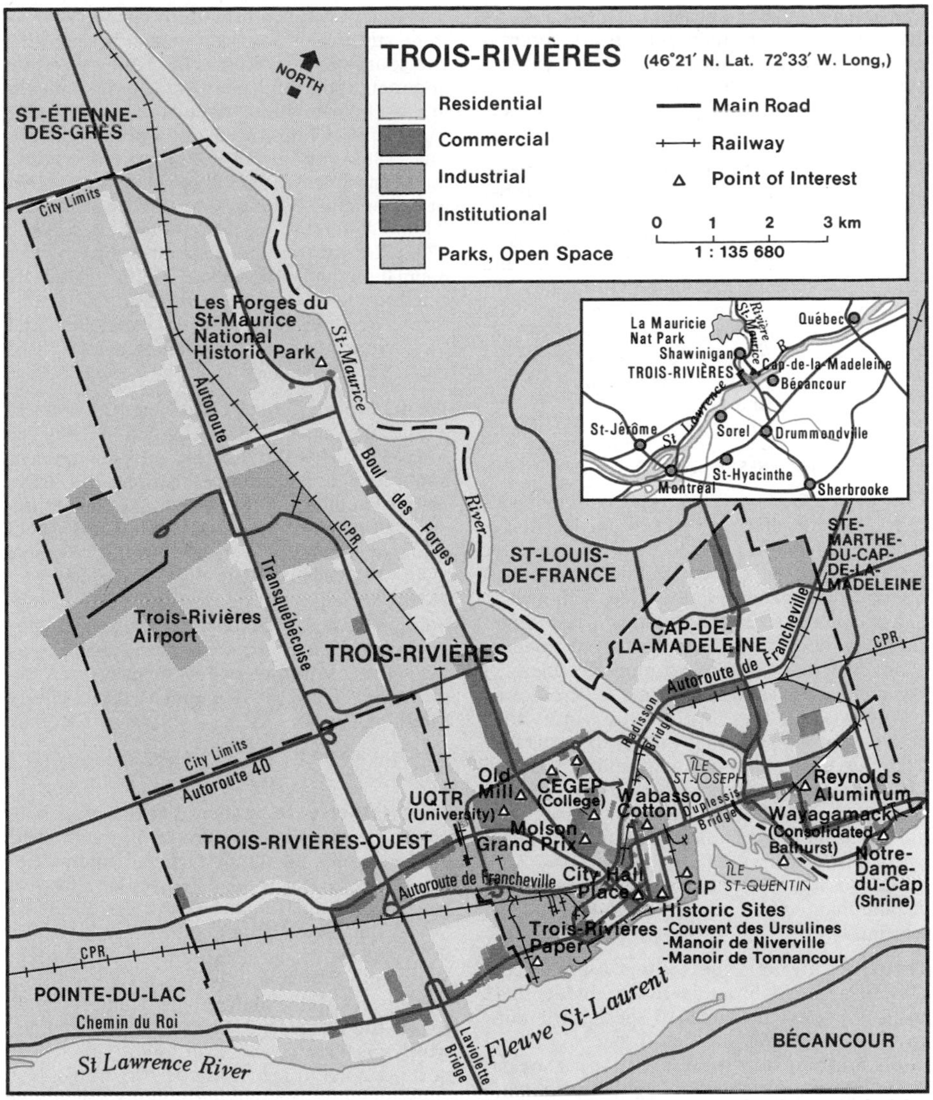
TROIS-RIVIÈRES (46°21′ N. Lat. 72°33′ W. Long.)
Residential
Commercial
Industrial
Institutional
Parks, Open Space
Main Road
Railway
Point of Interest
0 1 2 3 km
1 : 135 680
NORTH
ST-ÉTIENNE-DES-GRÈS
City Limits
Les Forges du St-Maurice National Historic Park
St-Maurice River
Autoroute
Boul des Forges
CPR
Transquébécoise
Trois-Rivières Airport
TROIS-RIVIÈRES
ST-LOUIS-DE-FRANCE
CAP-DE-LA-MADELEINE
STE-MARTHE-DU-CAP-DE-LA-MADELEINE
Autoroute de Francheville
Radisson Bridge
Autoroute 40
ÎLE ST-JOSEPH
Duplessis Bridge
UQTR (University)
Old Mill
CEGEP (College)
Wabasso Cotton
Reynolds Aluminum
Wayagamack (Consolidated Bathurst)
Notre-Dame-du-Cap (Shrine)
TROIS-RIVIÈRES-OUEST
Molson Grand Prix
City Hall
Place
ÎLE ST-QUENTIN
CIP
Historic Sites
-Couvent des Ursulines
-Manoir de Niverville
-Manoir de Tonnancour
Trois-Rivières Paper
POINTE-DU-LAC
Chemin du Roi
St Lawrence River
Laviolette Bridge
Fleuve St-Laurent
BÉCANCOUR
La Maurice Nat Park
Rivière St-Maurice
Shawinigan
TROIS-RIVIÈRES
Québec
Cap-de-la-Madeleine
Bécancour
St-Jérôme
St Lawrence
Sorel
Drummondville
Montréal
St-Hyacinthe
Sherbrooke

Rivières became the seat of local government, with a GOVERNEUR, king's lieutenant, major, court of royal jurisdiction and vicar general. In 1760 the town had 586 inhabitants.

Development The St-Maurice R played a major role in Trois-Rivières's history, being first used to transport furs from the northern forests. With the boom in forestry operations in the early 1850s, Trois-Rivières became an administrative centre, with several large sawmills and a major port for exporting timber. Then, with the development of hydroelectric power, the river's energy potential stimulated the development of the PULP AND PAPER INDUSTRY and made Trois-Rivières the world's capital for paper products around 1930. The pace of urbanization in the early 20th century was quite dramatic.

Cityscape Built on a sandy terrace overlooking the St Lawrence R, the early village was concentrated around the governor's manor, the Ursuline monastery and the Récollets' church. In the mid-19th century, industry began to spring up around the town, first along the shores of the St-Maurice and the St Lawrence rivers, then along the railway that skirted Trois-Rivières to the N. The Chemin du Roi, leading to Montréal, parallel to the St Lawrence R, was renamed rue Notre-Dame. Rue des Forges, running N to S, led to the FORGES ST-MAURICE, an early iron and steel works about 12 km to the N. In the early 20th century, working-class districts developed near the pulp and paper and textile factories. Postwar prosperity and the automobile encouraged the population to live farther from the centre. Urban expansion to the N annexed St-Michel-des-Vieilles-Forges in 1961. With the population spread and with the construction of shopping centres on the edge of the city, the downtown core declined commercially. This area is now under renovation. The terrible fire that ravaged Trois-Rivières in 1908 destroyed much of the old city, sparing only a dozen buildings from the French regime, among them the Ursuline monastery and the Tonnancour manor. A few beautiful early 19th-century buildings, including the old prison (1816) and the cathedral (1856), also survived. Trois-Rivières has nonetheless long been a modern city, with an avant-garde city hall (1967) and several high buildings that tower above the cathedral.

Population With the establishment of sawmills and the development of commercial and port activities 1850-60, the population of Trois-Rivières doubled. The population grew rapidly again in the early 20th century, with the opening of paper and textile mills and an influx of people from neighbouring parishes. So many people moved to the suburbs during the 1960s that in 1976 the city's population began to decline. The population of Trois-Rivières has always been predominantly francophone.

Economy When manufacturing became more diversified, especially into foodstuffs, clothing, metals and electrical appliances, the dominant pulp and paper and textile industries declined, and by 1961 provided slightly less than half the total manufacturing jobs. The tertiary sector has grown steadily, mainly through the establishment of government offices serving the regional population and the creation of UNIVERSITÉ DU QUÉBEC à Trois-Rivières in 1969.

Transportation As the major route penetrating the continent, the river continued to be the only link with the rest of the colony until construction of the Chemin du Roi was completed along the N shore in 1737. By the mid-19th century, a road network linked Trois-Rivières to the region's new parishes. In the late 1870s, the North Shore Railway linked the city directly to Québec C and Montréal. The port came under the control of the National Harbours Board in 1882. Its grain silos were erected in 1936. In 1968 Trois-Rivières was linked to the S shore by Laviolette bridge. The city has had a local airport since 1961.

Cultural Life The major cultural centre for the Mauricie region, the city has entertainment centres, art galleries, museums, a cultural centre and a municipal library. Visitors are attracted to its historic buildings, and the site of the forges has been developed by Parks Canada. The Québec National Archives has a regional branch here. The city has been a Catholic diocesan centre since 1852. Its role as an episcopal seat attracted several religious communities which took charge of education and hospital care before these responsibilities were assumed by the state in the 1960s. The city has a daily paper, *Le Nouvelliste* (1920), as

Aerial view of Trois-Rivières, Qué (*courtesy SSC Photocentre/photo by Michel Gagné*).

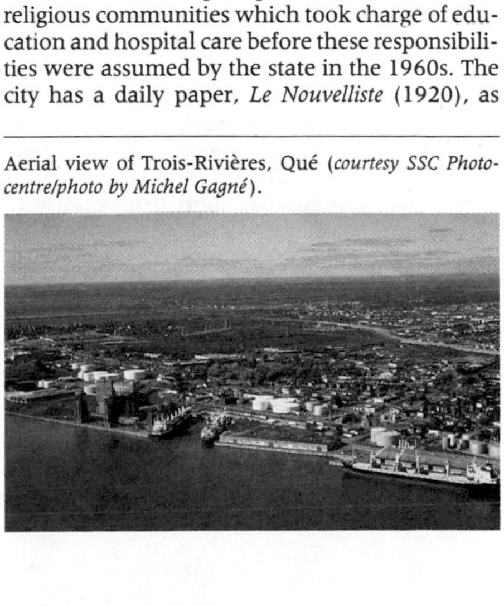

well as 3 TV and 4 radio stations. It has hosted a major agricultural exhibition for nearly a century. International canoeing races on the St-Maurice R finish at Trois-Rivières.

CLAIRE-ANDRÉE FORTIN, RENÉ HARDY AND
NORMAND SÉGUIN

Trotteur, Alexis Le, French Canadian designation of Alexis Lapointe, called le Trotteur because of his fantastic running ability. He lived in the Charlevois and Lac Saint-Jean regions of Québec. He could run over 240 km in a day and ran races with horses and even with trains. His stride was supposed to be 6 m long. Some said he had the legs of a horse, and an autopsy supposedly revealed that he had double joints and bones and muscles like a horse. He died around the beginning of the 20th century.

NANCY SCHMITZ

Trotting, *see* HARNESS RACING.

Troupes de la Marine (also known as independent companies of the navy, or colonial regulars), about 80 companies of 100 men each, est Dec 1690 as infantry for France and its colonies. About 30 companies were usually stationed in Canada and up to 20 at LOUISBOURG. The former gradually developed into the first permanent "Canadian" force. Initially composed entirely of Frenchmen, the companies came to be officered largely by Canadians. In the 18th century they became highly proficient in bush warfare, usually operating in small groups with militia and with friendly Indians in attacks on British forts and settlements. In 1758, during the SEVEN YEARS' WAR, the Louisbourg companies were taken prisoner by the British with the fall of that fortress. After the CONQUEST of 1760, many men settled in Canada, and many others repatriated to France went reluctantly. STUART R.J. SUTHERLAND

Trout, freshwater fishes, genus *Salmo*, of the SALMON family (Salmonidae). Worldwide, there are 6-7 species. In Canada, 3 species, the rainbow (*S. gairdneri*) and cutthroat (*S. clarki*) trouts, and the ATLANTIC SALMON (*S. salar*), are native; 2 others, the brown and golden trouts (*S. trutta, S. aquabonita,* respectively) have been introduced. Trouts are distinguished from other salmonids by black spots on the head and body and 7-12 anal fin rays. Trouts have both sea-run and freshwater forms, except golden trout, a California species, restricted in Canada to small, high-altitude lakes in western Alberta. All trouts spawn in streams. While some spend their lives in streams, young of most species migrate to lakes or to the sea, returning as adults to spawn in the natal stream.

Rainbow trout is native to western N America (northern Mexico to Alaska) and has been successfully introduced in temperate zones worldwide. It is one of 2 fish species considered domesticated (the other being common carp) and is the trout most commonly AQUACULTURED, with stock having spent at least 30 generations in captivity available. Trout have an excellent growth rate, take well to crowding in ponds or tanks, are fairly disease resistant and are in great public demand. They are popular sport fish because of fighting and jumping characteristics and because they readily take a shallow-water lure. Where sea-run populations called steelhead exist, they are most sought after in rivers when returning to spawn. Steelhead are large, up to 18 kg, and very strong.

Cutthroat trout, in Canada, is restricted to BC and southwestern Alberta. There are 2 subspecies: coastal cutthroat, with sea-run and freshwater forms, and freshwater Yellowstone or mountain cutthroat. The coastal cutthroat ranges throughout coastal BC and is larger (up to 8 kg)

than Yellowstone cutthroat. In Canada, Yellowstone cutthroat is restricted to southeastern BC and southwestern Alberta. Both subspecies are important sport fish, and stocking programs exist to assist in maintaining populations.

Brown trout, introduced to N America from Europe (1883), is now most common in Alberta and the 5 eastern provinces, although populations exist throughout southern Canada. It was the first salmonid species to be cultured (Germany, 1741). Brown trout has sea-run and freshwater populations and until the mid-1900s was heavily cultured and was used to stock lakes and streams. However, domestic rainbow stocks have replaced brown trout in most areas as the prime sportfishing trout. *See also* CHAR. E.D. LANE

Trout, Jennie (Jenny) Kidd, née Gowanlock, physician (b at Kelso, Scot 21 Apr 1841; d at Los Angeles, Calif 10 Nov 1921). She grew up near Stratford, Ont, and after her marriage in 1865 to Toronto publisher Edward Trout decided to become a doctor. As no Canadian medical school admitted women, she enrolled at the Woman's Medical College of Pennsylvania, graduating in 1875. That same year, on passing the Ontario registration exam, Dr Trout became the first Canadian woman licensed to practise medicine in Canada. A fervent promoter of women in medicine, she helped endow the Women's Medical College, Kingston, Ont, in 1883. CARLOTTA HACKER

Reading: Carlotta Hacker, *The Indomitable Lady Doctors* (1974).

Troyes, Pierre de, soldier (d at Niagara 8 May 1688). He arrived at Québec in Aug 1685 with reinforcements for the beleaguered colony. Departing on 20 Mar 1686, de Troyes led a force of 30 colonial regular French troops and 60 militia from Montréal overland to James Bay. Using the skills of the VOYAGEURS, the audacious expedition ascended the Ottawa R, portaged via Lks Timiskaming and Abitibi to the Abitibi R and descended on the astonished English at Moose Fort, which quickly succumbed on June 20. De Troyes next occupied Rupert House (Ft Charles) July 3 and with the captured English ship *Craven* took Ft Albany (July 26) before leaving Pierre Le Moyne d'IBERVILLE in charge and sailing back to Québec. In June 1687 de Troyes commanded one of the French companies led by Gov DENONVILLE into Iroquois territory (*see* IROQUOIS WARS). He was left in command at Niagara where he died of scurvy.

JAMES MARSH

Trucking Industry consists of persons and firms engaged in the business of owning and operating motor trucks to transport goods. The industry is composed mainly of 3 elements: contract, private and common carriage. A contract carrier transports goods for one or a limited number of consignors, according to contractual agreements specifying rates of compensation and other terms. A private carrier transports his own goods by his own motor vehicle, eg, raw materials to processing, finished products to market. It is estimated that private carriage is at least as large as common carriage in tonnage moved. The common-carrier (or for-hire) industry is composed of individuals and establishments that own and operate for-hire motor trucks for the transportation, by road, of any and all goods. Thus, unlike the private or contract carrier, the common carrier serves the general-shipping public. The common-carrier industry provides shippers with full-service, door-to-door delivery, with an enforceable legal obligation to provide service at a published rate to even the smallest hamlet in N America.

History The Canadian war effort provided a major impetus to commercial trucking. The enor-

mous demand for raw resources, manufactured goods, ships, aircraft and vehicles placed a great burden on Canada's total transportation system. A major labour shortage in the trucking industry developed and the federal government complied with a request from carriers that the industry be declared essential to the war effort, gaining recognition for the industry as a flexible and effective means of commercial transportation. After the war, expansion and improvement of the highway system made it possible for the trucking industry to become a vital part of Canada's TRANSPORTATION network.

Regulation and Operation Provincial governments determine most of the operating conditions and the regulatory economic environment for intraprovincial carriers, eg, driver qualifications, fuel taxes, vehicle weights, vehicle dimensions, rules of the road, vehicle inspection, securement of loads, vehicle licensing and mandated safety equipment. The authority of the federal government to regulate trucking was established (1954) by a Privy Council decision which stated that such jurisdiction applied to the entire operation of the journey when it crossed provincial or international boundaries. However, since no federal-government regulatory mechanism was in place, jurisdiction was delegated back to the provinces. The only guideline was that each province apply its laws equally to intraprovincial and extraprovincial traffic. As a result of this nonspecific mandate, economic regulation has developed with wide disparities among provinces. When companies or individuals use for-hire trucks to cross a provincial or international boundary, certain federal regulations supersede provincial laws. The federal government also regulates safety standards.

The common-carrier industry provides service among Canada's 52 metropolitan areas, with a population of 50 000 or more, and 4250 smaller centres. All of these points, plus cities in the US with a population of over 47 000, are accessible to shippers either by direct service provided by one carrier or by transferring from one carrier to another until final delivery. The shipper or consignee pays the total freight charges, and the carrier collecting these funds distributes them to each of the participating carriers. The annual operating revenue of the common-carrier segment of the industry was about $8.2 billion in 1985. The 5 commodities most commonly carried by for-hire trucks in Canada are sand, gravel and crude stone, pulpwood chips, logs and bolts, lumber and sawn timber and fuel oil—constituting almost 30% of total tonnage. Although the average distance for an intercity truck haul in Canada is about 482 km, the reliance on trucks to carry perishable goods over much longer distances has been increasing. Some carriers, specializing in long-distance movements, advertise that shipments leaving Toronto are scheduled for arrival in Vancouver less than 70 hours later.

In 1985 the 6270 for-hire establishments that grossed revenues for the year in excess of $100 000 operated 157 209 pieces of revenue equipment. These units travelled over 3.7 billion km and used nearly 2 billion litres of fuel, of which 91% was diesel. The rapid and continuing increase of fuel prices, beginning in 1973, with a concomitant rise in fuel taxes, has brought expenditures for fuel to unprecedented levels. On average, 10% of gross carrier revenue is now spent on fuel; in 1985 for-hire carriers spent over $846 million on diesel fuel and gasoline. As countermeasures, truck suppliers have been providing carriers with fuel-efficient vehicles, and suppliers of truck components have been producing air-drag reduction devices, radial tires, synthetic lubricants and modulated fans. Equally important are training programs for drivers, emphasizing conservation. The trucking industry is labour intensive: in 1985 common carriers paid their 98 694 employees nearly $2.68 billion.

Although provincial transport officials are responsible for their own highways, decisions concerning the establishment of specific regulations are often made only after consultation with regulators in other provinces. This is done through a permanent secretariat known as the Canadian Conference of Motor Transport Administrators. Although CCMTA's concerns are not confined to trucking, a great deal of work has been done to rationalize truck regulation in bonding requirements for drivers, cargo insurance, vehicle inspections, transportation of dangerous goods, and driver licensing. Probably the most significant accomplishment of the CCMTA is the introduction of a pro rata type vehicle-licensing system, under which carriers pay each jurisdiction a percentage based on the distance driven in that jurisdiction. Though there are significant provincial differences in the maximum axle and gross weights permitted, a 5-axle unit, the workhorse of the industry, may legally operate anywhere on designated Canadian highways with a gross of 36 400 kg.

It is estimated that 70% of manufactured goods moving between Canada and the US are carried by truck. Canadian carriers engaging in this international movement must, among other requirements, apply for US authorization and satisfy the requirements of both US and Canadian customs regulations.

Trudeau, Pierre Elliott, politician, writer, constitutional lawyer, prime minister of Canada 1968-79 and 1980-84 (b at Montréal 18 Oct 1919). Trudeau was born into a wealthy family, the son of a successful French Canadian businessman and a mother of Scottish ancestry. Educated at the Jesuit Collège Jean-de-Brébeuf, U de M, Harvard and London School of Economics, he also travelled extensively in his youth. Upon his return to Québec from a year's travels in 1949, he supported the unions in the bitter ASBESTOS STRIKE, a formative event in postwar Québec society. In 1956 he edited a book on the strike, to which he contributed an introduction and conclusion criticizing the province's dominant social, economic and political values.

After serving briefly in Ottawa as an adviser to the Privy Council Office in 1950-51, Trudeau returned to Montréal and devoted his energies to opposing the Union Nationale government of Maurice DUPLESSIS and agitating for social and political change. With other young intellectuals he founded the review CITÉ LIBRE. In this and other forums, Trudeau sought to rouse opposition to what he believed were reactionary and inward-looking elites. In the process, he picked up a reputation as a radical and a socialist, although the values he espoused were closer to those of liberalism and democracy.

After the Liberals' victory in the 1960 provincial election, the QUIET REVOLUTION fulfilled some of Trudeau's hopes for change. At the same time, it revealed a deep rift between Trudeau and many of his former colleagues who were moving toward the idea of an independent Québec. A law professor at U de M by the 1960s, Trudeau became a sharp critic of the contemporary Québec nationalism and argued for a Canadian FEDERALISM in which English and French Canada would find a new equality.

In 1965 Trudeau, with union leader Jean MARCHAND and journalist Gérard PELLETIER, joined the federal LIBERAL PARTY and were elected to Parliament. Trudeau was later appointed a parliamentary secretary to PM Lester PEARSON, and was

**Pierre Elliott Trudeau
Fifteenth Prime Minister of Canada**

Birth: 18 Oct 1919, Montréal, Qué
Father/Mother: Charles/Grace Elliott
Father's Occupation: Lawyer
Education: U de M; Harvard U; London School of Economics
Religious Affiliation: Roman Catholic
First Occupation: Lawyer
Last Private Occupation: Lawyer
Political Party: Liberal
Period(s) as PM: 20 Apr 1968 - 3 June 1979; 3 Mar 1980 - 30 June 1984
Ridings: Mount Royal, Qué, 1965-84
Other Ministries: Justice 1967-68
Marriage: 4 Mar 1971 to Margaret Sinclair (b 1948); divorced 1984
Children: 3 boys
Other Information: First PM born in 20th century. Full name: Joseph Philippe Pierre Yves Elliott Trudeau.

(*photo courtesy Karsh, Ottawa/Miller Comstock*)

named minister of justice in 1967. In the latter post, he gained national attention for his introduction of divorce law reform and for Criminal Code amendments liberalizing the laws on abortion, homosexuality, and public lotteries. He also established a reputation as a defender of a strong federal government against the nationalist demands of Québec.

He was persuaded to contest the Liberal leadership in 1968 and was elected on the fourth ballot; on 20 Apr 1968 he was sworn in as Canada's fifteenth prime minister. In the ensuing general election – which was dominated by "Trudeaumania" – his government won a majority, and thus he began a period in office which was to last longer than that of any other prime minister, save Mackenzie KING and Sir John A. MACDONALD.

The most dramatic event of his first government was the OCTOBER CRISIS of 1970, precipitated by the kidnapping of British diplomat James Cross and of Québec Cabinet minister Pierre LAPORTE by the terrorist FRONT DE LIBÉRATION DU QUÉBEC (FLQ). In response, Trudeau invoked the WAR MEASURES ACT, with its extraordinary powers of arrest, detention and censorship. Shortly after, Laporte was murdered by his abductors. Controversy over the appropriateness of these emergency measures and their effect on liberal democracy in Canada and Québec has continued to the present. Less dramatic, but of lasting significance, was the OFFICIAL LANGUAGES ACT, a central feature of Trudeau's new federalism. At the same time, he began to improve the position of Francophones in Ottawa. A growing antibilingual backlash in English Canada, however, was one result of these policies. Western Canada's growing alienation against a perceived lack of interest in western economic problems and in western perspectives on national issues also began in his first term. An important initiative in government brought about under Trudeau's direction was the attempt to centralize and nationalize decision-making under nondirect control of the PRIME MINISTER'S OFFICE and by CENTRAL AGENCIES such as the PRIVY COUNCIL OFFICE and TREASURY BOARD. Although very much along the lines of administrative reorganization in Washington and in other Western capitals, these changes proved controversial, leading critics to charge inefficiency and the undermining of the role of Parliament and Cabinet. In the 1972 election, Trudeau came close to losing office and was forced to form a MINORITY GOVERNMENT with the support of the NDP.

In 1971 Trudeau, hitherto a bachelor, married Margaret Sinclair, daughter of a former Liberal Cabinet minister. Their tempestuous marriage, beset by many well-publicized differences, finally ended in separation in 1977 and divorce in 1984, with Trudeau retaining custody of their 3 sons, Justin, Sasha and Michel.

After restoring a Liberal majority in 1974, Trudeau faced the effects of inflation. In an atmosphere of economic crisis, various expedients were tried, including mandatory WAGE AND PRICE CONTROLS in 1975. This economic crisis was compounded in 1976 when the PARTI QUÉBÉCOIS under René LÉVESQUE was elected to office, dedicated to Québec independence. In 1979 Trudeau and the Liberals suffered a narrow defeat at the polls. A few months later, he announced his intention to resign as Liberal leader and retire from public life. Three weeks after this announcement, the Progressive Conservative government of Joe CLARK was defeated in the Commons and a new general election was called. Trudeau was persuaded by the Liberal caucus to remain as leader and on 8 Feb 1980 – less than 3 months after his retirement – he was returned once again as prime minister with a parliamentary majority, thus accomplishing a remarkable resurrection.

Trudeau's last period in office as prime minister was eventful. His personal intervention in the 1980 QUÉBEC REFERENDUM campaign on SOVEREIGNTY-ASSOCIATION was significant. The defeat of the Parti Québécois's proposition was a milestone in his crusade against Québec separatism. In the wake of that victory, Trudeau pushed strongly for an accord on a new Canadian constitution. Unable to gain provincial agreement, he introduced into Parliament a unilateral federal initiative to "patriate" the BNA Act to Canada with an amending formula and an entrenched CANADIAN CHARTER OF RIGHTS AND FREEDOMS. There followed one of the epic federal-provincial battles of Canadian history, culminating in the final compromise and the proclamation of the CONSTITUTION ACT, 1982, on 17 Apr 1982. With the inclusion of entrenched minority language and education rights, and a charter of individual rights, Trudeau had thus fulfilled a goal he had set himself upon entering public life (*see* CONSTITUTION, PATRIATION OF).

In other areas, his 1980-84 government was less successful. Continued inflation and high levels of unemployment, along with huge federal deficits, cut deeply into his popular support. His government's National Energy Program, one of the major government interventions in the economy since WWII, further alienated the energy-producing regions in western Canada. A continuing problem that plagued his entire tenure of office was that of CANADIAN-AMERICAN RELATIONS. Trudeau often played an ambiguous role with regard to the US, but in his last period in office he moved towards a more nationalist position in economic relations with the US, and began to criticize its foreign and defence policies more freely than in the past. At the same time the policies of US Pres Reagan's administration were becoming more damaging to many of Canada's economic interests. In these years Trudeau devoted more and more time to the international stage, first to encouraging a "North-South" dialogue between the wealthy industrial nations and the underdeveloped countries, and then in 1983-84 to a personal peace initiative in which he visited leaders in several countries in both the eastern and western blocs to persuade them to negotiate the reduction of nuclear weapons and to lower the level of tension in the Cold War. These activities led to his being awarded the Albert Einstein Peace Prize. At the same time, his government was responsible for the decision to allow US testings of the Cruise missile, which roused widespread opposition from Canadians concerned about the worsening nuclear arms race.

Public opinion in Canada remained hostile to Trudeau and the Liberals from 1981 on. His personal style – sometimes charismatic, sometimes contemptuous of opposition, often mercurial and unpredictable – seemed to have become less of an electoral asset in difficult economic times. On 29 Feb 1984, Trudeau announced his intention to retire; on June 30 he left office, and his successor, John TURNER, was sworn in. In 1985 he became a Companion of the Order of Canada. His retirement has been relatively low profile, although in 1987-88 he went public to oppose strongly the MEECH LAKE ACCORD.

Trudeau's career as prime minister was one of electoral success, matched in this century only by Mackenzie King. Moreover, he served longer than every other contemporary leader in the Western world, becoming the elder statesman of the West. His achievements include the 1980 defeat of Québec separatism, official bilingualism, the patriated Constitution and the Charter of Rights. He was unable, however, to alleviate the alienation of western Canada or to end the conflict between federal and provincial governments. He left office much as he had entered it: a controversial figure with strong supporters and equally strong critics. That he was one of the dominant figures in 20th-century Canada is not in dispute.   REG WHITAKER

Reading: R. Gwyn, *The Northern Magus* (1980); C. Mc-Call-Newman, *Grits* (1983); G. Radwanski, *Trudeau* (1978). Trudeau's writings are collected in *Federalism and the French Canadians* (1968), *Approaches to Politics* (1970), *The Asbestos Strike* (1974) and *Pierre Elliot Trudeau: Lifting the Shadow of War* (1987).

Trudeau, Yves, sculptor (b at Montréal 3 Dec 1930). He studied at the École des beaux-arts in Montréal. Moving from stylized bronze spiral figures in the late 1950s, Trudeau's "iron and wood" creations of the 1960s became highly charged with symbolism. Sometimes anthropomorphic, sometimes of organic shapes, the works in this series demonstrate his progressive abandonment of figurative representation (*L'homme-révolté*, 1961). In the geometrical and abstract series "Murs fermés et ouverts" of the 1970s, compositions circumscribe space: wooden triangles appear on an uninterrupted surface, broken by a bend or a straight line, sometimes by a flat curve. These works, painted white to capture light and shadow, sometimes contain social or political graffiti. In 1984 a large sculpture symbolizing a ship under full sail was installed in Gaspé to commemorate the 450th anniversary of Jacques Cartier's landing.   LOUISE BEAUDRY

Trudel, Marcel, historian (b at St-Narcisse, Qué 29 May 1917), one of the masters of contempo-rary Québec historiography. He shaped generations of historians, first at Laval (1947-65) and then at Ottawa U. His demanding view of the profession of historian causes him to reject the formulas of "edifying history" and the bias of nationalist history. He strives for an even-handedness which is disturbed only by an occasional undercurrent of anticlericalism and his work is commendable for its erudition, precision and respect for primary sources. His overall vision of Canadian history is close to that of Arthur Maheux, Léon Gérin and Gustave Lanctot. A specialist in the French régime, he has a great many works to his credit, including the learned *Histoire de la Nouvelle France* (1963-83).   PIERRE TRÉPANIER

Trueman, Albert William, cultural and university administrator (b at Waverley, Penn 17 Jan 1902). As government film commissioner (head of the NATIONAL FILM BOARD), 1953-57, and director of the CANADA COUNCIL, 1957-65, he made major contributions to Canadian cultural policies, primarily by promoting the roles and influence of both agencies. He was also an experienced and skilled university administrator, serving as president of U of Manitoba (1945-48) and of U of New Brunswick (1948-53), and as principal and dean of University College, U of Western Ontario (1965-67). Though born in the US, he was educated in Canada and Britain and his early career was as a professor in Canadian universities. He published *A Second View of Things: A Memoir* in 1982.   PETER MORRIS

Truro, NS, Town, pop 12 124 (1986c), 12 552 (1981c), inc 1875, is located 100 km NE of Halifax on Cobequid Bay, MINAS BASIN. A land grant including the area was awarded in 1689 by Louis XIV, and ACADIANS were present as early as 1701, finally leaving in 1755 in the turbulent year of the expulsion. The town received its name in 1759 from New England settlers and likely honours Truro in Cornwall, Eng. Transports of settlers arrived in the 1760s and further development of the town began. A major railway centre since the days of the INTERCOLONIAL RY, Truro is a terminus for people travelling to most parts of NS. Metal foundries, machinery, printing and lumbering have bolstered the economy. The Brookfield Dairy Co, located here since 1920, is a major employer. Stanfield's Textile Mills, established 1868, still operates. In addition, Crossley Karastan Carpet Mills Ltd, Polymer International (NS) Ltd and Andres Wines Atlantic Ltd are located in Truro. Always a thriving farming area, Truro is home to an agricultural college. The NS Teachers Coll is also located here.   JANICE MILTON

Trust, The trust has its origins in the Middle Ages in the concept of "use." Property was conveyed to one person "to the use" or for the benefit of another. Through the use, a landowner could arrange for successive enjoyment of land and thus avoid the prohibition that land could not, until the 16th century, be conveyed by will. The use was also a method of avoiding the payment of feudal dues such as wardship, marriage and relief. It was thus an early tax-planning device. Since the Crown became the feudal lord to whom the dues were ultimately payable, Henry VIII persuaded Parliament in 1535 to enact the Statutes of Uses, which were intended to abolish the use. However, the courts decided that it destroyed only uses of real property where the trustee had no positive duties and that it did not affect uses of personal property. The uses which were not abolished by the statute became known as trusts and are the foundation of the modern law of trusts. The law of trusts is a unique achievement of the historically separate jurisdictions of law and equity. No directly comparable concept exists in the civil law system of Québec but the idea that a person may owe fiduciary obligations is well known to the civil law.

The major use of the trust has been for the administration of personal wealth. For example, a testator or testatrix might by will establish a trust of all his or her property, giving to the surviving spouse all the income for life with the capital to be distributed to the children equally on the death of the surviving spouse. The will might also provide a power to encroach on capital in case the income was not sufficient to maintain the spouse. In earlier times, most trusts were administered by family friends or solicitors. Today, where the trust property is substantial, an incorporated trustee, a TRUST COMPANY, will often be selected to administer the property. It is also possible to select one or more individuals to be trustees, together with a trust company. In addition the trust is now being used in many areas of business and commercial life as a security device, for pre-incorporation financial holding and for administering large pension funds.

A trust is an equitable obligation binding a person, called the trustee, to hold or manage property over which he has control for the benefit of persons, called beneficiaries. The person who creates the trust is called the settlor. The beneficiaries may include the settlor and any of the beneficiaries may enforce the equitable obligations which are imposed upon the trustee.

Trusts can be classified according to the way in which they were created. The most important kind of trust is the express trust which arises when the settlor has explicitly stated his or her intention to create a trust. It may be either *inter vivos* (created by a living person) or testamentary (created by the will of a deceased person). All testamentary trusts must comply with the formalities of the Wills Act and therefore must be in writing. Most express *inter vivos* trusts are also declared in writing. However, *inter vivos* trusts of personal property may be made orally but a written document is necessary for land.

At the other end of the spectrum is the constructive trust. It is imposed by the court, regardless of anyone's intent, as a remedial device usually to prevent unjust enrichment which would occur if retention of the property were permitted. For example, in the case of *Pettkus v Becker*, a 1980 Supreme Court of Canada decision, a "common-law" wife was awarded a one-half interest in property legally owned by her "husband" because of her contribution to the acquisition and maintenance of the property. The court felt it was unjust to allow the common-law husband to retain full interest in the land after he had benefited from her efforts on the land during their 19 years of cohabitation.

For an express trust to be valid, the "three certainties" must be satisfied – certainty of words, certainty of subject-matter and certainty of object. If there is a dispute about the validity of an express trust, the court must be convinced that the settlor intended to create a trust. There must also be certainty as to the property subject to the trust and certainty of object or beneficiaries of the trust. A trust is said to be completely constituted when the 3 certainties exist and the property has been transferred to the trustee. A trust may also come into existence by the owner declaring himself or herself to be trustee of the particular property for the specified beneficiaries. In this case, the settlor is also the trustee and no transfer of property is required for there to be a fully constituted trust. Such a trust is irrevocable in the sense that the settlor cannot get the trust property back unless in the trust instrument the settlor has reserved a power of revocation.

The trustee has a duty to account to the beneficiaries for the management of the trust property. The trustee must not let his or her personal interests conflict with the duties which are owed to the beneficiary. Therefore, a trustee may neither purchase trust property nor sell or lease his or her own property to the trust. A trustee may not obtain private advantage through dealing with the trust property. A rule, developed in the 17th century, excluded the trustee from receiving remuneration for services. However, the trust can expressly provide for payment to the trustee and, where it does not, the Trustee Acts of all the common-law provinces and the territories now enable the courts to award "fair and reasonable" compensation.

Another important duty of a trustee is to be impartial between beneficiaries. This duty is particularly important when there are income beneficiaries and capital beneficiaries. Maintaining an even hand means that the trustee has a duty to select suitable investments. Unless the trust deed provides otherwise, many Canadian jurisdictions limit the trustee to investments contained in the "legal list." This list emphasizes fixed interest securities and the conservation of wealth in terms of its nominal dollar value. Substantial inflation is bringing about a realization that beneficiaries cannot be protected by inflexible rules. We are likely to see more provinces following the example of New Brunswick, Manitoba and the territories in abolishing the legal list and permitting trustees to invest in any asset which a prudent person would select.

Trusts are also the vehicle for the creation of most future interests in property. This gives rise to a dilemma for the law in determining the balance between the rights of present and future generations. How long should present owners be able to tie up property through the creation of future interests when this means the property will be so encumbered that subsequent generations will not be able to deal with it as they wish. The compromise evolved by the courts and modified by many provincial legislatures is the Rule Against Perpetuities. This rule strikes down future interests which do not vest within a life or lives in being plus 21 years. GORDON BALE

Trust Company, a corporation that functions as a trustee, as well as providing regular BANKING services; they are the only corporations in Canada with the power to conduct fiduciary [Lat, *fiducia*, trust] business, eg, to act as executors, trustees and administrators of wills. The first Canadian trust company opened in 1872; by 1900 there were 14. Spawned by entrepreneurs, and encouraged by the government in an attempt to separate commercial banking and trust services in order to avoid CONFLICTS OF INTEREST, they prospered with the nation as a whole. In 1986 Canada's 57 trust companies (which, whether incorporated under provincial or federal charter, are regulated by the Department of Insurance in Ottawa or by comparable provincial bodies) had over 1500 branches, 640 real-estate offices, 45 000 employees and $220 billion in assets. Unlike banks, with whom they are in competition for expanded commercial lending power, trusts are usually closely held and are sometimes entirely private affairs; most big banks are required to limit ownership by one shareholder to 10%, but no such laws exist for trusts. Although the trust companies were at some disadvantage for years by not having direct access to the Bank of Canada clearing system, this

has now changed with the Canadian Payments System, and where retail deposits are concerned they are virtually on an equal footing with banks. Customer deposits are protected (to a certain maximum) by the Canada Deposit Insurance Corporation. Banks control 53% of the finance industry's total assets, while trust companies hold 20%. Various trust companies pioneered new product features: daily-interest chequing accounts, on-line interbranch banking, variable-rate mortgages and longer hours. While the largest trust companies have followed conservative investment strategies and hold financial ratings equal to the banks, from time to time the smaller, sometimes regional trust companies have experienced financial difficulties as a result of regional economic decline or imprudent investing. Canada is currently undergoing a major regulatory reform of all its financial institutions, the results of which should be a strong and viable trust group of companies and a competitive financial marketplace for the consumer. ERIC W. DALY

Tsetsaut were probably named from a TSIMSHIAN word used by the Gitksan for various Athapaskans in the interior of northern BC. There is scant information on their language, history and traditions, though there is some evidence that they were most closely related to the KASKA. For unknown reasons the Tsetsaut left the Plateau, moving W across the southern waters of the Stikine R and the northern headwaters of the Nass R as far as the Pacific coast. The main area they inhabited was in the vicinity of the Portland Canal. The Tsetsaut economy was based on inland game hunting and apparently they never adapted fully to the environment of the river systems or to the coast. The Tsetsaut were harassed and raided by their neighbours, particularly the TAHLTAN, and survivors were assimilated into the Nishga. When Franz BOAS visited them in 1894, their total number was 12, reduced from an estimated population of 500 just 60 years earlier. Today, there are no persons identified as Tsetsaut. The last speaker of the Tsetsaut language died around 1935. *See also* NATIVE PEOPLE: SUBARCTIC and general articles under NATIVE PEOPLE.
BERYL C. GILLESPIE

Reading: F. Boas, "Fifth Report on the Indians of British Columbia," *British Assn for the Advancement of Sciences, Annual Report* (1895); J. Helm, ed, *Handbook of North American Indians,* vol 6: *Subarctic* (1981).

Tsimshian The term Tsimshian (Tsim-she-yan meaning "People of the Skeena") is often broadly applied to all those northern BC Indian groups speaking languages of the Tsimshian language family: NISHGA (or Nisga'a), GITKSAN and the Coast Tsimshian. The latter, sometimes referred to as the Tsimshian Proper, included groups along the lower Skeena R from the Kitselas Canyon and Kitsumkalum (near Terrace) and the adjacent coast south to Milbanke Sound, including Port Simpson, Metlakatla (in the Prince Rupert area), Kitkatla, Hartley Bay and Kitasu. In 1887, a group of 825 Tsimshians following missionary William Duncan moved to a site near Ketchikan, Alaska, where they founded the settlement of New Metlakatla. Archaeological excavations in the harbour at Prince Rupert have unearthed the remains of cedar plankhouse villages that date back 5000 years; thus, the Tsimshians claim one of the oldest continuous cultural heritages in the New World. Tsimshian groups are also generally held to be related historically to the Penutian peoples of Oregon and California.

Like their neighbours, the Tlingit of Alaska and the Haida of the Queen Charlotte Is, the Tsimshian represent the Northwest Coast cultural area, characterized by TOTEM POLES and POTLATCH feasts at which wealth is distributed. Although aborigi-

nal culture patterns are being replaced, these people take pride in their heritage and many families still fulfil traditional obligations by hosting community ceremonial feasts to punctuate name-giving, marriage, divorce, adoption and funerals. Originally, descent was reckoned through the female line and each Tsimshian still recognizes him/herself as belonging to one of four phratries (tribes or totems: Frog or Raven, Wolf, Eagle, and Killer-whale or Fireweed). One belongs to the same phratry as one's mother and marries someone (in aboriginal times, the preferred mate was a cousin) from a different phratry than one's own. Hereditary chiefly titles are still maintained by both men and women for ceremonial purposes. Although few trap for a living these days, fishing remains an important subsistence activity. On the reserves, band projects provide most of the employment. J.V. POWELL and V. JENSEN

Reading: V.E. Garfield and Paul S. Wingert, *The Tsimshian Indians and Their Arts* (1966); Franz Boas, *Tsimshian Mythology* (1916).

Tsunami, Japanese term for destructive OCEAN WAVES affecting coastal zones of large water bodies, particularly the Pacific Ocean. Japan has probably suffered more from tsunamis than any other nation, but the Asian coast of the USSR and the Hawaiian Is are also known for destructive tsunamis. In 1964 the Good Friday, Alaska EARTHQUAKE tsunami caused property damage of several millions of dollars in the twin cities of Alberni and Port Alberni, BC. Tsunamis are not caused by TIDES and it is incorrect to call them tidal waves. They usually follow large, shallow earthquakes beneath the ocean but may be generated by other geophysical disturbances (eg, volcanic eruptions, landslides). Because the world's water bodies are either partly or completely confined within solid boundaries, all of them exhibit oscillations with fixed periods. A tsunami can set a water body into oscillation if at least some of its periods agree with or are close to the natural periods of oscillation of the water body. Tsunami waves are long waves; they radiate outward from their source and cross the ocean at speeds of hundreds of kilometres per hour. Their amplitude over the deeper part of the ocean is usually less than 1 m; their speed is proportional to the square root of the depth of the water. G.C. DOHLER

Reading: T.S. Murty, *Seismic Sea Waves, Tsunamis* (1977).

Tuberculosis Known – and dreaded – since Hippocratic times, tuberculosis affects primarily the lungs, the skeletal system, the kidneys and the lymph nodes, although all organ systems may be involved. Once SMALLPOX was controlled by vaccination in the 19th century, infection with the tubercle bacillus became *the* plague in Asian and European countries. Successive waves of immigrants brought the disease to Upper and Lower Canada in the 17th century and to the West by the mid-19th century. By 1900, the mortality rate in Canada had reached 180/100 000 population and the subsequent fall to only 2.5/100 000 at the end of the 1960s represents one of the most dramatic successes in disease control ever recorded.

Socioeconomic factors determined the prevalence of the disease in the unsanitary conditions which existed in medieval and renaissance times. However, once the infective nature of the disease was recognized a century ago, steps could then be taken to improve the hygienic conditions in overcrowded urban environments – where the poor could not afford proper diets and were forced to huddle in squalor – with the result that the mortality rate began to fall rapidly as early as the first decade of the present century. This remarkable decline in incidence, as well as in mortality rates, became abundantly clear before active surgical intervention (collapse therapy to rest the involved lung) was undertaken in the 1930s or truly effective antituberculous drugs made their appearance in the 1950s. Public health measures (eg, isolation of infective cases in sanitoria, public indoctrination in the principles of protective interpersonal contact, diagnostic screening by chest x-rays and skin testing, improved living conditions, and provision of a more adequate nutritional status to bolster the resistance of the host to the infection) obviously played an equally significant role in bringing the disease under control.

Inevitably, the aboriginal population of Canada was placed at particular risk when exposed to frequently destitute European trappers and settlers. These immigrants were thought to have developed a significant degree of immunity to the disease, following population exposure over many generations, whereas the Inuit and Indians were facing the challenge for the first time and had absolutely no resistance to rapidly progressive disease once they were infected. As late as the mid-20th century, the Inuit were reported to suffer the highest incidence of the disease in the world. However, striking evidence of the value of preventive measures was then declared. By aggressively combining case finding, supervised chemotherapy, BCG vaccination and chemoprophylactic programs, the sources of infections could be controlled and there has been a dramatic decline in disease incidence among the Inuit. It is now thought that tuberculosis can be successfully eradicated in Canada if continuing vigilance is maintained. Immigrants must be closely screened and preventive and therapeutic programs carefully pursued in high risk population groupings.
NORMAN C. DELARUE

Tuktoyaktuk, NWT, Hamlet, pop 929 (1986c), 772 (1981c), is located on the BEAUFORT SEA coast, E of the MACKENZIE R delta, 1135 air km NW of YELLOWKNIFE. The area is the traditional home of the whale-hunting Kittegaryumiut Inuit, who diminished owing to a series of epidemics in the late 1800s and early 1900s. The Inuit who settled at the site after it was established as a port of choice (Port Brabant) in 1934 were from the immediate area and from other parts of the North. It was given its present name (Inuktituk for "looks like caribou") in 1950. Today the community has a mostly wage-based economy, as it has grown to be a transportation, government and DEW Line maintenance centre and a base for oil and gas exploration. ANNELIES POOL

Tuktoyaktuk harbour, NWT. The hamlet has become a transportation centre for northern oil development (*photo by Hans Blohm/Masterfile*).

Tully, John Patrick, oceanographer (b at Brandon, Man 29 Nov 1906; d at Nanaimo, BC 19 May 1987). As oceanographer in charge of the Pacific Oceanographic Group, Nanaimo, BC (1946-65), Tully influenced the entire growth of West Coast oceanographic research, including studies in physical, chemical and biological oceanography. He is best known for his research in descriptive

oceanography and in his practical application of oceanography to contemporary military and industrial problems. His published works on estuarine mechanisms and physicochemical processes in the oceans earned him particular distinction. He was an MBE, received the Commemorative Medal of Albert I of Monaco and other medals (eg, Order of Merit, 1985), and in 1964 was made a fellow of the RSC. The Canadian Meteorological and Oceanographic Society now awards a J.P. Tully medal annually, and in 1985 the Canadian Dept of Fisheries and Oceans named a new scientific ship for him. T.R. PARSONS

Tully, Kivas, architect, civil engineer, politician (b at Garrarucum, Queen's County, Ire 1820; d at Toronto 24 Apr 1905). Architect of prominent early institutional buildings in Ontario, he also served as councillor and alderman for the City of Toronto, was a founding member and officer of the (Royal) Canadian Institute, and a mason. Tully immigrated to Canada in 1844, established a practice and, in 1868, was appointed architect and engineer of the Dept of Public Works of Ontario. Among his important works are the Customs House, Trinity Coll on Queen St, and the Bank of Montreal at Yonge and Front streets, all in Toronto, the Welland County Courthouse, asylums in London, Hamilton and Brockville, and engineering proposals for the Toronto and Georgian Bay Ship Canal and the Toronto Harbour Front and Railways. ANDREA KRISTOF

Tumpline [Algonquian *tump*, "pack strap"], a long leather strap or sling, broad at the middle and tapered at both ends, which crosses the chest or forehead and attaches to a pack or other load. It was used to PORTAGE loads of fur-trade goods.
JOHN ROBERT COLOMBO

Tuna, swift, elegant marine FISHES of class Osteichthyes, family Scombridae (MACKERELS). There are about 49 species in the family, including kingfishes, mackerels, tunas and bonitos. Strictly speaking, tunas are restricted to the tribe Thunnini which includes 3-9 genera, depending on the authority. For present purposes, 13 species of tuna in 4 genera (*Auxis, Euthynnus, Katsuwonus* and *Thunnus*) are recognized. Genus *Thunnus* contains 7 species: *T. alalunga* (albacore), *T. albacares* (yellowfin tuna), *T. atlanticus* (blackfin tuna), *T. maccoyi* (southern bluefin tuna), *T. obesus* (bigeye tuna), *T. thynnus* (bluefin tuna) and *T. tonggol* (longtail tuna). Tunas are wide-ranging, pelagic (open sea) fishes, inhabiting tropical and temperate waters worldwide. In Canada, 4 species occur in Pacific waters, 6 in Atlantic. Small species weigh under 9 kg but larger species may grow to weights of 45-679 kg. All tunas have hydrodynamically efficient, streamlined bodies and widely forked tails. Behind the second dorsal fin and the anal fin are a series of small finlets. Individual species are strikingly colourful. True tunas are unusual among fishes because they are warm-blooded and can maintain a body temperature of up to 10°C above surrounding waters through retention of heat from muscle contractions. Tunas are exceedingly active, ranging widely over the oceans and travelling thousands of kilometres on extensive MIGRATIONS. They consume large quantities of crustaceans, squids and fishes (up to 25% of their body weight daily) to meet their energy requirements. The commercial fisheries employ purse seines, trapnets, longlines and angling. In 1985 the landed value of the commercial tuna catch was $705 000. Tuna are canned or sold fresh. Bluefin tuna are trapped on Canada's East Coast, retained alive and fattened for shipment to Japan, where they are sold fresh for the sashimi market. During 1985 to 1987 much attention was given by Canadian news media to the inspection

Landing tuna at Hubbards, NS, early 20th century (*courtesy National Archives of Canada/PA-41868*).

problems at Canada's only tuna cannery at Chamcook, NB. The world's record rod-caught bluefin (679 kg) was caught off PEI in 1979; the record is still valid. W.B. SCOTT

Tundra [Finnish, *tunturi*], also called "barren land," large region of the Northern Hemisphere lacking trees and possessing abundant rock outcrops. In Canada, the southern boundary extends from the Mackenzie Delta to southern Hudson Bay and NE to Labrador. Many CLIMATE variables combine to determine the position of this boundary.

The tundra environment is characterized by the general presence of PERMAFROST (except beneath some lakes and rivers); short summers with almost continuous daylight; long winters and arctic "nights"; low annual precipitation (hence the name polar desert); strong winds and winter blizzards; discontinuous vegetation; unstable, wet SOIL conditions resulting from permafrost and frost action. Tundra plants have developed many adaptations for survival. Their low stature exploits the more favourable microclimate near the ground; small, leathery, hairy leaves prevent desiccation by evaporation. Perennial life habit, vegetative propagation, short reproductive cycle and effective seed dispersal by wind are common among tundra plants (eg, LICHENS, MOSSES, GRASSES, low shrubs). Many birds and some animals live in the tundra in summer, migrating in autumn (*see* ARCTIC ANIMALS). Tundra environments present many impediments to human activities. Buildings, pipelines, roads and airports must be so constructed that they can cope with cold climate and permafrost, and proper advance planning must precede resource development and waste disposal to avoid damage to ecosystems. The term "alpine tundra" has been used for areas above the TREELINE in mountains. Although alpine tundra resembles arctic tundra proper in some respects, the differences are both substantial and significant. *See also* PHYSIOGRAPHIC REGIONS.
J. TERASMAE

Reading: J.D. Ives and R.G. Barry, eds, *Arctic and Alpine Environments* (1974).

Tungsten, NWT, Settlement, pop 238 (1986c), 320 (1981c), is located in the SELWYN MTS, 700 air km W of YELLOWKNIFE. The name comes from 2 Swedish words meaning "heavy" and "stone." It is the site of Canada's largest TUNGSTEN-producing mine. The plant was built in 1960 but had to be rebuilt after a fire destroyed it a year later. The mine's operations are dependent on the price of its product. It suspended operations in 1963 and 1983. After the most recent closure (May 1986) the mine will remain closed until it is economically viable. ANNELIES POOL

Tungsten, or wolfram (W), silver-grey metallic element with the highest melting point of any metal (3410°C). Tungsten has a high density, high strength at elevated temperatures and extreme hardness. Its first important use, during the mid-1800s, was in the manufacture of high-speed steel. Tungsten steels are important to industry because they retain their hardness and strength at high temperatures. Sintered tungsten-carbide tools were developed in the 1920s, and account for about 60% of current tungsten consumption. Metallic tungsten is used in the ELECTRONICS INDUSTRY and for light-bulb filaments.

There are 4 important ore minerals of tungsten: scheelite, wolframite, ferberite and huebnerite, the first 2 being far more abundant than the others. Canada is the largest mine producer of scheelite in the Western world and will probably remain so as new Canadian deposits are brought into production. The largest tungsten deposits are located in the YT and the NWT (where there is a community named for the metal); smaller deposits are dispersed across the country. Wolframite was produced in NB, but mining was terminated in 1985 as a result of low prices and weak markets.

Most Canadian production of tungsten contained in ores and concentrates is exported to the US and western Europe. Canadian production of tungsten concentrate accounted for 20% of the tungsten concentrate traded on the world markets in the first half of the 1980s. There is also a relatively large domestic, tungsten-carbide tool industry based on imported tungsten. The metal-working and petroleum industries are the major users of tungsten-carbide tools. Major producers of tungsten, other than Canada, are the People's Republic of China, the USSR, Bolivia, the Republic of Korea and Australia.   DON LAW-WEST

Tunnels Unlike other mountainous countries such as Switzerland, and despite its size, Canada is not distinguished by well-known tunnels. It is possible to travel from sea to sea, from Halifax to Vancouver, by CANADIAN NATIONAL RAILWAYS, without going through any major tunnels, merely a few short ones west of Thunder Bay. There are, however, some notable tunnels in Canada, and some that are unique. Tunnels for coal mining in Cape Breton extend far out under the sea; the Granduc Mine in BC can only be reached by a 16.5 km tunnel under 3 glaciers. At NORTH BAY, the Canadian headquarters of NORAD are housed in an unusual set of great tunnels excavated in Precambrian bedrock, complete even to an underground powerhouse, approached through 2 ordinary access tunnels large enough to accommodate passenger buses.

Canada's oldest tunnel is at BROCKVILLE, Ont; it runs for 518 m from the waterfront, under the City Hall, below Market St. When the Brockville and Ottawa Railway was built in the 1850s, the contractors took the view that a railway, to be complete, had to have a tunnel. It was used first on 31 Dec 1860 and last in 1970, and is still there, with its great oak doors at each end.

No tunnels were required when the main line of the GRAND TRUNK RY was built from Montréal to Toronto in the 1850s, and only one very short tunnel was needed in the entire length of the INTERCOLONIAL RY (Halifax to Montréal) completed in 1876. But between 1889 and 1891, the first underwater railway tunnel in N America was built under the ST CLAIR R, linking the Grand Trunk Ry at SARNIA with the Grand Trunk Western Ry at Port Huron, to complete a through line between Toronto and Chicago. The tunnel was over 1800 m long between portals and was the first tunnel in N America to be built under compressed air, the first to be built with shields and only the second tunnel to be lined with cast-iron segments. When the CANADIAN PACIFIC RY was being built, a series of short tunnels along the N shore of Lk Superior could not be avoided, but the route through the mountains of the West was achieved without re-

sort to tunnelling. The resulting grades (up to 4%) made operation difficult and uneconomic as traffic increased, and so the Spiral Tunnels between Hector and Field were opened for use in 1909, reducing the maximum grade in that section to 2.3%. In 1916 the 5-mile (8 km) Connaught Tunnel was opened under ROGERS PASS to reduce grades and eliminate trouble from avalanches. In 1988 the longest railway tunnel in N America was expected to open. Through Mt Macdonald, it will duplicate the Connaught Tunnel to reduce grades for west-bound traffic.

Shorter tunnels, to give access to terminal facilities, were built in later years, such as the CNR tunnel under Capital Hill, Vancouver; the CPR access tunnel to Wolfe's Cove terminal at Québec; and the 4.8 km Mount Royal Tunnel, Montréal. Originally constructed to give the CANADIAN NORTHERN RY access to downtown Montréal, the Mount Royal Tunnel is now a part of the CNR, incorporated into the efficient complex of Montréal's Central Station.

Just as railway building in Canada passed its peak, new waterpower plants increased in number and size, often requiring tunnels for transferring water from impounding RESERVOIRS to penstocks and powerhouses. The twin 15.2 m diameter tunnels that convey water under the city of NIAGARA FALLS (90 m below the surface) for supplying the Sir Adam Beck powerhouse at Queenston are of special interest, as is the tunnel of the Kemano power plant of the Aluminum Co of Canada in BC which serves the smelter plant at KITIMAT. This tunnel conveys water from a new reservoir in the headwaters of the Nechako, a tributary of the Fraser R, through the mountains of the Coast Range, to a precipitate drop almost to sea level at the powerhouse (*see* ELECTRIC-POWER GENERATION).

One little-known but important tunnel in the West runs below the seabed of the First Narrows at Vancouver, conveying fresh water under pressure from reservoirs in the foothills of the Coast Range to supply the city of Vancouver. Tunnels for water supply and sewage disposal are to be found beneath the streets of all major Canadian cities. Beneath the streets of Ottawa, for example,

---

Some of the deepest and most spectacular tunnels are associated with hydroelectric developments, such as this one at the W.A.C. Bennett Dam, BC (*courtesy SSC Photocentre*).

are at least 160 km of such tunnels. One sewage collector tunnel along the N shore of the Island of Montréal is 48 km long. These are the "major" tunnels of Canada, unseen and generally unknown, but providing vital civic services. Underground railways necessitate large tunnels, also beneath city streets. The first section of the Toronto subway, almost all in tunnel, was opened in 1954 (*see* SUBWAYS AND LIGHT RAPID TRANSIT).

Canadian tunnelling expertise, largely gained in the tunnels required for metal-ore mining, was called upon in WWII when the Canadian Army was responsible for extending the labyrinth of tunnels that form a honeycomb beneath the Rock of Gibraltar. Completion of the major part of what is still the longest railway tunnel east of the Mississippi R, the Hoosac Tunnel in Massachusetts, was the successful work of 2 pioneer Canadian engineers, Walter and Francis SHANLY, in 1875.
ROBERT F. LEGGET

Tupper, Sir Charles, politician, diplomat, prime minister (b at Amherst, NS 2 July 1821; d at Bexleyheath, Eng 30 Oct 1915). He was the last survivor of the original FATHERS OF CONFEDERATION. Educated at Horton Academy (Acadia) and Edinburgh, Tupper returned to Amherst in 1843 to follow a successful medical career. (He was the first president of the Canadian Medical Assn, 1867-70.) In 1855 he sought a seat in the NS Assembly as a Conservative, dramatically winning Cumberland County from the popular Reform politician, Joseph HOWE. He soon entered the administration, serving as provincial secretary, 1857-60 and 1863-67. In May 1864 he became premier, championing Maritime or British N American union, which he did not feel to be incompatible goals. He was a delegate at the Charlottetown, Québec and London conferences but was unable to win approval for the Quebec Resolutions in the NS Assembly.

In 1867 he left provincial politics and won a federal seat as the only supporter of CONFEDERATION from NS. Although his claim for a Cabinet post was strong, he stood aside to allow others from NS to enter the ministry. He helped bring about the "better terms" settlement which led Howe into the Cabinet in 1869. In 1870 Tupper began his long ministerial career. He was successively president of the Privy Council (1870-72), minister of inland revenue (1872-73), and minister of customs (1873) in the first John A. MACDONALD government.

When the Conservatives returned to office, Tupper served as minister of public works (1878-79) and minister of railways and canals (1879-84) during the critical period of Pacific Railway construction. He became high commissioner to the UK in 1884, but returned to Ottawa to serve as minister of finance (1887-88). Resuming his duties in London, he became known as an outspoken advocate of imperial federation and preferential tariffs. Macdonald was not pleased with Tupper's views, but his political standing allowed him immunity from censure.

In Jan 1896 Tupper was recalled to Ottawa to serve as secretary of state in the failing government of Sir Mackenzie BOWELL. Having been passed over for the party leadership in favour of J.J.C. ABBOTT, J.S.D. THOMPSON and Bowell, Tupper finally became prime minister 1 May 1896. In a desperate attempt to stave off defeat in the House, Tupper and his colleagues had introduced remedial legislation to protect the educational rights of the French-speaking minority in Manitoba. Blocked in the Commons, Tupper and the Conservatives suffered a stunning general election defeat in June, as Québec's returns were decisive. He resigned on July 8, having served only 10 weeks as prime minister. He continued in Par-

Sir Charles Tupper
Sixth Prime Minister of Canada

Birth: 2 July 1821, Amherst, NS
Father/Mother: Charles/Miriam Lockhart
Father's Occupation: Clergyman
Education: U of Edinburgh, Scot
Religious Affiliation: Baptist
First Occupation: Physician
Last Private Occupation: Physician
Political Party: Conservative
Period(s) as PM: 1 May 1896 - 8 July 1896
Ridings: Cumberland, NS, 1867-84, 1887-96; Cape Breton, 1896-1900
Other Ministries: Privy Council 1870-72; Inland Revenue 1872; Customs 1873; Public Works 1878; Railways and Canals 1879-84; Finance 1887-88
Marriage: 8 Oct 1846 to Frances Morse (1826-1912)
Children: 3 boys, 3 girls
Died: 30 Oct 1915 in Bexleyheath, Eng
Cause of Death at Age: Heart failure at 94
Burial Place: Halifax
Other Information: Oldest to assume office. Shortest total duration. Second provincial premier to become PM. CB, 1867; KCMG, 1879; GCMG, 1886

(photo courtesy National Archives of Canada/C-10109)

liament as leader of the Opposition but was defeated in the election of 1900. On retirement he lived in Vancouver before moving to England in 1913. Tupper was a decisive figure in Canadian political life. As one of Macdonald's principal lieutenants, he had a real capacity for administration as well as a reputation for parliamentary bluff and bullying.   D.M.L. FARR

Reading: C. Tupper, *Recollections* (1914) and *Political Reminiscences* (1914).

Tupper, Sir Charles Hibbert, politician, cabinet minister (b at Amherst, NS 3 Aug 1855; d at Vancouver, BC 30 Mar 1927). Second son of Sir Charles TUPPER, he was educated at McGill and Harvard. He practised law in Halifax before being elected Conservative MP for Pictou, a seat he held until his retirement from public life in 1904. Appointed minister of marine and fisheries in 1888, he was the youngest member of a federal Cabinet to that time. Although opponents claimed he owed his rapid elevation to his father, Tupper proved to be a hardworking minister who gained a thorough understanding of the fisheries in Canada. As agent for Great Britain he contributed to the victory of Canada's case in the BERING SEA DISPUTE with the US, 1893. Called "bumptious" by

Sir John MACDONALD, Tupper showed himself to be a passionate, if argumentative, nationalist in advancing Canada's fishing interests. In 1894 he was promoted to minister of justice in the government of Sir Mackenzie BOWELL, where he drafted the unsuccessful remedial bill for the restoration of Roman Catholic schools in Manitoba (*see* MANITOBA SCHOOLS QUESTION). In Jan 1896 he resigned from Cabinet in protest against its ineffective leadership. From May to July 1896 he was solicitor general in the short-lived administration of his father. He practised law in Vancouver after his political retirement in 1904.   D.M.L. FARR

Turcotte, Ron, jockey (b at Drummond, NB 22 July 1941). One of 11 children, Turcotte was always a strong jockey because of his early years as a lumberjack in NB. Unemployment in 1959 sent him to Toronto where he obtained a job as a hotwalker at E.P. TAYLOR'S Windfields Farms. He recorded his first win in 1962 and was named Canada's top jockey that year and in 1963. In 1972 he rode Riva Ridge to victories in the Kentucky Derby and the Belmont Stakes. The following year he became the first jockey in 70 years to ride Kentucky Derby-winning horses in consecutive years: in 1973 he was aboard Secretariat, the first Triple Crown winner in 25 years. His career ended tragically on 13 July 1978 when he broke his back after falling from his horse at the Belmont track. Now confined to a wheelchair, he operates a restaurant and trains horses in NB. In 1986 he lost his lawsuit seeking more than $190 million for his 1978 fall.   J. THOMAS WEST

Turks Turkey is a republic of southeastern Europe and Asia Minor. Turkey in Europe is separated from Turkey in Asia (Anatolia) by the Bosporus, the Sea of Marmara and the Dardanelles which link the Black Sea to the Mediterranean. It is predominantly a Muslim country, with minorities of Kurds, ARMENIANS, GREEKS and Jews. The earliest Turkish immigrants to Canada are believed to have arrived in the 1880s. Estimates from the 1986 census place the Turkish population in Canada at just over 5000 (not including Armenians or Greeks). The main immigrations were in 1900-04 (156), 1906-14 (3922), 1915-55 (1262) and 1956-75 (5710). Of the last group, 43% settled in Québec, 43.5% in Ontario, 4.6% in BC, 4% in Alberta and 4% in the other provinces.

Social and Cultural Life Almost all Turks celebrate the Islamic religious holidays. The Turkish community is served by the periodical *Sesimiz* ("The Voice") established in 1964. Through their Cultural Association of Montréal, Turks enjoy a number of activities, eg, folk dancing, sports, social evenings, conferences, and a weekend school for their language, culture and heritage. Many other clubs and organizations exist as well.
                                FOUAD E. SHAKER

Turmel, Antoine, businessman (b at Thetford-Mines, Qué 25 Apr 1918). In 1945 Turmel joined Compagnie Denault Ltée as sales manager and later took over control of the company. In 1969 he negotiated the merger of 3 independent food companies (Denault Ltée, Couvrette et Provost, and Lamontagne Ltée) and formed Provigo Inc, one of the largest food chains in Canada. He retired from Provigo in 1985 and now sits on the boards of the National Bank of Canada, Canadian General Electric, Noranda Mines, Québec-Téléphone, Shell Canada, UAP Inc, Canada Development Investment Inc and Groupe La Laurientienne. He holds an honorary doctorate from Sherbrooke and in 1982 became an Officer of the Order of Canada.   JORGE NIOSI

Turnbull, Wallace Rupert, aeronautical engineer (b at Saint John 16 Oct 1870; d there 26 Nov

1954). From a wealthy family, he studied science at Cornell and in Germany to age 25 and worked at the Edison Lamp Works, Harrison, NJ, for 6 years. In 1902 he built the first wind tunnel in Canada at his private laboratory in Rothesay, NB, where he worked for the rest of his life, geographically remote but collaborating with aviation pioneers such as Alexander Graham BELL and J.H. PARKIN. Turnbull's research was recognized early – he won a medal from the Royal Aeronautical Soc in 1909 – but his greatest achievement was the variable-pitch propellor, tested in flight in 1927. This device adjusts the angle at which propellor blades cut the air and it became as essential to aviation as the gearbox is to the automobile. It provides for safety and efficiency at all engine speeds, for example, maximum power on takeoff and landings and economical cruising for long distances. It was independently perfected in several countries, so that Turnbull's work has been overlooked by most historians, perhaps because he licensed its manufacture and went on with other inventions. But his variable-pitch propellor (now in the National Aviation Museum, Ottawa) appears to have been the first to fly successfully.
                              DONALD J.C. PHILLIPSON

Turnbull, Walter James, public servant (b at Toronto 16 Sept 1896). As deputy postmaster general Turnbull directed the Post Office Dept with exceptional efficiency from 1945 to 1957 during a period of traumatic change in the transportation, volume and makeup of mail in Canada. He introduced "all-up" airmail service in 1948, making Canada the first country in the world to transport mail efficiently by air at regular postal rates. He computerized the money-order system and pioneered the development of mechanized mail sorting at Canada Post. He was the first public relations director of CANADA POST and from 1946 he led Canada Post's participation in the Universal Postal Union, culminating in his being, in 1957, the host and chairman of the only congress of that union to be held in Canada. Turnbull was also active in the Postal Union of the Americas and Spain in the late 1940s.
                                HERBERT L. GRIFFIN

Turner, David, soccer player (b at Edinburgh, Scot 11 Oct 1903). Turner came to Canada at age 11 and played junior soccer in Edmonton. A powerful player with an excellent shot and heading ability, he was one of Canada's top players in the 1920s and 1930s. At age 19 he moved west, playing for Vancouver St Andrews and Cumberland United. After one season as a professional in the US, he played for Toronto Ulster United, before enjoying his greatest success with the New Westminster Royals – Canadian champion in 1928, 1930, 1931 and 1936. Turner also played for Canada in 3 internationals against New Zealand in 1927.   COLIN JOSE

Turner, John Herbert, businessman, politician, premier of BC (b at Claydon, Eng 7 May 1834; d at Richmond, Eng 9 Dec 1923). A merchant in Halifax and Charlottetown, Turner moved in 1862 to Victoria, where in 1865 he established the firm of Turner, Beeton and Co. He was successively alderman and mayor of Victoria (1876-81); was elected to the BC legislature (1886); served as finance minister (1887-95); premier (1895-98), finance minister again (1900) and BC's agent general in London (1901-15). In both his business and political life, Turner epitomized the role of Victoria in late 19th-century BC; his firm was typically engaged in a wide variety of operations – salmon canning, importing, wholesaling, finance and insurance. Turner's premiership marked the final flowering of the Victoria business class in BC politics.
                      H. KEITH RALSTON AND MAIRI DONALDSON

Turner, John Napier, politician, lawyer, prime minister (b at Richmond, Eng 7 June 1929). Following the death of his father, Turner accompanied his Canadian-born mother to Canada in 1932. Educated in Ottawa private schools, Turner went west with his mother and stepfather, Frank Ross, at the end of WWII. After studies at UBC, Oxford and U of Paris, Turner joined a Montréal law firm, qualifying as a lawyer in Québec in 1954. Recruited by Lester PEARSON as a Liberal candidate in Montréal, Turner was elected to the Commons in 1962 (re-elected 1963, 1965). When redistribution abolished his seat, he moved in 1968 to an Ottawa constituency. He first entered the Cabinet as part of a post-election shuffle by Pearson in Dec 1965 and served in minor offices until becoming minister of consumer and corporate affairs in Dec 1967. In 1968 Turner ran for the Liberal leadership, won by Pierre TRUDEAU, making a respectable showing as an "anti-establishment" candidate and as the most prominent younger English-language minister. Trudeau appointed him minister of justice in July 1968, a position he held until Jan 1972. In this capacity Turner sponsored Criminal Code reform and special legislation that followed the 1970 OCTOBER CRISIS.

In 1972 Trudeau transferred Turner to the Department of finance. When the Trudeau government lost its majority in Nov 1972 Turner found it necessary to tailor policy to the demands of popularity, and tax reductions and pension increases followed. The government still ran a surplus, both in 1973 and 1974, but the overall effect of its policy was to stimulate inflation. Once the Trudeau government regained its majority in an election caused by the defeat of Turner's May 1974 budget in the Commons, Turner concentrated on restraining inflation, but policies had not yet been decided when, in Sept 1975, he suddenly resigned from Cabinet without explanation, quitting politics altogether in Feb 1976 to join a large Toronto law firm. He declined to contest the Liberal leadership in 1979 (a contest which was never held) after Trudeau's first resignation, but with the announcement of Trudeau's resignation in Feb 1984 Turner decided to try for the leadership, which he won on the second ballot on 16 June 1984, defeating Jean Chrétien. Becoming prime minister on June 30, Turner dissolved parliament on July 9. In the election that followed in early Sept, Turner directed a disorganized campaign which failed to recoup the Liberals' already massive unpopularity and they suffered a disastrous defeat, winning only 40 seats in the Commons. However, Turner, who was not able to convince voters that he represented innovation or decisive leadership, won his own seat in Vancouver Quadra. He left office 17 Sept 1984 and became Leader of the Opposition. This was the beginning of 2 years of discord in his own party, which was only temporarily quieted after the reconfirmation of Turner's leadership at a Liberal convention in Ottawa in Nov 1986. While Turner still faced the challenge of gaining wider acceptance of his leadership, his party rose to lead the polls through 1987. ROBERT BOTHWELL

Turner, Sir Richard Ernest William, KCMG, VC, DSO, businessman and soldier (b at Québec 25 July 1871; d there 19 June 1961). In 1891 he entered his family's wholesale grocery and lumber business. During the Battle of LELIEFONTEIN on 7 Nov 1900, Turner, a lieutenant with the Royal Canadian Dragoons, won the VICTORIA CROSS for deflecting a Boer attack on the Canadian guns, though wounded in the neck and arm (*see* SOUTH AFRICAN WAR). In WWI Brig-Gen Turner commanded Canada's Third Brigade, assumed temporary command of the 2nd Canadian Division

**John Turner
Seventeenth Prime Minister of Canada**

Birth: 7 June 1929, Richmond, Eng
Father/Mother: Leonard/Phyllis Gregory
Education: UBC; Oxford U, Eng; U de Paris
Religious Affiliation: Roman Catholic
First Occupation: Lawyer
Political Party: Liberal
Period(s) as PM: 30 June 1984 - 17 Sept 1984
Ridings: St-Lawrence-St George, Montréal 1962-68; Ottawa-Carleton, Ont, 1968-75; Vancouver-Quadra 1984-
Other Ministries: Consumer and Corporate Affairs 1967-68; Solicitor General 1968; Justice 1968-72; Finance 1972-75
Marriage: 11 May 1963 to Geills McCrae Kilgour (b 1937)
Children: 3 boys, 1 girl
Other Information: In office 80 days, shortest period for 20th-century PM. Rhodes scholar.

(*photo courtesy Gilbert Studios Ltd, Toronto*).

was promoted major-general in Sept 1915, and briefly commanded the Canadian Corps in Sept 1916. Controversy over responsibility for the St-Eloi setback in Mar-Apr 1916 deprived him of the command of the Canadian Corps. Instead he was made general officer of Canadian troops in the British Isles in Dec 1916, and was knighted and promoted to lt-gen in June 1917. He also received the Legion of Honour and the Russian White Eagle with Sword. CARMAN MILLER

Turner Valley, Alta, Town, pop 1271 (1986c), 1311 (1981c), inc 1930, located 40 km S of Calgary in the wide valley of the same name. It is named for the first settlers in the area, James and Robert Turner. The presence of oil was apparent through seepage, but it was not until May 1914 that Dingman No 1 came in – heralding the discovery of the first major gas and oil field in Alberta. Wells soon dotted the valley, and the petroleum activity was a bright spot in the otherwise bleak economy of Alberta in the 1930s. The field was depleted by the time the focus shifted N to LEDUC after WWII. ERIC J. HOLMGREN

Turnip (*Brassica rapa*, Rapifera Group), biennial VEGETABLE belonging to the Cruciferae family and grown in all provinces as a ROOT CROP. Native to Siberia, the turnip was introduced to England around 1550 and brought to America by the first settlers. The turnip is closely related to RUTABAGA but has a smaller, round, flat root, green downy leaves and white or yellow flesh. Various cultivars (commercial varieties) of white-fleshed and yellow-fleshed turnips are grown. A temperate-climate vegetable cultivated in spring or fall, the

turnip has a growing season of approximately 60 days. The turnip is prone to clubroot and black rot (fungus diseases) and is attacked by such parasites as the plant louse, flea beetle and cabbage fly. Served like spinach, the leaf is an excellent source of calcium, iron and vitamins A, B and C. The root contains calcium, potassium, sodium, and vitamins A and C. HUGUES LeBLANC

Turnor, Philip, surveyor, fur trader (b in Eng *c*1751; d at London, Eng 1799 or 1800). The first servant of the HUDSON'S BAY COMPANY employed specifically to survey and map its vast empire, he accumulated, in the course of his employment from 1778 to 1792, a considerable part of the information on the northern interior of N America published on Arrowsmith's map in 1795 (*see* CARTOGRAPHY). In 1789-90 he taught surveying to David THOMPSON and Peter FIDLER; and during his last assignment, to establish the position of Lake Athabasca and to find a route to it from the Saskatchewan R, he met Alexander MACKENZIE, whom he evidently persuaded to seek instruction in navigation before continuing his explorations. His enthusiastic evaluation of the great fur trading potential of the Athabasca region led to the establishment of the first HBC post there in 1793. STANLEY GORDON

Turtle (order Testudines or Chelonia), egg-laying, toothless REPTILE with limb girdles roofed over by a wide rib cage and fused to bony plates in the skin. The outer skin covering consists of horny, epidermal scales of keratin (sulphur-containing, fibrous protein). This basic body plan, a 3-layered box of ribs, skin-bones and hornlike scales, has remained unchanged over 200 million years and, with minor modifications, has been adapted for life in oceans, rivers, lakes, bogs, forests, grasslands and deserts. When Canada was ice covered and without reptiles, the greatest diversity of N American turtles was probably centered in the SE corner of the continent, where about 16 species occur today. After the ICE AGES, the major chelonian invasion of Canada was via the aquatic avenue of the Mississippi and Ohio rivers to southern Ontario. Subsequently a few species migrated into Québec and some even to chilly NS. Others ventured westward but were deterred by the cold, dry Prairies. On both coasts, migration northward involved crossing many rivers; only one species spread northwestward to BC and 4 species advanced eastward or northward to NB and NS. Over the past 3000-4000 years, a progressive, continental cooling has forced reptiles to move southward or become restricted to a single river valley, lake, bog or pond, where conditions suitable for survival still prevail. Thus, turtles have a tenuous toehold on the southern fringes of Canada, and locating these isolated pockets challenges both professional herpetologists and amateur naturalists.

The 8 native Canadian freshwater turtle species all occur in southern Ontario. The only non-Ontario species reported, the 14 cm northwestern pond turtle (*Clemmys marmorata*), is limited to BC and was probably introduced there. The other BC turtle is the 23 cm common western painted turtle (*Chrysemys picta belli*), an invader from the Prairies. This subspecies ranges from BC, across the southern Prairies into western Ontario. The species is represented by the midland painted turtle (*C. p. marginata*) in southern Ontario and Québec, and by the 18 cm eastern painted turtle (*C. p. picta*) in NB and NS. Most major categories of organism contain one or 2 species that can adapt to almost any natural or unnatural condition. Such is the painted turtle; the 43 cm snapping turtle (*Chelydra serpentina*) runs a close second, ranging from NS to Saskatchewan. These species not only occupy every natural body of water from lake to marsh, but even take over stagnant ditches, dams, fish ponds and farm water holes.

A floating log studded with basking, shiny black painted turtles is a common sight in many localities in southern Canada, except in turtleless Newfoundland and PEI. Snapping turtles, in contrast, are secretive. These sinister, 18 kg monsters prey on anything, dead or alive. Their population densities can be astounding, as professional hunters have demonstrated; this big, muscular turtle is commercial restaurant fare.

The terrestrial eastern box turtle (*Terrapene carolina carolina*), probably introduced in Canada, and the semiterrestrial wood turtle (*Clemmys insculpta*) can be poisonous if they have recently fed on toxic mushrooms, and should not be eaten. In Canada the 15 cm eastern box turtle, limited to Ontario's POINT PELÉE, may be either a relict population or a recent introduction. The 20 cm wood turtle is a truly northern species, ranging from Lk Superior to the Bay of FUNDY. Haunting riverbanks, grassy meadows and floodplain forests, it is partial to wild berries and earthworms. Painted turtles shed old scales as they grow. Wood turtles retain and add annual growth rings to each scale, and their age can be determined, much like that of a tree, by counting the rings.

The remaining species are limited to extreme southern Ontario, with a few adjacent Québec records. Turtles are best located through binoculars when they are basking or when just their heads project out of the water. The most distinctive head and neck (upper) and yellow (lower) of the 25 cm Blanding's turtle (*Emydoidea blandingi*). Partial to weedy bays, bogs and marshes, it eats fish, tadpoles, insects and crayfish. East of the Ontario-Québec boundary, it is limited to a thriving, very isolated, relict population in southern NS, centered in KEJIMKUJIK NATIONAL PARK.

Two small turtles, the 10 cm stinkpot or musk (*Sternotherus odoratus*) and the 13 cm spotted turtle (*Clemmys guttata*), have a scattered distribution over southern Ontario and, in the latter case, southern Québec. Both are easily overlooked. The dark brown musk turtle wanders about at the bottom of lakes, bogs and marsh pools searching for live or decomposing animal matter. It rarely basks and consequently becomes covered in algae and is very inconspicuous. The spotted turtle is a gregarious basker in spring but extremely shy. It frequents areas of swampy grass in woodlands and pools in marshes and bogs.

In larger lakes and rivers of southern Ontario, 2 large, rather specialized turtles occur, map turtle (*Graptemys geographica*) and eastern spiny softshell turtle (*Trionyx spiniferus spiniferus*). The pattern of maplike lines on the shell accounts for the map turtle's name. It has powerful jaws for crushing clams, etc. The softshell turtle frequents soft bottom areas where, befitting its flatfish shape, it lies in wait, half buried, ready to strike out at fish and crayfish. It has the typical bony casement, but the outer skin is a thick, rubbery pancake extending beyond the flattened body. Nostrils are peculiarly extended into a long, tubular snorkel which allows the turtle to remain buried yet reach the surface to breathe occasionally.

Four of the world's 6 species of sea turtles have been recorded in Canada, but these basically tropical and subtropical reptiles never nest on Canadian beaches. Reports over the past 100 years include 2 dead Pacific green turtles (*Chelonia mydas agassizi*), one washed ashore in BC, one in Alaska; 4 Atlantic ridley turtles (*Lepidochelys kempi*) washed up in NS; and a few Atlantic loggerhead turtles (*Caretta caretta caretta*) seen off the East Coast. Of an entirely different nature are regular reports of leatherback turtles (*Dermochelys co-*

The snapping turtle (*Chelydra serpentina*), which ranges from NS to Saskatchewan, weighs up to 18 kg. It preys on anything, dead or alive (*photo by Bill Ivy*).

riacea) near the Queen Charlotte Is and Vancouver I, along Labrador and Newfoundland coasts, and tangled in fishing nets off PEI, NB and NS. One of the largest living reptiles, it is nearly 2.5 m from snout to tail and sometimes weighs over 550 kg. In summer, it regularly haunts the cold Atlantic and Pacific coasts of Canada (also Scotland, Norway, Alaska and the USSR) hunting for its favourite food – giant lion's mane jellyfish. That it has a body temperature near 28°C (18° above the surrounding seawater) was discovered in Halifax in 1971. The leatherlike, oil-saturated, thick (5-7 cm) skin provides a sort of blubber layer that retains heat generated by muscular contractions.

J. SHERMAN BLEAKNEY

Tutchone of the southern Yukon Territory, who speak an Athapaskan language, numbered 1000-2000 in the 1980s. Traditionally, they exploited the vast plateau dissected by the YUKON R headwaters and flanked SW by the Coastal and St Elias mountains and NE by the Ogilvie and Selwyn ranges. They hunted caribou, moose, sheep and smaller game and also took various birds and freshwater fish. Some bands depended heavily on annual salmon runs. The fluctuating fauna and subarctic climate, characterized by warm summers and very cold winters, required a seminomadic way of life. Families gathered in spring and summer fish camps, at autumn meat camps, and tried to cluster for part of the winter near dried food supplies and at good fish lakes. By late winter, however, they had to scatter to find game and sometimes they starved (eg, RABBIT STARVATION). The 19th century FUR TRADE also encouraged winter trapping. A few Tutchone, influenced by the Coast Tlingit, had plank dwellings, but most lived in double lean-tos of brush or in domed skin tents. Since dog traction came only with white contact, belongings were limited to those which could be easily carried or made on the spot, such as the snares used to catch animals of all sizes. Some Tutchone had raw copper for making knives or arrowheads; the majority used bone and antler. Women made excellent birchbark containers and tailored skin clothing. People expressed themselves in singing, dancing, oratory and a rich store of oral traditions. Dietary and other observances marked birth, puberty and death. Both sexes learned how to maintain harmony with the powerful spirits of animals and other phenomena on whose good will the welfare of humans depended. SHAMANS enlisted spirit powers to locate game and cure illness.

Descent was reckoned through the female line and lineages were grouped into exogamous moieties. There was no formal political organization, although wealth-based rank began to develop in the 19th century as the result of trading and intermarriage with Tlingit, who were intermediaries between white coastal traders and interior Indians. Tutchone nearest the coast were incorporated into clans bearing Tlingit names.

The influx of whites during the KLONDIKE GOLD RUSH of the late 1890s and building of the ALASKA HIGHWAY in 1942 drastically altered Tutchone cul-

ture. The Indians have shifted to a dual economy based on wage labour as well as hunting, fishing and trapping. They have never signed a treaty (*see* INDIAN TREATIES) and, since 1970, have actively tried to clarify their legal status and settle LAND CLAIMS with the federal government. *See also* NATIVE PEOPLE: SUBARCTIC and general articles under NATIVE PEOPLE. CATHARINE McCLELLAN

Tutty, Patricia Lorraine, "Paddy," folksinger, musician, song-collector (b at Calgary 12 Apr 1953). A gifted instrumentalist, she began performing contemporary FOLK MUSIC with her sister in the late 1960s, and in 1975 became involved with the Regina Guild of Folk Arts where she first seriously studied and sang English and Celtic traditional music. After performing for a year with the folk trio *Barley Straw*, Tutty, as a solo artist, performed in folk clubs throughout Canada, also in 1978-79 travelling, singing and song-collecting in the British Isles. Returning to Saskatoon in 1979 Tutty helped form the Saskatoon Folk Music Assn and subsequently became an active member of the Canadian Folk Music Society. In 1983 she released her first cassette album, *Paddy Tutty*. Tutty has also recorded a record album, *Who Liveth So Merry* (1986). Tutty's growing popularity is an indication of the vitality of traditional Anglo-Celtic music in western Canada.

DAVID GREGORY

Tweedie, Lemuel John, lawyer, politician, premier of NB (b at Chatham, NB 30 Nov 1849; d there 15 July 1917). After developing an extensive law practice Tweedie served as surveyor general and provincial secretary before becoming Liberal premier in 1900. One of the most popular men ever to hold office as premier, his outgoing personality and entertaining oratory made him an institution on the Miramichi at the turn of the century. At the same time he was a shrewd and opportunistic political operator and an able lawyer. After 7 years in office he was lieutenant-governor until 1912. ARTHUR T. DOYLE

Tweedsmuir, John Buchan, 1st Baron, *see* BUCHAN.

25th Street Theatre of Saskatoon was founded in 1972 by U of Sask drama students, notably Andras Tahn, artistic director until 1983. The theatre developed primarily as a populist grassroots company, producing plays and collective creations on prairie subjects, but also as a venue for new plays from other regions. It is best known for *Paper Wheat* (opened 1977), a collective documentary collage on the history of the SASKATCHEWAN WHEAT POOL, which toured nationally in 1978 and 1979. Other premieres include Layne Coleman's *Queen's Cowboy* (1979); Andras Tahn's *Jacob Kepp* (1979); Jim Garrard's *Cold Comfort* (1981); Maria Campbell, Linda Griffiths and Paul Thompson's *Jessica* (1982); and Thelma Oliver's *Diefenbaker* (1983). DIANE BESSAI

24 Sussex Drive, in Ottawa, was designated as the official residence of the prime minister of Canada in 1950 and, in 1951, Louis St. Laurent became the first prime minister to live in the house. It was designed by J.M. Currier in 1867-68 as a Gothic Revival villa for his brother Joseph Merrill Currier, a prosperous mill owner and lumber manufacturer made wealthy by the tremendous 1860s boom in the lumber industry. In 1902 the house was sold to another lumber manufacturer, W.C. Edwards, who made substantial alterations to the house in 1907-08. Acquired by the federal government in 1943, this stone house was redesigned and given its present, formal appearance by the architectural firm of Allward and Gouinlock. The house is magnificently situated on the cliffs above the Ottawa R, in sight of the Parliament Buildings. JACQUELINE ADELL

RCMP officers in ceremonial uniform at the entrance of 24 Sussex Drive, home of the prime minister of Canada (*photo by Jim Merrithew*).

Twillingate, Nfld, Town, pop 1506 (1986c), inc 1962, is located on Twillingate Islands, NOTRE DAME BAY in NE Newfoundland. It was a summer base for hunting and fishing for the BEOTHUK as it had been for an earlier aboriginal people, the Dorset Eskimos. Twillingate, from the Breton place-name *Toulinguet,* was a French fishing station until the Treaty of UTRECHT, 1713. It became England's most northerly fishing settlement in the 1730s and was settled principally by migratory fishermen brought by merchants based in Poole, Eng, in particular the firm of John Slade. A strong resident merchant class developed a local fishery and in the 19th century Twillingate became one of Newfoundland's largest centres for the Labrador cod and seal fisheries. The modern town, now linked by causeway to insular Newfoundland, is a fish-processing and regional centre for smaller communities in the area.

JANET E.M. PITT AND ROBERT D. PITT

Two Solitudes, by Hugh MACLENNAN (Toronto, New York and Des Moines, 1945), is a novel whose title has become emblematic of Canada's most troubling legacy: the relations between English and French Canadians. Using historical settings within a mythological framework, MacLennan explores the tensions in these relations from WWI to 1939. The French Canadian realities are set in the parish of Saint-Marc-des-Érables, which is dominated by its priest, Father Beaubien, and by Athanase Tallard, a powerful but tragic figure ostracized by his church for trying to industrialize the village. Montréal, on the other hand, is dominated by characters such as

Huntley McQueen, a Presbyterian businessman from Ontario. Tallard's son Paul, at home in both languages but alienated from both cultures, embarks on an Odyssean quest for his own identity and for a vision of Canada as he struggles to write a novel which will define his own Canadian experience. It has been translated into French, as *Deux solitudes* (Paris, 1963), and Spanish, Swedish, Czech, Dutch and Estonian. NEIL BESNER

Typhus, *see* EPIDEMIC.

Tyrrell, James Williams, explorer, mine promoter (b at Weston, Canada W 10 May 1863; d at Bartonville, Ont 16 Jan 1945), brother of Joseph Burr TYRRELL. James was educated in civil engineering. He practised in Hamilton until 1893 when he embarked with his brother on a canoe trip across the interior of the Keewatin Dist from Lk Athabasca to Hudson Bay via the DUBAWNT R. His book describing the expedition, *Across the Sub-Arctics of Canada* (1897), is a classic of northern travel writing. In 1900 Tyrrell led a Dominion Lands Survey expedition through the Keewatin. He was later among the pioneer mine promoters in the Red Lk area of northern Ontario and became president of Tyrrell Red Lake Mines. DANIEL FRANCIS

Tyrrell, Joseph Burr, geologist, explorer, historian (b at Weston, Canada W 1 Nov 1858; d in Toronto 26 Aug 1957). Tyrrell explored the vast areas of western and northern Canada, consolidating information gathered by earlier explorers and filling in blank spots on the maps, especially in the NWT, while working for 17 years for the GEOLOGICAL SURVEY OF CANADA (1881-98). He explored the DUBAWNT and THELON rivers to CHESTERFIELD INLET under considerable hardship, discovered the rich dinosaur beds of southern Alberta and important coal beds at Drumheller, Alta, and Fernie, BC, and added knowledge to the geography, botany, entomology, mammalogy and ornithology of many regions. He later became a mining consultant, and then a miner in the Klondike and northern Ontario, eventually acquiring considerable wealth. Highly regarded both in the field and by government officials in Ottawa and Toronto, he was also involved in several historical publications, most notably in editing the diaries of Samuel HEARNE and David THOMPSON. He was president of the CHAMPLAIN SOCIETY and received many honours, including the RSC's Flavelle Gold Medal. A mountain, a lake in Alberta, as well as a town in Manitoba, bear his name; the establishment of the TYRRELL MUSEUM OF PALAEONTOLOGY at Drumheller in Sept 1985 provides an impressive monument to his discoveries a century earlier. MARTIN K. MCNICHOLL

Reading: A. Inglis, Northern Vagabond: The Life and Career of J.B. Tyrrell (1978); W.J. Loudon, A Canadian Geologist (1930).

Tyrrell Museum of Palaeontology, located in the BADLANDS along the Red Deer R near DRUMHELLER, Alta, is Canada's only museum dedicated solely to the study and display of prehistoric life. It is named after surveyor and explorer Joseph Burr TYRRELL, who discovered DINOSAUR

remains near the present museum site in 1884. The provincially funded facility had a capital cost of $30 million. It opened to the public on 25 Sept 1985. Exhibits in the Tyrrell's 4400 square metres of display space celebrate 3.5 billion years of life on Earth. More than 800 fossils are on permanent display. They come from all parts of the world and range in size from microscopic spores to some of the largest land animals the world has known. More than 30 dinosaur specimens can be seen in the main gallery. Included are skeletal reconstructions of large meat-eaters such as *Tyrannosaurus rex* and *Albertosaurus*, along with plant-eaters such as *Triceratops* and *Camarasaurus*. A grouping of duckbill dinosaurs includes babies, a nest of eggs, a juvenile and full-grown adults. Lifesize models of 4 dinosaurs known to have lived in Alberta some 64 million years ago dominate one exhibit. Videos, computers and other audio-visual programs provide information on the collection of fossils, continental drift, dinosaur extinction and other topics. A large window onto the Tyrrell Museum's preparation laboratory allows visitors to watch as fossils are being prepared for display. Other features include a fully enclosed prehistoric garden, interactive science

Centrosaurus and *Albertosaurus* skeletons and reconstructions of a Cretaceous (80 million years ago) feast in southern Alberta. The skeletons are now in the Tyrrell Museum, Drumheller (*courtesy Brian D.E. Chatterton*).

experiments and guided hikes in the surrounding badlands. Many public programs, including lectures, films, tours and demonstrations, are offered.

The Tyrrell Museum operates an intensive collection and research program in palaeontology. New specimens are found each year in nearby DINOSAUR PROVINCIAL PARK, where the museum operates its satellite field station. Further afield, the Tyrrell has participated in expeditions to the Canadian Arctic and the Gobi Desert. More than 80 000 specimens are currently held in the museum's collection. MONTY REID

Tyson, Ian, and Fricker, Sylvia, *see* IAN AND SYLVIA.

U-boat Operations threatened Canada's sovereignty in 2 world wars. German submarines (*Unterseeboote*) first laid mines off Halifax and attacked shipping in Aug 1918, and virtually unopposed by the unprepared naval service they sank 11 schooners and a trawler for a total of 2002 gross tons. U-boats returned to Canadian waters in 1942 during the Battle of the ATLANTIC, with improved technology and a dual strategic plan: attack single ships in order to prevent the formation of convoys and to pin down armed forces that might otherwise be deployed in European waters. Canada's commitment to alliance warfare overseas and to a convoy escort role in the Atlantic left limited resources for home defence. This weakness invited attack, and Germany's first strategic advance on N American shores began as Operation *Drumbeat* (*Paukenschlag*) on 13 Jan 1942. It faced a weak and inexperienced opposition. By Apr 1942, U-boats had sunk 198 ships (1 150 675 tons), half of them tankers. *Drumbeat* led to the Battle of the St Lawrence, a term coined at the time by the *Ottawa Journal*. Six independent U-boats penetrated the St Lawrence R and Gulf via the Cabot Str and the Str of Belle Isle by May-Oct 1942 and reached as far upriver as Rimouski, some 300 km from Québec C. In these waters, U-boats sank 3 Canadian warships (HMCS *Raccoon*, *Charlottetown* and *Shawinigan*) and 20 ships in convoy, including the SS *Chatham*, the first US troopship lost in the war. The sinking of the Sydney to Channel-Port Aux Basques ferry, SS *Caribou*, 14 Oct 1942 with the loss of 137 lives was considered the worst inshore disaster of the battle. The greatest tonnage, 9 ships, including *Chatham* and *Charlottetown*, was sunk by U-517, whose captain, Paul Hartwig, rose after the war to vice-admiral of Canada's NATO partner, the federal German navy. U-boat attacks in the St Lawrence fueled the CONSCRIPTION debate in the House of Commons, vitiated Québec-Ottawa relations, and forced the War Cabinet on 9 Sept 1942 to close the St Lawrence to all Allied shipping except the coastal trade. U-boats also undertook special missions (*see below*). U-262 attempted to embark escaped German prisoners of war from North Point, PEI, on 6 May 1943, while U-536 attempted a similar feat on 28 Sept 1943 at Pointe de Maisonette, NB. U-119 and U-220 laid mines off Halifax and St John's in June and Oct 1943 respectively. U-boats patrolled Canadian waters until war's end, and in the final phase destroyed the last 2 Canadian naval victims of the inshore war. U-806 sank HMCS *Clayoquot* on 24 Dec 1944, by the Halifax lightship, and U-190 sank HMCS *Esquimalt* on 16 Apr 1945 near the same spot. U-190 surrendered to Canada on 11 May 1945 and was commissioned in June of that year in the RCN as HMCS U-190. She was sunk ceremonially on 21 Oct 1947 where she had destroyed the *Esquimalt*. MICHAEL L. HADLEY

U-boat Landings

German submarines landed men in Québec and Labrador twice during WORLD WAR II. On the night of 8-9 Nov 1942 the spy Werner Janowski came ashore from U-518 near New Carlisle, Qué, and was almost immediately captured, later becoming an RCMP double agent. On 22 and 23 Oct 1943 the crew of U-537 landed an automatic weather station at Martin Bay, 32 km S of Cape Chidley, Labrador. The station transmitted data for about 3 months. Although sighted by casual visitors, it was not properly identified until July 1981. W.A.B. DOUGLAS

Reading: Michael L. Hadley, *U-boats Against Canada* (1985).

Uchucklesaht, a Nootka tribe of W Barkley Sd on the W coast of Vancouver I. Formerly a prominent tribe with extensive territories in E Barkley

Sd, the Uchucklesaht were decimated by disease and warfare in the early historic period, and their territory in the mid-19th century was confined to Uchucklesit Inlet. Today, the Uchucklesaht occupy their traditional village of Elhlateese. JOHN DEWHIRST

Ucluelet, BC, Village, pop 1512 (1986c), 1593 (1983c), inc 1952, is located on the W side of Vancouver I, 175 km NW of Victoria, at the western entrance to Barkley S. The name, meaning "safe landing place," was adopted in 1861. Nearby geographic features include Broken Islands, Long Beach and Florencia Bay (part of PACIFIC RIM NATIONAL PARK) and Amphitrite Point, the site of a lighthouse (built in 1905), the Canadian Coast Guard Vessel Traffic Management Centre and the Totino Marine radio station. Ucluelet's main industries are lumbering, fishing, tourism and government services. The third-largest fish-landing port in BC, it has a fine natural harbour. ALAN F.J. ARTIBISE

Ucluelet, a Nootka tribe of W Barkley Sd, Vancouver I. Their traditional territory includes Ucluelet Inlet, the Ucluth Pen and the outer coast northward to Green Point on Long Beach. The Ucluelet formerly consisted of several independent groups which amalgamated as a tribe as a result of prolonged warfare and decimation from disease after European contact. In the early historic period, Ucluelet groups gained additional territories through warfare. In *c*1790 they conquered the Namintaht for the rich salmon fishery on the Nahmint R. The Ucluelet, aided by Clayoquot with firearms, also took Effingham Inlet from the A'utsaht and the Hachaaht, now both extinct. Today, the Ucluelet live in their traditional village of Ittatsoo, across from the modern town of Ucluelet. JOHN DEWHIRST

Ukrainian Writing in Canada began in the 1890s with the first major wave of UKRAINIANS. The first story was written in 1897 by Nestor Dmytriw while he was visiting Calgary, and the first poem in 1898 by Ivan Zbura near Edmonton. From modest beginnings this literature developed and flourished in the genres of poetry, stories, novels and plays. After WWII, books of literary scholarship appeared.

The first period of Ukrainian writing, 1897-1920, was permeated with folklore. Zbura, Teodor Fedyk and Daria Mohylianka epitomized the pioneer poetry, which could hardly be distinguished from folklore. However, prose fiction by Sava Chernetskyj, Myroslav Stechyshyn, Pavlo Krat and Vasyl Kudryk had a higher level of creative achievement. These authors and others not only depicted hardships of pioneering but expressed the revolutionary flavour of struggles for a better life.

In the second period (1920-50) the Ukrainian writing in Canada broadened thematically and became more artistic. Ivan Danylchuk, born in Saskatchewan, published sophisticated poetry and Onufrij Ivakh (Honore Ewach) tried to philosophize in his works, paying attention to aesthetic expression, while Myroslav Ichnianskyj (Ivan Kmeta) poured out strong and impressionistic lyricism.

In prose fiction, Illia Kyrijak (Elias Kiriak) distinguished himself with his realistic trilogy *Syny zemli* (1939-45; tr and abridged as *Sons of the Soil*, 1959), a panorama of the life of settlers on the prairies. Oleksander Luhovyj also depicted Canadian life in his novel *Bezkhatnyj* (*Homeless*, 1946) and plays. Semen Kowbel and Dmytro Hunkevych were active in drama.

The third period opened with the arrival of political immigrants after WWII. In contrast to the previous realism, there appeared various literary trends and styles, including modernism. Mykyta Mandryka produced poetry with original images and the versified narrative *Kanada* (1961; tr Watson KIRKCONNELL as *Canada*, 1971). Canadian themes were prominent also in Ulas Samchuk's novel *Na tverdij zemli* (*On the Hard Soil*, 1967). Yar Slavutych, in his poems *Zavojovnyky prerij* (1968; tr R.H. Morrison as *The Conquerors of the Prairies*, 1974), pictured his impressions of settlers' life and the severity of the North. He has also written the long versified narrative "Moja doba" ("My Epoch"), in *Zibrani tvory* (*Collected Poems*, 1978).

Since the 1960s there has been a revival in Ukrainian literature in Canada. Among the active authors have been lyrical poets Borys Oleksandriv (pseudonym of Borys Hrybinsky), Bohdan Mazepa, Vira Vorsklo, Svitlana Kuzmenko and Teodor Matvijenko; patriotic bards Levko Romen, Dan Mur and Oleksa Hay-Holowko; the thinker in poetry Volodymyr Skorupskyj; the woman poet with preoccupations in ancient Ukrainian mythology, Larysa Murovych; and modernists Iryna Makaryk, Maria Revakovych, Marco Carynnyk, Danylo Struk and Oleksander Olijnyk. In prose fiction, Fedir Odrach, Ivan Bodnarchuk and Oleksander Smotrych have been extensively published. Mykola Kovshun has written drama and Oleh Zujewskyj has been very active in translating, besides writing symbolistic poetry. Orysia Prokopiw has translated much Ukrainian poetry into English and René Coulet du Gard into French.

Ukrainian authors in Canada formed their own literary society, which has published 8 volumes of the almanac *Slovo* (1970-87) and the *Antolohija ukrajins'koji poeziji v Kanadi, 1898-1973* (1975). Another almanac, with Canadian overtones, was *Pivnichne siajvo* (*Northern Lights*, 5 vols, 1964-71). Among books of literary scholarship, *Studia Ucrainica* (4 vols, 1978- 87) and *Ukrainian Shakespeariana in the West* (1987), which also includes translations, should be distinguished. The Ukrainian Academy of Arts and Sciences in Canada and the Shevchenko Scientific Society have regularly published their proceedings and other scholarly books. Despite the great variety of themes and significant ideas in Ukrainian writing, there are only some 15 Ukrainian Canadian authors whose artistic accomplishments place their literature on a level equal to that in Ukraine or higher. *See also* ETHNIC LITERATURE. YAR SLAVUTYCH

Reading: C.H. Andrusyshen and W. Kirkconnell, eds, *The Ukrainian Poets, 1189-1962* (1963); J. Balan, ed, *Identifications* (1982); M. Mandryka, *History of Ukrainian Literature in Canada* (1968); Yar Slavutych, comp, *An Annotated Bibliography of Ukrainian Literature in Canada, 1908-1986* (1987).

Ukrainians In the 19th century, the Russian Empire ruled 80% of Ukraine; the rest lay in the Austro-Hungarian provinces of Galicia, Bukovina and Transcarpathia. Serfs in Austria-Hungary until 1848 and in the Russian Empire until 1861, Ukrainians suffered from economic and national oppression. When attempts to establish an independent Ukrainian state from 1917 to 1921 collapsed, the greater portion of Ukraine became a republic in the USSR, while Poland, Romania and Czechoslovakia divided the remainder. Following WWII the western Ukrainian territories were annexed by the Ukrainian Soviet Socialist Republic. The Ukrainians constitute, after the Russians, the largest Slavic nation in Europe.

Migration and Settlement Isolated individuals of Ukrainian background may have come to Canada during the WAR OF 1812 as mercenaries in the DE MEURON and de Watteville regiments. It is possible that others participated in Russian exploration and colonization on the West Coast, or came with MENNONITE and other German immigrants in the 1870s, or entered Canada from the US. The first major immigration (170 000 peasants, primarily from Galicia and Bukovina) occurred between 1891 and 1914. Initiated by Ivan Pylypiw and Wasyl Eleniak, the movement grew after 1896 when Canada solicited agricultural immigrants from eastern Europe.

With the outbreak of WWI, immigration virtually ceased and Ukrainians were classified as "enemy aliens" by the Canadian government, although over 10 000 Ukrainians enlisted in the armed forces. Between the 2 world wars some 70 000 Ukrainians immigrated to Canada for political and economic reasons. They included war veterans, intellectuals and professionals, as well as peasants. Between 1947 and 1954 some 34 000 Ukrainians, displaced by WWII, arrived in Canada. Representing all Ukrainian territories, they were the most complex socioeconomic group. While the Prairie provinces absorbed the bulk of the first 2 immigrations, the displaced persons settled mainly in Ontario. Between 1955 and 1960 only 2768 Ukrainians immigrated to Canada, and approximately 500 per year have entered the country since. Today, over 80% of Ukrainian Canadians are native born.

By 1914 the Prairie provinces were marked by Ukrainian block settlements, extending from the original Edna [STAR] colony in Alberta through the Rosthern and Yorkton districts of Saskatchewan to the Dauphin, Interlake and Stuartburn regions of Manitoba. Later immigrants and migrants from the rural blocks developed modest Ukrainian urban communities that began around 1900. In 1986 the largest Ukrainian urban concentrations were in Edmonton (55 500), Winnipeg (47 860), and Toronto (46 120). By 1981, 59.1% of Ukrainian Canadians resided in the Prairie provinces and 25.3% lived in Ontario. Preliminary statistics from the 1986c estimated 420 210 Canadians of Ukrainian origin.

Economic Life Ukrainians homesteaded initially with limited capital, outdated peasant technology and no experience with large-scale agriculture. High wheat prices during WWI led to expansion based on wheat, but during the 1930s mixed farming came to prevail. Mechanization, scientific agriculture and out-migration in the Ukrainian blocks have since paralleled developments elsewhere in rural western Canada. Ukrainian male wage earners worked initially as city labourers, miners and railway and forestry workers, while women worked as domestics and as restaurant and hotel help. Discrimination and exploitation radicalized many Ukrainian labourers. As a group, Ukrainians benefited from occupational diversification and specialization only after the 1920s.

By 1971 the proportion of Ukrainian Canadians in agriculture had decreased to 11.2%, slightly above the Canadian average, and unskilled

workers to 3.5% of the Ukrainian male labour force. Compared with all Canadians, Ukrainians were overrepresented in manufacturing, construction and related occupations and underrepresented in semiprofessional and professional categories.

Social Life and Community The first Ukrainian block settlements and urban enclaves cushioned immigrant adjustment but could not prevent all problems of dislocation. Local cultural-educational associations, fashioned after Galician and Bukovinan models, maintained interest in the homeland and instructed the immigrants about Canada. Ukrainian Canadians assisted Ukrainian war victims after 1918 and interwar and postwar immigrants; 3 pioneer charitable societies still function.

National organizations emerged in the interwar years. The procommunist Ukrainian Labour-Farmer Temple Association (est 1924) attracted the unemployed in the 1930s. The Ukrainian Self-Reliance League (est 1927) and the Ukrainian Catholic Brotherhood (est 1932) represented Orthodox and Catholic laity, respectively. Organizations introduced by the second immigration reflected Ukrainian revolutionary trends in Europe. The small conservative, monarchical United Hetman Organization (est 1934) was counterbalanced by the influential nationalistic, republican Ukrainian National Federation (est 1932). Despite tensions, all groups publicized Polish pacification and Stalinist terror in Ukraine in the 1930s; only the Ukrainian Labour-Farmer Temple Association condoned the Soviet purges and the artificial famine of 1932-33 that killed 6 million people; its successor, the Association of United Ukrainian Canadians (est 1946), has declined steadily. In 1940, to unite Ukrainian Canadians behind the Canadian war effort, noncommunist organizations formed the Ukrainian Canadian Committee. It became a permanent coordinating superstructure with such political objectives as the admission of Ukrainian REFUGEES after 1945 and MULTICULTURALISM.

The major organizations introduced by the third immigration were the intensely nationalistic Canadian League for Ukraine's Liberation (est 1949) and the scouting Plast (est 1948). In the 1970s the Ukrainian Canadian Professional and Business Federation (est 1965) was politically significant, able to secure public benefits for the Ukrainian community.

Women's organizations have traditionally emphasized education, culture, handicrafts, museums and child rearing. Youth affiliates have had both ideological and social dimensions. Only 10-15% of Ukrainian Canadians belong to the organized community; others identify with its cultural but not its national-political goals.

Ukrainian Canadians have published nearly 600 newspapers and periodicals, most of which espouse a particular religious or political philosophy. English and bilingual publications partly compensate for the decline in Ukrainian-language readers, but many Ukrainian Canadians no longer find the ethnic press relevant.

Religion and Cultural Life While Ukrainians from Galicia were Eastern-rite Catholic (*see* CATHOLICISM), those from Bukovina were ORTHODOX. No priests immigrated initially, and other denominations tried to fill the religious and social vacuum. Until 1912, when they acquired an independent hierarchy, Ukrainian Catholics were under Roman Catholic jurisdiction. The Russian Orthodox Church worked among Orthodox immigrants but rapidly lost popularity after 1917. In 1918 Ukrainians who were opposed to centralization and latinization in the Ukrainian Catholic Church founded the Ukrainian Greek Orthodox Church of Canada. It became a metropolitanate

in 1951, the Ukrainian Catholic Church in 1956. Once central in preserving the language, culture and identity of Ukrainian Canadians, the 2 churches have seen their religious dominance, moral authority and social influence undermined by assimilation. In 1981 only 30.0% and 18.6% of Ukrainian Canadians belonged to the Ukrainian Catholic and Ukrainian Orthodox churches, respectively; 16.8% were Roman Catholic and 13.3% United Church adherents.

Most agricultural pagan-Christian rituals of Ukrainian peasant life were discarded with urbanization and secularization. Embroidery, Easter-egg ornamentation, dance, music and foods have won appreciation outside the Ukrainian Canadian group. Community archives, museums and libraries preserve the Ukrainian Canadian heritage, and they have recently been supplemented by public professional institutions.

Certain art forms have remained static while others have evolved. Dance ensembles have experimented with Ukrainian Canadian themes; Ukrainian Canadian country music has combined Ukrainian folk and western Canadian elements; and church architecture has skilfully integrated traditional Ukrainian with contemporary N American designs. The paintings of William KURELEK, inspired by his Ukrainian prairie pioneer experience, have been widely recognized. Numerous Ukrainian-language poets and prose writers have described Ukrainian life in Canada; George RYGA was one of few English-language writers of Ukrainian origin to achieve national stature. In the 1970s several films critically interpreted the Ukrainian Canadian experience.

Education After 1897 Ukrainians in Manitoba took advantage of opportunities for bilingual instruction under specially trained Ukrainian teachers. Bilingual schools operated unofficially in Saskatchewan until 1918 but not in Alberta. Criticized for retarding assimilation, they were abolished in Manitoba in 1916 despite Ukrainian opposition.

Vernacular schools expanded rapidly after 1916 to preserve the Ukrainian language and culture. Today, they reach only a fraction of youth; most schools exist in urban areas at the elementary level. Pioneer residential institutes provided Ukrainian surroundings for rural students pursuing their education and produced many community leaders. Four of 5 surviving institutes serve as Ukrainian Orthodox community centres and university residences.

Russification in Soviet Ukraine has spurred Ukrainian Canadians to seek public support for their language and culture. They have obtained Ukrainian-content university courses and degree programs, recognition of Ukrainian as a language of study and subsequently of instruction in Prairie schools, and a Canadian Institute of Ukrainian Studies (est 1976) at U of A. Ukrainian and Ukrainian Canadian studies have developed since the early 1950s.

Illiteracy, once prevalent, has almost disappeared. Ukrainian women were traditionally disadvantaged compared with Ukrainian men and Canadian women, and fewer Ukrainians have attended university than Canadians in more privileged groups. Today, however, educational levels generally reflect Canadian norms.

Politics Ukrainians originally entered municipal politics, and in rural areas where they came to control elected and administrative organs. William Hawrelak in Edmonton and Stephen JUBA in Winnipeg have been prominent mayors. The first Ukrainian elected to a provincial legislature was Andrew Shandro, a Liberal, in Alberta in 1913. In 1926 Michael Luchkovich of the United Farmers of Alberta became the first Ukrainian in the House of

Dancers at the Ukrainian Historical Village, near Edmonton, Alta (*photo by Harry Savage*).

Commons. Since then many Ukrainian candidates have been successful provincially and federally, and Ukrainians have been appointed to federal and provincial Cabinets. There have been 5 senators of Ukrainian origin. Stephen Worobetz was lieutenant-governor of Saskatchewan (1970-76).

During WWI approximately 6000 Ukrainians were interned as enemy aliens and those naturalized less than 15 years were disenfranchised. Ukrainians initially tended to vote Liberal, but their low socioeconomic status also drew them to protest parties, and later many approved the anticommunism of the Diefenbaker Conservatives. Increasingly, voting patterns reflect those of their economic class or region.

Group Maintenance Ukrainian Canadians form a mature ethnocultural group with little new infusion. Low organizational membership, decline in traditional religion, intermarriage and language loss have reduced the identifiable Ukrainian Canadian community. Overt discrimination has largely disappeared, and many Canadians of Ukrainian origin retain few distinctive ethnic values. Oppression in Ukraine has sustained Ukrainian community goals and group ties in Canada. Since the 1960s the Canadian born have countered assimilation by reviving interest in their heritage, aided by multiculturalism policies.

FRANCES A. SWYRIPA

Reading: J. Kolasky, *The Shattered Illusion: The History of Ukrainian Pro-Communist Organizations in Canada* (1979); M. Kostash, *All of Baba's Children* (1977); M.R. Lupul, ed, *A Heritage in Transition: Essays in the History of the Ukrainians in Canada* (1982); M.H. Marunchak, *The Ukrainian Canadians: A History* (2nd ed, 1983); J. Petryshyn, *Peasants in the Promised Land: Canada and the Ukrainians, 1891-1914* (1985); W.R. Petryshyn, ed, *Changing Realities: Social Trends among Ukrainian Canadians* (1980); H. Potrebenko, *No Streets of Gold: A Social History of Ukrainians in Alberta* (1977).

Ultra Vires-Intra Vires Ultra vires [Lat, "beyond the powers"] is used in CONSTITUTIONAL LAW by the courts who must decide the respective competences of Parliament and provincial legislatures. If one or the other, in enacting a law, goes beyond the jurisdiction allotted to it by the constitution, the court will declare that measure ultra vires. If not, the court will declare it intra vires [Lat, "within the powers"].

These 2 expressions also apply to ADMINISTRATIVE LAW, the law of local collectivities, corporate law, etc. Many bodies, eg, municipalities, school boards and corporations, have powers delegated to them by Parliament or provincial legislatures. These delegated bodies may, within their established limits, adopt regulations which, to be valid, must not exceed the limits prescribed by law.

GÉRALD-A. BEAUDOIN

Ultramontanism in Canada, as in Europe where it began during the French Revolution, was the theory of those who rejected any compromise by CATHOLICISM with modern thought, and

demanded the supremacy of religious over civil society. Its central tenet was an attachment to the person of the pope and belief in the doctrine of his infallibility.

Ultramontanism took root in Canada 1820-30, first in the Séminaire de Saint-Hyacinthe, strongly influenced by the ideas of Félicité de Lamennais, and in Montréal under the influence of its first Catholic bishop, Jean-Jacques LARTIGUE. This bishop opposed GALLICAN ideas and fought for freedom of the church and for religious supremacy in education. His successor, Mgr Ignace BOURGET, led ultramontane ideas to triumph in every field (theology, education, church-state relations, etc) in Montréal and throughout most of Catholic Canada. Ultramontanism, very strong in the 1860s, split into 2 groups. The extreme ultramontanes fought for the immediate application of ultramontane principles in the control of education, the reform of laws in conformity with canon law, and the surveillance of civil legislation by the episcopate, etc. The moderate ultramontanes, whom the extremists called "Catholic liberals," wanted a more prudent application of the principles, with compromise where necessary. The extremists, led first by Mgr Bourget and later by Mgr Louis-François LAFLÈCHE, mobilized journalists and conservative politicians, who recommended a *programme catholique* which would guarantee the supremacy of the church in political life. In following years, the extremists and the "programmists" led an antiliberal crusade, which had, as one consequence, the birth of the CASTORS in 1882. Despite the belief of ultramontanes in the state, ultramontanism became closely linked with those ideals within FRENCH CANADIAN NATIONALISM that pointed towards a church-dominated, self-contained society.

Direct intervention by extreme ultramontanists in politics was a failure, but ultramontane thought, with only slight modifications, pervaded philosophical and theological instruction in the *petits* and *grands* seminaries, in the SOCIAL DOCTRINE of the Canadian Catholic Church and in many of the episcopal directives from the second half of the 19th century until the 1950s. It took the QUIET REVOLUTION and the council of Vatican II to dismantle this ideological edifice.

NIVE VOISINE

Umiak Until recent times the chief means of summer water transport for coastal INUIT, the umiak was used for moving family and possessions to seasonal hunting areas and for whaling expeditions. The craft could hold more than 20 people and was 6-10 m in length and more than 1.5 m wide at the centre. Ownership was sometimes shared by 2 or more families. The frame was constructed of salvage driftwood or whalebone, and hide lashings on pegs of antler, ivory or wood held the boat together. Hides of bearded seal, sewn together with waterproof seams, were stretched to dry tightly around the frame. The umiak dates to THULE times (1000 AD) in the central Arctic and appeared in Greenland, Baffin I, Labrador, the Mackenzie Delta, Alaska and eastern Siberia.

RENÉ R. GADACZ

Reading: E.Y. Arima, *Report on an Eskimo Umiak Built at Ivuyivik, P.Q., in the Summer of 1960* (1963).

Underground Economy refers to economic transactions among individuals which are designed to escape detection – also referred to as the irregular economy. Technically, it includes all illegal transactions, eg, PROSTITUTION and drug transactions as well as evasions of TAXATION on otherwise legal activities. For example, a homeowner may hire someone to repair a roof. This is a legal transaction and is routinely reported when the person doing the repair declares the payment as income. However, the labourer may ask for

and receive cash payment in which case the income is not declared in order to evade tax. Individuals in various lines of work can potentially underreport income if payment is received in cash.

Law enforcement and taxation officials readily admit that there is a large underground economy but cannot agree on its size. Because of its very nature the size of the irregular economy is difficult to measure, but there is evidence to indicate that in Canada and elsewhere it has grown recently. Underground activities do not enter the official statistics on Gross Domestic Product (GDP). Those employed in the underground economy may be counted as unemployed in the official LABOUR FORCE statistics. If they hold a regular job and also work in the irregular economy, then the total quantity of labour input is incorrectly measured. Because current estimates suggest that the irregular economy may account for as much as 22% of reported GDP, and because the irregular economy is growing at a faster rate than GDP, these effects may be serious.

Because a large fraction of transactions in the underground economy appears to be in cash, measuring cash holdings is one method of estimating the extent of the transactions. Basically, this involves estimating the cash needed for regular transactions and then determining the difference between this amount and actual cash used. This method has been used to estimate the size of the underground economy in Canada, the US and other countries. These estimates explain the apparent paradox in the published data on cash holdings. Although it has been widely predicted that the growth in the use of CREDIT CARDS and electronic fund transfers would lead to a cashless society or one in which cash is less important, currency holdings have not declined. Economists assert that this results from the diversion of increasing quantities of cash for use in the irregular economy.

There are frequent references to the sale of drugs and other controlled commodities on "the black market," a term that aptly describes the illegal component of the underground economy. Officially, such transactions are unreported. However, there is another meaning to the expression black market. If a particular commodity is the subject of legal price controls, eg, food during wartime, then transactions at illegal prices are usually referred to as black-market transactions. An official report, if it is made, will indicate that the transaction took place at the legal rather than the actual price.

Legal activities conducted underground to escape taxation appear to be the fastest-growing component of the irregular economy, largely because of our tax system. The potential gains from illegal tax evasion are greater at high tax rates. If rising incomes push more people into higher tax brackets, and if there are no changes in the penalties or the degree of enforcement of tax laws, an increase in unreported income can be expected; this is exactly what has happened so far. The growth of the irregular economy has important implications for the Canadian tax system, which relies on self-assessment and involves relatively little direct scrutiny of individual tax returns by taxation officials. Continuing growth in unreported income will almost surely lead to changes in this system. If increasing amounts of taxation are being avoided through the irregular economy, the tax burden on reported activities will be higher. Taxation officials correctly worry that as taxpayers observe the growth of unreported income in the irregular economy more of them will be tempted to try to conceal income.

It has been observed that the growth of the underground economy has paralleled the growth of

INFLATION after the mid-1960s, although there is no concrete evidence to support this point. Inflation is an unlegislated tax which many economists regard as an important factor in reducing social cohesion. It may well be that this unlegislated tax rather than high rates of taxation explains the increase in failures to report income.

Even if estimates of the size of the underground economy are twice as high as the actual figure, it is clear that it is of greater importance in our economy than are most major industries. Unfortunately the growth of the underground economy also reflects a growth in disrespect for the law. This problem can be dealt with by auditing more tax returns and by increasing the penalties for nonreporting and other forms of tax evasion. Another alternative would be to lower tax rates, thereby reducing the incentive to evade taxation. The 1986 tax reform bill in the US lowered personal tax rates and similar tax legislation to reduce high marginal tax rates was introduced in Canada in 1988. **D.A. SMITH**

Underground Railroad, an informal network of safe houses and people who helped fugitive slaves pass from slave states in the US to free states or to Canada. It has been the object of much mythmaking, for not nearly so many fugitives passed along it, nor were there nearly so many whites involved, as is generally said. Although most fugitive slaves remained in the free states of the American North, perhaps 30 000 reached Canada. The "railroad," in operation roughly 1840-60, was most effective after the passage of the US Fugitive Slave Act in 1850, which empowered slave hunters to pursue fugitives onto free soil. This Act resulted in several efforts to kidnap fugitives who were in Canada to return them to Southern owners. *See also* SLAVERY. **ROBIN W. WINKS**

Underhill, Barbara Ann, figure skater (b at Pembroke, Ont 24 June 1963). She began pair FIGURE SKATING with Paul MARTINI in 1978 and they won the Junior world championships that year. They were Canadian champions 1979-83, and though they finished a disappointing 7th in the Feb 1984 Sarajevo Olympics, they rebounded to become World gold medallists at Ottawa a month later. Not competing since then, Underhill currently performs with Ice Capades. In 1984 she received a world champion award from the federal government and in 1985 was inducted into the Canadian Amateur Sports Hall of Fame. **TERESA MOORE**

Underhill, Frank Hawkins, historian, political thinker (b at Stouffville [Whitchurch-Stouffville], Ont 26 Nov 1889; d at Ottawa 16 Sept 1971). Describing himself as being born a "North York Presbyterian Grit," and thus an enemy of the establishment, he achieved his greatest fame as a commentator on the political events and controversies of his times. After studying at U of T and Oxford and serving as an officer in WWI, he taught history at U Sask until 1927 and then at U of T until 1955. An influential commentator on public affairs as well as a popular teacher, he wrote extensively for *Canadian Forum*. He was the first president of the LEAGUE FOR SOCIAL RECONSTRUCTION and the principal author of the CO-OPERATIVE COMMONWEALTH FEDERATION's Regina Manifesto of 1933. His public activities caused friction with U of T administration, and in 1941 he came close to being dismissed after openly predicting that Canada's ties with the UK would weaken as its ties with the US grew stronger (*see* ACADEMIC FREEDOM). Always more of a liberal than a socialist, an admirer of the US and a strong supporter of the Cold War, he was propelled towards the Liberal Party in the 1940s. In 1955 he was appointed

TOTAL EMPLOYMENT, CANADA
Millions of Persons

Source: Statistics Canada, Cat 71-001

curator of Laurier House, Ottawa, by the Liberal government, and he dedicated a volume of essays to L.B. PEARSON. In his last years he was associated with Carleton U. **GARTH STEVENSON**

Reading: R.D. Francis, Frank H. Underhill: Intellectual Provocateur (1986); F.H. Underhill, In Search of Canadian Liberalism (1960).

Unemployment The unemployed are those who want and are able to work but who have no work at present. They might alternatively be described as having no work, being available for work, and looking for a job or waiting for their work to resume or begin in the near future. For statistical purposes, Statistics Canada defines the unemployed more precisely as those who did not work in the LABOUR MARKET during the survey reference week (but may have done housework, etc), were available for work and had actively looked for work in the past 4 weeks, were on temporary layoff for 26 weeks or less and expected to be recalled by their employer, or were waiting for a new job to begin within 4 weeks. The unemployed are thus to be distinguished from the much larger number who are employed, on their own account or by an employer, or who, unlike the employed and the unemployed, are not in the labour force. The employed have jobs, although some may be temporarily absent from work because of illness, strikes, bad weather, etc. Those not in the labour force do not want to or cannot participate in the LABOUR MARKET. They include housewives, students, retirees, etc.

Measurement The official Canadian statistics on unemployment, as on the other categories mentioned, come from the monthly Labour Force Survey of Statistics Canada, a sample survey of some 56 000 representative households in the 10 provinces. (The Territories, Indian Reserves, the armed forces and residents of institutions are not covered.)

Some aggregative results from this survey are shown in the accompanying table. It will be seen that unemployment has risen on average since the mid-1960s, both in absolute numbers and as a percentage of the labour force (unemployment rate). The unemployment rate has not fallen below 7% since 1975, although it was consistently below that level earlier in the post-WWII period. Annual average rates of 3% to 5% were common before 1958 and from 1964 to 1969. From 1958 to 1963 and in the early 1970s, 5% to 7% rates prevailed.

Over most of the post-1975 period, employment also grew, but the labour force grew even more rapidly so that the number and fraction that were unemployed rose. In Aug 1981, employment declined, as did labour-force participation, and the fraction of the working-age population (those 15 years of age and over) that was employed. The unemployment rate rose steadily over the period to Dec 1982, reaching 12.9% seasonally adjusted (see below). This is thought to be the highest rate of unemployment since the 1930s. Similar increases in unemployment were observed in many other countries. In Canada, the rate declined to 11.1% by Dec 1983, 10.8% by Dec 1984, 9.3% by Dec 1986 and 7.9% by Dec 1987 (unadjusted; 8.1% seasonally adjusted).

Composition The annual averages, presented above, for the labour force as a whole conceal large variations within years, between regions and among different groups of people. Regular within-year variation or seasonality occurs as a result of a periodic influx of certain groups into the labour force, eg, students during vacation, and of marked seasonal patterns in certain industries, eg, agriculture, forestry, fishing, construction and tourism, which combine to produce regular seasonal fluctuations in the levels of unemployment and employment. For Canada as a whole, unemployment is typically at about the yearly average in May, falls gradually to some 90% of the average level in Oct and then rises to about 130% in Mar. Seasonal patterns for particular regions and demographic groups differ considerably. The numbers or rates are often seasonally adjusted to eliminate these regular fluctuations and to give a clearer picture of other month-to-month changes.

Regions and demographic (age-sex) groups differ also in their typical levels (rates) of unemployment. Traditionally, Québec and the Atlantic provinces have had higher rates than Ontario and the Prairies, but since the 1981-82 recession, while this general pattern persists, there have been marked differences between the provinces in recovery. Roughly speaking, unemployment rates have declined substantially in Ontario, Québec and Manitoba and changed little in the rest of the country. Women over 25 also have somewhat higher unemployment rates than men in that age bracket. Higher unemployment rates for young people are of long standing. The absolute differences, but probably not the percentage differences, have increased lately. Women's unemployment rates were likely lower than those of men in the 1950s and 1960s, but became higher in the 1970s as more women participated more regularly in the labour force. (Exact comparisons of detailed and pre- and post-1975 data are difficult because of substantial revisions in survey methods and definitions.) Some of the increase in overall unemployment rates in the 1970s might be attributable to the increasing number of young people and women in the labour force.

Similar differences in the incidence of unemployment exist between groups classified by occupation, industry, marital and family status, educational attainment, etc. Moreover, each of these classifications can be subdivided further (as can the age and geographic groupings), and 2 or more of them can be combined into various cross classifications.

Some of this detail is published regularly. The unemployed can also be classified by the duration of their unemployment up to the survey week, their reasons for leaving their last jobs, job search, type of work sought and activity immediately prior to looking for work. While the average duration of unemployment is short, the relatively few long spells account for a substantial, and likely increasing, share of unemployment.

Causes of Unemployment While specific occurrences of unemployment will, of course, have a multitude of causes, some progress can be made with classifying the general phenomenon according to cause and possible remedy. The general increase in unemployment in 1981-82 and similar episodes in the past are instances of cyclical unemployment resulting from a general decline in production and economic activity. They can be remedied by measures to stimulate the ECONOMY to a higher level of performance, although such policies must clearly be influenced by other attendant circumstances (*see* FISCAL POLICY; MONETARY POLICY). Thus, the preoccupation with INFLATION was almost certainly responsible for the reluctance of the authorities in Canada and elsewhere to embrace such policies to deal with the 1981-82 recession. It is also true, however, that economists have become less sanguine as to how easily the economy can be stimulated and at what cost to other objectives.

The seasonal unemployment, discussed above, is one of the components of frictional unemployment, a result of the normal operation of an economy. Other elements are contributed by the need to search for suitable jobs from time to time even when work is readily available. Thus, even when the economy operates at full capacity, there is always a positive level of frictional unemployment,

although there may be offsetting job vacancies. This must be so as long as the detailed composition of economic activity alters, firms start up and go out of business, people change jobs, enter and leave the labour force, move, etc. The unemployed are not a fixed collection of individuals but an ever-changing group, most of whom might be unemployed only briefly.

There is some evidence that the "normal" or average level of frictional unemployment has increased in the 1960s and 1970s, not only because of the demographic changes already noted and discussed further below but also because of changes in social legislation and possibly for other reasons. In particular, the major increases in the generosity of UNEMPLOYMENT INSURANCE in 1971 are said by a number of critics to have induced higher unemployment by making idleness and job search less costly and thus encouraging longer and less intensive search, greater readiness to change jobs and more seasonal and otherwise intermittent work. These trends may by now have been reversed by later amendments to the scheme.

Some have also pointed to higher minimum wages as leading to more difficulty for the relatively unskilled and unproductive in obtaining both work and on-the-job training. This last consideration made things especially difficult for new entrants, particularly the young. These were in any event experiencing difficulties because an unusually large number of them – a result of a bulge in births, ended their schooling and entered the labour force during the 1960s and early 1970s, putting pressure on the economy's capacity to absorb new, inexperienced workers. Youth unemployment rates have always been higher than the average – it is hardly surprising that the initial and early job searches should be more extensive – but they rose relatively over this period. That inflow has since declined. Some observers, notably Martin Feldstein, have interpreted this experience as the joint result of most N American schooling providing poor preparation for the world of work and the scarcity of on-the-job training, in part because of high minimum wages. In consequence, much of the work available to young people without special training was dead-end and monotonous. Employment instability and frequent unemployment resulted.

Measures to reduce frictional unemployment might include the provision of job market information and employment services, easing the transition from school to work, eg, by subsidizing

on-the-job training, redesign of educational and social policies, removal of barriers to entry into particular occupations, etc.

A final type of unemployment, more likely to be of long duration, is structural, that is, inherent in the structure of the economy itself. This is the result of a mismatching between the skills, location and other characteristics of job seekers and available jobs. Other causes of structural unemployment are technological changes, shifting product demands or a decline in a regional industry, such as the textile industry in the EASTERN TOWNSHIPS of Québec or the petroleum industry of the West in the mid-1980s. It might be remedied by provision of training and retraining, of mobility grants to workers and industries, of public or subsidized employment, etc.

As well as reducing unemployment, it is possible to ease its burden by providing insurance, welfare and other transfer payments or work sharing schemes. Some argued that since, recessions aside, unemployment is chiefly frictional, and prolonged or repeated unemployment is borne chiefly by secondary earners in families, the burden might not be great in any event. But this interpretation is contentious.

Reading: M. Gunderson, *Labour Market Economics, Theory, Evidence and Policy in Canada* (1980); S. Ostry and M.A. Zaidi, *Labour Economics in Canada* (1979); Royal Commission on the Economic Union and Development Prospects for Canada, *Report*, vol 2 (1985), *Studies*, vol 17 (1985), vol 18 (1986); Statistics Canada, *The Labour Force*.

Unemployment Insurance, government benefit payments during a period of UNEMPLOYMENT. In Canada, the unemployment insurance system is financed by premiums paid by employers and employees and by federal government contributions. As early as 1919 the Royal Commission on Industrial Relations had recommended a national program of unemployment insurance, but when the R.B. BENNETT government tried to introduce the Employment and Social Insurance Act in 1935, the Supreme Court of Canada and the Privy Council of Great Britain declared the Act unconstitutional on the grounds that it was an infringement of provincial authority. The first compulsory national unemployment insurance program was instituted in Aug 1940 (it came into operation July 1941) after a constitutional amendment gave the federal government legislative power over unemployment insurance. Unemployment rates in Canada reached levels of about 20% during the GREAT DEPRESSION and hastened the adoption of unemployment insurance, as did the mobilization effort of WWII. To aid the organization of the work force for war, employment bureaus were expanded and used to administer the unemployment insurance system.

To qualify for unemployment insurance benefits, applicants must show that they were previously employed for 20 weeks. To receive benefits, they must file a claim stating that they are without work, are willing to work and are registered at the Canada Employment Centre. Following a waiting period of 2 weeks (new claims only), individuals are eligible to receive 60% of average weekly insured earnings up to a maximum in 1988 of $339 per week. The number of weeks for which benefits can be claimed varies, depending on the length of previous employment, and the national and regional unemployment rate.

The unemployment insurance system is an important component of the economic safety net provided by government and there is little disagreement, in principle, that it has provided greater income security for Canadians. Among economists, however, there is substantial concern that specific features of the existing system

UNEMPLOYMENT RATE, CANADA
Percentage

Source: Statistics Canada, Cat 71-001

may create unemployment. For example, it has been argued that the relatively short qualifying period may encourage individuals who would not choose to work, were it not for the prospect of also collecting benefits, to enter the labour force; and that unemployment is higher than it should be among those employed in seasonal industries because it may be easier to collect benefits than to look for other work during the off-season. *See also* SOCIAL SECURITY; DISTRIBUTION OF POWERS; TRANSFER PAYMENTS.   D.A. SMITH

Unemployment Relief Camps In Oct 1932, at the end of the third year of the GREAT DEPRESSION, and on the recommendation of Maj-Gen A.G.L. MCNAUGHTON, chief of the general staff, PM BENNETT sanctioned the creation of a nationwide system of camps to house and provide work for single, unemployed, homeless Canadian males. The camps were placed under the Department of NATIONAL DEFENCE in consultation with the Department of Labour, and staffed with civilians. Occupants voluntarily entered the camps through the Employment Service of Canada and were free to leave at any time. In return for bunkhouse residence, 3 meals a day, work clothes, medical care and 20¢ a day, the "Royal Twenty Centers" worked 44-hr weeks clearing bush, building roads, planting trees and constructing public buildings. Critics argued that the federal government had established the camps in lieu of a reasonable program of work and wages. The most dramatic demonstration of this resentment occurred in Apr 1935, when 1500 men from BC camps went on strike and after 2 months' agitation in Vancouver set forth on the abortive ON TO OTTAWA TREK. By the time the camps were closed in June 1936, they had been home for 170 248 men who had been provided 10 201 103 man-days of relief. *See also* SOCIAL HISTORY, WORKING CLASS.   VICTOR HOWARD

Ungava Bay is a large, funnel-shaped bay that deeply indents the northern coast of Québec adjacent to LABRADOR. At its mouth, about 265 km wide, it opens into HUDSON STR. Leaf Basin at its SW extremity is noted for its high tidal range and its swift and dangerous tidal currents. Akpatok I in the bay's NW sector is remarkable for its forbidding coastal cliffs and extensive marine-abrasion platform, composed mainly of limestone, and its spectacular suite of raised beaches. Ice covers Ungava Bay from Nov until June, and its near-freezing waters are home to seal and arctic char, which are hunted and fished by the local Inuit population. Polar bear and walrus migrate from Hudson Str down the W coast on ice floes and may be seen in considerable numbers on Akpatok I in the summer.   J.T. GRAY

Ungava Inuit (New Québec Inuit) live along the shores of Ungava Bay, on the S shore of HUDSON

STRAIT and on the eastern coast of HUDSON BAY. They exploit the resources of the vast area N of the treeline, especially sea mammals in the coastal waters, and also move inland to hunt caribou and at times penetrate the traditional CREE and MONTAGNAIS-NASKAPI lands S of the treeline.

The term Ungava, meaning "towards the open water," was used to designate the Inuit band established at the mouth of the Arnaud (Payne) R. The Moravian Brothers, who established missions among LABRADOR INUIT, called the Inuit lands located to the west "Ungava"; the HUDSON'S BAY CO used the name widely in the 19th century, and the federal government then created the federal district of Ungava in 1895. Previously, these Inuit had no generic terms for themselves. Culturally close to the Inuit SE of Baffin I and to the Labrador Inuit, they nevertheless differ from these tribes in a number of linguistic and technological respects and in their social and religious customs. These distinctions have been accentuated by the acculturation and evolution of these Inuit as a result of the administrative division of their lands.

The Inuit of the northern part of Ungava, from Cape Smith to Killiniq Is hunted large sea mammals (arctic whale, walrus, belugas, bearded seals), had good transportation (UMIAK, kayak, dog teams), and lived in large warm IGLOOS built of snow; they had access to all coastal and inland resources; those in the southern reaches of Ungava lived on fish and small marine or land mammals. Archaeological remains and their oral history show that some bands lived permanently on the shores of the larger inland lakes (eg, Payne, Klotz and Nantais lakes) or on the coastal islands and archipelagos (Ottawa, Sleeper, Mansel and Nottingham Is).

Among the first Inuit in Canada to establish permanent contacts with Europeans, the Ungava were also the first to take charge of the administration and management of their development through INUIT CO-OPERATIVES and the JAMES BAY AGREEMENT; they also became renowned for the fine quality and abundance of their contemporary art (*see* INUIT ART). Though influenced by a strong SHAMAN tradition, they were Christianized by Wesleyan, Anglican and later Roman Catholic missionaries. A number of syncretic and messianic movements also marked their development. During the 1970s a dissident political movement opposed to the James Bay Agreement grew in the northwestern Ungava region. Two writers, Mitiarjuk de Kangirsujuaq (Wakeham Bay), author of the novel *Sanaaq*, and Thomassie Qumak of Povungnituk, author of an encyclopedia and an Inuit dictionary, have been instrumental in spreading Inuit culture through the written word. *See also* INUIT MYTH AND LEGEND; NATIVE PEOPLE: ARCTIC and general articles under NATIVE PEOPLE.
                                          B. SALADIN-D'ANGLURE

Reading: N. Graburn, *Eskimo without Igloos* (1969); L. Turner, *The Ethnology of the Ungava District* (1894, new ed 1979); M. Vézinet, *Les Nunamiut: Inuit au coeur des terres* (1980).

Ungava Peninsula, a large peninsula approximately 350 000 km^2 in area, washed by the waters of HUDSON BAY, HUDSON STRAIT and UNGAVA BAY, respectively. Peopled along the coastal fringe for centuries by Inuit communities, the interior is a vast, unpopulated, treeless plateau, which attains altitudes of 300 to 600 m. It is underlain by continuous permafrost which attains thicknesses of 200 to 600 m. Rich mineral wealth, mainly asbestos, nickel, copper, uranium and iron ores, has been discovered by recent geological exploration. This wealth remains largely untapped at present, because of the high costs of extraction and a poor world market. In 1950 a 500 m deep meteorite crater was discovered in the area.   J.T. GRAY

Unger, James, cartoonist (b at London, Eng 21 Jan 1937). After a chaotic employment history, Unger immigrated to Toronto in 1968 and became art director for the Mississauga *Times*. He won the Ontario Weekly Newspaper Association's Cartoonist of the Year Award 3 times. Unger's first attempt to syndicate his work through the *Toronto Star* was rejected, but in 1974 the Kansas-based Universal Press Syndicate contracted to distribute his one-panel cartoon. He moved to Ottawa to draw "Herman," the name UPS gave the cartoon, although Unger insists there is no such character. His black humour is expressed more by his drawing than by his bitterly sarcastic captions. "Herman" appears in more than 400 newspapers in 21 countries. After 2 "Herman" collections became best-sellers, Unger moved to the Bahamas to avoid Canadian income taxes. The first 4 Herman collections have sold over 1 million copies collectively.
                                          JOHN H. THOMPSON

Uniacke, James Boyle, lawyer, politician (b probably 1799, bap at Halifax 19 Jan 1800; d there 26 Mar 1858). As the son of Richard John UNIACKE, he enjoyed favoured status in NS politics and society. He became a lawyer and then entered the Assembly, representing Cape Breton County 1832-48, Halifax Township 1848-51 and Richmond County 1851-54, initially as a Conservative but after 1840 as a Reformer (Liberal). He was appointed to the Executive Council in 1838 and served intermittently in several important offices during the struggle for RESPONSIBLE GOVERNMENT, which culminated in 1848 with Uniacke serving as attorney general and nominal premier. He retired in 1854 to become commissioner of crown lands and surveyor general.   LOIS KERNAGHAN

Uniacke, Richard John, lawyer, politician (b at Castletown, Ire 22 Nov 1753; d at Mount Uniacke, NS 11 Oct 1830). After a turbulent early career in the Cumberland district of NS as a trader and a sympathizer with the American rebels, he returned to Ireland where he was admitted as an attorney. In 1781 he was named solicitor general of NS. By 1800 his was the province's largest legal practice; combined with his appointment (1784) as advocate general of the Vice-Admiralty Court, it secured his personal fortune. He also sat in the legislature (1783-93, 1798-1805) and served as Speaker (1789-93, 1799-1805). Named attorney general in 1797 he was appointed to the COUNCIL OF TWELVE in 1808, but his great ambition, the office of chief justice, eluded him. His forceful, conservative influence on contemporary politics, education and religion undoubtedly prolonged social dissension in NS, but his vision of colonial union and commercial independence for BNA marked him as a man ahead of his time.
                                          LOIS KERNAGHAN

Reading: B. Cuthbertson, *The Old Attorney General, a Biography of Richard John Uniacke* (1980).

Uniforms, garments of a similar ("uniform") pattern worn by a group of individuals to indicate their identity and function. Uniform clothing was used in ancient times and has been especially popular with the military since the emergence of standing armies in western Europe during the 17th century. Colonels of REGIMENTS found it convenient to require their troops to wear uniforms on which they could realize a profit from pay deductions, a system that lasted into the 1850s in the British army. Uniform colours varied greatly at first. In Canada, the first large body of uniformed men appeared in 1665 with the CARIGNAN-SALIÈRES REGIMENT dressed in brown coats lined with white and grey, black hats and buff and black ribbons. Nations soon standardized the basic coat colours, though there were many exceptions. The colonial infantry companies that garrisoned New France from 1683 to 1760 had grey-white coats, the French infantry colour, with blue linings and cuffs. From 1716, the buttons were brass, the vest, breeches and stockings were blue, and a gold-laced tricorn was worn. The army regiments sent to Canada from 1755 until the Conquest of 1760 had the same dress with differences in colours, eg, the La Sarre Regiment had a red vest, with grey-white coat linings and grey-white breeches.

The distinctively coloured cuffs, collars, linings and lapels became known as "facings" in the red-coated British infantry; most units also had lace patterns peculiar to each regiment. Shades of yellow, green, blue or buff were the usual facing colours. The impression that the whole British army was in red coats should be dismissed: artillery wore blue with red facings, as did some support services. Green was also adopted by some light infantry and rifle corps from the end of the 18th century, notably Queen's Rangers (1791-1802) who served in Upper Canada.

The militia of New France had no official uniform. Only the officers were expected to wear gorgets and swords. When the Americans besieged Québec in 1775, the town's militia provided itself with green coats with buff waistcoats and breeches, the first instance that a sizable body of Canadian militiamen took to wearing a uniform. During the WAR OF 1812 and the REBELLIONS OF 1837, militiamen wore what they could get until proper uniforms arrived from England. Apart from the British army and the militia, some units were raised in Canada and dressed as regular troops. Until the 1850s a few units composed of wealthy militiamen uniformed themselves splendidly at their own cost. Canadians feared hostilities during the AMERICAN CIVIL WAR and, in response to government encouragement, formed hundreds of companies. Rifle units usually wore green, artillery and cavalry blue in central Canada. On the Atlantic coast, the variety also extended to grey in many units. During the 1860s infantry units adopted scarlet with blue facings, rifle units green with red facings, artillery blue with red facings, and cavalry blue with buff facings. These are still the colours of the full-dress uniforms of most Canadian units. From the 1880s white pith helmets were popular. Highland dress also became established in several units. The SOUTH AFRICAN WAR brought khaki uniforms to the Canadian contingents, but tradition died hard and some newly raised western cavalry regiments could be seen in scarlet around 1910. With WWI and WWII, khaki and steel helmets (from 1916) became universal because the greatly increased accuracy of weapons made easy targets of brightly coloured uniforms. The Canadians usually adopted patterns similar to the British.

Royal Canadian Navy uniforms resembled those of the British Royal Navy from 1910, the distinction being "HMCS" instead of "HMS" on the caps. The Canadian Air Force first had dark blue dress in 1920 but adopted the British Royal Air Force's blue-grey in 1924. "RCAF" (Royal Canadian Air Force) replaced "RAF" on the uniforms, and all 3 services had "Canada" on the upper sleeve. With ARMED FORCES unification in 1968 came the "CF Green" uniform which was the subject of controversy until the reversion to separate uniforms since 1984.

Associated with smartness and efficiency in the 19th century, uniforms became the fashion in certain civilian occupations. Post office, customs, marine service, railway, steamship and hotel employees, prison guards and even milkmen were often dressed in dark blue. Nurses wore only white until recently. Policemen in Canada have usually worn dark blue, except for the famous

Soldier of the Troupes de la Marine, *c*1750 (left), uniform of the 58th Foot, 1759 (centre), and officer of the 4th Canadian Hussars, *c*1890 (right) (*courtesy Environment Canada, Parks*).

Infantryman of the 2nd Battalion, Canadian Expeditionary Force, 1916 (left), RCAF bomber crew, Europe, 1944-45 (centre), and RCN officer during the Battle of the Atlantic, 1943-44 (*courtesy Canadian War Museum/CMC/NMC*).

In 1984 new separate uniforms were introduced to replace the single "CF Green." Shown above are navy winter (2 on left), navy summer (3rd from left), air force (centre), army summer – parachute training (3rd from right) – and army winter (2 on right) (*courtesy Canapress Photo Service*).

scarlet of the ROYAL CANADIAN MOUNTED POLICE. The basic styling was of British inspiration, although American influence has lately been considerable.

RENÉ CHARTRAND

Reading: W.Y. Carman, *British Military Uniforms* (1957); D. Ross, *Military Uniforms from the Collections of the New Brunswick Museum* (1980); J.L. Summers and René Chartrand, *Military Uniforms in Canada, 1665-1970* (1981).

UniMédia (1988) Inc, is one of the 3 largest French-language newspaper chains in Québec. Wholly owned by Hollinger Inc (itself a holding company controlled by ARGUS CORP), UniMédia (1988) Inc publishes *Le Soleil* in Québec, *Le Quotidien* in Chicoutimi and *Le Droit* in Hull-Ottawa. Its other interests include newspaper and periodical distribution as well as printing of circulars. Prior to being purchased by Hollinger (June 1987), UniMédia Inc was controlled by Jacques Francoeur through Société générale de publications Inc.

Union Centrals, District and Regional, organizations which unite trade unions from different industries and occupations in the same city, province or region; usually formed in periods of intensifying industrial conflict, notably 1870-90, 1910-20 and 1935-50. The first and most persistent form of inter-union co-operation was the city-based labour council. In 1863 Hamilton's craft unions launched Canada's first trades assembly. The Toronto Trades Assembly followed in 1871, and eventually most large municipalities had such organizations, usually known as Trades and Labour Councils. Before WWII these were important, since they met frequently and could act promptly on workers' concerns. They were usually responsible for initiatives to create larger, regional labour federations or labour parties. By 1900 another form of city-based organization was appearing: councils of skilled workers in allied trades in the same industry, especially printing, construction and metalwork.

Regional labour organizations were generally of 2 types. The first were provincial federations of unions in the same industry. Coal miners formed the Miners' Mutual Protective Society in BC in 1877 and the Provincial Workmen's Association in NS 2 years later. Beginning in the 1880s, other groups of workers created similar regional bodies within the structure of their international unions, in an effort to establish common terms of employment. These declined or disappeared after WWI.

The other common form of regional labour organization was the provincial federation, which united various local and district bodies within one province. Administered by an executive board and typically with few or no full-time staff, it would meet annually to discuss wage earners' concerns and to plan common programs of action, including independent electoral campaigns. It would also make regular representations to provincial governments for labour legislation.

The first labour organization claiming national jurisdiction, the Canadian Labor Union, was actually regional, having no affiliates outside central Canada. Similarly the TRADES AND LABOR CONGRESS OF CANADA, which first met 1883, had no representation from outside Ontario and Québec until 1890, and it continued to be dominated by central Canada. At each TLC convention, provincial executives were elected to present the concerns of organized labour to their respective provincial governments.

The first distinct provincial federations were outside the TLC, and occasionally in opposition to its policies. BC's first provincial organizations were short-lived – the Workingmen's Protective Association, 1878-82, and the Federated Labor Congress, 1890-91. The Nova Scotia Provincial Workmen's Association (PWA) first expanded beyond the coalfields in 1881, reaching its broadest representation of workers 1899-1904. During the late 19th century the PWA published the *Trades Journal*, edited by Secretary Robert Drummond. After 1904 the association once again became purely a miners' union and later merged with the United Mine Workers of America.

The Labour Educational Association of Ontar-

UAW national director C.H. Millard with a group of union leaders in Hamilton, Ont, in 1946 during the steel strike (*courtesy National Archives of Canada/PA-120499*).

io, formed in 1903 outside the TLC structure, was a loosely knit body which promoted labour interests in southern Ontario, especially through the *Industrial Banner* edited by Secretary Joseph T. Marks. The association's fervent commitment to reform sometimes upset more narrow-minded Ontario trade unionists, and the TLC's provincial executive committee continued to assert its right to represent labour interests before the provincial government. The association had nonetheless assumed most of the functions of a provincial federation by WWI, and it organized the founding convention of the Independent Labor Party of Ontario in 1917.

Provincial federations chartered by the TLC were formed in BC in 1910, Alberta in 1911, New Brunswick in 1913 and Nova Scotia for the period 1919-21. The 2 western organizations quickly became focal points of opposition to the TLC's dominant policies, particularly in their open support of radical socialism and industrial unionism. The BC labour paper, the *BC Federationist*, edited by R.P. Pettipiece, led this radical sentiment. After WWI the 2 bodies supported the ONE BIG UNION, which dissolved the BC federation in 1920.

No new provincial federations appeared until 1935, when the TLC's rival, the All-Canadian Congress of Labour, chartered the NB Council of Labour. During the next 15 years, as the labour movement expanded dramatically and industrial unions were consolidated, provincial federations emerged in most provinces. Until 1956, however, there were separate provincial affiliates of the craft-unionist TLC and the industrial-unionist CANADIAN CONGRESS OF LABOUR: the TLC's Alberta and New Brunswick organizations were joined by parallel bodies in Québec in 1938, Ontario in 1946, Newfoundland in 1949, BC and Saskatchewan in 1953 and Nova Scotia and Manitoba in 1954; the CCL affiliates appeared in Nova Scotia in 1942, Ontario in 1943, BC in 1944, Saskatchewan in 1945, Alberta in 1948 and Québec in 1953. After the 1956 merger of the 2 national organizations, the separate provincial federations in each province amalgamated into a single labour body. The role of district and regional union centrals is now primarily political, representing workers' common interests to provincial governments, which hold most constitutional authority for LABOUR RELATIONS.   CRAIG HERON

Union Centrals, National (NUCs), organizations representing groups of trade unionists. Many 19th-century workers disliked being treated like commodities and protested the long hours, low wages, dangerous conditions and heightened insecurity of factory work. They formed local trade unions to protect themselves and to compete with employers for control over increasingly mechanized workplaces. In the 1870s and 1880s, when Canadian federal and provincial govern-

ments introduced laws affecting relations between workers and employers, trade unionists joined American NUCs or established their own to express their political interests. NUC conventions were called to advocate new labour laws, to discuss ways to exert political influence, and to impress public officials. Revenue came from members through dues based on each union's Canadian membership. NUCs helped organize workers into new unions, resolved disputes between dissident locals and often published labour journals. Annual conventions followed traditional rules of order and familiarized workers with bureaucratic procedures. Over the years a cadre of Canadian WORKING-CLASS leaders emerged from NUC conventions.

The CANADIAN LABOR UNION (1873-77), the first NUC, was largely responsible for the 1874 election to the Ontario legislature of D.J. O'DONOGHUE, the "father" of Canadian trade unionism. The most successful of the early NUCs, the TRADES AND LABOR CONGRESS of Canada (1883-1956) organized by O'Donoghue and others, demanded an 8-hour day, universal manhood suffrage, factory Acts, employers' liability laws, and arbitration of industrial disputes. By 1900 some Canadians wished the TLC to become an independent national labour body, but in 1902 an overwhelming majority of its members, responding to American leaders, joined the American Federation of Labor. Thereafter, it generally reflected the policies of its larger American associate.

The National Trades and Labor Congress (1902-08), the CANADIAN FEDERATION OF LABOUR (1908-27) and the All-Canadian Congress of Labour (1927-40) were NUCs composed largely of organizations expelled from or hostile to AFL-TLC affiliates. Lacking the TLC's resources, these NUCs won the adherence of relatively few Canadian workers. The WORKERS UNITY LEAGUE, directed 1930-35 by the Communist Party of Canada, attracted over 40 000 members and provided a cadre of militant labour leaders during the Depression. Québec's Catholic Church rejected AFL-affiliated unions and in 1921 established a church-controlled NUC. As clerical influence receded after WWII, that NUC's successor, the CONFEDERATION OF NATIONAL TRADE UNIONS (est 1960), began to resemble other NUCs. The CANADIAN CONGRESS OF LABOUR (1940-56) was launched by the American-based industrial unions with Canadian locals in steel, auto, electrical and other mass-production industries. These latter unions had been expelled from the TLC in 1939 upon AFL orders; their leaders generally supported the left-wing CO-OPERATIVE COMMONWEALTH FEDERATION.

During WWII NUC membership spiralled, aided by rapid industrialization, favourable government policies and Communist Party activists. Postwar difficulties, however, persuaded the American AFL and CIO to federate in 1955. A year later their Canadian affiliates, the TLC and CCL, merged into a new CANADIAN LABOUR CONGRESS. Promised complete freedom by the new American group, CLC leaders joined with the CCF in 1961 to form the NEW DEMOCRATIC PARTY to represent organized labour's interests in Canada. Canadian NUCs are vastly stronger (2.2 million members in the CLC; 220 000 in the CNTU) and more unified than a century ago. Canadian workers now toil under a panoply of protective laws. But NUC strength still varies greatly from province to province, well over half the work force is not yet enrolled in trade unions, and the NDP usually garners only a portion of the labour vote.   ROBERT H. BABCOCK

Reading: B.D. Palmer, *Working-Class Experience* (1983).

Union Centrals, Québec Québec has 4 groups of labour unions: the CONFEDERATION OF NATIONAL

TRADE UNIONS (Confédération des syndicats nationaux, CNTU), fd 1921 as the Canadian Catholic Federation of Labour; the Québec Federation of Labour (QFL), which includes international unions and national affiliates of the CANADIAN LABOUR CONGRESS; the Québec Teachers' Corporation (QTC); and the Confederation of Democratic Unions (CDU), formed in a June 1972 break-away from the CNTU.

The most important association in Québec is the QFL, the CLC's Québec wing, with about 320 000 members (1986). Its member unions belong either to international unions affiliated with the AFL-CIO and headquartered in the US, or to Canadian unions such as the CANADIAN UNION OF PUBLIC EMPLOYEES or the Canadian Union of Postal Workers. The QFL provides union information and education, and represents workers affiliated with the CLC to other intermediary bodies and to the Québec government.

The QFL was the result of the 1957 merger of the Provincial Federation of Labour of Québec (PFLQ) and the Federation of Industrial Trade Unions of Québec (FITQ). This merger followed the 1955 example of the union between the American giants, the AFL and the CIO, and of their Canadian counterparts, the TRADES AND LABOR CONGRESS and the Canadian Congress of Labour, into the CLC. The orientation of the new QFL was more strongly influenced by the INDUSTRIAL UNIONS of the FITQ than by the CRAFT UNIONS of the PFLQ. The federation kept its distance from the DUPLESSIS government, supported the NDP and took some militant stands (eg, the 1957 MURDOCHVILLE STRIKE).

The QFL changed significantly 1964-65, when Louis LABERGE became president and the position of permanent secretary-general was created. Threatened by the CNTU (in both membership and influence), the QFL toughened its criticism of the capitalist system and of governmental action, publishing such manifestos as *L'État, rouage de notre exploitation* (1971) and *Le combat inévitable* (1973). It participated in major strikes, including that at *La Presse* in 1971, the United Aircraft strike and the COMMON FRONT strikes. It accepted Québec nationalism and publicly supported the PARTI QUÉBÉCOIS in 1976 and 1981, although not in 1985. Since the economic recession of the early 1980s its militancy and its social critique have moderated. JACQUES ROUILLARD

Union des écrivains québecois (UNEQ) Founded in Montréal in 1977, this body brings together francophone and anglophone Québec authors and writers, defending their rights and promoting Québec books. UNEQ has negotiated a publishing contract with the Association des éditeurs québecois and has received authors' royalties from the Québec Ministry of Education for photocopies made of their works in educational establishments. As well as being a centre for consultation, information and research, UNEQ organizes tours, meetings and conferences while also carrying on its work with the Québec government to assure better distribution for writers and greater public recognition of their work. It regularly publishes a newsletter and a yearly directory of its members. In 1979 it published the *Petit dictionnaire des écrivains québecois*, containing a list of members. In 1983 it was revised and enlarged, and was republished as *Dictionnaire des écrivains québecois contemporains*. Led by an 8-person board of directors and run by a permanent office staff, UNEQ had 450 members in 1986. LUCIE ROBERT

Union Government In early 1917, during WORLD WAR I, recruitment for the CANADIAN EXPEDITIONARY FORCE fell to a very low level. PM Sir Robert BORDEN, opposed to any reduction in Canada's commitment to the war effort, announced

on 18 May 1917 that the government would introduce CONSCRIPTION to Canada. On May 25 he proposed to Liberal leader Sir Wilfrid LAURIER that the Liberals and Conservatives form a COALITION GOVERNMENT to carry through the measure. After Laurier rejected the proposal on June 6, Borden tried to strengthen his government by bringing in individual Liberals and prominent political independents. His early efforts met with little success. In late summer, however, the WARTIME ELECTIONS ACT and the Military Voters' Act appeared to increase the political prospects for a government supporting conscription. These Acts, together with strong pro-conscription sentiment in the English press and personal convictions that overrode party boundaries, made several Liberals and independents decide to accept Borden's suggestion. On Oct 12 Borden announced the formation of a Union government made up of 12 Conservatives, 9 Liberals or independents, and one labour representative. A general election in Dec 1917 gave the Unionists a large majority.

After its election victory, the Union government began to weaken. The end of the war in Nov 1918 destroyed the reason for unionism in the minds of many adherents. Many Unionists returned to the Liberal Party or joined the new PROGRESSIVE PARTY. Although the Union government was a coalition of varied political interests, many Canadians of non-British background still blamed Borden and the Conservative Party for conscription. The results of Unionist policies included an enduring Conservative weakness among French Canadians and many others of non-British descent – a weakness that contrasted with renewed Liberal strength in French Canada under Laurier's successor as Liberal leader, Mackenzie KING. With Borden's retirement in July 1920, Union government ended. JOHN ENGLISH

Union Nationale, originally a coalition of the Conservative Party and the ACTION LIBÉRALE NATIONALE, formed to contest the 1935 provincial election in Québec. The coalition's leaders were Maurice DUPLESSIS of the Conservative Party and Paul Gouin of the ALN. Narrowly defeated in 1935, the Union Nationale became a single party under Duplessis's leadership, and easily won the 1936 provincial election. Born during the Great Depression, the Union Nationale at first preached social, economic and political reform. It was defeated by the Liberal Party in 1939, after a campaign in which federal Liberals in Québec argued that they were the ones to protect French Canadians from CONSCRIPTION. The Union Nationale under Duplessis was elected again in 1944, having accused the Liberals, provincial and federal, of betraying Québec's rights. This nationalistic emphasis was to be characteristic of the party thereafter. The Union Nationale was completely dominated by Duplessis until his death in Sept 1959; it was then led by Paul SAUVÉ until his death less than 4 months later. It lost the 1960 election and has held power only once since then (1966-70). The death in 1968 of its leader, Daniel JOHNSON, was a heavy blow and the government of the new leader J. Jacques BERTRAND was defeated by a resurgent Liberal Party under Robert BOURASSA in 1970. Supplanted by the PARTI QUÉBÉCOIS as the nationalist party, the UN never won more than 20% of the vote in subsequent elections. Although still in existence to 1988, the party is no longer a political force in Québec: in the 1985 election it captured less than 1% of the vote.

The Union Nationale won its major support from rural voters, from small- and medium-scale businessmen and from unorganized labour. Anglophone voters distrusted the party and it had greater success in Québec City than in Montréal.

During the 1940s and 1950s, the size of its electoral funding, most of it donated by business, gave it a significant advantage over the Liberal opposition. This disappeared after the party's defeat in 1960 and the reform of electoral practices in Québec. *See also* FRENCH CANADIAN NATIONALISM. VINCENT LEMIEUX

Reading: Herbert F. Quinn, *The Union Nationale* (1970).

Union Station, Toronto, was designed by architects Ross and Macdonald, Hugh G. JONES and John M. LYLE for the GRAND TRUNK RAILWAY OF CANADA and CANADIAN PACIFIC RAILWAY. Design commenced in 1913 and construction began in 1914. The building was substantially finished by 1920, but the actual completion took place in 1927. The design and interior details of the building show the influence of the beaux-arts style, which greatly marked N American public architecture of the early 20th century. The building's long façade is divided into 7 sections, and the central portion is distinguished by a long Doric colonnade framed by 2 small projecting porticos. The façade ends in 2 slightly jutting sections with inset pilasters. The ground floor, designed by Lyle, includes a vast hall that contains the ticket windows and various services; it is notable for its huge proportions, vaulted ceiling, materials and colours, and the Canadian inspiration of its decoration. NATHALIE CLERK

Reading: R. Bébout, *The Open Gate: Toronto Union Station* (1972).

Unions, *see* CRAFT UNIONISM; INDUSTRIAL UNIONISM; LABOUR ORGANIZATIONS; LABOUR RELATIONS; REVOLUTIONARY INDUSTRIAL UNIONISM; UNION CENTRALS; WORKING-CLASS HISTORY; and articles on individual unions.

Unitarian Service Committee of Canada (USC Canada), was founded by Dr Lotta Hitschmanova in July 1945, with the assistance of the UUSC in Boston, Mass, and Unitarian churches across Canada, to help children in postwar Europe. Formal ties were dissolved in 1948, and from this date the organization has been independent and nondenominational. USC Canada administers a program of development assistance through local committees and nongovernmental organizations in Lesotho, Botswana, Swaziland and Mali in southern and N Africa, and Bangladesh, Nepal and Indonesia in Asia. Funds are raised from private individuals and organizations, and matching grants are received from the CANADIAN INTERNATIONAL DEVELOPMENT AGENCY (CIDA) and from the governments of British Columbia, Alberta, Saskatchewan and Manitoba. Free air time and advertising space donated by the media permit widespread appeals as well as a lower overhead. The national board of directors is elected by 10 branches across the country and its headquarters are in Ottawa. Hitschmanova (b at Prague, Czech 28 Nov 1909), who retired in 1982, is the recipient of many Canadian and international awards and honours. She received the 1979 ROYAL BANK AWARD and was made a Companion of the Order of Canada in 1980. In 1987 the Czechoslovak Assn of Canada awarded her the Masaryk Award, recognizing her outstanding achievement as a Czech in Canada.

Unitarians, adherents to a religious movement which originated in 16th-century Europe and whose members profess a holistic approach to religion. This has been theologically expressed in an emphasis upon the undivided unity of God, though many Unitarians now prefer to use nontheological language. The movement began within CHRISTIANITY but now brings together people from various religious traditions in a spirit of unity in diversity. Individual responsibility for faith and action is stressed, as are reason and personal experience as guides. Most early Unitarians in Canada came from Britain, though New Englanders constituted a strong influence in Montréal, where the first congregation was established in 1832. Throughout the 19th century this remained Canada's leading congregation, including in its membership such prominent politicians and merchants as Sir Francis HINCKS, John Young, Adam Ferrie and Luther Holton. Joseph WORKMAN, Canadian pioneer in psychiatry, was one founder of the Toronto congregation in 1845. Later a Unitarian movement developed among Icelandic settlers in Manitoba. The tradition of progressive leadership in social and cultural life continued in the 20th century, so that Unitarian influence on politics and society grew more rapidly than membership. Each of the 44 local societies (1987) is autonomous and is democratically organized, but in 1961 the Canadian Unitarian Council was formed to supplement denominational ties with the American and British movements. Worldwide links are maintained through the International Association for Religious Freedom. In 1987 the council reported approximately 5000 Unitarians in Canada.

PHILLIP HEWETT

Reading: Phillip Hewett, *Unitarians in Canada* (1978).

United Automobile Workers of Canada

Founded in 1937 as an affiliate of the UAW in the US, it won its first major victory in the famous OSHAWA STRIKE of 1937 and went on to become one of Canada's largest and most dynamic unions. Its leaders since 1937, Charles H. MILLARD, George BURT, Dennis MCDERMOTT and Robert WHITE, have consistently been among the most influential in the country, while its achievements for Canadian workers – the RAND FORMULA, guaranteed annual wage, health and safety standards, legal and medical clinics – were monumental collective-bargaining breakthroughs. No Canadian union was more unswerving in its support of the NDP and more generous in its support of progressive causes and movements. In 1986, dismayed by the actions and attitude of its parent organization in Detroit, Mich, the Canadian UAW, under the spirited leadership of Bob White, seceded and created the Canadian Auto Workers Union of Canada.

IRVING ABELLA

Reading: Irving Abella, *Nationalism, Communism and Canadian Labour* (1973).

United Church of Canada,

formed 10 June 1925 by union of the PRESBYTERIAN Church in Canada, the METHODIST Church (Canada, Nfld and Bermuda), the CONGREGATIONAL CHURCHES of Canada, and the General Council of Local Union Churches. This last represented a group of congregations, mainly in Saskatchewan, which had come together in anticipation of the larger union. A few Congregational churches and roughly one-third of the Presbyterians voted to stay out of the union. In 1968 the United Church was joined by the (eastern) Canada Conference of the Evangelical United Brethren Church (which originated in Methodist-style revivalism among German-speaking settlers in the US in the late 18th century), while the Western Canada Conference remained out. The United is Canada's largest Protestant church, with a confirmed membership of approximately 872 290 (1986). Since the mid-1960s membership has declined substantially. The most self-consciously Canadian of all churches, in principle it includes all ethnic groups. The bulk of its members are of British descent, however, and about 10 times as many live in Ontario as in Québec.

United Church policy, declared in its Basis of Union and reaffirmed 1935, is to be "not merely a united, but a uniting Church." Conversations

looking to union with the Anglican Church (*see* ANGLICANISM) of Canada began in 1944 and were broadened in 1969 to include the CHRISTIAN CHURCH (DISCIPLES OF CHRIST). Discussions broke down with the former body in 1975, and with the latter in 1984. Another joint committee is exploring closer relations with Roman CATHOLICS. The United Church has been committed to ecumenism from the outset and has been active in the CANADIAN COUNCIL OF CHURCHES and the World Council of Churches since their formation. It also participates in the World Alliance of Reformed Churches and the World Methodist Council.

The section on doctrine in the Basis of Union, with which candidates for ordination must express "essential agreement," is couched in the traditional language of EVANGELICAL Protestantism. In 1940 the church published an unofficial statement of faith that placed more emphasis on personal and less on legal relations with God. In 1969 it issued, as supplementary to more traditional statements, a creed intended to express the Christian faith in terms both ecumenically acceptable and readily understandable today. In practice the United Church embraces a wide spectrum of belief. "Liberal" views have tended to predominate, but recent years have seen a resurgence of conservative evangelicalism. CHARISMATIC RENEWAL is also influential.

Congregations are free to choose their own style of worship, which is usually informal, sometimes experimental, but seldom extemporaneous. The *Service Book* (1969) suggests orders of service and offers material for use on various occasions. The *Hymn Book* (1971) is jointly sponsored with the Anglican Church of Canada. In response to 20th-century liturgical developments, the tendency has been to greater care for logical sequence and to a heightened appreciation of the sacraments, and the black Genevan gown has been widely replaced by a variety of more colourful vestments. In recent years, the use of a lectionary has become more common.

Church government is conciliar, consisting of legislative bodies or "courts" in ascending sequence from 2414 pastoral charges through 97 presbyteries and 12 conferences to a biennial general council. Congregations elect their own officers, elders for spiritual affairs and stewards for financial matters. Regional and national bodies consist of laypersons and members of the order of ministry in approximately equal numbers. Although the higher courts determine church policy and legislate on matters of more than local concern, congregations are largely self-governing. By contrast, administration has been highly centralized in Toronto. The present trend is to decentralization; each conference now has its own staff and determines its financial priorities. Some members of the order of ministry are ordained, whereas others are commissioned to educational or other forms of service. Congregations normally choose their own ministers, although the church has some voice in appointments. Women may hold any office, including since 1936 the ordained ministry. There are now more than 430 ordained women, and in 1980 Dr Lois M. WILSON was elected the first woman moderator. Dr Robert B. MCCLURE, for many years a medical missionary in China, the Middle East and India, was the first lay moderator.

Voluntary organizations have always been most successful among women. In 1962 the long-established Woman's Missionary Society combined with the Woman's Association, which had specialized in local fund raising, to form United Church Women. At the time of its founding this was the largest women's organization in Canada, but dislike of sexual segregation has seriously eroded its appeal. The most successful program

for men has been AOTS ("As one that serves"), a semiofficial Christian service club. United Church Men, an organization more closely tied to the church, has not caught on to the same extent.

Theological education is carried out at 7 centres, usually in close association with other denominations. Other institutions help to equip lay persons for leadership or provide continuing education for ministers. The United Church inherited, chiefly from the Methodists, a tradition of involvement in secular education. Today, it has official relations of some kind with 12 universities, 3 residential colleges, and 7 secondary schools. Another Methodist legacy was RYERSON PRESS, which for many years under the editorship of Lorne PIERCE encouraged the development of Canadian literature, both religious and secular.

The United Church was brought into being largely by the conviction that only a strong, broad fellowship could meet the needs of Canada's scattered and diverse population. Accordingly, it has always accepted challenges that seemed to belong specifically to no other denomination, maintaining rescue homes, port chaplaincies, mission boats, hospitals in isolated areas, and ministries among various ethnic groups including native peoples, as well as aiding financially an unusually high proportion of isolated rural congregations. Overseas, the former pattern of mission fields supplied and directed from Canada has been replaced by one of partnership with indigenous churches, none of which represents precisely the same blend of denominational backgrounds as the United Church. Missionaries serve in various countries as need arises, always at the request and under the supervision of the receiving church.

The United Church is probably best known by most Canadians for its outspokenness on moral and social issues, often at the cost of alienating members. Dr James R. Mutchmor, secretary for evangelism and social service 1938-63, attracted much publicity by his denunciations of liquor, gambling and pornography, but also guided the church to progressive stands on such issues as LABOUR RELATIONS and the treatment of prisoners. Since his time there has been a shift from personal morality to social justice, which is now usually promoted in collaboration with other denominations. One of the United Church's persistent problems has been in holding together evangelism and social service, to each of which it is historically committed. On the whole it has been more effective in developing a prophetic critique of society than in inspiring the formulation of constructive theology, although there are signs of renewed interest in the resources inherent in its traditions.

See also MISSIONS AND MISSIONARIES; SOCIAL GOSPEL.

JOHN WEBSTER GRANT

Reading: S. Chambers, *This Is Your Church* (1982); John Webster Grant, *The Canadian Experience of Church Union* (1967); C.E. Silcox, *Church Union in Canada* (1933).

United Empire Loyalists' Association of Canada, The,

was incorporated on 27 May 1914. Its aims were to unite the descendants of families of the United Empire LOYALISTS; to perpetuate their spirit of loyalty; to collect memorabilia relating to the Loyalists; to construct and repair buildings and monuments perpetuating their memory; and to publish an historical and genealogical journal. *The Loyalist Gazette* is published semiannually, and the association headquarters are in Toronto, from which an educational service assists researchers of Loyalist history. About 24 branches have been established across Canada. Documentary proof of descendancy from a Loyalist family on either the paternal or maternal side entitles applicants to certified membership.

The association has been supported consistently by the patronage of the governors general of Canada. On 28 Mar 1972, when by royal authority Her Majesty's Kings of Arms granted the association armorial bearings and a badge, the organization was singularly honoured with 3 royal symbols: the crown in the shield and the Union Jack in the crest of the arms, and the royal cipher of George III in the badge. The motto is *Ducit Amor Patriae*.   MARGUERITE R. DOW

United Farmers of Alberta, a farmers' organization established Jan 1909 in Edmonton as an amalgamation of the Canadian Society of Equity and the Alberta Farmers' Association. The UFA was interested in rural economic, social and political issues. In 1913 it prompted the provincial Liberal government to organize the Alberta Farmers' Co-operative Elevator Co, which in 1917 joined with the Grain Growers' Grain Co to form United Grain Growers.

In 1915 it organized the United Farm Women of Alberta, which energetically campaigned for WOMEN'S SUFFRAGE (gained in Alberta in 1916) and struggled to secure better education and health services in rural Alberta. In 1916 the American NON-PARTISAN LEAGUE came to the province and encouraged direct political action by farmers. Close ties developed between the league and the UFA, which entered politics amid postwar unrest. The UFA was elected in 1921 and remained in office until 1935. It formed a cautious, pragmatic government which advanced educational and health services and tried to meet the financial and marketing needs of farmers, but it did not cope well with the GREAT DEPRESSION.

The most powerful early force in the UFA was Henry Wise WOOD, a charismatic farmer from Carstairs. He supported group government but refused to lead the UFA when it was elected. UFA premier 1921-25 was Herbert GREENFIELD, followed by John BROWNLEE (1925-34) and R.G. REID; Reid held office until the 1935 victory of SOCIAL CREDIT. After 1935 the UFA avoided direct political involvement but continued to provide supplies to members through local co-operatives. In 1948 it became the United Farmers of Alberta Co-operative Ltd, one of the strongest farmer-owned organizations in Alberta.   IAN MACPHERSON

United Farmers of Canada, a militant farmers' organization est 1926 as the United Farmers of Canada (Saskatchewan Section). It combined the radical Farmers' Union of Canada and the more conservative Saskatchewan GRAIN GROWERS' ASSOCIATION. During the late 1920s it led the unsuccessful but intense campaign for "the 100% pool," a system in which governments would market all grain. The UFC maintained strong educational programs for rural people, championed the cause of orderly marketing, and called for extensive reform of the educational and medical systems.

During the 1930s the UFC(SS) became dominated by radicals who favoured political action. It entered politics on a moderate SOCIALIST platform in 1931 and in 1932, along with the Independent Labour Party, formed the Farmer-Labour Group. In 1934 the Farmer-Labour Group became the Saskatchewan Section of the CO-OPERATIVE COMMONWEALTH FEDERATION. In 1938 the UFC (Alberta Section) was formed by radical members of the declining UNITED FARMERS OF ALBERTA. In 1943 the Alberta association, in an effort to gain broader support, reorganized as the Alberta Farmers' Union. The UFC(SS) was a powerful force until reorganization in 1949 as the Saskatchewan Farmers' Union. In 1960, along with farmers' unions from other provinces, it helped form a national farmers' union, in which the provincial unions held membership. In 1969 the provincial unions (except for Alberta) dissolved and the

NATIONAL FARMERS UNION became the national organization.   IAN MACPHERSON

United Farmers of Manitoba, fd 1920, an inclusive farmers' organization which replaced the Manitoba Grain Growers' Assn. It supported farmer candidates in the 1920 provincial election, and in 1922 its efforts helped elect John BRACKEN's UFM government (1922-42). In 1921 the UFM supported 12 successful candidates of the federal PROGRESSIVE PARTY but withdrew direct backing in 1924. It was financed by members and by occasional grants from farmers' companies. UFM membership varied from 15 700 in 1923 to 3700 in 1931. The rise of co-operative marketing bodies led to both the absorption of the Farmers' Union of Canada (Manitoba section) and the UFM's rejection of political affiliations by 1928. The United Farmers' goals of co-operative marketing, government intervention in transportation and the creation of a central bank were finally achieved, whereas basic alterations to the protective tariff, the operation of Cabinet government and party politics were not. In 1939 it became the Manitoba Federation of Agriculture; today it is the Manitoba Farm Bureau. *See also* GRAIN GROWERS' ASSOCIATIONS.   G.E. PANTING

United Farmers of Ontario, a farmers' educational, social and political organization formed Mar 1914 in Toronto. The UFO united several small Ontario co-operatives, the Grange and the Farmers' Association. Immediately after the founding of the UFO, the same farmers organized a "twin" company, the United Farmers' Co-operative, to buy supplies and sell produce for Ontario farmers. The UFO grew slowly until late in WWI, when labour shortages, inflated costs and a general dissatisfaction with existing political parties led to a rapid growth in membership. Auxiliary organizations, the United Farm Women and the United Farm Young People, helped to mobilize rural areas.

In 1919, with over 50 000 members, the UFO entered politics and won a plurality in the provincial election. E.C. DRURY, a Barrie farmer and longtime rural leader, was chosen premier. The UFO-labour coalition formed an honest and efficient, if unimaginative, administration that significantly improved rural education, transportation and hydroelectric services. After its defeat in 1923 the UFO declined steadily. Maintaining the enthusiasms of the early period proved difficult; many effective farm leaders were drawn to work with the United Farmers' Co-operative, and the destruction of the federal PROGRESSIVE PARTY was disheartening. During the 1930s, under the idealistic leadership of Agnes MACPHAIL, H.H. HANNAM and Leonard Harman, the UFO organized folk schools and supported the *Farmer's Sun* and the *Rural Co-operator*, and promoted orderly marketing. It briefly supported the CO-OPERATIVE COMMONWEALTH FEDERATION. In 1944 the UFO joined with other farm groups to form the Ontario Federation of Agriculture. In 1948 the United Farmers' Co-operative became the United Co-operatives of Ontario, today it is one of the largest farmer-owned companies in Canada.
                              IAN MACPHERSON

United Farmers of Quebec (Fermiers unis du Québec), fd 1920. PM Borden's decision to conscript farm youths caused a huge farmers' demonstration in Ottawa on 15 May 1918 and gave Québec farmers their first contact with the United Farmers movement in English Canada. By July some 20 local associations had sprung up in western Québec. In Sept the Interprovincial Union of Farmers was established as an umbrella for the local organizations. In Jan 1920, 300 farmers voted in Montréal to transform the union into the United

Farmers of Québec. In 1921 the United Farmers had some 5000 members in over 20 counties. That year they joined with the Union des cultivateurs du Québec (fd in 1919) to form the Parti fermier-progressiste du Québec (Progressive Farmers of Québec). They had the support of Joseph-Noé Ponton and his *Bulletin des agriculteurs*. Their detailed program followed the main lines of the progressive movement but also incorporated elements of Henri BOURASSA's nationalist movement.

The PFQ supported 21 candidates in the federal election of Dec 1921, but none was elected. The Liberals called them Conservatives in disguise, tools of that shameful symbol of CONSCRIPTION, Arthur MEIGHEN. Liberals swept the province; the farmers won a meagre 42 000 votes (11%). They never recovered from this defeat. The apolitical Catholic Union of Farmers was founded in 1924, becoming the dominant farmers' association and marking the end of the Progressive Farmers.
                              RENÉ DUROCHER

United Nations began in 1945 as a loosely coordinated international system of deliberatory bodies, functional agencies and temporary and permanent commissions with headquarters in New York, Geneva and elsewhere. In structure it resembles the LEAGUE OF NATIONS but with a more nearly universal membership. The term was first used 1 Jan 1942 when 26 nations pledged to continue fighting the Axis powers. As WORLD WAR II was drawing to a close, a UN Charter was drawn up by 50 countries, including Canada, in San Francisco. It was designed to promote international co-operation among sovereign states in which each would give up some of its sovereignty in the common interest of all nations to promote peace, security, economic development, social justice and fundamental human rights and freedoms. Much of this would be done through powerful functional agencies such as the International Monetary Fund, the International Civil Aviation Organization and the Food and Agriculture Organization, which were already being established and linked to the UN system. Because of the autonomy of these agencies and the smaller powers' resistance to great power dominance, the United Nations has remained adaptable to changing circumstances.

The main organs are the General Assembly of all 159 member states (1988), each having one vote; the Security Council of 15 members, in which 5 great powers have permanent seats and the power of veto; and the Economic and Social Council of 54 members. Although the Security Council was assumed to be stronger than the other organs, which only recommend, the power of any UN bodies to enforce decisions is limited by the need for consensus among members and their willingness to impose military or economic sanctions. The elected secretary general of the UN is bound by decisions of the constituent organs. After one effort to enforce its will in the KOREAN WAR, the Security Council has concentrated on peaceful settlement, including the provision of PEACE-KEEPING forces, in which Canadians have played a major role.

Although security was the founders' major consideration, economic and social questions now share the limelight. The UN's success in promoting decolonization and self-determination has led to the entry of a host of former colonies whose primary concern is with economic development and the devising of a new international economic order. Since 1945 enormous changes in science and technology have given international conventions, laws and infrastructures new dimensions that embrace such things as space law, commerce, travel, seabed mining, satellite communication, etc. Consequently, specialized agencies such as the World Health Organization and the UN High Commission for Refugees have in fact more rather than fewer issues to handle and the International Court of Justice has an agenda that goes far beyond the adjudication of political disputes.

The UN is essentially a network of institutions for multilateral diplomacy rather than a world government, and as such its achievements depend upon the collective strength of its members. That is why it has been unable to resolve such perennial problems as the escalating arms race, regional conflicts in the Middle East, Kampuchea and Cyprus, human rights violations in South Africa, the increasing gap between rich and poor and refugees.

The 1980s revealed signs of severe strains in the organization. Years of withholding assessed funds for programs which did not meet donor's expectations, together with irresponsible financial management and duplication combined to put its continued operation in jeopardy and, in agencies such as UNESCO, led to the withdrawal of the US and United Kingdom. Canada preferred to work from within to reform the organization rather than become a disengaged critic.

Along with restraint came some notable successes which served to bolster confidence in the UN system: a declaration on international TER-RORISM, a massive famine relief program for Africa; and the superpowers' use of the UN as a forum for reaching world opinion on arms control and the Iran-Iraq Gulf War.

For Canada, which was so active in the founding of most of the UN's organs, the UN remains its best hope for influencing the decisions of other nations through consensus building. It has been at the forefront in promoting universality of membership in the UN. While it may no longer be in a position to play the mediatory role that it did in resolving the SUEZ CRISIS of 1956, it is no less committed to peacemaking and has moved with the times to make its unique contribution of constructive internationalism through such means as verification procedures.

By population Canada ranks thirtieth in the world and among the Western industrialized nations it ranks seventh, but it is the fourth largest financial contributor to the UN system. Canada believes that in combination with other nations lies the best hope for dealing with global problems such as pollution, racial discrimination, hunger, sexual discrimination, and others that trouble and ultimately affect Canadians. However frustrating the UN system may at times appear, its essential purpose is being served as long as it provides the principal forum for discussing these issues and avoids the centuries-old effort to create a world order. *See also* EXTERNAL RELATIONS.

JOHN W. HOLMES AND DON PAGE

Reading: Canadians and the United Nations, 1945-1975 (1977); D. Roche, *United Nations: Divided World* (1984); *Canada and the United Nations* (1988).

United Nations Conference on Trade and Development (UNCTAD), est in 1964 as a permanent organ of the UN General Assembly to promote international trade, with an emphasis on speeding the economic development of developing nations. Total membership (1987) was 168 nation states, including Canada. It has attempted to secure remunerative, equitable and stable prices for primary commodities on which developing countries depend heavily for export earnings; to expand and diversify exports of manufactured products of developing countries; to establish equitable principles for control of restrictive business practices; to improve terms of aid and reduce debt problems of developing countries; and to reach an International Code on the Transfer of Technology.

The permanent machinery of UNCTAD consists of the Trade & Development Board which has 6 main committees (commodities; manufacturing; invisibles and financing related to trade; shipping; the transfer of technology; and economic co-operation among developing countries). The UNCTAD permanent secretariat, located in Geneva, Switz, is headed by a secretary-general.
GREGORY WIRICK

United Nations World Heritage Sites A convention concerning the protection of the world's cultural and natural heritage was launched by UNESCO in 1972. It aimed to recognize and protect sites around the world having outstanding universal significance because of their natural or cultural values. Designations require the co-operation of participating countries. To date, 100 states have signed the convention, agreeing to protect designated properties within their boundaries and to contribute to the World Heritage Fund, which was established to help preserve endangered sites. World heritage sites are selected by a committee according to established criteria.

As of Dec 1987, there were over 280 World Heritage Sites, including the Galapagos Is, the Egyptian Pyramids, the Grand Canyon and the Taj Mahal. To date, 10 areas in Canada have been designated. These are NAHANNI NATIONAL PARK (NWT), KLUANE NATIONAL PARK (YT), ANTHONY ISLAND (BC), DINOSAUR PROVINCIAL PARK (Alta), HEAD-SMASHED-IN BUFFALO JUMP Provincial Historic Resource (Alta), WOOD BUFFALO NATIONAL PARK (Alta/NWT), the BURGESS SHALE SITE (BC), Québec City historic area (*see* ARCHAEOLOGY IN QUÉBEC), L'ANSE AUX MEADOWS National Historic Park (Nfld) and GROS MORNE NATIONAL PARK (Nfld).
C.J. TAYLOR

United Steelworkers of America is the largest international union in Canada and the largest union of private-sector workers. It began in 1936 as the Steelworkers' Organizing Committee (SWOC), a creation of the fledgling Committee for Industrial Organizations (CIO) intended to sign up the thousands of unorganized workers in the American steel industry. SWOC soon persuaded previously independent unions of Canadian steelworkers in Sydney and Trenton, NS, and Hamilton and Sault Ste Marie, Ont, to join. Workers in a few other metalworking industries also formed SWOC locals. Some collective bargaining with 2 of the 3 primary steel companies began before WWII, but it took renewed organizing efforts during the war and a national steel strike in 1946 to consolidate the union's right to negotiate for the industry's workers in Canada. The union adopted its present name in 1942. Since the war it has broadened its membership base to take in workers in many different industries. By 1987 the union had about 160 000 Canadian members. The Canadian members have their own national office in Toronto and 3 district offices, for which they elect their own officers. The union has been a strong supporter of the NDP. In 1984 a Canadian, Lynn WILLIAMS, was elected president of the international union.
CRAIG HERON

Unity, Sask, Town, pop 2471 (1986c), inc 1919, is located in W central Saskatchewan 70 km SW of North Battleford. Settlement in the area commenced in 1904 and the townsite began developing when the railway arrived in 1908. It serves a large grain-growing area, and natural gas, salt, potash and oil have also been discovered in the district. The first attempt at potash mining in Canada was made at Unity. The extraction of salt and natural gas have proven more successful and contribute to the community's growth and stability.
DON HERPERGER

Université de Moncton was founded 19 June 1963 by the New Brunswick legislature in accordance with the recommendations of a royal commission. U de Moncton began with the amalgamation of 3 institutions, which agreed to suspend their charters in order to become affiliated colleges: Saint-Joseph (fd 1864), Sacré-Coeur (1899) and Saint-Louis (1946). As amended in 1977, the university's charter authorized campuses in each of New Brunswick's 3 francophone regions, in Moncton, Edmundston and Shippagan. Its academic programs are divided among 6 faculties (arts, science and engineering, administration, social sciences, education and postgraduate studies) and 4 schools (law, forestry, nutrition and family studies, and nursing).
CLEMENT CORMIER

Enrolment: Université de Moncton, 1985-86
(Source: Statistics Canada)

Full-time Undergrad	Full-time Graduate	Part-time Undergrad	Part-time Graduate
3 912	185	1 866	86

Université de Montréal, Montréal, Qué, was founded in 1876 and opened in 1878 as a branch of UNIVERSITÉ LAVAL of Québec. Its 4 schools were law, medicine, theology and arts. In 1920 the Montréal institution became a full and independent university known as Université de Montréal. For almost a century, U de M was a private, denominational university governed by the Roman Catholic Church. In 1967 the Québec government passed a bill making it a nondenominational university with a public character. In 1985-86, U de M was the largest Québec university, with a student enrolment of more than 50 000 in its 13 faculties, 60 departments, schools or institutes and affiliated schools of commerce (École des hautes études commerciales) and engineering (École polytechnique). It offers a wide range of undergraduate and graduate programs in all disciplines except agriculture and forestry. Research activities are being carried on in all academic units and in 20 specialized centres or groups; in 1985-86, the value of research grants made to the university and its affiliated institutions was close to $59 million.

In 1985-86, U de M awarded 4606 bachelor's degrees, 1403 master's degrees or graduate studies certificates and 858 PhD degrees.
RÉJEAN PLAMONDON

Enrolment: Université de Montréal and Affiliates, 1985-86
(Source: Statistics Canada)

Full-time Undergrad	Full-time Graduate	Part-time Undergrad	Part-time Graduate
19 300	4 488*	25 640	5 827

* Includes medical interns and residents

The Université de Montréal, founded in 1876, is the largest university in Québec, with 13 faculties and 60 departments, institutes and affiliated schools (*photo by Derek Caron/Masterfile*).

Université de Sherbrooke, Sherbrooke, Qué, is a French-language institution fd in 1954. Formed from the Séminaire St-Charles Borromée, the university expanded from its initial 3-faculty core (arts, law and science) to a 9-faculty body, plus a special continuing education unit. The university offers bachelor's, master's and doctoral programs in administration, arts, law, education, physical education and sports, medicine, theology, science and continuing education. Its broad range of programs, which focus on specific professional training and more general studies, attracts students from across Québec and overseas. It was the first university in Québec and the second in Canada to adopt a co-operative teaching system, now offered to more than 2800 students. It ranks second among Québec universities and among the top 14 Canadian universities in research expenditures (proportionate to size). The university has 2 campuses and offers a complete range of cultural and sports facilities.
MARC BERNIER

Enrolment: Université de Sherbrooke, 1985-86
(Source: Statistics Canada)

Full-time Undergrad	Full-time Graduate	Part-time Undergrad	Part-time Graduate
7 238	1 276*	3 926	611

* Includes medical interns and residents

Université du Québec, a multi-campus university, was founded on 18 Dec 1968 as Québec's first public university, its seventh university and its fourth in the French language. U du Q was conceived as a vital element in the reform of Québec's educational system which has seen, over a period of 10 years, a reorganization of the elementary, secondary and post-secondary (collegiate) levels. U du Q can have, according to the law, 3 major types of units: constituent universities, research institutes and superior schools. Each constituent bears a general responsibility for carrying out teaching and research activities with programs leading to the bachelor's, master's and doctoral

Enrolment: Université du Québec (total)
and Constituents, 1985-86
(Source: Statistics Canada)

Full-time Undergrad	Full-time Graduate	Part-time Undergrad	Part-time Graduate
Université du Québec*			
25 416	1 575	48 967	3 389
à Chicoutimi			
2 423	152	4 238	190
à Hull			
1 350	13	3 793	242
à Montréal			
14 868	968	17 985	1 599
à Rimouski			
1 338	69	3 785	135
à Trois-Rivières			
4 287	205	5 722	492
à Rouyn			
380	11	1 796	12
École de technologie supérieure			
598	—	640	—
École nationale d'administration publique			
—	77	80	500
Institut Armand-Frappier			
—	21	20	68
Institut national de la recherche scientifique			
—	39	—	111
Télé-université			
—	—	10 771	—

* Figures show totals of all constituent parts

degrees in most areas of the applied and pure sciences, business administration, the social sciences, the humanities and the arts. The superior schools and research institutes were devised as instruments of development for Québec academic and scientific communities, not only within U du Q but for the general public and other universities as well.

The U du Q system includes 6 constituent universities, in Montréal, Trois-Rivières, Chicoutimi, Rimouski, Hull and Rouyn; 2 research institutes, the Institut national de la recherche scientifique, with research centres throughout the province, and the INSTITUT ARMAND-FRAPPIER in Ville de Laval; and 2 superior schools, École nationale d'administration publique in Québec City and, specializing in the training and development of public administrators, École de technologie supérieure in Montréal. Also considered a unit of U du Q is the Télé-université, which offers study programs enabling students throughout Québec to study without having to go to a university campus (*see* DISTANCE LEARNING). By 1985-86 U du Q had given more than 99 400 diplomas and had an operating budget of $368 million (including sponsored research).
GILLES BOULET

Université Laval, the first francophone Roman Catholic university in N America, was founded 8 Dec 1852 in Québec City by priests of the SÉMINAIRE DE QUÉBEC, who named the institution after their founder, Mgr François de LAVAL. A century later the university gradually relocated to the present campus in Ste-Foy, a Québec City suburb. In 1988 the university had 12 faculties, 9 schools and 3 multi-faculty research centres.

The university originally consisted of the faculties of theology, medicine, law and arts, and served not only the area around Québec City but also the rest of the province. In 1876 the university established a satellite campus in Montréal with similar faculties. In 1919 this satellite became an independent university (*see* UNIVERSITÉ DE MONTRÉAL), the civil status of which was recognized 14 Feb 1920.

From 1852 to 1935, Laval administered education through its faculties. Québec's *collèges classiques* were affiliated with the Faculty of Arts. The bachelor of arts degree, which was awarded upon completion of college studies, was a prerequisite for admission to the faculties of theology, medicine and law. Beginning in 1907, the Faculty of Arts established a number of schools, some of which were subsequently recognized as faculties.

The Faculty of Theology drew students from Québec's Grand Séminaire and based its teachings on the directives of the Roman Congregation of Seminaries and Universities. Its professors, most of whom were graduates of the Roman universities, believed it their duty to espouse the most rigorously orthodox Roman Catholic Church doctrine in their teaching. Some professors of law and medicine had also received part of their education abroad, usually in Paris. It was not until the end of WWII that young doctors and law graduates planning a career in university teaching preferred instead to go to the US or London, and the university's law and medicine programs consequently became more closely associated with American and English programs than with those of France.

The graduate schools, which had links with the Faculty of Arts, were created in the early 20th century. In 1935 the graduate school of philosophy became the Faculty of Philosophy. Between then and 1965, 7 other schools left the Faculty of Arts to become separate faculties: science, literature, agriculture, social sciences, forestry, commerce and education.

In late 1968 a reform commission was estab-

Université Laval, Québec City, Qué, was founded in 1852 (*courtesy Environment Canada, Parks/Heritage Recording Services*).

lished to enable the university better to meet the needs of society, the requirements of university teaching and the aspirations of the student body. This commission drew up a new charter, which was adopted by the Government of Québec on 8 Dec 1970, but the charter could not be given force of law until complemented by new statutes. On 1 Sept 1971 the first statutes were laid out and the new charter promulgated, thus bringing into being the new Université Laval. The new university corporation was characterized by a democratic system at all levels, and emphasis was placed on the participation of all parties in planning and decision making. Undergraduate students are encouraged to play a role in deciding the shape of their education; postgraduate research students see the fruits of these efforts in well-organized seminars and laboratories.

Université Laval has resolutely committed itself to the quest for excellence and progressive thinking through the participation of students and professors, through liberalized study regulations and the thrust given to research.
PHILIPPE SYLVAIN

Enrolment: Université Laval, 1985-86
(Source: Statistics Canada)

Full-time Undergrad	Full-time Graduate	Part-time Undergrad	Part-time Graduate
17 452	3 800*	7 582	2 101

* Includes medical interns and residents

Université Sainte-Anne, Church Point, NS, was founded in 1890 by the Eudist Fathers. Instruction is in French. The only francophone university in Nova Scotia, Université Sainte-Anne is a liberal arts institution offering BA degrees with majors in French, English, history, psychology, sociology, commerce and Canadian studies; a BEd in French education; a bachelor of business administration with a specialization in small business management; a BComm degree; the first 2 years of the BSc degree; and diplomas in bilingual secretarial sciences, community development and computing science. The university is well known for its immersion programs. It has special research and teaching programs in Acadian language, culture and history, in Maritime studies, and in scientific programs of regional interest. The university has a publishing press, and its pedagogical resources centre creates, publishes and makes available books and learning materials in French for the primary and secondary schools of Nova Scotia. The university became nondenominational in 1971. The university had 172 full-time and 124 part-time students in 1985-86. Among its distinguished graduates are Laurent Beaudoin, president of the Bombardier Inc, and Jean-Louis Roy, former editor of *Le Devoir*.

University Universities are post-secondary institutions invested with degree-granting power. Canada's earliest universities had strong religious affiliations and were generally modelled on European institutions. The 3 King's Colleges (est at Windsor, NS, 1789; York [Toronto], 1827; and Fredericton, NB, 1828) were efforts to bring the ideals of the older English universities to Canada. They were residential, tutorial and Anglican. The more democratic ideals of the Scottish universities were evident in varying degrees in DALHOUSIE UNIVERSITY (Halifax, 1818), QUEEN'S UNIVERSITY (Kingston, 1841) and MCGILL UNIVERSITY (Montréal, 1821). The Methodist (Victoria College, Cobourg, Ont, 1841; MOUNT ALLISON UNIVERSITY, Sackville, NB, 1839) and Baptist (ACADIA UNIVERSITY, Wolfville, NS, 1838) institutions were designed to prepare men for the ministry and to supply education for lay members. Bishop's College which later became BISHOP'S UNIVERSITY was established by the Anglicans in 1843. Roman Catholics maintained their own ethos at the English-language ST FRANCIS XAVIER, established at Antigonish, NS, in 1855. LAVAL was established in 1852 by the SÉMINAIRE DE QUÉBEC, a college founded by Bishop LAVAL in 1663. Laval established a branch in Montréal in 1876, which became UNIVERSITÉ DE MONTRÉAL in 1920.

At the time of Confederation, 1867, 17 degree-granting institutions existed in the founding provinces. Four had a nondenominational basis (Dalhousie, McGill, New Brunswick, UNIVERSITY OF TORONTO); the remaining 13 were church related and controlled. Thirteen of the 17 had enrolments of about 100 students. One way of strengthening this multiplicity of small and financially insecure institutions was by consolidation. In 1868 the Ontario government, by withdrawing financial support, pressured its denominational universities to consider co-operation with the public sector. The 3 church universities that federated with U of T (Victoria College and St Michael's College in 1890; Trinity College in 1904) maintained university status and autonomy in instruction and staffing, but agreed to restrict their offerings to the sensitive and less costly liberal arts subjects (eg, classics, philosophy, English literature, history, modern languages, mathematics, science and theology); responsibility for instruction in all other areas and for the granting of degrees (except in theology) rested with the public university. The federative model, adopted by other Canadian universities in the course of their development, represents a Canadian solution to the problem of reconciling religiosity and secularism, diversity and economic pragmatism.

The western provinces adopted a policy of controlled university development from the beginning. In Manitoba this took the form of combining 3 existing church colleges – St-Boniface (Roman Catholic), St John's (Anglican) and Manitoba College (Presbyterian) – under one umbrella. Eleven years after the founding of UNIVERSITY OF MANITOBA (1877) a fourth college, Wesley College (Methodist), was affiliated. In each of the other 3 western provinces a single, public provincial university was created (UNIVERSITY OF ALBERTA, 1906, UNIVERSITY OF SASKATCHEWAN, 1907 and UNIVERSITY OF BRITISH COLUMBIA, 1908). The 3 western provinces adopted as their model the American state university, with its emphasis on extension work and applied research.

The growth of public higher EDUCATION raised the issue of university protection against government interference (see ACADEMIC FREEDOM). The pattern of university-government relationships adopted throughout much of Canada was influenced by the provincial University of Toronto Act of 1906, which established a bicameral system of university government consisting of a senate (faculty), responsible for academic policy, and a board of governors (citizens) exercising exclusive control over financial policy and having formal

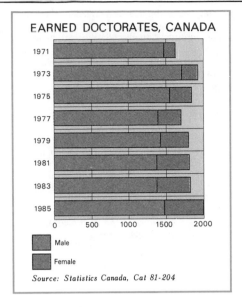

EARNED DOCTORATES, CANADA

Male

Female

Source: Statistics Canada, Cat 81-204

authority in all other matters. The role of the president, appointed by the board, was to provide a link between the 2 bodies and to furnish active institutional leadership. Other important developments in the early part of this century were the expansion of professional education beyond the traditional fields of theology, law and medicine and, to a more limited extent, the introduction of graduate training based on the German-inspired American model of specialized course work and the completion of a research thesis.

By 1939 the number of degree-granting universities in Canada had increased to 28, varying in size from U of T, with full-time enrolment of 7000, to those with fewer than 1000 students. There were 40 000 students, representing 5% of the population between ages 18 and 24. By 1985-86, 14.5% of the population between the ages of 18 and 24 were university students. Most universities were regional institutions; only McGill and Toronto had attained an international reputation for research. There was no systematic policy concerning higher education, and funding was established year by year. Except for the natural sciences, there was no federal or provincial grant agency providing regular support for graduate work and research. A few LEARNED SOCIETIES and academic journals had been established.

WWII marked the slow beginning of a new era in Canadian higher education. The war effort generated a high demand for scientific research and highly trained personnel (many of whom were imported into Canada) and this brought appreciation for the vital importance to the nation of the university sector. In the immediate postwar period the federal government began to provide some financial assistance to the universities to help them deal with the influx of veterans. As a result of a veterans' rehabilitation program, 53 000 veterans entered university between 1944 and 1951. When the expected return to much lower student enrolments failed to occur, the federal government, following the advice of the Massey Commission, became involved in 1951 in the regular provision of financial support to higher education (see NATIONAL DEVELOPMENT IN THE ARTS, LETTERS AND SCIENCES, ROYAL COMMISSION ON).

By the early 1950s the size of the university student population was twice that of 1940 and by 1963 another doubling had taken place. With much larger increases projected as a result of the BABY BOOM, provincial governments abandoned their initial strategy of trying to meet these increases by expanding existing institutions. The

single-university policy in the West was changed as existing colleges of the provincial universities gained autonomy as universities: UNIVERSITY OF VICTORIA (1963), UNIVERSITY OF CALGARY (1966), UNIVERSITY OF WINNIPEG (1967) and UNIVERSITY OF REGINA (1974). New university charters were granted to CARLETON UNIVERSITY (Ottawa, 1957), YORK UNIVERSITY (Toronto, 1959), UNIVERSITY OF WATERLOO (1959), and TRENT UNIVERSITY (Peterborough, 1963). Full-time undergraduate enrolments tripled, and part-time undergraduate and full-time graduate enrolments experienced close to a sixfold increase. Some 23 261 additional full-time university teachers were recruited. Because Canadian graduate programs had just started to expand, many university instructors recruited during the 1960s and the 1970s had received their graduate training abroad, particularly in the US and Britain. The costs of operating this expanded system increased even more dramatically.

The ambitious policy of university education initiated in the 1960s was not just a response to the pressure of numbers. It was motivated by the belief, borrowed from the US and endorsed by economists, that higher education was a key to economic productivity and would yield higher rates of economic returns both for individuals and for society. Social justice provided the second rationale. Improving EDUCATIONAL OPPORTUNITY was seen as a major means of accommodating rising social aspirations and of improving the social prospects of disadvantaged social, cultural and regional groups. Financial aid programs, aimed at removing financial barriers to university education, were introduced at both the federal and provincial levels. In 1986-87, 235 000 students received financial assistance under the Canada Student Loan Plan (see STUDENTS, FINANCIAL AID TO).

The Canadian higher-education systems of today are both similar to and different from those of the past. The most important reform in the organizational framework of higher education was undertaken in Québec with the introduction of the COLLÈGE D'ENSEIGNEMENT GÉNÉRAL ET PROFESSIONNEL (CEGEP), but in other provinces as well higher education had to come to terms with the rapid emergence of the COMMUNITY COLLEGE sector of post-secondary education. In some provinces systematic transfer arrangements between the 2 sectors (university and community college) have been established; in other provinces the 2 sectors operate as separate streams.

Today, Canada has 68 public degree-granting universities, 12 of which are in federation with another university. Canadian higher education has become a public-sector enterprise. Escalating costs have forced denominational universities, eg, Waterloo Lutheran University (which became WILFRID LAURIER UNIVERSITY) and Assumption University (which became UNIVERSITY OF WINDSOR), to sever their religious connections in order to qualify for public support. Another important development has been the provincialization of the system of higher education. While both the federal and provincial governments provide financial support, university policy is shaped by the provincial governments, particularly since 1966, when the federal government's program of direct grants to universities, begun in 1951, was replaced by a shared-cost contribution to the provincial governments. Other changes, introduced in 1977, reduced the direct financial role of the federal government even more and increased the discretionary power of the provincial governments in the allocation of federal support money.

The governance structure of most Canadian universities is still based on a 2-tier system, except in the case of Laval, U of T and ATHABASCA UNIVERSITY, where systems incorporating the powers of board and senate have been introduced. At most

	1962-63	1985-86
Full-time undergraduate enrolment		
Total	132 700	412 429
% Female	27.8	48.9
Part-time undergraduate enrolment		
Total	38 600	249 645
% Female	41.2	61.1
Full-time graduate enrolment		
Total	8 400	54 853
% Female	15.1	39.7
Bachelor's and first professional degrees		
Total	24 939	97 474
% Female	27.8	51.9
Master's Degree		
Total	2 755	15 194
% Female	18.1	42.0
Earned Doctorates		
Total	421	2 000
% Female	8.1	26.4
Full-time university teachers		
Total	9 983	35 171
% Female	11.5	17.0
Expenditures on university education (Millions$)	356	6 985

universities, however, the composition of the 2 governing bodies has changed. Although faculty still hold the majority of seats on the academic faculty councils and senates, membership now may include students, alumni and representatives of professional bodies. Similarly, faculty and students are often represented on boards of governors. One important power of the board has been taken away: until the 1950s, TENURE at most universities was held at the pleasure of the board, but this faculty right has become more firmly entrenched.

The contemporary Canadian university is a multipurpose organization striving to achieve a number of objectives simultaneously: teaching – the provision of a "liberal education" or general education; training – the transmission of expert knowledge required for high-level jobs; research – the creation of knowledge through basic scientific research and scholarship; public service – the provision of practical knowledge and science to society; and equalization of opportunity – the removal of all barriers that inhibit the motivated and academically capable person from receiving a university education.

The expansion of the 1960s was guided by the values of excellence, accessibility, service to society, autonomy and diversity. Faced with financial constraints and heightened international competition the optimistic assumption that all of these values could be simultaneously achieved has come under challenge. If it is important to develop a national strategy for higher education, how can such a strategy evolve within a stronger federal presence? Knowledge has become an important resource and both government and business want an important role in directing its use. How can this relationship be reconciled with the notion of academic freedom and of knowledge as a publicly available good? Can excellence only be achieved by the concentration of resources within universities? Demographic and social changes add to the problems the higher education system presently faces and will continue to encounter in the future. Among them are a shrinking 18-24-year-old age group and the increased participation by nontraditional groups (part-time university students).

Another problem faced by Canadian universities involves accessibility. Canadian participation rates have fared very well compared with other

nations; only the US and Sweden can claim higher participation rates for their 18-24-year-old age groups. Canadian data reveal, however, that educational expansion has not brought about a more equal representation by social class at university.   P. ANISEF AND J. LENNARDS

Reading: R.S. Harris, *A History of Higher Education in Canada 1663-1960* (1970); M. Ross, *The University* (1976).

University College, U of T (architects Frederick W. CUMBERLAND and William G. Storm, 1856-59), picturesque in its variety of silhouettes, colours, textures and carved details, eclectic in its rich amalgam of Norman, Romanesque, Anglo-French and Venetian forms, epitomizes the flamboyance and strength of the high-Victorian Gothic style. The architects, aided by their amateur colleague Gov Gen Sir Edmund HEAD, drew inspiration from the work of the Irish firm of Deane and Woodward, especially the contemporary Oxford University Museum. The erection of this vast college building 1856-59 signalled the achievement of a major 19th-century aspiration for a nondenominational institution of higher learning supported by government.

CHRISTINA CAMERON

University College of Cape Breton, Sydney, NS, was founded in 1974 by the amalgamation of the Sydney campus of ST FRANCIS XAVIER UNIVERSITY (est 1951) with the Nova Scotia Eastern Institute of Technology (fd 1968). Degree-granting status was obtained in 1982. The university works with the community and is committed to fostering both technology and theoretical learning. Liberal arts, business administration and science degrees, extensive continuing education programs, and diplomas in engineering, applied arts and technology are offered. The university had 1260 full-time and 734 part-time students in 1985-86.

LOIS KERNAGHAN

University Cup is awarded annually to the Canadian Interuniversity Athletic Union (CIAU) hockey champions. The trophy was presented by Queen's U and RMC of Canada – who were participants in the first organized intercollegiate hockey game played in Canada at Kingston, Ont, in 1885 – in recognition of the contribution made to the game of hockey by outstanding university players.

Teams from the CIAU's 3 regional conferences – Canada West, Ontario and Atlantic – compete for the trophy. Kingston was the site of the inaugural CIAU hockey championship in 1963 as Queen's and RMC co-hosted the national tournament. Over the course of its first 25 years, the format of the University Cup playoffs has varied. Originally a 4-team tournament, the playoffs have included 5- and 6-team tournaments, featuring conference champions, host and wild card teams, and progressive best-of-3 regional series between conference champions.

Of the 9 championship teams, 2 have dominated the University Cup playoffs: the Toronto Varsity Blues and Alberta Golden Bears have combined to win the Cup in 17 of the past 25 years. Clare Drake, the winningest coach in N American intercollegiate hockey history, with more than 600 victories, has coached Alberta to 6 titles.

STEVE KNOWLES

University Magazine, The (1907-20). A Montréal quarterly edited by Sir Andrew MACPHAIL, it succeeded the semiannual *McGill University Magazine* (1901-06). Notable for paying its contributors, the magazine was financially guaranteed by Macphail himself. Under his rigorous editorial direction it set a standard of excellence in English-speaking Canada while attaining a circulation of nearly 6000, a level no comparable Canadian quarterly has subsequently matched.

Macphail himself contributed 43 pieces of political comment and social criticism (without payment) and for him the magazine was a vehicle to advance "correct thought," by which he meant a Canada that was rural, traditional and, aside from Québec, overwhelmingly British. When these ideals seemed to be in irreversible decline and when at the same time he faced financial pressures, failing eyesight and a drastic decline in circulation owing to his 4-year absence during World War I, Macphail finally discontinued the magazine. *See also* LITERARY MAGAZINES.

IAN ROSS ROBERTSON

University of Alberta, Edmonton, Alta; fd 1906 at the first sitting of Alberta's Legislative Assembly. Classes started in Sept 1908 with 45 students and 5 faculty (H.M. TORY, first President, 1908-28). Degrees were conferred on the first graduating class in 1912 by Chancellor C.A. Stuart. The university grew rapidly until WWI, with the Faculty of Law being established in 1912 and the faculties of Applied Science (later Engineering) and Medicine in 1913. During this period the department (later faculty) of extension began its delivery of noncredit educational services to people in all parts of Alberta.

While use of extension's services, especially its lending library, grew constantly during the interwar years, it was in the 1960s that the university underwent its greatest period of expansion to over 15 000 students.

Throughout its history, U of A has maintained affiliation with several post-secondary educational institutions in Alberta: St Stephen's College (United Church), St Joseph's College (Roman Catholic), Camrose Lutheran College, Concordia Lutheran College and King's College. The university's divisions in Calgary and Lethbridge became universities in their own right in 1966 (UNIVERSITY OF CALGARY) and 1967 (UNIVERSITY OF LETHBRIDGE). The Faculté Saint-Jean, which was established in 1910 as a Juniorate of the Oblate Order, gained its current faculty status in 1978 and offers baccalaureate instruction in the French language.

The university is a recognized leader in several academic disciplines, with more than 20 research centres and institutes housed on campus. It is well known for basic and applied research in agriculture and is engaged in projects in several African and Asian countries. These projects relate to soil conservation and fertility, and plant and animal breeding and nutrition. Through the early contributions of K.A. CLARK, the university played a formative role in developing techniques for the recovery of oil from the Athabasca oil sands. In medicine, J.B. COLLIP helped develop INSULIN and, in organic chemistry, R. U. LEMIEUX was the first to synthesize sucrose.

University staff and students, especially in the Faculty of Medicine, receive indispensable support from the Alberta Heritage Foundation for Medical Research. University personnel also collaborate closely with members of the ALBERTA OIL SANDS TECHNOLOGY AND RESEARCH AUTHORITY and the ALBERTA RESEARCH COUNCIL, governed by the university from 1933 to 1942. Microelectronics and the application of advanced laser technology are primary areas of research in the university-based Alberta Microelectronic Centre and the Alberta Laser Institute. The university has achieved a high reputation in the humanities, social sciences and fine arts. Violet ARCHER taught theory and musical composition at the university from 1962 to 1978. The university was the first in Canada to establish a PhD program in physical education. In collaboration with the city of Edmonton, it hosted the WORLD UNIVERSITY GAMES in 1983, second in size and significance only to the Olympic Games.

HUB, a combined student residence and shopping mall on University of Alberta campus, Edmonton (*photo by Wilhelm Schmidt/Masterfile*).

The University of Alberta Press (est 1969) had published 83 books by 1987. The U of A plays a major support role in the preparation of *The Canadian Encyclopedia*, and in 1985 it published *The Collected Writings of Louis Riel/Les Écrits complets de Louis Riel*. The university's library is one of the better known research facilities in N America, with some 3 million titles covering every academic discipline. The university's main campus in south-central Edmonton is 89 ha in extent. The university owns and leases a further 5082 ha in 25 locations across Alberta, primarily for AGRICULTURAL RESEARCH and DEVELOPMENT.

W.H. JOHNS AND C.J. SIMPSON

Reading: W.H. Johns, *A History of the University of Alberta, 1908-1969* (1981).

Enrolment: University of Alberta, 1985-86
(Source: Statistics Canada)

Full-time Undergrad	Full-time Graduate	Part-time Undergrad	Part-time Graduate
20 619	3 205*	3 377	1 200

* Does not include over 400 medical interns and residents

University of British Columbia, Vancouver, was founded in 1908 by Act of the provincial legislature. Before UBC opened, higher education in BC was provided by denominational colleges affiliated with the universities of McMaster, Toronto and McGill. In 1910 a site at Point Grey was selected for the UBC campus. The outbreak of WWI delayed construction and UBC began operations at Fairview in 1915. Through its association with McGill, the university was provided with the nucleus of its first staff and basic curriculum in arts and science and engineering. In 1919, the Faculty of Agriculture was established; nursing and health programs began, leading to the first degree course in the British Empire. In 1920 honours courses, extension services and summer sessions were introduced, and McGill's Victoria College in Victoria became an affiliate of the university. In 1925 UBC moved to its permanent site on Point Grey. Expansion of the campus was virtually at a standstill during the 1930s. Academic expansion during this period included the establishment of a university extension department (1936) and the further development of work in forestry and commerce.

Military training for students was a feature of campus life during WWI and WWII. Many faculty members served in the armed forces or were involved in scientific research to aid the war effort. UBC enrolment rose dramatically following WWII from 3058 in 1944-45 to 9374 in 1947-48. Surplus army and air force camps provided several hundred temporary classrooms as well as faculty and student housing. In the postwar era several new buildings were erected. Four new faculties were established: law (1945), graduate studies (1948), pharmacy (1949) and medicine (1950); 2 established departments were elevated to faculty status: forestry (1951) and commerce (1957); and the provincial normal school was incorporated into the university as the Faculty of Education (1956).

Growth since the 1960s has made UBC one of Canada's largest anglophone universities. It has a campus of some 473 buildings. The UBC library, one of the largest in Canada, houses 2.5 million volumes, and UBC's computing facilities are among the most extensive in the country. During this period the university added the Faculty of Dentistry (1964), and schools of librarianship, rehabilitation medicine, and audiology and speech sciences. Expansion has also taken place in all of UBC's 12 faculties, 9 schools and 11 institutes and research centres. Special distinction has been achieved in forestry, biotechnology, computer science, Pacific Rim studies, the fine and performing arts, materials research, imaging research, biomedical imaging, environmental and ecological studies, pulp and paper engineering, genetics and international business research. Beginning in 1961, the university undertook construction on campus of an extensive health sciences centre which now comprises teaching and research buildings as well as an affiliated hospital complex of 600 beds for psychiatric, extended and acute care. UBC has become one of the major research universities in Canada, with sponsored research funding in excess of $60 million a year. An industry liaison program established in 1984 is active in all aspects of technology transfer.

A museum of anthropology, housing one of the world's leading collections of NORTHWEST COAST INDIAN ART and artifacts, and a 44 ha botanical garden are public facilities as well as teaching and research centres. UBC and other western Canadian universities co-operate in the operation of the TRIUMF cyclotron project, which produces high-intensity meson beams for basic physics research and cancer therapy, and in the Bamfield Marine Biological Station on Vancouver I, a major teaching and research centre in marine biology. UBC operates a 8900 ha research and teaching forest at Haney in the Fraser Valley and an AGRICULTURAL RESEARCH farm at Oyster River on Vancouver I. In 1985 the Pulp and Paper Research Institute of Canada (PAPRICAN) completed a laboratory on campus and a laboratory on the 52 ha Discovery Park adjacent to the campus. The Biomedical Research Centre, a joint project of the Terry Fox Medical Research Foundation and the Wellcome Foundation Ltd, opened in 1987.

The university has formal affiliation agreements with 3 campus theological colleges: Vancouver School of Theology (an amalgamation of Anglican and United Church colleges), St Mark's College (Roman Catholic) and Regent College. St Andrew's Hall (Presbyterian) offers residential accommodation, as does Carey Hall (Baptist), which also provides internship training and continuing education programs. The university has affiliation agreements with a number of hospitals in the Greater Vancouver area.

Enrolment: University of British Columbia, 1985-86
(Source: Statistics Canada)

Full-time Undergrad	Full-time Graduate	Part-time Undergrad	Part-time Graduate
17 779	3 292	4 789	1 103

University of Calgary, Calgary, Alta, was founded in 1966. U of C began in 1946 when Calgary Normal School became a branch of the Faculty of Education of the Edmonton-based UNIVERSITY OF ALBERTA. Gradually, introductory courses were offered in arts, science, commerce and engineering under the respective Edmonton faculties. Known as University of Alberta, Calgary Branch, it moved to its present campus in 1960. In 1963 department heads were established for the faculties of arts and science, education and physical education, and for a division of engineering. The university became fully autonomous in 1966. Subsequently, faculties of medicine, nursing, law, environmental design, social welfare, fine arts, general studies, humanities, management and social sciences have been added. Mount Royal College and Medicine Hat College have been affiliated with U of C since 1966.

B. BEATON

Enrolment: University of Calgary, 1985-86
(Source: Statistics Canada)

Full-time Undergrad	Full-time Graduate	Part-time Undergrad	Part-time Graduate
13 716	1 666	4 257	904

University of Guelph, Guelph, Ont, was founded in 1964. It has 7 academic colleges: arts, biological science, family and consumer studies (fd in 1903 as Macdonald Institute), physical science, social science, Ontario Agricultural College (fd 1874) and Ontario Veterinary College (fd 1862); and 2 university schools: rural planning and development, and part-time studies and continuing education. In addition to its traditional strengths in agriculture and VETERINARY MEDICINE the university now has excellent programs in the basic disciplines in the humanities, the social sciences and the physical and biological sciences; special programs include agricultural and biological engineering, human kinetics, gerontology, hotel and food administration and landscape architecture. Graduate and research interests include intervarsity programs in physics, chemistry and biotechnology (with U of Waterloo) and philosophy (with McMaster U). The university receives more than $37 million in research funding, $18 million of this from the Ontario Ministry of Agriculture and Food for agricultural research. The campus was established in 1874 when the Ontario School of Agriculture opened near Guelph on a 202 ha farm provided by the Ontario government. In 1880 it became Ontario Agricultural College and Experimental Farm. Ontario Veterinary College, founded by Andrew SMITH in Toronto, was acquired by the government and moved to Guelph in 1922. The Macdonald Institute, established as the Division of Home Economics at OAC, was financed by Sir William MAC-DONALD (founder of Macdonald College, Ste-Anne-de-Bellevue, Qué) as part of a movement led by Adelaide HOODLESS to promote domestic science in rural Canada. From 1888 until 1964 OAC was affiliated academically with UNIVERSITY OF TORONTO, as were OVC and Macdonald Institute from 1919. The University of Guelph was established in 1964 on the basis of the founding colleges. B. BEATON

Enrolment: University of Guelph, 1985-86 (Source: Statistics Canada)

Full-time Undergrad	Full-time Graduate	Part-time Undergrad	Part-time Graduate
9 612	438	1 925	179

University of King's College, Halifax, is Canada's oldest university. It was founded in 1789 by the Anglican Church at WINDSOR, NS, as an embodiment of LOYALIST political and religious principles. Degree-conferring status dates from 1802. King's remained classically oriented until 1920, when a disastrous fire forced realignment of educational approaches. King's, financially supported during this period by the Carnegie Foundation, moved to Halifax, where it has maintained a joint faculty of arts and science with DALHOUSIE UNIVERSITY since 1923. With the exception of its journalism program, all degrees are awarded in conjunction with either Dalhousie or the Atlantic School of Theology. King's had 521 full-time undergraduate and 16 part-time undergraduate students in 1985-86. LOIS KERNAGHAN

University of Lethbridge, Lethbridge, Alta, was founded in 1967. The university offers a liberal arts education leading to undergraduate degrees in arts and science, education, fine arts, management, music and nursing; a master's degree in education is also available. The continuing education division provides public-interest and credit courses at times and locations convenient to students across southern Alberta. In 1971 the university, which grew out of the University Section of Lethbridge Junior College (now Lethbridge Community College), moved to a new 185 ha campus designed by architect Arthur ERICKSON. Recent additions are the University Centre for the Arts (1981), which has outstanding facilities for

Dramatic view of U of Lethbridge, designed by architect Arthur Erickson (*photo by J.A. Kraulis*).

fine arts, drama and music, and the Max Bell Regional Aquatic Centre (1986), which has an Olympic-size pool and presents many opportunities for teaching and research in aquatic sports and for community-based aquatic activities. The university had 2648 full-time and 541 part-time undergraduate students in 1985-86.

University of Manitoba, Winnipeg, was founded in 1877, the first institution of higher education to be established in western Canada. At first it acted only as a degree-granting body for its 3 founding denominational colleges: St-Boniface College (Roman Catholic), St John's College (Anglican), and Manitoba College (Presbyterian). Wesley College (Methodist) became affiliated with the university in 1888, following by 6 years the privately founded Manitoba Medical College. In 1900 the university became a teaching institution by an Act of the provincial legislature. Thereafter, other colleges also received affiliated status: Manitoba College of Pharmacy (1902); Manitoba Agricultural College (1906); St Paul's College (Roman Catholic) and Brandon College (1938). Other forms of affiliation have continued to the present. In 1963 the nondenominational University College, the creation of historian W.L. MORTON, was completed; and in 1964 St Andrew's College, intended to train clergy for the Ukrainian Greek Orthodox Church, became an associated college. It was granted special affiliation status in 1981. In addition, the university recognizes the Canadian Mennonite Bible College and the Canadian Nazarene College, both in the Greater Winnipeg area, as "approved teaching centres." Altogether the system of affiliated colleges provides an accurate replication of the ethnic and religious diversity of Manitoba in the setting of higher education.

The university grew slowly after WWI but expanded greatly during the 1960s and early 1970s; it now offers programs in 20 faculties and schools. Especially noteworthy among its various contributions to knowledge have been the discovery of a treatment for, and control of, Rh disease and the genetic research that made possible the development of the hybrid cereal grain, TRITICALE.

A. BRIAN McKILLOP

Enrolment: University of Manitoba, 1985-86 (Source: Statistics Canada)

Full-time Undergrad	Full-time Graduate	Part-time Undergrad	Part-time Graduate
12 860	2 378*	6 379	1 519

* Includes medical interns and residents

University of New Brunswick, Fredericton, was founded in 1785 as the Provincial Academy of Arts and Sciences. It is a multidisciplinary institution noted particularly for engineering, forestry, science and the liberal arts. Modelled on the Tory and Anglican ideals of King's College, New York, the academy was tempered by its LOYALIST and wilderness beginnings. It was an early rival to King's College, Windsor, NS, and although enjoying provincial government support, it did not receive a charter until 1800, when it became the College of New Brunswick. In 1828 it received a royal charter as King's College and in 1859 was reconstituted as University of New Brunswick. Religious qualifications were abolished in 1846 and women were admitted in 1886. The early curriculum stressed a classical education, but by the mid-19th century progressive educators such as William Brydone JACK were introducing the newest scientific disciplines. Although financially limited, the institution was regarded as second only to UNIVERSITY OF TORONTO during the late 1800s.

Highlights of expansion included the introduction of forestry science in 1908 and, more recently, business administration, nursing and computer science. ST THOMAS U, an independent small liberal-arts university, has shared the Fredericton campus since its relocation from Chatham, NB, in 1964. A UNB campus opened in Saint John in 1964 and has about 2000 full- and part-time students. In 1973 the provincial Teachers' College was incorporated into the university in Fredericton. Prominent alumni include Bliss CARMAN, Sir Charles G.D. ROBERTS, Lord Beaverbrook (*see* Max AITKEN) and Anne MURRAY. LOIS KERNAGHAN

Enrolment: University of New Brunswick, 1985-86 (Source: Statistics Canada)

Full-time Undergrad	Full-time Graduate	Part-time Undergrad	Part-time Graduate
7 361	487	1 957	329

University of Ottawa, Ottawa, Ont, was founded in 1848. It is Canada's oldest and largest bilingual university. The university offers courses through the faculties of Administration, Arts, Education, Engineering, Health Sciences, Law (both common and civil), Science and Social Sciences. There is also a School of Graduate Studies, the Human Rights Research and Education Centre and the Institute for International Development and Co-operation. The U of O Heart Institute at Ottawa Civic Hospital is a leading cardiology centre and, in 1986, performed Canada's first artificial heart operation. U of O is heavily involved with business and government, in research, consulting and co-operative education programs. U of O began as the College of Bytown, founded by the Oblate fathers, and in 1861 became the College of Ottawa. In 1866, university status was granted by Parliament, making U of O the last university to receive its charter prior to the British N America Act, which made education a provincial responsibility. In 1965, U of O became a publicly funded, nondenominational institution, during a time in which it experienced rapid growth. The university is federated with St Paul U which offers degree programs in theology and canon law.

Enrolment: University of Ottawa, 1985-86 (Source: Statistics Canada)

Full-time Undergrad	Full-time Graduate	Part-time Undergrad	Part-time Graduate
11 262	1 832*	6 496	1 659

* Includes medical interns and residents

University of Prince Edward Island, Charlottetown, was established in Apr 1969 by the Legislature of PEI. UPEI is a public nondenominational institution created by the merger of 2 venerable institutions of higher learning, Prince of Wales College (est 1834), and St Dunstan's University (fd 1855). UPEI has undergraduate faculties of arts, science and education, and a school of business administration. It offers degrees in arts, science, business administration, education and music. It also offers a diploma in engineering and preparatory courses for agriculture, architecture, dentistry, law, medicine and veterinary medicine. A doctoral program in veterinary medicine has been offered since 1986. Enrolment has been fairly constant since UPEI's foundation. Ninety-one per cent of the student population is normally drawn from PEI, with 8% from other provinces and 1% from foreign countries. One-quarter of the students live in residence. The comparatively small number of students, and a satisfactory faculty-student ratio, has enabled the university to implement its central objective, the maintenance of personal and scholarly instruction. Over the years UPEI has preserved a close relationship with its principal constituency, the Island community. The university had 1768 full-time and 781 part-time students in 1985-86.

FRANCIS W.P. BOLGER

University of Regina, Regina, was founded in 1911 as Regina College by the METHODIST Church. In 1925 the college became affiliated with UNIVERSITY OF SASKATCHEWAN and began offering courses in arts and science. In 1934 it was transferred from UNITED CHURCH control to U Sask; degrees were granted after 1961. In 1965 the college moved to southeastern Regina, and university status was granted 1 July 1974. U of R offers degrees in arts, sciences, music, journalism, administration, engineering, education, social work and graduate studies, and programs in Canadian Plains studies, bilingual studies, human justice and co-operative work. U of R also has a Faculty of Physical Activity Studies and a Fine Arts College. In addition, the university offers courses at other Saskatchewan centres and provides correspondence, distance-education and satellite-televised instruction. Federated colleges include Campion College, Luther College and Saskatchewan Indian Federated College; affiliated institutes include Canadian Theological College and the Gabriel Dumont Institute of Native Studies and Applied Research. The Norman Mackenzie Art Gallery is affiliated to the university and is recognized nationwide not only for its collection but also for its innovative teaching methods.

NANCY BROWN FOULDS

Enrolment: University of Regina, 1985-86
(Source: Statistics Canada)

Full-time Undergrad	Full-time Graduate	Part-time Undergrad	Part-time Graduate
5 386	104	3 785	329

University of Saskatchewan, Saskatoon, was founded in 1907. In 1879 the Church of England (*see* ANGLICANISM) established Emmanuel College in Prince Albert to train "native helpers" in theology, classics and native languages. In 1883 it became known as "University of Saskatchewan." In 1907 the new province of Saskatchewan chartered U Sask as a nondenominational, co-educational institution. A 1032 ha tract, comprising a 146 ha campus, a university farm and experimental plots, was set aside in Saskatoon. In 1909 courses in arts and science were offered; Emmanuel College moved from Prince Albert to Saskatoon as an affiliate, and Rugby School in England donated a chapel for the new theological school. From 1912 to 1938 the university expanded, adding faculties of agriculture, engineering, law, pharmacy, commerce, medicine, education, home economics and nursing; graduate studies was added in 1946 and dentistry in 1965. In an effort to promote post-secondary education, several junior colleges were authorized to give university credit courses. Of these, Regina College, affiliated in 1934, had the most significant impact on the university's development: in 1959 it was given degree-granting status, becoming U Sask's second campus. Degrees were granted after 1961. It became autonomous in 1974 as UNIVERSITY OF REGINA. U Sask's program in agriculture has grown to include VETERINARY MEDICINE and 3 additional experimental farms totalling 1740 ha in area. Indian education and studies continue to

---

Enrolment: University of Saskatchewan, 1985-86
(Source: Statistics Canada)

Full-time Undergrad	Full-time Graduate	Part-time Undergrad	Part-time Graduate
11 395	911	3 874	421

---

be a particular interest of the university. In 1983 the Central Pentecostal College joined the other theological colleges affiliated with the university.

B. BEATON

University of Sudbury, *see* LAURENTIAN UNIVERSITY.

University of Toronto, Toronto, Canada's largest university, has a long and complex history. It was founded as King's College by royal charter in 1827 and was initially controlled by the colonial establishment and the Church of England. The church affiliation made it unpopular, and on 31 Dec 1849 the institution was secularized, becoming on 1 Jan 1850 the nondenominational University of Toronto. The Anglicans responded by creating Trinity College at Toronto in 1851 (actually opening in 1852). In the 1850s U of T was reorganized and UNIVERSITY COLLEGE was created as its teaching arm. Structural changes encouraged other colleges to federate with U of T: Victoria College (Methodist, fd 1841 in Cobourg, Ont) and St Michael's College (Roman Catholic, fd 1852 in Toronto by the Basilian Order) joined in 1890 and Trinity College in 1904, each of them retaining university status in order to continue granting degrees in theology. During this period some of Toronto's theological colleges also federated with the university. Knox College (fd 1844), a Presbyterian seminary, affiliated with the university in 1885 and federated in 1890. Wycliffe College (Anglican, fd 1877) became a federated college in 1889. Emmanuel College (Methodist, fd 1836) became affiliated with the university as a UNITED CHURCH OF CANADA seminary in 1925, the year the United Church came into existence. In 1969 Toronto School of Theology was created as an independent federation of 7 schools of theology, including the divinity faculties of Victoria (Emmanuel), St Michael's and Trinity universities and Knox and Wycliffe colleges. Within its own federation, U of T granted all but theology or divinity degrees, but since 1978, by virtue of a change made in U of T's charter, the university has granted theology degrees conjointly with TST's member institutions.

The reorganization of U of T in the 1850s had resulted in the abolishment of the faculties of law and medicine, but these were restored in 1887. The Royal College of Dental Surgeons (fd 1875) was affiliated with the university from 1888 until 1925, when it became the Faculty of Dentistry. Engineering students attended the School of Practical Science which was affiliated with the university from its inception in 1878 until 1887, when it amalgamated. The Conservatory of Music became an affiliate in 1896.

After the turn of the century the university expanded rapidly. New faculties included home economics (1906), education (1907), forestry (1907), social work (1914), nursing (1920), graduate studies (1922), hygiene (1926) and the School of Architecture (1948). Affiliate research

---

Hart House, built 1911-19 in the collegiate Gothic style, is the social, cultural and recreational centre of U of T (*photo © Hartill Art Associates, London, Ont*).

---

institutions such as the ROYAL ONTARIO MUSEUM (1914), Connaught Medical Laboratories (1914) and the David Dunlap Observatory (1935) played an important role in the development of the university. The building program during this period included Hart House, a social, cultural and recreational centre which was built between 1911 and 1919 and given to the university in 1919 by Vincent MASSEY.

Canada's evolution was reflected in the growth and diversification of the university. The University of Toronto Press was established in 1901, and it became a full-scale academic publishing house after 1945; by 1988, it was publishing 88 titles and 25 periodicals a year (*see* UNIVERSITY PRESSES). Graduate institutes in various areas of specialization were developed, the first being the Institute of Business Administration (1958). The Ontario Institute for Studies in Education (OISE) was founded in 1965 as a research and development institute and as a graduate school of education. In this latter capacity it serves as the dept of educational theory in U of T's School of Graduate Studies. By 1988, 22 graduate centres and institutes had come into existence to deal with subject areas as diverse as biomedical engineering, comparative literature, criminology, industrial relations and transportation. MASSEY COLLEGE, the only graduate college in U of T, was built and furnished by the Massey Foundation and opened in 1963 with Robertson DAVIES as master. The need to decentralize the university to meet the needs of metropolitan Toronto's growing population led to the development of 2 suburban campuses, Scarborough College (1964) and Erindale College (1966). The undergraduate college system was expanded at the central campus to include New College (1962) and Innis College (1964). YORK UNIVERSITY was affiliated with U of T from its creation in 1959 until it became fully independent in 1965.

The U of T has made important contributions in many areas of scholarship and research. The discovery of INSULIN and the development of Pablum, liquid helium, an artificial pancreas and the laser-beam image recorder took place at the university. The U of T is the home of many research projects in the arts and humanities, including the DICTIONARY OF CANADIAN BIOGRAPHY, Records of Early English Drama, the Dictionary of Old English and the editing of the works of John Stuart Mill.

Enrolment: University of Toronto, and Ontario Institute for Studies in Education, 1985-86*
(Source: Statistics Canada)

Full-time Undergrad	Full-time Graduate	Part-time Undergrad	Part-time Graduate
University of Toronto			
26 559	6 495	12 348	2 046
Ontario Institute for Studies in Education			
2	644	21	1 704

* Figures do not include "full-time equivalent" enrolment at constituent universities (Victoria, Trinity, St Michael's).

University of Toronto Quarterly began publication in Oct 1931 (though an undergraduate magazine of the same name appeared 1895-96). Its first editor, philosopher G.S. BRETT, wrote in an introductory foreword that it was "intended to be neither vocational nor technical"; it would, however, serve "scholarship and academic interests." Between 1935 and 1947 it was edited by A.S.P. WOODHOUSE, who firmly established its reputation as a leading international journal devoted to the humanities. For over 50 years *UTQ* has emphasized sound scholarship and the publication of Canadian scholars alongside international authorities. Perhaps its most distinctive feature is "Letters in Canada," an annual review of the previous year's publications in the arts and humanities, which first appeared in 1936. Since 1937 this has included French Canadian works, and it constitutes the longest continuous survey of francophone literature and scholarship. *See also* LITERARY PERIODICALS.   W.J. KEITH

University of Victoria, Victoria, was founded in 1903 as Victoria College and affiliated with MCGILL UNIVERSITY, offering first- and second-year arts and science courses towards a McGill degree. The opening of UNIVERSITY OF BRITISH COLUMBIA in 1915 resulted in the suspension of Victoria's university program. Five years later local pressure brought the college back into being, again as a 2-year institution but affiliated with UBC and offering the first 2 years of a BA at that university. Through the 1950s the college expanded its curriculum to a full degree program in basic arts and science. In 1961 it awarded its first bachelor's degree – a UBC degree but completed entirely in Victoria. Two years later it became independent, and soon afterwards moved to its present 115 ha campus. U Vic has Faculties of Arts and Science, Education, Engineering, Fine Arts, Graduate Studies, Human and Social Development, and Law. The university offers degrees in arts, science, education, law, engineering, nursing, fine arts, music, public administration and social work, and many of these programs include work at the master's and doctoral levels. U Vic's athletes compete both nationally and internationally, and by 1987 its men's basketball team had won 7 CIAU championships.   WALTER D. YOUNG

Enrolment: University of Victoria, 1985-86
(Source: Statistics Canada)

Full-time Undergrad	Full-time Graduate	Part-time Undergrad	Part-time Graduate
6 255	582	3 454	355

University of Waterloo, Waterloo, Ont, was founded in 1957 and received its Ontario charter in 1959. U of Waterloo began as a nondenominational engineering faculty associated with UNIVERSITY OF WESTERN ONTARIO in 1957, offering Canada's first co-operative education program, in which students spent alternating 4-month terms on campus (for academic studies) and at work in industry (for practical experience), on a year-round basis. Waterloo's "co-op" enrolment (8720 in 1987) is the second largest in the world. Waterloo's early association with local arts colleges, Waterloo College (Lutheran) and St Jerome's College (Roman Catholic), ceased in 1960 when University of St Jerome College became federated with U of Waterloo and Waterloo College became Waterloo Lutheran University (now WILFRID LAURIER U), a separate institution. Three other on-campus colleges are affiliated with Waterloo: Conrad Grebel (Mennonite), Renison (Anglican) and St Paul's (United). Waterloo acquired its campus in 1958 and expanded it in 1963 to a total of 405 ha. Waterloo now has undergraduate, graduate and research programs in 42 academic departments and schools, administered through 6 faculties: arts, engineering, environmental studies, human kinetics and leisure studies, mathematics and science. Waterloo enjoys an international reputation for COMPUTER SCIENCE research, and its mathematics enrolment (3680 in 1986-87) is probably the largest in the world. As a result of the university's reputation in

Enrolment: University of Waterloo, 1985-86
(Source: Statistics Canada)

Full-time Undergrad	Full-time Graduate	Part-time Undergrad	Part-time Graduate
14 481	1 316	6 848	443

computer expertise, Waterloo won the New Oxford English Dictionary project – a project which will produce a "computerized" Oxford English Dictionary in 1988.

University of Western Ontario, London, Ont, was founded in 1878 as Western University of London. Huron College, established in 1863 as an ANGLICAN theological school, provided the basis for the new university. In 1881 the first arts courses were given. In 1882 a group of London doctors formed a medical school which was affiliated with Western. A similar attempt in 1885 by London lawyers to organize a law school failed because the Law Society of Upper Canada had a monopoly on legal education in the province. After Western became nondenominational in 1908, it expanded steadily. The Institute for Public Health opened under university management in 1912 and became affiliated in 1917. The medical school became an integrated faculty in 1913. Extension and summer courses started in 1918, and Western opened one of the first French immersion courses in the summer of 1933. As the university grew, new faculties were added: music, graduate studies, business administration, nursing, law, engineering, education, dentistry, library and information science, physical education and journalism. In addition, new buildings were designed to complement the original modern Gothic architecture.

In 1919 the Ursuline Sisters had established Brescia College as a Roman Catholic affiliate, and that year Assumption College in Windsor affiliated with the university; it later evolved into UNIVERSITY OF WINDSOR. Similarly, Waterloo College of Arts became affiliated with Western in 1925; today, it is WILFRID LAURIER UNIVERSITY, and its science faculty has become UNIVERSITY OF WATERLOO. St Peter's College seminary of London affiliated with Western in 1939, and it eventually became an arts faculty, King's College. King's, Huron and Brescia colleges are all affiliates of Western.

B. BEATON

Enrolment: University of Western Ontario, 1985-86
(Source: Statistics Canada)

Full-time Undergrad	Full-time Graduate	Part-time Undergrad	Part-time Graduate
15 173	2 227*	5 373	654

* Includes medical interns and residents

University of Windsor, Windsor, Ont, was founded in 1962. The university began as Assumption College, fd in 1857 by Rev Pierre Point, pastor of Assumption Parish, to provide a liberal education. In 1858 it received its charter. It was directed by various Catholic religious orders until 1919. It was then affiliated with London's Western University (UNIVERSITY OF WESTERN ONTARIO), 1919-53. In 1956 it became Assumption University. Holy Names College for women became affiliated with Assumption in 1934 and merged with it in 1962. Essex College (nondenominational) was incorporated in 1954 to provide courses in science, mathematics, physics, geology and business administration. In 1962 University of Windsor was incorporated by the province. In 1963 and 1964 affiliation agreements were made with Holy Redeemer College, Canterbury College (Anglican) and Iona College (United Church). The university has faculties of arts, social science, science, business administration, education, engin-

Enrolment: University of Windsor, 1985-86
(Source: Statistics Canada)

Full-time Undergrad	Full-time Graduate	Part-time Undergrad	Part-time Graduate
7 282	559	4 380	367

eering, human kinetics, law, and graduate studies and research, and schools of social work, nursing, visual arts, dramatic art, music and computer science.   B. BEATON

University of Winnipeg, Winnipeg, was established in 1967 from the former United College, then a member college of UNIVERSITY OF MANITOBA and affiliated with the UNITED CHURCH OF CANADA. United College was founded in 1938 through the amalgamation of Manitoba College (fd in 1871 by the PRESBYTERIAN CHURCH) and Wesley College (fd in 1888 by the METHODIST Church). The University of Winnipeg is a public liberal arts and science institution, offering a full undergraduate degree program in arts, science and education, graduate degree programs in public administration, history, religious studies and theology, and a unique high-school program taught in a university environment by its Collegiate Division which enrols about 700 students. About half of the university's students study part-time in extensive continuing education programs, which offer credit and noncredit courses both on and off campus. The campus is located downtown and the city-oriented university provides a variety of educational, recreational and cultural services to the community, as well as urban research and education activities through its nationally renowned Institute of Urban Studies.   TOM W. ROBSON

Enrolment: University of Winnipeg, 1985-86
(Source: Statistics Canada)

Full-time Undergrad	Full-time Graduate	Part-time Undergrad	Part-time Graduate
3 008	10	4 280	14

University Presses Although university presses appeared in Europe in the 15th and 16th centuries and in the US in the last quarter of the 19th century, they are a recent development in Canada. Traditionally, Canadian scholars published abroad, with scholarly presses, trade publishers or foreign periodicals – and indeed they still do – because most trade publishers in this country lacked the expertise or the interest to tackle scholarly publishing, which is less profitable than textbooks and trade books.

While many of the day-to-day operations of a university press are similar to those of a trade publisher, the differences are more significant. To begin with, the university press is a specialized firm owned by a university or research centre, and its mandate is to issue scholarly books and periodicals. Occasionally it may issue textbooks, reference works and even books of a popular, commercial nature. Moreover, the recommendation to publish a manuscript is made by academic appraisers who are not connected with the press, in order to ensure an objective decision. Editing such manuscripts is a time-consuming, expensive task; and marketing is costly because of limited runs of books that are aimed at small, specialized, often international, audiences. Because its purpose is to disseminate knowledge, the university press cannot rely merely on profits from sales for its operating expenses, and therefore must turn to its university and to government agencies for funding.

University presses mushroomed in Canada after 1960. In that expansive decade, graduate and undergraduate enrolments climbed steadily, libraries increased their holdings, and faculty members were pressured to "publish or perish." However, by the late 1970s, university budgets had declined, library acquisitions were shrinking, and in fact the whole publishing industry was in a severe financial crisis. The future of many multivolume series, let alone individual monographs, was doubtful. The federal government then reconsidered its various funding programs for trade and scholarly publishing. A consultative group, established in 1976, recommended in *Canadian Scholarly Publishing* (1980) that more support be given to workshops on publishing, that more low-cost scholarly journals be subsidized, and that more attention be given to "parapublishing."

Since the 1940s federal funding has come from the Aid to Scholarly Publications Program (ASPP), which is now jointly administered by the Canadian Federation for the Humanities and the Social Science Federation of Canada; in 1986 ASPP provided about $920 000 for 150 books in the humanities and social sciences. Meanwhile, in 1985, Ottawa announced a major restructuring of financial support for trade and scholarly publishing, and the 1986 Nielson Task Force criticized the ASPP, which led to a reduction in its book budget.

The university presses themselves have streamlined their own operations. Many have shifted to computerized production and marketing. Some have centralized their distribution, as do SMALL PRESSES; others have arranged co-operative publishing and distribution with foreign university presses. Research that is continually revised – particularly both bibliographical and statistical projects – can be fed into a central data base for accessing, thus eliminating costly book editions.

The larger presses publish in many disciplines. The University of Toronto Press, the oldest (1901) and one of the 10 largest in N America, covers the humanities and the sciences among its 1020 in-print titles. It publishes 80-90 titles and 25 periodicals a year, and its sales are over $4 million. Its multivolume series include the *Collected Works of John Stuart Mill* and (in collaboration with Laval) the DICTIONARY OF CANADIAN BIOGRAPHY. McGill-Queen's University Press, which began as McGill in 1963 and amalgamated with Queen's in 1969, focuses on Canadian studies and publishes the Canadian Public Administration Series. The University of Alberta Press (1969), with 83 titles by 1987, concentrates on western Canadian history, general science and ecology. The Wilfrid Laurier University Press (1974) currently has 122 titles in print dealing with archaeology, military history and sociology/anthropology. The University of British Columbia Press (1971) emphasizes Canadian affairs and Pacific studies. Les Éditions de l'université d'Ottawa (1936), Les Presses de l'université Laval (1950), Les Presses de l'université de Montréal (1962) and Les Presses de l'université du Québec (1969) all deal with French Canadian civilization, literature, medieval studies, law, the social sciences, the physical sciences and engineering. Carleton University Press (1982) has published 146 titles, including the Carleton Library series, which focuses on Canada's history, society and institutions.

On the other hand, research centre presses confine their publications and periodicals to a narrower range of subjects. The Pontifical Institute of Medieval Studies (1939) in Toronto, with 214 titles in print, concentrates on the history and culture of the Middle Ages. The Ontario Institute for Studies in Education Press (1965) in Toronto publishes materials on education, curriculum and professional development. The Canadian Plains Studies Centre (1973) in Regina issues works on all aspects of the Canadian plains.

Fifteen of the more than 20 university presses belong to the Assn of Canadian University Presses. The sale of textbooks in Canada in 1985 totalled $505.8 million, of which nearly one-third was generated by Canadian-controlled firms. These figures include sales by trade publishers as well.

Despite these healthy figures, the university presses exist precariously. Editing and production costs are only one aspect of the problem in a country where funding, distribution and limited readership are factors never easily resolved. Yet the contribution of the university presses to Canadian and international culture is no less significant because few scholarly books are widely read. John Porter's *The Vertical Mosaic* (UTP, 1964) and Wallace Clement's *Canadian Corporate Elite* (by the Carleton Library Series, 1975) have had excellent sales. But more often scholarly books – eg, Harold Innis's *The Fur Trade in Canada* (1930) and *Empire and Communications* (1946) – have a seminal and indirect influence. Ultimately, scholars' ideas influence society itself when it perceives the universe through the printed word.

GEORGE L. PARKER

Upper Canada, the predecessor of modern ONTARIO, came into existence when the British Parliament passed the CONSTITUTIONAL ACT, 1791, dividing the old PROVINCE OF QUEBEC into LOWER CANADA in the E and Upper Canada in the W along the present-day Ontario-Québec BOUNDARY. The Act also established a government which would largely determine the colony's political nature and which, in practice, strongly influenced its social and economic character. The area that became Upper Canada was populated originally by Indians (eg, HURON, NEUTRAL, PETUN, ALGONQUIN). Samuel de CHAMPLAIN visited the region in the early 17th century, and was followed by other French explorers. Missionaries were particularly active in HURONIA, E and S of Georgian Bay (*see* STE MARIE AMONG THE HURONS). Through the FUR TRADE, the French were established in the area by the 18th century. Commerce and war provided the substantiation to the French claim. Permanent European settlement was scarcely a feature of the occupation, although the nuclei of what became modern TORONTO, WINDSOR, NIAGARA and KINGSTON were established.

During the SEVEN YEARS' WAR (1756-63) the French abandoned most of the region to the British, and upon the surrender of Montréal in Sept 1760, Britain effectively took over the territory which would later become Upper Canada. After the Treaty of PARIS (1763), the borders of Britain's new Province of Quebec were extended S into the Ohio Valley. When the AMERICAN REVOLUTION began, the permanent European population of western Québec consisted of a few French-speaking settlers around Detroit. By 1783 – the end of the American revolt – what had been a trickle of wartime LOYALIST refugees became a stream; 5000-6000 set a tone and fashioned an ideology that would influence much of Upper Canada's future.

The 2-century-old Loyalist myth has these sturdy people overcoming hardship and deprivation but, in fact, few refugees anywhere have been so privileged. Gov Sir Frederick HALDIMAND began Loyalist settlement initiatives, establishing disbanded army regiments in ranges of quickly surveyed townships stretched along the American frontier; in the event of war, these veterans were intended to form a defensive barrier. Three main areas were selected: along the St Lawrence, around Kingston and the Bay of Quinte, and in the NIAGARA PENINSULA. A fourth, near Detroit, was considered, but its scheduled surrender to the US postponed development. Land was granted in lots, with heads of families receiving 100 acres (40.5 ha) and field officers up to and eventually more than 1000 acres (405 ha). Clothing, tools and provisions were supplied for 3 years. Although there were difficulties, these favoured displaced persons did well, and many disgruntled Americans – some simply "land-hungry" – moved N to join them. By 1790 western Québec had a population of nearly 10 000.

The Loyalists who came to Upper Canada, mostly American frontiersmen, were well able to cope with the rigours of new settlements; moreover, they were not politically docile. Many had been in the forefront of political protest in the old American colonies, and although they had not been ready to take up arms for colonial rights, they were prepared to use every legal and constitutional means at their disposal to better their lives. It was their constitutional complaints that caused Britain in 1791 to modify the inadequate QUEBEC ACT of 1774.

The Constitutional Act was a clear response by London to the American Revolution. The excess of democracy that had permeated the southern colonies would not be allowed in the 2 new provinces of Upper and Lower Canada. A lieutenant-governor was established in each province, with an executive council to advise him, a legislative council to act as an upper house, and a representative assembly. Policy was to be directed by the executive, which was responsible not to the assembly but to the Crown. The Church of England (*see* ANGLICANISM) was to tie the colonies more firmly to Britain: in Upper Canada, a permanent appropriation of funds "for the Support and Maintenance of a Protestant clergy" was formally guaranteed by the establishment of one-seventh of all lands in the province as reserves, with the proceeds from sale or rental going to the church (*see* CLERGY RESERVES). Subsequent instructions established crown reserves, another seventh of the land, the revenue from which would be used to pay the costs of the provincial administration. Land ownership, the question that concerned most settlers, was to be on the British pat-

View of Kingston from Fort Henry, coloured aquatint by J. Gleadah, 1828. Kingston's early prosperity was based on its location as a transshipment point for the exports of Upper Canada (*courtesy National Archives of Canada/C-2041*).

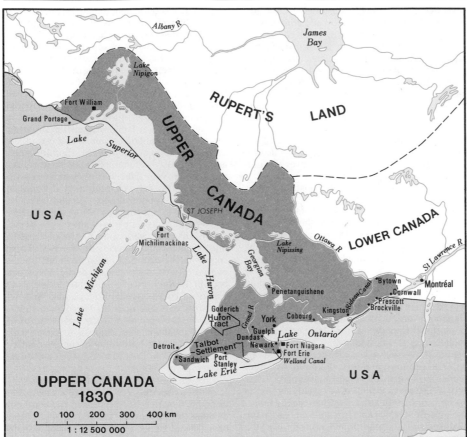

UPPER CANADA
1830

0   100   200   300   400 km

1 : 12 500 000

tern of freehold tenure. The SEIGNEURIAL SYSTEM was permanently eradicated in the upper province. The franchise was fairly wide, and the assembly numbered no fewer than 16 members while the Legislative Council was made up of 7.

The first leader of this new wilderness society was Lt-Gov John Graves SIMCOE, whose avowed purpose was to create in Upper Canada a "superior, more happy, and more polished form of government," not merely to attract immigrants but to renew the empire and by example to win Americans back into the British camp. Governmental institutions were established, first at Newark [Niagara-on-the-Lake] and then at the new capital at York [Toronto]. Simcoe used troops to build a series of primary roads, got the land boards and land distribution under way, established the judiciary, grandly abolished SLAVERY and showed a keen interest in promoting Anglican affairs. When he left the province in 1796 he could take pride in his achievements, although he had failed to convert Americans from republicanism and to persuade Britain to turn Upper Canada into a military centre. To Britain, Canada still meant Québec, and Simcoe's elaborate plans for the defence of a western appendage beyond the sea-lanes were unrealistic.

Upper Canada did not flourish under Simcoe's followers, the timid Peter Russell, the busy martinet Gen Peter Hunter, the scarcely busy Alexander Grant and the lacklustre Francis GORE. It was still a remote frontier of fragmented settlement; and land, the only real source of prosperity, had been carelessly carved up in huge grants by lax administrators. Politics began to emerge in provincial life, bearing the mark of the Constitutional Act, which, by its very nature, had created a party of favourites. Lieutenant-governors chose their executive and legislative councils from among men they could trust and understand, who shared their solid, conservative values: Loyalists or newly arrived Britons. These men (later called the FAMILY COMPACT) quickly became a kind

of Tory faction permanently in power. They could not conceive any brand of loyalty to the Crown apart from their own; when opposition arose, as it did frequently over money bills, those advocating extension of the shackled assembly's powers were branded, in exchanges of fiery rhetoric, as Yankee Republicans. But the influence of political critics such as Robert Thorpe, Joseph Willcocks and William Weekes, who were not merely "smoke-makers" but true parliamentary whigs, was to be washed away in the vortex of the WAR OF 1812.

During the war, Upper Canada, whose inhabitants were predominantly American in origin, was invaded, violated and, in parts, occupied. American forces were repulsed by British regulars assisted by Canadian militia. The war strengthened the British link, rendered loyalism a hallowed creed, fashioned martyr-heroes Sir Isaac BROCK and TECUMSEH, brought a certain prosperity, and appeared to legitimize the political status quo. Later commentators would find in it a touchstone for Canadian NATIONALISM and the explanation for much of Canada's persistent public, if not personal, anti-Americanism.

The war ended Upper Canada's isolation. American immigration was formally halted, but Upper Canada received an increased number of British newcomers – some with capital. The economy continued to be tied to Britain's declining MERCANTILISM, and the wheat trade gained primacy among Upper Canadian farmers. Still, the province remained capital-poor: for example, the Welland Canal Co, a public works venture, had to look abroad for investors. The expense of administering the growing colony increased substantially in the early 1820s. Schemes to reunite the 2 Canadas were occasionally considered. In 1822 an effort was made to adjust the customs duties shared with Lower Canada to provide the upper province, which had no ocean port, with a larger share of revenue.

Revenues remained inadequate and the prov-

ince was plunged into debt, unable to pay the interest on its own badly received debentures without further borrowings. The establishment of the BANK OF UPPER CANADA (1821) and other banks failed to bring real fiscal stability, and neither did the contributions of the massive British-based colonization venture, the CANADA COMPANY. In fact, Canada Co payments were used to defray the salaries of government officials (the civil list) and thus the assembly was sidestepped in its desire to control government revenues.

The War of 1812 consolidated the political control of the province's ruling oligarchy, whose leading light was Anglican Archdeacon (later bishop of Toronto) John STRACHAN. Many commentators have labelled the Family Compact corrupt, although recent evidence suggests that the group was rigorous and methodical in its administration and thorough in its investigation of irregularities. It had a strong sense of duty to development, as shown by its unswerving support of public works such as the WELLAND CANAL. But an oligarchy, enlightened or not, was an anachronism in an age in which democracy was becoming the fashion.

By 1820 opposition in the province was becoming sophisticated but had not yet taken the form of disciplined parties. Some agitators such as Robert GOURLAY, the celebrated "Banished Briton," had earlier dramatized popular grievances in martyrlike fashion. Until the mid-1830s the major impulse of opposition was frequently conducted by more moderate and whiggish politicians such as Dr William BALDWIN, Robert BALDWIN and Rev Egerton RYERSON. Reformer William Lyon MACKENZIE sometimes wanted Upper Canada to be a kind of Jeffersonian dream and envisaged a province composed of yeomen-farmers wedded to the soil, firmly patriotic and ready to become British-American minutemen. At the same time he never failed to laud technological advances. He, like the compact he so vigorously opposed, was actually a stranger to the forces and values that eventually dominated the 19th century: moderate liberalism and increasing industrialism. His REBELLION OF 1837 misfired because, like so many politicians after him, he failed to understand the basic, moderate political posture of Upper Canadians. The rebellion marked the nadir of Upper Canada's never buoyant fortunes. Political chaos was accompanied by economic disaster as the panic of 1837 swept Anglo-American finance and the province found itself over a million pounds in debt.

Mackenzie's violent posturing and his poorly supported rebellion turned out to be unnecessary, since gradual reforms were already under way in both the colony and Britain. The inadequacies of the rigid Constitutional Act were by now apparent. For battered post-rebellion Upper Canada the impetus for real political change could only come from Westminster, although it might be accelerated by advocates in the province, as was later shown by the brief but powerful government of Robert Baldwin and Louis LAFONTAINE. Some immediate change came through the efforts of the earl of DURHAM in 1838. As governor general he spent only a few days in Upper Canada, but he found time for a short, formal visit to Toronto and an interview with Baldwin. He also received sound counsel from his advisers, especially Charles Buller, all of which he placed in his report (*see* DURHAM REPORT).

Durham set in motion a scheme that had long been considered: the reunification of Upper and Lower Canada. By 1838 Upper Canada had a diverse population of more than 400 000 and stretched W from the Ottawa R to the head of the Great Lakes. It was still a rough-hewn and somewhat amorphous community, poorly equipped with schools, hospitals or local government. Durham, from his lofty imperial perch, argued that a reunion of the provinces would swamp the French of Lower Canada in an English sea and, more important, that the economic potential of both colonies would be enhanced and they would thus be less burdensome to Britain. All this Durham insisted would easily be advanced under RESPONSIBLE GOVERNMENT, whereby the Cabinet is rendered responsible to the assembly rather than to the Crown. The errors of the Constitutional Act could be exorcised and unruly politics temporized without fear of further revolts. Britain approved the union, although the granting of responsible government would take almost a decade more. On 10 Feb 1841 Upper Canada's short, unhappy history came to an end. The relationship with its French-speaking counterpart would remain to be worked out under the new legislative union. Meanwhile, Upper Canadians could make some claim to having a collective past and, with the prospects of a rapidly increasing population and improving agricultural opportunities, a collective future. *See also* PROVINCE OF CANADA. ROGER HALL

Reading: G.M. Craig, *Upper Canada* (1963).

Upper Canada College (UCC) is the most highly regarded independent school for boys in Canada. Situated in Toronto, it is the oldest private school in Ontario, having been founded in 1829 by Sir John Colborne, lt-gov of Upper Canada. Established by a representative of the Crown, UCC retains close ties with the monarchy. The enrolment consists of almost 1000 day and boarding students in grades 3 to 13. UCC is very selective in its admission requirements and is known for high academic standards and a vigorous and extensive extracurricular program in which all boys participate. The college is controlled by a 29-member board of governors; its endowment is valued at $8.8 million and gifts from all sources in 1986 amounted to more than $900 000. Over the past 150 years, UCC's graduates have attained positions of distinction in government, business, the professions and the arts. Since 1907, 22 graduates have been named Rhodes scholars.

Upper Canada Village, developed during the 1950s and 1960s near Morrisburg, Ont, a replica of a 19th-century community that might have existed along the St Lawrence R. It includes a pioneer farm, general store, doctor's house, tavern, blacksmith shop, school, sawmill, cheese factory and woollen mill. Many original buildings have been moved to the site from nearby, eg, Crysler's Hall, restored to 1846, and Cook's Tavern, restored to 1835. The buildings are authentically furnished and demonstrate to the visitor various aspects of early life in UPPER CANADA. Guides in

Church at Upper Canada Village, Morrisburg, Ont (*photo by Malak, Ottawa*).

period costumes explain the history and also demonstrate the way of life of the region's original inhabitants.

The ST LAWRENCE SEAWAY project, beginning in 1954, called for the flooding of a large portion of the old river "front," one of the first areas to be settled in Ontario. To save some of this heritage and develop the new riverbank area, in 1955 the Ontario government established the Ontario-St Lawrence Development Commission. This sponsored the creation of Upper Canada Village to preserve representative buildings and memorialize life as it was along the front. The commission also developed 800 ha of adjacent parkland and relocated the old monument commemorating the 1813 battle of CRYSLER'S FARM. C.J. TAYLOR

Uranium (U), the heaviest of naturally occurring elements, is metallic and radioactive. It is a hard, dense, malleable, silver-white metal which is never found in nature in its metallic state; it always occurs in combination with oxygen as oxides or silicates. Uranium oxide was first identified in 1789 by M.H. Klaproth in the MINERAL pitchblende, but its distinctive property of radioactivity was discovered much later (1896) by Henri Becquerel. The subsequent discovery in 1898 of the elements polonium and RADIUM led to the development of the radium industry. Uranium was recovered as a by-product of radium until 1939 but found little use except as a ceramic colouring agent. Important developments in nuclear PHYSICS led to the realization that uranium atoms could be split to release large amounts of energy. It was soon recognized that this energy could be harnessed to produce ELECTRIC POWER and nuclear weapons. Demand for uranium began with the initiation in 1942 of an Allied nuclear-weapons program, the Manhattan Project. Major uranium-producing industries were developed in the early 1950s, principally in the US, Canada and S Africa. Peak levels of production were attained by 1959. Production declined precipitously during the early 1960s, and its anticipated revival, based on the demand for uranium for NUCLEAR-POWER generation, was slow to materialize. It was not until the mid-1970s that price levels and market activity were sufficient to prompt significant expansion of exploration and development, and by the late 1970s the industry had been firmly re-established. In the early 1980s, production levels declined again in some countries, particularly the US, in response to lower than expected increases in uranium demand. However, over the longer term, steady growth in nuclear power and related uranium requirements is anticipated. The US, Canada and S Africa account for some 75% of the Western world's total production to 1986. Other important producing countries have been Australia, France, Zaire and, more recently, Niger and Gabon.

Uranium was first discovered in Canada, during the middle of the last century, on the north shore of Lake Superior. However, Canada's first economic uranium discovery is attributed to Gilbert LABINE, who in 1930 identified the Port Radium deposit at Great Bear Lake, NWT, exploited initially for its radium content. Important discoveries were subsequently made in the URANIUM CITY area of northern Saskatchewan (late 1940s) and, more significantly, in the ELLIOT LAKE area of northern Ontario (early 1950s). Credit for the latter goes to geologist Franc Joubin, who was backed by financier J.H. HIRSHHORN. Most of Canada's production has come from these 2 areas. Beginning in the early 1970s,

the focus of Canada's uranium exploration effort turned to the Athabasca Basin area of northern Saskatchewan, where several important, relatively rich deposits have been discovered and developed. It is expected that the Elliot Lake and Athabasca Basin areas will remain the principal sources of Canadian production to at least the turn of the century. About 85% of Canada's production is exported to the US, Japan and western Europe. Canada is the world's largest exporter and, in 1984, replaced the US as the largest producer of uranium. R.M. WILLIAMS

Uranium City, Sask, UP, pop 171 (1986c), 2507 (1984 est), is located 50 km S of the provincial boundary with the NWT and 75 km E of the Saskatchewan-Alberta border. The FUR TRADE was the dominant economic activity until the 1930s when gold was discovered in the Beaverlodge Lk area. From 1938 until the mid-1940s gold was mined in the area. In 1946 URANIUM exploration was initiated and Eldorado Mining & Refining Ltd began production in 1953. In 1952 a townsite named Uranium City was established and in 1956 a special local government jurisdiction was created. A thriving mining community developed and continued in existence until Eldorado announced that it was closing its operations. Since the termination of mining and milling operations in 1982 the community has experienced economic collapse and depopulation. DON HERPERGER

Urban and Regional Planning In broadest terms, urban and regional planning is the process by which communities attempt to control and/or design change and development in their physical environments. It has been practised under many names: town planning, city planning, community planning, land use planning, and physical environment planning. The object of planning is the "physical environment," which is taken to mean land and all its uses, along with everything that has tangible existence on or beneath the land surface. Planning also includes the manner and style by which buildings are laid out in a city, and the design of public places.

Physical environments are partly natural and partly man-made. A satisfying man-made or "built" environment is the ultimate goal of planning, but relations between natural and built environments, and interactions between people and their environments, are also of vital concern. Human activities can have negative impacts upon the natural environment, just as certain natural conditions are hazardous to human well-being. Planners are equally concerned to protect natural environments from the adverse effects of human use (eg, water pollution), and to protect people from "risk" environments (eg, flood zones).

To plan the physical environment means to impose some deliberate order upon it, with the aim of achieving a desired standard of environmental quality. Environmental quality is the heart of planning practice, although there is no universal agreement about the characteristics of a "good" or well-ordered environment. Different cultures have tended to value environmental qualities differently and to organize their environments in different ways. Many factors influence the choice of qualities that are most desired at a particular time and place. Each community, through social and political processes, must set its own standards of a good physical environment. Also, people's needs, tastes and economic circumstances influence the quality of environments that are planned and built.

A variety of issues fall within the scope of urban and regional planning, depending partly on the geographical scale of the planning area. Regional planners will be concerned with such matters as the protection of farmland or other valued resource sites (eg, forests, mineral deposits, seashores, lakeshores); the preservation of unique natural or historical features; the locations of highways and other transport facilities, such as PIPELINES or airports; and the growth prospects of communities located throughout the region. If the region is organized around a large city, the planners must also take account of the problems caused by the city's expansion, and its impact upon the surrounding countryside and nearby towns.

For cities and towns, planning issues are of 2 general kinds. First there is a need to think ahead to accommodate the city's growth – deciding which lands should be built on and when, and whether they should be used for residential development, for industry or for some more specialized function, such as a shopping centre or playing fields. Eventually, more detailed plans will also be required to determine the layout of every piece of land. The street network has to be designed; sites have to be reserved for schools and parks, shops, public buildings and religious institutions; provision has to be made for transit services and utilities; and development standards have to be set and design ideas have to be tested to ensure that the desired environmental quality is achieved.

A second group of issues concerns those parts of the community that are already developed. Planners will distinguish between areas where change is not desired and those where change is either unavoidable or judged to be needed. In the former case, the concern is for maintaining the built environment at its existing quality, regardless of pressures for change. This applies particularly to inner-city neighbourhoods which face pressures for apartment redevelopment or for streets to be widened to permit through traffic. In the latter case, the problem is to facilitate the changes that are considered most desirable. In one situation this may mean that a deteriorating area has to be upgraded; in another it may mean that buildings have to be demolished to allow their sites to be used in a new and different way. The problems of rapidly changing downtowns, of outdated industrial and warehousing districts, and of inner-city neighbourhoods experiencing a complex mix of social and physical changes all have to be dealt with by planners and public authorities. So, too, must special issues such as HERITAGE CONSERVATION, the relocation of railway tracks, the provision of rapid-transit facilities, and the special housing needs of different groups of people.

Even under conditions of little or no growth, such as many Canadian cities experienced in the 1980s, urban environments go on changing. As cities age, it becomes more difficult and more expensive to maintain environmental quality. People's needs and desires change as well, and the built environment must be constantly adapted. Special restoration or revitalization programs may be undertaken to try to draw business back to declining shopping districts and stimulate the local economy. Yet investment funds, both public and private, are in shorter supply than in times of economic growth. For Canadian planners, coping with the special problems of slow growth is one of the current issues.

Social and Political Foundations Like all types of planning (eg, REGIONAL DEVELOPMENT PLANNING; NATIONAL CAPITAL COMMISSION; URBAN DESIGN), planning cities and regions finds its rationale in the belief that a controllable future offers more promise than an uncontrolled one, and that a planned environment provides better opportunities for all people to enjoy their community setting. Urban and regional planning is but one of many approaches adopted by society for achiev-

ing the security, comfort and long-term betterment of its members. This does not mean that all plans are prepared by governments, or that all planners are public servants, but it does mean that planning systems are usually designed to ensure that the needs of the entire community are properly considered. Plans come from many sources – from individuals, private corporations and public agencies – all of which have special ends or interests to pursue. In the "planned" community a higher level of forethought and public control is imposed, not to prevent these individual plans from being realized but to ensure that they harmonize with one another and with the overall needs of the community.

It is rarely possible to demonstrate that an action taken in anticipation of the future will benefit an entire community. It is also difficult to show that a single public interest can be served. More commonly, planning is a matter of trying to decide which of many competing interests is more deserving, while also trying to treat everyone in a fair and lawful manner. Should a city council allow a shopping centre to be built in a residential area? An issue like this raises questions about personal rights and freedoms, and about the powers and obligations of public authorities. Hence, the ultimate planning decisions are political decisions, since politics is society's way of settling the conflicts that arise within a community.

Planning, then, is a way by which communities determine how they would like their environment to be. What kinds of benefits can they then look forward to? Official definitions in Canada have generally responded to this question by describing planning as a type of CONSERVATION. It is aimed at the wise use and management of community resources, a critical one being land. The idea that land is both a private commodity and a community resource is controversial, but Canadian law has established that there is a legitimate community interest in the development of any land. Large amounts of public money have to be spent on such things as transport facilities, water treatment plants, schools and parks. The community assumes most of the responsibility for ensuring that land is developed in ways that will allow these public services to function efficiently. This is taken to mean that the development of land should yield the greatest possible public benefit for the lowest possible public cost. Yet the measurement of benefits and costs is no easy matter. For example, deciding upon the "best" use of land on the outskirts of a city depends on estimating what values to attach to such benefits as an increase in the supply of new houses or an attractive residential environment, and how to weigh these benefits against a different set of costs, such as long journeys to work or the loss of prime agricultural land.

Origins of Planning in Canada The close connection between conservation and urban and regional planning began with the COMMISSION OF CONSERVATION in the years before WWI. At this time, Canada was caught up in a wave of reform enthusiasm that drew its inspiration from several international sources – from the British town planning movement; from the progressive reform movement in the US, with its attacks on political corruption and public mismanagement of all kinds; from the housing reform movements in both countries; and from the CITY BEAUTIFUL movement, which offered the ideal of well-ordered cities, with handsome buildings and public spaces, as symbols of the progress of industrial civilization. All across Canada, groups of citizens organized themselves into "city planning commissions" and "civic improvement leagues" (*see* URBAN REFORM). Yet it was not until the Commission of Conservation developed an interest in

PUBLIC HEALTH that these concerns were given national prominence. The commission viewed the health of the people as the greatest of all resources. Town planning, as it was then called, was thought to be one way of ensuring a healthy and productive population. The first British planning Act of 1909, and the Garden City ideals advanced in the UK by Ebenezer Howard, were seen as the model for achieving the development of healthy, attractive communities in Canada.

The person chiefly responsible for drawing out the importance of the British example was Dr Charles HODGETTS, adviser to the Commission of Conservation from 1910 to 1920. Hodgetts was keenly aware of the unhealthiness of the houses in which many working-class families lived in Toronto and other industrial cities. He believed that better standards of city layout and housing design would eliminate these problems. He organized an international city planning conference in Toronto in 1914. That same year he secured the appointment of Thomas ADAMS, one of the most eminent British planners of the day, as the commission's town planning adviser.

Adams regarded planning as a combination of art and scientific procedure, requiring the most rigorous analysis of human needs and problems and the natural conditions of an area before a land development plan could be drawn up. He agreed with Hodgetts about the importance of healthy living conditions and better design standards, but his conception of a well-planned environment went beyond that. Adams represented the "city-efficient" or "city-functional" school of planning. Different parts of the city should be designed to suit their special functions: residential areas provided with all the amenities and services that go with healthy community life; industrial areas well served by railways and other transport facilities; business areas and civic centres designed to satisfy all the commercial and public needs of a modern community; and the whole city arranged to allow communications to be carried out safely and conveniently. In addition, land should always be allocated to its "best" use and never wasted; the special characteristics of each site should be incorporated into detailed development plans; public facilities, such as community centres or hospitals, should always be accessibly located for the people who have to use them; and private land development and public works programs should be co-ordinated and scheduled to economize on public expenditures and to prevent costly mistakes. These principles persist in Canadian planning.

Adams repeatedly travelled across Canada, carrying out planning studies and analysing land-use and settlement problems. In 1919 he founded the Town Planning Institute of Canada. Interested persons from any profession were admitted as members. Initially, they were mostly civil engineers or land surveyors, along with some landscape architects and municipal officials. The institute sought to promote research, to disseminate new knowledge and the results of planning experiences, and generally to advance planning ideas and set a high standard of planning practice. It was also hoped that the subject of planning would be introduced into university programs. The GREAT DEPRESSION brought an end to most planning activity in Canada. The Town Planning Institute was disbanded in 1932 and not revived until some 20 years later. Among the notable planning practitioners of this early period were Noulan CAUCHON, Frederick Todd, Horace SEYMOUR and Howard Dunington-Grubb. Many towns and cities drew up master plans, among them Ottawa, Vancouver, Calgary, Saint John and Halifax; and many interesting garden suburbs and new towns were planned.

Planning Law and Administration Another of Adams's contributions was his "model planning legislation," which he spent much time urging provincial governments to adopt. Planning law establishes rules and procedures by which communities can act on matters affecting their physical environments. He also believed that rural communities were as much in need of planning as urban ones. Not only did they have grave environmental and fiscal problems of their own, but town and country were so closely dependent on each other that they could not be separated for land-use planning purposes. This marked the beginning of regional planning in Canada.

In 1914 only 3 provinces had planning statutes: NS, NB and Alberta. By 1925 every province except Québec had a statute of some kind, although professional planners thought they were all inadequate. For one thing, the Acts did not make it mandatory that municipalities should prepare plans; for another, they did not provide for provincial governments to take an active part in planning. Municipal governments also tended to be critical, because they were mainly interested in having stronger powers to regulate construction and land development. The new American technique of ZONING looked particularly attractive, and the city of Kitchener adopted Canada's first zoning bylaw in 1924. Not until 1925, when BC adopted its first planning statute, was zoning recognized in planning law. Other provinces followed suit, but the most complete statute of this early period was Alberta's Town and Rural Planning Act of 1929. Canadian planning law has evolved continually since then, and the modern administrative systems of urban and regional planning are far larger and more complex than anyone could have foreseen in 1929. The pattern set by Alberta can be seen in the statutes now in effect, all of which date from the late 1970s and early 1980s.

The essential purposes of all provincial and territorial planning Acts are to secure the orderly, coherent growth and development of municipalities, based on sound forethought and considerations of public interest; to bring about and conserve physical environments, including buildings and other works, which are satisfying to human needs and community concerns; to regulate how private and public lands may be used; and to allow for public participation in planning decisions. In addition to their planning Acts, all provinces provide for other types of planning and environmental or land-use regulation not conferred specifically on the municipalities – in statutes dealing with energy, environment, forestry, heritage protection and parks. The province of Québec, for example, has an Act to protect agricultural lands (La Loi sur la protection du territoire agricole); Alberta has a Special Areas Board to plan for and administer over one million ha of public lands in agricultural use; the PEI Development Corporation undertakes comprehensive land planning with powers to acquire, sell and lease lands for several kinds of purposes; Manitoba operates an Interdepartmental Planning Board for the planning and management of the province's crown lands. The federal government performs planning functions for Canadian crown lands through many statutes and a number of Cabinet policies, such as the Federal Policy on Land Use and the Federal Environmental Assessment and Review Process.

Thus, in an overall sense, regional land use plans in Canada come about through the co-ordinated administration of many laws within a province, through co-ordination between provincial and federal laws, and by co-ordinative policies among neighbouring jurisdictions. These and municipal planning activities are all support-ed by modern information systems, such as computerized MAPPING and data analysis operations, the Canada Land Use Monitoring Program, and Statistics Canada's census data on population, housing and business activity.

All municipalities maintain some kind of data monitoring system to aid both long-range forecasting and planning policy decisions. The larger cities in Canada use computerized information systems for the planning of TRANSPORTATION systems and for monitoring certain environmental changes such as AIR POLLUTION, and for conducting studies or forecasts on land use, population, building construction, etc.

Provincial planning Acts spell out what municipalities or regional authorities must and may do. Generally speaking, an Act provides for 5 basic measures. First the municipality is to prepare a "general plan," sometimes called the "official plan" or the "plan d'urbanism." This plan sets down the policies that will govern where and when developments on land can take place. It usually includes statements on the community's social, economic and quality-of-life goals, and the fiscal requirements of the public works (eg, sewers, roads) that will be required. The plan describes by maps, drawings and written texts the various communities and land use districts, and the guidelines for building developments. A second set of plans, in more detail, may also be prepared for special areas, such as plans for heritage conservation or redevelopment of inner city neighbourhoods, or for industrial parks. The remaining 3 measures in a planning Act are legal and administrative instruments for implementing a general plan: a "land use" or "zoning" bylaw, subdivision controls, and a building permit process. Before a building permit is issued, the plot of land must first be part of an approved subdivision of land, while specified rules for the type and amount of building space allowed and the requirements of architectural features must be adhered to. Subdivision control governs the process of converting raw land into building plots of adequate size and shape, while zoning establishes the detailed range and limitations of use to which a plot can be put.

Planning laws limit an owner's rights in private property in order to secure benefits for the community as a whole. These benefits include such things as the safety and health of persons; convenience, amenities and agreeable environments for the public; acceptable standards of private and public living and work places; and reasonable burdens of public expenditures that have to be incurred when land is developed. Planning law in some provinces also allows municipalities or the provincial government to prevent the destruction of heritage properties and natural environments, or to force property owners to undertake measures that enhance the architectural, aesthetic, landscaping features, or the convenience to users, of any buildings proposed for construction. The balance struck between freedom to use one's land and requirements imposed by public authority depends on the prevailing social values of the community of the day. Moreover, all planning Acts in Canada now require that citizens be heard before major land planning decisions are made, and there is always a right of appeal by the property owners affected.

The province confers responsibility upon urban municipalities to carry out planning in their areas. Rural areas and towns are frequently organized for regional planning around a "regional district" created by decree of the provincial government. In some jurisdictions, the municipalities of selected metropolitan areas have been grouped together in order to create a special, "second tier" planning administration (for exam-ple, Québec City and Montréal, Toronto, Greater Vancouver, Winnipeg). In the latter cases, the metropolitan administration performs broad policy planning and the co-ordination of major public services and works; detailed plans and development regulation are left to the constituent municipalities.

The foregoing planning arrangements apply to Canada's privately owned lands. These constitute, however, only some 10% of the Canadian landmass; or, on a provincial basis, as much as 75% (NS) or as little as 6% (BC) of the land. The planning and environmental management of provincial and federal crown lands falls to the various departments and agencies of the governments. In most instances, special "integrative" administrative mechanisms have been established to further a comprehensive approach to planning the use of crown lands and the wise development and conservation of resources underneath or upon them.

New Towns are a specialized aspect of planning. The term refers to the comprehensive planning, zoning and land subdivision of a community, executed before the arrival of any residents. Typically one-industry resource-development towns of small size (fewer than 5000 people), Canada's new towns are mainly located in remote areas (eg, KITIMAT, BC, Matagami, Qué, THOMPSON, Man, and Tumbler Ridge, Sask). Since 1946 nearly 200 new towns have been founded in Canada, with a population of about 700 000. Most of the early examples (1900-20) were not laid out by planners and did not benefit from imaginative site planning. Adams and others began applying the ideas of Garden City, master plans and zoning to new resource towns in the 1920s (eg, TÉMISKAMING, Qué, KAPUSKASING, Ont, Arvida, Qué, CORNER BROOK, Nfld, Port Alice, BC). In the post-WWII period, planners of RESOURCE TOWNS began to pay attention to the acute social and leisure activity problems associated with small, isolated and "closed" communities. Further advancements were made in devising new forms for town layout and housing, making these fundamental components of a new town plan more adapted to the rugged site conditions and cold climate environments. A notable recent example of progressive new town planning is Fermont, Qué, designed by Norbert Schoenauer and built by the Québec-Cartier Mining Co. The overall plan is compact, and both the street layout and housing construction serve as screens against the harsh winter winds. Many of the single-family houses are oriented for passive solar heating. The town's commercial and entertainment centre is fully enclosed within an extensive building complex that also includes apartment dwellings.

Community Planning and Social Policy Arguments persist about the appropriate role and purposes of planning as an instrument for social betterment. It is not that the basic goals of efficiency and orderly urban development are under challenge; the real question is whether order and efficiency should be the only goals. In its beginnings in Canada, and in the early American and European reform movements, town planning had offered the promise of something altogether more radical. It was to be part of the antidote to the enormous social costs of the Industrial Revolution, a sweeping movement of social reform in which the building of better cities would contribute to the building of a better civilization. At a more practical, humanitarian level, this meant that each community should assume some obligation to care for the victims of economic development and of the progress of urban industrial areas.

The main impact of these ideas in Canada began to be felt in the 1950s, although there were earlier signs of concern. Prominent social reformers, such as J.S. WOODSWORTH in Winnipeg and Claire Casgrain in Montréal, made no small contribution to the progressive advancement of the Canadian planning movement. It took the Great Depression of the 1930s, followed by the desire for national reconstruction after WWII, however, for housing reform and physical planning to be linked effectively as instruments of social policy. One of the first indications of this trend appeared in 1935, in the chapter on housing in *Social Planning for Canada* compiled by the LEAGUE FOR SOCIAL RECONSTRUCTION. The author was a young British-born architect, Humphrey CARVER, who was to become one of the most distinguished Canadian planners. Carver argued that all Canadians had a right to live in safe, healthful, comfortable houses and neighbourhoods, even if they could not afford them, and that the state had a responsibility to ensure that good housing conditions were available to everyone. He argued, as Hodgetts and Adams had done, that it was necessary to build better communities to create a physical and social environment conducive to a decent way of life. Carver's argument was developed further in "Housing and Community Planning," a study released in 1944 as part of the final report of the Committee on Post-War Reconstruction, set up by the federal government in 1941.

This study was largely the work of 2 men, C.A. Curtis, an economist who chaired the housing subcommittee, and Leonard MARSH, the committee's research adviser. In a manner reminiscent of Adams's most famous report, *Rural Planning and Development* (1917), Curtis and Marsh described the ills of uncontrolled urbanization and slum conditions. They drew attention to the extensive occurrence of wasteful and unsightly suburban developments. They urged the government of Canada to embark upon a comprehensive national program for social betterment and community development, in which housing, planning and public education would figure prominently. Consequently, in 1944 the federal government made sweeping changes to the National Housing Act to promote the construction of new houses, the repair and modernization of existing houses, and the general improvement of community environments.

In 1946 the Central Mortgage and Housing Corporation (now CANADA MORTGAGE AND HOUSING CORPORATION) was created to implement the new national housing policy. This policy was subjected to further refinement over the next 20 years or so, through a series of amendments to the National Housing Act (NHA), which provided a major spur to urban planning activity in the postwar period. For the first time there was a national planning agency with strong regulatory and financial power. Through its role as an insurer of residential mortgages CMHC exerted a great deal of control over the design of Canadian suburbs (*see* DEVELOPMENT INDUSTRY). Through its direct grants for housing for low-income families and other disadvantaged groups, CMHC has influenced the social geography of Canadian cities. And through its various urban renewal programs, from the slum clearance and redevelopment schemes of the 1950s and 1960s to the neighbourhood rehabilitation projects of the 1970s, CMHC has been a major force for environmental change in inner city areas.

CMHC's policies and programs have generated their own share of controversy over the years, but the NHA has always held a clear social objective: all Canadians should have access to a decent standard of housing. The "decent standard" must be defined by society, while the community at large assumes part of the cost of raising everyone's en-

vironment to an acceptable condition. This principle is well accepted in Canada today and underlies numerous social programs of federal and provincial governments alike. Yet the question arises: Is physical planning (and land use regulation) a proper instrument for redistributive purposes? On the one hand, the provincial planning statutes largely ignore the issue; their statements of purpose are usually limited to "the economical and orderly development of land," or some such phrase. On the other hand, in the actual planning decisions that are taken, day in and day out, questions of rights and justice are constantly in the forefront, and many Canadian communities have adopted physical planning policies that indeed serve redistributive ends. In general, though, Canadian planners are still struggling to reconcile the social reform ideals that were such a powerful force at the turn of the century with the simpler notion of "proper" use of land.

Planning Profession and Education With the growth of cities after 1945, the Canadian planning profession was revitalized and developed quickly. It is not just that planners were needed in greater numbers than before; the specialized tasks performed in modern planning agencies became far more diverse. In addition to the traditional principles of city layout, land subdivision and architectural arts, planners had to learn about urban sociology and human behaviour, management sciences, data analysis and forecasting, municipal and planning law, and environmental sciences. Educational programs were established after 1947, for which the federal government and CMHC provided invaluable assistance. In 1944, Marsh and others suggested to the deputy minister of finance, W.C. Clark, that provision be made in NHA to fund research, professional training and public education. Clark inserted a Part V into the Act, entitled "Housing Research and Community Planning." Parliament authorized $5 million to begin implementing Part V, and has continued its support ever since.

Over the years CMHC has funded much research and has numerous practical planning studies in partnership with provincial or municipal governments or with the universities. It has awarded hundreds of scholarships for Canadian students to learn urban and regional planning. CMHC has also sponsored a variety of informative magazines (eg, *Community Planning Review, Habitat, Living Places*), and Part V funds made possible the establishment of the Community Planning Assn of Canada in 1946. The CPAC is a nongovernment organization that seeks to increase citizen awareness and understanding of community planning and community involvement in planning matters.

NHA funds were also used to help introduce degree-granting planning programs in the universities, partly by grants to the first planning schools: McGill (1947), Manitoba (1949), British Columbia (1950) and Toronto (1951). A French-language program was commenced at U de Montréal in 1961. Several other universities introduced planning programs in the 1960s and 1970s, and a total of 18 are now accredited by the Canadian Institute of Planners (CIP). A number of the later programs were titled "Environmental Design" or "Environmental Studies," an indication of the expanding breadth and multidisciplinary nature of the modern planning profession. U of Waterloo, Ryerson Polytechnical Institute, U du Québec and Institut de Montréal offer 4-year undergraduate degrees, while other approved programs are at the graduate level. Initially, when urban or civic design was emphasized in the planning curriculum, architects and engineers made up the majority of planning students. This pattern changed as planning programs

underwent transformations in social outlook and professional scope. By the late 1950s training in one of the social sciences (eg, geography, sociology or economics) became an equally common route into planning, and this background was further expanded to include the managerial and environmental sciences in the 1960s and 1970s.

In 1949, 45 persons practised planning in Canada. In 1988 the Canadian Institute of Planners counted some 3300 members. They serve in many roles encompassed by private consultancies, various departments of the provincial and federal governments, municipal and regional authorities, crown corporations, resource industries, and the land development industry. Two years of supervised work experience after obtaining a planning degree are required for admission into the profession. The CIP is a national affiliation of institutes, one in each of the provinces and territories. Besides regulating the professional conduct of its members and supervising standards of practice, the institute carries out programs of public education, and occasionally advises governments on legislation and environmental issues. Approximately one-third of the institute's financial resources go to support a professional journal, *Plan Canada*. Most of the provincial affiliates of the CIP publish a journal on current planning matters (eg, the *Alberta Journal of Planning Practice*).

Unlike the architecture and engineering professions, where professional practice and the use of titles are strictly regulated by provincial legislation, planning is generally not regulated. In 2 provinces only, BC and Saskatchewan, provincial enactments reserve the title of "planner" to those persons accredited by the provincial affiliate of CIP. Even here, and in all other provinces and territories except Québec, any person or private company may practise planning. Québec restricts the right to practise planning to persons granted a licence through the Corporation des urbanistes du Québec, an affiliate of CIP. Over the years, institute members in virtually all provinces have endeavoured to persuade governments to accord their profession an exclusive right to practise planning. Yet opinion among professional planners within CIP is divided about the desirability of legislation that would have to prescribe, in a finite manner, where a privileged practice of planning should begin and end in relation to other licensed professions. This doubt is explained by the fact that planning cannot be yet described as a discipline founded upon a discrete body of knowledge and skills. Indeed, as planning has attached itself to an increasingly broad range of urban, regional and environmental management affairs, it has become an "interdisciplinary" profession that embraces highly qualified people from many disciplines.

WILLIAM T. PERKS and P.J. SMITH

Reading: A.F.J. Artibise and G.A. Stelter, eds, *The Usable Urban Past: Planning and Politics in the Modern Canadian City* (1979), and *Shaping the Urban Landscape: Aspects of the Canadian City-Building Process* (1982); Canada, Dept of Environment, *Report of the Interdepartmental Task Force on Land Use Policy* (1980); H. Carver, *Compassionate Landscape* (1975); J.B. Cullingworth, *Urban and Regional Planning in Canada* (1987); L.O. Gertler, *Regional Planning in Canada* (1972); Gertler, ed, *Planning the Canadian Environment* (1968); S.M. Makuch, *Canadian Municipal and Planning Law* (1983); William T. Perks, "Canada," in N. Patricios, ed, *International Handbook of Land Use Planning* (1985); Perks and I.M. Robinson, eds, *Urban and Regional Planning in a Federal State: The Canadian Experience* (1979); P. Rutherford, ed, *Saving the Canadian City* (1974).

Urban Citizen Movements are community groups that are often organized around concerns about land use and the way planning decisions are made in local government. These concerns can be summed up respectively by the familiar slogans "Protect our neighbourhood" and "Open up city hall." Community groups have been a feature of urban political life since MUNICIPAL GOVERNMENT began in Canada in the 1840s, but such groups have been particularly prominent during times of economic boom such as the period from the mid-1960s up to the economic recession of 1980-83. Typically, such groups become organized or revitalized when a neighbourhood, often an older inner-city area, is threatened by a development proposal, particularly for an expressway or high-density building (see CITY). When high-density (and perhaps high-rise) office or apartment development is proposed for a lower-density residential neighbourhood, the property development company, municipal council and municipal staff (especially the planning department) become targets of protest. The developer and city hall are also the focus of community groups' activities when expressways or other major roadworks are planned. Because most provinces provide a legal procedure for appealing municipal planning decisions, community groups often take their cases to provincial bodies such as the Alberta Local Authorities Board and the Ontario Municipal Board. Sometimes community groups appeal decisions made by such bodies, making their appeal to provincial Cabinets or courts of law. Another tactic sometimes employed by community groups is to run their own candidates in civic elections, particularly if the groups find that existing municipal councillors are not receptive to written or oral presentations made by the groups. As well as perceived threats to the stability of existing neighbourhoods, community groups have also called for more open decision-making processes because of having experienced difficulty in getting access to information or because decisions are sometimes made in closed meetings or behind the scenes. Especially in recent years, community groups have gone beyond the traditional concerns of opening up decision-making processes and resisting threats to the stability of existing neighbourhoods (sometimes called the NIMBY syndrome, meaning Not In My Back Yard) to include broader questions of policy such as group homes, environmental pollution, day-care facilities and racial discrimination in recruitment to police forces. After a lull, the citizen movement in Canada has again become prominent in efforts to stabilize neighbourhoods, to change the ways decisions are made, and to change the policies of local government. DONALD HIGGINS

Urban Design can be applied to the whole city (as in KITIMAT), to well-defined units of the city (as in Don Mills in Toronto) and to individual streets and clusters of buildings. The earliest extant examples of urban design in Canada are designs for the whole city. Québec City is a compact, fortified city, paying respect in its design to church and state, and acknowledging its existence to the St Lawrence R. Old Montréal, despite demolition and building, preserves the form of the 18th-century street pattern, crowned by Place d'Armes on the height of land at its centre. Halifax derives its visual character from a generous orthogonal grid of streets laid out by British military engineers.

Since the rapid growth of cities at the end of the 19th century, cities have been planned rather than designed, and the term urban design is applied to parts of a city in which there has been particular emphasis on the visual aspect of the streets and open spaces. Ottawa is perhaps the only Canadian city in which, during the 20th century, design of the urban fabric was considered on a large scale. The visual focus in every new city in the West was on the city hall and legislative buildings (see GOVERNMENT BUILDINGS). The street was an important urban-design element; most towns had their Main St, and Sherbrooke St in Montréal and University Ave in Toronto were grand avenues.

After WWII, when cities grew rapidly, there was less concern for the design of the urban environment than for the design of individual buildings. However, in the new, extensive residential areas there were notable attempts to design the whole environment. Don Mills exemplified these new communities, with curved, treed streets and widely spaced buildings. Later, Flemingdon Park in Toronto answered a demand for higher density with tighter massing of buildings and a harder edge to its streets and paths.

The design of the metropolitan downtown entered a new era with the building from 1956 to 1965 of PLACE VILLE MARIE in Montréal. The project combined retail stores with corporate office space and a major banking hall; introduced the idea of a building complex in which public circulation and access are designed 3-dimensionally, so that entrances are at several levels; made pedestrian connections underground with the public transportation system; and created a plaza for public use. Contrary to fears that business would be diverted from downtown, Place Ville Marie has competed with suburban centres and has helped revitalize the downtown core.

The paved civic space had not been an important element in Canadian cities, except in the old French cities of Québec. In the early 1960s both private and public projects began to recognize their function, which is quite distinct from park use. For lunch breaks or for public gatherings, celebrations, exhibitions and protests, these plazas or squares created new views in the city and displayed buildings in their entirety as objects. At the same time, a populist movement emerged in the cities, with a demand for paths exclusive to pedestrians and the closing of some streets to automobiles, as on Sparks St Mall in Ottawa.

Many commercial projects have now been built with a plaza on the street or enclosed by buildings. The Toronto Dominion Bank complex in Toronto exemplifies the straight-sided group of towers set in a paved plaza. Commerce Court, Toronto, is a skilful grouping of new buildings that complement the ornate 1931 bank headquarters and enclose a serene courtyard. It introduced another element to contemporary urban design: the plaza which is only glimpsed from the street and provides a pedestrian route through the city block. The TORONTO CITY HALL, on Nathan Phillips Square, and Robson Square in Vancouver are examples of such public buildings.

The year 1967 was important for urban design in Canada; the celebration of the Canadian Centennial prompted expressions of national and civic pride in new community buildings and parks and also focused attention on a frequently neglected architectural heritage (see HERITAGE CONSERVATION; PUBLIC ART). EXPO 67 also played a significant role as a demonstration of urban-design elements, of elegant street furniture, and of the total composition of paths, spaces and buildings to create a memorable image. In 1971, when the Vincent Massey Awards for Excellence in the Urban Environment were instituted, entries varied from tree-planting programs, housing enclaves, and historic street preservation to promenades.

Designing the city at different levels (on street, below and above ground level) was a response both to a harsh climate and to the demands of circulation in the downtown core. Besides enclosed pedestrian ways between buildings, it produced large-scale indoor gathering places or atria. The extensive underground pedestrian ways in Montréal and Toronto link atria in much the same way that streets link squares. Place Desjardins in Montréal was similarly designed for public gatherings. HUB at U of Alberta is essentially an elevated indoor street, lined with service outlets and stores on the first-floor level and with student housing above and below. One of the largest and most acclaimed of these indoor urban designs is EATON CENTRE in Toronto, a multilevel street lined with stores and services, connected to the subway and to other city blocks under a great vaulted glass roof. Atria add another dimension to the design of cities, particularly when the connection to the street is generous. The weather-protected city changes the views of the city, besides affecting its appearance. In Calgary the system of glazed bridges crossing the streets between buildings (known as Plus 15) becomes a feature in the design of the street and also offers a new vantage point from which to view the streets. However, the misapplication of this device as a connector of buildings without regard to streetscape and views can be disastrous in terms of urban design. A notable example is the pedestrian bridge across Rideau St in Ottawa, which reduces the scale of this important street, obscures the view of Parliament and reduces the sense of arrival at the central space of Confederation Square.

The visual aspect of the city changes with the economy and with cultural custom and fashion. As industry left the city centre and as the railways and harbours declined, underutilized and derelict properties created an opportunity for new design of city sectors. Since 1970, downtown railway property has been the subject of urban design competitions, as in Regina and Toronto. With increasing leisure time and the demand for entertainment and consumer goods, the old working waterfronts are being converted to housing, shopping and marinas, with an emphasis on public open space and pedestrian access to the water edge. Halifax, Toronto and Québec C present the most extensive examples of recent urban design on the waterfront which is based on an openness of the ground plane and unconfined views. EXPO 86 in Vancouver provided the opportunity for similar new design of the waterfront, with some major semipublic buildings remaining as a legacy of the exhibition. Even in smaller towns, a "window" on the waterfront is now considered a desirable amenity.

Cultural change of the late 1960s which promoted populism and the subsequent affluence of the 1970s combined to change the public attitude to streets and public places — no longer merely to pass through but to linger in. Sidewalk cafes appeared with attendant shrubbery and light standards; benches, trees and planters were installed on the sidewalks; and small pockets of wasteland between buildings were converted to miniparks. These measures served to soften the contemporary city image but generally lacked the scale of significant street design. The planters, benches, quaint lamp standards and potted trees of Sherbrooke St in Montréal tend to make an obstacle course of the sidewalk. By comparison, the large shade trees with which it formerly was lined gave Sherbrooke St the scale and grandeur which is appropriate to a principal street of a major city.

Populism, conservation of natural heritage, and later an interest in fitness and exercise, focused interest on parkland, tree planting, walking and bicycle trails. Examples are the Lachine Canal park in Montréal (also a declining industrial area) and the ravine system of walks in Toronto. These pedestrian paths add another dimension to the design of the city, since they do not follow the road system and consequently the urban scene is perceived in a different way. Wascana Centre in Regina is a noteworthy example of urban design of the 1970s which focuses on an artificial lake and park, around which are grouped public buildings, in the tradition of the garden cities movement.

In the wake of skyscrapers, megaprojects, plazas and atria came a growing concern for the older fabric of the city, for the preservation of historic buildings and for housing. Consequently an increasing number of projects were designed on a modest scale, rehabilitating and preserving the heritage of familiar streets. From the steep, picturesque streets of St John's, Nfld, to Bastion Square in Victoria, in many cities and towns and along innumerable main streets, there has been greater recognition of the worth of the urban image. *See also* LANDSCAPE ARCHITECTURE.

BLANCHE LEMCO VAN GINKEL

Reading: H. Carver, *Cities in the Suburbs* (1962); R.W. Collier, *Contemporary Cathedrals: Large-Scale Development in Canadian Cities* (1974); L.O. Gertler, ed, *Planning the Canadian Environment* (1968); G. LePape, ed, *Land Use and Development/Développement et aménagement du territoire* (1975); H. Spence-Sales, *Beautifying Towns/L'embellissement urbain* (1966).

Urban Effect on Climate is one of the best examples of unintentional modification of the atmosphere by humans (*see* CLIMATOLOGY). The construction of every building, road and parking lot creates a new, local microclimate. Taken together with the AIR POLLUTION resulting from human activities, these changes constitute the local effect of a settlement upon its CLIMATE. In Canada such effects have been observed in villages with as few as a thousand inhabitants, as well as in metropolitan areas, and in all climatic regions. Both land surface and air are altered by urbanization. Buildings change the geometric arrangement of the land surface, creating a rigid, rough system of blocks and street "canyons," especially in the centre of cities. This changes the airflow over the city and creates traps for incoming and outgoing radiant energy. Construction materials alter the rate of heat and the rate of water uptake and loss by the surface. Changes in the composition of the air are produced by the release of heat, water vapour and pollutants from combustion of fuels and other activities. Pollutants may alter both the transfer of radiation and the growth of CLOUD droplets.

All of the climatic elements (sunshine, temperature, humidity, wind, etc) are affected by the presence of the city. The impact is discernible on an annual basis and over a period of years as a city grows, but it is usually best displayed on individual days during fine weather (clear skies and light winds). For example, pollution decreases the amount of solar energy in Montréal by about 9% annually, but on individual days the decrease may be as great as 25%. A "heat island" often exists in a city centre because it is warmer than the surrounding countryside. In most large cities in Canada the annual heat-island effect is 1-2°C, but on occasion it is much larger. On clear, calm summer evenings the heat island can be as large as 5-6°C in Brandon, 6-7°C in St-Hyacinthe, 9-10°C in Hamilton, 10-11°C in Vancouver and 11-12°C in Winnipeg, Edmonton and Montréal. The latter values are some of the largest in the world. Even during arctic nights, towns such as Inuvik have a heat island. The relative humidity is almost always lower in a city (because of the warmth), but the actual amount of moisture is often greater, especially at night and in winter. In Prairie centres such as Edmonton, the winter release of water vapour from the combustion of natural gas used for heating gives greater humidity and the possibility of ice FOG at temperatures below about -30°C. Ice fog is also an unpleasant feature of high-latitude settlements such as Inuvik. Winds are generally reduced in the city except around tall buildings where "jetting" may be a problem.

Cities also induce their own breeze circulations. Little is known about the effects of Canadian cities on precipitation. Foreign research would suggest that cities enhance summer precipitation, but the heat island may melt some of the snowfall before it is registered.

T.R. OKE

Urban Reform, a loosely knit set of municipal government and citizen group initiatives, from the late 1890s to the end of WWI and from the late 1960s to the mid-1970s, aimed at improving city life. The first reforms showed a political emphasis that favoured vesting authority in the hands of supposedly apolitical experts. A distrust of local democracy, a feeling that government had to be made secure for people of proven talent, underlay structural reform in local government.

Occasionally, preference for rule by "the best men" led to new local government bodies of appointed, rather than elected, members. Reformers equated proven ability with business success or – as professions such as urban planning, accounting and public health expanded – with appropriate training.

New MUNICIPAL GOVERNMENT bodies seldom usurped the mayor and council, but a modest tampering with the tradition of civic government by council and its standing committees came with the 1896 introduction of the Toronto Board of Control. It was eventually elected by a city-wide vote, thereby evading ward politics, and had special authority in fiscal matters. Among the cities adopting it were Winnipeg (1906), Ottawa (1907), Montréal (1909), Hamilton (1910) and London (1914). A more extreme change teamed a city manager with a mayor at the head of municipal administration. In 1904 Edmonton hired a "city commissioner," the equivalent of a city manager. Similar arrangements were made in Saint John, NB (1908), and Regina, Saskatoon and Prince Albert, Sask (1911-12). Long after the reform period, the city manager scheme was adopted in many Québec municipalities, and in Halifax and Victoria.

The real devolution of power by elected representatives to civic bureaucrats occurred in the administration of new civic services, as increased PUBLIC OWNERSHIP led to the management of transit systems and electric-power distribution by appointed commissions; other commissions were established for parks and urban planning. Municipal ownership was not a novel concept. From the 1850s to the 1870s, Canadian cities had either sponsored publicly owned waterworks or assumed control from private companies. Streetcar lines in the 1870s and 1880s and electric-generating and distributing firms in the 1890s had entered into franchise contracts with cities to operate on municipal rights-of-way. But the reputation of this private franchise approach was tarnished by consumer grievances about fares, rates and levels of service. In many Prairie cities municipal ownership accompanied booster campaigns. By 1914 Edmonton's progressive image was enhanced by municipal ownership of a full range of urban services: electricity, streetcars and telephones. In Montréal local businessmen ran private utilities that withstood reform criticism; in Vancouver the streetcars and power network of the British Columbia Electric Railway were British owned. Although municipal ownership was a reform cause across Canada, its outcome confirmed the nation's regional identities.

PUBLIC-HEALTH concerns before the early reform period had taken the form of ad hoc reactions to sporadic EPIDEMICS. The advance of the germ theory of disease in the 1880s, and the concurrent growth of government collection of vital statistics, helped foster vigorous public-health campaigns. Most cities relied upon voluntary agencies and a modest public-health budget until the late 1920s. In some communities medical health officers asserted the considerable authority placed in their hands by provincial health Acts and city bylaws passed between 1900 and 1920, working to eliminate outdoor privies, overcrowded dwellings, adulterated food and contaminated water supplies. Other reformers were keenly patriotic and religiously inspired to do good works (*see* SOCIAL GOSPEL); playground movements arose to instil British character, virtue and cleanliness among foreign children. Settlement houses run by pioneering social workers (including Winnipeg's All People's Mission, run for a time by J.S. WOODSWORTH) similarly sought to "improve" immigrants. If such social programs were condescending, they nevertheless served practical ends: a playground was safer than a street, and the settlement houses held classes in conversational English.

Owing to the great population growth of urban Canada from 1900 to 1920, housing became a reform concern. Recognizing a need to remedy inadequate housing, many groups discussed the feasibility of forming philanthropic housing companies. Most plans were shelved in the 1913 depression, and the frail philanthropic impulse was swept aside in WWI.

Urban planning also began in the first era of urban reform, originating from a concern about shabby streets and a lack of civic grandeur. City governments or citizens' groups commissioned planners to draft sketches of a CITY BEAUTIFUL, with neoclassical civic buildings, park boulevards, broad avenues and realigned railways. But the war dampened optimism; transition towards an interest in health, housing and the efficient layout of services occurred toward the end of the reform era. Thomas ADAMS, hired in 1914 as planning adviser to the COMMISSION OF CONSERVATION (1909), campaigned for provincial planning Acts to bolster the authority of municipal planning agencies; he also supervised reconstruction after the 1917 HALIFAX EXPLOSION.

Political changes during this complex reform era increased the authority of civic experts, but it is doubtful whether this upgraded civic affairs; politicians and administrators clashed and citizens became confused by the array of agencies. Despite improvements effected by health officers, urban planners and social workers, these challenges to neighbourhood or ward-level political decisions did not entirely extirpate old practices. Moreover, although many successful ideas from the United States and England influenced Canadian action, Canada experienced modest reform achievements.

The second reform period had a similarly international dimension, in this instance the widespread reaction in Western democracies against centralized and bureaucratic authority, and rejection of the tenet that "bigger is better." In Canadian cities, neighbourhood groups mobilized to halt expressways, demolition and renewal projects, and high-rise invasions of the urban core. *City Magazine* was a major voice of the movement in the 1970s. Political style was another feature. Toronto Mayor John Sewell (1978-80) had all the elements of a reformer: identification with community activism and a distrust of nonelected agents of civic authority. There were crusades to save neighbourhoods and defeat drastic land-use changes; some utilized self-interest for a defence of property values. In many cities, action came too late to save remarkable older structures or venerable residential areas. Nevertheless the second and short-lived reform movement affected the way politicians, planners and the middle class perceived the city. Restoration rather than demolition became fashionable; the domination of ur-

Little Champlain St, Québec City, c1900-10 (*courtesy National Archives of Canada/PA-43301/Notman*).

ban planning by the requirements of the automobile was challenged. *See also* HERITAGE CANADA FOUNDATION; HISTORIC SITE; URBAN AND REGIONAL PLANNING.   JOHN WEAVER

Reading: C. Armstrong and and H.V. Nelles, *Monopoly's Moment: The Organization and Regulation of Canadian Utilities, 1830-1930* (1986); A.F.J. Artibise and G.A. Stelter, eds, *The Usable Urban Past* (1979); H. Kaplan, *Reform, Planning and City Politics* (1982); P. Rutherford, ed, *Saving the Canadian City* (1974) and "Urban Reform," *Urban History Review* 2, 76 (1976); John Weaver, *Shaping the Canadian City* (1977).

Urban Studies, the study of Canada's urban development in all its diverse aspects, including the evolution of communities (urban history); city-building processes (urban geography, urban economics, planning, architecture); urban politics and government (urban political science); and urban society (urban sociology and anthropology, urban demography).

Before the 1960s urban studies were dominated by geographers. In Québec, Raoul Blanchard and his students published numerous urban studies in the 1930s, 1940s and 1950s, while Jacob Spelt, Donald Kerr, J. Wreford Watson and others examined urban development in Ontario. Most studies concentrated on individual communities or regions and adopted one of 2 approaches: studies that singled out the urban aspects of the man-environment system, resulting in systematic studies of individual phenomena (urban-economic geography); and synthetic studies that attempted to achieve a holistic appreciation of the many interrelated phenomena that evolved over time to give a unique, urban character to the landscape (historical urban geography).

By the early 1970s many other disciplines had become involved in urban studies, and distinct subdisciplines emerged rapidly. This trend was marked by the establishment, for example, of the Centre for Urban and Community Studies at U of Toronto, the Institute of Urban Studies at U of Winnipeg, and the Institut national de la recherche scientifique (INRS) – urbanization in the U du Québec system. Activity in universities was not restricted to research centres; it also included the introduction or expansion of urban studies courses and teaching programs, and substantial growth in schools of URBAN AND REGIONAL PLANNING.

In government, distinct ministries of urban affairs at the provincial level were formed or expanded, and the federal Ministry of State for Urban Affairs was established (1971). These departments supported research and added to the well-established research programs of such bodies as the CANADA MORTGAGE AND HOUSING CORPORATION (CMHC) and the Canadian Council on Urban and Regional Research (CCURR). Several

important projects were undertaken during the 1970s, including the publication of the Urban Profiles Series (1974-75) and the Urban Prospects Series (1975-76).

The urban studies environment was bolstered as well by the appearance of a variety of new journals, newsletters and magazines, including *Urban Focus* (1972), published by the Institute of Local Government; *Urban History Review/Revue d'histoire urbaine* (1972), published by the National Museum of Man; *Urban Reader* (1973), published by the city of Vancouver; *Urban Forum* (1975), published by CCURR; and *City Magazine* (1974), a commercial venture undertaken by Toronto publisher James Lorimer. In 1977 Micromedia of Toronto began to produce a quarterly index of publications in the urban studies field entitled *Urban Canada/Canada urbain.*

The increasing concern over urban issues was also evident at the municipal level. The Federation of Canadian Municipalities either undertook or sponsored urban research, while individual communities organized formal city archives. Preservation of the built urban heritage was another characteristic of the 1970s as many communities established committees and departments and passed by-laws dealing with preservation and conservation (*see* HERITAGE CONSERVATION; HERITAGE CANADA FOUNDATION).

Despite all this activity, no dominant theoretical or interpretative trends emerged in urban studies in the 1970s or early 1980s. Hundreds of books and articles were published, particularly at the community and regional levels. Books included N.H. Lithwick, *Urban Canada: Problems and Prospects* (1970); J. and R. Simmons, *Urban Canada* (1974); G. Nader, *Cities of Canada,* (2 vols, 1975-76); J.N. Jackson, *The Canadian City: Space, Form, Quality* (1973); L. Stone, *Urban Development in Canada* (1967); D.J.H. Higgins, *Urban Canada: Its Government and Politics* (1977); J. Lorimer and E. Ross, *The City Book* (2 vols, 1976-77); L.O. Gertler, *Planning the Canadian Environment* (1968); G.A. Stelter and A.F.J. Artibise, eds, *The Canadian City* (1977) and *Canada's Urban Past* (1981).

By the early 1980s the attention devoted to urban issues was beginning to wane as a result of the recession and because many of the earlier initiatives had not – in the minds of politicians, at least – fulfilled their early promise. Thus the federal urban ministry was disbanded in 1979, several provincial urban ministries were reduced, urban research institutes foundered, and several urban studies journals and newsletters died. But although there was a notable decline in interest in urban studies, there remained a solid core of specialists. *See also* CITY; URBAN DESIGN; URBAN REFORM; URBANIZATION.   A.F.J. ARTIBISE

Urban Transportation With the spread of industrialism and the growing size of cities, it was no longer possible for many city dwellers to live within walking distance of work. Urban transportation has become increasingly important as our cities continue to grow.

Early attempts to solve the urban transportation problem were made in other countries. In 1819, for example, Paris benefited from the operation of a system of horse-drawn stagecoaches. In the next decade, omnibuses began operating in New York City and in London, England. The development of railways for intercity passenger transportation in the 1820s and 1830s was quickly followed by their adaptation for use in cities. Steam locomotives were unsuitable for urban use as they scared horses and were dirty, so most of the early street railways used horses or mules for propulsion. Toronto had horse-drawn trams in operation by 1845, Montréal by the 1860s, and

Early streetcar, Ste-Catherine St, Montréal (*courtesy Notman Photographic Archives*).

soon after other Canadian cities introduced these vehicles.

Horse-drawn trams were a vast improvement, but they were far from ideal transportation. Heavy loads could not be hauled, and horses were expensive and required frequent rest periods; they also polluted the streets. Numerous attempts were made to substitute mechanical power for muscle power: the invention of the first successful electric railway in 1879 by Dr E.W. von Siemens in Germany led to a revolution in transportation. German, US and British inventors were soon busy perfecting the electric streetcar. One of the first full-scale examples of the new technology was built at the Toronto Industrial Exposition of 1885. This short line introduced another important invention, the trolley pole, which permitted the efficient and safe collection of electric power from overhead wires. Commercial use followed, and Canada was one of the first countries to exploit fully the technological advances. The first electric railway line in Canada was established in Windsor, Ont, and opened 28 May 1886 using 1.5 miles (2.4 km) of track. Another electric streetcar system was opened the following year in St Catharines, Ont, with several systems following in the next few years. Ultimately, most Canadian cities and their adjoining suburbs, located in every province except PEI, had STREET RAILWAYS.

Although the streetcar provided an effective service when there was no alternative, its era was over almost as soon as it began. The development of the AUTOMOBILE eventually resulted in most Canadians having access to cheap and convenient TRANSPORTATION. The motor vehicle also revolutionized public transportation, as BUSES came into general use in the 1920s. Although slower and less comfortable than streetcars, motorbuses provided street railway companies with the means of facing increasing competition from the automobile.

To combine the good features of both streetcars and motorbuses, experiments were made with trolleybuses, which ran on rubber tires but drew their power from overhead lines. Windsor was the first Canadian city to try the new mode, with the Lincoln Road route being opened on 5 May 1922. Toronto also experimented with trolleybuses, opening a route in June 1922. Both of these experiments were abandoned by 1926, but the trolleybus replaced many streetcars after WWII.

The automobile continued to divert traffic from the street railway monopolies throughout the

1920s. The Depression of the 1930s brought further reductions in traffic, and many street railways were abandoned during this period, as the rolling stock deteriorated. With little capital available, bus manufacturers persuaded some street railways to opt for motorbuses. Transit systems in the largest cities, particularly Toronto, Montréal and Vancouver, purchased new streetcars and modernized their equipment.

WWII saw a dramatic resurgence of all forms of public transportation, as supplies of gasoline, tires and spare parts, as well as new cars, were severely restricted. By 1945 most public transit systems in Canada were worn out and required extensive new investment. The return to peace permitted more automobiles to be purchased, and the end of wartime emergencies saw a general decline in the demand for public transport. The decision was made in most cities to abandon all streetcar services, replacing them with modern trolleybuses and motorbuses. After the 1959 closure of the Montréal and Ottawa systems, only Toronto operated streetcars.

An important addition to Canadian urban transportation was the opening of Toronto's Yonge St subway in 1954. SUBWAYS provide high passenger capacities, as their trains operate on protected rights-of-way totally separated from interference by other traffic.

Significant improvements to private transportation were also made possible in the 1950s through the construction of expressways. The dramatic postwar increase in automobile ownership put pressure on conventional street systems, and the average time required to make a particular journey by either automobile or public transit actually increased. Expressways are intended to remove motor vehicles from local streets, placing them on separate rights-of-way, avoiding other traffic. As with subways, traffic on expressways moves at high speeds, permitting greater capacity. Both subways and expressways have severe disadvantages and cannot be universally applied as solutions to transportation problems. One disadvantage shared by subways and expressways is the extremely high cost of construction. Both forms consume large amounts of scarce land, although land used by subways can be built over once the subway is completed.

Despite the number of expressways constructed, traffic congestion continued to grow in Canadian cities in the 1960s and 1970s. A dramatic increase in the price of oil, as well as increases in parking and other costs, started a return to public transit. Many systems were rejuvenated with new equipment, and passengers once again began to use public transportation. Most transit expansion in this era depended on motorbuses and conventional rail-based systems. As the subway systems in Toronto and Montréal were extended, other cities looked for cheaper solutions to their transportation problems. Light Rail Transit provides most of the advantages of subways at less cost, and LRT lines were opened in Edmonton (1978), Calgary (1981) and Vancouver (1986).

Administration, Planning and Finance No less dramatic than the change in technology has been the change in the administrative, financial and planning structures of urban transportation. Careful planning and scheduling of manpower and equipment are required to provide services at the times passengers wish to travel. Vehicles must be maintained; supervisors must ensure that the vehicles adhere to predetermined schedules and that every passenger pays the fare. These activities are co-ordinated by transportation management. In the early days of public transportation, these organizations were usually privately owned concerns which operated in the expectation of profit. Fares collected were expected to cover all costs

Aerial view of the Decarie Métropolitain Blvd interchange in Ville St-Laurent, Qué. Expressways became dramatic additions to the urban landscape in the 1950s and 1960s (*courtesy SSC Photocentre*).

and to provide a reasonable return on invested capital. Many cities even charged the private companies a franchise fee for the privilege of using their streets, and imposed other requirements on the transit systems. Other cities had a more direct involvement in the provision of transportation. In some cases, no suitable private company could be found to construct a streetcar system, and in other cities local residents were reluctant to give a private company a profitable monopoly.

In 1909 municipally owned streetcars began to operate in Calgary, and in 1911 the first streetcars in Saskatchewan, also municipally owned, began service in Regina. In 1921 the newly created Toronto Transportation Commission took over and extended the networks of both privately and municipally owned street railway companies. Private ownership remained important in other cities, however, with Halifax, Winnipeg and Vancouver, among others, being served by privately owned companies until the 1950s or later.

Whether ownership was private or public, all early transportation systems were operated with the expectation of profit, or at least with the aim of meeting expenses. Within a few years, some systems found it difficult to achieve this goal. Streetcar services had to be provided not only throughout the day, but on weekends and evenings when there were relatively few riders available. Large amounts of equipment and manpower had to be reserved for the journeys to and from work.

As riders started to drift away from public transportation to private automobiles, the financial problems of the transit systems accelerated. Fewer riders meant that higher fares had to be charged to cover operating costs. Higher fares resulted in even fewer riders. Attempts to cut costs were not totally effective, particularly as transit-system operating costs started to rise dramatically. In 1960 the average Canadian transit passenger brought a profit of 1.7¢ per trip, but by 1971 this profit had disappeared with an average net cost per passenger of 0.7¢. Losses have increased so that the average cost per passenger on transit systems was 38.1¢ in 1980 and 52¢ in 1985.

This reversal of the profitability of urban transportation systems caused planners to revise their thinking. The problems encountered by freeway systems in meeting urban transportation needs made it obvious that support of public transit systems was a viable, less costly alternative. By deliberately deferring or cancelling roadway construction projects and by introducing measures to support transit systems, automobile travel in our

cities was made relatively unattractive in comparison to public transit. Innovative traffic management measures, such as "bus-only" lanes and streets, and transit-operated traffic signals, provided cheap ways of accelerating transit schedules. Buses required no downtown parking spaces and, per passenger, consumed less roadway space than that required by automobiles. There was virtual unanimity across the country in the 1970s that public transportation should receive some form of subsidy to attract more passengers and to allow public transit to compete on a fair basis with the private car. Many of the traffic management measures undertaken specifically to aid buses in their travels through city streets have also assisted automobiles, as conflict between buses and other vehicles slows the speed of all traffic.

Having made the commitment to support public transit services, urban planners found that direct control over the type and quality of services enabled them to achieve innovations in the actual design and layout of cities and suburbs. The provision of transit service to a particular area was an added amenity which attracted development. If the transit service was permanent, such as a subway, LRT or trolleybus line, the attraction would be even stronger than that of a motorbus route which could be easily moved to another location without warning. Subway lines in Toronto and Montréal, although underground, can be readily identified from the air by the high-density developments around many stations. Residential areas can be made more attractive if there is a commitment to provide an alternative, reliable, permanent transit service. The development of the False Creek community in Vancouver saved thousands of dollars per housing unit by restricting garage space and by providing a frequent bus service as an alternative to second and third family cars. Even in remote suburbs, which are often difficult to serve effectively by public transit, steps are now being taken to provide walkways at the ends of cul-de-sacs, thereby bringing public transit within easy walking distance of all houses in the subdivision.

The trend towards public transportation was reinforced in the 1970s when automobile fuel and parking costs in major cities rose dramatically. Many Canadians turned to public transit for the first time in their lives as a result of the energy crisis; others moved to individual means of transportation, by foot, bicycle or motorcycle. Some transit companies experimented with special bus services to enable handicapped people to use public transport. Although the automobile still has a major role in urban transportation, it is unlikely that it will ever regain its popularity of the 1950s and 1960s.

In 1985 the 86 members of the Canadian Urban Transit Assn operated 10 599 motorbuses, 1640 subway cars and computer train coaches, 611 trolleybuses, 439 light rail vehicles and streetcars, and 73 intermediate capacity coaches (eg, Skytrain in Vancouver). Among them, these vehicles operated 691 million revenue km, carried 1.4 billion paying passengers and earned $936 million in revenue. They consumed 327 million L of diesel fuel, 4.1 million L of gasoline and 567 million kWh of electricity. Nearly 35 000 persons were employed in the industry.   JOHN M. DAY

Reading: H.W. Blake, The Era of Streetcars and Interurbans in Winnipeg (1974); Canadian Urban Transit Assn, Transit Fact Book, 1981 (1982); J.F. Due, The Intercity Electric Railway Industry in Canada (1966); C.K. Hatcher, Saskatchewan's Pioneer Streetcars (1971) and Stampede City Streetcars (1975).

Urbanization, a complex process in which a country's organized communities become larger, more specialized and more interdependent. Urbanization is the result of many variables – economic, technological, demographic, political, etc – and it is inevitably accompanied by other changes in society. Some 76.5% of Canada's population lives in urban areas (1986). In this respect it ranks 16th in the world, behind such countries as Belgium, Australia, Israel, the UK and Japan, but far ahead of the USSR, Pakistan, India and China. Despite its overall high national level, an important characteristic of Canadian urbanization is its regional variation reflecting in part economic development differences among the provinces. Since 1881, Ontario, Québec and British Columbia consistently maintained the highest levels of urban concentration.

Canada became an urban nation relatively early in its history. The urbanization process has passed through 4 major phases and, in the 1970s, entered a fifth stage. The earliest began with the founding of Québec in 1608. Urban development was mercantile or colonial in nature and was characterized by imperial (French and British) control over location, function and growth. Functionally, urban places – notably Québec City, Montréal, Halifax and St John's – tended to be administrative or military centres. Economically, they were entrepôts, collection agencies for colonial staples and distribution centres of manufactured goods from the mother country. A characteristic of these mercantile forms was their lack of significant connections with other towns in the colonies, for the primary connection was the overseas metropolis. Another common feature of urban centres during this period was a dependence on water transport, powered by wind and sail. In terms of form, the mercantile town reflected imperial needs and designs.

The second phase began in the early 1800s and was marked by the increasing control of commercial interests – rather than imperial – over urban development. In the sphere of economic activity, the outstanding characteristic of this period was a move away from an exclusive reliance on staples export to a new concern for regional and interregional commerce and small scale artisanal production for a local or regional market. Several cities began to assume metropolitan functions by dominating their immediate region. A third as-

Jasper Avenue, Edmonton, 1890 (*courtesy Provincial Archives of Alberta/E. Brown Coll/B4755*).

Jasper Avenue, Edmonton, from 99th Street, *c*1912. Urban growth, brought by the railway and nearby agricultural settlement, was dramatic 1890-1912 (*courtesy Provincial Archives of Alberta/E. Brown Coll/B4818*).

pect of the economic reorientation of this period was the use of new technologies in transportation, notably the application of steam to shipping, to railways and to the means of production. The form of cities in this era is not readily definable, but a number of features distinguish them from both their predecessors and successors. While there was now an absence of central direction in shaping cities, there was nonetheless a semblance of order and regularity. Transportation routes and the provision of services – such as water and sewers – often determined the direction of development. Commercial cities were also characterized by a sorting out of the city's functions (residential, commercial, etc) and people, the latter by class and ethnicity.

The third phase, which began with the industrial era in the 1870s and lasted until the 1920s, saw the development of a national urban system that tended to concentrate power in major central Canadian cities, notably Montréal and Toronto. The political economy of this industrial era was marked by the emergence of industrial capitalism and its counterpart, the industrial working class. The extent and nature of urban development was dependent on major improvements in the technological capacity of Canada. Science and engineering were systematically applied to transportation, communications, building methods and production. The outstanding physical characteristics of cities were the enormous spatial expansion of the suburbs and the tall office towers of the central core. The social landscape of cities was affected by the changing scale of development. A

Percentage of Canadians in Urban Centres, 1851-1986					
Year	*%*	*Year*	*%*	*Year*	*%*
1851	13.1	1901	34.9	1951	62.4
1861	15.8	1911	41.8	1961	69.7
1871	18.3	1921	47.4	1971	76.1
1881	23.3	1931	52.5	1981	75.8
1891	29.8	1941	55.7	1986	76.5

kind of giantism prevailed, from the size of suburbs and the height of the buildings in the central core to the organization of new business enterprises and the building of enormous factories. Land use was increasingly specialized.

A fourth era of development began around the 1940s and extended in most senses to the 1970s. The corporate era was characterized by the technology of the automobile and truck, an economic orientation away from industry to service functions, and spatial decentralization of population and activities. Canada's population grew rapidly and corporate concentration in all sectors of the economy tended to centralize growth in major cities. In terms of form, the corporate city was characterized by 5 features: corporate suburbs developed by the private sector; high-rise apartments; suburban industrial parks; downtown office towers; and regional shopping centres.

By the late 1970s a new "post-urbanization" era was beginning to be identifiable in urban development. The crises in energy and high interest rates, and a variety of other factors, began to have an affect on urbanization patterns and suggested that Canada was entering a new era. Since the beginning of the 1970s, the population of the old urban cores and the central districts have levelled off or even declined, while that of peripheral areas around cities has increased considerably. The city, which has until the 1970s consistently attracted the rural population, is now losing population to the rural areas. Along with many countries in the industrialized world, Canada has entered a "post-urbanization" era. Of Canada's 12 provinces and territories, only 4 experienced greater growth in urban rather than rural areas between 1976 and 1981. Urban Canada was losing ground to "exurbia," but by the 1986 census, 8 of the 10 provinces had experienced modest growth in their urban areas. Canada's population is avoiding the very large and very small urban concentrations in favour of medium-sized cities. More and more Canadians are settling outside metropolitan areas, choosing the urban fringe areas. The increase in Canada's rural population thus does not indicate a return to farming; rather, people are seeking out "rural" environments that are close to a city. In the 1980s, slower economic growth led some municipalities to annex adjoining lands to increase their tax base. For example, in 1982 Edmonton's land area was effectively doubled through annexation, a process which

Percent of Population Urban, Canada and Provinces, 1851-1986													
Source: Censuses of Canada, 1871-1986													
	1871	*1881*	*1891*	*1901*	*1911*	*1921*	*1931*	*1941*	*1951*	*1961*	*1971*	*1981*	*1986*
BC	9.0	18.3	42.6	46.4	50.9	50.9	62.3	64.0	68.6	72.6	75.7	78.0	79.2
Alta	–	–	–	16.2	29.4	30.7	31.8	31.9	47.6	63.3	73.5	77.2	79.4
Sask	–	–	–	6.1	16.1	16.8	20.3	21.3	30.4	43.0	53.0	58.1	61.4
Man	–	14.9	23.3	24.9	39.3	41.5	45.2	45.7	56.0	63.9	69.5	71.2	72.1
Ont	20.6	27.1	35.0	40.3	49.5	58.8	63.1	67.5	72.5	77.3	82.4	81.7	82.1
Qué	19.9	23.8	28.6	36.1	44.5	51.8	59.5	61.2	66.8	74.3	80.6	77.6	77.9
NB	17.6	17.6	19.9	23.1	26.7	35.2	35.4	38.7	42.8	46.5	56.9	50.6	49.4
NS	8.3	14.7	19.4	27.7	36.7	44.8	46.6	52.0	54.5	54.3	56.7	55.1	54.0
PEI	9.4	10.5	13.1	14.5	16.0	18.8	19.5	22.1	25.1	32.4	38.3	36.3	38.1
Nfld	–	–	–	–	–	–	–	–	43.3	50.7	57.2	58.6	58.9
Canada	18.3	23.3	29.8	34.9	41.8	47.4	52.5	55.7	62.4	69.7	76.1	75.8	76.5

added approximately 100 000 new "residents" to Edmonton's population by 1986.

Recent trends seem to suggest that the decline of the monocentred metropolis in favour of a polycentric urban field will continue, with serious consequences for large centres and urban cores. Yet the city as a focus of cultural, economic and transportation relations probably has a future in Canada. One indication of this, evident by the early 1980s, was a growing concern to preserve or create identifiable symbols of a community in the forms of historic buildings or significant space. And Canadians still continue to identify with urban places in a traditional manner – even if they live in exurbia – suggesting a good deal of continuity in how society perceives place.

A.F.J. ARTIBISE AND G.A. STELTER

Reading: G. Nader, *Cities of Canada* (2 vols, 1975-76); J. and R. Simmons, *Urban Canada* (1974); G.A. Stelter and A.F.J. Artibise, eds, *The Canadian City* (1984); Stelter and Artibise, *Power and Place: Canadian Urban Development in a North American Context* (1985).

Urgent Ethnology involves recording on sound tapes, films, photographs and in writing the rapidly vanishing languages and cultures of the Inuit, Indian and Métis peoples of Canada. Recent decades have seen a dramatic increase in the pace of social and cultural change, and the traditional cultures of Canada's original inhabitants are closer to extinction than at any other period in our history. Research priority is given to those aspects of language and culture that are undergoing the most rapid change and require immediate documentation to prevent their being lost. This knowledge is of special importance to people of native ancestry who wish to maintain their cultural identity. Such knowledge is also essential for a complete understanding of Canadian history and PREHISTORY.

Contract research conducted by the National Museum of Man (CANADIAN MUSEUM OF CIVILIZATION) was given a higher profile after 1960 by the Ethnology Division, which initiated the Urgent Ethnology Program in 1972. Research projects cover all cultural regions of Canada including the Prairies, northeastern woodlands and the Subarctic. Fieldwork stresses ethnomedicine, ethnobotany (*see* PLANTS, NATIVE USES), material culture and mythology. There have also been projects in art, cultural ecology, music, individual life histories and genealogy. A major emphasis has been on ethnolinguistics. Nowhere is the infringement of acculturation felt more than in oral tradition, including language itself. As nearly as can be determined, 53 native languages survive in Canada, though only 3 have more than 5000 speakers (*see* NATIVE PEOPLE, LANGUAGES). Of the remainder, two-thirds are spoken by fewer than 1000 speakers and may disappear in less than 2 generations. Some are represented by fewer than 10 speakers and must now be regarded as extinct.

An urgent ethnology program requires not only actual ethnographic fieldwork but also the contributions of a knowledgeable archival and technical staff. The program of the Canadian Museum of Civilization has included preservation of the voluminous correspondence and archival collection of Edward SAPIR and Diamond JENNESS, early Canadian ethnologists. At the technical level, scientific work includes the preservation and restoration of quickly deteriorating film, such as movies of Copper Eskimo life, shot between 1913 and 1918 by the CANADIAN ARCTIC EXPEDITION. As more natives move to large modern communities, as the number of camps on the land dwindle each year and as the number of men and women knowledgeable in the old ways diminish, the importance of urgent ethnology increases.

RENÉ R. GADACZ

Reading: J.G. Taylor, *A National Programme for Urgent Ethnology* (1977).

Urquhart, Anthony Morse, "Tony," painter, sculptor (b at Niagara Falls, Ont 9 Apr 1934). He studied art at the Albright Art School and U of Buffalo. In 1961 he joined a group of London, Ont, artists, including Greg CURNOE and Jack CHAMBERS, who advocated a regional approach to art. Drawing from his own experiences, Urquhart works in a style that makes explicit reference to the underlying complexities and paradoxes he sees in the local landscape. In his boxed landscape sculptures of the 1960s he achieved a surreal juxtaposition of savage and primordial relationships with the actual and familiar. The constructions become at once a personal interior space and a universal collective landscape. A 1984 show held in Toronto focused on death, a persistent theme in his work.

KATHLEEN LAVERTY

Ursuline Convent, Québec City. First occupying this site in 1642 under the leadership of MARIE DE L'INCARNATION (who had established a convent first in the lower town in 1639), the Ursuline Sisters gradually (1686-1902) erected this complex of buildings dedicated to the education of young girls. The St-Augustin, Ste-Famille and kitchen wings, the largest surviving pre-1700 structures in Canada, have features characteristic of this early period, such as the steep medieval roofs with 2 rows of dormers, massive chimneys, rubble masonry protected by stucco, or *crépi*, and segmentally arched windows with small-paned casements. Although the original church was destroyed by fire, the Ursulines managed to save the magnificent altarpiece and pulpit carved by members of the LEVASSEUR FAMILY dynasty, 1732-36, a masterpiece that attests to the highly skilled craftsmanship available in New France.

CHRISTINA CAMERON

Ursulines St Angela Merici founded the Company of St Ursula (Brescia, Italy 1535) for the instruction, education and protection of young girls. Not a religious institute, it drew women who made a vow of chastity and lived together as a family (a novel arrangement for young women in those days). Of various canonical natures, these foundations continued, as monasteries, congregations, etc, and all claimed connection with the founder and called themselves Ursulines. Today therefore we find enclosed nuns (some living in centralized institutes, some not), sisters (living in about 60 religious congregations) and secular Ursulines (most of them living in companies of St Ursula, as in the 16th century). The Ursulines who came to Québec in 1639 with the blessed MARIE DE L'INCARNATION were enclosed nuns. Having spread throughout French Canada, they now live in an institute which had 675 members in 1986. There are also the Ursulines of Chatham (1860), Prelate (1912), Bruno (1913), Tildonk (1914) and the Ursuline Sisters of the Agonizing Heart of Jesus (1965).

MICHEL THÉRIAULT

Utilities, often described as businesses so "affected with the public interest" that they must be regulated by government regarding entry into (and exit from) the market, rate charges to customers, rate of return allowed to owners, and for the requirement to serve all customers within their area of operation (*see* REGULATORY PROCESS). Businesses engaged in the production and distribution of electricity, the distribution of natural gas, the distribution of water, telecommunications (particularly telephone service) and pipelines (gas, oil, commodities) are considered public utilities. Cable-television service is also described by some as a utility. In earlier times, railways, grain elevators, ferries and privately owned bridges were considered public utilities.

Utilities may be owned by private investors or by governments through, for example, CROWN CORPORATIONS. Distribution of electricity is provided by provincial crown corporations in most provinces, while that of natural gas to businesses, households and pipelines are almost entirely privately controlled. Telephone services in the 3 Prairie provinces are provided by crown corporations, but in the rest of Canada by privately owned firms (subject to government regulation).

Rationale for Government Intervention The most common argument for regulating public utilities is that such businesses are subject to very important economies of scale; that is, the unit cost of supplying a product or service declines as output increases. Because a large enterprise can more easily spread these costs over many customers to lower the per unit cost, natural monopolies are created. While a monopoly may result in greater efficiency, its power may be used to exploit consumers (businesses and households) in at least 2 ways. First, prices may be set well above the total costs of production, allowing the utility owner to earn excess profits. Second, the utility may engage in discriminatory pricing, eg, charging different customer groups different prices when the cost of serving each group is the same. In response to these potential problems, government regulators often control entry to the extent of granting a monopoly franchise for a specific market area to one firm, but the regulators are responsible for ensuring that rates charged by the utility are "just and reasonable" and are "not unduly discriminatory or unfair" to different classes of customers.

It is also argued that since public utilities supply essential services to industries and households, all those willing to pay the price must have access to such services. Regulation is therefore necessary to ensure the maintenance of essential services.

Moreover, utilities are capital intensive, ie, the value of their assets is several times their annual revenues and the incremental costs of serving additional customers (up to a point) are small once the utility's network is in place. The 3 largest electric utilities in Canada (which are among the 5 largest nonfinancial enterprises in Canada measured by assets) control assets of 5 to 6 times their annual revenues. The ratio for telephone companies is much lower (3 to 1) while the ratio of total assets to annual revenues for natural-gas distributors and pipelines is about 2 to 1.

In most cases, utilities provide a nonstorable commodity or service which must be available to the customer on demand. For example, electricity must flow into the house when the lights are turned on; otherwise it has little value. Customers cannot store the product to accommodate fluctuations in demand. Moreover, most utility customers cannot obtain alternative sources of supply. While large-scale industrial buyers can, in time, find alternative sources of supply, households have less opportunity to switch if prices are too high or service is poor.

The rationale for regulating utilities is not constant, and a utility's status may evolve over time. For example, railways, until the growth of truck and airline transport just before WWII, were considered public utilities. Rapid technological change has severely undermined the argument for the monopoly-supply of another utility: long-distance telecommunications services. While entry of competitors into the market in Canada has been limited to nonvoice services, federal regulators in the US have permitted competition in the supply of long-distance voice services. Even the status of local-exchange telephone service, considered a classic natural monopoly, is threatened by cellular radio and by direct transmission to satellites that bypass the local exchange.

Alternative Forms of Intervention Government

intervention takes 2 forms. First, governments can assume public ownership of the means of production through the creation of crown corporations. As owners, governments can establish the firm's prices directly and determine the conditions of service. Public ownership, however, does not necessarily entail control over entry. Second, governments can leave ownership of utilities in private hands while establishing a regulatory agency (commission or board) to monitor and control the utilities' activities. Public ownership is chosen more on practical than ideological grounds and has often been adopted after private ownership has prevailed for years. For instance, the fact that provincial crown corporations paid no federal corporate income taxes was a major determinant in the nationalization of electricity in both BC and Québec in the early 1960s.

It is important to note that public ownership has not been used as a substitute for government regulation. With very few exceptions (Saskatchewan Telephone, HYDRO-QUÉBEC), government regulation has been imposed on both publicly and privately owned utilities.

Regulation of Public Utilities Governments regulate utilities through specialized agencies (eg, CANADIAN RADIO-TELEVISION AND TELECOMMUNICATIONS COMMISSION, the National Energy Board and the various provincial public utilities commissions), which receive their mandates directly from government through statutes specifying many of the rules by which they operate. Most regulatory agencies operate in a quasi-judicial fashion (*see* ADMINISTRATIVE TRIBUNAL), their most important task being to make impartial decisions on matters such as the level of rates or tariffs, the allowed rate of return the owners may earn, and entry into the relevant markets.

The decisions of such agencies are usually subject to appeal to Cabinet. The agencies themselves are less independent than their American counterparts, and their role in policymaking is usually more restricted.

First, an agency decides who is allowed to operate in a given market, such as the extension of a pipeline into a new territory; when the decision was taken to build the gas pipeline from Montréal to Halifax, the NEB chose Trans-Québec and Maritimes Pipelines from among various candidates. Second, the agency must decide to whom the service is available upon demand, the implication being that utilities are not free to withdraw the service, once it is established, without the regulator's approval. Most of the work of utility regulators, however, involves determining the prices a utility is allowed to charge for its services. In establishing "just and reasonable" rates, the agency must determine the total amount of revenue that the enterprise may receive and how much the various classes of customer must pay for a service. Through public hearings the agency seeks to determine the normal costs incurred by the utility in providing the required level of services, in particular, what level of capital expenditure is deemed appropriate and what should be the allowed rate of return on the company's "rate base" (usually the depreciated value of plant and equipment used to provide the commodity or service). In this respect, the agency must regulate monopoly profits while ensuring that the rate of return is sufficient to attract and retain capital in the enterprise. Once the overall level of revenues has been determined, the agency must ensure that no class of customers is treated unfairly, eg, in the case of telephone regulation, a perennial question is how much businesses (as opposed to households) should pay per month for local-exchange service.

Problems with Utilities and Their Regulation The regulation of utilities by quasi-independent agencies is a time-consuming process subject to considerable criticism. First, because utilities appear able to pass higher costs on to their customers, they are not forced to be as efficient as enterprises that have to contend with competition. Second, some classes of customer may pay rates that are lower than the real costs of the services they receive, while other classes bear the difference; there is evidence that such cross-subsidization is part of the design of telephone regulation in Canada, eg, long distance versus local exchanges. Third, it is frequently argued that consumer interests are not well represented before utility regulators and that they are insufficiently taken into account in the regulators' decisions. Fourth, technological change provides opportunities either to substitute the discipline of the competitive market for the regulation of utilities or to make greater use of competition in some degree to ensure that such firms are as efficient as possible and are responsive to changing economic conditions, yet regulators are reluctant to make greater use of competition. Fifth, utility regulators are accused of devoting too much time to establishing the allowed rate of return rather than to determining whether the utility's actual production costs are the lowest attainable (which involves the difficult task of judging whether the utility has adopted the most appropriate new technology). Sixth, in establishing the prices that utilities may charge, regulators usually focus on historical average cost of "embedded capital" (ie, many hydro dams were built 30 years ago) rather than on the current level of incremental costs. *See also* ELECTRIC UTILITIES.   J.T. BERNARD

Utrecht, Treaty of, an agreement between Britain and France concluded 11 Apr 1713 at Utrecht in the Netherlands as part of the series of treaties ending the WAR OF THE SPANISH SUCCESSION. The treaty recognized Queen Anne as the legitimate sovereign of England and officially ended French support for the claims of the Jacobite party to the British throne. Territorially, it resulted in major concessions by France in N America. France agreed to restore the entire drainage basin of Hudson Bay to Britain and to compensate the Hudson's Bay Co for losses suffered during the war. In addition, France agreed to cede all claims to Newfoundland and to evacuate its base there at Plaisance (Placentia), although French fishermen retained certain rights on the Newfoundland coasts (*see* FRENCH SHORE). Moreover, ACADIA, whose capital of Port-Royal (Annapolis Royal) had been captured by a New England expedition in 1710, was to pass to Britain, although France continued in possession of a part of the territory (modern New Brunswick) because of differences of interpretation in the size of the territory. Lastly, France retained Cape Breton I, where it began to construct the fortress of LOUISBOURG and Île Saint-Jean (Prince Edward Island).

STUART R.J. SUTHERLAND

Uxbridge, Ont, Township, pop 11 895 (1986c), 11 210 (1981c), is located 68 km NE of Toronto on Hwy 47. Its first settler in 1804 was S.S. Wilmot, but most date settlement from 1806 with the arrival of Dr Christopher Beswick. Both Quakers, they were soon joined by Scots, Germans and Pennsylvania Dutch. Incorporated as a town in 1885, its principal economic activity in the 19th century was as a service centre for local agriculture. The municipality was reputedly one of the first in Ontario to own its own waterworks. The town of Uxbridge was amalgamated in 1974 with the townships of Scott and Uxbridge to form a new township in the Regional Municipality of Durham. Residents of note include local manufacturer Joseph Gould, an ally of William Lyon MACKENZIE, who named the settlement after Uxbridge, Eng. Lucy Maud MONTGOMERY, author of the "Anne" series, wrote more than half her published works while residing in Leaskdale, a hamlet just N of the town.   GERALD STORTZ

VE-Day Riots, 7-8 May 1945 in Halifax and Dartmouth, NS, began as a poorly co-ordinated celebration of the WORLD WAR II Victory in Europe. This rapidly declined into a rampage by several thousand servicemen (predominantly naval), merchant seamen and civilians, who drank, smashed and looted their way through downtown Halifax. Dartmouth suffered on a smaller scale. Although a subsequent federal inquiry expediently blamed lax naval authority, the true causes lay in bureaucratic confusion, insufficient policing and antipathy between the military and civilians, fueled by the presence of 25 000 servicemen who had strained Halifax wartime resources to the limit.   LOIS KERNAGHAN

Reading: S.R. Redman, *Open Gangway: The (Real) Story of the Halifax Navy Riot* (1981).

Vachon, Joseph Pierre Romeo, pilot, airline executive (b at Ste-Marie-de-la-Beauce, Qué 29 June 1898; d at Ottawa 17 Dec 1954). After service in the RCNVR during WWI, Vachon joined Laurentide Air Service in 1921 and in 1924-25 performed an aerial survey of Québec's North Shore. After flying with the Ontario Provincial Air Service (1925-27), he was hired by Canadian Airways to open an airmail route along the North Shore, work for which he was awarded the MCKEE TROPHY in 1937. In 1938 he joined TRANS-CANADA AIRLINES as deputy manager of the eastern division, and he was named a member of the federal Air Transport Commission on its creation in 1944. In 1960 a park named for him was laid out on the site of Québec City's first airfield, and in 1968 the Vachon Award was created to honour outstanding contributions to aeronautical engineering in Canada.   STANLEY GORDON

Vadeboncoeur, Pierre, essayist (b at Strathmore, near Montréal, 1920). A man of thought and action who became a full-time writer fairly late in life, Vadeboncoeur has in the last 20 years contributed several major works to the literature of ideas. After studying law and economics, he worked in business, freelance journalism and translation. During the 1949 ASBESTOS STRIKE he allied himself with Jean MARCHAND, P.E. TRUDEAU and Gérard PELLETIER and, especially, with the workers. He became an employee of the Catholic trade union association which in 1960 became the Confédération des syndicats nationaux (*see* CONFEDERATION OF NATIONAL TRADE UNIONS).

A contributor to magazines CITÉ LIBRE, LIBERTÉ, *Socialisme* and PARTI PRIS, Vadeboncoeur's first important article was "La Ligne du risque," about Paul-Émile BORDUAS and the creative artist as a prophet of liberty. The essay gave both title and tone to a somewhat disparate collection published in 1963. The tone of the collection *Lettres et colères* (1969) echoed that of the great French Catholic pamphleteers. He also brought together polemical articles about Québec nationalism, *Un Génocide en douce* (1976) and *Chaque jour, l'indépendance* (1978). *Indépendances* (1972), however, is not a political thesis but a cultural essay about youth and youth movements after Marcuse and the events of May 1968 in Paris. *Les Deux Royaumes* (1978) explores the problem inherent in any system, attacks reason for its authoritarianism, and defends intuition, meditation and spirituality. Other books by Vadeboncoeur are *L'Autorité du peuple* (1965), *Un Amour libre* (1970), *La* DERNIÈRE HEURE ET LA PREMIÈRE (1973), *Trois Essais sur l'insignifiance* (1983), *L'Absence* (1985), a personal essay dealing with love, art and literature, and *Essais inactuels* (1987).
                LAURENT MAILHOT

Vaillancourt, Armand J.R., sculptor (b at Black Lake, Qué 4 Sept 1932). He studied at the École des beaux-arts in Montréal. An inventor of

new techniques, he uses modern materials such as welded metal. He sees himself as a sculptor and social activist, committed to the battle to free Québec's political prisoners. The symbolic figurative elements in some of his work stems from this conviction: a hand outstretched to the sky is a sign of despair, an expression of social injustice. The intensity of his symbolism lies in the interaction of the formal tensions of his works and is reinforced by their gigantic form. In wood or bronze, the play between his triangular, tubular or cubic geometric forms reflects strength and compression, mass and dynamism. Vaillancourt has produced many sculptures for particular settings, including *Je me souviens*, a fountain sculpture (1969-71); Embarcadero Plaza, San Francisco; and *Justice!* (1983), Palais de Justice de Québec, Québec. More recently he has progressed towards a smaller scale in an effort to harmonize sculpture with nature.
                LOUISE BEAUDRY

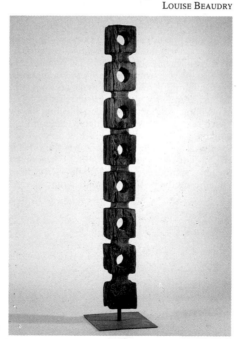

Burntwood, wood sculpture by A.J.R. Vaillancourt, 236.2 cm high (*courtesy National Gallery of Canada*).

Val-d'Or, Qué, Town, pop 22 252 (1986c), 21 371 (1981c), (greater Val-d'Or c35 000), inc 1968, is located 95 km SE of Rouyn-Noranda in northwestern Québec's Abitibi region, near the source of the Rivière Harricana, one of the major rivers flowing N to James Bay. The name is linked to the gold rush, second in scale only to the Klondike, which took the area by storm in the

mid-1930s. The town was originally made up of 2 separate municipalities. The first, Bourlamaque, founded in 1934 by the Lamaque Mining Co, was a COMPANY TOWN for many years. The other, Val-d'Or, was incorporated as a village in 1935 and a town 2 years later, and began as a bustling goldrush town. For many years, the twin centres were known as Val-d'Or-Bourlamaque. A third town, Lac Lemoyne, was formed in 1958. In 1968 the 3 towns amalgamated under the name Val-d'Or; it was now the largest municipality in the Abitibi-Témiscamingue region.

Val-d'Or prospered from the dozens of gold mines discovered in the vicinity. Despite several mine closures, its economy has been based largely on 2 of the richest gold-bearing mines in Québec, (Sigma and Lamaque), located within the town's limits. Although Lamaque has been temporarily closed, numerous other mines are operating in the vicinity which have been in production for almost 50 years. The lumber business is also important to the economy of Val-d'Or; the forests of the Abitibi region provide 65% of the lumber produced in Québec. An industrial park, created in 1972, provides some 3000 jobs in numerous industries. Val-d'Or is also a service centre, with the third-busiest airport in Québec. The first 65 log cabins built beside the Lamaque mine in 1934 are still in their original state, and in 1978 this section of the town was designated a historic site. The Bourlamaque Miners' Village commemorates the gold rush that brough Val-d'Or into existence. The town has a music conservatory, a large hospital and offers university services.
                BENOÎT-BEAUDRY GOURD

Valdes Island is one of a range of islands on the outer edge of the GULF ISLANDS in the Str of GEORGIA, off the SE coast of Vancouver I, BC. The long, narrow island is heavily wooded and has a few farms. An Indian reserve occupies a third of it and there are several native burial grounds. In the 1920s it provided a refuge for the cult leader BROTHER TWELVE, who ruled a colony there and is rumoured to have left behind buried gold when he fled. The name refers to a Spanish mariner who explored the area in the 1790s.   DANIEL FRANCIS

Valente Case, The A judge of the Provincial Court of Ontario declared that he had no jurisdiction to hear a case under the Highway Traffic Act of Ontario because he did not preside over an independent court in the sense of s11(d) of the CANADIAN CHARTER OF RIGHTS AND FREEDOMS. In his view, the structures and administration of the court are such that there is not a sufficiently clear separation between the executive and the judiciary. On 19 Sept 1985, the Supreme Court ruled that the judge did enjoy judicial independence. Impartiality is a state of mind. Independence is a question of status vis-à-vis the executive. The test is the following: Can the court reasonably be seen as independent? There are 3 essential conditions for an independent judiciary in the sense of s11(d) of the Charter: judges have the security of tenure; judges enjoy financial security; and the court has institutional independence in administrative matters which directly affect the functioning of the judge. The Supreme Court declared that these 3 conditions were satisfied.
                GÉRALD-A. BEAUDOIN

Vallerand, Jean, composer, critic, administrator, teacher, violinist (b at Montréal 24 Dec 1915). His career as a critic began on *Le Canada* in 1941, followed by *Montréal-Matin*, *Le* DEVOIR, *Le Nouveau Journal* and *La* PRESSE. During the 1940s and 1950s, he composed incidental music for more than 50 radio dramas on the CBC, where he later became head of musical broadcasts. His opera *Le Magicien* was performed over 100 times across the country during the JEUNESSES MUSICALES DU CANADA 1961-62 tour. Secretary general and teacher at the Conservatoire de musique de Montréal 1942-63, Vallerand also taught at U de M 1950-66. Other positions he has held include cultural attaché for Québec in Paris, director of the Service des arts d'interprétation of the Québec Ministère des affaires culturelles and director of the Conservatoire de musique et d'art dramatique du Québec. HÉLÈNE PLOUFFE

Valleyfield, Qué, City (official name: Salaberry-de-Valleyfield), pop 27 942 (1986c), 29 574 (1981c), inc 1904, is located on the S shore of the ST LAWRENCE R, at the NE extremity of Lac St-François. The townsite was part of the seigneurial land granted to Charles de BEAUHARNOIS, governor of New France from 1726 to 1747. Construction of the Beauharnois Canal (1842-54) attracted many immigrants to the town. A sawmill and a large paper mill were established in the 1850s. A cotton mill (the future Montreal Cotton Co) opened 1875 and dominated the activity and growth of this small industrial town until WWII.

Valleyfield draws its labour force from the local population and its history is marked by often violent labour disputes (*see* COMPANY TOWNS). Originally (1874), it was called Salaberry, in honour of Charles d'Irumberry de SALABERRY. Through popular usage, the name "Valleyfield" was added by the economically elite anglophone minority (in memory, it is said, of a Scottish paper mill). Served by railway since 1885, Valleyfield became an episcopal seat in 1892. An important commercial and industrial centre, its activities today are diversified: ocean shipping, hydroelectric production, rubber manufacturing, zinc refining, chemical products, textiles and foodstuffs. Each summer it hosts N America's biggest speedboat regatta. SYLVIE TASCHEREAU

Vallières, Pierre, writer (b at Montréal 22 Feb 1938). Vallières was a journalist in Montréal before joining the FRONT DE LIBÉRATION DU QUÉBEC (FLQ) in 1965. Convinced that Québec could survive only as an independent, socialist nation, and impressed by the example of Latin American revolutionaries, he pressed the FLQ to use violence to achieve their ends. A series of bomb blasts in Montréal resulted, and when his associates were arrested Vallières fled to New York, where he was arrested in 1966 and imprisoned. Deported to Canada in 1967, he spent 4 years in jail, writing his memoir, *Nègres blancs d'Amérique* (1968, tr *White Niggers of America*, 1971), and reassessing his convictions. In 1971 he renounced violence and endorsed the PARTI QUÉBÉCOIS as the best means to independence. In 1980 he repudiated them as well, publishing his belief that Québec was doomed to assimilation. In 1984, after experiencing a revelation, he joined a Franciscan-influenced religious order. STANLEY GORDON

Van den Bergh, Sidney, astronomer, cosmologist (b at Wassenaar, Netherlands 20 May 1929). After completing studies at Princeton (1950), Ohio State U (1952) and U of Göttingen (1956), Van den Bergh assumed a faculty position at Ohio (1956-58) before moving to Toronto (1958). At the David Dunlap Observatory, U of T, he played a key role in expanding the facilities, developing computer techniques, multicolour photometry and other innovations. Although he has contributed to lunar studies and studies of other aspects of our own solar system, his real forte is with extragalactic studies on which he has published original findings and major reviews on nebulae, star clusters, variable stars, supernovae and recently a revision to the perceived age of the universe (*see* COSMOLOGY). In 1977 he was appointed director of the Dominion Astrophysical Observa-

tory, Victoria, taking office in 1978. Since 1982 he has also served as president and chairman of the board of the Canada-France-Hawaii Telescope Corp in Hawaii. In Mar 1986 he and fellow astronomer C.J. Pritchet obtained remarkable images of some of the jets of Halley's Comet. A COMET he discovered in 1974 bears his name.
MARTIN K. MCNICHOLL

van Ginkel, H.P. Daniel, "Sandy" (b at Amsterdam, Netherlands 10 Feb 1920) and **van Ginkel, Blanche,** née Lemco (b at London, England 14 Dec 1923), architects and planners van Ginkel Associates, Toronto. The firm is distinguished for the first rehabilitation plan for Old Montréal, for urban design and transportation planning for such cities as New York, Montréal and Calgary, and for numerous studies for development in the Canadian Arctic. Well established as an architect in Europe, Sandy van Ginkel immigrated to Canada in 1957 and established a practice with his wife in Montréal; he has served as chief planner for Stockholm and for EXPO 67 in Montréal and has taught at several universities. Blanche van Ginkel, educated at McGill and Harvard, worked at the Atelier Le Corbusier, Paris (1948) and was dean of architecture at U of T (1977-82). ANDREA KRISTOF

Van Horne, Sir William Cornelius, railway official (b at Chelsea, Ill 3 Feb 1843; d at Montréal 11 Sept 1915). Van Horne's formal education ended at age 14, when he began his railway career as a telegrapher with the Illinois Central Railroad in 1857. He worked for several American railways and by 1880 he was general superintendent of the Milwaukee Road. Van Horne was appointed general manager of the CANADIAN PACIFIC RAILWAY on 1 Jan 1882, and he used his excellent managerial skills to improve the organization of construction on the prairie section, which was complete from Winnipeg to Calgary by Aug 1883. Van Horne's drive and determination were responsible for the rapid completion of the main line between Montréal and Port Moody (*see* RAILWAY HISTORY).

Van Horne succeeded George STEPHEN as president of the CPR in 1888. He regarded the Canadian Pacific as a transportation and communications system. At his insistence, the company de-

---

Sir William Van Horne, brilliant railway manager whose drive and determination were largely responsible for the rapid completion of the CPR (*courtesy National Archives of Canada/C-8549*).

veloped a telegraph service and entered the express business. He launched the famous Empress line of Pacific steamships in 1891 – fast, luxurious vessels which ran between Vancouver and Hong Kong, carried mail for the British government and increased tourist and freight traffic between Canada and the Orient. Van Horne was also the founder of CP Hotels; as an amateur architect he helped plan the Banff Springs and Château Frontenac hotels. He negotiated the famous CROW'S NEST PASS AGREEMENT, which substantially reduced freight rates on Prairie grain and flour. After his retirement from the presidency in 1899, he promoted the building of a railway in Cuba. Van Horne was a complex personality: a brilliant railway manager, a gourmet and a man with tremendous intellectual curiosity. He was awarded a knighthood in 1894. JOHN A. EAGLE

Reading: P. Berton, *The Last Spike* (1971); W. Vaughan, *The Life and Work of Sir William Van Horne* (1920).

Van Steenburgh, William Elgin, entomologist, scientific administrator (b at Havelock, Ont 24 Dec 1899; d at Ottawa 14 Apr 1974). He grew up in the US, working in the W Virginia mining industry as a young man. With an MA (1927) and a PhD (1931) from U of T, Van Steenburgh worked on biological control of fruit pests for the Canada Dept of Agriculture 1927-39. An active member of the militia, he became director of artillery for Canada in 1943 and later developed the armaments establishment at Valcartier. Between 1947 and 1956, he played an important part in the expansion of Agriculture Canada's research laboratories. As director general of scientific services and deputy minister of mines and technical surveys 1956-66, he promoted the Polar Continental Shelf Project, furthered the Canadian Upper Mantle Project, reorganized the Canadian Committee on Oceanography and helped to establish the BEDFORD INSTITUTE OF OCEANOGRAPHY.
ERIC L. MILLS

Vancouver, the largest city in British Columbia and third largest in Canada, lies on a peninsula in the SW corner of the province's mainland. The surrounding waterways – Burrard Inlet, the Strait of GEORGIA and the FRASER R respectively – provide an excellent, sheltered deep-sea port, convenient access to the Pacific Ocean, and an easy route to the rich agricultural lands of the Fraser Valley and the interior.

Settlement Archaeological evidence indicates that coastal Indians settled at Locarno Beach by 500 BC and at Marpole about 400 BC. The English sailor Capt George VANCOUVER and the Spaniards Galiano and Valdes met off Point Grey in 1792 but Europeans paid little attention to the area until the 1860s when 3 Englishmen pre-empted land and built an unsuccessful brickyard. In the 1870s several entrepreneurs established logging camps, sawmills and 3 small settlements on the shores of Burrard Inlet.

Development, Economy and Transportation Vancouver began when CPR VP, William VAN HORNE, announced that the company would extend its line 20 km westward from the statutory terminus, Port Moody, in order to take advantage of a better harbour and terminal site. The provincial government gave the CPR over 2500 ha of crown land at the new terminus and private owners donated land. On 6 Apr 1886 the provincial legislature incorporated the city of Vancouver, a name that Van Horne had suggested in honour of the English explorer. Ratepayers elected M.A. MacLean, a real-estate dealer, as the first mayor. Then, on June 13, a clearing fire blew out of control, claimed at least 11 lives, destroyed ramshackle buildings and drew invaluable publicity when residents rebuilt immediately. The CPR, the largest single landowner, recognizing the value of

Population: 431 147 (1986c), 413 952 (1981cA);
1 380 729 (1986 CMA), 1 268 183
(1981 CMA)

Rate of Increase (1981-86): (City) 4.2%; (CMA) 8.9%

Rank in Canada: Third (by CMA)

Date of Incorporation: 1886

Land Area: (City) 112.94 km²; (CMA) 2786.26 km²

Elevation: 87 m

Climate: Average daily temp, July 16.9°C, Jan 2.9°C;
Yearly precip, rain 1203.0 mm, snow 54.7 mm;
Hours of sunshine 1872.2 per year

orderly growth, did not "boom" its land. Private real-estate developers, eg, David Oppenheimer (mayor, 1888-91) advertised the city and, through cash bonuses and tax concessions, attracted industries such as BC Sugar Refinery.

The continent-wide depression of the mid-1890s temporarily checked growth, but during the 1897-98 KLONDIKE GOLD RUSH excitement, prosperity returned to Vancouver. By the turn of the century it had displaced Victoria, the provincial capital, as the leading commercial centre on Canada's West Coast. Transpacific ships, including the Canadian Pacific's Empress liners, called regularly; coastal steamship companies, including CP Navigation and Union Steamships, made Vancouver their headquarters; and eastern businesses established their Pacific coast branches in Vancouver. The prewar economic boom expanded markets for such BC products as fish, minerals and lumber. Most lumber was sold on the Prairies. Nevertheless, Vancouver wholesalers complained that the lack of direct rail connections and discriminatory freight rates put them at a disadvantage relative to Calgary and Winnipeg in securing the trade of BC's interior. In response, the provincial government offered aid to new railways, including the Pacific Great Eastern.

The beginning of worldwide economic depression in 1913 and of war in 1914 severely reduced trade, retarded railway development and, coupled with declining resources, ended much of the mining boom in the Kootenay and Boundary districts. Nevertheless the Vancouver Stock Exchange (1907) survived and remains active in financing BC and Alberta developments, especially of the more speculative kind. During the 1920s growth resumed and Vancouver replaced Winnipeg as the leading city in western Canada. Cheap ocean transport through the Panama Canal opened new markets for BC lumber on the American E coast and made Europe more accessible. The province's successful campaign for freight-rate reduction enabled Vancouver to become a grain-exporting port. The port itself expanded greatly and came under the jurisdiction of a federal agency, the National Harbours Board, in 1936. The export grain trade held up remarkably well during the Great Depression of the 1930s, but the city suffered extensive unemployment, especially since the unemployed of western Canada regarded Vancouver, with its mild climate, as a "mecca." Unrest among the unemployed caused several incidents, including the reading of the Riot Act by Mayor G.G. MCGEER in 1935 (*see* ON TO OTTAWA TREK). The outbreak of WWII and the development of war industries, particularly shipbuilding, ended unemployment but sharply reduced the grain trade. Trade grew once shipping became available again after the war, especially after Canada began selling large quantities of wheat to China in 1961. By 1963 Vancouver ranked first among Canadian ports in tonnage. Demand around the Pacific Rim for other western Canadian products, notably lumber, potash and coal, has led to the construction of specialized port facilities and the extension of the port as far E as Port Moody and S to the Roberts Bank coal

Canada Place, one of the most dramatic new buildings in Vancouver, BC, and the adjacent Pan Pacific Hotel (*photo by Al Harvey/Masterfile*).

terminal (1970). Because of the importance of the Pacific Rim, CP Air (now Canadian Airlines International; *see* PACIFIC WESTERN AIRLINES) had established its headquarters in the city in 1949 and, along with other international and domestic carriers, uses the Vancouver International Airport, which the federal government expanded significantly after buying it from the city in 1961. Vancouver also expanded its role as the head office centre for such provincial corporations as BC Forest Products, Cominco and MACMILLAN BLOEDEL; a variety of smaller firms; the major provincial labour unions; and the regional offices for national enterprises such as the chartered banks. The BANK OF BRITISH COLUMBIA (chartered 1966) has its head office there. Vancouver was in the spotlight in 1986 when it hosted Expo 86, an international exposition devoted to transportation. The show was opened by the Prince and Princess of Wales, and ran from May 2 to Oct 13. It had over 20 million visitors.

VANCOUVER
Employment by Industry, 1986

% of total workers

Bar chart showing percentage of total workers by industry:
- Primary Industries: ~1%
- Manufacturing: ~12%
- Construction: ~5%
- Transportation, Communication and Other Utilities: ~10%
- Retail and Wholesale: ~20%
- Finance, Insurance and Real Estate: ~8%
- Services: ~37%
- Public Administration: ~6%

Total does not add to 100% because some estimates are not available and some workers are unclassified

Source: Household Surveys Div, Statistics Canada

Cityscape The backdrop of mountains, the proximity of the sea and the presence within the city limits of such wilderness areas as Stanley Park long lulled Vancouver residents into a feeling that none of their doings could seriously impair the city's natural beauty. The original surveyors, many of them CPR employees, showed little imagination as they generally laid out streets according to a grid pattern that made few allowances for such natural features as steep slopes. Apart from establishing fire limits and attempting to keep noisome industries on the outskirts, the city made few efforts to direct land use until the late 1920s when it commissioned the American firm, Harland Bartholomew and Associates, to draw up a town plan. The city adopted some of its suggestions, such as a comprehensive zoning regulation, but could not really enforce these rules until after WWII. Nevertheless, clear land-use patterns emerged. More affluent residents, for example, have always tended to live W of Cambie Street where developers subdivided land into large lots; the less affluent lived to the E where lots had sometimes as little as 7.5 m frontages.

Since the 1960s the city's older core has undergone a considerable transformation. City planners studied land-use proposals; civic politicians debated and redesigned some of them; and private developers financed much of the new building. Downtown, a forest of 20- to 40-storey-high office and hotel towers, including the Bentall, Royal, Pacific and Vancouver centres, have replaced the 2- and 3-storey retail blocks of pre-WWI vintage. Architecturally, among the most interesting newer buildings are the Provincial Court House, the Robson Square Conference Centre, Canada Place and VANCOUVER ART GALLERY. As a landmark, Canada Place includes the 500-room Pan Pacific Hotel (1983-86), built for Expo 86 and now a trade facility and cruise ship terminal. Cutting across much of the city until it goes underground downtown is the elevated Skytrain (1986) which links the city with Burnaby and New Westminster and will extend to Surrey.

A dramatic indication of the city's post-industrial status is False Creek, off English Bay. From the city's earliest days this area, with its easy access to trackage and water transport, was the site of rail yards, sawmills, machine shops and related industries. Indeed, Vancouver was unique among N American cities of comparable size for the importance of first-stage resource processing in its economy. By the 1950s, changing technology in the lumber industry and the obsolescence of old plants turned False Cr into a decaying industrial centre. After much study and controversy, the city decided to develop False Cr town houses and apartments in 1976. Nearby Granville I – created as an industrial site in 1915 when the eastern part of False Cr was filled to provide land for the terminus and yards of the Canadian Northern Ry

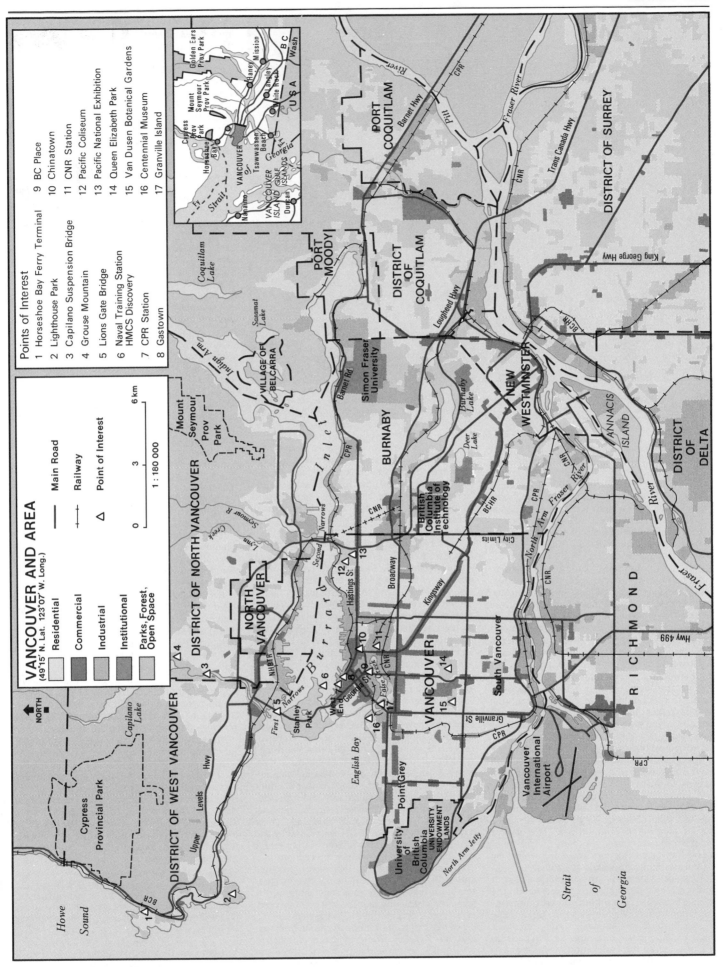

VANCOUVER AND AREA
(49°15' N. Lat. 123°07' W. Long.)

Residential
Commercial
Industrial
Institutional
Parks, Forest, Open Space

Main Road
Railway
Point of Interest

0   3   6 km

1 : 180 000

NORTH

Points of Interest

1 Horseshoe Bay Ferry Terminal
2 Lighthouse Park
3 Capilano Suspension Bridge
4 Grouse Mountain
5 Lions Gate Bridge
6 Naval Training Station HMCS Discovery
7 CPR Station
8 Gastown
9 BC Place
10 Chinatown
11 CNR Station
12 Pacific Coliseum
13 Pacific National Exhibition
14 Queen Elizabeth Park
15 Van Dusen Botanical Gardens
16 Centennial Museum
17 Granville Island

DISTRICT OF WEST VANCOUVER

DISTRICT OF NORTH VANCOUVER

NORTH VANCOUVER

Cypress Provincial Park

Howe Sound

Capilano Lake

Upper Levels Hwy

Mount Seymour Prov Park

Coquitlam Lake

Sasamat Lake

Indian Arm

VILLAGE OF BELCARRA

PORT MOODY

PORT COQUITLAM

DISTRICT OF COQUITLAM

Barnet Hwy

Lougheed Hwy

Simon Fraser University

BURNABY

Burnaby Lake

Deer Lake

NEW WESTMINSTER

DISTRICT OF SURREY

King George Hwy

Trans Canada Hwy

Fraser River

Pitt River

CPR

CNR

BCHR

ANNACIS ISLAND

DISTRICT OF DELTA

British Columbia Institute of Technology

VANCOUVER

Kingsway

Broadway

Hastings St

Second Narrows

First Narrows

Stanley Park

Burrard Inlet

English Bay

West End

False Creek

Point Grey

University of British Columbia

UNIVERSITY ENDOWMENT LANDS

South Vancouver

Granville St

Vancouver International Airport

North Arm Jetty

North Arm Fraser River

RICHMOND

Hwy 499

Fraser River

Strait of Georgia

Lynn Creek

Seymour R

Mount Seymour Prov Park

NHBTR

City Limits

CPR

CNR

BCHR

Georgia St

(inset map)

Golden Ears Prov Park

Mount Seymour Prov Park

Cypress Prov Park

Horseshoe Bay

Haney   Mission

Langley

White Rock

Tsawwassen Beach

Georgia Strait

VANCOUVER ISLAND

GULF ISLANDS

Nanaimo

Duncan

B C

U S A

Wash

Fraser River

View of Vancouver from the south (*courtesy Colour Library Books*).

(now CN) and the Great Northern Ry (now Burlington Northern) – has become home to a public market, art school, theatres and restaurants. On the N side of the creek, on land formerly occupied by the CPR yards, the provincial government opened a 60 000-seat sports stadium in 1983, the first stage in the BC Place development, planned to include stores, office towers, recreational space and up to 19 000 residential units; it was also the site of EXPO 86.

Whereas the downtown and False Cr are being almost completely redeveloped, the city's oldest residential neighbourhood, east-end Strathcona, has been largely rehabilitated. Traditionally a working-class neighbourhood, it is home to many ethnic groups, of whom the most important are the CHINESE. In the late 1950s the city began demolishing some of the poorest dwellings and replacing them with public-housing projects. After a successful protest against a proposed freeway, local residents persuaded the senior governments to provide funds to rehabilitate existing facilities rather than undertaking further renewal projects. In the West End, private developers, encouraged by new zoning regulations, began in the 1960s to build high-rise apartment blocks in place of the apartment and rooming houses that had been carved out of the large homes of the city's early well-to-do residents. By 1971 the West End was noted for the density of its population. Paradoxically, Vancouver had once prided itself as a city of owner-occupied, single-family detached homes. Most homes (and this is still true of most neighbourhoods outside the West End) were of wood-frame construction, often influenced by California architectural style (*see* HOUSE).

Population Vancouver's most significant growth spurts occurred during its first 5 years and in the decade before WWI, resulting primarily from immigration from the British Isles and Ontario. The expansion of the 1920s, which saw Vancouver attain its status as the third-largest city in Canada, is explained by the annexation of the adjacent bedroom municipalities of Point Grey and S Van-

couver in 1929, natural increase, renewed immigration from Britain and the beginning of significant migration from the Prairies. After a brief wartime and postwar spurt, the rate of population growth tapered off. The 1976 census recorded an absolute decline in the city proper, while the population of Greater Vancouver passed the one million mark for the first time. High real-estate values in the city led young families to live in suburban municipalities, especially BURNABY, COQUITLAM, DELTA, North Vancouver City and Dist, RICHMOND and SURREY.

From 1901 (the first year for which statistics are available) to 1951, people of British ethnic origin – many of them Canadian born – formed three-quarters of the population and dominated the elite. After WWII new immigrants made Vancouver more cosmopolitan. In 1979 the school board reported that nearly 40% of the children in elementary school did not speak English as a first language. Pupils of Chinese, Italian and East Indian background were most numerous. Until after WWII, the largest and least accepted ethnic group was the Asians, mainly Chinese and JAPANESE. An anti-Chinese riot in 1887, an anti-Asian riot in 1907, the tension surrounding the KOMAGATA MARU incident of 1914, and the 1942 decision of the federal government to evacuate all Japanese, including about 8600 city residents, from the coast demonstrates the hostility that Vancouver residents, like other British Columbians, felt towards Asians. With the postwar easing of immigration barriers, an increasing number of ethnic Chinese have come to Vancouver. Although Chinatown flourishes, Chinese reside throughout the city and participate fully in its life. Those Japanese who returned to the coast have blended into the city. Immigrants of South Asian ethnic origin have experienced a mixed reception.

Government and Politics Vancouver is unique among BC municipalities in having its own charter, but it remains very much a creature of the provincial legislature, which must approve every charter amendment. Until 1935 the city was governed by a mayor and aldermen chosen from various wards. When the province abolished the ward system, only the aldermen seriously objected. Taking advantage of the at-large system, the

CO-OPERATIVE COMMONWEALTH FEDERATION in 1936 ran a slate of aldermanic candidates and elected 3. The existence of party politics at city hall was confirmed in 1937 with the formation of the Non-Partisan Association (NPA), a loose amalgam of Conservatives and Liberals. The NPA has been dominant in civic politics although it was challenged in 1972 by The Electors Action Movement (TEAM) and recently by several left-wing groups, of which the most important is the Committee of Progressive Electors (COPE). In 1986, however, a revived NPA won 23 of the 27 elected city offices.

Vancouver's first experience with METROPOLITAN GOVERNMENT occurred in 1913 with the formation of the Vancouver and Dist Joint Sewerage and Drainage Board. Metropolitan agencies concerned with water, public health and regional planning appeared later. The growth of suburban municipalities encouraged the provincial government to create an elected body, the Greater Vancouver Regional Dist (1967), which has taken over most functions of the earlier agencies and added such responsibilities as capital finance, building regulations, housing and air-pollution control.

Cultural Life Vancouver has long enjoyed a variety of cultural activities. The Art, Historical and Scientific Assn (one of the first groups organized) established a museum 1894. In honour of the 1958 BC centennial, the city built a new museum, a Maritime Museum and, with funds from lumberman H.R. MACMILLAN, a planetarium. As soon as the CPR opened an opera house in 1891, Vancouver became a regular stop for touring concert artists and theatrical companies. As well as supporting local amateur musical and dramatic groups, the city also has such professional bodies as the VANCOUVER SYMPHONY ORCHESTRA (until operations were suspended in the 1987-88 season), the Vancouver Opera Assn and the Playhouse Theatre Centre. The last was one of many professional theatrical companies that mushroomed in the 1960s and 1970s. All 3 used the Queen Elizabeth Theatre, a civic auditorium opened in 1959, but the symphony played in the restored Orpheum Theatre. Since Oct 1983 the Vancouver Art Gallery (est 1931) has been located at the Old Courthouse, a larger site than its previous home and redesigned by architect Arthur ERICKSON.

Institutions of higher learning have also stimulated the arts. The Vancouver area has 2 public universities, UNIVERSITY OF BRITISH COLUMBIA (fd 1908) and SIMON FRASER U (fd 1963); several regional colleges, including Vancouver Community College (1965); and the BC Institute of Technology (1964). Two daily newspapers, the SUN and the PROVINCE, a number of specialized newspapers and journals, more than 20 local and ethnic newspapers, a host of radio stations, 4 TV stations and easy access to American TV via cable provide information and entertainment.

The Vancouver area offers many opportunities for outdoor recreation, including skiing and year-round boating, golfing and diving. Within the city are 159 parks of which the largest and most important is Stanley Park. Amateur teams participate in most sports and the BRITISH COLUMBIA LIONS football team and the VANCOUVER CANUCKS hockey team play in major professional leagues. The Lions play their home games at BC Place; the Canucks use the Pacific Coliseum, located on the Pacific National Exhibition grounds. PATRICIA E. ROY

Reading: C. Davis, *The Vancouver Book* (1976); L.J. Evenden, ed, *Vancouver: Western Metropolis* (1978); H. Kalman, *Exploring Vancouver 2* (1978); R.A.J. McDonald and J. Burman, eds, *Vancouver's Past: Essays in Social History* (1986); Patricia E. Roy, *Vancouver: An Illustrated History* (1980).

Vancouver, George, naval officer, explorer (b at King's Lynn, Eng 22 June 1757; d at Petersham, London, Eng 12 May 1798). Vancouver was with James COOK on his expeditions to the South Seas (1772-75) and the NORTHWEST COAST (1776-80). In 1790 an expedition was planned to explore that coast. Preparations were delayed by news that the Spaniards had seized British property at NOOTKA SOUND but were resumed, under Vancouver's command, after a convention had been signed with Spain in Oct. Vancouver was charged with 2 missions: to receive back the properties alleged to have been seized at Nootka and to explore the coast from California to Cook Inlet, Alaska. He reached the coast in Apr 1792. In Aug he met the Spanish commissioner BODEGA Y QUADRA at Nootka; negotiations were friendly but futile, and the matter of the seized properties had to be referred to London and Madrid. The summers of 1792, 1793 and 1794 were spent exploring the coast, including the intricacies of Puget Sd and the whole of the mainland coast of BC. The intervening winters were spent in the Sandwich Is [Hawaii]. After his return to Eng in Sept 1795 he set about revising his journal, published in 1798 as *A Voyage of Discovery to the North Pacific Ocean and Round the World.* In it he claimed with justice that his survey, one of the greatest of its kind, had removed "every doubt" about the existence of a NORTHWEST PASSAGE to the Atlantic "within the limits of our researches."

W. KAYE LAMB

Vancouver, Mount, elev 4828 m, situated in the YT's St Elias Mts, rises SE of Mt LOGAN between 2 immense glacier systems, Hubbard and Seward. A large massif, it supports 4 summits and measures 24 km from NW to SE at its base. Its SE summit, 4792 m, is a boundary peak between Canada and Alaska, only 32 km from the sea. The highest (NW) peak was first climbed June 1949 by N. Odell, W. Hainsworth, R. McCarter and A. Bruce Robertson. The SE summit, the highest unclimbed summit left in Canada by 1967, was climbed by a joint US-Canadian team to commemorate the Alaskan and Canadian centennials. It was renamed Good Neighbour Peak.

GLEN BOLES

Vancouver Art Gallery, founded in 1931, has a collection of about 4000 paintings, sculptures, photographs, prints, drawings and objects, largely of contemporary Canadian art. One of the collection's strongest elements is the Emily CARR bequest, and a gallery is devoted to an ongoing display of her work. The original gallery was a small art deco building on West Georgia St. It housed a modest collection of British works purchased for the Vancouver Art Gallery by Sir Charles Holmes, and featured an exhibition schedule devoted largely to British art trends. In 1938 the gallery was occupied by unemployed men protesting government policy, but no paintings were damaged.

After the war, Vancouver's modernists, Lawren HARRIS among them, set the gallery on a new course. A renovation and expansion in 1950 gave the building the look of the international style, and in the 1960s the gallery became well known for its open and innovative programs under Doris Shadbolt and Tony Emery. In 1983 the gallery moved into larger quarters in the old courthouse which had been renovated by Arthur ERICKSON. Only recently has the gallery had an acquisitions budget, which is now one of the largest in Canada, and besides having an active exhibition program, the gallery also maintains a library, a slide library and education programs. Between 1976 and 1984, the gallery published *Vanguard*, a magazine of Canadian art criticism. The gallery also played a role in the early 1970s in establishing the Pacific Cinémathèque and Video Inn.

SCOTT WATSON AND W. HOLMES

Vancouver Canucks, HOCKEY team. The Vancouver Canucks had been members of the Western Hockey League since 1946. For a price of $6 million, they joined the NATIONAL HOCKEY LEAGUE on 22 May 1970. They played their first home game on 9 Oct 1970 in the 3-year-old, 15 564-seat Pacific Coliseum, and went on to accumulate 56 points for a sixth-place finish in the 7-team East Division under coach Hal Laycoe and general manager Bud Poile. In 1974 team ownership was transferred from the Medicor Corporation of Minneapolis to a group of Vancouver businessmen headed by Frank Griffiths. The Canucks best regular-season performance to date occurred in 1974-75, when they finished atop the Smythe Division with 86 points in 80 games. In 1982 they made a surprising advance through the playoffs but lost in 4 straight games to the New York Islanders in the STANLEY CUP final.   DEREK DRAGER

Vancouver International Festival was held for a few weeks each summer 1958 to 1968. Established and directed by Nicholas Goldschmidt, until 1962, the festival was unashamedly elitist, looking to European and American artists. Modelled on Edinburgh and Salzburg, concerts and opera predominated. The first performance was of *Don Giovanni*; Herbert von Karajan, Bruno Walter and Joan Sutherland appeared. Theatre included the Comédie Française and Lister SINCLAIR's *The World of the Wonderful Dark*. Achievements in 1960-61 included *Noye's Fludde* (Benjamin Britten) in Christchurch cathedral, 1200 in attendance at Glenn GOULD's all-Schoenberg program, and a $25 000 profit from a tattoo at Empire Stadium. Financial and artistic policies, however, were constantly criticized.

Four men had short periods as artistic director 1963-68: Dina Yannopoulos, William Crawford III, Hugh Pickett and Gordon Hilker. The festival now tried, in a fumbling, inconsistent way, to be more local, more popular and cheaper: "International" was dropped in 1965 and productions of *West Side Story, The Most Happy Fella* and *Oliver* succeeded. 1968 saw the Joffrey Ballet; the pre-Broadway *And Now, Noel Coward*; and a symphony concert drawing 8000 to the new Coliseum. Despite the successes, the deficit reached $322 000 and the festival was terminated.

MALCOLM PAGE

South Beach in Pacific Rim National Park, Vancouver I *(photo by Bill Brooks/Masterfile).*

Vancouver Island, BC, 31 284 km², the largest island on the W Coast of N America, is about 460 km long and 50-80 km wide and stretches parallel to the BC mainland. It is separated from the mainland by the GEORGIA, Queen Charlotte and Johnstone straits and from the US by JUAN DE FUCA STR. With the QUEEN CHARLOTTE IS, it forms part of a partially submerged chain of the Cordillera and is a continuation of the US coastal mountains. Its coastline is very rugged, especially on the W where there are several fjordlike inlets – the longest being Alberni Inlet and Muchalat Inlet – that cut into a heavily forested, mountainous interior, with mountains averaging 600-1000 m. Higher peaks include GOLDEN HINDE (2200 m), Elkhorn Mt (2194 m) and Mt Colonel Foster (2133 m). In contrast to this mountainous core are the coastal lowlands, which form an almost encircling belt. They are most pronounced in the N and E where the Nahwitti and Nanaimo lowlands form part of a coastal trough stretching from SE Alaska to the Puget Depression in Washington state. The Island has numerous freshwater lakes, the largest being Nimpkish, Cowichan, Buttle, Sproat, Great Central and Campbell. Its climate is damp but mild, with precipitation ranging from 3.8 m in the western flanks of the mountains to less than 0.8 m in the SE Nanaimo Lowland. Much of the precipitation returns to the Pacific through a series of rapid-flowing, deeply incised, relatively short rivers, such as the Nanaimo and Campbell. The Island is most heavily populated in the SE, where the city of VICTORIA is located.

Although the archaeological record is still incomplete, it is clear that Indians have occupied the Island for several thousand years. A tribal, village society evolved, with an economy based on fishing, collecting and hunting. The abundant marine and forest resources along the coasts supported a culture rich in oral tradition and artistic expression. Two main linguistic families, Salishan and Wakashan, developed and continue to exist. Traditionally, villages comprised stoutly constructed cedar longhouses and were usually situated in sheltered coves or a short distance upriver from the ocean. During the hunting season tribes migrated through well-defined territories. In the early 19th century the native population was about 15 000. Owing to disease, it declined to about 5600 in 1881, remained around 5000 until the 1950s, but increased to more than 7000 by the 1970s.

Spanish, Russian, French, British and American explorers and traders began penetrating the waters of the NE Pacific in the 18th century. Britain gradually ousted the others, however, through the activities of its trading companies, the Royal Navy's presence, and negotiation and threat in Europe. The voyage of James COOK and George VANCOUVER's circumnavigation and hydrographic survey of the Island 1792-94 provided the basis for increased British penetration. The diversity of PLACE-NAMES with which the Island and its surrounding islands and waters abound are a permanent record of this exploratory period. In 1843 the HBC sent James DOUGLAS to the Island to select a site for a fort, and a small settlement at the southern tip developed around Fort Victoria. The Treaty of Washington (1846; *see* OREGON TREATY) established the Island as British territory; it was made a British crown colony in 1849. It united with the mainland BC colony in 1866, and the united colony entered the Dominion of Canada as the province of BRITISH COLUMBIA in 1871.

The European population grew slowly until the 1860s, when the discovery of gold on the mainland and coal on the Island led to a significant increase. Some of those disappointed in the goldfields turned to farming and coal mining and joined a growing trickle of settlers carving out homesteads on the narrow eastern lowlands. Besides Victoria, early settlement centered on the Duncan area of the Cowichan R valley and the COURTENAY-Comox region, both attractive and fertile valleys. Although the forest was an obstacle to the pioneer farmer, its sheer quantity and high quality stimulated the growth of lumber mills at points accessible to tidewater, such as PORT ALBERNI (1861) and Chemainus (1862). The Esquimalt and Nanaimo Ry (1886) provided the basis for expanding the Island's lumber and mining industries. By 1900 the population had grown to around 51 000, with nearly 90% concentrated in the Victoria-NANAIMO region. After 1900 the pace of development increased rapidly as immigration continued and the mining and lumbering industries developed. Nanaimo expanded and new coal mines were opened at CUMBERLAND, LADYSMITH and Union Bay. Population growth slowed between 1921 and 1941, as little suitable land for agricultural development remained; the exhaustion of the best coal deposits left further development to the expansion of the forest industry. The potential for tourism was also becoming apparent as transportation facilities improved and as the attraction of the Island as a retirement area grew.

The postwar era saw a new surge of growth associated with the increased activity of the forest-products industry, with new or expanded mills at Port Alberni, Crofton, CAMPBELL RIVER and Gold River. The province also became more actively involved in developing and managing the economy, and Victoria, the capital, benefited from expanded government functions. Recent elements of growth have been highway and hydroelectric-power construction, modernization of the ferry system, expansion of military bases and the continued growth of tourism.

The majority of the Island's residents live in Greater Victoria, DUNCAN, Nanaimo, Port Alberni, Courtenay, Campbell River and numerous small towns and villages. Most urban settlements owe their origins and early growth to resource extraction or processing. Since about 1900, those centres possessing both accessibility, as ports or railway stations, and more than one resource

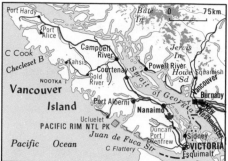

continued to grow, and gradually made the transition from single-enterprise company towns. Victoria's early lead was lost with the growth of Vancouver, which had the advantage of a rail connection to the east. Others stagnated or became ghost towns. Throughout the first half of the 20th century over 77% of the Island's population was of British origin. The CHINESE formed the largest ethnic minority, followed by Scandinavians, JAPANESE and NATIVE PEOPLE.

ALAN F.J. ARTIBISE

Reading: C.N. Forward, ed, *Vancouver Island: Land of Contrasts* (1979); M.A. Ormsby, *British Columbia: A History* (1958).

Vancouver Island Coal Strike began on 16 Sept 1912 when miners at Cumberland declared a "holiday" to protest the firing of Oscar Mottishaw. Canadian Collieries, recent purchaser of the Dunsmuir Mines, locked them out and hired Chinese and recruits from Britain and the US as strikebreakers. The issues were safety (gas explosions had killed hundreds) and union recognition. Other Island employers, Western Fuel and Pacific Coast Collieries, had followed the pattern set by Robert and James DUNSMUIR in vigorously resisting any union, especially those from the US. By spring 1913, 3500 miners from Nanaimo, Extension, S Wellington and Ladysmith were off work, the United Mine Workers of America providing leadership and strike pay. That summer, a fourth company, the Vancouver and Nanaimo Coal Co, settled with its employees, but not before rioting had broken out in all the coal towns. Peace was restored when the BC government sent in 1000 militiamen, but many strikers spent the second winter in jail. Withdrawal of strike pay in the summer of 1914 and the beginning of WWI ended the confrontation. By then the mines were running at almost pre-strike capacity using newly hired labour. After the war, while the rest of N America witnessed a dramatic expansion in the activity of organized labour, there was none whatsoever on Vancouver I. Union recognition did not come until 1938, 6 weeks after the largest mine on the Island had shut down forever.

LYNNE BOWEN

Vancouver Playhouse Theatre Co began its first season in 1963, and the next year began a tradition of commissioning original works. Five to 7 plays have been presented annually in a September-to-April season at the 647-seat Vancouver Playhouse, which adjoins the large Queen Elizabeth Theatre, and sometimes an additional 3 or 4 plays are staged elsewhere. George RYGA's *The Ecstasy of Rita Joe* (1967, publ 1970) was the Playhouse's greatest success. The artistic directors have been Michael Johnston (1963), Malcolm Black (1964-67), Joy Coghill (1967-69), David Gardner (1969-71), Paxton Whitehead (1971-73), Christopher Newton (1973-79), Roger Hodgman (1979-82), Walter Learning (1982-86), Guy Sprung (1987-88) and Larry Lillo (1988-). The company offers Canada's only 2-year conservatory acting school program. *See also* THEATRE, ENGLISH-LANGUAGE.

MALCOLM PAGE

Vancouver Symphony Orchestra began in 1930, when an earlier Vancouver orchestra was revived. During its inaugural season, the VSO gave 4 concerts, all under conductor Allard de Ridder, 1930-40. A series of guest conductors led the orchestra until Jacques Singer was appointed music director, 1947-52. Under Irwin Hoffman, 1952-64, a protégé of Serge Koussevitzky, the orchestra moved from its home in the Orpheum Theatre to the new Queen Elizabeth Theatre in 1960. Meredith Davies, 1964-70, revitalized and rejuvenated the orchestra, and Kazuyoshi Akiyama was music director from 1972 to 1985, when he was succeeded by Rudolph Barshai. The orchestra toured Japan in 1974, Canada in 1976 and the US in 1978. In 1977 it moved back to the renovated Orpheum Theatre. By 1984-85, with a season of some 43 weeks and nearly 190 concerts, the VSO was regarded as one of Canada's major orchestras. However, falling support, internal dissension and a debt totalling $1.7 million brought the orchestra to financial crisis and it suspended operations in Jan 1988.

BARBARA NOVAK

Vander Zalm, Wilhelmus Nicholaas Theodore Marie, "Bill," premier of BC, horticulturalist, businessman (b at Noordwykerhout, Holland 29 May 1934). In 1947 he moved to the Fraser Valley with his family. After completing high school he sold bulbs and in 1956 bought a nursery business. He invested in real estate and developed Fantasy Garden World, a theme park in Richmond, BC, before entering municipal politics. While serving as an alderman (1965-68) and as mayor (1969-75) in Surrey, Vander Zalm unsuccessfully sought provincial and federal office as a Liberal. In 1974 he joined the Social Credit Party, and in 1975 he was elected an MLA for Surrey. While serving successively as minister of human resources (1975-78), municipal affairs (1978-82) and education (1982-83), he was noted for his outspokenness; eg, he attacked ablebodied welfare recipients who refused "to pick up a shovel," described Cabinet colleagues as "gutless" for rejecting proposed land-use legislation, and complained about bilingual cereal boxes. After a temporary withdrawal from politics, Vander Zalm won the Social Credit leadership in July 1986 and succeeded William R. BENNETT as premier. Although the Opposition accused him of having no policies, the charismatic Vander Zalm led the Social Credit Party to an overwhelming victory in the election of 22 Oct 1986. He was a strong supporter of the federal FREE TRADE initiative and in 1988 vigorously opposed access to abortion in BC.

PATRICIA E. ROY

Vanderburg, Helen, synchronized swimmer (b at Calgary 12 Jan 1959). Vanderburg was the first Canadian to dominate international SYNCHRONIZED SWIMMING. A member of the national team from 1971 to 1979, she won 11 Canadian solo, duet and figure titles. Until 1978, Canadian entries in international competition had consistently come in second, behind the US, although Vanderburg and Michele Calkins won the duet in the 1977 Pan-Pacific Games. But in 1978, Vanderburg achieved a remarkable breakthrough, winning Canada's first world championship gold medals, in solo and duet. In 1979, Vanderburg demonstrated that she was the best synchronized swimmer in the world, completing an unprecedented sweep of all major championships: solo and duet in the Pan-American Games, solo in the Pan-Pacific Games, and solo and duet in the FINA Cup (in 1979, her duet partner was Kelly Kryczka). Vanderburg has received many honours: the Elaine Tanner Trophy (twice), 1979 Canadian woman athlete of the year, and induction into Canada's Sports Hall of Fame. Vanderburg retired from competition in 1979.

BARBARA SCHRODT

Vanderhaeghe, Guy Clarence, writer (b at Esterhazy, Sask 5 Apr 1951). A young, emerging writer of note, Vanderhaeghe already has a Gov Gen's Award to his credit, for his short-story collection *Man Descending* (1982). Vanderhaeghe studied education and history at the universities of Regina and Sask, respectively, and later worked as an archivist, researcher and high-school teacher in the 1970s. He then turned to writing as his full-time concentration and has since served as writer-in-residence at the Saskatoon Public Library (1983-84) and U of Ottawa (1985-86). Besides contributions to magazines and articles, Vanderhaeghe has produced *The Trouble with Heroes, and Other Stories* (1983) and *My Present Age* (1984), a dark comedy and successful first novel.   MARLENE ALT

Vanderpant, John, photographer (b Jan van der Pant at Alkmaar, Netherlands 11 Jan 1884; d at Vancouver 24 July 1939). A major influence on Canadian photography in the 1920s and 1930s, he established a distinctive style that emphasized light and form and generally shunned popular manipulative processes. After being a photojournalist for a Dutch magazine, he came to Canada in 1911. He opened a studio in Okotoks, Alta, and after WWI moved to BC, eventually settling in Vancouver, where he set up a commercial portrait studio. He began exhibiting in international salons, quickly achieving acclaim and winning awards around the world; his solo exhibitions toured the US, Great Britain and Europe. A fellow of the Royal Photographic Soc of Great Britain, he also wrote and lectured widely. His Robson Street gallery, opened in 1926 with Harold Mortimer-Lamb, was a centre for music, poetry and painting.   JOAN M. SCHWARTZ

Vanier, Georges-Philéas, governor general 1959-67 (b at Montréal 23 Apr 1888; d at Ottawa 5 Mar 1967). Educated at Loyola and Laval, he was called to the Québec Bar in 1911. He enlisted in 1915 and after winning the Military Cross and DSO he became a founding officer of the Royal 22e Regiment, of which he later became commanding officer (1926-28). After WWI he entered the diplomatic service and represented Canada at the League of Nations, in London, and at many international conferences. In 1939 he became Canadian minister to France, and in 1943 minister to all allied governments in exile in London. He returned to France in 1944 as ambassador and served there with great distinction until his retirement in 1953.

Maj-Gen Vanier was installed as governor general on 15 Sept 1959. His years in office were turbulent ones because of a difficult economic situation, a succession of minority governments and the rise of violence and SEPARATISM in Québec. But he won the affection and admiration of Canadians by his concern, manifested in his inspiring

Governor General Georges Vanier and Her Excellency Mrs Vanier during a sports event at Camp Fortune (*courtesy National Archives of Canada/C-75936*).

public addresses and wide travels across the country, for the poor and the humble, for youth and for the family. A tall, impressive man who moved with great dignity and composure, he was profoundly religious and brought a spiritual and moral dimension to his office. His wife Pauline (née Archer) won equal respect and contributed much to the success of his term.
                    JACQUES MONET, S.J.

Reading: R. Speaight, *Vanier: Soldier, Diplomat, and Governor General* (1970).

Vanier, Jean, spiritual leader, worker with the handicapped (b at Geneva, Switz 28 Sept 1928). The son of Georges VANIER, governor general of Canada, and Pauline Vanier (née Archer), he served in the British and Canadian navies 1945-50. He studied and taught philosophy and theology in France, and then in 1964 established a home for handicapped men living with him in Trosly-Breuil, France. Called L'Arche (the ark), it was the first of many; by 1986 there were 13 in France, 23 in Canada, 9 in the US, 4 in India, 2 in Africa and numerous others around the world. Vanier is widely esteemed for his leadership of spiritual retreats and for several books, including *Tears of Silence* (1970), *Eruption to Hope* (1971), *Followers of Jesus* (1976) and *Community and Growth* (1979). His writings and way of life challenge people to share life with the disadvantaged, in the belief that each person has a unique value as a human being. He was named Companion of the Order of Canada (1987).   MAC FREEMAN

Vanier Cup Winners 1967-87

1967	Alberta	1978	Queen's
1968	Queen's	1979	Acadia
1969	Manitoba	1980	Alberta
1970	Manitoba	1981	Acadia
1971	Western Ontario	1982	UBC
1972	Alberta	1983	Calgary
1973	Saint Mary's	1984	Guelph
1974	Western Ontario	1985	Calgary
1975	Ottawa	1986	UBC
1976	Western Ontario	1987	McGill
1977	Western Ontario		

Vanier Cup, so named after Gov Gen Georges VANIER (1959-67), was first awarded in 1965 to the winner of an invitational football game called the Canadian College Bowl. The game's founder was Peter Gorman, a Toronto businessman who gave the game a charity focus by pairing it with the Canadian Save the Children Fund. A previous attempt at a Canadian interuniversity championship had been made in 1959 when U of Western Ontario and UBC had met for the "Canadian championship" at Varsity Stadium. In 1967 the Canadian Intercollegiate Athletics Union (CIAU) accepted the Vanier Cup game as its championship, the culmination of western and eastern semifinal play-off games. In 1982 the game became known as the Vanier Cup, and the date set for the second last Saturday in Nov at the end of a week-long program of activities. The 4 leagues competing for the Vanier Cup are the Western Intercollegiate Football League (WIFL), the Ontario Universities Athletic Association (OUAA), the Ontario-Québec Intercollegiate Football Conference (OQIFC) and the Atlantic Universities Athletic Association (AUAA).
                    FRANK COSENTINO

Varley, Frederick Horsman, painter (b at Sheffield, Eng 2 Jan 1881; d at Toronto 8 Sept 1969). In early life he spent much time in the English countryside and became intensely spiritual, finding God in nature, not in the church. He received a solid art education, first at the Sheffield School of Art (1892-1900), then the Académie

*Vera, c*1930, oil on canvas by F.H. Varley (*courtesy National Gallery of Canada*).

royale des beaux-arts in Antwerp, Belgium (1900-02) where he studied original paintings by Rubens. After unsuccessful starts at careers as an illustrator and art teacher in England, Varley immigrated to Canada in 1912. Through Arthur LISMER, a Sheffield friend who had moved to Canada a year earlier, he found employment as a commercial illustrator in Toronto and befriended Tom THOMSON and Frank CARMICHAEL.

In 1918 Canadian War Records commissioned Varley to illustrate the war in Europe. He painted several portraits in England and made 2 trips to France. The 4 large war scenes that resulted were critically acclaimed and brought him to the forefront of painters in Canada. In May 1920 Varley became a founding member of the GROUP OF SEVEN. He did not share the Group's enthusiasm for the Ontario landscape, however, and during the early 1920s attempted to make a living as a portraitist. The family of Vincent MASSEY commissioned several, but Varley made little money and in 1926 began to teach at the Vancouver School of Decorative and Applied Arts.

During the next 10 years he painted hundreds of landscapes in oil and watercolour, marked by fine draftsmanship, exotic colour, unusual vantage points, and after 1933 by metamorphosis of forms. In 1933, he and J.W.G. MACDONALD opened their own school, the BC College of Arts. Though it was well attended, it closed after 2 years, a victim of the Depression. By 1936 Varley was broke, and moved to Ottawa to try to resume his career as a portraitist. During the next 9 years he drifted between Ottawa and Montréal, making few paintings, except in 1938 when he travelled to the Arctic on the government supply ship *Nascopie*. In 1944 he returned to Toronto and, in 1948-49, taught at the Doon Summer School of Fine Arts near Kitchener. In 1955 he made a sketching trip to Cape Breton, and in 1957 the first of several more painting trips to BC. Romantic and independent, Varley was known as the "gypsy" of the Group of Seven. His gifts as a colourist, draftsman and intimate observer of life are best displayed in both his drawings and small watercolours.   CHRISTOPHER VARLEY

Reading: Christopher Varley, *F.H. Varley* (1981).

Vaudreuil, Philippe de Rigaud de Vaudreuil, Marquis de, governor general of New France 1703-25 (b probably near Revel, France *c*1643; d at Québec C 10 Oct 1725). Vaudreuil served in the French army with the Mousque-

taires from 1672 and distinguished himself in campaigns in Flanders. He was appointed commander of the troops in Canada in 1687 and took part in campaigns against the IROQUOIS (*see* IROQUOIS WARS). He followed CALLIÈRE in the governorship of Montréal 1698-1703 and then as governor of New France from 1703 until his death. When Vaudreuil took over, the colony was at war with its southern neighbour and its Indian alliances were threatened because of the collapse of the beaver trade and the French withdrawal from the western posts. In his conduct of the war, Vaudreuil tried to preserve the 1701 peace with the Iroquois while encouraging the Abenakis to harass the eastern New England settlements. After the Treaty of UTRECHT, 1713, he worked through a network of highly effective Indian agents to reassert New France's control of the western FUR TRADE by establishing posts in Iroquois territory, and around the Great Lakes and upper Mississippi drainage area. He continued to exploit the Abenaki alliance to contain the spread of Massachusetts. He was a popular governor who through tenacious work and sometimes ruthless tactics guided New France through a critical era. His success was due in part to the lobbying of his Canadian-born wife at the French court.
MARY McDOUGALL MAUDE

Reading: Y. Zoltvany, *Philippe de Rigaud de Vaudreuil* (1974).

Vaudreuil, Pierre de Rigaud de Vaudreuil de Cavagnial, Marquis de (sometimes Vaudreuil-Cavagnial), officer, last governor general of New France 1755-60 (b at Québec C 22 Nov 1698; d at Paris, France 4 Aug 1778), son of Philippe de Rigaud de VAUDREUIL. He followed his father into the TROUPES DE LA MARINE and the colonial service. After rising through the ranks, he was governor of Trois-Rivières 1733-42. He then succeeded BIENVILLE as governor of Louisiana 1742-53, where his governorship brought a degree of economic stability to the colony. In 1755 he was appointed to succeed DUQUESNE as governor general of New France – the only Canadian-born to hold that position. His overall responsibility for military affairs during the SEVEN YEARS' WAR was complicated by the decision to reinforce the Marine troops and militia in New France with 6 regular army infantry battalions, commanded in succession by Baron Dieskau, MONTCALM and LÉVIS. This split command seriously impeded French efforts to pursue the war: Vaudreuil advocated Canadian-style guerrilla warfare on the frontiers while Montcalm preferred a defensive stance concentrating on the centre of the colony and the European-style battle. After Montcalm's defeat in the Battle of the PLAINS OF ABRAHAM, Vaudreuil left instructions with J.B.N.R. de RAMEZAY to surrender the town under certain conditions, orders he was later unable to countermand in time to stop the action. Vaudreuil planned the 1760 operations with Lévis, but despite the latter's successful defeat of the British at the Battle of STE-FOY, the arrival of the English fleet in the spring forced withdrawal again to Montréal. Unable to see any alternative that would not bring suffering to the population, Vaudreuil surrendered the colony at Montréal on Sept 8 after negotiating terms that protected the Canadians in their property, laws and religion but did not allow the troops the honours of war. He was strongly criticized for his action by the French military and the court. He was arrested a few months after Intendant François BIGOT and tried in the famous *affaire du Canada*, but was completely exonerated in Dec 1763.
MARY McDOUGALL MAUDE

Vaughan, Robert Charles, railway executive (b at Toronto 1 Dec 1883; d at Montréal 5 Jan 1966). Vaughan joined the CPR as messenger in 1898. He moved on to the GRAND TRUNK RY and to the CANADIAN NORTHERN RY in 1902, rising rapidly to become VP of CANADIAN NATIONAL RYS during the 1920s and 1930s and president 1941-50. Chairman of the Defence Purchasing Board in WWII, Vaughan was created CMG in 1946. He was governor of Montréal General Hospital, president and chairman of Commonwealth International Corp and Commonwealth International Leverage Fund Ltd, and a director of several others.
J. LINDSEY

Vaughan, Sir William, colonial promoter, author (b at Carmarthen, Wales 1575; d at Llangyndeyrn, Wales Aug 1641). Vaughan was one of the earliest advocates of Newfoundland as a practical and economically suitable place for English settlement. In 1616 he purchased the southern Avalon Peninsula from the London and Bristol Co and the next year sent out WELSH colonists to Renews. This colony, and further attempts at Trepassey in the 1620s and 1630s, met with failure. Vaughan also wrote 2 of the earliest promotional works about Newfoundland's value to Great Britain, *The Golden Fleece* (1626) and *The Newlanders Cure* (1630).
BERT RIGGS

Vegetable, herbaceous plant of which all or a part is eaten, raw or cooked. Vegetables are a valuable source of protein, vitamins, minerals, trace elements and fibre. All vegetables are high in carbohydrates, which contribute to their unique taste. They are most prized when eaten shortly after harvest, either fresh or cooked.

In Canada, at least 53 species or botanical varieties of vegetables are grown: one is a MUSHROOM; 52 are SEED PLANTS (listed below according to family grouping).

Gramineae (GRASS family): *Zea mays* var. *praecox*, popcorn; *Z. mays* var. *rugosa*, sweet CORN.

Liliaceae (LILY family): *Asparagus officinalis*, ASPARAGUS.

Amaryllidaceae (amaryllis family): *Allium cepa*, ONION; *A. cepa* (Aggregatum Group), shallot; *A. ampeloprasum*, leek; *A. sativum*, garlic; *A. fistulosum*, Welsh onion; *A. schoenoprasum*, chive.

Polygonaceae (BUCKWHEAT family): *Rheum rhabarbarum*, RHUBARB.

Chenopodiaceae (goosefoot family): *Beta vulgaris*, BEET; *B. vulgaris* (Cicla Group), chard; *Spinacia oleracea*, SPINACH.

Cruciferae (mustard family): *Brassica oleracea* (Acephala Group), KALE and collards; *B. oleracea* (Gemmifera Group), BRUSSELS SPROUTS; *B. oleracea* (Capitata Group), CABBAGE; *B. oleracea* (Botrytis Group), BROCCOLI, CAULIFLOWER; *B. oleracea* (Gongylodes Group), KOHLRABI; *B. napus* (Napobrassica Group), RUTABAGA or swede; *B. juncea*, mustard greens; *B. rapa* (Rapifera Group), TURNIP; *B. rapa* (Pekinensis Group), pe-tsai Chinese cabbage; *B. rapa* (Chinensis Group), pakchoi Chinese cabbage; *Nasturtium officinale*, watercress; *Amoracia rusticana*, horseradish; *Raphanus sativus*, RADISH.

Leguminosae (PEA or PULSE family): *Pisum sativum*, garden pea; *P. sativum* var. *arvense*, field pea; *P. sativum* var. *macrocarpon*, edible-podded pea; *Vicia faba*, broad or FABA BEAN; *Phaseolus vulgaris*, green BEAN; *P. coccineus*, scarlet runner bean; *P. limensis*, Lima bean; *Vigna radiata*, mung bean.

Umbelliferae (parsley family): *Daucus carota* var. *sativus*, CARROT; *Foeniculum vulgare*, fennel; *Petroselinum crispum*, parsley; *Apium graveolens* var. *dulce*, CELERY; *A. graveolens* var. *rapaceum*, celeriac; *Pastinaca sativa*, PARSNIP.

Solanaceae (NIGHTSHADE family): *Solanum tuberosum*, POTATO; *S. melongena*, EGGPLANT; *Lycopersicon esculentum*, TOMATO; *Capsicum annuum* (Cerasiforme Group), PEPPER.

Cucurbitaceae (gourd family): *Cucurbita pepo* var. *pepo*, PUMPKIN, acorn SQUASH; *C. pepo* var. *melopepo*, bush summer squash; *C. maxima*, winter squash; *C. moschata*, winter crookneck squash; *Citrullus lanatus*, watermelon; *Cucumis sativus*, CUCUMBER; *Cucumis melo* var. *cantalupensis*, cantaloupe; *Cucumis melo* (Reticulatus Group), muskmelon.

Compositae (composite family): *Cichorium intybus*, witloof, chicory; *C. endivia*, ENDIVE; *Tragopogon porrifolius*, salsify; *Lactuca sativa*, LETTUCE; *Helianthus tuberosus*, Jerusalem artichoke; *Taraxacum officinale*, DANDELION.

Only about 16 of the species listed are widely grown in Canada; 5 or 6 species account for the bulk of all vegetables produced. Vegetables are sometimes classified as cool-season and warm-season types or by their edible parts: for example, flowers – cauliflower, broccoli; leaves – cabbage, lettuce, spinach; shoots – asparagus; leaf stalk (petiole) – rhubarb, chard; roots – beet, carrot, potato, onion; fruit – tomato, pepper, squash.

Cultivation

Vegetable production ranges from highly intensive row cropping to very extensive types of production. Although good soil is beneficial, the grower often finds it more important to use light sandy soils in order to get an early start on the season. Vegetable crops recover from seasonal or short-period DROUGHTS less efficiently than most other horticultural crops; thus, a source of water for irrigation during dry spells is necessary. All vegetable-growing operations, from precision seeding to ultimate harvest, handling and packaging, are rapidly becoming fully mechanized. Every mechanical or chemical WEED-control method is used. Insects and PLANT DISEASES are closely monitored, and crop losses are minimized by use of chemical PESTICIDES. Many growers have built storage facilities for long-term storage of crops such as potatoes, onions, carrots and cabbages. Canada's long winter season makes it imperative that all vegetables capable of storage in the living state be stored in prime condition.

Areas and Yields The potato is the most widely cultivated vegetable in Canada. Excluding potatoes, Ontario ranks first in vegetable production, both in yield and area; Québec comes second, followed by BC, the Prairie region and the Atlantic region. Ontario also has the greatest potential for increasing production. When potato production is included, Ontario is still in front, but the Atlantic region is second, followed by Québec, the Prairie region and BC. Relatively few sites in Canada have the moderate, reasonably long growing season necessary for vegetable production. Moving from W to E these areas are the lower Fraser Valley, BC; the irrigated area of southern Alberta; the Red and Assiniboine river valleys of Manitoba; the southern Great Lakes rim area of Ontario; the St Lawrence Valley and the muck areas of SW Québec; the St John River Valley, NB; the Annapolis Valley, NS; and most of PEI.

Canadian yields of vegetable crops are comparable to those of similar crops grown in the US or Europe. However, unlike our southern neighbours, we grow only a single vegetable crop on the same land in a year; therefore, total yields usually reflect only one harvest. We compensate by growing vegetables in greenhouses, where our yields of tomatoes and cucumbers are as high as those anywhere in the world. In Canada, maximum yields of carrots, onions, cabbage, celery and lettuce are obtained from muck or organic soils, where adequate summer heat prevails. Upland soils for similar crops are slightly less productive, because the water supply is not usually as constant as on muck. Examples of good yields of

In Canada, there are at least 53 species or botanical varieties of vegetables; 16 are widely grown, and 5 or 6 of these account for the bulk of all vegetables produced (*artwork by Claire Tremblay*).

major crops would range as follows: potatoes, 9-16 t; tomatoes, 18-23 t; canning peas, 1-2 t; sweet corn, 4-5 t; carrots and onions, 16-20 t.

Value and Processing Vegetables grown in Canada (1986) contribute about 3% of the total farm gate value. Unlike many other agricultural products, their value increases 5-7 fold as the farmgate value is increased by grading, washing, packaging, transportation, wholesaling and eventual retailing. Whenever vegetables are not immediately consumed, they should be rapidly cooled to retard loss of quality. If summer or field heat is not quickly reduced, vegetables soon lose their desirability. To retain maximum taste and food value, vegetables can be hydrocooled, vacuum cooled, covered with ice, canned or processed, quick-frozen after a brief blanching period and stored, freeze-dried to remove all water in the tissue, or dehydrated under high temperatures. In addition, vegetables handled by any of these means can also be converted to soups, chips, condiments or flakes. Managers of produce departments of modern supermarkets recognize that well-handled, attractively displayed produce carries the greatest unit profit in the store.   I.L. NONNECKE

Vegetable Oil Industry is made up of companies that manufacture oils and their by-prod-

ucts, such as linseed, SOYBEAN and CANOLA oil cake and meal. This industry, the youngest sector of Canada's FOOD AND BEVERAGE INDUSTRIES, did not exist before the early 1940s, as most of Canada's edible oil needs were met by imports. WWII provided the impetus for development, as most of the Allied nations, facing a critical shortage of imported fats, particularly vegetable oils, increased efforts to fill their needs domestically. Soybeans were grown for the first time in southern Ontario; commercial SUNFLOWER production began in Manitoba and Saskatchewan, and a new seed, Black Argentine rapeseed, was planted for the first time. The initial reason for growing rapeseed was to provide desperately needed high-quality marine lubricants for the Allied fleets. After the war, interest in OILSEEDS (especially rapeseed) almost disappeared. In the case of rapeseed, existing varieties were not well suited to producing oil for human consumption or meal for animal feed. The seeds contained high levels of 2 undesirable components, erucic acid (associated with heart lesions in laboratory animals) and glucosinolate (which causes enlarged thyroid glands and poor feed conversion in livestock). However, Canadian agricultural and food scientists, working for the federal Dept of Agriculture and several Canadian universities, began an intense research program, and their accomplishments were remarkable. By 1956 the first improved rapeseed oil for human consumption was being manufactured; by the early 1960s erucic acid had been almost completely re-

moved; and by the early 1970s the glucosinolate content had been dramatically reduced. The new rapeseed varieties, now called canola, were fully accepted in the world's oilseed markets. The achievement was one of Canada's most spectacular AGRICULTURAL RESEARCH success stories. Canola oil and meal have achieved international recognition as an excellent source of human food and livestock feed; canola now provides most of the vegetable oil consumed in Canada. Export sales of edible vegetable oils are now worth about $500 million a year and will unquestionably increase substantially in future. Similar research, which is being done on soybeans to develop varieties that can be grown in cooler areas of Canada, has resulted in a steady increase in Canadian soybean production. Research has begun on reducing the erucic acid and glucosinolate content of mustard seed to create a new oilseed crop, and on using mustard meal as livestock feed.

Statistics Canada figures indicate that, in 1986, 11 oilseed crushing plants were in production: Ont had 3 plants, Man, 2; Sask, 1; and Alta, 5. In 1983 Canada Packers Inc of Toronto started a new $20-million crushing plant in Hamilton, Ont, one of the most advanced in the world. The industry produced 158 000 t of soybean oil and 633 000 t of canola oil in the 1986-87 crop year. The industry had a 1986-87 crop-year output of 731 000 t of soybean meal and 892 000 t of canola meal. The value of factory shipments in 1986 was $732.1 million, up dramatically from $62.8 million in 1961. Cost of materials and supplies in 1986 amounted to $636.5 million. The industry is represented by the Institute of Edible Oil Foods in Toronto and is also involved with the producer organization, the Canola Council of Canada in Winnipeg. It must comply with regulations administered by Agriculture Canada, Health and Welfare Canada, and Consumer and Corporate Affairs Canada.   ROBERT F. BARRATT

Vegetarianism describes the diet (eg, roots, green vegetables, cereals, seeds, fruit and nuts, and perhaps eggs and dairy products) of those who abstain from food from animal sources. Many Canadians have chosen a vegetarian diet for economic or religious reasons or because of its legendary benefits. Semivegetarians have eliminated only red meat from their diet and may substitute for it poultry, fish, milk or eggs. Those who eat no meat are called "lacto-ovo" (milk and eggs) vegetarians. Milk and eggs provide the necessary protein, plus B vitamins and minerals. For those who cannot tolerate lactose, cheese and fermented milk products can be used. "Lacto vegetarians" have eliminated eggs, but a substitute source of iron and other nutrients must be found.

Total vegetarians ("vegans") avoid all animal by-products, and some eat only fruit or raw food. Vegetarian diets that exclude all animal by-products might result in nutritional deficiencies. For example, diets of "vegans" are low in vitamin B_{12} but contain enough folic acid to mask the early signs of vitamin B_{12} deficiency until irreversible damage to neural tissues in the spinal cord (known as "vegan back") occurs. Protein balance in the vegetarian diet is also a potential problem if the essential amino acids are missing. The Zen macrobiotic diet (an extreme form of cult vegetarianism, where only brown rice is consumed in the final stage of the dietary regime) reflects the greater health risks. In the long-term, Zen macrobiotic converts may suffer scurvy, hypoproteinemia, anemia, hypocalcemia and emaciation or starvation with accompanying loss of kidney function. Pregnant and lactating Zen macrobiotics are particularly vulnerable to these nutritional deficiencies. However, vegetarianism generally leads to poor health only in those individuals who completely ignore the need for a balanced diet. Careful planning and a basic knowledge of nutrient sources and requirements are necessary to achieve this balance (*see* CANADA'S FOOD GUIDE). M.T. CLANDININ

Vegetation Regions are geographical areas characterized by distinct plant communities. Community composition, determined primarily by climate (eg, temperature, precipitation, sunlight), may be affected by factors such as geology, soil composition and erosion, water drainage patterns and human interference. Each vegetation region supports a characteristic animal community which may affect its composition. The principal regions represented in Canada are as follows.

Arctic Tundra

The arctic tundra is the second-largest vegetation region in the country. It covers a greater range of latitude than any other yet is little understood because of its remoteness and sparse human population. The Arctic is treeless because of its low summer temperatures (a mean of less than 11°C in the warmest month) and short growing season (1.5-3.5 months). The transition from boreal forest to tundra, termed forest-tundra, consists of ribbons or islands of stunted black and white spruce trees in a sea of tundra vegetation. Only a few birch and quaking aspen reach this far North. The major environmental factors which limit plant growth and distribution are cold soils with an active layer in summer of 20-60 cm above the permafrost; varying depth of winter snow; low levels of soil nutrients, especially nitrogen and phosphorus; and soils that can be very dry (on ridges) or very wet (in lowlands) in summer.

The Arctic is often divided into the Low Arctic of the mainland and the High Arctic of the Northern Dist of Keewatin and ARCTIC ARCHIPELAGO. The Low Arctic is characterized by nearly complete plant cover and abundant, low and dwarf woody shrubs. Major plant communities include tall (2-3 m) shrub tundra of alder, scrub birch and willows, along rivers, streams, steep slopes and lake shores; low (30-60 cm) shrub tundra of willow, dwarf birch, dwarf heath shrubs, numerous sedges and small herbaceous species and abundant lichens and mosses, on medium-drained slopes; tussock sedge, dwarf heath shrubs, mosses and lichens on poorly drained soils of low rolling hills; and various combinations of sedges, a few grasses and herbs, and abundant mosses in poorly drained soils of flatlands. These latter areas are the summer habitat of many waterfowl. Hills of tussock sedge and low shrub tundras are the summer rangelands of barren ground caribou and the year-round home of lemming, ptarmigan, fox and wolf.

In the High Arctic, vegetation is sparser and the wildlife it supports is more limited because of

Low shrub-tussock tundra south of Tuktoyaktuk, NWT. Dominant plants include dwarf birch, willows, cottongrass, dwarf heath species, lichens (*courtesy Lawrence Bliss*).

colder summers (2-5°C warmest month), shorter growing season (1.5-2.5 months), and low precipitation (100-200 mm). In lowlands, limited areas of sedge-moss tundras occur, decreasing in extent N of 74° N. About 50% of the land consists of scattered clumps of very dwarf shrubs (1-3 cm high) of willow and mountain avens, with small cushion plants (species of draba, saxifrage, chickweed, poppy), and abundant lichens and mosses; or areas of lichens, mosses, scattered clumps of grasses and rushes, and cushion plants. These lands (polar semideserts) can support small scattered herds of muskox and Peary's caribou, with waterfowl in lowland lakes.

At higher elevations (above 100 m) in the southern and central islands and at lower elevations in the more northerly islands, the abundance of surface, frost-shattered rock and small pockets of fine soil result in truly barren land (polar deserts). Here flowering plants and mosses grow only where large snowbanks provide meltwater. Elsewhere, tiny scattered flowering plants grow with essentially no lichens or mosses.

L.C. BLISS

Boreal Forest or Taiga

The boreal forest encircles the Northern Hemisphere south of the treeless tundra. This, Canada's largest vegetation region, has forests and woodlands dominated by a relatively few cold-tolerant conifers: species of spruce, fir, pine and larch. Poplars and birches are also common, but more so in the south than in the north. The terrain is characterized by numerous lakes, extensive peatlands, and podzol soils on uplands. The continental climate with short, cool summers and long, cold winters is subarctic. The boreal forest can be traced to near the end of the Miocene (5.3-11.2 million years ago) when the trees which today typify the North first appear in the fossil record. Probably they evolved at upper altitudes in the mountains, spread to lowlands as the climate cooled, and replaced the Arcto-Tertiary forest, fragments of which still survive in the southern US, southern Europe and SE Asia.

In N America, the bulk of the boreal forest is in Canada, with extensions into Alaska and the Lake states. The southern subzone has a strong, broadleaf component of aspen and birch which, with jack pine, white spruce and balsam fir, forms upland mixed-wood stands. Associated tall shrubs and herbaceous plants reflect the relatively favourable climate and soils, except on peatlands, where black spruce and larch dominate. In western Canada, mixed woods grade into the grasslands through a belt of aspen parkland; in the East, the transition to the richer forests of the Great Lakes-St Lawrence Region is marked by a variety of temperate hardwoods and evergreens. The middle boreal subzone is the pulpwood forest par excellence, dominated by dense stands of spruce, pine and fir. On infertile soils, under the closed-crown conifers, feather mosses and small, winter-green herbs are characteristic. Aspen and birch are prominent where soils are richer, especially following logging and fire. The northernmost subzone, the Subarctic, constitutes almost one half of the boreal zone. The Low Subarctic bears extensive lichen woodland: a savannah of spruce or pine scattered through a handsome carpet of lichens. The High Subarctic includes both forest-tundra near the treeline, where patches of spruce and larch on low areas alternate with treeless uplands, and the shrub-tundra, extending beyond treeline to the tree-species line.

Throughout the boreal forest, peat accumulates in depressions. Fen peat forms along drainageways, its presence being indicated by

Boreal forest and bog at Heart Lake, NWT (*courtesy Provincial Museum of Alberta*).

alder, willow, larch and sedges. Bogs are raised above fens and are identified by acid sphagnum hummocks, dwarf evergreen shrubs (especially Labrador tea) and black spruce. In the Subarctic, all bogs contain permafrost; the larger ones, scarred by thaw pockets, are called peat plateaus. The influence of fire is evident almost everywhere. Burning favours the invasion of sprouters (aspen and balsam poplar), wind-dispersed seeders (birch), and closed-cone conifers (jackpine and black spruce). Such trees flourish in pure or mixed stands where fires are frequent. Areas less subject to burning support forests of white spruce and, the least fire-resistant of boreal trees, balsam fir. J. STAN ROWE

Pacific Coastal

The Pacific Coastal region, which ranges from nearly 48° N latitude to 55° N, may be divided into 4 distinct growing zones, reflecting the great variation in temperature, length of growing season and average precipitation (650-3000 mm per year). Significant rainfall shadows, caused by mountain ranges on Vancouver I and the Queen Charlotte Is, can produce further climatic variation on the eastern flanks of the mountain ranges and in associated, mainland coastal areas.

Vegetation of the outer coasts of island archipelagoes and the exposed coasts of the mainland is predominantly coniferous forest consisting of Douglas fir, western hemlock, yellow cypress, Sitka spruce, shore pine, western red cedar and occasionally western yew. The principal deciduous hardwoods are red alder and Scouler willow. Douglas fir is absent from the Queen Charlotte Is.

The Georgia Strait area on the E coast of Vancouver I and the adjacent mainland have a drier, Mediterranean climate. Here, coastal vegetation must persist through a hot, dry period lasting up to 8 weeks. The vegetation is characterized by a colourful spring flora with several, annual, herbaceous species. Arbutus, western flowering dogwood and Garry oak reach their northern limits in this region. Arbutus is the only native broad-leaved evergreen tree in Canada. Pacific dogwood is the PROVINCIAL FLORAL EMBLEM of BC. Other forest species include Douglas fir, western hemlock, grand fir, bigleaf maple, western red cedar and bitter cherry.

The predominant undergrowth shrubs of the outer-coastal forest are salal, salmonberry, and several species of genus *Vaccinium* (eg, bilberries and huckleberries). These shrubs, notably salal, often form impenetrable thickets on exposed headlands. In the drier, inner-coastal areas, thimbleberry, red elderberry, Nootka rose, ocean spray, snowberry, western sword fern and deer fern are common in the undergrowth. Specialized plant communities are associated with the beaches. Most are cobble or shingle beaches with a prominent driftwood zone containing large logs of the forest tree species. Fine sand beaches occur, most commonly in the southern portion of the Canadian Pacific coast. Common plants in the driftwood zone are American wild dune grass, beach pea, giant vetch, common cleavers, bluejoint small reed grass, tufted hair grass, Pacific coastal strawberry and sea plantain.

The Pacific coastline is highly dissected by many fjordlike inlets. Salt marsh vegetation is found at the head of such inlets. Common plants of these marshes are various species of alkali grass, seaside arrow grass, pickleweed, springbank clover, salt-marsh starwort, and sedges such as *Carex lyngbyei* and *C. obnupta.* Grasses found in these communities are spike bent grass, red fescue, tufted hair grass and meadow barley. Occasional, but conspicuous, flowering plants include Douglas's aster, western buttercup, entire-leaved gumweed and *Apargidium boreale.* Soft rushes form conspicuous, herbaceous clumps in these marsh lands.   ROY L. TAYLOR

Cordillera

The Canadian Cordillera can be divided into 12 zones (distinguished by a certain macroclimate, zonal vegetation and soil) which can then be grouped into 7 regions and 4 formations. The variations are staggering: regions represented range from alpine tundra to cool, mesothermal rain forest and include 5 of the 8 major Canadian forest zones.

Alpine Formation contains only the Alpine Region comprising the Alpine Tundra Zone, which extends through YT, Mackenzie Dist, BC and Alberta. Mean temperature of the warmest month is 0°-10°C. Mean total precipitation is 700-3500 mm, 76-80% in snowfall. Vegetation consists of mainly herbaceous plants, mosses, liverworts, lichens and very low shrubs (eg, arctic willow).

Microthermal Coniferous Forest Formation is characterized by cold, forest climates which are meagrely to moderately forest productive. The mean temperature of the coldest months is well below 0°C; the mean of the warmest months, above 10°. Snow covers the ground for more than one month. The formation includes 4 forest regions: Pacific Coastal Subalpine, Interior Cordilleran Subalpine, Boreal Montane and Cordilleran Montane Temperate.

The Pacific Coastal Subalpine Forest Region contains only the Mountain Hemlock Zone which, in Canada, occurs along the Pacific coast. Underneath the snowpack, the ground does not freeze. Mountain hemlock, Pacific silver fir and Alaska yellow cedar are characteristic tree species. The most characteristic shrubs are mountain juniper, Alaskan, Cascade and oval-leaved blueberries, red mountain heather, copper bush, coastal Douglas fir, Sitka mountain ash, Sitka alder, and deer fern.

The Interior Cordilleran Subalpine Forest Region is characterized by having ground that is often frozen before snowfall. Two zones are recognized. The first, the Engelmann Spruce-Subalpine Fir Zone, occurs in BC and Alberta. Typical tree and shrub species include Engelmann spruce, subalpine fir, lodgepole and whitebark pines, subalpine larch, trembling aspen, mountain juniper, white-leaved rhododendron, coastal Douglas fir, shrub and water birches, Sitka alder, devil's club, Oregon boxwood, black huckleberry, oval-leaved blueberry, grouseberry, Sitka mountain ash and Utah honeysuckle. The second zone, Spruce-Willow-Birch Zone, occurs in BC, north of 57°10′ N latitude and extends to 70° N latitude (YT and Mackenzie Dist). Elevations are: southwest, 950-1550 m; southeast, 1100-1750 m; north, sea level. In northern Alberta, this zone is centered around the Caribou Mts at elevations above 700 m. In the summer, days are long or

Timberline in winter, near Smithers, BC. Subalpine firs are limited in their growth by climatic conditions (*photo by Tom W. Parkin/Pathfinder*).

have pronounced twilight, and temperatures remain above freezing. Typical vegetation includes white and black spruces, mountain juniper, shrub birch, green alder, many willows and Northern Labrador tea.

In the Boreal Montane Forest Region, the ground is solidly frozen before snowfall. Mean temperature is above 10°C for 3-4 months, below 0° for 5-7 months. Summer is hot at its peak; winter very severe. Elevations are montane, ie, below subalpine elevations. Two zones occur. The first, the Boreal White-and-Black-Spruce Zone, is found in BC, Alta, YT and NWT, in the latitude of 54-69° N. Elevations range from sea level in the North to 1100 m in BC. In Alberta, growth of trees is poor (except on alluvial soils) because the growing season is short, the winter very severe, and the ground deeply frozen. Permafrost occurs in lenses in central parts and is continuous in the North. Common tree species include white and black spruces, lodgepole and jack pines, larch, subalpine fir, mountain and creeping junipers, trembling aspen, balsam poplar, paper, water, Alaska, shrub and swamp birches, and thinleaf and green alders. Common shrubs include dwarf and bog blueberry, mountain cranberry, leatherleaf, etc. High moors are common. In the second zone, the Sub-boreal Spruce Zone, the mean temperature is below 0°C for 5 months. The zone occurs in BC, between 52°30′ and 57°10′ N latitudes, and at montane elevations. Compared to the Boreal White-and-Black-Spruce Zone, winter is milder, growth of trees better, especially because low moors are common. High moors are rare and free of permafrost. Tree species are, essentially, as in the Boreal White-and-Black-Spruce Zone, except that Engelmann spruce, black cottonwood and Sitka alder are present; Alaska birch, green alder and creeping juniper are absent. Shrub species include devil's club, black huckleberry, and oval-leaved blueberry.

The final forest region, the Cordilleran Montane Temperate Forest Region, has a mean temperature above 10°C for 4-5 months, below 0° for 3-5 months. Three zones are distinguished. The Cariboo Aspen-Lodgepole Pine Zone occurs only in the central part of interior BC, between 51°10′ and 54°15′ N latitude, elevation 510-1200 m. The number of conifers is limited by the severe winters and dry, hot summers. Common tree species include lodgepole pine, white spruce, interior variety of Douglas fir, Rocky Mountain and mountain junipers, trembling aspen, black cottonwood, paper and water birches, and thinleaf and Sitka alders. Pine grass is common. The Interior Western Hemlock Zone which, in BC, occurs between 49° and 54°10′ N latitude at elevations of 360-1260 m, is the wettest and most productive temperate forest zone in the BC interior. Vegetation includes the interior variety of Douglas fir, western hemlock, western white and lodgepole pines, western red cedar, western larch, grand fir, En-

gelmann spruce, mountain juniper, black cottonwood, trembling aspen, paper, water, shrub and swamp birches, Sitka and thinleaf alders, devil's club, Oregon boxwood, Oregon wintergreen, globe and oval-leaved blueberries, black huckleberry, Utah honeysuckle and American skunk cabbage. The Interior Douglas Fir Zone occurs mainly in BC and very little on the eastern slopes of the Rocky Mts in Alberta, between 49° and 53°10′ N latitude, at elevations of 300-1350 m. It is the second-warmest interior zone in BC. Vegetation includes interior variety of Douglas fir, ponderosa, lodgepole and western white pines, grand fir, western larch, western red cedar, Rocky Mountain and mountain junipers, creeping juniper, trembling aspen, paper and water birches, redstem and snowbush ceanothus, pine and wheat grasses, and several needle grasses. In Alberta, many of the plant indicators are very rare or are lacking.

Semiarid Cold Steppe Formation encompasses dry climates in which evaporation exceeds precipitation and no surplus of water remains to maintain a constant groundwater level. This formation includes only the Cordilleran Cold-Steppe-Savanna Forest Region with only the Ponderosa Pine-Bunchgrass Zone. The mean temperature is above 10°C for 5-7 months, below 0° for 2-3 months. The long frost-free period (207-260 days) allows orchards to develop if artificial irrigation is provided. The zone lies across southern BC between 49° and 51° N latitude, at elevations of 270-750 m. It includes the Fraser, Thompson, Nicola, Similkameen, Okanagan and Kootenay (most southern part) river valleys. The strongest rain shadow effects in BC are caused by the Western Coast Cordilleras. Limited growth of trees occurs, mainly ponderosa pine in savanna stands. After overgrazing and fires, bluebunch wheat grass, rough fescue, needle grasses and several bluegrass species are replaced by prairie sage brush in cooler areas and by Big Basin sage brush in warmer areas, and by arrow-leaved balsamroot, 2 prickly pear cactus species, rabbitbrush, several milk vetch species and many other steppe plants. Poison ivy, smooth sumac and tall Oregon grape grow at the bottom of coarse talus slopes.

Mesothermal Forest Formation contains only the Pacific Coastal Mesothermal Forest Region. Winter is mild with Jan mean temperature usually above 0°C. Vegetation includes western hemlock, western red cedar, Sitka spruce, red alder, bitter cherry, black cottonwood, cascara sagrada, salal, evergreen and red huckleberries, western swordfern, deer fern and American skunk cabbage. The region is divided into 2 zones. In the first, the Coastal Douglas Fir Zone, the relative dryness results from the rain shadow effect of insular mountains on Vancouver I. Vegetation includes coastal varieties of Douglas fir, grand fir, western red cedar, Garry oak, arbutus, lodgepole pine, western flowering dogwood, broadleaf and vine maples, Vancouverian variety of trembling aspen, long-leaved Oregon grape, common and trailing snowberry, western trumpet and hairy honeysuckles, and salal. The second zone is the Coastal Western Hemlock Zone, the wettest in BC. In the North, heavy snowfall protects the ground from freezing. Mean temperature is above 10°C for 4-7 months, below 0° for 0-3 months. Sitka spruce, western red cedar, amabilis fir, Alaska yellow cedar and western hemlock have the best production here. The coastal variety of Douglas and grand firs (both only in the southern parts of the zone) grow best in the drier subzone, where Douglas fir may reach 100 m tall in its best habitats, when 300 years old. Lodgepole pine and Labrador tea are common in sphagnum bogs. Salal forms impenetrable thickets. Among the

Short-grass prairie near Swift Current, Sask. The grasses of the dry prairie areas of SW Sask and SE Alta are highly drought resistant (*photo by Bill Brooks/Masterfile*).

many long hanging epiphytes (plants deriving moisture and nutrients from air and rain) which live on woody plants, *Isothecium stoloniferum* is the most common. *See also* BIOGEOCLIMATIC ZONE.

V.J. KRAJINA

Prairie

Prairie is a natural grassland found in semiarid to subhumid climates. Plants are perennials, mostly grasses, associated with sedges, forbs (nongrasslike herbaceous plants) and a few dwarf shrubs. Before European settlement, this vegetation occupied valleys of southern interior BC, and much of southern Man, Sask and Alta, from Winnipeg to Calgary and from the US border to Saskatoon and Edmonton. The nature of grassland vegetation depends on climate and soil. Precipitation increases eastward from the Rocky Mts; temperature decreases northward. Both factors are affected by increasing elevation in the foothills of Alberta, on the valley slopes of BC, and in elevated locations across the southern Canadian prairies.

Climatic differences have caused the formation of 3 grassland soil zones. Brown soils of the driest area, southwestern Saskatchewan and southeastern Alberta, are populated by relatively drought-resistant grasses, particularly common spear grass, western wheat grass and blue grama. In the adjacent, dark brown soils (east, north and west), principal species are short-awned porcupine grass and northern wheat grass. These zones comprise the mixed prairie. Fescue prairie occupies black soils in Alta and western Sask, between mixed prairie and northern forest, giving way eastward to the true prairie of southern Man. The principal grass of fescue prairie is rough fescue; in true prairie, bluestems and porcupine grass are most important. In BC, bluebunch wheat grass, occupying semiarid valley floors (lower grassland), changes to a type of vegetation dominated by rough fescue (upper grassland). Usually, 2-3 grass species contribute 70% or more of the vegetation; the number of associated species varies widely, diversity increasing with moistness of habitat. Mixed and true prairie extend southward

to Texas, with considerable change in species composition; fescue prairie and BC grassland (palouse prairie) extend only into the adjacent states.

In the black soil zone, forest penetrates prairie where the local climate is moister and cooler than average (north-facing slopes, edges of sloughs, and elevated areas), so that grassland and forest intermingle to form the aspen grove region within fescue and true prairie. In BC, the margin between open grassland and forest is a savanna (grassland with scattered trees) with Douglas fir as the main tree. The character of grassland varies locally with soil texture. In dune sand, various specialized grasses abound (eg, sand grass, sand dropseed and Indian rice grass). In saline flats, salt grass, alkali grass and wild barley dominate. Similarly, the wet slough environment results in a cover of various grass species (eg, slough grass, spangle top, bluegrasses), sedges, bulrushes and cattail.

At the end of the 19th century, rangeland grazing by domesticated livestock was the principal agricultural use made of the prairies. The cultivated area increased rapidly 1900-30; today, about 55% of the area E of the mountains is under crop or summerfallow, representing 65% of cultivated land in Canada. The high fertility of prairie soils is depleted by tillage. It was estimated that, by the 1980s, 33-50% of organic matter in cultivated prairie soils had been lost (*see* SOIL CONSERVATION). The large tracts of uncultivated grassland, mostly community pasture or crown land leased by ranchers, are grazed by domesticated livestock. GRASSLANDS NATIONAL PARK Reserve, Sask, was established to ensure survival of some native prairie.

ROBERT T. COUPLAND

Eastern Temperate Forests

The most northern expression of the extensive temperate forests of southeastern N America, this region is dominated by deciduous, broad-leaved trees. In favourable southern climates, deciduous leaves are most efficient, but they are energy-consuming because they must be renewed annually. A shorter growing season and harsher climate favour replacement by less efficient but less energy-demanding needle-leaved evergreens. Therefore, the zone may be divided into the

Southern Deciduous Forests and the more northerly Deciduous-Evergreen Forests.

The summer green character is most prominent in extreme southern Ontario where 80 different tree species grow naturally (now largely displaced by agriculture). Within this region, many dominance patterns occur because of local variations in soil moisture, soil type and microclimate. In drier environments of the Southern Deciduous Forests, black, red and white oak predominate and shagbark hickory, hop hornbeam, beech, red maple and white pine are strong associates. In mesic (moist) environments sugar maple and beech dominate in association with red elm, black maple, black cherry, white ash and basswood. In wet lowlands and bottomlands, white elm and red and silver maple are major forest components, growing with black walnut, white and green ash, bitternut hickory, cottonwood, pin oak, box elder and black willow. In Canada, many southern species occur only in this region (eg, flowering dogwood, chestnut and Hill's oaks, sweet pignut, pignut and kingnut hickories, sweet chestnut, red mulberry, sassafras, tuliptree, Kentucky coffee tree, hackberry, cucumber magnolia, sycamore, sour gum and honey locust). White pine and pencil cedar are associated evergreens in dry environments; hemlock is the only other significant conifer, in moist forests. Left undisturbed, the trees in these forests grow to great size (40 m) and great age (500 years).

The Deciduous-Evergreen Forests are often referred to as mixed forests; however, pure evergreen or deciduous types are also prevalent. Thus, in the broad triangle from Michipicoten to North Bay, Ont, and Ste-Agathe, Qué, with outliers west of Thunder Bay, at Lac Saint-Jean and in Gaspé, the drier sites support forests of jack pine, red or white pine in association with largetooth aspen, red oak, beech, paper birch, trembling aspen and hemlock. Moist forests are composed of sugar maple as an almost overriding dominant or in association with beech (south), basswood, hop hornbeam, yellow birch or hemlock. These terminal forests are remarkably similar to those on mesic sites southward. Wet environments support monodominant forests or admixtures of white elm, silver maple (southward), red maple (northward), white cedar or black willow. Associated species include green and black ashes and larch.

Northward, evergreen elements are more dominant. Stands of pine, white cedar, tamarack and, occasionally, black spruce become prominent parts of the forest scene. Successional forests are also frequent. Extensive stands, often of a single species (eg, trembling aspen, paper birch, jack, red or white pines), result from frequent fires. Trees are frequently short-lived and vulnerable to wind, disease and fungus attack. Except for white and red pine and maple, the forests seldom achieve great age or size.

In summer, deciduous forests are too shady for growth of significant ground cover; however, in spring, flowering plants with short reproductive cycles are abundant. These WILDFLOWERS provide welcome contrast to the monotony of winter snow and the sombre majesty of the mature forests, but far more spectacular is the brilliant display of colour before leaf-fall.

PAUL F. MAYCOCK

Atlantic Coastal Region

The vegetation of this region reflects also the human activity of the area. The island of Newfoundland lies at the eastern limits of the Boreal Forest Region. The Island's forests are dominated by conifers, particularly white and black spruce and balsam fir. Larch and other deciduous spe-

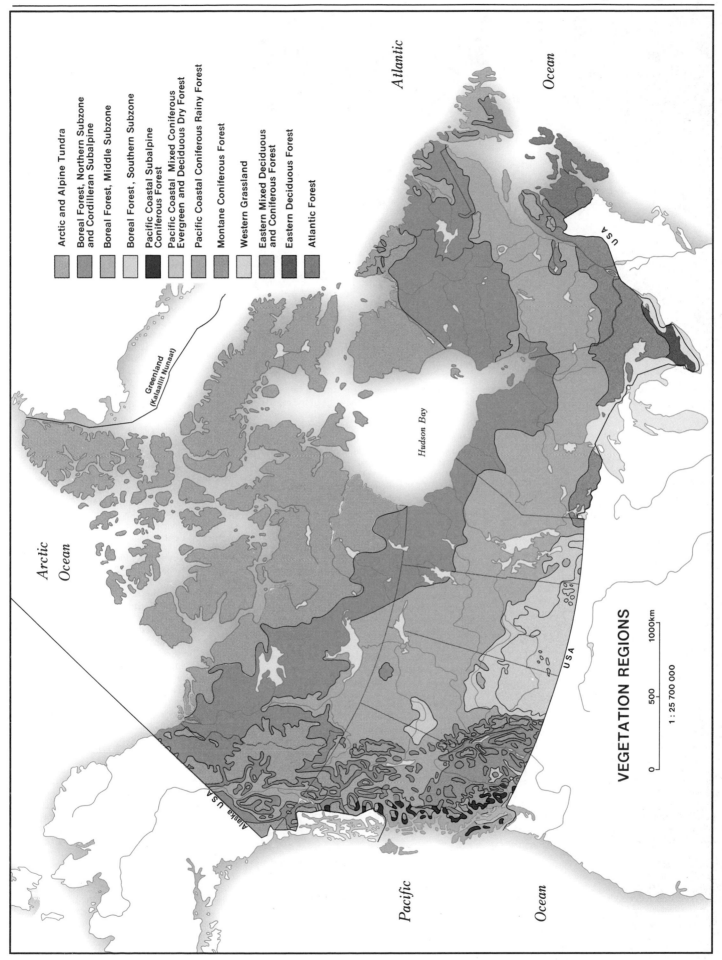

Arctic and Alpine Tundra

Boreal Forest, Northern Subzone
and Cordilleran Subalpine

Boreal Forest, Middle Subzone

Boreal Forest, Southern Subzone

Pacific Coastal Subalpine
Coniferous Forest

Pacific Coastal Mixed Coniferous
Evergreen and Deciduous Dry Forest

Pacific Coastal Coniferous Rainy Forest

Montane Coniferous Forest

Western Grassland

Eastern Mixed Deciduous
and Coniferous Forest

Eastern Deciduous Forest

Atlantic Forest

VEGETATION REGIONS

1 : 25 700 000

0   500   1000km

Atlantic   *Ocean*

Arctic Ocean

Pacific   *Ocean*

Hudson Bay

Greenland
(Kalaallit Nunaat)

USA

Alaska U.S.A.

Algae bloom on lake in Big Salmon Range, YT (*courtesy Boreal Institute for Northern Studies, U of Alberta*).

cies have been reduced in abundance by diseases and pests such as white pine blister rust and beech bark disease. Unless they are maintained, the cleared or burnt-over areas are recolonized by stands of white spruce and balsam fir. Such relatively pure stands have been plagued by problems common to monoculture situations, such as insect attacks, in this case by the spruce budworm.

Wind, cool temperatures and abundant precipitation are characteristic of the maritime climate. Along sea coasts, forests are usually dwarfed and large areas of peatland and heath occur, particularly in NS and Newfoundland. Peatlands are areas of poor drainage and low productivity, dominated by sphagnum, sedges, heath shrubs, stunted black spruce and larch. Heaths are found along the coasts, on hilltops and in other areas where forests have difficulty becoming established. They are areas of short, shrubby vegetation which are usually dominated by crowberry, bilberries, dwarf birches, junipers and other dwarf or prostrate shrubs. Forest growth improves in inland valleys and in many parts of NB because of better soils and more protected situations. However, the woodland flora is less rich than it is farther south. The growth of blueberries, an important crop of the region, is promoted by controlled burning which reduces competition from other species and keeps the blueberry plants pruned, thus increasing yield. There are some saltmarshes and freshwater marshes, particularly in the Bay of FUNDY area.

The vegetation of the Atlantic Coastal Region has a rugged character with a marked contrast between the sombre coniferous forests and mounds of brightly coloured wildflowers along roadsides during summer and autumn. It is a mosaic of natural, man-altered, and man-made habitats that is a product of glacial history and human colonization. PETER J. SCOTT

Coastal Marine Flora

A coastal marine flora comprises spermatophytes (flowering plants) and thallophytes (non-vascular, spore-producing plants, eg, algae and lichens) that live in or at the edge of the sea. The highly indented Canadian coastline provides many habitats for marine plants, from sheltered estuaries and lagoons to rocky shores exposed to open ocean. The composition of the flora varies with habitat. Some algae and lichens live just within reach of wave spray; other algae occur as deep as sufficient light for photosynthesis penetrates (about 75 m on the Atlantic coast and slightly less in more turbid Pacific waters). Intertidally, plants are distributed according to resistance to temperature extremes, desiccation, strong illumination, and wave impact, and according to their ability to compete with other species for space. In northern and eastern Canada, the capacity of plants to withstand ice cover and abrasion is a determinant. Paradoxically, confined, shallow coastal waters in Canada may attain summer temperatures of 28°C or higher, and may support more southerly, warm-water species that can tolerate cold winters.

In Canada, marine flowering plants may be dune and beach-dwellers adapted to a dry habitat (eg, sea rocket), saltmarsh species tolerant of periodic flooding by tides (eg, cordgrass), or truly marine and usually submerged sea "grasses" (eg, eelgrass and surf-grass). Marine spore-producing plants are much more numerous, the most conspicuous and diverse being benthic (attached to substratum) algae. They range from microscopic aggregates of a few cells to some of the tallest plants known and are grouped into 3 main colour classes: red, brown and green. A fourth group, the BLUE-GREEN ALGAE, is widespread and often abundant. It consists chiefly of microscopic forms, poorly documented because of taxonomic difficulties.

The richest Canadian marine algal flora occurs on the Pacific coast, where about 480 species are recognized (66% red, 21% brown, 13% green). This profusion is due to equable ocean temperatures and the upwelling of nutrient-rich water. Diversity is at times spectacular, as in the 16 genera of kelps, of which cold-water species may reach 30 m in length.

In Atlantic Canada, with cold Arctic currents and severe winter conditions, a markedly differ-ent and less diverse algal flora of about 345 species occurs (39% red, 37% brown, 24% green). Lesser diversity allows greater density of individual species, and exposed Atlantic shores usually show striking vertical zonation of a few dominant algae. Subtidal kelp forests off NS have an unusually high growth rate compared to many other marine and terrestrial ecosystems; however, much of the subtidal algal flora has been overgrazed by sea urchins, and prospects for recovery are unclear. About 75 taxa are common to both Atlantic and Pacific shores.

The Canadian Arctic, with low temperatures and limited sunlight, has a meagre algal flora of 170 species (32% red, 38% brown, 30% green). Arctic algae appear to be peculiarly adapted to photosynthesize with minimal light and temperature, although heterotrophy (by absorption and metabolism of organic substances dissolved in sea water) has been suggested as a means of subsistence. Incidence of annual species decreases at higher latitudes, and the intertidal flora is sparse or absent. *See also* SEAWEEDS. C.J. BIRD

Vegreville, Alta, Town, pop 5276 (1986c), inc 1906, is located in the parkland region of east-central Alberta 100 km E of Edmonton. The post office and hamlet on Birch Cr, which emerged in the midst of French Canadian settlement after 1894, was named to honour the western Canadian career of Father Valentin Vegreville OMI. English-speaking and European settlers filled in local homestead land before the Canadian Northern Railway arrived in 1905. Vegreville moved immediately to the new railway townsite, some 8 km to the northeast. The French and UKRAINIAN concentrations were noticeable from the start in distinctive churches, schools, community halls and residential clusters. The Ukrainian Pysanka Festival is a modern tradition: the town boasts a giant *pysanka* (Easter egg), unveiled in 1978. Serving a rich agricultural region specializing in grains and some livestock, Vegreville has been the site of the provincial government's Alberta Environmental Centre since 1981. CARL BETKE

Veniot, Peter John, "Pierre," journalist, politician, premier of NB 1923-25 (b at Richibucto, NB 4 Oct 1863; d at Bathurst, NB 6 July 1936). First elected MLA for Gloucester in 1894 he resigned in 1900 to become Bathurst collector of customs. Hired in 1912 to reorganize the provincial Liberals, he was re-elected in 1917 and as minister of public works undertook extensive road-building projects. He succeeded W.E. FOSTER as premier in 1923 and supported public ownership of the provincial hydro system and the Maritime Rights Movement. The first Acadian NB premier, he was recognized as the leader of Acadian Liberalism. Following the defeat of his party in 1925, he ran successfully as MP for Gloucester and was appointed postmaster general by PM KING. He sat as an MP until his death. DELLA M.M. STANLEY

Verchères, Marie-Madeleine Jarret de, heroine (b at Verchères, Qué 3 Mar 1678; buried at Ste-Anne-de-la-Pérade 8 Aug 1747). Daughter of an officer and seigneur, François Jarret de Verchères, in 1706 she married another officer and seigneur, Pierre-Thomas Tarieu de La Pérade. By age 21 she was famous for the story of her defence 7 years earlier, in 1692, of the family fort, a story subsequently published by historians Bacqueville de La Potherie and CHARLEVOIX. However, at about age 54, seeking a favour from France after other eyewitnesses had disappeared, the heroine told a new version, one full of exaggerations and lies. (In this one, she did not flee from one Iroquois, she evaded 45 who were firing at her.) This new version, being more dramatic, is the one favoured by most history books. MICHELINE D'ALLAIRE

Verigin, Peter Vasilevich, also Veregin, religious leader (b at Slavyanka, Russia 29 June 1859; d near Grand Forks, BC 29 Oct 1924). He became leader of the pacifist Russian sect of DOUKHOBORS in 1886 and in 1887 was exiled to Siberia. Influenced by the doctrines of the Christian anarchist novelist, Leo Tolstoi, he clandestinely instructed his followers to abandon meat and alcohol and to resume their historic resistance to military service. Persecution resulted, many Doukhobors were exiled in inhumane conditions to Georgia, Russia and, in 1898-99, more than 7000 were admitted to Canada. Verigin followed in 1903. He encouraged his people not to take the oath of allegiance required by the government to secure the land granted to them. When Doukhobor farms were seized, he led his followers, the Christian Community of Universal Brotherhood, to the Kootenay area of BC where, on purchased land, he attempted to create a self-supporting, self-governing commune. An able organizer, he placed the community on a good economic footing, but he struggled with the authorities over such matters as compulsory education. Verigin died in a train explosion of undetermined cause. After his death, the Christian Community fell into financial and organizational disarray. Verigin's powerful and imaginative personality had enabled the Doukhobors to weather their difficult first decades in Canada and to retain their special identity as a sect of Christian pacifist communists. GEORGE WOODCOCK

Vermilion, Alta, pop 3766 (1981c), 3879 (1986c), inc 1906, is located on the Vermilion R 190 km E of Edmonton. Although squatters occupied land near the river in the late 1890s, it was the Dominion Lands Survey of 1902 which ushered in a wave of homesteaders to the area. A small settlement called Breage soon emerged but was moved several kilometres W with the coming of the Canadian Northern Railway in 1905. The settlement was then named Vermilion (Cree for red clay deposits), after the river, and grew so rapidly that it was incorporated as both a village and a town in 1906. Although a fire wiped out most of the business district in 1918, Vermilion has remained the prosperous centre of a rich mixed-farming district. The town's major attraction, the Vermilion School of Agriculture (since 1975, Lakeland College), has offered training in agricultural science since 1913. DAVID LEONARD

Vermilion Pass, elev 1651 m, is situated between Boom and Storm mountains on the BC-Alberta border, 42 km W of Banff. It takes its name from the mineral springs of iron oxide located along the VERMILION R, 9 km SW of the pass, where Indians gathered material for war paint and decoration. Sir James HECTOR's party of the PALLISER EXPEDITION was the first group of non-natives to cross the pass in Aug 1858. GLEN BOLES

Vermilion River, 70 km (from its headstream to its confluence with the Kootenay R), rises in the Continental Ranges on the BC-Alberta border at the N end of KOOTENAY NATIONAL PARK. Fed by Tokumm Cr, it drains in a southerly direction, eventually emptying into the Kootenay R. It takes its name from mineral springs, located 9 km SW of VERMILION PASS, where Indians obtained iron oxide for decorative purposes and body paint. For most of its length, the river is paralleled by the 105 km Banff-Windermere Hwy. Like many mountain rivers, the Vermilion features instances of potholing and abrasion. DAVID EVANS

Verner, Frederick Arthur, painter (b at Hammondsville [later Sheridan], UC 26 Feb 1836; d at London, Eng 16 May 1928). After study at Heatherly's Art School, London, in 1856, Verner enlisted in the 3rd West York Regiment. On his

F.A. Verner, *Hudson's Bay Officials Leaving Brûlé Portage* (1876) (*courtesy Glenbow Museum, Calgary*).

return to Canada in 1862, he earned his living as a photographer. In time he became a painter of Indians, seeking accuracy in his subjects. He was present with Manitoba's Lt-Gov Alexander MORRIS in 1873 at the signing of the North West Angle Treaty, Lk of the Woods (Treaty No 3). The sketches he made there were the basis for many of his later paintings. He also carefully studied the buffalo (one sketch, now at the National Gallery of Canada, was made in Buffalo Bill's show in London 1892) and used these sketches for buffalo canvases such as *The Last of the Herd*. His mellow vision conveyed an image of the Canadian West as a secret garden, an oasis of calm and quiet, rather than the tragic battlefield portrayed by many American painters. He moved to London, Eng, in 1880. JOAN MURRAY

Vernon, BC, City, pop 20 241 (1986c), 19 987 (1981c), greater Vernon *c* 42 000, inc 1892, is located between the N end of Okanagan Lk and Kalamalka Lk. The area was first visited by David Stuart, a fur trader working for the Pacific Fur Co, in 1811, but missionaries built the first settlement in the 1840s. Several large ranches were established in the vicinity in the 1880s and fruit growing started in the 1890s. The townsite was a camp on the fur-trade trail, and the northern terminus for lake steamers was at nearby Okanagan Landing. The town was not connected to the main rail line until the 1890s, when a branch was built to Sicamous, on the CPR. In 1906 a major irrigation canal was built around the Vernon valley. The population swelled with over 10 000 recruits during WWI, as Vernon was the largest military camp in BC. Today, Vernon is a prosperous marketing and distribution centre for the northern OKANAGAN VALLEY; most of the valley's vegetables are grown in the area. Lumber, canning and tourism are important industries, and the military camp is still in operation.

The city centre is built on relatively flat land; much of the residential section is on glacial terraces and valley slopes. There is a branch of Okanagan College at nearby COLDSTREAM, on Kalamalka Lk. The Salish Indian name for Vernon was *hun-cul-deep-moose chin*, meaning "jumping over place"; it was named (1887) for Forbes George Vernon, chief commissioner of lands and works for BC, and one of the city's pioneers. JAMES MARSH

Verrazzano, Giovanni da, explorer (b at or near Florence *c*1485; d in the W Indies *c*1528). Several years before Jacques CARTIER, he established a French claim in N America. A rarity among early explorers, he was of distinguished lineage and was well educated in Florence, then a centre of geographic and navigational science. He moved to Dieppe, France, to pursue a maritime career and set sail westward from there in 1523 under the French flag. He made landfall around 1 Mar 1524 at or near Cape Fear (33°50' N lat). He sailed S and then N to avoid the Spaniards, coasted N past New York Bay and the coast of Maine and likely departed from the E coast of Newfoundland (about 50° N lat), arriving back at

Dieppe 8 July 1524. Although he mistakenly believed that he saw the Pacific Ocean across a narrow peninsula near Cape Hatteras, he was the first to recognize that the coast from Florida to Newfoundland was contiguous and belonged to a New World. On a second voyage in 1528, he rowed ashore to one of the Caribbean islands, likely Guadeloupe, and was slain and eaten by cannibals. JAMES MARSH

Verrier, Étienne, military engineer (b at Aix-en-Provence, France 4 Jan 1683; d at La Rochelle, France 10 Sept 1747). After 17 years with the engineer corps, Verrier served at LOUISBOURG as chief engineer 1724-45. During these years he planned and revised the layout of the town, completed the bastioned enceinte, with its ornate town gates, the barracks with clock tower and governor's wing, the hospital, the lighthouse, 2 harbour batteries and harbour installations, and designed an unbuilt parish church. Son of a master sculptor, Verrier had a flair for architecture. Militarily he was somewhat less successful. Although his fortifications facilitated a spirited defence against overwhelming odds during the siege of 1745, his advice to abandon the Royal Battery to the enemy is difficult to understand. Verrier's plans and reports, together with archaeological data, have provided the basis for much of today's reconstruction at the Fortress of Louisbourg National Historic Park. F.J. THORPE

Reading: J. Fortier and O. Fitzgerald, *Fortress of Louisbourg* (1979).

Verrier, Louis-Guillaume, lawyer, teacher, attorney general of the Conseil Supérieur of New France (b at Paris, France 19 Oct 1690; d at Québec C 13 Sept 1758). He is noteworthy for his service as attorney general, the chief law officer for the colony (1728-58), for his survey of notarial deeds (1730-32) and exhaustive register of landed property in the colony (1732-40), and especially for his establishment, in 1733, of Canada's first structured program of LEGAL EDUCATION. Descended from a family of Parisian jurists and himself a lawyer in the *parlement* of Paris, this impecunious bachelor earned the reputation, following his immigration to Québec in 1728, of being a meticulous scholar and compulsive bibliophile. The quality of his law-school graduates moved Louis XV in 1741 to rescind a 1678 ordinance prohibiting lawyers from practising in New France. As a result a literate and active group of schooled advocates emerged who played an important role in the post-Conquest affirmation of SEIGNEURIAL tenure and the COUTUME DE PARIS, and in the 1785 restructuring of Québec's legal profession. G. BLAINE BAKER

Versailles, Treaty of, 28 June 1919, the peace settlement imposed on Germany after WORLD WAR I, drawn up at the Paris Peace Conference and signed near the French capital at Versailles. The treaty broke up and redistributed the German Empire and required substantial reparation payments from it. Canada had little impact on the final shape of the treaty, but PM Sir Robert BORDEN led a successful fight for separate Dominion representation at the conference and separate signatures on the treaty. He believed passionately that Canada, with 60 000 war dead, had paid the price of such recognition. In addition to representation in its own right, and along with the other Dominions and India, Canada was represented on the British Empire delegation, a fact that increased Canada's prestige and the opportunities for making its views known. However, when it came to signing the treaty, the British PM did so for the entire empire, the Dominions included, thus reducing the importance of their hard-won individual signatures. Canada's involvement reflected the ambiguity of its position in the world. Canada remained subordinate to Britain, in fact and in the perception of other nations, but her emerging international personality had been recognized. The treaty also made provision for a LEAGUE OF NATIONS, providing another vehicle for the advancement of Canada's national status.

NORMAN HILLMER

Vertebrate, member of the subphylum Vertebrata of the phylum Chordata. Vertebrates are bilaterally symmetrical ANIMALS with an internal skeleton of bone or cartilage consisting of, at least, a vertebral column and skull. The eyes (if present) and olfactory and feeding structures are always grouped in a distinct head region at the front of the body. At some stage, or throughout life, there is a series of gill slits behind the head, passing from the digestive tract to the outside. These are supported by skeletal bars in their walls. Usually, there are also appendages assisting in movement and manipulation of the environment, ranging from the median fins and tails of fishes to the specialized arms and hands of humans. The body covering may range from smooth, mucus-covered skin to a solid shell of bony armour, or to insulating fur or feathers.

The earliest evidence of vertebrates consists of fragmentary FOSSILS of the external armour of jawless fishes from the late Cambrian period (505-523 million years ago). Vertebrates apparently remained rare, scattered, and limited to jawless fishes until the appearance of the first jawed fishes in the late Silurian period (408-421 million years ago). In the next 50 million years, during the Devonian period, all major groups of living fishes and the first AMPHIBIANS appeared. The first REPTILES appeared at the beginning of the Pennsylvanian period (about 300 million years ago). The earliest identifiable reptilian ancestors of MAMMALS constitute one of the oldest distinct groups of reptiles, first appearing in the Pennsylvanian period, although mammals themselves date from the late Triassic period (208-230 million years ago). BIRDS, the youngest vertebrate class, apparently arose from small DINOSAUR ancestors during the Jurassic period (144-208 million years ago).

Aquatic, fishlike vertebrates comprise 5 of the 9 classes and about half of the nearly 40 000 living species. This probably reflects the greater age of fishlike groups and the relative stability of marine habitats over long periods, compared to freshwater or terrestrial habitats. Among terrestrial vertebrates, reptiles have shown the widest variety of body plans and adaptations, but birds have the most living species (9000). Mammals have about 4000 and amphibians about 3000 living species.

Vertebrates attain the largest sizes of all animals. They are more capable of efficient, rapid, sustained movements and have the most complex body organizations. These characteristics are interrelated and derive from the basic vertebrate body plan. The internal skeleton provides the necessary strength to anchor muscles and support the body, and is proportionally lighter than the external skeletons or shells of INVERTEBRATES. It allows for growth without the periodic moulting of a rigid external skeleton, and it increases the mechanical efficiency of muscles. Vertebrates are able to regulate their physiological processes. All (except hagfish, the most primitive vertebrates) regulate the dissolved salt concentrations and water content of their bodies. They also exert some control over their body temperatures, either by selecting environments in which they can gain or lose heat as required (ectothermy), as in FISH, amphibians and reptiles; or by regulating metabolism to produce heat internally (endothermy), as in birds and mammals.

Large size and increased activity have led to the

Classification of the Superclass Gnathostomata
(Numbers refer to living species worldwide and in Canada)

Class	Subclass	Examples	Habitat
Placodermi*		placoderms	mostly marine, open water to bottom feeders (late Silurian to late Devonian)
Chondrichthyes	Elasmobranchii c740; 51	sharks, skates, rays	mostly marine, open water to bottom feeders, coastal to deep sea
	Holocephali c30; 4	chimaeras	marine, bottom feeders, coastal to deep sea
Osteichthyes	Acanthodii*	acanthodians	mostly marine, probably open water (middle Silurian to early Permian)
	Sarcopterygii 7; 0	lobe-finned fishes	mostly freshwater, in shallow, standing water, frequently stagnant and subject to drying
	Actinopterygii c20 800; c880	ray-finned fishes	freshwater and marine, all aquatic habitats
Amphibia	Labyrinthodontia*	labyrinthodonts	freshwater marshes, semiaquatic (late Devonian to late Triassic)
	Lepospondyli*	lepospondyls	freshwater, aquatic to semiaquatic; some were eellike or snakelike (early Mississippian to early Permian)
	Lissamphibia c3 260; 40	living amphibians	freshwater, aquatic to terrestrial, burrowing to tree climbing
Reptilia	Anapsida c220; 12	stem reptiles,* turtles	aquatic, freshwater or marine to terrestrial, some desert dwellers
	Synapsida*	mammallike reptiles	semiaquatic to terrestrial (late Pennsylvanian to early Jurassic)
	Euryapsida*	plesiosaurs and relatives	marine, probably surface dwelling, coastal (Permian to late Cretaceous)
	Ichthyopterygia*	ichthyosaurs	marine, probably open water; some fed on squid
	Archosauria c25; 0	dinosaurs*, flying reptiles*, crocodilians	semiaquatic to terrestrial; crocodilians are semiaquatic, freshwater and marine.
	Lepidosauria c5 575; 30	tuatara, lizards, snakes	mostly terrestrial, burrowing to climbing; few marine forms
Aves	Archaeornithes*	toothed birds	terrestrial (late Jurassic)
	Neornithes c9 000; c420	modern birds	terrestrial to semiaquatic, flying to flightless
Mammalia	Prototheria 3; 0	Mesozoic mammals, monotremes	terrestrial to semiaquatic
	Metatheria c250; 1	marsupials	terrestrial
	Eutheria c3 800; c200	placental mammals	terrestrial in virtually all habitats; some also aquatic, from freshwater to open sea; some flying

* Extinct

development of systems which allow vertebrates both to take in food, oxygen, water and salts and to excrete metabolic wastes more rapidly than invertebrates can. The gills of aquatic species, or lungs of terrestrial species, have large surface areas through which oxygen can be absorbed and carbon dioxide lost. The kidneys act as filters for the removal of metabolic wastes and the regulation of water and salt in the body. The digestive system includes mechanisms to increase efficiency of feeding and of breaking up food so that digestion will proceed more rapidly. The intestinal walls have large surface areas through which nutrients can be absorbed. Finally, the closed, high-pressure circulatory system carries substances throughout the body.

All of these must function together to produce the co-ordinated activity required for survival. Co-ordination is supplied by the central nervous system, using information from the surroundings, which is collected by the sensory system. Throughout vertebrate evolutionary history, changes in habitat or activity have been accompanied by changes in the structure and function of body systems. An increase in swimming speed in a fish, for example, will cause increased size of muscles and the bones to which they are an-

chored. However, higher muscle activity also requires a greater flow of nutrients and oxygen, which affects the digestive, respiratory and circulatory systems. The increased production of wastes requires adaptation of the excretory system, and the changing needs of all of these together will affect the sensory and nervous systems, which supply information and co-ordination for the body as a whole.

The subphylum Vertebrata is divided into 2 superclasses. The first, Agnatha or jawless fishes, includes the lampreys, hagfish and extinct ostracoderms. About 40 species of lampreys occur worldwide (11 in Canada), while there are about 30 species of hagfish (3 in Canada). The second subclass, Gnathostomata, includes all jawed vertebrates. The table summarizes the major classes of jawed vertebrates. The outlines of classification are generally accepted; however, changes may occur as a result of continuing taxonomic studies.

K.W. STEWART

Vertical Mosaic, a term used by sociologist John PORTER to convey the concept that Canada is a mosaic of different ethnic, language, regional and religious groupings unequal in status and power. Porter published his book, *Vertical Mosaic: An*

Analysis of Social Class and Power in Canada, in 1965. "Mosaic" is often contrasted with the American concept of "melting pot." The Canadian John Murray Gibbon, in his book *The Canadian Mosaic* (1938), disapproved of the American melting-pot policy, according to which immigrants and their descendants were discouraged from maintaining close ties with their countries and cultures of origin and instead were encouraged to assimilate into the American way of life. Many Canadians pointed with pride to the alternative Canadian policy of encouraging immigrants and their descendants to maintain important aspects of their ancestral cultures. Porter's view was that in income, occupation and education, this supposedly beneficial policy worked to the advantage of some ethnic groups and to the disadvantage of others.

Porter's book revealed that some groups (eg, those of British origin) have better incomes, education and health than others (eg, those of eastern and southern European origin). Native Indian and Inuit people were the most disadvantaged. According to Porter, this vertical arrangement also applied to power and to influence in decision making. In the bureaucratic, economic and political spheres, those of British origin are overrepresented among the ELITES.

Since 1965 several studies have shown that the picture sketched by Porter has been modified only slightly, ie, there has been some lessening of the economic gap between ethnic groups, and people of French origin are better represented in the political and bureaucratic spheres. The economic elite, still dominated by those of British origin, has changed very little. The book earned Porter the prestigious American Sociological Assn's McIver Award.   FRANK G. VALLEE

Reading: W. Clement, *The Canadian Corporate Elite* (1975); J. Heap, *Everybody's Canada* (1974).

Verville, Alphonse, plumber, socialist, MP, president of the Trades and Labor Congress of Canada (b at Côte-St-Paul [Montréal], Canada E 28 Oct 1864; d at Montréal 20 June 1930). Verville left Montréal at age 18 to work in Chicago, where he became a member of the International Plumbers' Union. Returning to Montréal in 1893, he actively promoted international unionism there. He then became president of the Plumbers' Union and of the Conseil des métiers et du travail de Montréal, and was president of the TLC (1904-10). A supporter of the political labour movement, Verville was elected federal MP for Maisonneuve under the Parti ouvrier banner in 1906.   JACQUES ROUILLARD

Verville, Jean-François Du Verger de, military engineer (b at Paris, France *c*1670-75; d at Valenciennes or Paris, France 1729). Verville designed the landward front of fortification of the fortress of LOUISBOURG, including the citadel barracks, as well as the Royal and Island batteries; he drew the first plan of the town. Born into a family of architects, Verville served 12 years as a military engineer in Europe prior to his secondment in 1716 to Île Royale [Cape Breton I]. His plan for Louisbourg provided for 3 interdependent batteries and a bastioned front to defend the town against attack, respectively from the harbour and the swampy land to the W. After Verville's recall in 1725 his design, despite evident structural flaws, served as the basis for Étienne VERRIER's Louisbourg.   F.J. THORPE

Vesak, Norbert, choreographer (b at Port Moody, BC 22 Oct 1936). Controversial because of his penchant for flashy choreography, trendy subjects and lavish visual effects, Vesak was resident choreographer at VANCOUVER PLAYHOUSE Theatre 1964 before founding Western Dance The-

atre (1969-71). He created 2 popular works for the ROYAL WINNIPEG BALLET – *The Ecstasy of Rita Joe* (1971), a multimedia work featuring Dan GEORGE which was commissioned by the Manitoba Indian Brotherhood and based on George RYGA's play, and *What to Do Till the Messiah Comes* (1973), whose "Belong" pas de deux became ballerina Evelyn HART's signature piece and won a gold medal for choreography at the Varna International Ballet Competition 1980. An official choreographer with the Royal Winnipeg for a short time in the 1970s, Vesak later directed the Metropolitan and San Francisco Opera ballets while creating dances for many companies.   PENELOPE DOOB

Vetch (genus *Vicia*), semivining, herbaceous plant of the legume family, which produces good-quality hay. The 150 species are widely distributed worldwide. Most vetches originated in the Mediterranean region and some species were introduced into Canada by the earliest immigrants. Three species are now grown in Canada: *V. villosa*, hairy vetch; *V. pannonica*, Hungarian vetch; *V. sativa*, common vetch. Vetches have compound leaves, purple, pink or, rarely, white flowers. They form seed pods which explode on ripening. Vetches have tendrils and climb up tall, growing plants or fences. They occur commonly in pasture and in uncultivated fields in moist temperate areas of Canada. When planted early in June, vetches produce a hay crop in the year of seeding. If planted in Sept, they overwinter, producing a crop the following year. Vetch is now of little economic importance and commercial seed is scarce; however, historically, vetches have been used as an emergency FORAGE CROP, alone or with OATS or PEAS. Vetches produce hard seeds and may form dark green patches in uncultivated fields.   WALTER R. CHILDERS

Veterans, *see* WAR VETERANS.

Veterans Affairs, Department of, est 1944, upon division of the Department of Pensions and National Health. Made solely responsible for administering pensions and benefits for Canada's servicemen and women, it first had to develop a rehabilitation and re-establishment program for those returning from WWII. Legislation was enacted during the war to deal with hospital treatment, education, insurance, civil-service job preference, welfare, allowances and loans, pensions and land settlement. Although some programs have lapsed, the department's activities have increased owing to the advancing age of veterans. DVA continues to manage special programs providing aging veterans and their dependants with medical care and financial assistance. Pensions and allowances are administered by 3 associated agencies: Canadian Pension Commission, War Veterans Appeal Board, and Bureau of Pensions Advocates.   GLENN T. WRIGHT

Veterans' Land Act, passed 20 July 1942, following a Canadian tradition dating from the 17th century of settling ex-soldiers on the land. In 1919 a Soldier Settlement Act had provided returned WWI veterans who wished to farm with loans to purchase land, stock and equipment. Over 25 000 took advantage of the scheme, although many had to abandon their farms between the wars because of heavy debts and adverse farming conditions. The VLA, designed to overcome some of the problems inherent in the 1919 plan, gave WWII veterans choices. With only a small down payment, ex-servicemen could purchase land with the help of a government loan; additional funds were available for livestock and equipment. Repayment terms allowed settlers time to re-establish themselves without incurring heavy financial obligations. Veterans were also encouraged to settle small rural or sub-

urban holdings as part-time farmers or to substitute commercial fishing for full-time farming. In 1950 the VLA began to provide loans to veterans who wished to construct their own homes. Under the Veterans' Land Administration, a branch of the Department of VETERANS AFFAIRS, over 140 000 ex-servicemen had sought assistance before new loans were terminated in 1977. GLENN T. WRIGHT

Veterinary Medicine, the SCIENCE dealing with health and disease in VERTEBRATES, has application to 4 broad domains: domestic animals, wildlife, comparative medicine and PUBLIC HEALTH. In Canada in 1987, there were approximately 5700 professionally active veterinarians; this number will rise by 250 annually. Veterinarians are distributed in roughly equal numbers in private rural practice, private urban practice and institutional employment, but the proportion in urban practice is rising. Veterinary education requires at least 2 years of university preveterinary training, followed by 4 years of professional instruction. Postgraduate training in clinical or research programs is undertaken by 10-20% of veterinary graduates. The veterinary curriculum is similar to that of human MEDICINE. The veterinary profession is organized nationally in the Canadian Veterinary Medical Association and in each province as a provincial association.

Clinical veterinary medicine, including food-animal, small-animal and equine practices, or some mixture of these specializations, provides primary health care to an owner's animals. In rural settings, veterinarians deal with all types of animals, most being food animals. In urban centres, many veterinarians practise exclusively on pets or HORSES. Veterinarians practise singly, in partnerships or in corporations, depending on personal preferences. Income derives from fees charged to clients. Veterinary practitioners must be licensed by a provincial authority, normally the provincial veterinary association, upon successful completion of appropriate examinations.

Food-Animal Practice involves dairy and beef cattle, pigs, sheep, goats and poultry (*see* ANIMAL AGRICULTURE). Animals are treated on the farm or in a large-animal hospital. Food-animal practice may be subsidized by provincial or municipal governments. Subsidies vary from hospital grants, as in Manitoba, to direct assistance in paying professional fees, as in Québec, which has the only "veticare" scheme in N America. In NB all food-animal veterinarians are employed by the province. Veterinarians dealing with poultry disease tend to specialize and are usually employed by government or private industry.

Small-Animal Practice deals most commonly with DOGS and CATS but can also include rabbits and rodents (eg, mice, gerbils), birds (eg, budgerigars, parrots, finches), fish and more unusual animals (eg, primates, reptiles).

Federal, provincial and municipal governments employ veterinarians to provide services that protect animal and human health. Under the departments of agriculture, health, environment and wildlife, veterinarians conduct laboratory diagnosis, field investigation, food and animal inspection, administration, research and extension education. University veterinarians teach and do research in veterinary medical science. Most are employed in Canada's colleges of veterinary medicine. A few are also located in faculties of agriculture or medicine or departments of biology and in specialized research institutions such as the Veterinary Infectious Disease Organization (VIDO), U Sask. A few veterinarians find employment in industry, particularly in companies producing or selling PHARMACEUTICAL and BIOLOGICAL PRODUCTS. Their work includes research, sales, administration and extension of both advice and information to veterinarians in animal-related industries.

The growth of knowledge and technology in veterinary science is motivating some veterinarians to specialize in a branch of veterinary science (eg, internal medicine, pathology, dermatology, microbiology, radiology) or in a class of animal (eg, laboratory animals, food animals, horses, small pets). To specialize, a veterinarian must have appropriate practical experience, must undertake formal postgraduate training and must pass rigorous examinations. Most specialists are employed by institutions. Many practising veterinarians confine their work to one or a few species, but this limitation is not considered specialization, in the formal sense, by the profession.

Domestic Animals

Food Animals In Canada about one-half of the cash income from farms comes from animals or animal products. The protection of the health of this resource is the responsibility of practising veterinarians and appropriate government agencies. Food-animal practitioners are concerned with the treatment and prevention of indigenous diseases in animals on individual farms. Their primary objective is the economic benefit of the owner; thus, treatment must be economically sensible or must be imperative because of humane considerations. In food-animal practice, the major emphases are on prevention of disease and on reproductive management for optimal productivity (*see* ANIMAL BREEDING). Practitioners must be skilled in diagnosis, surgery, livestock reproduction practices, use of drugs, and analysis of production data. Preventive medicine involves monitoring the health of individual animals and of the herd by measuring, recording and analysing production performance.

Agriculture Canada is responsible for major legislation protecting Canada's livestock from diseases identified by law as reportable, and for excluding from Canada exotic diseases such as foot-and-mouth and African swine fever. International travel and transportation of animals is a constant threat because of the risk of introducing exotic, contagious animal diseases. The department's enviable record in controlling such diseases gives Canada's livestock access to world markets. Federal programs also seek to control or eradicate important indigenous diseases, eg, rabies, tuberculosis, brucellosis (contagious abortion). A milestone was reached in 1985 when the Canadian domestic cattle population was declared free of brucellosis. Federal veterinarians also ensure the quality and safety of food-animal products, eg, through meat inspection (*see* FOOD LEGISLATION).

Major health problems in livestock include high neonatal mortality from intestinal and respiratory diseases, poor reproductive efficiency and suboptimal production associated with subclinical disease and mismanagement. Veterinary research in food-animal disease and health maintenance is conducted principally by the federal government and the universities. Government research gives priority to detection and control of contagious diseases, especially those reportable by law. An example of an important Canadian contribution to the control of animal disease worldwide is a vaccine against neonatal diarrhea in calves, caused by certain strains of the bacterium *Escherichia coli*. Developed by VIDO, the vaccine was marketed by a Canadian firm. New technology in reproduction (eg, embryo transfer, freezing embryos) promises to make livestock production more efficient and to promote more rapid genetic improvement.

Companion Animals or Pets There are several

million pets in Canada. Health services are provided almost entirely by private practitioners who must build up their own hospitals or clinics and employ animal-health technicians and other support staff. Facilities accommodating 50-100 animals and providing equipment for surgery, radiology, laboratory diagnosis and various other specialties are common. The capital investment required to establish a hospital is substantial. Small-animal medicine is similar to human medicine, since pet animals are normally kept for a natural life span and succumb to the infirmities of old age as well as to disease. There are fewer economic constraints on medical treatment of pets in comparison to food animals.

Work and Recreation Animals The health care of domestic animals used in recreation or work is a major field of veterinary medicine. Canadian society is highly mechanized; consequently, animals have a limited role in performing work. In recent years, horses have increased in number: a few are still used as draft animals and for herding cattle, but most are used for recreation and sports (*see* HARNESS RACING; THOROUGHBRED RACING). These athletes of the animal world are prone to injuries and to problems associated with racing or other sports activities. Many veterinarians confine their practice to horses and become skilled at dealing with their special problems, for example, lameness. Dogs are used for a number of chores: herding sheep, pulling sleds and providing surrogate eyes or ears for handicapped individuals. Their occupational health needs are met by small-animal practitioners.

Fibre and Furs Sheep, the only significant animal fibre producers in Canada, are attended by veterinarians, usually in preventive medical programs. Several other animal species provide woollike fibres that can be used to make clothing. In Canada the native MUSKOXEN produce a high-quality fibre called *qiviut*. In the future, northerners may manage muskoxen in some form of semi-domestication to allow the harvesting of *qiviut*. Veterinary researchers are studying the muskox with a view to its more intensive management.

Fur-bearing animals are raised across Canada. Economically important species are MINK and FOX. Disease control is crucial to the success of FUR FARMING, since the relatively close confinement of a large number of animals makes them vulnerable to various highly contagious diseases, eg, distemper, parvovirus intestinal infection. The latter was first described at Fort William and bears this name. Mink have provided an important example of how animals serve as monitors of chemical POLLUTION. The poor reproductive performance developed by ranch mink fed a diet of fish from Lk Michigan was shown to be caused by PCBs (polychlorinated biphenyls) in the fish. This incident was the first indication that PCBs and related compounds were a biological hazard.

Wildlife

In Nature Wildlife, including animals, fish and birds, is an especially rich component of Canada's natural environment. In addition to its intrinsic value, wildlife provides food, clothing and economic benefits, particularly to native people, and is a major source of recreation for naturalists and hunters. Wild animals also serve as monitors of environmental problems. Veterinary medicine is among the professions taking an active interest in health and disease in these populations. Wild animals are important in the epidemiology of certain animal and human diseases (eg, rabies, tularemia) because they act as disease reservoirs. For example, tuberculosis and brucellosis are present in BISON in WOOD BUFFALO NATIONAL PARK.

In Captivity The health and reproductive per-

formance of ZOO animals are the principal concerns of zoo veterinary medicine, an emerging practice specialty. High population density and unnatural feeding conditions make zoo animals particularly vulnerable to disease and poor reproductive performance. Canada's zoos and aquariums employ veterinarians full- and part-time.

Fish and Aquatic Species Health management of FISH or other marine food sources in nature and in captivity is an emerging concern. Confinement of fish in ponds or by mechanical devices to give high population densities puts them at increased risk from infectious disease. The emergence of fish farming (AQUACULTURE) as an economically viable industry depends on an assured supply of disease-free stock. In Canada various aquatic habitats are adaptable to fish farming, including ocean waters, streams, lakes and prairie sloughs.

Public Health, Laboratory Animals and Comparative Medicine

Public-health veterinarians help ensure a wholesome supply of food of animal origin. This complex government responsibility involves the detection of infectious agents and undesirable chemicals (eg, feed additives, drugs, environmental pollutants) in meat, milk and eggs. Zoonoses are diseases transmissible from animals to humans. Over 200 such diseases may exist in wildlife (eg, rabies, western encephalitis, tularemia, plague) or in domestic animals (eg, tuberculosis, brucellosis). Veterinarians help protect humans from zoonoses, eg, through the immunization of dogs against rabies. The veterinary profession informs the public about other potentially dangerous factors in the relationship between animals and man, eg, the connection between rabies and stray dogs.

Laboratory animals are widely used in medical research and in the identification and investigation of hazards to human health. The care and use of such animals has become an area of specialization. Laboratory animals provide natural and experimental models of human or animal diseases and their study is essential to a better understanding of disease. A primary concern of those working with laboratory animals has been the assurance of high standards of humane care. The Canadian Council on Animal Care has been very successful in working toward this end (*see* ANIMAL ISSUES; HUMANE SOCIETIES).

Comparative medicine is the study of phenomena that are basic to diseases of all species, through research into natural and experimental disease. Insights gained can be extrapolated to diseases of individual species, including man. Veterinarians and others in the field have recognized many naturally occurring animal diseases that may be used as models for similar or identical conditions in human or other animals. Such model diseases may be numerous because the phenomena of disease causation are similar throughout the animal kingdom. The study of experimental disease in animals has facilitated major advances in medicine, eg, the elucidation of germ theory and the discovery of insulin. Comparative medicine is also responsible for the discoveries that arthropods act as vectors of infectious disease and that viruses cause cancer. The transmission by ticks of a protozoan disease of cattle (Texas fever) was the first demonstration that such a phenomenon was possible, and it led to an understanding of the transmission of malaria and other diseases by mosquitoes and other arthropods. That viruses can cause cancer was first demonstrated in chickens and subsequently recognized in many animals. A Canadian contribution to comparative medicine was the discovery of a mycotoxin in 1922 by Francis SCHOFIELD of

Veterinary students use a flashlight to examine the oral cavity of a steer (*courtesy Western College of Veterinary Medicine*).

the Ontario Veterinary College. He found that mold growing on damp sweet clover produced a toxin which caused a fatal bleeding disorder in cattle. This toxic material, dicoumarol, a powerful blood anticoagulant, is now used medicinally in humans. Many other mycotoxins have since been described. The discovery of dicoumarol also portended the discovery of other biologically active materials produced by molds, eg, antibiotics.
N.O. NIELSEN

Reading: K. Aspinwall, *First Steps in Veterinary Science* (1976).

Veterinary Medicine, Education There are 4 veterinary colleges in Canada. In general, 6 years of training are required to earn a veterinary degree: 2 years of preveterinary courses, which may be taken at a number of institutions of higher learning; and 4 years of specialized professional education at one of the veterinary colleges. Veterinary courses include anatomy, BIOCHEMISTRY, embryology, epidemiology, physiology, pharmacology, toxicology, microbiology, IMMUNOLOGY, pathology, clinical medicine and surgery. There have been major construction and expansion programs at all 4 colleges in recent years and approximately 260 veterinarians graduate yearly. In 1928 the first woman graduated from a Canadian veterinary college. In 1986 about 53% of graduates were women. Veterinary colleges carry on research on diseases of food-producing and companion animals, and of fish, birds and wildlife, and on problems in biomedical science. There are 250-300 graduate students in the Canadian veterinary colleges.

Ontario Veterinary College (OVC), Guelph, is the oldest in Canada. Until 1965 it was affiliated with the U of T and graduates received their degrees from that university. In 1965 OVC became one of the colleges forming UNIVERSITY OF GUELPH. Until 1963, when the Western College of Veterinary Medicine was founded, OVC was the only veterinary college for English Canada, serving students from all provinces. Most students now come from Ontario, although there are generally a few from Québec. OVC grants Doctor of Veterinary Medicine (DVM), MSc, Phd and DVSc degrees. Postgraduate diploma courses are also given. Enrolment in the DVM course is *c*100 annually.

Atlantic Veterinary College was established in 1983 at UPEI in Charlottetown and serves the 4 Atlantic provinces, from which it derives most of its students. The first class of 50 students started in 1986 and will graduate in 1990. Degrees obtainable are DVM and MSc. Diploma and doctoral programs are planned. Diseases of aquatic species related to aquaculture will be a significant program at AVC in addition to traditional veterinary programs.

Faculty of Veterinary Medicine, UNIVERSITÉ DE MONTRÉAL is located in St-Hyacinthe, Qué. Before

moving there in 1947, the school was for many years located in OKA, Qué, where it formed part of an agricultural-veterinary educational centre financed by the Québec Dept of Agriculture and operated by the Trappists. With the move to St-Hyacinthe, it became the direct responsibility of the Québec Dept of Agriculture until 1969 when it became a U de M faculty. Considerable development in staff and facilities has taken place. The only French-language veterinary college in N America, it offers the DMV and MSc degrees. Postgraduate diploma courses are also given. About 70 undergraduates register yearly.

Western College of Veterinary Medicine (WCVM) was established at Saskatoon in 1963 as part of U Sask. The first veterinarians graduated in 1969. The second of the English-speaking veterinary colleges in Canada, it serves the 4 western provinces and the territories. Degrees obtainable are the DVM, MVSc, MSc and PhD. Diploma courses are offered at the postgraduate level. About 70 undergraduates enter each year.
J. FRANK and R.G. THOMSON

Veterinary Medicine, History of The healing of ANIMAL and human ailments has been a preoccupation of man for centuries. Human MEDICINE became professionalized much before veterinary medicine, which did not become institutionalized until the opening of veterinary schools in France at Lyons (1761) and Alfort (1766). Graduates probably did not come to Canada, immigration from France having been halted by the British CONQUEST in 1760. In England the veterinary art was formally established in 1791, the year in which provision was made to create the colony of UPPER CANADA. Graduates of the Edinburgh Veterinary College, founded in 1823 in Scotland, are the first known veterinary practitioners in Canada with a diploma from a chartered school. Probably the only veterinary surgeon in the colony of NB in 1851 was M.A. Cuming of Saint John, an 1846 graduate of Edinburgh.

Veterinary Education Farriers, without specialized veterinary training, outnumbered trained persons before and long after 1866 – the year in which the graduation of persons in Canada who had received formal training in a diploma course began (*see* BLACKSMITHING). Andrew SMITH, an 1861 graduate of the Edinburgh college, established the first formal course in Toronto (1862). From 1866 to 1908 (when the Ontario Veterinary College was acquired by the provincial government), over 3000 graduates completed the 2-year diploma course. Many of the graduates were from the US and did not remain in Canada; consequently, Canada continued to suffer from a lack of veterinary surgeons. Andrew Smith's college, moved from Toronto in 1922, continues today as the Ontario Veterinary College, UNIVERSITY OF GUELPH.

In 1866, a second private college with high admission standards was established in Montréal by Duncan MCEACHRAN. It eventually became a faculty of McGill University, closing in 1903 from lack of funds. The French-speaking college which arose from this English-speaking one has been in continuous operation since 1886. Founded by V.T. DAUBIGNY it united in 1894 with 2 other Québec schools to form the School of Comparative Medicine and Veterinary Science of Montréal. The school was moved to the Trappist Agricultural Institute of OKA, Qué, in 1928 and taken over by the Québec government and moved to St-Hyacinthe in 1947. It is affiliated with U de Montréal. A college founded in 1895 in association with Queens U, Kingston, Ont, was short-lived, closing in 1899. A fourth college, the Western College of Veterinary Medicine, established at U of Sask in 1963, admitted its first class in 1965.

Veterinary Associations The advent of the Ontario Veterinary College and its "educated" professionals was followed by a demand that society recognize these qualifications and services in preference to those of the empiric farrier. In 1874 through the aegis of Professor Smith, the Ontario Veterinary Medical Association was founded. It was incorporated as the Ontario Veterinary Association (OVA) in 1879. Veterinary associations were formed in Man (1881), Qué (1902), Alta (1906), BC (1907), Sask (1908-09), NS (1913), NB (1919) and PEI (1920). Each body was autonomous, recognized by provincial legislation established under Section 92, BRITISH NORTH AMERICA ACT, 1867. Each formulated bylaws to govern its membership and especially to decide who should be admitted to practice by virtue of holding a recognized diploma. The 1871 census showed 247 "Farriers and Veterinary Surgeons," most residing in Ontario, the remainder in NS and NB. The North-West Territories had virtually no veterinary surgeons. Veterinary medicine thus developed along provincial lines, characterized for many years, and in some instances to the present day, by narrow provincialism. This attitude was probably related to low fees, the fear of professional opposition from recent graduates, and an inability to take a broad view of the profession. It meant that little or no interest developed in a national association. Furthermore, the American Veterinary Medical Association, founded in 1863, filled the needs of the affluent who could afford to travel to its annual meetings.

Between 1871 and 1911 the number of veterinary surgeons increased to 1150: Ontario, 50%; western Canada, 30%; the eastern provinces, 20%. Empiricism continued to flourish despite efforts by provincial associations to confine the treatment of farm animals to their membership. In the early 1890s, veterinary dental schools in Toronto gave instruction to anyone who could pay for the brief instruction and diploma. Instructors were not necessarily veterinary surgeons. In 1896 the Veterinary Science Company of London, Ont, was established and through the London Veterinary Correspondence School ran a course in veterinary medicine and surgery. Besides a home-study course, the school provided a textbook and diploma which it led recipients to believe was qualification to practise anywhere in Canada. Provincial legislation closed the school in 1921, but before then 77 editions of the text were published and diplomas were issued worldwide. For many years the provincial associations had to cope with the demands of London school "graduates" who unsuccessfully sought membership and practice privileges.

After WWII, the subject of the formation of a national veterinary association surfaced in western Canada. The need became evident when the federal government disbanded the Royal Canadian Army Veterinary Corps (RCAVC) without consulting the profession. There was no national group to lobby against disbanding. In addition, displaced veterinarians from Europe were immigrating to Canada, and provincial associations were uncertain about their standards. A national association was needed to speak for the profession and to act as an examining body to screen immigrant veterinarians and to establish reciprocity among provincial examining boards.

In 1912 the British Columbia Veterinary Medical Association (BCVMA) had proposed a national body and by about 1920 most of the provinces were sympathetic. In 1921 a Canadian Veterinary Council was formed with representatives from each provincial association; however, at a conference in Ottawa that year, a draft bill to enact a Dominion association faltered on provincial misunderstanding. In 1923 a Canadian National Veterinary Association was founded by individuals attending a national meeting in Montréal, but this association died quietly for lack of funds and provincial support. The Western Canadian Veterinary Association (WCVA), formed in the 1930s, became dormant until 1945, mainly because of problems related to reconciling provincial autonomy with national registration. The problem was a draft clause which would give a national association the right to permit recognized graduates to practise anywhere in Canada. A Dominion Veterinary Council, which was formed (1943-44) to try again to organize a viable national association, promoted a Dominion body within which provinces would retain the right to set examinations. This council succeeded in starting provincial discussions but held only one meeting. In 1945 a revived Western Canada association proposed a national association and skirted the sensitive areas of national registration and a national examining board. Largely through the efforts of Albertan B.I. Love, as representative of the WCVA, the thoughts of presidents of the eastern Canadian associations began to crystallize and by Apr 1946 plans had been developed for a national body. On 30 June 1948 the Act to incorporate the Canadian Veterinary Medical Association received royal assent.

Mounted Police Veterinarians The mounted police force, enacted by legislation in 1873 to police the North-West Territories, "marched" west from Toronto in June 1874, by train, accompanied by 244 HORSES under the care of John Luke Poett, veterinary surgeon from Stratford, Ont. Poett, an 1860 Edinburgh graduate, had practised in Ontario since 1869, first in London, then in Stratford. One of the first veterinary surgeons in the Territories and the first graduate veterinary surgeon of the force, Poett served under a commission 1874-77 and 1884-95, latterly as a staff sergeant.

The NORTH-WEST MOUNTED POLICE (NWMP) became the arm of the federal government responsible for the enforcement of disease control in domestic animals arriving in the Territories with settlers from the US. Initially, control of contagious diseases was mainly related to horses but it soon extended to cattle. In 1884, Poett inspected nearly 2800 imported cattle for evidence of skin diseases and contagious pleuropneumonia. In 1895, 9 other qualified veterinary surgeons belonged to the force. These men were responsible for the health of the horses (782 in 1895) and acted as inspectors of imported animals until the number of veterinarians in the Territories reached a level which permitted their employment in lieu of NWMP veterinarians (about 1896).

Two veterinary surgeons took care of the horses of the government forces suppressing the NORTH-WEST REBELLION. One of these, J.G. RUTHERFORD, an 1879 graduate of OVC, left his newly opened practice in Portage la Prairie to become a commissioned officer in the Winnipeg Field Battery and veterinary surgeon for General Middleton's forces. Subsequently, he practised in Portage, became a politician (provincial and federal government) and then founder of the Health of Animals Branch, Canada Dept of Agriculture, with the title Veterinary Director General (1902).

Army Veterinarians Before 1910 no veterinary corps existed in the Canadian Army; veterinary surgeons were noncommissioned officers or regimental officers with mounted and artillery units. In 1910 the Army Veterinary Service (AVS) was established, consisting of qualified veterinary surgeons with commissioned rank, supported by personnel of other ranks. This service, part of the Canadian Militia, consisted of the Canadian Permanent Army Veterinary Corps (CPAVC), veterinary officers gazetted to the corps, and NCOs and

privates enlisted therein; the Canadian Army Veterinary Corps (CAVC), veterinary officers gazetted to the corps and detailed for duty with mounted corps of the Active Militia; and the short-lived Regimental Veterinary Service (RVS), consisting of officers then on the regimental staff of mounted corps.

The Army Veterinary Service thus had a permanent force and a militia group of officers, each responsible to the quartermaster general of the Canadian Militia. The senior officer of the CPAVC administered the service. Beneath him were the principal veterinary officers of military districts or divisions. There was a Veterinary Remount Establishment and schools for training enlisted men. In 1912 the Militia Council published regulations specifying the duties and functions of all officers, veterinary schools and hospitals, and other facets of the Canadian Army Veterinary Service. When WWI began, the groundwork had been established for the employment of veterinary surgeons, and within 3 months of the outbreak Canadian veterinarians were en route to England with troops and horses. In addition, a Remount Service had begun to purchase horses to supply currently formed army units and to replace losses overseas.

Canadian veterinarians enlisted in both the Canadian and British Army Veterinary Corps, each corps eventually being awarded the title Royal in recognition of war service. About 300 Canadian veterinarians served varying periods during 1914-18, mainly in Europe but also in India, Egypt, Mesopotamia and Russia. Several received decorations for preserving the lives of horses while under severe enemy attack. Mobile sections removed horse casualties to evacuation stations, which sent severely injured animals to base hospitals for surgical and other treatments. Mange hospitals were essential to control and suppress outbreaks of that debilitating parasite. On the conclusion of hostilities, a few veterinary officers remained in Europe until 1920 in order to aid in the disposal of horses, either as human food or as work animals in Belgium and Italy. In 1915, because of a severe shortage of veterinary officers for the British army, some Canadian veterinary students (final year) had been permitted to forgo final examinations if they enlisted in the British corps as second lieutenants. A few took advantage of this, were graduated in absentia and were in England as fully fledged veterinary officers about 3 weeks after enlisting. The veterinary personnel of the Canadian Expeditionary Force (1914-18), 72 officers and 756 other ranks had cared for 24 000 horses by the time the war ended.

In 1929 the RCAVC establishment was 12 officers and 38 other ranks, in 6 detachments. The CAVC consisted of 100 officers and 55 other ranks, in 11 sections. With replacement of horses by motorized vehicles, a veterinary establishment was no longer needed. In 1940 both corps were disbanded, and during WWII very few veterinarians served in a capacity related to their veterinary qualifications. The majority of those serving belonged to a group concerned with biological warfare; their work remains classified. Technological warfare caused the demise of the army veterinary surgeon in Canada, but not in Britain or the US.

C.A.V. BARKER

Veterinary Medicines Industry Industrial VETERINARY MEDICINE is that sector of the veterinary profession concerned with the research, development, manufacture and marketing of veterinary drugs. The industry is composed of 2 segments: biologicals, ie, drugs derived from living organisms, including vaccines and serums; and PHARMACEUTICALS, ie, other drugs, including antibiotics, steroids, anthelmintics (deworming compounds)

and anesthetics. The research, development and application of pharmaceuticals has differed from that of biologicals. With few exceptions, pharmaceuticals have been developed primarily to treat human diseases, and their application in veterinary medicine has been a sequel to their use as human drugs. Biologicals are disease specific and species specific drugs, and this exclusivity has resulted in the development of a veterinary biologicals industry discrete from its human counterpart.

Canada has made a number of significant contributions to the veterinary biologicals industry; for example, ERA rabies vaccine, used throughout the world, was developed by CONNAUGHT LABORATORIES Ltd, Toronto. ERA vaccine is a live, attenuated (ie, weakened) vaccine that contains a strain of rabies VIRUS modified so that it will induce immunity in animals for up to 5 years, after a single injection. The vaccine has been conclusively demonstrated to be safe in a wide variety of animal species. In 1979 the Veterinary Infectious Disease Organization (VIDO) in Saskatoon developed a vaccine to protect calves against calfhood diarrhea caused by the bacterium *Escherichia coli*. This vaccine is unique in that it confers protection against disease-producing strains of *E. coli* by employing hairlike projections (pilli) on the surface of the cell as the immunizing agent. The antibodies produced by the mother in response to these pilli, which are passed to the calf in the colostrum (precursor of milk) during the first 5 days of life, prevent *E. coli* bacteria from attaching to the inner surface of the intestinal wall, a process which is necessary for the organism to produce disease. The first federally licensed vaccine in N America against Marek's disease, a cancerous complex affecting young chickens, was another Canadian contribution. Other Canadian innovations include an orally administered vaccine to protect swine against erysipelas (St Anthony's Fire), and a commercial technique for immunizing young chickens.

The world veterinary drug market was a $9.2-billion industry in 1986, of which Canada had a 1.9% share. The US, Japan and the UK are the leading countries in the industry. Drugs used as feed additives constitute over 75% of the Canadian market; biologicals make up the remainder. The Canadian industry is served primarily by a handful of manufacturers (Canada Packers Inc, Dispar Veterinary Products Ltd, Langford Inc, Sanofi Animal House and Vetrepharm Inc).

M.J. WALCROFT

Vézina, Georges, hockey player (b at Chicoutimi, Qué Jan 1887; d there 26 Mar 1926). He tended goal for MONTREAL CANADIENS 1910-25 without missing a game. He was noted for his composure under fire, once stopping 78 of 79 shots in a game. He collapsed during a game on 28 Nov 1925 and died 4 months later of tuberculosis. The Canadiens donated the VÉZINA TROPHY to the NHL in his honour.

JAMES MARSH

Vézina Trophy is awarded to the goalkeeper voted most valuable to his team. Up until the 1981-82 season, it was awarded annually to the goalkeeper(s) who had played a minimum 25 games for the team that had allowed the fewest goals during the regular NATIONAL HOCKEY LEAGUE season. It was first presented in 1926-27 in memory of Georges VÉZINA. Jacques PLANTE won, or shared, the trophy 7 times, Bill DURNAN 6, Ken DRYDEN 5 and Terry SAWCHUK 4. The goalie(s) on the team giving up the fewest goals are now awarded the William M. Jennings Award. The Vézina is now awarded to the "most valuable" goalkeeper, who is not necessarily the one who allows the fewest goals.

JAMES MARSH

VIA Rail Canada Ltd was established as a CROWN CORPORATION in 1978 after a brief history as a CN subsidiary. Financed by the federal government, it operates all intercity passenger railway services in Canada. The corporation's board of directors reports to TRANSPORT CANADA.

In 1981 VIA cancelled or reduced numerous routes in an attempt to make passenger service more efficient. Services in parts of the country were seriously affected and the Liberal government was widely criticized. A non-confidence vote over the issue in Oct 1981 was won by the government. Many of the services were reinstated by the new Conservative government elected in 1984. With head offices in Montréal, in 1986 VIA Rail had operating revenue of $671 million, assets of $719 million and 5370 employees, and carried over 6 million passengers. *See also* RAILWAYS, CONTEMPORARY.

Vickers, Jonathan Stewart, Jon, tenor (b at Prince Albert, Sask 29 Oct 1926). Vickers sang in church choirs and in Gilbert and Sullivan and Victor Herbert operettas, and in 1950 became a scholarship student at the Royal Conservatory of Music, Toronto. His professional career began almost immediately with concert, oratorio and operatic engagements throughout eastern Canada, followed by CBC radio successes. His international career began in 1957 with performances in New York in *Fidelio* and *Medea* and a 3-year contract with the Royal Opera House, Covent Garden, London, Eng. Towering performances at Bayreuth, Dallas, Vienna, Milan and Buenos Aires followed, and Vickers was soon in demand throughout the operatic world. An outstanding performer of the dramatic and Heldentenor repertoire, and in his time the world's greatest interpreter of the role of Siegmund in Wagner's *Die Walküre*, he has made numerous recordings and films, including those in association with Herbert von Karajan in the Salzburg festivals. His approach to his operatic roles includes the study of the composer's philosophy and emotional intent, as seen particularly in his favourite role, Britten's *Peter Grimes*. By his own choice Vickers has performed infrequently in Canada but he has appeared at EXPO 67, the National Arts Centre, the Guelph Spring Festival, and with the Toronto Symphony and the Opéra du Québec. A Sas-

Tenor Jon Vickers as Othello at the Vienna State Opera, Vienna, Austria, Oct 1975 (*courtesy National Archives of Canada/PA-137106/Walter Curtin*).

Parliament Buildings, Victoria, BC (*photo by M.G. Kingshott/Valan*).

katchewan tour in 1977 was climaxed by a concert in Prince Albert in the church where he sang as a boy. He peformed in *Peter Grimes* in Toronto in 1984 and in Handel's *Samson* in Covent Garden in 1985-86. Vickers was made Companion of the Order of Canada in 1969 and in 1976 received the MOLSON PRIZE.   MABEL H. LAINE

Victoria, queen of the United Kingdom of Great Britain and Ireland and empress of India (b at Kensington Palace 24 May 1819; d at Windsor Castle 22 Jan 1901). She succeeded her uncle George IV in 1837 at age 18. She was an ardent imperialist and took an intense interest in her colonial subjects. No individual has been more honoured than Queen Victoria in the names of Canada's public buildings, streets, populated places and physical features. Victoria College in Toronto, Royal Victoria Hospital in Montréal, Victoria General Hospital in both Halifax and Winnipeg are among the notable public institutions named for her. Among Canada's 280 postal divisions, more than half have at least one thoroughfare identified by the name Victoria, most named to honour her. In 1831 John ROSS, while searching for the Northwest Passage, entered a small bay on the E side of Boothia Pen and named it Victoria Harbour for the young princess. Subsequently, she formally granted him permission to use her name for this remote and minor water feature in Canada's Arctic. From then on, explorers, mapmakers and administrators assigned the name Victoria to a multitude of geographical features all over the Canadian map, where her name appears more than 300 times.

On the occasions of the golden (1887) and diamond (1897) anniversaries of her reign many features were named for her. And long after her death, Queen Peak in northern BC was named for her in 1933 because of its association with nearby Victoria Peak and Consort Park.

The best-known place named for the British monarch is the city at the tip of Vancouver I. In 1843, the Hudson's Bay Co resolved to name the new fort overlooking the Strait of Juan de Fuca for the beloved queen, but Fort Albert was locally assigned to it. Subsequently, a terse message from London compelled the use of Fort Victoria. The townsite of VICTORIA was established in 1851-52, and in 1868 the growing city became the capital of the colony of British Columbia. Alberta also had a Victoria northeast of Edmonton, where George MCDOUGALL had established a mission in 1862, and the Hudson's Bay Co had set up a post in 1864. In 1887, to avoid confusion with other Victorias, the name of this small community was

changed to Pakan, the nickname of a Cree chief. The village of Empress, NE of Medicine Hat, was named in 1913 in commemoration of the queen's imperial title received from Parliament in 1876 when Disraeli was prime minister. The marquess of Lorne and his wife, Princess Louise (the queen's daughter), wanted to give the name Victoria to the capital of the North-West Territories in 1882, but wisely chose the other half of her Latin title, Regina. In 1905 it became the capital of the new province of Saskatchewan. Manitoba has a rural municipality and a lake named Victoria, and another municipality called Victoria Beach. Ontario has at least 47 distinct features with her name: one county, one township, 14 populated places and 31 physical features. In fact, one does not travel far in Ontario before encountering Victoria Corners, Victoria Square, Victoria Harbour, Victoria Springs, Victoria Lake or just plain Victoria. Evidence of Victoria is less apparent in Québec, although the second-largest place in Canada with her name is in that province. Victoriaville, a town of more than 21 500 people, was named for the queen in 1861. There are as well 7 physical features in Québec with the name Victoria, including Grand lac Victoria at the head of the Ottawa R, S of Val-d'Or.

The Atlantic provinces have 29 places and features with the name Victoria. Among these are a county in each of NB and NS. Victoria is an attractive seaside village in PEI, where there are also places called Victoria Cross and Victoria West. Newfoundland has a Victoria, a town of nearly 2000; it lies on the west side of Conception Bay about 50 km NW of St John's.

The 2 northern territories have 22 features with the name Victoria. Among them are Victoria I, Canada's second-largest island (after Baffin) in the Arctic Archipelago, and Victoria and Albert Mountains on Ellesmere I. *See also* PLACE-NAMES.
                                                   ALAN RAYBURN

Victoria, capital of British Columbia, is situated on the southern tip of VANCOUVER I, about 100 km S of Vancouver. Occupying a peninsular site, Victorians view the bordering Juan de Fuca and Haro straits, backed by the Olympic Mts of Washington to the S and the Gulf Is to the E, with the majestic, volcanic peak of Mt Baker in the distance. The metropolitan area is characterized by a number of low hills interspersed with relatively flat areas, and is bordered on the W by the fjordlike

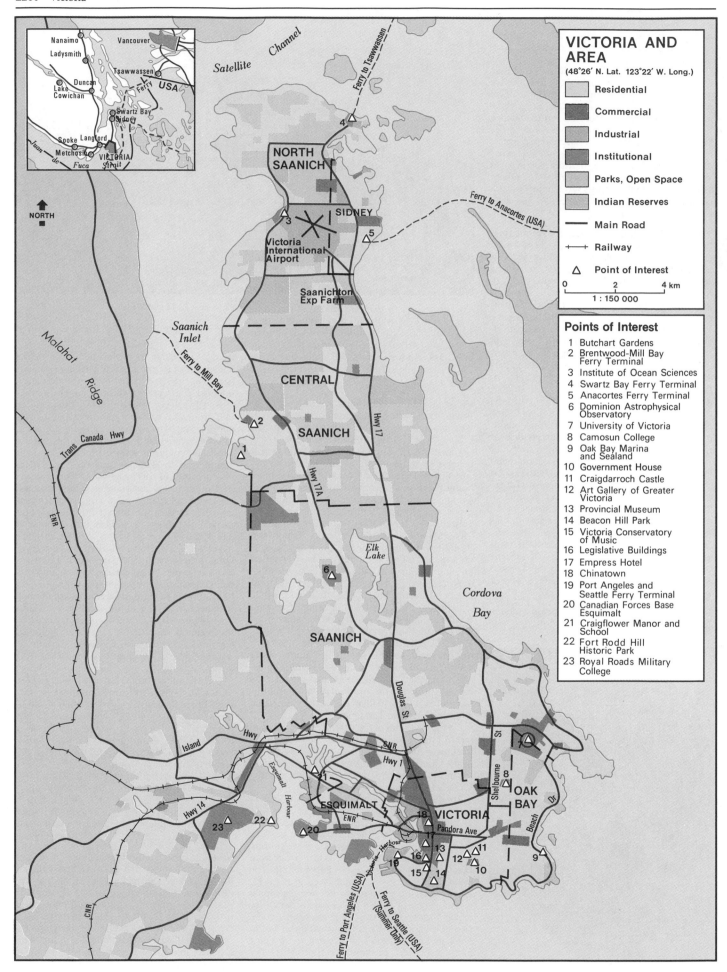

Inset map (top left):
Nanaimo
Ladysmith
Vancouver
Tsawwassen
Duncan
Lake Cowichan
Ferry
USA
Swartz Bay
Sidney
Sooke
Langford
Metchosin
VICTORIA
Juan de Fuca Strait

NORTH

VICTORIA AND AREA
(48°26' N. Lat. 123°22' W. Long.)

Residential
Commercial
Industrial
Institutional
Parks, Open Space
Indian Reserves
——— Main Road
—+— Railway
△ Point of Interest

0   2   4 km
1 : 150 000

Points of Interest
1 Butchart Gardens
2 Brentwood-Mill Bay Ferry Terminal
3 Institute of Ocean Sciences
4 Swartz Bay Ferry Terminal
5 Anacortes Ferry Terminal
6 Dominion Astrophysical Observatory
7 University of Victoria
8 Camosun College
9 Oak Bay Marina and Sealand
10 Government House
11 Craigdarroch Castle
12 Art Gallery of Greater Victoria
13 Provincial Museum
14 Beacon Hill Park
15 Victoria Conservatory of Music
16 Legislative Buildings
17 Empress Hotel
18 Chinatown
19 Port Angeles and Seattle Ferry Terminal
20 Canadian Forces Base Esquimalt
21 Craigflower Manor and School
22 Fort Rodd Hill Historic Park
23 Royal Roads Military College

Map labels:
Satellite Channel
Ferry to Tsawwassen
Ferry to Anacortes (USA)
NORTH SAANICH
SIDNEY
Victoria International Airport
Saanichton Exp Farm
Saanich Inlet
Ferry to Mill Bay
Malahat Ridge
Trans Canada Hwy
EMR
CENTRAL SAANICH
Hwy 17
Hwy 17A
Elk Lake
Cordova Bay
SAANICH
Douglas St
Island Hwy
CNR
Hwy 1
Esquimalt Harbour
ESQUIMALT
ENR
Hwy 14
Shelbourne St
OAK BAY
Beach Dr
VICTORIA
Pandora Ave
Victoria Harbour
Ferry to Port Angeles (USA)
Ferry to Seattle (USA) (Summer Only)
CNR

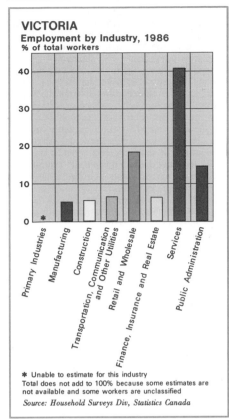

VICTORIA
Employment by Industry, 1986
% of total workers

* Unable to estimate for this industry
Total does not add to 100% because some estimates are
not available and some workers are unclassified
Source: Household Surveys Div, Statistics Canada

Saanich Inlet and the richly forested higher elevations of Malahat Ridge and the Vancouver I ranges. Greater Victoria comprises the following incorporated area: the cities of Victoria (66 303, 1986c) and Colwood, the municipalities of Saanich (pop 82 940, 1986c), Oak Bay (17 065, 1986c), Esquimalt (15 972, 1986c), Central Saanich (11 475, 1986c) and North Saanich (7247, 1986c), the town of Sidney (8982, 1986c) and the district of Metchosin, as well as the unincorporated districts of Langford and View Royal.

Settlement The site of Victoria was chosen for settlement in 1843 by James DOUGLAS, chief factor of the HBC's Pacific coast headquarters at Ft Vancouver (Vancouver, Wash), near the mouth of the Columbia R. A boundary settlement between the US and British N America was anticipated, and in the event that the 49th parallel was extended to the Pacific, which did occur in 1846, the HBC wanted an alternative fur-trading headquarters site under development. The smaller harbour of Victoria was chosen over that of Esquimalt for the establishment of Ft Victoria (named after Queen VICTORIA) because it was bordered by extensive tracts of level to gently sloping land suitable for agriculture.

Development Victoria remained a small community of less than 1000 population until it burgeoned as the supply centre and jumping-off point for the Fraser GOLD RUSH of 1858. It was incorporated as a city in 1862. The commodious ESQUIMALT Harbour nearby was designated as a naval base by the British Admiralty in 1865 and still performs this role today as CFB Esquimalt.

Population: 66 303 (1986c), 64 379 (1981c); 255 547 (1986 CMA), 241 450 (1981 ACMA)
Rate of Increase (1981-86): City 3.0%; CMA 5.8%
Rank in Canada: Fourteenth (by CMA)
Date of Incorporation: City 1862
Land Area: City 18.78 km²; CMA 1951.11 km²
Elevation: 19 m
Climate: Average daily temp, July 16.3°C, Jan 3.1°C; Yearly precip 872.9 mm; Hours of sunshine 2058.7 per year

Victoria's political capital function remained through the successive stages as capital of the colony of Vancouver I, then of the amalgamated colony and the later province of British Columbia (1871). As the dominant urban centre in BC, Victoria was unchallenged until the rise of Vancouver following the arrival of the CPR at Burrard Inlet in 1886. By the turn of the century Vancouver had taken over many of the shipping, commercial and manufacturing functions of Victoria, and the capital city gradually settled into its modern role as a government, naval, tourist and retirement centre.

Cityscape The narrow, doglegged Victoria Harbour and its long extension, Gorge Waters, constitute a picturesque, human-scaled focus for the city. The inner harbour is flanked by the impressive provincial legislative buildings completed in 1898 and CP's Empress Hotel (1908). Recent planning developments have capitalized on the unique, old-world charm of this area by establishing an extensive public walkway along much of the harbour front. Another effective planning emphasis has been the rehabilitation of the "old town" area of Victoria, including a redefinition of Chinatown, complete with the colourful and decorative Gate of Harmonious Interest marking its entrance. In addition to redevelopment of the inner harbour and the Songhees Pen, a new Victoria Conference Centre is to be attached to the Empress Hotel and a proposed Eaton's Centre is to cover about 2 city blocks.

Population Compared with other large Canadian cities, Victoria's metropolitan area population is older and more strongly of British origin, despite the infusion of other ethnic groups through postwar immigration. Both the city and metropolitan area had the highest proportion of population 65 and over among their Canadian counterparts, 25.3% and 17.9%, respectively, in 1986. Although rates of natural increase are low, the metropolitan population has had a growth rate above the national metropolitan average since the mid-1960s, owing to strong in-migration from other parts of Canada.

Economy and Labour Force The prominence of government and tourism in Victoria's economy results in high proportions of the labour force being engaged in public administration, personal services and retail trade. The lack of a well-populated hinterland on the narrow southern tip of Vancouver I has constricted the growth of wholesale trade, and Victoria's isolation from major mainland markets has proven to be a strong disadvantage for manufacturing. Some industries have shifted to the mainland in recent years. Sawmilling and shipbuilding are the leading industries that remain.

Transportation Ferry connections with the mainland have always been of the utmost importance to Victorians. The CP Steamships service from Vancouver to Victoria was replaced in 1960 by the provincially owned BC Ferry operating from Swartz Bay, N of Victoria, to Tsawwassen, S of Vancouver. Other services include the Washington state ferries from Sidney to Anacortes, Black Ball transport from Victoria to Port Angeles, and the summer service of BC Steamship from Victoria to Seattle. There is also a Victoria-Seattle hydrofoil service. Air transportation especially mitigates the isolation of Island life: Air Canada, Airspeed Aviation, Air BC, Burrard Air, Canadian Airlines International, San Juan Air, Skylink, Time Air and Wardair all have scheduled services from Victoria International Airport. As a shipping port, Victoria has declined in importance, and its function as terminus of the Esquimalt and Nanaimo Ry is a minor one.

Government and Politics Recent mayors and city councils have been concerned with the preserva-

tion of Victoria's role as the retail core of the region, but have at the same time successfully resisted attempts by developers to create a high-rise downtown in the image of many business-oriented Canadian cities. A number of functions, including regional parks, trunk sewers and hospital services, are carried out by the Capital Regional District, although police and fire protection remain under local municipal control. The Greater Victoria Water District is controlled by the 4 core municipalities of Victoria, Saanich, Oak Bay and Sidney.

Cultural Life Victoria is well endowed with educational and fine-arts institutions. The UNIVERSITY OF VICTORIA (fd 1963), grew out of Victoria College (1903), which was originally affiliated with McGill and subsequently with UBC. Other institutions include Royal Roads Military College, Camosun College and the Victoria Conservatory of Music. The Provincial Museum and Butchart Gardens (20 km NW) are leading attractions for visitors. The Art Gallery of Greater Victoria, the Victoria Symphony Orchestra and the Bastion Theatre have enhanced the city's reputation in the arts.   C.N. FORWARD

Reading: C.N. Forward, ed, *Residential and Neighbourhood Studies in Victoria* (1973); H.D. Foster, ed, *Victoria: Physical Environment and Development* (1976); H. Gregson, *A History of Victoria, 1842-1970* (1977).

Victoria Cross, instituted 1856 by Queen Victoria, is the COMMONWEALTH's premier military decoration for gallantry. It is awarded in recognition of the most exceptional bravery displayed in the presence of the enemy, although in rare instances the decoration has been given to mark other courageous acts. The first recipients saw action in the Crimean War. Among them a Canadian lieutenant, Alexander Roberts DUNN, won the VC for heroism during the charge of the Light Brigade at the Battle of Balaklava. Over the years, Canada's recipients (living and posthumous) have totalled 93, including Canadians who were attached to the forces of other Commonwealth countries and some non-Canadians serving in Canadian units. The decoration is in the form of a bronze cross

Victoria Cross, the Commonwealth's premier decoration for gallantry (*courtesy National Museums of Canada/Canadian Museum of Civilization/K71-95*).

patée bearing the royal crest and the words "For Valour." The ribbon is dark crimson. The awarding of the medal was dropped in 1972 when the Canadian bravery awards were created; however, in Apr 1987 Brian Mulroney's Conservative government asked the deputy director of the Chancellory of Canadian Orders and Decorations to consider its reinstatement. *See also* HONOURS.

CARL LOCHNAN

Victoria Day is a legal holiday throughout Canada remembered as "the twenty-fourth of May, the Queen's Birthday." It celebrates, in fact, the birthdays of Queen Victoria and Queen Elizabeth II. Victoria Day was established as a holiday in Canada West in 1845, and as a NATIONAL HOLIDAY to turn the queen's birthday into an occasion to salute the British Empire resulted in its association from the 1890s on with EMPIRE DAY. Since 1952 Victoria Day has been observed on the first Monday preceding May 25.

JOHN ROBERT COLOMBO

Victoria Island, NWT, 217 290 km², second-largest island in Canada, lies in the ARCTIC ARCHIPELAGO directly N of the arctic mainland. It is surrounded by Amundsen Gulf to the W, Viscount Melville Sound to the N and M'Clintock Channel in the E. BANKS I lies across the narrow Prince of Wales Str in the NW. The island is largely composed of sedimentary rock. There is a belt of Precambrian rock on the W coast and another on the S coast, veined with copper formerly used by the Inuit. The E side is a flat lowland that rises to prominent cliffs on the Wollaston Pen in the N. The glacial landforms are more complex than those on any of the other arctic islands. The rivers of the lowlands follow gently wandering courses and there are numerous lakes. The rock formations as well as the shape of the S coast closely resemble those of CORONATION GULF immediately to the S.

The island was first sighted in the SW by John RICHARDSON of the second FRANKLIN Expedition in 1826. In 1839 P.W. DEASE and Thomas Simpson named the island for the newly crowned queen. The NW peninsula later took the name of her consort, Prince Albert. John RAE of the HBC examined the shoreline (1851) from Prince Albert Sound to Pelly Pt, travelling by toboggan. The island received the attention of the Canadian Arctic Expedition under V. STEFANSSON in 1915 and 1917, and Diamond JENNESS – for whom the western peninsula is named – made a study of the COPPER INUIT. The HBC established posts at Cambridge Bay, Walker Bay and Holman I in the 1920s.

JAMES MARSH

Victorian Order of Nurses for Canada is a national nonprofit, community-health organization that provides NURSING care in the home, particularly for the elderly and chronically ill. Organized by Lady ABERDEEN in 1897 to commemorate Queen Victoria's Diamond Jubilee, the VON's initial aims were to provide visiting nursing services to districts without access to medical facilities and to establish cottage hospitals in isolated areas. The VON established 44 such hospitals, but by 1924 all had been taken over by other authorities and home nursing service became the main focus of VON activities. Since then the functions of the VON have evolved in response to changes in Canadian society and new home nursing needs. During 1986, over 2000 VON staff working out of 70 local branches made 3 092 934 visits to 134 503 patients, of which over 70% were over the age of 65. There are now 72 local branches and 9 provincial branches. Fees paid through provincial government health-care insurance provide the main source of funding in most provinces and additional revenue is obtained from local governments and the United Way.

JEAN E. DRYDEN

Victory Loans, Canadian government appeals for money to finance the war effort in WWI and WWII. The first domestic war loan was raised in Nov 1915, but not until the fourth campaign of Nov 1917 was the term "Victory Loan" applied. The First Victory Loan, with an issue of $150 million, 5.5% 5, 10 and 20 year gold bonds (some as small as $50), was quickly oversubscribed, collecting $398 million, or about $50 per capita. The Second and Third Victory Loans were floated in 1918 and 1919, bringing another $1338 million. In WWII, following the slow-moving second war loan of 1940, the Victory Loan returned with the panoply of colourful posters, patriotic pleas and vast sales apparatus which had become familiar in WWI. There were 9 Victory Loans dating from 15 June 1941 to 1 Nov 1945, having total cash sales of almost $12 billion, about 52% from corporations and the rest from individuals.

NORMAN HILLMER

Victoriaville, Qué, Town, pop 21 587 (1986c), 21 838 (1981c), inc 1860, is located on the Rivière Nicolet in the Piedmont Appalachians, 117 km SW of Québec C and 60 km NE of Drummondville. Originally called Demersville, its name was changed in 1861 to honour Queen VICTORIA. In the early days, the town was only a small train station on the GRAND TRUNK RY line between Québec C and Richmond, Qué. Today, it is renowned for its furniture and clothing industries and has become a major agricentre for marketing local produce. Its industrial park houses a prosperous group of metal-product machinery plants.

JEAN-MARIE DUBOIS AND PIERRE MAILHOT

Video Art Video is an independent, personal television, created outside commercial channels, using small-format $\frac{1}{2}''$ or $\frac{3}{4}''$ magnetic tape (as opposed to the 1" or 2" tape of commercial TV) and simplified recording equipment. In the late 1960s, when the first low-cost portable videotape cameras came onto the market for consumer use, these "portapaks" were taken up by artists and community organizers as a medium with the qualities of television yet without the costly and restrictive format requirements of commercial systems. Art tapes of the late 1960s and early 1970s related closely to the current art issues and nonproduct emphasis of conceptual art and performance. The first tapes were extremely simple, usually produced by the artist alone for closed-circuit screening in studios or at the artist-run "alternate" galleries then being established with CANADA COUNCIL support. From the beginning, the major centres for video art – Vancouver, Toronto, Montréal, Halifax – each had a different character. Vancouver turned to video (about 1969) to record performances and events associated with Intermedia (1967-71), a group of artists working in different media. By 1973 the artist-run Satellite Video Exchange Society (Video Inn) and Western Front were established as production and viewing centres, growing partly out of the important Matrix International Video conference held that year. Vancouver has continued to see a double purpose for video, in both performance and community collaboration, with increased interest in developing technologies.

Toronto has been oriented to individual expression through video, with artists conscious of international art issues working independently. The first workshops were organized in 1970 at A Space, an artist-run facility. The A Space equipment, now separately incorporated as Charles Street Video, provides sophisticated editing facilities around-the-clock for $\frac{3}{4}''$ colour productions, and Trinity Square Video is the source for production equipment, studio recording time and workshops, as well as recently improved editing/audio facilities and screening rooms, and information on new technologies such as TELIDON.

Many Montréal artists viewed video politically as a tool for social change. The works produced at Vidéographe, which was begun in 1970 in co-operation with the National Film Board's "Challenge for Change" program, developed a video documentary form based somewhat on the film model. *Pea Soup* (1978, 94 minutes) by Pierre Falardeau and Julien Poulin is exemplary, a composite portrait of Québecois street culture, as is *Chaperons rouges* (*Little Red Riding Hood*, 1979) by Helen Doyle and Hélène Bourgault, an anti-rape dramatization. Vidéo Véhicule, originating at the artist-run gallery Véhicule Art in the early 1970s and now operating as PRIM (Productions Réalisations Indépendants de Montréal Inc), has generated some individual art piecement operative work coming from Coop vidéo de Montréal remains dominant, while some younger artists have become interested in rapid edits and dazzling special effects.

Video art in Halifax began in the late 1960s, chiefly structuralist and formal works created at the NOVA SCOTIA COLLEGE OF ART AND DESIGN. NSCAD's tapes by both staff and students reached their peak from 1971 to 1973, a fine example being *Shuffle* by Douglas Waterman. Production continues at the college, though many video artists in eastern Canada have moved to the Centre for Art Tapes, an artist-run exhibition facility established in Halifax in 1978.

Video has changed greatly in its first 20 years, in the 4 main centres and the many smaller cities producing tapes. Toronto, with its emphasis on single-channel works (as distinct from multi-monitor pieces or installations) and strong statements by individuals, has also assumed a high profile through the sheer volume of production. A significant development in the mid-1970s was the use of narrative, exemplified by Colin Campbell ("The Woman from Malibu" series, 1976) and Lisa Steele (*A Very Personal Story*, 1974). General Idea originated "found-formats," playing ironically on commercial idioms, in their *Pilot* (1977) for TVOntario. Both these threads are seen elsewhere, as in Eric Metcalfe/Dana Atchley's *Crime Time Comix Presents Steel and Flesh* (1980), produced in Vancouver. In all centres developing technologies have offered an increasingly attractive challenge; new tapes often reflect these new opportunities. Distribution of these noncommercial, independent tapes remains problematic, but the descriptive catalogues and fee schedules developed by Art Metropole (est in Toronto in 1974) or database information of V Tapes (est in Toronto 1980) may provide solutions. By 1980 the $\frac{3}{4}''$ colour cassette had become the standard for production and circulation of artists' tapes in Canada, the US and Europe.

The Vancouver Art Gallery, the Art Gallery of Ontario and the National Gallery of Canada have substantial videotape collections, and Canadian artists have been included in important exhibitions and festivals around the world, including "Projekt 74" (Cologne, West Germany, 1974), Documenta 6 and 8 (Kassel, West Germany, 1979; 1987), São Paulo Bienal (Brazil, 1977), Biennale di Venezia (Italy, 1980), "OKanada" (Berlin, East Germany, 1983), and at the Museum of Modern Art in New York.

In Canada, artists are considering opportunities for broadcast and other communications options as they are developed, to expand their audiences beyond the museum and artist-run gallery circuit. Canadian video is recognized as having developed a unique visual language and personal communication in both form and content.

PEGGY GALE

Reading: Art Gallery of Ontario, *Videoscape* (1974); Peggy Gale, ed, *Video by Artists* (1976); R. Payant, ed, *Vidéo* (1986); E. Town, ed, *Video By Artists 2* (1986).

Vietnam War had its roots in the French colonial conquest of Indochina in the mid-19th century and in the nationalist movements that arose to oppose it. At the end of WWII, on 2 Sept 1945, the Democratic Republic of Viet-Nam was proclaimed an independent country by Ho Chi Minh; Hanoi was its capital. The French attempt to reconquer Vietnam met with defeat in the valley of Dien Bien Phu on 2 May 1954. The July Geneva Agreements provided for a cease-fire and a provisional military demarcation line at the 17th parallel, pending nationwide elections for reunification in July 1956. Western efforts to divide the country permanently by creating a Vietnamese republic in Saigon, coupled with the refusal to hold the promised elections, led to rebellion in the S, massive US military intervention and the ensuing civil war.

The failure of US policy became apparent in Feb 1968 when 525 000 American soldiers were unable to stop the insurgents' Tet Offensive. In Jan 1973 the Paris Peace Accords were signed, upholding the unity and territorial integrity of Vietnam and providing for the orderly withdrawal of US troops, the release of 200 000 civilian detainees and POWs and the organization of free and democratic elections in S Vietnam. The refusal to implement these last conditions provoked an armed insurrection and on 30 Apr 1975 Saigon fell. The cost of the war was staggering: 1.7 million dead, 3 million wounded and maimed, and 13 million refugees. The US dropped 7 million tons of bombs, 75 million litres of herbicide and lost 10 000 helicopters and warplanes. Some 56 000 US soldiers were killed and another 303 000 were wounded. The direct cost of the war was $140 billion; indirect costs are estimated at $900 billion.

During the years 1954 to 1975 Canada served on 2 international truce commissions and provided medical supplies and technical assistance. Canadian diplomats were involved in negotiations between Washington and Hanoi and successive Canadian governments, both Liberal and Conservative, maintained that Ottawa was an impartial and objective peacekeeper, an innocent and helpful bystander negotiating for peace and administering aid to victims of the war. However, Cabinet papers, confidential stenographic minutes of the truce commissions as well as top-secret American government cables revealed Canada to be a willing ally of US counterinsurgency efforts.

Canada's record on the truce commissions was a partisan one, rooted in the presumption of Hanoi's guilt and Saigon's innocence and designed to discredit N Vietnam while exonerating S Vietnam from its obligations to uphold the Geneva Agreements. Canadian delegates engaged in espionage for the US Central Intelligence Agency and aided the covert introduction of American arms and personnel into S Vietnam while they spotted for US bombers over N Vietnam. Canadian commissioners shielded the US chemical defoliant program from public inquiry, parlayed American threats of expanded war to Hanoi, and penned the reports legitimating both the rupture of the Geneva Agreements and the US air war over N Vietnam. Ottawa would later assert that these actions were necessary to counterbalance the activities of the Eastern bloc countries with whom they shared membership on the truce commissions.

Canadian aid during the war went only to S Vietnam, $29 million 1950-75, routed through the COLOMBO PLAN and the Canadian Red Cross. Although humanitarian in appearance, Canadian assistance was an integral part of the Free World Assistance Program, co-ordinated by the US Department of State with the International Security Office of the Pentagon as the point of

contact. In the field, Canadian capital assistance was regulated by the US-RVN Health Defense Agreement and administered by the International Military Assistance Force Office in Saigon. On a number of occasions, Ottawa stopped the shipment of ecumenical medical relief to civilian victims of the war in N Vietnam.

At home, 500 firms sold $2.5 billion of war materiel (ammunition, napalm, aircraft engines and explosives) to the Pentagon. Another $10 billion in food, beverages, berets and boots for the troops was exported to the US, as well as nickel, copper, lead, brass and oil for shell casings, wiring, plate armour and military transport. In Canada unemployment fell to record low levels of 3.9%, the gross domestic product rose by 6% yearly, and capital expenditure expanded exponentially in manufacturing and mining as US firms invested more than $3 billion in Canada to offset shrinking domestic capacity as a result of the war. The herbicide "Agent Orange" was tested for use in Vietnam at CFB Gagetown, NB. US bomber pilots practised carpet-bombing runs over Suffield, Alta, and North Battleford, Sask, before their tours of duty in SE Asia. And the results of the only successful peace initiative to Hanoi – that of Canadian diplomat Chester RONNING – would be kept from public knowledge in order not to harm official US-Canadian relations. Ten thousand young Canadian men fought in the US armed forces in the war. At the same time 20 000 American draft-dodgers and 12 000 army deserters found refuge in Canada. *See also* AMERICANS; Sherwood LETT; James B. SEABORN.   VICTOR LEVANT

Reading: Victor Levant, *Quiet Complicity: Canadian Involvement in the Vietnam War* (1986).

Vietnamese, *see* SOUTHEAST ASIANS.

Viger, Jacques, journalist, author, militia officer, civil servant, politician, (b at Montréal 7 May 1787; d there 12 Dec 1858). Viger is known primarily for having been the first mayor of Montréal, but he also played an important role as a civil servant and as an intellectual, through his learned works and his collections. His career beginnings are poorly known. An editor of the Québec paper, *Le Canadien*, for a period of months (1808-09), he next appears as an active militia officer in the War of 1812. For the rest of his life he was involved with military functions through the militia. In 1814 he was given the position of inspector of the roads, streets, alleys and bridges of the city and parish of Montréal, a position he held until 1840. He was therefore responsible for the upkeep of the streets and for the development and physical maintenance of the city. When a first municipal charter was bestowed upon Montréal, he was mayor from 1833 to 1836, but due to the rebellion the charter was not renewed, and it was undoubtedly his patriote sympathies which lost him his inspector's position in 1840. Viger was always interested in learned works. He filled all 43 volumes of his monumental *Saberdache* with many miscellaneous memories, such as details from the campaign of 1812 or correspondence. He collected numerous documents and books and was one of the founders of the Société historique de Montréal (1858).   JEAN-CLAUDE ROBERT

Vigneault, Gilles, singer-songwriter, poet, publisher (b at Natashquan, Qué 27 Oct 1928). Like Félix LECLERC, Vigneault revitalized the Québec *chanson* and helped make Québec culture known abroad. After studying at Laval he founded in 1959 Éditions de l'arc to distribute his writings. The next year he began singing his own songs. Despite his hoarse voice and awkward appearance, he could always touch his audience with the poetry, sincerity and youth that emanated from his person and his work. His rousing song

Gilles Vigneault revitalized Québec *chanson* and helped make Québec culture known abroad. His rousing song "Mon Pays" became a virtual anthem in Québec (*courtesy Canapress Photo Service*).

"Mon Pays" (1964) became virtually an anthem for Québecois and swelled his popularity at home and abroad.

Vigneault has appeared in various great Canadian halls (several times with the Orchestre symphonique de Montréal at the Montréal Place des Arts, and at the National Arts Centre, Ottawa, as well as at Toronto's Massey Hall) and in Europe (France, Switzerland, Poland, Belgium and Luxembourg). He started his own record label, Le Nordet (Éditions du vent qui vire). Among the awards he has received are the Prix Denise-Pelletier (1983) and the Prix de l'Académie Charles-Cros (1984). In 1986 he was made a Chevalier de la Légion d'honneur of France.   HÉLÈNE PLOUFFE

Ville-Marie, Catholic utopian colony fd 17 May 1642 on Montréal I by the Société Notre-Dame de Montréal, under the governship of Maisonneuve, to bring Christianity to the Indians; but located in a key region for the development of agriculture and the FUR TRADE. Assisted by recruits sent in 1653 and again in 1659, the little colony sank its roots and withstood Iroquois incursions. In 1663 it was taken over by the Seminary of St Sulpice in Paris, which already supplied its priests. The settlers, from the first preoccupied with the fur trade, lived to see the Roman Catholic ideal of Ville-Marie fade before the realization of a commercial MONTRÉAL. *See also* MISSIONS AND MISSIONARIES.
   DALE MIQUELON

Ville-Marie, Qué, Town, pop 2621 (1986c), 2651 (1981c), inc 1962, is located on Lk TIMISKAMING near the Québec-Ontario border. It took shape at the end of the 19th century, developing around the Oblate mission settlements and the forestry company posts that had been exploiting the large pine forests of the Lac Témiscaming basin for several decades. The Oblate mission was established in 1836 near Fort Témiscaming, built in 1686 by fur traders. After 1885 settlement of the land around the lake by families from the older regions of Québec led to the establishment of Ville-Marie. The name dates from 1896 and honours the patron of the Oblates of Mary Immaculate, indicating the Oblates' role in the development of the region. Ville-Marie was made a village in 1897. The major town of rural Québec's Témiscamingue region, it has strong ties with the towns of HAILEYBURY and NEW LISKEARD on the Ontario shore of the lake.   BENOÎT-BEAUDRY GOURD

Villemaire, Yolande, teacher, writer (b at St-Augustin-des-Deux-Montagnes, Qué 28 Aug 1949). After studying dramatic arts at UQAM, where she received her BA (1970) and MA (1974), she taught creative literature at the Rosemont CEGEP. Her work (poems, literary criticism, radio dramas, novels) moves from its experimental days, in such reviews as *Hobo/Québec* and *Cul-Q*, to the development of a neorealism acclaimed by the critics with the appearance of *La Vie en prose* (Prix des Jeunes Écrivains of the *Journal de Montréal*, 1980) and *La Constellation du cygne* (Grand Prix of the *Journal de Montréal*, 1985). This book, on the boundary between political commitment and esotericism, contributes to the creation of a N American mythology. Founder of the Rose Sélavy writers' helix and the Ombre jaune international telepathy network, she has moved into the dramatic arts with her performances in Montréal and New York, where she occupied the Québec studio in 1985.

LUCIE ROBERT

Villeneuve, Gilles, auto racer (b at Berthierville, Qué 18 Jan 1950; d at Zolder, Belgium 9 May 1982). In his brief career Villeneuve was Canada's finest high-speed racer. He first showed his penchant for speed by guiding motorized sleds at breakneck speeds, winning the N American championship in 1971, the Québec crown in 1972 and the Canadian title in 1973. Villeneuve used his earnings from snowmobile racing to enter Formula Ford competition, winning the 1973 Québec crown. He progressed to Formula Atlantic (FA) races in 1974 but broke his leg at his debut at Mosport, Ont. Undaunted, he returned in 1975 to score one victory and rank 5th overall in the standings. In 1976 he dominated Canadian and American FA competition, winning 9 of 10 races. Another Canadian championship followed in 1977 as he entered Can-Am class racing. Villeneuve's success brought an offer to join the Ferrari team on the world circuit. His initial grand prix triumph occurred at Montréal and in 1979 he scored further victories at Kyalami, Long Beach, Calif; and Watkins Glen, NY. He also finished 2nd in the Canadian Grand Prix, and was runner-up to teammate Jody Scheckter as the world's finest grand prix racer. He won 6 of the 67 races he drove for Ferrari in Formula One. Villeneuve was killed in a high-speed qualifying race for the Belgian Grand Prix following a collision with another car at 250 km/h. Montréal's Grand Prix circuit has been named for him. *See also* AUTOMOBILE RACING.

BOB FERGUSON

Villeneuve, Jean-Marie-Rodrigue, Oblate priest, Roman Catholic archbishop of Québec, cardinal (b at Montréal 2 Nov 1883; d at Alhambra, Calif 17 Jan 1947). After studying philosophy and theology, he began a teaching career and became active in nationalist circles, with Abbé Lionel GROULX. Named first bishop of Gravelbourg (Sask) in 1930, he became the 20th bishop of Québec in 1932, the 10th archbishop, and, in 1933, the fourth Canadian cardinal. While head of the Québec church, Cardinal Villeneuve continued to teach, using his homilies, talks and academic presentations, and spread his ideas through brochures and books. At the same time he also gave new impetus to CATHOLIC ACTION, liturgical renewal and Marist piety; he ran his diocese firmly and was the uncontested leader of Québec and Canadian bishops. Despite his taste for grandeur and a certain stubbornness, he liked to mingle with the crowds that greeted him.

Although his episcopacy faced the serious problems of the Great Depression — strikes, debates about the nature of Catholic Action and relations with public authorities — he skilfully found solutions that were acceptable to his colleagues. He was less successful with his position on the war. Convinced that "Hitler and Nazism are a catastrophic threat to our Christianity and our rights," he yielded to pressure from federal politicians and was increasingly sympathetic to total war, a position that appalled some bishops, the nationalist circles and a good many French Canadian Catholics. To save unanimity and avoid scandal, he agreed to some concessions. Yet the tensions that remained were indicative of the upheaval that was beginning to shake Québec.

NIVE VOISINE

Vimy Ridge, battle fought 9-14 Apr 1917 during WORLD WAR I. The long, low ridge formed a key position linking the Germans' new HINDENBURG LINE to their main trench lines leading N from HILL 70 near Arras, France. Both British and French forces had tried unsuccessfully to take the ridge earlier during the war. In spring 1917 the task was given to the Canadian Corps, commanded by British Lt-Gen Sir J.H.G. BYNG.

After careful training and rehearsal, and supported by almost 1000 artillery pieces, the Canadians attacked along a 6.4 km front on 9 Apr 1917. It was the first time the Canadians attacked together, and they achieved a magnificent victory, sweeping the Germans off the ridge. By Apr 14 they had gained more ground, more guns, and more prisoners than any previous British offensive had done. Canadian casualties mounted to 10 602, of which 3598 were killed. Nevertheless the sense of achievement and national pride created by this success gave the Canadians a great feeling of self-confidence. The Canadian Corps was to gain recognition as an elite corps.

R.H. ROY

Reading: Pierre Berton, *Vimy* (1986).

Memorial to the Canadian dead, Vimy Ridge, France (*courtesy Veterans Affairs Canada*).

Vinland, *see* NORSE VOYAGES.

Violence, Political, refers to the use of physical force to achieve or prevent political or economic change. In this specific sense, Canada (as compared to the US) has been a "peaceable kingdom." There has been no bloody revolution or massive civil war and very little of the "lawless West." The incidence of individual crimes of violence has also been very much lower. Nevertheless, Canadian history records a great deal of violence, especially collective violence, eg, that used in war, in the maintenance of "order" (*see* AID TO (OR OF) THE CIVIL POWER) and as a tool of political method. War and a concern with military defence in the name of "survival" or "protection of national interests" have been instrumental in Canadian history since the founding of New France. Violence characterized the turbulent relations between the settlers and the IROQUOIS, and the response to American attacks and border harassments in the 1770s, 1812-14, and during the 1830s (*see* HUNTERS LODGES) and the 1860s (*see* FENIANS). Canada was also involved in the SOUTH AFRICAN WAR, WORLD WAR I and WORLD WAR II, the KOREAN WAR (1950-53) and the United Nations PEACEKEEPING activities of the 20th century. Canada's membership in NATO and in NORAD symbolizes its recognition that military strength (however secured) is the chief expression of power in international affairs, although the Canadian government has occasionally rejected requests by her senior allies to contribute military support to what it considered imperial wars. Sir John A. MACDONALD refused to authorize a Canadian contingent to support a British expedition to the Sudan in 1885; similarly, pressure from the US for at least token support for the intervention in Vietnam was resisted in the 1960s. In both cases and in others like them it might be argued that Canada was hypocritical; in the first by accepting the insurance of Pax Britannica and Pax Americana without paying premiums, and in the second by profiting from the Defence Production Sharing Agreement in the US.

Debates on defence, from the militia bills of the 1860s through the Laurier-Borden struggle over naval contributions to imperial and national defence (*see* NAVAL AID BILL) to 20th-century CONSCRIPTION crises and the issues resulting from membership in a nuclear-based alliance system, have significantly affected the political process in Canada and the evolution of Canada's Constitution and domestic cultural relations. For example, Mackenzie KING's role in bringing about the BALFOUR REPORT and the STATUTE OF WESTMINSTER, as well as his reliance on Ernest LAPOINTE in all matters concerning Québec, resulted directly from his perception of the impact of military commitments upon domestic politics and upon Canada's international status.

The tortuous and little-examined history of collective violence within Canada reveals a nation that paradoxically combines a national attachment to the notion that only legally constituted government is legitimate (and that it may legitimately use force to maintain order) with an apparent belief that a healthy society must expect political and economic competition to generate violence. The 19th and early 20th centuries were pockmarked with incidents of physical intimidation at the polling booth, and with violence among competing lumber and railway interests and between strikers and militiamen. Political discourse has occasionally been tinged with violence, eg, Joseph HOWE of Nova Scotia once suggested irately that someone would shortly "hire a blackfellow to horsewhip a lieutenant-governor," and some Canadians tend to honour historical leaders of violent political dissent such as W.L. MACKENZIE, L.J. PAPINEAU and Louis RIEL. Religious and cultural antipathies have often sparked violent confrontations; in 1871 a large militia force was required to ensure the removal of the body of rationalist Joseph Guibord from a Protestant to a Catholic cemetery in Montréal. Anti-Asian riots erupted in Vancouver in the early 20th century, and anti-Semitic melées in Toronto and Montréal occurred in the mid-1930s.

In Canada attitudes toward political and cultural violence and those toward individual violence are linked by the perception that social order is an absolute prerequisite of both individual and political liberty. In principal constitutional statements it is declared that "good government" is inseparable from "peace and order," comparatively strict controls on the possession of handguns are maintained, and a broad reserve of executive authority is endorsed to prevent or suppress the use of violence as a political method. Retention of the 1914 WAR MEASURES ACT for use in time of "real or apprehended" insurrection allows suspension of habeas corpus by order-in-council. Attempts to replace the Act with more restricted emergency powers legislation have failed – although in early 1985 the new Conservative government in Ottawa indicated a willingness to implement the recommendation of the McDonald Commission for legislation which would provide emergency powers short of those in the War Measures Act. Replacement legislation was introduced in late 1987.

The reaction of Canadians to political trials and collective violence seems to be characterized by a stringent suppression of violence when it occurs or is threatened and lenience toward the instigators once the crisis has been weathered. During the REBELLIONS OF 1837 in UPPER CANADA only 2 rebels were executed; in LOWER CANADA 12 were hanged, and these only after a second attempt on their part in 1838 and because of fears of American intervention. The AMNESTY ACT pardoned the rebels in 1849.

Confidence in the evolving constitutional system has bred tolerance of basic constitutional dissent, allowing political actions which might otherwise be violently suppressed. In 1939 J.S. WOODSWORTH could support his vote in the Commons against the declaration of war with the statement that if any of his sons were "willing to take his stand on this matter, if necessary, face a concentration camp or a firing squad, I shall be more proud of that boy than if he enlisted for war."

Pronouncements of Canadian courts reveal much about Canadian attitudes towards violence. Chief Justice John Beverley ROBINSON of Upper Canada, who had fought under Brock at Detroit and Niagara, explained to Samuel LOUNT and Peter MATTHEWS why, having pleaded guilty, they must be hanged for their part in the 1837 rebellion: "You were not the tenants of rigorous and exacting landlords; you were not burthened with taxes for the State, further than the payment perhaps of a few shillings in the year, to support the common expenses of the district in which you lived;...regularity and industry would always have ensured you a competency....You lived in a country where every man who obeys the laws is secure in the protection of life, liberty and property....In a country in which you [Lount] have been admitted to the honourable privilege of making laws to bind your fellow subjects, it was due from *you* to set an example of faithful obedience of public authority." (It was also Robinson's view, however, that "some example should be made in the way of capital punishment.")

Stressing the interrelationships of order, liberty and obedience of law, Robinson made clear that violence might be justified only if the avenues of constitutional redress of grievance were demonstrably closed. They appeared to be closed in 1869-70 when Riel's use of force secured provincial status for Manitoba (*see* RED RIVER REBELLION). Yet when Riel's successful "provisional government" executed the Orangeman Thomas SCOTT this raised an insuperable obstacle to the clemency which would probably have characterized the response to the second Métis rebellion in 1885 (*see* NORTH-WEST REBELLION). Nevertheless the Regina jury recommended Riel to "the mercy of the Crown," apparently attaching weight (as did opponents of the federal government then and later) to Riel's plea that "I have acted reasonably and in self-defence, while the Government, my accuser, being irresponsible and consequently insane, cannot but have acted wrong." Sir John A. Macdonald's decision not to commute Riel's death sentence suggests that prejudice and racism increases the potential for violence. This was certainly the case when fierce anticonscription rioting swept Québec City in the spring of 1918.

The conviction that the state can employ force to suppress the use of violence as a political tool has been exploited by class-biased governments in Canada to impede the protest or organization of workers. In 1935 in Regina police were ordered to break up a large group of unemployed men headed for Ottawa to demand job-creating action by the government, and rioting resulted (*see* ON TO OTTAWA TREK). The most dramatic instance of this kind, however, occurred earlier (1919) during the WINNIPEG GENERAL STRIKE. The strike leaders, representing some 30 000 workers who supported demands for union recognition and wage increases to match the sharply rising living costs, had pursued a rigorous policy of nonviolence. Shaken by the ability of the strikers to halt peacefully the city's economic life, business and professional leaders along with civic, provincial and federal authorities pronounced the strike an attempt to overthrow constituted authority and proclaimed that revolutionary violence was imminent. Violence was, in fact, instigated when police and soldiers were ordered to disperse a "silent parade" that had been organized by the strikers and WWI veterans to protest the arrest of their leaders on charges of sedition. When the strike collapsed, 8 leaders were brought to trial; one was acquitted and the others were sentenced to imprisonment for terms ranging from 6 months to 2 years. Perhaps the most interesting aspect of this complicated interaction was the evident opinion of a majority of Winnipeggers that the assumptions of the authorities had been ill-founded.

Three convicted strike leaders were elected to the Manitoba legislature in 1920 while still in prison. F.J. Dixon, acquitted on a charge of seditious libel, topped the polls in Winnipeg, while J.S. Woodsworth, similarly charged, was elected MP in 1921. Collective violence by the state was condemned. In the same period the New York state legislature expelled 5 duly-elected members of the Socialist Party of America on the grounds that socialism was "absolutely inimical" to the interests of the state.

The relationship of violence to constituted authority was also at the heart of the 1970 OCTOBER CRISIS in Québec. In Winnipeg and Montréal the governments concerned declared their apprehension of insurrection; in Montréal the FRONT DE LIBÉRATION DU QUÉBEC had actually declared its belief in violence as a means of reconstituting society and it had a record of bombing, murder and kidnapping. When the federal government proclaimed the War Measures Act following the kidnapping of British Trade Commissioner James Cross, and when both the RCMP and the army were given extraordinary powers of search, arrest and detention, many people endorsed the stern measures; after the murder of Québec Labour Minister Pierre LAPORTE and the release of Cross, the emergency orders were withdrawn and any persons who could prove damages resulting from an arbitrary arrest which failed to culminate in legal charges were offered compensation. Charges that the 2 levels of government were motivated largely by perceptions of political advantage led to 2 major investigations, but the controversy over means and ends that ensued will probably not modify traditional attitudes toward violence and the role of the state.

KENNETH MCNAUGHT

Reading: M. Friedland, ed, *Courts and Trials* (1975); Desmond Morton, *Canada and War* (1981); P. Ward, *White Canada Forever* (1978).

Violet (Violaceae), family of annual or perennial herbaceous plants widely distributed throughout temperate and tropical regions. Tropical species may reach tree size. Roughly 500 species of genera *Viola* (violets, pansies) and *Hybanthus* (green violets) alone occur worldwide. The 35 species of *Viola* native to Canada are found in abundance in woods, prairies and marshes from the Atlantic to the Pacific and N to the treeline. One green violet species (*H. concolor*) occurs in southern Ontario. Some violets produce 2 kinds of flowers. In spring, colourful flowers (eg, purple, blue, white) are produced for POLLINATION by insects. Green, petalless, self-pollinating flowers are produced in summer. These are more fruitful and ensure seed set if earlier flowers were affected by cold. Many species are popular as ORNAMENTALS, mainly for rock gardens and shaded areas, where they prefer moist, rich soil. The hooded or purple violet (*V. cucullata*) has a rich purple flower and a rosette of heart-shaped leaves. It has been the PROVINCIAL FLORAL EMBLEM of NB since 1936.

CÉLINE ARSENEAULT

Virden, Man, Town, pop 3054 (1986c), 2940 (1981c), inc 1904, is located 278 km W of Winnipeg on the Trans-Canada Hwy. Large-scale agricultural settlement began in the area in the 1880s, encouraged by construction of the CPR. Virden began as a railway camp on Gopher Creek in 1882, and became a transportation, processing and service centre for surrounding farms started by settlers from Scotland, England, Ontario and Nova Scotia. Evidence concerning the origin of the name is contradictory. It may derive from settlers who were relatives of Lord Mount STEPHEN, whose home in Scotland had this name, or from the German town of Verden, home of the wife of the duke of Manchester. A BRITISH COMMONWEALTH AIR TRAINING PLAN flying school was located here during WWII. In 1951 the province's first commercially productive oil zone was discovered, leading to development of the Daly field W of Virden. Virden-Roselea and North Virden-Scallion, now known jointly as the Virden Field, were discovered in 1953. Wells even appeared within the town, where the population doubled in the oil boom which followed. The Virden Field has accounted for 75% of Manitoba's cumulative oil production since the 1950s. While it is still the largest producer, its relative importance has declined. In 1986, its output was 320 573 cubic metres or 39% of Manitoba's total oil production. Today, agricultural and retail services and a modest manufacturing sector are also part of Virden's economy.

D.M. LYON

Reading: I. Clingan, *The Virden Story* (1957).

Vireo (Vireonidae), family of small, basically olive green, insectivorous and partly frugivorous songbirds with repetitive, persistent songs (sometimes musical, often harsh). The 43 known species, restricted to the New World, are related to the cosmopolitan SHRIKE and CROW. Vireos spread northward from the American tropics, 8 species reaching Canada. Seven of these breed here, excluding Bell's vireo (*V. bellii*), which occurs, rarely, in spring at Point Pelée, Ont. The only permanent resident is Hutton's vireo (*V. huttoni*) which lives in broad-leaved coniferous forests in extreme southwestern BC. The thicket-dwelling white-eyed vireo (*V. griseus*) breeds in extreme southern Ont. The yellow-throated vireo (*V.*

flavifrons) inhabits mixed forest from SE Qué to SW Ont and occurs locally in SE Man. Solitary vireos (*V. solitarius*) frequent boreal forest transcontinentally N to Fort Simpson, NWT. The abundant red-eyed vireo (*V. olivaceus*), of mixed forests, ranges across Canada to 64° N lat, NWT. The Philadelphia vireo (*V. philadelphicus*), vocally similar to red-eyed vireo, inhabits deciduous woodland from SW Newfoundland to central BC. The warbling vireo (*V. gilvus*) prefers deciduous woodland from SW Québec to the West Coast. Vireos build distinctive, pensile nests in trees and shrubs, breeding May-July; clutches contain 3-5 eggs. J.C. BARLOW

Virus, the smallest form of life (20-300 nanometres), is structurally and functionally unique. The size of viruses is such that they do not contain enough genetic material to code for the proteins they require for reproduction, nor do they have ribosomes needed to synthesize these proteins. Therefore, being obliged to enter permissive host cells that assist them to reproduce, they are obligate intracellular parasites implicated in DISEASES of humans, other animals and plants.

In Canada, specialists in microbiology, MOLECULAR BIOLOGY, BIOCHEMISTRY, IMMUNOLOGY and other biological sciences are engaged in interdisciplinary research to identify, describe and control disease-causing viruses. Research into human viral disease is carried out primarily in the universities and hospitals, and is funded largely by federal grants, co-ordinated through the MEDICAL RESEARCH COUNCIL OF CANADA. Some research funds are also supplied by provincial agencies. Agriculture Canada and certain of the universities (notably U of Saskatchewan, through the Veterinary Infectious Disease Organization) operate extensive programs on viral diseases of animals. Work on plant viruses is done in Agriculture Canada RESEARCH STATIONS and in plant pathology laboratories connected to university departments of botany or biology, within science or agriculture faculties throughout the country.

Structure and Function

The mature virus organism (virion) consists of viral genes contained in a protective protein shell (a capsid). Viral genes may be deoxyribonucleic acid (DNA) or ribonucleic acid (RNA); genetic RNA is unique to viruses. RNA viruses include enteroviruses (eg, causing poliomyelitis), rhinoviruses (common cold), rhabdoviruses (rabies), paramyxoviruses (measles), orthomyxoviruses (influenza) and almost all plant viruses. DNA viruses include papavoviruses (warts), adenoviruses (acute respiratory disease), herpesviruses (cold sore, infectious mononucleosis, chicken pox), poxviruses (smallpox, cowpox), hepatitis B, and many viruses that infect bacteria (bacteriophages) and insects. Virions are functionally very limited and serve mainly to protect the viral genetic material (genome) from adverse environmental factors outside the host cell and to facilitate its entry into compatible host cells. Specific types of viruses take advantage of the resources of particular host cells. Bacteriophages (bacteria eaters), named by Canadian virologist Felix d'Herelle in 1917, prey only on bacteria and have specific preferences for particular bacterial species. Similarly, plant-specific viruses (discovered by Russian botanist Dimitri Ivanovsky in 1892) and animal-specific viruses (discovered by Friedrich Loeffler and Paul Frosch in 1898) have preferred host cells. Such preferences may stem from the origins of viruses, which are thought by some theorists to be degenerate, subcellular, self-replicating particles.

Viruses infect cells by fusion, endocytosis or injection. In viruses of a certain structure, the viral envelope fuses with the cell membrane of a host cell and the virus genome it contains is introduced into the cell. In endocytosis the host cell engulfs the virus, engulfment being triggered by contact with a viral particle, and the nucleic material is released from the capsid. Injection, a technique copied in laboratory GENETIC ENGINEERING, is used on bacteria only. The virus attaches itself to the bacterial cell wall and injects its nucleic acid, leaving the capsid outside the wall. Once inside the host cell, the viral nucleic acid and any enzymes participate in replicative activity.

Following "uncoating," the viral DNA or RNA may integrate itself into the genome of the host cell or may immediately initiate replication through a cytolytic (ie, cell-degenerating) infection, depending on the type of virus. In the case of integration, the host cell undergoes changes during which it acquires many of the properties of CANCER cells. The virus genome, being integrated, is conserved and replicated along with the host genome. The virus may, however, initiate a "lytic" infection, ie, replicating the mature virion which is then capable of infecting another host cell. The association between viruses and some tumours in humans is well documented, and viruses are known to cause many cancers in other VERTEBRATE species.

Cells undergoing a lytic virus infection frequently have their own synthetic processes inhibited but produce hundreds of identical copies of the infecting virion. The replicative strategies employed by RNA viruses are diverse and complex, depending upon whether the virus genome can function directly as messenger RNA, which instructs host cell ribosomes (cell organelles through which protein synthesis occurs) to make viral enzymes and proteins, or whether messenger RNA must be synthesized on the viral genetic template, before protein and enzyme synthesis can proceed. Most DNA viruses replicate in the nucleus of the host cell, using host-cell proteins to synthesize messenger RNA on the virus's DNA template. Assembly of the virus is a complex and still poorly understood process. RNA viruses may assume simple spherical forms, complicated forms with enveloping membranes, and other special structures. DNA viruses may assemble in "factories" in the host-cell cytoplasm or be "budded off" from the host-cell membranes. Viruses that acquire outer membranes from the membrane of the cell's nucleus or cytoplasm incorporate virus-coded glycoproteins into these membranes, before the final assembly of the mature virion.

Viruses cause major diseases in plants and animals, but there are few effective methods for cure. Plant breeding may yield strains resistant to viruses, but this avenue of approach is unavailable to humans. Recently, some antiviral chemicals have shown promise as antibiotics; however, this control technique is of relatively limited application as the life processes of the virus are so intimately bound up with those of the host cell that it is difficult to kill the one without destroying the other. More successful efforts have been directed towards the development of vaccines for preventing viral disease. Properly administered, such vaccines have resulted in the worldwide eradication of smallpox and the virtual disappearance of poliomyelitis, measles and rubella from specific populations. In all Canadian provinces, PUBLIC HEALTH authorities maintain vaccination programs directed especially at small children. It remains to be seen, however, if the elimination of these traditional scourges of man can be maintained. *See also* BIOLOGICAL PRODUCTS INDUSTRY; PHARMACY; VETERINARY MEDICINE. K.R. ROZEE

Vivier, Claude, composer (b at Montréal 14 Apr 1948; d at Paris, France 7 Mar 1983). He studied at the Montreal Conservatory with Gilles Tremblay (composition) and Irving Heller (piano), then in Europe with Gottfried Michael Koenig, Hans Ulrich Humpert, Karlheinz Stockhausen and Paul Méfano (composition and electroacoustics). During his brief but prolific career, he composed some 40 works. He made his name with *Prolifération* (1969). His passion for languages — he was fluent in 7 – plus his many trips to Europe and Indonesia greatly influenced his writing. He excelled in compositions for the human voice: *Chants, Love Songs, Lonely Child, Wo bist du licht!* and his opera *Kopernicus*.

Vivier's touching music seeks to convey a humanitarian message. In Montréal, he founded Les Evénements du neuf (1978) with José Evangelista. In 1981, the Canadian Music Council named him the composer of the year. Ignoring his friends' warnings, he frequented dangerous milieux and died violently, murdered in his Paris apartment. He received posthumously one of the 2 awards of the referendum concert organized in Paris by the Colonne orchestra (1984).

HÉLÈNE PLOUFFE

Voaden, Herman Arthur, playwright, director, educator, editor (b at London, Ont 19 Jan 1903). English Canada's most significant pre-WWII playwright following the departure of Merrill DENISON to the US in 1931, Voaden developed a unique nonrealist, multimedia playwriting and production style, which he termed "symphonic expressionism," 1932-43. Influenced by the paintings and cultural nationalism of the GROUP OF SEVEN, his "symphonic theatre," a fusion of realistic and poetic choral speech, music, dance and nonrealistic lighting and setting, was the primary stylistic alternative to the prevailing realism in Canadian theatre production. His most important dramatic works include *Rocks* and *Earth Song* (1932), *Hill-land* (1934), *Murder Pattern* (1936), *Ascend As the Sun* (1942) and the realistic *Emily Carr* (1960). Following the suspension of regular theatre production because of WWII, Voaden began a second career as a national arts lobbyist. As first president, Canadian Arts Council (1945-48), national director, Canadian Conference of the Arts (1966-68) and president, Canadian Guild of Crafts (1968-70), he helped to secure government support for the arts in Canada. In 1987 he attended a performance of a revival of *Murder Pattern* in Toronto. ANTON WAGNER

Vogt, Augustus Stephen, "A.S.," choral conductor, educator, administrator (b at Washington, Ont 14 Aug 1861; d at Toronto 17 Sept 1926). After studies in Boston and Leipzig, Vogt, a church organist, choirmaster, piano and organ teacher, founded the TORONTO MENDELSSOHN CHOIR in 1894. Soon one of the continent's finest, his choir was renowned for *a cappella* work and for annual festival performances with leading orchestras. Appointed principal of Toronto Conservatory in 1913, he retired from conducting in 1917 to devote all his time to administration. From 1918 until his death he was dean of U of T's music faculty. BARCLAY McMILLAN

Voice of Women, since 1960 a voluntary nonpartisan organization with members in every province of Canada, has opposed violence and war and promoted DISARMAMENT and peace. To this end VOW has organized extensive educational campaigns, lobbied all levels of government, held meetings and conferences including 2 international women's peace conferences, and sent representatives to other countries to consider the mutual concerns of women and to promote action. Regular meetings take place in many centres, and VOW initiates and supports campaigns with other groups. VOW is a member group of the

NATIONAL ACTION COMMITTEE ON THE STATUS OF WOMEN and PROJECT PLOUGHSHARES, and has a representative on the federal government's Consultative Group on Disarmament and Arms Control. *See also* PEACE MOVEMENT; WOMEN'S INTERNATIONAL LEAGUE FOR PEACE AND FREEDOM. KAY MACPHERSON

Vokes, Christopher, Chris, soldier (b at Armagh, Ire 13 Apr 1904; d at Toronto 27 Mar 1985). He was one of the few Canadian generals to emerge from WWII with a high reputation as an operational commander. Son of a British soldier, Vokes attended schools in Kingston, Ont, graduated from Royal Military College in 1925 and McGill (BSc) in 1927, joined the Royal Canadian Engineers, completed staff college in England in 1935 and, when war came, rose rapidly in command and staff appointments. He led the 2nd Canadian Infantry Brigade in the Sicily campaign in 1943 and took over 1st Canadian Division in November to lead it through the brutal house-to-house fighting at ORTONA and north to the Hitler Line. In Nov 1944, he was switched to command 4th Canadian Armoured Division and commanded it during the bitter Hochwald Forest battle and into Germany. At war's end, Vokes commanded the Canadian Army Occupation Force. In that role, he commuted the death sentence passed on Kurt Meyer, an SS general, by Canada's only WAR CRIMES trial. In the postwar years, Vokes commanded the army's Central Command and then Western Command before retiring to Oakville, Ont, in 1959. While judged by Gen Montgomery as no better than "a good plain cook" as a tactician, Vokes was a tough, hard-driving divisional commander who met the tough objectives set for his 1st Division. No intellectual, he was one of the ablest products of Canada's tiny pre-1939 army. Command, Vokes insisted, "is often not *what* you do but the *way* you do it." DESMOND MORTON

General Bernard Law Montgomery (right) congratulating Major-General Christopher Vokes on the capture of Ortona by the 1st Canadian Infantry Division, Vasto, Italy, 20 Dec 1943 (*courtesy National Archives of Canada/ PA-132783*).

Volcano, an opening in the crust of a planetary body through which liquid, gaseous or solid material is expelled; also the structure formed by eruption of this material. Most terrestrial volcanoes expel magma, a mixture of molten rock and dissolved gases (eg, water vapour, carbon diox-

ide, sulphur dioxide). The Earth's volcanic belts are located above zones of anomalously high temperature (700-1400°C) where magma is produced by partial melting of solid material in the crust and upper mantle. These areas commonly occur along crustal plate margins at depths of 10-50 km (*see* PLATE TECTONICS). Basalt is the principal magma of diverging plate boundaries such as the oceanic spreading ridges; basalt, andesite, dacite and rhyolite characterize volcanic arcs along converging plate margins. The relatively low density of magma causes it to rise through fractures into regions of lower pressure where dissolved gases expand and propel it toward the surface. Magma trapped in shallow reservoirs may solidify to form subvolcanic intrusions or may undergo chemical change before resuming its ascent. Evacuation of such reservoirs sometimes causes overlying rocks to collapse, leaving steep-walled, circular depressions (calderas). Groundwater heated by magma may discharge as hot mineral SPRINGS, as geysers or as fumaroles, or steam may escape in explosive bursts (phreatic eruptions) which commonly precede eruptions of magma. Magma reaching the surface may issue as molten lava or as solid, pyroclastic ejecta (bombs, blocks, lapilli, ash).

Eruptive behaviour depends on the magma's temperature, composition and gas content, and on whether the vent is on land (subaerial), under water (subaqueous) or beneath ice (subglacial). Subaerial eruptions of characteristically fluid basalt are usually accompanied by fire fountains of incandescent globules thrown out of the vent by expanding gas. The globules fall back around the vent, building a pyroclastic cone, but most of the magma spreads in the form of thin lava flows which may build broad shields or lava plateaus. Escape of gases is restricted in viscous andesite, dacite and rhyolite magma. The trapped gases may inflate the melt into a porous froth (pumice) or may escape explosively, tearing apart the stiff, enclosing magma and hurling ash and pumice fragments from the vent. In these Plinian eruptions (named for the Roman scholar Pliny the Younger, who witnessed the event), columns of hot gases carry plumes of fine ash high into the atmosphere to be spread for hundreds of kilometres. Dense mixtures of hot gases, ash and pumice sometimes form fluidized flows (eg, ash flows, pyroclastic flows, glowing avalanches) which sweep rapidly down the flanks of an erupting volcano. Lava associated with such eruptions is commonly so viscous that it clings to the slopes in short, thick flows. These alternate with pyroclastic deposits to form steep-sided, composite cones with the classical symmetry of Mt Fuji. Extremely viscous lava, containing little gas, may pile up over its vent into bulbous lava domes or may project from the vent as crumbling spines of incandescent, nearly solid rock. Lava that enters water from a subaqueous vent is quenched, resulting in a glassy rind that may fracture into a pile of fragments or act as a viscous skin enclosing molten lava. In shallow water, magma thrown from a subaqueous vent by expanding gas is quenched to solid ejecta which accumulates as a tuff ring. In contrast, lava from vents on the deep ocean floor issues quietly, its dissolved gas held in solution by enormous hydrostatic pressure. Ejecta from subglacial vents may accumulate on the ice as supraglacial cones which collapse when the ice melts. Alternatively, lava may thaw a hole in the ice and there accumulate to form a steep-sided, flat-topped table mountain (tuya).

The deeply eroded remnants of ancient volcanic belts are found in volcanically inactive regions such as the Canadian Shield. In Canada, geologically young volcanoes are confined to the Western CORDILLERA. The Garibaldi belt of southwestern BC includes many supraglacial and sub-

Volcanic cinder cone in northwest BC. The Aiyansh lava flow is the youngest in Canada (200 years ago) (*photo by Tom W. Parkin/Pathfinder*).

glacial volcanoes. Lava plateaus and shield volcanoes dotted with pyroclastic cones cover much of central BC; and composite volcanoes, such as Mt Edziza, form a belt extending from northern BC into the southern YT. No historical record of an eruption in Canada exists, but native legends and radiometric dating suggest that the Aiyansh lava flow near Terrace, BC, was extruded about 200 years ago. The explosive eruption in 1980 of Mt St Helens, Washington, left nearly 400 km² of total devastation. Eruption forecasting, based on the detection of precursor events such as seismic activity, tilting and heating of ground and emission of gases, may soon provide a warning to people living in areas threatened by an impending eruption. Volcanoes are not unique to the Earth. The dark maria of the moon are lava plains formed by the eruption of basalt. Olympus Mons, a Martian shield volcano 700 km across and 27 km high, is the largest volcano in the solar system. Io, an inner moon of Jupiter, is the most volcanically active body yet identified in the solar system. Its numerous volcanoes produce a dark lava (probably basalt) and a lighter material believed to be molten sulphur. *See also* GEOLOGICAL REGIONS; GEOTHERMAL ENERGY. J.G. SOUTHER

Reading: M.B. Lambert, *Volcanoes* (1978).

Vole, common name for several RODENTS of family Arvicolidae, found only in the Northern Hemisphere. They have stout bodies, short legs and tails, and ears nearly hidden by moderately long hair. Genus *Microtus* (about 55 species) is most widespread and diverse; 11 *Microtus* species occur in Canada (including woodland, prairie, singing, montane, Townsend's, root, long-tailed, rock, chestnut-cheeked and creeping voles). Meadow voles (*M. pennsylvanicus*), commonly called field mice, occur throughout Canada, in grasslands, forests and low arctic tundra. Red-backed voles (*Clethrionomys*), most abundant in forests, also occur on the prairies and on tundra W of Hudson Bay. Heather voles (*Phenacomys*), found across the boreal forest, are rare; sagebrush voles (*Lagurus curtatus*) are confined to dry grasslands of SW Sask and SE Alta. Voles range in size from 15-20 g (red-backed voles) to 200 g (large Richardson's water vole, *M. richardsoni*). Many make prominent runways and above-ground, grassy nests. They remain active and may breed under the snow cover. Females of many species become fertile immediately after giving birth, bearing litters at close intervals; they may have 2 or more litters in the summer of their own birth. Voles rarely survive more than one winter. Many species undergo cycles of abundance and scarcity, peaking every 3-4 years. They can cause serious losses of hay and cereal crops, and damage fruit trees and ornamental shrubs. W.A. FULLER

Volkoff, Boris Vladimirovich, dancer, choreographer (b Boris Vladimirovich Baskakoff at Schepotievo, Russia 24 April 1900; d at Toronto 11 Mar 1974). Volkoff studied at the Bolshoi dance school, Moscow. He arrived in Toronto via the Soviet Far East, China and the US to become BALLET master and dancer at the Uptown Theatre in 1929, and in 1930 he established the Boris Volkoff School of the Dance. Through recitals, performances and lectures Volkoff introduced many to dance and built an audience. In 1936 he and his dancers won a Tanz-Spiele medal at the Berlin Olympics, dancing 2 of his ballets with Canadian themes. By 1939 this group had evolved into the Canadian Ballet. He commissioned and choreographed *The Red Ear of Corn* (1949), a Canadian theme ballet to a score by John WEINZWEIG. In 1951 he donated his studio and dancers to help the nascent NATIONAL BALLET OF CANADA. Volkoff also taught at the Toronto Skating Club and revolutionized choreography for FIGURE SKATING. He designed the first ice ballet for the club in 1934 and choreographed and produced its ice ballets for 14 seasons. His students include Melissa HAYDEN and Barbara Ann SCOTT.

Vollenweider, Richard Albert, scientist, limnologist, environmentalist, teacher (b at Zurich, Switz 27 June 1922). He is known for providing a generalized theoretical framework of the relationship between nutrient enrichment and eutrophication (process by which water becomes rich in dissolved nutrients and deficient in oxygen) of fresh waters. In a fundamental reform of the dominant limnological thinking of the time, he discarded the idea that predictions could only be made on the basis of individual lake studies. He provided the first generalized predictions of a lake's trophic (nutritional) state from quantitative data on the lake's nutrient load and hydrology. His work found direct application at the end of the 1960s when the effects of urbanization, industrialization and intensification of agriculture after WWII resulted in excessive nutrient enrichment of runoff and severe problems due to overgrowth of plant life in rivers, lakes and reservoirs. The Organization for Economic Cooperation and Development, Paris, France, appointed Vollenweider chief co-ordinator of a worldwide scientific effort 1966-81. Over this period he was responsible for documenting his approach, directing technical reports on methodology, regional reports of quantitative results, a summary synthesis report and finally a test of all results using information on more than 200 Canadian LAKES. These documents provide a sound basis for water management to alleviate or prevent eutrophication. It was through his involvement in the INTERNATIONAL JOINT COMMISSION that the limit was set for phosphorus loading to the Laurentian Great Lakes as stated in the 1972 Water Quality Agreement Act, thus avoiding severe eutrophication of the world's largest supply of fresh water. Vollenweider has been senior scientist since 1973 at the Canada Centre for Inland Waters, Burlington. He has travelled throughout the world on assignments with UNESCO and has directed major programs for preservation of the Adriatic Sea and Lake Maricaibo. In 1986, Vollenweider was awarded the Tyler Prize (a US award, considered equivalent to a Nobel Prize in environmental science) and in 1987 the Naumann-Thiennemann Medal by the International Limnological Society (*Societus Internationalis Limnologiae*).

LORRAINE L. JANUS

Volleyball is a team sport played by 6 players on a side. The playing court, 18 m x 9 m, is divided by a centre line. Above the centre line is an extended net, placed 2.43 m high for men, and 2.24 m high for women. The goal of the game is to send the ball, according to the regulations, over the net to the floor of the opposite court. Service, initiated

Ex-voto painting, *Mme Riverin and her four children* (1703), by D. de Richeterre (*courtesy Basilique-Ste-Anne-de-Beaupré*).

within the service zone by the right back player, puts the ball into play. Each team is entitled to contact the ball 3 times (in addition to the touch on the block) to prevent the ball from touching the floor of its own court. Players, except blockers, are not allowed to contact the ball twice consecutively. The ball remains in play until it touches the floor, walls, ceiling, any other object or until a player commits a fault. Points are scored only by the serving team. The team that scores at least 15 points or more, with an advantage of 2 points over its opponent, wins a set (game). The team that wins 3 sets (games) wins the match.

Volleyball was developed in the US in the last decade of the 19th century. As the game developed from being recreational to being a highly competitive sport, skills grew more sophisticated and intricate tactics of attack and defence evolved. It is played competitively around the world and has been an Olympic sport since 1964.

Volleyball was introduced to Canada in 1900 through the YMCA, and intercity competitions began shortly after. The Canadian Volleyball Assn was formed in 1953. Championship tournaments were launched in eastern Canada and then nationally. Toronto Central Y' Estonians were men's champions 1953-59; Montreal International Y' Latvians were the first women's champions (1953). In international competition, Canadian teams qualified for the 1976 and 1984 Olympics. The Canadian men's team scored impressive wins over the world-leading Soviet team in 1984 and later finished fourth at the 1984 Los Angeles Olympics.

LORNE SAWULA

Voltigeurs, light infantry corps recruited among French-speaking Canadians in Lower Canada immediately prior to the WAR OF 1812 and commanded by a Canadian lt-col in the British army, Charles de SALABERRY. In Nov 1812 the Voltigeurs, posted first to the Eastern Townships, helped repel an American army. During Oct-Nov 1813 they helped turn back a 2-pronged American advance on Montréal from the west, participating in the battles of Châteauguay and CRYSLER'S FARM. The following spring they returned to the Eastern Townships, and in Aug participated in a feeble attack on Plattsburgh, NY. Although the original corps was disbanded 24 Mar 1815, a regiment in today's armed forces bears its name.

ROY MacLAREN

Von Gencsy, Eva, dancer, teacher, choreographer (b at Budapest, Hungary 11 Mar 1924). She trained and performed as a ballet dancer in Hungary and Austria before immigrating to Canada in 1948. As a principal dancer with the Winnipeg (later ROYAL WINNIPEG) Ballet 1948-53 and Les Ballets Chiriaeff in Montréal 1953-57, Von Gencsy contributed to the beginnings of 2 of Canada's 3 major ballet companies. She then turned to jazz as a medium for personal expression, performing and teaching, and in 1972 founding Les BALLETS JAZZ DE MONTREAL where she remained as artistic director and choreographer until 1979. Her choreography has a distinctive ballet-jazz style for which she is known internationally.

JILLIAN M. OFFICER

Votive Painting The term "ex voto" comes from the Latin "*ex voto suscepto*" meaning "in pursuance of a vow." It may be used in reference to a painting, a plaque or any object placed in a church or chapel to commemorate a vow or to express thanks for a favour received. This practice, a religious gesture made in the face of death or a simple expression of gratitude to the Divinity, has existed since the beginning of time and was introduced into New France with the arrival of the French colonists. The STE-ANNE-DE-BEAUPRÉ historical museum (across from Île d'Orléans) houses Canada's largest collection of votive paintings, dedicated to St Anne, the patron saint of sailors. These paintings date back to the 17th and 18th centuries, each telling a particular story.

Congratulatory ex-votos, offered for a favour received, are the most common. They include the *Ex-voto de Saint-François*, the *Ex-voto du Saint-Esprit de Québec*, the *Ex-voto à Sainte Anne et à Saint Antoine*, the *Ex-voto des cinq naufragés*, the *Ex-voto d'Iberville*, the *Ex-voto de Monsieur Edouin* (all kept

Voyageurs at Dawn (1871), by Frances Ann Hopkins (*courtesy National Archives of Canada/C-2773*).

at Ste-Anne-de-Beaupré) and the *Ex-voto de l'Aimable Marthe* kept at Notre-Dame-des-Victoires. To attract the protection of the divine power, the donor may offer a propitiary ex-voto before the event, as in the *Ex-voto de Madame Riverin*. Commemorative ex-votos, such as the *Ex-voto de Louis Prat*, serve as a reminder of a past event. Ex-votos may also be offered out of simple devotion. Usually the saint is depicted in the upper part of the painting and the event for which the ex-voto is offered is shown in the lower part. The artist makes no link between the scene and the sacred person, and the 2 parts are often disproportioned.

In the past, votive paintings were sometimes considered of little artistic value and, having lost their significance for priests in charge of pilgrimage sites, many recorded examples have disappeared, including the *Ex-voto de Saint-François* offered by Antoine Lamorille and Capt Pierre d'Astaritz after their ship was dismasted on 29 Sept 1732. Marble plaques began to appear in Canada in the mid-19th century and gradually replaced the ex-voto artworks. Votive paintings conserved today are important not only to our country's history, but also because few examples dating from the 17th and 18th centuries are found elsewhere.   NICOLE CLOUTIER

Reading: Ex-voto marins dans le monde de l'antiquité à nos jours (1981); F.M. Gagnon, Premiers peintres de la Nouvelle-France (1976); J. Russell Harper, Painting in Canada (1977).

Voyageur, an adventurer who journeyed by canoe from Montréal to the interior to trade with Indians for furs. At the close of the 17th century, the term was applied to selected COUREURS DE BOIS, hired by Montréal merchants to arrange and sustain trading alliances with Indian bands. The term later included all FUR-TRADE participants: the merchant (BOURGEOIS), his clerk (*commis*) and con-

tracted servants (*engagés*). Today, the term "voyageur" suggests the romantic image of men paddling the canoes in the fur brigades which traversed much of the continent, living lives full of perilous adventure, gruelling labour and boisterous cameraderie.   JOHN E. FOSTER

Vulture, large, long-winged, bald-headed BIRD OF PREY, normally abundant in warmer latitudes. Graceful in flight, it glides and circles for extended periods. The one Canadian representative, turkey vulture (*Cathartes aura*), belongs to the family Cathartidae (New World vultures). It breeds from southernmost Canada to southern S America, inhabiting all but heavily forested terrains. Usually, 2 eggs are laid on the ground, among rocks or in caves. Incubation lasts 30-41 days. As carrion feeders, vultures are threatened in most parts of the world by the general decline in numbers of wandering herds of wild and domestic herbivores and by sanitary practices involving the removal or burning of dead animals.   R.W. FYFE

W.D. Lawrence, 2548 ton square-rigged sailing ship built in 1874 in Maitland, NS. It was designed and built by William Dawson Lawrence, who earned substantial profits from the ship until 1883, when he sold it to a Norwegian. Renamed the *Kommander Sven Foyn,* the windjammer continued in profitable service until 1897, when it was stranded in the English Channel. It finished as a barge in W Africa.   JAMES MARSH

Wabana, Nfld, Town, pop 4057 (1986c), inc 1950, is located on the N end of Bell I in Conception Bay and is the principal community on the island. The community grew up around the site of iron-ore mines opened in the 1890s and is said to have been named by a mining official for an Abenaki word meaning "place of first light." The community grew as a mining town and service centre for the island until the closing of the mines in 1966. Its population dropped quickly after the closure, but lately the decline has slowed. Since the 1960s, Wabana has been the site of the island's hospital and vocational school, and recently of a fish plant and a community co-operative which has engaged in diverse projects for the town.   ROBERT D. PITT

Wacousta; Or, The Prophecy: A Tale of the Canadas, novel by John RICHARDSON, was published in London and Edinburgh in 1832; and in Montréal in 1868, as *Wacousta; Or the Prophecy. An Indian Tale.* Numerous editions appeared under various titles. Many of them were pirated (eg, Waldie's Select Circulating Library edition, Philadelphia, 1833), and many were abridged. Richardson frames his novel within PONTIAC'S 1763 siege of forts Detroit and Michilimackinac, but at the story's centre is the gory and protracted development of Wacousta's revenge upon the British commander, Colonel De Haldimar, who had betrayed Wacousta by marrying his fiancée years earlier in Scotland. Wacousta (formerly a fellow soldier and friend of De Haldimar) is a Herculean savage, made monstrous by his bitterness, who advises Pontiac in his plans to capture the forts. The novel is at once a Gothic romance and a blood-soaked tragedy. *Wacousta's* complex publishing and editing history, and the story of Richardson's tortured life as well, have interested as many critics and bibliographers as the novel itself has. *Wacousta* was translated into German in 1858.   NEIL BESNER

Waddington, Geoffrey, conductor, administrator (b at Leicester, Eng 23 Sept 1904; d at Toronto 3 Jan 1966). He learned the violin while growing up in Lethbridge, Alta, where he made his conducting debut before age 12. Waddington joined the Toronto Conservatory's faculty in 1922, simultaneously beginning a career as a radio musician. He joined the CBC in 1947, founded the CBC Symphony Orchestra in 1952 and remained its music director until 1964. In this most influential position, he continually sought out the country's best performing talent for national and international exposure and regularly commissioned new music from Canadian composers.   BARCLAY MCMILLAN

Waddington, Miriam, née Dworkin, poet (b at Winnipeg 3 Dec 1917). Educated in Winnipeg, Ottawa, Toronto and Philadelphia, she received her BA (1939) and MA (1968) from U of T. In 1945 she received her MSW from the U of Penn, and she worked as a caseworker and teacher of social work in the 1940s and 1950s. She has written 12 books of poetry. *Green World* (1945), her first book, marked her association with First Statement poets of Montréal such as Ronald Sutherland, Irving LAYTON and A.M. KLEIN. She changed her profession from social work to teaching English in the mid-1960s, lecturing at

York U from 1964. Her books of poetry include *The Season's Lovers* (1958), *The Glass Trumpet* (1966), *The Price of Gold* (1976), *The Visitants* (1981) and *Collected Poems* (1986). She is also the author of a critical study on A.M. Klein (1970). In 1972 she edited *John Sutherland: Essays Controversies and Poems* and in 1974 *The Collected Poems of A.M. Klein.* She has written articles and reviews for numerous publications in Canada and abroad. Her poems have been translated and published in the Soviet Union, France, Greece, Hungary, Japan, Roumania, S America and China. *Driving Home,* her seventh volume of poetry, won the J.I. Segal Prize in 1972. In 1982 she published her first collection of short stories, *Summer at Lonely Beach.* Writing out of her Russian-Jewish secular heritage, she has a highly lyrical voice which speaks honestly and sometimes brutally. Waddington has achieved a prominent place in Canadian letters by successfully transforming being female and Jewish into powerful, positive forces in her poetry and fiction. In 1974 she delivered the annual E.J. Pratt memorial lecture at Memorial U in Newfoundland. She has had 3 writer-in-residence appointments: U of Ottawa (1974); Windsor Public Library (1983); and Metro Toronto Public Library (1986). Waddington has read her poetry at numerous universities, is both visiting lecturer and exchange poet, and among other honours and awards she has received 2 honorary doctorate degrees (Lakehead U, 1975; York U, 1985).   SHARON DRACHE

Waddington, Mount, elev 4019 m, the highest mountain in BC's COAST MTS, rises near the head of Knight Inlet, 282 km NW of Vancouver. Standing only 39 km from the tidewater, it nourishes at least 5 valley glaciers over 16 km long. Known earlier as Mystery Mt, it was named after English-born industrialist Alfred Waddington, whose dream of a road to the Cariboo goldfields went unrealized. The main summit was climbed 1933 by F. Weissner and W. House.   GLEN BOLES

Waffle, a group established in 1969 as a caucus within the NEW DEMOCRATIC PARTY. Its members' choice of name was self-consciously ironic. It issued a Manifesto for an Independent Socialist Canada which demanded that Canadian public ownership replace American private ownership; subsequent Waffle statements called for Québec's right to self-determination and for an independent Canadian labour movement. Its politics were militantly socialist and nationalist, a Canadian manifestation of widespread and diverse political ferment, which included opposition to the VIETNAM WAR, the support of NEW LEFT politics on the campuses of N America and Europe, and a burgeoning women's movement. University professors Mel Watkins and James Laxer were the

Waffle's national leaders; in 1971 Laxer was the runner-up to David LEWIS for the leadership of the federal NDP. The Waffle was also organized provincially, particularly in Ontario and Saskatchewan. Purged from the Ontario NDP in 1972, it became a separate political group. It disintegrated in 1974, except for a surviving remnant in Saskatchewan. Many of its members slowly drifted back into the NDP.   MEL WATKINS

Wage and Price Controls are comprehensive government restrictions on the maximum rate at which wages and prices may increase during a specified time period. Wage and price controls can be distinguished from other types of government price and wage intervention by 2 characteristics. First, they are adopted for the purpose of controlling overall INFLATION, rather than to achieve some specific economic efficiency or economic equity goal (in contrast, for example, to minimum wage legislation). Second, they affect many sectors of the economy rather than focusing on one particular market, unlike programs such as agricultural price supports. Controls are a type of incomes policy (ie, any government policy that has a direct effect on overall price and wage setting in the economy). Other examples of incomes policy include voluntary wage and price guidelines and tax incentives to encourage lower rates of wage and price increase.

Many nations, including Canada, instituted a system of both price controls and rationing during WWII to prevent the profiteering and skyrocketing prices that might otherwise have resulted from wartime shortages (*see* WARTIME PRICES AND TRADE BOARD). These measures were largely abandoned in the postwar era. However, during the 1950s and 1960s a number of European countries experimented with income-policy interventions, including wage and price controls. Controls were primarily used as an attempt to combat inflation, and stimulative monetary and fiscal policies were used to reduce unemployment. The experiences with this type of policy combination were largely unsuccessful. The buoyant demand conditions created by high money-supply growth rates and various government spending and taxation initiatives either made the controls themselves unworkable and ineffective or created substantial latent inflationary pressure that was manifested when controls were finally lifted. This was also largely the fate of an American trial with controls in the early 1970s.

Subsequently, economists have realized that if controls are to be successful, they must be viewed as a complement to, rather than a substitute for, restrictive monetary and fiscal policy. While high inflation can eventually be controlled by significant lowering of money-supply growth rates, the process may be long and may involve painfully high UNEMPLOYMENT. Controls are seen by some economists as a means of overcoming the strong momentum of high price and wage increases and hence easing the transition to lower inflation.

Canada's only experience in peacetime with controls occurred 1975-78 in response to the exceptionally high inflation rates of 1974-75. The federal Anti-Inflation Act established a 3-year controls system. Wage guidelines were binding on all firms with 500 or more employees, on all federal employees, and (with the agreement of the majority of provincial governments) on most other public-sector employees. Profit-margin controls restricted the price and cost markups of large firms. Although the magnitude of the effect of the legislation is debatable, empirical analysis has generally supported the claim that the controls program did reduce inflation below the level that otherwise would have prevailed.   RONALD G. WIRICK

Wagner, Barbara Aileen, figure skater (b at Toronto 5 May 1938). Wagner and partner Robert PAUL formed the outstanding Canadian figure skating team that dominated the international pairs event 1957-62. They started skating together in 1952 in Toronto. In their first international experience at the 1956 Cortina Olympics they placed sixth. Following the retirement of Canada's Frances Defoe and Norris Bowden, they won the Canadian, N American and world championships in 1957. They performed flawlessly in winning the 1960 Squaw Valley, Calif, Olympics pairs event; all 7 judges awarded them first place. As professionals, they skated with ice shows until Wagner's marriage in 1964. She became a coach and teacher, serving as principal coach of the Ice Follies. BARBARA SCHRODT

Wagner, Claude, lawyer, judge, politician (b at Shawinigan, Qué 4 Apr 1925; d at Montréal 11 July 1979). At first active in legal circles as a crown prosecutor, professor of criminal law and judge in the Sessions Court, he confirmed his reputation as a staunch advocate of "law and order" while serving as minister of justice (1964-66) in Jean LESAGE's administration. Elected in a 1964 provincial by-election (Montréal-Verdun), he resigned in 1970 to become again a judge in the Sessions Court. He was elected Progressive Conservative MP for St-Hyacinthe in the federal elections of 1972 and 1974, and ran for the PC leadership in 1976, coming second to Joe CLARK. He resigned his seat in Apr 1978 when named to the Senate. DANIEL LATOUCHE

Wagner, Virgil Edwin, football player (b at Belleville, Ill 27 Feb 1922). Wagner entered the CANADIAN FOOTBALL LEAGUE as an original MONTREAL ALOUETTE in 1946, and as a high-scoring running back led the Als to the Big Four Title that first year, tying for the league scoring championship with Joe KROL. Wagner won the scoring title the next 3 years as well and is still the only man to win 4 consecutive eastern scoring titles. His scoring prowess brought instant credibility to the new franchise and helped the team earn a trip to its first GREY CUP appearance in 1949, where Wagner scored 2 touchdowns to help beat the CALGARY STAMPEDERS. Wagner played 5 more seasons with the Als. He won the Jeff Russell Memorial Trophy in 1947 as the Big Four's outstanding player and his career mark of 79 touchdowns was a new CFL record. He was inducted into the Canadian Football Hall of Fame in 1980. PETER WONS

Wah, Fred, poet, editor, teacher (b at Swift Current, Sask 1939). An influential figure in postmodern Canadian poetry, best known to date for his book *Waiting for Saskatchewan* (1985). Wah was educated at UBC where he founded, edited and wrote for *Tish* magazine. After his return to the Kootenay area of BC in 1967, he taught at Selkirk College and then the ill-fated David Thompson U Centre, where he was head of the creative writing program. He has also been a contributing editor to *Open Letter* since its founding in 1965, and in 1980 edited the selected poems of Daphne MARLATT, *Net Work*. His own selected poems, *Loki is Buried at Smokey Creek*, were published that same year. Wah's poetry is influenced by his experiments with language, his interest in jazz and the magical geography of the Kootenay area. His other books include *Among* (1972), *Pictograms From the Interior of BC* (1975), *Breathin' My Name with a Sigh* (1981), *Owner's Manual* (1982) and *Music at the Heart of Things* (1987). In 1985 he won the Gov Gen's Award for poetry for *Waiting for Saskatchewan*. MARC CÔTÉ

Wainwright, Alta, Town, pop 4665 (1986c), 4266 (1981c), inc 1910, is located 200 km SE of Edmonton. The first settlement, Denwood, established in 1906, was moved in its entirety to a railway divisional point 4 km away in 1908. This new site was named for William Wainwright, second VP of the Grand Trunk Pacific Ry. It developed as the administrative and distributing centre of an extensive farming area. Oil and gas were discovered 1922 and are piped from some 400 wells. In 1909 Bison Recovery Park was established nearby, but the BISON were moved elsewhere and the park was converted to CFB Camp Wainwright during WWII. A few bison were returned in 1980. The Wainwright Museum features a reconstructed post office (c1900), and an early oil rig is preserved in Petroleum Park. The weekly newspaper is the Wainwright *Star-Chronicle*. ERIC J. HOLMGREN

Walbran, John Thomas, ship's officer, historian, writer (b at Ripon, Eng 23 Mar 1848; d at Victoria 31 Mar 1913). He sailed the world until 1888, when he joined the coastal service of the Canadian Pacific Navigation Co. Three years later he became captain of the Canadian government steamship *Quadra* and travelled the BC coast, 1891-1903, engaged in fisheries protection and lighthouse supply. Walbran's *British Columbia Coast Names* (1909, repr 1971), as well as a directory of PLACE-NAMES, is a rich store of information on ships, fur traders, explorers and missionaries. ERIC J. HOLMGREN

Waldo, Carolyn, synchronized swimmer (b at Montréal 11 Dec 1964). SYNCHRONIZED SWIMMING is a relatively new sport at which Canadians consistently excel in international competition, and Waldo has been recognized as the world's best. Starting at the age of 11, within 5 years she had won her first junior title in duet. In 1982 she joined the Calgary Aquabelles, and since then has won many honours and medals at various levels. Waldo swept the 1986 world championships in Madrid with 3 gold medals, by retaining the individual gold medal (first to register 200 points), pairing with Michelle Cameron to take the duet title, and helping the Canadian contingent to win the team event. She was named female athlete of the year for 1987 by Canadian Press. GERALD REDMOND

Walhachin The turn of the century in British Columbia was a time of economic prosperity. The optimism associated with this prosperity enabled land speculators to attract upper-class Englishmen to purchase land and settle at Walhachin. The British Columbia Development Corp developed a 2000 ha benchland property along the S Thompson R, W of Kamloops, in 1908-09 and built a planned community surrounded by orchards. However, Walhachin as a viable orchard-based settlement was destined not to succeed. The soil was inadequate, the climate harsh, the extensive gravity irrigation system inappropriate, and the settlers inexperienced and lacking the necessary commitment.

Within weeks of the outbreak of WWI, Walhachin was credited with having the highest enlistment rate per capita of any Canadian community. The prospect of returning to their familiar aristocratic roots was more attractive to the settlers than enduring the deprivations of remaining on Canada's western frontier. At war's end, only a few returned. Today, only the ghosts of abandoned irrigation flumes, relic homes and the skeletal remains of fruit trees remain of the romantic western adventure. NELSON A. RIIS

Walkem, George Anthony, lawyer, judge, politician, premier of BC 1874-76; 1878-82 (b at Newry, Ire 15 Nov 1834; d at Victoria 13 Jan 1908). Educated in the Province of Canada, Walkem moved to BC in 1862, was a member of the colonial Legislative Council (1864-70) and after 1871 sat in the provincial legislature. Associated with Amor DE COSMOS in the Confederation League before BC joined CONFEDERATION, he became attorney general in De Cosmos's Cabinet and succeeded him as premier. The 2 Walkem administrations were dominated by the struggle with Ottawa over the failure to begin the Pacific railway in the time set out in the Terms of Union. Walkem led the fight with vigour but with an irascibility that forfeited him community support once construction of the CPR began. He ended his career as a justice of the Supreme Court of British Columbia (1882-1904). H. KEITH RALSTON AND BETTY WILCOX

Walker, Sir Byron Edmund, banker (b in Haldimand County, Canada W 14 Oct 1848; d at Toronto 27 Mar 1924). With little education, Walker took 18 years to rise from a discount clerk to general manager of the Canadian Bank of Commerce in 1886; he was president 1907-24. He showed great organizational talent in developing the first set of written regulations for dividing a bank into the complex array of departments that have come to characterize modern banking. His greatest public notice came in 1911 when, although a Liberal, he opposed the policy of RECIPROCITY with the US announced by the Laurier government, because it would weaken ties with Great Britain. Thus began the surge of IMPERIALISM that led to the defeat of the trade agreement and the government. Walker had helped to found *The Round Table Quarterly* (1910) to promote discussion of imperial issues. A man of wide interests, he was an adviser to the National Gallery, a founder of the CHAMPLAIN SOCIETY, and a fellow of the Royal Society. D.N. SPRAGUE

Walker, David Harry, army officer, novelist (b at Dundee, Scot 9 Feb 1911). Raised in Scotland and England, Walker was aide-de-camp to Canadian Gov Gen John BUCHAN 1938-39, a POW in Europe 1940-45, and comptroller to the viceroy of India 1946-47. A major with an MBE, he retired in 1948 to write full-time in St Andrews, NB. The popular *Geordie* (1950) tells of a small Scottish boy who takes a body-building course and wins an Olympic gold medal. *The Pillar* (Gov Gen's Award 1952) depicts POW life. *Digby* (Gov Gen's Award 1953) tells how a weary N American tycoon is rejuvenated during a Rabelaisian visit to Scotland. *Where the High Winds Blow* (1960) portrays the rise of an entrepreneur in the Canadian North, while NB settings dominate *Mallabec* (1965), *Pirate Rock* (1969) and *Ash* (1976). *Black Dougal* (1973), an adventure thriller, is in part set in Québec, while *The Lord's Pink Ocean* (1972) portrays the survivors of a worldwide biochemical disaster. His 20 books include 5 for children and adolescents. In July 1987, he was named a Member of the Order of Canada. His memoirs, *Lean, Wind, Lean*, were published in 1984. JOHN R. SORFLEET

Walker, Edmund Murton, entomologist (b at Windsor, Ont 5 Oct 1877; d at Toronto 14 Feb 1969). After studies in natural sciences and medicine at Toronto, Walker studied in Berlin, then joined the dept of biology at U of T (1904), became head of zoology in 1934 and retired in 1948. He was largely responsible for the extensive invertebrate collection of the ROYAL ONTARIO MUSEUM, founding the collection in 1914 and serving as assistant director 1918-31 and honorary director 1931-69. His many publications include a 3-vol treatise on the Odonata of Canada and Alaska and editorship of the *Canadian Entomologist* (1910-20). His discovery with T.B. Kurata of "ice-bugs" (*Grylloblatta*) on Sulphur Mt, Alta (1913), resulted in the naming of a new order of insects (*see* ICE-WORM). He served many local and

international nature, zoological and entomological associations in various capacities, and was honoured by the RSC's Flavelle Medal (1960).
MARTIN K. MCNICHOLL

Walker, Hiram, distiller, businessman (b at East Douglas, Mass 4 July 1816; d at Detroit, Mich 12 Jan 1899). Though Walker lived in Canada for only 5 years (1859-64), he built a distillery, a new town and a major railway line. In 1856 he began buying land around what became Walkerville (now part of Windsor, Ont) and in 1859 built the Windsor Distillery and Flouring Mill, which produced high-quality, refined, branded whiskies. By 1910 Walker's Canadian Club Whisky, introduced in 1884, had become Canada's top export whisky. Walker's business interests included wheat and flour trade with the US, hog and cattle fattening and the development of the Lk Erie, Essex and Detroit River Ry, completed in 1885 and providing transportation for Essex County produce and lumber to the American market.   DON SPENCER

Reading: William F. Rannie, *Canadian Whisky* (1976).

Walker, Horatio, painter (b at Listowel, Canada W 12 May 1858; d at Ste-Pétronille, Qué 21 Sept 1938). A member of the Canadian Art Club from 1908, Walker painted habitant life on Île d'Orléans, Qué. He received his early training at Toronto's Notman-Fraser photographic studios before moving to the US. By the mid-1880s he was spending his winters in New York and his summers at Île d'Orléans. His interpretation of Québec farm life is extremely sentimental and reminiscent in style of the French Barbizon painter Jean-François Millet. In a thick, brown impasto, the paintings depict the pious life of toiling peasants, set against glowing skies. This American Barbizon style brought Walker high prices for paintings such as *Oxen Drinking* (1899), many medals and awards, and a reputation during his lifetime as one of Canada's senior painters.
DOROTHY FARR

Noce canadienne (1930), oil on canvas by Horatio Walker *(courtesy Musée du Québec, photo by Patrick Altman).*

Walker, James, policeman, businessman (b at Carluke, Canada W 14 Apr 1848; d at Calgary 31 Mar 1936). He joined the NWMP in 1874 and was given command of the Battleford (Sask) detachment in 1879. While there he served as Indian agent and was the first civilian justice in the North-West Territories. In 1880 he resigned and in 1883 began a successful sawmill and lumber business in Calgary. He chaired the committee that secured Calgary's incorporation (1884), served on school and hospital boards, and installed Calgary's first telephone. He organized provincial boy scout and cadet corps, and the 238th Forestry Battalion during WWI. At Calgary's centennial (1975), Walker was also named "Citizen of the Century" for his outstanding service.   ROBERT M. STAMP

Walker, Norma Ford, née Ford, human geneticist (b at St Thomas, Ont 3 Sept 1893; d at Toronto 9 Aug 1968). Her academic life was spent entirely

at U of T, from which she graduated in 1918. She completed a PhD in entomology in 1923 under the direction of Edmund Murton WALKER, whom she married in 1943, and as a faculty member became interested in human genetics. She established her reputation as an authority on multiple births with her research on the DIONNE QUINTUPLETS. In addition to her university position, she was associated with the Hospital for Sick Children, Toronto, and was the first director of the hospital's department of genetics. Walker's publications in genetics contributed to knowledge of a number of genetic disorders of childhood and to the application of dermatoglyphics to clinical diagnosis. Through her work and that of her graduate students, who included the first appointees in human genetics at several Canadian universities, Walker has had a lasting influence on the national development of human genetics as an academic discipline and in relation to medicine.
MARGARET W. THOMPSON

Walking Buffalo, Tatânga Mânî, or George McLean, Stoney leader, Indian statesman, philosopher (b in Bow R Valley near Morley, Alta 20 Mar 1871; d at Banff, Alta 26 Dec 1967). Walking Buffalo was present at the signing of Treaty No 7 (1877) and became the most famous protégé of the Methodist missionaries John MCDOUGALL and John McLean. He witnessed the disappearance of the BISON, the building of the CPR and the evolution of tribal lands into provinces. Educated at the McDougall Orphanage at Morley and in Red Deer and Winnipeg, he worked briefly as a blacksmith and as a scout for the NWMP, then as an interpreter. He was councillor for the Bearspaw band of the Stoney Indians 1907-12 and chief 1912-16. Active in the Banff Indian Days and the CALGARY STAMPEDE, Walking Buffalo was a leader in the Morley United Church. Attracted to the moral rearmament movement in 1934, he was an ambassador for world peace until his death.
IAN A.L. GETTY

Wallace, William Stewart, librarian, editor, historian (b at Georgetown, Ont 23 June 1884; d at Toronto 11 Mar 1970). He was educated at Toronto and Oxford and served in WWI as major in the CEF, battalion adjutant and commanding officer of Khaki College (*see* KHAKI UNIVERSITY), Shorncliffe. He became assistant librarian at U of T in 1920 and was librarian 1923-54. He was general editor of the university program of scholarly publishing 1923-32 and though he served in a number of capacities in library affairs and teaching, he spent the greater part of his time editing and writing. He was the first editor of the CANADIAN HISTORICAL REVIEW (1920-30) and made it the chief vehicle for historians in English Canada. He was editor of the CHAMPLAIN SOCIETY 1923-43 and honorary editor of the Royal Society of Canada 1937-45. His *The Dictionary of Canadian Biography* (1926) was enlarged in 1945 and revised under the title *The Macmillan Dictionary of Canadian Biography* (1963). He was general editor and wrote most of the articles for the *Encyclopedia of Canada* (6 vols, 1935-37). These reference works were of inestimable value in Canadian studies. In all, Wallace published more than 30 books and hundreds of articles. After retiring at age 70, he was proprietor of Dora Hood's Book Room. He was distinguished and honoured in both of his fields and in his own mind drew no distinction between them.   ROBERT H. BLACKBURN

Wallaceburg, Ont, Town, pop 11 367 (1986c), 11 506 (1981c), inc 1875 (village), 1896 (town), located on Sydenham R, 53 km S of Sarnia. Settled in the 1830s, it was named for Scottish patriot Sir William Wallace. Lumbering was the basis of its early economy. As it was connected by water to

the Great Lakes, steamboat building also became important. At the end of the 19th century, logging declined and the town became known for its glass manufacturing and sugar-beet industry. Glass products still highlight the local economy, along with metal goods, plastics and auto accessories, from an extensive tool-and-die industry. The canning of farm products is also a principal enterprise.   DANIEL FRANCIS

Walleye (*Stizostedion vitreum vitreum*), moderately large, predatory, freshwater fish of the family Percidae (order Perciformes). Other common names include yellow walleye, pickerel, yellow pickerel, pikeperch, doré or doré jaune. Walleyes should not be confused with true PICKERELS, family Esocidae. Walleyes have a bluntly pointed head, a mouth well armed with teeth and 2 dorsal fins (the first with sharp spines, the second without). Their eyes are specially adapted to low light intensities. Walleyes are bright golden to brownish green, with darker markings; the lower tip of the caudal fin is milk white. They occur in fresh waters from the mouth of the Mackenzie R to near the Gulf of Mexico. In Canada they are found from southern Québec to northeastern BC and N to the mouth of the Mackenzie R. Walleyes are adapted to prey on other fishes. This is probably the most economically important species of fish in Canada's inland waters, being prized summer and winter for its delicious white flesh. The closely related sauger (*S. canadense*) is somewhat smaller and has a more restricted range (Québec to Alberta). It is also a popular sport fish.
E.J. CROSSMAN

Walmsley, Thomas, writer (b at Liverpool, Eng 13 Dec 1948). A high-school dropout and sometime heroin addict, Walmsley developed his craft at Vancouver's New Play Centre in the mid-1970s to become the Canadian theatre's foremost chronicler of the lower depths. His 6 plays, as well as 2 books of poetry and a novel, describe an urban subculture self-victimized by violence, drugs, alcohol and abusive sex. Dividing his time between Toronto and Vancouver, Walmsley has made a powerful impact with such brutally naturalistic plays as *The Jones Boy* (1977) and *Something Red* (1978), and the comedy *White Boys* (1982). A new play, *Mr Nice Guy,* co-written with Dolly Reisman, was produced in Toronto in 1986.
JERRY WASSERMAN

Walnut (*Juglans*), genus of trees of the walnut family (Juglandaceae). The roughly 15 known species are widely dispersed through temperate and tropical regions. The 2 species native to Canada (butternut and black walnut) are found only in the East. Walnuts average 20-30 m high and have horizontally spreading branches. The large, compound leaves consist of 15-23 leaflets. The edible kernel, enclosed in a leathery or woody hull, is used as a table nut, for flavouring desserts (eg, ice cream) and for walnut oil. A yellow dye may be obtained from the fresh bark and from the husk of the fruit itself. Walnuts, usually in scattered stands, may grow in dry areas but prefer fertile, moist, well-drained soil. They are particularly common in shallow valleys and in alluvial plains bordering waterways. The hard, lustrous dark wood, used primarily for veneer, cabinetmaking, panelling and boat building, was common in pioneer times but is now rare.   ESTELLE LACOURSIÈRE

Walrus (*Odobenus rosmarus*), massive, seallike MAMMAL with disproportionately small head and huge neck. The feet are flippers, and hind feet can be turned forward for movement ashore. Upper canines project downward as tusks up to 36 cm long. A mass of quill-like whiskers appears on the muzzle. Males average 3 m in length and 900 kgs in weight; females are 9% shorter and 16% lighter. The skin is thick, much folded and creased, with a sparse coat of coarse hair. The colour is cinnamon to grey, with pink in the folds and on the abdomen. There is a thick blubber layer. Walrus, generally associated with the ice edge and arctic seas of 40 m or less in depth, occur from Siberia to Greenland, but in Canada are confined to the eastern Arctic. They feed on invertebrates (primarily bivalves and molluscs). Some males take to killing seals and may scavenge. Breeding is polygamous, occurring Jan-Mar. Gestation is 15-16 months and most births occur from mid-Apr to June; nursing continues for over a year and, at most, pups are produced in alternate years. The killer whale is the only serious predator. European whalers almost exterminated walrus between 1650 and 1850, and there has been only partial recovery. About 500 are taken by Canadian Inuit annually, formerly for dog food, now mainly for ivory. *See also* ENDANGERED ANIMALS.

IAN McTAGGART-COWAN

Walsh, James Morrow, police officer, territorial commissioner (b at Prescott, Canada W 22 May 1840; d at Brockville, Ont 25 July 1905). As inspector in the North-West Mounted Police 1873-83, he gave his name to FORT WALSH. He dealt firmly but fairly with SITTING BULL and his followers, who had crossed into Canada in 1876 after the defeat of Custer at Little Bighorn (Montana), and he became friendly with the Sioux chief. In 1883 he established the Dominion Coke, Coal and Transportation Co in Winnipeg. With the onset of the KLONDIKE GOLD RUSH he returned to the force as superintendent and was commissioner of the Yukon District 1897-98. ERIC J. HOLMGREN

Walter, Arnold Maria, musicologist, educator, administrator (b at Hannsdorf, Moravia 30 Aug 1902; d at Toronto 6 Oct 1973). Immigrating to Canada in 1937, Walter became one of the most farsighted and influential leaders of Canadian MUSIC EDUCATION, effective in establishing programs to develop both musical talent and audiences receptive to it. In 1946 he established an opera school at the Toronto Conservatory. Under his direction (1952-68), the faculty of music at U of T attained international stature, its research library one of the continent's most comprehensive.

BARCLAY McMILLAN

Walters, Angus, fishing captain (b at Lunenburg, NS 9 June 1882; d there 11 Aug 1968). Walters went to sea in 1895, beginning as a deckhand for his father, who had pioneered LUNENBURG's involvement with the banks fishery. His ability to find fish and to get the most speed out of his vessel led to his selection in 1920 as skipper of the BLUENOSE, then under construction. Walters bought a controlling interest and insisted on certain structural modifications. Under his command, the schooner achieved fame on the Grand Banks and in the International Fisherman's Trophy races 1921 to 1938. He and his ship became inseparable in the popular imagination, but the decline of the salt fishery and the outbreak of WWII forced the retirement of both vessel and captain in 1939. Walters bought out the other shareholders, but was then forced to sell the *Bluenose* in 1942. The loss of the vessel and his death marked the end of an era in Canada's fishing tradition. LOIS KERNAGHAN

Walton, Dorothy Louise, née McKenzie, badminton player (b at Swift Current, Sask 7 Aug 1909; d at Toronto 17 Oct 1981). An outstanding all-round athlete at U of Sask, she earned her BA and MA degrees before moving to Ontario in 1932. From 1936 to 1940 she dominated Canadian women's badminton and was never ranked below sixth in tennis. Her career culminated in her winning the All-England Badminton Championship in 1939 and being acclaimed world champion; no other Canadian has won that title.

JOHN J. JACKSON

Wampum, made of white and purple Atlantic coast seashells, had considerable value to Indians in eastern Canada for ornament and ceremony and to non-Indians for currency, particularly in the 17th and 18th centuries. Wampum was threaded on string or woven into belts and sashes. Particular patterns symbolized events, alliances and people, and wampum was used to form relationships, propose marriage, atone for murder or ransom captives. Wampum was closely linked with the FUR TRADE in eastern Canada, where it was used as a trade good. Before Confederation, 1867, some Indian groups indicated their assent to certain INDIAN TREATIES by presenting wampum to crown officials. RENÉ R. GADACZ

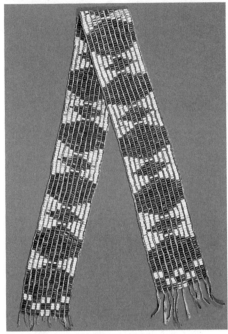

Wampum belt (*courtesy National Museums of Canada/Canadian Museum of Civilization/S75-620*).

Wangersky, Peter John, oceanographer (b at Woonsocket, RI 26 Aug 1927; naturalized Canadian 1975). Substantial contributions to OCEANOGRAPHY in Canada have come from Wangersky's research and teaching in chemical and biological oceanography. His degree in chemistry and subsequent work at the Scripps Inst, U Calif, and with the US Fish and Wildlife Service equipped Wangersky for further study at Yale. After positions at Miami and Yale, he joined Dalhousie as professor of chemistry in 1965, and then moved to the fledgling Institute of Oceanography in 1968, serving as chairman of the department and director of the institute 1977-80. His major research has illuminated patterns of distribution and dynamics of organic carbon in the sea. A sustained interest in theoretical ecology began with pioneer work on time lags in population equations and has led to novel analyses of marine communities. Wangersky's former students are widely placed in universities and government laboratories. IAN A. McLAREN

Wapiti (*Cervus elaphus*), largest-bodied, most highly evolved Old World DEER, is also known as the American elk. Its name is Shawnee for "white rump." Wapiti came to N America via BERINGIA late in the Ice Ages but expanded their range and population only after the extinction of the American megafauna about 11 000 years ago. By 1835 they had disappeared from their eastern range (Ontario and Québec). Locally (Manitoba to the Peace R district and eastern BC), the wapiti remains common and is an important game animal. Although valued for its hide by native people, the wapiti was not a favourite food animal and played no great role in aboriginal economics. Wapiti are social, tending towards life in open terrain. Males and females segregate, with females maximizing security from predation and bulls maximizing access to forage. Stags are larger than hinds. In rut, bulls advertise with loud, clear buglings (the most vocal deer in Canada), and by soaking themselves with urine. Dominant wapiti bulls form their respective female harems. The gestation period is relatively long, some 240 days; calves are born in June. Wapiti have been domesticated in Siberia and China where the antlers are used for medicinal purposes. VALERIUS GEIST

War Artists Canada's first official war art program, known as the Canadian War Memorials Fund, was established by Lords Beaverbrook (Max AITKEN) and Rothermere under the aegis of the Canadian War Records Office of the Canadian Army during WWI. From its inception in 1916 to its conclusion in 1919, the fund hired more than 80 artists of British, Australian, Yugoslavian and Canadian nationality to produce canvases, works on paper and sculptures depicting Canada's participation in the Great War. None of the resulting 800 works recording the farm and factory workers on the home front and the war-torn landscape of France and Flanders were exhibited during the hostilities. But at the war's end a large portion were shown in London, New York, Ottawa, Toronto and Montréal. These exhibitions not only demonstrated that Canada had produced a visual record of the war that was second to none but also that the country possessed a group of artists who offered a unique vision of the war through such canvases as F.H. VARLEY's *For What?* and A.Y. JACKSON's *Screened Road "A"* (*see* photo next page).

During WWII Canada did not have an official war art program until 1943. Created largely through the efforts of Vincent MASSEY and the director of the National Gallery of Canada, H.O. McCurry, the Canadian War Art Program came under the jurisdiction of the Department of National Defence. Only Canadian artists serving in the armed forces were employed. On a smaller scale than the Canadian War Memorials Fund — only 30 artists were given war artist commissions — the record nevertheless included Canadian activities in N Africa, off the Alaskan coast at Kiska, in the N Atlantic and the Pacific, as well as in Canada, Britain and Europe. Unlike WWI, paintings were exhibited during the war — sometimes directly behind fighting operations — in an attempt to inform civilians and military personnel alike of Canada's contribution to the war. Taken as a whole, the collection, totalling more than 1000 works, was less concerned with depicting the land than the men and machines, as Lawren P. HARRIS's *Tank Advance, 1944* and Charles F. COMFORT's *Dead German on the Hitler Line* suggest.

Canada had no war artists to record military activities in the Korean War or peacekeeping operations in the Congo. In 1967, however, the Canadian Armed Forces Civilian Artists Program was established by the Department of National Defence. It sent civilian artists to, among other places, Vietnam, Europe and the Middle East to ensure that the representation of Canada's armed forces begun during WWI was continued. Some 2 dozen artists have contributed to date; among them are Robert Hyndman, Mary Leach and Graham Wragg. MARIA TIPPETT

Screened Road "A" (unfinished), oil on canvas, by A.Y. Jackson (*courtesy Canadian War Museum/CMC/NMC/8188*).

War Brides This term gained popular currency during WWII to describe women who married Canadian servicemen overseas and then immigrated to Canada after the war to join their husbands. It is now also used to describe women who had similar experiences after WWI. By the end of 1946, 47 783 wives with 21 950 children had come to Canada. The vast majority (44 886) were from Great Britain, with much smaller numbers coming from Holland, Belgium, France and elsewhere. Some 80% married soldiers, whereas 18% married men in the RCAF and the remainder married men in the navy. The Canadian government provided the war brides with free sea and rail passage from their original homes to their destinations in Canada, as well as daily food allowances and free access to medical care on boats and trains. Many of the war brides were unprepared for the conditions they found in Canada, but most stayed and adjusted to a new way of life.

REBECCA PRIEGERT COULTER

War Criminals, Commission of Inquiry on (Deschênes Commission), established 7 Feb 1985. In response to charges that Joseph Mengele and other alleged Nazi war criminals had attempted to enter or were resident in Canada, a commission under Judge Jules Deschênes of the Superior Court of Québec was asked by the federal government to discover whether there were war criminals in Canada, when and how they obtained entry, and what action might be taken to bring them to justice. The commission reported 30 Dec 1986 after compiling and examining 3 lists of suspects: a master file of 774 names, an addendum of 38 and a group of 71 German scientists and technicians. In the majority of cases the commission found that the accused was either not in Canada or that there was no *prima facie* evidence that the individual had participated in war crimes. Mengele, it was concluded, had not attempted to enter Canada. In Dec 1987, 3 months after the Criminal Code was amended to allow for prosecution, the first charges were laid against Imre Finta, for crimes allegedly committed in Hungary during WWII. NORMAN HILLMER

War Measures Act, statute (1914) conferring emergency powers on the federal Cabinet, allowing it to govern by decree when it perceives the existence of "war, invasion or insurrection, real or apprehended." The Act was proclaimed in force, with detailed regulations limiting the freedom of Canadians, during both world wars. More limited emergency legislation, the offshoot of War Measures, was applied during demobilization after WWII, and during and after the KOREAN WAR in the 1950s. The only use of the War Measures Act in a domestic crisis occurred in Oct and Nov 1970 when a state of "apprehended insurrection" was declared to exist in Québec and emergency regulations were proclaimed in response to 2 kidnappings by the terrorist FRONT DE LIBÉRATION DU QUÉBEC (*see* OCTOBER CRISIS). Afterwards PM Pierre Trudeau pledged to refine and limit the application of the Act in internal crises, but by the time of the Liberal defeat in 1984 the Act had not been modified. The government of Brian Mulroney introduced legislation to replace War Measures with a more detailed and limited emergency law late in 1987. DENIS SMITH

War of the Austrian Succession, 1739-48, actually 2 wars, one fought in Europe, the other, also known as King George's War, fought in the colonies. Between 1713 and 1739 French overseas trade had increased astronomically, while that of Britain stagnated. Particularly at issue was trade with the Spanish Empire, which France dominated. Britain, determined to oust the French from this vast market, declared war on Spain (the so-called War of Jenkins's Ear) on 19 Oct 1739. War with France would quickly have followed but for the outbreak of hostilities between the continental powers in Europe upon the accession in Oct 1740 of Maria Theresa to the Imperial Habsburg (Austrian) throne.

Britain and France were drawn into this conflict on opposing sides. It proved a disaster for both. A British army was soundly defeated 11 May 1745 at Fontenoy, Flanders (now in Belgium), by the French and driven off the continent. Overseas, French maritime trade was eventually ruined by the Royal Navy, and Canadian war parties ravaged British frontier settlements in NS, NY and New England. A combined British-New England expedition captured LOUISBOURG in June,

but the Anglo-American force was no more able to conquer Canada than the Canadians were able to conquer New England. In May-June 1748 the Treaty of Aix-la-Chapelle ended the war but settled nothing. Britain exchanged Louisbourg for Madras, India, which then went to France. The Netherlands were ceded to Austria, and Silesia to Prussia. The powers were all dissatisfied with their respective allies, and so made changes: on the eve of the SEVEN YEARS' WAR Prussia was allied with Britain, Austria with France. W.J. ECCLES

War of the Spanish Succession (Queen Anne's War), 1702-13, was a general European war that also involved the colonies of the major powers. The war was caused by conflicting claims to the Spanish throne after the death of the childless King Charles II. The accession of the grandson of King Louis XIV of France to the Spanish throne as Philip V antagonized England and Holland, which were in growing competition with France, and Holy Roman Emperor Leopold I, who had claimed the succession on behalf of his son.

European war broke out in 1702, with Holland, England and most of the German states aligned against France, Spain, Bavaria, Portugal and Savoy. The conflict spilled over into the N American colonies of France and England, as ACADIA and New England exchanged bloody local raids. French forces destroyed the English settlement at Bonavista, Nfld, in 1704 and captured St John's in 1708. The English gained control of PORT-ROYAL and with it Acadia in 1710, but the following year a British fleet was wrecked in the St Lawrence in an abortive attempt to sail on Québec. The Treaty of UTRECHT (1713) settled a number of succession disputes between England and France and granted considerable territory to England; France retained Île St-Jean [PEI] and Île Royale [Cape Breton], but ceded Acadia and Newfoundland to the English and restored to them the Hudson Bay drainage basin. The treaty is acknowledged as the end of French expansion and the rise of the British Empire.

JAMES A. OGILVY

War of 1812 On 18 June 1812, at the height of the Napoleonic conflict (*see* NAPOLEONIC WARS), the US declared war on Great Britain and struck at the only British possession on the continent: Canada. Most of the battles that followed took place along the international border. The war ended in stalemate. The Treaty of GHENT, signed 24 Dec 1814, solved nothing, since the reasons for the war – British high-handedness on the high seas, including searching American ships during the Napoleonic blockade and IMPRESSMENT – had been rendered academic by France's defeat. Yet Canada owes its present shape to negotiations that grew out of the peace, while the war itself – or the myths created by the war – gave Canadians their first sense of community.

The British and Canadians were badly outnumbered by the Americans but better prepared for war, thanks to the prescience of Maj-Gen Isaac BROCK, administrator of UPPER CANADA. If the enemy could move up the traditional Champlain-Richelieu invasion route, seize Montréal and cut the lifeline between Upper and Lower Canada, the war would be as good as over. Brock thought this impossible because his Indian allies, under the Shawnee war chief TECUMSEH, had the American NW frontier in a ferment. The Americans would thus first try to secure their left flank. The bloodless British capture of a key US post at Michilimackinac I in Lk Huron, on July 16, and of Detroit, Aug 16, frustrated that strategy and gave the British control of Michigan territory and the Upper Mississippi. At this point Thomas Jefferson's remark that the capture of Canada was "a mere matter of marching" returned to haunt

Washington. Having lost one army at Detroit, the Americans lost another at Queenston Heights (see QUEENSTON HEIGHTS, BATTLE OF), Oct 13, after their militia stood on its constitutional guarantee and refused to cross into Canada. But Brock was killed – an irreparable loss. A new American army under William Henry Harrison struggled up from Kentucky to try to retake Detroit. One wing was so badly mauled at Frenchtown, 22 Jan 1813, by a force of British, Canadians and Indians under Lt-Col Henry PROCTOR, that further attempts at invasion that winter were abandoned. The only Americans in Canada were prisoners of war.

British strategy was to act defensively and allow the invaders to make mistakes. Gov Sir George PREVOST husbanded his thin forces carefully, a sensible precaution given the US's overwhelming numerical superiority. As the campaign of 1813 opened, the invaders determined to seize Kingston to cut the link between the Canadas. But a weakness of resolve diverted the attack to the lesser prize of York [Toronto]. The Americans briefly occupied the town, burning the public buildings and seizing valuable naval supplies destined for Lk Erie; but the British, by burning their half-completed warship, frustrated the enemy's plan to appropriate it and change the balance of naval power on Lk Ontario. Neither side totally controlled that lake for the balance of the war. The Americans abandoned York and on 27 May 1813 their fleet seized FT GEORGE at the mouth of the Niagara R. The British army escaped, however, repulsing the advance of the enemy up the Niagara peninsula by winning the battles at Stoney Creek and Beaver Dams (see BEAVER DAMS, BATTLE OF; STONEY CREEK, BATTLE OF), and driving the Americans back into the enclave of the fort. For all of that season the Niagara peninsula was a no-man's-land of marauding parties. Finally, worn down by sickness, desertion, and the departure of short-term soldiers, the

American command evacuated Ft George on Dec 10 and quit Canada. On leaving, the militia burned the town of Newark [NIAGARA-ON-THE LAKE], an act that drove the British to brutal retaliation at Buffalo. These incendiary reprisals continued until Washington itself was burned the following Aug.

The US fared better on the western flank. The British tried and failed to take Harrison's stronghold at Ft Meigs on the Maumee R. A struggle for control of Lk Erie followed. The 2 rival fleets, both built of green lumber on the spot, met Sept 10 at PUT-IN-BAY. The British were hampered by the American seizure of naval supplies at York the previous spring and by the loss, early in the battle, of several senior officers. American commodore Oliver Hazard Perry, a bold seaman, used unorthodox tactics to turn defeat into victory and become the first man in history to capture an entire British fleet. Erie became an American lake, Detroit was abandoned, and the British retreated up the Thames R. At Moraviantown (see MORAVIANTOWN, BATTLE OF) Harrison defeated Proctor. Tecumseh died in the battle, an event signalling the end of the northwestern Indian alliance. But Harrison, his lines extended, could not follow up his victory; his Kentuckians were eager to get back to their farms at harvest time.

Meanwhile, the US was mounting a 2-pronged attack designed to take Montréal, but this was so halfhearted that it was foredoomed to failure. On the Châteauguay R on Oct 26, a handful of French Canadian VOLTIGEURS under Lt-Col Charles de SALABERRY drove an American army of 4000 back across the border (see CHÂTEAUGUAY, BATTLE OF). At CRYSLER'S FARM (near Morrisburg, Ont) on Nov 11, Lt-Col Joseph Wanton Morrison's regulars won a resounding victory over James Wilkinson's superior force, which also quit Canada. Thus the 1813 campaign ended with the Americans in possession of Ft AMHERSTBURG on the Detroit R, and the

British holding the 2 American forts, Niagara and Michilimackinac.

The following year the Americans again crossed the Niagara, seized Ft Erie on July 3, and defeated the British at Chippawa on July 5, but failed to retake Ft George. The bitter battle of LUNDY'S LANE followed on July 25 within earshot of the Niagara cataract. Fought in the pitch dark of a sultry night by exhausted troops who could not tell friend from foe, it ended in stalemate. The Americans withdrew to Ft Erie. Here they badly mauled the forces of the new British commander, Lt-Gen Gordon Drummond, when he attempted a night attack (Aug 14-15). With both sides exhausted a 3-month standoff followed. Finally, on Nov 5, the Americans again withdrew. Meanwhile, NS Lt-Gov Sir John SHERBROOKE led a force from Halifax into Maine, capturing Castine on Sept 3. By mid-month British forces held much of Maine, which was returned to the US only with the signing of the peace treaty.

In the west, the Canadian voyageurs took Prairie du Chien on the Upper Mississippi and beat off an American attack on Michilimackinac I, capturing 2 warships on Lk Huron. In the east, the story was different. With Napoleon defeated, the British army now outnumbered the thin American force at Plattsburgh on Lk Champlain. Prevost marched S with 11 000 of Wellington's veterans but his hesitancy to attack – he was no Brock – together with the Sept 11 defeat of the hastily built British fleet in Plattsburgh Bay by the American commodore, Thomas Macdonough, caused Prevost to abort the ground attack and withdraw (see PLATTSBURGH, BATTLE OF). That single action tipped the scales, forcing the British peace negotiators at Ghent to lower their demands and accept the status quo. Had Prevost succeeded, much of upper NY state might be Canadian today. On the other hand, if the Americans had won the battle of Stoney Creek, or taken Montréal, much

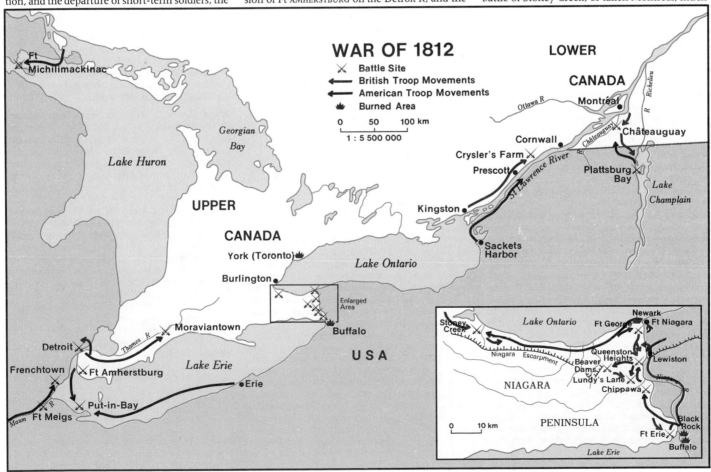

of Ontario and Québec – perhaps all – might now be under the Stars and Stripes.

Washington had expected the largely American population of Upper Canada to throw off the British yoke as soon as its army crossed the border. This did not happen. Lured northwards by free land and low taxes, the settlers wanted to be left alone. Nor was it wise after such a bitter war to advocate American political ideals, such as democracy and republicanism. Thus the British and LOYALIST elite were able to set Canadians on a different course from that of their former enemy. And the growing belief that they, the civilian soldiers, and not the Indians and British regulars, had won the war – more mythic than real – helped to germinate the seeds of nationalism in the Canadas. *See also* NIAGARA HISTORIC FRONTIER; FORT HENRY. PIERRE BERTON

Reading: Pierre Berton, *The Invasion of Canada* (1980) and *Flames Across the Border* (1981); G.F.G. Stanley, *The War of 1812* (1983).

War Veterans Canadian humorist Stephen LEACOCK wrote of war veterans in 1938: "When the war ends they are welcomed home under arches of flowers with all the girls leaping for their necks, and within six months they are expected to vanish into thin air, keep out of the public house and give no trouble." The comment, made with another war imminent, summed up Canada's rather shabby treatment of veterans of the Great War of 1914-18. Canadians made amends after WORLD WAR II with generous rehabilitation programs, generally recognized as the best in the world, though with oversights such as long-delayed grants for PRISONERS OF WAR.

Canada has had war veterans since 1759 when 6 militia battalions took part in the unsuccessful defence of Québec. The brunt of the fighting in the WAR OF 1812 was done by British regulars, but Canadian militiamen were employed, as they were later in the 1837 uprisings in Lower and Upper Canada (*see* REBELLIONS OF 1837) and in the FENIAN RAIDS on Canada in 1864, 1866 and 1870. The militia of the Northwest Field Force fought against Louis RIEL in the 1885 NORTH-WEST REBELLION – a widow of a force member was still receiving a pension in 1987 – and Canada contributed voyageurs to the NILE EXPEDITION in 1885 and contingents to the SOUTH AFRICAN WAR of 1899-1902. Canada was heavily engaged in the 2 world wars and sent land, sea and air contingents to the KOREAN WAR 1950-53 for United Nations action.

A favourite method of rewarding veterans in Canada has been the land grant, or scrip. Veterans of the Fenian raids were given 160-acre grants on the Canadian prairies. In 1931, 160 surviving members of the North-West Mounted Police who had served in the 1885 Northwest Field Force were awarded $300 each in lieu of scrip to which they had been entitled but had never received.

Canada expends nearly $1.5 billion a year in war pensions, mainly for survivors' disabilities. The number of veterans in Canada was about 708 000 in 1987, of whom 32 300 are women and about 11 000 merchant seamen. The veteran population is expected to decline to 206 000 by the turn of the century and to fewer than 200 by 2031, barring future wars. At 1 June 1987, the average age of surviving WWI veterans was 90 and of WWII veterans 67. Recipients of allowances for "burned-out" veterans included 2 from the S African War, 1989 from WWI, 45 522 from WWII and 2354 from the Korean War. Total number of recipients of these allowances was 83 872, including widows and orphans. Another 142 167, including dependants, were receiving pensions for war disabilities. Of these, more than 95 000 were veterans, or nearly 1 in 7 for all surviving veterans.

The first and second world wars came so close together that veterans of the first recognized what had gone wrong with rehabilitation plans for them (financing for soldier settlement on farms was niggardly) and corrected them for veterans of the second. Nearly all legislative proposals, including the 1943 suggestion for creation of a veterans affairs department, came from veterans themselves. It helped that scores of MPs, including those in the Cabinet, were veterans. As a result, 50 000 WWII veterans attended university, while 96 000 other veterans received benefits for farming, fishing, small holdings and businesses, and housing.

Chief veterans' advocate is the ROYAL CANADIAN LEGION, founded in 1926 through amalgamation of 10 veterans' groups, 50 independent regimental societies and 790 other units, 20 000 members in all. Today the legion numbers more than 600 000 in 1800 branches, having replenished its ranks by taking in spouses, sons and daughters, and associate members. In its early days, the legion was the spur for veterans' legislation and a leading voice for national public broadcasting, Canadian film, Canadian history textbooks and public housing. It has always looked after its own, especially in hard times, but now assists a much wider community as the biggest service organization in Canada. DAVE MCINTOSH

Warbler, name applied to several groups of birds, primarily the New World wood warblers (family Emberizidae), and Old World warblers (Muscicapidae) of which only 2 species commonly breed in Canada (*see* KINGLET). About 37 of the approximately 115 species of wood warbler nest in Canada. Many have bright yellow plumage which gives them the name wild canary, a term also applied to American goldfinches (*Carduelis tristis*). In spring males are usually brightly coloured; females have duller plumages, as do males in fall. Warblers are mostly small, active birds. Their sharp, pointed bills are ideal for probing for insect prey, though some species also catch insects by aerial pursuit. Flycatchers often have flatter bills with bristles at the base. Exceptions to the usual cup-shaped nests in shrubs and forks of trees include the dome-shaped ground nest of the ovenbird (*Seiurus aurocapillus*); the hole nest of the prothonotary warbler (*Protonotaria citrea*); and the hanging, lichen-based nest of the northern parula (*Parula americana*). The brown-headed cowbird (*Molothrus ater*), a significant brood parasite of several species, poses a significant threat to the rare Kirtland's warbler (*Dendroica kirtlandii*). Several species have evolved mechanisms which reduce cowbird parasitism, eg, the well-known habit of the yellow warbler (*D. petechia*) of building new nests on top of old. In Canada wood warblers are widespread, breeding virtually everywhere S of the treeline and forming spectacular mixed-species flocks during migration, especially in the East. Most Canadian breeding species belong to genus *Dendroica*. Kirtland's warbler, until recently thought to breed only in a restricted area of Michigan, is now believed to nest in Ontario and possibly Québec. Two other widespread genera of several species are *Vermivora* and *Oporornis*, the latter known as "skulkers" of low brush. The creeperlike black-and-white warbler (*Mniotilta varia*), the black-masked, marsh-dwelling common yellowthroat (*Geothlypis trichas*), the flycatching American redstart (*Setophaga ruticilla*), the thrushlike, ground-dwelling ovenbird, the northern waterthrush (*Seiurus noveboracensis*) and 2 species of *Wilsonia* are also widespread. More restricted breeders include Louisiana waterthrush (*Seiurus motacilla*) and prothonotary and hooded warblers (*Wilsonia citrina*) of S Ontario, northern parula of southern Manitoba E

Yellow warbler (*Dendroica kirtlandii*) (*artwork by Claire Tremblay*).

through the Maritimes, yellow-breasted chat (*Icteria virens*) of S Ontario and local valleys of southern BC, Alberta and Saskatchewan. Warblers' insectivorous diets make them economically important to humans, especially species which help to control spruce budworm.

MARTIN K. MCNICHOLL

Warburton, Alexander Bannerman, historian, politician, premier of PEI 1897-98 (b at Charlottetown 5 Apr 1852; d there 14 Jan 1929). Warburton practised law in Charlottetown and won election as a Liberal to the provincial legislature in 1891. He was named premier on 27 Oct 1897 but resigned 1 Aug 1898 following his appointment as a judge in June 1898. He held that post until Oct 1904. An MP, 1908-11, he returned to the bench as a judge of probate in 1920 and served until his death. Warburton is best remembered for his 2 landmark histories of PEI. P.E. RIDER

Ward, Maxwell William, aviator, businessman (b at Edmonton 22 Nov 1921). He joined the RCAF in 1940 and served as a flight instructor during WWII. He worked as a bush pilot after the war and made an outstanding contribution to the service of the northern frontier by air. In 1946 he organized Polaris Charter Co Ltd, based in Yellowknife, NWT. With a single-engined DH 83C de Havilland Fox Moth, he carried supplies and passengers throughout the Subarctic. In 1953 he returned to Yellowknife with a newly formed company, Wardair Ltd, which pioneered the air transport of heavy equipment to the Far North. In 1962 he was operating 6 aircraft in the North and had acquired a DC-6A, which provided the company with an opportunity to test the market for transatlantic charter flights. He obtained a licence to operate international air charters in 1961, changed the company name to Wardair Canada Ltd (now WARDAIR INTERNATIONAL LTD), and moved his head offices to Edmonton. By the mid-1970s Wardair had developed into Canada's largest international air charter carrier. He was awarded the MCKEE TROPHY in 1973 for his contributions to aviation, and has received honorary degrees from U of A (1979), York U (1981) and Athabasca U (1987). JAMES MARSH

Ward, Norman, political scientist, author, teacher (b at Hamilton, Ont 10 May 1918). Identified with U of Sask, Ward's reputation as a scholar is national and international. For 4 decades his prodigious writings on Parliament, its officers and members have informed Canadians of their pre-eminent national institution, while a score of federal and provincial commissions, committees and task forces have benefited from his academic rigour. The clarity of his prose derives from a parallel career as author of articles on etymology and linguistics and as a humorist; in this last capacity he has written 3 books (*Mice in the Beer* was awarded the Stephen Leacock Memorial Medal for humour in 1960). Wearing his scholarship lightly, his writings have provided a model of the thorough researcher for several generations of students and young academics.

DAVID E. SMITH

Reading: John C. Courtney, ed, *The Canadian House of Commons: Essays in Honour of Norman Ward* (1985).

Wardair International Ltd, with head offices in Toronto, is an international and domestic airline incorporated in Alberta in 1953 as Wardair Ltd. Initially a bush charter airline based in Yellowknife, NWT, the name was changed in 1962 to Wardair Canada Ltd. It became a public company in 1967. In 1972 the company formed 2 subsidiaries, Canada UK Travel (now Wardair (UK) Ltd) and International Vacations (Intervac), to solicit passengers and operate tour packages. In 1976 the company name was changed to Wardair International Ltd. The company has since expanded, and in 1986 was granted permission to run regular scheduled flights to domestic and foreign locations. In 1986 it had sales of $491.1 million (ranking 177th in Canada), assets of $456.4 million (ranking 171st) and 2664 employees. Its major shareholder is Max WARD, founder of the company.

DEBORAH C. SAWYER

Wardner, BC, UP, pop 111 (1986c), 119 (1981c), is located at the opening of the KOOTENAY R into Lk Koocanusa. The lake was formed recently, after completion of the Columbia R Treaty Dam at Libby, Montana, and flooding of the original townsite has reduced Wardner to the status of a post office. It was founded in 1897 by an American fortune hunter, James F. Wardner, as a construction camp on the Crow's Nest Pass Ry. A large sawmill operated there, drawing logs from the Kootenay and Bull river drainages. Today, Wardner has limited dairying and ranching on some of the best rangeland in the region, but the farming area has declined 19% because of flooding by Lk Koocanusa. At Kootenay Trout Hatchery, 8 km N, some 8 million trout and char of various types are bred yearly.

WILLIAM A. SLOAN

Ware, John, "Nigger John," horseman, rancher (b near Georgetown, SC 1845; d near Brooks, Alta 11 Sept 1905). Freed from slavery on a southern cotton plantation at the close of the American Civil War, Ware drifted west, eventually finding work on a ranch near Fort Worth, Tex. As an experienced cowhand by the late 1870s, he was employed driving herds of Texas cattle northward along the Western Cattle Trail to the distant ranges in Wyoming and Montana territories. After helping to bring 3000 head of Montana cattle to the North West Cattle Company ranch in the foothills SW of Calgary in late Sept 1882, Ware found that experienced cowboys were much in demand in this northernmost edge of the ranching frontier. He remained and worked for several of the large cattle companies before starting his own ranch in the foothills in 1890. In face of increasing settlement in 1900, Ware moved to a new ranch site along the Red Deer R east of Brooks. Here, 5 years later, a riding accident caused Ware's untimely death. The large crowd which assembled to pay their last respects marked Ware's stature in ranching and confirmed that his commonly used nickname, "Nigger John," was not intended pejoratively.

DAVID H. BREEN

Warren, Jack Hamilton, public servant, banker (b in Howard Twp, Ont 10 Apr 1921). Service with the Royal Canadian Navy during WWII and the Dept of External Affairs from 1945 preceded Warren's appointment to the General Agreement on Tariffs and Trade, 1960-64, and to the Dept of Trade and Commerce, where he was deputy minister, 1958-60, 1964-71. He resumed his diplomatic career in 1971, becoming high commissioner to the UK (1971-74) and ambassador to the US 1975-77, before his appointment as Canada's ambassador and chief spokesman at the Multilateral Trade Negotiations. He was vice-chairman of the board of the Bank of Montreal, 1979-86, when he became a trade consultant to the province of Québec.

ANNE HILLMER

Warren, Sir Peter, naval officer (b *c*1703; d at Dublin, Ire 29 July 1752). He commanded the Royal Navy at the 1745 siege of LOUISBOURG, where he was made governor. Warren recommended the deportation of Acadians and the fortification of Chebucto (Halifax) as early as 1739. While serving under Admiral Anson in 1747, his squadron defeated the French off Cape Ortegal. From the declining Catholic gentry of Ireland, he married into a prominent New York mercantile family and made a great fortune from war, part of which he invested in New England, New York and S Carolina, before buying land and lending money in Ireland and England. He was MP for Westminster 1747-52.

JULIAN GWYN

Warren, Vincent de Paul, dancer, teacher (b at Jacksonville, Fla 31 Aug 1939). During his 18 years with LES GRANDS BALLETS CANADIENS, Warren became one of the most accomplished dancers in the company's history. A fine interpreter of roles from the traditional story-ballets, he also excelled in contemporary works, a number of which were choreographed for him. Warren was trained and began his career in the US. He was a member of Les Grands Ballets Canadiens 1961-79, except for 1970-71 when he performed with the Théâtre français de la danse in Paris and the Cologne Opera Ballet. Since 1979 he has taught ballet and dance history in Montréal, primarily at the school of Les Grands Ballets.

MICHAEL CRABB

Warren, William Robertson, lawyer, politician, judge (b at St John's 9 Oct 1879; d there 31 Dec 1927). He became the sixteenth prime minister of Newfoundland, July 1923-Apr 1924, upon the resignation of Richard SQUIRES. A barrister in St John's at age 21, he was a Liberal member of the Assembly by 1903, Speaker 1909-13 and Squires's minister of justice from 1919. Warren and 3 other ministers quit the Cabinet following the 1923 elections amid accusations of misspending of government funds before the elections. Squires resigned and the party chose Warren as leader and prime minister. Warren immediately determined to investigate the charges and instituted a public inquiry, led by Thomas Hollis Walker. The report, presented Mar 1924, found misconduct in public spending, and several arrests followed. In spite of these actions, Warren's former supporters moved a motion of no confidence and the government fell. Warren continued in the Assembly until 1926 when he was appointed to the Supreme Court.

ROBERT D. PITT

Wartime Elections Act In 1917 PM Sir Robert Borden's Conservative government feared that CONSCRIPTION, introduced in May to bolster the Canadian fighting forces in WORLD WAR I, was unpopular and that Canadians not of British descent would combine to defeat the government in the upcoming general election. On Sept 20, after an angry debate, Parliament passed the Wartime Elections Act disfranchising citizens of enemy-alien birth naturalized after 31 Mar 1902, except when such citizens had a son, grandson or brother on active duty. The Act also granted the vote to the wives, mothers and sisters of serving soldiers, as well as women serving in the armed forces. The Act undoubtedly increased support for Borden's party but was not a factor in the 1917 election. In the long run, Conservative support among some ethnic groups was affected negatively.

JOHN ENGLISH

Wartime Home Front The 2 world wars of the 20th century were total wars that involved the whole nation, and the "home front" became a critical part of the war effort. In WORLD WAR I farmers broke new land and, with state assistance, began to mechanize their operations; the latter was one attempt to make up for the shortage of farm help caused by enlistment and by the drift of workers to cities in search of employment in the war industry. Schemes were devised to send city teenagers into the country to assist with the harvest (a mixed blessing). At the same time the booming war factories were in desperate need of skilled tradesmen, too many of whom had been allowed to enlist before their greater value at home had been recognized. One result was that large numbers of women were brought into war factories, and "aliens," often unacceptable for military service because of their nationality, took factory jobs. Another result of the labour scarcity was that wages rose – although not as much as the cost of living – but because conditions in the plants were often terrible, labour unrest was widespread.

The hothouse atmosphere of war fostered other strange growths. PROHIBITION was a popular measure because it seemed to be a sacrifice that could help the war effort. WOMEN'S SUFFRAGE was widely seen as a reward to Canadian women for their help in the war effort. The income tax, an inconceivable measure in 1914, by 1917 had become necessary to help the state finance the staggering costs of total war. Even price controls and controls on coal and steel could be justified on the grounds of necessity.

The war had changed much, not least the attitudes of the public. If Prohibition was popular in Canada, it seemed mean-spirited when an attempt was made to apply it to soldiers at the front. But some attitudes died hard. For example, the puritanical morality of the day could scarcely deal with the explosion of venereal disease the war produced. One study attributed the spread of social diseases to the factory girl who saw "women largely predominating in the city" and felt "she must push forward and not miss her chance at romance." As a result of loose behaviour, she became "a disintegrating social force" who spread disease to middle-class men who might in turn infect their wives. The woman, not the man, seemed to be to blame, an attitude that persisted into WWII.

The home front during WORLD WAR II was much better organized than it had been in WWI. In late 1941 the WARTIME PRICES AND TRADE BOARD, est in Sept 1939, was given charge of a sweeping system of WAGE AND PRICE CONTROLS. This made the rising costs of WWI an impossibility and, while not everyone was pleased by controls, the public could see the fairness of the system. This was true also with the use of the nation's manpower. The institution of National Selective Service in early 1942 effectively controlled the destiny of all men and women, told them who could join up and who could not, where they could work, and when they could change jobs. The WPTB also devised

Parachute Riggers, oil on canvas, by Paraskeva Clark (*courtesy Canadian War Museum/CMC/NMC/14086*).

major rationing schemes that distributed meat, butter, oil and gas, and other scarce goods. Inevitably there was black marketeering, but most people regarded it as a social crime.

The shortage of consumer goods meant that workers, earning good wages for the first time after 10 years of the Great Depression, had little to buy, and the state acted to acquire as much of the people's savings as possible. In WWI the minister of finance had been astonished at how much money war bond campaigns raised; in WWII the sums were vastly greater as individuals and companies, in addition to paying higher taxes than ever before, put their money at the service of the war effort. Even school children were urged to purchase war savings stamps, each showing a tank or airplane, for 25 cents. Children also did their bit by collecting cooking fat, bones or milkweed, all of which were necessary for the war effort, while their parents planted victory gardens on waste patches of land or contributed their old pots and pans for melting down into weaponry.

Opinion surveys demonstrated that by 1944 Canadians had become supporters of a continuation of wartime controls into the peace. That was undoubtedly a reflection of their concern for the future and their fear of renewed depression, but it was also a striking vote of confidence in the fairness of the system the federal government had created. The relatively smooth transition to peace also showed the care with which Ottawa had planned. J.L. GRANATSTEIN

Reading: M.J. Lennon, *On The Homefront* (1981); D. Read, ed, *The Great War and Canadian Society* (1978).

Wartime Information Board, est 9 Sept 1942, succeeded the Bureau of Public Information, which had been formed early in WWII to issue certain information on the course of the war to the public. By 1942 the government believed that its troubles over CONSCRIPTION derived from inadequate publicity. In Aug, Cabinet approved the creation of a largely autonomous information board. Charles Vining was WIB chairman until Jan 1943, when educator Norman A.M. MACKENZIE succeeded him. The real power on the board was held by its general manager, John GRIERSON, who promoted the war as a vehicle for social change. The approach naturally created some political controversy. In 1944 Grierson was succeeded by A. Davidson DUNTON, who followed Grierson's general direction until the end of the war. The board influenced the public's interpretation of the war, and pioneered systematic public-opinion polling in Canada. JOHN ENGLISH

Wartime Prices and Trade Board, est 3 Sept 1939 by the Canadian government immediately before the onset of WORLD WAR II, and initially responsible to the Dept of Labour. Its creation reflected the government's concern that WWI conditions of inflation and social unrest should not return. Until Aug 1941 the board's work seemed ineffective in restraining Canadian wartime inflation. It then became the responsibility of the Dept of Finance. On Oct 18 its powers were enormously expanded when PM Mackenzie KING announced a price freeze and the "stabilization" of wages and salaries. To manage the large bureaucracy required to supervise the program, the government selected Donald GORDON, a prominent banker. Gordon attracted competent administrators from private industry and quickly built up an effective system in which businessmen administered the industries they knew best. A public-relations campaign urged Canadians to exercise restraint in wage demands and consumer demand. Canadians supported the board's aims until 1943, when labour officials became critical of its arbitrariness, farmers complained about discrimination and business tried to escape price ceilings. The board and the government kept the controls patched together through subsidization, social-security schemes, promises of postwar reforms and strategic political retreats. The board played a major role in postwar decontrol until Gordon resigned in 1947. Although there is much about it that can be criticized, the board's major achievement, a mere 2.8% increase in prices between Oct 1941 and Apr 1945, was a sign of its remarkable overall effectiveness. JOHN ENGLISH

Washington, Treaty of, negotiated in 1871, came into effect in 1873. Canadian PM Sir John A. MACDONALD was one of 5 commissioners chosen to represent British interests, but he held little power during the deliberations. The issues were the American claim for losses stemming from the ALABAMA's depredations; the American desire to resume use of Canadian and Newfoundland inshore fisheries, denied 1818-54 and after the 1866 lapse of the RECIPROCITY Treaty; ownership of the San Juan Is in the Str of Georgia; and restitution to Canada for FENIAN raids, 1866-70. The Americans refused to have the last item on the agenda. Some Americans hoped Britain would cede Canada in the negotiations. However, the treaty was settled in a series of arbitrations in Washington: the *Alabama* claims were settled in 1872 in Geneva for $15.5 million; the San Juan Is question was resolved by Germany, which gave them to the US; and the US was admitted to the Canadian inshore fishery for 12 years, in return for free entry to the American market for Canadian fish and $5.5 million. Britain eventually compensated Canada for the Fenian raids, with a $2.5-million loan guarantee. P.B. WAITE

Waskahegan Trail, a 400 km regional hiking trail developed in the Edmonton, Alta, area. It began as a Centennial project to promote hiking opportunities in the Edmonton, WETASKIWIN, CAMROSE, FT SASKATCHEWAN and ST ALBERT areas. Similar in concept to the BRUCE TRAIL in Ontario, it follows public land as much as possible but has access across private lands by way of landowner agreements and easements. It connects numerous small communities in the Edmonton region and passes through picturesque Alberta countryside, including ELK ISLAND NATIONAL PK and Miquelon Lake Provincial Pk, highlighting a typical aspen parkland ecosystem. BART DEEG

Wasp, term properly applied to stinging Hymenoptera of the superfamilies Vespoidea, Sphecoidea and Scolioidea. In common usage, a number of parasitic and gall-forming hymenopterans are also referred to as wasps. These insects generally have an abdomen somewhat narrowed at the base, a body covered with simple hairs (contrasting to the branched hairs of BEES) and an ovipositor (egg-laying organ) that may be modified into a sting. Most wasps have 2 pairs of membranous wings; some forms are wingless. Wasps vary in size from tiny parasites less than 1 mm long to large predators 35 mm long. Some 550 species of stinging wasps are found in Canada. If parasitic and gall wasps are included, this number is more than doubled. Wasps are distributed throughout the country. Such a large and diverse insect group exhibits great variation in life-styles and habitats. Gall wasps (family Cynipidae) form characteristic galls on plant leaves and stems, in which their larvae feed and develop. Many wasps are parasites and place their eggs in or on the bodies of their insect hosts. Velvet ants (Mutillidae) are parasites of ground-nesting wasps and bees. These brightly coloured, hairy wasps have wingless females which can give a very painful sting. Mud daubers (Sphecidae) gather pellets of mud which they fashion into nest cells and provision with spiders as food for their young. Included in the Vespidae are perhaps the best known of this group, the social wasps. The familiar paper nests constructed by these insects house complex societies of from a few dozen to over a thousand individuals. Most wasps are beneficial, being parasites or predators of other insects. Some parasitic forms are reared and released for the biological control of INSECT PESTS. *See also* HORNET. M.V. SMITH

Waste Disposal Although the term SOLID WASTE refers to a wide range of discarded materials (from kitchen scraps to mine tailings), the component known as refuse has the greatest potential for environmental contamination. Refuse comprises solid wastes consisting of household garbage and commercial rubbish produced, usually in equal parts, by the residents and merchants of a community. If simply left to decay, refuse can become a serious threat to community health, both as a direct source of human illnesses and as an attractant to disease-carrying organisms. Therefore, many Canadian communities collect refuse from its source and deliver it to a waste-disposal site.

Many smaller towns and villages cannot afford a refuse collection service or a proper waste-disposal site. Because small communities are prevalent in Canada, improperly operated dumps outnumber the better-operated facilities used by larger communities. In most provinces the garbage dump is regarded as unacceptable. As they are on fire most of the time, they are a fire hazard, threatening users of the site, nearby fields, forests and buildings, and resulting in considerable damage each year. Dumps are also an ideal feeding ground for rats and other disease-carrying animals, and attract dangerous mammals as well as flocks of birds, which may pose a hazard to nearby airfields.

Major Canadian cities now use an improved method of waste disposal called sanitary landfilling. At a sanitary landfill, refuse is spread in thin layers, on the ground or in a trench, by a mobile compaction vehicle. Then a layer of clean soil is spread and compacted over the layer of refuse. Hence a series of alternating layers (refuse, soil, refuse) is built up until the trench is filled or a mound created. As cities expand, landfill once on the outskirts is surrounded by housing developments and industrial parks. It may be reclaimed for other uses (eg, in several cities the old dump is now a park).

Incineration is the most common method of refuse treatment in Canada. Some incinerators must handle 200 or more truckloads of refuse daily; hence, units capable of continual operation are needed. Newer, "starved air" incinerators are so efficient that special air-pollution control devices are not required. Some incinerators are equipped with boilers that use heat from burning garbage to produce hot water or steam, which can be used to heat buildings or operate machinery.

Up to 50% of refuse is said to be reusable; thus RECYCLING may offer the greatest potential for reducing the growing volumes of waste. In recent years, there has been a move to community recycling programs. Over 500 000 households in Ontario already receive curbside collection of recyclables; in 1988 it is projected that the figure will be over one million. In Alberta, the program has just been initiated in some communities. *See also* HAZARDOUS WASTES.   R.C. MACKENZIE

Wasteneys, Hardolph, professor of biochemistry (b at Richmond, Eng Apr 1881; d at Toronto 1 Feb 1965). As a boy Wasteneys went to Australia and found employment in government laboratories dealing with water purification. He moved to California about 1909 to study this subject further. From 1910 to 1916 he was a technician with Jacques Loeb, famous physiologist at the Rockefeller Inst for Medical Research in NY. His work with Loeb resulted in his only university degree, a PhD from Columbia in 1916. He joined the dept of biochemistry, U of T in 1918 and succeeded Andrew Hunter as head in 1928. He and his students did some pioneering studies on protein synthesis and he encouraged the development of research in his department. His own main interests in later years turned to social service and humanitarian directions.   DAVID B. SMITH

Water (H$_2$O) occurs in the atmosphere and above and below the Earth's surface as a liquid, solid or gas. It is continually changing state (eg, by freezing/thawing, evaporation/condensation) and location (eg, by gaseous, liquid or GLACIER flow). All water is involved in a continuous hydrologic cycle, of which evaporation into the atmosphere from oceans, lakes, rivers and land surfaces, and transpiration through plant leaves may be considered the first phase. This moisture is transported, often great distances, by winds and is precipitated, as rain or snow, upon water and land surfaces.

Worldwide, over two-thirds of precipitation falling on land surfaces is evaporated and transpired back into the atmosphere. In Canada less than 40% is evaporated and transpired; the remainder, called the water yield, enters into streamflow. In the drier plains, only 10-20 mm of the 300-400 mm of precipitation enters streamflow, largely from drift snowmelt and from heavy rains in some years. In west-facing coastal ranges of the West Coast, where annual precipitation is 3000-7500 mm, approximately 500-600 mm is evaporated and transpired, and 80-95% runs off. In far northern areas where little heat is available, only 100-200 mm is evaporated or transpired and 100-500 mm enters streamflow. The proportion of runoff increases in rocky, paved, fallow and elevated (cooler) areas, where there is little moisture storage, vegetative cover or heat for much evapotranspiration. Small coastal and mountain areas in the West have very high yields; larger areas in the East and in parts of the North have moderately high yields; lower yields occur in the southern plains and in some interior valleys of the western Cordillera.

Water may be drawn for use from rivers, lakes and groundwater supplies. It may also be put to uses (eg, HYDROELECTRICITY, fishing, navigation, recreation, wildlife habitat), which involve little consumption of water. Canada is fortunate in having relatively abundant supplies. Withdrawal uses involve only 1.3% of the total; consumptive uses

only 0.1%. We are in no danger of running out of water, although there are regional deficiencies and problems of quality. Partly because of these abundant supplies, flooding and drainage problems are relatively large. Canada's history is closely related to LAKE and RIVER use. Exploration and development were largely along water TRANSPORTATION routes and the early FUR and TIMBER trades were river oriented. Water transport dominated early commerce. With CANAL development, bulk movement far into the continent became possible, and canal transportation remains very important today. Farm IRRIGATION was and is a major factor in agricultural development in the drier southwestern plains of the Prairie provinces and the southern interior of BC, and supplemental irrigation is expanding into more humid areas. Water power and, later, hydroelectric site developments were major bases for industrial development. Urban and industrial demands have grown rapidly and most cities and industries are river and lake oriented. Commercial and recreational fishing are significant, but WATER POLLUTION, dams and other man-made changes have had largely negative effects on these activities. Wildlife and recreational demands are important and have also suffered from human activities. Environmental enhancement is possible but not widely undertaken, even to compensate for damage done. Water conservation measures are not yet widely employed, but the growing costs of obtaining high-quality water and avoiding stream WATER POLLUTION are resulting in an increased recycling of water.

Provincial Profiles

Water supply and demand patterns vary greatly from province to province.

British Columbia has the greatest flow, half coming from the one-sixth of the province's area occupied by the Coast and Island ranges. Some interior valleys are very dry, but surpluses from adjoining mountain areas can be used for irrigation and other purposes. For the province as a whole, supply exceeds consumptive use by over 1600 times, but water shortages are present locally. The major conflicts are between nonwithdrawal users such as hydroelectric developments and salmon fisheries. To protect the salmon industry, dam development has not proceeded on some rivers (eg, lower and middle Fraser). Pollution is a growing problem and the costs of control are now a major part of pulp and paper and mineral development.

Alberta, with only 2% of the supply, in drier years has over 50% of the consumptive use demand for Canada. Well over half of Canada's irrigated land and most of the secondary recovery of oil and gas (involving the pumping of water into the geological formations to replace these fuels) are in Alberta. Substantial expansion of BITUMEN development, involving evaporation of large quantities of water from tailings ponds, might increase Alberta's share of Canadian consumptive demand. The problem is accentuated since almost all of the irrigation, urban and industrial demand and some of the mining demand is in southern Alberta, while most (87%) of the water supply is in the north (Arctic rather than Hudson Bay or Gulf of Mexico drainage). Moreover, by agreement with Saskatchewan, Manitoba and Canada, one-half of the southern flow is allocated to downstream use. In the near future, dry-year demand may exceed supply, and political pressure for massive interbasin transfers is growing.

Saskatchewan, with much less irrigation and oil, is trying to expand with a limited water supply in the S. POTASH mining demands are large, and mines and municipalities are served increasingly by canal and pipeline systems. Quality issues in the Qu'Appelle Valley are as acute as anywhere in Canada, largely because there is so little flow to

assimilate and dilute wastes. Tertiary treatment of municipal wastes in the southern plains is relatively advanced. Thermal and hydroelectric power alternatives are varied, and environmental concerns and multiple-use management are well developed. Prairie sloughs, which are part of a major migratory waterfowl habitat, need protection and enhancement.

Manitoba Hydroelectric power has been dominant in water planning for the province, but drainage, flood damage limitation and a significant potential for irrigation development are of strong interest. The supply issue is less critical, partly because of the large amount of water that flows into the province from the W, E and S. Environmental issues are prominent, including some relating to the Garrison Project development in North Dakota and the possible dumping of saline waters or southern fish and other organisms into the province's rivers and lakes.

Ontario had long considered its water resources to be unlimited and indestructible. They are abundant, but by the 1960s it had become apparent that river and lake water quality had been severely damaged by industrial, municipal and other pollutants. The GREAT LAKES and connecting rivers had received more pollution from the more populous and highly industrialized American side than from Canadian sources, and joint programs for reducing pollution were instituted. Ontario is coping with the problem through tertiary treatment of most municipal and industrial waste; through the use of multiple-purpose development for withdrawal and on-stream uses and for river control; and through river-basin management, including the institution of conservation measures. Supplemental irrigation in dry periods is becoming more widespread for tobacco fields, orchards and market gardens, where quality control as well as yield increase is important. Urban and industrial uses are large, but most of the water used for washing, cooling and other purposes is returned to streams. Thermal power plant (coal and nuclear based) return flow is potentially damaging to fish, but this heated water can also be a resource. Consumptive use is small and water shortages are not a problem.

Québec has abundant supplies and a long history of water use. Nonwithdrawal uses (eg, hydroelectric power, navigation, fishing, recreation) are very important. Urban and industrial use is large and there has tended to be a greater reliance upon the natural assimilative capacities of streams in waste disposal than there has been in most parts of Canada. Waste treatment is needed and is slowly being instituted. The hydroelectric power potential has been large and, with development in northern basins (eg, Manicouagan and La Grande Rivière), over half of it has been realized. Navigation on the St Lawrence is limited by ice in winter, but the shipping season is being extended, especially for downstream ports. Drainage for agricultural development is widespread and some drainage for forest site improvement is under way. Flooding is a problem, especially in spring when snowmelt supplies are augmented by heavy rains.

Atlantic Provinces are relatively humid with little need for irrigation. Problems of flooding and drainage relating to seasonal oversupply are more common. Water yields are high and rivers are large, relative to basin areas. Waterpower, followed by hydroelectric power, has long been a basis for industry. Recreational and commercial fishing, navigation (limited by sea ice in most winters and most areas) and some withdrawal uses are significant. Pollution is a problem, but streams, tides and coastal ocean currents have been used to dilute and assimilate wastes and the problem is not as acute as in some water-short areas.

Territories The measurement data of the last few decades in the YT and the NWT are for much larger rivers than might be expected to be present with the limited precipitation recorded. This may be the result of unrepresentative precipitation records (the settlement stations are in the drier areas); furthermore, gauge undercatch is normal, especially for blowing snow. With low evapotranspiration, the greater part of the precipitation enters streamflow. Many of the problems of water use relate to frost and PERMAFROST and some communities have insulated corridors for water and sewage. River navigation is still very important; actual hydroelectric development represents only a small part of the potential; withdrawal uses are small. Recreational uses are growing and wildlife concerns are of growing importance.

With increasing competition for limited supplies of pure water, the need for integrated multiple-purpose management and for conservation will grow. Canadian pressure upon supply is much less than in the US where the total supply for the coterminous 48 states is only 40% as large as that of Canada (70% with Alaska); in the US, withdrawal demand in 1975 was 27% of the supply, consumptive demand was 8.5%, and much more of the supply was polluted to varying degrees. Regional shortages are much greater than in Canada, but the demand for interbasin transfers from Canada will continue to be negligible for many decades. There are cheaper alternative supplies in the US; costs of transfer would exceed the value of most products that might be produced; the willingness to subsidize irrigation is declining; and the political, legal, environmental and other problems would be formidable. In the future there could be some transfer, but only if mutually beneficial arrangements, with environmental enhancement at least equalling the minimal damage required, can be worked out. Irrigation is one of the less likely recipients because it is a low-return use, unable to cover the costs of major transfer, and greater increases in agricultural production can be obtained by other cheaper means.

A.H. LAYCOCK

Water-Borne Disease, any illness resulting from ingestion of or contact with water. Like food-borne diseases, water-ingestion illnesses are either infections or intoxications. Organisms responsible for infections are bacteria, eg, SALMONELLA (causing salmonellosis), *Shigella* (shigellosis) and *Vibrio cholerae* (cholera); viruses, eg, rotavirus, Norwalk-type agent and hepatitis A virus; or parasites, eg, *Entamoeba* (causing amebiasis), *Dracunculus* (Guinea worm disease) and *Giardia* (giardiasis). These organisms usually occur in water contaminated with sewage (eg, especially bird and mammal excrement) or by infected persons or animals. Intoxications are invariably chemical in nature (eg, copper, lead, insecticide poisonings) and usually occur as a result of the leaching of metal into water (from pipes or containers) and through the accidental spillage or seepage of chemicals into water supplies. The illnesses can either be acute or chronic, depending on the contaminating conditions and the volume of water consumed. Illnesses acquired through contact with water are caused by bacteria, eg, *Leptospira* (causing leptospirosis), *Chlamydia* (swimming-pool conjunctivitis) and parasites, eg, *Schistosoma* (causing swimmer's itch and bilharziasis).

According to the World Health Organization, most diseases in the world are associated with water. Fortunately, this is not the case in Canada. Documentation of water-borne disease in this country, however, is very limited: only a few outbreaks are reported each year, and it is recognized that many more occur without being investigated. From data available since 1973, typhoid (caused by *Salmonella typhi*) has been associated with water in a camp and a municipal system using inadequately chlorinated water from a lake.

Streamflow Originating Within and Passing Through Canada[a]			
	Originating (km³)	%	*Passing Through*[b] (km³)
YT	140	4.2	165
NWT	700	20.8	890
BC	800	23.7	870
Alta	69	2.0	137
Sask	56	1.7	73
Man	94	2.8	172
Ont	325	9.6	500
Qué	780	23.2	1 060
NB	46	1.4	67
NS	45	1.3	45
PEI	3.5	0.1	3.5
Nfld	310	9.2	310
Canada	3 368 500	100.0	4 292 500

[a] Estimates based upon Water Survey of Canada data with minor corrections based on later data. Totals for NWT and BC, especially, require upward revision.

[b] The amount originating within the province or territory (the water yield), plus that originating elsewhere and passing through. Because of duplication, totals are less meaningful.

Shigellosis and hepatitis were reported mainly from northern rural communities, eg, Indian and Inuit settlements. Giardiasis is becoming more recognized as a cause of severe diarrhea; the parasite is sometimes isolated from tourists travelling abroad, but more often from residents of small communities with no water-filtering systems. Animals such as BEAVER regularly excrete the *Giardia* organism into water. The parasites survive chlorination but can be filtered out. Occasional intoxications have occurred, eg, through water remaining in newly soldered copper pipes. Water-contact disease is rarely documented and is not considered common in Canada. Swimmer's itch, however, can become a problem with bathers in some lakes, and wounds of swimmers have been invaded by *Vibrio parahaemolyticus* (which can also cause food-borne disease) in the ocean off BC. Whirlpool baths have occasionally been contaminated with *Pseudomonas aeruginosa*, causing itchy rashes and ear infections in bathers. Concern about WATER POLLUTION (whether the result of toxic chemicals or fecal material) is increasing in Canada. For example, swimming beaches in major cities are often closed because of high fecal coliform bacteria counts and risk of infection through water-contact diseases.

EWEN TODD

Water Distribution System, a provincially regulated network used to distribute water from a central location to a location of end use. While the most complex distribution systems are those required to supply urban areas, fairly extensive systems are also used in some areas to supply irrigation water to orchards and to vegetables and other crops. Elaborate distribution systems may also be required within a major industrial plant (eg, steel mill, petroleum refinery) or commercial complex (eg, large shopping centre, office building).

Nearly 80% of Canada's population is classifed as "urban," and the distribution of water to this group of users is a major task. Most of Canada's larger cities are located on or near a major river system or lake, which provides water for distribution. Since river systems extend across provincial, territorial or national boundaries, some degree of intergovernmental co-operation is required in water management; for example MACKENZIE RIVER BASIN COMMITTEE, Prairie Provinces Water Board, and International St Croix River Board of Control. Some cities obtain their water from a relatively distant but more reliable source (for example, Winnipeg's water comes via aqueduct from Lake of the Woods, 150 km away); groundwater supplies the needs of other cities, notably Kitchener-Waterloo.

Canadian cities developed urban water distribution systems quite early: Toronto and Kingston had pumping stations by 1841 and 1850, respectively; gravity systems were operating even earlier in Saint John, NB, and Halifax, NS, in 1838 and 1848. By the 1870s, the water supplies of most large cities were steam pumped. Although the amount of water used for fire protection is small compared to other uses, the high rate of water flow needed in fire fighting is often the most important factor to be considered in designing the system. The system's main components are pumping stations to create and maintain pressure, reservoirs to store water and aid in pressure equalization, and a network of pipes to convey the water to users.

Distribution systems for farm IRRIGATION typically consist of a network of canals or pipes. With pipe systems, pumps are used to maintain sufficient hydraulic head to operate spray irrigation equipment, and valves are used to control flow in the pipes. With canal systems, a combination of gravity, pumps, weirs and gates are used to distribute and control the flow of water through the system. In Canada the Prairie provinces have the largest area under irrigation, 559 954 ha; British Columbia is next with 117 811 ha; the rest of Canada has 29 860 ha of irrigated land. Irrigation systems may be privately developed or may be put in place with the assistance of provincial or federal governments (*see* PRAIRIE FARM REHABILITATION ADMINISTRATION).

Before the environmental movement of the late 1960s, water agencies built more and larger dams and conveyance facilities to meet the demand for water; but rising costs and growing public opposition to such projects forced planners to explore other means of supplying the demand. Most solutions are aimed at efficient use of water, since waste is a major problem. Canada's per capita water-use rates are among the world's highest. Research shows that economic pricing and conservation can save impressive quantities of water. The Federal Water Policy (1987) endorsed user fees to regulate water demand and production costs. The policy also prohibited large-scale export as a threat to the environment and to Canada's future needs. D.W. DRAPER AND FRANK QUINN

Water Flea, tiny crustacean that swims with jerky movements. The "fleas," found in almost any drop of pond water, use powerful strokes of their antennae for propulsion. These branchiopods belong to the suborder Cladocera, a cosmopolitan, freshwater group of about 400 species. The water flea feeds on phytoplankton and detritus, filtered through bristles on its appendages. Sexes are separate; the female broods eggs in a dorsal chamber. Population sizes are highly seasonal and adverse times are passed in dormant stages. Numerous aspects of cladoceran biology are studied in Canada: there is high commercial potential in their cultivation for fish food.

V. TUNNICLIFFE

Water Lily (Nymphaeaceae), large family of freshwater plants characterized by large, shield-shaped leaves and showy blossoms. They are mostly tropical or subtropical. Four genera and 9 species are native to Canada, of which 3 species are important. *Nuphar variegatum*, yellow pond lily, cow lily or spatterdock has yellow, globular flowers. It occurs as far N as the YT and is widespread throughout Canada. White or pygmy water lily (*Nymphaea tetragona*) is found in northern Canada. Sweet or fragrant water lily (*Nymphaea odorata*), the most beautiful of the 3, has waxy, white flowers, 10-15 cm across. It is found in ponds and quiet streams from southeastern Canada to Florida. All are edible and were an important emergency food for Indians, the rhizome be-

Water shield (*Brasenia schreberi*), a member of the water lily family (*photo by Barbara K. Deans/Masterfile*).

ing boiled, baked or dried, and the seeds roasted and ground into a highly nutritious flour. The root, because of its astringent, antiseptic and demulcent properties, was used externally for healing sores and internally for inflammation and dysentery. GILLIAN FORD

Water Pollution occurs when discharges of energy or materials degrade water for other users. Population growth and industrialization have resulted in POLLUTION of inland and marine waters. Water pollution can be classified according to the nature of pollutants, the sources releasing them and the water bodies into which they are discharged. Water pollution is measured by the concentration of pollutants in the water body and their effects on other water uses. Six categories of pollutants are recognized.

Pathogens are disease-causing bacteria, VIRUSES and protozoa, usually from human sewage. As pathogen numbers increase, so does the risk to human health.

Biochemical Oxygen Demand (BOD) is created by organic wastes decaying in the water body. Major sources of BOD are PULP AND PAPER mills and municipal sewage. If dissolved oxygen is depressed to zero, all fish die and anaerobic (ie, without oxygen) decomposition generates noxious gases (eg, hydrogen sulphide).

Nutrients, particularly nitrogen and phosphorus, enrich waters and accelerate the aging of lakes and streams (eutrophication). The resultant rich plant growth often prohibits recreational activities, and PLANKTON blooms depress oxygen levels. Major sources of nutrients are municipal sewage and urban and agricultural runoff.

Toxic Materials can affect the health of aquatic organisms and their consumers, and of those drinking contaminated waters. Toxicants include heavy metals (eg, LEAD, MERCURY), chlorinated hydrocarbons (eg, DDT, PCBS), polycyclic aromatic hydrocarbons (eg, benzopyrene) and phthalates (eg, dibutyl phthalate). They originate from many sources as a result of the large quantities of chemicals used in industries. Mixtures of toxic materials can be toxic even if their individual concentrations are below lethally toxic levels. Oil pollutants are toxic and may also smother aquatic organisms and cause the death of birds, attracted by the appearance of calm water, by destroying the waterproofing properties of their plumage.

Acidification, particularly of lakes, results from precipitation of sulphur and nitrogen oxides emitted by industries and automobiles (*see* ACID RAIN).

Temperature Changes from waste heat discharges (eg, from NUCLEAR POWER PLANT cooling waters) can cause pollution when their elevation reduces dissolved-oxygen levels, accelerates eutrophication, affects ecological processes and blocks migration paths of fishes.

Controls The most cost-effective measure of pollution control depends on the particular pollutant and its source. Pathogens are usually con-

trolled by the disinfection (frequently using chlorine) of municipal sewage and domestic water supply (*see* WATER TREATMENT). High costs usually inhibit collecting runoff for disinfection. BOD can be reduced by treating municipal and industrial wastes (eg, in settling and stabilization lagoons and activated sludge plants) to decrease oxygen demand before the effluent is discharged; treatment of runoff is often too costly. Nitrogen and phosphorus are controlled most cost-effectively by regulation of the product (eg, phosphorus-free detergents) and by land-use regulations (eg, fertilizer limitations). Specialized treatment processes can remove them from municipal and industrial wastes.

Toxicants cannot be controlled except at great cost at the point of entry into the water but must be regulated earlier in production. Different toxicants present different regulatory possibilities and problems. For example, PCBs (polychlorinated biphenyls) have to be controlled at the point of manufacture to limit dispersal; valuable materials (eg, chromium, lead) can be recycled economically; some toxicants can be replaced by nontoxic substitutes (eg, replacement of cyanide rinses in electroplating). Municipal and industrial treatment processes generally place toxic materials in sludges, which must then be treated or stored. Acidification can be prevented effectively only by controlling discharges of both nitrogen and sulphur oxides into the atmosphere. Temperature changes can be prevented only by dissipating heat into the atmosphere by air cooling.

Canada's rich endowment of fresh and marine water is threatened by regional shortages (eg, southern Saskatchewan and Alberta) and by serious pollution (eg, Great Lakes). Although pollution from pathogens, BOD and waste heat may be relatively easily reversed, eutrophication and oil spills are more difficult, and acidification and toxicity may be irreversible. Thus, control policies at all levels of government are increasingly emphasizing the regulation of toxicants and the early detection and prevention of pollution.

ANTHONY H.J. DORCEY

Reading: M. Keating, *To the Last Drop: Canada and the World's Water Crisis* (1986); P.H. Pearse, F. Bertrand and J.W. MacLaren, *Currents of Change* (1985).

Water Polo is a sport played in water, generally a swimming pool, by 2 teams of 13 players each (7 per team in the field of play at one time), with the object of propelling a ball through the opposing goal. The name derives from the original game started in England about 1870, where players rode floating barrels, or "horses," and struck at the ball with a stick. This aspect was soon abandoned and the game became popular in Great Britain, with teams from the north of England dominating. England won the water-polo event at several early Olympic Games 1900-20; since the 1930s, Hungary, the Soviet Union and Yugoslavia have dominated international competition. Canada gained prominence in men's water polo at the 1976 Olympic Games with many excellent matches against the world leaders, including a 6-6 draw with defending world and olympic champions, the Soviet Union. Canada has established itself as the third power in the Western Hemisphere behind the US and Cuba. In the 1987 Pan-Am Games, Canada's men's team narrowly missed a bronze medal. Women's water polo gained "official status" at the international level in 1986 with its inclusion in the World Aquatic Championships in Madrid. Canada has an excellent reputation in international women's water polo. In 1981 Canada was the top women's water polo nation in the world. Water polo, in its various forms, is enjoyed all across Canada by approximately 10 000 participants. The Canadian

Water Polo Assn was formed in 1964; Water Polo Canada is now the national governing body.

JACK BODDINGTON

Water Skiing is a sport in which competitors plane and jump on water skis while being towed by a speedboat. The sport was derived from snow SKIING and aquaplaning and was started in the US by Ralph Samuelson in 1922. It is perhaps the fastest-growing, all-family competitive sport. Competition is divided into 3 events – slalom, tricks (figures) and jumping. In Canada, it is also arranged in age categories. Water skiing caused a sensation when it was first introduced in Canada in the 1930s. The sport became more widely known in Canada after an appearance of the Cypress Gardens skiers at the CANADIAN NATIONAL EXHIBITION waterfront shows in 1948. The Canadian Water Ski Assn was founded in 1949, and Canada's first national championship was held that year. Canada has hosted 3 world championships, in 1953, 1967 and 1979. Canada first sent a full team (6 skiers) to the 1958 world championships held at Cypress Gardens, Fla, and has since climbed to second place in the world (1979, Toronto). Canadian world champions have been Charlie Blackwell (slalom, 1953); Carol Ann Duthie (overall, jr girls, 1953); George ATHANS, Jr (overall, 1971, 1972 and 1973); Joel McClintock (overall, 1979); Pat Messner (slalom, 1979); Judy McClintock (tricks, 1985) and Jaret Llewellyn (figures, jr mens, 1986-87).

Since 1971, Canadians have won 5 world titles in the men's division, and the Canadian team has placed no less than fourth in the world. The junior team won the gold medal at the 1987 world junior cup in Sherbrooke, Qué. Water skiing has been a participating sport in every Canada Summer Games and was approved as an Olympic category sport in 1981.

Reading: G. Athans, Jr, and C. Ward, *Water Skiing* (1975).

Water Treatment, the physical and chemical processes used to ensure water's quality for its intended use. Minimum standards for drinking water are set by environmental agencies while industries have their own guidelines.

Physical characterisititics, such as temperature, colour, turbidity (clarity or transparency), odour and taste, are measures of aesthetic acceptability and palatability, the oldest criteria for judging water quality. Micro-organisms, such as pathogenic and coliform organisms, are chemically eliminated to prevent WATER-BORNE DISEASES, but the chemicals must also be monitored because they can be detrimental to human health. Other chemical characteristics include the degree of acidity or alkalinity (the cause of scaling on pipes and household cookware), and concentrations of dissolved solids and oxygen. For example, some prairie natural waters have total-dissolved-solids (TDS) concentrations higher than 1000 mg/L, while the maximum level for Canadian drinking water is 500 mg/L and many industry processes require concentrations which are below 200 mg/L. Concentrations of various radionuclides which may originate from natural sources, nuclear accidents or NUCLEAR POWER generation, are also monitored.

Several physical and chemical processes are available for water treatment. The most common physical processes are screening, flocculation, sedimentation, filtration and adsorption. Distillation and reverse osmosis are used primarily in industrial water treatment. Chemical processes include aeration, coagulation, softening, pH adjustment, ion exchange and disinfection. Disinfection can be accomplished by chlorination, the addition of ozone, heating, exposure to ultraviolet light and the addition of bromine or iodine compounds (for industrial applications). Chlorination is the most common method. An effective germicide, chlorine is also beneficial in colour removal, taste and odour control, suppression of algal growths and the precipitation of iron and manganese.   D.W. DRAPER

Reading: M.S. Babbitt et al, *Water Supply Engineering* (1962); Health & Welfare Canada, *Guidelines for Canadian Drinking Water Quality 1978* (1979).

Waterfall, phenomenon which occurs when water flowing in a river channel encounters a vertical or near-vertical drop in the channel bed. A cascade occurs when the drop results in a series of small falls; rapids occur where the river is steep and turbulent and the water remains in contact with the bed; and a cataract when a waterfall has a large volume of flow. Waterfalls can be classified according to nature of origin.

Geological Discordance Falls result from a natural discordance in the river profile caused by geological faulting, glaciation, uplift plateaus, springs emanating from canyon walls, or earthquakes. Twin Falls near Yoho Glacier, BC, and NIAGARA FALLS, Ont, are examples.

Erosion Falls Cap-rock falls and vertical barrier falls are typical erosion waterfalls, formed by differential erosion that occurs where erosion-resistant rocks are underlain by or adjoin softer rocks. A cap-rock fall is formed when a surface layer of hard rock rests on a softer layer. Water flowing over the hard rock cap erodes the face of the softer rock underneath, undermining the cap which eventually breaks and tumbles into the river at the foot of the fall or immediately downstream. Over time, a fall of this kind may degenerate to a long cascade. Alexandra Falls on the Hay R, NWT, is a cap-rock fall. When a layer of very hard igneous rock, extending vertically through great thicknesses of softer rock, lies across a river channel, the erosive force of flowing water will not significantly affect the igneous rock but will wear down the softer rock, especially in the area immediately downstream from the igneous rock. A vertical barrier fall is eventually formed at the face of the vertical layer of hard rock. Little Falls on the Pigeon R, S of Thunder Bay, Ont, is an example.

Tidal Falls are typified by the reversing falls originating from the ebb and flow of ocean tides.

Helmcken Falls, 137 m high, on the Murtle R, BC, have carved an impressive cauldron out of the layers of lava (*photo by J.A. Kraulis*).

Horsethief Creek Falls in the Purcell Mts, BC (*photo by Pat Morrow*).

A rock shelf across a narrow point where a river empties into the ocean forms a waterfall at low TIDE because the water level in the river above the shelf is then higher than sea level. When sea level rises with the incoming tide to the point where it is higher than the river level upstream from the rock shelf, the seawater forces its way upstream against the flow of the river and through the narrow point in the channel. The resulting rapids, whirlpools and eddies create the impression that the falls have actually reversed. A notable example occurs on the SAINT JOHN R at Saint John, NB, where the very high tides of the Bay of FUNDY create the reversing effect. Other reversing falls in Canada are at Wager Bay, Ford Lk and Barrier Inlet, Hudson Str, both located in the Northwest Territories.

Duration Geologically speaking, all waterfalls are transient because their erosive power makes them self-destructive. This erosion is noticeable within a human lifetime at certain falls, eg, Horseshoe Falls on the Canadian side of the NIAGARA R. The crest of this waterfall has retreated approximately 335 m (roughly one metre per year) since its position was first recorded by Louis HENNEPIN in 1678. Since its beginning with the retreat of the last ice sheet about 10 000 years ago, the Niagara R has eroded a stretch of channel approximately 12 km long, creating the spectacular Niagara gorge. Along the bed of the Niagara R, downstream from the falls, there is evidence of plunge pools, cut during periods when the position of the crest was stable.

When a waterfall undercuts itself and large blocks of rock drop from the scarp (face), the material tends to accumulate at the foot, gradually turning the falls into rapids. The American Falls on the Niagara R are a good example of this process; the relatively rapid erosion is caused largely by the effects of large volumes of water falling from a high plateau. By contrast, there are some very high falls where erosion is much slower because water flow is small and the water is dispersed to a fine mist during its descent. The oldest falls, thought to be many millions of years old, result from water descending from high plateaus. The world's highest waterfall (with a

single, vertical drop of 807 m), Angel Falls, Venezuela, is an example.

Height There are various interpretations of what constitutes the height of a waterfall. Most waterfalls start with a series of rapids; the water then goes over the crest and drops vertically or nearly vertically, ending up as a cascade tumbling over accumulated debris. The heights shown in the table refer to the vertical or near-vertical drop from the crest to the top of the debris. The highest waterfall in Canada and sixteenth-highest in the world is Takakkaw Falls (dropping 503 m) which carries snow and ice melt from the Daly Glacier, BC.

Significance Waterways were the highways of Canada's early explorers; waterfalls were obstacles to transportation along these routes and had to be bypassed, usually by overland portages. Townsites were often established near a large falls on a navigable river and they marked the terminus of a portage. Later, canals were constructed, eg, the WELLAND CANAL bypassing Niagara Falls. Waterfalls serve as natural barriers that prevent undesirable aquatic life from migrating to upper portions of a watershed. For example, before construction of the Welland Canal, lampreys were unable to move upstream from Lk Ontario. Waterfalls also mark the sites of hydroelectric-power concentrations; in Canada many have been developed for this purpose. Many Canadian and foreign visitors view these spectacular natural attractions, drawn by the awesome power of falling water and the majestic settings.   P.I. CAMPBELL AND I.A. REID

Principal Canadian Waterfalls

Name	Vertical drop (m)	Location
Alexandra Falls	32	Hay R, NWT
Aubrey Falls	33	Mississagi R, Ont
Barrow Falls*	27	Barrow R, NWT
Big Beaver Falls*	19	Kapuskasing R, Ont
Brandywine Falls*	61	Brandywine Creek, BC
Bridal Veil Falls	122	Bridal Creek, BC
Calcaire, Chute du*	22	Caniapiscau R, Qué
Christoper Falls*	23	Opasatika R, Ont
Churchill Falls	75	Churchill R, Nfld
Della Falls*	440	Vancouver I
Dog Falls	47	Kaministikwia R, Ont
Elizabeth Falls*	34	Fond du Lac R, Sask
Grand Falls	43	Exploits R, Nfld
Granite, Chute au*	21	Caniapiscau R, Qué
Helmcken Falls*	137	Murtle R, BC
High Falls	24	Onaping R, Ont
Hunlen Falls*	253	Atnarko R, BC
Kakabeka Falls	47	Kaministikwia R, Ont
Louise Falls	20	Hay R, NWT
Marengo Falls*	61	Marengo Creek, NWT
Montmorency, Chute	76	Montmorency R, Qué
Muhigan Falls*	19	Muhigan R, Man
Muskrat Falls*	15	Churchill R, Nfld
Niagara Falls		Niagara R, Ont
Horseshoe Falls	57	
American Falls	59	
Ouiatchouane, Chute	79	Ouiatchouanish R, Ont
Panther Falls*	183	Nigel Creek, Alta
Parry Falls*	40	Lockhart R, NWT
Partridge Falls*	21	Pigeon R, Ont
Pigeon Falls*	27	Pigeon R, Ont
Rideau Falls	12	Rideau R, Ont
Schist Falls*	24	Pukaskwa R, Ont
Schistes, Chute aux*	18	Caniapiscau R, Qué
Scott Falls	27	Unknown R, Nfld
Shawinigan, Chutes*	46	St-Maurice R, Qué
Smoky Falls	24	Mattagami R, Ont
Steephill Falls*	21	Magpie R, Ont
Takakkaw Falls	503	From Daly Glacier, BC
Tasinigup Falls*	15	Burntwood R, Man
Thomas Falls	30	Unknown R, Nfld
Twin Falls	274	Twin Falls Creek, BC
Tyrrell Falls*	26	Lockhart R, NWT
Virginia Falls*	90	S Nahanni R, NWT
Wawaitin Falls	38	Mattagami R, Ont
Wilberforce Falls*	49	Hood R, NWT

* Not readily accessible

Waterfowl, general term used for members of the family Anatidae, composed of closely allied species commonly known as DUCKS, geese and SWANS. The group has a worldwide distribution and contains flightless species as well as others capable of long migrations. Some species, eg, northern pintail (*Anas acuta*), have very wide distribution; others are restricted to a few ponds on remote islands. Waterfowl range in size from pygmy geese, averaging 300 g when fully grown, to N American trumpeter swans, exceeding 13 kg and having a wingspread of 250 cm. Scientists divide waterfowl into 3 subfamilies, 2 of which are found in N America. The third, the primitive Australian Anseranatinae, contains the magpie geese, which are not true geese. In late summer as many as 80-100 million waterfowl are found in N America. Three species of swan, 7 of geese and 28 of ducks breed in Canada. Unfortunately, one species native to eastern Canada, the Labrador duck, is now extinct. *See also* GOOSE. F.G. COOCH

Waterloo, Ont, City, pop 58 718 (1986c), 49 428 (1981c), is the smaller of twin cities in central SW Ontario, 110 km W of Toronto (*see* KITCHENER-WATERLOO). Waterloo shares many general characteristics of social and economic development with Kitchener, yet continues a separate evolution.

First settled by Mennonites in 1806, it was incorporated as a village in 1857 (pop *c*500), as a town in 1876 (pop *c*1700) and as a city in 1947 (pop 10 736). While it was growing in the village-town stage, the people, their houses and their places of employment remained concentrated in a core area, where all mingled daily and virtually everyone was generally known and recognized. The sense of community solidarity learned at this time has continued. The great majority of the people were of German origin and spoke German. The proportions of the religious censuses of 1861 and 1871 held good for a generation: 54% Lutheran, 9% Roman Catholic, 6% Mennonite.

Waterfowl (from right foreground to background): whistling swan, Canada goose, green winged teal, pintail, mallard (*artwork by Claire Tremblay*).

The town thrived under energetic leadership. The town counsellors were virtually a board of trade, and the same sort of people filled church boards, parks and cemetery committees, as well as directing in commerce, insurance and manufacturing. The local specialization in the insurance industry began in the 1860s with Farmers' Mutual Fire and Ontario Mutual Life.

The SEAGRAM COMPANY LIMITED distillery took shape and prospered in the 1870s, providing a measure of security and co-ordination for the community, as the family, in addition to extensive charities, seeded capital into trust, insurance, furniture, music and other companies. Waterloo remembers band festivals from the 1920s to 1940s, drawing entries broadly from eastern N America. The Waterloo Music Society has been realizing public music since 1882.

Population increased fivefold 1948-81, diluting German characteristics and dispersing the central core. New suburbs pressed boundaries outward as industries and head offices relocated. The expansion of WILFRID LAURIER U, and the mushrooming development of UNIVERSITY OF WATERLOO have made a deep impact on post-WWII growth in this distinctive self-conscious community. *See also* statistical table at KITCHENER-WATERLOO. PAUL CORNELL

Waterton Lakes National Park (est 1895, 525 km²) is situated in Alberta, 276 km SW of Calgary on the Canada-US border. In 1932, this park was united with Montana's Glacier National Park to create the world's first international peace park. The setting is spectacular. In less than a kilometre, the dry rolling hills of the prairies soar to icy peaks nearly 3000 m high. The 3 Waterton Lakes, nestling between 2 mountain ranges, are over 150 m deep. Because the park embraces both prairie and mountain, there is a great variety of plant and animal life. Antelope and coyote roam the grasslands; mountain goat, bighorn sheep, grizzly bear and marmot frequent alpine meadows and barren ridgetops. The area, once a Blackfoot stronghold, was discovered by Europeans in the late 1850s during fur-trade expeditions. In the early 1900s Alta's first oil well was drilled near Cameron Creek. The park provides facilities for tent, recreational-vehicle and primitive winter camping, and has numerous trails.

LILLIAN STEWART

Watkin, Sir Edward William, businessman (b at Salford, Eng 26 Sept 1819; d at Rosehill, Eng 13 Apr 1901) was a proponent of the federation of the British N American colonies, a key figure in the reorganization of the Hudson's Bay Co which led to its 1869 agreement with the Canadian government, and president of the Grand Trunk Ry 1861-63. He devoted most of his life to railway work in England, but in 1861 he was commissioned by the directors of the Grand Trunk Ry to reorganize the affairs of that company, and by the Colonial Office to report on the feasibility of federating the British N American colonies. He was created a knight bachelor in 1868, and a baronet of the UK in 1880. T.D. REGEHR

Watkins, John B.C., scholar, diplomat (b at Norval Station, Ont 1902; d at Montréal 12 Oct 1964). A Scandinavian specialist at U Man, he joined the Dept of External Affairs in 1946. Because he spoke fluent Russian, he was sent to Moscow as chargé d'affaires, 1948-51. He was minister to Norway, 1952-54, then returned to Moscow as ambassador, 1954-56. He served as assistant undersecretary of state for external affairs and as ambassador to Denmark. Western intelligence suspected him as a security risk because of alleged homosexual contacts in the USSR and, under questioning, he suffered a heart attack and died. ROBERT BOTHWELL

Reading: J. Watkins, *Moscow Despatches: Inside Cold War Russia*, eds, D. Besky and W. Kaplan (1987).

Watmough, David Arthur, writer (b at London, Eng 17 Aug 1926). One of western Canada's finest fiction writers, Watmough's literary reputation rests on his series of linked, semiautobiographical stories concerning Davey Bryant, a homosexual everyman whose frustration, acute self-consciousness and sense of "lovelessness" in the homophobic societies of Europe and N America underscores the complexity, ambiguity and occasional violence of ordinary human relationships in the 20th century. Seven volumes of the Bryant cycle have appeared, including *No More into the Garden* (1978), *The Connecticut Countess* (1984) and *The Year of Fears* (1987). Since the stories are written as a mature man's recollection of his past, and since they are intended to be read as parts of a single, extended work, comparisons with Proust are inevitable; as autobiographical writing they have been ranked with that of Dylan Thomas. STANLEY GORDON

Watson, Edward A., veterinarian, pathologist, researcher (b in Devon, Eng 2 Jan 1879; d at Victoria 12 Mar 1945). He came to Canada in 1896 and graduated from the Ontario Veterinary College in 1904. In charge of the Lethbridge (Alta) Animal Pathology Laboratory 1906-15, he carried out important research on dourine, a disease of horses. He was chief of the pathology division of the federal Dept of Agriculture 1919-42 and established the Animal Diseases Research Inst. Watson was a persistent and dedicated laboratory worker and researcher. His work in dourine is but one example of his many studies on animal diseases. His many ideas, born of an international outlook on science, formed the basis for veterinary research in Canada. *See also* VETERINARY MEDICINE. J.F. FRANK

Watson, Helen Griffith Wylie, née McArthur, nursing administrator (b at Stettler, Alta 11 July 1911; d at Guelph, Ont 15 Dec 1974). A graduate of U of A, Watson received her first practical experience as a public-health nurse at an isolated settlement in the Peace River country during the

2284 Watson, Homer Ransford

Depression. In 1946 she joined the RED CROSS SOCIETY, eventually becoming national director of nursing services. She served as president of the Canadian Nurses' Assn 1950-54 and was active internationally with the Red Cross. In 1954 she was awarded the Florence Nightingale Award for her work in Korea – the highest award of the International Red Cross. An Officer of the Order of Canada, she retired in 1971. DANIEL FRANCIS

Watson, Homer Ransford, painter (b at Doon, Canada W 14 Jan 1855; d there 30 May 1936). Virtually self-taught, Watson spent 1874-76 in Toronto working with John A. Fraser and Henri Perré and in New York absorbing the influence of George Inness and the Hudson River School. Later in Europe he met Sir George Clausen and Whistler, and admired Millet, the Barbizon painters and Constable. Internationally famous at the peak of his career, Watson developed a landscape style marked by honesty of purpose and a focus on the moods of nature. Many of his canvases depict the countryside around Kitchener, the trees, fields of grain, grazing cattle – the "Land of Thrift" much prized in pioneer society. He began exhibiting in 1878 but the purchase of his *The Pioneer Mill* for Queen Victoria at the first Royal Canadian Academy of 1880 brought early acclaim. Many significant canvases were completed by the end of the century: *Cornfield* (1883), *The Flood Gate* (1900) and *After the Rain* (1883). His patrons included Lord Strathcona, James Ross, Oscar Wilde and many affluent Canadians. He and Edmund Morris founded the Canadian Art Club in 1907 hoping to replace imported European with Canadian canvases. Watson was president of the Royal Canadian Academy, 1918-21. J. RUSSELL HARPER

Watson, John, philosopher (b at Glasgow, Scot 25 Feb 1847; d at Kingston, Ont 27 Jan 1939). Canada's foremost early philosopher, he was a charter member of the Royal Soc of Canada and author of 8 books and over 200 articles. He arrived at Queen's in Kingston, Ont, in 1872. Hegelianism influenced much of Watson's writings, which in turn affected the development of religious and political ideas in Canada. He is the only Canadian philosopher ever to be invited to give the prestigious Gifford Lectures in Edinburgh, Scot. These lectures were published in the 2-volume *The Interpretation of Religious Experience* (1910-12) – a landmark in Canadian philosophical history. Watson's main philosophical interest was the metaphysics of religion and he proposed a rational interpretation of Christianity in *Christianity and Idealism* (1896). By focusing on reason he provided a commonality around which people could unite, and thus helped build the intellectual foundations of the UNITED CHURCH OF CANADA (formed during his later years). His first books were about the German philosopher Kant. *Kant and his English Critics* (1881), *The Philosophy of Kant* (1888) and *The Philosophy of Kant Explained* (1908) were classics in the field and are still consulted by Kantian scholars. During those same years Watson wrote texts that introduced hundreds of students to PHILOSOPHY. His clear style and unique commentary contributed to the popularity of his publications. In the aftermath of WWI Watson wrote *The State in Peace and War* (1919), urging world government based on tolerance and multicultural integration. Canada's cultural pluralism and peaceful emergence as a nation influenced his thinking. He advocated fair living conditions for all and rewards for individual effort. ELIZABETH A. TROTT

Watson, Ken, curler (b at Minnedosa, Man 12 Aug 1904; d at Winnipeg 26 July 1986). When he skipped his Strathcona Cup (Man) Rink to victory in the 1949 Macdonald Brier, Watson became the first to win the coveted Tankard 3 times (with a career Brier record of 25 and 2). Beginning in 1923 at the Manitoba Bonspiel, he won 32 major bonspiels, including an unprecedented 6 grand aggregates in succession (1942-47). An innovative strategist, he helped develop the sliding delivery and was a supreme exponent of the draw game. Watson also served as an administrator of CURLING at several levels and was a successful author – *Ken Watson on Curling* sold nearly 150 000 copies. GERALD REDMOND

Watson, Patrick, television producer and host, filmmaker, author, actor, communicator (b at Toronto 23 Dec 1929). After receiving an MA from U of T, he abandoned his plans for an academic career and accepted a number of CBC assignments before joining the production staff of "Close-Up" in 1957. From 1960 to 1964 he produced the weekly "Inquiry" from Ottawa. This was followed by 2 years as co-producer (with Douglas Leiterman) and co-host (with John DRAINIE and Laurier LAPIERRE) of the popular THIS HOUR HAS SEVEN DAYS (1964-66), which firmly established his status as national celebrity. Since then he has served as host, writer and producer on a large number of programs, including "The Watson Report" 1975-81, culminating in the 10-part international co-production "The Struggle for Democracy" scheduled for completion in 1988. He has also been a host on the PBS "Live From Lincoln Centre" and on CBC-TV's "Venture." Watson's skills range from piloting airplanes to performing his own adaptation of *The Book of Job* on the stage (1984). His best-known book is the psychological thriller *Alter Ego* (1978).
ERIC KOCH

Watson, Sheila, née Doherty, novelist, critic, teacher (b at New Westminster, BC 24 Oct 1909). Publication of Watson's novel The DOUBLE HOOK (1959) marks the start of contemporary writing in Canada. She attended UBC and later completed a PhD at U of T under Marshall MCLUHAN. A distinguished scholar of the early modernist period in Britain, specializing in the works of Wyndham Lewis, Watson taught school in the BC interior and later taught at U of A. She is married to Wilfred WATSON, with whom she retired to Vancouver in 1980. Her *Four Stories* appeared in 1979, and one other story, *And the Four Animals,* in 1980. Her critical articles were collected in a special issue of *Open Letter* (1974). She was the founding editor of the periodical *White Pelican* (1971-75), and a volume of essays in her honour, *Figures in a Ground,* appeared in 1978. *Five Stories* and *The Collected Works of Miriam Mandel* (ed by Watson) were published in 1984.

The Double Hook is Watson's only novel; it presents in concise, symbolic terms a drama of social disintegration and redemption, set in an isolated BC community. Watson has said of the novel that it is "about how people are driven, how if they have no art, how if they have no tradition, how if they have no ritual, they are driven in one of 2 ways, either towards violence or towards insensibility – if they have no mediating rituals which manifest themselves in what I suppose we call art forms." These themes are presented in a style which itself balances on a "double hook": it is simultaneously local and universal, realistic and symbolic. Writers such as Robert KROETSCH have seen in the image of the double hook a balancing of opposites that is a fundamental characteristic of Canadian culture. Watson made possible, through her intellectual daring, the sophistication she assumed in her readers and her sceptical care for the nature of language itself, the development of contemporary writing in Canada. She was awarded the Lorne Pierce medal by the RSC in 1984. STEPHEN SCOBIE

Watson, Wilfred, poet, playwright, professor emeritus of English literature at U of A (b at Rochester, Eng 1 May 1911). A highly innovative writer, Watson influenced 1960s theatre in Canada; his number-grid verse is significant to prosody and to poetry performance. His first book, *Friday's Child* (1955) won the British Council and the Gov Gen's Awards for poetry. Its mythological, literary and religious imagery and intense energy persist in his later work. In the 1960s, Watson turned to drama, producing 10 plays, mostly in verse (including *Cockrow and the Gulls,* produced 1962; *O Holy Ghost DIP YOUR FINGER IN THE BLOOD OF CANADA and write, I LOVE YOU,* 1967; *Let's murder Clytemnestra, according to the principles of Marshall McLuhan,* 1969), the immediate influence of which was considerable. A close reader of Marshall MCLUHAN (they co-authored *From Cliché to Archetype,* 1970), Watson believes the world of multimedia produces multiconsciousnesses, demanding a theatre of "radical absurdity" in which realistic settings and action are replaced by "multi-environments." Much of his work is political allegory. In the 1970s he returned to poetry: *The Sorrowful Canadians* (1972) counterpoints type fonts, refrains and "voices." With *I Begin with Counting* (1978) and *Mass on Cowback* (1982), he developed number-grid verse, using a vertical grid of 9 numbers with 17 slots for words, syllables or phrases. By stacking the grids, Watson writes a "score" for the performance of multivoice poems, which exist not on the page but in transformations from visual to auditory forms. His 1983 work, *Gramsci x 3* (produced 1986), though partly "docudrama," is characterized by absurdity, continual experimentation with verse forms, satire alternating with lyricism, and an energy and exaltation that transcends the horrors it depicts. Watson's *Collected Poems* (1986) and *Collected Plays* (1987) bring together his most important work. SHIRLEY NEUMAN

Watson, William, "Whipper Billy," professional wrestler (b at Toronto 25 June 1915). It is claimed that he won 99% of his 6300 matches during a 30-year career. He was popular in the Toronto area and frequently drew capacity crowds. In 1947 he briefly held professional wrestling's world title, and he was the perennial Commonwealth champion. A 1971 automobile accident forced his retirement from the ring. Pursuing a long-standing interest, he began to work full-time on behalf of crippled children. Watson acted as fund-raising chairman for the Ontario Soc for Crippled Children and served on Ontario's Advisory Council for the Disabled between 1976 and 1982. J. THOMAS WEST

Watson Lake, YT, Town, pop 826 (1986c), 748 (1981c), is located at kilometre 1018 of the ALASKA HIGHWAY, 459 km SE of Whitehorse. It is named after Frank Watson, a pioneer trapper and prospector who settled in the area in 1898 en route to the Klondike. During construction of the Alaska Hwy, the townsite was moved 12 km from the lake to a location near the highway. Watson Lake became an important communication centre after the construction of a major airport (1943), and remains a transportation hub, linking roads from BC with main routes to the interior and to the NWT. By the highway is a growing "forest" of signs of faraway places begun by a homesick soldier in 1942. H. GUEST

Watt, Charlie, Inuk leader (b at Ft Chimo, Qué 29 June 1944). Energetic and dynamic, Watt has helped lead the Inuit through a time of rapidly increasing political sophistication. He founded the Northern Québec Inuit Assn in 1972 and the following year helped establish the Labrador Inuit Assn. He was a negotiator for the JAMES BAY

AGREEMENT, signed in 1975, and was founding president of Makivik Corp, the successor to NQI and the first Inuit development corporation. His belief that the Inuit should have a voice in national affairs led him to help create the Inuit Committee on National Issues in 1979, and he worked unsuccessfully toward greater recognition of native rights in the CONSTITUTION ACT, 1982. He was sworn into the Senate in 1984. JOHN BENNETT

Watters, James C., coal miner, trade unionist, socialist (b at Edinburgh, Scot 1869; d at Victoria 1947). As founding president of the BC Federation of Labour (1910), Watters played an important though ultimately unsuccessful role in labour's 1917 anticonscription coalition. As president of the TRADES AND LABOR CONGRESS, he hoped to rally Québec, ethnic minorities, moderate Liberals and moderate socialists behind the campaign to stop the CONSCRIPTION law of Robert BORDEN's Conservative, later Liberal-Conservative, wartime administration. Socialists and trade unionists, especially in western Canada, did forge a common front with Sir Wilfrid LAURIER during the Dec 1917 national election. No Liberal-Labour candidate, however, was elected and at the 1918 TLC convention Watters lost the presidency he had held since 1911. By 1920 he was reduced to attempting to mediate between conservatives and socialists in the labour movement. When this failed, he drifted into obscurity.
ALLEN SEAGER

Wawa, Ont, Algoma District, pop 3972 (1986c), 96 km N of Sault Ste Marie. Originally called Michipicoten, the original economic activity was gold prospecting, but iron-ore deposits proved to be the source of major economic activity. Area mines supply Algoma Steel in the Soo. Settlement began as early as 1647, when fur traders established a trading post in the area, and the name Wawa, adopted in the 1890s, comes from the Ojibwa word for "wild goose." The name was changed briefly in the 1950s by railways and the post office was named Jamestown after Sir James DUNN. However, the local usage did not change and the name Wawa was restored in 1960.
GERALD STORTZ

Waxman, Albert Samuel, "Al," TV and movie performer, director (b at Toronto 2 Mar 1935). As title character of CBC TV's situation comedy "King of Kensington" 1975-80, he became one of Canada's most familiar actors. Later roles in TV dramas have brought critical praise. Waxman studied acting in New York in 1959, performed in Hollywood films, and directed short subjects and full-length Canadian movies before his CBC TV role, which earned him an ACTRA award 1976. A stunning performance as an unemployed labourer in "The Winnings of Frankie Walls" won the coveted Earle Grey Award 1981. He has since starred in the American TV series "Cagney and Lacey" and is active in fund-raising and charitable activities across Canada. ALLAN M. GOULD

Waxwing (Bombycillidae), family comprising 8 species, including the true waxwings, the hypocolius of the Middle East and the silky-flycatchers of southwestern US and Central America. True waxwings (3 species) are small passerines (perching birds), 15-19 cm long. They inhabit subarctic and temperate regions of the Northern Hemisphere and are migratory. In Canada, 2 species occur, cedar waxwing (*Bombycilla cedrorum*) and bohemian waxwing (*B. garrulus*). They have very soft plumage dominated by rich fawn or soft grey coloration, with shadings of chestnut. Waxwings have a black throat and band across the eyes. The secondary wing feathers often have waxy, red tips from which the name is derived. Wings and tail are grey. The bill

is short, thick, slightly notched and hooked. The crest is prominent. Waxwings are gregarious, particularly during the nonbreeding season. They eat insects which they may catch in flight but, in season, feed primarily on berries, fruits and flowers. They build a bulky nest consisting of an open cup of twigs, moss and grass lined with hair, down or feathers. Clutches, of 3-7 ash grey or bluish eggs, marked with dark brown, are incubated mainly by the female. Young are fed by both parents. HENRI OUELLET

Wayman, Thomas Ethan, poet, editor, teacher (b at Hawkesbury, Ont 13 Aug 1945). Wayman is an ardent spokesman and advocate of the workplace, and thus has a unique voice in Canadian poetry. Raised in Prince Rupert and Vancouver, Wayman received his BA from UBC (1966) and his MFA from U of California in Irvine (1968). He currently teaches at the Kootenay School of Writing, Vancouver, where he makes his home. From 1970 to 1974, Wayman laboured at construction, demolition and factory jobs, experiences which he has transferred into his writing, as he consistently argues that daily work is one of the central concerns of life, and that it should therefore be – along with love, death and nature – a central concern of artists as well. In an unpretentious and colloquial style, he has produced 9 volumes of poetry, largely on the importance of work, including *Waiting for Wayman* (1973), *The Nobel Prize Acceptance Speech: New and Selected Wayman Poems* (1981) and *Counting the Hours: City Poems* (1983). He has also edited 3 anthologies of poems about work, *Inside Job* (1983) contains 4 of his essays on the importance of contemporary work writing. His latest work is *The Face of Jack Munro* (1986).
DONNA COATES

Wayne and Shuster, comedy team composed of John Louis Wayne (b at Toronto 28 May 1918) and Frank Shuster (b at Toronto 5 Sept 1916). They met at Harbord Collegiate, Toronto, where they performed in annual revues. After receiving BAs in English from U of T, they were both studying for MAs when WWII intervened. After enlisting in the infantry, they were soon reunited, writing and performing for *The Army Show*. Following the war, they returned to Canada and worked together on radio (by 1947 they had their own show on CBC) and later on television. In 1950 they began appearing as guests on various American TV programs, including a record 67 performances on "The Ed Sullivan Show." Although their wide-ranging skits, described as "an amiable mixture of slapstick, pantomime, visual tricks, sheer corn and sometimes ingenious twists on classic situations," have not always met with critical approval, the comedy team has remained popular and has won several international awards. Despite their popularity in the US, Wayne and Shuster remained based, personally

Comedians Johnny Wayne (left) and Frank Shuster (*courtesy National Archives of Canada/MISA/CBC Coll/ #12438*).

and professionally, in Toronto, repeatedly resisting pressure to pursue greater wealth and fame south of the border. CHARLES DOUGALL

Short-tailed weasel (*Mustela erminea*) (artwork by Claire Tremblay).

Weasel, small, long-bodied, carnivorous mammal of family Mustelidae. Three occur in Canada: short-tailed weasel, ermine or stoat (*Mustela erminea*); long-tailed, and least weasels (*M. frenata, M. rixosa,* respectively). Genus *Mustela* also includes MINK, black-footed FERRET and the introduced European ferret. Weasels have dark brown upper-bodies and tails; creamy white underparts. They assume a white winter coat in northern regions. In the FUR INDUSTRY no distinction is made among the coats of the 3 species; all are marketed as ermine. The weasel's head is bluntly pointed; ears, small and rounded. The long, slender body has a thick neck and short feet. Next to WOLVERINES, least weasels, the smallest species, are the rarest mammals in eastern Canada. They occur throughout mainland Canada from interior BC to northern Ontario and Québec. They prefer coniferous forest or tundra but also inhabit marshes, meadows and broken woodlands. Long-tailed weasels, the largest species, occur from S America to about 49° N lat and are found in southern BC, the Prairies, Ontario, Québec and NB. They prefer mixed hardwood forest but also inhabit other forests or open country, always near water. The short-tailed weasel, widespread in the Northern Hemisphere, occurs throughout Canada in habitats including tundra, boreal forest, meadows and riverbanks. All species take small mammals and insects; long-tailed and short-tailed weasels also take young rabbits and larger rodents. Long-tailed weasels breed in July-Aug; 4-9 young are born 205-237 days later. Delayed implantation of the embryo accounts for the long gestation. Short-tailed weasels mate in March; gestation lasts about 30 days; the single litter averages 6 young. Least weasels bear 2-3 litters annually, each of 3-6 young; gestation lasts about 35 days. Males may assist females in hunting food for young. As efficient killers of mice, weasels are useful to farmers, except when they take poultry. They do not make good pets. C.S. CHURCHER

Weather is defined as the atmospheric conditions prevailing at a specific place and time; CLIMATE is the characteristic weather, including average and extreme conditions, over months, seasons and years. METEOROLOGY is the study of the motions, processes and phenomena of the atmosphere. Although people have always been fascinated and challenged by weather and climate, scientific weather observation and the development of meteorology as a physical science only became possible after the invention of the thermometer and barometer in the 17th century. In the 1980s over 150 national meteorological services collaborate, through the World Meteorological Organization, in exchanging meteorological information several times daily around the globe. *See also* CLIMATE SEVERITY.

Weather Forecasting attempts to predict the air temperature, humidity, WIND speed and direction, precipitation, CLOUDS, etc, that will occur at a given place or region at a particular time in the future. The atmosphere may be seen as a massive air machine which moves heat and moisture from place to place. Weather is a product of this machine. The workings of the atmosphere follow physical laws, ie, the laws of thermodynamics, motion, conservation of mass and energy, etc, which are very complex to apply (*see* PHYSICS). Since the Earth is almost spherical and spins on its own axis, the laws of motion cannot be described in simple terms. Some deviations from spherical shape, especially mountains and MOUNTAIN RANGES, create still more problems. In addition, most SOLAR ENERGY reaches the Earth in a band near the equator; the atmosphere and the oceans play a major role in distributing this excessive heat northward and southward, and this process further affects the various physical laws. As well, oceans have a different effect on the bottom part of the atmosphere than land does; and forests, lakes, plains, tundra, cities, etc, all have their own special effects on the atmosphere.

Most modern meteorologists attempt to cope with physical processes by expressing them mathematically, ie, by creating mathematical models of the atmosphere. Powerful computers are then used to solve problems. As computers become more powerful, the models can be made more complex and, often, more accurate. During the 1960s and 1970s, improved atmospheric models permitted useful forecasts projecting much further into the future than had been possible before; by 1980, forecasts extended 5 days into the future. All of the world's weather services are co-operating to push weather predictions out to 2 weeks by the end of the century. Weather forecasting usually involves the following stages: observation of what is now happening at many places; analysis of the observations to create a comprehensive picture of what is now happening at various places in the atmosphere; projection of this picture into the future (prognosis); interpretation of that future picture to determine the temperature, humidity, wind, precipitation, etc, to be expected at the time represented by that picture.

Meteorologists who are more interested in a shorter time range (1-2 days) often bypass the mathematical model and use their knowledge of how one weather event follows another. These observations are the basis of much weather lore relating the appearance of the sky, the timing of precipitation, the recent history of the wind or the trend in pressure to predictions of what will happen next. Others observe animal behaviour or consider how people are affected (eg, painful joints, migraine headaches) to make their, often correct, predictions. Severe local storms (eg, showers, damaging windstorms, thunderstorms with HAIL, TORNADOES) are of great interest, but because of their very short life cycles, usually tens of minutes from birth to death, observation by RADAR and extrapolation is usually the only effective approach to prediction.

National or continental boundaries are irrelevant to weather forecasting. This fact has made METEOROLOGY a truly international science. The World Meteorological Organization (WMO), part of the UNITED NATIONS structure, co-ordinates meteorological activities throughout the world. One of the organization's main programs, the World Weather Watch (WWW), attempts to provide the information analysis and exchange required by all national weather services to create weather forecasts. The principal elements of WWW are the Global Observing System, which provides the weather observations required for forecasting; the Global Telecommunications System, which makes the observations available to all countries needing them for weather forecasting; and the Global Data Processing System, which analyses the observations and carries out the prognosis function on behalf of countries lacking these capabilities. All countries benefit from the elements of the WWW; without it Canadian meteorologists could not be reasonably sure that they would get the weather observations required for forecasting, or that weather observations made in Canada would reach other countries needing them.

In Canada weather forecasting is carried out in the same way as in other scientifically advanced countries. Weather observations from all around the Earth's surface, from balloons released at many locations around the globe, and from SATELLITES, radar, aircraft and ships are transmitted freely to all countries over the Global Telecommunications System. These data are analysed in the Canadian Meteorological Centre in Montréal to create a mathematical picture of the present condition of the atmosphere over the Northern Hemisphere. This picture is provided to Canadian meteorologists in the form of a series of weather maps for the surface and for various higher levels. (Before 1990 the Canadian model may well cover the whole globe, since what happens in the Southern Hemisphere has an effect over Canada beyond the fourth or fifth day.) Next, the mathematical model is run in a computer in a series of short time steps, some as brief as 6 minutes. New series of charts are provided to meteorologists for specific intervals out to the end of the model run. The results of the model are then translated into weather forecasts. There is a great deal of research under way into using the model to give a direct prediction of the various elements of the weather; but, until that research bears fruit, weather forecasts will continue to be made by forecasters. Many aspects of the forecast are not done well automatically, largely because it is not yet possible to create mathematical models that are as complex as the atmosphere itself.

J.A.W. McCULLOCH

Reading: R.A. Hornstein, *The Weather Book* (1980); J.G. Navarra, *Atmosphere, Weather and Climate* (1979).

Weather Observations Weather in Canada ranges from the extreme cold of the Arctic to tornadoes and other severe weather in the southern regions; from the storms and fog of the Atlantic to the dry heat and majestic thunderstorms of the prairies. Weather observing in Canada is equally varied, challenging and interesting.

Weather observations are based on a definition of present weather as "state of the atmosphere with respect to heat or cold, wetness or dryness, calm or storm, clearness or cloudiness." In addition to elements implied by the definition there are also measurements needed to feed the weather forecast process. These traditional observations are those of sky state, wind, air temperature, and the water content of the air as humidity, haze, fog and precipitation, along with their induced factors of visibility and environmental icing, all observed from the Earth's surface. The human observer can be assisted in observing the weather by

Canadian Weather Records

	Canada	World
Highest maximum air temperature	45.0° Midale and Yellow Grass, Sask, 5 July 1937	58.0° Al'azizyah, Libya, 13 Sept 1922
Lowest minimum air temperature	-63.0° Snag, YT, 3 Feb 1947	-89.2° Vostok, Antarctica, 21 July 1983
Coldest month	-47.9° Eureka, NWT, Feb 1979	
Highest sea-level pressure	106.76 kPa, Mayo, YT, 1 Jan 1974	108.38 kPa, Agata, Siberia, USSR 31 Dec 1968
Lowest sea-level pressure	94.02 kPa, St Anthony, Nfld, 20 Jan 1977	87.64 kPa in eye of Typhoon June (Pacific Ocean 17°N, 138°E), 19 Nov 1975
Greatest precipitation in 24 hrs	489.2 mm, Ucluelet Brynnor Mines, BC, 6 Oct 1967	1869.9 mm, Cilaos, La Réunion Is, 15 March 1952
Greatest precipitation in one month	2235.5 mm, Swanson Bay, BC, Nov 1917	9300 mm, Cherrapunji, India, July 1861
Greatest precipitation in one year	8122.4 mm, Henderson Lake, BC, 1931	25 461.2 mm, Cherrapunji, India, Aug 1860-July 1861
Greatest average annual precipitation	6655 mm, Henderson Lake, BC	11 770 mm, Tutunendo, Colombia
Least annual precipitation	12.7 mm, Arctic Bay, NWT, 1949	0.0 Arica, Chile – no rain for 14 years
Greatest average annual snowfall	1433 cm, Glacier, Mt Fidelity, BC	
Greatest snowfall in one season	2446.5 cm, Revelstoke/Mt Copeland, BC, 1971-72	31 102 mm, Paradise, Mt Rainier, Wash, Feb 1971-Feb 1972
Greatest snowfall in one month	535.9 cm, Haines Apps No 2, BC Dec 1959	
Greatest snowfall in one day	1181.1 cm, Lakelse Lake, BC, 17 Jan 1974	1930 mm, Silver Lake, Colo, 14-15 Apr 1921
Highest average annual no of thunderstorm days	34 days, London, Ont	322 days, Bogor, Indonesia
Heaviest hailstone	290 g, Cedoux, Sask	1.02 kg Gopalganj Dist, Bangladesh, 14 Apr 1986
Highest average annual wind speed	36 km/h, Cape Warwick, Resolution Island, NWT	
Highest wind speed for 1 hr	201.1 km/h, Cape Hopes Advance (Quaqtaq), Qué, 18 Nov 1931	371 km/h Mt Washington, NH, 12 Apr 1934
Highest average hours of fog	1890 hr, Argentia, Nfld	

an array of equipment, appropriately sited and applied. Temperature is measured by liquid in glass thermometers or electronic thermometers. Air humidity is measured with wet- and dry-bulb temperature comparisons or by hair hygrographs, or more recently with dew-point or infrared sensors. Wind speed and direction are commonly measured by rotating cup-wheels and vanes. Precipitation is observed visually and collected in open gauges for later measurement of volume or mass. Surface air pressure, for forecast and aviation purposes, is measured by balancing the weight of air against a column of mercury, or by more recent electronic techniques using evacuated aneroid capsules. Pressure changes over the previous 3 hours are also reported for forecast purposes. More complex instrumentation supports the meteorological observer where special interests must be satisfied. Cloud heights for aviation operations were first estimated by the observer. More commonly they are now measured by a number of techniques, culminating in the laser range-finding ceilometer. Visibility is estimated by optical instruments that measure the local degree of obscuration. Icing sensors and snow accumulation sensors are still in development. Electronic thermometers infer profiles of soil temperature for the agriculturalist, who also measures solar radiation, precipitation and evaporation from soil and other surfaces.

Upper-Air Observations of temperature, humidity and wind as functions of height or pressure were introduced half a century ago as a service to aviation and as an aid to improving forecasts. Balloons carry instrument packages, transmitting their information to surface equipment. There are presently more than 30 installations operating twice daily spread over the entire landmass of Canada. A few also carry special instrument packages to measure OZONE in the upper atmosphere. Canada has recently pioneered the use of operational upper-air systems, from the decks of commercial freighters on the N Pacific between Japan and Canada, to provide routine information over present data-sparse areas.

Remote Sensing of meteorological elements is becoming more common. Weather radar has been developed to warn of severe storm developments and to estimate the precipitation falling over wide areas. There are now 13 weather radars operated by the Government of Canada over the more densely settled areas of Canada. Two more are Doppler radars which also measure the wind within storms. Experimental systems are now being engineered to sense upper-air elements remotely, either from the Earth's surface or from satellite. Powerful, vertically pointed Doppler radars are also being developed to measure the profile of upper winds.

Earth Satellites have emerged as valuable meteorological observers. Early satellites flew low over the Earth in an orbit over the poles and transmitted pictures back to any receiver within operating range. These pictured the development and decay of weather systems twice a day over any area of the country. With special sensors these orbiting satellites have also been able to observe ocean temperatures, surface winds and wave height and measure the profile of atmospheric temperature above the Earth's surface. There are plans to place radars on satellites to measure high altitude winds and to map the ice fields in Canada's northern waters. Satellites are also parked in stationary positions over the equator and picture the cloud formations over large areas. In addition, they serve as communication relays from remote areas, from aircraft and from ships. There are hundreds of environmental measurement stations in Canada reporting through satellite to 2 centres set up to receive the satellite signals.

Network Observations provide a routine base of information for many classes of users, including the forecast and climatological services of the Atmospheric Environment Services (AES), of other world services affiliated with the World Meteorological Organization, and of private meteorology in Canada and around the world. There are 350 locations where observers of the AES and air traffic services of the Dept of Transport provide hourly or more frequent observations. Observations are provided by lake and oceangoing ships, from sites of the provincial Departments of Agriculture in Canada, from hydrological services, grain elevator companies, educational institutions and other sources. The pride of the AES is its network of more than 2000 volunteer weather observers. These observers are equipped with basic instruments to provide observations of daily maximum and minimum temperatures and precipitation and notes on the general character of the weather.

Automatic Weather Stations are increasingly providing meteorological observations. There are over 100 automatic weather stations operating in Canada. These automatic stations are providing observations in specific applications, eg, from northern locations and automated lighthouses. More capable weather stations are being procured to automate information for aviation and sensors are being developed for a wider range of weather elements. Other automatic stations are located in buoys or on ships. In one program a line of buoys is released between Hawaii and Alaska to drift with the ocean currents in towards the BC coast. Observations from automatic stations are reported through commercial wire services, through telephone call-up or data services, or through the satellite collection and retransmission services of American meteorological satellites and the French Argos system. The latter can also locate the positions of drifting buoys.

Canadian Observational Challenges are those associated with operating at low temperatures, both people and equipment, and with the measurement of snow and associated elements. The outdoor equipment must operate in the presence of freezing rain, rime icing and hoarfrost and down to -60°C in some areas of Canada. In unattended locations automatic weather stations must survive this cold and find a source of electrical power for their operation. Either heat is provided to take the chill off the electronics, or electronics are designed to operate at the lowest temperatures. For power there are special batteries, perhaps buried for protection against extreme cold, and solar panels to recharge them when the long winter night is over. The measurement of snow, of visibility in falling and blowing snow, and the accumulation of snow on the ground, are challenges shared with other polar nations. Rain and snow are collected in a reservoir of glycol antifreeze and weighed automatically. In mountainous regions snow accumulations can be measured with surface mounted hydraulic snow pillows. WILLIAM L. CLINK

Weathering processes cause the disintegration of rock materials in the Earth's uppermost layer. These mechanisms provide vital links between organic and inorganic elements of ecosystems and thus are crucial for the maintenance of life on Earth. Although in reality weathering processes are highly interactive, they may be grouped into 2 main types: mechanical (ie, physical) and chemical. Mechanical processes break up rock masses into fragments but cause no fundamental mineral alterations. Disintegration may be triggered in many ways. The long-term unloading of rock that was originally formed at great depths below the Earth's surface often produces sheetlike cracks

(dilatation joints). Intense heating of rock may set up expansion stresses sufficient to split boulders and separate sheets or flakes. Frost wedging is effective where there are freeze-thaw cycles, rapid subfreezing temperature declines, and significant free water in cracks and pore spaces. Particularly in forest environments, plant roots promote rock wedging by their penetration and growth; burrowing animals also contribute to the decomposition of earth materials. Salt weathering, by the growth and thermal expansion of salt crystals in rock and soil interstices, is probably of some importance in coastal zones, and possibly in polar desert ecosystems like those of Canadian higharctic latitudes.

Fragmented rock materials formed by mechanical weathering are normally larger than clay particles. These materials constitute major sources of sediment for later erosion, transportation and deposition under the impetus of gravity, wind, water or ice. To varying degrees, these relatively coarse-textured rock fragments also aid in the development of a soil cover at the Earth's surface. As mechanical weathering progresses through geologic time, increased surface areas per-unit volume of rock are developed. Chemical weathering processes are assisted by the consequent exposure of new minerals to their attack.

Chemical weathering involves the decomposition or rotting of rock by mineral transformations and by partial resyntheses of secondary weathering residues (including clay minerals). The major processes of chemical weathering are hydration-dehydration and hydrolysis (involving action of water), oxidation (involving oxygen), carbonation (activity of carbon dioxide dissolved in water), chelation (combination with a metal), fixation, reduction and solution. As the conversion of primary to secondary minerals continues, clay minerals accumulate in soil. These minerals are extremely important in the functioning of soil systems, particularly as base-exchangers between vegetation and mineral soil constituents. The amount and dominant types of clay minerals present in different soils also exert strong controls on water quality and transmission. Some clay minerals expand greatly when water saturated; others are comparatively water stable. Partly because of this and other weathering effects, slope stability generally declines as rock decomposition intensifies, the clay content of subsoil materials increases and rock shear strength below the soil is diminished by rotting. Many types of slope failure are directly attributable to the long-term effects of subsurface weathering processes (*see* LANDSLIDE, ROCKSLIDE).

Thus, weathering may be viewed as simultaneously performing a range of destructive and constructive functions. The destructive facets of rock decay through time provide the constructive skeleton of soil development (pedogenesis) and replenishment. In Canada, good expressions of deep, relatively intense chemical weathering occur in the warmest, moist environments of western BC and southern Ontario.

Many factors help determine the combinations of dominant weathering, sedimentary and pedogenic processes typifying different regions. Prevailing climate and vegetation types are of paramount importance. Wherever severe water shortages, extreme temperature regimes, or both, occur, many chemical weathering processes are inhibited and mechanical weathering achieves greater prominence. In Canada such ecosystems are best exemplified by high latitude tundra and by regions above the treeline in alpine zones. Even on stable sites in these areas, soil development is meagre because weathering processes are not able to produce significant soil-clay complexes. Predominant vegetation types have a closely reciprocal relationship with soils and weathering. Species which are not particularly base demanding, but which produce abundant organic acids, will concentrate leaching in the topsoil. Only the most resistant primary minerals, such as quartz, can repel the onslaught of organic acids, and secondary weathering products (including clays) are moved to some depth below the topsoil. Many boreal forest soil types are related to this general weathering regime.

Mineral susceptibility to chemical attack is highly variable, but rocks with high proportions of quartz are generally more resistant to weathering than others. Thus, the geologic setting of particular regions partially controls the effectiveness of the weathering processes (*see* GEOLOGICAL REGIONS). Geologic "inheritance" may assume great importance: certain types of sedimentary environments favour accumulation of clays; others concentrate quartz-rich sands or gravels. Further, because much of Canada has only recently (in geologic time) emerged from the covering masses of Pleistocene ice sheets (*see* GLACIATION), weathering and other pedogenic processes have had only a few thousand years in which to work. *See also* LANDFORM REGIONS.   BRUCE RAINS

Weaver, Robert, literary editor (b at Niagara Falls, Ont 6 Jan 1921). Weaver grew up in Niagara Falls and Toronto, and before graduating from U of T worked briefly for a bank and in the RCAF and the army. Appointed program organizer in the Talks and Public Affairs Department of the CBC in 1948, Weaver created programs such as "CBC Stage," "CBC Playhouse," "Canadian Short Stories," and "CBC Tuesday Night" (later the popular "Anthology") and provided much-needed outlets for Canadian talent. He founded the TAMARACK REVIEW, a leading literary quarterly (1956), and co-edited the *Oxford Anthology of Canadian Literature* (1973). He is perhaps best known as editor of numerous anthologies in both verse and prose, including the *Canadian Short Stories* editions (1952, 1960, 1968, 1978, 1985) and *The Anthology Anthology: A Selection from Thirty Years of CBC Radio's "Anthology."* Although he took early retirement from the CBC in 1985, he continues to oversee its annual literary competition and was appointed fiction editor of *Saturday Night* in 1988. He is an unflagging inspirational voice, offering constant encouragement to writers through frequent conversations and faithful correspondence.   DONNA COATES

Weaving Long before loom weaving was developed, woven and coiled baskets were made from grasses, twigs, root fibres and leaves readily collected from indigenous plants and worked with the hands. Basketry forms have changed little to the present day. Spinning was first used in the production of simple ropes, cords and fishing lines and, later, to create yarns. More complex forms of weaving gradually evolved from basketry and a new tool, the loom, was developed. The loom allowed the interlacing of fibres to make a continuous web (or fabric) composed of 2 sets of threads at right angles to one another: warp threads, stretched under tension down the length, and weft threads, interlaced across the width. In primitive looms the tension on the warp is created by weighting the threads with stones, just as primitive spinning uses a drop spindle under the force of gravity. As the requirements of the loom (stronger threads) brought about changes in yarns (simple and compound) and vice versa, these simple devices developed into modern TEXTILE technology. Tapestry weaving coincided with the invention of loom weaving, but tapestry is worked on a loom of different type. In tapestry the weft threads cover the warp in a discontinuous fashion. Early tapestries often told a story in pic-

tures; modern ones rarely do so. Early settlers in Canada brought advanced weaving skills with them and their home industry satisfied the community's textile needs. INDUSTRIALIZATION caused a decline in home spinning and weaving, but interest has renewed in recent years. There are an estimated 7000 or 8000 weavers in Ontario, Québec and BC, and weavers' guilds exist in most large communities in Canada.

Since the 1960s some craftsmen have moved away from traditional weaving into "art fabric," experimenting with traditional techniques but using a wide range of materials in the production of unique works. They usually sell through galleries, or their work is commissioned for public places and private homes. Two notable weavers, principally in tapestry, Joanna Staniszkis of BC and Micheline Beauchemin of Québec, have been recipients of the Saidye Bronfman award for excellence in CRAFTS.

From PREHISTORY, Canadian Indians and Inuit had a knowledge of basketry, a craft, like weaving, usually undertaken by women. The Salishan peoples of the Northwest Coast have had a long history of textile manufacture, using mountain-goat hair, fireweed and woolly dog hair; most famous are the CHILKAT BLANKETS (*see* NORTHWEST COAST INDIAN ART). Native Canadians have revived many of these skills, including basketry, in recent years. The NOOTKA of Vancouver I plait grass, cherry and cedar baskets; the INUIT of Great Whale R make lidded baskets of lime grass, often incorporating soapstone knops; the Micmac, Maliseet and Ontarian Indians customarily use split ash. The Salish weavers of BC are unique in re-establishing a flourishing home industry, using locally grown wool and natural dyes in their own authentic tradition. All this work, and that of many other talented weavers across Canada, is sought after and the economic effect is considerable, although it may only be a supplementary income for many because of the time, care and skill that are still the hallmarks of the dedicated weaver.
                                  DEIRDRE SPENCER

Webb, Phyllis, poet, broadcaster (b at Victoria 8 Apr 1927). Author of several books of poetry and one of broadcast scripts, essays and reviews, Webb is a writer of stature in Canadian letters. Her work is brilliantly crafted, formal in its energies and humane in its concern. In Webb's poetry there is a sadness about the pomposities of human nature, variegated with a visionary sympathy with natural life and landscape, and with the human impulse toward freedom. Webb's political activities, her work as a public-affairs broadcaster and her interest in political theory infuse her work with a concern for public life.

Webb attended UBC (BA) and McGill. Her first collection of poems appeared in *Trio* (1954). *Even Your Right Eye* was published in 1956, and in 1957 she won a grant enabling her to study drama and theatre in France. In 1962, *The Sea Is Also a Garden* appeared, followed by *Naked Poems*, a series of intense, haiku-like poems, in 1965. From 1964 to 1969, Webb worked at CBC Toronto, first in public affairs and then, 1967-69, as executive producer of the program "Ideas." Returning to the West Coast in 1969, Webb eventually took up permanent residence on Saltspring I. In 1971, her *Selected Poems 1954-65* was published. *Wilson's Bowl* (1980) is an important collection of poems written during the 1970s. *Talking* (1982) is a collection of some of Webb's reviews, articles and CBC broadcasts, and a new selection of poems, *The Vision Tree*, appeared the same year. *Water and Light*, a series of poems corresponding with the ghazal form of Persian poetry, was published in 1984. She has taught at UBC, U Vic, U of A and the Banff Centre.   SHARON THESEN

Webb Zerafa Menkès Housden Partnership, est 1961, has offices throughout Canada, the US, the Middle East, Europe and New Zealand and ranks as the largest Canadian architectural firm and the third largest in N America. Earning fees of about $20 million a year, the firm has contributed to the transformation of many Canadian cities, with its designs for the corporate headquarters of major oil companies, insurance companies and banks. Among its many projects are the Royal Bank Building, Toronto (1976); City Hall, Calgary (1985); Waterfront Park, Phase I, Halifax (1988); Canada Place, Edmonton (1988), and Maison des Coopérant, Montréal (completion in 1989). In its more than 25-year history, the firm has been awarded virtually every architectural award available.

Weber, Anna, folk painter, fraktur artist (b in Earl Twp, Lancaster County, Pa 3 June 1814; d in Woolwich Twp, Waterloo County, Ont 12 Oct 1888). Weber immigrated to UC in 1825 and, following the death of her parents, moved from one Mennonite family to another until her own death. She painted watercolour panels for friends in traditional German heraldic styles that incorporated motifs of tulips, doves, peacocks and horses. Simple and rich in religious overtones, these works are fine examples of Canadian folk paintings. Many are still preserved by descendants of the original owners.   J. RUSSELL HARPER

Webster, John Clarence, physician, historian, nationalist (b at Shediac, NB 21 Oct 1863; d there 16 Mar 1950). Educated in Shediac and at Mount Allison and Edinburgh universities, from 1890 to 1896 he was an assistant instructor at Edinburgh and Berlin. He was assistant gynaecologist 1896-99 at Royal Victoria Hospital in Montréal and lecturer at McGill. While in Montréal he co-operated with Lady ABERDEEN in the founding of the VICTORIAN ORDER OF NURSES. Webster left Canada to take up the appointment of professor of obstetrics and gynaecology at U of Chicago Rush Medical Centre (1899) with accompanying hospital appointments. He retired to Shediac in 1919 and began an entirely new career. Fascinated with history since his youth, he now took up the field full time. He amassed a library on N American history, and then collected some 9000 artifacts and visual representations of that history. In 1922 he was asked to become a member of the Historic Sites and Monuments Board. He remained on the board until 1949, becoming its chairman in 1940. His major historical work, *Acadia at the End of the Seventeenth Century*, still sells well. In 1935, for his services to Canada, he was made a Commander of the Order of St Michael and St George and awarded the Order of Merit by King George V. By the time of his death, he had received awards and honours from kings, governments and universities in Great Britain, France, Italy, the US and Canada.   GERALD THOMAS

Webster, John Edgar, "Jack," journalist, broadcaster (b at Glasgow, Scot 15 Apr 1918). He was pre-eminent among British Columbia public affairs broadcasters for his knowledge of the province's affairs, his probing and pugnacious approach to his interview subjects, and his ability to make news himself. Late in 1947, he immigrated to Canada and worked on the Vancouver *Sun* until 1953. That year he began a program on CJOR radio called "City Mike." During this period his hard-hitting daily reports on a police scandal in Vancouver created a sensation. In 1963 Webster found his metier in an "open line" radio program. By championing those with grievances against authority, Webster became in effect an ombudsman, helping, for example, to bring about improvements in the care of severely retarded children, to improve the legal aid system, and to better the administration of care for the elderly. In 1978, when Webster was planning to retire, he was offered a daily open line show on BCTV. He has repeated his success on television. He retired from the show in May 1987 but made known his intention to continue making occasional TV appearances while working on his autobiography. During that same month, he was inducted into the Canadian News Hall of Fame. CHUCK DAVIS

Webster, Lorne Campbell, financier (b at Montréal 19 Sept 1928). Educated at Lower Canada College and McGill, Webster started his business career with the family fuel-oil company, Canadian Import. In 1968 he founded his own firm, Prenor Group, a holding company with major investments in insurance (through Canadian Provident, Northern Life, Paragon and Personal insurance companies), trust services (with the General Trust of Canada and North America Trust), real estate (through Armand DesRosiers Inc) and investment management (with Bolton Tremblay). Webster has also been a director of the Bank of Montreal, Domtar, Murphy Oil, Quebecor, Dale-Ross Holdings and several other companies. JORGE NIOSI

Webster, Norman Eric, journalist (b at Summerside, PEI 4 June 1941). Educated at Bishops College School and then at Bishops U, Webster won a Rhodes scholarship to Oxford. Returning to Canada, he joined the *Globe and Mail* and served successfully in the newspaper's bureaus in Québec C and Ottawa. He then worked as editor of the Saturday supplement, the *Globe Magazine* (now defunct), before leaving for a stint as Beijing [Peking] correspondent. It was in the unlikely role as the paper's commentator on Ontario provincial affairs that he won a faithful following during the 1970s, before undertaking a stint as European correspondent. He then joined the editorial staff and has been editor-in-chief since 1983. Webster also served as a financial angel to the magazine *Saturday Night*, enabling it to survive one of its periodic spasms of fiscal trouble. In 1987 he sold his interest in the magazine to Conrad Black. ROBERT BOTHWELL

Weeds are plants growing where humans do not want them. Their undesirable qualities are varied: they deprive crop plants of sunlight, water and mineral nutrients; can be poisonous to humans or domestic animals; act as hosts for plant diseases, destructive insects and other pests; contaminate milk or other agricultural products; bear spines or thorns; cause allergies such as hay fever. Weeds are found not just in agricultural areas but also in forests, lakes, recreational areas, roadsides and all other sites of human activity.

Weeds belong to virtually all plant families. They include algae, primitive vascular plants (eg, field horsetail, *Equisetum arvense,* and bracken fern, *Pteridium aquilinum*), low creeping annuals (eg, purslane, *Portulaca oleracea*), tall coarse herbs (eg, lamb's-quarters, *Chenopodium album*), vines (eg, field bindweed, *Convolvulus arvensis*), parasites (eg, dodder, *Cuscuta*), shrubs (eg, common barberry, *Berberis vulgaris*) and trees (eg, Manitoba maple, *Acer negundo*). Weeds have the following attributes: rank, vigorous growth; rapid maturation; vigorous regrowth after damage; abundant seed production; intermittent germination of seeds over many years; underground spread of roots or rhizomes. No single weed excels in all these attributes, but all have several.

In agriculture, weeds are estimated to cause more losses than destructive insects and plant diseases combined. Until the mid-1950s, the principal means of control was cultivation. Increasingly sophisticated cultivators, first horse drawn and then tractor drawn, made the task easier, but

much of the labour involved in crop production was for weed control. The development, early in the century, of seed-cleaning plants where weed contaminants were removed from crop seeds, was a major step in weed control. The Canada Seeds Act classifies crop seeds according to weed seed content. Grain exports must have less than a specified minimum content of weed seeds, and seeds of species designated as noxious are subject to the most stringent rules.

Chemical Control of Weeds began around 1950 with widespread use of 2,4-D. At present in Canada, more than 100 chemicals are licensed for sale as herbicides. Millions of dollars are spent on them annually, but this sum is less than would otherwise be spent on weed removal from fields and harvested crops. Federal and provincial legislation is designed to ensure that herbicides are marketed and applied safely. Modern farmers attempt integrated weed control by a combination of chemical means and tillage. The advent of chemical herbicides has modified, but not eliminated, the weed problem. Across the prairies, infestations of weeds (eg, wild mustard, *Sinapis arvensis*) have been reduced, but species tolerant of common herbicides (eg, green foxtail, *Setaria viridis*) have greatly increased. Similar shifts in weed populations involving various species have occurred in other agricultural regions. In the 1970s, herbicide-resistant forms of several common weeds began to appear. Lamb's-quarters, common groundsel (*Senecio vulgaris*) and redroot pigweed (*Amaranthus retroflexus*) all now have forms that are resistant to the popular triazine herbicides.

Biological Control of Weeds usually involves the introduction of an insect or a fungus species to control an introduced weed, and has been attempted in many parts of Canada. In the interior of BC, Saint-John's-wort (*Hypericum perforatum*) has been controlled by beetles. In the same area, the reduction of knapweeds (*Centaurea*) by both insects and fungi is being tried. The targets are usually perennial species in uncultivated land.

Canada's largest and most important agricultural area encompasses the southern part of the Prairie provinces. In cultivated land in Saskatchewan and Manitoba, the most abundant weed (in a 1976-79 survey) was green foxtail; second and third were wild oats (*Avena fatua*) and wild buckwheat (*Polygonum convolvulus*). Other common weeds of Canadian agricultural land are dandelion (*Taraxacum officinale*), Canada thistle (*Cirsium arvense*), common milkweed (*Asclepias syriaca*), leafy spurge (*Euphorbia esula*), pigweeds (*Amaranthus*), sow thistles (*Sonchus*) and ragweeds (*Ambrosia*).

Weeds of other habitats include poison ivy (*Rhus radicans*) in woodlands, and common plantain (*Plantago major*) and white clover (*Trifolium repens*) in lawns. The introduced submerged aquatic weed, Eurasian water milfoil (*Myriophyllum spicatum*), poses a multifaceted problem in lakes, canals and streams across southern Canada, much as our native elodea (*Elodea canadensis*) did in Europe in the 1800s. Weeds may have desirable qualities. White clover is a useful pasture plant. Sweet clovers (*Melilotus*) are dangerous roadside weeds because they attract bees near passing cars and obscure road signs, but they are valuable short-term hay and pasture plants and are a source of honey. *See also* INSECTS, BENEFICIAL; INSECT PESTS; PESTICIDES.

PAUL B. CAVERS

Reading: G.A. Mulligan, *Common Weeds of Canada* (1976).

Weekend Magazine began publication in Sept 1951, distributed free of charge with 9 daily NEWSPAPERS across the country. *Weekend* offered high-

quality colour reproduction to advertisers, good photographs, feature stories and recipes to readers, and a profit-making supplement that boosted circulation for the newspaper publishers. By the 1960s *Weekend Magazine* was carried in 41 newspapers with a circulation over 2 million, and it was the most popular ADVERTISING vehicle in the nation. Colour television and the turn away from general-interest periodicals hurt the magazine, and it got thinner each year. By 1979 it had been merged with *The Canadian*, and in 1982 *Today*, the successor supplement, ceased publication. *See also* MAGAZINES. J.L. GRANATSTEIN

Weightlifting has been an Olympic sport since the first modern Games in 1896. It also figures in the Commonwealth, Pan-American, Asian, Mediterranean and African Games. Counting more than 120 nations, the International Weightlifting Federation is one of the largest federations in the world. There are approximately 1200 members of the Canadian Weightlifting Federation.

This spectacular indoor sport is composed of 2 events: the snatch and the clean and jerk. In the snatch, the athlete lifts the bar to arms' length in one continuous motion. In the clean and jerk, he lifts the bar to his shoulders, then jerks it overhead to arms' length. The athlete is allowed a total of 3 attempts in each event. The best snatch is added to the best clean and jerk to give a total result. Medals are awarded in each event, with the overall winner being determined by the total. Competitors are divided into 10 bodyweight categories, ranging from 52 kg to plus 110 kg. (However, these divisions are to be reviewed at the 1988 Olympic Congress in Seoul, S Korea.) In case of a tie, the lighter athlete is declared the winner. Both events, which demand great speed, balance, flexibility and strength, are performed on a 4 m square platform before 3 judges. A team is composed of a maximum of 10 athletes. The apparatus used in competition is standardized by the IWF and all equipment is manufactured to metric specifications.

The legendary figure of early Canadian weightlifting was strong-man Louis CYR, who in competition resulting from his open challenge to any man in the world was undefeated. Among his many outstanding feats were lifting 250 kg with

Louis Cyr, the legendary figure of early Canadian weightlifting (*courtesy National Archives of Canada*).

one finger and lifting (in Boston in 1895) 4337 pounds (1967 kg) on his back – claimed to be the greatest weight ever lifted by one man. In formal competition G. Gratton won a silver medal at the 1952 Helsinki Olympic Games, Doug HEPBURN won the world heavyweight championship in Stockholm 1953 and Jacques Demers won a silver medal (75 kilo class) at the 1984 Los Angeles Olympics. In the 1987 Pan-Am Games, Canadian weightlifters won 2 gold, 3 silver and 3 bronze medals. The gold medals were won by Denis Garon of Québec and Daniel Bolduc of Montréal in the heavyweight and superheavyweight divisions respectively.　　　　RICHARD CAMPION

Weights and Measures, terms which traditionally referred to standards of mass (or weight), length and volume. Over the past few thousand years such standards have frequently been introduced throughout the world for trading and tax purposes. However, as measurement is one of the most fundamental aspects of science and engineering, the term now embraces a much wider gamut of units. The development and dissemination of measurement standards has become the science of metrology. To the original basic units of mass and length (volume is a derived unit) have been added other "base units": time, temperature, electric current, luminosity, and the somewhat esoteric amount-of-substance unit. These base units and a large number of derived units are rigorously defined in the International System of Units (Système International d'Unités, or SI), a version of the metric system, formulated by and under the aegis of the International Bureau of Weights and Measures (BIPM). First adopted in 1960, the SI is not invariant but evolves slowly in the interests of greater precision, convenience or internal consistency. Virtually all of the world's scientific work is reported in SI units; construction, engineering and commerce substantially use or will use the system in all major countries except the US and Great Britain, which still largely use the British imperial system.

In 1965 the British government expressed its intention to convert to the SI over a 10-year period; in 1972 the US Senate favoured a voluntary 10-year conversion, but because of a procedural point this suggestion was not endorsed by the House of Representatives. In both countries progress towards metrication has been sporadic and a completion date cannot plausibly be forecast for either. Canada has been converting from the imperial system to SI since 1971; the process is now (1988) largely completed but with residual, and visible, exceptions in retail trade and advertising.

Canada's former measurement system derived mainly from the imperial system, with some contribution from a French measurement system. The imperial system was codified in its first reasonably "scientific" form in 1838, following a complex history. A number of imperial units (eg, foot, mile) can be traced back to the Roman Empire; however, their magnitude has fluctuated with time and locality. R.E. Zupko's *A Dictionary of English Weights and Measures, from Anglo-Saxon Times to the Nineteenth Century* contains entries for some 3000 measurement units with 25 000 nu-

merical variations. In 1884 the UK (hence Canada, as a colony) became an adherent of the Convention of the Metre, by which the BIPM had been established in 1875. The UK was thus a participant in the first distribution by the BIPM of national prototype metre bars and kilogram masses in 1889. Canada became an adherent to the convention in its own right in 1907. A Canadian, J.C. MACLENNAN, was a member of the International Committee of Weights and Measures (CIPM) from 1929 to 1935. This committee is charged with the direction and supervision of the BIPM, including its metrological laboratories at Sèvres on the outskirts of Paris. There has been a Canadian presence on the CIPM continuously since 1951; one of them, L.E. Howlett, served as CIPM president for the period 1964-68. No country is represented on the CIPM; the 18 members (not more than one per country) are elected in a personal capacity. Their task is to monitor and foster metric-based metrology in all nations adhering to the Convention of the Metre (47 in 1988).

Since 1951 Canadian CIPM members have all been members of the NATIONAL RESEARCH COUNCIL. NRC's Division of Physics maintains or realizes the country's primary standards of measurement and many derived standards. Standards disseminated to laboratories and industries requiring the highest precision are calibrated at NRC. The reference standards for trade (periodically calibrated at NRC) are in the custody of the Dept of CONSUMER AND CORPORATE AFFAIRS and constitute the legal basis for all local standards employed in the application of the Canadian Weights and Measures Act (1971) to commercial or trade transactions (*see* CONSUMER STANDARDS). In 1982 Canada joined the International Organization of Legal Metrology (OIML, est 1955). The OIML is concerned only with the application of metrology to trade, eg, in establishing uniformity in international trading practices.

All major industrial countries support national standards laboratories equivalent to that of NRC, eg, the National Bureau of Standards in the US and the National Physical Laboratory in the UK. Elaborate control and comparison procedures ensure measurement consistency among national laboratories. For nations such as Canada, measurement standards are now secure, and adequate monitoring has reduced fraudulent measure to an incidental problem. This achievement

eluded all efforts until well into the 20th century. The reasons for failure were many, but the major one was undoubtedly human cupidity. Today's relatively happy situation is one of the benefits of modern technology coupled with a technological infrastructure so pervasive that we now take it for granted.

International System of Units (SI)

The following descriptions of the 7 SI base units and the 2 SI supplementary units include 1987 estimates of reproducibilities. These estimates are based on measurements of the highest quality made at various places and times, and are applicable to measurements at unit magnitude.

Some SI Derived Units with Special Names

Quantity	Unit (Symbol)	Derivation
Mechanical		
force	newton (N)	$(m \cdot kg)/s^2$
pressure	pascal (Pa)	N/m^2
energy, work	joule (J)	$N \cdot m$
power	watt (W)	J/s
frequency	hertz (Hz)	cycles/s
Electrical		
electrical potential	volt (V)	W/A
electrical resistance	ohm (Ω)	V/A
electric charge	coulomb (C)	$A \cdot s$
electric capacitance	farad (F)	C/V
magnetic flux	weber (Wb)	$V \cdot s$
magnetic flux density	tesla (T)	Wb/m^2
inductance	henry (H)	Wb/A
Light		
luminous flux	lumen (lm)	$cd \cdot sr$
illuminance	lux (lx)	lm/m^2
Nuclear and X-Ray Dosimetry [1]		
activity (of radionuclide)	becquerel (Bq)	disintegrations/s
absorbed dose	gray (Gy)	J/kg
dose equivalent	sievert (Sv)	J/kg

[1] Relations to the earlier curie, rad and rem are as follows: one curie is 3.7×10^{10} Bq; one rad is 0.01 Gy; one rem is 0.01 Sv

Some non-SI Units in Use in North America

Unit (Symbol)	Definition	Approximate SI Value
Length		
parsec (pc)		3.086×10^{16} m
light-year		9.461×10^{15} m
astronomical unit (AU)		1.496×10^{11} m
nautical mile	1.852 km	
mile (mi)	8 furlongs, 1760 yd	1.609 km
furlong	220 yd	201.2 m
arpent	180 Paris feet	58.47 m
yard (yd)	3 ft	0.9144 m
Paris foot	12.789 in	0.3248 m
foot ("ft" or ')	12 in	0.3048 m
inch ("in" or ")	25.4 mm	
Area		
acre	(1/640) mi² or 4840 yd²	4047 m²
arpent de superficie	32 400 square Paris feet	3419 m²
hectare (ha)	1000 m²	
Mass (Weight)		
Avoirdupois:		
tonne	1 Mg	
long ton	2 240 lb	1.016 t
short ton	2 000 lb	0.907 t
long hundredweight (cwt)	112 lb	50.80 kg
short hundredweight (cwt)	100 lb	45.36 kg
pound (lb)	0.453 592 37 kg	
ounce (oz)	(1/16) lb	28.35 g
dram (dr)	(1/16) oz	1.772 g
grain (gr)	(1/7000) lb	64.80 mg
Troy (or Apothecary):		
pound (lb t)	12 oz t	0.3732 kg
ounce (oz t)	20 dwt	31.10 g
pennyweight (dwt)	24 gr	1.555 g
Capacity		
barrel (bbl)	36 gal	163.7 L
barrel [US] [1]	42 gal [US]	159.0 L
bushel (bu)	4 pk	36.37 L
bushel [US]	8 gal [US]	30.28 L
peck (pk)	2 gal	9.092 L
gallon (gal)	4.54609 L	
gallon [US]	231 cu in	3.785 L
quart (qt)	(1/4) gal	1.137 L
pint (pt)	(1/2) qt	568.3 mL
litre (L or l)	10 dm³	
Miscellaneous		
British thermal unit (Btu) [2]		1 055 J
Btu per hour		0.2931 kW
calorie [3]		4.184 J
carat	200 mg	
fahrenheit (°F)	(t)°F=(9/5) (t)°C + 32	
horsepower [4]	550 ft·lb/sec	745.7 W
knot	1 nautical mile per hour	0.5144 m/s

[1] This is the barrel used by the oil industry
[2] Based on the heat required to heat one pound of water 1°F
[3] Based on the heat required to heat one gram of water 1°C. The "food calorie" used by dieticians is a kilocalorie
[4] Here lb refers to the force pound-weight, not to the mass pound. The correct, but very seldom used, formulation is 550 ft·lb·g/s, where g is the acceleration due to gravity

SI Prefixes

Factor	Prefix	Symbol	Factor	Prefix	Symbol
10^1	deca	da	10^{-1}	deci	d
10^2	hecto	h	10^{-2}	centi	c
10^3	kilo	k	10^{-3}	milli	m
10^6	mega	M	10^{-6}	micro	μ
10^9	giga	G	10^{-9}	nano	n
10^{12}	tera	T	10^{-12}	pico	p
10^{15}	peta	P	10^{-15}	femto	f
10^{18}	exa	E	10^{-18}	atto	a

Imprecision will increase at substantially greater or smaller magnitudes; thus, while a mass of one kilogram can be determined to within about 2 parts in 10^9, masses of a gram can be determined only to within 3 parts in 10 million (3 in 10^7); those of a tonne, to within one part per million (1 in 10^6).

Length When adopted in 1799, the metre (m) was fixed as one ten-millionth part of a quadrant of the Earth's meridian. In 1983 it was defined as the distance light travels in a vacuum in one 299 792 458th of a second. Reproducibility is 2 parts in 10^{11}.

Mass The unit of mass is the kilogram (kg), not the gram (g). When adopted in 1799, the kilogram was defined as the mass of a cubic decimetre of water. Since 1889 it has been the mass of the international prototype kilogram, a platinum-iridium artifact kept at Sèvres. Reproducibility is 2 parts in 10^9.

Time The second (s), traditionally one 86 400th of a mean solar day, was established in 1960 as one 31 556 925.9744th of the tropical year 1900. In 1968 it was defined in terms of the frequency radiated from the transition between specified energy levels of the cesium-133 atom. Measurement accuracy is 5 parts in 10^{14}.

Electric Current The ampere (A) was defined in 1881 in terms of the force between magnetic poles (a purely theoretical concept); in 1908 as a more reproducible "international ampere" in electrolytic terms. Since 1948 the "absolute ampere" has been defined in terms of the force between parallel, current-carrying conductors. However, in practice electric units are maintained in terms of the ohm and the volt. Reproducibility is 1 part in 10^7.

Temperature (kelvin, K) is the only base unit that is "intensive" rather than "extensive" (ie, 2 temperatures cannot be added together to give their sum). This characteristic presents certain measurement difficulties. The present International Practical Temperature Scale of 1968 evolved from the "hydrogen temperature scale" of 1889; it is likely to be superseded in 1990. Measurements are accurate to within 0.0002 K at room temperature. Significant celsius equivalents are 273.15 K = 0°C and 373.15 K = 100°C.

Amount of Substance The mole (mol) is a quantity which serves to connect the macroscopic SI units to measurements used in chemistry and atomic physics. A 1902 convention using oxygen-16 as a standard was superseded in 1960-61 by one using carbon-12; the latter standard was incorporated into the SI in 1971. The mole is the amount of substance which contains as many elementary particles (atoms, molecules, ions, etc; the precise ones under consideration must be specified) as there are atoms in 0.012 kg of carbon-12. In some circumstances, relative atomic weights can be determined to one part in 10^7. The absolute value of the mole is known to about 1 part per million (1 in 10^6).

Luminous Intensity The candela (cd) is one of various "standard candles" which have been in use since before 1800. The candela (then called "new candle") was first defined in 1946 in terms of the freezing temperature of platinum. The present definition is a monochromatic (f = 540 x 10^{12} Hz) radiant intensity of 1/683 watt per steradian. Reproducibility is 3 parts per thousand.

Plane Angle The radian (rad) is the plane angle between 2 radii of a circle that cut off (from its circumference) an arc equal in length to the radius. Thus a full circle (360 arc degrees) is an angle of 2 π rad. Measurement accuracy is 5 x 10^{-7} rad or 0.1 arc second.

Solid Angle The steradian (sr) is the solid angle which, having its vertex at the centre of a sphere, cuts off an area of the surface of the sphere equal to that of a square with sides of length equal to the radius of the sphere. Thus the solid angle of an entire sphere is 4 π sr.

The SI is essentially a decimal system, ie, units are related by factors of 10, expressed in prefixes attached to the unit name. Many quantities derived from the base units and which could be expressed in terms of those units are more conveniently designated by special names and symbols. Some non-SI units are used with the SI because they are in worldwide use (eg, hour, knot, nautical mile). Others, eg, the hectare, tonne and litre are not SI units but are used conjointly with the SI for convenience. H. PRESTON-THOMAS

Weinzweig, John Jacob, composer, educator, administrator (b at Toronto 11 Mar 1913). A pioneer of 20th-century composing methods in Canada – the first Canadian to explore 12-tone technique – he created a body of music indispensable to the Canadian repertoire and influenced several generations of young composers who were his students. When he graduated from U of T in 1937, Weinzweig's interest in contemporary composition drew him to the Eastman School of Music in Rochester, NY, for graduate studies. In 1939 he began to teach at the Toronto Conservatory and became composition professor at U of T in 1956, continuing there until his retirement in 1978. Deeply committed to the concerns of career composers, Weinzweig played an important part in the establishment of several support organizations, including the Canadian League of Composers (1951) and the Canadian Music Centre (1959). Weinzweig's ballet suite, *Red Ear of Corn* (1949), is probably his best-known work, though the series of *Divertimenti* (1946-) for various solo instruments and string orchestra offer a more representative view of his music. In 1974 he was made an Officer of the Order of Canada. In 1988 a monograph on Weinzweig was to be released as part of the Canadian Music Centre series.

BARCLAY MCMILLAN

Reading: Peter Such, "John Weinzweig," *Soundprints* (1972).

Composer John Weinzweig (*photo by Ruth Kaplan*).

Weir, Walter C., mortician, politician, premier of Manitoba 1967-69 (b at High Bluff, Man 7 Jan 1929; d at Minnedosa, Man 17 Apr 1985). A Progressive Conservative, Weir was elected to the Manitoba legislature in 1959. He served consecutively as minister of municipal affairs and then as minister of highways under Duff ROBLIN. Of great personal charm, he was popular among his caucus and Cabinet colleagues, and their support enabled him to secure the party leadership in 1967.

More conservative than his predecessor, Weir braked the pace of reform established by Roblin. In fact the principal aspects of his brief administration were government restraint, caution about medicare and opposition to federal proposals for constitutional reform and official bilingualism. Misjudging the public mood in 1969, he called an election ahead of schedule and was beaten by the NDP. Widely blamed for the Tory defeat, Weir retired from politics soon after the Manitoba Conservatives set up a process of leadership review in 1970. During the Sterling LYON premiership, he served as chairman of a government commission on local taxation. GEOFFREY LAMBERT

Weldon, Richard Chapman, educator, politician (b at Sussex, NB 19 Jan 1849; d at Dartmouth, NS 26 Nov 1925). His education was unusually broad for his day: BA (1866) and MA (1870) from Mount Allison; he received his doctorate in international law from Yale at age 23. Returning to Mount Allison, he was appointed professor of political economy and mathematics, but after a year took leave to study public law at Heidelberg. Thus equipped he became a pioneer in legal education, being co-founder of Dalhousie Law School in 1883 and its first dean 1884-1914. Dalhousie was the first university law school in the common-law provinces; under Weldon's guidance it offered a systematic and liberal course of instruction, in contrast to the haphazard program of legal apprenticeship then prevalent. A prominent Conservative, he was MP, 1887-96, and a friend of Sir John THOMPSON. D.H. BROWN

Welfare State is a term that was apparently first used in the English language in 1941 in a book written by William Temple, Archbishop of York, England. For many years after, postwar British society was frequently characterized (often pejoratively) as a "welfare state," but by the 1960s the term commonly denoted an industrial capitalist society in which state power was "deliberately used (through politics and administration) in an effort to modify the play of market forces." For Asa Briggs, the author of this definition in an article appearing in *The Welfare State* (1967), there are 3 types of welfare state activities: provision of minimum income, provision for the reduction of economic insecurity resulting from such "contingencies" as sickness, old age and unemployment, and provision to all members of society of a range of social services. By this definition, Canada became a welfare state after the passage of the social welfare reforms of the 1960s (*see* SOCIAL SECURITY).

Richard Titmuss, one of the most influential writers on the welfare state, noted in *Essays on the Welfare State* (1959) that the social welfare system may be larger than the welfare state, a distinction of particular importance in Canada, where the social services component of the welfare state is less well developed. In addition to occupational welfare, there is a range of services provided by parapublic, trade union, church, and nonprofit institutions. These are often funded by a combination of state and private sources.

Social Welfare and Social Philosophy To some writers, the expansion of the welfare state is a central political focus of SOCIAL DEMOCRACY because of the contribution of welfare state policies and programs to the reduction of inequality, the expansion of freedom, the promotion of fellowship and democracy, and the expression of humanitarianism. In Canada such a view of the welfare state appeared in the LEAGUE FOR SOCIAL RECONSTRUCTION'S *Social Planning for Canada* (1935) and in the reports of social reformers, such as Leonard MARSH's classic, *Report on Social Security for Canada* (1943), written for the wartime Advisory Committee on Reconstruction. Politically, this view has been expressed in the platforms of the NEW DEMOCRATIC PARTY (NDP) and its predecessor the CO-OPERATIVE COMMONWEALTH FEDERATION (CCF), and practised most notably by the postwar CCF government in Saskatchewan. However, it is the modern liberal conception of the role of the state in the provision of social welfare that has been dominant.

In 20th-century liberalism, as practised in Canada and elsewhere, the responsibility for well-being rests with either the individual or the FAMILY, or with both. Simultaneously, there is a clear acceptance that capitalist economies are not self-regulating but require significant levels of state intervention to achieve stability. In relation to Briggs's definition, there is an emphasis in liberalism on the first 2 of the 3 welfare state activities: minimum income and social insurance. The necessity to develop a more cautious and residual social welfare state has been the theme of a number of major statements and reports by British writers J.M. Keynes and William Beveridge, and of the Canadian Report of the Royal Commission on Dominion-Provincial Relations (1940), the postwar White Paper on Employment and Income (1945) and the more recent federal Working Paper on Social Security in Canada (1973). It is an approach expressed in Mackenzie KING's *Industry and Humanity* (1918), Harry Cassidy's *Social Security and Reconstruction in Canada* (1943), and also in Tom KENT's *Social Policy for Canada* (1962), which presaged the period of high social reform, 1963 to 1968.

The modern conservative conception of the welfare state is guided by the principles of 19th-century liberalism, ie, less government equals more liberty, from which follows the defence of individual pursuit of self-interest and the unleashing of competitive forces operating through private markets (*see* CONSERVATISM). The reduction of inequality, often held to be a goal if not a result of the welfare state, is considered antithetical to the pursuit of freedom and to material progress.

Consequently the modern welfare state is criticized from the conservative perspective. In particular, it is often argued that social expenditures have become too heavy a burden for the modern state and that state expenditures on social programs divert resources from private markets, thus hampering economic growth. According to the conservative conception, the welfare state has discouraged people from seeking work and has created a large, centralized, uncontrolled and unproductive bureaucracy. Proponents of this view argue that the welfare state must be cut down and streamlined, and that many of its welfare activities should be turned over to charity.

This view of the welfare state is supported in Canada by members of the federal Progressive Conservative Party and BC's Social Credit Party. The idea of the conservative welfare state had its clearest expression in Charlotte WHITTON's *The Dawn of Ampler Life* (1943) commissioned by John BRACKEN, then Conservative Party leader, to criticize the social democratic views incorporated in Marsh's *Report on Social Security for Canada*; it also appears in the work of the FRASER INSTITUTE, in the West in the writings of former Alberta premier E.C. Manning and, in Québec, in the publications of the Semaines sociales du Canada.

The re-examination of contemporary capitalist societies begun in the 1960s has produced a Marxist interpretation of the welfare state. From this point of view, a major role of the modern state is the provision of an appropriately trained, educated, housed and disciplined labour force available to employers when and where necessary. To accomplish this the welfare state becomes involved in the regulation of women, children and the family through laws affecting marriage, divorce, contraception, separation, adoption, and child support (since the family is the institution directly concerned with the preparation of present and future generations of workers) and in provisions for employment, education, housing, and public and private health.

Development of a Welfare State in Canada

Social welfare in Canada has passed through roughly 4 phases of development, that correspond to 4 phases of the country's economic, political and domestic development.

The Early Period: 1840-1890 In the early period of capitalist development, the activities of the state, initiated in response to POVERTY and disease, were largely regulatory in nature. Social welfare, considered a matter that was primarily of local and private concern, consisted of the provision of relief, the care of the insane and of handicapped and neglected children (*see* CHILD WELFARE), and the incarceration of lawbreakers. After Confederation, the provision of social welfare services continued to be irregular and piecemeal, depending in part on the philanthropic inclinations and concerns of the upper class – in particular of those upper-class women who viewed charitable activities as an extension of their maternal roles and as an acceptable undertaking in society. Reform of this system was predicated on the notion that the family was the basis of economic security. The institutionalization of the family and the social reproduction of labour, which began with legislation to enforce alimony, to regulate matrimonial property and marriage, and to limit divorce and contraception, was expanded with limitations on hours of work for women and children. Compulsory EDUCATION and PUBLIC HEALTH regulations were developed primarily in response to the spread of disease and fears of social unrest. Provincial governments began to support charitable institutions with regular grants.

The Transitional Phase 1891-1940 Although the primary concern of the Canadian state remained the promotion of profitable private economic development, particularly through support of "infrastructural" institutions, the state also came to be associated with the provision of a plentiful supply of appropriately skilled labour through the regulation of the relations of capital and labour, and the maintenance of the family. This was largely achieved by the use of state mechanisms to maintain stability in the economy and in the family, and to do both at the least cost and risk to employers. During the same period charity workers and private charity organizations began to consolidate and to battle ideologically and, generally, unsuccessfully for control of social welfare.

The appearance of legislation compelling children to attend school and providing public authorities with the power to make decisions in relation to "neglected" children was part of a growing number of state interventions to regulate social welfare. INDUSTRIAL RELATIONS legislation was also passed in the first decade of the 20th century, allowing the state to intervene in the relations between labour and capital.

The first piece of compulsory contributory social insurance legislation in Canada, the Workmen's Compensation Act, was passed in Ontario in 1914. During WWI, 2 important events speeded the development of an interventionist welfare state: demands for the support of injured soldiers and demands for the support of the families left behind. Both demands led to the establishment of a Dominion scheme of pensions and rehabilitation and, in Manitoba, to the first mothers' allowances legislation (1916). Several provinces followed with mothers' allowance legislation of their own, but by war's end, after the incorporation of many thousands of women workers into the wartime labour force, mothers' allowances were the justification used to remove women workers who were single parents from the labour force and to provide them with minimum support. The postwar era also ushered in the first (and brief) Dominion scheme to encourage the construction of housing, but it had died by 1924. While there was considerable debate during the 1920s about whether to establish permanent unemployment, relief and pension schemes, the only result was the passage of the 1927 OLD-AGE PENSION legislation, and this was in part the result of the efforts of J.S. WOODSWORTH and a small group of Independent Labour members of Parliament.

It was the traumatic economic conditions of the GREAT DEPRESSION that forced a change in social philosophy and state intervention. In 1930, with hundreds of thousands of Canadians unemployed, the newly elected Conservative government under R.B. BENNETT legislated Dominion Unemployment Relief. By 1935 the Conservative Party's stern resistance to change in the face of an economic catastrophe and Bennett's continuing reliance on the so-called natural "restorative" powers of capitalism were replaced by advocacy of social reform in BENNETT'S NEW DEAL legislation. Although the package was set aside the same year by the returned government of Mackenzie King and although the courts subsequently determined that the federal government did not have the power to pass such legislation, the necessity for major social intervention was reaffirmed in the report of the Royal Commission on Dominion-Provincial Relations, created by King to examine the constitutional and social questions posed by the Depression. In consequence, the Unemployment Insurance Act was passed in 1940 and the Tax Rental Agreement in 1941.

The Interventionist Phase 1941-1974 marks the arrival of what is conventionally called the welfare state. By the beginning of WWII, the economic and political lessons of the Depression had been well learned. People increasingly accepted the expanded role of the state in economic and social life and expected this to continue after the war. Nevertheless, the postwar Liberal government largely ignored reports on social security, health insurance and public housing; instead, King settled on a political compromise, which at first boiled down to the establishment of family allowances. In all other areas the Liberal government moved to dismantle the apparatus of state intervention that had been constructed during the war. The state was to aid private enterprise rather than providing directly for economic security. During the postwar period, Dominion hospital grants, the provision of old-age pensions and old-age security, the first permanent program for the funding of relief, and permanent programs for the funding of higher education and vocational rehabilitation were introduced.

The Liberal Party was defeated in 1957 but was returned as a reform-minded MINORITY GOVERNMENT under L.B. Pearson in the early 1960s on a cyclical economic upsurge. Influenced by the American "war on poverty" and by the necessity to maintain the political support of the NDP, Pearson's Liberal government presided over the introduction of 3 major pieces of social legislation that constituted the last major building blocks of a welfare state in Canada: Medicare, the Canada Pension Plan and the Canada Assistance Plan. To these were added the Guaranteed Income Supplement, the increase in post-secondary education funding, and the consolidation of hospital, medicare and education grants through the

Established Programs Financing Act (*see* INTERGOV-ERNMENTAL FINANCE). The reorganization of income tax and family allowance, and the expansion of public, co-operative and nonprofit housing, and of unemployment insurance provisions in the early 1970s were additional reform measures. Lastly, there were important reforms in the late 1960s in legislation controlling divorce, ABORTION and the availability of contraceptives, all of which had an important impact on the family.

The Fourth Phase: Erosion and the Future of Welfare, 1975- In the 1970s, state expenditures automatically increased with parallel increases in unemployment, in the AGING of the population, and in the broader use of medical services. The impact of these automatic mechanisms has become increasingly evident since 1975 when the economy began to decline after 10 years of growth. At the same time, revisions to the tax system, eg, indexation and the expansion of corporate tax write-offs, meant a reduction in tax revenue.

In the late 1970s and early 1980s rising inflation and the growing demands of large numbers of newly unionized white-collar workers, particularly public-sector workers, increased demands on expenditure. These conditions ushered in an attack on the state, both as employer and as spender. Corporations and governments advocated cutbacks in expenditures and layoffs of public-sector workers. The resulting unemployment was intended to reduce the power of the labour movement, particularly in the public sector, and help to moderate wage increases. Even as inflation dropped in the mid-1980s attacks continued on public expenditure, justified by a need to reduce the public debt.

The attempts to reduce welfare state expenditures have included changing eligibility standards for unemployment insurance, welfare, etc; "privatizing" social programs by contracting out responsibility for social services (particularly those relating to children and the aged); shifting the burden of medical-care financing through the use of premiums and user fees; and decreasing social-program budgets relatively if not absolutely. The election of a new Conservative government in 1984 renewed the debate over "universality"; the minister of health announced a commitment to universal payment of pensions, but changes were made to deindex family allowances partly in the late 1980s and early 1990s. There has also been fierce conflict among federal, provincial and municipal governments over which level of government will finance social programs. Provincial reductions in social budgets (eg, in Ont, NS and BC) throw the burden onto municipal governments or onto para-public agencies, or onto the family. Since 1975, as a result of these changes, welfare state structures have eroded. The existence of FOOD BANKS is striking evidence of the changes. State intervention schemes are still designed to deal with unemployment as a "contingency," an unusual occurrence, and not as the regular feature of economic and social life that it has become. This fact will no doubt exert considerable pressure on future welfare state policy. ALLAN MOSCOVITCH

Reading: National Council of Welfare, *Welfare in Canada* (1987); Allan Moscovitch, "The Rise and Decline of the Canadian Welfare State," *Perception* (Nov 1982); Moscovitch and J. Albert, eds, *The "Benevolent" State: The Growth of Welfare in Canada* (1987); Moscovitch et al, *The Welfare State in Canada: A Selected Bibliography 1840-1978* (1983); G. Riches, *Food Banks and the Welfare Crisis* (1986).

Welland, Ont, City, pop 45 054 (1986c), 45 448 (1981c), inc 1917, located in the Niagara Peninsula, 20 km S of St Catharines. It grew up where the WELLAND CANAL crossed the Welland R, and was the seat of Welland County from 1856 until regional government was established in 1970. Welland experienced industrial growth after 1900 when its canal and railway advantages were supplemented by hydroelectric power from NIAGARA FALLS. Welland is home to the Niagara College of Applied Arts and Technology, and is the centre of French education in the Niagara region. With construction of a bypass channel (1973), inner Welland became surrounded by canal channels, and the abandoned channel became a recreational waterway. The city's present industries include the manufacture of stainless and other steels, agricultural implements and large-diameter pipes. JOHN N. JACKSON

Welland Canal, 43.5 km long, crosses the Niagara Peninsula of SW Ontario, from Port Weller on Lk Ontario to PORT COLBORNE on Lk Erie, overcoming a height difference of 99.4 m between the 2 lakes, and bypassing the turbulent Niagara R and NIAGARA FALLS. A part of the ST LAWRENCE SEAWAY since 1959, the canal has 7 lift locks along its northern length, and one guard lock near the southern entrance. Locks 4, 5, and 6 comprise the world-famous series of twinned flight locks, with a length of almost 1249.7 m and a rise of 42.5 m. The canal has a depth of 8.2 m, a surface width generally of 94.5 m and 152.4 m along the Bypass Channel at Welland. Maximum vessel dimensions are length, 222.5 m; breadth, 23.2 m; draught, 7.9 m; and height above water level, 35.5 m. The canal is crossed by 11 lift-bridges, 3 tunnels, one high-level bridge, and a seasonal pedestrian ferry. Cargo tonnes have increased from 25 million t in 1959 to a maximum of 66.2 million t in 1979. Thereafter, recession has caused decline. About 42.7 million t of cargo were handled in 1985, principally grain (19.2 million t), iron ore (6.2 million t), coal (5.6 million t) and other bulk cargoes (8.8 million t). Of the 3941 vessel transits, 2881 were in lake vessels and 1060 were in oceangoing vessels; an estimated 72% of vessel transits were in Canadian-owned vessels by country of registry. A lifeline of trade and commerce into the inland heart of N America, the first Welland Canal opened in 1829, an achievement attributed primarily to a St Catharines businessman, William Hamilton MERRITT. A series of major new construction works have been undertaken at various times, often on different routes. Remnants of the Second Canal (opened 1845) and the Third Canal (opened 1887), and the modern or Fourth Canal (opened 1932) with a 13.4 km bypass at Welland (opened 1973), may be viewed. The Welland Canal created and expanded communities along its length, and has been a primary factor in their urban form and industrial development. JOHN N. JACKSON

The Welland Canal bypasses the Niagara R and Niagara Falls, overcoming a height difference of 99.4 m between lakes Ontario and Erie (*photo by John Reeves/Masterfile*).

Wells, George Anderson, bishop, scholar, lecturer (b at Clarke's Beach, Nfld 18 Nov 1877; d at Toronto 10 Apr 1964). Wells was a fisherman, sealer, labourer, and a trooper in the SOUTH AFRICAN WAR before continuing his education at various American institutions. Ordained a minister of the Church of England in 1910, he was a chaplain during WWI and chaplain of the fleet during WWII. He was awarded the CMG in 1918. He became bishop of the Cariboo diocese in 1934 and was assistant bishop to the bishop of Toronto 1946-51. J. ROGERS

Welsh The principality of Wales (incorporated into England by the Act of Union of 1536) has always been overshadowed by England, Ireland and Scotland. One historian has commented that the Welsh "apart from their language, lacked practically every attribute of a nation except for the perverse and persistent belief that they were one." Wales's population (less than 3 million in 1988) has turned to emigration as a means of advancement.

If one ignores the improbable voyage of Madoc (the quasi-historical Welsh prince who supposedly discovered N America *c* 1170) but accepts the probability that Welshmen sailed with John CABOT from Bristol on his epic voyage of 1497, a 500-year-old Welsh connection with Newfoundland and Cape Breton I can be accepted. Another unsubstantiated view claims that Welsh seafarer John Lloyd (John the Skillful) reached Hudson Bay as early as 1475. In 1612 Sir Thomas BUTTON, a Welsh naval officer in command of HMS *Resolution,* searched unsuccessfully for the NORTHWEST PASSAGE and for Henry HUDSON. A Welsh settlement was established on the southern Avalon Peninsula in 1617 by Sir William VAUGHAN, an ardent supporter of colonial expansion. Despite the failure of the venture, Vaughan wrote 2 books promoting Newfoundland and thereby provided 2 of the earliest works about English N America. In 1759, at the siege of Québec, a Major Gwillim served under Gen James WOLFE. His daughter (Elizabeth SIMCOE) later married the first lt-gov of Upper Canada. Explorer David THOMPSON, although English-born, was of Welsh descent. In the early 18th-century, eastern coastal waters were plagued by the puritanical Welsh pirate and slaver Bartholomew ROBERTS, and the volatile Acadian population of Nova Scotia was experiencing British rule under the sincere and practical Gov Richard PHILIPPS.

Welshmen serving in the British forces in British N America during the AMERICAN REVOLUTION, the WAR OF 1812 and the REBELLIONS OF 1837 stayed on. There was a specific area of Welsh settlement along Lake Erie that absorbed the immigrants of the 18th and 19th centuries. A second wave of immigration was precipitated by the Cariboo gold rush in BC in 1862. Welsh immigration figures for the 20th century are more detailed and, just as for their ENGLISH, IRISH and SCOTS cousins, reflect the ebb and flow of economic depressions and world tensions. After David Lloyd George's visit in 1899, the Canadian West was endorsed as a good prospect for immigrants. In 1902 a third wave of immigrants – the "Patagonian Welsh," so named for their 35-year sojourn as a Welsh colony in Argentina – were relocated in Saskatchewan. The all-time high for Welsh immigration was in 1906, when 5018 settlers arrived. Immigration increased following WWI, and again from 1926 to 1929. Immigration was also high in 1946 (1294) and after the Suez Crisis in 1957 (2629). Overall, from 1900 to 1950, more than 50 000 Welsh came to Canada.

Since 1960, Welsh immigration has been slight but steady, representing a small percentage of British immigration. In the 1961 census, 143 942 people claimed Welsh descent. In the 1971 census, this figure was reduced to 74 415 (perhaps because many of Welsh descent were recorded as being English). By 1981, only 46 620 people

(0.2%) claimed Welsh descent; the Welsh were not counted separately in the 1986 census. The largest grouping of Welsh (1981 figures) is in Ontario (17 400), followed by BC (10 950), Alta (8510), Sask (2630), Man (2455), NS (1500), Qué (1170), NB (1055), Nfld (525), PEI (190), the YT (140) and the NWT (105). If at all, they have tended to consolidate in the mining areas of Ontario, BC, Alberta and the Maritimes. Their presence is evident in such place-names as Newport and Pontypool (Ont), Cardiff (Alta) and Bangor (Sask).

Religion (METHODISM, Presbyterianism) and language were important to early Welsh settlers. Some communities developed around a Welsh-speaking nucleus and a Welsh-speaking preacher; however, these characteristics rarely survived the next generation. Most Welsh cultural activities are carried out at the local community level. There has never been a national society for the preservation of Welsh culture. However, they do maintain some of their cultural organizations and historic festivals. Most major Canadian cities have a St David's society – named after the patron saint of Wales – and some have Welsh choirs (eg, Montréal, Ottawa, Toronto and Edmonton). St David's Day, March 1, is celebrated by Welsh Canadians, and there are also traditional Welsh festivals of *Gymanfa Ganu* and the *eisteddfod,* which celebrate music, song and poetry.

The contribution of Wales to the development of Canada is impressive. Welsh and Welsh Canadians who have left their imprint on Canada, from both past and present, include missionaries Peter JONES and James EVANS; artist Robert HARRIS; scientists Stanley J. HUGHES and George L. PICKARD; philosopher George S. BRETT; writers Sir Charles G.D. ROBERTS and Robertson DAVIES; administrator Leonard W. BROCKINGTON; athlete Diane JONES KONIHOWSKI and cartoonist Yardley Jones.   DAVID EVANS

Reading: C. Bennett, *In Search of the Red Dragon: The Welsh in Canada* (1985); P. Thomas, *Strangers from a Secret Land* (1986).

Welsh, Harry Lambert, physicist, educator (b at Aurora, Ont 23 Mar 1910; d at Toronto 23 July 1984). He was educated and spent his career at U of T, except for 1931-33 in Göttingen and 1943-45 in Ottawa as lieutenant-commander of naval operational research. Welsh began his outstanding research in molecular spectroscopy with the discovery of pressure-induced absorption in 1949. His laboratory became a world-recognized centre, with new developments in light scattering and pioneering studies of liquid and solid hydrogen and of molecular complexes. As chairman of the U of T department of physics 1962-68, he played a major role in its development as one of the major science departments in Canada. He published almost 200 scientific papers and received many awards, including the Order of Canada and fellowship in the Royal Society of London. The U of T's annual H.L. Welsh Lectures in Physics, inaugurated on his retirement in 1978, attract international scholars. BORIS P. STOICHEFF

Wesbrook, Frank Fairchild, physician, educator (b in Brant County, Ont 12 July 1868; d at Vancouver 20 Oct 1918). Having obtained his arts and medical degrees at U of Man 1890, he did postgraduate work in London, Dublin and Marburg, Germany. Elected to a studentship at Cambridge in 1892, he spent 3 heady years amid brilliant fellow students in the laboratory of the eminent physiologist Michael Foster. He was then asked at age 27 to occupy the chair of pathology at U of Minn. Dean of medicine by 1906, he began publishing hard-hitting papers on medical and general university education. With his postgraduate student Moses Barron he was a forerun-

ner of Frederick G. BANTING in the field of DIABETES as it relates to changes in the pancreas. In 1913 Wesbrook was invited to Vancouver to become founding president of UBC. The ensuing 2 years were occupied in selecting a faculty of international distinction, in trying to extract from a debt-ridden provincial government a basic budget, and in developing "the Promised Land" at Point Grey as a campus. Despite the outbreak of WWI and recurrent illness attributable to Bright's disease, he established the vigorous university that is his legacy.   WILLIAM C. GIBSON

Weslock, Nick, golfer (b at Winnipeg 13 Dec 1917). He is one of the true students of golf, having absorbed lessons from many of the world's great amateurs and professionals in a career that has given him 4 Canadian amateur championships, 7 Ontario open championships and 8 Ontario amateur championships. Weslock has also been Canadian senior champion 6 times and Ontario senior champion 11 times. He left Winnipeg at age 5 and after living in Windsor and Hamilton, Ont, moved to Detroit, Mich, in 1947. He became a naturalized US citizen in 1956 and returned to Canada as a landed immigrant in 1959. Weslock has represented Ontario in provincial matches 25 times. He has also represented Canada as a member of the Eisenhower world cup team 5 times and as Commonwealth team member 5 times.   LORNE RUBENSTEIN

Wesson, John Henry, "Jack," farmer, farm leader (b near Sheffield, Eng 24 Aug 1887; d at Regina 13 Nov 1965). Wesson immigrated to Canada in 1907 and homesteaded near Maidstone, Sask. He joined the Saskatchewan Grain Growers' Assn and became well known for his public speaking, musical ability and sense of humour. An early enthusiast for the pooling movement, he was elected one of the first directors of the SASKATCHEWAN WHEAT POOL (est 1924). He was elected VP of the pool in 1931 and, because of president Louis C. Brouillette's illness, gradually assumed more responsibilities before becoming president in 1937, holding office until 1960. Under his leadership, the pool led campaigns for the CANADIAN WHEAT BOARD, the protection of Canadian agriculture and the expansion of the CO-OPERATIVE MOVEMENT. Wesson served as the first president of the Canadian Federation of Agriculture (1936-40) and was the leader of the 1942 Farmers March on Ottawa protesting low prices for produce.   IAN MACPHERSON

West Coast Longshore Strikes, 1923 and 1935 On 8 Oct 1923 the 1400 members of the International Longshoremen's Assn (ILA) in Vancouver struck for higher wages. The Shipping Federation imported strikebreakers, housed in the CPR ship *Empress of Japan,* while an armed launch and 350 armed men guarded the waterfront. The longshoremen gave up on Dec 10. Refusing further dealings with the ILA, the Shipping Federation took over the dispatch of the work force, formerly controlled by the union, and set up a company union, the Vancouver and District Waterfront Workers Assn. This evolved into a genuine union, and on 4 June 1935 became involved in the strike-lockout of 1935, resulting from union struggles to regain control of dispatch and to unite with other longshoremen in the region. The conflict led to the "Battle of the Ballentyne Pier" on June 18, when mounted police charged 1000 longshoremen. Following the imprisonment of union leaders, the strike ended on Dec 9.   JOHN BELLAMY FOSTER

West Coast Trail, on W coast of VANCOUVER I, follows the 72 km route of the historic lifesaving trail between the communities of Bamfield and Port Renfrew, BC. This trail was constructed by

The indoor skating rink at West Edmonton Mall, the largest shopping centre in the world (*photo by Roman Spalek/Reflexion*).

the federal government in the early 1900s so that rescuers could assist shipwrecked sailors on this section of coast, known as the "graveyard of the Pacific." The trail is a challenge for the experienced hiker and can be completed in 6-10 days. Although some sections are wide and easy, following scenic, sandy beaches, the south portion remains strenuous, with fast-moving streams, vertical ladders and steep gullies.   BART DEEG

West Edmonton Mall, world's largest shopping mall, located in the western suburbs of Edmonton. It contains more than 800 stores and services, including 11 major department stores, 110 food outlets, 7 amusement parks, a chapel, 10 bird aviaries, a bingo hall, 25 saltwater aquariums, 19 movie theatres and a night club. Fantasyland Hotel (1986) contains 354 rooms. The indoor amusement park, called Fantasyland, contains water rides, a miniature train and a 14-storey high roller coaster. An NHL-sized rink is occasionally used by the Edmonton Oilers for practice. The first phase, which opened in 1981, contained 225 stores, but it was "phase 2," with the addition of the rink and Fantasyland, which combined a carnival atmosphere with retailing. Phase 3 opened in 1985 and brought the total area to 483 271 sq m; it featured a water park with slides and artificial surf and a marine environment with dolphins, sharks, submarines and a replica of Columbus's ship *Santa Maria.* The mall was built by Triple Five Corp Ltd, which is owned by the Ghermezians. It has had a profound effect on the concept of retailing and has been emulated elsewhere, although crucial questions about the financial viability of such enterprises have yet to be proven. While the mall provides 16 000 jobs, critics claim that it has already had a deleterious effect on Edmonton's development, drawing attention and badly needed business from downtown. It has become, however, Edmonton's most identifiable and controversial symbol.

West Indians The large and visible presence of West Indians in Canada is a fairly recent phenomenon. A group of 556 Jamaicans arrived in Canada in 1796 after an unsuccessful British attempt to enslave them in Jamaica (*see* BLACKS), but early contacts between Canada and West Indians were few. Large-scale immigration of West Indians really began in the 1960s, and by 1973 accounted for almost 13% of all immigration to Canada. Today the West Indian population of Canada is about 200 000. In all, 5630 West Indians arrived in Canada in 1984, the majority from Haiti and Jamaica.

English-speaking West Indians are from Antigua, Grenada, Bahamas, Barbados, Jamaica, Trinidad and Tobago, Montserrat, St Lucia, Virgin Islands, St Kitts-Nevis, Dominica, St Vincent; French-speaking West Indians are from Haiti, Martinique and Guadeloupe; and Spanish speakers are from Puerto Rico, Cuba and the Dominican Republic.

There have been 3 major periods of West Indian immigration. From 1900 to 1960, Canada accepted about 21 500 West Indians, only 33% of whom were placed under the ethnic-origin heading of "Black." The slight increase in West Indian immigration from 1945 to 1960 corresponds with postwar economic expansion and the West Indian Domestic Scheme (1955-60). The second period, from 1960 to 1971, corresponds with the "liberalization" of the Canadian Immigration Act. In this period Canada accepted about 64 000 West Indians. The increased migration was part of an international movement in which Canada, in response to slow European emigration, began to depend increasingly on labour from the Third World. The last period, which began in the early 1970s, coincided with the economic recession. Except for 1973 and 1974 (unusual years because of the Addressment of Status Program that helped many persons regularize their status), immigration from the West Indies has generally declined. West Indian immigration fell from 10% of total immigration in 1975 to 6% in 1979.

Before 1960, most immigrants came from the British colonies, especially from Barbados, Jamaica, Trinidad, and Bermuda. From 1973 to 1979, Jamaica provided 48% of the immigration, Trinidad 19% and Haiti 18%. West Indians are concentrated overwhelmingly in the major urban centres of Québec and Ontario. Between 1973 and 1980, 96% of Haitian immigrants to Canada settled in Québec, particularly in Montréal. Of the English-speaking immigrants in the same period, 80% settled in Ontario, primarily in Toronto, but also in Kitchener, Waterloo and Windsor. Almost 11% from the same group settled in Montréal and 8.6% chose to establish themselves in the West, particularly in Alberta and BC.

Economic Life From the early 1900s, West Indian immigrants have contributed to Canada's economic life by providing cheap labour. Between 1900 and 1945, they were employed primarily on farms or in mines and factories. They also worked as mechanics and domestics or as waiters, porters, clerks, etc. In the 1960s, thousands of skilled workers came to fill a burgeoning job market, particularly in education, health services and office work. Between 1962 and 1966, almost 33% of immigrants sought work in the professional and technical categories. Because of the savings in labour-training costs and the productivity of the new arrivals, Canada was one of the beneficiaries of this Third World "brain drain."

In the late 1970s, there was a marked change in immigration eligibility categories (fewer independants, more sponsored applicants) and in labour qualifications (education and training). At the same time, employers continued to hire temporary workers in agriculture and in the services sector. West Indian immigrants have included a minority of family entrepreneurs and highly educated and qualified professionals, who form a small, separate bourgeoisie, and a majority of taxi drivers, factory workers, building superintendents, domestics, etc, whose working conditions are unstable and difficult.

Social and Cultural Life The West Indian community is not homogeneous. Class distinctions cut across regional differences which stem as much from the identity of the European countries that divided up the West Indies in previous centuries as from each island's individual history. The principal cleavage, however, is linguistic. Haitians moved en masse to Québec (Montréal) whereas anglophone West Indians chose Ontario (Toronto). Where the 2 groups coexist, as in Montréal, they have relatively little contact with each other. Where the language is the same, other

A Bahamian woman and fellow revellers participating in Toronto's Caribana parade (*courtesy Gera Dillon*).

differences come into play, eg, religion and social class. West Indians have fought a number of battles in Canada over school issues. Many associations have instituted transition programs to deal with the problems experienced by young West Indians in adapting to various school programs. These programs are also meant to give children a better knowledge of their origins and to counter prejudice in Canadian society. Courses in Creole have also been established for some Haitian immigrants. Montréal has become one of the main publishing centres for Haitian literature, which deals with both memories of home and the difficulties of immigrant life. Haitian painting and sculpture have also appeared in Québec.

In the West Indian community the nuclear family is part of an extended family group spread over several major N American cities, and ties are often maintained with the country of origin. Aside from the family, the Protestant church plays an important role both in welcoming new arrivals and in helping persons in difficulty. Montréal's Haitians meet in masonic lodges, where they indulge in an original form of spirituality, some of which stems from Haiti's voodoo practices.

Jamaican immigrants introduced Rastafarianism to Canada. Originally (1933) a messianic movement in which Haile Selassie (who before he became emperor was called Ras Tafari) was believed to be the god of the blacks who comes to overthrow the white world (Babylon), Rastafarianism has since had considerable influence on the entire Jamaican society. Jamaicans also introduced "reggae" music, which originated in the ghettos of Kingston, Jamaica. A blend of African musical traditions and rhythm and blues, reggae was born during the 1960s and spread to England and America. Trinidadians introduced calypso and the carnival. Held each year at the beginning of the summer in Montréal and Toronto, the carnival has become a symbol of identity for the entire Canadian West Indian community.

Politics The political battles of West Indians in Canada have been waged over improved working conditions, pervasive racism in employment, education and accommodation, the right to immigrate, and the right to participate in the political life of their mother country and of Canada. Anglophone West Indians have long fought through what is now the Order of Sleeping Car Porters, and have tried to affiliate this labour organization with the International Brotherhood of Sleeping Car Porters (AFC-CIO). Since the early 20th century, West Indians have fought on behalf of women's issues through the Coloured Women's Club. The National Congress of Black Women, a more recent organization, includes anglophone and francophone women from Canada, the West Indies and other countries.

To defend the interests of blacks and to fight racism at various levels, a number of organizations were established, uniting blacks of Canadian and West Indian origin. Among these was the

Canadian League for the Advancement of Colored People, inspired by the large American organization. Between the 2 wars, the Universal Negro Improvement Association, founded by Marcus Garvey, a Jamaican and one of the great black American leaders, led a different black movement advocating a return to Africa and nonintegration. This association gave rise to a string of satellite organizations in Canada.

At the end of the 1960s, student and youth organizations mobilized against the existing school system. This movement was influenced by the Black Panther movement in the US, the national liberation struggles throughout the world and the incident at Sir George Williams U [CONCORDIA U], Montréal, in 1968-69 when several black students, protesting against the racist grading system of a professor, attacked a computer. The Black United Front has been founded in Nova Scotia.

Haitian organizations in Québec have been active in the fight against the Duvalier regime in Haiti, the deportation of Haitians in 1974 and 1979, and have established information, emergency, literacy and other services. Haitians have also exerted enough pressure on the government that political refugee status is given more freely to Haitian and Latin American immigrants.

M. LABELLE, S. LAROSE, V. PICHÉ

Reading: K. Levitt, *Canada-West Indies Economic Relations* (1967) and *The Canadian Family Tree* (1979); R. Winks, *The Blacks in Canada* (1971).

West Vancouver, BC, District Municipality, pop 36 266 (1986c), 35 728 (1981c), area 9893 ha, inc 1912, is located on the N shore of Burrard Inlet, bounded by Howe Sound on the W, North Vancouver on the E and the Hollyburn, Strachan and Black mountains on the N. Until 1912 it was known as the West Capilano region of the Dist of NORTH VANCOUVER. West Vancouver is a mountainside community bisected by 19 major creeks, with rich coastal vegetation and a temperate climate typical of the Lower Mainland. The municipality is governed by an elected council and 6 aldermen. West Vancouver is primarily a residential suburb, with most of its residents employed in other parts of Metropolitan Vancouver; 80% of the labour force commutes across Lion's Gate Bridge each day. In 1988 Revenue Canada figures showed that its residents had the highest per-capita income in Canada. It grew slowly after incorporation (pop 700), until the catalyst of British Pacific Properties investments set off a residential boom after WWII. Growth was rapid up to and including the 1960s, but future expansion is greatly limited by topography and by very high real-estate prices. Manufacturing exists only on a small scale, but tourism is important. Two scenic highways, the Upper Levels and Marine Drive, traverse the area, whose attractions include exclusive residential districts, Hollyburn Ridge (a year-round alpine recreation area), Lighthouse Park and Horseshoe Bay. The area is noted for its salmon fishing, its rugged coastline and numerous outdoor recreation spots. ALAN F.J. ARTIBISE

Western Settlement, *see* PRAIRIE WEST.

Westlock, Alta, Town, pop 4532 (1986c), inc 1916, located 80 km NW of Edmonton. Originally part of land owned by the Westgate and Lockhart families, hence the name Westlock, the town was formed with the coming of the railway in 1913. Although situated at the crossroads of highways leading N to resource rich areas, farming is still the major industry in an area that was once described in a survey as having the highest yield for the lowest cost for crops on the N American continent. In addition to rail and road links, Westlock also has its own airport, hospital and radio station. BLAIR CHING

Weston, Willard Garfield, food merchant, manufacturer (b at Toronto 26 Jan 1893; d there 22 Oct 1978). The son of biscuit manufacturer George Weston, he developed the family business into one of the largest food conglomerates in Canada. He became a VP of GEORGE WESTON LTD in 1921, and was elected president and general manager upon his father's death in 1924. By 1928 he had started the international expansion of the firm, first to the US in 1929, then in 1933 to the UK, where he soon became England's largest biscuit manufacturer. He moved to England in 1933 and was elected to the British House of Commons but never gave up his Canadian citizenship. The Weston conglomerate, now run by his sons W. Gordon Galen (b Eng 29 Oct 1940) and Garry (b 1927), controls retail and food manufacturing companies in the US, Canada, UK, Australia, S Africa, New Zealand, W Germany and Ireland. Galen, who heads Canadian operations, used his own funds to build up a chain of supermarkets in Ireland while still in his twenties and became involved in real estate and department stores. After his father's death, Galen reorganized the conglomerate by restructuring the flagging Loblaws and pruning other operations. Recent acquisitions include Holt Renfrew (1986). JORGE NIOSI

Reading: C. Davies, *Bread Men: How the Westons Built an International Empire* (1988).

Westport, NS, Village, pop 350 (1986c), 356 (1981c), inc 1946, is located at the southern tip of Digby Neck, on the eastern side of BRIER I, western NS. Originally known as Brier I Settlement, it was named Westport in 1839 because of its location. Two New Englanders were its sole occupants until the arrival of LOYALISTS in 1783. With the best cod and pollock grounds in the Bay of FUNDY located here, fishing is the principal industry. A cod-liver-oil factory was established in 1880. A memorial plaque in the town commemorates the solo voyage of Capt Joshua SLOCUM around the world (1895-98) in an 11 m long sloop. Brier I is becoming quite well known among bird-watchers for the variety of species of land and seabirds concentrated here during migration. It is also a good place for lapidary enthusiasts to collect agate. JEAN PETERSON

Westville, NS, Town, pop 4271 (1986c), 4522 (1981c), inc 1894, is located near the Middle R, 8 km SW of NEW GLASGOW. Originally called Acadia Village, it was renamed Westville in 1868, 2 years after the Acadian Coal Co discovered coal. In 1868, 3 mines were in operation and a railway was built to join the mines to the INTERCOLONIAL RY. Coal from these mines supplied ironworks in a nearby town or was shipped elsewhere. The town's prosperity peaked in 1910, when coke ovens, a coal washer and a brick plant were also in operation. By 1953 the only mine in operation was the Drummond. Demands for Westville coal declined and by 1969 only a little over 100 men were working. Today, most residents work in the nearby towns of New Glasgow or Stellarton. There is some manufacturing and a small service industry. HEATHER MacDONALD

Wetaskiwin, Alta, City, pop 10 071 (1986c), 9597 (1981c), inc 1906, distribution centre and headquarters for the Battle River Regional Planning Commission, is located 70 km S of Edmonton. The town began (1891) as Siding 16 on the Calgary-Edmonton Ry and was a point of departure for early, predominantly Scandinavian, homesteaders. A CPR branch line was built eastward in 1906, and the town grew as wheat farming and cattle ranching prospered in the area. The Reynolds Alberta Museum, scheduled to open in the early 1990s, will contain over 900 artifacts depicting technological developments in trans-

portation, industry and agriculture in Alberta. The city has one weekly newspaper, the Wetaskiwin *Times Advertiser,* and also a local radio station and an airstrip. Its name is Cree for "hills (or place) of peace," referring to the nearby Peace Hills. ERIC J. HOLMGREN

Wetmore, Andrew Rainsford, jurist, politician, premier of NB 1867-70 (b at Fredericton 16 Aug 1820; d there 7 Mar 1892). Born into a distinguished Loyalist family, Wetmore's father, George Ludlow Wetmore, was the last New Brunswicker killed in a formal duel (20 Oct 1821). Andrew Wetmore went into law. He joined the anti-Confederationists for the 1865 electoral victory, expecting the attorney generalship. Refused that office, he moved to the Confederationists to be "certain to have been right at least once," even though he was considered a "political weathercock" for his move. The 1867 mass exodus of NB politicians to Ottawa propelled Wetmore to the premiership and the attorney general's office. He was also promised the Supreme Court. Under him provincial affairs were chaotic, and his elevation to the NB Supreme Court (1870) was the occasion for political realignment under firmer leadership.
CARL M. WALLACE

Weyburn, Sask, City, pop 10 153 (1986c), 9523 (1981c), inc 1912, is located on the SOURIS R in southeastern Saskatchewan, about 75 km from the international boundary. Weyburn became a village in 1902 as the result of a heavy inflow of Americans. There are 2 versions as to how it received its name. Most people prefer the romantic one, which concerns a party of thirsty Scots working their way west on a hot summer day. One member was said to have exclaimed "wee burn" upon seeing the Souris R for the first time. The second, and more practical, version contends that the city got its name from a railway construction contractor who named the site after his brother-in-law. In the 1950s the Weyburn oil field was discovered in the area and since then oil has played a very significant role in the city's economy. Agricultural production continues to be its dominant industry. DON HERPERGER

Whale, common name for large, aquatic or marine MAMMALS of order CETACEA, which inhabit all oceans. Whales range from about 30 kg for some of the smaller dolphins to over 150 t for the blue whale. Whales belong to 2 suborders: Mysticeti, baleen or toothless whales; and Odontoceti, toothed whales (smaller kinds of which are called DOLPHINS or porpoises). Canadian waters are rich in whale fauna (8 species of mysticetes, about 25 species of odontocetes), and the commercial search for these animals was significant in early exploration (*see* WHALING). Because of overexploitation, several species are rare, eg, bowhead (*Balaena mysticetus*), an arctic mysticete; right whale (*Eubalaena glacialis*), a temperate

zone mysticete; humpback (*Megaptera novaeangliae*), known for its haunting "song"; and blue whale (*Balaenoptera musculus*), largest animal ever known. The grey whale (*Eschrichtius robustus*) was extirpated in the N Atlantic and depleted in the N Pacific. Today, however, its migration along the N American Pacific coast is one of the world's great wildlife spectacles. The cosmopolitan sperm whale (*Physeter catodon*), the largest odontocete, preys mainly on squid and usually remains in deep water. Adult bulls seasonally visit high latitudes; females and young remain in temperate or tropical waters. The beaked whales (family Ziphiidae) are rare in coastal areas, but Baird's beaked whale (*Berardius bairdii*) off the BC coast, and the northern bottlenose (*Hyperoodon ampullatus*) off NS, have been hunted by shore-based whalers.

Since the 1972 moratorium on commercial whaling in Canada, whale watching has become popular. Several species, especially BELUGA, fin and minke whales (*Delphinapterus leucas, Balaenoptera physalus, B. acutorostrata,* respectively) and blue whales, occur along the N shore of the St Lawrence estuary. Pilot (*Globicephala melaena*), humpback and fin whales are the main attractions off Newfoundland; right whales in lower Bay of FUNDY; killer whales (*Orcinus orca*) and grey whales off BC. *See also* ENDANGERED ANIMALS and illustration on page 2297.
R. REEVES AND E.D. MITCHELL

Whaling About 33 WHALE species occur in Canadian waters, of which about 13 have been commercially significant. The earliest exploited were the relatively easily hunted right, bowhead and grey whales. As the numbers of these species declined, humpback and sperm whales became the preferred prey. Later still, when technological advances made it feasible, the very fast blue, fin and sei whales were taken. The first whalers in Canada were native people, the INUIT of the Far North and the NOOTKA of Vancouver I who hunted for subsistence. As early as the 16th century, BASQUE seamen from France and Spain sailed to the Gulf of ST LAWRENCE, where large numbers of whales congregated each summer to feed. In the 18th century, British and American ships cruised the Atlantic seaboard. In the 19th century, Canadians entered the field, establishing a whaling station in Newfoundland, and taking whales as part of a deep-sea fishery operation from Gaspé. Norwegian whalers entered the area toward the end of the century, establishing stations in Newfoundland, Labrador and the Gulf of St Lawrence. Beginning in the 1830s American whalers cruising N to the Bering Sea hunted whales migrating along the Pacific coast. A local Canadian industry was established for a brief period (1868-72) at harbours on Vancouver I and in the Gulf of Georgia. From 1905 at least one company operated at any given time (excluding the period 1942-47) until 1967 when the last Canadian West Coast whaling company (the Western Canada Whaling Co) ceased whaling.

Whaling began in the DAVIS STR region of the Arctic in the 17th century. Dutch, German, English and Scottish whalers largely confined their efforts to the eastern (Greenland) side until the expeditions of John Ross (1818) and W. Edward PARRY (1819) crossed Baffin Bay and showed the way to LANCASTER SOUND. The northernmost extent of whaling was Ellesmere I. The most important area for autumn whaling was CUMBERLAND SOUND. The peak of whaling activity was from 1820 to 1840, when there were sometimes almost 100 vessels in the Davis Str area; in some years the catch exceeded 1000 whales.

Ordinarily, arctic whaling voyages lasted a single summer; ships arrived in Davis Str in Apr and

Whales of Canada

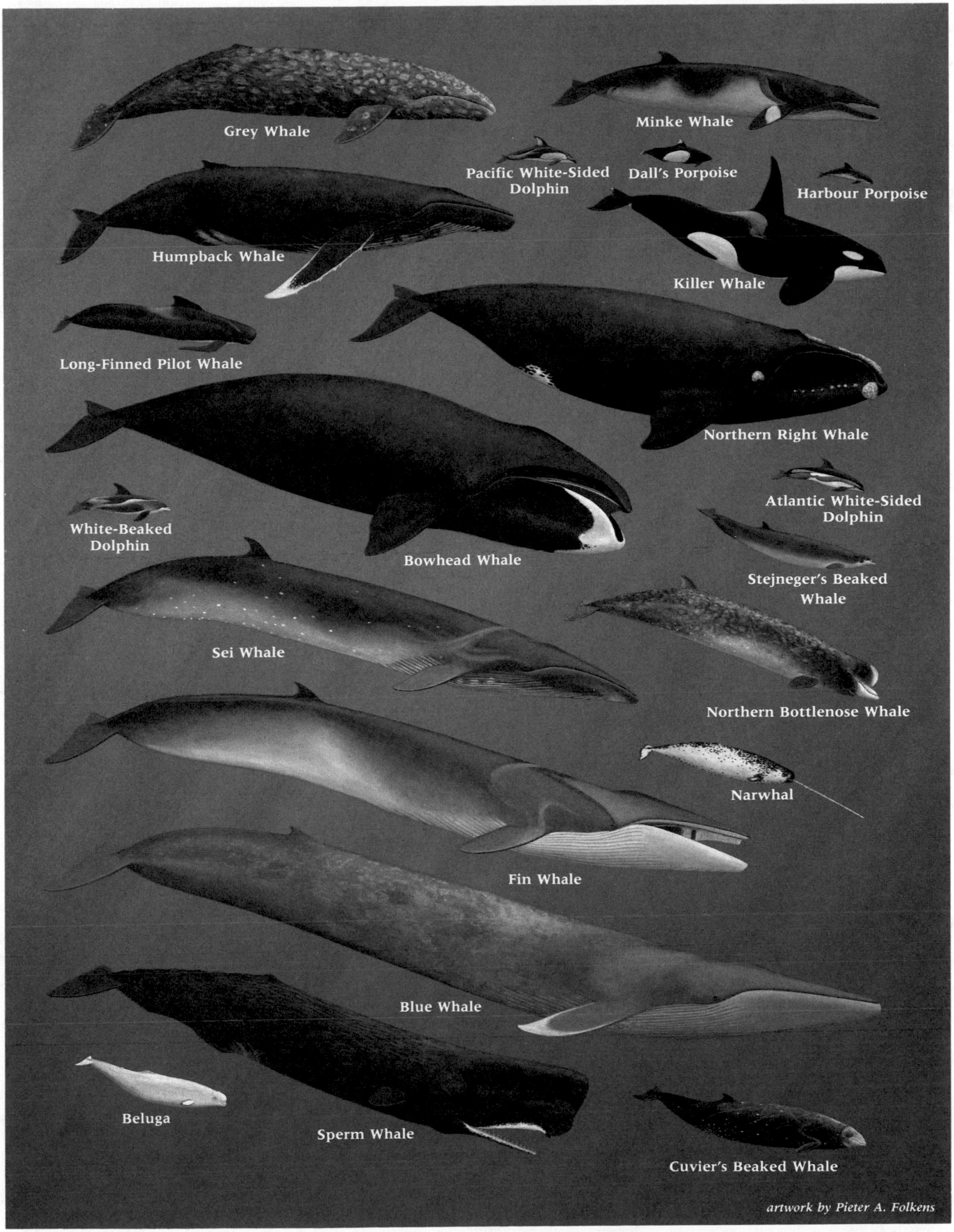

Grey Whale

Minke Whale

Pacific White-Sided Dolphin

Dall's Porpoise

Harbour Porpoise

Humpback Whale

Killer Whale

Long-Finned Pilot Whale

Northern Right Whale

White-Beaked Dolphin

Atlantic White-Sided Dolphin

Bowhead Whale

Stejneger's Beaked Whale

Sei Whale

Northern Bottlenose Whale

Narwhal

Fin Whale

Blue Whale

Beluga

Sperm Whale

Cuvier's Beaked Whale

artwork by Pieter A. Folkens

tried to begin the return journey by Oct. However, on many occasions vessels were trapped by ice and either imprisoned through the winter or sunk.

While British whalers dominated the Davis Str grounds, US ships opened the NW corner of Hudson Bay (1860) and after 1889 pushed past Point Barrow in the BEAUFORT SEA. By the late 1890s vessels had penetrated Amundsen Gulf. Compared to the eastern Arctic, whaling in the Beaufort Sea was of short duration (1889-c1914). These areas were so inaccessible that whalers extended their visits over a year, spending the winter months frozen in sheltered harbours to get an early start in spring. The population of whalers was not large: at most, 500 seamen wintered in the Beaufort Sea and 200 in Hudson Bay. Wintering did not begin on Baffin I until the 1850s and it was not until later in the century that permanent shore stations, such as Kekerton and Blacklead I on Cumberland Sound, were established. However, the impact of the whalers on the Inuit was profound. Natives were employed as pilots, hunters, dog drivers and seamstresses, and were eager to procure European trade goods. Liquor was imported and violence increased. Contact between whalers and Inuit at shore stations inevitably resulted in the spread of alien diseases. Epidemics of measles, typhus and scarlet fever swept through the native populations. At the beginning of the 20th century an entire people, the SADLERMIUT of Southampton I in Hudson Bay, were wiped out. The influx of whalers placed a great strain on arctic resources. Caribou herds were decimated to provide meat for the ships' crews. As supplies of meat and leather dwindled, and as tastes changed, many Inuit came to rely on food and clothing traded from the whalers. Some native people were employed on the ships as hunters or crewmen and increasingly the economic life of the Inuit was changed.

The activities of foreign whalers in the Arctic stimulated the Canadian government to assert sovereignty over the ARCTIC ARCHIPELAGO. Officially, these islands had belonged to Canada since 1880, but no presence had been established and foreign whalers continued to operate in the Arctic without any regulation. By 1900 suspicions were growing that the US planned to annex the area, using the activities of American whalers as a pretext. Detachments of North-West Mounted Police were established (1903) to collect customs, regulate the liquor traffic, impose whaling licences and maintain order.

Whales have been valued for different products at different times. The Inuit used all of the whale: skin, blubber, flesh and internal organs were eaten; baleen and bones were used for buildings, furniture and innumerable smaller items; oil provided heat and light. Europeans were more wasteful. Initially, oil extracted from blubber was used in street lamps and for soap. By the late 19th century, coal gas and petroleum products replaced animal oil as an illuminant, but it continued to be used in margarine, paints and varnishes, and as a lubricant. The waxy spermaceti produced by sperm whales was used for candles, lubricants, cosmetics and shoe polish. In Canadian waters, the most important whale was the bowhead, which supplied baleen (whalebone), a substance which hangs in long, curtainlike strips from the roof of its mouth. A large bowhead might produce over 700 strips. By the end of the 19th century, it became common practice to remove baleen and discard the carcass. This flexible substance was used for a range of products including buggy whips, skirt hoops, umbrellas, carriage wheels, corset stays and fishing rods. It was replaced in the 20th century by spring steel and plastics. Whale meat has been used for human consumption,

chiefly in Japan and Norway, and for animal food.

At first commercial whalers armed with handheld harpoons and lances pursued the animals in small boats. The harpoon was thrust into the whale and the animal was allowed to run out line. "Nantucket sleigh rides" occurred when all the line had run out and the whale was "tethered" to the boat. When the whale was exhausted, the whalers moved in for the kill. New weapons were introduced in the middle of the 19th century. The shoulder gun fired an explosive missile with a time fuse which detonated inside the animal. The harpoon gun, a cannonlike weapon mounted at the bow of the boat, fired a barbed harpoon with an explosive charge attached. Such weapons transformed the hunt from a contest to a slaughter. The steam engine was first applied to whaling ships in the 1850s. By 1870, most of the Davis Str fleet had converted to steam and American whalers in the Beaufort Sea quickly followed suit. The increased speed, power and maneuverability allowed whalers to carry the hunt farther from home ports and reduced dangers of ice and storm.

In the Canadian Arctic, commercial whaling had all but ceased by the outbreak of WWI. Whale stocks were depleted to the point of extinction and the demand for baleen had decreased. Along the BC coast, however, and in Newfoundland and NS, whaling continued from several landbased stations with catcher boats pursuing and killing whales and towing the carcasses to land for processing. Whaling entered a new phase internationally in 1925 with the introduction of factory ships. More recently, helicopters and SONAR have been used, especially by the USSR and Japan, to locate whales, which are then chased by catcher boats and processed aboard factory ships. Annual catches rose dramatically: in the late 1930s more than 50 000 whales were taken annually. After formation of the International Whaling Commission (IWC) in 1946, the killing of several species was banned completely and quotas were established to control exploitation of the rest. In 1972, the federal government ordered a halt to all whaling operations based in Canadian ports. The last West Coast company had stopped whaling in 1967; thus the government order affected only 2 shore-based operations in Newfoundland and one in NS. The Inuit are still allowed to take whales. As a result of conservation measures, some whale stocks have shown signs of recovery. In the 1930s, the bowhead was thought to be on the brink of extinction and was declared an ENDANGERED ANIMAL. Recent studies indicate that it has survived and may be recovering slowly in some areas.

Canada was a member of the IWC but withdrew from the organization in 1982. The commission had achieved some significant success; however, because member nations are not bound to conform to its recommendations, the commission can be only as effective as the whaling nations allow. Decisions have often been tempered by the desire to keep nations in the organization, where some control is possible, rather than outside, where their activities would be totally unregulated. Canada disagreed with efforts in 1980 to declare a moratorium on commercial whaling because in the absence of a clear and scientifically justified recommendation for such action from the commission's scientific committee, it felt that conservation requirements could be met under the commission's management procedure which provides for selective moratoria (zero quotas). Canada's position on the moratorium issue earned a great deal of criticism from anti-whaling groups. Nevertheless, a moratorium announced in 1982 took effect 1 Jan 1986. Although no longer a member of the IWC, Canada continues to

ban commercial whaling in its territory and continues to co-operate with the commission's scientific committee. *See also* WILDLIFE CONSERVATION AND MANAGEMENT.   DANIEL FRANCIS

Reading: J.N. Tønnessen and A.O. Johnsen, *The History of Modern Whaling* (tr 1982).

Wheat, common name for members of genus *Triticum* of the GRASS family (Gramineae) and for the CEREAL grains produced by these grasses. Wheat is the most important cereal in the world: with rice and maize it accounts for about 73% of world cereal production. Canada is the world's sixth-largest producer and one of the largest exporters of wheat, producing annually an average of over 25 billion t and exporting about 19 billion t. Cultivated forms evolved from natural crossings of wild species, followed by domestication and selection by humans. Wheat was domesticated in SW Asia over thousands of years and spread across Asia, Africa and Europe. Introduction to the New World took place in the late 15th and 16th centuries. The most important modern cultivated species (ie, cultivars) are common and durum wheats, usually given the binomial designations *T. aestivum* and *T. turgidum* var. *durum*, respectively.

History In Canada, wheat probably was first grown at PORT-ROYAL in about 1605; the first exports were made in 1654. Although personnel at some HUDSON'S BAY COMPANY posts experimented with wheat, and the settlers at the RED RIVER COLONY had some success in 1815, the early years in western Canada were precarious ones for wheat farmers. Many cultivars from Europe were tried: some were winter wheats that could not survive Canada's severe winters; others were spring wheats that matured too late for the short growing season. The cultivar Red Fife, developed in Ontario, became very popular because of its good yield and excellent milling and baking qualities. By about 1870 Red Fife was very popular on the prairies but it, too, froze in the fields in years with early frosts. Later investigations have revealed that Red Fife is actually the central European cultivar Galician.

William SAUNDERS, first director of the Dominion Experimental Farms, was interested in plant breeding. His son, Sir Charles SAUNDERS, took over the wheat-breeding work in 1903 and developed the cultivar Marquis (*see* MARQUIS WHEAT) from a cross, made some years earlier, between Hard Red Calcutta and Red Fife. He had a small increase plot (12 plants) of Marquis in 1904, but it took several years to verify that it matured earlier than Red Fife and had excellent yield and superior milling and baking qualities. It was distributed in the spring of 1909 and quickly became very popular throughout Canada. Western wheat production was increasing rapidly at this time: 2 million t, 1904; 3.7 million t, 1906; 7.7 million t, 1913. Red Fife and Marquis made Canada famous for its high-quality hard red spring wheat. Marquis was later adopted as the statutory standard of quality for this class of wheat, a position it held until 1987.

Protection Stem rust (*Puccinia graminis tritici*) is a FUNGUS disease disseminated by spores, which can be carried by wind for thousands of kilometres. In Canada, epidemics in 1916, 1927 and 1935 caused losses estimated at about 3.6, 3.3 and 3.2 million t of grain. The Dominion Rust Research Laboratory was set up in Winnipeg in 1925 to investigate stem rust and develop resistant cultivars. Renown, their first cultivar, distributed in 1936, has been followed by several other important cultivars (eg, Selkirk, Manitou, Neepawa); however, the Thatcher cultivar, developed in Minnesota and licensed in Canada in 1935, became the dominant form for many years. A new physiologic race of stem rust (15B) became epidemic from 1953 to 1955, causing losses of at least 8 million t of grain. Since that time, stem rust has caused little loss, but leaf rust (*P. recondita*) has been a problem because of its rapid changes in virulence. Cultivars resistant to both rusts are available. In Alberta and western Saskatchewan, rust was rarely a problem, but drought and wheat-stem sawfly (*Cephus cinctus*) were. The sawfly, which occurs mainly in the Swift Current, Sask, to Lethbridge, Alta, area, cuts stems so that the heads fall on the ground and cannot be harvested. Resistance has been obtained by developing cultivars with solid stems, eg, Rescue (licensed 1946). RESEARCH STATIONS in the area have since developed a number of resistant cultivars with better yield and quality. They also work on developing drought-resistant cultivars.

Production Within Canada, wheat is the most important cultivated crop (grown on over 13 million ha). Only one class of durum is grown, amber durum (spring); however, there are several classes of common wheat, based on seed hardness and colour, and on sowing time (autumn or spring). About 18% of Canada's 293 000 farms are classified as wheat farms, and wheat contributes about $2.5 billion (1%) to Canada's GROSS DOMESTIC PRODUCT. Soft white winter wheat is grown on an area of some 500 000 ha, mainly in Ontario; over 925 000 t are produced annually, of which about 60% is exported. The protein content is usually 9-10%, and this class is used for cake and pastry flour and breakfast cereals. The flour, mixed with hard wheat flour, produces an all-purpose flour.

Saskatchewan alone grows about 60% of Canada's wheat. Production on the PRAIRIES usually amounts to about 3 times domestic consumption; therefore, the industry is export oriented. The area devoted to common wheat averaged 11.3 million ha over the 1983-87 period; durum wheat averaged 1.8 million ha. The protein levels of prairie wheats are usually 12-15%. Durum wheat is used for the production of semolina for pasta products, and hard red spring wheat is used for bread. Wheat contains gluten protein, which forms minute gas cells that hold carbon dioxide during fermentation, allowing dough to rise and resulting in light bread. Importers of Canadian wheat often blend it with weaker wheats before using it for bread. For this reason, much effort goes into maintaining the strength and mixing qualities of Canadian wheat. Maintenance involves controlling cultivars grown and applying a comprehensive grading system. *See also* COMMODITY INSPECTION AND GRADING.   A.B. CAMPBELL

Wheeler, Anne, filmmaker, producer, director, writer (b at Edmonton 23 Sept 1946). Educated at U of A, Wheeler had some experience as an actress before making her first film in 1971. She made documentaries for the NFB as a free-lancer in the late 1970s and joined the board's Prairie region as a staff member 1978-81. From this period dates *A War Story* (1981), a documentary-docudrama based on her father's diaries as a Japanese POW, which received deservedly high acclaim. Subsequently, she has made a number of short dramatic films, notably *A Change of Heart* (1984; scripted by Sharon Riis), and has recently moved successfully into feature films with *Loyalties* (1986, also scripted by Riis) and *Cowboys Don't Cry* (1988, based on a book by Canadian children's novelist Marilyn Halvorsen). Her films are distinguished by a sensitivity to human problems, both social and personal, by a fundamental clear-eyed optimism and (in her fictional work) by a remarkable ability to get the best from actors.   WILLIAM BEARD

Wheeler, Arthur Oliver, surveyor, mountaineer (b at Lyrath, Ire 1 May 1860; d at Banff,

Alta 20 Mar 1945). Qualifying in 1881 as Ontario land surveyor and Dominion land surveyor, Wheeler worked on surveys throughout the W with the federal government and privately. He pioneered in photogrammetry, developed by E.G. DEVILLE. A founder of the ALPINE CLUB OF CANADA in 1906, he was a tireless promoter of the Rockies and Selkirks and participated in many first ascents.   ERIC J. HOLMGREN

Wheeler, Kenneth Vincent John, jazz trumpeter, composer (b at Toronto 14 Jan 1930). After studying music in Toronto, Wheeler moved to London, Eng, in 1952, rising to prominence in Britain in the 1960s, and in the European avant-garde in the 1970s. His association from 1971 to 1976 with American reedman Anthony Braxton brought him back to perform in N America. He is recognized as a major figure in jazz, and his extensive discography includes recordings with John Dankworth, Braxton, Globe Unity, and the co-operative trio Azimuth, as well as several of his own records (*Gnu High, Deer Wan, Around 6, Double, Double You*) after 1973. Wheeler spends the summers teaching at the Banff Jazz Workshop in the Banff Centre.   MARK MILLER

Wheeler, Lucile, alpine skier (b at Montréal 14 Jan 1935). She started skiing at age 2. In 1956, after 5 winters of rigorous training at Kitzbühel, Austria, with coach Pepi Salvenmoser, she won Canada's first Olympic ski medal, a bronze in the downhill. In 1958 she shattered a European monopoly of world ski championships by winning both the downhill and giant slalom titles, thereby inspiring Canada to begin sending a national ski team to Europe the following year. Her honours include Canada's Outstanding Athlete of the Year (1958).   MURRAY SHAW

Wheeler, Seager, plant breeder, farmer (b on the Isle of Wight, Eng 1869; d at Victoria 15 Dec 1961). After starting work at age 11, Wheeler immigrated to Saskatchewan in 1885, working on farms near Moose Jaw and Saskatoon until 1897, when he bought his own farm near Rosthern. In 1904 he began selective breeding of spring wheat, developing such popular varieties of the time as Early Triumph, Kitchener, Red Bobs and Supreme. He was 5 times the world champion hard spring wheat grower between 1911 and 1918, a fact used by agents of the Canadian government in the US to promote settlement of the Canadian Prairies. He also developed hardy fruits and other crops, winning several awards. Some of his techniques were documented in his 1919 *Wheeler's Book on Profitable Grain Growing.*   MARTIN K. McNICHOLL

Whelan, Edward, journalist, politician (b at Ballina, Ire 1824; d at Charlottetown 10 Dec 1867). In 1831 Whelan immigrated with his mother to Halifax, where he was apprenticed in 1832 in the printing office of Joseph HOWE. After his schooling in Halifax, he arrived in Charlottetown in 1843, already having had editorial experience. He established his own semiweekly Reform newspaper, the *Palladium,* which he discontinued in 1845 for financial reasons. Next year, at age 22, he was elected to the Assembly and in 1847 commenced the weekly *Examiner,* which he continued to publish, with some interruptions, until his death. An exceptionally able writer with a brilliant satiric pen and keen insight into character, Whelan was the leading journalistic spokesman for the Reformers in their struggle for RESPONSIBLE GOVERNMENT and a solution to the LAND QUESTION. In the mid-1860s he strongly supported CONFEDERATION, which was one reason for his first electoral defeat in Apr 1867. He seems not to have recovered from the ensuing bitterness and died that Dec.   IAN ROSS ROBERTSON

Whelan, Patrick James, tailor, convicted assassin (b in Ireland *c*1840; hanged at Ottawa 11 Feb 1869). Arrested within hours of the assassination of Thomas D'Arcy MCGEE on 7 Apr 1868, and formally charged with the murder 2 days later, Whelan persisted in his denial of guilt throughout a trial marred by bad procedure, and he repeated his denial on the scaffold at his public execution. The case remains controversial. Although FENIAN terrorists were popularly believed responsible for McGee's death, no proof was ever found that Whelan was a Fenian; and since the testimony that placed him at the scene of the crime can be discredited, there seems reason to doubt that he was in fact the assassin.   STANLEY GORDON

Reading: T.P. Slattery, *They Got to Find MEE Guilty Yet* (1972).

Whelk, common name for a carnivorous marine SNAIL which may be included with the Buccinid, Muricid or Purpurid families. Whelks are advanced prosobranch gastropod MOLLUSCS possessing a heavy, spindle-shaped shell with a siphonal groove. Arising from the latter is a sensory siphon that whelks use for the detection and tracking of prey. Several muricids are pests on oysters and, because of this, their biology and control have been extensively investigated. The Eastern oyster drill (*Urosalpinx cinerea*) and the Japanese oyster drill (*Ocenebra japonica*) have caused extensive damage to East and West Coast oyster fisheries, respectively. Oyster drills employ an auxiliary boring organ, located in the foot, to perforate the shell of their prey. The organ secretes enzymes that dissolve the organic matrix of the oyster's shell causing it to collapse, a process analogous to the collapse of a brick wall when mortar is removed. The proboscis bears a small, toothed feeding organ, a radula, which is inserted through the shell hole to feed on the victim's flesh. Separate sexes occur and copulation leads to production of lidded egg cases. Cannibalism within the egg cases results in the emergence of a few vigorous snails.   PETER V. FANKBONER

Whitby, Ont, Town, pop 45 819 (1986c), 36 698 (1981c), is located on Lk Ontario, 48 km E of Toronto. It was first known as Perry's Corners, after Peter Perry, a dynamic early settler. It was also known as Windsor, but was renamed Whitby in 1848 after a seaside town in Yorkshire, Eng. Whitby was made the county town for Ontario County in 1852 and was incorporated as a town in 1855. The former town of Whitby and township of Whitby amalgamated in 1968 to form a new municipality called the Town of Whitby. In Jan 1974 the County of Ontario was dissolved and Whitby became one of 8 area municipalities in the new Regional Municipality of Durham. With its excellent harbour, the Whitby-Port Perry Ry (1869) and road connections, Whitby's primary 19th-century economic activity was as a transportation centre; it had some of the finest grain-handling facilities on the N Shore of Lake Ontario. By 1871, however, it had been eclipsed by both Oshawa and Toronto. Whitby was in William Lyon MACKENZIE's riding and he held so many pre-1837 meetings in the town square that it became known as "radical corners." Other notables included local editor and Liberal organizer W.H. Higgins, whose letter to Archbishop Lynch of Toronto helped spur Ontario's "No Popery" campaign. A Senior "A" hockey team, the Whitby Dunlops was one of the last Canadian teams to win the world championship (1958).   GERALD STORTZ

Reading: L.A. Johnson, *History of the County of Ontario* (1973).

Whitchurch-Stouffville, Ont, Town, York County, pop 15 135 (1986c), 47 km NE of Toronto. The area of Whitchurch Twp was the site of several Indian villages. The first European settlement took place in the 1790s. Stouffville (originally Stouffersville or Stoversville) was named after Abraham Stouffer who arrived in 1805. Initially the affairs of Stouffville were administered by the township which was incorporated in 1851. However, the village soon became the dominant commercial centre in the region and inaugurated its own council in 1877. Despite the separation there continued to be an interdependence between the 2 and the sharing of utilities such as water supply and early telephone service. The present union was achieved in Jan 1971, at which time York Region, of which the town is part, was also formed. The town continues as a light industrial, commercial and primarily residential centre.   GERALD STORTZ

White, George, né Weitz, producer, director, librettist, lyricist, actor, dancer (b at New York City, NY 1890; d at Hollywood, Calif 10 Oct 1968). A "Runyonesque" Broadway showman, often presumed Canadian because his family moved to Toronto when he was 7, he played harmonica while selling newspapers at King and Bay streets and ran away before he was 18. He made his Broadway debuts acting in *The Echo* (1910) and dancing in *The Ziegfeld Follies* (1911). He came to prominence as the author-producer of *Scandals of 1919*, in which he starred. Until 1931 *George White's Scandals* were a virtually annual New York event. His extravaganzas featured showgirls and comedians, while popularizing Harlem jazz, "the blues," and the Charleston and Black Bottom dances. There were additional *Scandals* in 1935 and 1939, and a final nightclub version in 1963. Three editions (1934, 1935, 1945) were filmed.
                    DAVID GARDNER

White, James, geographer (b at Ingersoll, Ont 3 Feb 1863; d at Ottawa 26 Feb 1928). He was educated at RMC and in 1884 he was employed as an assistant topographer in the GEOLOGICAL SURVEY OF CANADA, where he carried out numerous surveys in Ontario, Québec and the Rocky Mts. He was appointed geographer and chief draftsman in 1894 and in 1899 became geographer and then chief geographer at the Dept of the Interior. White's contributions to Canadian geography over the next decade are truly remarkable. He expanded the staff, which allowed him to produce better general reference maps, and was responsible for the production of the first edition of the *Atlas of Canada* (1906). This was the second national atlas to be produced in the world. Other important publications included *Altitudes in Canada* (1901) and *Dictionary of Altitudes in Canada* (1903). In 1909 he resigned his position as chief geographer to become the secretary of the COMMISSION OF CONSERVATION, and in 1913 chairman and deputy head. In 1921 White became technical adviser to the minister of justice, and in this capacity he was responsible for the preparation of maps and other evidence in the LABRADOR BOUNDARY DISPUTE, which was brought before the Privy Council in London in 1926. White was a long-standing member and chairman (1927) of the Geographic Board of Canada. He also chaired the Advisory Board of Wild Life Protection (Canada) from its inception in 1917 and played an important part in the adoption by Canada and the US of the Migratory Birds Convention.
                    DANIEL MACKAY

White, Robert, labour leader (b at Upper Lands, N Ireland 28 Apr 1935). He came to Canada at age 13. He worked for Hay and Co in Woodstock, Ont, and by 1959 had become president of the UNITED AUTOMOBILE WORKERS Local 636. He was appointed UAW international representative and

in 1964 co-ordinator of organizing staff. In 1972 he became assistant to UAW director, Dennis MCDERMOTT. He travelled across Canada to mobilize protests against the federal wage-control program. He led the UAW opposition to corporate demands for wage concessions. Firmly believing that the Canadian wing of the UAW should act primarily in the interest of its 120 000 Canadian workers, White led the Canadian members in a strike and eventually a secession movement from the American UAW. He continued to lead the Canadian Auto Workers, and was also VP of the New Democratic Party. His autobiography, *Hard Bargains: My Life on the Line*, was published in 1987.

White-Collar Crime consists of occupational crime and corporate crime. Occupational crime refers to offences committed against legitimate institutions (businesses or government) by those with "respectable" social status. It includes the embezzlement of corporate funds, tax evasion, computer crime and expense-account fraud. Corporate crime refers to offences committed by legitimate institutions to further their own interests and includes conspiring to fix the prices of goods or services, the dumping of pollutants, the payment of kickbacks by manufacturers to retailers, misleading advertising, selling unsafe drugs, etc.

In Canada, most occupational crime is prohibited under the Canadian CRIMINAL CODE, which is enforced by municipal or provincial POLICE, a complicated procedure because the suspects are often employees of the institutions from which they are stealing, and the employers either do not discover the theft quickly or prefer to avoid publicity by not reporting the loss. The culprit may be fired or asked to make restitution. Corporate crimes are prohibited by a wide variety of federal, provincial and municipal laws. Enforcement is the responsibility of government inspectors who generally have fewer powers than police to detain suspects and search for evidence. Contrary to common belief, corporate crimes cause far more financial harm, and many more personal injuries (some leading to death) than do traditional crimes such as theft, robbery and assault.

The Combines Investigation Act (s36.37), renamed the Competition Act as of 19 June 1986, prohibits advertising special sales when prices have not been reduced, making false claims about what a product can accomplish, and selling used cars as new ones and a myriad of other acts. According to the federal Ministry of Consumer and Corporate Affairs, these are common crimes, and the ministry receives more complaints than it can investigate, so it chooses only the most serious and significant for prosecution. Compared to other Western countries, fines are low and enforcement infrequent. Many charges are laid annually under the false advertising provisions of the Act, but fines are small, usually less than $400 per charge. Excluding these sections, there have been 89 other prosecutions under the Combines Investigation Act from 1952 to 1975. Of these, 8 were acquitted and 2 were dismissed at a preliminary hearing. Twenty-two defendants (individuals and corporations) were served only with Order of Prohibition (a device whereby judges tell guilty parties not to repeat the offence) whereas 57 defendants were convicted and fined amounts ranging from $300 to $50 000 (averaging $7500 per case). Illegal combines can net the offending companies several million dollars per year in profits, so such fines are unlikely to be effective deterrents.

Other laws directed at corporate crime include the Food and Drugs Act (preventing the sale of contaminated food and drugs); Hazardous Products Act (preventing the sale of dangerous items);

Weights and Measures Act (preventing dishonest scales); Environmental Protection Acts, both federal and provincial; laws to protect the investor against unscrupulous promoters and brokers; and laws to ensure that workers are not exploited, eg, by being forced to work 18-hour days in unventilated facilities. However, these laws are not always stringently enforced; in general, authorities use persuasion first, and criminal sanctions as a last resort; when cases do go to court, they take longer, are more likely to be appealed by the defendant and to lead to an acquittal or withdrawal by the CROWN, and are less likely to lead to imprisonment than comparable Criminal Code cases; both judges and laymen are uncertain whether individuals and corporations convicted for acts against consumers, employees, rivals or the environment are truly criminals.

Laws against occupational crime do not include most kinds of computer crime, such as breaking computer codes and copying confidential records. However, the Copyright Act is at present being amended so that it will cover computer software.

Legal reform is needed to enforce laws against corporate crime. In 1986 the maximum fine for conspiracy offences was increased to $10 million (an important if symbolic step, since judges traditionally do not assess fines anywhere near the maximum allowable amount for corporate crimes); and banks and crown corporations engaging in commercial activities are now subject to the competition laws. Together with the 1976 amendments extending the laws to prohibit price fixing by professionals, setting heavier sanctions for misleading advertising and prohibiting deceptive selling practices, such as bait and switch and pyramid sales, the laws on competition have been thoroughly revised. It remains to be seen whether or not this will lessen its frequency or modify the harm corporate crime does. Attempts to strengthen environmental protection or MINIMUM WAGE laws have frequently been defeated by corporate threats to close up shop, eliminating badly needed jobs; and the public, not realizing the damage caused by corporate crime, has been slow to demand reform.   LAUREEN SNIDER

White Paper, a government document which outlines both government policy on an issue and possible future action, including legislation. It is sometimes a reaction to the report of a ROYAL COMMISSION or TASK FORCE. The Trudeau government, after its experience with the White Paper on Tax Reform, discovered that White Papers provided elites, rather than the public, with access to decision making and publicity. There has often been confusion about whether a White Paper has expressed government intentions or whether its purpose has simply been to raise an issue for discussion, like a GREEN PAPER. White Papers can be withdrawn with less embarrassment than legislation can.   C.E.S. FRANKS

White Pass, elev 889 m, sits on the Alaska-BC boundary, approximately 125 km S of Whitehorse, YT. In 1887 the federal government sent William Ogilvie to survey the 141st meridian national boundary where it crosses the Yukon R; members of his party found the pass. It was named for Thomas White, then minister of the interior. After the KLONDIKE gold strike (1896), thousands crossed White Pass 1897-98 to reach the goldfields at Dawson City. The narrow-gauge WHITE PASS AND YUKON RY (closed since 1982), from Skagway to Whitehorse, and a recently completed highway traverse the pass.   GLEN BOLES

White Pass and Yukon Railway, at 175 km long, was the steepest pitched railway in Canada.

Work began in 1898, at the height of the KLONDIKE GOLD RUSH, to provide transportation from Skagway, Alaska, to WHITEHORSE, YT. Building of the narrow gauge railway was an extremely difficult engineering feat, requiring extensive blasting, tunnels and precarious bridging. Thirty-five of the 35 000 who men worked on construction were killed. The summit of WHITE PASS was reached in Feb 1899 and the "last spike" was driven at Carcross on 29 July 1900. The gold was exhausted by the time work was complete, though the line struggled along carrying passengers and freight. The mining boom in the Yukon revived the railway, as lead-zinc was hauled from Faro, Mayo and Clinton Creek. The shutdown of the WP&Y in 1982, as a result of the collapse of the mining boom, deprived Whitehorse of some employment and its sea rail link.   JAMES MARSH

White Rock, BC, City, pop 14 387 (1986c), 13 550 (1981c), inc 1957, when it separated from municipality of SURREY, is 48 km by road SE of Vancouver and is bounded on the N, E and W by Surrey. It began as a recreational resort on the shores of Semiahmoo Bay. A boulder on the beach was painted white as a navigation mark by sailors. The bay's fine beach was famous for its swimming, fishing and boating. Cottages were built along the waterfront in the early 1900s and slowly a community developed, with a post office and general store, schools, waterworks and a hospital being established. Retail trade and services are its leading sources of employment, but it is primarily a residential, retirement and cultural community. White Rock has one newspaper and active summer theatre companies.

ALAN F.J. ARTIBISE

Whiteaves, Joseph Frederick, paleontologist, zoologist (b at Oxford, Eng 26 Dec 1835; d at Ottawa 8 Aug 1909). Whiteaves visited Canada in 1861 and stayed permanently from 1862. As museum curator and recording secretary of the Natural History Society of Montreal 1863-75, he studied modern freshwater and marine invertebrates and Ordovician fossils of the St Lawrence area of Québec. He joined the GEOLOGICAL SURVEY OF CANADA in Montréal, becoming zoologist in 1883. Whiteaves published more than 100 papers on Canadian paleontology and zoology, on Paleozoic and Mesozoic fossils from NB, Ontario, Manitoba, Alberta and BC and on modern marine and nonmarine fauna from all areas of Canada. Whiteaves was an original Fellow of the Royal Society of Canada (1881). M.J. COPELAND

Whitecourt, Alta, Town, pop 5737 (1986c), inc 1959, is located near the confluence of the McLeod and Athabasca rivers, 177 km NW of Edmonton. The Grand Trunk Ry survey led to this spot in 1903, and although the railway did not immediately follow, the survey line facilitated the emergence of a tiny settlement named Saquitawah (Cree for "meeting of the waters"). The community, composed mainly of trappers, was soon renamed Whitecourt after Walter White, who delivered mail to the district from Greencourt until a post office was established in 1910. With the building of the first of 3 sawmills in 1919, and the arrival of Canadian National Rys 2 years later, Whitecourt became a major lumbering centre. Oil and gas discoveries in the region, and the completion of Highway 43 in the mid-1950s brought further growth, and in 1971 Whitecourt was incorporated as a town. Recent developments (eg, a new pulp mill and a medium-density fibre-board plant at Blue Ridge, 30 km E) have increased Whitecourt's stature in the forestry industry.   DAVID LEONARD

Whitefish, common name for several freshwater fishes of class Osteichthyes, family Salmo-nidae (SALMON), subfamily Coregoninac (sometimes elevated to family rank). Whitefishes are widely distributed throughout the Northern Hemisphere. In Canada, 3 genera and 18 species are found, including 3 species of genus *Prosopium* (round, mountain and pygmy). Genus *Coregonus* includes the whitefishes proper and the ciscos (formerly classified in genus *Leucichthys*). White-fishes tend to be bottom feeders, with the snout overhanging the lower jaw and a few gill rakers for sifting large food particles. Ciscos feed in midwater, have a lower jaw at least as long as the upper, and many gill rakers for sifting small food items. There is considerable confusion concerning the relationships of species within genus *Coregonus*, but it includes at least 3 species of whitefish and 11 of cisco (5 found only in the Great Lakes). In southern Canada, most species, marketed as "chubs," are confined to lakes. In the North, river and even anadromous (seagoing) populations are common. The latter may undertake long journeys, eg, migrating over 1000 km in the Mackenzie R. The third genus, *Stenodus*, includes a single species, inconnu (*S. leucichthys*), the largest of the whitefishes (up to 150 cm long and over 28 kg). The inconnu preys on other fishes and has a pike-shaped body and a large mouth with a projecting lower jaw. It occurs in large lakes and streams but, in Canada, is confined to the Mackenzie drainage and areas west. Lake whitefish (*C. clupeaformis*) is Canada's most important commercial freshwater species, although catches have declined over the last 20 years, particularly in the Great Lakes, because of environmental degradation and overfishing. Several species of ciscos were formerly fished commercially in the Great Lakes, but are now much depleted and no longer commercially exploited. Several species of whitefish remain important in native food fisheries. Whitefishes are not important for sport, although angling for mountain whitefish (*P. williamsoni*) is gaining popularity in BC and Alberta.   PETER J. MCCART

Whitehorse, capital city of YUKON TERRITORY, pop 15 199 (1986c), 14 814 (1981c), inc 1950, is located at kilometre 1470, just off the ALASKA HIGHWAY, about 105 km N of the BC border. The city lies mainly on the W side of the YUKON R on a 600 m wide river plain backed by a steep scarp and a plateaulike summit 60 m above. Nestled in a protected valley, Whitehorse enjoys a moderate climate for the North, with warm, dry summers. Long hours of summer daylight (almost 20 hours in June) offset a short growing season and dark winters. Whitehorse is about 2070 km by road from Edmonton.

History Located at the head of navigation on the Yukon R, in 1898 Whitehorse became a temporary stopping point – past 2 major obstacles on the river, Miles Canyon and the Whitehorse Rapids – for prospectors during the KLONDIKE GOLD RUSH. In 1900 it became a permanent settlement, based on transportation and services, with the completion of the WHITE PASS AND YUKON RAILWAY from Skagway, Alaska. The community grew around the point where the railway and river met, on the western bank of the river. Since 1900 the White Pass and Yukon Route Corp has helped the city and territory develop by providing ser-

Whitehorse, capital city of Yukon Territory, originated as a temporary stopping point for prospectors bound for the Klondike (*photo by Fred Bruemmer*).

vices and employment. Apart from its railway, the corporation established the British Yukon Navigation Company, which built riverboats and operated them to DAWSON until 1954.

A short-lived copper boom in the Whitehorse copper belt ended in 1920. Throughout the 1920s and 1930s, the corporation promoted the tourist industry and Whitehorse became an outfitting and takeoff base. In 1935 it established the British Yukon Aviation company to transport mail, freight and passengers from its base in Whitehorse. From an estimated 2000 after the gold rush, Whitehorse's population dropped by 1941 to about 750.

During WWII Whitehorse played a significant role as a key link in the N-S transportation system supporting the war effort. About 30 000 American and Canadian servicemen and civilian workers expanded the facilities of the Northwest Staging Route (a series of airfields across the Northwest), which acted as the air link; built the 2400 km ALASKA HWY, and constructed the CANOL PIPELINE from NORMAN WELLS, NWT, and an oil refinery at Whitehorse. After the war, the Alaska Hwy was opened to civilian traffic and replaced the Yukon R as the dominant transportation route. Whitehorse became the headquarters of the Northwest highway system. In 1953 the territorial capital was moved from Dawson to Whitehorse, adding the government sector to the city's economic base.

Economy In the 1950s the federal government initiated a road-construction and financial-aid program to stimulate the territory's mining economy. As a result silver production expanded at Mayo, and copper and lead-zinc production started at Faro. By the end of the 1950s an integrated ship-train-truck containerized transportation system was moving ore through Whitehorse to external markets. The shutdown of mines in the Yukon, notably Faro in 1982, had an adverse effect on the city, and the WP&Y rail operations were ended in 1982. However, the Faro mine reopened in 1986, gold mining began at nearby Mt Skookum, and the world's largest TUNGSTEN reserve was found at Mae Pass.

Improved accessibility also directly affected Whitehorse's economy through the tourist industry. Since 1960 there has been an average annual growth rate of 12%. In 1987 an estimated 400 000 people visited the territory, bringing revenues of around $82 million. Much of the optimism for the future is based on the tourist potential of the compelling northern landscape.

Cityscape Whitehorse's original townsite, surveyed on a conventional grid pattern, evolved into 3 functional zones: commercial and retail located on Main and Front streets, residential N and S of Main Street, and the railway and docking facilities between Front St and the Yukon R. The industrial area, including mining company offices, lies N of the city, while government offices dominate blocks on the edge of the commercial area, located in the city centre. Its colourful past is preserved in the restored riverboat *Klondike* and the Anglican log church built in 1900. A new $40-million facility for Yukon College is to be completed in 1988.   PAUL M. KOROSCIL

Whiten, Colette, sculptor (b at Birmingham, Eng 7 Feb 1945). In 1972 she graduated from the Ontario College of Art, recipient of the Governor General's Medal, and exhibited her first cast piece, a wooden structure filled with fibreglass molds of her friends' arms and legs, documented by photographs and slides to record the creative process. Her figures are concerned with the nature of human existence, with human interaction (particularly power relationships) and with the process of art. Since 1975 her focus has shifted to an intimate exploration of the nature of identity and the duality inherent in the cast image (*September, 1975*). Since 1986, Whiten has reassessed the nature of the art object and of art making and has turned in her investigation of power, in this case images of political power and everyday violence, to a series of small-scale meticulously stitched works. A show of her needlepoint was held at a Toronto gallery in early 1987.
                                                    JOYCE ZEMANS

Whiteshell Provincial Park (est 1961), 105 km E of Winnipeg, Man, by the Trans-Canada Highway, is Precambrian SHIELD country. Glaciation acting on the 2.5-billion-year-old rocks, has formed many lakes and granite outcrops. West Hawk Lk, the deepest in Manitoba (111 m), is believed to have been created by a METEORITE. Most of the area is forested, with both coniferous and deciduous species; numerous wetland plants occur (eg, lilies, wild rice). Mammals include black bears, moose, deer, coyotes, beavers and mink. Bird life is varied, Canada geese being especially abundant at the Alfred Hole Sanctuary. Indian presence can be traced archaeologically to 3000 BC and is revealed in petroglyphs at Bannock Point. In 1732 the LA VÉRENDRYE expedition traversed the area via the Winnipeg R; other explorers (eg, MACKENZIE, THOMPSON, HENRY, KANE) followed. The transcontinental railway was built in the 1880s and sporadic mining, logging and farming occurred. In the 1920s, the area's recreation potential was recognized, cottages were developed and, in 1931, a Forest Reserve was established. The park is accessible by several roads, although the NE section remains a roadless wilderness. Resort facilities are available at Falcon Lk and West Hawk Lk. Activities include motorboating, fishing, swimming, camping, horseback riding and interpretation events and, in winter, downhill and cross-country skiing and snowmobiling. Many canoe routes, day-use or interpretive hiking trails, and the 60 km Mantario wilderness trail are available.   JOHN S. MARSH

Whiteway, Sir William Vallance, lawyer, politician, premier of Newfoundland 1878-85, 1889-94, 1895-97 (b near Totnes, Eng 1 Apr 1828; d at St John's 24 June 1908). Whiteway came to Newfoundland in 1843 and began a legal career in 1852. He entered politics in 1859 and achieved prominence as a leading confederate in the late 1860s. Defeated in the anticonfederate landslide of 1869, he later returned to the Assembly, becoming solicitor general in 1874 and premier in 1878. Ambitious and energetic, Whiteway worked to develop the Newfoundland economy. His instrument was a trans-island railway, begun in 1881. The policy was controversial, and Whiteway found himself maneuvered out of office in 1885 by a mercantile party that favoured more attention for the trou-

bled fishing industry. He was triumphantly re-elected in 1889 as leader of the Liberal Party, and again in 1893 on a platform stressing railway building and economic progress. However, the filing of petitions alleging corrupt electoral practices against Whiteway and 16 other Liberals precipitated a major political crisis and his government's resignation in Apr 1894. He regained the premiership in 1895 but was defeated in the 1897 election. Soon after, he was replaced as Liberal leader by Robert BOND. Whiteway's principal legacy is the Newfoundland railway, though his assertion of colonial rights on the FRENCH SHORE is historically important. He was among the first Newfoundland politicians to cast the political process in class terms.   J.K. HILLER

Whitney, Sir James Pliny, lawyer, politician, premier of Ontario 1905-14 (b in Williamsburg Twp, Canada W 2 Oct 1843; d at Toronto 25 Sept 1914). After breaking a 33-year Liberal hold upon the province, he headed an administration noteworthy for its reforms and its creation of an enduring political machine. Son of a blacksmith, Whitney was a staunch Conservative long before being called to the bar in 1876. He won the provincial riding of Dundas in an 1888 by-election, and never yielded it. Chosen leader of the Ontario party in 1896, he inherited a dispirited body weakened by religious controversy, a shortage of promising men and a poor organization. As Opposition leader, he rebuilt the Tories and healed most of the wounds, while constantly berating the governing Liberals and slowly shaping a party platform. In office, his administration began Ontario's publicly owned hydroelectric power system, set U of T on a firm financial foundation, passed ground-breaking workmen's compensation legislation, created new bureaucratic forms such as the Ontario Ry and Municipal Board, and enacted tough but fair liquor legislation. On the negative side, his government produced Regulation 17 governing the use of French as a language of instruction in some Ontario schools; this sparked a bitter controversy with Franco-Ontarians that did nothing for national unity as WWI approached (*see* ONTARIO SCHOOLS QUESTION).   CHARLES W. HUMPHRIES

Whitton, Charlotte, social worker, politician, feminist (b at Renfrew, Ont 8 Mar 1896; d at Ottawa 25 Jan 1975). Whitton was one of this century's most colourful and controversial women. Pugnacious and energetic, she is best remembered as Ottawa's flamboyant and outspoken mayor during the 1950s and 1960s. Her more significant accomplishments, however, occurred during her earlier career as the director and driving force behind the Canadian Council on Child Welfare (later the Canadian Welfare Council and the CANADIAN COUNCIL ON SOCIAL DEVELOPMENT) from 1920 to 1941. Whitton joined the fledgling council after a brilliant academic career at Queen's during WWI. In the 1920s she crusaded relentlessly for professional standards in the care of juvenile immigrants and neglected and dependent children. During the Depression, she became a key adviser on federal unemployment relief policy. An arch social conservative, however, Whitton's opposition to more liberal spending on the unemployed in the 1930s placed her increasingly on the margins of Canadian SOCIAL WORK.

After resigning from the Welfare Council in 1941, Whitton championed women's equality in politics and the workplace. However, her views on women, as on the WELFARE STATE, were contradictory. She opposed more liberal divorce laws and criticized married women who worked. Elected as a controller to Ottawa's municipal council in 1950, Whitton became Canada's first woman mayor in 1951. She was re-elected mayor

in 1952 and 1954, and again in 1960 and 1962. Defeated in 1964, Whitton continued as an alderman until her retirement from politics in 1972. Her tenure as mayor was notable chiefly for her stormy verbal and, in one celebrated instance, physical battles with hostile male colleagues.
                                            JAMES STRUTHERS

Reading: P.T. Rooke and R.L. Schnell, *No Bleeding Heart: Charlotte Whitton a Feminist on the Right* (1987).

Who Has Seen the Wind (Toronto and Boston, 1947), a novel by W.O. MITCHELL, tells the story of a prairie boy's initiation into the mysteries of life, death, God, and the spirit that moves through everything: the wind. The novel's greatest strengths lie in its sensitive evocations of Brian O'Connal's "feeling," sometimes associated with his various experiences of death, sometimes with a child's fundamental, inarticulate but insistent curiosity to discover the world within and beyond himself. Brian learns about life and death in town and on the prairie: the town is the setting for social conventions, institutions and hypocrisies; and on the prairie is a natural order throughout which the wind metes out its invisible imperatives, chief among them change and death. Vibrant with the serious comedy of children's dialogue, rich with poetic descriptions of the prairie in all its guises, *Who Has Seen the Wind* articulates a universal theme in a classically western Canadian voice. The novel has been translated into French as *Qui a vu le vent* (Montréal, 1974) and into several other languages; it was also made into a successful movie.
                                            NEIL BESNER

Wholesale Trade Wholesalers either sell goods for resale to retailers (*see* RETAIL TRADE), to industrial, commercial, governmental, institutional and professional users or to other wholesalers. They also act as agents in connection with such sales. Firms engaged in wholesaling, as well as retailing, contracting, service trades, manufacturing, etc, are considered to be primarily wholesalers whenever they derive a larger gross margin (the difference between total sales and the cost of goods sold) from wholesale trade than from any other activity. Wholesalers include primary-product dealers, eg, those engaged in the wholesaling of grain, livestock, fish, leaf tobacco, raw furs and so on; wholesale merchants, who buy and sell goods on their own account (that is, they take legal title to them); agents and brokers, who buy and sell goods for others on commission; manufacturers' sales branches and offices, which are wholesale businesses owned for wholesaling their own goods; and petroleum-bulk tank plants and truck distributors who specialize in the distribution of petroleum products.

Wholesalers perform basic marketing functions for the firms from which they purchase and for the firms to which they sell. They anticipate customers' needs and demands, carry inventories, deliver merchandise, extend credit, provide market information, provide consulting services and purchase merchandise. For manufacturers, the wholesaler may offer to sell and store merchandise, may finance the production by purchasing in advance, may reduce credit by screening customers and may provide marketing information. In order to be successful, the wholesale firm must offer these functions at a lower cost than manufacturers or retailers. In Canada wholesalers are successful because of the great number of small- and medium-sized manufacturers and retailers who cannot perform such functions as effectively, partly because of the country-wide distribution of cities and partly because of the great distances between manufacturing and intermediate and retail centres.

Types of Wholesalers Merchant wholesalers, agents and brokers, and manufacturers' sales branches are the 3 major types of wholesalers. Specialized wholesalers include co-operative marketing associations, petroleum-bulk plants, terminals, and liquified-petroleum (LP) facilities. There are about 22 000 merchant wholesaling firms in Canada which are either full-service wholesalers who perform all of the marketing functions or limited-line or -service wholesalers. Electrical, hardware and pharmaceutical wholesalers, for example, who sell all of the products in the category are full-service wholesalers. Limited-line wholesalers, by contrast, only carry narrow lines such as paint or electric motors; they also include cash-and-carry firms which do not provide credit or transportation to their customers. Agents and brokers (eg, auction companies, agricultural commission merchants, manufacturing agents, food brokers, selling agents, and export and import agents and brokers) specialize in exchange functions and are organized by product lines; they make their profits by commissions. Manufacturers' sales branches are wholesale businesses established by manufacturers which often sell the products of other suppliers as well – an important type of wholesaling in Canada. All of the types of wholesaler operate in most of the different product categories. For merchant wholesalers the most important lines of trade are food, petroleum products, and machinery and equipment; for agents and brokers, the most important areas are farm products, petroleum products, apparel, and dry goods.

Wholesale trade at the federal level comes under the Competition Act, which regulates mergers and monopolies, specialization agreements, export agreements, price discrimination, delivered prices (that is, forcing the customer to pay a delivered price regardless of where or how the manufacturer delivers the merchandise), reciprocal buying and resale price maintenance (pressuring customers to sell at a price set by the wholesaler).

Over several decades the dominant position of independent wholesale middlemen in the marketing system has declined because manufacturers and retailers have grown in size. The functions of the wholesaler are now performed either by manufacturers or by customers or retailers largely because, in their attempt to become price competitive, retailers have gone directly to manufacturers to purchase at lower prices. However, wholesalers have also failed to adapt to market conditions. Independent wholesalers will continue to dominate in the sale of industrial goods, machinery and petroleum products sold primarily to agricultural segments. In these areas, they have been able to specialize and adapt to the vast distribution of customers throughout Canada. The independent wholesaler will decline in importance in the marketing of retail goods, especially food items. This is a nationwide phenomenon, especially where wholesalers have been affected by large chain retailers. A primary area of growth for all types of wholesaler in Canada is in the export trade. RONALD SAVITT

Whoop-up, a shortened form of "whoop it up" which means to celebrate boisterously. It recalls FT WHOOP-UP, the fort built in 1869 by American fur traders in what is now southern Alberta. The fort, which was the centre of the illegal exchange with the Indians of whisky for buffalo hides, was abandoned when the NORTH-WEST MOUNTED POLICE came West in 1874. JOHN ROBERT COLOMBO

Whooping Crane (*Grus americana*), standing almost 1.5 m high, is the tallest N American bird. Adults may weigh 7.5 kg and have a 2.2 m wingspan. They are impressive in their pure white plumage with black wing tips, long black

Whooping crane and chick (*courtesy Environment Canada, Parks/Prairie & Northern Region*).

legs, black moustachelike markings and red crown. In their first summer and fall, juveniles are predominantly cinnamon and white. After their first birthday, they are almost indistinguishable from adults. Whooping cranes, indigenous to N America, number about 136 wild birds and are officially classified as ENDANGERED ANIMALS. In 1941 only 15 wild migratory birds remained, and conservation measures and joint management by the Canadian and US Wildlife Services and other organizations were instituted. In 1987, 132 wild birds, including an all-time record of 25 juveniles, migrated from their only breeding range, in WOOD BUFFALO NATIONAL PARK, to their winter range in the Aransas National Wildlife Refuge on the Texas coast. From 1984 to 1987, 28 to 32 pairs nested in Wood Buffalo and were watched by Canadian Wildlife Service biologists. Whoopers nest and raise their young in inaccessible bogs and bulrush marshes. In some years, dry weather destroys nesting and feeding habitat, and wolves may take some young, leaving only a few juveniles to begin the 3900 km migration with their parents. En route, hazards such as powerlines may endanger them, particularly if the birds are flying low during poor weather conditions. They spend the winter feeding and resting. During late Mar and early Apr the northward migration begins. They arrive the last week in Apr. Two eggs (rarely one or 3) are laid in a large nest of bulrushes. Eggs are incubated by both parents and reddish brown chicks hatch after 29-30 days. Usually, only one chick survives. Each year since 1975, a small number of surplus eggs have been removed and placed in nests of greater sandhill cranes (*G. canadensis tabida*) in Idaho. The foster parents hatch and rear the whooper chicks. It is hoped that these whoopers will mate with their own kind to form a new, self-perpetuating population. At least 25 Idaho-raised whoopers have adopted the migration pathway of their foster-parents, and the 2 species winter together in New Mexico. Two viable, geographically separate populations would greatly reduce the danger of extinction. E. KUYT

Whyte Museum of the Canadian Rockies, The, aims to foster the culture of the Canadian Rockies and to collect, preserve, exhibit and make available for research and education materials related to the Rockies' cultural heritage. Peter Whyte, a Banff native, met Catharine Robb, a member of a distinguished New England family, at the School of the Museum of Fine Arts in Boston, where they were both students in the late 1920s. After their marriage in 1930, they moved to Banff, built a log home and studio along the banks of the Bow R and dedicated their lives to painting the landscape, activities and native people of the mountains. Their collection of art and historical materials related to the area grew rapidly and in 1958 they set up a foundation to ensure its survival. In 1968 a museum building was con-

structed adjacent to their home with their collection forming its nucleus. Peter died in 1965 and Catharine in 1979, after which the museum was named in their honour and was expanded to incorporate their home and other historic buildings on the site. The Whyte Museum of the Canadian Rockies consists at present of a gallery, containing a permanent collection of art relating primarily to the Canadian Rockies; an archives, where the documentary history of the mountains of western Canada is preserved and made available for research; and a heritage collection, which collects and exhibits cultural history artifacts and historic homes and cabins of the region. TED HART

Wiarton, Ont, Town, pop 2054 (1986c), 2074 (1981c), inc 1894, located at the head of Colpoys B on GEORGIAN BAY, 225 km NW of Toronto. The site of 17th-century French missions, it was first settled in 1866 and was named for Wiarton Place, near Maidstone, Eng, birthplace of Sir Edmund HEAD, governor general when the area was surveyed. Logging predominated until WWI. Nestled at the base of the ruggedly picturesque BRUCE PENINSULA, it is now a service centre for the tourist industry and the site of major airport facilities. DANIEL FRANCIS

WIC (Western International Communications Ltd), controlled by Frank Griffiths and the Owen family, is one of western Canada's largest media companies. Its broadcasting holdings include 9 radio stations in Vancouver, Calgary, Winnipeg and Toronto, and in television a 59% interest in British Columbia Television Co (BCTV), which owns CHAN-TV, Vancouver, and CHEK-TV, Victoria, stations which provide CTV television service for all of BC. Western, through BCTV, has a 51.4% interest in Canadian Satellite Communications Inc, which provides television services via satellite to rural and remote regions of Canada (*see* SATELLITE COMMUNICATIONS). Other interests include broadcast commercial production, sales and promotion operations. Total revenues in 1987 were $95 million. PETER S. ANDERSON

Wickananish, or Wikinanish, meaning "having no one in front of him in the canoe," Nootka chief (*fl* 1788-93). Wickananish was the leading chief at Clayoquot Sound, on the W coast of Vancouver I, during the period of initial European contact. Because trading vessels visited Clayoquot Sound less frequently than Nootka, Wickananish was not as well known as MAQUINNA but he was certainly as wealthy and powerful as his neighbour. Wickananish had achieved prominence in Nootka society according to traditional patterns and then, with the coming of the white man, he was able to consolidate and enhance his position by controlling the local maritime FUR TRADE. ROBIN FISHER

Wickett, Samuel Morley, political economist, leather-goods manufacturer (b at Brooklin, Ont 17 Oct 1872; d at Toronto 7 Dec 1915). A graduate of U of T (1894), he was one of the first Canadians to pursue advanced studies in economics in Europe (Austria, Germany), where the traditions of state planning so impressed him that he became Canada's foremost advocate of employing professional administrators at all levels of government. A pioneer in urban studies and reform, and a lecturer in POLITICAL ECONOMY at U of T (1898-1905), he launched a monograph series on Canadian municipal government and helped found the Toronto Bureau of Municipal Research (1913-82). Elected an alderman in 1913, he prepared a transportation committee report recommending the establishment of a Toronto metropolitan region for planning urban services. He went into business in 1905 and led the CANADIAN MANUFACTURERS' ASSN in its unsuccessful efforts to secure technical education and a nonpartisan tariff board. Stressing the need for data upon which to base rational decisions, he lobbied for a statistical bureau in Ottawa. Like other Canadian businessmen concerned about urban problems in the period 1895 to 1914, Wickett was an elitist who distrusted popular democracy and opposed extending the franchise. It was exposure to the German ideals of state service and planning based on statistics that made his contributions unique. *See also* URBAN AND REGIONAL PLANNING.

JOHN WEAVER

Wicks, Alfred, "Ben," cartoonist, television personality, writer (b at London, Eng 1 Oct 1926). Wicks immigrated to Calgary in 1957. Working as a milkman and a militia bandsman, he sold cartoons to *The Saturday Evening Post* and the Calgary *Albertan*, launching a career that has made him Canada's most prolific and allegedly best-paid cartoonist. Wicks's cartoons went into syndication after he joined the Toronto *Telegram* in 1966. Since 1975 he has drawn both one-panel gags and a daily strip, "The Outcasts," which combines political comment with humour. To enable binational circulation, Wicks draws both US and Canadian versions of the strip. His art is crude ("Actually, I'm rotten at drawing," he admits cheerfully) but his satire trenchant; 12 books of Wicks cartoons have been published. He was host of "The World of Wicks" on Global TV and has contributed articles to several magazines.

JOHN H. THOMPSON

Widmer, Christopher, surgeon, medical educator, medical administrator (b at High Wycombe, Eng 15 May 1780, d at Toronto 3 May 1858). Widmer was a dominant figure in Upper Canadian medicine from the 1820s almost until his death. After serving on the medical staff in Spain and Portugal in the Peninsular War (1808-14) and in Canada (1814-17), he settled at York [Toronto]. In 1819 he was appointed to the Medical Board of Upper Canada, and presided over this and successor regulatory boards (1822-58), leading the push for high standards of medical practice and education. He was influential in the founding of the Toronto General Hospital, the provincial lunatic asylum and the King's College (U of T) medical school. In 1853 Widmer was briefly chancellor of the university, elected in a vain protest against government plans to close the medical school. In politics he was conservative, until late in 1836, when he became a prominent ally of W.W. and Robert BALDWIN. From 1843 to 1858 he served on the legislative council of Canada. Fiercely energetic, profane of speech, a reputed atheist and philanderer, Widmer remained a brilliant surgeon until remarkably late in life.

PAUL ROMNEY

Wiebe, Rudy Henry, writer (b at Speedwell, near Fairholme, Sask 4 Oct 1934). Wiebe has written impressive novels not only about his own people, the MENNONITES, but about other minority ethnic groups living close to the land. Born in a small Low-German-speaking community in northern Saskatchewan 4 years after his parents emigrated from Russia, Wiebe was the youngest of 7 children and did not learn English until he went to school. He attended high school in Coaldale, Alta, and later U of Alberta. His first novel, *Peace Shall Destroy Many* (1962), set in a community similar to that in which he had grown up, began as an exercise for his MA. It is a powerful problem novel concerned with the split between pacifist principles and the urge to violence in the hero and in the congregation in which he lives during WWII. On publication it caused bitter controversy among Mennonites. It was followed by *First and Vital Candle* (1966), set in an Indian com-

munity in northern Ontario and dealing didactically with moral and religious issues. In 1970, his first "epic" novel, *The Blue Mountains of China*, presented a saga of the Mennonite people dispersed yet enduring in Russia, Paraguay and Canada. Wiebe then turned to historical fiction. *The Temptations of Big Bear* (1973) is a long, intricate novel centered on the Plains Cree chief (*see* BIG BEAR). It won a Gov Gen's Award. *The Scorched-Wood People* (1977) is set in the same period and offers an interpretation of Louis RIEL from the viewpoint of the Métis. Both books are based on detailed historical research, and each offers a sympathetic but not idealized portrait of a complex and controversial figure. His latest novel, *My Lovely Enemy* (1983), combines his interest in Mennonite and Indian subjects; it is a daring, experimental book involving a radical theology of love.

Wiebe has also published 3 volumes of short stories, *Where Is the Voice Coming From?* (1974), *Alberta/A Celebration* (1979) and *The Angel of the Tar Sands* (1982); a play, *Far as the Eye Can See*, written in collaboration with Theatre Passe Muraille (1977); a novella, *The Mad Trapper* (1980), based on the RCMP hunt for Albert Johnson, and, with Bob Beal, *War in the West: Voices of the 1885 Rebellion* (1985), an illustrated collection of documents and memoirs.

Wiebe holds a bachelor of theology degree from the Mennonite Brethren Bible College, Winnipeg (1962), and for 18 months edited the *Mennonite Brethren Herald*. In 1967 he began teaching English and creative writing at U of Alberta. He is remarkable for the ambitious scope of his fiction, his treatment of important moral issues, and a craggy style which, though sometimes ungainly, frequently results in an eloquence that is both appropriate and evocative. Wiebe was awarded the Royal Society of Canada's Lorne Pierce Medal in 1987.

W.J. KEITH

Reading: W.J. Keith, *Epic Fiction* (1981) and, ed, *A Voice in the Land: Essays by and about Rudy Wiebe* (1981).

Rudy Wiebe has written impressive novels about his own people, the Mennonites, as well as about others who live close to the land (*photo by Jorge Frascara*).

Wieland, Joyce, artist, filmmaker (b at Toronto 30 June 1931). Wieland studied at Central Technical School, Toronto, and in 1960 held her first exhibition of paintings at the Isaacs Gallery, Toronto, where she showed paintings in an abstract expressionist genre, as well as drawings and cartoons, and later her constructions. From 1962 to 1970 she and her then-husband, artist Michael SNOW, lived in New York where she became an

Joyce Wieland, *The Artist on Fire* (1983), oil on canvas (*courtesy Robert McLaughlin Gallery, Oshawa*).

important figure in the experimental film world, with such award-winning films as *Rat Life and Diet in North America* (1968) and *La Raison avant la passion* (1967-69). She is known for her feature-length film *The Far Shore* (1976). Passionately concerned with the aesthetic perspective of the woman artist, Wieland draws inspiration from Canadian history, politics and ecology and she has worked in a variety of media (painting, drawing, construction, quilting, embroidery and film). In 1971 the National Gallery of Canada organized "True Patriot Love," its first major exhibition of a living Canadian woman artist. Recently in her paintings she has turned to visionary landscape and figurative imagery. In Apr 1987 the Art Gallery of Ontario mounted a major travelling retrospective of Wieland's work, and in Sept 1987 she was awarded the visual arts award from the Toronto Arts Awards Foundation. Her commissions include *Barren Ground, Cariboo*, for the Spadina Subway (Toronto) and *Défende la terre*, for the National Science Library (Ottawa).

JOYCE ZEMANS

Wiens, Clifford Donald, architect (b at Glenn Kerr, Sask 27 Apr 1926). Raised on a Mennonite farm, Wiens studied painting with A.Y. JACKSON at the BANFF CENTRE FOR CONTINUING EDUCATION, studied agriculture at U of Sask, and machine tooling at the Moose Jaw Technical School before graduating from the Rhode Island School of Design in 1954 and founding his own firm in Regina in 1957. Saskatchewan's most respected architect, Wiens has received numerous awards, and his distinguished body of work, from rural schools to the 1983 CBC headquarters in Regina, reflects both corporate modern architecture and a broader expressionist movement.

TREVOR BODDY

Wiesner, Karel, chemist, educator (b at Prague, Czech 1919; d at Fredericton 28 Nov 1986). Wiesner studied chemical engineering in Prague, receiving his doctorate in 1945 for research in polarography at Bulovka Hospital. He studied in Switzerland before coming to UNB in 1948 where he developed Canada's leading school of natural products chemistry. His former students are found at most of the major chemistry schools in Canada. In 1957 he was elected a fellow of the RSC and in 1963 received the highest honour of the Chemical Institute of Canada. He authored more than 200 papers in organic chemistry, and made major contributions in the fields of alkaloids, terpenoids and steroids.

W.A. AYER

Wigwam, an Algonquian domed or conical dwelling prevalent in the eastern half of N America. The circular framework of poles was covered with bark or reed mats. A hole in the roof allowed the smoke from the fire to escape. The wigwam was occupied by one or more families.

RENÉ R. GADACZ

Wilcox, Charles Seward, businessman (b at Painesville, Ohio 16 Mar 1856; d at Hamilton, Ont 6 June 1938). Wilcox attended Dartmouth College and Yale U, graduating in 1879, the same year as Canada's NATIONAL POLICY tariff gave substantial new protection to the iron and steel industries. The tariff induced a group of Cleveland, Ohio, capitalists to purchase the rolling mill of the former Great Western Ry in Hamilton. The firm took over the Hamilton Blast Furnace Co (1899) and Wilcox was appointed general manager of the new enterprise, known as the Hamilton Steel and Iron Co, which in 1910 became a principal component of the major Canadian merger creating the Steel Company of Canada (*see* STELCO INC). Wilcox was appointed the company's first president, and he insisted on delaying dividends on common shares in order to build up the company's capacity and financial situation. He stepped down from the presidency in 1916 but remained chairman of the board. A prominent corporate executive and philanthropist, Wilcox conducted his business and public life in model fashion for a man of his class and time. He held directorships in several Canadian corporations, including the Royal Bank and National Trust.   JOHN WEAVER

Wild Animals I Have Known (New York, 1898), Ernest Thompson SETON's most famous collection of animal stories, reprinted numerous times and translated into at least 15 languages, is reputed to be one of the best-selling books of any Canadian writer. Seton was a lifelong naturalist, scientist, painter and illustrator; the first edition of *Wild Animals* appeared with "two hundred drawings by the author." For some critics, Seton is one of the originators of the realistic animal story; to others his stories exemplify the Canadian writer's tendency to depict animals as victims (*see* SURVIVAL). Seton's best-known story, "Lobo, The King of Currumpaw," is representative in its dramatic but meticulous recreation of a particular animal and its notorious exploits, as well as in its presentation of the wolf's tragic end at the hands of man. *Wild Animals I Have Known* established Seton with a wide public as a keen-eyed naturalist and a natural storyteller.   NEIL BESNER

Wild Rice, a true GRASS (*Zizania aquatica*, family Gramineae or Poaceae), grows in marshlands and along waterways from Manitoba to the Atlantic Ocean in southern Canada, and over much of the eastern US. Botanists recognize several varieties; some treat these as 3-4 separate species. An annual with stalks up to 3 m high, wild rice bears long, thin grains in loose, drooping clusters. When ripe, grains drop readily and can be harvested by bending laden stalks into a boat and flailing them. They were and are an important food for Indians, who sow and harvest the crop, particularly in the Great Lakes region. Wild rice, one of the few wild plant foods harvested and marketed in Canada, can be purchased throughout the country. Large quantities are exported annually. The nutty-flavoured grains, an ideal dressing for wild game, are good in casseroles and other dishes. Today, wild rice is increasing in importance as a cash crop. The 2 major growing areas in Canada are Manitoba and Ontario. In 1986 Canada exported 204 t ($1.36 million), mainly to the US (149 t). *See also* PLANTS, NATIVE USES.   NANCY J. TURNER

Reading: William G. Dore, *Wild-Rice* (1969).

Wildflowers include all flowering plants growing without cultivation. In popular use, the term refers mainly to the numerous nonwoody (herbaceous) plants and smaller shrubs with showy flowers. Plants with inconspicuous, petalless flowers, eg, the GRASSES and the superficially similar SEDGES, are not usually recognized as wildflowers. There are approximately 4000 species of

Wildflowers: 1. Milkweed (*Asclepias syriaca L.*), 2. Buttercup (*Ranunculus acris L.*), 3. Bunchberry (*Cornus canadensis L.*), 4. Heal-all (*Prunella vulgaris L.*), 5. Chicory (*Cichorium intybus L.*), 6. Goldenrod (*Solidago*), 7. Blue-eyed grass (*Sisyrinchium L.*), 8. Blue flag (*Iris versicolor L.*) (*artwork by Claire Tremblay*).

flowering plants in Canada, of which about 3000 may be considered wildflowers. About one-quarter of these have been introduced from other regions of the world. These introduced WEEDS differ from most native wildflowers mainly in their ability to spread rapidly into disturbed habitats and agricultural lands. Their prolific growth and often harmful or objectionable properties make many of them unwanted aliens. Some native wildflowers, such as milkweed (*Asclepias*) and locoweed (*Oxytropis*), can also be considered weeds since they commonly grow in fields and pastures in considerable numbers and may cause livestock poisoning. The common names of many wildflowers (eg, locoweed) make reference to some property of the plant or its use in native cultures and folk medicine. Names such as may apple (*Podophyllum*), fairy-spuds (*Claytonia*), wild ginger (*Asarum*) and miner's lettuce (*Montia*) refer to the edible nature of the plant or its parts. Others like heal-all (*Prunella*), liverleaf (*Hepatica*) and toothwort (*Dentaria*) refer to a belief in the curative power of the plant, specific to the part of the body recorded in the name.

Distribution Some of the most widespread native wildflowers in Canada are the plants of the coniferous boreal forest. Within this broad belt, extending from Newfoundland to the YT, are found such common wildflowers as twinflower, mitrewort, bunchberry and Labrador tea. Because of the relatively uniform conditions beneath this evergreen canopy throughout the growing season, no obvious displays of seasonal flowering occur. Within the deciduous and mixed deciduous-coniferous forests of the Great Lakes and the St Lawrence R valley, an array of showy, woodland wildflowers heralds the arrival of each new growing season. These perennial herbs, many of which are members of the lily, buttercup and saxifrage families, come to flower and set seed before the unfolding new leaves of the canopy overhead shade the forest floor. As summer progresses, the wildflowers of the forest clearings, meadows, riverbanks and lakes gradually come to flower. In the shortening days of fall, the numerous and sometimes confusing members of the daisy family (Asteraceae or Compositae), such as the asters and goldenrods, carpet the fields and pastures in a final splash of colour. In central Canada, nearly all of the original prairie is now gone, plowed to accommodate expanding agricultural needs. The common grasses and characteristic wildflowers such as the prairie lily, blue-eyed grass and coneflower are now found mainly along roadsides and railway lines, or in coulees and sandy areas. The prairie crocuses, prairie lilies and wild roses have also proved adaptable. The coniferous forests of the western mountains share many wildflowers with the boreal forest. Other flowers, such as Lyall's saxifrage and heartleaf arnica, are strictly alpine. Still others, such as the woolly fernweed, are arctic-alpine in distribution, ie, they range widely through the Arctic and extend southward throughout the mountains in suitable habitats. Although both the dry, interior montane forest and the wet, coast forest of BC have distinctive species of wildflowers, perhaps the showiest displays of western wildflowers occur in the alpine meadows. On sheltered slopes and in moist depressions fed by melting snow, lush growths of tall herbs flower in profusion, while on the drier rocky and turfy slopes and exposed ledges dwarfed rosette and cushionlike plants hug the ground and bask in the bright, high-altitude sunlight of the brief alpine summer.

Beyond the treeline, the number of flowering plants decreases rapidly to as few as about 300 species for all of the arctic islands. The most abundant growths of arctic wildflowers occur in sheltered and moist tundra habitats, where the shallow soil is saturated with meltwater that has been prevented from draining by permafrost not far below the roots of the plants. Among the clumps of tundra grasses and sedges occur such plants as the arctic lupine, Lapland rosebay and arctic white heather. Low year-round precipitation makes most of the high arctic islands into rock deserts. Here, plants with rosette or cushionlike growth (eg, arctic poppy, purple saxifrage, mountain avens and large-flowered wintergreen) flower in seepage areas, boulder fields, and on gravel beds wherever adequate moisture is present. Arctic wildflowers survive in the rigorous climate with its short summer by taking advantage of the nearly continuous daylight of the low arctic sun and the warm air temperatures close to the ground. In spite of this, many plants cannot always produce flowers and must rely on "vegetative growth," including the formation of bulbils in place of seeds, as in the nodding saxifrage, to ensure their continued survival. *See also* individual species entries. ERICH HABER

Reading: R.G.H. Cormack, *Wildflowers of Alberta* (1977); M. Ferguson and R.M. Saunders, *Canadian Wildflowers Through the Seasons* (1982); T. Fitzharris, *Wildflowers of Canada* (1986); H. Flygare and G.W. Scotter, *Wildflowers of the Canadian Rockies* (1986).

Wildlife Conservation and Management
Wildlife comprises those forms of animal life that are not domesticated. Individual members of wild species held tame in captivity are still considered "wildlife" as they are not genetically different from those remaining in a wild state. Wildlife conservation and management is the protection and use of wild-animal populations and of the land necessary to support them to ensure that productivity and ecological balance are maintained in perpetuity, while social benefits are realized. Human activity has become one of the most significant influences on the abundance and well-being of wildlife.

The first European explorers and settlers in N America found wildlife in abundance. This wealth was recognized as having immediate commercial value, with FISHERIES and the FUR TRADE being the first widespread exploitive activities. As further exploration revealed the vast, sparsely populated expanse of land, it was believed that natural resources were unlimited; hence, there was no apparent need to practise CONSERVATION. Wildlife, fish and timber were free for the taking for personal use, or could be converted into a monetary return. The practical result of this attitude became apparent in the latter half of the 19th century. WAPITI once roamed to their eastern limit in Ontario. Land development and uncontrolled harvest had extirpated them in that area by 1850. Wild turkey disappeared well before 1900, but only with the extinction of the once abundant PASSENGER PIGEON was there sufficient concern to cause the passage of wildlife conservation laws. While concern and consequently protective legislation developed in eastern Canada, western and northern Canada were still held to be boundless frontiers. Wapiti rapidly diminished on the prairie; by 1890 only scattered, remnant populations remained throughout their former western range. In the 1820s BISON teemed in millions, defying counting, across the N American plains. Their numbers remained significant to the late 1870s but, by 1885, they were almost gone.

The people of Canada, however, still believed in the myth of unlimited land and wildlife. Government and people were preoccupied with economic prosperity, transcontinental railways and Confederation. The BRITISH NORTH AMERICA ACT (1867) assigned resource-management responsibilities to governments; wildlife is obvious by its omission, being lumped under "matters of private and local nature." Wildlife enthusiasts of the 1880s solemnly predicted the extinction of most large N American mammals, but the next 2 decades marked a significant turning point in wildlife history in Canada. Following Confederation and the assumption of resource-management control by the original provinces, a move was made to develop wildlife conservation laws. The first national park in Canada, BANFF NATIONAL PARK (est 1885), was not created to protect wildlife, although this became one of its significant functions. The concept led to the creation of Bison Recovery Park at Wainwright, Alta, and WOOD BUFFALO NATIONAL PARK, Alta and NWT.

International concern for the well-being of migratory birds slowly gained support and led to the signing, between Great Britain (on behalf of Canada) and the US, of the Migratory Birds Convention Treaty (1916). This treaty led to the passage of the Canada Migratory Birds Convention Act in Aug 1917. In 1919 the Canadian government convened the first national wildlife conference among various government representatives. The first BIRD SANCTUARY in N America (and perhaps the Western Hemisphere) was created at Last Mountain Lk [Sask] in 1887; however, the declaration establishing it remained essentially unrecognized until after the signing of the Migratory Birds Convention Treaty. Land and population protection through park and sanctuary creation became a common solution, although not always without heated argument and dispute. Sanctuaries have been created by federal and provincial governments in key locations throughout the country. Some notable coastal island sanctuaries for seabirds have been declared on Bird Rocks, PERCÉ ROCK and Bonaventure I in the Gulf of St Lawrence, while many inland sanctuaries have also been recognized. These areas were to protect against overharvesting but they have come to reflect protection of original habitats as well.

Between 1900 and 1960 considerable success was achieved in wildlife conservation. The banning of commercial killing of wildlife over vast areas, combined with favourable climatic trends, has allowed for dramatic recovery. Bison were returned from the brink of extinction. The WHOOPING CRANE population was protected from hunting, and its nesting and wintering areas have been safeguarded. Whitetailed DEER now flourish in regrowth forests and in fringe agricultural areas. Wapiti, aided by transplanted populations, have regained strength in the mountain regions and in the localized areas of the prairie that are associated with parks. SEA OTTERS have responded to protection from commercial overharvest. BEAVER have returned from dangerously low levels to become a problem species, causing damage where populations are not controlled. Through protection, northern tundra MUSKOXEN have shown a dramatic recovery, as have prairie grassland PRONGHORN.

Wildlife Management Wildlife management in Canada is a reflection of legislation which can be divided into that concerning fisheries and marine mammals and that dealing with other forms of wildlife. The Fisheries Act of Canada provides that all fishes and marine mammals in Canadian waters are the responsibility of Canada's Department of Fisheries and Oceans (DFO). The DFO actively protects and manages marine mammals (seals, whales, walrus, etc) and offshore fisheries. Marine fish and mammal populations are viewed primarily as a commercial resource. Legal harvesting seasons and quotas on lobster, salmon and other species reflect the continued monitoring of populations and harvest. Harvest management, together with pollution-control laws, is designed to maintain healthy, viable populations. The industry depends on the sustained yield of a quality product.

To provincial and territorial governments are delegated the active responsibility for inland freshwater fisheries, subject to federal laws. These fisheries are largely managed as a recreation resource for sportfishing but also have significant commercial value. The Great Lakes and the larger lakes of the northern and prairie regions support sizable industries, including the export trade. Fisheries research is conducted by both levels of government, often in concert with various universities.

Birds, land mammals, amphibians, reptiles, etc, make up the second major group. Migratory bird conservation is managed in an unusual manner, being conducted co-operatively by federal and provincial governments under the authority of the Canada Migratory Birds Convention Act. This law also ensures international co-ordination. Migratory birds include WATERFOWL, cranes, SHOREBIRDS, SEABIRDS and birds generally grouped as songbirds and insect eaters. Other land-related wildlife is managed and protected primarily by provincial laws, when possible in co-operation with the federal government. Nongovernmental conservation organizations and individuals play an increasingly active role in wildlife management and general wildlife education.

Population surveys are conducted regularly on a wide variety of wildlife to allow management agencies to monitor population trends and distribution. Surveys may be conducted on the ground or from aircraft, often with the aid of photographic techniques. The harvest of wildlife is monitored and recorded for comparison with other population information, in an effort to ensure the maintenance of optimal populations. Less visible forms have defied accurate monitoring techniques. Sample counts, conducted mainly by volunteer conservation organizations, provide some insight into the well-being of these species.

The Canadian native peoples have been granted special-use rights to wildlife through a varied and complex process of treaties and laws (see INDIAN ACT, LAND CLAIMS). While the continuance of existing rights has been assured by the CONSTITUTION ACT, 1982, the exact rights of individuals residing in different areas or being of diverse ancestry remains unclear. Supreme Court of Canada rulings have clarified the rights in some areas, but others remain unresolved, thus posing serious limitations to individual resource users and management agencies.

Just as humans and domestic livestock require food, shelter and space in order to survive, so do the various forms of wildlife. Efforts are made by all Canadian wildlife agencies to preserve and protect key wildlife areas on government lands. Government agencies and nongovernmental groups operate programs for the purchase of unique wildlife lands from private individuals. If many species are to be maintained at desirable levels, a means must be found of encouraging the management of all lands in accordance with an awareness of wildlife needs. Government wildlife agencies and public groups have formed the Committee on the Status of Endangered Wildlife in Canada (COSEWIC), which encourages and commissions studies on rare and ENDANGERED ANIMALS or on species of unknown status. Recommendations of the committee encourage increased protection as required. Through its membership in the Convention on International Trade in Endangered Species (1973) (CITES), Canada is involved with most conservation-minded countries of the world in the protection of endangered species. Canada's increasingly urban society moves most people away from direct in-

A wildlife veterinarian works with biologists to weigh a drug-immobilized moose (*courtesy Dr J. Haigh, W.C.V.M., University of Saskatchewan*).

teraction with wildlife. Thus, there is need for an increasing effort toward wildlife conservation and toward management education, information, and interpretation programs.

Conclusion Recovery of wildlife, primarily from 1920 to 1970, has reflected societal concern which demanded active management programs. Public and nonprofit organizations such as the CANADIAN WILDLIFE FEDERATION, CANADIAN NATURE FEDERATION, DUCKS UNLIMITED (Canada), World Wildlife Fund (Canada) and the Nature Conservancy of Canada, at the national level, and their provincially based affiliates, have played a significant role in concert with government conservation agencies (eg, the CANADIAN WILDLIFE SERVICE of Environment Canada). However, populations have returned only to those areas that remain suitable for their production. Habitats suitable for population production have been the key ingredients of conservation programs. Populations will not return where land has been modified from its natural state through agriculture or through industrial and urban development.

While many forms of wildlife are more abundant in the 1980s than they were in 1870, a number of species have continued to decline to threatened levels or are in danger of extinction. Wetland drainage permanently removes the habitat required by many species. POLLUTION of rivers and estuaries renders them unfit for wildlife survival. ACID RAIN from industrial effluent stacks, automobiles and urban areas continues to sterilize vast tracts of the land and waterways of eastern Canada. Marine birds and mammals increasingly face the threat of offshore oil spills and general pollution of the oceans. The direct threat of uncontrolled harvest, so devastating in the 19th century, has been replaced by the indirect, insidious but permanent threats of environmental degradation that are characteristic of the 20th century. If society wishes to maintain wildlife in its variety and abundance, a place for wildlife must be maintained in land-use planning and environmental management.

The uses and value of wildlife to society are varied. Wildlife is one part of the equation which, together with vegetation and the nonliving ENVIRONMENT, constitutes the "balance of nature," ie,

the set of complex natural processes on which human survival depends. A country fit for wildlife is a country fit for people. Wildlife is a direct source of food and other products for many Canadians. While this value is most apparent in northern regions, it is also significant in southern Canada. Coastal and inland commercial fishing, based on naturally reproducing populations, is a significant industry. The wild FUR INDUSTRY provides a direct source of income for thousands, representing the highest continuing economic return of any resource in mid-northern regions. These harvest uses not only give direct economic return but, provided their management is biologically sound, also keep populations in balance with their food supply, preventing overpopulation and dramatic losses from starvation and disease.

Wildlife is a basic component of outdoor recreation and part of the national heritage of all Canadians. Wildlife reflects the condition of the environment and constitutes a "barometer" for measuring environmental change. Throughout Canada, wildlife is the legal property of all Canadians. Its ownership is entrusted in law to the stewardship of the various governments. Sound conservation and management of all wildlife is thus the rightful concern and responsibility of all Canadians. GORDON R. KERR

Reading: J. Foster, Working for Wildlife: The Beginning of Preservation in Canada (1978); R. Vontobel, Man and Wildlife in a Shared Environment (1982).

Wildlife Preserve, an area of land or water set aside from development or recreational use to protect wildlife and habitats. Wildlife preserves are found, under extremely varied conditions, in virtually every part of the world. In Canada, they are established federally, provincially and privately to protect a rare species from extinction or to provide a sanctuary for species that are important for hunting or tourism. Most of southern Canada is too heavily populated for large, new wildlife preserves to be feasible, but pressure is being put on governments to set aside large preserves in northern Canada before habitats or species are eliminated. The educational facilities provided by wildlife preserves are in part responsible for the growing awareness of CONSERVATION. For example, the Prairie Wildlife Interpretation Centre, near Swift Current, Sask, combines excellent educational facilities with the opportunity to see native PRAIRIE flora and fauna.

Canadian conservation had its start in the later 1800s, when the extinction or near-extinction of the passenger pigeon, Labrador duck, great auk, wild turkey, elk and bison in the East, and the drastic reduction of large mammals in the West (bison, pronghorn, elk) and the North (muskox), caused Canadians to press for wildlife preserves. The first preserves were national parks in the West where land was, as yet, unsettled. These were established primarily for tourism. To save the bison, WOOD BUFFALO NATIONAL PARK was established on the Alberta/NWT border (1922), and bison from Montana were settled there. In Saskatchewan and Alberta, 3 national sanctuaries were established (1914-15) to counteract habitat alteration caused by farming, which was endangering the pronghorn. These were so successful that they were abolished by 1947 because the pronghorn no longer needed protection. Muskoxen were saved, first through game laws, then by the establishment of the Thelon Game Sanctuary, NWT (1927). In Sept 1986 Canada's first national wildlife area was established at Polar Bear Pass, Bathurst I, NWT, formerly an International Biological Programme (IBP) site.

Today, wildlife preserves protect many different plants and animals. For example, Ducks Unlimited (Canada), a private waterfowl conservation organization, has secured and developed more than 1.5 million hectares of WATERFOWL habitat across Canada, thanks, in part, to Canadian landowners who provide land free of charge. Long Point Provincial Park, Ont, is visited by many kinds of waterfowl and is home to at least 5 rare or endangered species of reptiles and amphibians. POINT PELÉE NATIONAL PARK, Ont, is a world-renowned stopping point for songbirds during migration. Birds of prey, rare in much of N America, are relatively common in western and northern Canadian preserves. Several preserves in British Columbia's QUEEN CHARLOTTE ISLANDS are refuges for the peregrine falcon; others, in the East, protect marine birds (eg, cormorants, kittiwakes, gannets and razorbills) (see BIRD SANCTUARIES AND RESERVES). A recently developed form of wildlife preserve, and one for which Canada, with its many lakes and extensive coastline, has a great potential, is the aquatic preserve, intended to protect aquatic wildlife and habitats. Fathom Five Provincial Park, Tobermory, Ont, is the best Canadian example. Such preserves, even more than terrestrial ones, are prone to recreational overuse. Motorboating, scuba diving and even swimming cause considerable disturbance in aquatic ecosystems, including the habitats of nesting waterfowl. In Sept 1986, Environment Canada, Parks, released its marine parks policy.

Preserves are often in jeopardy from human exploitation. If an area is popular for recreation, campers and hikers may trample and degrade vegetation; their campsites sometimes cause FOREST FIRES. There may be pressures to permit logging, use as rangeland, oil exploration and drilling, or mining. Roads through a preserve result in animals being killed by vehicles. POLLUTION from spraying timber with insecticides or pollution from distant industries (eg, acid rain) can affect both plants and animals. Controversy about the rights of native peoples to use land and wildlife resources will have a bearing on the future of preserves (see LAND CLAIMS). These problems mean that the establishment of a preserve is only the beginning, and management should ensure that conditions remain suitable for preservation. A.I. DAGG AND D.S. SLOCOMBE

Reading: A.I. Dagg, *Canadian Wildlife and Man* (1974); J. Foster, *Working for Wildlife: The Beginning of Preservation in Canada* (1978); Wildlife Habitat Canada, *The Status of Wildlife Habitat in Canada: Problems, Issues and Opportunities* (1986).

Wilfrid Laurier University, Waterloo, Ont, was founded in 1959. The Evangelical Lutheran Seminary of Canada was established in Oct 1911 in Waterloo because most Ontario Lutherans lived in the area and because of a gift of 2 ha of land from the Waterloo Board of Trade. To provide post-secondary courses, in 1924 the Lutheran Church founded Waterloo College of Arts, which was affiliated with UNIVERSITY OF WESTERN ONTARIO, 1925-60. In 1959, when UNIVERSITY OF WATERLOO was being incorporated, plans were made for Waterloo College of Arts to become its arts faculty. However, the Lutheran Church did not want the college to lose its denominational character. Instead the college and the Lutheran seminary were chartered as Waterloo Lutheran U in 1960. The Mennonite Brethren College of Arts was affiliated with Waterloo Lutheran, 1961-71. In 1973 the university was transferred to the province and became Wilfrid Laurier University. Waterloo Lutheran Seminary remains an affiliate of the nondenominational university and in 1986 established the Institute for Christian Ethics. WLU Press, established in 1974 to produce moderately priced academic publications, annually publishes about 20

books and 8 academic journals in the humanities and social science areas. The university offers undergraduate degrees in arts and science, music, and business and economics; masters degrees in arts and sciences, business and economics, and social work; and a doctoral program in social work.

Enrolment: Wilfrid Laurier University, 1985-86 (Source: Statistics Canada)			
Full-time Undergrad	*Full-time Graduate*	*Part-time Undergrad*	*Part-time Graduate*
4 332	311	2 387	295

Wilgress, Leolyn Dana, public servant (b at Vancouver 20 Oct 1892; d at Ottawa 21 July 1969). Entering the Trade Commissioner Service in 1914, Wilgress served in Russia, Romania, England and Germany 1916-32, when he was appointed director of the Commercial Intelligence Service in Ottawa. He was one of Canada's key trade negotiators in the 1930s, becoming deputy minister of trade and commerce in 1940. An indifferent administrator, he happily returned to the USSR as minister, 1942-44, and ambassador, 1944-46. Even as the COLD WAR took hold, Wilgress remained moderate on East-West issues. Among other postings he was chairman and one of the principal architects of the GENERAL AGREEMENT ON TARIFFS AND TRADE 1948-51 and 1953-56, high commissioner to the UK 1949-52, undersecretary of state for external affairs 1952-53 and permanent representative to NATO, 1953-55. He published his *Memoirs* in 1967. NORMAN HILLMER

Wilkie, William, merchant, radical (b at Halifax *c*1795; d unknown). The son of a sea captain, Wilkie went into business just as the War of 1812 ended. Peacetime Halifax experienced acute economic dislocation and, provoked by slumping trade and rising taxes, Wilkie turned to protest. In 1820 he published a pamphlet alleging that distress derived from elitism, extravagance and corruption within government. Remedial action, he suggested, required extreme measures, including assassination. Seeking to intimidate protestors, the authorities charged Wilkie with sedition. Convicted by the Supreme Court, he went to prison and then disappeared into self-imposed exile. Although a failure, Wilkie won the sympathy of many and his denunciation of oligarchy would eventually be revived by the campaign for RESPONSIBLE GOVERNMENT. D.A. SUTHERLAND

Wilkinson, Anne, née Gibbons, writer (b at Toronto 21 Sept 1910; d there 10 May 1961). A member of the family of William OSLER, Wilkinson grew up in London, Ont, and was educated privately. She is known chiefly for her poetry, which is sensuous and wittily intellectual. She is included in many anthologies and contributed to many small magazines. In 1951 she published her first book, *Counterpoint to Sleep.* A second volume, *The Hangman Ties the Holly,* appeared in 1955. Wilkinson was founding editor (1956) and generous patron of *The* TAMARACK REVIEW, in which was published posthumously an autobiographical fragment about her childhood, "Four Corners of My World," also included in *The Collected Poems* (1968). Besides her poetry, she published *Lions in the Way: A Discursive History of the Oslers* (1956) and *Swann and Daphne* (1960), a modern fairy tale for children. JEAN WILSON

Willan, James Healey, composer, organist, choir director, educator (b at Balham [London], Eng 12 Oct 1880; d at Toronto 16 Feb 1968). A dominant figure in Canadian musical life for over half a century, Willan influenced several generations of composers, organists, choir direc-

tors, singers and audiences through his teaching and example. After immigrating to Canada in 1913 he taught at the Toronto Conservatory (1913-36) and U of T (1937-50). From 1921 until his death he was organist-choirmaster of the Anglican Church of St Mary Magdalene. Apparently uninfluenced by musical innovations of the times, Willan's compositions reflect variously the enthusiasms of his boyhood and training – Anglo-Catholic liturgy, choral music of Tudor and contemporary English masters, the rich romanticism of Brahms and Wagner. He composed operas, symphonies, concertos and music for band, piano, organ, choir and solo voice – in all some 800 works. The *Introduction, Passacaglia and Fugue* (1916) for organ and *An Apostrophe to the Heavenly Hosts* (1921) for unaccompanied choir represent Willan's most opulent style, contrasting with the more austere liturgical music most frequently performed. Willan was made a Companion of the Order of Canada in 1967. BARCLAY McMILLAN

Reading: F.R.C. Clarke, *Healey Willan: Life and Music* (1983).

Willcocks, Joseph, officeholder, journalist, politician, army officer (b at Palmerston, Ire 1773; d at Ft Erie, Upper Canada 4 Sept 1814). A keen observer of Irish and local politics, Willcocks initially eschewed participation in UC in favour of a "genteel income" as an office holder. In 1807 he was removed from office by reason of "general and notorious bad conduct," whereupon he established the *Upper Canada Guardian; or, Freeman's Journal* (Niagara-on-the-Lake). Elected to the Assembly in 1807, 1808 and 1812, and leader of the coalition of interests that formed the Opposition, he was an 18th-century Whig, concerned to "check the progress of inordinate power, and keep alive the sacred flame of a just and rational liberty." Motivated more by political principle than self-interest, Willcocks, after a period of active loyalty during the WAR OF 1812, joined the Americans in 1813, raising the Company of Canadian Volunteers "to assist in changing the government of this province into a Republic." He was killed in action. ROBERT L. FRASER

Williams, Eleazer, Protestant Episcopalian minister, pretender to the French throne (b at Lk George, NY, about 1788; d at St Regis Reservation, NY 28 Aug 1858). Williams was an Iroquois of mixed Indian and white ancestry from the Caughnawaga Reserve near Montréal. The young Mohawk fought on the American side in the WAR OF 1812 and remained in the US. After many years as an Indian missionary, Williams began presenting himself as the lost Bourbon dauphin. J.H. Hanson of New York City published *The Lost Prince* on Williams's behalf in 1854. Shortly before the Caughnawaga Mohawk's death in 1858 his extraordinary claim had been disproven. His biography of his real father, *Life of Te-ho-ra-gwo-ne-gen, alias Thomas Williams,* appeared in 1859. DONALD B. SMITH

Williams, James Miller, manufacturer, politician (b at Camden, NJ 14 Sept 1818; d at Hamilton, Ont 25 Nov 1890). Immigrating to Canada in 1840, he was a successful carriage and railway-car builder at London, Ont, and Hamilton. Engaged in oil production and refining in Lambton County after 1857, Williams is considered the father of the oil industry in Canada. Claims that Williams drilled the first oil well in N America are shared with E.L. Drake of Pennsylvania. He was a member of the Ontario Legislature 1867-79 and registrar of Wentworth County 1879-90. EDWARD PHELPS

Williams, Lynn, union leader (b at Springfield, Ont, 21 July 1924). A minister's son, he received a degree in economics from McMaster U and served in the Canadian Navy during WWII. In 1947 he took a job at a Toronto plant and joined the USWA. His first union job was as an organizer with the CANADIAN CONGRESS OF LABOUR, and in 1956 he joined the staff of the USWA in the Niagara Pen area. Under his leadership, USWA doubled its membership in the area. During the 1960s, Williams became involved in bargaining, labour education and politics. He was director of the 130 000-member District 6 based in Toronto (then second largest in the union) 1973-77, when he was elected temporary acting international secretary. He was elected temporary acting president of the USWA on 17 Nov 1983, and following a bitterly fought election was sworn in as fifth president of the union 1 Mar 1986, thus becoming the first Canadian ever to head the United Steelworkers of America and one of the few non-US citizens to lead a major US union. CRAIG HERON

Williams, Percy Alfred, runner (b at Vancouver 19 May 1908; d there 29 Nov 1982). As a child Williams suffered from rheumatic fever, which left him with a damaged heart. But just a year out of high school, the 59 kg runner became the sensation of the 1928 Amsterdam Olympics, winning gold medals in the 100 and 200 m sprints against the fastest field ever assembled. He had previously tied the world mark of 9.6 seconds over 100 yards and, following the Olympics, clinched his domination of the world's top stars by going unbeaten in a spectacular series of indoor races in New York, Chicago, Boston and Philadelphia. Williams's Olympic double is the most brilliant solo achievement by any Canadian in international TRACK AND FIELD competition.

BRIAN S. LEWIS

Percy Williams at the 1928 Amsterdam Olympics, where he won gold medals in the 100 m and 200 m sprints (*courtesy Canada Sports Hall of Fame*).

Williams, Sir William Fenwick, army officer (b at Annapolis Royal, NS 4 Dec 1800; d at London, Eng 26 July 1883). A British officer on loan to the Turkish army, Williams became a hero in 1855 when he led the determined, though unsuccessful, defence of Kars against Russia during the CRIMEAN WAR. From 1859 to 1865, as commander

in chief in BNA, he organized preparations for defence against the US during the AMERICAN CIVIL WAR although the British government doubted his capacity to command should an invasion occur. Valuing his charm and popularity, however, the British made him lt-gov of NS (Nov 1865-Oct 1867) so that he could use his influence to counter provincial opposition to CONFEDERATION.

ROGER SARTY

Williams Lake, BC, City, pop 10 280 (1986c), 8362 (1981c), inc 1929, is located in the Cariboo country of central BC, 545 km NE of Vancouver. Williams Lake received its name from the adjacent lake, named in 1860 after Chief William of the Sugar Cane Indian Reserve. The Shuswap Indian name for the location, "Columneetza," means "the gathering place of the lordly ones." The highway, the railway and enlarged airport facilities have been essential in the city's development, especially in recent years. Its economy was long based primarily on agriculture, as the service centre and market for the numerous cattle ranches of the great Cariboo and Chilcotin plateaus. In recent decades forestry, logging and lumbering have overtaken ranching in importance. Mining, tourism, service industries and government offices give a varied economic base for the city. Williams Lake is also the home, every July, of the famous Williams Lake Stampede.

JOHN R. STEWART

Williamson, Curtis Albert, painter (b at Brampton, Ont 2 Jan 1867; d at Toronto 18 Apr 1944). A founding member 1907 and secretary 1908-09 of the Canadian Art Club and member of its executive council 1910-15, Williamson brought Dutch subject matter and technique to Toronto in the 1890s. Nicknamed "the Canadian Rembrandt," and known primarily as a portraitist, he also painted genre scenes, interiors and landscapes, typically in a dark tonal style developed after more than 10 years of painting in France and Holland following a brief period of study in Paris (1889). He returned to Toronto in 1904, and that year was awarded a silver medal at the St Louis Universal Exposition. Williamson's later work is more loosely painted and in a higher key. Notable among his portraits is that of Frederick BANTING. CHRISTINE BOYANOSKI

Williamson, John Thoburn, geologist, diamond-mine owner (b at Montfort, Qué 10 Feb 1907; d at Mwadui, Tanganyika, E Africa 7 Jan 1958). After receiving a doctorate in geology from McGill in 1933, he began mining exploration in Northern Rhodesia [Zambia] but soon switched to Tanganyika [Tanzania]. Williamson was one of many N American geologists in SE Africa whose role in the development of mining was fundamental. Six years of prospecting, much of it as an impoverished independent geologist, were finally rewarded by a diamond strike in 1940 near Lk Victoria. Retaining ownership himself, Williamson became a significant force in the world diamond market. A lifelong bachelor, he lived simply at the mine and developed it as a model property, noted for humane labour practices. He became a benefactor of Makerere University, Uganda. ALAN JEEVES

Willingdon, Freeman Freeman-Thomas, 1st Marquess of, governor general of Canada 1926-31 (b at Ratton, Eng 12 Sept 1866; d at London, Eng 12 Aug 1941). After a period as an MP (1900-10) and terms as governor of the Indian provinces of Bombay (1913-18) and Madras (1919-24), Willingdon was governor general of Canada 1926-31 and viceroy of India 1931-36. The British Conservative government did not favour Willingdon as a suitable candidate to be Canadian governor general, claiming that he had

less general ability, knowledge of affairs and public appeal than others. But King George V, whom Willingdon had served both as lord-in-waiting and tennis partner, intervened to request that his name be included on the list sent to Canada, and Canadian PM KING promptly chose Willingdon, a fellow Liberal. Thin and grandfatherly, he brought a sense of humour and an air of informality to his duties. He was the first governor general to act solely as the king's agent and the first to visit the US in his capacity as head of state. He initiated the Willingdon Arts Competitions for excellence in music, literature, painting and sculpture, and privately worried about the "peaceful penetration" into Canada of American media and economic influences. NORMAN HILLMER

Willis, John Walpole, judge (b in Eng 4 Jan 1793; d in Worcestershire, Eng 10 Sept 1877). Willis arrived in Upper Canada in 1827 to take office as puisne justice of the court of King's Bench. His arrogant conduct soon offended the political establishment, and he quarrelled with John Beverley ROBINSON over the Assembly's failure to pass legislation establishing a court of chancery, in which the imperial government had intended Willis to preside. When, at the Home District Assizes of Apr 1828, the journalist Francis Collins accused Robinson of political bias in the conduct of criminal prosecutions, Willis supported Collins and rebuked Robinson in public for mishandling his duties as attorney general. In June 1828 Willis publicly proclaimed that the court of King's Bench had often been informally constituted, implying that most of its proceedings since its founding in 1794 were invalid. Suspended by Lt-Gov Sir Peregrine MAITLAND, Willis was later exonerated on technical grounds. Subsequently he held judicial appointments in Demerara and in Australia, where he was again dismissed after quarrelling with the lt-gov of New South Wales. Willis was a conceited snob who lent himself to an important political cause out of vanity. His dismissal precipitated the first public campaign for RESPONSIBLE GOVERNMENT and reinforced the demand for an independent colonial judiciary. PAUL ROMNEY

Willison, Sir John Stephen, journalist, historian, imperialist, publicist (b at Hills Green, Canada W 9 Nov 1856; d at Toronto 27 May 1927). Willison's extraordinary public career stretched from 1881 until his death. In Toronto he edited the Liberal *Globe* 1890-1902; the independent, then Conservative *News* 1903-17; and *Willison's Monthly* 1925-27. He reported Canada to the British elite in *The Times* 1909-27. In turn he was an intimate adviser of prime ministers Wilfrid LAURIER and Robert L. BORDEN. His biography of Laurier (1903) and his *Reminiscences* (1919) remain charming and insightful. His conversion to IMPERIALISM was evident in his writings and through his membership in the empire-wide ROUND TABLE MOVEMENT. An early free trader, he became president of the protectionist Canadian Reconstruction Assn 1918-21.

RICHARD T. CLIPPINGDALE

Williston Lake, 1660 km², is the largest freshwater body in BC. Created in 1968 as the reservoir of the W.A.C. Bennett hydroelectric dam on the PEACE R, it was named for Ray Williston, BC minister of lands and forests 1956-72, who encouraged the development of a pulp economy from the unused forest resource in interior BC, coincident with government hydroelectric energy projects. Spruce forests around the lake supply pulp mills and sawmills at the district municipality of MACKENZIE, an "instant town" on the Parsnip Reach of Williston Lk. The lake is used to transport timber to the mills. PETER GRANT

Weeping willow (*Salix babylonica*), showing male flowers (left) and female flowers (right) (*artwork by Claire Tremblay*).

Willow (*Salix*), genus of trees and shrubs of willow family (Salicaceae). About 300 species occur worldwide, chiefly in the Northern Hemisphere; in Canada, some 54 native species (7 or 8 reaching tree size) are known, plus numerous forms of subspecific rank. Identification is complicated because plants are dioecious (ie, male and female flowering catkins occur on different plants) and the catkins frequently appear before the leaves. Leaves are simple, alternate and usually long and pointed; flowers are petalless. Distribution is transcontinental; some of the smallest woody plants, eg, dwarf willow (*S. herbacea)*, extend the genus range to the High Arctic. Introduced species include the large, popular weeping willow (*S. babylonica*). Willows are widely grown for ornament, as shelterbelt plantings, and sometimes for waterside erosion control. The tough, flexible young branches are wickerwork material (osier). Like the ancient Greeks, Canadian Indians used the bitter inner bark, which contains salicylic acid, as a painkiller and to reduce fever. Although the wood is soft, it is used by artisans in the weaving and crafting of rustic furniture. ROGER VICK

Willson, David, religious leader (b in Dutchess County, NY 7 June 1778; d at Sharon, Canada W 16 Jan 1866). Having disagreed with the Quakers in 1812, he formed his own sect, the Children of Peace, promoting peace, love and equality among all people. Like other dissident leaders of his time, he turned a backwoods settlement into a cohesive community, strong in faith, charitable and dedicated to education. Lovers of music, they had a band, a choir and the oldest extant barrel organ built in Upper Canada. Their temple is an architectural gem, rich in symbolism. Willson wrote many hymns and sermons, and some political treatises, especially around the time of the 1837 Rebellion. JEAN MCFALL

Willson, Thomas Leopold, "Carbide," inventor (b 1860; d at New York C 20 Dec 1915). Propelled by curiosity, Willson was a chronic inventor gifted in both recognizing the potential of his discoveries and funding their development. He obtained over 70 patents in Canada. The earliest concern electric dynamos and their application in ALUMINUM production and domestic lighting. He moved to the US, where he discovered a process for the production of bulk calcium carbide and acetylene gas in 1892. Willson then returned to Canada to participate in carbide concerns and to

promote early hydroelectric development. He also patented several marine devices using acetylene. Finally, intrigued with triple phosphates and their fertilizer and paper product potential, "Carbide" mortgaged his assets to American J.B. Duke to obtain development capital. He lost the gamble, and then died. Willson's carbide discovery laid a basis for development of the electrochemical industry. MARGARET CARTER

Wilmot, Lemuel Allan, politician, lawyer, judge (b in Sunbury Co, NB 31 Jan 1809; d at Fredericton 20 May 1878). A brilliant, flamboyant orator, Wilmot used his skills in the courtroom, in the NB Assembly and in public speeches, often in support of Methodism. While appearing to be a Reformer in his fights against the privileges of the old system, Wilmot aggressively sought those advantages for himself. Never defeated between 1834 and 1851, he rattled off the catch phrases of RESPONSIBLE GOVERNMENT while never understanding the principle. An effective provocateur, Wilmot was eventually appointed attorney general in 1848 when he abandoned all pretence of support for Reform. He sought and received an appointment to the Supreme Court in 1851, creating a serious crisis in government. A competent if controversial judge, Wilmot was never promoted. His public support of CONFEDERATION was considered unethical, but the success of the movement led to his becoming NB's first native-born lieutenant-governor (23 Jan 1868-15 Nov 1873). CARL M. WALLACE

Wilmot, Montagu, British army officer, governor of Nova Scotia (d at Halifax 23 May 1766). An officer from 1730, Wilmot served almost exclusively in Nova Scotia 1746-66 and was at the siege of LOUISBOURG in 1758 as a regimental commander. Appointed lieutenant-governor of NS Mar 1763, he was advanced to governor May 1764, both appointments won by patronage. Unfortunately, he was plagued by illness and lacked sufficient willpower to govern effectively. During his term the province suffered from a postwar depression, caused in part by sharply reduced British government spending and, in addition, 2.5 to 3.5 million acres (1.0-1.4 million ha) were granted away, often to speculators who did little to improve their acquisitions. Generally regarded as weak, Wilmot died in office.
STUART SUTHERLAND

Reading: J.B. Brebner, *The Neutral Yankees of Nova Scotia* (1969).

Wilmot, Samuel, pisciculturist (b at Belmont Farm, Clarke Twp, West Durham, Upper Canada 22 Aug 1822; d at Newcastle, Ont 17 May 1899). Wilmot became interested in the new practice of artificially hatching fish as a means of saving the Lk Ontario salmon and in 1865 established a small hatchery on his farm. Although his effort to save the salmon failed, the hatchery itself succeeded. The government leased his hatchery in 1868 and Wilmot was superintendent of fish culture 1876-95. Active in local government and agriculture as well, in 1879 he was president of the Ontario Agricultural and Arts Assn. Wilmot established 15 hatcheries across Canada. His designs were widely copied in N America, and in 1883 a working model of his hatchery won a gold prize at the International Fisheries Exhibition. In 1891 and 1892 Wilmot conducted extensive inquiries into the fisheries of Ontario and BC. *See also* AQUACULTURE. A.B. MCCULLOUGH

Wilson, Alice Evelyn, paleontologist (b at Cobourg, Ont 26 Aug 1881; d at Ottawa 15 Apr 1964). Educated at Toronto and Chicago, Wilson spent all her professional career, 1909-46, with the GEOLOGICAL SURVEY OF CANADA, from museum assistant to geologist. She was the recognized au-

thority on the Paleozoic formations of eastern Ontario, which she recorded for distribution, stratigraphy and structure. She described the fossils, mostly of Ordovician age, in numerous papers and monographs. Through lectures, field trips, publications and museum exhibits she brought geology to the general public, especially the children. In 1937 she was elected a fellow of the Royal Soc of Canada, the first woman to receive that honour. LORIS S. RUSSELL

Wilson, Bertha, née Wernham, lawyer, judge (b at Kirkcaldy, Scot 18 Sept 1923), first woman appointed to the SUPREME COURT OF CANADA. Educated at U of Aberdeen she immigrated to Canada with her husband, Presbyterian minister John Wilson. She was admitted to Dalhousie Law School in 1954 and was called to the NS Bar in 1957 and of Ontario in 1959. She practised law 1958-75 with the large Toronto firm Osler, Hoskin and Harcourt where she specialized in legal research and opinion writing on a wide range of subjects for the other lawyers. She was appointed to the Ontario Court of Appeal in Dec 1975 and captured public attention by her imaginative and humane decisions in cases involving human rights, ethnic and sex discrimination, matrimonial property, child custody and the access of citizens to information about themselves collected by government and police. In 1982, after intense feminist pressure to name a woman to the Supreme Court, Wilson was appointed. Since then she has participated in several Supreme Court decisions, one of the most momentous of which is probably striking down Canadian ABORTION law in early 1988. JENNIFER STODDART

Wilson, Bill, politician, administrator, (b at Comox, BC 6 Apr 1944). Educated at U Vic (BA, 1970) and UBC (LLB, 1973), Wilson was the leading theorist in BC Indian politics 1970-81 and was influential in every major development. Although initially active in both the Union of BC Indian Chiefs and the BC Assn of Non-Status Indians (BCANSI), he advocated reducing the role of these organizations in favour of a return to unity of all Indians at the level of the traditional Indian tribes or nations. He was founding president of the United Native Nations (1976-81), the renamed BCANSI which sought support of all BC Indians and encouraged tribal political development. In 1982-83 he was vice-president of the Native Council of Canada, attaining national prominence as its spokesman at the 1983 First Ministers Conference. He chose not to seek re-election, and returned to his own Kwagulth (Kwakiutl) nation to become co-ordinator of the Musamagw Tribal Council. PAUL TENNANT

Wilson, Cairine Reay, née Mackay, Canada's first woman senator, philanthropist (b at Montréal 4 Feb 1885; d at Ottawa 3 Mar 1962). Wilson was active in the organization of Women's Liberal clubs and youth groups during the 1920s. A member of the Liberal establishment, she was appointed to the Senate on 20 Feb 1930. She was president of the LEAGUE OF NATIONS SOC in Canada 1936-42 and Canada's first woman delegate to the UN in 1949. As chairman of the Canadian National Committee on Refugees 1938-48, she was outspoken against ANTI-SEMITISM in Canada.
HARRIET GORHAM

Wilson, Sir Daniel, scientist, author, educator (b at Edinburgh, Scot 5 Jan 1816; d at Toronto 6 Aug 1892). Wilson was a man of many talents. He was educated at Edinburgh U, studied art briefly with William Turner, wrote essays for *Chambers' Journal,* published a history of Oliver Cromwell, and was fascinated with antiquity during his Scottish years. In 1847, while secretary of the Scottish Antiquarian Soc, he published *Memorials* of *Edinburgh in the Olden Time* (illustrated by the author); 4 years later appeared *The Archaeology and Prehistoric Annals of Scotland*, in which was coined the word "prehistory."

In 1853 Wilson was appointed professor of history and English at the yet-to-be-constructed UNIVERSITY COLLEGE in U of T. He contributed to the design of the building, was a major defender of the "provincial university" against denominational attack and became president of University College (nondenominational) in 1880. During these years Wilson continued his scientific research, especially in the emerging field of ethnology. He became a major interpreter in Canada of the scientific consequences of the work of Charles Darwin. While he accepted the extension of geological time and the evolution of species, Wilson rejected – as did his colleague J.W. DAWSON at McGill – the notion of natural selection as unproven speculation, and insisted upon innate differences between man and animal, largely on religious grounds. Wilson's 2-vol *Prehistoric Man: Researches into the Origin of Civilisation in the Old and New World* (1862), a masterpiece of 19th-century ethnology and erudition, was meant to disprove natural selection. One of the best-known scholars in Canada, Wilson was president of the ROYAL SOCIETY OF CANADA (which he helped found in 1882) in 1885.

Much of Wilson's energy was taken up with university administration. In the 1880s he sought to preserve the best interests of U of T and University College in the face of a movement to federate denominational colleges with the provincial university. He opposed the notion, but accepted political and economic realities, and became the first president of U of T under the Federation Act of 1887. His last years were plagued by bitter animosities and professorial bickering within the university community.   A. BRIAN MCKILLOP

Reading: A. Brian McKillop, *A Disciplined Intelligence* (1979).

Wilson, Ethel Davis, née Bryant, novelist, storywriter, essayist (b at Port Elizabeth, S Africa 20 Jan 1888; d at Vancouver 22 Dec 1980). Wilson's small but impressive literary output has earned her an important place in Canadian literature. The only child of an English Wesleyan minister missioned in S Africa, Wilson was orphaned at 10 and sent to Vancouver to live with her maternal grandmother and several aunts. She received her education at private schools in Vancouver and England, graduating from the Vancouver Normal School in 1907. She taught in several city schools until her marriage in 1927. Wilson's delight and fascination with her adopted homeland permeates her work, and she is one of the first Canadian writers to capture truly the rugged and unsurpassed beauty of the BC landscape. Yet this strong sense of place, evoked in her unpretentious and lucid style, is never merely regional, as her characters consistently struggle with the paradox of the human condition – the intense desire for personal freedom versus the strong need for responsible and harmonious integration with others. Wilson's early stories were published in British magazines in 1937, but she quit writing until after WWII. *Hetty Dorval* (1947) established her reputation, and was followed quickly by *The Innocent Traveller* (1949, which is not strictly fiction but a family chronicle in which Wilson herself figures as the character Rose), *The Equations of Love* (1952), SWAMP ANGEL (1954), *Love and Salt Water* (1956) and *Mrs. Golightly and Other Stories* (1961). Her last stories and essays appeared in 1964. In 1961 Wilson received the Canada Council Medal, in 1964 the Lorne Pierce Medal from the Royal Society of Canada, and in 1970 the Order of Canada Medal of Service.   DONNA COATES

Reading: D. Stouck, ed, *Ethel Wilson: Stories, Essays and Letters* (1988).

Wilson, Jean, speed skater (b at Glasgow, Scot 19 July 1910; d at Toronto 3 Sept 1933). After winning international honours, she died of the muscular disease myasthenia gravis. Wilson started SPEED SKATING when she was 15. A strong, natural skater, by 1931 she was able to challenge the sport's reigning queen, Lela BROOKS, and prior to the 1932 Winter Olympics established herself as N American champion. At the Olympics in Lake Placid, in which speed skating was a demonstration event, she won the 500 m event. Although she set a world record in the 1500 m in her preliminary heat, she was closely beaten by America's Kit Klein in the final. She fell while leading the 1000 m race. Within months of the Olympics, she entered hospital and battled her rare disease for a year before succumbing at age 23.   J. THOMAS WEST

Wilson, John Armistead, civil servant, aviation pioneer (b at Broughty Ferry, Scot 2 Nov 1879; d at Ottawa 10 Oct 1954). Trained as an engineer, he became interested in the potential of aviation while in the Department of Naval Services in WWI. As secretary of the Air Board (1920-22) and later controller of civil aviation (1922-41), Wilson guided the national policies which led to the use of aircraft in the remote regions of Canada. Later he was closely involved in planning the Trans-Canada Airways, the flying-club movement, air mail service and transoceanic flying. He was director of the selection, surveying and construction of aerodromes used by the RCAF for the BRITISH COMMONWEALTH AIR TRAINING PLAN and other wartime needs.   W.J. MCANDREW

Wilson, John Tuzo, geophysicist (b at Ottawa 24 Oct 1908). After obtaining U of T's first BA in geophysics (1930), Wilson attended Cambridge (1932, 1940) and Princeton (1936), and worked with the GEOLOGICAL SURVEY OF CANADA (1936-39). He was professor of geophysics at U of T 1946-74 and principal of Erindale Coll 1967-74. He is internationally respected for work on glaciers, mountain building, geology of ocean basins, and structure of continents; his greatest contribution lies in his explanation of PLATE TECTONICS. He also pioneered the use of air photos in geological mapping and was responsible for the first glacial map of Canada. While searching for unknown arctic islands in 1946-47, Wilson became the second Canadian to fly over the North Pole, a site he revisited in 1982. He has served on the NRC (1958-64), the Defence Research Board of Canada (1960-66), and the Science Council of Canada (1977-83). Besides his academic work, Wilson has written for popular audiences, including 2 books on China that helped reopen relations between China and Western countries. In 1935 he became the first person to ascend Mt Hague in Montana, following the example of his mountain-climbing parents. Mt Tuzo in the Rockies bears his mother's name. After "retirement" in 1974, Wilson combined his science and public interests as director general of the ONTARIO SCIENCE CENTRE (1974-85), remained at U of T as a distinguished lecturer (1974-77) and professor emeritus (1977) and was chancellor of York (1983-86). In 1988, in addition to preparing an autobiography, he was involved in a number of writing and research projects.

Recognition of his contributions to geophysics has included his election as president of the International Union of Geodesy and Geophysics (1957-60), and medals or awards from the RSC (1955) and various physics, geology and geography organizations. He is a Companion of the Order of Canada.   MARTIN K. MCNICHOLL

Wilson, Lois Miriam, née Freeman, United Church minister (b at Winnipeg 8 Apr 1927). Ordained after 15 years as a homemaker, Wilson shared team ministries with her husband Roy, successively in Thunder Bay, Hamilton and Kingston, Ont. The success of Town Talk, a multimedia program for involving the citizens of Thunder Bay in the discussion of community concerns, first brought her to public notice. Wilson was elected president of the Canadian Council of Churches in 1976 and moderator of the United Church of Canada in 1980, the first woman to hold either office. In 1983 she was elected one of the 7 presidents of the World Council of Churches. Also in 1983, she became co-director of the Ecumenical Forum of Canada. She has been instrumental in awakening in the United Church an increased concern for co-ordinated action to eliminate poverty and promote peace throughout the world. In 1984 she became a Member of the Order of Canada, and in 1985 she received the Pearson Peace Prize and World Federalists Peace Award.   JOHN WEBSTER GRANT

Wilson, Michael Holcombe, politician (b at Toronto 4 Nov 1937). Brought up in Toronto's comfortable Rosedale district, he attended Upper Canada Coll and U of T. In 1961 he joined the investment firm of Harris and Partners Ltd; apart from 2 years in the Dept of Finance, 1964-66, he remained in the Toronto investment business for 18 years, becoming executive VP of Dominion Securities, 1973-79. He was elected to the Commons as Conservative MP for Etobicoke Centre in 1979, and was minister of state for international trade in the short-lived CLARK government. He ran for the PC leadership in 1983; disappointed by his first-ballot showing, he threw his support to Brian MULRONEY. Wilson became minister of finance in 1984. Astute, solid and hard-working, he was widely regarded as one of the most successful Cabinet ministers in the Mulroney government. Wilson was also instrumental in the Conservatives' attempt at reforming Canada's TAXATION structure and in the negotiations for the loosening of trade barriers between Canada and the US (*see* FREE TRADE).   NORMAN HILLMER

Wilson, Montgomery, "Bud," figure skater (*fl* 1926-64). Wilson was the first Canadian to place in the top 3 in the world championships, coming 2nd in 1932. He also won the Olympic bronze medal that year. His reign as Canadian men's champion (1929-34 and 1938-39) was not equalled until Brian ORSER in the 1980s, and he held the N American championship 1929-39. Competing in pairs (his principal partner, Constance Samuel, became his wife), he won the Canadian championship 6 times between 1926 and 1934. After retiring he appeared in skating club carnivals. He later taught at the Boston Skating Club 1949-63 and, after 1964, at Michigan State University.   BARBARA SCHRODT

Wilson, Richard Albert, educator, author (b near Renfrew, Ont 18 Mar 1874; d at Vancouver 2 Jan 1949). Born on a farm in rural Ontario, he spent nearly the first half of his life working his way through school. He was 27 by the time he received his BA from Queen's U in 1901, and then, in quick succession, he earned his MA, 1902, his teaching certificate, 1903, and PhD, 1906, all from Queen's. He completed his education while teaching English in secondary schools, and after graduating became Principal of Regina Normal School in 1912 and then professor of English language and literature at U of Sask in 1915. In 1937, 3 years before he retired from U of Sask, Wilson collated his lecture notes and published a book entitled *The Birth of Language: Its Place in World Evolution and Its Structure in Relation* *to Space and Time.* In various English and American editions 1937-49, the book won critical accolades and popular acclaim, selling more than 100 000 copies. The book conjectures about the role played by language in the evolution of humankind, opposing Darwin's "mechanistic" views by emphasizing linguistic creativity. For Wilson, language is "the completely efficient instrument for the elaboration of the space-time world of free mind." Virtually unaware of the developing science of LINGUISTICS, Wilson espoused a more modern view than was then current, giving central importance to mentalism and language universals. In Wilson's obituary, the literary editor of the *Globe and Mail*, William Arthur DEACON, said "It is a fair guess that the late Professor Emeritus Wilson was the only Canadian so far, to write a book likely to affect, in time, the outlook of all human beings." When Wilson died the book went out of print, and it was largely forgotten until 1980 when the Canadian Linguistic Assn published the first Canadian edition to commemorate its silver anniversary.   J.K. CHAMBERS

Wilson, Ronald York, painter (b at Toronto 6 Dec 1907; d there 10 Feb 1984). A commercial artist, he first painted portraits of people caught in nervous moments: musicians playing to a table in a nightclub (1944), teenagers at the Saturday night hop (1945), the dressing room of a burlesque house (1946), young telegraph messengers talking to each other (1947) or a ballet class. But with the late 1950s Wilson made the change to abstraction, a move that isolated him from contemporaries such as Carl SCHAEFER but which proved central to his future. Like his early paintings, his abstractions, with their witty shapes, give a general impression of gaiety and constant movement. His colour sense changed for the better: now more gorgeous, it is at its best with blue and black, or as in certain geometrical abstractions, in brown stripes. His landscapes, large and French style, convey a sense of scale. Sometimes they seem to brood, recalling certain early abstractions of Paul-Émile BORDUAS.   JOAN MURRAY

Wiman, Erastus, journalist, businessman (b at Churchville, UC 21 Apr 1834; d on Staten I, NY 9 Feb 1904). Wiman made his reputation in Toronto as a commercial reporter for the *Globe* and the Board of Trade, as publisher of his own market and trade reviews, and, from 1860, as a reporter and manager for R.G. Dun's Mercantile Agency in Toronto and Montréal. He left Canada in 1866 to become Dun's New York C manager, but he retained a partnership in the Canadian agency, Dun, Wiman and Co, and personal and business ties. In the 1880s Wiman emerged as an enthusiastic advocate of commercial union with the US, writing and speaking on both sides of the border. The story told in his autobiographical *Chances of Success* (1893) ended in the same year with the loss of his fortune, invested in the development of Staten I, and of his position as general manager of the Dun firm, upon Dun's discovery that he had diverted company funds to his own use.
     WENDY CAMERON

Winch, Ernest Edward, trade unionist, politician (b at Harlow, Eng 22 Mar 1879; d at Vancouver 11 Jan 1957). He was a vigorous and dogmatic radical in his early years in the BC labour and socialist movements, active in supporting the ONE BIG UNION and rather suspicious at first of the doctrinal soundness of the central Canadian and academic reformers who associated with him in the formation of the CO-OPERATIVE COMMONWEALTH FEDERATION in 1932. Winch became somewhat more moderate in his politics after his election as CCF MLA for Burnaby in 1933, a seat he held continuously until his death. He became a reso-

lute advocate for immediate reform, exposing abuses and inadequacies in BC's social welfare and correctional institutions and taking a special interest in the problems of the aged. His son **Harold Edward** (b at Loughton, Eng 18 June 1907), who was elected CCF MLA for Vancouver E in 1933, became provincial party leader in 1938 and served as leader of the Opposition 1941-53. When the CCF was defeated in the controversial election of 1953, which saw W.A.C. BENNETT come to power, Harold abandoned provincial politics for the House of Commons, where he represented Vancouver E until his retirement in 1972.   STANLEY GORDON

Wind is the motion of air relative to the rotating surface of the Earth. Winds are caused by differences in atmospheric pressure: the greater the difference, the stronger the wind. The horizontal component of a wind is much greater than its vertical component; therefore, winds are usually thought of as moving horizontally. On a nonrotating Earth, air would move directly from areas of high pressure to those of lower pressure, ie, warm air would rise at the equator and flow poleward, as cold polar air sank and flowed towards the equator. However, in Canada, as elsewhere in the Northern Hemisphere, winds are deflected to the right of the path of motion by the Coriolis effect, a force resulting from the Earth's rotation. This deflection produces the prevailing westerly winds. In the atmosphere, between about 1.2 and 1.6 km, winds tend to blow parallel to rather than across the lines of equal pressure (isobars). These winds, known as geostrophic winds [Gk *geo*, "earth," *strophikos*, "turned"], are balanced because they are acted upon equally by the horizontal pressure force and the horizontal Coriolis effect. Gradient winds have the same direction as geostrophic winds, but move more quickly in cyclonically curved, counterclockwise paths (low pressure areas), and more slowly in anticyclonically curved, clockwise paths (high pressure areas). Near the ground, friction reduces wind speed and deflects the wind towards lower pressure. Consequently, winds converge and lift in lows. The result is bad weather. In high pressure systems they diverge. The subsidence which accompanies divergence leads to clear weather.

Winds play a major role in the heat and moisture balance of Canada. They pick up moisture from the oceans and lakes and distribute it across the country as precipitation. They transport heat from the oceans and from southerly latitudes into the interior and bring down cold air from the Arctic to the rest of the country and beyond. In Canada, wind speed is strongest in the North. Resolution I, NWT, has the greatest average annual wind speed in the country (35.5 km/h). The average in the prairies is about 18 km/h, compared to 14 km/h for the rest of the country. Some of the strongest winds in the country are hurricanes and tornadoes. Regional and local winds occur in many parts of the country. Mountain and valley winds (downslope and upslope, respectively) are found in interior BC. In coastal areas and around the Great Lakes, land and sea/lake breezes alternate; land breezes occur at night, sea/lake breezes during the day. CHINOOKS are warm, dry, gusty, foehn-type winds, ie, winds which blow down alpine valleys. They occur in southern Alberta.

Strong winds can cause damage to life and property. Canada's worst natural disaster in recent history occurred in Edmonton 31 July 1987 when a series of tornadoes struck the city. Twenty-seven people died and hundreds were injured. Property damage was estimated at over $250 million. The cooling effect of winds is familiar to most Canadians. Although this effect is present at all temperatures, it is most strongly felt in cold

weather. Wind chill results from the transfer of heat, primarily by convection, from the warmer human body to the colder atmosphere. The stronger the wind the greater the heat loss. Wind chill is expressed as the number of watts of energy lost per square metre of surface (W/m^2) or as the still air temperature which would cause the same heat loss (°C). *See also* DISASTERS; HURRICANE HAZEL; TORNADO.   L.C. NKEMDIRIM

Wind Energy is ENERGY obtained from moving air. The motion results from the heating and cooling of the Earth; thus, wind energy is an indirect form of SOLAR ENERGY. It is normally turned into useful energy by the action of WIND currents on moving surfaces such as the sails of a ship or the blades of a windmill. Wind energy is one of the oldest forms of energy used to supplement human muscle. Windmills and other spinning wind-energy devices – more accurately known as wind turbines – were used for grinding grain by the 7th century AD, and were in wide use for this purpose and for pumping water by the Middle Ages; they were brought by the French to Canada in the 17th century and were commonly used for grinding grain. Ships have used sails for at least 3000-4000 years. Before the advent of rural electrification systems, wind turbines were also used to generate electricity on farms in N America, notably on the Canadian prairies.

The advantage of wind-energy systems is that they tap an inexhaustible energy source that has no competing uses; hence, there is no fuel cost. The disadvantage is that wind conditions are unpredictable: they are subject to gusting and becalming, to daily and seasonal variations in strength, and to interactions with local topographic features. To meet a continuous demand such as a community's lighting and heating, a wind-energy system must either be integrated with other energy sources or include a means of storing energy for use during calm periods. If the demand is not continuous (eg, in agricultural water systems or unscheduled water transportation) wind energy can be employed very usefully. The reawakening of interest in wind-energy conversion systems is the result of increasing energy demands and the relatively high costs of conventional energy sources. New wind-energy conversion equipment uses advanced AERODYNAMIC features, modern structural design and new materials. The revival encompasses not only land-based systems but also commercial marine applications. New sail configurations have been devised to improve ship performance dramatically. However, the greatest effort has been focused on land-based generation of ELECTRIC POWER using high-speed wind turbines.

Applications The areas of Canada with the prime potential for wind-energy applications are those where there is a coincidence of good wind-energy sites with nearby energy users. Such a combination minimizes the size of wind turbine required for a given output, the capital cost of the energy-transmission system required and the associated transmission losses. Areas of maximum wind energy availability in Canada tend to occur on the E and W coasts, in a portion of northern Manitoba and in the southern portions of Alberta and Saskatchewan. The greatest potential appears to be for ELECTRIC-POWER GENERATION to serve nearby population centres and rural communities. Where circumstances permit, the electricity would be fed into existing electrical distribution grids. This is the type of system that utilities such as Newfoundland and Labrador Hydro and Saskatchewan Power Corp are using experimentally. Fairly large-scale water-pumping applications may also be feasible in Alberta and Saskatchewan for irrigation. Special cases where wind energy appears to be particularly attractive occur in very isolated areas that have high conventional energy costs, eg, some northern communities. In these cases wind-turbine generators will almost certainly be combined with, for example, power from internal-combustion engines to provide a continuous and reliable supply. The alternative, using wind-turbine generators to charge batteries, appears to be too costly for large-scale plants. Additional opportunities for Canadian industry may arise from the export of wind-energy systems to other countries.

The most recent developments in wind-energy applications relate to the generation of electrical power. This use arises from the prior existence in many areas of electrical-distribution grids, as well as the general convenience and flexibility of electrical power. Direct uses of mechanical energy produced by wind turbines are primarily for water pumping. At present, wind-turbine-driven water pumps are typically small machines, used mostly for watering stock. In the future, larger machines may be produced for IRRIGATION pumping and other applications. One possibility is pumped-storage systems in which water pumped from a low elevation to a reservoir at a higher level is allowed to flow back through a hydroelectric turbine.

Turbine Characteristics Different turbine characteristics are required for each type of application. Most electrical-power generators, or alternators, tend to require a relatively high speed of rotation. Consequently, turbines that run fairly fast, with the tips of the rotor moving 3-10 times the wind speed, are generally preferable to low-speed turbines because less gearing is required between the shaft of the wind turbine and the armature of the generator. A relatively low running speed is generally favoured for wind turbines that are directly coupled to water pumps or other mechanical loads. A striking feature of wind turbines intended for high-speed operation is the low rotor solidity, that is, the very small blade area in proportion to the turbine rotor's total projected area. Low-speed turbines feature a high solidity (either a small number of relatively broad blades or a large number of narrower ones). All modern high-speed turbines and most of the low-speed units incorporate blades designed on airfoil principles. Some inefficient low-speed machines depend on a drag effect, as does a square-rigged sailing ship. The foregoing remarks apply equally to wind turbines that are arranged with horizontal or vertical axes of rotation.

Typical horizontal-axis high-speed wind turbines have either 2 or 3 blades and resemble aircraft propellors. The blades of these machines are commonly arranged to vary in pitch automatically to optimize performance under conditions of varying wind speed. The most common high-speed vertical-axis turbine is the Darrieus rotor, named for its inventor. This machine is also known as an "egg beater" because of its characteristic appearance.

The most common form of low-speed machine is the horizontal axis, multibladed form often found on farms. The turbine is usually connected, via a crank, to a reciprocating water pump. A related design is the multibladed "bicycle-wheel" turbine, an example of a relatively low-speed turbine used for electrical-power generation. A simple vertical-axis design, often used for water pumping, is the split-cylinder configuration known as the Savonius rotor, after its originator. In this turbine each of the 2 or 3 rotor blades consists of a semicylinder offset radially from the axis of rotation. The design relies, in part, on a drag effect for its operation. It is not, therefore, a particularly efficient configuration, but is relatively simple to make.

Old windmill on Highway 1 near Tompkins, Sask. Modern wind technology has streamlined the design of wind turbines (*photo by G.J. Harris*).

General advantages of wind turbines are the complete absence of air pollution and a high energy-conversion efficiency. Well-designed wind turbines can recover up to 60-80% of the kinetic energy from the flow passing through their rotors. However, the low energy density available in the wind typically restricts output to a range 0.1 to 0.8 kW/m^2 (kilowatts per square metre) of the rotor's projected area. The result is a large machine size in relation to output; for example, in a machine rated at 5 MW ($MW = 10^6$ W), a high output for a single wind turbine, the rotor diameter can be as large as 100 m. This size problem results in the use of clustered machines, known as wind farms, to extract large power outputs from individual sites. Another problem with wind-energy systems is the variability of wind strength, which leads to substantial fluctuations in power since output is roughly proportional to the cube of the wind speed. Furthermore, all wind-energy conversion devices incur additional costs because they must be capable of withstanding storms.

In N America the main organization promoting the use of wind energy is the American Wind Energy Assn, Washington. In Canada the corresponding group is the Canadian Wind Energy Assn, Ottawa. The Solar Energy Society of Canada, Winnipeg, also supports work in the field. The NATIONAL RESEARCH COUNCIL OF CANADA has promoted research into wind energy since the 1960s. In 1984 construction began on the world's largest Darrieus-type wind turbine at Cap-Chat on the Gaspé Pen. Project Éole, a joint HYDRO-QUÉBEC and NRC enterprise, erected a turbine 110 m tall at a cost of $35 million. The turbine was designed and built by Canadian industries. A predecessor of Éole was the 230 kW wind turbine erected in the Magdalen Is, Qué. It was built by Indal Technologies Inc, Mississauga, Ont, which has subsequently developed a 500 kW commercial variant of this experimental machine.   J.A.C. KENTFIELD

Reading: J. Park, *The Wind Power Book* (1980).

Windigo, the spirit believed by the Algonquian to take possession of vulnerable persons and cause them to engage in various types of antisocial behaviour, most notably cannibalism. People are most susceptible when isolated in the woods (akin to being "bushed") for some considerable time. The resultant psychosis is well documented and is the subject of medical and psychological research.   CAROLE CARPENTER

Windmill, Battle of, was an incident in the raids across the Canadian frontier by the American-based HUNTERS LODGES. On 12 Nov 1838

Colonel Nils Von Schoultz, a Finn (mistakenly identified as a Pole) ran the schooner *Charlotte* aground some miles below Prescott, and took up a position in a 6-storey stone windmill and several stone houses nearby. A small vessel, the *Experiment,* cut Schoultz off from the US, while a force of 70 marines came by steamer from Kingston and about 700 militia arrived from the surrounding counties. These forces drove "the Hunters" from their outworks but could make no impression on the windmill. After 2 days of minor operations, Col Henry Dundas arrived with 4 companies of the 83rd Regiment, 2 eighteen-pounders and a howitzer. When resistance collapsed, on Nov 16, 137 invaders, including Schoultz, were taken prisoner. Hunters' losses were estimated at 80, and British and Canadian losses were 16 dead and 60 wounded.   HEREWARD SENIOR

Windsor, Nfld, Town, pop 5545 (1986c), 5747 (1981c), inc 1942, is located in N-central Newfoundland, adjacent to the pulp and paper town of GRAND FALLS. When a pulp and paper mill was constructed by 1909 on the route of the trans-insular railway at Grand Falls, a new settlement called Grand Falls Station grew up parallel to the railway. In contrast to the Anglo-Newfoundland Development Co town of Grand Falls, Grand Falls Station, renamed Windsor (possibly for the royal house of Windsor), grew without benefit of planning and services. In 1942 it was the second municipality in Newfoundland, after ST JOHN'S, to be incorporated. Municipal and community facilities followed, remedying some of the town's problems caused by rapid settlement and growth. Since the beginning, Windsor has been economically dependent upon Grand Falls.

JANET E.M. PITT AND ROBERT D. PITT

Windsor, NS, Town, pop 3665 (1986c), 3646 (1981c), inc 1878, is located in central NS, at the mouth of the Avon and St Croix rivers. Its short distance from HALIFAX (66 km) has long made Windsor a town of commuters. It was first settled by ACADIANS in 1684 and was called Pisiquid, a name of Micmac origin. The English township of Windsor (after Windsor, Eng) was established 1764, and wealthy Halifax businessmen and politicians were granted land here. During the AMERICAN REVOLUTION, troops were kept at Windsor's Ft Edward to ensure the loyalty of Annapolis Valley residents. Following the war, many LOYALISTS came to the town. They farmed, traded and opened shops, disrupting the pastoral luxury of the big Windsor estates. In 1789 Bishop Charles INGLIS established UNIVERSITY OF KING'S COLLEGE, the oldest university in Canada. It is now located in Halifax.

Windsor thrived during the 1800s, gaining sawmills, furniture and fertilizer factories, a foundry, tannery, cotton mill and plaster mine. The arrival of the first train to Windsor in 1858 tied the town closer to Halifax. Today, Windsor is mainly residential. Light manufacturing and tourism are the main industries. Visitors may see the remains of Ft Edward and "Clifton," the home of Judge Thomas Chandler HALIBURTON, the famous 19th-century author and creator of Sam Slick.   HEATHER MACDONALD

Windsor, Ont, Canada's southernmost city, is located on the DETROIT R in the extreme SW corner of the province. Lying directly S of Detroit on the rich agricultural peninsula nestled between Lakes ERIE and ST CLAIR, Windsor is an international gateway through which millions of foreign visitors enter the country each year. Windsor has grown from the coalescing of a chain of separate communities along the Detroit R and Lk St Clair and from spreading inland to the south, and today its Census Metropolitan Area includes the towns

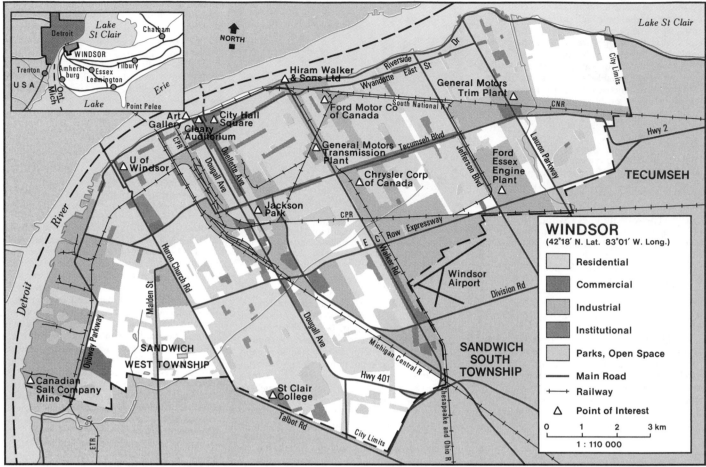

WINDSOR
(42°18' N. Lat. 83°01' W. Long.)

- Residential
- Commercial
- Industrial
- Institutional
- Parks, Open Space
- Main Road
- Railway
- △ Point of Interest

0   1   2   3 km
1 : 110 000

of Tecumseh, Essex and Belle River; the village of St Clair Beach; and the townships of Sandwich W and S Maidstone, Rochester and Colchester N.

Settlement The area was visited by Jesuit missionaries and French explorers in the 17th century, and permanent settlement followed Cadillac's founding of Detroit. The first land grants for settlement were made in 1749. French settlers were augmented by English-speaking LOYALISTS in the 1780s. By the 1820s the introduction of steamships on Lk Erie, the opening of the Erie Canal and WELLAND CANAL and regular stage service from the E stimulated frontier expansion westward. The ferry connection with Detroit led to the establishment of a small hamlet around the ferry dock. Known variously as the Ferry, Richmond and south Detroit, the community in 1836 agreed upon Windsor with its Loyalist and British associations.

Development With the arrival of the GREAT WESTERN RAILWAY in 1854 the village was incorporated; it reached town status 4 years later. Initially, there were barriers to international commerce and travel, eg, a difference of gauge between US and Canadian railways, but in the 1860s standardized gauges and the development of huge ferries capable of transporting entire trains allowed cargoes and passengers to pass directly across the river. By then Windsor had also become a service centre for the surrounding agricultural area. The railway network was completed in 1910 with the opening of a railway tunnel under the river.

Industrial activity began upriver in Walkerville, a company town (inc 1890) developed by Hiram WALKER around his distillery. In 1904 Ford Motor Co of Canada was established just E of Walker's distillery, creating the industry that would become the area's economic lifeline. Through the early 20th century, Ford, General Motors, Chrysler and a host of long-forgotten au-

to companies and parts plants helped make the area the "Auto Capital of the British Empire." With hundreds of American firms taking advantage of favourable tariff policies, the area experienced unparalleled prosperity and optimism. The new auto age was capped by the opening of the Ambassador Bridge (1929) – the world's longest international suspension bridge – and the Detroit-Windsor Auto Tunnel (1930) – the only international vehicular tunnel in the world.

Cityscape The French system of land division had encouraged a stringing out of settlement along the Detroit R. Over time communities were established (Sandwich) or sprang up around some function such as the ferry dock (Windsor), a distillery (Walkerville) or an auto maker's plant (Ford City). The transformation of the industrial base by the auto industry attracted rapid population growth and increased demands for administering the metropolitan area as a single functioning unit. Plans for zoning, waterfront beautification and other urban improvements were lost on those whose priorities were rebuilding the city's tax base and providing new employment. The short-sighted, development-at-all-costs view resulted in a disillusioning experience with riverfront development, but the community learned a lesson. As a result there has been a heightened community commitment to the riverfront and its protection.

Population From 21 000 in 1908, population grew to 105 000 in 1928. This rise was almost entirely due to employment offered in the automobile industry. This industrial work force was young, had a high male to female ratio and a high percentage of foreign born. Another attraction was the opportunity of employment in Detroit; in 1927 over 15 000 Windsor residents held jobs there. During the Depression unemployment reached 30% of the work force, immigration

ceased and the area suffered an outmigration. WWII production of war materials and postwar demand for automobiles meant employment and population gains, but from 1953 to 1962 the number of auto workers dropped to nearly half. In 1965 following a major territorial annexation and the signing of the Autopact, employment was high and there was a continual immigration from many lands. The ITALIANS were the largest postwar group and perhaps the most visible, but the Asian population has grown recently. Slightly more than half of the population is Catholic.

A considerable boost was given to the eroding French culture by official national bilingual and bicultural policies with support from Ontario's educational policies. Designated an official bilingual district, Windsor is served by French-language radio and television and by École secondaire l'Essor.

Economy and Labour Force Windsor is Canada's fifth-largest manufacturing centre. Since its inception the auto industry has set wage and employment patterns for the area. Chrysler, Ford and General Motors continue to invest heavily in Windsor which augurs well for its future. Chrysler has head offices in Windsor and is the city's largest employer. Windsor also has significant employment in construction, transportation, trade and service industries. Much of the food and beverage industry consists in processing locally grown farm products. Windsor's best-known processor is Hiram Walker and Sons, Ltd, makers of Canadian Club Whisky. Windsor is also Ontario's fifth-ranked tourist and convention centre.

Transportation Located in the heart of N America, Windsor is a transportation centre and Canada's busiest port of entry. It is served by 5 railways, 4 provincial highways and the Macdonald-Cartier Freeway (401) connecting with Toronto and Montréal. A deepwater port near the centre

Population: 193 111 (1986c), 192 078 (1981cA); 253 988 (1986 CMA), 250 885 (1981 ACMA)

Rate of Increase (1981-86): City .5%; CMA 1.2%

Rank in Canada: Fifteenth (by CMA)

Date of Incorporation: City 1892

Land Area: City 119.87 km²; CMA 861.66 km²

Elevation: 190 m

Climate: Average daily temp, July 22.2°C, Jan -4.9°C; Yearly precip 848.8 mm; Hours of sunshine 1995 per year

point of the ST LAWRENCE SEAWAY, the city is also served by the Windsor International Airport.

Government and Politics In the early 20th century, the border community was swept by municipal reform currents from both Canada and the US and experimented with at-large elections, reduction of wards and councillors and commission government.

The entry of labour into municipal politics occurred in 1918 when the local Trades and Labor Congress ran a slate that captured one-third of the council seats. Though labour faltered in the prosperous 1920s, this form of union political action reached its apex in the 1935 election of George Bennett, a trade unionist and CCF member, but it was short-lived. Much of labour's strength was siphoned off in Windsor by 2 remarkable Liberal mayors – David Croll and Arthur Reaume – who dominated local politics from 1930 to 1954. The economic crisis of the 1950s marked the return to dominance of the structural reformers who implemented city manager government. A very politicized ward system was re-established in 1979 on the assumption that the "city interest" was insensitive to special groups and neighbourhood concerns. Currently there are 5 wards and 10 councillors serving 3-year terms.

Cultural Life Windsor's reputation as a community devoted to the arts is increasingly being recognized. The Art Gallery of Windsor has attained national status; the Cleary Auditorium and Convention Centre is the city's major centre

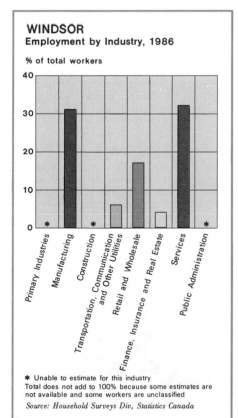

WINDSOR
Employment by Industry, 1986

% of total workers

[Bar chart with y-axis labelled in percentages from 0 to 40. X-axis categories: Primary Industries (*), Manufacturing, Construction (*), Transportation, Communication and Other Utilities, Retail and Wholesale, Finance, Insurance and Real Estate, Services, Public Administration (*)]

* Unable to estimate for this industry
Total does not add to 100% because some estimates are not available and some workers are unclassified

Source: Household Surveys Div, Statistics Canada

for the performing arts and houses the Windsor Symphony and the Windsor Light Opera. Windsor's stock of interesting and diverse historic architecture includes the Hiram Walker Historical Museum, Mackenzie Hall and Willistead Manor.

Windsor's tradition in higher education began with the establishment in 1857 of Assumption College, which became UNIVERSITY OF WINDSOR (incorporated 1962), a nondenominational, provincially supported university. St Clair College of Applied Arts and Technology, fd in 1967, continues a tradition begun early in this century by F.P. Gavin, a pioneer in technical education.

Windsor's special relationship with Detroit is marked by the Windsor-Detroit International Freedom Festival – a week of co-operative activities and events topped off with a gigantic fireworks display on the Detroit R. Windsor has one major newspaper, the daily Windsor *Star*, owned by the Southam chain.   LARRY L. KULISEK

Reading: E.J. Lajeunesse, *The Windsor Border Region* (1960); N. Morrison, *Garden Gateway to Canada* (1954); T. Price and Larry L. Kulisek, *Windsor: An Illustrated History* (1985).

Windsor Strike, 12 Sept-20 Dec 1945, at the WINDSOR, Ont, plant of Ford Motor Co. The walkout of some 17 000 workers was the first and most significant of the many strikes occurring immediately after WWII as Canada's unions attempted to capitalize on their great wartime advances. But most companies were determined to limit organized labour's gains. There was really only one strike issue at Ford: union recognition. The UNITED AUTOMOBILE WORKERS demanded it; the company refused to grant it. "Union shop and checkoff" had been the union's slogan for some time. Negotiations had lasted for almost 2 years, and the plant had been subject to many wildcat strikes during the war. The company, with the help of the provincial government, desperately strove to break the strike. Police attempts to break through the picket line were thwarted by strikers who blockaded all the streets in downtown Windsor, surrounding the plant with their cars – parked, locked and abandoned.

On Dec 13 both parties agreed to binding arbitration under Mr Justice Ivan RAND of the Supreme Court of Canada. In his arbitration award rendered 29 Jan 1946, he denied the UAW's demand for a union shop and condemned both the union and the company for their behaviour. Most importantly, he provided for a compulsory checkoff of union dues for all employees in the bargaining unit whether they were union members or not. Finally, he developed a system of financial penalties, to be drawn from union dues, which would be levied against the union in the event of a wildcat or illegal strike, based on the duration of the strike. This arbitration ruling, later known as the RAND FORMULA, became widely used in collective bargaining in Canada.   IRVING ABELLA

Wine Industry The cultivation of GRAPES to produce wine occurs in only 2 areas of Canada: southwestern Ontario and the OKANAGAN VALLEY of BC. The 55 km long belt of the NIAGARA PENINSULA, in which 80% of the nation's wine grapes are grown, and the Okanagan, reaching down to the Similkameen vineyard pocket near the US border, are well within the North Temperate Zone, in which the world's major vineyards are located. The number of degree-days (a method of scientifically recording the amount of warmth required to ripen the grape and increase its sugar content) is higher than that of all German vineyards and, in the Niagara Pen, close to that of Bordeaux, France. However, low winter temperatures and the risk of late May frosts that damage blossoms have necessitated the use of exceedingly hardy

vines. This factor is the main difference between Canadian viticulture and that of all other parts of the world, except New York state.

In Canada, historically, the basis of wine has been grapes from N American *Vitis labrusca* vines; in Europe *V. vinifera* vines are used. However, there has been a dramatic change in the past decade, and today 70% of the wine in Canada is made from hybrids of vinifera vines. The presence of wild native labrusca vines spurred the first attempts at wine making; Seneca, Tuscarora and Cayuga used them before European contact, and Paul LE JEUNE's *Relation* of 1636 records that early Jesuit missionaries made sacramental wine. The first wine was made for commercial sale in 1811 by a German mercenary, Joseph Schiller, who used vines growing on the banks of the Credit R, 32 km W of present-day Toronto. Forty-six years later, Porter Adams was the first to plant vines. He did so near St David's (in what is now the heart of the Niagara grape-growing region) on land deeded to him by the family to which Laura SECORD belonged.

Throughout the 19th century, wine making was a cottage-industry. Grapes were grown in many areas, eg, Pelée I, Essex County and plots near Brantford. However, in 1873 George Barnes started a larger winery at St Catharines that is still operating. A year later, Thomas Bright and a partner began what is today Canada's largest winery. The wild blue Concord grape accounted for 70% of all production and ensured a predominance of red wines. The wine was invariably "fortified" with spirits to produce port or sherry, a practice that continued until the 1960s.

Two significant developments occurred during the 1920s. First, the BC wine industry was started on Vancouver I to make use of surplus loganberries. The industry then expanded to irrigated lakeside grape plots in the arid Okanagan; however, there have never been enough local grapes for winery demands, and a large tonnage is imported annually from the US. Second, the sale of domestic wine was permitted in Ontario during PROHIBITION, leading to the creation of a multiplicity of wineries, many producing drink of dubious quality. As a result, when Prohibition ended, wine making, marketing and sale came under strict regulation by provincial liquor commissions, beginning in Ontario. Today testing of both domestic and imported wines is more faithfully and aggressively conducted, for both quality and safety reasons, than anywhere in the world, and Ontario is exploring further improvements in wine standards for 5 categories: varietal, vintage, estate bottled, superior wines and champagne.

A few winemakers, such as the redoubtable Adhemar F. de Chaunac, and crossbreeding specialists, like those at Ontario's Vineland Horticultural Station, realized that improvements in wine could only come from doing more research, from using hybrid or vinifera vines and from aging the wines. However, they worked virtually "in the wilderness" for 3 decades because most Canadians were not wine drinkers and those who were preferred the cheapest products with high alcohol content. Life-style changes, including concerns about health, the increase in women drinkers and the availability of wine with meals affected the industry radically. Beginning in the 1960s, tastes changed and consumption increased. In 1964 the Canadian per capita wine consumption for all ages was 2.4 L; by 1986 it was 8.8 L. This figure is far below the 78.4 L and 73.3 L of France and Italy, respectively, but is comparable with the per capita consumption in Britain (10.4 L). Perhaps more important, the proportion of per capita consumption represented by light table wines (under 14% alcohol by volume) increased from 33% in 1968 to 73% in 1986.

In the 1980s dry white table wines became extremely popular at home and in restaurants and wine bars in major cities. Canadian products battle imports from 45 countries but are becoming more popular because, after 25 years of experimentation, they have been developed from hybrid grapes (eg, the Siebel group) and high-quality viniferas (Cabernet Sauvignon, Pinot Noir, Gewürztraminer). Small Ontario and BC "estate" wineries now specialize in these higher-quality wines. The large wineries continue to make sparkling wines, sherries and ports and the so-called "coolers" (of less than 7% alcoholic content), in addition to the traditional reds.

Standards of production (from crushing and pressing to clarification) have also improved. Many wine makers come to Canada after rigorous European oenological training. Grape harvesting by machine to reduce labour costs is common. New cellarage of the highest hygienic standards has been added. Canadian wines in 1986 won more than 200 gold, silver and bronze medals in international competitions. Canadian wine making has become scientific and has spread: wineries now exist in 8 provinces. In 1986 there were 46 wineries in Canada, producing products valued at more than $256 million. Canadian vintners are concerned about the industry's inability to achieve a 50-50 import-domestic market share of liquor-board listings. In 1983 domestic wines made up 37% of liquor-board listings; this figure was 38% in 1986. The industry is represented by the Canadian Wine Institute.   PERCY ROWE

Winisk River, 475 km long, rises in Wunnummin Lk in the Kenora Dist of northern Ontario, and flows E and NE into HUDSON BAY. The name is from a Cree word meaning "groundhog" or "woodchuck." The river drains an area of 67 300 km², most of it uninhabited.   DANIEL FRANCIS

Winkler, Man, Town, pop 5926 (1986c), 5046 (1981c), inc as Village 1906 and Town 1954, is located in the Pembina Valley region, 115 km SW of Winnipeg and 22 km N of the US international boundary. Settlement in the Winkler area began in 1882 and the CPR established a siding there on land owned by Valentine Winkler, a businessman and politician, in 1892. Nearby were agricultural villages in the NW part of the West Reserve, one of 2 areas in Manitoba set aside in the 1870s for Mennonite immigrants from southern Russia. Favourable soil and climate, combined with the farming expertise of these religious settlers, helped develop one of Manitoba's richest farming regions. Winkler grew as a trade, service and processing centre for the agricultural sector and, after WWII, as a regional retail and industrial centre. Industrial production includes recreational vehicles, mobile homes, agricultural machinery, metal and plastic products, and manufactured homes. Among the town's facilities are a regional shopping centre (1985), a radio station, a municipal airport, a museum and a recreation complex.   D.M. LYON

Reading: F. Brown, *A History of the Town of Winkler, Manitoba* (1973).

Winnipeg, capital and largest city of Manitoba, is located at the confluence of the RED R and ASSINIBOINE R, 100 km N of the Minnesota border. Lying midway between the Atlantic and Pacific oceans, it has been called "Bull's Eye of the Dominion" and situated where the Canadian SHIELD gives way to the prairie, "Gateway to the West." The name derives from the Cree name for the lake 65 km N, *win-nipi,* meaning "murky water."

Settlement The area was frequented by Cree hunters, and attracted fur traders as early as 1738, when LA VÉRENDRYE built Ft Rouge at the "forks."

Winnipeg, corner of Portage Avenue and Main Street, 1872 (*by permission of the British Library*).

Other activity in the area was related to the activities of Forts Gibraltar and Garry, but the nucleus of the future city of Winnipeg was related to the construction of a general store by Henry McKenney in 1862. His store was built where the furrunners' trail coming down the Assiniboine R to Fort Garry crossed the trail running down the Red R — in present-day Winnipeg the corner of Portage and Main. Until 1873, when Winnipeg was incorporated as a city, the settlement remained a relatively unimportant part of the larger RED RIVER COLONY. When the first city council meeting was held in 1874, the city had a population of 3700 and was little more than a collection of shacks.

Development Winnipeg's strategic geographical location made it the natural focus for the western extension of the transcontinental railways. With the completion of the CPR (1885), the city was launched into a period of growth and prosperity unequalled in Canadian urban development. A flood of immigrants, high wheat prices, plentiful capital and improved dry-land farming all contributed to sustained growth. The city became the wholesale, administrative and financial centre of the West. By 1911 Winnipeg ranked fourth in Canada in manufacturing.

This meteoric rise had peaked by 1914, when the city entered recession. The WINNIPEG GENERAL STRIKE (1919) left scars, and the Great Depression plunged business, manufacturing, wholesale trade and the mail-order business into sharp decline. Factories closed and unemployment soared. Not until WWII did the city lift out of its stubborn depression. Conditions improved greatly in the postwar years, but growth was steady, compared to the frenzied pace earlier this century. In the interim, the development of oil, gas, coal and potash shifted economic power westward. Winnipeg's previous monopoly of the marketing of agricultural products and distribution of goods has been challenged by Regina, Saskatoon, Edmonton and Calgary. The city's traditional resources have sustained its commerce and its position as the largest city on the Prairies, but its recent fortunes pale in comparison with its rivals.

Cityscape River lots and fur-trade routes shaped early street patterns, and later the dominant feature was the railway, which physically di-

vided the city in 2: the "North End" was the home of most of the city's Slavs and Jews; the prosperous and politically dominant Anglo-Saxons were concentrated in the W and S. Commerce centered at Portage Ave and Main St, and after 1886 industry moved from the riverbanks to the rail lines. Early ARCHITECTURE was in the indigenous form, called "Red River Frame," composed of vertical and horizontal logs. Early public buildings and better houses were built of limestone in imported styles, and after the railway arrived, Winnipeg began to resemble other cities of the time. Prosperity brought greater pretensions, notably the famous "gingerbread" city hall, a picturesque Victorian fantasy. Much of the city had to be rebuilt after the disastrous Red River Flood (1950), and shopping centres began to proliferate. During the 1960s and 1970s, Winnipeg changed steadily, though not as dramatically as places like Calgary. Nonetheless, almost the entire urban landscape was remade. New industrial parks housed relocated industries. A new city hall, convention centre and a Centennial Centre, including a planetarium, concert hall and museum, were completed. Numerous high-rise hotels, banks and office buildings altered the skyline. A dramatic new building spree got under way in 1985 under the auspices of the North Portage Development Corp, an arm's-length body funded by all 3 levels of government. The NPDC is responsible for changing the face of a stretch of Winnipeg's famous Portage Ave by the construction of more than 180 000 m² of retail and commercial space and more than 1000 units of housing. The first major phase of this project was completed in 1987 and plans call for additional buildings to be constructed as the market demands. In addition, in 1986, the 3 levels of government also revealed major plans to revitalize Winnipeg's CN East Yards area, thus opening this waterfront site to Winnipeggers for the first time in many decades.

Population Winnipeg changed in several distinct stages, from a small, compact, ethnically homogeneous community to a large, sprawling, cosmopolitan city. With the exception of a sharp increase in the early 1880s, growth was steady and resulted primarily from immigration from Britain and Ontario. These early groups established a dominance that persisted until after 1945, despite the arrival of other "foreigners." In contrast, the growth from 1900 to 1913 was phenomenal, and by 1911 Winnipeg was the third-largest city in Canada. Rapid growth placed strains on the city, which faced serious problems of public health and the provision of services. But the most serious problem was the conflict of values between the charter groups and the immigrants, many of whom were Slavs and Jews who did not fit into the Anglo-Canadian mold and as a result experienced overt discrimination, ranging from residential segregation to job discrimination and destruction of their property. A deeply preju-

A panoramic view of a prosperous, thriving Winnipeg in 1913 (*by permission of the British Library*).

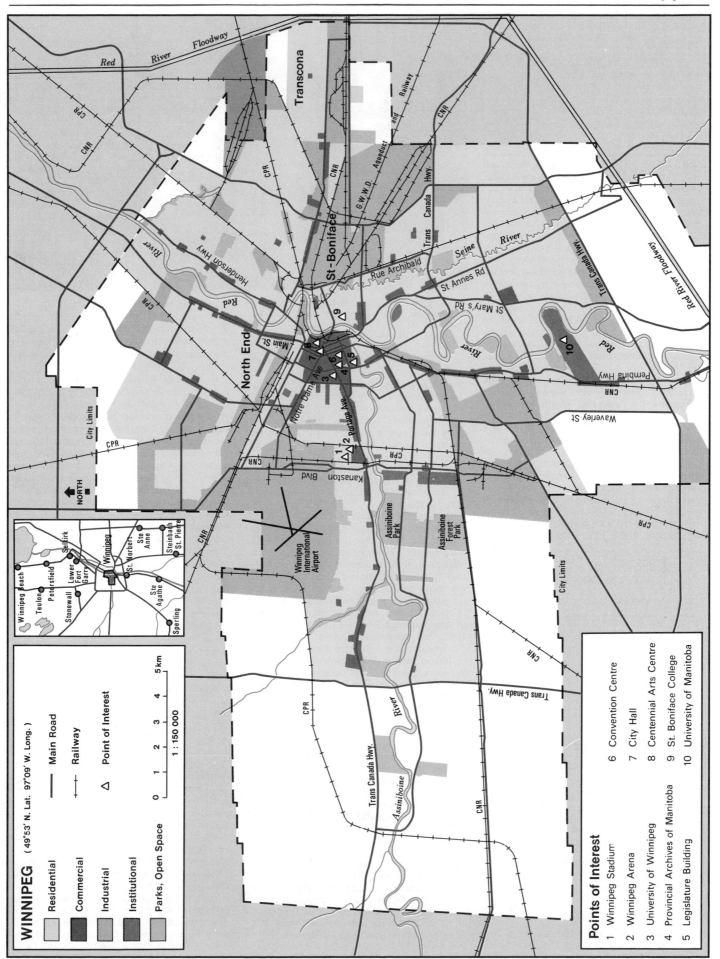

WINNIPEG (49°53' N. Lat. 97°09' W. Long.)

Residential	— Main Road
Commercial	+— Railway
Industrial	△ Point of Interest
Institutional	
Parks, Open Space	

0 1 2 3 4 5 km
1 : 150 000

Points of Interest

1 Winnipeg Stadium
2 Winnipeg Arena
3 University of Winnipeg
4 Provincial Archives of Manitoba
5 Legislature Building
6 Convention Centre
7 City Hall
8 Centennial Arts Centre
9 St. Boniface College
10 University of Manitoba

Population: 594 551 (1986c), 564 473 (1981c); 625 304 (1986 CMA), 592 061 (1981 ACMA)

Rate of Increase (1981-86): City 5.3%; CMA 6%

Rank in Canada: Seventh (by CMA)

Date of Incorporation: City 1873; under Unicity 1973

Land Area: City 571.60 km²; CMA 3294.82 km²

Elevation: 239 m

Climate: Average daily temp, July 19.6°C, Jan -19.3°C; Yearly precip 525.5 mm; Hours of sunshine 2321.4 per year

Winnipeg, Manitoba's capital and its largest city; view of the Legislative Building (*photo by Douglas J. Fisher/Masterfile*).

diced majority saw the immigrants as a threat, and by 1920 Winnipeg was a city of isolated and frequently bitter ethnic groups. Tensions eased as immigration declined 1920-60 and as natural increase played a greater role. The decrease in hostilities was apparent when Stephen JUBA, a Ukrainian, was elected mayor in 1956. Juba was joined by increasing numbers of other non-Anglo-Saxons on city council and also in other public positions.

After 1960 the population of the city proper actually declined as surrounding municipalities grew. The region was recognized as one city with the creation of Unicity (1972), which also included the large concentration of Francophones from ST-BONIFACE. Winnipeg has become more cosmopolitan with each succeeding decade, with recent increases in Italians, Indians and Métis; young members of these groups have shown renewed interest in their native language and culture. Since 1970, an annual week-long festival, called Folklorama, has celebrated Winnipeg's cosmopolitan character.

Economy Winnipeg dominates Manitoba's economy, containing half the provincial population and 68% of its employees, producing 83% of its manufactured goods and accounting for 62% of its retail sales. It is still pre-eminently a transportation centre, and much of its industry is geared to the transportation systems. Secondary manufacturing has traditionally been seen as the key to expansion, and prairie settlement has given impetus to consumer industries. Recently,

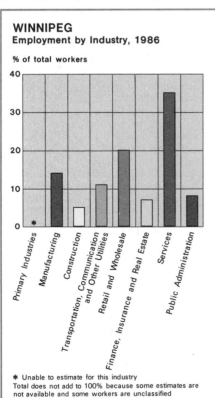

WINNIPEG
Employment by Industry, 1986

% of total workers

* Unable to estimate for this industry
Total does not add to 100% because some estimates are not available and some workers are unclassified
Source: Household Surveys Div, Statistics Canada

the large increases in employment have been in the public and private service industries. The provincial and federal governments support a large public service, and Winnipeg has remained a financial and insurance centre. The city has a long tradition of "boosterism." In 1906 the Winnipeg Development and Industrial Bureau was organized to promote manufacturing and commerce. It became the Industrial Development Board (1925) and operated until 1979, when a new group – Winnipeg Business Development Inc – was formed to attract high-technology industry to the city.

Government and Politics Until 1920 Winnipeg was governed by a mayor and 14 aldermen from 7 wards. In 1920, after the general strike, the ward system was, in effect, gerrymandered by business interests to prevent labour representatives from gaining control of city government. The move worked, for although a few radical mayors and aldermen were elected, the so-called "Citizens' League" retained a majority on council. The powerful Board of Control, created in 1907, was representative of the URBAN REFORM movement of the time. The mayor and 4 controllers, elected annually, carried out the executive work. The board was disbanded in 1918.

The next attempt at reform did not take place until the 1960s when Winnipeg was moved into the forefront of N American cities by first creating a metropolitan form of government and then moving to a unified, single level of government. Although the division of the region into a number of separate jurisdictions made it difficult to provide services and administer community affairs, it was not until the 1950s that the first step was taken towards REGIONAL GOVERNMENT. In 1960 the Metropolitan Winnipeg Act was passed, creating a new alignment of 7 cities, 5 suburban municipalities and one town. The Metropolitan Corp of Greater Winnipeg was given sole authority over planning, zoning, building, flood control, transportation, etc. Many of the municipalities were unhappy with the format.

In 1972 the provincial government replaced the area municipalities with a 50-member city council that controlled an urban territory with a population of 550 000. With the formation of Unicity, Winnipeg became the first large N American city to move beyond the stage of split-level metropolitan government to a single administration. The original

Unicity format has been studied extensively, and in 1977 further reforms were undertaken, reducing the council in size from 50 to 29 members. A second major review was undertaken in 1984-85 and a series of new reforms were introduced by the provincial government in 1987.

Cultural Life Winnipeg is a major cultural centre of the Prairie provinces and has long held a reputation as a thriving community of literature, sport, religion, ethnic organizations, music, education and art. There has been an outpouring of novels either set in Winnipeg or written by novelists who had spent considerable parts of their lives in the city. Works by such noted writers as Jack Ludwig, John Marlyn, Dorothy LIVESAY, Adele WISEMAN, Margaret LAURENCE and Patricia Blondel have some strong link with the city. The city is the home of the acclaimed ROYAL WINNIPEG BALLET, the WINNIPEG SYMPHONY ORCHESTRA, Rainbow Stage, the Winnipeg Art Gallery and the MANITOBA THEATRE CENTRE – one of the most important regional theatres in N America. The Assiniboine Park Zoo, the Manitoba Museum of Man and Nature, the Provincial Archives of Manitoba, the Royal Canadian Mint and Lower Fort Garry (*see* FORT GARRY, LOWER, a historic restoration located just N of the city) are also major attractions. The Manitoba Music Festival, held each spring in the city, is the largest music festival to be held in Canada. In sports Winnipeg is noted especially for curling and football. Between 1947 and 1971, Winnipeg rinks won the Canadian curling championship 8 times while the WINNIPEG BLUE BOMBERS have won the GREY CUP 8 times between 1935 and 1987. In 1972 the WINNIPEG JETS joined the World Hockey Assn, and then the National Hockey League in 1979. In 1967 Winnipeg was host to the fifth Pan-American Games, leaving the city with many new sports facilities, including the Olympic-size Pan-Am Swimming Pool (which includes the Aquatic Hall of Fame and Museum of Canada), a cycling velodrome, a high-school stadium, a track facility and a rifle range.

Winnipeg is the location of UNIVERSITY OF MANITOBA (fd 1877), UNIVERSITY OF WINNIPEG (fd 1871, as Manitoba College), St-Boniface College (fd 1818) and the more recent Red River Community College. There are, as well, numerous private schools and special facilities, such as the Manitoba School for the Deaf. The city has one major newspaper, the WINNIPEG FREE PRESS (the rival *Winnipeg Tribune* ceased publication in 1980), one daily tabloid, the Winnipeg SUN, several TV stations and numerous radio stations.

A cosmopolitan city of many diverse groups, Winnipeg has a wide variety of ethnic clubs and organizations, synagogues, cathedrals, religious colleges and institutes. ALAN F.J. ARTIBISE

Reading: Alan F.J. Artibise, *Winnipeg: An Illustrated History* (1977); Artibise and E.H. Dahl, *Winnipeg in Maps, 1816-1972* (1975); Artibise and G.A. Stelter, *Canada's Urban Past: A Bibliography and Guide to Canadian Urban Studies* (1981); R.C. Bellan, *Winnipeg's First Century: An Economic History* (1978); T.J. Kuz, ed, *Winnipeg, 1874-1974: Progress and Prospects* (1974); P.L. Sloane et al, *Winnipeg: A Centennial Bibliography* (1974); T.R. Weir, *Atlas of Winnipeg* (1978).

Winnipeg, Lake, 24 400 km², elev 217 m, estimated maximum depth 18 m, sixth-largest freshwater lake in Canada, is located in central Manitoba. Extending 416 km N-S, it drains approximately 984 200 km² of land by way of the SASKATCHEWAN, RED-ASSINIBOINE and WINNIPEG river systems. This drainage basin extends from the foothills of the Rockies across Alberta, Saskatchewan and Manitoba to the rolling metamorphic uplands of Ontario's Precambrian SHIELD. In the S it extends along the Red R to the headwaters of the Mississippi, including large parts of the states of Minnesota and N Dakota. Lk Winnipeg discharges its waters into the NELSON R, which flows to HUDSON BAY at an average annual rate of 2066 m³/s. Since the construction of a lake-outlet control structure at Jenpeg, Man, the monthly discharge has been maintained between 25 000 m³/s and 183 300 m³/s. The control structure maintains lake levels at about 217 m and assures an adequate supply of water for the numerous hydroelectric generating stations on the Nelson.

The lake lies in a lowland basin that was scoured out of the limestone and shale bedrock by continental glaciers during the ice ages. When the glaciers finally melted, about 12 000 years ago, a large lake, Glacial Lk AGASSIZ, filled the entire basin. It gradually drained and exposed a flat plain that extends from the Manitoba Escarpment in the W to the rocky edge of the Precambrian Shield in the E. Today the glacial lake bottom constitutes the Manitoba Lowlands and is occupied by Lks Winnipeg, WINNIPEGOSIS and MANITOBA.

English explorer Henry KELSEY (1690) may have been the first European to see the "murky waters" (*win-nipi*) and adopted this Cree Indian name for the vast freshwater body. The lake soon became an important transport link between the Hudson Bay port of York Factory and the fur-trade hinterlands of the Red-Assiniboine watershed. In 1812 Lord Selkirk's boats traversed the length of Lk Winnipeg on their way to founding the RED RIVER COLONY at the junction of the Red and Assiniboine rivers. Later the lake gave its name to this community, which later became the capital of the new province of Manitoba.

On long and relatively narrow lakes such as Lk Winnipeg, interesting wind and wave effects occasionally take place. When prevailing northerly winds blow along the length of Lk Winnipeg, they exert a horizontal stress on its surface. Surface waters move in the direction of the wind and pile up along the windward S shores – a phenomenon known as a setup or wind tide. Setups greater than 1 m above normal lake levels have been recorded along many of southern Lk Winnipeg's recreational beaches, and the associated high waves with their uprush effects have caused considerable storm damage, backshore flooding and shoreline erosion. The highest setups occur in the fall, when the northerly winds are strongest. If the winds die down suddenly, the waters rush northward, then slosh back and forth in a process called seiching. R.A. McGINN

Winnipeg Blue Bombers, football team. Winnipeg had been represented in interprovincial play by several different teams since 1911 (the Winnipeg Tigers appearing in the 1925 GREY CUP), but the Winnipeg Rugby Football Club was not established until 1930. They were christened the Blue Bombers in 1935, the year they became the first western team to win the Grey Cup, defeating the Hamilton Tigers 18-12. Led by the great Melvin "Fritzie" HANSON, this squad returned to the national final in 1937 and 1938, losing both times but winning in 1939 and 1941. The postwar years saw 5 western championships (1945-47, 1950, 1953) but no Grey Cup victories. In 1957 Winnipeg's golden era under coach Bud Grant began. In 10 seasons (1957-66) he took the Blue Bombers to 6 Grey Cups, winning 4 (1958, 1959, 1961, 1962) and losing 2 (1957, 1965), all against the HAMILTON TIGER-CATS. The next victory came in 1984, again against Hamilton. Winnipeg Stadium, the community-owned Bombers' present home, was opened in 1953. DEREK DRAGER

Winnipeg Commodity Exchange The WCE was established in 1887 as the Winnipeg Grain Exchange – the name was changed in 1972 – by western farmers and grain merchants to provide a marketplace for the expanding agricultural production of the Canadian prairies. For its first 18 years, the WCE operated strictly as a cash market, ie, a marketplace for grains that have already been grown (as distinct from a "futures market" in which contracts are traded for the delivery of grain at a later date). In this capacity, WCE provides meeting rooms, communications facilities and rules of trade for the grain and produce grown in the West.

In 1904 the WCE established a futures market for wheat. Other futures markets were opened later for oats and flaxseed (1904), barley (1913) and rye (1917). Wheat futures trading was discontinued in 1942. Rapeseed (CANOLA) futures trading opened in 1963, gold in 1972, feed wheat for domestic use in 1974; silver, Government of Canada bonds and Treasury bill futures markets opened in 1981. Lumber is also traded.

The WCE is the only agricultural commodities exchange and futures market in Canada. A voluntary, nonprofit, unincorporated association, its 330 members (farmers, elevator companies, grain processors' merchandisers, exporters, overseas importers and the general public) represent virtually every group with an interest in Canadian grains. The CANADIAN WHEAT BOARD is also a member.

The futures markets of the WCE are used by the grain industry for price protection and price discovery. Through the process known as "hedging," producers, handlers and users of grain buy and sell futures contracts to protect themselves against the possibility that prices will change. They trade in an open, competitive auction on the trading floor in Winnipeg, trying to obtain the best price they can for the grain they own or the grain they need to buy later. The market prices established through this process are used throughout the grain industry (*see* GRAIN HANDLING AND MARKETING).

Publications of the WCE include *The Winnipeg Commodity Exchange,* booklets on each of the futures contracts, *Using the Grain Markets, The Winnipeg Gold & Silver Markets* and *The Interest Rate Futures Markets.* K.S. KEARNS

Reading: A. Levine, *The Exchange: 100 Years of Trading Grain in Winnipeg* (1987).

Winnipeg Free Press Founded as the *Manitoba Free Press* by W.F. Luxton in 1872, the newspaper displayed a distinct Liberal preference from its earliest days. It was purchased in 1898 by Clifford SIFTON, a prominent Liberal politician and Cabinet minister, and thereafter was the organ of the Liberal Party on the Prairies. In 1901 Sifton appointed a young journalist from Montréal, John W. DAFOE, as editor. Even after Sifton's departure from the Laurier Cabinet in 1905, the *Free Press* continued to support Laurier, and in 1911 it opposed its owner's personal preference by championing Laurier and reciprocity with the US. Owner and newspaper were reunited in 1917, when the *Free Press* backed UNION GOVERNMENT and CONSCRIPTION. During the 1920s, however, Dafoe and Sifton returned to the Liberal fold to support Mackenzie King and his government.

During this period the *Free Press* was a generally profitable enterprise and ran a highly successful farm weekly. Dafoe also began to gather together a skilled group of journalists. Employing such men as A. Grant DEXTER and Bruce HUTCHISON, Dafoe's paper was the best-informed in Canada during periods of Liberal government. The *Free Press* was also notable for its coverage of foreign affairs. In 1931 the paper became the *Winnipeg Free Press;* 2 years earlier, when Sifton died, it had passed into the hands of his children. Dafoe remained the dominant influence at the *Free Press* until his death in 1944. Although the *Free Press* employed some distinguished journalists as editors afterwards, George FERGUSON, Hutchison and Tom KENT, it tended to become less distinctive and more profitable. In 1980 it absorbed its long-standing rival, the *Winnipeg Tribune,* and confirmed its dominance in the Winnipeg newspaper field. In 1987 its daily circulation was 169 339, with a Saturday circulation of 229 246. *See also* JOURNALISM; NEWSPAPERS. ROBERT BOTHWELL

Reading: R. Cook, *The Politics of John W. Dafoe and the Free Press* (1963); D. Hall, *Clifford Sifton,* 2 vols (1981, 1984).

Winnipeg General Strike, 15 May-25 June 1919, Canada's best-known general strike. Massive unemployment and inflation, the success of the Russian Revolution (1917), a wave of strikes across Canada and rising REVOLUTIONARY INDUSTRIAL UNIONISM all contributed to postwar labour unrest. In Mar 1919 in Calgary western labour leaders met to discuss the creation of ONE BIG UNION. In Winnipeg on May 15, when negotiations broke down between management and labour in the building and metal trades, the Winnipeg Trades and Labor Council called a general strike. At stake were the principle of collective bargaining, better wages and the improvement of often dreadful working conditions. Within hours almost 30 000 workers had left their jobs. The almost unanimous response by working men and women closed the city's factories, crippled its retail trade and stopped the trains. Public-sector employees such as policemen, firemen, postal workers, telephone operators and employees of waterworks

Great War Veteran's Assn parade lining up on Broadway to march on the Legislative Building, during the Winnipeg General Strike, 4 June 1919 (*courtesy National Archives of Canada/C-48334/Brown Brothers, NY*).

and other utilities joined the workers of private industry in an impressive display of working-class solidarity. The strike was co-ordinated by the Central Strike Committee, composed of delegates elected from each of the unions affiliated with the WTLC. The committee bargained with employers on behalf of the workers and co-ordinated the provision of essential services.

Opposition to the strike was organized by the Citizens' Committee of 1000, created shortly after the strike began by Winnipeg's most influential manufacturers, bankers and politicians. Rather than giving the strikers' demands any serious consideration, the Citizens' Committee, with the support of Winnipeg's leading newspapers, declared the strike a revolutionary conspiracy led by a small group of "alien scum." The available evidence failed to support its charges that the strike was initiated by European workers and Bolsheviks, but the Citizens' Committee used these unsubstantiated charges to block any conciliation efforts by the workers.

Afraid that the strike would spark confrontations in other cities, the federal government decided to intervene; soon after the strike began, Senator Gideon Robertson, minister of labour, and Arthur MEIGHEN, minister of the interior and acting minister of justice, went to Winnipeg to meet with the Citizens' Committee. They refused requests from the Central Strike Committee for a similar hearing. On their advice, the federal government swiftly supported the employers, and federal employees were ordered to return to work immediately or face dismissal. The Immigration Act was amended so that British-born immigrants could be deported, and the Criminal Code's definition of sedition was broadened. On June 17 the government arrested 10 leaders of the Central Strike Committee and 2 propagandists from the newly formed One Big Union. Four days later, a charge by Royal North-West Mounted Police into a crowd of strikers resulted in 30 casualties, including one death. "Bloody Saturday" ended with federal troops occupying the city's streets. Six of the labour leaders were released, but Fred Dixon and J.S. WOODSWORTH were arrested. Faced with the combined forces of the government and the employers, the strikers decided to return to work on June 25.

The General Strike left a legacy of bitterness and controversy. In a wave of increased unionism and militancy across Canada, sympathetic strikes erupted in centres from Amherst, NS, to Victoria, BC. Seven of the arrested leaders were unfairly convicted of a conspiracy to overthrow the government and sentenced to jail terms from 6 months to 2 years; the charges against J.S. Woodsworth were dropped. Almost 3 decades passed before Canadian workers secured union recognition and collective bargaining. *See also* RAND FORMULA; WORKING-CLASS HISTORY.

J. NOLAN REILLY

Reading: David J. Bercuson, *Confrontation at Winnipeg* (1974); A. Ross McCormack, *Reformers, Rebels and Revolutionaries* (1977).

Winnipeg Grain Exchange, *see* WINNIPEG COMMODITY EXCHANGE.

Winnipeg Jets, HOCKEY team. An original WORLD HOCKEY ASSOCIATION (WHA) franchise (1972), the Winnipeg Jets brought instant credibility to the league by signing NHL superstar Bobby HULL in their first year. They also pioneered the importation of European hockey players to N America, beginning with the 1974 acquisition of Swedish stars Anders Hedberg and Ulf Nilsson. They won 3 out of the 7 WHA championships, including the final one in 1979. Under majority owner and president Michael Gobuty, their home base, the Winnipeg Arena, was expanded to 15 250 seats upon their 1979 entry into the NHL's Smythe Division, but merger conditions also stripped them of 10 players. They won only 29 games in their first 2 NHL campaigns but rallied under since-departed coach Tom Watt for a second-place finish in 1981-82. Since then, the Jets have relied on centre Dale Hawerchuk to carry their offence (531 points in his first 399 games). In the 1984-85 season the team finished fourth overall in the 21-team NHL.

DEREK DRAGER

Winnipeg River, 813 km long (to head of Firesteel R), issues from the N end of LK OF THE WOODS and flows NW to Lk WINNIPEG. The name is from the Cree *win-nipi,* meaning "murky water." After its discovery by Jean-Baptiste de LA VÉRENDRYE (*c*1732) the river was a major link in the FUR-TRADE route between Lks Superior and Winnipeg. Both the NWC and HBC built forts on the river, but traffic dwindled after the merger of the 2 companies in 1821. The river has a heavy, rapid flow and was first used for power by a lumber mill at Pine Falls (1870). Its first hydroelectric power was fed to pulp mills at KENORA, Ont, in 1892, and the first hydroelectric plant on the Manitoba reach began construction at PINAWA, 1902. Today, 6 generating stations harness all but a few metres of the river's 106 m drop. The once turbulent river, with its 26 portages, is now placid, though still frequented by boats and canoes. Since 1965 its water has been used to cool organic coolant in the Whiteshell Nuclear Research Establishment.

JAMES MARSH

Winnipeg Symphony Orchestra gave its first performance on 16 Dec 1948 in the Winnipeg Auditorium under conductor Walter Kaufmann. He was succeeded in 1958 by Victor FELDBRILL who, in the next decade, regularly programmed Canadian works and established the WSO as a full-time symphony orchestra. In 1968 the WSO moved to the Manitoba Centennial Concert Hall and appointed George Cleve as conductor. Piero Gamba was music director 1971-80 and in 1979 led the gala concert at Carnegie Hall. In 1983 Kazuhiro Koizumi became director. In addition to its 36-week, 60-performance season (1987-88), it is the official orchestra for the Manitoba Opera Assn and ROYAL WINNIPEG BALLET.

BARBARA NOVAK

Winnipegosis, Lake, 5370 km², 195 km long, elev 254 m, maximum depth 12 m, Canada's eleventh-largest lake, is located in W-central Manitoba. It drains approximately 49 825 km² of western Manitoba and eastern Saskatchewan, drawing most of its waters from the Manitoba Escarpment – in particular Riding Mt, Duck Mt, Porcupine Hills and the Pasquia Hills – and discharging them through the Waterhen R at an average annual rate of 80.9 m³/s into Lk MANITOBA, and thence into Lk WINNIPEG. Its interesting name is derived from 2 sources: *win-nipi,* Cree for "murky waters," and the suffix *osis,* meaning "little."

R.A. McGINN

Winnipeg's Contemporary Dancers is a modern dance repertory company which was until 1983 under the artistic direction of its founder, Rachel Browne. First formed in 1964, it became fully professional in 1970. Until the late 1970s it was generally known as Contemporary Dancers. Although Browne's own choreography, amounting to more than 25 pieces, has been presented by the company throughout its existence, since 1984, when Ted Robinson became director, WCD has produced more radical dance theatre, much of it Robinson's creation. The company, consisting generally of about 10 dancers, performs throughout Canada and has made several tours abroad.

MICHAEL CRABB

Wintemberg, William John, archaeologist (b at New Dundee, Ont 18 May 1876; d at Ottawa 25 Apr 1941). Wintemberg worked as a compositor and later a coppersmith before his varied and dedicated antiquarian activities led to an association with the Ontario Provincial Museum. In 1911 he was hired as a part-time field-worker by the Victoria Memorial Museum (later National Museum of Canada) and subsequently as a preparator, assistant archaeologist and finally associate archaeologist (1937) at that institution. Wintemberg's archaeological surveys and excavations ranged from Ontario to Newfoundland despite his delicate health. His prolific and model publications established the foundation for much of the prehistory of eastern Canada, in particular, concerning the prehistoric Iroquoian farmers of Ontario.

J.V. WRIGHT

Reading: N. Swayze, *Canadian Portraits: The Man Hunters* (1960).

Winter, Sir James Spearman, politician, prime minister of Newfoundland 1897-1900 (b at Lamaline, Nfld 1 Jan 1845; d at Toronto 6 Oct 1911). Winter began his political career in 1873 and entered Sir William WHITEWAY's Cabinet as solicitor general in 1882. In 1885 Winter, then grand master of the ORANGE ORDER, resigned, expecting to become leader of a new Protestant party. He was disappointed but became a dominant influence as attorney general in Sir Robert THORBURN's 1885-89 administration. Defeated in 1889, Winter became a Supreme Court judge in 1893. He resigned from the bench to lead the Tory Party to victory in the 1897 election. His administration soon ran into severe problems and was defeated in 1900. In 1909 Winter helped present Newfoundland's case in the N Atlantic fisheries dispute to The Hague tribunal.

J.K. HILLER

Wintergreen is the common name for smooth, low-growing, woodland, herbaceous plants in genus *Pyrola* of the wintergreen family (Pyrolaceae). These plants were known to the Cree as "beaver's ears" because of their small, round, evergreen leaves. Nine of the 12 known species are native to Canada. The name also applies to the closely related genera: *Chimaphila* (pipsissewa),

The volatile oil of the wintergreen plant is used in perfumes (*photo by Mary W. Ferguson*).

with 3 species in Canada; and *Moneses* (one-flowered wintergreen), with one species in Canada. Also widely known as wintergreen is genus *Gaultheria* of the related heath family (Ericaceae). *Gaultheria* contains about 100 species worldwide, mostly in the Andes, and 5 native to Canada. Of these, the name wintergreen is most frequently used for *G. procumbens*, which has persistent leaves and dainty pink or white, urn-shaped flowers, followed by scarlet, berrylike capsules. This plant's volatile oil contains methyl salicylate (oil of wintergreen) which is used in perfumery; it was once valued in the treatment of rheumatic disorders but is now largely replaced by safer, synthetic formulations. ROGER VICK

Wintering Partner (also "winterer"), inland trader and shareholder, most notably in the NORTH WEST COMPANY. The wintering partner system evolved in New France, where fur merchants divided their profits with associates conducting the trade. Elected only from among clerks trained as apprentice traders and motivated by profit and participation in corporate decision making, NWC wintering partners were proprietors of the departments they managed. Considered the key to the company's geographic and commercial expansion, this system of management was adopted by such rival firms as the XY COMPANY, the PACIFIC FUR COMPANY and HUDSON'S BAY COMPANY. *See also* FUR TRADE. JEAN MORRISON

Winters, Kenneth Lyle, music encyclopedist, critic, broadcaster (b at Dauphin, Man 28 Nov 1929). Co-editor with Helmut KALLMANN and Gilles POTVIN of the authoritative ENCYCLOPEDIA OF MUSIC IN CANADA (1981), he was particularly responsible for the text of the English-language version. Winters began his career as a boy soprano and became a versatile musician, a baritone soloist, organist, choir director, composer, teacher and musical administrator. He was music and dance critic of the Winnipeg *Free Press* 1956-66 and of the Toronto *Telegram* 1966-71. Since 1956, Winters has appeared frequently as a music commentator on CBC Radio. BARCLAY MCMILLAN

Winters, Robert Henry, politician, businessman (b at Lunenburg, NS 18 Aug 1910; d at Monterey, Calif 10 Oct 1969). Educated at Mt Allison U and Massachusetts Inst of Technology, Winters joined Northern Electric in Montréal in 1934. He became a lt-col in the army in WWII. Elected to the House of Commons for Lunenburg 1945 as a Liberal and re-elected in 1949 and 1953, he sat in the Cabinet 1948-57. Defeated in the 1957 election, Winters entered private business and was president and chairman of Rio Algom Mines 1963-65. At Lester PEARSON's urging, he re-entered politics. He was elected in the 1965 election (York West) and was rewarded with the post of minister of trade and commerce. Narrowly defeated by Pierre TRUDEAU in the contest for the Liberal leadership after Pearson's resignation, Winters retired from politics. He was president and director of Brazilian Light and Power Co Ltd in 1968-69. ROBERT BOTHWELL

Winton, Henry David, journalist (fl 1830-85? at St John's). Outspoken editor of the St John's *Public Ledger*, a Protestant, mercantile journal, Winton originally supported representative government but soon felt the system to be ineffective, owing greatly to the influence of "an ignorant, a vicious and a political priesthood." Thus began his vocal crusade against religion in politics, often degenerating to one of mud-slinging, which aroused the active opposition of the Catholics, who reciprocated with equal fervour. In May 1835 he had his ears cut off by a band of 4 men, supposedly fishermen he had insulted some years earlier for assembling to protest the truck system

used by merchants. A substantial reward failed to apprehend the guilty. This did not temper Winton's pen, and on a later Christmas night his house was surrounded by a mob, which he had to call garrison troops to disperse. During election riots in 1860-61, which culminated in deaths, Winton advocated the termination of the entire representative system, calling the Assembly an "impossible mob." TONY HOLLIHAN

Wise, Jack Marlowe, painter (b at Centerville, Iowa 27 Apr 1928). During his art training at New Orleans, at Washington U and Florida State U, Wise absorbed the prevailing abstract expressionist style of painting. He moved to Mexico and from 1958 to 1961 taught batik in a workshop at San Miguel de Allende. In 1963, conscious of a need to restructure his approach to art, he immigrated to Canada and farmed in BC. When he returned to painting it was as a miniaturist dedicated to the microcosmic patterning of archetypal images. Wise's paintings since that time have been essentially icons, with the mandala, the mystic circle, as dominant image, though lately he has shown a tendency to turn to formalized landscape. Like many contemporary BC artists, Wise was related to Asian art traditions. In 1966 he studied with Tibetan painting masters in India, who taught that the ultimate answers lay within oneself. With much virtuosity he combined eastern and western religious symbols in paintings reflecting the great archetypes that dominate the human unconscious. He has taught at the Victoria College of Art and U of C, and in recent years has moved from place to place in the interior and on the coast of BC, where he now lives in Victoria, painting and occasionally lecturing. In Mar 1985 his show "The Internal Landscape" was mounted at U of C. GEORGE WOODCOCK

Wiseman, Adele, author, educator (b at Winnipeg 21 May 1928). Wiseman was raised and educated in Winnipeg, where she received her honours BA from U Man (1949). She was reader and tutor in that university's English department (1949-55) and won the Chancellor's Medal for the best short story (1948-49). She has published 2 novels, *The Sacrifice* (1956), for which she won the Gov Gen's Award, and *Crackpot* (1974), winner of the J.I. Segal Award for the best Canadian novel in English on a Jewish theme. Wiseman's Russian-Jewish parents fled Ukraine pogroms in the 1920s and immigrated to Canada. Their escape and subsequent New World adjustment influenced Wiseman's fiction. Her novels, set in Winnipeg's North End, are concerned with survival, and Wiseman successfully weaves the restrictions of the urban Jewish ghetto with the unlimited freedom of the prairie landscape. Wiseman has also published *Old Markets, New World* (1964), her reminiscences of the Winnipeg Farmers' Market, accompanied by Joe Rosenthal's drawings of Toronto's Kensington market. The book won the bronze medal at the Leipzig Book Fair. In 1978 she published a play, *Testimonial Dinner and Old Women at Play*, a holistic examination of creativity as seen through the craft of her own mother's doll making. She has published one children's story, *Miko and the Crickets* (1986) and one collection of essays, *Memoirs of a Book-Molesting Childhood* (1987). She was a full-time lecturer and then assistant professor in the English department at Macdonald College of McGill 1964-69, and she has had 8 writer-in-residence appointments, most recently at Western (1986-87). SHARON DRACHE

Wiseman, Clarence Dexter, general of the SALVATION ARMY (b at Moreton's Harbour, Nfld 19 June 1907; d at Toronto 4 May 1985). Wiseman was commissioned as an officer in the Salvation

Army in 1927. During WWII he became the senior SA representative with the Canadian Armed Forces Overseas. He held several positions 1945-67, including chief secretary of Canada and Bermuda, territorial commander of East Africa and principal of the International Training College in London, Eng. He became territorial commander of Canada and Bermuda (1967) and was elected general of the Int Salvation Army (1974). Wiseman retired in 1977 and published his autobiography, *A Burning in My Bones* (1980) and *The Desert Road to Glory* (1982). AUBREY VINCENT

Witch Hazel, the common name for a family (Hamamelidaceae) of trees or shrubs, refers especially to members of the genus *Hamamelis*. Four species of *Hamamelis* are found in E Asia, 2 are native to N America. *H. virginiana* (witch hazel or snapping hazel), a fall-flowering shrub, is native to Canada, growing in woods in Qué, NS, NB and Ont. The plant grows to 5 m, and flowers are bright yellow with 4 long thin petals. Spring-flowering Chinese witch hazel (*H. mollis*), introduced from China in the 1890s, is a popular ORNAMENTAL in milder regions of Canada. Witch hazel may be called "hazel" because the leaf shape resembles that of true hazels (genus *Corylus* of the birch family). "Witch" may come from the use of *Hamamelis* branches for divining rods, although true hazels, not *Hamamelis* plants, were traditionally associated with witches. A leaf and bark extract of *H. virginiana* was a common remedy among N American Indians and was introduced to Europe in 1736. It was used for soothing inflammations and bruises, and for treating hemorrhoids, congestions and tumours; its astringent and soothing properties are still appreciated for external application. GILLIAN FORD

Southern witch hazel (*Hamamelis virginiana*), with flowers and fruits (*artwork by Claire Tremblay*).

Withers, Ramsey Muir, soldier, public servant (b at Toronto 28 July 1930). An engineering graduate of RMC and Queen's, Withers was commissioned in the Signal Corps in 1952 and served with the Royal 22nd Regiment in Korea in 1952-53. An effective, articulate organizer with a crisp manner and open personality, he was promoted brigadier in 1970, the first officer commissioned after WWII to reach that rank, and became the first commander, Northern Region Headquarters (Yellowknife). This was followed by senior management assignments at headquarters, 1973-76, and command of the Canadian Forces in Europe, 1976-77. He was vice-chief and then chief of the defence staff, 1977-83, excelling in the bureaucracy of flowcharts, management systems and political awareness. He was deputy minister of the Dept of Transport 1983-88 before entering private business. NORMAN HILLMER

Wix, Edward, Church of England clergyman, missionary (b at Faulkbourne, Eng 1 Feb 1802; d at Swanmore, Isle of Wight, Eng 24 Nov 1866).

Wix graduated from Oxford in 1824 and was ordained in 1825. He first served as a missionary in Nova Scotia but moved to Newfoundland where he was appointed archdeacon in 1830. He spent the next 8 years travelling around the Island, preaching, raising funds and organizing the Church of England. After a 6-month missionary tour along the S and W coasts of Newfoundland in 1835, he published *Six Months of a Newfoundland Missionary's Journal* (1836). Wix was the driving force behind fund raising for St Thomas's Church, St John's, which opened in 1836. In Oct 1838 he returned to England. His appeals to church officials in England undoubtedly led to the appointment in 1839 of the first Church of England bishop of Newfoundland, Aubrey George Spencer.

JOHN PARSONS

Wolf, largest wild member of the dog family. Living wolves belong to the Holarctic species *Canis lupus* (except red wolf, *C. rufus* of the Texas Gulf Coast). The grey wolf is the largest, weighing 25-45 kg, and has a distinctively massive head with a strong forehead. It resembles a German shepherd dog, usually with a greyish coat (black or almost white individuals exist). Northern forms are largest in N America. Wolves were common in N America in forests, tundra and prairies but are now restricted to wilder northern regions. They live in packs (usually 3-7) with a dominant male and his breeding bitch. Breeding starts at about 2-3 years. Litters of about 7 (4-13) pups are born after 63 days gestation. The bitch whelps in a den, either a burrow or natural shelter. The pack protects and brings food to the nursing mother. Wolves are shy, usually nocturnal and elusive. They hunt deer, caribou, moose, wapiti and, in summer, smaller game. Their only enemy, man, hunts them for sport and to protect livestock, and has extirpated them from the settled parts of N America, where coyotes or feral dogs replace them.

The genus *Canis,* of which wolves, coyotes and dogs are the most familiar forms, derives from the small, fox-sized Miocene N American canid *Cynodesmus.* By Early Pleistocene times (about 1.5 million years ago), *Canis* was widespread in N America, Asia and Europe. During the Late Pleistocene, about 10 000 years ago, wolves were tamed to become dogs. Dogs differ structurally from wolves in having shorter faces, smaller and more crowded cheekteeth, and higher foreheads. Early dogs were smaller than most wolves, and subsequent selective breeding has produced dogs of many sizes and conformations. Dogs also possess a posteriorly recurved coronoid margin to the ascending process of the lower jaw, which all wolves lack, except for the Chinese *C. l. chanco* known from Mongolia and China. This form of the coronoid is characteristic of omnivorous carnivores (bears, raccoons, etc) and has been interpreted to suggest that the smaller omnivorous ancestor to *C. l. chanco* was preadapted to living with man, as it could share his diet.

Tamed wolves, or ones that associated with man, are first recorded with Late Paleolithic mammoth hunters at Mezine, Ukraine, during the last ice age. The oldest dogs are reported from Palegawra Cave, Iraq, and the Mallaha and Hayonim sites, Israel, at about 10 000 BC, with the oldest dated N American record from Jaguar Cave, New Mexico, at about 6400 BC. A jaw recovered from the Old Crow Basin, Yukon Territory, may be of Late Pleistocene age and thus as old as or older than the other records. Dogs became common about 2900 BC at Pan p'o, China, and from about 100 AD onwards in N America. No evidence exists for deriving dogs from N American wolves, although husky bitches may

Wolf (*Canis lupus*), the largest wild member of the dog family; the grey wolf can weigh 25-45 kg (*photo by Hälle Flygare*).

be bred with wolves (*C. l. lycaon*) to maintain larger size, stamina and hardiness.

C.S. CHURCHER

Wolfe, James, British army officer, commander of the British expedition that took Québec in 1759 (b at Westerham, Eng 2 Jan 1727/28; d at the Battle of the PLAINS OF ABRAHAM 13 Sept 1759). One of the legendary figures of Canadian history, Wolfe has become known as the man whose defeat of MONTCALM in 1759 marked the beginning of British rule in Canada. He saw fighting in both Flanders and Scotland, and gained a notable reputation before going to N America in 1758 as a senior officer in Jeffery AMHERST'S expedition against LOUISBOURG. During the siege, Wolfe, a charismatic figure, played a distinguished and active role, which influenced his selection as commander of the expedition against Québec planned for 1759. Yet for most of the 1759 campaign he made little headway, partially because of his vacillation and limited ideas.

Wolfe's assault on the strong MONTMORENCY position of July 31 was a bloody failure, and neither the bombardment of Québec nor the destruction of neighbouring settlements had any real effect. He was ravaged by illness, and his relations with 3 senior officers, Robert MONCKTON, George TOWNSHEND and James MURRAY, and with the navy were marked by sharp disagreements. But when in Aug his subordinates proposed landing above Québec he began to plan an amphibious landing that would cut the enemy's supply lines and force

General James Wolfe, *c*1742, portrait by Joseph Highmore (*courtesy National Archives of Canada/C-3916*).

a battle. A midnight passage of the St Lawrence and a series of fortunate strokes saw his force established on the Plains of Abraham on Sept 13. Montcalm's forces attacked, but the better-trained British force routed the French in a short action. Wolfe himself was mortally wounded but lived long enough to hear of his victory. His reputation in both Britain and Canada survived until this century, when several works questioned the consistently favourable picture hitherto drawn of him. *See also* SEVEN YEARS' WAR.

Reading: C.P. Stacey, *Québec, 1759* (1959).

Wolfville, NS, Town, pop 3277 (1986c), 3235 (1981c), inc 1893, is located on MINAS BASIN, 75 km NW of Halifax. Once part of the Acadian district of Les Mines (Minas), the site was known as *Mtaban* ("mud-cat-fish catching-ground") to the Micmac, and Mud Creek and Upper Horton to the Connecticut emigrants who settled Horton Township after the deportation of the ACADIANS. The route of the Halifax-Annapolis Road and the natural harbour encouraged settlement at this site. The name was changed to Wolfville in 1830, in honour of Judge Elisha DeWolf, one of 3 De-Wolf second cousins who were among the original grantees in 1761. With the decline of shipbuilding E of the harbour, Wolfville became a New England-style university town. Established as a BAPTIST academy (1828) and college (1838), ACADIA U (1891) is now nondenominational but closely associated with the Maritime United Baptist Convention. With 40 main buildings and more than 3200 full-time students (1985-86), it is the main local employer and the cultural, political and recreational centre for the town and its agricultural surroundings. Founded in 1765-66 and reorganized solely as a Baptist church in 1778, Wolfville United Baptist Church has the oldest continuing Baptist congregation in Canada. The easy pace of life in the town has attracted numerous senior citizens and a small counterculture colony. Many descendants of the original New England settlers remain. DEBRA McNABB

Wollaston Lake, 2681 km², elev 398 m, lies in the wooded SHIELD country of NE Saskatchewan. To the NW it drains via the Fond Du Lac R into ATHABASCA and the MACKENZIE R system; to the NE it drains via the Cochrane R into REINDEER LK and the CHURCHILL R system. Discovered by Peter FIDLER about 1800, it was used by fur traders as a link between the 2 watersheds. It was named in 1821 by arctic explorer John FRANKLIN after the English chemist William Hyde Wollaston.

DANIEL FRANCIS

Wolseley, Garnet Joseph Wolseley, 1st Viscount, soldier (b at Golden Bridge House, Ire 4 June 1833; d at Menton, France 25 Mar 1913). Wolseley served with the British army in India, the Crimea and China. In 1861 he was sent to Canada as assistant quartermaster general, becoming deputy quartermaster general in 1865. In 1870 he commanded the expedition to the Red River (*see* RED RIVER EXPEDITION), where his organizational skills won plaudits. After 1871 he alternated between the War Office and field command (*see* NILE EXPEDITION) and was commander in chief of the British army 1895-1900. His autobiography, *The Story of a Soldier's Life,* appeared in 1903.

J.M. BUMSTED

Wolverine, or carcajou (*Gulo gulo*), largest of the WEASELS, resembles a powerful, miniature bear. Adult males weigh about 14 kg; females, 9 kg. Fur is usually dark brown; head and tail are slightly lighter than the body. Usually, 2 tan stripes run from the neck along the sides, meeting at the tail. Wolverine fur is preferred for trimming parka hoods because outer hairs shed frost without wetting. The wolverine is a rare animal in Canada.

Wolverine (*Gulo gulo*) on snow (*photo by Leonard Lee Rue III/DRK Photo*).

They are now absent from the southeast and the prairies, rare in the East, and sparse in western and northern regions. They are known for travelling long distances (up to 112 km in 24 hours). In Alaska adult males have been found to have territories of up to 770 km²; females, 355 km². Wolverines are normally solitary except when breeding or raising young. Mating occurs May-July; implantation is delayed and the 2-5 young are born Feb-Mar. The wolverine's supposed strength, ferocity, and ability to raid traplines and cabins have become legendary. The powerful teeth and jaws are adapted for crushing frozen meat. Wolverines are better scavengers than hunters. In winter they eat mainly carrion; in summer, berries and vegetation as well. Wolverines do best in sparsely populated areas with abundant ungulate populations. BC provides about one-third of all pelts (300-500) taken in Canada annually. Exploitation by man is the most important external factor influencing abundance and distribution. STEPHEN HERRERO

Woman's Christian Temperance Union in Canada originated in Owen Sound, Ont, in 1874. Under the influence of Letitia Youmans of Pictou, Ont, the temperance union idea spread and a national WCTU was organized in 1885, with Youmans as president. Believing that the abuse of alcohol was the cause of unemployment, disease, poverty and immorality, the WCTU campaigned for the legal PROHIBITION of all alcoholic beverages. In addition, it promoted such reforms as female suffrage, sex hygiene and mothers' allowances. National and provincial prohibition legislation, approved during WWI, was a highlight for the WCTU. The defeat of these laws and the adoption of government control of alcoholic beverages during the 1920s heralded the decline of the organization. In 1987 there were 2473 members in 76 branches. *See also* TEMPERANCE MOVEMENT.
NANCY M. SHEEHAN

Reading: L. Kealey, *A Not Unreasonable Claim: Women and Reform in Canada, 1880s-1920s* (1979).

Women and Education Although women have always been well represented in schools as students and teachers, it is possible, by examining women's participation in schooling, to understand how that participation has both reflected and produced the unequal position of women in society. Prior to 1850, middle-class families tended to hire governesses and tutors to educate their children at home. Some pioneers ran their own schools; for example Anne Langton (1804-93) ran a small informal school with her brother at Fenelon Falls. By 1871, with the establishment of the free provincial public schools, the number of girls enrolled in Ontario schools approximated that of boys. Most post-secondary education for female students was available only at private colleges, which provided special instruction in the

personal, social and domestic proprieties. The curriculum was designed to train women in "the arts and graces of life" and to prepare them to become schoolteachers.

Teaching has always provided employment opportunities for women (*see* TEACHING PROFESSION). In the early 19th century, Canadian women taught children in private domestic settings, in so-called "dame" schools, while men dominated the public schooling. By mid-century, women began to be employed in public schools, and by 1900 elementary school teaching was done almost entirely by women. In 1872 the BC superintendent of education declared that a woman's mission was "predominantly that of an educator," specifically of infants and young children. The change occurred largely because women could be hired at lower wages than men, at a time when the cost of an expanding school system weighed heavily on taxpayers. The change both caused and reflected an increasing acceptance of the participation of middle-class women in work outside the home and an ideology that emphasized women's special abilities to nurture and educate children.

While teaching provided new employment opportunities for many women (many prominent women suffragists entered the work force as teachers) it also reaffirmed the secondary position of women. Women teachers, paid less than men, were kept in the lower ranks and were supervised by male administrators. They were mainly young women, who left or were let go when they married and who rarely gained seniority or administrative responsibility.

Women teachers in 1985-86 had generally won equal salaries with men and could no longer be laid off simply because they marry or have children. Women comprise about 50% of all teachers in the public schools, which breaks down to 33% of all teachers in secondary schools, 70% of those in elementary schools and more than 95% of those in kindergarten. Only 17% of university teachers and 6% of full professors are women.

According to a 1984 report from the Commission on Canadian Studies, discrimination against women in Canadian universities is still a "national disgrace." The commission's report, titled *Some Questions of Balance*, was prepared for the Association of Universities and Colleges of Canada. Commissioners Thomas SYMONS and James Page claim that women are deterred by discriminatory practices and attitudes from participating in many areas of higher education and research. Women university teachers hold lower academic ranks and receive lower pay at every academic rank and in almost every age group. The many (over 32) major university reports commissioned in the 1970s and early 1980s to investigate problems facing women have had virtually no effect, the commission reported, on hiring, promotion, tenure and salary differentials. Employment equity legislation, as proposed by the Abella Commission and introduced by the federal government in 1986 and by some provincial governments, may provide a base for addressing these problems in the 1990s. Some universities have signed agreements to implement employment equity.

Girls and boys enjoy formally equal schooling. Canada's public-school system has always been overwhelmingly coeducational, but for reasons of convenience and cost, rather than a belief in the similar needs of male and female students. Girls have tended to stay in school longer than boys and to do better academically. It was only in 1950 that the number of males in school in the 15-19-year-old age group began to surpass that of females. The number of Canadian women

who have graduated from high school still surpasses the number of men. In community colleges, women received 55% of the diplomas granted in spring 1986 compared to 54% in 1973. In universities, on the other hand, women comprised 16% of undergraduate enrolment in 1920, almost 20% from 1930 to 1960, 35% by 1970, and almost 50% by 1986. Women were 60% of part-time students at university and part-time students are increasing as a percentage of all students. Women received 53% of the bachelor and first professional degrees granted in Canada in 1986, up from 40% in 1973. Women are making their largest gains at the university level.

Despite the evidence of women's achievements in school, the opportunities offered women in the educational system are often circumscribed by the view that women belong in the home and in traditionally female jobs. Analyses of textbooks, teaching materials, films and readers used in schools (*see* CURRICULUM DEVELOPMENT) have consistently revealed that women are underrepresented and are portrayed in traditional ways. While publishers and ministries of education have begun, in the 1980s, to screen new materials for evidence of bias, old materials are still being used. Women's-studies courses and materials have been developed to provide a balanced representation of women in the curriculum, but while most universities now offer women's studies as an option, materials conveying the experience of women are rarely available at high-school or elementary-school levels.

Studies of teachers' attitudes toward sex roles and their interactions with students have also revealed that male and female students are treated differently, eg, male students receive both more praise and more criticism. Teachers reward traditionally "masculine" behaviour in boys and "feminine" behaviour in girls.

Male and female students often study different courses, particularly in the higher grades. In a system of academic electives, girls are more likely to drop out of mathematics, physics and chemistry than boys, and they are more likely to avoid industrial arts altogether. A 1984 report from the Science Council of Canada noted the low participation of girls in physical science courses and recommended changes in curriculum, teaching methods and CAREER COUNSELLING to ensure greater involvement of girls in science and technology education. Girls comprise the majority of students in home economics, business education and languages.

At the community-college level in 1985-86 women comprise more than 90% of the student body in nursing, rehabilitative medicine and secretarial science; more than 80% in library and SOCIAL WORK; and more than 50% in education and the fine and applied arts. In universities, they are underrepresented in engineering, forestry, dentistry, architecture, computing science, law, business, science and medicine. These patterns are changing somewhat, especially at the university level, where increasing numbers of women are enrolling in professional faculties dominated by men; but in 1986 women are still represented by only about one-third of the enrolment in law, 40% in medicine and 44% in business, and 10% of the enrolment in engineering. These patterns of differential enrolment contribute directly to the maintenance of a sexually segregated work world.

These patterns of differential enrolment contribute directly to the maintenance of a sexually segregated work world. Moreover, women with the same educational credentials as men get paid less when they go to work. Women with university degrees earned $21 512 in 1985; men with university degrees earned $37 089.

Guidance and career counsellors have also been criticized for their tendency to encourage girls to enter traditional fields. Feminist counsellors urge that more attention be paid to the fact that female students must plan for many years of work outside the home, must learn assertiveness and must examine the issue of sex-role stereotyping. The discussion and changes in schools generated by a renewed attention to women's place confronts parents, teachers and administrators with new dilemmas.

The notion that the school should reflect the community's standards sometimes conflicts with the notion that schools must provide equal opportunities for all students. Those who believe women belong in the home are opposed to those who believe women should have the same education and opportunities as men. JANE GASKELL

Reading: Jane Gaskell, "Equal Educational Opportunity for Women" in *Canadian Education in the '80s* (1981); J. L'Espérance, *The Widening Sphere* (1982).

Women and Health In Canada women are the greatest users of the health-care system, primarily because of their roles as child-bearers and child-raisers, but also because on average a woman's life expectancy in Canada exceeds a man's by approximately 7 years. Women also occupy over 75% of jobs in the health and medical fields, although they are occupationally segregated into the low-status and low-paying positions. Although the number is rising as graduate interns enter the profession, in 1987 only 14% of practising physicians and surgeons in Canada were female. Slightly less than half of the accepted applicants to Canadian medical schools are women.

Despite the inferior occupational status of women in the field of health care and the low percentage of female doctors, women have always played an important role in health care. Historically, mothers were the primary health resource of families, and women healers who derived their knowledge from apprenticeship and oral tradition were essential to the development of both native and white settlements. With their knowledge of herbs and medicinal plants, these women were the people most likely to be consulted in medical emergencies. Midwives, who assisted women during pregnancy and childbirth, were very important members of most early Canadian communities.

Religious sisters from Europe who helped meet the physical and spiritual welfare of Canada's new inhabitants (*see* NURSING) also played a significant role in early Canadian medical history. Canada's first hospital (1639), HÔTEL-DIEU in Québec City, was founded and run by nuns of the nursing order AUGUSTINES hospitalières. Emily STOWE, the first Canadian woman with a medical degree (1867) to practise medicine in Canada, was forced to study at the New York Medical College for Women, because women were not allowed into medical schools in Canada. Emily Stowe's daughter Augusta was the first woman to graduate in medicine in Canada (1883), having been permitted to study at the Toronto School of Medicine in 1879.

By the mid-19th century, partly as a result of efforts of the male medical profession to convince legislators and the general public that care traditionally provided by women (midwives and lay healers) could be better provided by technically trained doctors, many women, particularly in urban areas, were forced out of their traditional roles as health-care providers.

Midwifery was officially outlawed in various provinces. In the contemporary Canadian health-care system, the important positions of power and decision making are held primarily by men, which tends to influence the kind of health care

women receive. For example, there has been increased medical intervention in the birth process, reflected in the rising rate (from 8% to 15% in the 1970s; 19% in the mid-1980s) of Caesarean section deliveries. To the concern of many women, this operation, considered a "last resort" procedure some 25 years ago, is now viewed by many obstetricians as a standard measure and is, according to some critics, indiscriminately used.

A recent study by the Addiction Research Foundation revealed that women are twice as likely as men suffering from the same complaints to be prescribed tranquillizers. Doctors tend to send men, but not the women, for additional tests or X rays, which suggests that women's complaints are likely to be taken less seriously than men's. Women have also attempted to draw attention to the fact that many female health problems result from social, occupational and environmental factors, and are therefore related to women's status in society. A recent report of the Canadian Advisory Council on the Status of Women focused on some occupational health hazards (chemical, biological, physical and those affecting mental health) to which women in particular were vulnerable. Some of the health hazards associated with these occupations are fatigue, noise, and exposure to solvents, detergents, mercury, radiation, asbestos, beryllium, lead, trichloroethylene, resins, methylene chloride, silicone, and anesthetic gases. Research has indicated that certain levels of exposure to these health hazards are harmful not only to women but to fetuses.

With the rise of the women's movement in the late 1960s and early 1970s, and as a result of growing dissatisfaction with current medical attitudes and the rise of medical technology, women began to speak out against ABORTION laws, hazardous drugs, BIRTH-CONTROL methods, paternalistic medical care, and the increased medicalization of the BIRTHING PRACTICE. Women's health centres, self-help groups, RAPE crisis centres, birth-control and venereal disease clinics, and patient advocacy groups have been formed. A prototype for women's health groups is the Vancouver Women's Health Collective, established in 1972 to provide for women "a critique of, but not a substitute for the traditional health-care system." The group is structured as a collective. It maintains an extensive resource library on women's health, conducts self-help groups, offers birth-control counselling and publishes material on a variety of health issues. Since 1986, a broad-based co-ordinating committee of women's health activists from across Canada has been working to develop a Canadian Women's Health Network. The network functions as an information-sharing group as well as being active in lobbying and advocacy for better health care for Canadian women.
ANNE ROCHON FORD

Women and the Law Traditionally, laws in Canada upheld the STATUS OF WOMEN as dependants. In the 20th century, as women increasingly demanded a new legal position, laws seen as symbols of inferiority became the subject of controversy. In the 1970s many women, like those in the earlier suffrage campaigns, again became aware that the law would have to be reformed if they were to achieve autonomy and equality within Canadian society (*see* WOMEN'S SUFFRAGE).

Under the French regime, important posts in the army and the government were, by custom, granted only to men. Under the British regime, women were usually excluded by law from holding public office until the beginning of the 20th century. Certain criminal laws applied only to women, such as infanticide, or involved women as victims, such as laws concerning rape or seduc-

tion under promise of marriage. Different punishments were meted out, depending on the sex of the offender. In prostitution, for example, punishment inevitably fell upon the prostitute (almost always a woman).

It is in the area of FAMILY LAW that women have been treated most clearly as dependants. In NEW FRANCE, where 25 was the legal age of majority, a woman usually passed from the control of her father to that of her husband when she married. A husband's permission was necessary for a wife to engage in business, or even to administer or sell property which she had owned before marriage. French law, however, provided that half of the common property belonged to the wife and her heirs on marriage dissolution, whereas British law gave a husband wide authority over his wife's property and made no provision for division of assets. Although Married Women's Property Acts were passed in the late 19th century in most common-law provinces, giving women the right to control their own property, the laws made no provision for the equitable division of property held by the spouses in case of marriage breakdown or death. Nor did they improve the economic situation of women (*see* WOMEN IN THE LABOUR FORCE).

By the end of the 19th century, many women and some men were questioning the severe restrictions of rights for female citizens. A loophole in the law allowing some women, particularly in LOWER CANADA, to exercise the franchise had been specifically removed by the 1850s throughout Canada. Feminists argued for a fuller participation of women in public life, on the grounds both of moral justice and because "feminine virtues" might help bring about needed reforms. After a lengthy campaign, women in Manitoba, Alberta and Saskatchewan gained the right to vote in 1916, and in Ontario and BC the following year. On the federal level, the vote was first given to relatives of enlisted men in 1917 and then broadened to all women in 1918. The other provinces followed suit by 1922, with the exception of Québec, where women were denied the vote until 1940.

Women recognized that the ability to use or challenge existing laws was one of the keys to raising their status. In 1897 Clara Brett Martin was admitted to the Law Society of Upper Canada. In 1929, 5 women from Alberta successfully challenged the law that excluded female citizens from becoming senators (*see* PERSONS CASE). However, women were slow to enter the legal profession and, by 1988, only about 18% of practising Canadian lawyers were female. In 1982 Bertha WILSON was appointed as the first woman to the SUPREME COURT OF CANADA, followed by Claire L'Heureux-Dubé in 1987.

The report of the Royal Commission on the Status of Women in 1970 recommended a new agenda for legal reform that would reflect more accurately the changing reality of women's lives (*see* WOMEN'S MOVEMENT). Homemakers and mothers became increasingly aware that their tasks gave them almost no legal right to financial security. Inequities in matrimonial property laws that did not recognize the wife's contribution to marriage were crystallized in the MURDOCH CASE. By the early 1980s most provinces had rewritten their family law to allow better recognition of women's unpaid contribution to marriage.

By the 1970s approximately one half of Canadian women were in the paid labour force, though, overall, women in 1986 earned 66% of what men earned. In a drive for fairer labour legislation, especially legislation recognizing equal pay for work of equal value, women's groups and unions proposed affirmative action programs to counteract employment policies that were intentionally or inadvertently discriminatory to women. Parental and pregnancy benefits became an important issue as, increasingly, women remained in the paid work force during childbearing years. After 1971 Canada's unemployment insurance scheme provided for limited pregnancy benefits for workers, but the Bliss case (1979) showed how inadequate its provisions were when the Supreme Court of Canada ruled that if a worker, otherwise entitled, was denied benefits because of pregnancy, it was not because she was a woman. In 1983 amendments were made to the Unemployment Insurance Act concerning parental benefits to eliminate this problem.

Sexual harassment on the job was first considered by federal and provincial human rights commissions in the 1970s and, by the early 1980s, unions began to insist that employers enforce policies against it. In 1984 legislation providing redress for victims of sexual harassment was introduced into Canada's Labour Code.

In the 1970s and 1980s the issue of violence claimed public attention, particularly among women. The double sexual standard was mirrored dramatically in the Criminal Code laws on RAPE, which permitted questions as to the victim's, but not the accused's, previous sexual history and encouraged defence counsel to argue that the women had consented. In 1982 major changes to the Criminal Code addressed the situation where the victim of a sexual assault was, in effect, put on trial along with the accused. The legal concept of rape was replaced by one of sexual assault and violence. Domestic violence, which is almost always against women and children (*see* CHILD ABUSE), has long been considered a private matter in Canada. Although wife beating is a form of assault and punishable under the Criminal Code, social attitudes and prejudices have meant that police were reluctant to intervene in domestic disputes. The courts hesitated to find a husband guilty of beating his wife without a third-party witness. In the late 1970s WOMEN'S ORGANIZATIONS drew public attention to wife and child battering and to the fact that laws on the books were not being applied. Across Canada, law enforcement agencies began to intervene in cases of domestic assault. It soon became evident, however, that simply punishing the offenders was not in itself a long-term solution. In many cases, the woman was dependent on the man and feared for the welfare of the family if he was sent to prison. Women's shelters, therapy and public campaigns against family violence were some of the alternate approaches developed.

In the 1970s women became more conscious of their legal rights, or lack of them, than ever before. As courts and lawyers are prohibitively expensive for most women, the recently formed federal and provincial human rights commissions proved to be an alternate and less expensive way of dealing with individual complaints of discrimination. The Bliss case, dealing with pregnancy discrimination, as well as the earlier LAVELL and Bedard cases, dealing with discrimination against female Indians on the basis of their sex, pointed out to Canadian women how inadequate were the existing constitutional guarantees against sexual discrimination. It was cases such as these, as well as a growing consciousness of the need for stronger legal measures against discrimination, which fueled the successful drive by women for better guarantees in the new CANADIAN CHARTER OF RIGHTS AND FREEDOMS (1982). Section 15 of the Charter, which came into force in Apr 1982, attempted to provide the broadest possible definition of equality rights, while specifically allowing affirmative action programs. The Charter, women hoped, would provide a new standard of equality against which laws in Canada could be measured. In 1983 the Constitution Act guaranteed aboriginal rights to male and female persons. Section 12 of the Indian Act (loss of status upon marrying a non-Indian) was repealed in 1985. However, the federal and the provincial governments retained the right to suspend the Charter's provisions for a specific time period and it remains to be seen, given the provincial right to "opt out" and resistance to equality generally, whether optimism is justified. *See also* ABORTION; MEECH LAKE ACCORD; NATIVE PEOPLE, LAW; PORNOGRAPHY.

JENNIFER STODDART

Reading: A. Bayefsky and M. Eberts, eds, *Equality of Rights in the Canadian Charter of Rights and Freedoms* (1984); A. Doerr and M. Carrier, eds, *Women and the Constitution in Canada* (1981); L. MacLeod, *Wife Battering in Canada* (1980).

Women and War During war, through circumstances or by design, women defended their homes and communities, cared for the wounded, prepared wartime materials and provided physical, economic and moral support. In countering the effects of external threat or pressing for military advantages, their work was vital.

Oral legends of Indian women as warriors, healers, strategists and spies acquired substance in written records about Molly BRANT's role as a spy and adviser to the British during the American Revolution and John ROWAND's encounter in 1844 with "the Queen of the Plains" and her war party of 1000 men and 200 women. In New France, women such as Francoise-Marie Jacquelin, better known as Madame de LA TOUR, and Marie-Madeleine Jarret de VERCHÈRES took command against attackers while others such as Jeanne MANCE cared for the wounded. Marie, wife of Louis HÉBERT, not only nursed the sick during the English siege of Québec in 1629 but worked with the other women to ensure the survival of the colony. Laura SECORD during the War of 1812 and Cornelia De Grassi in the Rebellion of 1837 carried messages through enemy lines.

Most often women were nameless and faceless participants. Those accompanying the French and English military forces of the 18th and 19th century cooked, laundered, sewed and administered to the sick, and if necessary assisted in wartime operations. Those settled in communities protected their property from marauders and when battles raged on their doorsteps, prepared ammunition, food and medicines. Not until the 1885 North-West Rebellion did women receive official recognition as part of a military force in the field, and then in what was considered to be their most acceptable active wartime role of NURSING the wounded. Civilian nurses also accompanied the Yukon Field Force of 1898 and the Canadian contingent to the South African War.

By the 20th century, factors including the distance of the conflicts and restrictive ideas about women's abilities combined to prevent direct action by women as combatants. Nonetheless, during both WWI and WWII, women organized for home defence, outfitting themselves in uniforms, and training in rifle shooting, military drill and other appropriate skills. By 1941, when the first 2 women's services were created as auxiliaries to the air force and the army, many of the new recruits were drawn from the more than 6000 members across the country.

It was the growing wartime bureaucracy that opened the way for women as officially recognized members of the armed forces outside of nursing. Initially, civilian women filled military clerical positions to release ablebodied men for combat, but in WWII, the advantages of having servicewomen under military control and discipline became apparent. By war's end, the RCAF (Women's Division), the CANADIAN WOMEN'S ARMY CORPS and the Women's Royal Canadian Naval Service had proved their worth.

While a few women produced ammunition in factories during the S African War, WWI and WWII witnessed the most conspicuous movement into wartime industry. In 1917 there were about 35 000 women in munitions factories in Ontario and Québec. By 1943, about 261 000 women were involved in the production of war goods, accounting for more than 30% of the aircraft industry, close to 50% of the employees in many gun plants, and a distinct majority in munitions inspection (*see* WOMEN IN THE MILITARY).

Always women have worked to ensure a thriving, or at least a surviving, home economy. During WWI and then WWII, they produced and conserved food; raised funds to finance hospitals, ambulances, hostels, aircraft; and volunteered their services inside and outside the country. Primarily through groups, including the FEDERATED WOMEN'S INSTITUTES OF CANADA, the IMPERIAL ORDER DAUGHTERS OF THE EMPIRE, the YOUNG WOMEN'S CHRISTIAN ASSN and the Canadian Red Cross Society, they joined forces to sustain the nation.

Whatever the conventional role for women in the social order, war required all the resources of the community and provided a period when roles could be more flexible. At the same time, especially during WWI and WWII, the emphasis on the temporary nature of women's contributions ensured that their wartime efforts did not challenge the established system and that they reverted to conventional female roles after the hostilities. In war, women's labour was essential, but in peace expendable. NANCY MILLER CHENIER

Women in the Labour Force Women are considered LABOUR FORCE participants only if they work outside the home. Women have been expected to be in the labour force only until they marry; this reflects the historical, idealized notion of a society in which the man is the breadwinner and the woman the homemaker. This notion of the FAMILY has not been a reality in the past and is not so today, since more than half of all married women work outside the home; but the idea that women belong in the home has had a significant effect on the conditions under which they participate in the labour force (*see* MARRIAGE AND DIVORCE). That participation is characterized by segregation and low pay. The majority of women in the labour force have always been isolated in "female" occupations, called such because they are often extensions of the work women do at home and because the vast majority of the people doing them are women (*see* STATUS OF WOMEN). Some occupations have changed over time and new ones have come into existence, but various occupations are still defined as women's work. Today women have one unpaid job in the home and one low-paid job in the labour force. Women have always been responsible for work in the home and in the labour force and they have always been paid lower wages than men; they have been paid less both when their jobs are not the same as those of men but could be seen as equally valuable and when the work is exactly the same (*see* WORK). Women earned 52.8% of what men earned in 1911, 58% in 1971 and 66% in 1986.

History of Female Labour At the end of the 19th century the factories replaced families as the main productive unit. Factory work involved long hours, low wages and often brutal working conditions. For example, young girls worked for 60 hours a week for 80 cents, or less than 2 cents per hour. In 1901 women comprised 13% of the total labour force and the female labour-force participation rate (FLFPR, defined as that proportion of working-age female population with jobs or looking for jobs) was 14% (this refers to women who worked for pay; many women worked but were not paid). The majority of women were employed as servants, dressmakers, teachers, seamstresses, tailors, housekeepers, launderers, milliners and saleswomen. During the first half of the 20th century the number of jobs available to women was limited and strong sentiment existed against married women working outside the home. Men feared that the cheap labour of large numbers of women would undercut their wages; employers and moral reformers were concerned that work would impair the femininity and high moral standards of women and distract them from their true calling as wives and mothers. During WWI, women replaced men who had joined the armed services, but the labour shortage was not severe enough to warrant their large-scale employment. Although women did men's jobs, they did not receive men's wages. At the end of the war, women were strongly encouraged to leave the work force and married women employed by government were legislated out of it. By 1921, 65% of all women workers were in clerical, domestic service and professional (mainly teaching and nursing) occupations.

In the early part of the 20th century, women's fight for equality focused on political rights and was characterized by the suffrage movement. The right to the federal vote was finally won in 1918, and by 1922 women had won the right to vote in all provinces except Québec where the struggle continued until 1940. In 1929 women were recognized as "persons" eligible to hold a seat in the Canadian Senate (see PERSONS CASE). The expansionary period of the 1920s was cut short by the Great Depression, but production and employment expanded enormously with WWII and once again employers hired single and then married women to do men's jobs, once again for lower wages. Incentives, eg, free government nurseries and income-tax concessions, were provided to attract married women into the labour force. At the end of the war the incentives were withdrawn and married women were again encouraged and in some cases regulated out of the labour force. This time, however, many stayed and found employment in the expanding number of "female" jobs in the service industries.

The greater numbers of women entering the labour force presented male-dominated trade unions with a dilemma. Trade unionists feared the competition from "unskilled" female labour and were concerned as well with maintaining the traditional role of women. Simultaneously, they were interested in protecting all workers, including women. Women workers, however, with or without the support of the trade-union movement, have traditionally fought for higher wages and better working conditions (see WORKING-CLASS HISTORY).

The 1950s were a time of rapid economic expansion. Changes in the productive process, emphasis by government and private industry on construction and on research and development, expansion in health, welfare and educational services, and the need to advertise, sell and finance new products all created new jobs for women. By 1951 women comprised 22% of the total labour force and the FLFPR was 24%. As the economy developed and as labour's productivity increased, consumer goods, cheaper in price, became available to more people. Mass consumption of these goods was imperative to the economic system. By mid-20th century many families, to be able to afford more goods and to educate their children, needed 2 income earners. Because young people were staying in school longer, married women entered the labour force to help their families raise their STANDARD OF LIVING. Between 1951 and 1986 the FLFPR of married women rose from

Female Workers over 16 years of age
without dependants
(Source: *Annual Report of the Ontario Bureau of Industries*, 1889).

Average number of hours/week worked	54
Average number of days/year worked	259
Average wages/year from occupation	$216.71
Cost of clothing	$ 67.31
Cost of board and lodging	$126.36
Total cost of living	$214.28
Surplus	$ 2.43

11% to 56%. Since the 1950s there has been a steady increase in part-time work and by the mid-1980s the number of part-time jobs, which have few benefits and little security, had expanded enormously; 71% of these were filled by women, the majority of whom were married. Women continued to earn lower wages than men and in 1978 the average wage rate for full-time women workers was 58% of that of the average wage rate for men workers. The vast majority of women were still employed in clerical, sales, service, teaching and medicine and health occupations. By 1986 women comprised 43% of the total labour force and the FLFPR had risen to 55%. Women continue to work predominantly (60% in 1984) in the nonprofessional clerical, sales and service occupations.

From 1971 women organized to demand greater equality in wages and working conditions, and to gain recognition of their social, economic, legal and political position in society. The women's movement of the 1960s had made many women aware of their right to independence and control of their own lives. Women joined unions and other organizations in greater numbers. The women's movement also raised and debated issues such as wages for HOUSEWORK and pensions for housewives. Considerable agreement existed in a wide range of areas: the prohibition of discrimination in employment policies on the grounds of gender or marital status; affirmative action; equal pay for work of equal value; maternity leave and benefits; adequate day-care facilities; provision for health and safety; and protection against sexual harassment in the workplace. By the mid-1980s the majority of mothers with children 5 years and under are in the labour force and the crisis in child-care services is a major issue. As the need for the 2-income earner family increases so too does the demand for parental leave and quality day care programs that recognize women's role in the labour force and men's role in child rearing and household work.

During the deep recession of the 1980s, real wages and consequently the standard of living have generally been declining, bringing into sharp focus the connection between women's unpaid work in the home and their underpaid work in the labour force. For example, the number of single-parent households headed by women has grown steadily in recent years, but the traditional notion, which has not changed, that there is a male breadwinner to support every household reinforces the occupational segregation and low wages of women in the labour force. As a result many employed, female single parents do not earn enough to live on after child care and other costs of working outside the home are deducted. The percentage of female-headed families (the majority of them single-parent families) with incomes below the poverty line increased from 18% in 1969 to 37% in 1985. An increasing number of elderly women also live in poverty; because most of these women worked all their lives in the home they have no work-related pension of their own. Husbands' pension plans seldom provide adequate protection for their surviving wives.

Government restraint has increased unemployment and decreased necessary services in health, welfare and education. Unemployment rates are higher than at any time since the Great Depression and the development of microelectronic technology will likely result in greater unemployment for women and will strand many women at home in "high-tech" sweatshops – a modern incarnation of the traditional piece-rate work for which little legislation exists. Without adequate government services, the care of the elderly, the disabled and the unemployed will once again fall on the shoulders of women, who are still generally considered responsible for this work. It appears therefore that women's work in the home is expanding, although it is increasingly necessary for women to be income earners, either as sole supporters of single-parent families or as members of 2-parent families. In this context, women's struggle for equality becomes even more difficult. Yet the struggle continues, as many women try to reach the goal of a society where women and men equally combine and share work and family responsibilities.

Achieving this goal would require major social, political and economic changes in order to create structures such as parental leave and child-care programs that support women and overturn existing structures such as labour force segregation and low wages that are disadvantageous to women. It would also require changes in attitudes that divide work in the labour force and work in the home into "women's" work and "men's" work.

M.P. CONNELLY

Women in the Military Until WWII the role of women in the Canadian forces was limited to NURSING services. The heavy casualties sustained by the Canadian Expeditionary Force in Europe during WWI required the development of a very large medical service. In its ranks served 3141 nursing sisters, of whom 2504 went overseas on the staffs of military hospitals in England, Egypt, Greece and on the western front in France and Belgium, where they also served in casualty clearing stations close behind the battle lines.

The tiny peacetime military nursing service of the 1920s and 1930s underwent great expansion again during WWII. By 1945, 4480 nursing sisters had served in the Royal Canadian Army Medical Corps and in the medical services of the RCN and the RCAF. During the war, the demands of women for a larger role, shortages of manpower, and the example of the British armed forces brought the further employment of Canadian women in many military trades that had previously been male preserves. Following the organization of the CANADIAN WOMEN'S ARMY CORPS and the Royal Canadian Air Force (Women's Division) in 1941, and the Royal Canadian Naval Women's Service in the next year, a total of 45 423 women entered the wartime forces. They served as clerical, administrative, communications and other kinds of support personnel, thereby releasing men for combat. Their success is reflected in the enthusiastic report of a senior air-force officer that they were "just as valuable as men and I would like to have as many as you can possibly spare." Like the members of the medical services, they saw duty in the rear areas of fighting theatres.

In 1946 the 3 women's services were disbanded, leaving only a small number of nursing sisters in uniform. That changed as the Cold War deepened and the Canadian forces expanded once more. In 1951 the reserve elements of all 3 services began to recruit women, as did the regular RCAF and, subsequently, in 1954-55, the regular army and navy, although in much smaller numbers than the 3000 women then in the air force.

By 1966, however, reductions in the size of the Canadian forces, automation in trades staffed by women, and difficulties in recruiting, at least partly because of the limited careers available to women, reduced their total number in the regular services to fewer than 900. That was the low point. Since then the changing role of women in Canadian society has made their increased participation in the armed forces, and their equality with men in both career opportunities and terms of service, a government priority. As of Feb 1988 there were 8099 women in the regular forces, 9.4% of its total strength (in addition, as of Dec 1987, 4391 women constituted 17.5% of the strength of the reserve forces). To compare, during WWII women made up something less than 5% of the Canadian forces. Although women are still not eligible for combat duty, near-combat roles, on aircraft of various types, on naval support ships and in army units operating immediately behind the front lines, have recently been approved *See also* WOMEN AND WAR.   ROGER SARTY

Women's International League for Peace and Freedom, fd 1915 in The Hague, the Netherlands, by women active in the WOMEN'S SUFFRAGE movement in Europe and N America. These women wished to end WWI and seek ways to ensure that no more wars took place. The league came to Canada in the early 1920s on the initiative of socially and politically conscious women such as Dorothy Steeves and Laura Jamieson, founders of the Vancouver branch. Branches were also formed in Toronto, Edmonton and Winnipeg. In Toronto J.S. WOODSWORTH's wife, Lucy, was an active member. Agnes MACPHAIL was probably the best-known member, serving for a number of years as honorary president. In the West, Violet MCNAUGHTON, a journalist and ardent supporter of the concerns of both women and farmers, played a key role in promoting the organization and in uniting other groups concerned with peace and DISARMAMENT.

In Canada the league was involved in promoting peace education and conducting campaigns for disarmament and against militarism in general. The protest against cadet training in the schools was one of its most persistent campaigns. WILPF also conducted a study into school textbooks, which, members felt, glorified war and paid insufficient attention to the values of co-operation and harmony. In 1931 the international body initiated a petition campaign for universal disarmament; 491 000 signatures were collected in Canada. Just before and during WWII the Toronto branch worked to help REFUGEES settle and learn English. But the league declined during the 1940s and 1950s, in part because of renewed militarism and fear engendered by WWII and the subsequent COLD WAR. Only the Vancouver branch remained after the mid-1950s, and with a greatly reduced membership. However, in the late 1970s a branch was formed in Ottawa and membership again began to grow across the country. *See also* PEACE MOVEMENT.

DEBORAH POWELL

Women's Labour Leagues (WLL) emerged in Canada prior to WWI. Modelled on the British Labour Leagues, auxiliaries to the Independent Labour Party, their purpose was to organize women workers and support the trade-union movement. After a period of limited growth, they were rejuvenated in 1923-24 by the COMMUNIST PARTY OF CANADA. Under the direction of Florence Custance, the leagues grew to 37 locals in 1927, and the Federation of WLLs published the monthly paper *The Woman Worker*, which discussed women's issues from a Marxist perspective. League members were usually working-class housewives, sometimes wage-earning

women, and many were Finnish, Yiddish or Ukrainian speaking. The WLL platform, radical for its time, included demands for equal pay, maternity care and birth control. Although the WLLs were not successful in unionizing women, they did educational work, raised money for the Communist Party and the labour movement, and developed their members' understanding of socialism. In 1930 they were advised to join the WORKERS UNITY LEAGUE, and subsequently some faded away, although a few functioned until the 1940s.

JOAN SANGSTER

Women's Movement Since the end of the 19th century Canadian women have been organizing to redefine their place in society, to demand equality and justice. Through legal and political means, the women's movement has allowed Canadian women to obtain a certain formal equality. Parallel to this slow conquest of equal rights, the life-style of Canadian women, as for women in most other Western countries, has undergone profound changes. Goods and services traditionally produced in the home are now available for purchase by consumers; and these technological developments, together with the growth of the service sector, have facilitated the increasing participation of women in the labour market, so that by the 1980s the majority of Canadian married women had a paying job. Serious inequalities in the relative position of men and women in society remain, however. The federal government in 1967 set up the Royal Commission on the STATUS OF WOMEN to examine the situation, and in its 1970 report the commission made 167 recommendations for greater equality of women.

The late 1960s in Canada, as throughout the Western world, saw the emergence of a new women's movement. This new feminism rejected all limits to the equality of women's rights and showed that equality in daily life cannot be obtained through simple legal, political or institutional modifications. Women were greatly influenced by books and articles by feminists such as Kate Millett, Germaine Greer, Gloria Steinem, and Shulamith Firestone and by publications such as *Women Unite: An Anthology of the Women's Movement* (1972) and Margaret Anderson's *Mother Was Not a Person* (1973). These writers held that society's major power relationship was one of domination and oppression of women by men. The existing body of social relationships, along with the very functioning of society, was analysed and criticized.

In the late 1960s, discovering that "sisterhood is powerful," women from Vancouver to Halifax began forming groups. The Vancouver Women's Caucus was organized in 1968 and published *The Pedestal* from 1969 to 1973. The Montréal Women's Liberation Movement was founded in 1969, the Front de libération des femmes du Québec published a feminist manifesto in 1970, and the Centre des femmes edited the first French-language radical feminist periodical, *Québécoises deboutte!* (1971-75). At first, some were consciousness-raising groups, but others quickly turned to concrete action, providing abortion services, health centres, feminist magazines, militant theatre, day-care, shelters for battered women and rape crisis centres, and organizing for equal pay. By the end of the 1960s Canadian society had begun to adjust to the rebirth of a major social movement, the women's movement.

Social movements, which can be loosely defined as conscious collective efforts to change some aspects of the social order, are difficult to describe with precision. Major social movements contain within themselves many subgroupings which may differ in important ways. The women's movement, for example, includes liberal,

radical and Marxist feminists, lesbian separatists, and those who view lesbianism as one life-style among others; although these groupings debate vigorously on a number of issues, they do agree on the basic need to improve the situation of women. The women's movement has been working for social justice for women along many different fronts, including politics, culture, the mass media, law, education, health, the labour force and the home. Organizations of every size and from every region participate. Some concentrate on self-help; some on working for general social change. While in the beginning, in the early 1970s, the movement seemed to consist of smaller radical groups, the movement's base has gradually expanded to incorporate women of diverse opinions and from all parts of Canadian society, including welfare mothers, professional, business and executive women, native women and immigrant domestic workers. Large, well-established organizations have also adopted feminist practices and the women's movement itself has now generated a number of autonomous organizations.

The women's movement uses diverse methods to promote its goal of social justice for women. Public events, including lectures, entertainment in various forms and leafletting, are arranged to "raise consciousness" and disseminate information. Protest actions, such as demonstrations, marches, vigils and petitions, are organized. Government, political parties and particular agencies, institutions and employers are lobbied for reform. Action often takes the form of first establishing a committee (caucus, interest group) on the status of women, then documenting existing inequities, formulating proposals for improvement, and finally lobbying for their implementation. In response, the federal and various provincial governments have established advisory councils on the STATUS OF WOMEN as well as other bureaucratic mechanisms, and municipalities and educational and health institutions have set up councils or units specifically for women.

Another important activity of the women's movement centers on publication, ranging from informal flyers to posters to highly academic volumes, and including children's books, self-help manuals and newspaper columns. These contributions are published through mainstream outlets as well as through an emerging network of feminist presses.

The women's movement has been effective in organizing action on particular issues, employing a multitude of means and involving a coalition of groups and individuals. Issues generating mass efforts include, for example, the right to choice in obtaining a legal abortion, the entrenchment of sex equality in the CANADIAN CHARTER OF RIGHTS AND FREEDOMS in 1982, PORNOGRAPHY, and threats to the ENVIRONMENT, CIVIL LIBERTIES and peace (*see* PEACE MOVEMENT).

In sum, women have broken their isolation and have set up groups and organizations across the country, or have joined existent organizations. Since the late 1970s co-operation among the various groups has intensified. Some of the national groups include the NATIONAL ACTION COMMITTEE ON THE STATUS OF WOMEN, Canadian Research Institute for the Advancement of Women, CANADIAN CONGRESS FOR LEARNING OPPORTUNITIES FOR WOMEN, Canadian Assn for the Advancement of Women in Sport, Canadian Day Care Advocacy Assn, Charter of Rights Coalition, Fédération des femmes canadiennes-françaises, Indian Rights for Indian Women, Media Watch, National Congress of Black Women, NATIONAL COUNCIL OF WOMEN, VOICE OF WOMEN, Women in Science and Engineering, and many more. Such groups consist mainly of women from the anglophone provinces, for

French Canadian women tend to align themselves on linguistic rather than truly "national" lines. Thus, Québec has a whole series of counterpart organizations to the "national" ones mentioned above, eg, Fédération des femmes du Québec and L'Association feminine d'éducation et d'action sociale. These groups and organizations define to some extent the structure of the feminist movement in Canada. While a majority of Canadian women as well as men are in sympathy with the goal of social justice for women, much of the actual work falls to "front-line" feminist organizations, some of which appear to be more or less permanent and others more ad hoc groups which surface only to confront specific tasks.

There is no overall leadership structure for the movement, although there are some individuals who have been highly visible at different times and for different issues. The movement stresses the importance of issues over the personalities involved and rejects the notion that a few women can speak on all issues for all women. The main point is that women desire to speak for themselves, and they may speak from a multitude of theoretical and political orientations. Ideological debates over tactics and theory are ongoing.

Changing the Social Structure Creating a just society for women means the elimination of sexism in all areas and particularly in the legal system, in the organization of social production, in the perception and treatment of women's bodies, and in the arts, sciences, education and the mass media.

Most progress has been achieved in the legal area. Among the earliest targets for action were the various FAMILY LAWS. In 1973 the MURDOCH CASE, in which an Alberta farm wife was denied a half interest in the farm that she and her husband had built up together over a 25-year period because her work was seen simply as the fulfilment of her wifely duties, raised awareness about the injustices of family laws. Since that time, all provinces have reformed their family laws in the direction of greater equality between spouses, and some provinces more than once. Another legal decision in the LAVELL CASE (1973) involved an Indian woman who had lost her Indian status and privileges upon marriage to a non-Indian. The discriminatory aspects of the Indian Act have been removed as of June 1985, but social problems remain. Since that time, women who lost Indian status because they married a non-Indian can reclaim their lost status as can their first-generation children. However, this does not carry with it automatic membership in an Indian band. Indian bands had until June 1987 the option to develop membership codes. As of now, children will have automatic Indian status only if both their parents are registered Indians.

One of the primary concerns of the women's movement has been the securing of appropriate rewards for WORK performed by women. In this context, "work" includes both paid and unpaid work, and involves the realization that the 2 are inextricably linked. It was the women's movement that first emphasized that work done within the home is, indeed, work, and should be regarded as such. The Wages for HOUSEWORK movement has been instrumental in focusing attention on this issue. Out of this concern have sprung campaigns as well as one federal commission and one parliamentary committee for good DAY CARE, maternity and paternity benefits in employment, and some recognition in both the pension system and in cases of divorce of work performed by the housewife.

In the paid labour force, concern focused initially on equal pay for equal work. More recently, the demand for equal pay for work of equal value has prompted comparisons of dissimilar jobs in order to establish fair pay scales for jobs requiring similar skills, efforts and responsibilities. The Royal Commission on Equality in Employment (Abella Commission), which tabled its report in 1984, made a number of recommendations for sweeping changes, which in 1987 are still working their way through the system. A few employment equality programs try to overcome historical discrimination by facilitating the promotion of women into levels and types of occupation from which they have so far been excluded. There has also been a concern to recognize the contribution of wives who work in partnership with their husbands in nonincorporated businesses, so that wages paid to the wife can be rated as such for tax and legal purposes. Under pressure from unionized women, many unions are now including equal pay and other women's issues among their demands (*see* WOMEN IN THE LABOUR FORCE).

The most controversial field of feminist action is the attempt to affirm women's right to control over their bodies, eg, with respect to fertility, sexual relationships, sexual violence, and medical power over women's health. The most fiery demonstrations have been about the control of ABORTION, a struggle which began in the late 1960s. Dr Henry MORGENTALER, who supported the establishment of free-standing abortion clinics, was at the centre of the debate. After several court trials, he was finally acquitted in Québec, where abortions in family-planning clinics became possible. The abortion question flared up again in the 1980s. In 1983 Dr Morgentaler opened abortion clinics in Toronto and Winnipeg. Morgentaler was prosecuted and acquitted by jury. The Crown appealed and ordered a new trial. At that point, Morgentaler appealed to the Supreme Court of Canada. In early 1988 in a landmark decision the Supreme Court voted to strike down Canada's abortion law. The decision paved the way for new legislation but it also meant that abortion policy varied greatly from province to province.

The abortion debate has had its corollary in a re-evaluation of medical practices and initiatives in the field of contraception. It includes such questions as: Is it necessary for women alone to carry its burdens? Why are they the only ones to suffer the side effects of contraceptives? Why has research into male contraception been so slow? Why do doctors so commonly perform hysterectomies on menopausal women? Such questions have led feminists to produce written and visual health "kits," to open self-help health clinics, and to champion alternative medicine and the removal of pregnancy and childbirth from medical structures. Some militant groups in the women's movement concentrate on regaining women's control over childbirth and winning the right for midwives to practise (*see* WOMEN AND HEALTH).

With the rapid changes that are occurring in the field of reproductive technologies, and the social arrangements concerning them, the whole issue of women's control over their reproductive processes has taken on a new dimension and urgency. On the one hand, certain techniques such as in-vitro fertilization, embryo transfer, etc, open the possibility for women to have children who before were not able to do so. On the other hand, these same techniques and other social arrangements raise problems of a type and magnitude that did not exist before. Medical doctors are now, in many cases, a third party to the process of reproduction and literally hold the power to determine the genetic makeup of a new human being. Laws concerning the ownership of gametes (eggs and semen) and practices of handling them (to whom does the sperm of a dead donor belong?; can one experiment on human embryos?; can such manipulated embryos be implanted in women?) either do not yet exist or have been insufficiently elaborated. Recent developments in what has been called surrogate motherhood arrangements (in fact, preconception contracts for the production of a child) threaten to make pregnancy a commercial, judicially controlled activity in which women do not have the right to refuse certain medical treatments. This poses a threat to women's rights over their own bodies that previously did not exist. This subject has increasingly become a matter of great debate for the feminist movement.

Male control over women's bodies has also traditionally expressed itself through violence. New halfway houses for battered women have opened in several cities, and analyses and reports on this hitherto forbidden topic are published in newspapers and magazines. RAPE, the chief representation of aggression against women, has escaped from the silence which formerly surrounded it. Rape-crisis centres have existed in major cities since 1973; a lobby has been organized to press for changes in the law; each fall urban women parade to demonstrate their right to use the streets safely at night; and every year thousands of Canadian women take courses in self-defence. Violent pornography is strongly denounced and the Canadian Coalition Against Media Pornography is an increasingly active lobby group.

The new feminism has also affected the arts, creative activities, education and the mass media. Discussions about women are analysed, evaluated and dissected, with the result that women are using new languages, images and methods of analysis.

Women's writing in the last few years has seen an unprecedented and revitalizing explosion. Women now talk about what it is to be a woman. They talk about things that were previously private, hidden or mythologized, such as rape, incest and family violence. Some writings focus on the denunciation of oppression; others "celebrate the differences" and talk about maternity, mothers' daily work, children, marriage, the family, the relationship of women to nature and love between women. Female writers such as Nicole BROSSARD, Louky Bersianik, Madeleine Gagnon, Denise Boucher, Margaret ATWOOD, Alice MUNRO, Jane RULE and many others mark a turning-point in Québec and Canadian literature. Theatrical production includes such acclaimed feminist plays as *La Nef de sorcières* (1976), written by a feminist collective, Boucher's *Les Fées ont soif* (1978) and Betty Lambert's *Jenny's Story* (1982). Feminist theatre troupes have existed since the 1970s and feminist plays are now in the repertory of various small or institutional theatres.

In the mass media, feminist journalists and the work of feminist groups have had some effect in generating higher awareness of women as readers and newsmakers. Columnists in several major newspapers and periodicals now write from an explicitly feminist perspective. Nevertheless, the relationship between the women's movement and the mass media remains strained, as the media sometimes misrepresent the movement. As a result, a feminist press has developed, with its own media production and distribution system.

Politically committed humorists, rockers and women performers challenge audiences. Female producers at the NATIONAL FILM BOARD have made several documentaries, including the major series "En tant que femmes" (1973) as well as *Mourir à tue-tête* (1979) and *Not a Love Story* (1981). Video has always been open to women: in 1975, to honour International Women's Year, feminist video production and distribution centres opened in 8 Canadian cities. Some still exist and each year they produce material or fictional work which is distributed through community and educational circles.

A great effort has been put into eliminating sexism in education. WOMEN'S STUDIES are now an accepted part of many curricula. In 1983 the SOCIAL SCIENCES AND HUMANITIES RESEARCH COUNCIL created a committee for facilitating the equal treatment of the sexes in social science and humanities research. It produced a pamphlet, Eichler and Lapointe, *On the Treatment of the Sexes in Research* (French reference is Lapointe and Eichler, *Le Traitement objectif des sexes dans la recherche*), which argues that good research must be nonsexist. In general, integrating women into our thought processes is now widely seen as important and legitimate, although the process of doing so has just begun.

Conclusion In the time since its re-emergence, feminism has had a major impact on our society. Ultimately, creating social justice for women involves a profound restructuring of society and of the way people think and experience the world. By stressing that "the personal is political," the women's movement has made the social inequality of women a public and not merely a private problem. This accomplishment is its single most important contribution. The scope of the task has been defined; its full implementation has yet to be achieved.   MARGRIT EICHLER AND MARIE LAVIGNE

Reading: M. FitzGerald et al, *Still Ain't Satisfied: Canadian Feminism Today* (1982); L. Gagnon, *Vivre avec les hommes: un nouveau partage* (1983); P. Kome, *The Taking of Twenty-Eight: Women Challenge the Constitution* (1983); A. Miles and G. Finn, *Feminism in Canada: From Pressure to Politics* (1982); V. O'Leary and L. Toupin, *Québécoises deboutte!: une anthologie de textes du Front de libération des femmes et du Centre des femmes*, 2 vols (1982); Royal Commission on Equality in Employment, *Report* (1984); Royal Commission on the Status of Women in Canada, *Report* (1970).

Women's Organizations In the early 19th century affluent women grouped together at the local level for charitable and religious purposes. They set up refuges and orphanages to help needy women and children, and worked for their churches through ladies' auxiliaries. By the end of the 19th century this activity had expanded to include a myriad of reform organizations, now increasingly interdenominational and secular, such as the WOMAN'S CHRISTIAN TEMPERANCE UNION, the YOUNG WOMEN'S CHRISTIAN ASSOCIATION and the NATIONAL COUNCIL OF WOMEN. Unlike the earlier groups, these organizations were national in extent and appealed to a much broader segment of Canadian womanhood. They sought to improve society and were willing, in specific instances, to use the power of the state through compulsory legislation to effect reforms. Their focus, however, had not really altered, since these societies also concentrated their efforts on helping needy women and children.

The women who joined such organizations felt a responsibility to become involved in society. For the most part they accepted women's domestic role, but were convinced that their position necessitated a more public stance since increasingly society impinged on family life. This seemed particularly true in urban areas where alcoholism, prostitution, delinquency and disease were prevalent. Rural women anticipated the challenge of urbanization and, in addition, wanted to overcome the problems of isolation and depopulation. Farmers' organizations in the early decades of the 20th century accepted women's auxiliaries and associations as an integral part of the farmers' movement. Women's institutes became so successful that they were established throughout the world (*see* FEDERATED WOMEN'S INSTITUTES OF CANADA). In addition to the women's organizations which were instrumental in nature, many others existed which were expressive, designed solely for the benefit of their member-

National Council of Women group at Rideau Hall, Ottawa, Ont, Oct 1898. Lord and Lady Aberdeen are at centre; Lady Marjorie Gordon at left (*courtesy National Archives of Canada/PA-28033*).

ship. Some, such as reading and musical associations, catered to the woman at home, but others represented the specific needs of professional women such as teachers and nurses (*see* WOMEN IN THE LABOUR FORCE).

By 1912 it was estimated that one out of every 8 adult women in Canada belonged to a women's group, making the women's organizational movement a significant force in Canadian society. However, it was not a movement which appealed to all women. Joiners were, in the main, middle aged, middle class, English-speaking and Protestant. French-speaking and Roman Catholic women found the Catholic church with its sisterhoods and groups a rich source of organizational life. Not until the early 20th century did these women organize such societies as the Fédération nationale St-Jean-Baptiste, which agitated for change in society, along the same lines as English-speaking and Protestant initiatives. Nevertheless, religious inspiration and influence remained crucial to a greater degree for them than for English-speaking Canadians.

The work of the various organizations, especially the instrumental ones, was impressive. They made the public aware of the needs of working women, the deficiencies of the educational system, the problems of intemperance, the existence of the double standard of morality between men and women, and the abysmally high infant mortality rate in some Canadian cities. Women's participation in these groups helped change the image of Canadian women. By joining together, women experienced the power of collective action and the joys of sisterhood. They also learned how to be administrators and fund raisers. In encountering resistance to reform, they came face to face with their own powerlessness as women. They learned that because they lacked the right to vote, politicians would not listen to them and certainly would not respond to their requests. This encouraged them to support WOMEN'S SUFFRAGE, an issue that brought about a concerted effort on the part of many women's organizations in the second decade of the 20th century.

After women gained the right to vote at the federal level in 1918, there was no longer one issue which joined the various women's groups and they lost some of their visibility and appeal. In the

1920s energies were taken up with church union and the peace movement (*see* WOMEN'S INTERNATIONAL LEAGUE FOR PEACE AND FREEDOM). Young women were not attracted by the organizational movement, preferring to explore their potential individually. With the emergence of the WOMEN'S MOVEMENT in the late 1960s a new organizational impetus emerged. Added to the older groups were new ones, many of which were self-directed. They concentrated their activities on increasing women's awareness of their subordinate status in society. Out of this awareness developed specific groups for native women, working women, ethnic women and lesbian women. In addition, the NATIONAL ACTION COMMITTEE ON THE STATUS OF WOMEN emerged as a political voice and lobby for Canadian women. Once again public attention was focused on the collective action of women. However, this time their concern has not been the acceptance of one reform but a fundamental shift in the way women are treated and perceived by society.   WENDY MITCHINSON

Reading: E. Collins et al, *Fifty Years of Achievement: Federated Women's Institutes in Ontario* (1948); E. Forbes, *With Enthusiasm and Faith: History of the Canadian Federation of Business and Professional Women's Clubs, 1930-1972* (1974); J.P. Harshaw, *When Women Work Together: A History of Young Women's Christian Association in Canada, 1870-1966* (1966); M.Q. Innis, *Unfold the Years: A History of the Young Women's Christian Association in Canada* (1949); L. Kealy, ed, *A Not Unreasonable Claim* (1979); Wendy Mitchinson, "Women's Missionary Societies in Nineteenth Century Canada," *Atlantis* 2 (spring 1977), and "The YWCA and Reform in the Late Nineteenth Century," *Histoire Sociale* 12 (Nov 1979); V. Strong-Boag, *The Parliament of Women: The National Council of Women of Canada, 1893-1929* (1976).

Women's Studies is a generic term for a diverse and growing field of knowledge, which is sometimes described as feminist studies, nonsexist scholarship or, less often, feminology. Women's studies is characterized by a multitude of subfields (eg, psychology of women, sociology of women) which share 2 basic concerns: that knowledge be generated and taught which is relevant to women; that knowledge generated and taught in the past was often sexist, based on a male perspective of the world. United by a commitment to these central concerns, women's studies also embraces differences which further guarantee the dynamic quality of this new field of study. A sexist bias is reflected even in everyday language, which often utilizes male terms (he, workman's compensation, etc) to express general as well as sex-specific facts. Sexist biases are also embedded in the most basic assumptions on which science is based; eg, until recently economics has treated housework as nonwork, and rarely has history studied the lives of women with the same attention as it looked at the lives of men.

Women's studies cuts across all disciplines in the social sciences and humanities, and embraces a diversity of perspectives, methodologies and tactics. There is an interdisciplinary flavour to the work, although some of the most important work is done within specific disciplines: anthropology, history, psychology, sociology, political science, theology, economics, linguistics, literature, philosophy and, more recently, the natural sciences.

Women's studies in Canada were started around 1970, usually being developed and taught at the university level. Community support from the WOMEN'S MOVEMENT was at times crucial in establishing and maintaining academic programs. By the 1980s most universities in Canada had some courses in this area, and several offered degree programs with a major in women's studies. Instruction in women's studies now spans the entire educational spectrum, from primary grades to graduate school as well as adult noncredit courses.

People involved in women's studies organized conferences and founded periodicals and organizations devoted to this growing field of study. As a consequence there is now a community of feminist scholars, dispersed all across the country and working in different disciplines. Resistance to women's studies on the part of academics who themselves do sexist research has not yet vanished, but the scholarship generated in the years since women's studies began clearly establishes its validity and significance. In 1984 the secretary of state announced the establishment of 5 chairs in women's studies, which have since been awarded to Mount Saint Vincent U, Halifax, U Vic, Carleton U and U of O (a joint chair), U of Winnipeg and U Man (a joint chair) and U Laval.

The first Canadian periodical dedicated to the discipline was the *Canadian Newsletter of Research on Women*, later renamed *Resources for Feminist Research*. Founded in 1972, it lists information on current research projects across the country. Three other important journals are *Atlantis, Canadian Woman Studies* and the *International Journal of Women's Studies*. The first 3 journals are bilingual. The most important organizations concerned with some aspect of women's studies are the Canadian Research Institute for the Advancement of Women (1976), Canadian Congress for Learning Opportunities for Women (1976) and the Canadian Women's Studies Association (1982), founded with the specific goal of fostering women's studies in high schools, colleges and universities.   MARGRIT EICHLER

Reading: Le Collectif Clio, *L'Histoire des femmes au Québec* (1982); Corrective Collective, *Never Done: Three Centuries of Women's Work in Canada* (1974); Margrit Eichler, *The Double Standard* (1980); Eichler and J. Lapointe, *On the Treatment of the Sexes in Research* (1985); Groupe de recherche multidisciplinaire féministe, *Approches et methodes de la recherche féministe* (1986); G.H. Nemiroff, ed, *Women and Men* (1987); Linda Rasmussen, Lorna Rasmussen, C. Savage and A. Wheeler, eds, *A Harvest Yet to Reap* (1976); M. Stephenson, ed, *Women in Canada* (1977); V. Strong-Boag and Beth Light, eds, *True Daughters of the North: Canadian Women's History: An Annotated Bibliography* (1980); S.M. Trofimenkoff and A. Prentice, eds, *The Neglected Majority* (1977); J. Vickers, *Taking Sex into Account* (1984).

Women's Suffrage In the 19th century, female property holders could demand municipal voting rights on the principle of "no taxation without representation." Propertied women in Québec voted unchallenged between 1809 and 1849, when the word "male" was inserted into Québec's franchise Act. What Québec women lost,

Ontario women soon gained: from 1850, women with property, married or single, could vote for school trustees. By 1900 municipal voting privileges for propertied women were general throughout Canada. But most 19th-century Canadians, women as well as men, believed that the sexes had been assigned to "separate spheres" by natural and divine laws that overrode mere man-made laws, and this stood squarely in the way of achieving votes for all women as a democratic right.

At the provincial level, public debate in Ontario began among members of the Toronto Women's Literary Club, a screen for suffrage activities created 1876 by Dr Emily Howard STOWE, Canada's first woman doctor. She and her daughter, Dr Augusta STOWE-GULLEN, spearheaded Ontario's suffrage campaign for 40 years. In 1883 the club became the Toronto Women's Suffrage Association, then in 1889 the Dominion Women's Enfranchisement Association – a national group in name only. Despite numerous petitions and bills, Ontario's lawmakers, confident that they had public opinion behind them, repeatedly blocked changes. Suffrage groups were thus forced to undertake long years of public education. Valuable support came in the 1890s from the WOMAN'S CHRISTIAN TEMPERANCE UNION, whose leaders saw votes for women as necessary in achieving PROHIBITION. In 1910, the respected and influential NATIONAL COUNCIL OF WOMEN spoke out for suffrage.

The WCTU was also active in Manitoba, where women's suffrage had first been proposed in 1870 by the Icelandic community. Among Manitoba's early leaders were Mrs M.J. Benedictssen, Mrs A.V. Thomas, Dr Amelia Yeomans and Mrs J.A. McClung. McClung's daughter-in-law, Nellie MCCLUNG, later became the Prairie movement's dominant figure. Between 1912 and 1915 there was a sharp, concerted campaign. Then on 28 Jan 1916 Manitoba women became the first in Canada to win the rights to vote and to hold provincial office. They were followed by Saskatchewan on Mar 14 and Alberta on Apr 19. BC approved women's suffrage on 5 Apr 1917, and Ontario suffragists, after many years of struggle, celebrated their hard-won victory on Apr 12.

Meanwhile, pressure was mounting on federal politicians. In the controversial WARTIME ELECTIONS ACT of 1917 the federal vote was extended to women in the armed forces, and to female relatives of military men. At the same time thousands of loyal citizens, naturalized after 1902, were disenfranchised. It was not an honourable victory for Canadian women.

On 24 May 1918 all female citizens aged 21 and over became eligible to vote in federal elections, regardless of whether they had yet attained the provincial franchise. In July 1919 they gained the complementary right to stand for the House of Commons, although appointment to the Senate remained out of reach until after the PERSONS CASE of 1929. Throughout the preceding debates, the compelling argument in women's favour was their service, sacrifice and proven competence during WWI – just as Prairie women had gained provincial rights largely on their record in helping to settle and build the country. Although democratic right did have a place in the argument, service was the keynote.

The provincial franchise for Nova Scotia women came on 26 Apr 1918 after a lacklustre campaign. The cause was even less popular in New Brunswick, which approved women's suffrage on 17 Apr 1919. PEI, with practically no popular agitation, changed its franchise Act on 3 May 1922, and Newfoundland women gained the vote on 13 Apr 1925. In NS, PEI and Newfoundland, the right to stand for provincial office accompanied voting rights, but New Brunswick

avoided that radical step until 9 Mar 1934. In Québec, under the courageous leadership of Thérèse CASGRAIN, the struggle continued until 25 Apr 1940, when women finally achieved the provincial counterpart to the federal vote they had been exercising for over 20 years.

Compared to the flamboyance and occasional violence of British, French and American suffrage campaigns, Canada's was peaceable and urbane, with humour, reason and quiet persistence. Canadian women have generally remained outside politics, and with the exception of municipal politics, only a small handful have so far been elected to provincial legislatures or to the House of Commons, or appointed to the Senate. In the 1984 federal election, the greatest number of women (27) were elected to the House of Commons and the greatest number (6) subsequently became Cabinet ministers. Canadian women only began to consider careers in politics seriously in the 1970s, having learned in the preceding half century that winning the vote was only a first step in a movement, far from over, for fundamental political and social change.   SUSAN JACKEL

Reading: C.L. Bacchi, *Liberation Deferred?* (1983); C.L. Cleverdon, *The Woman Suffrage Movement in Canada* (1950).

Wood, Edward Rogers, financier (b at Peterborough, Canada W 14 May 1866; d at Toronto 16 June 1941). Originally a telegraph operator, Wood joined the Central Canada Loan and Savings Co in 1884. He later became managing director and VP, and was elected president in 1914. Out of Central Canada came Dominion Securities Corp, one of the largest investment houses in Canada, incorporated in 1901 by Senator George A. COX, Henry PELLATT and Wood, who eventually became its president. He was also a VP of National Trust; Brazilian Traction, Light and Power; Canada Life Assurance; and the Canadian Bank of Commerce; and a director of Massey-Harris; Mexican Light and Power; Canadian Barcelona Traction, Light and Power; International Paper; Toronto Savings and Loan; and Canada Northern Power Corp.   JORGE NIOSI

Wood, Henry Wise, farmer, farm leader (b on a farm near Monroe City, Mo 31 May 1860; d at Calgary 10 June 1941). A member of a prosperous family with farms in Missouri and Texas, Wood became an expert stockman while a teenager. He belonged to the Campbellite Church, a Christian sect that emphasized the New Testament, the brotherhood of man, a democratic congregational system and the need for Christian ethics in economic activities. Educated in local schools and Christian College (Canton, Mo), Wood was an earnest student of agrarian reform. He observed the Alliance and Populist movements in Missouri during the 1890s and agreed essentially with their programs for rural economic and social organization, but he disagreed with their attempt to develop into a conventional political party.

In 1904 he visited Alberta, "the Last Best West," and a year later purchased a wheat farm near Carstairs. He joined the Society of Equity, an early farm association, and in 1909, its successor, the UNITED FARMERS OF ALBERTA. In 1914 Wood became a director of the UFA; in 1915 he was elected vice-president and was president 1916-31.

Wood emerged as one of the most powerful agrarian and political figures in Alberta from 1915 until his death. Devoting nearly all his time to visiting UFA locals, he preached the need for a strong, broadly based farm organization so that rural people could offset the growing power of bankers, industrialists and professionals. He gradually developed a theory of group government, in which occupational groupings would be the framework for political organization. Although originally a Liberal, Wood reluctantly became convinced that direct farmer involvement in politics was needed to protect rural interests. He helped develop the federal PROGRESSIVE PARTY platform as it evolved from the programs of the Canadian Council of Agriculture at the end of WWI. He also played a key role in the entry of the UFA into politics during 1919 and 1920. When the UFA candidates elected a majority in 1921, Wood declined to become premier but continued to play a powerful role in determining the government's policies and programs.

During the early 1920s Wood became increasingly involved in the wheat-marketing question. In 1920 the federal government had ended its control over grain marketing begun in 1917. Western farm organizations, fearing high marketing costs and low prices, frantically sought orderly marketing under provincial or federal government control. Wood was a central figure in these attempts, although he personally preferred marketing through farmer-owned co-operatives. When attempts to involve government failed, therefore, Wood became a leader in the wheat pool movement which swept rural Alberta in 1923-24.

Wood's influence among Prairie farmers was based on a widespread respect for his sincerity, religious conviction and devotion to the farmers' cause. A gifted orator with a powerful personality, he was a cautious leader who never embraced new issues prematurely, and he was effective as a conciliator.   IAN MACPHERSON

Reading: W.K. Rolph, *Henry Wise Wood of Alberta* (1950).

Wood, Josiah, businessman, politician, lt-gov of NB 1912-17 (b at Sackville, NB 18 Apr 1843; d there 13 May 1927). A graduate of Mt Allison Coll (MA 1866) and a lawyer, Wood inherited his father's wholesaling, lumbering and shipping firm in 1875. During the 1880s he diversified into manufacturing, directing a sugar refinery, a cotton mill and other industries in nearby Moncton, NB. Wood secured government subsidies for a railway between Sackville and the Northumberland Str. It was completed in 1886, and he served as president until 1913. A Conservative, he was MP for Westmorland, NB, 1882-95 and became a leading advocate of tariff protection for Canadian industry. He was appointed to the Senate in 1895, resigning in 1912 to become lieutenant-governor of NB. He retired in 1917. Wood was a generous benefactor of the Methodist Church and Mt Allison College.   DEAN JOBB

Wood, Sharon Adele, mountaineer, guide (b at Halifax 18 May 1957). In pursuit of a passion that began with an introductory climbing class in Jasper, Alta, when she was 17, Wood achieved international recognition in the spring of 1986 when she became the first woman from the Western Hemisphere to stand atop Mt Everest. Known as a strong, aggressive climber, she had previously accumulated an impressive portfolio of difficult ascents, including the Kane Face of Mt Robson; Mt Logan (as part of the first all-woman team to negotiate the peak); the Cassin Ridge on Mt McKinley; and a new route on the S face on Aconcagua. Her climb on Everest was as a member of the Canadian Everest Light Expedition, a 12-person, non-Sherpa-supported assault on the mountain's W ridge. On May 20, the last day of the climb, Wood and her partner, Dwayne CONGDON, overcame severe winds and 695 vertical m of rock, snow and ice to reach the summit at 9:00 PM. When not on one of her own climbs, Wood teaches the sport to others. She is also a helicopter ski guide.   BART ROBINSON

Wood, William Burke, actor-manager (b at Montréal 26 May 1779; d at Philadelphia, Pa 23 Sept 1861). He was the first native-born N American to achieve notable success in the theatre; Wood's parents had immigrated to Canada before the American Revolution and returned to NY *c* 1784. At 19, Wood made his acting debut in Annapolis, Md, with Thomas Wignell's company. Over the years he found favour as a polished comedian. Wignell's troupe was based at the Chestnut St Theatre, Philadelphia, which Wood eventually managed for 16 years (1810-26). He introduced many indigenous plays and wrote *Personal Recollections of the Stage* (1855).
                                    DAVID GARDNER

Wood, William John, labourer, artist (b near Ottawa 26 May 1877; d at Midland, Ont 5 Jan 1954). Although isolated from the contemporary artistic centres of his day, and obliged to work as an unskilled labourer for most of his life, Wood nonetheless pursued an intense lifelong interest in art, especially etching, through which he expressed his immediate experience of life in Midland in a bold, personal style. This style, evolved from familiarity with impressionism and the Swedish etcher Anders Zorn, attracted the attention of the GROUP OF SEVEN, with whom he exhibited on several occasions. Wood was a member of the Soc of Canadian Painter-Etchers and Engravers, the Canadian Soc of Graphic Art and a founding member of the Canadian Group of Painters.   CHRISTINE BOYANOSKI

Wood Buffalo National Park (44 840 km²), Canada's largest park, was established in 1922 to protect the last herd of wood BISON. Straddling the Alberta/NWT border, it includes 3 major environments: fire-scarred forested uplands; a poorly drained plateau etched with meandering streams and pocked with bogs; and the Peace-Athabasca delta, a water world of sedge meadows, marshes and shallow lakes. The park provides excellent habitat for a variety of wildlife. The bison herd has grown from fewer than 500 to over 5000. Moose, caribou, wolves and black bear are also plentiful. In the wetlands, muskrat, beaver and mink thrive; in the forests, fox, lynx, ermine and red squirrels. Waterfowl abound in the Delta. Over one million ducks, geese and swans pass through on MIGRATION; many remain to nest. The park is famous as the only nesting site for WHOOPING CRANES. The area has been inhabited by humans since the retreat of the glaciers. In recent centuries, nomadic Cree, Chipewyan and Beaver bands were integral to this ecosystem. Their descendants occupy the park and carry on fishing, hunting and trapping activities. LILLIAN STEWART

Salt plains in Wood Buffalo National Park, Alta, Canada's largest park (*courtesy Environment Canada, Parks/ Prairie & Northern Region*).

Wood Gundy Inc Founded in Toronto in 1905, the company evolved into a full-service international investment dealer with its head office in Toronto and offices in London, New York, Paris,

Tokyo, Hong Kong, Barbados and Shanghai. In Canada in 1986 the firm maintained 35 offices, located in 28 cities. The company was a leading underwriter and distributor of government and corporate securities in Canada and abroad. It was also prominent in mergers and acquisitions and in providing financial advisory services. With membership in all major stock exchanges in N America and an active participant in the European markets, it provided comprehensive facilities as agent and principal in bond, stock and money market transactions for institutional and retail investors supported by investment and economic research and professional investment management. The company was adversely affected by the stock-market crash of Oct 1987. Since early 1988 it has been 65% owned by the Canadian Imperial Bank of Commerce.   ARTHUR E. GREGG

Wood Mountain, elev 1000 m, is located about 135 km SW of MOOSE JAW, Sask, near the FORTY-NINTH PARALLEL. It is underlain by sedimentary rocks that were not eroded by downcutting rivers because of their position between drainage systems. Flat-topped hills, dissected by coulees, rise some 400 m above the surrounding prairie. Métis settled on the slopes of *Montagne de bois* in 1870, building houses from the plentiful poplar trees. In 1871 the HBC trading post at Wood Mt became the prairie depot of the Boundary Commission. Use of the area by whisky runners and horse thieves prompted the NWMP to purchase the depot in 1876 and maintain a post until 1918. Over 5000 Dakota Sioux and their leader, SITTING BULL, took refuge in this area after the Battle of the Little Bighorn in 1876. A provincial historic park was established in 1965. The only known sources of helium in Canada exist around Wood Mt and SWIFT CURRENT.   DAVID SAUCHYN

Woodcock, name given to 4 species of SHOREBIRDS of the SANDPIPER family (Scolopacidae). Woodcock occur in open woodlands with damp soil. Their characteristic long, straight bills are very flexible at the tip and can be opened below the soil surface to grasp prey (earthworms). The skull is much modified to accommodate the large eyes; hence, the ear openings are located under instead of behind the eyes as in other birds. American woodcock (*Scolopax minor*), the only species in Canada, breed in eastern N America from southern Canada to southern Texas, and winter in southern US.   A.J. BAKER

Woodcock, George, author, essayist, man of letters (b at Winnipeg 8 May 1912). Although most widely known as a literary journalist and historian, Woodcock has exerted a strong influence on political thinking as well as on cultural matters. He spent virtually all his first 37 years in England, and it was there that he was trained in British literary journalism, whose facility he transferred to the Canadian scene after his repatriation in 1949. Residence in the UK also meant that Woodcock was heir to the British radical tradition with its sense of historical continuity and its feeling that leftward progress is achieved partly by progress in the arts. His political beliefs are based on ANARCHISM, ie, the mutual non-involvement of the state and the individual — an ideology he gave voice to in the 1930s and 1940s through such editorial ventures as the magazines *Now* and *Freedom*. But when he sat down to write *Anarchism* (1962), his historical account of the movement, he did so with a sense that he was composing its obituary. The book, however, helped rekindle the principles of anarchism. Since then, Woodcock has been the pre-eminent figure in English-speaking anarchist circles and his book the movement's bible.

He began his writing life as a poet, with such

works as *The Centre Cannot Hold* (1943), and has returned to poetry in his later years, but poetry of a very different sort, bearing stylistic traces of Margaret ATWOOD and other Canadian poets whom he has long championed. Over the years he has also written many prose books – so many and on so many different subjects that they have tended to obscure his views even while boosting his reputation. Yet most of them can be fitted into various categories which, taken together, show both the breadth and the single-minded dedication of his life's work. First there are the purely political writings, such as his works on anarchists and pacificists, including *The Anarchist Prince: A Biographical Study of Peter Kropotkin* (1950) and *The Doukhobors* (1960) both co-authored with Ivan Avakumovic; *Pierre-Joseph Proudhon* (1956); and *Gandhi* (1971). Closely related are works combining history and travel, such as *Faces of India* (1964), *South Sea Journey* (1976) and *The Canadians* (1979), the latter being aimed at non-Canadians. More important are Woodcock's works of literary criticism, such as the books about his near contemporaries, eg, *Dawn and the Darkest Hour: A Study of Aldous Huxley* (1972) and *Thomas Merton, Monk and Poet* (1978). The best known of such works is *The Crystal Spirit* (1966, Gov Gen's Award), about George Orwell, who was Woodcock's cohort or antagonist in a number of early struggles. Also a part of Woodcock's literary criticism are his works on modern Canadian writers, eg, *The World of Canadian Writing* (1978) and *Northern Spring* (1986). Much of such material has its provenance in the quarterly journal, *Canadian Literature*, which Woodcock had founded at UBC in 1959 and edited until 1977. *Letters to the Past* (1982) and *Beyond the Blue Mountains* (1987) are volumes of autobiography, and *Taking It to the Letter* (1985) is a selection of his correspondence. DOUGLAS FETHERLING

Woodenware, or treen, simple, small objects made entirely of wood, usually by home craftsmen who were their own carpenters, joiners, carvers and turners. Normally, woodenware was made from a single piece of wood (block or plank, rough or milled), cut, hollowed or turned but rarely joined. Treen is always functional and utilitarian, of good form, made with simple techniques and easy to use. Wooden utensils, especially those associated with the preparation, serving and storage of food, are considered to be treen; ornamental objects (eg, carved figures, panels) are not.

In early Canada, treen items replaced costly and often unobtainable domestic objects normally made in Europe of glass, earthenware, stoneware, porcelain, china, silver or pewter. Even a pitchfork could be made of hardwood, the tines formed by making 2 parallel cuts and by using steam to bend the pieces. Wood was used because of its many practical qualities: it was durable, easily worked, recyclable and, most important, always available. The objects, worked one at a time during the long pioneer evenings, were made in the same useful shapes for hundreds of years. The familiar forms were copied from European models that remained unchanged from generation to generation. Great care was taken in selecting wood suitable for the purpose at hand, in order to provide the desired shape, colour, grain, strength or ornament. It was also very important to select the appropriate woodworking technique.

Canadian forests provided a good variety of hardwoods (eg, ash, birch, cherry, walnut, maple) and softwoods (eg, cedar, basswood, spruce, pine, poplar). New-felled timber, cut in planks, was usually left to season for at least one year before being used.

Hardwoods were used for objects in which weight and durability were important. For example, the hard, dense grain of maple, which can be lathe turned, was ideal for ladles, stirrers, breadboards, butter prints, spoons, mashers and rolling pins. Maple was often used in mallets because it could withstand constant pounding. Ash and hickory, exceptionally resilient hardwoods which can be bent without breaking, were steamed into hoops, box and wheel rims, and even bootjacks. The springiness of ash was extremely useful in the handles of mashers, mallets, hammers and axes because it was able to absorb the shock of each blow. Small bundles of fine birch twiglets or smooth hickory rods could be used as an eggbeater.

The bowls were made using a variety of techniques and methods. An adze or chisel could be used to hollow out the shape of a bowl; some bowls had handles carved right into the body of the piece. Bowls might also be made by lathe turning, using well-seasoned wood. Maple and ash were commonly used for turned bowls, but burls, abnormal protruding growths found on many hardwood species, were prized for use for carved or lathe-turned bowls. Although the attractive, erratic, dense grain of the burl was hard to work, it seldom split, and its resistance to water was useful. Their rarity is one reason why burl bowls have survived and are still prized.

Softwoods were employed in lightly used utensils. Pine, a lightweight, odourless and tasteless wood, was often selected for kitchen utensils. Maple sugar molds, introduced in Québec in the 18th century, were sometimes made of pine because its softness allowed it to be carved. A spoon or stirring rod could easily be whittled out of softwood and was easily replaced.

Carving was rarely done, because embellished decorating would be secondary to the utilitarian purpose of a treen item, although wood with an unusually figured grain was sometimes selected particularly for its decorative qualities. Pieces such as butter prints or maple sugar molds were exceptions; their carved decoration helped identify the product and make it more attractive to the user. "Print butter" was much sought after.

It is easy to detect the touch of the maker in a piece of treen. The variety of rolling pins, for example, shows that there was no single style; there would be as many variations of an object as makers. The rough-hewn rolling pin could be as functional as the smoothly sanded lathe-turned rolling pin. Each piece had small individual details; a handle might be grooved around its edge, or the knobs might be of varying shapes. It is easy to see these details as unselfconscious additions, produced quickly by the tool at hand, just before the rolling pin came off the lathe.

The maker of a woodenware object was also its user and the objects often reflect this close relationship. The maker could create an object according to his needs without taking any shortcuts in technique or material. Thus, beauty of form and love of craftsmanship were never divided from the utility of an object of treen. The work would express the craftsman's pride and reveal his cultural tradition. The object would be used until it was worn out, at which point it would be discarded and a new one made. Surviving examples of treen found today are thus among the most recent made and date only from the later 19th century. Human irreverence for objects of treen is not the only reason there are so few surviving examples. Wood is a vulnerable material which rots and warps, burns readily and wears with use. The use of woodenware began to diminish with the coming of industrialization in the 19th century. It became impractical to produce commonplace objects in wood when these items were so readily

and cheaply available in other, hardier materials.
CAROL BAUM

Woodhouse, Arthur Sutherland Piggott, teacher, scholar, humanist (b at Port Hope, Ont 27 Sept 1895; d at Toronto 31 Oct 1964). He was educated at U of T and Harvard, taught for 5 years at U of Man and joined the Faculty of English at U of T in 1928. He subsequently became head of the department at University College (1944-64) and head of the graduate department of English. An advocate of "historical criticism," he demonstrated his scholarship in a long series of essays on the work of John Milton, which led to *The Heavenly Muse* (1972). His contribution to the history of ideas includes studies in the Puritan revolution (*Puritanism and Liberty*, 1938), studies of nature and grace as intellectual framework in Renaissance literature, and studies of the evolution of the Romantic doctrine of the imagination. He fostered the growth of the humanities in Canada by writing in their defence, by editing the UNIVERSITY OF TORONTO QUARTERLY, and by administrative action. Three times president of the Humanities Research Council of Canada, he worked effectively for the support of pure research. The clarity, strength and zest of his scholarship were evident in his teaching. HUGH MACCALLUM

Woodpecker (Picidae), large family of climbing birds comprising 204 species. Thirteen woodpecker species occur in Canada. These are red-bellied, red-headed, Lewis's, hairy, downy, white-headed, three-toed, black-backed and pileated woodpeckers (*Centurus carolinus, Melanerpes erythrocephalus, Asyndesmus lewis, Picoides villosus, P. pubescens, P. albolarvatus, P. tridactylus, P. arcticus* and *Dryocopus pileatus,* respectively); yellow-bellied, red-breasted and Williamson's sapsuckers (*Sphyrapicus varius, S. ruber, S. thyroideus*); and northern flicker (*Colaptes auratus*). Woodpeckers have almost worldwide distribution. Most species are nonmigratory; however, many found in Canada migrate. Their flight is strong, rapid and undulating. These birds vary in length from 8 to 60 cm. Plumage can contain black, white, yellow, red, brown or green, in various combinations, and they often have red or yellow on the head. Many species are barred, spotted or streaked, especially on underparts; several have a prominent crest.

Woodpeckers are heavy bodied and have moderately long, rather rounded wings, and round or wedge-shaped tails. The chisel-shaped bill is strong and usually straight. Nostrils are hidden under tufts of bristlelike feathers. Usually, legs are short and strong with 2 toes in front and 2 behind. A few species (2 occur in Canada) have 3 toes, 2 in front and one behind. The toes have strong, sharp, downward-curving nails, allowing the birds to cling to vertical tree trunks or to undersides of branches. Stiffened, pointed tail feathers provide support when the birds climb up and down trees.

Woodpeckers rarely perch. They are primarily arboreal, although some species such as the northern flicker spend much of their life on the ground. With chisellike bills, woodpeckers dig into tunnels in wood where larvae of wood-boring insects live. Sapsuckers bore series of holes in the bark of deciduous trees to obtain running sap. Certain species (eg, northern flicker) secure ants by a sticky secretion of the salivary glands that covers the long, extensible tongue. Most species eat berries in season; some even snap insects in flight.

Woodpeckers excavate a cavity in a tree trunk or branch, rarely in a bank, for nesting. White eggs (2-8), laid on a layer of wood chips, are incubated by both parents. Young are naked at hatching and remain in the nesting cavity until ready to

Pileated woodpecker (*Dryocopus pileatus*) (*artwork by John Crosby*).

fly. They are cared for by both adults. Woodpeckers have a loud voice and a variety of call notes. They also drum with the bill, particularly during nesting season and when they have found a particularly resonant surface. They are very useful in destroying wood-boring larvae. Studies show that trees in which they dig holes contain larvae of wood-boring insects, even if they appear insect free. HENRI OUELLET

Woodstock, Ont, City, seat of Oxford County, pop 26 386 (1986c), 26 183 (1981c), inc as a city 1901, located on the Thames R, in the heart of SW Ontario. In 1792 Sir John Graves SIMCOE, impressed with the elevated terrain, designated the area as a potential townsite. The first settler, Zacharias Burtch, arrived in 1800, but a townsite was not surveyed until 1833 and 1834. A number of Sutherlandshire Scots arrived in 1830, followed by a group of retired army and navy officers from England. In 1834 British Adm Henry Vansittart, who had provided 700 acres in the area, arrived and named the village in honour of Woodstock, Oxfordshire, England, where he had been educated. It became seat of Oxford County in 1839. The census of 1851 placed the population at 2112 and Woodstock was officially proclaimed a town. A major point in development came in 1853, with the arrival of the GREAT WESTERN RY; rail connection to Toronto came in 1880. Located in the heart of a rich farming area, the town was a milling centre in its early years. Industries included rope, woollens, barrels, soap, candles, harnesses, carriages, furniture and organs. The Woodstock Iron Works were established in 1842. Standard Tube, still in operation, was established in 1905; it was the site of Canada's first electrical resistance welded tubing. The industrial variety, which prompted the town to dub itself the "Industrial City," has continued to include batteries, electric generators, hosiery, fire engines, reed organs, auto parts, etc. The yellow-brick town hall (built 1851-52) is a national historic site and houses a museum. DANIEL FRANCIS

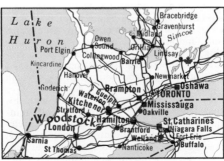

Woodstock, NB, Town, pop 4549 (1986c), 4649 (1981c), inc 1856, shire town of Carleton County, is located 103 km up the SAINT JOHN R from Fredericton, at the mouth of the Meduxnekeag R. It was possibly named for the community of the same name in Oxfordshire, Eng. The disbanded troops of the 2nd battalion of Delancey's were the initiators of Woodstock's development. Despite its LOYALIST tradition, the ethnic mix of the community rapidly changed and by the mid-19th century the town was the site of a riot between members of the Loyal Orange Order and Roman Catholics. By the beginning of the 20th century Woodstock was the site of sawmills, tanneries, harness shops, carriage factories, woodworking plants, a woollen mill, a canning factory and several foundries. With the development in the 1960s of a head pond for the Mactaquac Power project, much of the town's recreational area, on islands in the Saint John, was destroyed; new facilities have since replaced these. FRED FARRELL

Woodsworth, James Shaver, Methodist minister, social worker, politician (b at Etobicoke, Ont 29 July 1874; d at Vancouver 21 Mar 1942). First leader of the CO-OPERATIVE COMMONWEALTH FEDERATION (CCF), he was the best known of the reform-minded SOCIAL GOSPEL ministers and led many of them into the politics of democratic socialism. Woodsworth moved to Brandon, Man, in 1885 where his father became superintendent of Methodist missions in the Northwest. Ordained in 1896, he spent 2 years as a Methodist circuit rider in Manitoba and a further 2 years studying at Victoria College and Oxford.

Observing the grim results of industrial capitalism in Canada and Britain, Woodsworth concluded that his church's stress upon personal salvation was wrong. Moving from middle-class pulpits to a city mission, All People's, Winnipeg, he worked with immigrant slum dwellers 1904-13. At the same time he wrote extensively, expounding the "social gospel" – a creedless movement calling for establishment of the Kingdom of God "here and now." By 1914 he had become a controversial supporter of trade-union collective bargaining and an ardent democratic socialist – on Fabian and British Labour Party lines. He was also adamantly pacifist, seeing war as a product of capitalist and imperial competition, and he was fired from a governmental social-research position in 1917 for openly opposing CONSCRIPTION. In 1918 he resigned the ministry in protest against church support of the war. To support his young family he joined a longshoremen's union and worked for a year on the Vancouver docks.

In June 1919 Woodsworth was arrested in Winnipeg and charged with seditious libel for editorials written during the WINNIPEG GENERAL STRIKE. Following the arrest of 10 strike leaders on June 17 and "Bloody Saturday," June 21, when a nonviolent protest parade was broken up by mounted police and soldiers, Woodsworth had written about "Kaiserism" in Canada. The case was dropped although the charges, including Woodsworth's citing of 2 relevant verses from Isaiah, were never formally withdrawn. His popularity assured by his role in the strike, Woodsworth plunged with renewed zeal into the organizing work of the Manitoba Independent Labour Party. With a platform modelled on that of the British Labour Party, the ILP succeeded in electing Woodsworth to the House of Commons in 1921 for Winnipeg North Centre, with the slogan "Human Needs before Property Rights." While details of organization and policy would change, Woodsworth's principles remained constant as he held Winnipeg North Centre until his death in 1942.

In Parliament Woodsworth moved a resolution each session calling for replacement of capitalism's competitive profit motive with public and co-operative ownership of the means of production and distribution. Knowing his "co-operative commonwealth" would not arrive instantly, he worked tirelessly to promote immediate changes to benefit those who suffered most under the market system. Vigorously rejecting the shortcut of revolution, and any association with the new Communist Party, Woodsworth became a master of parliamentary procedure and used the Commons as a public platform. In so doing he helped establish a multiparty political system and his own reputation as the "conscience of Canada." He documented the government's hostility to labour; its timorous approach to the LEAGUE OF NATIONS; its antiquated procedures for parliamentary divorce; its refusal to enact promised social-security measures; and its compliant support of banking and other corporate legislation. In 1926 he demonstrated the worth of the parliamentary process when he bargained his vote (and that of one colleague) in return for a promise from the politically insecure PM Mackenzie KING to enact an OLD-AGE PENSION plan. Introduced in 1927, the plan was the cornerstone of Canada's social-security system.

Woodsworth collaborated in the 1920s with a "GINGER GROUP" of more radical Progressives. When the Depression struck, they joined with various labour and socialist groups to found a federal socialist party. At Regina in 1933 the new party adopted a democratic socialist manifesto and chose Woodsworth as its leader under the banner of Co-operative Commonwealth Federation. By 1935 the CCF had attracted the interest of a number of academics and professionals who joined together in the LEAGUE FOR SOCIAL RECONSTRUCTION and supported both the CCF and the lively political journal CANADIAN FORUM. Woodsworth was the spokesman for these people and for the unionists and farmers who looked to the CCF. Although the 1935 election sent only 7 CCFers to Ottawa, that little group included such political dynamos as T.C. DOUGLAS, and the party had become the official opposition in both BC and Saskatchewan.

For Woodsworth the tragedy of the Depression was increasingly overshadowed by the impending horror of WWII and he gave his attention to Canada's international position. Inside the CCF he faced the growing concern of some of his colleagues that Hitler's threat could only be met by force. Believing that war breeds only war he strove to persuade the government to declare Canada's right to neutrality. He failed, as he did in the CCF National Council in Sept 1939 which gave limited support to a Canadian declaration of war. "M.J." COLDWELL stated the official CCF position in the special parliamentary session while Woodsworth was permitted to explain his dissent. Reviewing the interwar period and repeating that war settles nothing, Woodsworth declared: "I rejoice that it is possible to say these things in a Canadian parliament under British institutions. It would not be possible in Germany, I recognize that… and I want to maintain the very essence of our British institutions of real liberty. I believe that the only way to do it is by an appeal to the moral forces which are still resident among our people, and not by another resort to brute force." He alone rose to record his opposition to the declaration of war. In 1940 Woodsworth won his last election with a sharply reduced majority. He was already weakened by a stroke and died in the spring of 1942. KENNETH McNAUGHT

Reading: G. MacInnis, *J.S. Woodsworth, A Man to Remember* (1953); Kenneth McNaught, *A Prophet in Politics* (1959); J.S. Woodsworth, *The Strangers Within Our Gates* (1908, repr 1972) and *My Neighbor* (1910, repr 1972).

Woodward, Charles, merchant, politician (b in Wentworth County, Canada W 19 July 1842; d at Vancouver 2 June 1937). After failing as a farmer and having mixed success as a merchant on Manitoulin I and at Thessalon, Ont, Woodward decided that Vancouver offered better opportunities. On 1 Mar 1892 he began selling boots, shoes and groceries. He added other lines and in 1902 incorporated Woodward Department Stores Ltd. In 1926 he opened a branch in Edmonton, Alta. Woodward always took an interest in public life. In 1924, after he was a millionaire and 2 of his sons had taken on many management responsibilities, Woodward ran as a Liberal candidate in the provincial election. He became senior member for the city but often clashed with the Liberal government of John OLIVER and J.D. MACLEAN over timber policy, the Pacific Great Eastern Ry and Vancouver's lack of representation in the Cabinet. Today a grandson, Charles Namby Wynn Woodward (b at Vancouver 1924), is chairman of the board and CEO of Woodward Stores Ltd, which had in 1986 annual sales of $1.1 billion and assets of $396 million. Charles ran the company until 1979 and now devotes much of his time to ranching; he owns Canada's largest ranch (Douglas Lake, BC).

PATRICIA E. ROY

Reading: D.E. Harker, The Woodwards (1976).

Work At different times in different cultures, work has been thought of as divine punishment, as an activity unworthy of free citizens, as the best possible way to accomplish the will of the Creator, or as the best possible way to earn a living. In modern Canadian society, work as the central activity around which social life revolves has been challenged in recent decades. The reduction in work hours, growing concerns about major changes in TECHNOLOGY and their impact on the form and content of work, and strong signs of dissatisfaction with work indicate that "work" may be on the threshold of a new era. Until the 20th century Canada was a traditional RURAL SOCIETY in which work was directly related to the production of life's staples but was also important in the individual's social life. The purposes and circumstances of farming activities of production were part of the general organization of society. The independent workers (farmers or artisans) often owned their own means of production, organized their work as they wished and sold their produce themselves.

Despite the independence and the nature of the work (both of which distinguished farmers from shop or factory workers), traditional farmers still did arduous and demanding work with rudimentary tools. The result of their labours depended largely on the caprices of temperature and climate; they were often as bound to local merchants and moneylenders for funds to acquire land, animals, etc, as were workers in town to their employer. Many farmers, to earn money to cover their farming expenses, became seasonal employees.

Work in the other resource industries was no easier. The early FUR TRADE demanded great endurance, and the portages were strewn with the graves of VOYAGEURS who expired under their heavy loads. Forestry work attracted rural youth, peasants and immigrants, but it was seasonal and required great physical endurance (*see* TIMBER TRADE HISTORY). The workers lived in primitive lodgings and worked long days on meagre rations (beans, fresh beef, salted bacon and lard were not introduced to the menu until the 1850s). In the spring, the work was dangerous and demanded great agility. The drivers (raftsmen) worked 16-hour days, often in icy water up to their waists. This was also the age when squared logs were floated in log booms down the Ottawa and St Lawrence rivers to Québec City, a voyage of about 2 months.

Fishing was another seasonal activity with long hours for highly variable results that depended on the whims of climate and the availability of fish. Earnings fluctuated with the market, making it hard for fishermen to survive without supplementary work in agriculture or forestry (*see* FISHERIES HISTORY).

In secondary industry, it was the age of the independent producer of commodities, such as furniture, and of the establishment of carding houses, sawmills, flour mills, breweries and distilleries, tanneries and foundries. The work was usually done in small shops employing 3 or 4 men, eg, the proprietor, a master artisan, one or 2 companions and a few apprentices. Employer-employee relationships were paternalistic, especially in the APPRENTICESHIP system. For 3-10 years, the apprentice was bound by a contract under which his master was virtually his father. The apprentice could not absent himself without his master's permission, could not marry and was sworn to keep the secrets of his master's trade. In return, the master had to provide the apprentice with food, lodging and an acceptable amount and quality of education. However, the apprenticeship system became a form of bonded labour rather than a craft-training program accompanied by moral and educational supervision. As the masters accumulated capital, increased their production demands and took on more apprentices to do the dirty and often unskilled work required in the shop, apprentices experienced only the tyranny of their obligations and resented their masters' inadequate or totally nonexistent compliance with their own responsibilities.

Qualified artisans, who prior to the 20th century comprised about 10% of the urban labour force, formed a well-paid workers' aristocracy whose social status was closer to that of the middle class. A craftsman earned twice as much as a day-labourer, 4 times as much as a domestic servant. WOMEN IN THE LABOUR FORCE and children in the labour force were the most poorly paid, and one worker in 5 lived in extreme poverty.

A working-class culture had already appeared in the FOOTWEAR INDUSTRY and TEXTILE INDUSTRY and among the French Canadian workers who floated the log booms to Québec City and workers (usually IRISH) in the canal-building construction camps. Work conditions were hard, hours long. Monthly salaries were low and were often paid in the form of chits that could only be used in the company store, where the price of merchandise was invariably inflated. Entrepreneurs frequently disappeared without paying the labourers, who were generally charged high rents for miserable quarters where the hygiene standards often led to EPIDEMICS of cholera, fever and other illnesses.

Work and the Industrial Revolution In Canada, as in other Western countries, the development of a free-market ECONOMY that accompanied industrialization drastically altered the nature of work for most individuals. Work lost its intrinsic value and became a way to earn a living, a commodity to buy and sell like other goods. The evolution of society progressively eliminated the direct relationship between the productive effort of individuals and the consumption of goods and services.

As Canada's rural economy, based on self-sufficiency, changed to an industrial economy characterized by an increasingly more sophisticated and complex system of production and exchange, production enterprises themselves were transformed, the number of occupations increased, work conditions and organization changed, and work took on a new meaning in relationship to the other activities of life.

In the mid-19th century, with the development of means of TRANSPORTATION (CANALS, RAILWAYS) and the appearance of the steam engine, the first factories and large businesses appeared in the major urban centres (Montréal, Hamilton, Toronto) in the tobacco and textile industries, in foundries, and in the railway-supplies business. The demand for unskilled labour (especially for construction gangs) and the numbers of skilled workers (eg, carpenters, bricklayers, tailors, and foundry and leather workers) grew rapidly. At this time the traditional enterprises, eg, small stores, offices, craft and manufacturing shops (businesses in which several craftsmen and apprentices still did handwork), were still very important. These enterprises were still unspecialized; each worker created the product from start to finish. Employer-employee relations remained largely personal; production continued to be primarily determined by commissions received.

The turning point came in the last third of the 19th century with the introduction of the factory system, in which workers were considered a cost of production. To minimize costs, businesses tried to "rationalize" production by eliminating the freedom of the small workshop, by closely regulating working hours, increasing the work pace and reducing skill levels where possible. The system, which spread everywhere, was based on techniques of co-ordination, supervision and discipline of the work force.

Workers laboured under a harsh system of disciplinary measures (eg, they were forbidden to talk, to leave their posts, to be late) and of punitive ones (fines, dismissals, physical abuse), which were later complemented with more sophisticated techniques of persuasion, manipulation and economic incentives. The "sweatshop system" (which still exists), under which maximum labour was extracted from workers for minimum salary and in conditions where the usual rules of health and comfort were ignored, appeared at this time, especially in the textile and food industries. This system was linked with contract and subcontract labour carried out in the workers' homes.

The new system of exploitation was described in the Royal Commission on the Relations of Labour and Capital (1889): meals taken at the work post; lack of job security; poor protection against the belts, pullies and steam engines; lack of compensation for victims of industrial accidents; crowded and unhealthy conditions; authoritarian discipline; widespread child labour; frequent unemployment; and permanent material insecurity.

The processes of concentration, centralization and bureaucratization of businesses accelerated after the turn of the century with the increase in the size of businesses and industries. The work process became even more rationalized and specialized. Companies needed more administrators, managers and intermediaries and clerical help. Furthermore, the increasing mechanization, fragmentation and simplification of work created a growing demand for unskilled labour. This heavy demand was met by the use of IMMIGRANT LABOUR for the most unpleasant, dirty, dangerous and ill-paid positions. Many immigrants were (and are) "BUNKHOUSE MEN," the do-anything labourers found in isolated regions, employed in the big construction camps for railways, hydroelectric dams and industrial projects, and in lumber camps.

The COMPANY TOWN appeared along with this rapid development of primary (especially mining) and secondary (textiles, pulp and paper, etc) industries. In these new industrial centres, which sprang up like mushrooms, the employer controlled not only the work but also all the other institutions and material facilities necessary to the life of the population: housing, stores, water and sewage systems, etc. These centres were concentrated in Ont, Qué and BC.

The factory system, which by 1920 had virtually eliminated craft production, underwent at this time a particularly marked refinement of its policies and methods of co-ordination, supervision and work specialization through the introduction of the scientific administration of work and the techniques of mass production. Under this scientific administration, work was characterized by a more complex division of labour, based on the increased separation of the conceptualization of work (mental work) and its execution (manual work), by the assignment of a specific task to each worker through very precise selection procedures, by the simplification and compartmentalization of tasks, by the regulation of the rhythm of work, by economic incentives, and by an increase in foremen and managerial cadres.

The objective of this new system was to reduce as much as possible the real control over work processes (methods, standards, pace) which skilled industrial workers had retained despite the new managerial policies. Mass-production techniques (essentially the assembly line introduced by Henry Ford in the AUTOMOTIVE INDUSTRY) reinforced the principles of precision, economy, continuity, speed and repetition.

Workers reacted in a variety of ways to the profound changes in work and working conditions. Individually, they resorted to industrial sabotage, insubordination, absenteeism, occupational mobility, the refusal of work; collectively, they used demonstrations, such as the WINNIPEG GENERAL STRIKE, the ON TO OTTAWA TREK during the GREAT DEPRESSION, pickets, various forms of STRIKE, and above all the formation of LABOUR ORGANIZATIONS. A federal law of 1872 had removed workers' associations from the provisions of criminal law, but not until almost 30 years later were federal laws protecting workers adopted (eg, the 1900 Conciliation Act on voluntary conciliation and ARBITRATION, and the federal Industrial Disputes Investigation Act of 1907 concerning inquiries into industrial disputes). Among the first laws regulating working conditions were the manufacturing laws adopted in 1884 in Ontario and in 1885 in Québec; those concerning work by women and children adopted in Québec in 1910; and those concerning work-related accidents adopted in Québec in 1909 and in Ontario in 1914.

Most of these early protective laws were hard to apply and often inoperative because of highly inadequate and almost toothless inspection services; but once workers' unions were recognized, LABOUR LAW developed into an increasingly complex institutional apparatus and labour laws were progressively improved and broadened. SOCIAL SECURITY legislation also developed considerably in the postwar years.

Work Today

The development of increasingly large and concentrated factories and businesses was marked by extensive mechanization and automation which greatly eased the physical burden of work. However, the physical environment of modern work exposes workers to the risks of poor ventilation, excessive heat and noise, dust and air POLLUTION, and exposure to toxic gas, acids and radioactive substances (*see* OCCUPATIONAL DISEASES). Also, despite its diversity, work is characterized in most cases by repetitive, meaningless, narrow and specialized tasks which require little skill and training and involve little responsibility. Semiskilled workers who may have developed certain skills while learning a specific task in a specific context usually find these skills worthless if they change jobs.

Whatever the workplace – a small business with paternalistic employer-employee relations or a large one where authority is bureaucratic and

impersonal – most workers must follow orders and directives telling them the purpose of their work, its methods and pace, and even behaviour patterns that are only indirectly related to the work itself.

Working for oneself (eg, in SMALL BUSINESS) has always been an attractive way to escape the problems associated with wage labour, but the joys of such an escape are often illusory. For many, the dream ends in bankruptcy; for the successful minority, it takes long hours of hard, stubborn work and many disillusionments.

Almost half of the active and experienced LABOUR FORCE in Canada now belongs to nonmanual occupational groups; known as the tertiary sector, it includes office workers, specialized cadres and technicians, administrators, salespeople and commercial workers. The growth in this sector has been most sustained and impressive among office workers, administrators, and specialized workers and technicians. This growth has been attributed to the increased size of businesses and multinational activities, the growing complexity of financial activities, the increased importance of marketing, and the growth in the creation and processing of information.

Until the 1920s, clerical work was not as mechanized or rationalized as manual labour, but since then and especially since WWII, office and saleswork has been progressively mechanized, specialized, downgraded and simplified. Most of it is now carried on in the impersonal world of the major corporations where a clear gap exists between employees and supervisors. The so-called "professional" nonmanual occupations (administrators, specialized cadres and technicians), which offer the most interesting work and should have retained considerable autonomy, have also been affected. The very idea of the professions has been changed. Because of the prestige associated with those who carry out professional activities in Canada, many nonmanual occupational groups have tried to win social and governmental recognition for their activities (eg, real-estate salespeople, hairdressers). The traditional idea of profession has been so extended that observers speak of the "professionalization" of the labour force. In fact, the attributes of professional activities (the knowledge and abilities required to exercise the profession, the nature of the professional activity, the nature of the relationship between the professional and the client, and professional autonomy) have lost much of their specific character or have been transformed.

Traditionally the acquisition of specialized knowledge through lengthy training constituted the essential element of a profession. But the average training level for workers and the training and apprenticeship requirements in many occupations (eg, airline pilots) have risen considerably as a result of industrial and technological progress and their corollaries (eg, rising educational levels in the population, increased job specialization). The idea of service is no longer exclusive to the professions, and because of technological developments, many of these specialized service activities have become as difficult to conduct and evaluate, and as weighted with consequence for the eventual clients and for society, as the traditional professional activities.

In the past, the typical professional-client relationship (modelled on the medical profession) was based on confidentiality, the total responsibility of the professional, and the unique and specific nature of each professional decision. These elements are no longer part of most professional activities. The client is often not a person but a business, a group or an institution, and the question of confidentiality occurs in a different context. As well, professionals are now often

salaried employees and are no longer the only people privy to confidential information or involved in decision making.

Finally, the idea of professional autonomy, whereby practitioners work for themselves in private practice (only 10% of those with professional training), has been shattered by the increasing phenomenon of salaried professionals (eg, engineers, doctors and lawyers) and by the appearance of professions composed largely of employees of businesses, establishments or institutions. In these cases, professionals who are in specialized cadres or are technicians are subject to a bureaucratic organization of their work. Their authority and professional autonomy is further reduced by their obedience to the political objectives (in the public sector) or the profit objectives (in the private sector) of their employers. These professionals, whose numbers and central role in production are constantly growing, remain caught between their knowledge and skills on the one hand and, on the other, their narrow sphere of activities and their limited freedom. It is therefore not surprising that some groups, eg, doctors, engineers, teachers, nurses, have virtually abandoned professional objectives (and with them at least part of their control over their labour) and have formed their own labour unions.

Employers are caught up in rapid technological change and constant market shifts that require them to adapt rapidly to changes in products and services. As they did in the past, they seek solutions to labour problems through new forms of work organization; however, today these forms include quality-of-life programs designed to give more room to workers' desire for autonomy, responsibility, creativity and conviviality. Tasks have been upgraded and workers' groups have been given greater autonomy, eg, semiautonomous production circles. Some employers have eliminated time clocks, have introduced flex-time and shortened hours, and have designed programs (eg, suggestion programs, various joint consultative committees on issues such as productivity, welfare, health and job security) to increase the workers' participation and interest in their work. Profit-sharing and other forms of financial participation have also been tried. The goal of all these efforts is to increase the workers' identification with the company and their motivation and thus increase productivity. These new organizational forms have not been widely applied and the advantages for workers are still unclear. Essentially, the wage-earning system remains unchanged.

Finally new forms of employment have developed in which the position of workers is generally precarious, eg, part-time, free-lance or contract work, interim work and shared jobs. These kinds of employment use the condition or needs of certain categories of workers (eg, working mothers, students, handicapped and older workers), to meet the needs of businesses (decreased labour costs and more flexible response to production fluctuations) and of the governmental authorities (spreading available employment over more workers).

The present preoccupation with working conditions marks a change in perspective towards various aspects of work, eg, organization of work, interpersonal relations, and HEALTH and safety. There is less attention to the purely functional concept of work and more recognition that the quality of a wage earner's working life affects off-the-job quality of life as well.

Youth and Work Between 1953 and 1984, the number of young people (under 25 years) in the labour force grew from 1.3 million to 2.8 million, but by 1987 it had declined to 2.3 million. In hard economic times, because of their inexperience and lack of seniority and training, they are usually the first to be laid off. Thus they have a disproportionately high UNEMPLOYMENT rate. They also have the highest rate of job mobility, though it is often involuntary. Those who voluntarily change jobs (the best educated, the unmarried or the young married without children) usually do so for experience. But for many, job changes are an expression of their unhappiness with modern work – both its intrinsic aspects and its material conditions. Many young people, children of a more liberal society, tend to challenge traditional forms of authority in the workplace. Better educated than their elders and accustomed to a higher standard of living, they seek more demanding and more enriching work which will use the capabilities developed by their education.

Work, Education and Training Not so long ago, the (usually limited) training received at school would see people through their professional careers. They entered the work force young, having undergone an apprenticeship which often began in the family and continued on the job. Today, given the social demand for general and diversified education and the need for skilled labour, a diploma is essential. Young people are entering the labour force at a later age all the time.

During the prosperous 1950s and 1960s, a diploma was the passport to the more interesting jobs. Since 1970, and especially in a period of economic crisis, the diploma no longer guarantees a job in a given occupational category. Educational level is often used as a pretext for stricter selection and the assurance of the individuals' ability to adapt to the procedures of the organization of production. Young people now enter the work force in more difficult conditions, and many of them must make do with occasional and part-time work. Moreover, their prior training offers less guarantee of career advancement. Technological progress, office reorganization, the shift toward employment in the tertiary sector, unemployment or its threat, the possibility and the attractions of job mobility, and the search for a higher standard of living are all incentives leading adults in ever-greater numbers to seek supplementary training at some stage in their working life.

While this training can be found in educational institutions, businesses (especially the biggest ones) have also begun offering professional training to increase the productivity of their work force. These courses are usually short, focusing on a particular task or job function and dealing with immediate needs. They are largely controlled by the corporation, and usually favour managers and professionals over unskilled labourers.

Women and Work The proportion of women in the labour force has risen from 20% in 1921 to more than 56% by late 1987. This rapid growth is mainly due to the rising number of working wives (11% in 1951; 53% in 1987).

The growing number of working women may have a profound long-term effect on the nature and organization of work itself, but so far the repercussions are limited and the structure of female jobs has remained static. Women are usually found in traditionally "female" occupations (eg, office work, sales, teaching, hospital services and light industry). Those who venture into traditionally male strongholds still suffer discrimination. Working conditions in female jobs are usually characterized by longer work hours, unusual shifts, lack of job security, and systematic pay and benefits discrimination in those jobs (which comprise the majority) not covered by collective agreements. Although they are usually better educated than men, women generally hold junior positions and dead-end jobs.

The explosion in part-time work (at the present rate, by the year 2000 more than half of all workers will have part-time jobs) has occurred in such a way that most of the people so employed are women. The concentration of women in precarious jobs and in the tertiary sector largely explains their higher unemployment rate (in late 1987, 47.3% of the unemployed though only 40% of the working population) and the fact that they are especially threatened by the technological changes being wrought by the microelectronic revolution.

Various legislative measures (eg, against job discrimination, in favour of maternity leave), passed because of pressure from the women's movement and from trade unions, have improved conditions for women who already work and are an incentive for more women to seek salaried employment. But major improvements are still needed, especially in the application of these laws. The idea of women working outside the home is better accepted today, but traditional attitudes have not disappeared. Recently, a poll revealed that the majority of men and women still feel that a woman's place is in the home.

Work and Retirement Because of the sharp rise in life expectancy, more attention is being paid to the relationship between work and the quality of life in retirement years. The nature and conditions of work and its level of remuneration have a determining influence not only on workers' standard of living during retirement (especially on their income) but also on their state of physical and mental health. These preoccupations have intensified in the last 20 years because of the strong trend toward earlier retirement.

Several factors have caused this trend, eg, the establishment of obligatory retirement at age 65 and universal public PENSION programs and voluntary private ones; the desire for more active lives outside the job; and the rise in incomes that allows more people to retire before age 65. As well, competition in the labour market and the effects of technological change mitigate against employing older workers. Lowering the retirement age has become a popular way of reducing the labour force. Governments and businesses have introduced early-retirement incentive programs, the former to fight unemployment and the latter to reduce the numbers and costs of their labour forces.

Yet for both economic and social reasons, a counter trend has recently developed against obligatory retirement. Social-security measures have failed to assure most workers and their dependents of a satisfactory level of material security. In the mid-1970s, more than half the retired people in Canada needed a guaranteed income supplement to stay above the POVERTY line. Moreover, the rapid AGING of the population raises the problem of insufficient pension funds. From the social point of view, retired workers find themselves socially isolated, marginalized, and insecure. The abolition of obligatory retirement (Québec was the first province to do so) allows staggered retirements that better respect the needs, circumstances and hopes of individual workers.

Work and Technology The application of information technologies based on microelectronics in communications (ie, the switching and transmission of information) in business through word-processing machines and in manufacturing through robotics has amounted to a technological revolution (*see* COMPUTER COMMUNICATIONS; COMPUTERS AND SOCIETY; OFFICE AUTOMATION).

The productivity gains being realized in the quantity and structure of employment will undoubtedly cause a significant reduction in clerical and low-ranking specialized jobs in the tertiary sector, the sector most affected by these changes and the most important sector (accounting for more than 60% of Canada's labour force) in modern economies. These losses will likely be only partially balanced by the creation of new specialized and professional jobs in the industries producing and using the new technologies. Though the professional structure in place since the turn of the century will undergo profound changes, it is very unlikely that Canada will be left with only 2 kinds of workers, ie, those who push the buttons and those who invent the programs and technologies. It is more likely that workers in the traditional trades and operators will be replaced by technicians and workers specialized in maintenance, tooling, information technologies and electronics. The move to an information age could therefore lead to greater uniformity of skills (*see* INFORMATION SOCIETY).

The content and organization of work will also be affected. In the past, technological progress had contradictory effects: reduced physical labour and increased salaries versus highly specialized jobs and increased job pace and controls. Today's changes will also have contradictory effects which may well accentuate trends from the past. The new technologies will make it possible to eliminate many repetitive, dangerous manual jobs and to create new tasks connected with the control, supervision and maintenance of automatons. However, the technologies may also increase the compartmentalization and repetitive nature of some tasks which until now could not be simplified and downgraded. It is also possible that there will be tighter controls over workers and a faster job pace, an increased sense of isolation on the job because of reduced interaction, and new health and job-security problems (eg, stress-producing conditions, different types of fatigue and physical ills from radiation exposure). Finally, the new technologies could lead to the development of work teams, to job decentralization into smaller work units, work at a distance (eg, working at home), increased use of contract workers, and more flexible and shorter hours.

Future of Work Work is both an instrumental activity (ie, it creates social status and personal independence) and a liberating, creative activity through which individuals may shape and express their own identities. In Canadian society today, work for most people is almost entirely instrumental. Can it also become a free and creative activity? The changes now underway may cause work to lose its exclusively instrumental nature and to take on new significance within a socioeconomic balance where the relationships of production, which are based on the private ownership of the means of production, will be replaced by relationships based on principles of co-determination or social self-management.

More probably, however, organized work will remain instrumental in nature. If so, it is possible that the production and consumption cycle will be perpetuated; increased productivity will allow higher wages and increased consumption; and organized work will remain a central activity. On the other hand, organized work may remain instrumental but may lose its central position in society. Productivity gains might lead to shorter work hours, leaving more time for other activities, including independent or self-chosen work. This work would consist of the production of goods and services for personal use, or for exchange outside the organized market. People's desire for part-time work is an expression of their desire for greater control over their own time. Further reduction in organized working hours (eg, the 32-hour week) may lead people to pay more attention to their other activities, particularly to work of their own choosing, rather than simply to recreation. *See also* WORKING-CLASS HISTORY.

CAMILLE LEGENDRE

Workers' Compensation, legislation designed to provide benefits, medical care and rehabilitation services to individuals who suffer workplace injuries or contract OCCUPATIONAL DISEASES. Prior to workers' compensation legislation, workplace accidents were dealt with entirely under the common law (see TORT). In practice, this meant that workers could sue employers with some probability of success only if they could establish employer negligence. In the absence of a more widespread compensation plan, many trade unions maintained their own accident funds but these covered only a minority of the labour force. In 1889 the Royal Commission on the Relations of Labour and Capital reported the high level of injury among workers and condemned the oppressiveness of working conditions in many industries. It made many important recommendations to improve working conditions, but the federal government claimed that to act upon them would constitute an infringement of provincial authority. The premise of modern workers' compensation legislation is that some level of injury is inevitable and that compensation should be provided without regard to responsibility. The Ontario Workmen's Compensation Act of 1914 was the first Canadian statute to accept this principle. It served as a model for provincial legislation in NS (1915), BC (1916), Alberta (1918) and NB (1918). Workers' compensation Acts now exist in all Canadian jurisdictions and provide medical rehabilitation services as well as financial benefits.

The range of workers covered under compensation varies from province to province. Initially, only workers in hazardous industries were included, but now the law applies to almost every industry and 70-90% of workers are covered. In most jurisdictions, however, agricultural labourers, domestic workers, casual workers and outworkers are not covered by the legislation, although in some provinces inclusion can be obtained by application or other special means. Benefit levels are based on previous earnings with the general formula being that 75% of wages are replaced by compensation payments up to a legal maximum. Financing procedures and contribution rates to workers' compensation funds vary, but in all jurisdictions the fund is financed exclusively by employer contributions. These contributions are calculated on the probability of accident in different industrial groupings. For example, firms in industries with very few accidents and with few employees drawing compensation benefits might pay as little as 25¢ per $100 of payroll, while other firms in industries that record more accidents and more claims on the system might pay $15 per $100 of payroll. The system is similar to an insurance policy in which high-risk customers pay higher premiums.

Workers' compensation plays a major role in alleviating hardship caused by injuries or death, but because its major contribution is the provision of compensation to individuals after accidents occur, it is only part of a broader set of policies aimed at reducing accidents and producing a safer work place. See also LABOUR POLICY; INDUSTRIAL RELATIONS.
                                                           D.A. SMITH

Workers' Educational Association, was founded in Toronto in 1918 by university professors and trade unionists interested in providing, on the model of the British WEA, noncredit evening classes for working people. In its heyday during the 1930s and 1940s, funds from provincial and federal sources, the Carnegie Foundation, the labour movement, and tuition fees enabled the WEA in centres across Canada to offer courses on such subjects as economics, current events, labour history and collective bargaining.

In the early 1950s, the organization shrank drastically in the face of competing programs in adult education and opponents who erroneously labelled the WEA "communist dominated."
                                                           IAN RADFORTH

Workers Unity League (WUL) This national trade union federation was formed in 1929 on the initiative of the COMMUNIST PARTY OF CANADA in line with the decision of the Communist International (Comintern) in 1928 that communists break with their previous policy of working inside existing labour parties and labour unions to push for more militant stances. The new policy stressed the need for revolutionary organizations independent of the existing "class collaborationist" labour leadership. The WUL was the major labour organization in Canada during the early Depression period. It attempted to organize semiskilled and unskilled as opposed to crafts workers. Particularly active among miners and lumber workers, it also enjoyed support among industrial workers in southern Ontario and among unemployed organizations. It was disbanded in 1935 when the international communist line shifted back to calls for a united labour front, this time in the face of the international fascist threat. Though its membership never exceeded 40 000, the WUL accounted for most strikes in the early 1930s and its organizers went on to provide many key organizers for the CIO-CCL unions.   ALVIN FINKEL

Working-Class History is the story of the changing conditions and actions of all working people. Most adult Canadians today earn their living in the form of wages and salaries and thus share the conditions of dependent employment associated with the definition of "working class." The Canadian worker has been a neglected figure in Canadian history and, although Canadians have always worked, working-class history has received little attention. Until recently, the most common form of working-class history has been the study of the trade union, or labour, movement (unions are organizations formed by workers in order to strengthen their position in dealing with employers and sometimes with governments). Although the development of organized labour provides a convenient focus for the discussion of working-class history, it is important to remember that most working people, past and present, have not belonged to unions: in 1987 only 37.6% of all nonagricultural paid workers in Canada belonged to unions. However, because unions have often pursued goals designed to benefit all workers, the labour movement has won a place in Canadian society. Canadian workers have contributed in many ways to the development of Canadian society, but the history of working people, in their families, communities and work places, is only gradually becoming part of our view of the Canadian past. Canadian historians have often studied the various Canadian cultural and regional identities, but the working-class experience is now proving to be one of the unifying themes in Canadian history (see WORK).

English Canada

The working class emerged during the 19th century in English Canada as a result of the spread of industrial capitalism in British North America. At the time, it was common for many Canadians to support themselves as independent farmers, fishermen and craftworkers. Entire families contributed to the production of goods (see CHILDHOOD, HISTORY OF). The growing differentiation between rich and poor in the countryside, the expansion of resource industries (see RESOURCE USE), the construction of canals and railways, the growth of cities and the rise of manufacturing all helped create a new kind of work force in which

Knights of Labor procession, King Street, Hamilton, Ont, 1885 (*courtesy National Archives of Canada/PA-103086*).

the relationship between employer and employee was governed by a capitalist labour market and where women and children no longer participated to as great an extent. COMPANY TOWNS, based on the production of a single resource such as coal, emerged during the colonial period and provided a reserve of skilled labour for the company and a certain degree of stability for the workers. When violence erupted, the companies' responses varied from closing the company-owned store to calling in the militia. DOMESTIC SERVICE (servants, housekeepers, etc) emerged as the primary paid employment for women. CHILD LABOUR reached its peak in the late 19th and early 20th centuries, supplemented by IMMIGRANT CHILDREN brought from Britain by various children's aid societies. The workers were often cruelly exploited, and for any worker, job security and assistance in the event of illness, injury or death were almost nonexistent.

For most of the 19th century, unions were usually small, local organizations. Often they were illegal: in 1816 the Nova Scotia government prohibited workers from bargaining for better hours or wages and provided prison terms as a penalty. Nevertheless, workers protested their conditions, with or without unions, and sometimes violently. Huge, violent strikes took place on the Welland and Lachine canals in the 1840s. Despite an atmosphere of hostility, by the end of the 1850s local unions had become established in many Canadian centres, particularly among skilled workers such as printers, shoemakers, moulders, tailors, coopers, bakers and other tradesmen. The labour movement gained cohesiveness when unions created local assemblies and forged ties with British and American unions in their trade. In 1872 workers in Ontario industrial towns and in Montréal rallied behind the NINE-HOUR MOVEMENT, which sought to reduce the working day from up to 12 hrs to 9 hrs. Hamilton's James Ryan, Toronto's John HEWITT and Montréal's James Black led the workers. Toronto printers struck against employer George BROWN, and in Hamilton, on 15 May 1872, 1500 workers paraded through the streets. The ambitiously titled CANADIAN LABOR UNION, formed in 1873, spoke for unions mainly in southern Ontario. It was succeeded in 1883 by the TRADES AND LABOR CONGRESS OF CANADA, which became a lasting forum for Canadian labour. In Nova Scotia the Provincial Workmen's Association (1879) emerged as the voice of the coal miners and later spoke for other Maritime workers. The most important organization of this era was the KNIGHTS OF LABOR, which organized more than 450 assemblies with more than 20 000 members across the country. The Knights were an INDUSTRIAL UNION which brought together workers regardless of craft, race (excepting Chinese) or sex. Strongest in Ontario, Québec and BC, the Knights were firm believers in economic and social democracy, and were often critical of the developing industrial, capitalist society. Key Knights included A.W. WRIGHT, Thomas Phillips THOMPSON and Daniel J. O'DONOGHUE.

By the late 19th century the "labour question" had gained recognition. The Toronto printers' strike of 1872 led PM Sir John A. MACDONALD to introduce the Trade Unions Act, which stated that unions were not to be regarded as illegal conspiracies. The Royal Commission on the Relations of Labour and Capital, which reported in 1889, documented the sweeping impact of industrialization in Canada, and the commissioners strongly defended unions as a suitable form of organization for workers: "The man who sells labor should, in selling it, be on an equality with the man who buys it." Another sign of recognition came in 1894 when the federal government officially adopted LABOUR DAY as a national holiday falling on the first Monday in Sept.

The consolidation of Canadian capitalism in the early 20th century accelerated the growth of the working class. From the countryside, and from Britain and Europe, hundreds of thousands of people moved to Canada's booming cities and tramped through Canada's industrial frontiers (*see* BUNKHOUSE MEN). Most workers remained poor, their lives dominated by a struggle for the economic security of food, clothing and shelter; by the 1920s most workers were in no better financial position than their counterparts had been a generation earlier. Not surprisingly, most strikes of this time concerned wages, but workers also went on strike to protest working conditions, unpopular supervisors and new rules, and to defend workers who were being fired. Skilled workers were particularly alarmed that new machinery and new ideas of management were depriving them of some traditional forms of workplace authority.

Despite growing membership, divisions appeared between unions, and this limited their effectiveness. The most aggressive organizers were the CRAFT UNIONS, whose membership was generally restricted to the more skilled workers. Industrial unions were less common, though some, such as the United Mine Workers, were important. The American Federation of Labor (fd 1886, *see* AFL-CIO) unified American craft unions and, under Canadian organizer John FLETT, chartered more than 700 locals in Canada between 1898 and 1902; most were affiliated with the TLC. At the TLC meetings in 1902 the AFL craft unions voted to expel any Canadian unions, including the Knights of Labor, in jurisdictional conflict with the American unions, a step which deepened union divisions in Canada. The attitudes of government were also a source of weakness. Though unions were legal, they had few rights under the law. Employers could fire union members at will, and there was no law requiring employers to recognize a union chosen by their workers. In strikes employers could ask governments to call out the troops and militia in the name of law and order, as happened on more than 30 occasions before 1914 (*see*, for example, FORT WILLIAM FREIGHT HANDLERS STRIKE). With the creation of the Dept of Labour in 1900, the federal government became increasingly involved in dispute settlement. The Industrial Disputes Investigation Act (1907), the brainchild of William Lyon Mackenzie KING, required that some important groups of workers, including miners and railwaymen, must go through a period of conciliation before they could engage in "legal" strikes. Since employers were still free to ignore the unions, dismiss employees, bring in strikebreakers and call for military aid, unions came to oppose this legislation.

Men and women workers in a textile plant, c1908 (*courtesy City of Toronto Archives/James Coll 137*).

One of the most important developments in the prewar labour movement was the rise of REVOLUTIONARY INDUSTRIAL UNIONISM, an international movement which favoured the unification of all workers into one labour body to overthrow the capitalist system and place workers in control of political and economic life. The INDUSTRIAL WORKERS OF THE WORLD, founded in Chicago in 1905, rapidly gained support among workers in western Canada such as navvies, fishermen, loggers and railway workers. The "Wobblies" attracted nationwide attention in 1912 when 7000 illtreated immigrant railway workers in the Fraser Canyon struck against the CANADIAN NORTHERN RY. A number of factors, including government suppression, hastened its demise during the war.

WWI had an important influence on the labour movement. While workers bore the weight of the war effort at home and paid a bloody price on the battlefield, many employers prospered. Labour was excluded from wartime planning and protested against CONSCRIPTION and other wartime measures. Many workers joined unions for the first time and union membership grew rapidly, reaching 378 000 in 1919. At the end of the war strike activity increased across the country: there were more than 400 strikes in 1919, most of them in Ontario and Québec. Three general strikes also took place that year, in Amherst, NS, Toronto and Winnipeg. In Winnipeg the arrest of the strike leaders and the violent defeat of the strike demonstrated that in a labour conflict of this magnitude the government would not remain neutral (*see* WINNIPEG GENERAL STRIKE). In 1919 as well, the radical ONE BIG UNION was founded in Calgary, raised from the ashes of the IWW. It soon claimed 50 000 members in the forestry, mining, transportation and construction industries. Despite the formation of the OBU and the COMMUNIST PARTY OF CANADA, the 1920s remained a period of retreat for organized labour. The exception was the coal miners and steelworkers of Cape Breton I, who, led by J.B. MCLACHLAN, rebelled repeatedly against one of the country's largest corporations (*see* CAPE BRETON STRIKES).

The 1930s marked an important turning point for workers. The biggest problem of the decade was unemployment. In the depths of the GREAT DEPRESSION more than one million Canadians were out of work, about one in 4 workers. Emergency relief was inadequate and was often provided under humiliating conditions (*see* UNEMPLOYMENT RELIEF CAMPS). Unemployed workers' associations fought evictions and gathered support for UNEMPLOYMENT INSURANCE, a reform finally achieved in 1940. One dramatic protest was the ON TO OTTAWA TREK of 1935, led by the former Wobbly Arthur "Slim" EVANS, an organizer for the National Unemployed Workers' Assn. The Depression demonstrated the need for workers' organizations, and by 1949 union membership exceeded one million workers. Much of the growth in union organization came in the new

mass-production industries among workers neglected by craft unions: rubber, electrical, steel, auto and packinghouse workers. The communist-supported WORKERS UNITY LEAGUE (1929-36) had pioneered industrial unionism in many of these industries. The OSHAWA STRIKE (8-23 Aug 1937), when 4000 workers struck against General Motors, was among the most significant in establishing the new industrial unionism in Canada. Linked to the Congress of Industrial Organizations in the US, many of the new unions were expelled by the TLC and formed the CANADIAN CONGRESS OF LABOUR (CCL) in 1940.

Early in WWII the federal government attempted to limit the power of unions through wage controls and restrictions on the right to strike (*see* WARTIME PRICES AND TRADE BOARD; NATIONAL WAR LABOUR BOARD), but many workers refused to wait until the war was over to win better wages and union recognition. Strikes such as that of the Kirkland Lake gold miners in 1941 persuaded the government to change its policies. In Jan 1944 an emergency order-in-council, PC 1003, protected the workers' right to join a union and required employers to recognize unions chosen by their employees. This long-awaited reform became the cornerstone of Canadian INDUSTRIAL RELATIONS after the war, in the Industrial Relations and Disputes Investigation Act (1948) and in some provincial legislation.

At the end of the war a wave of strikes swept across the country. Workers achieved major improvements in wages and hours, and many contracts incorporated grievance procedures and innovations such as vacation pay. Some industrywide strikes attempted to challenge regional disparities in wages. The Ford strike in Windsor, Ont, between Sept 12 and 29 Dec 1945, began when 17 000 workers walked off the job. The lengthy, bitter strike resulted in the landmark decision by Justice Ivan C. RAND which granted a compulsory check-off of union dues (*see* RAND FORMULA; WINDSOR STRIKE). The check-off helped give unions financial security, though some critics worried that unions might become more bureaucratic as a result.

By the end of the war Canadian workers also had become more active politically. The labour movement had become involved in politics after 1872 when the first workingman (Hamilton's Henry Buckingham Witton), was elected to Parliament. In 1874 Ottawa printer D.J. O'Donoghue was elected to the Ontario legislature, and in 1888 A.T. Lépine, a Montréal leader of the Knights of Labor, was elected to Parliament. Labour candidates and workers' parties were often backed by local unions. In 1900 A.W. PUTTEE, a LABOUR PARTY founder, and Ralph SMITH, TLC president, were elected to Parliament. The SOCIALIST PARTY OF CANADA appealed to the radical element. During the war, policies such as conscription encouraged unions to increase their political activity at the provincial and federal levels. In the 1921 federal election, labour candidates contested seats in all 9 provinces; OBU general secretary R.B. RUSSELL was defeated, as was Cape Breton's J.B. McLachlan, but Winnipeg's J.S. WOODSWORTH and Calgary's William IRVINE were elected. The social catastrophe of the Great Depression increased the appeal of radical politics; Communist Party support increased, and the CO-OPERATIVE COMMONWEALTH FEDERATION was founded. During the 1940s the CCF became the official opposition in BC, Ontario and Nova Scotia, and in 1944 the first CCF government was elected in Saskatchewan. By the late 1940s the CCF and the Communist Party had a combined membership of 50 000.

The new rights of labour and the rise of the WELFARE STATE were the decisive achievements of the

1930s and 1940s, promising to protect Canadian working people against major economic misfortunes. The position of labour in Canadian society was strengthened by the formation of the CANADIAN LABOUR CONGRESS (1956), which united the AFL and the Canadian Congress of Labour and absorbed the OBU. The CLC was active in the founding of the NEW DEMOCRATIC PARTY, and, despite the emergence of the Confederation of Canadian Unions (1975) and the Canadian Federation of Labour (1982), it continues to represent about 60% of union members. Steady growth in government employment during this period meant that by the 1970s one in 5 workers was a public employee. With the exception of Saskatchewan, which gave provincial employees union rights in 1944, it was not until the mid-1960s, following an illegal national strike by postal workers (*see* POSTAL STRIKES), that public employees gained collective bargaining rights similar to those of other workers. By the 1980s, 3 of the 4 largest unions in Canada were PUBLIC-SERVICE UNIONS, whose growth has increased the prominence of Canadian over American-based unions in Canada. Several major industrial unions, including the Canadian Auto Workers, have reinforced this trend by separating from their American parent unions. Another significant change has been the rise in the number of female workers. By 1987, the female LABOUR FORCE participation rate was over 56%. Women made up more than 42% of the labour force and about 35% of union membership. The change was reflected in the growing prominence of women union leaders and in concern over issues such as maternity leave, child care, sexual harrassment and equal pay to women workers for work of equal value.

Despite the achievements of organized labour, the sources of conflict between employers and employees have persisted. Determined employers have been able to resist unions by using strikebreakers and by refusing to reach agreement on first contracts. Workers have continued to exert little direct influence over the investment decisions that govern the distribution of economic activity across the country. In collective agreements such issues as health, safety and technological change have received greater attention, but the employer's right to manage property has predominated over the workers' right to control the conditions and purposes of their work. Governments have often acted to restrict union rights: on occasion, as in the 1959 NEWFOUNDLAND LOGGERS' STRIKE, individual unions have been outlawed, and during the 1960s and 1970s governments turned with increasing frequency to the use of legislated settlements, especially in disputes with their own employees. Despite the intervention of the welfare state, many workers have continued to suffer economic insecurity and poverty. The capitalist labour market has failed to provide full employment for Canadian workers, and during the 1980s more than one million Canadians were regularly reported unemployed; especially in underdeveloped regions such as Atlantic Canada, many workers have continued to depend on part-time, seasonal work and to provide a reserve pool of labour for the national economy. Most working people today are more affluent than their counterparts were in the past, but the distribution of the national income has not changed significantly in favour of working people. DAVID FRANK

Québec

As in other parts of Canada, the history of working-class Québec has only recently received serious study, and research has concentrated on the trade-union phenomenon. Before the industrialization of Québec (about 1870-80), most businesses were small and crafts-oriented. In 1851 there were only 37 companies employing more than 25 workers. Salaried employees were rare, although there were some in the TIMBER TRADE, construction, and canal and railway earthworks. A few trade unions began a precarious existence after 1827. Montréal craft unions united 3 times in larger associations: in 1834, to win a 10-hour day; in 1867, to form the Grand Association; and in 1872, to win a 9-hour day. But each lasted only a few months and few unions withstood the 1837 economic crisis. Québec workers gave other signs of their presence as well. There were over 80 strikes from 1840 to 1880. The CO-OPERATIVE MOVEMENT, through life and health mutual-assurance funds, expanded rapidly after 1850 among the working class. These early signs of worker consciousness demonstrate the workers' desire to create alliances in response to the insecurities of factory work and urban life, and also the workers' rejection of the capitalist labour market in which they were treated as commodities.

Manufacturing activities overtook commerce around 1880. The industrial bourgeoisie now dominated, and the state adopted the objectives of this new social class. MONTRÉAL's population doubled, 1871-91, as the city became Canada's industrial and financial capital. Workers' solidarity and sense of social class both increased. Trade unionism reached more and more workers, thanks to international unions and the Knights of Labor. The number of unions in Québec jumped from 22 in 1880 to 136 in 1901 and to 491 in 1931. About 12 000 workers belonged to unions in 1901 and some 72 100 (10.3% of all Québec wage earners) in 1931.

Unlike other international unions which stressed the economic betterment of members within their own companies, the Knights proposed a total reform of industrial society, including the abolition of wage-earning and the introduction of co-operatives and small-scale ownership. Their activities helped in the formation of the national TLC and in Québec led to the creation of central workers' councils in Montréal (1886) and Québec City (1890). These organizations gave workers a political voice which, in the period 1886-1930, called for electoral reform, free and compulsory education, social legislation and the nationalization of public services. Their representatives, though not revolutionary, reflected a view of society which nevertheless differed greatly from that of the other social classes. Some workers, impatient with government reluctance to adopt pro-worker legislation, moved into party politics, at first within traditional parties and then in the Parti ouvrier (fd 1899). Of 38 candidates, 5 were elected provincially and federally before the Parti joined the CCF in 1933.

The international unions set up their own central council in Montréal in 1897, and a provincial federation in 1937 which became the main union body in Québec. Their greatest challenge came from the Catholic unions. The QUÉBEC SHOE WORKERS' STRIKE (23 Oct-10 Dec 1900) was the first direct intervention in a labour conflict by the clergy, and the first step towards the creation of Catholic unions. The church recognized workers' rights to form unions, but insisted on clerical involvement. The Catholic unions were formed in 1907 in various dioceses under the guidance of the clergy, who feared the "socialist" and anticlerical leanings of the international unions. The Catholic unions established a central in 1921 and gradually adopted many of the methods and principles of international unionism (*see* SOCIAL DOCTRINE OF THE ROMAN CATHOLIC CHURCH). As Québec workers became better organized, they increasingly used strikes to gain their objectives. There were 1073 strikes from 1881 to 1940, a wave that peaked with 134 in 1919-20 alone. Thus it was that after 1880 the working class affirmed its existence as it brought its claims to the level of society as a whole. The trade-union movement, to which most of the organized workers belonged, expressed its claims as part of a larger plan for social reform. The middle class, especially the clergy, tried to control this rising force. Federal and provincial governments both met some demands but remained true to liberal capitalism.

In the Great Depression, worker unrest forced governments to reconsider their function. Having been guardians of public order, they now became guardians of economic and social order as well. They tried to stabilize economic growth and adopted some of the social legislation demanded by the unions, including (Québec dates) OLD-AGE PENSIONS (1936), MINIMUM WAGE (1937), unemployment insurance (1940), FAMILY ALLOWANCE (1944), hospital insurance (1960) and health insurance (1970). Pressure from the trade-union movement played a part, as rapid growth gave the unions increasing influence. The population of workers unionized rose from 10.3% in 1931 to 26.5% in 1951 and 37.7% in 1976. Craftsmen, who had formed the bulk of organized workers at the turn of the century, were joined by skilled and semiskilled workers and, in the 1960s, by teachers and employees in the public sector. During this period the Catholic unions (which secularized themselves in 1960; *see* CONFEDERATION OF NATIONAL TRADE UNIONS) accounted for about 30% of union membership, the international unions for about 40%.

The massive unionization of civil servants radicalized the union movement, especially the CNTU and the Québec Teachers Corp, which promoted a socialist view of society and supported Québec independence. The substance of this socialism, which will have a democratic tone, still remains to be fully defined. The establishment of political action committees outside the Québec UNION CENTRALS led to a municipal political party in Montréal in 1970 and, in 1981, to a socialist movement which aspired to become an official provincial party. In Québec the catalyst for partisan political activity was not the Depression but the QUIET REVOLUTION, followed by the ideological transformation of union centrals during the 1960s.

The volatile ideological dimension of Québec unionism produced more militant conflicts. Québec had proportionately fewer strikes than Ontario in the 1950s but lost twice as many man-days per 100 workers in 1961-79, largely through public-sector strikes. The existence after 1970 of a "common front" (a combined force of labour bodies) for each negotiation with government led to major clashes. There were some spectacular strikes in the private sector, against *La Presse* (1971), United Aircraft (1974-75) and the Commission de Transport de la Communauté urbaine de Montréal (1974), and the general strike protesting WAGE AND PRICE CONTROLS (1976). These followed in the tradition of the great postwar strikes: the ASBESTOS STRIKE (1949) and those at Louiseville (1952) and MURDOCHVILLE (1957).

The Québec labour movement's postwar history divides into 2 phases. The first was dominated by battles against the DUPLESSIS government's reactionary policies (1944-59) and the birth of a vision of society which was to take shape during the 1960s. The second phase, which began with the Quiet Revolution and continued into the 1980s, was marked by a strengthening of progressive forces. But the economic recession of 1981-82 put the trade unions and socialist forces on the defensive. The high level of unemployment weakened their power and the Québec govern-

2340 Working-Class History

ment, in the grip of financial difficulties, abandoned its social concerns to give priority to revitalizing the economy through private enterprise. The neoconservative policies which inspired it tended towards a retreat of the role of the state in the economy and the erosion of social policies. The popular forces, only being able to count on such a strong militancy of their members, turned out badly in the face of this trend.

JACQUES ROUILLARD

Historiography

Each period in the recording of Canadian labour history paralleled specific concerns associated with the practical struggles of the time. In 19th- and early 20th-century Canada, workers were not prominent subjects of scholarly production. Royal commissions provided copious evidence of the conditions of work and of labour's attempts to organize, and a few advocates of the working class offered their evaluations of Canadian workers' emergence as a social and political force. But concern with workers was a pragmatic one with explicit political purposes, and when studies were commissioned, as with, for example, R.H. Coats's 1915 examination of the cost of living, they were related directly to the perceived needs of the moment. Between 1929 and 1945 in Britain and the US the study of labour history was channelled into examinations of political activity, the growth and consolidation of unions, and the gradual winning of collective bargaining rights, improved wages and better conditions. In Canada, individuals associated with an emerging social-democratic milieu had similar concerns and were advocates of public ownership, an active state and the preservation of civil liberties. Leading this moderate socialist contingent was historian Frank UNDERHILL, and associated with him were social scientists, economists and researchers at both McGill and the University of Toronto, including Frank SCOTT, Eugene FORSEY and Stuart Jamieson. Forsey eventually produced *Trade Unions in Canada 1812-1902* (1982), an important overview of the institutional development of Canadian unionism in the 19th century, and Jamieson published *Times of Trouble* (1968) on strike activity, 1900-66. But in the 1930s and 1940s such figures played a more political role, sustaining the LEAGUE FOR SOCIAL RECONSTRUCTION and helping the Co-operative Commonwealth Federation. Often it seemed as though the academic advocates of SOCIALISM regarded labour as the passive recipient of the social reform they sought to stimulate. Those associated with social-democratic thought eased labour into scholarly discourse and defined the character of working-class studies. They regarded the labour movement as one of the forces upon which they could rely for support, but they had little intrinsic interest in labour as a class. The study of labour thus encompassed concern with unions, with labour's political activity, and with appropriate and humane leadership and reforms that only the CCF could offer.

After WWII labour history first began to be written in Canada. Often, especially among professional historians, it was a by-product of other concerns. "George Brown, Sir John Macdonald, and the 'Workingman'" in the *Canadian Historical Review* (1943), by Donald CREIGHTON, indicated how concerns with central political figures might provide a footnote to labour's as-yet untold story. D.C. Masters's *The Winnipeg General Strike* (1950) was purportedly part of a projected exploration of SOCIAL CREDIT in Alberta. J.I. Cooper published "The Social Structure of Montréal in the 1850s" in the CANADIAN HISTORICAL ASSOCIATION's *Annual Report* (1956), which took a preliminary step to-

ward the exploration of workers' everyday lives.

Most studies of Canadian workers were not actually done by historians. Political scientist Bernard Ostry wrote on labour and politics of the 1870s and 1880s. The most innovative work came from economist and economic historian H.C. Pentland (*Labour and Capital in Canada (1650-1860)*, 1981), whose studies challenged conventional wisdom, and from literary critic Frank Watt. They argued that labour had posed a fundamental criticism, through physical struggles and journalistic attacks on monopoly and political corruption, of 19th- and early 20th-century Canadian society well before the upheaval at Winnipeg and the appearance of the SOCIAL GOSPEL and the CCF. Such studies probably had less force in the universities than among historically minded associates of the Communist Party, who penned histories of early Canada and Canadian workers. Within the established circles of professional historians Kenneth McNaught exerted a far greater influence. McNaught was a product of the social-democratic movement of the 1940s, and attained significance not so much for what he wrote – which, in labour history, was rather limited – but because he taught a number of graduate students who pushed labour history into prominence in the 1970s. McNaught's work stressed leadership in the experience of Canadian workers, and he was drawn to the institutional approach of labour-economist Harold Logan. Logan had been active in teaching and writing labour economics since the 1920s, and he produced the first adequate overview of Canadian trade-union development in *Trade Unions in Canada* (1948). His writing in the 1930s and 1940s emphasized the struggle within the Canadian labour movement between CCF followers and associates of the Communist Party. Logan's arguments against communism, together with the practical confrontations of the period, molded social-democratic intellectuals in specific ways: for example, anti-Marxism (equated with opposition to the Stalinist Communist Party) was forever embedded in their approach to Canadian labour. Their horizons seemed bounded by the study of institutions, social reform and the question of proper leadership of the progressive movement and labour itself. McNaught's *A Prophet in Politics* (1959), which was a biography of J.S. WOODSWORTH, father of Canadian social democracy and a central figure in the history of radicalism, was the exemplary study in this genre.

In 1965 Stanley Mealing published "The Concept of Social Class in the Interpretation of Canadian History" (*Canadian Historical Review*, 1965). He concluded that little historical work in Canada had been directed toward workers' experience and that the main interpretive contours of our history would not be dramatically altered by attention to class. Important studies of the Communist Party, the CCF-NDP, early radicalism and labour's general political orientation soon appeared. By the early 1970s studies of such major working-class developments as the rise of the Congress of Industrial Organizations, the consolidation of the AFL before WWI, western labour radicalism and the Winnipeg General Strike were under way or had appeared in print. They were followed by examinations of the One Big Union, the government response to immigrant radicalism, and conditions of life and labour in early 20th-century Montréal.

Leading figures in this proliferation of working-class studies were Irving Abella, David Bercuson, Robert Babcock, Ross McCormack and Donald Avery. Their work, in conjunction with labour studies undertaken by social scientists such as Paul Phillips, Martin Robin, Leo Zakuta, Gad Horowitz and Walter Young, as well as histo-

rians Desmond Morton and Gerald Caplan, served to establish labour history as a legitimate realm of professional historical inquiry. Their labour histories were written, perhaps unconsciously, out of the social-democratic concerns of the 1940s: leadership, decisive events, conditions demanding reform, the nature of ideology and the evolution of particular kinds of unions. Labour-history courses were taught for the first time, a committee of the Canadian Historical Assn was created, and a journal, *Labour/Le Travailleur*, was launched in 1976. In 1980 Desmond Morton and Terry Copp published *Working People*, an illustrated history of Canadian workers.

After 1975 a new group of historians emerged, uninfluenced by the social democracy of the 1940s and attracted to the MARXISM of the late 1960s and early 1970s. These historians were first struck with the general importance of theory, and looked to a series of debates within Western Marxism after 1917 for the nature of class structure and the character of subordination of the working class in capitalist societies. Second, many drew inspiration from American and British studies (by E.P. Thompson, Eric Hobsbawm, David Montgomery and H.G. Gutman) that appeared in the 1960s and heralded a break with earlier histories of labour. Finally the emergence of women's history provided a third and complementary influence, which forced consideration of the process through which labour was reproduced in the family and was socialized into a particular relationship to structures of authority and work.

Generally speaking, those who were fashioning labour history in the early 1980s were united in their commitment to write the SOCIAL HISTORY of the working class. If labour's institutions, political activities and material conditions of life were of essential importance in this broad social history, so too were hitherto-unexplored aspects of the workers' experience: family life, leisure activities, community associations, and work processes and forms of managerial domination affecting both the evolution of unions and the lives of unorganized workers. In all of this work there is a concern with working-class history as an analysis of the place of class in Canadian society. Class is conceived as a reciprocal, if unequal, relationship between those who sell their labour and those who purchase it. Some studies have concentrated on the structural, largely impersonal, dimensions of class experience (the size of working-class families, the numbers of workers associated with particular sectors of the labour market, the rates of wages and levels of unemployment), whereas other works have concentrated on the cultural activities of workers and the conflicts they have waged at the work place or in the community.

Some published works by this generation of historians – including Joy Parr's *Labouring Children* (1980), an examination of the labouring experiences of pauper immigrant children; Bryan Palmer's *A Culture in Conflict* (1979), a discussion of skilled labour in Hamilton in the late 19th and early 20th centuries; Gregory Kealey's *Toronto Workers Respond to Industrial Capitalism 1867-1892* (1980), a similar study of Toronto workers; and *"Dreaming of What Might Be"* (1982), an examination of the Knights of Labor in Ontario, 1880-1900, by Kealey and Palmer – attempt detailed explorations of working-class experience. A host of articles and postgraduate theses attest to the treatment of subjects that a previous labour history never envisaged: ritualistic forms of resistance, patterns of craft inheritance among shoemakers, the place of the family economy in Montréal in the 1870s and 1880s, the riotous behaviour of early canallers, the significance of the life cycle among Québec cotton workers, 1910-50, the effects of mechanization and skill-dilution upon metalworkers in the WWI era, the nature of life in coal communities, or the role of literacy, housing, tavern life and the oral tradition among specific groups of workers. This work must be placed beside studies of such vital areas of working-class life as unions and labour politics. It is unclear how significantly the developing work will revise the general contours of labour history or, more importantly, how it will affect larger interpretations of Canadian society.

Three recently published anthologies of essays on Canadian working-class history reveal different ways of looking at labour's past. D.J. Bercuson's *Canadian Labour History: Selected Readings* (1987) brings together articles that lay stress on the 20th-century history, episodic conflict and strike action, and union formation. *On the Job: Confronting the Labour Process in Canada* (1986), edited by C. Heron and R. Storey, indicates both the strengths and limitations of a sociologically inspired attention to the labour process. Finally, Bryan Palmer's *The Character of Class Struggle: Essays in Canadian Working-Class History* (1987) organizes a series of essays around the general theme of the persistence of class struggle, broadly defined, within Canadian society, rooting this class struggle within distinct periods of capitalist development. BRYAN D. PALMER

Reading: I. Abella and D. Millar, *The Canadian Worker in the Twentieth Century* (1978); M.S. Cross, ed, *The Workingman in the Nineteenth Century* (1974); Eugene Forsey, *Trade Unions in Canada 1812-1902* (1982); Jean Hamelin, ed, *Les Travailleurs québécois 1851-1896* (1973); F. Harvey, ed, *Le Mouvement ouvrier au Québec* (1980); S. Jamieson, *Times of Trouble* (1968); H.A. Logan, *Trade Unions in Canada* (1948); D. Morton with T. Copp, *Working People* (1980); Bryan D. Palmer, *Working-Class Experience* (1983); I. Radforth, *Bushworkers and Bosses: Logging in Northern Ontario 1900-1980* (1987); J. Rouillard, *Les Syndicats nationaux au Québec de 1900 à 1930* (1979), *Histoire de la CSN 1921-81* (1981) and *Histoire du mouvement ouvrier au Québec* (1984).

Workman, Joseph, psychiatrist, educator (b near Lisburn, Ire 26 May 1805; d at Toronto 15 Apr 1894). He immigrated to Montréal in 1829 and received his MD from McGill in 1835. For a time he ran a successful hardware business in Toronto, but in 1846 he accepted an invitation to teach at Dr John ROLPH's Toronto medical school, lecturing first on midwifery and later on materia medica. After resigning in 1853, he was appointed medical superintendent of the newly opened Provincial Lunatic Asylum in Toronto, a position he retained until his retirement in 1875. Workman was the author of numerous papers on insanity, its etiology and treatment, and he often appeared as an expert witness at criminal trials. He was undoubtedly Canada's most distinguished and able mid-19th-century alienist, a fact recognized by his colleagues, to whom he was known affectionately as "the Nestor of Canadian alienists." THOMAS E. BROWN

World Hockey Association, professional HOCKEY league established 1971 (first season of play was 1972-73) to challenge the NATIONAL HOCKEY LEAGUE. Canada was well represented in the new league, with teams in Ottawa, Québec City, Edmonton and Winnipeg. The signing of NHL superstar Bobby HULL by the WINNIPEG JETS gave the league credibility and in its second season the Houston Aeros signed Gordie HOWE to play with his sons Mark and Marty. The financially troubled league disbanded in June 1979 and Winnipeg, Québec, Hartford and EDMONTON OILERS were taken into the NHL. FRANK POLNASZEK

World Literacy of Canada (WLC) Founded in 1955, WLC is a nonprofit, voluntary, international development organization working overseas and in Canada in support of self-help adult LITERA-CY programs. It was the first nongovernmental organization in Canada, and one of the first anywhere to support literacy, nonformal education and development programs overseas, especially in India, Africa and the Caribbean. For many years, its primary project was Literacy House in India. Since 1976, WLC has supported 3 training programs in India, and has participated in a number of events on literacy in Canada. This international experience led WLC to undertake the first extensive study of adult basic education in Canada, published in 1976 and released at the first national conference on adult basic education, organized primarily by WLC. Out of its 1977 annual conference held in Ottawa, came the Movement for Canadian Literacy. WLC's 3 honorary presidents have been Dr Frank Laubach, Dr (Mrs) Welthy Fisher and currently Dr Robert MCCLURE. Through its contacts in other countries, WLC supports self-help and development programs for the poor and illiterate. It publishes a newsletter called *Worldlit*. JAMES A. DRAPER

World Soundscape Project A research and educational endeavour founded (1969, fully functional by 1971) by Canadian composer R. Murray SCHAFER at Simon Fraser U. The project was concerned with all aspects of sound environments, with emphasis on raising public awareness of sound, documenting environmental sound and its changing character, and establishing the concept and practice of soundscape design as an alternative to noise pollution. Activities have included extensive field recordings made across Canada and Europe, archival and educational work, and the publication of many documents and works on tape. Most important are Schafer's *The Book of Noise* (1970), *The Music of the Environment* (1973) and *The Tuning of the World* (1977), as well as project documents which include *A Survey of Community Noise By-laws in Canada* (1972), *The Vancouver Soundscape* (1974), the radio series *Soundscapes of Canada* (1974), *Five Village Soundscapes* and *European Sound Diary* (1977) and the *Handbook for Acoustic Ecology* (1978). Although the project has not continued as a group effort, courses in acoustic communication and soundscape studies are still taught at SFU. Individual composers, however, continue to develop soundscape themes, such as in the "Soundwalking" series of radio programs by H. Westerkamp, and through tape compositions. BARRY D. TRUAX

World University Games were first held in conjunction with the Congress of the International Student's Federation (CIE) in Warsaw, Poland, in 1924. They were the brainchild of Frenchman Jean Petitjean and attracted some 60 students, mainly from Great Britain, Poland and France. Between 1927 and 1939 the Games were held in various European locations: Rome (1927), Paris (1928), Darmstadt, Germany (1930), Turin, Italy (1933), Budapest (1935), Paris (1937) and Monte Carlo (1939). After 1928 the Games began to attract many Olympic competitors and champions. The 1933 Games in Turin had manifest political overtones – the host country's victory seemingly reflecting the strength of its Fascist government – and pushed the Games to the forefront of the athletic world. By 1937 some 26 nations were represented by over 1500 athletes contending for honours in 12 sports.

The CIE organized postwar Games in Paris (1947) and Budapest (1949) before the International University Sports Federation (FISU), founded in 1948, took over. The Games have since been held in Luxembourg (1951), Dortmund, West Germany (1953), San Sebastian, Spain (1955), Paris (1957), Turin, Italy (1959), Sofia, Bulgaria (1961), Port Allegre, Brazil (1963), Budapest (1965), Tokyo (1967), Moscow (1973), Sofia (1977), Mexico City (1979), Bucharest (1981), Edmonton, Alta (1983), Kōbe, Japan (1985) and Zagreb, Yugoslavia (1987). Since the 1950s, the Games have attracted world-class competitors such as the Press sisters (USSR), Harry JEROME (Canada), David Hemery (Great Britain), Tommie Smith (US) and Alberto Juantorena (Cuba), and have become second only in prestige and importance to the Olympics.

At the Edmonton Games, over 3500 athletes from 74 countries competed in 10 sports, the primary focus being track and field, swimming and basketball. DAVE BROWN

World War I On 4 Aug 1914 Britain's ultimatum to Germany to withdraw from Belgium expired. The British Empire, including Canada, was at war, allied with Serbia, Russia, and France against the German and Austro-Hungarian empires. Prewar Canada had a regular army of only 3000, but 60 000 militia had trained in 1913; most provinces, including Québec, insisted on military training in their schools, and defence spending had risen sixfold since 1897.

The war united Canadians at first. The Liberal opposition urged PM Sir Robert BORDEN's Conservative government to take sweeping powers under the new WAR MEASURES ACT. Minister of Militia Sam HUGHES summoned 25 000 volunteers to train at a new camp at Valcartier near Québec; some 33 000 appeared. On Oct 3 the first contingent sailed for England. Much of Canada's war effort was launched by volunteers. The Canadian Patriotic Fund collected money to support soldiers' families. A Military Hospitals Commission cared for the sick and wounded. Churches, charities, women's organizations and the Red Cross found ways to "do their bit" for the war effort. In patriotic fervour, Canadians demanded that Germans and Austrians be dismissed from their jobs and interned (*see* INTERNMENT), and pressured Berlin, Ont, to rename itself Kitchener.

At first the war hurt a troubled economy, increasing unemployment and making it hard for Canada's new, debt-ridden transcontinental railways, the Canadian Northern and the Grand Trunk Pacific, to find credit. By 1915, military spending equalled the entire government expenditure of 1913. Minister of Finance Thomas White opposed raising taxes. Since Britain could not afford to lend to Canada, White turned to the US.

Also, despite the belief that Canadians would never lend to their own government, White had to take the risk. In 1915 he asked for $50 million; he got $100 million. In 1917 the government's Victory Loan campaign began raising huge sums from ordinary citizens for the first time. Canada's war effort was financed mainly by borrowing. Between 1913 and 1918 the national debt rose from $463 million to $2.46 billion.

Canada's economic burden would have been unbearable without huge exports of wheat, timber and munitions. A prewar crop failure had been a warning to prairie farmers of future droughts, but a bumper crop in 1915 and soaring prices banished caution. Since many farm labourers had joined the army, farmers began to complain of a labour shortage. It was hoped that factories shut down by the recession would profit from the war. Manufacturers formed a Shell Committee, got contracts to make British artillery ammunition, and created a brand new industry. It was not easy. By summer 1915 the committee had orders worth $170 million but had delivered only $5.5 million in shells. The British government insisted on reorganization. The resulting IMPERIAL MUNITIONS BOARD was a British agency in Canada, though headed by a talented, hard-driving Cana-

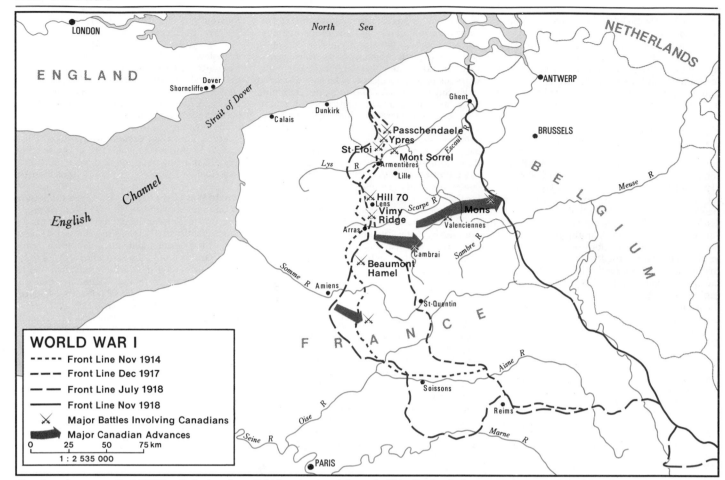

WORLD WAR I
- - - - - - - Front Line Nov 1914
- - - - - Front Line Dec 1917
- - - Front Line July 1918
——— Front Line Nov 1918
✕ Major Battles Involving Canadians
➤ Major Canadian Advances

0   25   50   75 km

1 : 2 535 000

dian, Joseph FLAVELLE. By 1917 Flavelle had made the IMB Canada's biggest business, with 250 000 workers. When the British stopped buying in Canada in 1917, Flavelle negotiated huge new contracts with the Americans, now in the war.

Unemployed workers had flocked to enlist in 1914-15. Recruiting, handled by prewar militia regiments and by civic organizations, cost the government nothing. By the end of 1914 the target for the CANADIAN EXPEDITIONARY FORCE was 50 000; by summer 1915 it was 150 000. During a visit to England that summer, PM Borden was shocked with the magnitude of the struggle. To set even the British an example of earnestness, Borden used his 1916 New Year's message to pledge 500 000 soldiers from a Canadian population of barely 8 million. By then volunteering had virtually dried up. Early contingents had been filled by recent British immigrants; enlistments in 1915 had taken most of the Canadian-born who were willing to go. The total, 330 000, was impressive but insufficient. Recruiting methods became fervid and divisive. Clergy preached Christian duty; women wore badges proclaiming "Knit or Fight"; more and more English Canadians complained that French Canada was not doing its share. This was not surprising: few French Canadians felt deep loyalty to France or Britain. Those few in Borden's government had won election in 1911 by opposing imperialism. Henri BOURASSA, leader and spokesman of Québec's nationalists, initially approved of the war but soon insisted that French Canada's real enemies were not Germans but "English-Canadian anglicisers, the Ontario intriguers, or Irish priests" who were busy ending French-language education in the English-speaking provinces. In Québec and across Canada, unemployment gave way to high wages and a manpower shortage. There were good economic reasons to stay home.

Canadians in the CEF became part of the British army. As minister of militia, Hughes insisted on choosing the officers and on retaining the Canadian-made ROSS RIFLE. Since the rifle had serious faults and since some of Hughes's choices were incompetent cronies, the Canadian military had serious deficiencies. A recruiting system based on forming hundreds of new battalions meant that most of them arrived in England only to be broken up, leaving a large residue of unhappy senior officers. Hughes believed that Canadians would be natural soldiers; in practice they had many costly lessons to learn. They did so with courage and self-sacrifice. At the second Battle of YPRES, Apr 1915, a raw 1st Canadian Division suffered 6036 casualties, and the Princess Patricia's Canadian Light Infantry a further 678. The troops also shed their defective Ross rifles. At the St Eloi craters in 1916, the 2nd Division suffered a painful setback because its senior commanders failed to locate their men. In June the 3rd Division was shattered at MONT SORREL though the position was recovered by the now battle-hardened 1st Division. The test of battle eliminated inept officers and showed survivors that careful staff work, preparation, and discipline were vital. Canadians were spared the early battles of the SOMME in summer 1916, though a separate Newfoundland force, 1st Newfoundland Regiment, was annihilated at Beaumont Hamel on the disastrous first day, July 1. When Canadians entered the battle on Aug 30, their experience helped toward limited gains, though at high cost. By the end of the battle the Canadian Corps had reached its full strength of 4 divisions.

The embarrassing confusion of Canadian administration in England and Hughes's reluctance to displace his cronies forced Borden's government to establish a separate MINISTRY OF OVERSEAS MILITARY FORCES based in London to control the CEF overseas. Bereft of much power, Hughes resigned in Nov 1916. The Act creating the new

ministry established that the CEF was now a Canadian military organization, though its day-to-day relations with the British army did not change immediately. Two ministers, Sir George PERLEY and then Sir Edward KEMP, gradually reformed overseas administration and expanded effective Canadian control over the CEF.

While most of those forces were with the Canadian Corps or with a separate Canadian cavalry brigade on the Western Front, Canadians could be found almost everywhere in the Allied war effort. Young Canadians had trained (initially at their own expense) to become pilots in the British flying services. In 1917 the ROYAL FLYING CORPS opened schools in Canada, and by war's end almost a quarter of the pilots in the Royal Air Force were Canadians. Two of them, Maj William A. BISHOP and Maj Raymond COLLISHAW, ranked among the top air aces of the war. An independent Canadian air force was authorized in the last months of the war. Canadians also served with the Royal Navy and Canada's own tiny naval service organized a coastal submarine patrol. Thousands of Canadians cut down forests in Scotland and France, and built and operated most of the railways behind the British front. Others ran steamers on the Tigris R, cared for the wounded at Salonika (Thessaloniki), Greece, and fought Bolsheviks at Archangel and Baku (see RUSSIAN CIVIL WAR, CANADIAN INTERVENTION IN).

British and French strategists deplored such diversions from the effort on the Western Front. It was there, against the main German forces, that war must be waged. A battle-hardened Canadian Corps was a major instrument in this war of attrition. Its skill and training were tested on Easter weekend, 1917, when all 4 divisions were sent forward to capture a seemingly impregnable VIMY RIDGE. Weeks of rehearsals, stockpiling, and bombardment paid off. In 5 days the ridge was taken. The able British commander of the corps, Lt-Gen

Sir Julian BYNG, was promoted; his successor was a Canadian, Lt-Gen Sir Arthur CURRIE, who followed Byng's methods and improved on them. Instead of attacking Lens in the summer of 1917, Currie captured the nearby HILL 70 and used artillery to destroy wave after wave of German counterattacks. As an increasingly independent subordinate, Currie questioned orders, but he could not refuse them. When ordered to finish the disastrous British offensive at PASSCHENDAELE in Oct 1917, Currie warned that it would cost 16 000 of his 20 000 men. Though he insisted on time to prepare, the Canadian victory on the dismal, water-logged battlefield left a toll of 15 654 dead and wounded.

A year before, even the patriotic leagues had confessed the failure of voluntary recruiting. Business leaders, Protestants, and English-speaking Catholics such as Bishop Michael FALLON grew critical of French Canada. Faced with a growing demand for conscription, the Borden government compromised in Aug 1916 with a program of national registration. A prominent Montréal manufacturer, Arthur Mignault, was put in charge of Québec recruiting and, for the first time, public funds were provided. A final attempt to raise a French Canadian battalion, the 14th out of 258 battalions in the CEF, failed in 1917.

Until 1917 Borden had no more news of the war or Allied strategy than he read in newspapers. He was concerned about British war leadership but he devoted 1916 to improving Canadian military administration and munition production. In Dec 1916 David Lloyd George became head of a new British coalition government pledged wholeheartedly to winning the war. An expatriate Canadian, Max AITKEN, helped engineer the change. Faced by suspicious officials and a failing war effort, Lloyd George summoned premiers of the Dominions to London. They would see for themselves that the Allies needed more men. On Mar 2, when Borden and his fellow premiers met, Russia was collapsing, the French army was close to mutiny, and German submarines had almost cut off supplies to Britain.

Borden was a leader in establishing a voice for the Dominions in policymaking and in gaining a more independent status for them in the postwar world. Visits to Canadian camps and hospitals also persuaded him that the CEF needed more men. The triumph of Vimy Ridge during his visit gave all Canadians pride but it cost 10 602 casualties, 3598 of them fatal. Borden cancelled plans to expand the corps but he returned to Canada committed to conscription. On 18 May 1917 he told Canadians of his government's new policy. The 1914 promise of an all-volunteer contingent had been superseded by events.

Many in English-speaking Canada — farmers, trade union leaders, pacifists — opposed conscription, but they had few outlets for their views. French Canada's opposition was almost unanimous under Henri Bourassa, who argued that Canada had done enough, that Canada's interests were not served by the European conflict, and that men were more needed to grow food and make munitions. Borden felt such arguments were cold and materialistic. Canada owed its support to its young soldiers. The Allied struggle against Prussian militarism was a crusade for freedom. There was no bridging the rival points of view. To win conscription, Borden offered Laurier a coalition. The Liberal leader refused, sure that his party could now defeat the Conservatives. He also feared that if he joined Borden, Bourassa's nationalism would sweep Québec. Laurier misjudged his support. Many English-speaking Liberals agreed that the war was a crusade. A mood of reform and sacrifice had led many provinces to grant votes to women and to prohibit the sale or use of liquor (*see* TEMPERANCE). Although they disliked the Conservatives, many reform Liberals like Ontario's Newton Rowell believed that Borden was in earnest about the war and Laurier was not. Borden also gave himself 2 political weapons: on 20 Sept 1917 Parliament gave the franchise to all soldiers, including those overseas; it also gave votes to soldiers' wives, mothers and sisters, as well as women serving in the armed forces, and took it away from Canadians of enemy origin who had become citizens since 1902. This added many votes for conscription and removed many certain Liberal voters from the lists. On Oct 6 Parliament was dissolved. Five days later, Borden announced a coalition Union government pledged to conscription, an end to political patronage, and full WOMEN'S SUFFRAGE.

Eight of Canada's 9 provinces endorsed the new government, but Laurier could dominate Québec, and many Liberals across Canada would not forget their allegiance. Borden and his ministers had to promise many exemptions to make conscription acceptable. On Dec 17, Unionists had won 153 seats to Laurier's 82, but without the soldiers' vote, only 100 000 votes separated the parties. Conscription was not applied until 1 Jan 1918. The MILITARY SERVICE ACT had so many opportunities for exemption and appeal, that of more than 400 000 called 380 510 appealed. The manpower problem continued.

In Mar 1918 disaster struck the Allies. German armies, moved from the Eastern to the Western Front after Russia's collapse in 1917, smashed through British lines. Fifth British Army was destroyed. In Canada, anticonscription riots in Québec on the Easter weekend left 4 dead. Borden's new government cancelled all exemptions. Many who had voted Unionist in the belief that their sons would be exempted felt betrayed.

The war had entered a bitter final phase. On 6 Dec 1917 the HALIFAX EXPLOSION killed over 1600, and it was followed by the worst snowstorm in years. Across Canada, Sir Thomas White's (minster of finance) heavy borrowing finally led to runaway inflation. Workers joined unions and struck for wages. Food and fuel controllers now preached conservation, sought increased production and sent agents to prosecute hoarders. Public pressure to "conscript wealth" forced a reluctant White in Apr 1917 to impose a Business Profits Tax and a War Income Tax. An "anti-loafing" law threatened jail for any man not gainfully employed. Federal police forces were ordered to hunt for sedition. Socialist parties and radical unions were banned. So were newspapers published in the "enemy" languages. Canadians learned to live with unprecedented government controls and involvement in their daily lives. Food and fuel shortages led to "Meatless Fridays" and "Fuelless Sundays."

In other warring countries, exhaustion and despair went far deeper. Defeat now faced the western Allies, but the Canadian Corps escaped the succession of German offensives. Sir Arthur Currie insisted that it be kept together. A 5th Canadian division, held in England since 1916, was finally broken up to provide reinforcements. When Borden went to England in spring 1918, the Canadian Corps was the strongest formation of its size on the British front. Borden was furious at the mismanagement of the war. He condemned the waste of Passchendaele but he agreed that the British army would have to be husbanded and rebuilt for a victory that might have to wait until 1920. He argued that the Russian front must be revived and was obliged to offer Canadian troops to help Britain in seeking the overthrow of the new Bolshevik government.

To help restore the Allied line, Canadians and Australians attacked near Amiens on 8 Aug 1918 (*see* AMIENS, BATTLE OF). Shock tactics, using airplanes, tanks, and infantry, shattered the German line. When resistance thickened, Currie was among those who advised switching to new lines of attack. In Sept and early Oct the Canadians attacked again and again, suffering heavy casualties but making advances thought unimaginable. The Germans fought with skill and courage all the way to Mons, the little Belgian town where fighting ended for the Canadians at 11 AM (Greenwich time), 11 Nov 1918. More officially, the war ended with the Treaty of VERSAILLES, signed 28 June 1919.

The CEF lost 60 661 dead. Many more returned from the war mutilated in mind or body. In autumn 1918 almost as many Canadians died from the effects of a worldwide influenza epidemic. Both tolls fell heavily on the young and energetic. The survivors found that almost every facet of Canadian life, from the length of skirts to the value of money, had been transformed by the war years. Governments had assumed responsibilities they would never abandon. The income tax would survive the war. So would government departments later to become the Department of VETERANS AFFAIRS and the Department of Pensions and National Health.

Overseas, Canada's soldiers had struggled to achieve, and had won, a considerable degree of autonomy from British control. Prewar dreams of imperial federation perished with Borden's own experience in 1917 and 1918. Canada's direct reward for her sacrifices was a modest presence at the Versailles conference and a seat in the new

Canadian troops in France during WWI. Endless shelling created a desolate landscape of mud and death (*courtesy City of Vancouver Archives*).

LEAGUE OF NATIONS. However, the deep national divisions between French and English created by the war and especially by the CONSCRIPTION crisis of 1917 made postwar Canada fearful of international responsibilities. Canadians had done great things in the war but they had not done them together.   DESMOND MORTON

Reading: E. Armstrong, *The Crisis of Quebec, 1914-1918* (1974 reprint); Pierre Berton, *Vimy* (1986); W.R. Bird, *Ghosts Have Warm Hands* (1968); M. Bliss, *A Canadian Millionaire* (1978); R.C. Brown, *Robert Laird Borden*, vol II (1980); D.G. Dancocks, *Legacy of Valour* (1986) and *Spearhead to Victory: Canada and the Great War* (1987); W.A.B. Douglas, *The Creation of the National Air Force* (1986); D.J. Goodspeed, *The Road Past Vimy* (1967); J.L. Granatstein and J.M. Hitsman, *Broken Promises* (1977); Desmond Morton, *A Peculiar Kind of Politics* (1982), and *Canada and War* (1981); G.W.L. Nicholson, *Canadian Expeditionary Force 1914-1919* (1964); J.A. Swettenham, *To Seize the Victory* (1965); J. Thompson, *The Harvests of War* (1978); B. Wilson, *Ontario and the First World War, 1914-1918* (1977); S.F. Wise, *Canadian Airmen and the First World War* (1980).

World War II Memories of WWI – the tragic loss of life, the heavy burden of debt, and the strain on the country's unity imposed by CONSCRIPTION – made Canadians, including politicians of all parties, loath to contemplate another such experience. The general mood was isolationist. Initially PM Mackenzie KING warmly supported British PM Neville Chamberlain's policy of appeasing German leader Adolf Hitler, and when Chamberlain postponed war by sacrificing Czechoslovakia in the Munich Crisis of Sept 1938 King thanked

him publicly, and Canadians in general certainly agreed. Nevertheless, the shock of this crisis likely turned opinion towards accepting war to check the advance of Nazism. Only gradually did the progress of events, notably Nazi aggression, alter this mood to the point where Canada was prepared to face taking part in another great war. King himself had no doubt that in a great war involving the UK, Canada could not stand aside.

When the German attack on Poland on 1 Sept 1939 finally led Britain and France to declare war on Germany, King summoned Parliament to "decide," as he had pledged. Declaration of war was postponed for a week, during which Canada was formally neutral. The government announced that approval of the "Address in reply to the Speech from the Throne," which stated the government's decision to support Britain and France, would constitute approval of a declaration of war. On Sept 9 the address was approved without a recorded vote, and war was declared the following day. The basis for parliamentary unity had in fact been laid in Mar, when both major parties accepted a program rejecting conscription for overseas service. King clearly envisaged a limited effort and was lukewarm towards an expeditionary force. Nevertheless, there was enough pressure to lead the Cabinet to dispatch one army division to Europe. The Allies' defeat in France and Belgium in the early summer of 1940, and the collapse of France, frightened Canadians. The idea of limited and economical war went by the board, and thereafter the only effective limita-

tion was the pledge against overseas conscription. The armed forces were rapidly enlarged, conscription was introduced June 1940 for home defence (*see* NATIONAL RESOURCES MOBILIZATION ACT), and expenditure grew enormously.

The army expanded until by late 1942 there were 5 divisions overseas, 2 of them armoured. In Apr of that year FIRST CANADIAN ARMY was formed in England under Lt-Gen A.G.L. MCNAUGHTON. In contrast with WWI, it was a long time before the army saw large-scale action. Until summer 1943 the force in England was engaged only in the unsuccessful DIEPPE RAID (19 Aug 1942), whereas 2 battalions sent from Canada had taken part in the hopeless defence of HONG KONG against the Japanese in Dec 1941. Public opinion in Canada became disturbed by the inaction, and disagreement developed between the government and McNaughton, who wished to reserve the army for a final, decisive campaign. The government arranged with Britain for 1st Canadian Infantry Division to join the attack on Sicily, July 1943, and subsequently insisted upon building its Mediterranean force up to a 2-division corps (by adding the 5th Division). This produced a serious clash with McNaughton, just when the British War Office, which considered him unsuited for field command, was influencing the Canadian government against him. At the end of 1943 he was replaced by Lt-Gen H.D.G. CRERAR.

The 1st Division was heavily engaged in the Sicilian campaign as part of the British Eighth Army, and subsequently took part in the Dec

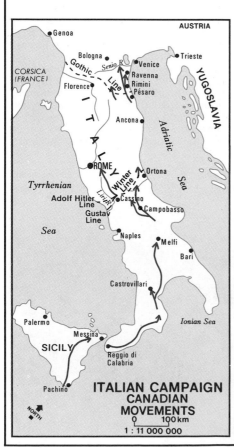

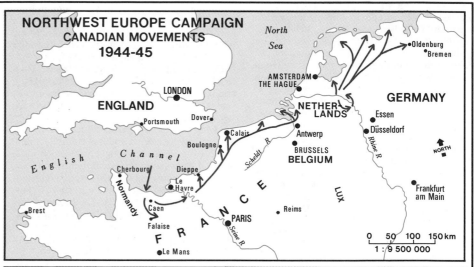

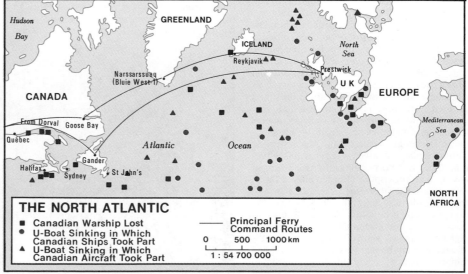

1943 advance up the mainland of Italy, seeing particularly severe fighting in and around Ortona (*see* ORTONA, BATTLE OF). In the spring of 1944 Canadians under Lt-Gen E.L.M. BURNS played a leading role in breaking the Hitler Line barring the Liri Valley. At the end of Aug the corps broke the Gothic Line in the Adriatic sector and pushed on through the German positions covering Rimini, which fell in Sept. These battles cost Canada its heaviest casualties of the Italian campaign. The final phase of Canadian involvement in Italy found 1st Canadian Corps, now commanded by Lt-Gen Charles FOULKES, fighting its way across the Lombard Plain, hindered by mud and swift-flowing rivers. The corps' advance ended at the Senio R in the first days of 1945. The Canadian government, so eager to get its troops into action in Italy, had soon begun to ask for their return to join the main Canadian force in NW Europe. Allied policy finally made this possible early in 1945, and the 1st Corps came under the First Canadian Army's command in mid-Mar, to the general satisfaction of the men from Italy. All told, 92 757 Canadian soldiers of all ranks had served in Italy, and 5764 had lost their lives.

In the final great campaign in NW Europe, beginning with the NORMANDY INVASION (code name Operation *Overlord*) on 6 June 1944, First Canadian Army under Crerar played an important and costly part. Since the 1st Corps had been sent to Italy, its place had to be filled by British and Allied formations. The army's central kernel, however, was the 2nd Canadian Corps, under Lt-Gen G.G. SIMONDS, who had commanded the 1st Division in Sicily; it was normally composed of the 2nd and 3rd Canadian Infantry Divisions and the 4th Canadian Armoured Division. Throughout, the army was part of the 21st British Army Group commanded by Gen Sir (later Field-Marshal Lord) Bernard Law Montgomery. In the landing phase only the 3rd Division and the 2nd Canadian Armoured Brigade were engaged, fighting under the Second British Army. These formations landed on D-Day, experiencing bitter fighting then and subsequently. On July 11 Simonds's corps took over a section of the line near Caen, but Crerar's army did not become operational (on the extreme left of the Allied line, where it remained for the rest of the campaign) until July 23. On the 31st its front was extended to include the Caen sector.

The Canadian formations played a leading part in the breakout from the Normandy bridgehead in Aug, fighting against fierce opposition to reach Falaise and subsequently to close the gap south of it through which the enemy was retiring to avoid being trapped between the British and Canadians coming from the north and the Americans approaching from the south. Falaise was taken on Aug 16 and on the 19th the Allies finally made contact across the gap. The next phase was one of

Marshalling of the "Hallies," oil on canvas, by Paul A. Goranson, showing Halifax bombers of No 419 (Moose) Squadron, preparing for a raid, at their base in County Durham, Eng, in the spring of 1943 (*courtesy Canadian War Museum/CMC/NMC/11402*).

pursuit towards the German frontier. First Canadian Army, with the 1st British Corps under command, cleared the coastal fortresses, taking in turn Le Havre, Boulogne, and Calais. Early in Sept the British took Antwerp, but the enemy still held the banks of the Scheldt R between this much-needed port and the sea, and the Canadians fought a bitter battle to open the river through Oct and the first week of Nov.

The first major Canadian operation of 1945, the Battle of the RHINELAND, was to clear the area between the Maas and the Rhine rivers; it began Feb 8 and ended only Mar 10 when the Germans, pushed back by the Canadians and the converging thrust of the Ninth US Army, withdrew across the Rhine. The final operations in the west began with the Rhine crossing in the British area on Mar 23; thereafter, First Canadian Army, still on the left of the line, liberated E and N Netherlands and advanced across the N German plain (*see* LIBERATION OF HOLLAND). When the Germans surrendered on Field-Marshal Montgomery's front on May 5, the 2nd Canadian Corps had taken Oldenburg, and the 1st Canadian Corps was standing fast on the Grebbe R line while, by arrangement with the Germans, food was sent into the starving W Netherlands. The entire campaign had cost the Canadian Army 11 336 fatal casualties. Some 237 000 men and women of the army had served in NW Europe.

The war effort of the Royal Canadian Air Force was deeply affected by its management of the BRITISH COMMONWEALTH AIR TRAINING PLAN. Great numbers of Canadians served in units of Britain's Royal Air Force, and the growth of a national Canadian air organization overseas was delayed. Nevertheless, by the German surrender, 48 RCAF squadrons were overseas, virtually completely manned by Canadian officers and men. A landmark was the formation of No 6 (RCAF) Bomber Group of the RAF Bomber Command on 1 Jan 1943. It grew ultimately to 14 squadrons. It was commanded successively by Air Vice-Marshals G.E. Brookes and C.M. MCEWEN. Bomber Command's task was the night bombing of Germany, a desperately perilous job calling for sustained fortitude. Almost 10 000 Canadians lost their lives in this command. Canadian airmen served in every theatre, from bases in the UK, N Africa, Italy, NW Europe and SE Asia. Squadrons in N America worked in antisubmarine operations off

the Atlantic coast and co-operated with US air forces against the Japanese in the Aleutian Is. At one time or another 7 RCAF squadrons served in the RAF's Coastal Command over the Atlantic. RCAF aircraft destroyed or had a part in destroying 23 enemy submarines. In the NW Europe campaign of 1944-45, the RCAF deployed 17 squadrons, 15 of them in No 83 Group of the RAF's Second Tactical Air Force. During the war 232 632 men and 17 030 women served in the RCAF, and 17 101 lost their lives.

The Royal Canadian Navy was tiny in 1939, but its expansion during the war was remarkable: it enlisted 99 688 men and some 6500 women, and it manned 471 fighting vessels of various types. Its primary task was convoy, protecting the troop and supply ships across the Atlantic. It carried an increasing proportion of this burden, fighting grim battles sometimes of several days' duration with U-boat "wolfpacks." Its vast expansion produced some growing pains; in 1943 measures had to be taken to improve its escort vessels' technical equipment and in some cases the crew training. During the war it sank or shared in sinking 29 enemy submarines. After the Atlantic Convoy Conference in Washington in Mar 1943 the Canadian NW Atlantic Command was set up, covering the area N of New York City and W of the 47th meridian; a Canadian officer, Rear-Adm L.W. MURRAY, was responsible for convoys in this area. Apart from their main task in the Battle of the ATLANTIC, Canadian naval units took part in many other campaigns, including supporting the Allied landings in N Africa in Nov 1942; and to the Normandy operations of June 1944 the RCN contributed some 110 vessels and 10 000 men. During the war it lost by enemy action 24 vessels, ranging from the "Tribal" class destroyer *Athabaskan*, sunk in the English Channel in Apr 1944, to the armed yacht *Raccoon*, torpedoed in the St Lawrence in Sept 1942 (*see* U-BOAT OPERATIONS). In personnel, the navy had 2024 fatal casualties.

Canada's industrial contribution to victory was considerable, though it began slowly. After

Canadian soldiers in action in *The Hitler Line*, by Charles Comfort (*courtesy Canadian War Museum/CMC/NMC/12296*).

the Allied reverses in Europe in 1940 British orders for equipment, which had been a trickle, became a flood. In Apr 1940 the Dept of MUNITIONS AND SUPPLY, provided for in 1939, was established with C.D. HOWE as minister. In Aug 1940 an amended Act gave the minister almost dictatorial powers, and under it the industrial effort expanded vastly. Various CROWN CORPORATIONS were instituted for special tasks. New factories were built, and old ones adapted for war purposes. Whereas in WWI Canadian production had largely been limited to shells (no weapons were made except the ROSS RIFLE), now a great variety of guns and small arms was produced. Many ships, notably escort vessels and cargo carriers, were built; there was large production of aircraft, including Lancaster bombers; and the greatest triumph of the program was in the field of military vehicles, of which 815 729 were made. Tanks were produced, chiefly of components imported from the US. More than half the material produced went to Britain. Britain could not possibly pay for all of it; so Canada, in the interest of helping to win the war, and keeping her factories working, financed a high proportion. At the beginning of 1942 a BILLION-DOLLAR GIFT was devoted to this purpose. The next year a program of MUTUAL AID to serve Allied nations generally, but still in practice mainly directed to the UK, was introduced. During the war Canadian financial assistance to Britain amounted to $3 043 000 000.

Canada had a limited role in the development of atomic energy, a fateful business that was revealed when atomic bombs were dropped on Japan in Aug 1945. Canada had an available source of uranium in a mine at Great Bear Lk, which led to Mackenzie King's being taken into the greater Allies' confidence in the matter in 1942. That summer the Canadian government acquired control of the mine. A team of scientists that had been working on the project in England was moved to Canada. Tension developed between Britain and the US, but at the Québec Conference of Sept 1943 an Anglo-American agreement was made that incidentally gave Canada a small share in control. A Canadian policy committee decided in 1944 to construct an atomic reactor at Chalk River, Ont. The first reactor there did not "go critical" until after the Japanese surrender. Canada had no part in producing the bombs used against Japan, unless some Canadian uranium was used in them, which seems impossible to determine.

Canada had no effective part in the higher direction of the war. This would have been extremely difficult to obtain, and King never exerted himself strongly to obtain it. It is possible that he anticipated that doing so would have an adverse effect upon his personal relations with British PM Winston Churchill and American Pres Franklin D. Roosevelt which he considered very important to him politically. The western Allies' strategy was decided by the Combined Chiefs of Staff, a purely Anglo-American committee. Its most important decisions were made in periodical conferences with political leaders, 2 of which were held at Québec. Even to these King was a party only as host. Although Canadian forces were employed in accordance with the Combined Chiefs' decisions, it is a curious fact that Canada was never officially informed of the institution of the committee at the end of 1941. Even formal recognition of Canadian sovereignty was minimal; although the directives of the Allied commanders for the war against Japan were issued in the names of the US, Britain, Australia and New Zealand, the directive to Gen Dwight D. Eisenhower, supreme commander in NW Europe, under whom large Canadian forces served, made no mention of Canada.

Celebrating VE Day, Montréal, c8 May 1945 (courtesy National Archives of Canada/PA-152318).

Canadian relations with the US became notably closer during the war. From the moment King resumed office in 1935 he had cultivated his connection with Roosevelt. During the first months of the war there was little contact, but the fears aroused by early German victories immediately produced a rapprochement. On 18 Aug 1940 King and Roosevelt, meeting at Ogdensburg, NY, announced an agreement (not a formal treaty) to set up a PERMANENT JOINT BOARD ON DEFENCE, which met frequently thereafter to discuss mutual defence problems. In 1941 Canada's balance of payments with the US became serious, largely because of the difficulty of financing imports from the US resulting from Canada's industrial production for Britain. It was solved by the Hyde Park Declaration on Apr 20. Nevertheless, King sometimes worried over what he saw as a danger of the US absorbing Canada. A reaction to American activity in the Canadian North (eg, the building of the ALASKA HIGHWAY in 1942) was the appointment in 1943 of a Special Commissioner for Defence Projects in the Northwest, to reinforce Canadian control in the region.

The worst political problems that arose in Canada during the war originated in the conscription question, and King had more difficulties in his own Liberal Party than with the Opposition. The election of 26 Mar 1940, before the war reached a critical stage, indicated that the country was happy with a limited war effort and gave King a solid majority. French Canada's lack of enthusiasm for the war and its particular opposition to conscription were as evident as in WWI (voluntary enlistments in Québec amounted to only about 4% of the population, whereas elsewhere the figure was roughly 10%). By 1942 agitation for overseas conscription in the English-speaking parts of the country led King to hold a plebiscite on releasing the government from its pledge. The result was a heavy vote for release in every province but Québec. Nevertheless, there was still little active enthusiasm for conscription in English Canada; when Arthur MEIGHEN returned to the Conservative leadership and advocated overseas conscription he failed to be elected even in a Toronto constituency. But the atmosphere changed after casualties mounted.

After the Normandy campaign in 1944 a shortage of infantry reinforcements arose and Minister of National Defence Col J.L. RALSTON told Cabinet that the time for overseas conscription had come. King, who had apparently convinced himself that there was a conspiracy in the ministry to unseat him and substitute Ralston, dismissed Ralston and replaced him with McNaughton. The latter failed to prevail on any large number of home-defence conscripts to volunteer for overseas service, and King, finding himself faced with resignations of conscriptionist ministers, which would have ruined his government, agreed to send a large group of the conscripts overseas. Québec reluc-

tantly accepted the situation, preferring King's to any Conservative administration, and he was safe again until the end of the war.

Canada had little share in making the peace. The great powers, which had kept the direction of the war in their own hands, did the same now. The so-called peace conference in Paris in the summer of 1946 merely gave the lesser Allies, including Canada, an opportunity of commenting upon arrangements already made. Canada signed treaties only with Italy, Hungary, Romania and Finland. With Germany divided and the eastern part of the country dominated by the USSR, there was never a German treaty. In 1951 Canada, like other Western powers, ended the state of war with Germany by royal proclamation. That year a treaty of peace with Japan, drafted by the US, was signed by most Allied states, including Canada (but not including the communist powers).

The financial cost of the Canadian war effort was astronomical. Expenditure for the fiscal year 1939-40 was a modest $118 291 000. The next year it rose to $752 045 000; in the peak year, 1943-44, it was $4 587 023 000. The total through the fiscal year 1949-50, for the 11 years beginning 1939-40, was $21 786 077 519.12. Other costs due to the war have continued to accumulate. During the war, 1 086 343 Canadian men and women performed full-time duty in the 3 services. The cost in blood was smaller than in WWI, but still tragic: 42 042 lost their lives.

The significance of WWII in Canadian history was great, but probably rather less than that of WWI. National unity between French and English was damaged, though happily not so seriously as in WWI. The economy was strengthened and its manufacturing capacity much diversified. National pride and confidence were enhanced. The status as an independent country, only shakily established in 1919, was beyond doubt after 1945. Canada was a power in her own right, if a modest one. On the other hand, it had been made painfully clear that "status" did not necessarily imply influence. A MIDDLE POWER had to limit its aspirations. Real authority in the world remained with the big battalions, the big populations, and the big money.   C.P. STACEY

Reading: J.A. Boutilier, ed, *The RCN in Retrospect 1910-1968* (1982); D.J. Goodspeed, ed, *The Armed Forces of Canada, 1867-1967* (1967); J.L. Granatstein, *Canada's War* (1975); D. Morton, *A Military History of Canada* (1985); J.W. Pickersgill and D.F. Forster, *The Mackenzie King Record* (1960-70); J. Schull, *The Far Distant Ships* (1950); C.P. Stacey, *Arms, Men and Governments* (1970), *Six Years of War* (1955), *The Victory Campaign* (1960) and *Canada and the Age of Conflict*, vol II (1981); G.N. Tucker, *The Naval Service of Canada*, vol II (1952).

Worthington, Edward Dagge, physician (b at Ballinakill, Ire 1 Dec 1820; d at Sherbrooke, Qué 25 Feb 1895). In 1847 Worthington pioneered the use of general anesthesia in Canada. Using an inhalation apparatus he built himself, he performed major operations and assisted at births while his patients were under the influence of first ether and later chloroform. He practised for over 50 years in Sherbrooke, was a military surgeon, a governor of the College of Physicians and Surgeons of Lower Canada, and helped found the Canadian Medical Assn in 1867. He also contributed many articles to contemporary medical journals. In addition to his MD from St Andrews (Scot), Worthington was awarded honorary degrees from Bishop's and McGill.   J.T.H. CONNOR

Worthington, Frederic Franklin, "Worthy," army officer, engineer, adventurer (b in Scotland 1890; d at Ottawa 8 Dec 1967). Orphaned at 11, he became the ward of a half-brother (later murdered by Villista irregulars) in Mexico, later going to sea and, as a "sailor of fortune," briefly commanding the tiny Nicaraguan navy in 1907. His earlier life in Mexico led him to sympathize with the ideals of Francisco Madero, for whose cause he fought during the revolution. At the start of WWI, he joined the Canadian Motor Machine Gun Brigade and was promoted to battery commander in France. He joined the peacetime Permanent Force of the Armed Forces, developing his doctrine of firepower plus mobility. In WWII, Maj-Gen Worthington founded the Canadian Armoured Corps and designed the prototype for the Sherman tank, used so successfully by the Allies in N Africa and Europe. Resigning his commission in 1947, he was appointed the first civil defence co-ordinator, a position which he held until 1957, stepping down to enter the business community. ALLAN E. LEVINE

Worthington, Peter John Vickers, soldier, journalist, publisher, author (b at Fort Osborne Barracks, Winnipeg 16 Feb 1927). The son of F.F. WORTHINGTON, he served in the RCN and RN in WWII, and as a PPCLI lieutenant in the Korean War. After earning his BA and bachelor of journalism at UBC and Carleton, respectively, he was a roving reporter for the Toronto *Telegram* from 1956 to 1971, capably covering many coups, wars and revolutions. He obtained an important "scoop" on witnessing Jack Ruby's 1963 shooting of Lee Harvey Oswald in Dallas and he worked briefly with the Biafran army during the Nigerian civil war. Worthington was the cofounder and outspoken editor in chief of the Toronto *Sun* from 1971 until 1982, when he entered politics. Losing his bid to be the PC candidate in Toronto Broadview-Greenwood, he ran unsuccessfully as an independent; 2 years later, he won the PC nomination but lost the election. Worthington has for several years been the editor of *Influence*, one of Canada's new crop of innovative and informative magazines. ALLAN E. LEVINE

Wrangel Island lies in the Arctic Ocean 200 km N of the coast of eastern Siberia. Discovered in 1849, it was named in 1867 after Baron Wrangel, the Russian governor of Alaska. Though uninhabited, it served for 6 months in 1914 as a refuge for the crew of the KARLUK, wrecked during the CANADIAN ARCTIC EXPEDITION of that year. Members of the crew claimed the island for Canada, and the expedition's commander, Vilhjalmur STEFANSSON, who had never seen it, conceived the idea that it might become the centre of a northern empire – the base to the riches of the polar basin – and should be Canadian territory. In 1922 the Canadian government claimed the island, but after protests from the Soviet government the claim was quickly dropped. W.R. MORRISON

Wren (Troglodytidae), family of small, mainly brown, insectivorous songbirds, characterized by chunky bodies, tails that are often erect, and forceful rather than musical songs. The family, comprising 60 species, apparently originated in the American tropics and spread N to Canada. The northernmost species, winter wren (*Troglodytes troglodytes*), extends into Eurasia. Of the 8 species in Canada, 4 have limited ranges: Bewick's wren (*Thryomanes bewickii*), southwestern BC; canyon wren (*Catherpes mexicanus*), Okanagan Valley; rock wren (*Salpinctes obsoletus*), southern BC to southern Sask and rarely Man; Carolina wren (*Thryothorus ludovicianus*), southern Ont. Winter wrens inhabit boreal and transitional conifer forests across Canada. House wrens (*Troglodytes aedon*), native to more southern, broad-leaved woodland and scrub habitats, penetrate only a short distance N of the US border, except near the Rockies, where they reach 58° N at Ft Nelson, BC. The marsh wren (*Cistothorus palustris*) is found in cattail marshes transcontinentally, reaching its

northern limit at Lk Athabasca. Sedge wrens (*C. platensis*) occupy wet sedge meadows. They occur only very locally in eastern N America. In Canada, they are common only in Man but occur locally in Alta. All are migratory, except in southern, coastal BC. All species build enclosed nests. Woodland wrens use tree holes (or nest boxes) and dense brush piles; winter wrens especially favour crannies among upturned roots of fallen trees. Marsh and sedge wrens construct spherical nests of grasses in low, wetland vegetation, often over water. Rock and canyon wrens use cliff crannies and rock piles. Initially, males build several nests, only one of which is used. This occurs especially with marsh and sedge wrens. Clutches average 5-6 eggs (range 4-8). The winter wren's song is one of the longest (5-6 sec) and highest-pitched among Canadian birds. Songs of other species are much shorter and of lower pitch. A.J. ERSKINE

Marsh wren (*Cistothorus palustris*) (*photo by Tim Fitzharris*).

Wrestling is so natural to man and so ancient that its precise origins are impossible to trace. Prehistoric man wrestled first for survival and eventually for sport; in fact, drawings on cave walls portray a form of freestyle wrestling. Wall paintings in Egyptian tombs from about 3400 BC depict matches that show an amazing similarity in moves to those practised today. Homer's *Iliad* describes a wrestling match between Odysseus and Aïas at burial festivities during the Trojan War (c 1200 BC), and records show wrestling as one of the original Olympic sports.

In early times there seem to have been as many styles or forms of wrestling as there were villages or towns. Modern competition has brought with it standardized rules and forms. Although many folk styles are still practised, there now exist 3 official world-championship styles recognized by the world governing body, FILA (Fédération internationale de lutte amateur): Greco-Roman, with holds above the waist only; freestyle, which allows the wrestlers to use any part of their body in executing their techniques; and Sambo, which incorporates many moves from the martial arts. Wrestling is a sport of strength, speed and the scientific application of both. Thus, there are no points for defence but only for attack – and then only if some degree of command is gained over the opponent. The points scored vary from one to

4, according to the degree to which command over the opponent is established. A wrestling match consists of two 3-minute rounds with a one-minute rest period in between. The match is terminated before the 6-minute term in the event of a fall, a 12-point difference in score, a disqualification or a default.

The most commonly practised style in Canada is freestyle. Since freestyle rules are used in all university and high-school competitions, it is not surprising that Canadians have generally distinguished themselves in this form at the international level. Canadian medallists in OLYMPIC GAMES competition include D. Stockton with a silver and Jim Trifunov with a bronze (1928); D. McDonald (silver, 1932); Joe Schleimer (bronze, 1936); and Bob Molle with a silver and Chris Rinke with a bronze (1984). World championship medallists for Canada are G. Bertie (bronze, 1973); C. Davis (silver, 1982); and Clark Davis with a silver and Pat Sullivan with a bronze (1985). Canadians have excelled at COMMONWEALTH GAMES competitions, notably in 1930 when they won all 7 gold medals. Earl McCready, who in 1930 won every amateur wrestling championship in Canada, the US and British Commonwealth, and Trifunov, a 10-time Canadian champion, have been elected to Canada's Sports Hall of Fame. In the 1987 Pan-Am Games Canada won one gold medal (Doug Cox), 4 silver and 7 bronze.

Since the first Canadian amateur wrestling championships were held at Toronto's Argonaut Rowing Club in 1901, the sport has grown considerably in Canada. In 1969 the Canadian Amateur Wrestling Assn was formed and amateur wrestling was touted as the fastest-growing sport in the country. Canadian wrestlers now regularly place high in this very competitive sport and Canada has achieved an excellent reputation for the quality of its wrestling officials and administrators. The fact that Canada has hosted the world wrestling championships twice since the inception of the CAWA is a further testament to the high regard in which Canada is held in this sport.

The sport of wrestling is now generally called amateur wrestling to distinguish it from professional wrestling (*see* WRESTLING, PROFESSIONAL), which is more a spectacle than a sport. WILLIAM F. DOWBIGGIN

Wrestling, Professional is perhaps the oldest professional sport competed in by man. In fact wrestling has been a livelihood of the rich and poor alike for centuries. Many great athletes have made their fame and fortune thanks to the appeal of this sport. Modern professional wrestling in Canada and the US, however, has taken a turn towards entertainment. It is now more important to be colourful than to be athletically superior. Perhaps Gene Kiniski is the best-known Canadian professional wrestler of our time. On 7 Jan 1966 Kiniski defeated veteran champion Lou Thesz 2-falls-to-one to become the world professional heavyweight champion. Kiniski, an ex-Edmonton Eskimo football star, had already gained prominence by defeating the British Empire champion "Whipper Billy" WATSON. Other Canadian world champions include Dan McLeod of Montréal who, fighting under the name of George Little, won a world championship in 1902. In 1908 Miss May Cullen of Toronto defeated the world women's champion winning a purse of $25. "Whipper Billy" Watson became the world light heavyweight champion in 1947, lost the title in 1948 and regained it in 1956. Other Canadian professional wrestlers popular in N America include Yukon Eric, who lost an ear in one of 15 grudge matches with "Killer Kowalski"; Edouard Carpentier, nephew of world boxing champion Georges Carpentier; and the recently retired Maurice "Mad Dog" Vachon.

WILLIAM F. DOWBIGGIN

Wright, Alexander Whyte, journalist, labour leader, politician (b at Elmira, Ont 17 Dec 1845; d c1919). After some business attempts in southwestern Ontario, he became a journalist and newspaper editor in the 1870s. Although a Conservative and prominent advocate of the NATIONAL POLICY, he endorsed currency and labour reform. He believed in the primacy of workers, farmers and productive manufacturers, and in the 1880s became a prominent KNIGHTS OF LABOR leader, first in Toronto and then in the US, becoming secretary of the order and editor of the *Journal of the Knights of Labor,* 1889-93. Returning to Ontario after the order's virtual collapse in 1893, he served as a royal commissioner to investigate sweatshop labour for the Tory federal government (1895). He edited a Toronto Tory labour paper 1909-14 and later was made vice-chairman of the Ontario Workmen's Compensation Board. A talented writer and orator, Wright was both charlatan and reformer and undoubtedly the best Canadian example of a mediator between the working class and the traditional political party.

GREGORY S. KEALEY

Wright, Cecil Augustus, "Caesar," educator (b at London, Ont 2 July 1904; d at Toronto 24 Apr 1967). Called Canada's most influential law teacher and the architect of LEGAL EDUCATION in Ontario, Wright taught at Osgoode Hall Law School from 1927, becoming dean in 1948. In 1949, when the Law Society of Upper Canada rejected changes in legal education for which he had been campaigning for years, he and most of the teaching staff at Osgoode Hall resigned. Wright, Bora LASKIN and John Willis then converted the undergraduate law department at U of T into Ontario's first professional university law school, and Wright served as its dean 1949-67. He wrote many articles, edited an important book on tort law, the *Canadian Bar Review* and several law reports, arbitrated labour disputes, provided legal advice to many lawyers, and strove to increase awareness of N American legal thought.

C. IAN KYER

Wright, Sir Charles Seymour, physicist (b at Toronto 7 Apr 1887; d at Victoria 1 Nov 1975). He attended Upper Canada College and U of T, and won a scholarship for postgraduate study in physics at Cambridge. He worked at the Cavendish Laboratory (1908-10) and was accepted as physicist and glaciologist with the British Antarctic Expedition (1910-13) under Capt Robert F. Scott. Wright was navigator for the sledge team that in Nov 1912 found the tent containing the bodies of Scott and his companions, who had died on their return from the S pole. He worked for the intelligence division of the British army during WWI, and served in the research arm of the British navy (1919-47), assuming the post of director of scientific research in 1934. He directed the work of a 600-member scientific team that developed, among other things, the allied radar system, and was knighted for this work in 1946. He retired to Canada in 1947 but remained a naval research consultant to Canada, Britain and the US and lectured at UBC. He returned to the Antarctic several times in the early 1960s as a guest of the US government. DEAN BEEBY

Wright, Eric Stanley, writer, teacher (b at London, Eng 4 May 1929). Immigrating to Churchill, Man (1951), and graduating from U Man (Hons BA, 1951) and U of T (MA, 1961), Wright has taught at Ryerson Polytechnical Institute. His series of award-winning crime novels, featuring a low-key but ironic hero, middle-aged Insp Char-

lie Salter of the Metropolitan Toronto Police Force, presents a cross-section of the Canadian urban social strata. Each book investigates a particular world as well as a mystery: academia in *The Night the Gods Smiled* (1983), the antique business in *Smoke Detector* (1984), innocents abroad in *Death in the Old Country* (1985), the world of singles in *A Single Death* (1986) and a PEI mystery in *A Body Surrounded by Water* (1987).

MARYLYNN SCOTT

Wright, Joseph, Sr, oarsman (b at Toronto 13 Jan 1864; d there 18 Oct 1950). In 1950 Wright was named Canada's outstanding oarsman of the half-century. In 1885 he stroked a Toronto Argonaut crew to victory at the US Nationals. Twenty years later he led the Argonauts to victory at the Royal Canadian Henley Regatta. In all, he won 137 national titles. One of the most famous rowing coaches in the world, he looked after U of Penn crews 1916-26, and coached his son Joe Jr to victory at the prestigious Diamond Sculls in 1928. Wright was successful at many other sports. He won the Canadian amateur heavyweight wrestling championship at 35, and at 44 played football on the senior Argonaut team.

J. THOMAS WEST

Wright, Philemon, lumberman (b at Woburn, Mass 3 Sept 1760; d at Hull, Qué 2 June 1839). The founder of HULL and the man who initiated the Ottawa Valley TIMBER TRADE, Wright came to Canada in 1800 as the leader of a small group from Massachusetts who settled at the present site of Hull. He intended to develop a community of independent farmers, but lack of income forced him into the timber trade in 1806 in order to provide cash for the settlement and a winter occupation. That year he floated the first raft of square timber from Ottawa to Québec. The growth of the trade ensured Wright continued predominance in the social, economic and political life of Hull.

CHRISTOPHER G. CURTIS

Wright, Robert Ramsay, zoologist, educator (b at Alloa, Scot 23 Sept 1852; d at Droitwich Spa, Eng 6 Sept 1933). Educated at Edinburgh U (MA 1871, BSc 1873), Ramsay Wright gave up a position on the CHALLENGER EXPEDITION to become professor of natural history (later biology) at U of T in 1874 and remained there for 38 years. He exerted a tremendous personal influence on the teaching of biology in Canada and on a generation of students. He emphasized instruction in the laboratory and developed a large teaching museum in the new Biological Building (1889); his own research ranged from parasitology to catfish anatomy. Wright was also a leading figure in the reestablishment of the Faculty of Medicine at U of T in 1887, where his former pupils A. B. MACALLUM and J. P. MCMURRICH later continued his work of applying biology to medicine. Interested in fisheries, he was a member of the Biological Board of Canada (later the FISHERIES RESEARCH BOARD) 1901-12, and then retired to Oxford to study classics. SANDRA F. MCRAE

Writers' Union of Canada (fd 1973) Prose writing in Canada, especially the writing of fiction, had certain problems associated with it until recently. Readership was small: until the late 1960s, readers shunned most Canadian fiction as second best, and most companies were reluctant to publish it unless an English or American publisher could be involved. Lingering puritanism limited subject matter, and conservatism of taste limited publishing opportunities for avant-garde texts. There were few writers' agents, and writers had either to go to the US or Britain for agents who were unfamiliar with Canada, or to do without. The vast distances between cities meant that writers seldom met, nor was a reading circuit

available to them. Prose writers frequently lived isolated lives, receiving scant recognition for their work – if it appeared at all. It was common for writers with serious ambitions to leave the country. Like the other arts, fiction was considered a frill of dubious value by most of Canadian society.

By the 1970s, growing national self-awareness and confidence translated into a larger audience for fiction and nonfiction prose. The indigenous share of the trade book business increased to 25%. Publishing houses established in the 1960s contributed to this new growth, as did a more entrepreneurial and Canadian-centered spirit in older houses such as MCCLELLAND AND STEWART. Soon writers as well as audiences realized they had something of value – and therefore something to lose. Foreign domination was now seen as a threat, and royal commissions were set up by Québec (1971) and Ontario (1973) to investigate the publishing industry.

Out of the Ontario commission hearings grew the idea for a union of Canadian writers. The union initially comprised a small number of authors who felt that writers must work as a unified group if they were to gain any measure of control over the economic conditions influencing them. A planning conference was held in Dec 1972, and the Writers' Union of Canada was officially founded in Nov 1973. Since the LEAGUE OF CANADIAN POETS (fd 1966) already existed, the union limited itself to prose writers who had published a trade book within the past 7 years, or had a book still in print. It did not, and does not, include journalists and playwrights, who have their own organizations (PERIODICAL WRITERS ASSOCIATION OF CANADA and the PLAYWRIGHTS UNION OF CANADA). Since 1973 many provincial writers' organizations have been formed to deal with matters that cannot be well handled by a national organization. The union finances itself through membership dues and fund-raising drives. It receives some federal and provincial grant money, especially for its annual general meeting. In 1988 its membership was about 600.

The union has done extensive work on contracts and retains a lawyer to give advice in negotiations; its Grievance Committee helps to resolve problems with publishers; it runs a manuscript-evaluation agency; it gives advice on tax matters; it acts as a clearing house for information and distributes a monthly newsletter. It organizes around particular issues, such as book dumping (the practice of importing from abroad remaindered copies of books by Canadians which are sold at reduced prices while the Canadian edition is still in the stores at full price); through the union's efforts this practice has reached the attention of the public and the government, the latter having announced its commitment to stopping the practice. Union committees work on matters of COPYRIGHT protection, liaison with publishers and librarians, and CENSORSHIP and repression issues. One major objective – the establishment of a "Public Lending Right" fee which would reimburse writers for multiple use of their works through libraries – was achieved in 1986.

But one of the most important achievements of the union is to have fostered a spirit of professionalism and self-respect among writers. This organization, founded by writers for writers, has enabled them to meet and know one another and to take collective responsibility for decisions which affect the ways in which they are seen and treated. Since the 1960s the public's image of the Canadian writer has changed – though the change is incomplete – from defective freak to acceptable member of society, and the union has reflected and fostered that change. *See also* LITERATURE AND POLITICS.

MARGARET ATWOOD

Wrong, George MacKinnon, historian (b at Grovesend, Elgin County, Canada W 25 June 1860; d at Toronto 29 June 1948). Educated at U of T, Wrong was ordained a priest of the Church of England upon his graduation in 1883. He lectured in ecclesiastical history and liturgics at Wycliffe 1883-92 and in history at U of T 1892-94. From 1894 until his retirement in 1927 he was professor of history and head of the department. He promoted history as a distinct discipline, and Canadian history as a legitimate field of study. In 1896-97 he founded the *Review of Historical Publications Relating to Canada* (since 1920 the CANADIAN HISTORICAL REVIEW) and in 1905 he co-founded the CHAMPLAIN SOCIETY. He wrote numerous monographs and texts on Canadian history, the best being *A Canadian Manor and Its Seigneurs* (1908). Formal in habit and something of an anglophile in taste, Wrong influenced a generation of students.   M. BROOK TAYLOR

Wrong, Humphrey Hume, diplomat (b at Toronto 10 Sept 1894; d at Ottawa 24 Jan 1954). Grandson of Edward BLAKE and son of historian George WRONG, Hume Wrong was raised in privileged circumstances. He attended U of T, was denied enrolment in the Canadian Expeditionary Force because of a blind eye, enlisted in the British Expeditionary Force, and served at the front before being invalided home. He studied history at Oxford and was hired in 1921 to teach history in his father's department at U of T. In 1928, Vincent MASSEY, a family friend, called Wrong to Washington as first secretary in the new Canadian legation, and Wrong spent the next decade there learning the craft of diplomacy. Service at the League of Nations, in London, in Washington once more, and in Ottawa for 3 critical wartime years followed. As Norman ROBERTSON's closest colleague, Wrong devised and honed the idea of functionalism, a principle which argued that in those areas in which Canada had the resources of a great power – food, minerals, air power – she should be treated like a great power. Functionalism became the basis of Canadian wartime policy, and to it must be credited much of the gains in Canadian influence and prestige. Wrong was posted to Washington as ambassador in 1946. There he had great influence, resolved financial problems, and did the actual day-to-day negotiation of the North Atlantic Treaty. In 1953 he returned to Ottawa as undersecretary but died before he could take up the reins.   J.L. GRANATSTEIN

Reading: J.L. Granatstein, *The Ottawa Men* (1982).

Wrongful Dismissal, *see* EMPLOYMENT LAW.

Wyle, Florence, sculptor (b at Trenton, Ill 24 Nov 1881; d at Newmarket, Ont 14 Jan 1968). Settling in Canada in 1913, she was considered by contemporaries to be Canada's finest academic sculptor. Reclusive, she was happiest working quietly in her studio in the converted Toronto church that she shared for over 50 years with Frances LORING. Early premedical studies in Chicago had given her the profound respect for anatomical perfection that was evident in her work as a sculptor. Also a poet (*Poems*, 1958), her lyrics reflected her love of nature. As a founding member (1928) of the Sculptors' Soc of Canada, she fought for recognition of Canadian SCULPTURE and was the first woman sculptor accorded full membership in the Royal Canadian Academy of Arts. While her public commissions were successful, such as the fine memorial in relief to nurse Edith Cavell on the grounds of the Toronto General Hospital, she is best remembered for her smaller, more intimate, studio sculptures, especially her studies of children and animals.
REBECCA SISLER

Wyman, Anna, née Roman, dancer, choreographer, teacher and director (b at Graz, Austria *c* 1928). As founder and choreographer of her own Vancouver dance company, Wyman has become a noted figure in Canadian modern dance. She studied ballet and contemporary movement in various European cities and danced in Austria until 1948. Wyman moved to England in 1952 where she taught and opened her own school. Immigrating to Canada, she established the Anna Wyman School of Dance Arts in Vancouver in 1968 and the Anna Wyman Dancers in 1970 (professional debut 1971) which became the AN-NA WYMAN DANCE THEATRE in 1973. She has choreographed 39 works for her company and has led it on many overseas tours.   MICHAEL CRABB

Wyn Wood, Elizabeth, sculptor (b at Orillia, Ont 8 Oct 1903; d at Toronto 27 Jan 1966). She made a significant contribution to Canada's cultural life, primarily through her modernist interpretation of the Canadian landscape in sculpture, but also through teaching at Central Technical School, Toronto, and through her involvement with the Federation of Canadian Artists and the Canadian Arts Council (as organizing secretary 1944-45, chairman of the International Relations Committee 1945-48 and VP 1945-48). Just as the GROUP OF SEVEN (several of whom taught her at the Ontario Coll of Art in the 1920s) translated their experience of the Canadian landscape into paint, Wyn Wood was innovative in expressing similar artistic concerns through fashioning modern materials (notably tin) into pared-down designs composed of juxtaposed masses in space. Her later work shows a greater social concern as she turned to figural subjects and received a number of important major public commissions in Ontario, such as the Welland-Crowland War Memorial (1934-39), fountains and panels in the Rainbow Bridge Gardens (1940-41), a monument to King George VI (1963) at Niagara Falls, and the Simcoe Memorial at Niagara-on-the-Lake, Ont (1953).
CHRISTINE BOYANOSKI

Wynyard, Sask, Town, pop 2079 (1986c), inc 1911, is located 150 km N of Regina. The area was originally settled in 1905 by a group of ICELANDERS and the CPR selected the site as a divisional point in 1908. The province soon designated Wynyard as a judicial centre for the Touchwood Hills-Quill Lakes area. At present, the main industry, Plains Poultry Ltd, operates a poultry-eviscerating plant and hatchery in the town. The town also serves as an agricultural service centre for the area. The QUILL LAKES, immediately N of Wynyard, cover an area of 230 square miles (611 square km). The Potash Corp of Saskatchewan has established a plant at Big Quill Lake near Wynyard to extract potassium sulphate from the water.

DON HERPERGER

XY Company (New North West Co), named after the marks used to distinguish its bales of goods from those of the NORTH WEST COMPANY, was a product of conflicts between NWC agents (led by Simon MCTAVISH) and NWC winterers, following the company's reorganization in 1795. In 1797-98, Montréal partners who did not join the 1795 agreement became a focal point for uncommitted or alienated winterers, and in 1798 they fielded an opposition that reached as far as Athabasca. In 1800 Alexander MACKENZIE joined the new concern, which then became popularly known as "Alexander Mackenzie & Co." Rivalry became intense and costly. The use of liquor in the trade rose sharply; more employees were needed and were able to sue for higher wages in both firms. When McTavish's death in July 1804 removed a focus of personal hostilities and disaffection, the NWC and XYC negotiated a coalition. Their agreement of 5 Nov 1804 created a newly powerful and monopolistic NWC of 100 shares, 75 to be held by the old Nor'Westers and 25 by the former XYC partners. JENNIFER S.H. BROWN

Yachting refers to races of watercraft using sail power only. Competitors are required to complete a prescribed course in the shortest possible time, passing marker buoys in the correct order and on the correct side. It is believed that the sport has Dutch origins. It was introduced to England by Charles II following his exile in Holland and the word itself comes from the Dutch *jaght*. Although the first recorded race took place in 1610, the International Yacht Racing Union, which governs the sport in the world, was not formed until 1906.

Yachting competition takes place with a wide variety of SAILING craft and under quite varied conditions. Races are organized for the smallest of dinghies on lake courses and for oceangoing vessels with substantial crews taking several days to complete the course. Olympic yachting, however, is confined to 6 classes: Tornado, catamarans crewed by 2 people; Flying Dutchman, centreboard dinghies weighing 174 kg with spinnakers and a crew of 2; 470, the same as Flying Dutchman, but the boat weighing 188 kg; soling, a keel yacht with a 3-man crew; Finn, one person sailing a centre-board dinghy; and Tempest, keel yachts with a 2-man crew. There are 7 races in each class and competitors record their 6 best results. The sailor or crew with the lowest number of points is the winner, since a first-place finish earns zero points – points being accumulated on a graduated scale for less favourable placings.

In Canada, yachting traces its origins to Kingston, Halifax and Toronto. The Kingston Boat Club was formed in 1826, but with the establishment of the Royal Nova Scotia Yacht Squadron (later Halifax Yacht Club) in 1837 came the founding of the country's oldest continuous club in the sport. In 1854 the Royal Canadian Yacht Club was formed in Toronto, and by 1892 the sport had spread across Canada with the founding of the Royal Victoria Yacht Club. Three

Yacht Race, Halifax (1850), oil on canvas, by John O'Brien (*courtesy National Gallery of Canada*).

years later, the Canada Cup races were established as a perpetual challenge series between yachts from Canada and the US on the Great Lakes.

Although the Canada Cup has generally been won by the Americans, more recent years have brought Canadian domination, starting with the win by *Evergreen* in 1978. One of the most glorious chapters in Canadian yachting was written by the BLUENOSE out of Lunenburg, NS, which dominated the races for the Halifax *Herald's* International Fisherman's Trophy from 1921 until her retirement in 1938.

Besides the *Bluenose*, Canadians have enjoyed many other international successes in yachting. Canadian sailors won Olympic silver and bronze medals in 1936 and a bronze medal in the soling class in 1972. In 1959 Walter Windeyer of Toronto won the world Dragon Class championship. In 1977 and 1979 Glen Dexter of Lunenburg, NS, and his crew of Andreas Josenhans and Sandy Macmillan won the world soling championship. In 1982 Terry Neilson won the world Flying Dutchman championship. Much attention was focused on Canada's unsuccessful challenge (1983) for the prestigious America's Cup for 12 m yachts – a natural interest for a nation bounded by 2 great oceans with thousands of freshwater lakes in between. In the 1987 Pan-Am Games Canada won medals in 5 out of 6 classes, including one tie for gold with the US in the star class.
J. THOMAS WEST

Yaffe, Leo, educator, nuclear scientist, university administrator (b at Devil's Lake, N Dak 6 July 1916). In 1952 Yaffe established a productive nuclear chemistry research laboratory at McGill. He has contributed richly to measurements of beta radiation, neutron- and proton-induced reactions, nuclear isomer ratios, and analysis of archaeological artifacts, all described in over 150 publications. He was director of Research and Laboratories (1963-65) of the International Atomic Energy Agency, Vienna; chairman, Dept of Chemistry (1965-72) and vice-principal, administration (1974-81) of McGill; and president (1981-82) of the Chemical Inst of Canada. He has been the recipient of many honours. In 1984 he was made professor emeritus at McGill.
MARIO ONYSZCHUK

Yahk, BC, UP, pop 169 (1986c), 172 (1981c), is located on the Moyie R near its passage into Idaho State, 65 km SW of Cranbrook and 40 km E of Creston. In prehistoric times the area was a crossroads, as Interior Salishan people to the S met the Lower Kootenay Indians from the W via Goat R and the Upper Kootenays. The Dewdney Trail was built on the latter 2 trails in 1865. The modern era began with the establishment of the Crow's Nest Pass Ry 1898. A large CPR tie-mak-

ing camp was built close by. In recent years, logging, some sawmilling and post-making have supported the area. WILLIAM A. SLOAN

Yanofsky, Daniel Abraham chess grandmaster (b at Brody, Poland 26 Mar 1925). He came to Canada at an early age and developed a talent for chess, winning his first tournament at 12. He qualified for the Canadian Olympiad team for the 1939 world team championships in Buenos Aires, where he received a special prize for best score on Board 2. He played in many European tournaments and in 1953 won the British championship. His career in Canada includes 9 Canadian championships, 1941-79, and 10 appearances on the Canadian national team, most recently in 1980 at Malta. He received the grandmaster title in 1964 for his performance on Board 1 for Canada at the Olympiad in Tel Aviv. Yanofsky is one of only 3 Canadians to hold the international grandmaster title. He continued to compete until 1986. Yanofsky is a lawyer and was on the Winnipeg City Council until 1986. LAWRENCE DAY

Yarmouth, NS, Town, pop 7617 (1986c), 7475 (1981c), is located at the entrance to Yarmouth harbour at the western tip of NS. Called *Kespoowuit* ("land's end") by the Micmac, and Port Fourchu by CHAMPLAIN, it was settled first by ACADIANS, later by settlers from New England (1761). During the AMERICAN REVOLUTION settlers began to arrive from Massachusetts, the beginning of Loyalist immigration to NS. Settlement in the Chebogue area had by 1810 moved to Yarmouth, which became the administrative and commercial centre. The shipbuilding industry, which began about 1764, had by the 19th century expanded into an impressive merchant fleet. By 1879 Yarmouth reached its peak as a shipbuilding port, being the second-largest port of registry, in tonnage, in Canada. Today the economy of the town is based largely on fishing, fish processing, dairy processing and the production of textiles, knitted goods and wood products. The first township in NS to introduce municipal incorporation (1856), Yarmouth was reincorporated 1890 after repeal in 1858.

As well as being the commercial and industrial centre of southwestern NS, Yarmouth is also its transportation centre, with 2 ferries to Maine. The discovery of a "runic stone," similar to a Norse cemetery stone, near Yarmouth harbour has caused considerable speculation and study suggesting the early presence of Norsemen in the area. Artifacts held by the Yarmouth County Museum serve as reminders of the days when it was a major seaport. JEAN PETERSON

Yarrow, common name for some 200 species of herbaceous plants of genus *Achillea* of the Compositae (Asteraceae) family; 3 species occur in Canada (*Achillea millefolium*, *A. ptarmica*, *A. sibirica*). Common yarrow (*A. millefolium* var. *lanulosa*), also known as milfoil, is an erect, aromatic perennial with rhizomes (underground stems). It grows across Canada in grassy places and roadsides from BC to Nfld, N to Great Bear Lk. The genus was named for the Gk hero, Achilles, who was supposed to have used the plant to heal his soldiers' wounds. *Lanulosa* comes from Lat *lana*, "wool." The leaves grow alternately up the densely hairy, 30-100 cm stem and are finely divided with a feathery appearance [Lat *millefolium*, "thousand leaf"]. Flowers, borne in flat clusters of numerous flowerheads, are composite structures.

Yellowish disc florets (3-10) make up the central part, which is surrounded by 5 petal-shaped ray florets. They bloom from May to October. Yarrow has a dry, one-seeded fruit. Throughout the ages, yarrow has been used to stop blood flow, hence one common name, "nosebleed." Blackfoot used it to aid childbirth, for gastroenteritis and liver trouble, as a diuretic, and for sore throat and skin troubles. *A. ptarmica* (sneezeweed) occurs across Canada, from southern BC to PEI. *A. sibirica* is found from the YT to eastern Québec, including central BC. *See also* PLANTS, NATIVE USES.

BERYL HALLWORTH

Yeast, group of unicellular fungi with at least 450 known species. Most yeasts are ascomycetes which multiply by budding in various ways or by transverse fission, and may form ascospores in a naked ascus (saclike cell). They may form pseudomycelium or true mycelium. Some yeasts are basidiomycetes (Ustilaginaceae); some of these produce red or yellow carotenoid pigments (*Rhodotorula* spp). All reproduce asexually by budding, and sexually by formation of teliospores. Classification at genus level is based on the morphology of the spores and vegetative cells and, at species level, by the ability to metabolize different sugars and related compounds. Major genera include *Schizosaccharomyces* (fission yeasts), *Saccharomyces*, *Kluyveromyces*, *Hansenula*, *Pichia*, *Candida*, *Rhodotorula* and *Cryptococcus*, the latter 2 being basidiomycetes. Although not as widely distributed as bacteria, yeasts occur in terrestrial and aquatic environments worldwide in association with plants and animals. A few are pathogenic: *Candida tropicalis* and *Cryptococcus neoformans* cause infections in humans; *Candida albicans* causes thrush and vaginitis. Patients treated with immunosuppressants are particularly susceptible to yeast infections. One yeast species is pathogenic for cotton. The best-known yeast is *Saccharomyces cerevisiae* (common bread, brewing and wine yeast), used for leavening and brewing for thousands of years, although its role was unsuspected until the work of Pasteur. It is a source of B vitamins and a valuable research tool for biochemical and genetic investigations. Other species have been used in biotechnological processes: treatment of wood pulp wastes, production of food and fodder yeast (single cell protein), production of SCP from whey and petroleum, production of gums (mannans), polyhydroxy alcohols (glycerol) and glycolipids. Yeasts may act as spoilage agents: *Rhodotorula*, spoiling olives; *Debaryomyces*, preserved meats; and some *Pichia*, mayonnaise and sauerkraut. Yeasts that are sugar tolerant can cause explosive bursting of fondant-centered chocolates and spoilage of fruit-flavoured yogurts. *Schizosaccharomyces octosporus* often grows on dried dates, figs and raisins, without impairing their quality.   J.F.T. SPENCER

Yellowhead, William, or Musquakie, Ojibwa chief (d at the Rama Reserve, Lk Simcoe, Canada W 11 Jan 1864). During the WAR OF 1812 Yellowhead, then in his thirties or forties, fought for the British. He had his jaw shattered by a musket ball. Succeeding his father as head chief of the Lk Simcoe Ojibwa in 1817, he participated in the surrender the following year of 1 600 000 acres of their territory. He converted to Methodism in the late 1820s but later became an Anglican. As head chief he kept the great wampum belt which recorded the final peace between the Ojibwa and their hereditary enemies, the Six Nations Iroquois.   DONALD B. SMITH

Yellowhead Pass, elev 1133 m, crosses the continental divide between Alberta and BC, 25 km W of JASPER. The Miette R flows E from the pass to meet the Athabasca R at Jasper. Yellowhead Lk, on the W side, empties into the Fraser River. Yellowhead Pass was first called Leather Pass, because the HBC obtained moose and caribou hides through the pass 1826-28; it was supposedly later named for a blond Iroquois trapper, Pierre Bostonais, nicknamed "Tête Jaune," who hunted and trapped in the area. It provided a route to the Cariboo goldfields 1862. It was originally proposed by Sandford FLEMING as the route for the CPR, but was rejected. However, early this century both GRAND TRUNK PACIFIC and CANADIAN NORTHERN RY installed trackage over the pass – in some places side by side. Today the CNR and Yellowhead Hwy traverse the pass, which in 1985 was officially designated a Canadian historic site.

GLEN BOLES

Yellowknife (Redknives, Copper) were a BAND of the Athapaskan-speaking CHIPEWYAN associated with the region encompassed by the Coppermine and Yellowknife rivers, the NE shore of Great Slave Lk, and NE into the Barren Grounds. From the first direct contact with European traders in the 17th century until their amalgamation with other Chipewyan and DOGRIB, every account has described them as similar to Chipewyan in language and culture. Their distinctiveness and separate name is largely based on European perception. Early in the 17th century, traders were anxious to make contact with the Indians associated with copper, thus the name Copper Indians. Samuel HEARNE travelled inland to Yellowknife territory, 1770-72, and dispelled the idea of rich copper deposits.

The Yellowknife were the main providers and guides for the Franklin Expedition, 1819-22. Their leader at this time, Akaitcho, acquired respect from the Europeans as a strong and competent leader. To the neighbouring native groups, he was a bullying, cruel leader with a reputation for plundering and killing. In 1823 the Dogrib made a revenge attack on a Yellowknife camp, killing most of the group. Devastated by European diseases, the Yellowknife soon thereafter ended their raids on INUIT groups, initiating a period of relatively peaceful relations between them and their neighbours.

In 1900 the Yellowknife were still acknowledged as a distinct group (estimated population 200) when they signed Treaty No 8 at Ft Resolution along with other natives of the area (*see* INDIAN TREATIES). Before this date, however, they began to merge with neighbouring Chipewyan and Dogrib. By the 1960s Dogrib and Chipewyan were not aware of any group called Yellowknife but could recount vivid stories about Akaitcho, whom they both considered to be Chipewyan. *See also* NATIVE PEOPLE: SUBARCTIC.   BERYL C. GILLESPIE

Yellowknife, NWT, City, inc 1970, pop 11 753 (1986c), 9483 (1981c), is located on the N arm of GREAT SLAVE LK, 966 air km N of Edmonton. Nestled on the jagged rocks of the northern Canadian SHIELD, Yellowknife is the capital and only city of the NWT, headquarters of the territorial government and other territory-wide organizations, and is the base for tours to more remote areas of the North. It is also the home of 2 gold mines. The population is a mix of DENE, INUIT and whites of varied nationalities.

History Named after the YELLOWKNIFE band who moved into the area in the late 1700s, the first settlement was a trading post established in 1789 by Alexander MACKENZIE. But the city's real history is the story of a GOLD rush. Although gold was first discovered in the late 1890s by miners on their way to the KLONDIKE, the rush only began here in 1934. By 1936 Yellowknife was a boom town and by 1940 had a population of 1000. Development was halted briefly during WWII, but regained momentum after the war. At that time

the Giant Gold Mine, which is still operational, was established. The second gold rush was aided by the construction of a road from the S. By the end of 1947, gold mines were again producing on a large scale. Even greater growth in the mining industry is projected for 1988. Creation of a hydroelectric dam on the nearby Snare R in 1948 alleviated the former problem of power shortages. The first mayor was elected in 1953. Prior to 1967 the NWT were administered from Ottawa; that year Yellowknife was named capital of the NWT and the NWT's commissioner and territorial government offices were established in the city.

Townscape Like many other northern communities, Yellowknife boasts an old and a new town. The former, wrapped around Back Bay, is a picturesque collection of old gold-rush buildings and includes a Dene village, called Rainbow Valley for its brightly coloured houses. The new town, with its high-rise office buildings, hotels and apartments, is the most modern of NWT settlements. Each year in March, Yellowknifers enjoy Caribou Carnival, a 3-day festival celebrating the end of winter. The city is also the home of the Prince of Wales Northern Heritage Centre. In May 1984 the 313-seat Globe Theatre of the Northern Arts and Cultural Centre officially opened; since its first season, beginning in Sept 1984, it has presented a variety of entertainment from the Royal Winnipeg Ballet to local drama.   ANNELIES POOL

Yeo, James, shipbuilder and owner, entrepreneur (b at Kilkhampton, Eng 1789; d at Port Hill, PEI 25 Aug 1868). Beginning as an agent for a Devonshire merchant, he established his own transatlantic commercial enterprise between PEI and N Devon, Eng. By 1833 he was the pre-eminent individual in Prince County and, by the mid-1840s, the most powerful businessman in the colony. At mid-century, he was engaged in agriculture, fishing, lumbering, merchandising and shipbuilding, while his son William had established facilities for shipbuilding and repair at Appledore in N Devon. Entering the Legislative Assembly in 1839, Yeo was a powerful member of the government from the late 1850s.

GERRY PANTING

Yew is the common name for evergreen CONIFERS, genus *Taxus*, of the yew family (Taxaceae). Yews are unusual conifers in that seeds are not borne in cones but occur singly and are enclosed by a red, fleshy, berrylike structure (aril). Pollen cones and seeds usually occur on different plants. POLLINATION occurs in spring and seeds mature in fall. The flat, needlelike leaves are 2-3 cm long. There are about 10 species of yew, all in the Northern Hemisphere; 2 in Canada. Canada yew or ground hemlock (*T. canadensis*) is a low-spreading shrub which grows from Manitoba eastward. Western yew (*T. brevifolia*) is a shrub or TREE in moist areas of southern and western BC. The hard, reddish wood is prized for wood carving and making archery bows, but yew has minor commercial importance in Canada. English and Japanese yew are popular introduced ORNAMENTALS. The leaves, bark and seeds are toxic. *See also* PLANTS, NATIVE USES.   JOHN N. OWENS

Yoho National Park (est in 1886, 1300 km²). With 28 mountain peaks towering more than 3000 m, it is aptly named after the Cree word meaning "awe." Situated in the ROCKY MOUNTAINS, Yoho has BANFF and KOOTENAY national parks as its eastern and southern boundaries. It is a park of steep, glacier-carved valleys, thundering WATER-FALLS (Takakkaw is Canada's highest), turquoise glacial lakes and icy peaks. Crystal caves, natural bridges and HOODOOS add to the spectacular alpine landscape. In the high alpine meadows there are pika, marmot and grizzly bear. Moose, wolverine, marten and elk live lower down in subalpine forests. From the park's many shallow lakes and wetlands to the rocky peaks, a great variety of bird life soars, flits and hops, including golden eagles, white-tailed ptarmigan and Clark's nutcrackers. Yoho was initially discovered in the course of the search for a route to the Pacific. KICKING HORSE PASS provides the route through which trains traverse the Rockies. Services are available in the towns of Field and Golden, BC.   LILLIAN STEWART

York, Derek, geophysics professor and science writer (b at Normanton, Yorkshire, Eng 12 Aug 1936). A leader in the field of potassium-argon dating of rock, he was a foreign principal investigator for NASA during the Apollo missions to the moon. He came to U of Toronto in 1960 from Oxford, where he had earned a DPhil in earth sciences. His first book, *The Earth's Age and Geochronology*, written with R.M. Farquhar (1972), was translated into Chinese, and a subsequent book, *Planet Earth* (1976), into Japanese and Italian. In 1985 he won the past president's medal of the Geological Association of Canada for research in earth sciences and was elected a fellow of the Royal Society of Canada. He began writing science articles for *The Globe and Mail* in 1980 and in 1986 won the Royal Society's Bancroft award for his contribution to public understanding of the earth sciences.   JUDITH KNELMAN

York Boat, named for the HUDSON'S BAY CO's York Factory; one of 3 types of inland boats (the others being scows and sturgeon-heads) used by the HBC, and the most suitable for lake travel. Boatbuilders recruited from the Orkney Is built the first boat about 1749, for use on the Albany R. In competition inland with the NWC on the Saskatchewan R in the 1790s the York boat offered the HBC a distinct advantage, since it carried twice the cargo of a *canot du nord* (*see* CANOE) with the same number of crew; it was less easily damaged by ice and was safer in storms. The typical boat had a 9.1 m keel and overall length of 12.6 m, beam 2.7 m and inside depth of 0.9 m. It carried 6 to 8 tripmen and a cargo of over 2700 kg. By the late 18th century the HBC had boat-building stations from James Bay to Ft Chipewyan, and in 1795 York boats were first built at Ft Edmonton. In the early 20th century York boats were of 3 sizes, "60 pieces" (2700 kg), "100 pieces" (4535 kg) and "120 pieces" (5440 kg). By the 1920s the York boat had passed from service.   JOHN E. FOSTER

The York boat was the basis of the HBC transportation system. It was durable, stable and required less skill than a canoe. It was propelled by oars, as shown here, or a square sail (*courtesy Hudson's Bay Co*).

York Factory, Man, a trading post located on the N bank at the mouth of the HAYES R and perma-

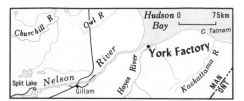

nently established in 1684 by Gov George Geyer of the HUDSON'S BAY COMPANY. It is the oldest permanent settlement in the province. Until the British were awarded possession by the Treaty of UTRECHT in 1713, ownership shifted between France and Britain. The comte de Lapérouse sacked and burned it in 1782. Tapping the trade of the entire North-West through the SASKATCHEWAN R system, the factory was the most important of all the HBC's posts. All goods going into the West and all furs coming out of the interior passed through York Factory and until 1774 the volume of trade there exceeded that of all the other bay posts. Trade declined after 1774, as the HBC expanded its inland operations, but it remained the principal transportation depot; and in 1821 became headquarters of the Northern Dept. After 1850, when transportation costs through the US became almost two-thirds cheaper, the factory declined rapidly in importance. It was reduced by 1870 to a coastal trading post and the local environment was not able to support the post and its population of Europeans, Métis and Indians. Forest clearance and overhunting of local game increased the cost of operating the post, while local fur returns also became marginal. York Factory's role as headquarters was terminated in 1873 and the post continued to decline until it was closed in 1957. Title was transferred in 1968 to National Historic Sites. All that remains today at the site is a small clearing, the large depot and an outbuilding. The depot was built in the early 19th century and has survived on the PERMAFROST because of a number of engineering innovations. The large columns and beams were joined in ways to make allowance for heaving and settling and a series of drainage ditches were dug beneath the building to carry off surface water. Archaeologists have uncovered the remains of earlier structures and camping areas of the visiting Indians and the site promises a harvest of artifacts. However, the extreme climate and the encroaching river are relentlessly destroying the entire site.
                                        FRITS PANNEKOEK

York University, Toronto, was founded in 1959 and took as its name Toronto's early name. Instruction is principally in English but is bilingual at Glendon College. Founded in response to the rapid growth of Toronto's metropolitan area, York was conceived in the 1950s with support from the North Toronto YMCA, which was interested in the promotion of adult education, and from major business and professional establishments. York was originally an affiliate of UNIVERSITY OF TORONTO and maintained that connection 1959-65. In 1961 it moved to the Glendon campus, and the main campus of 243 ha in suburban Downsview opened in 1965. York expanded rapidly in the 1960s, establishing new faculties and programs such as Atkinson College for part-time degree studies, the Centre for Research in Experimental Space Science, the Institute of Social Research and the Faculty of Administrative Studies. Osgoode Hall Law School, established

Enrolment: York University, 1985-86 (Source: Statistics Canada)			
Full-time Undergrad	Full-time Graduate	Part-time Undergrad	Part-time Graduate
18 266	1 595	12 178	1 447

1862 by the Law Society of Upper Canada, became affiliated with York in 1968, merging an older Toronto institution with a new one. More recently added research units include Joint Centre on Asia Pacific Studies and Joint Program in Transportation (both with U of T); Centre for Research on Latin America and the Caribbean; LaMarsh Research Program on Violence and Conflict Resolution; and Centre for International and Strategic Studies.   B. BEATON

Yorkton, Sask, City, pop 15 574 (1986c), 15 339 (1981c), inc 1928, is located about 175 km NE of Regina. The city acts as a regional service centre for the surrounding rich prairie parkland, known for its good agricultural production, particularly in grain crops. The community's beginnings can be traced back to 1882 with the York Farmers' Colonization Co, a block settlement group from York County, Ont. Originally known as York City, the village was established 4 km NE of its present site and was intended to serve the York colony. In 1884, with the establishment of a post office, the settlement was renamed Yorkton. With the coming of the railway in 1889, the village was moved trackside to its present site. Although the York colony eventually faded, large numbers of immigrants from across Europe settled in the area. Of particular significance were the early UKRAINIANS and DOUKHOBORS who formed a large portion of the population. Today the city performs commercial, transportation and government functions. Points of interest to visitors include a branch of the Western Development Museum, the Godfrey Dean Cultural Centre and the dome paintings of the St Mary's Ukrainian Catholic Church.   MARK RASMUSSEN

Reading: Yorkton: York Colony to Treasure Chest City (1982).

Youmans, Letitia, née Creighton, temperance worker (b in Hamilton Twp, UC 3 Jan 1827; d at Toronto 18 July 1896), founder of the WOMAN'S CHRISTIAN TEMPERANCE UNION in Canada. Educated at the Burlington Ladies' Academy, she graduated in 1847 and taught there for 2 years. She then went to the Picton Ladies' Academy and became its preceptress in the spring of 1850, marrying later that year. In 1868 she became increasingly involved in Sunday school and TEMPERANCE work. As a result of both these interests, she attended the CHAUTAUQUA Assembly in 1874 where she met leaders of the American women's temperance crusade. She returned to Canada and formed the second Canadian woman's temperance group, at Picton in Dec 1874. (A similar organization had formed in Owen Sound just previous to this.) Through her efforts, WCTUs spread across the country and in 1885 a national WCTU was formed with Youmans as first president. She continued in this position until 1889 when she resigned owing to ill health. An invalid, she remained honorary president until her death. Her autobiography, *Campaign Echoes*, appeared in 1893.   WENDY L. MITCHINSON

Young, George Paxton, philosopher, educator (b at Berwick upon Tweed, Eng 9 Nov 1818; d at Toronto 26 Feb 1889). He was educated at Edinburgh U, studying for ordination in the Presbyterian ministry, and was appointed minister of Knox Church, Hamilton, Canada W, in 1850.

Subsequently professor of both "Logic, Mental and Moral Philosophy" and "Evidences of Natural and Revealed Religion" at Knox College, Toronto, 1853-64, he resigned from this position, and from the Presbyterian ministry, because of his commitment to reason, rather than theological creed, as the foundation of ethics. From then until 1868 he was inspector of grammar schools for Ontario; his annual reports were instrumental in laying the foundations of the Ontario high school system.

Young spent the remainder of his life as a philosopher and teacher of PHILOSOPHY, first at Knox College, which invited him to return in 1868, and from 1871, as professor of logic, metaphysics and ethics at the nondenominational University College at U of T. Young's influence on University College students was enormous. He had come to advocate a system of idealism similar to that of Thomas Hill Green in England (but antecedent to it), and his ethical system, compatible with, but not dependent upon, Christian revelation, struck a responsive chord in students faced with the intrusion of evolutionary naturalism.

A. BRIAN MCKILLOP

Young, John, businessman, journalist, politician (b at Falkirk, Scot 1 Sept 1773; d at Halifax 6 Oct 1837). Young had a brilliant career at Glasgow U and wished to study medicine. His father refused further support so he began a career in business. Immigrating to Halifax in 1814 he established John Young and Company, even selling goods in Castine, Maine, following the British occupation of the town in 1814. Best remembered for a series of essays on agriculture, published under the name "Agricola" in the *Acadian Recorder* (1818-22), he pointed out the need for agricultural reform and his articles led to the formation of the Provincial Agricultural Soc with Young as secretary. He and 2 of his sons later became members of the NS Assembly. Ambitious, he had the ability to reconcile his own goals with the public interest. He believed people to be motivated by self-interest, and his own career suggests that this was so.

R.A. MACLEAN

Young, Neil Percival, rock singer, songwriter, guitarist (b at Toronto 12 Nov 1945), son of journalist Scott Young. After early years with Winnipeg and Toronto rock bands (The Squires, Mynah Birds), Young became a founding member 1966-68 of the folk-rock band Buffalo Springfield in Los Angeles, Calif. Thereafter he pursued a solo career while maintaining an informal association (1969-74) with the group Crosby, Stills and Nash. His most popular songs include "Heart of Gold," "Tell Me Why," "Only Love Can Break Your Heart" and "Lotta Love." In the last 12 years he has recorded more than 20 albums, one of the most recent of which was *Life* (1986).

MARK MILLER

Reading: Johnny Rogan, *Neil Young* (1982); Scott Young *Neil and Me* (1984).

Young, Reynold Kenneth, astronomer, professor (b at Binbrook, Ont 4 Oct 1886; d at Peterborough, Ont 24 Dec 1977). He was astronomer at the Dominion Observatory in Ottawa 1913-18 and at the Dominion Astrophysical Observatory in Victoria, BC, 1918-24, professor at U of T 1924-45 and director of the David Dunlap Observatory in Richmond Hill, Ont, 1935-45. Young's research was primarily in the field of stellar radial velocities, the velocities of stars in the line of sight. His work helped place Canada among the world leaders in radial velocities. His unique contribution was his guidance in the design and construction of the 1.88 mm telescope at the David Dunlap Observatory, where he planned and developed a far-reaching program of fundamental astro-

physics. Copies of the telescope have been mounted in Egypt, South Africa, Japan and Australia.

PETER M. MILLMAN

Young, Sir William, lawyer, politician, judge, philanthropist (b at Falkirk, Scot 8 Sept 1799; d at Halifax 8 May 1887). A political opportunist, Young maneuvered his career to achieve 2 goals: the office of premier and that of chief justice. He entered the NS legislature in 1836 as a Reformer (Liberal) and achieved prominence defending Reform journalists in several heated libel cases. He tailored his political climb, hoping to become first premier under RESPONSIBLE GOVERNMENT in 1848, but lost to J.B. UNIACKE, whom he succeeded in 1854. Young's leadership was not outstanding, and was marred by indecision, flagrant patronage and growing religious-political turmoil. In 1860 he resigned to accept the pinnacle of his aspirations — the office of chief justice. His later life was marked by great philanthropy, which brought power and acclaim to a man once described as "so tricky a character that he probably never ate his dinner without a stratagem."

LOIS KERNAGHAN

Young Men's Christian Association, worldwide private voluntary organization that offers a wide range of educational, social and recreational services. Founded in London, Eng, in 1844 by George Williams, it spread rapidly to other cities where groups of young men wished to protect themselves against the temptations of modern urban life. The first N American association appeared in Montréal in 1851 and a Canadian National Council was organized in 1912. The YMCA's original goal was the spiritual improvement of young men and for many years it was closely tied to the Protestant evangelical churches. Today, it serves people of both sexes and all ages, walks of life, races and religions. The Canadian YMCA has promoted physical education, camping, adult education, youth services, and international development projects. In 1986, 262 372 Canadians held memberships in the YMCA, while 1.4 million used its available services. *See also* YOUNG WOMEN'S CHRISTIAN ASSOCIATION.

DIANA PEDERSEN

Young Women's Christian Association cooperates closely with the YOUNG MEN'S CHRISTIAN ASSOCIATION in many Canadian communities but has retained its distinct identity. Two organizations providing religious fellowship and boardinghouse accommodation to young women were created in England in 1855, and amalgamated in 1877. The rapid growth of the YWCA as an international movement was linked to the increasing concentration in cities of large numbers of young unmarried women seeking employment, especially in factories. The first Canadian branch was organized in Saint John, NB, in 1870, and a national body was created in 1895. Sharing the Protestant evangelical orientation of the YMCA, early YWCA programs combined attempts to increase the employment and educational opportunities available to young women, with a concern for their physical and moral welfare. The Canadian YWCA today is actively working to improve the social, legal and economic position of all Canadian women. Some half million Canadians annually make use of YWCA facilities in one way or another.

DIANA PEDERSEN

Youville, Marie-Marguerite d', née Dufrost de La Jemmerais, founder of the Sisters of Charity of the Hôpital Général of Montréal (b at Varennes, Qué 15 Oct 1701; d at Montréal 23 Dec 1771). Educated by the Ursulines of Québec, in 1722 Marie-Marguerite married François d'Youville of Montréal who died in 1730. She raised 2 children and continued the family busi-

ness although she had experienced a religious "conversion" and had withdrawn from society in 1727. Ten years later, she and 4 other women formed a lay group dedicated to charity and took simple vows. Called "tipsy women" because of the d'Youvilles' alleged profits from brandy trafficking, in 1747 they were put in charge of the bankrupt Hôpital Général of Montréal, founded in 1692 by François Charon de La Barre. They reorganized it into a hospice for aged men and women, foundlings, orphans and "fallen women." In 1750 civil and ecclesiastical authorities decided to unite it with the Hôpital Général of Québec, but the Sulpicians interceded in Paris and, on 3 June 1753, Louis XV gave the community legal status and title to the hospital. In 1755 the women finally began their life as the Sisters of Charity of the Hôpital Général, or GREY NUNS (*Soeurs grises*). They developed various enterprises including farms, an orchard, a mill and a bakery to finance their work. During the smallpox epidemic of 1755 and the Seven Years' War, their institution truly became a hospital. Mère d'Youville faced disappointments, however; her family returned to France at the Conquest, her hospital burned in 1765, and after years of failing health she died in 1771. Many Montréalers attested to her prophetic gifts and miraculous healing powers. On 3 May 1959, her spirituality and sacrificial life were officially recognized by Rome. She was the first Canadian-born person to be beatified, a step on the way to canonization (sainthood). She was designated Blessed and by papal order could be venerated throughout Canada and in her religious order.

CORNELIUS J. JAENEN

Ypres, first series of major battles fought by Canadian troops during WORLD WAR I, officially lasting from 22 Apr to 25 May 1915. On 22 Apr 1915 a greenish yellow cloud of chlorine gas almost 7 km long was carried by a light NE wind toward the Allied trenches near Ypres (now Ieper), Belgium. It was the first effective gas attack on the Western Front. Without gas masks, the French and Algerians in the trenches were forced to retreat, choking, gasping, and dying as the chlorine affected their lungs. A wide gap opened to the attacking Germans, and 1st Canadian Division, together with British troops, rushed in to halt the enemy's advance. In a week of fierce fighting and bitter counterattacks involving further use of gas, the German thrust was brought to a halt. Although they suffered over 6000 casualties, the Canadians' courage and ability in the face of this new weapon of war won them recognition as first-class troops. FREZENBERG RIDGE was part of this Ypres series of battles.

R.H. ROY

Yugoslavs Yugoslavia is the land of the South Slavs. It occupies 255 084 km² of the Balkan peninsula. It is a classical example of a modern, multicultural, multilingual and multireligious society, with many nations and nationalities. It is a relatively new nation, created in 1918 as the Kingdom of Serbs, Croats and Slovenes and renamed Yugoslavia in 1929. After the Nazi occupation in 1941, the country was divided into 11 parts. In 1945, in the wake of mass resistance, civil war and revolution, it was recreated as a new Yugoslavia, ie, a federative republic. Today, it is a state with 2 alphabets (Latin and Cyrillic), 3 major religions (Orthodox, Roman Catholic and Muslim) and 3 major languages (Serbo-Croatian, Slovenian and Macedonian). It consists of 6 republics, the largest of which, Serbia, contains 2 autonomous regions. Although these contain considerable ethnic minorities, the Serbs, with 42% of Yugoslavia's total population, represent the largest of its component nations. The next in number are Croatians, Muslims, Slovenes, Albanians, Macedonians, Yugoslavs of mixed parentage and Montenegrins, a historical offshoot of the original Serbian ethnic group. With such an unusually complex ethno-cultural makeup, Yugoslavia is truly one of the most heterogeneous multicultural states of Europe. Pressured for centuries by internal and external upheavals and economic problems and in search of better opportunities elsewhere, the Southern Slavs and their compatriots began to migrate overseas as early as the first half of the 19th century. They participated in the Yukon gold rush euphoria as well as in British Columbia's early fishing and forestry industries. Some of the more entrepreneurial ran rooming (or "transition") houses in Victoria. Most Yugoslav pioneers in Canada were for a long time migratory labourers, moving from one distant job opportunity to another.

Migration and Settlement WWI greatly stimulated Canada's industrial development and, by offering more stable employment opportunities, led to the eventual settlement of former migrants. Canadians of South Slavic origin have been identified in companies' archives throughout the country. In WWII, Canadian war industries provided unprecedented job opportunities, particularly in the large urban centres of Ontario. The Yugoslav immigrants began to accumulate modest amounts of basic capital, some of which later grew into considerable fortunes.

Social and Cultural Life Along with economic developments, various cultural and recreational associations came into being. Many of these contributed to the organization of all-Canadian efforts against the fascist forces in Europe and to war relief in both their adopted country and their country of origin. Alas, the fratricidal war and revolution in wartime and postwar Yugoslavia produced a bitter echo among Canadians of Yugoslav origin and led to a serious fragmentation of their communities along ethnoreligious and ideological and political lines.

In the 1981 census 64 835 persons are declared as "Yugoslavs" (not otherwise stated). This represents 52% out of the total 124 640 individuals whose ethnic background is one of several national groups of Yugoslavia. The statistical breakdown of the major national groups from Yugoslavia, according to the 1981 census, is as follows: Croats 34 765, Serbians 8600, Slovenians 6395 and Macedonians 10 045. The 1986 census estimated 51 205 Yugoslavs, 32 215 of whom lived in Ontario.   VLADISLAV A. TOMOVIĆ

Reading: Lovett F. Edwards, "The Yugoslav Idea," *Yugoslavia* (1971).

Yukon Field Force (1898-1900), composed of 203 officers and men drawn from all 3 branches (cavalry, artillery and infantry) of the Permanent Force of the Canadian Militia. It was sent to the Yukon, to be based at Ft Selkirk with a detachment at Dawson, as a symbol of Canadian sovereignty and as a support for the civil power in maintaining law and order in the territory during the KLONDIKE GOLD RUSH. Half the force was withdrawn in Sept 1899 and the remainder, restyled the Yukon Garrison, left a year later.
     BRERETON GREENHOUS

Yukon River, 3185 km long (of which 1149 km lie in Canada), fifth-longest river in N America, rises in Tagish Lk on the northern BC border, flows N and NW across the YUKON TERRITORY into Alaska, where it flows in a great westward arc to Norton Sound on the Bering Sea. It has a DRAINAGE area of about 800 000 km² and an average discharge of 2300 m³/s where it crosses into Alaska. Four principal tributaries, draining a vast area of the YT, feed the river in Canada. The Teslin R (393 km) rises in Teslin Lk, on the BC border, and joins the Yukon N of Lk Laberge. The Pelly R (608 km) rises in the SELWYN MTS to the E and de-

Five Fingers Rapids on the Yukon River, N America's 5th-longest river (*photo by Hans Blohm/Masterfile*).

scends to the Yukon at Fort Selkirk. The White R (320 km) drains the glacial waters of the SW, and the Stewart R (644 km) rises in the mountainous area to the E, in the mining region of Mayo and Keno Hill. In Alaska the major tributaries are the Porcupine R (721 km), which rises in the NW Yukon Territory, the Tanana from the S, and the Koyukuk from the N.

The Yukon is a slow-moving, braided stream, and is shallow except when swollen by spring waters. Its gradient is even and there are few rapids; those at Miles Canyon, which proved so treacherous to the Klondike prospectors, have been drowned by a hydroelectric development. From Fort Selkirk to DAWSON, the river is sprinkled with wooded islands and its long, wide stretches are bordered by mountains. Past Dawson, the valley becomes narrow and then, as it enters Alaska, widens into the broad interior plateau called the "Yukon Flats."

The river mouth was known to Russian fur traders by 1831. The upper reaches were explored by HBC trader Robert Campbell, who explored the Pelly R and established a post at Fort Selkirk on the Yukon in 1848. John Bell of the HBC reached the river via the Porcupine R in 1846. For 3 months of the year, the Yukon is navigable from its mouth to WHITEHORSE (some 2860 km). Steamers plied the river in the 1860s, and there were at least 20 in service in 1900, at the height of the KLONDIKE GOLD RUSH. Today the steamers are antique and the area is served by road and air.

The Yukon basin is believed to be the chief migration route of America's original settlers (*see* PREHISTORY). However, it remains sparsely populated. Several thousand native people maintain their traditional life-style, being at least partly dependent on hunting and trapping. The forest cover of small conifers supplies local needs, but growth is too slow for a viable forestry industry; there is little agriculture. The isolation and scenic beauty of the river attracts tourists. The name Yukon was first applied to the river and is from the Loucheux word *Yu-kun-ah,* meaning "great river."   JAMES MARSH

Yukon Territory takes its name from the Loucheux Indian name *Yu-kun-ah* for the "great river" which drains most of its area. Lying in the NW corner of Canada's continental mainland, isolated by rugged mountains, it shares a common border and many characteristics with its American neighbour, Alaska. Historically, it is in-

delibly associated with the great KLONDIKE GOLD RUSH.

Land and Resources

Geographically the bulk of the Yukon is a subarctic plateau interspersed by mountains. The major exception is the Arctic Coastal Plain, a narrower eastward continuation of the same region in Alaska, which slopes down to the BEAUFORT SEA from the British Mts inland.

Geology The Yukon constitutes the northernmost part of the Cordilleran region. It is geologically very complex but includes 3 parallel sectors oriented NW-SE. In the E, folded sedimentary Paleozoic and Mesozoic formations are set off sharply from the Mackenzie Valley by great faults. The middle sector includes sedimentaries, metamorphics and volcanics ranging from Precambrian to Mesozoic age. Massive plutonic Mesozoic and Tertiary granites make up the core of the western sector.

Surface The geologic structure is reflected in a similar physiographic subdivision into plateau and mountain regions, all of which continue westwards into Alaska. In detail there are significant variations within each major physiographic region. The high central Yukon Plateau, at an average elevation of 1200 m, is interrupted frequently by local mountain areas and deep valleys – many of the latter strikingly aligned NW-SE, reflecting the structure. The 2400 m Ogilvie Mountains on the N, separate it from the Porcupine Plateau, which is delineated on the N and E by the British and Richardson Mountains, respectively. On the E the Yukon Plateau is bounded by the Selwyn and Mackenzie mountains. On the S an area of lower terrain near the 60th parallel separates it from the mountainous areas of northern BC. In the SW Yukon the spectacular St Elias and Coast mountains include Canada's highest mountains, many over 4600 m, with Mt LOGAN (5950 m) the highest in Canada. Many are covered by extensive permanent ice caps – the largest nonpolar icefields in N America – and effectively cut off direct access to the Pacific Ocean despite its relative proximity.

Water Approximately 75% of the territory is drained by the YUKON R system, including the Porcupine R basin N of the Ogilvie Mountains. The 2 major exceptions are the Peel R, which drains a lesser plateau in the NE, and the LIARD R in the lower-lying plain sector in the SE. These rivers drain into the MACKENZIE R to the E. Included in the Yukon headwaters are magnificent elongated glacial lakes along the eastern edge of the St Elias Mountains. The Yukon includes a large area in

Yukon Territory

Capital: Whitehorse
Motto: None
Flower: Fireweed
Largest Urban Centres: Whitehorse, Dawson, Watson Lake, Mayo-Elsa
Population: 23 504 (1986c); rank twelfth; 1.9% increase from 1981-86; 7.6% increase from 1976-86.
Languages: 90% English; 2.5% French; 7.5% Other
Entered Confederation: 13 June 1898
Government: Territorial – Commissioner, Executive Committee, Legislative Council of 16 members; federal – one senator, one member of the House of Commons; the Minister of Indian Affairs and Northern Development is responsible for directing the Commissioner in the administration of the territory
Area: 482 515 km²; including 4481 km² of inland water; 4.9% of Canada .
Elevation: Highest point – Mount Logan (5951 m); lowest point – sea level at arctic shore
Value of Mineral Production: $183.5 million (1986)
Electric Power Produced: 766 GWh (Yukon and NWT) (1985)
Sales Tax: None (1987)

the N and NW that was never covered by Pleistocene ice sheets, despite its northern latitude. PERMAFROST is continuous N of the Porcupine R, and discontinuous but widespread through the rest of the territory. As in the NWT, the latter condition results in finely balanced biotic conditions and poses problems for construction and ground transportation.

Vegetation All the Yukon except the Arctic Coastal Plain and the higher mountains lies below the TREELINE but approximately 40% is not treed, and only 12% is productive forest. The area S of Dawson is fairly well forested, at least in the river valleys, with the best stands in the moist eastern sectors, especially the Liard valley. It forms part of the boreal forest region, including such trees as spruce, pine, aspen, poplar and birch.

Climate The climate of the Yukon is continental, with its mountain ramparts sealing it off from most direct contact with the moderating Pacific Ocean. Winters are very cold most of the time, with the lowest temperature ever recorded in Canada (-63°C) at Snag, NW of Kluane Lk, in Feb 1947. At times, Pacific air may edge into the SW sectors resulting in short intervals of milder temperatures. Summers are warm and frequently hot (35°C has been recorded at Dawson) but cooler air from the Arctic can push southward. Precipitation is generally low because the high mountains in the SW seal off access to the moister air.

Resources Yukon's big game animals, furbearers, birds and fish have sustained Yukon's native people for thousands of years, and continue to do so, especially in remote communities such as Old Crow. Yukon's wildlife resources, which fall under the jurisdiction of the territorial government, are also valued by other residents and by tourists, particularly big game hunters. The Yukon has some of N America's largest populations of grizzly bears and dall sheep. Moose, black bears and wolves are other important species. The Yukon provides critical habitat for migratory birds, such as trumpeter swans and birds of prey. The barren-ground Porcupine caribou herd, estimated at 165 000 animals, migrates between Alaska, the Yukon and the Northwest Territories. Pacific

salmon ascend the Yukon R and its tributaries from Norton Sd, in Alaska.

Minerals, such as gold, zinc, lead and silver, remain the territory's most economic nonrenewable resources. Difficult access and rugged terrain have deterred mineral development in the past; however, the Yukon now has a highly developed road system with year-round access to tidewater. New government assistance programs have also spurred exploration and development. It has been estimated that about 9200 MW of hydro power resources are available in the Yukon, primarily on the Yukon R and its tributaries; however, development would involve flooding many of the valleys in which wildlife resources and population are located.

Conservation Yukon's historic and spectacular scenic attractions are important tourism resources. KLUANE NATIONAL PARK in the SW includes Canada's highest mountain, Mt Logan, and part of what has been called the largest nonpolar ice field in the world outside the Arctic and Antarctic, as well as grizzly bears and dall sheep. Efforts to balance development and conservation are being

Open-pit mines near Faro, YT. The fate of mining has fluctuated in the 1980s (*photo by Richard Harrington*).

incorporated in a conservation strategy now being planned by the Yukon government. The first territorial park was established in 1987 on Herschel I, and includes archaeological sites of early aboriginal residents as well as whaling era artifacts. The North Yukon National Park was established in July 1984, under the terms of the Inuvialuit Land Claim, to protect critical habitats of the Porcupine caribou herd and certain species of migratory birds. The caribou herd and other wildlife populations of the area are valued subsistence resources for northern aboriginal people.

A federal-territorial agreement to manage the herd was signed in 1985; 2 years later Canada and the US signed an international treaty for the conservation of the herd. There is growing pressure within the US, however, to allow oil and gas leasing within the herd's calving grounds in Alaska, in the Arctic National Wildlife Refuge.

People

Urban Centres Nearly three-quarters of all Yukoners live in 4 centres, and 2 out of 3 live in WHITEHORSE. Whitehorse (pop 15 199, 1986c), the territorial capital, is the transportation, business and service centre for the territory. DAWSON CITY was the capital until 1951 and has dwindled to a population of 896, based on gold mining in the area and on tourism. FARO (pop 400) developed in response to the nearby Anvil zinc-lead mine, and Watson Lk (pop 826) on the ALASKA HIGHWAY is the service centre for the SE Yukon. Elsa, the company town for the Keno Hill mine, now has a population of 294.

Ethnicity Yukon Indians comprise approximately 25% of the population of the territory. In 1987, 4716 resided in 13 bands. Although there are 6 small Indian reserves in Yukon only a few are occupied and the Indian Act reserve system has never been highly developed. Yukon Indians live side by side with non-native residents in every community in Yukon and form the majority of the population in more remote villages. Since 1973 Yukon Indians have been negotiating a comprehensive LAND-CLAIM settlement in Yukon involving both status and non-status Indians. The Agreement in Principle for the Yukon Indian Claim was approved by the federal Cabinet on 17 Apr 1984.

Transient Population One of the characteristics of both the Yukon and the NWT is the transient nature of much of the non-native population. Many workers, attracted by high wages, plan to stay for a short time and return "outside." The labour force includes a disproportionate number of young single men and recent immigrants. Many companies encourage married workers through assistance in family housing.

Economy

Primary resource extraction has always been the foundation of the Yukon economy. Furs, the original trading commodity, continue to be harvested and exported. Although of declining importance to the economy overall, the fur harvest remains a vital source of income. During a brief but hectic period at the turn of the century an active Arctic WHALING industry was based on Herschel I, the only sheltered harbour along the Yukon's Arctic coast. The economy is vulnerable to reversals in mining, which comprises about 40% of the territory's economic base. The closure of all major mines in the Yukon in the 1980s because of depressed world markets and depleting resources resulted in a serious economic crisis and a decline of population. By 1986, the situation had begun to rebound with the reopening of the Yukon's major lead-zinc mine and the setting of a 30-year record in placer gold production. In 1987, the placer industry achieved a 70-year record and a large hardrock gold mine went into production. A second hardrock mine began producing gold ore in early 1988.

Farming was significant at the time of the gold rush, but it subsequently was negligible because of high costs, low profits, marginal soil, climatic restrictions, topography and improved transportation which lowered the price of agricultural imports. Aided by new technologies and favourable government policy, agriculture has shown slow but steady growth in the 1980s. Forestry has been of limited importance, but with the 1987 reactivation of a large sawmill by the newly formed Yukon Development Corporation, lumber production is expected to increase significantly. The area and rate of growth of the territory's merchantable timber are restricted by environmental conditions. Fish are important to the diet of many Yukon native people. There is some sportfishing, fish and caviar processing and aquaculture.

The manufacturing sector is steadily contributing more to the territorial economy. Yukon-made goods include furniture, vinyl windows, trusses, printed materials, chocolates, clothing, handicrafts and gold nugget jewellery.

Commercial production of the territory's renewable resources, in forestry, agriculture, fishing, trapping and sport hunting, has not exceeded $10 million in recent years. However, subsistence fishing and hunting, carried out primarily by Yukon's aboriginal people, represents a vital economic activity, especially in the smaller, rural communities.

Mining The emphasis in mining has shifted since WWII from gold to zinc, lead and copper in the 1960s-70s and back to gold during the mine closures of the early 1980s. Zinc now accounts for about 45% of mining production value in the territory; lead, 20%; placer gold, 15%; and hardrock gold, 7%. Placer gold production dropped off after the first decade of the 20th century, but much higher gold prices in recent years have resulted in renewed activity. There are currently about 200 placer operations in the Yukon. Silver and coal have been mined since the turn of the century. A former asbestos mine at Clinton Creek, W of Dawson, closed in 1978 when ore was exhausted. Many potential new mines exist (eg, tungsten and lead-zinc in the MacMillan Pass area NE of Ross R on the NWT border) but development costs in isolated northern areas are quite often prohibitive.

Tourism Tourism has become an increasingly important industry. Along with government, it largely sustained the Yukon economy during the recent slump in mining. Tourism is the second most important industry in the Yukon. Visitors are drawn by the Yukon's colourful GOLD RUSH history, its native heritage and its scenic and wildlife attractions. Dawson contains many reconstructed buildings and artifacts from its flamboyant era at the turn of the century. Recently, American and Canadian national parks services have co-operated in developing the Klondike Gold Rush International Historical Park, including the Chilkoot Trail through the SW mountains from Skagway, Alaska. Whitehorse puts on an annual winter festival, "Sourdough Rendezvous," and Dawson celebrates Discovery Day. The territory also hosts the ARCTIC WINTER GAMES every 6 years.

In 1987, there were 498 000 visitors to the Yukon (a large percentage passing through on their way to or from Alaska), with an estimated expenditure of about $100 million. Registered outfitters in 22 big-game guiding areas provide for hunters. Other tourist services and campground facilities are available along the Yukon highways. Kluane National Park headquarters is

The Richardson Mts form a boundary between the YT and NWT (*photo by Richard Harrington*).

located at Haines Junction. Native arts and crafts are of growing importance to the local economy.

Transportation Transportation in the Yukon was based upon the Yukon R system until the construction of the Alaska Highway in WWII. Shallow-draught, stern-wheeler STEAMBOATS operated seasonally from gold rush days; the main route was between Dawson and Whitehorse where rapids made the latter the effective head of river navigation. Limited transportation by sleigh or coach was available on winter roads during the closed season. The 177 km narrow gauge WHITE PASS AND YUKON RAILWAY was constructed from tidewater at Skagway, Alaska, through the rugged Coast Mountains to Whitehorse, and was particularly important in exporting minerals from the territory until it was shut down in Oct 1982. The transportation pattern and local population distribution were radically altered during WWII. Construction of the Alaska Highway between Dawson Creek, BC and Fairbanks, Alaska, in 1942 included 1014 km through the Yukon via Watson Lk and Whitehorse. There are now over 4700 km of roads in the territory. In 1978 completion of the Haines Road from Carcross and Whitehorse provided the Yukon with its first road access to the Pacific at Skagway, Alaska. In 1979 the Dempster Highway was completed between Dawson and Inuvik in the Mackenzie R Delta. Originally conceived as part of the government's "roads to resources" program, the Dempster Highway has helped reduce prices in the Delta area and has encouraged tourism.

New airport facilities were constructed through the southern Yukon during WWII as part of the NORTHWEST STAGING ROUTE from the US to Alaska. Airports and airstrips are now available at most Yukon settlements, including Old Crow in the north. The Whitehorse airport is by far the most important, providing daily scheduled and charter links with Alaska, southern Canada (via Vancouver and Edmonton) and the "lower 48" American states.

Pipelines to transport Arctic Alaskan gas overland to the US inevitably would have to cross the Yukon. The Alaska Highway pipeline proposed in the late 1970s has been delayed by political pressures within the US, and because of heavy financial costs and an overabundance of gas in the world market (*see* MACKENZIE VALLEY PIPELINE).

Energy The Yukon assets of the federal Northern Canada Power Commission were transferred

to the new publicly owned Yukon Energy Corp in 1987. Installed electrical generating capacity is 107 MW, with 77 MW hydro and 30 MW thermal. The major hydro power facilities are at Whitehorse (40 000 kW installed capacity), Aishihik (31 200 kW) and Mayo (6150 kW).

Government and Politics

The Yukon moved towards self-government earlier than the NWT. The first territorial government consisted of a federally appointed commissioner (James WALSH being the first) and a similarly appointed council, located in Dawson City. Unlike the NWT councils from 1905 to 1967, Yukon's appointed officials were all resident in the territory. As early as 1899 the Act was amended to provide for 2 elected members of council to be added, and in 1902, 3 more. In 1908 a fully elected council of 10 members was established. Dwindling population resulted in the council being abolished in 1918; in the face of local protest it was reinstated in 1919, but only as a 3-member elected council. The office of commissioner disappeared after 1916 as its duties were assumed by the gold commissioner of the territory. Further changes did not occur until after WWII when the territory's population increased. In 1948 legal provision was made for the reappointment of a commissioner as chief executive officer of the Yukon, along with the installation of several other appointed territorial officers. In 1951 the council was increased to 5 elected members, and subsequent additions have expanded it to 16. From 1970 to 1979 the federally appointed commissioner chaired an executive committee consisting first of appointed officials and representatives of the legislative assembly (former council) and in its later stages of the deputy commissioner and 5 elected members from the legislative assembly. In 1979 an executive council of 5 elected members functioning as a Cabinet superseded the former executive committee; it now reports to the government leader instead of to the commissioner. (Party politics were introduced to the Yukon assembly for the first time in 1978.) Like provincial governments, the Yukon government is responsible for such things as education, social services, tax collection, most highways and community services. Unlike the provinces, however, the Yukon has no authority over natural resources, with the exception of wildlife; royalties derived from resource development are paid to Ottawa. Resource management programs, including those in forestry, mines and land, are gradually being transferred or devolved from the federal to

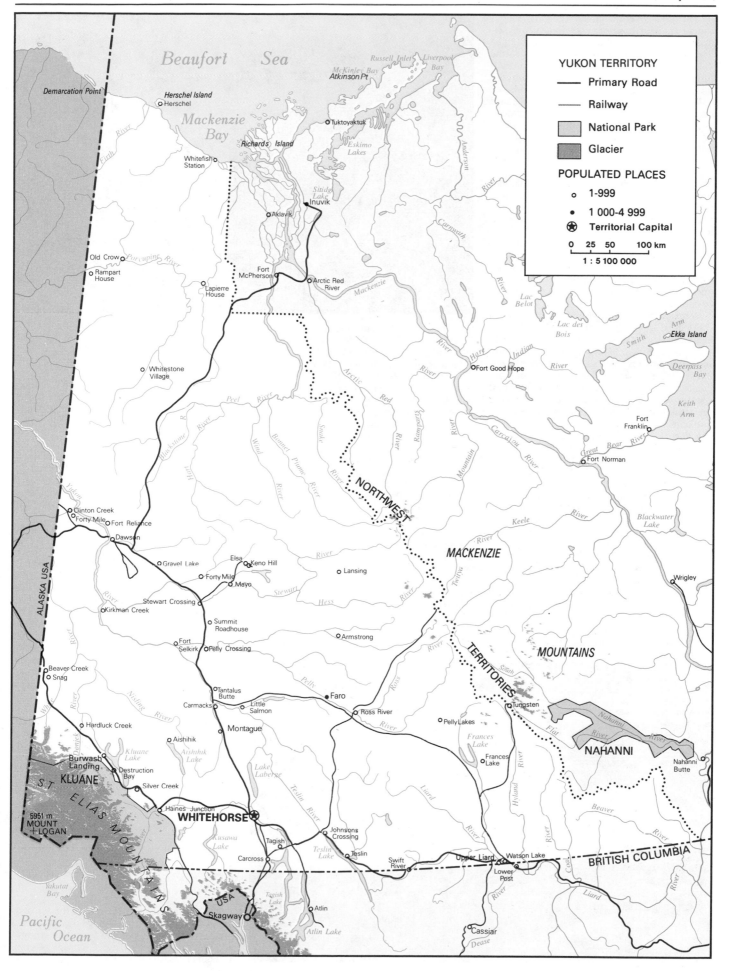

Beaufort Sea

Demarcation Point

Herschel Island
○ Herschel

Mackenzie Bay

Richards Island

○ Whitefish Station

McKinley Bay
Atkinson Pt

Russell Inlet
Liverpool Bay

○ Tuktoyaktuk

Eskimo Lakes

Sitidgi Lake
● Inuvik

○ Aklavik

Anderson River

○ Old Crow

○ Rampart House

Porcupine River

Fort McPherson

○ Lapierre House

○ Arctic Red River

Mackenzie

Carnwath

River

Lac Belot

Lac des Bois

● Fort Good Hope

Smith Arm

Ekka Island

○ Whitestone Village

Peel River

Blackstone R

Wind River

Bonnet Plume River

Snake River

Arctic Red River

Rampart River

Carcajou River

Fort Franklin

Great Bear River

Keith Arm

Deerpass Bay

NORTHWEST

Hart River
Indian River
Mountain River

● Fort Norman

Blackwater Lake

○ Clinton Creek
○ Forty Mile ○ Fort Reliance
● Dawson

MACKENZIE

Keele River

ALASKA USA

○ Gravel Lake

Elsa ○ ○ Keno Hill
○ Forty Mile
○ Mayo

○ Lansing

River

Stewart River
Hess River

Twitya River

River

MOUNTAINS

○ Wrigley

○ Kirkman Creek

Stewart Crossing

○ Summit Roadhouse

○ Armstrong

Pelly River

Ross River

TERRITORIES

Tungsten ●

○ Fort Selkirk
○ Pelly Crossing

○ Beaver Creek
○ Snag

River

Tantalus Butte
Carmacks ○
○ Little Salmon

● Faro

○ Ross River

○ Pelly Lakes

South Nahanni River

NAHANNI

○ Hardluck Creek

○ Aishihik

Montague

Nisling River

Aishihik Lake

Kluane Lake

Lake Laberge

Frances Lake
○ Frances Lake

Hyland River

Flat River

Nahanni Butte ○

Burwash Landing
○ Destruction Bay
○ Silver Creek

KLUANE

ST ELIAS MOUNTAINS

5951 m
MOUNT
+ LOGAN

○ Haines Junction

Dezadeash River

Kusawa Lake

⊛ WHITEHORSE

Tagish ○

Carcross ○

Teslin River

Teslin Lake

○ Johnsons Crossing

○ Teslin

○ Swift River

Liard River

Beaver River

Upper Liard ○ ● Watson Lake

Lower Post ○

Coal River

Liard River

BRITISH COLUMBIA

Yakutat Bay

USA

Tagish Lake

○ Atlin

Atlin Lake

Skagway ○

Pacific Ocean

○ Cassiar

Dease

YUKON TERRITORY
━━━ Primary Road
─── Railway
▨ National Park
▨ Glacier
POPULATED PLACES
○ 1-999
● 1 000-4 999
⊛ Territorial Capital
0 25 50   100 km
1 : 5 100 000

the territorial government. Such negotiations are concurrent with those for a native land claims settlement. Yukoners and other northerners argue that the recently proposed amendments to the Canadian Constitution (*see* MEECH LAKE ACCORD) deny them a role in determining their future constitutional status and in achieving provincehood.

Judiciary In 1987 the Yukon Territorial Court consisted of a chief judge and 2 territorial judges, located in Whitehorse. There are 41 justices of the peace appointed by the commissioner at 15 locations in the territory. The judge of the Supreme Court of the Yukon Territory is ex officio judge in the NWT and vice versa, and sits on the Court of Appeal in both territories as well. The remainder of the Supreme Court judges are selected from various provincial courts; the remainder of the Court of Appeal justices are from the British Columbia Court of Appeal.

Local Government At the local administrative level there is one city in the Yukon (Whitehorse), 3 towns (Dawson, Faro, Watson Lk), 4 villages (Mayo, Haines Junction, Teslin and Carmacks), one hamlet (Elsa) and another 10 unincorporated communities.

Health The territorial government shares with the federal government the responsibility for health service. Modern hospitals are located in Whitehorse, Mayo, Faro, Watson Lk and Dawson. There are 2 nursing stations, 12 health centres and 3 health stations staffed by one or more public health nurses in the smaller communities. Clinics, dental services and a wide range of more specialized medical and social services are also available.

Politics The 2 major political issues are native land claims and provincial status. The native Indians of the Yukon have never signed treaties with the federal government. Their Council for Yukon Indians continues to prepare its case for a land claims settlement, also with federal government financial assistance. Provincial status has recently become a serious issue, as territorial citizens are now concerned that as a result of the Meech Lake Constitutional Accord, their provincial aspirations are seriously threatened.

Education

There are 25 public schools serving the needs of 4800 students from kindergarten to grade 12

while post-secondary education programs are delivered through Yukon College's main campus in Whitehorse and its network of 13 community campuses in 12 communities. The Yukon schools curriculum is based on the BC curriculum with modifications to reflect local interests. Native Indian language programs are also offered as are French immersion, French first language and standard French courses. Students can obtain their first 2 years of university-level education through Yukon College or they can enrol in specialized diploma and trade programs. Financial assistance is available for students who pursue their post-secondary education in approved institutions outside the Yukon.

Cultural Life

Aboriginal native culture in the Yukon has been severely altered by the whaling era at Herschel I, the Klondike Gold Rush, the construction of the Alaska Hwy and modern communications. There has been a recent renaissance in native cultural traditions and crafts.

Arts The MacBride Museum and the Old Log Church Museum in Whitehorse are open part of the year, and museums in Dawson City, Keno, Burwash and Teslin are open during the summer. A Yukon Arts Council provides administrative

Dawson, YT, located on the E bank of the Yukon R, came into existence at the time of the Klondike Gold Rush (*photo by John deVisser/Masterfile*).

support for cultural organizations and sponsors a program bringing artists into the schools, as well as annual art exhibitions and concerts. The Territorial Library and Archives are located in Whitehorse, with library branches in Dawson City, Elsa, Faro, Haines Junction, Mayo, Watson Lake, Teslin and Carcross. The territorial art gallery maintains a collection of work by Yukon and Canadian artists, as well as sponsoring regular local and touring exhibitions. There is a theatre in Whitehorse and a new arts centre will be built in 1989.

Communications Three newspapers are published in the Yukon Territory, including one daily and one weekly in Whitehorse. Three radio stations and one TV station are located in Whitehorse, with CBC Radio, CHON-FM and CKRW serving most communities by microwave. Live TV is generally available by means of satellite. Telephone and telex services are available throughout the Yukon (*see* COMMUNICATIONS IN THE NORTH).

Historic Sites Archaeological sites near Old Crow and in the northern Yukon attest to the presence of humankind in the territory for thousands of years. Physical evidence of ancient aboriginal life precedes that of early European contact, such as the abandoned fur trading and mining sites at Fort Selkirk and Forty Mile on the Yukon River. The bowhead whaling industry and later the fur trade resulted in settlement at Herschel I on the north coast, recently designated as the Yukon's first territorial park. The Klondike River area has Dawson City at its heart. Until WWII the Yukon's lakes and waterways were the primary means of travel in the Yukon. This is reflected by the hundreds of sites located along their length, and by the few beached sternwheelers left from the heyday of river travel. Watson Lake's signposts, started by a homesick American GI in 1943, help tell the story of the construction of the Alaska Hwy.

History

The Yukon Indians all belong to the Na-Dene linguistic phylum. They included the Nahanni in the E (with Kaska, Goat and Mountain groups), and several groups in the S and W (Teslin, Tutchone, Tagish, etc). The latter had a greater

Near Old Crow, YT, 112 km inside the Arctic Circle (*photo by Hans Blohm/Masterfile*).

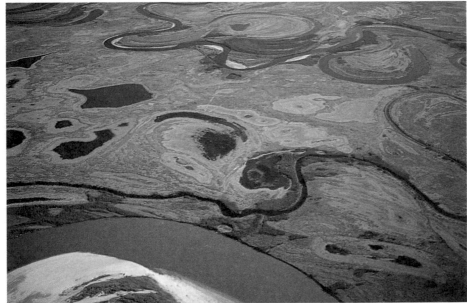

variety of food sources, including salmon, but were often dominated by the fierce coastal Tlingit, to the extent that some adopted their language. In the central and northern Yukon, the KUTCHIN occupied the basin of the Yukon R downstream from the mouth of the Pelly R, including the Porcupine R area to the N, and also the Peel R basin in the NE.

Exploration The first lasting contact was made in the 1840s by fur traders of the HBC, using maps and information from early explorers such as Sir John FRANKLIN, who reached Yukon's arctic shore in 1825. Robert Campbell pushed westwards from the Mackenzie R system by way of the upper Liard onto the Pelly R and John BELL moved into the Yukon interior via the Porcupine R. Traders in the interior and whalers on the N coast were followed by missionaries and the North-West Mounted Police in communities such as Fort Selkirk and at Herschel I.

By the late 19th century, gold prospectors in growing numbers pushed northwards from the Cassiar and Omineca mountains of northern BC. Crossing onto the Yukon watershed they worked their way along the various rivers. Others moved inland from the Bering Sea, following up the Yukon R from its mouth by stern-wheeler. Several centres of gold mining developed, often for only a brief period. Forty Mile, almost astride the Alaskan boundary, was one. George Carmack's discovery of gold on Bonanza Creek, a tributary of the Klondike R, on 17 Aug 1896, however, marked the beginning of what is often considered the world's greatest gold rush. Thousands of newcomers poured into this hitherto remote corner of Canada, transforming the Yukon permanently. Most of the goldseekers arrived by way of Skagway and the upper Yukon R. Others tried the "Overland Route" from Edmonton, via the Peace or Mackenzie rivers, but few reached their destination. Still others sought an all-American route via Valdez, Alaska, hoping to avoid Canadian government regulations. Dawson came into existence to serve the influx, at the junction of the Klondike and Yukon rivers, with the actual mining up the nearby creeks. In one month, in 1898, it grew into the largest Canadian city W of Winnipeg, developing a complete range of services, including water, sewerage, electricity and telephones. At its peak, the population has been estimated at 40 000. The Yukon was made a separate territory, Dawson named its capital, and a well-integrated transportation system was established through much of the territory. Whitehorse came into existence as the point where transshipping from rail to river took place, but Dawson was the dominant centre. Between 1897 and 1904, it is estimated that over $100 million in gold was recovered from the creek gravels. The population of Dawson began to decline almost immediately. Newcomers seeking easy riches were soon discouraged and were lured by reports of other gold discoveries (eg, Nome, Alaska in 1899). By 1906 the most easily worked placer mines were finished, leaving claims to be mined by large companies using expensive dredges.

Development Yukon's economy shifted from gold to other minerals beginning in 1913 when its first hardrock mine started silver and lead production at Keno Hill in the central Yukon. A mill was later established at nearby Elsa with services in the community of Mayo. High fur prices made trapping an important seasonal activity in the 1930s for native people and prospectors, in the absence of any other industry. The WWII construction of the Alaska Highway, and the Canol pipeline and road expedited new mineral exploration activity as well as bringing people, services, industries and tourists to the Yukon. With the highway came a permanent non-native popula-

tion that outnumbered Yukon's indigenous peoples for the first time. Yukon's capital was transferred from Dawson to Whitehorse in 1953, 2 years after the initial announcement. In 1957 a major hydroelectric plant was built in Whitehorse. The largest economic development in the postwar years was the opening of a major open-pit lead-zinc mine and town at Faro in 1969. Low metal prices and the recession in the mid-1980s resulted in mine closures throughout the Yukon, and increased government efforts to strengthen other economic sectors such as tourism and renewable resource development. The mining sector rebounded in 1986 with the reopening of the Faro mine, followed by the opening of 2 new hardrock gold mines. The Yukon government began a major economic development planning strategy in 1986 involving all economic and social sectors.   WILLIAM C. WONDERS

Reading: P. Berton, *Klondike* (1958); K.S. Coates and W.R. Morrison, *A History of the Yukon* (1988); L.-E. Hamelin, *Canadian Nordicity: It's Your North Too* (1979); K.M. Lysyk et al, *Alaska Highway Pipeline Inquiry* (1977); C. McClellan, *Part of the Land, Part of the Water* (1987); W.G. MacLeod, *The Dempster Highway* (1979); D.H. Pimlott et al, eds, *Arctic Alternatives* (1973); K.J. Rea, *The Political Economy of the Canadian North* (1968); William C. Wonders, ed, *The North* (1972); M. Zaslow, *The Opening of the Canadian North, 1870-1914* (1971).

Zeidler, Eberhard Heinrich, architect (b at Braunsdorf, Germany 11 Jan 1926). He is the most successful Canadian exponent of building technology as the central theme for architectural design. Trained at the Bauhaus, Weimar, E Germany, and the Technische Hochschule, Karlsruhe, W Germany, Zeidler immigrated to Canada in 1951. He joined Blackwell and Craig in Peterborough, Ont, and the successor firm, now Toronto based, is Zeidler Roberts Partnership/Architects. The technological themes displayed by Zeidler's work include structural and mechanical services (especially exposed air-handling ducts) and movement and communication systems. McMaster University Health Sciences Centre (1972) combined regular geometric building modules, marked by glazed service and circulation towers, internally exposed steel trusses, ducts and an automated materials delivery system to create a building reminiscent of a child's giant construction set. The display of mechanical efficiency is made more palatable to occupants by colourful interiors, generous greenery and interior courtyards. Other works include Ontario Place, Toronto (1967-71), and EATON CENTRE, Toronto (1974-81, with Bregman and Hamann), the Walter C. Mackenzie Health Sciences Centre, Edmonton (1975-86), the master plan for the $700 million Yerba Buena Gardens in San Francisco (1980-84), Queen's Quay Terminal, Toronto (1979-83) and Canada Place for Expo 86, Vancouver. In 1986 he was awarded the gold medal of the Royal Architectural Inst of Canada for his contribution to Canadian architecture and its reputation abroad. In late 1987 he received a Toronto Arts lifetime achievement award.
                    MICHAEL MCMORDIE

Zeisberger, David, Moravian clergyman (b near Ostrava, Czech 11 Apr 1721; d in Ohio 17 Nov 1808). Beginning in the 1740s he carried on Moravian missionary work among the Indians of Pennsylvania and founded a settlement in Ohio. The pacifism of his creed brought him and his converts under suspicion during the AMERICAN REVOLUTION and many were killed. In 1786 he founded New Salem (near Milan, Ohio), but was forced to evacuate in 1791 and moved with his followers to a grant along the Thames R, near present-day Thamesville, Ont. He established a flourishing agricultural colony, called Fairfield in

English. However, defections weakened the colony and he reluctantly accepted the encouragement of the Moravian bishop in the US to set up a new colony at Goshen, Ohio. Descendants of Zeisberger's converts still live on the remainder of his Thames R colony, called the Moravian Indian Reserve. He left a valuable legacy of writings on native culture and language.   JAMES MARSH

Zimmerman, Samuel, businessman (b in Huntington County, Pa 17 Mar 1815; d near Hamilton, Canada W 12 Mar 1857). The best-known railway contractor of his time, he was notorious for his free-wheeling business methods and political connections. Coming to Canada about 1842, he became a contractor during the rebuilding of the WELLAND CANAL and then on a series of railway projects. In co-operation with American engineers Roswell Benedict and Ira Spaulding, he acquired the contracts, in some cases through the use of bribery, to build the eastern division of the Great Western, the Cobourg and Peterborough, the Port Hope Lindsay and Beaverton railways and part of the Woodstock and Lake Erie Railway, which was intended to form part of a Zimmerman controlled "Southern" line connecting the Detroit and Niagara rivers. He also acquired extensive real-estate holdings at Niagara Falls, Toronto, Hamilton and elsewhere as well as his own bank, a hotel, mills, a foundry and lake steamers.

Zimmerman was widely believed to be the richest man in Canada. He was famous for his lavish hospitality to politicians of all kinds and as a lobbyist for railway legislation he wished to see passed. He was at the height of his activity and influence when he died in a railway accident in which a Great Western train crashed into the frozen Desjardins Canal.   J.K. JOHNSON

Zinc (Zn), bluish white metal of low to intermediate hardness, which melts at 419°C and is estimated to comprise about 0.013% of the Earth's crust. Zinc usually occurs as the MINERAL sphalerite. Brass, produced by colouring copper with the zinc mineral calamine, was in use 3000 years ago, but zinc was first identified as a metal in the 16th century. Production began in Europe in the 18th century; and in Canada in 1916 at TRAIL, BC, when Cominco Ltd opened a small electrolytic plant, using ore from the Sullivan Mine. Production was hampered because the complex lead-zinc-iron ore was difficult to treat. In 1920 the differential flotation method was successfully used to separate out lead and zinc concentrates, marking the beginning of substantial zinc production in Canada. In 1987 about 30 mining operations produced about 1.45 million tonnes of zinc, in concentrates which are either refined in Canada or exported; the value was just over $1.7 billion. Zinc mines are located in every province and territory except Alberta, NS and PEI. As well as the original Sullivan Mine, Cominco operates Polaris, the world's northernmost mine.

The total of 705 000 t of refined zinc is produced annually at Trail, BC; VALLEYFIELD, Qué; Hoyle, Ont; and FLIN FLON, Man. Zinc production involves roasting, leaching, electrowinning and melting (*see* METALLURGY). Canada, the world's largest zinc producer, contributes about 25% of the Western world's supply. About 85% of production is exported as refined metal or concentrates; major customers are the US and UK for metal, and Japan, Belgium, the US and Germany for concentrates. Zinc is used principally to galvanize iron and to prepare alloys such as brass and German silver. The next most common use is in die-cast products, eg, small electrical appliances, tools, toys, automobile door and window handles, carburetors, etc. Rolled zinc metal is used in dry-cell batteries and for roofing; zinc oxide is used in paints and as a catalyst in rubber manufacture.   M.J. GAUVIN

Zoning is the term used to describe the control by authority of the use of land, and of the buildings and improvements thereon. Areas of land are divided by appropriate authorities into zones within which various uses are permitted. Any buildings to be constructed thereon are designated for certain uses and their size, location and appearance are regulated. Zoning is thus at the heart of development control by which responsible governments spell out both their immediate and long-range land use goals (*see* URBAN AND REGIONAL PLANNING).

In Canada the control of land and its uses is a provincial responsibility. It is derived from the constitutional authority over "property and civil rights" granted to the provinces under the BNA Act of 1867 and carried forward in the Constitution Act, 1982. The zoning power relates to "real property," or land and the improvements constructed thereon that become part of the land itself (in Québec, "*immeubles*"). Each province has established municipalities and regions that are empowered to control the use of land within their boundaries. Provision has also been made for control of land use in unorganized areas of the province. In both areas provincial tribunals are the ultimate authority for appeal and review. In Ontario a recent amendment permits the provincial government to affect the exercise of this power in that the official plans must comply with provincial policy statements.

Each municipality may enact bylaws to control the use of land within its boundaries. Plans are made by the municipality, and the land area is divided into zones, each zone being set apart for certain defined uses. Plans are based on geographic features and existing development such as harbours, railways, highways, buildings and land use. Bylaws are then enacted to restrict the use of land in the defined areas to those uses established by the planning process.

There are many uses for land: agricultural; forest; highways; parks; industrial (abattoirs, factories, warehousing, etc); commercial (from corner groceries to high-rise office complexes); residential (from single homes to high-rise apartments and to condominiums). Each use ascribed to an area sets the value on the land affected and establishes the profile of a municipality. Their common aim is to allow uses that do not harm one another to be clustered together in the same zone, while keeping "incompatible" uses apart in their separate zones. On the outskirts of cities, by contrast, land may be held under a general zoning category that simply indicates that it is scheduled for development one day. The detailed zoning map cannot be drawn until a detailed development plan has been approved. Some of the outlying land may also be zoned for agricultural use or for a green belt, if it is not needed for urban development in the foreseeable future or if the municipal government wishes to prevent the city from expanding farther onto rural land (*see* NATIONAL CAPITAL COMMISSION). In rural municipalities, zoning is mostly used to protect agricultural land from urban or industrial development.

In addition to separating incompatible uses, the main objective of zoning is to control the intensity with which land is used. In residential districts, for example, there will often be a limit on the number of dwelling units that can be built per acre or hectare. Lot dimensions will also be regulated, and there is an obvious difference in the intensity of development between use zones that permit detached houses on 20 m frontages and those permitting row houses on 5 m frontages. Where the bylaw provides for high-density devel-

opment, it establishes this density by defining the floor-space index (fsi) that will be permitted on the parcel being dealt with. For example, in a downtown core all land may be zoned commercial with an fsi of 8:1. This means that the office building to be constructed thereon can have 8 times the land area of the parcel as floor space. This could result in an 8-storey building covering the entire lot or, taking into account setbacks from streets or neighbouring buildings, or special designs with patios, etc, could even result in a 16- to 20-storey tower. Many urban municipalities now offer "incentive zoning" or "bonusing" to encourage developers to add features to their buildings. For example, in return for constructing an enclosed garden or an elevated walkway to an adjacent building, a developer may be allowed to exceed the fsi for the district (*see* DEVELOPMENT INDUSTRY; URBAN DESIGN).

Power is given to departments of government to "designate" a use of land; in Québec a line is drawn called a "homologated line," which puts the owner on notice that a special use may be made of some property – a highway, a road widening, a public park – and that nothing can be done on the land so affected until the final decision is made. The value of the land is established as of the date of designation.

Traditional zoning has often been criticized for its inflexibility, but techniques like incentive zoning indicate that municipal governments in Canada are willing to look for more flexible approaches to the regulation of land use. Another example is the transfer of development rights. Under this technique the right to a particular type of development may be transferred to a site that does not have the appropriate zoning, on condition that the use of the original site is not changed. This is especially important if the original site is zoned for more intensive use but is occupied by a building that the city council would like to preserve for either historic or architectural reasons (*see* HERITAGE CONSERVATION).

In practice, zoning has been most effective at preventing change in stable, homogeneous districts. It has created the greatest difficulty when applied to areas of mixed land use or to areas where there are great pressures for change. In the former case there are 2 standard approaches, though both are controversial. The first is "spot zoning," or picking out single sites for a class of use that is incompatible with the surrounding uses. A factory in a residential district would be an extreme example. The alternative approach, which is generally preferred, is to classify the factory as a "nonconforming use." This means that it can remain, on condition that there is no change in the industrial use and no alterations to the buildings. Eventually, it is expected that the factory will be closed, allowing the site to be put to a compatible use.

In areas under development pressure, it is difficult to determine in advance the exact zoning that will be required. The needs of communities and of landowners and developers are in constant flux. As a consequence, particularly in rapidly growing cities, there is a continual demand for amending bylaws to change the use classifications of particular parcels of land. On one side there is pressure from developers who want sites to be "up-zoned" to permit redevelopment for more intensive use, such as apartments or office towers. On the other, community groups have organized to request "down-zoning" to prevent further redevelopment and to preserve whatever remains of their original neighbourhood.

As can be seen from these examples, zoning is often a contentious political issue that has to be settled by public debate and sometimes by court decisions. The need for land-use controls is now

well accepted in Canada, however, and has gained strength from the increasing awareness of the public that land is owned in trust for future generations and is not owned for immediate profit. This is also reflected in the awareness by citizens and public authorities of their respective rights and duties. In many Western societies, notably in Europe, there is little freedom for an owner of land to control its use. In Canada, too, owners have given up certain rights, or have had them taken away, on the grounds that the good of the community now and in the future is more important than the individual's rights. Thus, our laws are becoming more stringent and the planning of land use enters the life of every citizen.

EILEEN MITCHELL THOMAS

Reading: M.A. Goldberg, *Zoning: Its Costs and Relevance for the 1980s* (1979); S.M. Makuch, *Canadian Municipal and Planning Law* (1983).

Zoology is the study of ANIMALS. Zoologists have many interests: some study form (morphology) or function (physiology), from gross to molecular levels; behaviour (ethology); association (ecology); or distribution (zoogeography); and some specialize in one kind of animal.

Early History People have always been interested in other animals and have needed their company. Among the earliest artifacts are images of animals scratched on bone or stone, or painted on cave walls. Aristotle (384-322 BC) provided the most comprehensive ancient commentaries on nature in his treatises. His understanding of man in nature pervaded his philosophy, which in turn dominated Western culture beyond the Renaissance, with the result that man's zoological knowledge has vastly influenced his own behaviour. Following Aristotle, there was a pause in the accumulation of knowledge, lasting nearly 2000 years. Information became codified and dogmatic; argument took the place of experiment. Not until the Renaissance did curiosity and skilled, systematic observation of nature become widespread. Andreas Vesalius (1514-64), relying on his own senses, revivified the study of anatomy; William Harvey (1578-1657) demonstrated blood circulation by experimental means. Skilled dissectors made detailed explorations of animal structure and development. These and other workers made zoology an active science. Perhaps the greatest encyclopedic work of the time was the 44-volume *Histoire naturelle* of Georges de Buffon (1707-88), which provided a basis for the further exploration of nature which followed, literally, as the fleets of Europe set out to discover the world. The culmination of efforts to find relationships among living things and name them in a universally agreed upon manner was reached with the publication (1758) of the 10th edition of *Systema Naturae* by Carolus Linnaeus. Thus the ever-growing collections could be systematically stored and catalogued, available for study and synthesis.

19th Century European science began to take on a clear form in the 19th century. Disciplined empiricism came to be expected of scientists, with the solution of problems leading to the posing of more advanced questions, to more critical and imaginative searching, and to more profound understanding. Comparative morphology, in the broadest sense, dominated zoology in the 19th century. J.B. Lamarck and Georges Cuvier, studying chiefly INVERTEBRATES and VERTEBRATES, respectively, established the pattern of such studies and showed the relationships of FOSSILS to recent forms. Using the microscope, zoologist Theodor Schwann and botanist Matthias Schleiden recognized in 1838-39 that cells occurred in all living things, and so established the first of the great unifying principles of BIOLOGY, the cell theory. This in turn spurred improvements in the microscope and in techniques of microscopy. During the last half of the century, microanatomical studies revealed the nature of egg and sperm and fertilization, the mechanisms (mitosis and meiosis) of cell division and the early progress of embryonic development.

Concurrently, physiology was firmly established as a rigorous experimental science. Great hope was held for the understanding of life on the basis of the laws of physics and chemistry. Among physiologists, Claude Bernard takes pre-eminence because of his grand generalization that an animal will maintain, as far as possible, a balanced function internally, unaffected by wide fluctuations of its external environment (homeostasis).

Perhaps the most significant event in zoology during the 19th century was the formal expression, in 1858-59, of the theory of EVOLUTION by natural selection by Charles Darwin and A.R. Wallace. Evolution is the second unifying principle of biology. Darwin was the first great ecologist and the greatest synthesizer of the 19th century, equally at home studying animals and plants. Among other things, he recognized that the same forces govern the histories of both plants and animals, so closely indeed that many are said to have co-evolved.

20th Century The third great unifying principle, that of the mechanism of heredity, ie, the theory of the gene, belongs essentially to the 20th century. The initial statement was made in 1866 by Gregor Mendel, on the basis of his work with plants, but it was not until 1900 that his results were appreciated. Afterward, the development of GENETICS took place rapidly, the study of animals and micro-organisms contributing importantly to its growth. In 1953 James Watson and Francis Crick described the physical nature of the genetic materials, nucleic acids.

It is difficult and, in many respects, quite artificial, to divide biology into zoology and BOTANY. The overwhelming generality of the unifying principles apply equally to all organisms. Together, they lay the foundation for understanding the processes and potentialities of life, the basis of structure, and the external and internal mechanisms of adaptive change.

In the 20th century, zoology has followed several paths. Development, the mysterious process that leads to the final form of an animal, has been the subject of intense research, starting in the 19th century and culminating, for a time, in the 1920s in the work of Hans Spemann. His demonstration of the phenomenon of embryonic induction and the concept of the organizer (cell masses in the embryo which regulate the development of nearby tissues) provided the basis for most of the work that has followed. A significant part of the work has been biochemical, and this is true in other areas of study, such as physiology (eg, respiration, enzyme kinetics), genetics (eg, nature of gene), evolution (eg, biochemical attributes of species) and ecology (eg, sources of energy). Similarly, biomathematical analysis is becoming increasingly sophisticated and widely used, particularly in a field such as ecology, which more than any other has grown out of natural history but which is trying to produce hypotheses about environmental associations that are rigorously quantitatively testable. It, too, has become an experimental science, simultaneously giving rise to current interest in and concern for the ENVIRONMENT. This influence must be added to the direct effects which zoology continues to have on other primary concerns, eg, AGRICULTURE and medical science.

Zoology in Canada Part of the impetus to explore N America came from John Cabot's report (1497) of vast congregations of fish near its E coast. Nicholas DENYS published *Description géographique et historique des costes de l'Amérique septentrionale* (1672), based on experience around the Gulf of ST LAWRENCE. Between 1660 and 1725, first Claude Perreault, then Michel SARRAZIN, dissected and described numerous animals, including beaver, muskrat, wolverine and moose. Later explorers sent back descriptive natural histories which led to the opening of the North West for the FUR TRADE. In England, Thomas Pennant published *Arctic Zoology* (1784-87), based on collections made by explorers such as Samuel HEARNE. The best known of the early studies was *Fauna Boreali-Americana* (1829-37) by John RICHARDSON, who was surgeon and naturalist on Franklin's first 2 expeditions (1819-22 and 1825-26) and later commander of the Franklin search expedition of 1848-49. P.H. GOSSE began his career in Newfoundland and the Eastern Townships of Québec; his first work was *The Canadian Naturalist* (1840), written as he sailed home. In 1849, Moses Perley began an analysis of the NB fishery. In 1852, the federal government appointed Pierre FORTIN to control the Gulf of St Lawrence FISHERIES. These were the beginnings of fishery science in Canada. Biological stations were established in 1908 at St Andrews, NB, and Nanaimo, BC. The Biological Board of Canada, created in 1912, evolved into the Fisheries Research Board of Canada in 1937. The FRB, synonymous with excellence in fisheries research, was incorporated into the Department of Fisheries and Oceans in 1979.

The universities have been active, both in cooperation with fisheries and marine studies, and in more academic zoology. Natural history, as a separate science department, was established at University of Toronto in 1854, and at McGill and Queen's in 1858. Now, nearly every Canadian university has a zoology or biology department offering graduate study. Almost every field of zoology has outstanding practitioners. These have included Abbé Léon PROVANCHER, whose collections and descriptions provided a basis for the immensely important entomological studies for which Canada is noted; J.P. MCMURRICH, noted for work on subjects ranging from sea anemones to humans; A.G. HUNTSMAN, whose persistent curiosity and immense energy sparked many lines of research in fisheries; E.M. WALKER, one of the most influential entomologists in Canada; R.A. Wardle, godfather to a generation of parasitologists; William ROWAN, whose experiments with birds set the stage for important studies of photoperiodicity as an agent governing animal behaviour; J.B. COLLIP, endocrinologist, of insulin and parahormone fame; J.R. Dymond, influential in initiating systematic fish studies in Canada; W.A. Clemens, who, working both with the FRB and universities, played a vital role in developing zoology on the West Coast; Helen BATTLE, acclaimed teacher and investigator of the physiology, embryology, morphology and ecology of marine organisms; Donald RAWSON whose insights into the structure of lakes continue to excite limnological research; W.E. RICKER, leader in the analysis of fish populations; William Hoar, who set the standard for comparative physiology; C.P. LEBLOND, perhaps Canada's leading practitioner of electron microscopy and cellular analysis; and Douglas Pimlott, articulate advocate of environmental concerns. The list represents only a very small fraction of those who have made important contributions. Today, Canadian zoologists are at the forefront in studies of comparative respiratory and endocrine physiology, neurobiology, population analysis, PARASITOLOGY and vertebrate PALEONTOLOGY.

Extensive collections of organisms are held by the National Museum of Natural History, Ottawa; Royal Ontario Museum, Toronto; and the Entomology Research Institute, Ottawa. Provincial, local and university museums also are important, often especially for local fauna. MOLLUSCS, FISHES, BIRDS and MAMMALS are very well described for Canada in a number of readily accessible books. The Biological Survey of Canada, supported by the National Museum, is developing descriptions and distributions in Canada of as many more groups of organisms as possible. Under this aegis the Entomological Society of Canada has published *Canada and its Insect Fauna* (1978) and *Arctic Arthropods* (1981).

Zoology in Canada is served by the Entomological Soc of Canada (founded 1863), the Canadian Soc of Zoologists (founded 1961), and the Canadian Soc of Environmental Biologists, which began in 1959 as the Canadian Soc of Wildlife and Fishery Biologists. There are also provincial and local natural history clubs; groups dealing with special fields, eg, the Soc of Canadian Limnologists, and university activities, eg, the Canadian Committee of University Biology Chairmen; and professional organizations, eg, Assn des biologistes du Québec; the Alberta Soc of Professional Biologists. The Canadian Federation of Biological Societies, which comprises 8 specialist societies, including those for physiologists, biochemists and cell biologists, provides a bridge between zoology in the broad sense and its medical applications. The Biological Council of Canada includes the Entomological Soc and the Canadian Soc of Zoologists among its constituents. The council and the federation represent the needs of biological sciences to the federal government.

Scientists are cosmopolitan; they communicate with and depend on colleagues from around the world. There are literally thousands of journals specializing in biology; many of these are used by Canadian zoologists. But among the world's leading journals for zoology are the *Canadian Journal of Fisheries and Aquatic Sciences,* which first appeared in 1901 as *Contributions to Canadian Biology,* and the *Canadian Journal of Zoology,* a publication of the NATIONAL RESEARCH COUNCIL, which began as the *Canadian Journal of Research* in 1935; both are published monthly. Other important journals are *Le naturaliste canadien* (from 1868), *The Canadian Entomologist* (from 1868), *The Canadian Field-Naturalist* (from 1887), *Quaestiones Entomologicae* (from 1965) and *Syesis* (from 1968). Opportunities for careers in zoology continue in Canada as Canadians develop farm and fishery resources, learn to appreciate the environment, advance medical research and contribute generally to an understanding of the history of life. *J.R. NURSALL*

Zooplankton, weakly swimming animals belonging to many phyla (primary divisions of the animal kingdom), which, as larvae or adults, exist wholly suspended within a water body. The marine zooplankton is dominated by copepod CRUSTACEANS, found in great numbers in all oceans. The following organisms appear in lesser quantities in the zooplankton: euphausiid crustaceans (eg, krill), chaetognaths (arrow worms), pteropods (small gastropod MOLLUSCS), tunicates (protochordates), ctenophores (comb jellies) and JELLYFISH. Animals that are planktonic for only part of their lives include clam, crab and barnacle larvae, and fish eggs and larvae. Hundreds of species occur in Canadian waters but few exclusively. Locomotion is by movement of structures resembling oars, wings or fins; by cilia (hairlike appendages); or even by jet propulsion. Zooplankton range from zooflagellates a few micrometres long, to large jellyfish. Most feed on smaller particles, including phytoplankton (microscopic plants), using sievelike devices which may function like flypaper rather than sieves because viscous forces prevail in water at such small scales of motion. Other planktonic animals are omnivores or carnivores. Several steps in the food chain can occur within the PLANKTON if the dominant primary producers are very small (under 1 μm), eg, cyanobacteria (*see* BLUE-GREEN ALGAE). Because energy is lost at each step, the elaborate food webs characteristic of warmer, offshore waters usually do not produce commercially exploitable quantities of fish. Japanese and Russian researchers have tried to improve on the chain by harvesting krill for human consumption. Krill and copepod crustaceans added to the diets of AQUACULTURED salmon, trout, etc, improve flesh colour.

Zooplankton occur everywhere in fresh or salt water if oxygen is present. Usually, more and larger specimens representing fewer species are found near shore, near the surface and at high latitudes. Fewer, smaller, more diverse plankton occur offshore. Adaptations for pelagic (open sea) existence may include gas-filled floats, but most animals probably adjust their internal ionic composition to regulate buoyancy. Elaborate fans of setae (bristles) or tentacles probably serve for feeding, for flotation and as sensors. Where light penetrates, animals are often transparent to avoid detection by prey or predators.

Near the surface, blue pigment, offering camouflage and protection from ultraviolet light, is common. In the twilight zone, farther down, animals are darker and frequently possess light-producing organs (photophores) or produce light-emitting (bioluminescent) secretions. Bioluminescence may countershade the animal when seen from below, or may confuse predators or serve as an intraspecific recognition signal, but its adaptive role remains in dispute. The daily migrations, often of hundreds of metres, made by many zooplankters are little understood, although reduced predation at night is advantageous to herbivorous forms seeking near-surface phytoplankton concentrations.

Exclusively marine and largely planktonic comb jellies and arrow worms are important zooplankters; comb jellies because of their numbers and predatory impact; arrow worms because of their value as indicators of water quality. Comb jellies, jellyfishlike animals which swim with 8 rows of comb plates, capture food with entangling colloblasts (adhesive cells). Most are bioluminescent. Larvae of most species have tentacles; in some adults, tentacles act as a net to capture other zooplankton. Arrow worms belong to a coelomate phylum of uncertain affinities. Most are transparent ambush-predators, capturing other zooplankton with 8-12 pairs of bony, raptorial spines. R.J. CONOVER

Zoos or zoological gardens are facilities exhibiting wild and domesticated ANIMALS for purposes of education, recreation, conservation and research. Zoological gardens can be conventional, dense-occupancy zoos or open animal parks and game farms. They can incorporate AQUARIUMS exhibiting FISH and other aquatic life forms. Often, aquariums, oceanariums and sealife parks are independent, specialized, public facilities.

History People have always kept captive wildlife. Nomadic peoples maintained few species, but with the emergence of sedentary societies, animal collections became larger and more commonplace, eg, in Egypt, Assyria and China 3000-1000 BC, and later in Greece and Rome. Augustus Caesar (63 BC-14 AD) maintained a menagerie of over 3500 animals, a collection larger than any Canadian zoo. The famous menagerie of the Aztec ruler Montezuma II (*c*1480-1520 AD) employed 600 keepers. When

Keeper washing African elephant (*courtesy Metropolitan Toronto Zoo*).

monarchies were replaced by parliamentary governments, many private collections became public zoos; eg, the menagerie of Louis XVI, at Versailles, was moved to the Jardin des Plantes (1794). Many zoological gardens have evolved in the last 200 years. The *International Zoo Yearbook* (1988) lists 812 zoological facilities, but is not exhaustive. The roster of *Canadian Zoos, Game Farms and Aquariums 1988*, published by the Canadian Assn of Zoological Parks and Aquariums (est 1975), notes 56 facilities.

Objectives Private zoos brought prestige and enjoyment to their owners and entertainment to their guests. Early public zoos emphasized recreation, later coming to serve modern objectives of education, CONSERVATION and research. During the first half of the 20th century, zoos commonly attempted to show a wide variety of species in rows of cages, giving animal inventories the character of stamp collections. The concentration of species offered a broad spectrum for taxonomic (systematic classification) study and, by its diversity, considerable entertainment to viewers, but the approach has become outdated, and the zoos have been redesigned to foster a better understanding of animal psychology, behaviour and

wildlife appreciation. The artificial environment of a zoo must accommodate the physical and psychological needs of animals; exhibits must provide seclusion, sight barriers, camouflage, opportunities for hierarchical positioning, and stimulus to prevent boredom and stereotyped behaviour. The reduction of obvious barriers (for example, bars, fences) is important. Many modern exhibits contain animals through their physical and behavioural limitations, using water moats, dry moats, electric fences, light zones, etc. Glass barriers are used to provide an unobstructed view. Many exhibits have off-exhibit facilities (for example, maternity dens, sleeping boxes, treatment enclosures) that are often equipped with closed-circuit television for behavioural monitoring. Urban environments are in sharp contrast to undisturbed natural ecosystems, and zoological gardens serve as a link and catalyst to nature appreciation. Zoos are engaged in various international conservation programs. International studbooks are maintained for many endangered species. The American Assn of Zoological Parks and Aquariums adopted a Species Survival Plan (1981) which has the committed support of participating zoos. Zoos have become wildlife producers, not wildlife users as in former times. Today, few animals are collected from the wild for zoos. Most zoos operate extensive rescue and animal orphanage programs. Rehabilitated specimens are returned to their native habitats or are exhibited and traded with other zoos.

With diminishing wild habitats, countless species of animals become endangered, even extinct. Zoos propagate various species in captivity, and some species now depend on captive management for survival. Relatively few species can be perpetuated in captivity: only about 350 of 4050 mammal species have had consistent multiple-generation reproductions in captivity.

Objectives are now focused on general conservation, establishment of self-sustaining populations, specialized education programs and presentation of wildlife in natural habitat settings.

Zoo Management Zoos have become complex operations. Animal husbandry, research and development, education and interpretation, VETERINARY MEDICINE, public relations, food services, horticulture, facility maintenance, security, marketing, general administration and finance are all important. Many zoos are subsidized by municipal or provincial funding; direct federal funding is less common. Other facilities operate commercially; shareholders receive profits after operating expenses and capital development costs are covered. Commonly, zoos have the support of zoological societies – volunteer, usually tax-exempt, nonprofit organizations; involvement ranges from interested affiliation to managing authority. Major zoos are found in larger cities. The Riverdale Zoo in Toronto (est 1887) was Canada's first. The Metro Toronto Zoo, Canada's largest, opened in 1974; Stanley Park Zoo, Vancouver, 1888; Assiniboine Park Zoo, Winnipeg, 1905; Calgary Zoo, 1917; Moose Jaw Wild Animal Park, 1929; Provincial Wildlife Park, Shubenacadie, NS, 1947; Vancouver Aquarium, 1956; Jardin Zoologique de Montréal, 1957; Valley Zoo, Edmonton, 1959; Aquarium de Québec, 1959; Aquarium de Montréal, 1967; African Lion Safari, Rockton, Ont, 1969; Parc Safari

Africain, Hemmingford, Qué, 1972; and Salmonier Nature Park, near Holyrood, Nfld, 1978. Canadian zoos range from very modest collections to facilities exhibiting more than 3000 animals of over 400 species. Costly housing requirements during the winter season may limit the number of exotic species. More than 15 million visitors are estimated to visit Canadian zoos annually.   PETER KARSTEN

Zouaves Between Feb 1868 and Sept 1870, 7 contingents of Canadians enrolled in the papal army to help defend Rome from the Italian troops who wanted to bring about Italian unification. The last contingent of 114 recruits left too late and had to turn back, for Rome surrendered on Sept 16. About 390 Canadians served as pontifical troops. Their departure for Rome put the government in an embarrassing position since they were off to fight in a country with which Great Britain and Canada were not at war. The movement might have been forbidden but for George-Étienne Cartier, who stood up for the Zouaves because he feared that such an action would alienate the clergy and voters of Québec. Most of the Canadian Zouaves were educated young men recruited in Québec. The organizational committee set up by Bishop Ignace BOURGET of Montréal had recruited them for their moral qualities, because the main goal was to create an elite able to oppose the propagation within Québec of liberal ideas formally condemned by the pope. Freedom of speech and conscience, popular sovereignty and the separation of church from state – such were the grand ideals which the Zouaves were to combat. Upon their return, they formed an association which still exists and whose objectives gradually adapted to the main concerns of the Roman Catholic Church.   RENÉ HARDY

Zurakowski, Janusz, aviator (b at Ryzawka, Russia 12 Sept 1914). Raised in Poland, he joined

the Polish Air Force in 1937, escaped to England and took part in the Battle of Britain. In 1945 he tested Britain's first jet fighter. In Toronto, he became Avro Aircraft's chief development pilot in 1952. Zurakowski broke the sound barrier in an AVRO CF-100 – the first Canadian aircraft to reach that speed – and made the first flight of the AVRO ARROW (CF-105), an advanced supersonic jet, exceeding 1600 km/h on the seventh flight. He was awarded the MCKEE TROPHY in 1958.

                                                     JAMES MARSH

Janusz Zurakowski, Avro Aircraft's chief test pilot, shown here after the first flight in the Avro Arrow, 25 March 1958 (*courtesy National Archives of Canada/ C-61731*).

INDEX

This unique and comprehensive index should be viewed as a list of search paths in which the reader is urged to *complete* a search by reading not only the text of the referenced article but also by looking again in the index for the same article title used as a heading. The process is similar to that used in a more conventional index except that search paths are more easily found in this index. It is not printed in a format of headings, sub-headings, and sub-sub-headings but is intended to be used as though it were.

Anyone wishing to find all the information about religion in the encyclopedia should first read the article **Religion** (page 1849, column c) and then return to the index heading **Religion**. There, one is referred to articles about various religions, including Christianity. This list becomes, in effect, a series of sub-headings. Upon locating the index heading **Christianity** one is referred to a list of articles on the Christian religions and related topics. These should be seen as sub-sub-headings of **Religion**. Thus, it is emphasized, by continually returning to the index for further direction, the reader will, at length, locate all the available information on a chosen topic.

The index is alphabetized using the word-by-word method in which the space between words has significance for multiple-word headings. Therefore, headings such as **New Fairfield**, **New Forest pony** and **New France** are grouped together and precede headings such as **Newcastle**, **Newcastle Art Club** and **Newfoundland**. Also, for convenience, all variations of St, Ste, St-, etc are listed as if spelled Saint, and Mac, Mc and M' are all listed as if spelled Mac.

All article titles are listed as headings in the index and can be identified as titles wherever the heading includes a page number. For example, the entry **Abalone 1b:** is an article beginning on page 1 column b, and further information about the Abalone can be found on page 1371c of the **Mollusc** article. **Abasand Oils Ltd:** has no article of its own but is mentioned on page 233c of **Bitumen**.

Anthologie de la littérature québécoise, L':
Dionne, René **599b**;
Essay in French **722a**;
Literature in French – Scholarship and Teaching **1231b**
Anthologie de la poésie canadienne-française:
Sylvestre, Joseph Jean Guy **2105b**
Anthologie thématique du théâtre québécois au XIXe siècle:
Theatre, French-Language **2144c**
"Anthology":
Weaver, Robert **2288a**
Anthology Anthology, The:
Weaver, Robert **2288a**
Anthology of Canadian Music:
Music Composition **1413c**
Anthology of Canadian Poetry:
Poetry in English **1697b**
Anthony Island Provincial Park **80b**
Anthozoa:
Cnidaria **446b**
anthracite:
Coal **446c**
Anthracosauria:
Amphibian **71c**
anthrax:
Disease, Animal **605a**
Anthropoïdes, Les:
Bessette, Gérard **209c**
Anthropological Papers:
Archaeology **94a**
Anthropology **80c**:
Archaeology **91c**;
Mumming **1402a**;
Sapir, Edward **1929b**
Anthropology, Applied **83b**
Anthropology, Linguistic **83c**
Anthropology, Physical **83c**
anthropometry:
Anthropology **80c**
Anthropometry of the Saulteaux, Cree, and Chipewyan Indians:
Grant, John Charles Boileau **927b**
anti-Americanism:
Arctic Sovereignty **113b**;
Diefenbaker, John George **594c**;
Imperialism **1050a**;
Upper Canada **2226b**
anti-Asianism:
British Columbia **275b**;
Japanese **1105a**;
Prejudice and Discrimination **1741b**
antibiotics:
Bacteria **159b**;
Disease, Animal **604b**;
Fungus **855b**;
Medicine, Contemporary **1327c**;
Medicine, History of **1330c**;
Microbiology **1349a**;
Mold **1369c**;
Veterinary Medicine **2257a**
antibodies:
Allergies **64c**; **65b**
anti-Catholicism:
Canada First **326a**;
Gavazzi Riots **877b**;
Orange Order **1583a**
anticommunism:
Communist Party of Canada **475a**;
Fascism **752a**
Anticosti, Île d' **84b**:
Bayfield, Henry Wolsey **188a**;
Endangered Plants **697a**;
Gamache, Louis-Olivier **870a**;
Karst Landform **1128c**;
Lighthouses **1213c**;
Peat **1636a**
Anticosti Basin:
Petroleum **1650a**
anti-dumping duties:
General Agreement on Tariffs and Trade **879c**
Anti-Dumping Tribunal:
Finance, Department of **772a**;
Footwear Industry **805a**
Anti-Gallic Letters:
Essay in French **721a**
anti-Germanism:
Immigration **1046c**
Antigonish, NS **84b**
Antigonish harbour:
Antigonish, NS **84b**

Antigonish Movement **84c**:
Tompkins, James John **2166a**
Antigonish Review:
Literary Magazines in English **1220b**
Antiguans:
West Indians **2294c**
anti-Indianism:
Native People, Economic Conditions **1449c**
Anti-Inflation Act (1975):
Anti-Inflation Act Reference **85a**;
Wage and Price Controls **2270c**
Anti-Inflation Act Reference **85a**
Anti-Inflation Board **85a**:
Labour Relations **1159b**;
Pepin, Jean-Luc **1641b**;
Political Participation **1709b**
"anti-loafing law":
World War I **2343b**
Antimony **85a**
Antiochian Orthodox Church:
Arabs **90b**;
Orthodox Church **1590a**
Antiochian Rite Catholic Church:
Catholicism **382b**
antipersonnel mines:
Armaments **115b**
Antiphonaire, L':
Aquin, Hubert **89c**
Antiphonie:
Morel, François **1388c**
Antiquarian Booksellers Association of Canada/Association de la librairie ancienne du Canada:
Books, Antiquarian **250c**
antiques:
Furniture, Country **861a**
Anti-Reciprocity Movement **85b**
Anti-Semitism **85b**:
Arcand, Adrian **91b**;
Fascism **752a**;
Jews **1110c**;
Prejudice and Discrimination **1741a**
antisepsis:
Malloch, Archibald Edward **1288b**
antiseptic:
Mint **1364c**
antiseptic surgery:
Malloch, Archibald Edward **1288b**
antispasmodic:
Mint **1364c**
"Anti-Strikebreakers Act":
Johnson, Pierre-Marc **1114a**
antisubmarine operations:
Armed Forces **117a**; **117c**; **118c**;
Atlantic, Battle of the **142a**;
Cameron, William Maxwell **319c**;
Canadair CL-28 Argus **328c**;
Defence Research **581b**;
Helicopter **976c**;
Keys, David Arnold **1134a**;
Klein, George Johnn **1143b**
antivivisection movement:
Animal Issues **78a**
Antoft, Susan:
Rowing **1891a**
Antoinette de Mirecourt:
Leprohon, Rosanna Eleanor **1202c**;
Novel in English **1535c**
Antolohija ukrajins'koji poeziji v Kanadi, 1898 to 1973:
Ukrainian Writing **2206c**
Anville, Jean-Baptiste Bourguignon, Duc d':
Cartography, History of **371a**;
Le Loutre, Jean-Louis **1191c**
Anyox, BC **86a**
Anything is Possible:
di Michele, Mary **592a**
AOTS (As one that serves):
United Church of Canada **2215c**
apartments:
House **1013a**; **1013b**;
Housing and Housing Policy **1016a**;
Real Estate **1830c**
apatite:
Mineral **1355b**; **1356a**
Aperture Synthesis Telescope:
Observatory **1552b**

Aphid **86a**:
Ant **80b**;
Asparagus **135a**;
Berries, Cultivated **207b**; **207c**;
Insect Pests **1071c**;
Kale **1125b**;
Kohlrabi **1145c**;
Lettuce **1203c**;
Melon **1333c**;
Plant Disease **1688c**;
Plum **1694c**;
Tobacco **2164c**
Api 2967:
Gurik, Robert **947a**
apiculture:
Beekeeping **196c**
APL (A Programming Language):
Computer-Assisted Learning **479c**;
Computer Science **482b**
Aplacophora:
Mollusc **1371c**
Aplodontidae:
Mammals **1290a**
aplowite:
Mineral Resources **1358a**
Apocalypsis:
Music Composition **1413b**
apocalyptic perfectionism:
Anabaptists **72a**
apocalypticism:
Anabaptists **72a**
Apodiformes:
Bird Classification and Evolution **228c**
Apohaqui, NB:
McKenna, Frank Joseph **1269a**
Apostasies, Les:
Gagnon, Jean-Louis **868a**
Apostles of Infinite Love:
New Religious Movements **1481b**
Apostolic Church of Pentecost:
Pentecostal Movement **1640c**
Apostrophe to the Heavenly Hosts:
Willan, James Healey **2308c**
apothecary weight:
Weights and Measures **2290c**
Apothéose de Christophe Colomb:
Bourassa, Napoléon **260c**
Appalachian geosyncline:
Great Lakes **934c**
Appalachian highlands:
Chaudière, Rivière **399c**;
Earthquake **640c**;
Grosse Île **941b**;
Lake **1166a**;
Lennoxville, Qué **1202a**;
Long Range Mountains **1241c**;
Maritime Provinces **1306a**;
Mégantic, Lac **1331b**;
Mégantic Hills **1331c**;
Mineral Resources **1358b**;
Mountain Range **1398a**;
Newfoundland **1483c**;
St Lawrence River **1920a**;
Thetford-Mines, Qué **2149c**
Appalachian Orogen:
Geological Regions **887c**
Appalachian Piedmont:
Arthabaska, Qué **128c**;
Drummondville, Qué **629c**;
Victoriaville, Qué **2262b**
Appalachian Region:
Physiographic Regions **1674c**;
Spring **2064a**
Appaloosa:
Horse **1008b**
Appaloosa, The:
Furie, Sidney **861a**
Appassionata:
Maheux-Forcier, Louise **1286a**
Appeal **86a**
Appel de la race, L':
Novel in French **1539c**
Appel de la terre, L':
Potvin, Damase **1731b**
"Appelez-moi Lise":
Payette, Lise **1631b**
appendectomy:
Groves, Abraham **944a**
Appetite for Life, An:
Autobiographical Writing in English **147b**;
Ritchie, Charles Stewart Almon **1873c**
Apple **86b**:
Agriculture History **37c**;
Annapolis Lowlands **79b**;
Autumn Colours **152b**;
Botany **255b**;

Crab Apple **529a**;
Crop Research **542c**;
Domestic Utensils **611b**;
Fruit Cultivation **851a**;
Gibb, Charles **898c**;
McIntosh, John **1268a**;
Okanagan Valley **1563a**;
Pioneer Life **1679b**
apple bark borer:
Beetle **198b**
Apple in the Eye, The:
Drama in English **622b**
apple maggot:
Crop Research **543a**
apple scab:
Crab Apple **529a**;
Fungus **855a**;
Plant Disease **1688c**
Apple Tree Landing, NS:
Canning, NS **354c**
Applebaum, Louis **86b**:
Jews **1111b**
Applebaum-Hébert Commission:
Federal Cultural Policy Review Committee **753c**;
Theatre, English-Language **2141b**
Appleby College:
Massey, Raymond Hart **1312c**
Appleyard, Peter **86c**
applied mathematics:
Mathematics **1314a**
Applied Microelectronics Institute:
Nova Scotia Research Foundation Corporation **1535a**
Applying Philosophy:
Lodge, Rupert Clendon **1238a**
Appraisals of Canadian Literature:
Literature in English – Theory and Criticism **1228b**
Apprenticeship **86c**:
Engineering **704a**
Apprenticeship Act (1928) (Ont):
Apprenticeship **87a**
Apprenticeship Act (1935) (BC):
Apprenticeship **87a**
Apprenticeship Act (1936) (NS):
Apprenticeship **87a**
Apprenticeship in Early Canada **87b**:
Art Education **126a**;
Clocks and Watches **442a**
Apprenticeship of Duddy Kravitz, The **88a**:
Film **767a**;
Humorous Writing in English **1026c**;
Kotcheff, William, "Ted" **1147c**;
Richler, Mordecai **1869a**; **1869b**
Apprentis-Sorciers, les:
Drama in French **623b**;
Germain, Jean-Claude **895b**
Apprentissage d'Arahé, L':
Children's Literature in French **415a**
Apps, Charles Joseph Sylvanus **88b**
Apps, Michael:
Soaring **2021c**
Apricot **88b**:
Okanagan Valley **1563a**;
Poisonous Plants **1702b**
April, Jean-Pierre:
Popular Literature in French **1717c**
April, Raymonde:
Photography **1665c**
April Wine:
Popular Music **1719a**
Aqjangajuk Shaa **88c**
Aquaculture **88c**:
Biological Product **222c**;
Char **395c**;
Irish Moss **1092c**;
Malpeque Bay **1288c**;
Mussel **1422c**;
Newcastle, Ont **1482c**;
North Vancouver, BC **1510c**;
Oyster **1599b**;
Rockwood, Man **1882a**;
Trout **2196c**;
Veterinary Medicine **2256c**;
Wilmot, Samuel **2310b**;
Zooplankton **2362a**
aquafer:
Esker **719a**;
Saskatchewan **1932c**
aqualung:
Diving, Underwater **607a**
Aquarian Conspiracy, The:
New Religious Movements **1481b**

Au milieu, la montagne:
Novel in French **1541a**
Au milieu du corps l'attraction s'insinue:
Beausoleil, Claude **192b**
"Au pays de Neufve-France":
Perrault, Pierre **1645b**
Au pays de Zom:
Groulx, Gilles **941c**
Au pays des côtes:
Acadia **9a**
Au pied de la pente douce:
Lemelin, Roger **1201a**;
Pleure pas, Germaine **1694b**
Au plus fort la poche:
Acadia **8c**
Au Retour des oies blanches:
Theatre, French-Language **2145a**
Au Saint-Germain-des-Prés:
Julien, Pauline **1122a**
Aube assassiné, L':
Croatians **541b**
"Auberge des chercheurs d'or, L'":
Radio Drama, French-Language **1818b**
Auberge des Gouverneurs, L':
Gatineau, Qué **876b**
aubergine:
Eggplant **673b**
Aubert de Gaspé, Philippe-Ignace-François **143c**
Aubert de Gaspé, Philippe-Joseph **144a**:
Aubert de Gaspé, Philippe-Ignace-François **143c**;
Casgrain, Henri-Raymond **377b**
Aubert de la Chesnaye, Charles:
Compagnie du Nord **477b**;
Rivière-du-Loup, Qué **1876b**
Aubert de Lalonde Gayon, Thérèse:
St-Georges, Qué **1913a**
Aubert-Gallion, Qué:
St-Georges, Qué **1913a**
Aubigny, Lower Canada:
Lévis, Qué **1205a**
Aubin, Napoléon:
Essay in French **721c**;
Humorous Writing in French **1027b**
Aubin, Napoleon:
Printmaking **1757c**
Aubin de L'Isle, Gabriel:
St-Georges, Qué **1913a**
aubretia:
Flowers, Cultivated **793b**
Aubrey Falls:
Waterfall **2282c**
Aubry, Claude:
Children's Literature in French **414a**; **414b**
Aubry, Jérôme:
Couture, Joseph-Alphonse **528b**
Auburn, Romaine and Tom:
Magic **1285c**
Aubut, Françoise **144a**
Aubut, Lise:
Arsenault, Angèle **121a**
Aubut, Marcel:
Québec Nordiques **1807b**
Aucoin, Johnny:
Acadia **8a**
Auction, The:
Brown, Daniel Price Erichsen **288a**
Aucune créature:
Charbonneau, Robert **396a**
Audet, Jean-Paul:
Molson Prize **1373b**
"Audience":
Radio Drama, English-Language **1818a**
Audit Bureau of Circulations:
Magazines **1283a**
auditing:
Accounting **11b**;
Corporation Law **521b**
Auditor General Act (1977):
Auditor General of Canada **144b**
Auditor General of Canada **144a**:
Langton, John **1174c**
Auditory Impairment **144b**:
Disability **600b**;
Education, Special **667b**;
Mining Safety and Health **1363a**;
Noise **1502a**
Audley, Gordon:
Speed Skating **2057c**
Audubon, John James:
McCulloch, Thomas **1258b**

Aue, Walter:
Chemistry Subdisciplines **404b**
Auerbach, Herbert C.:
Centaur Theatre Co **386b**
Augé, Pierre:
Guitar **945c**
auger:
Tools, Carpentry **2167a**
Auger, Gilles:
Conductors and Conducting **488a**
Auger, Roger:
Theatre, French-Language **2146c**
Auger de Subercase, Daniel d' **145a**
August Nights:
Hood, Hugh John **1006b**
Augustine burial mound:
Prehistory **1739c**
Augustines de la Miséricorde de Jésus **145a**
Augustines hospitalières:
Augustines de la Miséricorde de Jésus **145a**;
Christian Religious Communities **421c**;
Hôtel-Dieu **1011b**;
Nursing **1546c**
Augustus **145a**
Augustyn, Frank **145a**
Auk **145b**:
Bird Classification and Evolution **228c**;
Great Auk **932c**;
Murre **1407c**;
Puffin **1788b**;
Razorbill **1830a**
Auk Redivivus: Selected Poems:
Johnston, George Benson **1114c**
auklet:
Auk **145b**
Aukuras drama group:
Theatre, Multicultural **2147a**
Auld, Georgie:
Jazz **1106c**
"Auld Lang Syne":
Lombardo, Guy **1239b**
Auliciems, A.:
Climate Severity **439b**
Aulnaies, Rivière des:
Saint-Jean, Lac **1913b**
Aulneau, Jean-Pierre:
La Vérendrye, Jean-Baptiste Gaultier de **1153a**;
Lake of the Woods **1167b**
Aulneau Peninsula:
Lake of the Woods **1167b**
Ault Foods Ltd:
John Labatt Corporation **1112c**
Auntie's Knitting a Baby:
Children's Literature in English **413a**
Aurora:
Jackman, Arthur **1101a**
Aurora, Ont **145b**
aurora borealis:
Northern Lights **1514c**
Aurora Borealis:
Collier, Ronald William **460a**
Aurora Range:
Torngat Mountains **2168b**
aurora trout:
Endangered Animals **695b**
Aurore, L':
Literature in French – Criticism and Theory **1230b**
Aurore, l'enfant martyre:
Drama in French **622c**;
Theatre, French-Language **2144c**
Auschwitz:
Jewish Writing **1110a**;
Judaism **1119b**
Austin, Horatio T.:
Arctic Exploration **110c**;
Franklin Search **839a**;
Prince of Wales Island **1754c**
Austin Airways:
Air Transport Industry **44b**;
Aviation **154c**
Australian and New Zealand Association for Canadian Studies:
Canada and Australia **323b**;
Canadian Studies **350b**
Australian-Canadian Studies:
Canada and Australia **323b**
Australian Cattle Dog:
Dog **609a**

Austrians **145b**:
Croatians **541a**;
Fur Industry **856a**;
Internment **1084a**;
Serbs **1981b**;
Skiing **2009b**;
Slovenes **2012a**
Austronesian language family:
Language **1174c**
"authors":
Games **872a**
Authors and Their Milieu **145c**
Authors' Bulletin:
Literary Magazines in English **1219c**
autism:
Education, Special **667b**
Autobiographical Writing in English **146c**:
Backwoods of Canada, The **159a**;
In Search of Myself **1050c**;
Roughing It In The Bush: or, Forest Life In Canada **1888c**
Autobiographical Writing in French **147c**
Autobiographies, Political **148b**
Autobiography:
Russell, Benjamin **1902c**
Autobiography:
Galt, John **870a**
Autobiography of a Nobody:
Autobiographical Writing in English **147b**
Autobiography of Oliver Goldsmith, The:
Goldsmith, Oliver **910b**
autocratic monarchy:
Monarchism **1373c**
autogyro:
Helicopter **976c**
Automated Light Rapid Transit:
New Westminster, BC **1482b**;
Subways and Light Rapid Transit **2090b**
Automatic Pilot:
Drama in English **622c**;
Ritter, Erika **1874a**;
Theatre, English-Language **2140c**
Automatic Train Control:
Railways, Track and Yards **1825b**
automation:
Office Automation **1559a**;
Postal Strikes, CUPW **1728c**;
Robotics **1881a**
Automatistes, Les **149a**:
Ferron, Marcelle **760a**
Automobile **149a**:
Baillairgé Family **164a**;
Bricklin automobile **269a**;
Frontenac automobile **850a**;
Metric Conversion **1346c**;
Platinum **1693a**;
Pollution **1714c**;
Roads and Highways **1877a**;
Rubber Products Industry **1898c**;
Safety Standards **1908a**
automobile accidents:
Automobile **149c**;
Disasters **603a**;
Impaired Driving **1049a**;
Injury and Prevention **1068a**; **1068c**
Automobile Associations **149c**
automobile insurance:
Insurance **1073b**;
Manitoba **1299a**;
Saskatchewan **1935b**
Automobile Insurance Act (Qué):
Delict **582b**;
Parti Québécois **1624c**
Automobile Racing **150a**
automobile theft:
Crime **536a**
automobile tire. *See* tire, pneumatic
Automotive Industry **150c**:
Canada-US Automotive Products Agreement **328b**;
Chrysler Canada Ltd **425a**;
Dofasco Inc **608a**;
Ford Motor Company of Canada, Limited **805c**;
General Motors of Canada Limited **879c**;
Redcliff, Alta **1838a**;
Saskatchewan **1935a**

Automotive Industry, Royal Commission on the:
Automotive Industry **151a**
Automotive Parts Technology Centre:
Automotive Industry **151b**
Autonomous Living Movement:
Disability **601a**
Autonomy Bills **151c**
Autopact:
Canada-US Automotive Products Agreement **328b**
autopsy:
Funeral Practices **853c**;
Murray, John Wilson **1407a**
Autorité du peuple, L':
Vadeboncoeur, Pierre **2238a**
Autoroute du Canton de l'est:
Sherbrooke, Qué **1990b**
Autour d'Ainola:
Music Composition **1413c**
Autour de la perception:
Hébert, Pierre **975b**
A'utsaht:
Ucluelet **2206b**
autumn:
Indian Summer **1056a**
Autumn Blaze white ash:
Ornamentals **1588c**
Autumn Colours **151c**
autumn equinox:
Buddhism **293b**
Autumn Flame maple:
Autumn Colours **152a**
Autumn Nocturn:
Symonds, Norman **2106b**
Autumn Sonata:
FitzGerald, Lionel LeMoine **787c**
Aux frontières de la science:
Seguin, Fernand **1975b**
Aux marges du silence:
Morel, François **1389a**
Aux quatre coins des routes canadiennes:
Children's Literature in French **414a**
"Aux 20 heures":
Radio Programming **1820a**
Auxiliary Active Air Force:
Armed Forces **117c**
Auyuittuq National Park **152c**:
Pangnirtung, NWT **1611c**
av Paul, Annette **152c**
Avakumovic, Ivan:
Woodcock, George **2332a**
Avalanche **153a**:
Disasters **601c**;
Rogers Pass **1884b**
Avalée des avalés, L':
Ducharme, Réjean **630c**;
Novel in French **1541b**
Avalon, Isthmus of:
Avalon Peninsula **153c**;
Come by Chance, Nfld **463b**;
Placentia Bay **1684c**
Avalon Channel:
Grand Banks **923a**
Avalon colony:
Calvert, George, 1st Baron Baltimore **319a**
Avalon Peninsula **153c**:
Bay Bulls, Nfld **187c**;
Cape Race **358c**;
Fossil Animals **826c**;
Goulds, Nfld **915a**;
Masterless Men of Newfoundland **1313b**;
Newfoundland **1485c**;
Vaughan, Sir William **2246b**
Avalon Telephone Co:
Telephones **2124a**
Avalon Wilderness Reserve:
Parks, Provincial **1619c**
Avalon Zone:
Geological Regions **887c**
Avant le chaos:
Grandbois, Alain **925b**
Avare, L':
Roux, Jean-Louis **1890a**
Avco Financial Services Canada Ltd:
London, Ont **1239c**
"Ave Maris Stella":
Acadia **7a**
Avec ma vie:
Poetry in French **1699c**
Avec ou sans amour:
Martin, Claire **1310a**;
Novel in French **1541a**

Barrie, Ont **181b**:
Disasters **603c**;
Plastics-Processing Industry **1690b**;
Queen's Plate **1812b**;
Religious Building **1853b**;
Rosenfeld, Fanny, "Bobby" **1887b**;
Rubber Products Industry **1898c**;
Theatre, English-Language **2142c**; **2143a**;
Tornado **2168a**
Barrie, Robert:
Barrie, Ont **181b**
Barrie Collegiate Institute:
Gallie, William Edward **869b**
Barriefield, Ont:
Kingston, Ont **1138c**
Barrier Inlet:
Waterfall **2282b**
Barrington, NS **181c**:
Canada and Australia **323a**
Barrington Bay:
Cape Sable Island **359a**
Barrington Meeting House:
Barrington, NS **181c**;
Religious Building **1852a**
Barrington Passage:
Barrington, NS **181c**
Barrister **181c**
Barristers' Society of New Brunswick:
Associations **137a**
Barrow, Francis J.:
Pictographs and Petroglyphs **1676a**
Barrow, John **181c**
Barrow River and Barrow Falls:
Waterfall **2282c**
Barrow Strait:
Arctic Archipelago **110a**;
Arctic Exploration **110b**;
Cornwallis Island **518c**;
Kellett, Sir Henry **1130c**;
Lancaster Sound **1169c**;
Parry Channel **1623c**
Barrow's goldeneye:
Duck **631b**
Barry, Anne Meredith:
Printmaking **1759b**
Barry, Fred:
Theatre, English-Language **2142c**
Barter **181c**
Barter Island:
Mackenzie Inuit **1271c**
Bartholomew Green 1751 Association Inc:
Magazines **1284b**
Bartlett, N.:
Chemistry Subdisciplines **404c**
Bartlett, Robert Abram **182a**:
Karluk **1128a**
Bartlett, William:
Musicology **1420c**
Bartlett, William Henry **182b**:
Hotel **1010c**
Bartlett pear:
Pear **1634c**
Bartocci, Gianni:
Italian Writing **1099a**
Barton Myers Associates:
Myers, Barton **1423c**
Bartram, Ed:
Printmaking **1759b**
baryon:
Physics **1670b**
Bas-Canada, 1791-1840, Le:
Ouellet, Fernand **1597c**
basalt:
Annapolis Lowlands **79b**;
Geological Regions **885c**; **887b**;
Greenstone **938a**;
Igneous Rock **1041b**;
Sedimentary Rock **1973c**;
Volcano **2267b**
Baseball **182b**:
Kinsella, William Patrick **1139c**;
Montreal Expos **1383b**;
Toronto Blue Jays **2172b**
Basement Cage Press:
Private Presses **1762b**
Basford, S. Ronald:
Morgentaler, Henry **1389b**
BASIC (Beginner's All-Purpose Symbolic Instruction Code):
Computer-Assisted Learning **479c**;
Computer Science **482b**;
Language **1174b**

Basic Nutrition:
McHenry, Earle Willard **1267a**
basic oxygen process:
Algoma Steel Corporation Limited **62c**;
Dofasco Inc **608a**;
Iron and Steel Industry **1093c**
Basidiomycotina:
Mycorrhizae **1423b**
basil:
Condiment Crops **487a**;
Herbs **980c**
Basile, Jean **183c**
Basilian Press:
Catholicism **382c**
Basilian Sisters:
Catholicism **382b**
Basilians **184a**:
Saint Thomas University **1924c**
Basin Head Fisheries Museum:
Prince Edward Island **1753b**
Basinski, Zbigniew Stanislaw **184a**
Basketball **184a**
Basketball Canada:
Basketball **184b**
basketry:
Abenaki **2c**;
Indian Art **1054b**; **1054c**;
Northwest Coast Indian Art **1517b**;
Weaving **2288a**; **2288b**
basking shark:
Fish **778a**;
Shark **1987c**
Basque language:
Port au Choix, Nfld **1724b**;
Port au Port Peninsula **1724c**
Basques **184b**:
Red Bay **1835a**
Basques, Île aux:
Bird Sanctuaries and Reserves **230b**;
Trois-Pistoles, Qué **2194c**
Bass **184c**:
Huron, Lake **1031a**
bass clarinet:
Orchestral Music **1583b**
Bass Saxophone, The:
Ethnic Literature **728a**;
Škvorecký, Josef **2010c**
Bassano, Alta:
Brooks, Alta **286c**
Bassett, Carling Kathrin **185a**
Bassett, Douglas:
Bassett, John White Hughes **185a**;
Baton Broadcasting Incorporated **186c**
Bassett, John:
Bassett, John White Hughes **185a**
Bassett, John White Hughes **185a**:
Toronto Maple Leafs **2173b**
Bassin de Chambly:
Chambly, Qué **392c**
Basso, Guido:
Appleyard, Peter **86c**;
Jazz **1106c**
bassoon:
Orchestral Music **1583b**
basswood:
Beekeeping **197b**;
Canoe, Dugout **355a**;
Vegetation Regions **2250c**
Bastedo, Frank Lindsay:
Saskatchewan **1936b**
Bastien, Gabriel:
Popular Literature in French **1718a**
Bastien, Hermas:
Philosophy **1658b**
Bastien Brothers Inc:
Footwear Industry **804c**
Bastion Square:
Hunt, Tony **1029b**;
Urban Design **2232a**
Bastion Theatre:
Theatre, English-Language **2139a**;
Victoria, BC **2261c**
Bat **185a**:
Animals in Winter **78c**
Bata, Thomas:
Bata, Thomas John **185b**
Bata Ltd:
Barter **182a**;
Bata, Thomas John **185b**;
Footwear Industry **805a**

Bataille de Sainte-Foy, La:
Légaré, Joseph **1199b**
Batawa, Ont:
Bata, Thomas John **185b**
Batchelor, George:
Dorion, Jean-Baptiste-Éric **613b**
Bateau bleu, maison verte:
Acadia **9b**
Bateman, Robert McLellan **185b**
Bates, Bob:
Lucania, Mount **1251a**
Bates, Donald:
Canadian Physicians for the Prevention of Nuclear War **348c**
Bates, John Seaman **185c**
Bates, Maxwell **185c**:
Printmaking **1759a**
Bates, Mona:
Music History **1417c**
Bates, Patricia **185c**:
Printmaking **1759a**
Batfish **185c**
Bath, Ont:
Frontenac **850a**;
McDowall, Robert **1263c**
bathtub race:
Nanaimo, BC **1425a**
Bathurst, Henry, 3rd Earl of:
Bathurst Island **186b**;
Bathurst Island **186b**
Bathurst, NB **186a**:
Acadia **8b**;
New Brunswick **1472c**
Bathurst harbour:
Bathurst, NB **186a**
Bathurst Inlet **186a**
Bathurst Inlet, NWT:
Bathurst Inlet **186a**
Bathurst Island **186b**:
Brooman Point Village **287a**;
Northwest Territories **1521a**;
Queen Elizabeth Islands **1812a**
Bathurst Mines Ltd:
Bush Flying **302c**
batik:
Indonesians **1060a**
Batiscan, Rivière:
St Lawrence Lowland **1919a**;
Technology **2120a**
Batoche, Sask **186c**:
Métis **1345c**;
Red Cross Society **1835b**;
Smyth, Sir Edward Selby **2018a**
Baton Broadcasting Incorporated **186c**:
Media Ownership **1321c**
Batson, Alfred:
Soldiers of Fortune **2044a**
Batstone, Harry, "Red":
Football **803a**
battalion:
Regiment **1840b**
Battalion of Incorporated Militia:
Regiment **1840c**
battered women and children:
Child Abuse **409a**;
Crime **536a**;
Criminology **540c**;
Foundations **831b**;
Status of Women **2074b**;
Women and the Law **2325a**
batteries:
Antimony **85a**;
Cadmium **314a**;
Electric-Power Development **677c**;
Lead **1192c**
Battle, Helen Irene **186c**
Battle for the Mind:
New Religious Movements **1480c**
Battle Harbour, Nfld:
Grenfell, Sir Wilfred Thomason **938a**;
Macpherson, Cluny **1281c**
Battle of Beaver Dams Park:
Thorold, Ont **2154b**
Battle of Foxtrap, The:
Burke, Johnny **299c**
Battle of Mule Run and Other Offenses:
Essay in English **720c**
Battle of the Long Sault, The:
Film **765c**
Battle River:
Battleford, Sask **187a**;
North Battleford, Sask **1509c**;
Stettler, Alta **2078b**
Battle River Crossing, North-West Territories:
Ponoka, Alta **1715c**

Battle River Regional Planning Commission:
Wetaskiwin, Alta **2296a**
"Battlefield of Batoche, The":
Purdy, Alfred Wellington **1791a**
Battleford, Sask **187a**:
Big Bear **215c**;
Poundmaker **1732b**;
Print Industry **1756a**;
Walker, James **2272a**
Battleford National Historic Park:
Battleford, Sask **187a**
Battling Malone:
Hémon, Louis **977c**
Batty Bay:
Kennedy, William **1132a**
Baudry, Edouard:
Radio Drama, French-Language **1818b**
Bauer, David William **187a**
Bauer, Robert, "Bobby":
Bauer, David William **187a**;
Schmidt, Milton Conrad **1946c**
Bauer, Stephen:
Bicycling **214a**;
Cycling **559c**
Bauer, Walter:
German Writing **895c**
Bauer skates:
Footwear Industry **804c**
Bauhin, C.:
Botany History **255c**
Baum, Gregory:
Philosophy **1662b**
Baumann, Alex **187b**
Baumé scale:
Maple Sugar Industry **1303b**
bauxite:
Aluminum **67a**;
Mineral Resources **1360c**
Bavasi, Peter:
Toronto Blue Jays **2172b**
bawdy house:
Prostitution **1768c**
Bawlf, Sam:
Expo 86 **738c**
Bawtree, Michael:
Drama in English **621c**
Baxter, (Elaine) Ingrid:
Art, Contemporary Trends **123c**;
Baxter, Joseph Iain Wilson **187c**
Baxter, John Babington Macaulay **187c**
Baxter, Joseph Iain Wilson **187c**:
Art, Contemporary Trends **123c**
Bay Bulls, Nfld **187c**
Bay d'Espoir **187c**:
Place-names **1683c**
Bay Fiord:
Fosheim Peninsula **826b**
bay lynx:
Bobcat **245b**
bay mussel:
Mussel **1422c**;
Seashell **1969c**
Bay Roberts, Nfld **188a**
Bay St George Community College:
Community College **476c**;
Newfoundland **1489b**
Bay Street Academy:
Macdonald, John **1260b**
Bàyefsky, Aba **188a**:
Illustration, Art **1043c**
Bayeur family:
Musical Instruments **1419c**
Bayfield, Adam Henry:
Science **1950c**
Bayfield, Henry Wolsey **188a**:
Cartography, History of **372a**;
Georgian Bay **894a**
Bayley, Charles:
Moose Factory **1387b**
Bayley, Cornwall:
Foreign Writers on Canada in English **809a**
Bayonets in the Streets:
Gellner, John **878b**
Bays, Lake of:
Huntsville, Ont **1030b**;
Muskoka Lakes **1421c**
Bayshore Shopping Centre:
Shopping Centre **1995c**
Bayside, NB:
McCain, H. Harrison **1256a**
Bazalgette, Ian Willoughby **188a**
Bazemore, A.W.:
Neuroscience **1467a**
BC Arts Council:
Lowther, Patricia Louise **1249c**

black guillemot:
  Auk **145b**;
  Auyuittuq National Park **152c**;
  Terra Nova National Park **2132a**
black gum:
  Autumn Colours **152a**
Black Hallelujah:
  Symonds, Norman **2106b**
black-headed grosbeak:
  Grosbeak **941a**
black heart:
  Celery **383c**
Black Hole **236a**:
  Israel, Werner **1098c**;
  Science and Society **1954b**
black huckleberry:
  Vegetation Regions **2249a**
Black Huntsman, The:
  Layton, Irving Peter **1191a**
black ice:
  Ice **1037a**;
  Iceberg **1038b**
Black Island:
  Hecla, Man **975c**
Black Jews:
  Africans **22a**
black knot:
  Plum **1694c**
Black Lace:
  Salverson, Laura **1928b**
Black Lake, Qué:
  Mineral Resources **1360a**;
  Vaillancourt, Armand
    J.R. **2238a**
Black Lake (Sask):
  Cree Lake **533b**
black-legged kittiwake:
  Bird Sanctuaries and Re-
    serves **230a**;
  Gull **946a**
black lung disease:
  Coal Mining **449a**;
  Mining Safety and Health **1363a**;
  Occupational Diseases **1553b**
Black (Manicouagan) River:
  Manicouagan Réservoir **1290c**
black maple:
  Maple **1302c**;
  Vegetation Regions **2250c**
black market:
  Underground Economy **2208c**
Black Mountain:
  West Vancouver, BC **2295c**
Black Night Window:
  Exploration and Travel Litera-
    ture in English **737a**;
  Newlove, John **1492a**
black nightshade:
  Nightshade **1500a**
black oak:
  Oak **1549a**
Black Pioneer Rifle Corps:
  Blacks **238b**
Black Pioneers:
  Peters, Thomas **1647b**
black poplar:
  Poplar **1716b**
Black Powder:
  Deverell, Rex **590b**;
  Drama in English **622a**;
  Globe Theatre **906c**
black raspberry:
  Berries, Wild **208c**
black rat:
  Rat **1828c**
black rat snake:
  Snake **2018b; 2019a**
Black Report:
  Theatre Education **2148a**;
  2148b
Black Rock:
  Best-Sellers in English **210a**
black root rot:
  Tobacco **2164c**
Black Rose, The:
  Costain, Thomas Bertram **524a**
black rot:
  Grape **927c**;
  Turnip **2203c**
black sea bass:
  Bass **184c**
black slug:
  Slug **2012a**
black soils:
  Soil Classification **2038c**;
  Vegetation Regions **2250a**
black spot:
  Rose, Cultivated **1886c**

black spruce:
  Forest Fire **812c; 813a**;
  Forest Harvesting **813c**;
  Spruce **2064b**;
  Treeline **2191b**;
  Vegetation Regions **2248a**;
    2248c
black star:
  Black Hole **236a**
black swift:
  Swift **2103a**
black-tailed deer:
  Deer **580a**
black-tailed prairie dog:
  Grasslands National Park **931a**;
  Prairie Dog **1734c**
black tern:
  Tern **2131c**
Black Theatre Canada (Toronto):
  Theatre, English-
    Language **2139c**;
  Theatre, Multicultural **2147b**
Black Tusk:
  Coast Mountains **449c**;
  Garibaldi Provincial Park **873c**
Black United Front:
  Oliver, William Pearly **1565a**;
  West Indians **2295c**
black walnut:
  Endangered Plants **697b**;
  Furniture, English, Scottish and
    American **864a**;
  Vegetation Regions **2250c**;
  Walnut **2272c**
Black Watch (Royal Highland
    Regiment) of Canada:
  Allan, Sir Hugh Andrew Mon-
    tagu **64a**;
  Regiment **1841a**
Black Welsh cattle:
  Beef Cattle Farming **196a**
black widow spider:
  Spider **2058b**
black willow:
  Vegetation Regions **2250c**
Blackbeard:
  Oak Island **1549c**
blackberries:
  Berries, Wild **207c**
Blackbird **236b**:
  Bird Distribution and Habi-
    tat **229b**
Blackburn, Maurice:
  Music History **1418c**;
  Opera **1579a**
Blackburn, Robert:
  Encyclopedia **694b**
blackcap:
  Berries, Wild **208c**
Blackduck culture:
  Brockinton **285b**;
  Rainy River Burial
    Mounds **1826b**
Blackfeet:
  Blackfoot Nation **237a**;
  Peigan **1637b**
blackfin tuna:
  Tuna **2200b**
Blackfish:
  Literary Magazines in Eng-
    lish **1220a**
Blackfoot **236c**:
  Bearberry **189b**;
  Dickens, Francis Jeffrey **592c**;
  Dumont, Gabriel **633c**;
  Sun Dance **2095a**
Blackfoot Crossing (Bow River):
  Blackfoot **237a**;
  Crowfoot **545b**
Blackfoot-English dictionary:
  L'Heureux, Jean-Baptiste **1206b**
Blackfoot language:
  Blackfoot **236c**;
  High River, Alta **986a**;
  L'Heureux, Jean-Baptiste **1206b**
Blackfoot Nation **237a**:
  Blackfoot **236c**;
  Blood **242a**;
  Peigan **1637a**;
  Potts, Jerry **1731c**;
  Rocky Mountain House National
    Historic Park **1882b**
Blackfoot Reserve:
  Blackfoot **237a**;
  L'Heureux, Jean-Baptiste **1206b**
blackheaded duck:
  Duck **631b**
blackjack:
  Gambling **870a; 870b**

"Blackjack":
  Lost Lemon Mine **1244a**
Blacklead Island:
  Baffin Island **161b**;
  Hantzsch, Bernhard Adolf **960c**;
  Whaling **2298a**
blackleg:
  Animal Agriculture **77a**;
  Beef Cattle Farming **196b**
blackleg:
  Kale **1125b**;
  Kohlrabi **1145c**
"blackout" nickel:
  Coinage **456c**
Blacks **237b**:
  Africans **21b**;
  Baseball **183b**;
  Education, History of **666c**;
  Genetic Diseases **880b**;
  Immigration **1046b; 1047a**;
  Jazz **1106c**;
  Langford, Sam **1173c**;
  Lucan, Ont **1250c**;
  New Brunswick **1470a**;
  Orthodox Church **1591b**;
  Prejudice and Discrimina-
    tion **1741c**;
  Theatre, English-
    Language **2137b**;
  West Indians **2295a**
Blacks Harbour, NB:
  Grand Manan Island **923c**;
  Resource Towns **1861a**
blacksmith tokens:
  Coinage **456c**
Blacksmithing **238c**
blackspot:
  Perch **1642b**;
  Pike **1677c**
Blackstone, Milton:
  Hart House String Quartet **965b**
Blackstone formation:
  Sedimentary Rock **1973c**
blackstripe top minnow:
  Endangered Animals **695b**
Blackwater (West Road) River:
  Carrier **366c**
Blackwell, Charlie:
  Water Skiing **2281c**
Blackwell and Craig:
  Zeidler, Eberhard Hein-
    rich **2359b**
Blackwood, Algernon:
  Foreign Writers on Canada in
    English **809b**;
  Theosophy **2149b**
Blackwood, David Lloyd **239c**:
  Printmaking **1759b**
Blackwood, Robert:
  Furniture, Country **861b**
bladderwort:
  Carnivorous Plants **365c**
Bladen, Vincent Wheeler **239c**
Blades, Ann **239c**:
  Children's Literature in Eng-
    lish **413a**
Blain, Maurice:
  Cité libre **427b**
Blaine Lake, Sask:
  Horner, John Henry **1007b**
Blainville, Qué:
  Automotive Industry **151b**
Blainville, Thérèse de:
  Place-names **1683b**
Blair, Andrew George **239c**
Blair, Duncan Black:
  Ethnic Literature **726b**
Blair, Sidney Robert **239c**
Blairmore, Alta:
  Crowsnest Pass Strike,
    1932 **547c**;
  Czechs **560c**;
  Mineral Resources **1360a**;
  Revolutionary Industrial Union-
    ism **1866c**
Blais, Aristide:
  French in the West **847a**
Blais, Marie-Claire **240a**:
  Novel in French **1541b**;
  Poetry in French **1700b**
Blais, Roger:
  Film **767c**
Blaise, Clark **240a**
Blake, Catherine Hume:
  Blake, William Hume **241a**
Blake, Edward **240b**:
  Canada First **326a**;
  Cronyn, Benjamin **542a**;
  Judicial Committee of the Privy
    Council **1120c**;

Lash, Zebulon Aiton **1179c**;
  Laurier, Sir Wilfrid **1183c**;
  Political Campaign **1707b**;
  Schull, Joseph **1950b**;
  Wrong, Humphrey Hume **2349a**
Blake, Hector, "Toe" **240c**
Blake, Margaret Cronyn:
  Blake, Edward **240b**
Blake, William Hume **240c**
Blake, William Hume:
  Essay in English **720a**;
  Maria Chapdelaine **1305b**
Blakeley, Phyllis:
  Musicology **1420c**
Blakeney, Allan Emrys **241a**:
  Constitution, Patriation of **498a**
Blakeny, C.H.:
  Canadian Travellers
    Abroad **351b**
Blakiston, Mount:
  Blakiston, Thomas Wright **241a**
Blakiston, Thomas Wright **241a**:
  Palliser Expedition **1610a**
Blakiston Creek:
  Blakiston, Thomas Wright **241a**
Blanc, John:
  Soldiers of Fortune **2044b**
Blanc Reservoir:
  St-Maurice, Rivière **1923b**
Blanc-Sablon, Qué:
  Labrador Boundary Dis-
    pute **1160c**
Blancard, Roseline:
  Acadia **8c**
Blanchard, Hiram **241b**
Blanchard, Raoul:
  Geomorphology **892a**;
  Physical Geography **1667a**;
  Urban Studies **2233a**
Blanche, Rivière:
  Henderson, Alexander **978a**
Blanche forcée:
  Beaulieu, Victor-Lévy **191c**
Blanchet, François **241b**
Blanchet, François-Norbert:
  Exploration and Travel Litera-
    ture in French **737c**
Bland, John **241b**
Bland, Salem Goldworth **241b**:
  Academic Freedom **5b**
Blanding's turtle:
  Turtle **2204a**
Blaney, Justine:
  Bolt, Carol **246b**
blanket:
  Chilkat Blanket **415b**;
  Davidson, Florence Eden-
    shaw **571a**
Blanket society:
  Kootenay **1146b**
Blanket-Stiff:
  Exploration and Travel Litera-
    ture in English **736c**
Blankstein, Cecil Nat:
  Green, Blankstein, Russell **936c**
Blanshard, Richard:
  Douglas, Sir James **615a**
Blasco, Steve:
  Breadalbane **267c**
Blaser, Robin **241c**:
  Bowering, George **262c**
Blaskowitz, Karol:
  Poles **1704a**
blasphemous libel:
  Law and the Press **1188c**
blast furnace:
  Iron and Steel Industry **1093c**
Blasted Pine, The:
  Humorous Writing in Eng-
    lish **1026c**
Blatchly, William D.:
  Graphic Art and Design **928b**;
  Printmaking **1758a**
Blatter, Robert:
  Architectural Styles **99a**;
  Architecture, Development
    of **104a**
Blenheim apricot:
  Apricot **88c**
Blennerhasset, Margaret:
  Poetry in English **1696a**
Blessure au flanc du ciel:
  Croatians **541b**
Blessures, Les:
  Poetry in French **1699c**
Bleu, Mont:
  Laurentian Highlands **1182c**
Blewchamp, Anna:
  Dance, Modern **567b; 567c**
Blewett, George John **241c**

blewointment:
Literary Magazines in English **1220a**
Bley, Paul **241c**
Bligh, Stanley:
Music Criticism **1414a**
Bligh, William:
Canada and Australia **322c**
blights:
Barley **178c**;
Carrot **367a**;
Celery **383c**;
Chestnut **407b**;
Fungus **854c**;
Plant Disease **1688c**
"Blind Faith":
Television Drama, English-Language **2126b**
Blind Organization of Ontario . . .:
Blindness and Visual Impairment **242a**
"blind pig":
Prohibition **1765b**
Blind River **241c**:
Mining **1362b**
Blind River, Ont:
Hirshhorn, Joseph Herman **990b**
Blindness and Visual Impairment **242a**:
Disability **600b**;
Ophthalmology **1579c**
Blinkety Blank:
McLaren, Norman **1274c**
Bliss, Michael:
Biography in English **221a**;
Business History **306a**
Bliss Carman:
Biography in English **220c**
Bliss Carman Poetry Society:
Fiddlehead, The **762b**
Bliss case:
Women and the Law **2325a**
blister beetle:
Beetle **198b**
Blitzkrieg:
Drama in English **622b**
Blizzard **242b**
bloat:
Legume **1200c**
Bloc populaire canadien **242b**:
Chartrand, Michel **398c**;
Gouin, Paul **914b**
"block parents":
Police **1705a**
Blockhouse Island:
Brockville, Ont **285b**
Blodgett, Edward Dickinson **242c**
Bloedel, Stewart and Welch:
MacMillan, Harvey Reginald **1279c**
Bloem, Jan Jacques:
Sculpture **1963a**
Bloemfontein, Battle of:
South African War **2048b**
Blonde d'Aquitaine cattle:
Beef Cattle Farming **196b**
Blondel, Maurice:
Philosophy **1660a**
Blondel, Patricia:
Winnipeg, Man **2318c**
"Blondin":
Niagara Falls **1497a**
Blondin, Marie-Esther Sureau dit:
Sisters of St Anne **2007c**
blood:
AIDS **41a**;
Biological Product **222c**;
Black Fly **236a**;
Disease, Animal **604a**;
Genest, Jacques **880a**;
Leech **1197b**;
Medicine, Contemporary **1327b**;
Mosquito **1393c**;
Ocean Industry **1556a**
Blood **242c**:
Folk Dance **797a**;
Red Crow **1835c**;
Tailfeathers, Gerald **2109b**
Blood, Sweat and Tears:
Clayton-Thomas, David **435b**
Blood Brothers:
Children's Literature in English **412b**
blood fluke:
Mollusc **1371b**
Blood is Strong, The:
Festival Lennoxville **761a**;
Sinclair, Lister Shedden **2006c**
Blood of Others, The:
Héroux, Denis **983a**

Blood Relations:
Drama in English **621c**;
Pollock, Sharon **1713b**
Blood Relatives:
Héroux, Denis **983a**
blood transfusion:
AIDS **41b**;
Bethune, Henry Norman **211b**;
Connaught Laboratories Limited **491b**;
Medicine, Contemporary **1328a**;
Red Cross Society **1835b**
blood worm:
Annelida **80a**
Bloodflowers:
Ethnic Literature **726c**
bloodroot:
Biogeography **219c**
Bloody Falls **243a**:
Coppermine River **515a**
Bloody Mary:
Poetry in French **1701b**
Bloody Run, Battle of:
Pontiac **1715c**
"Bloody Saturday":
Winnipeg General Strike **2320a**
Bloom, M.:
Physics **1668a**
Bloomfield, Leonard:
Folklore **800a**
Bloomsdays:
Theatre, English-Language **2140a**
Bloor Street United Church:
Pidgeon, George Campbell **1676c**
Bloore, Ronald **243a**
blossom-end rot:
Tomato **2165c**
blow fly:
Fly **793c**
blowball:
Dandelion **568c**
Blown Fingers:
Thomas, Audrey Grace **2151a**
Blue:
Mitchell, Joni **1367c**;
Popular Music **1718c**
Blue, Ben:
Canadian Expatriates in Show Business **337c**
blue ash:
Ash **134b**
Blue Book:
Budgetary Process **294b**
blue butterfly:
Butterfly **308b**
Blue Champagne:
Musical Theatre **1420b**
Blue cheese:
Cheese and Cheesemaking **400b**;
Mold **1369c**
blue-collar workers:
Social Class **2024a**
Blue Dolphin expedition:
Hamilton Inlet **958b**
Blue Ensign:
Keane, Abraham **1130a**
blue-eyed grass:
Wildflowers **2306a**
blue flag:
Lily **1215c**
blue-flowered alfalfa:
Alfalfa **61a**
blue fox:
Fur Farming **855c**
blue gas:
Coal Gasification **448a**
blue goose:
Cape Dorset, NWT **358c**;
Soper, Joseph Dewey **2047a**
blue grama:
Alberta **50c**;
Biogeography **219c**;
Vegetation Regions **2250a**
Blue-green Algae **243b**:
Fossil Plants **828b**;
Lichen **1211c**;
Sedimentary Rock **1974a**;
Vegetation Regions **2252b**
blue-green mold:
Cheese and Cheesemaking **400b**
blue grosbeak:
Grosbeak **941a**
blue grouse:
Grouse **943a**;
Migration **1351a**
blue jay:
Jay **1106b**;
Migration **1351a**

blue mold:
Tobacco **2164c**
Blue Mondays:
Fennario, David **757c**
Blue Mountain:
Bruce Trail **290b**
Blue Mountain pottery:
Collingwood, Ont **460a**;
Nepheline Syenite **1466a**
Blue Mountains of China:
Wiebe, Rudy Henry **2304b**
blue mussel:
Mussel **1422c**
Blue Ontario Hemingway Boat Race, The:
Donnell, David **613a**
Blue Pete: Half Breed:
Best-Sellers in English **210b**
Blue Quills Indian College:
St Paul, Alta **1923c**
Blue Ridge, Alta:
Whitecourt, Alta **2301a**
blue shark:
Shark **1987c**
Blue Sky, The:
Donnell, David **613a**
Blue Snake, The:
Dance on Television and Film **568c**;
Desrosiers, Robert Guy **589b**
blue-spotted salamander:
Salamander **1926a**
blue spruce:
Spruce **2064c**
blue walleye:
Endangered Animals **694c**; **695b**
Blue Water:
Shipman, Ernest G. **1993c**
blue whale:
Crustacean **549a**;
Endangered Animals **695a**;
Mingan, Îles de **1361a**;
Whale **2296b**;
Whaling **2296c**
blueback herring:
Herring **983c**
Bluebeard's Egg:
Atwood, Margaret Eleanor **143b**
Bluebell **243c**
blueberries:
Autumn Colours **152a**;
Berries, Cultivated **207b**;
Berries, Wild **207c**;
Crop Research **542c**;
Mistassini, Lac **1367b**;
Newfoundland **1487a**;
Vegetation Regions **2249a**; **2252a**
Blueberry Festival:
Mistassini, Qué **1367a**
Bluebird **243c**
bluebunch wheat grass:
Vegetation Regions **2249c**; **2250a**
bluefin tuna:
Aquaculture **89b**;
Notre Dame Bay **1526a**;
Sportfishing **2059b**;
Tuna **2200b**
Bluefish Caves **243c**
Bluefish River:
Bluefish Caves **243c**
Bluefre plum:
Plum **1694c**
"bluegrass" music:
Country and Western Music **526a**
bluegrasses:
Grasses **930c**;
Vegetation Regions **2249c**; **2250b**
Bluejay Dance:
Kootenay **1146b**
bluejoint small reed grass:
Vegetation Regions **2249a**
Bluenose, The **244a**:
Literature in English **1224a**;
Rugs and Rug Making **1900a**;
Stamp Collecting **2067b**
Bluenose caribou herd:
Horton Plain **1009a**
Bluenose Ghosts:
Children's Literature in English **412c**
Bluenose Lake:
Horton Plain **1009a**
"blueschists":
Metamorphic Rock **1340c**

bluestem:
Endangered Animals **695a**;
Vegetation Regions **2250a**
bluetongue virus:
Midge **1350b**
Bluffton, Alta:
Christian Religious Communities **422c**
Blumenau, Alta:
Stettler, Alta **2078b**;
Swiss **2104a**
Blumenfeld, Hans **244a**
Blumenort, Man:
Hanover, Man **959c**
Blumhart, William-Edmond:
Presse, La **1744b**
Blyth Festival **244b**:
Theatre, English-Language **2141b**
Blyth Memorial History Show:
Blyth Festival **244b**
Blythe, Alan:
Popular Music **1718b**
BMEWS:
Radar **1817b**
BMI Canada Ltd:
Champagne, Claude **392c**;
Music Composition **1413c**;
Music Publishing **1419b**
BMI Canada Ltd Award:
Gellman, Steven **878a**
B'nai B'rith:
Jews **1111a**;
Judaism **1120a**
B'Nai B'rith National Humanitarian Award:
Manning, Ernest Charles **1301a**
board games:
Chess **406b**;
Games **871b**
Board of Admiralty:
Admiralty **16a**
Board of Agricultural Education (Alta):
Education, Technical **668b**
Board of Agriculture (NS):
Lawson, George **1190c**
Board of Broadcast Governors:
Broadcasting, Radio and Television **284a**;
Canadian Radio-television and Telecommunications Commission **349b**;
Juneau, Pierre **1122a**;
Television Programming **2127c**
Board of Commissioners of Public Utilities (NS):
Regulatory Process **1847c**
Board of Education (NS):
Murdoch, Beamish **1405a**
Board of Grain Supervisors:
Agriculture and Food Policy **35c**
Board of Health (Ont):
Bryce, Peter Henderson **291a**;
Health Policy **971c**;
Hodgetts, Charles Alfred **999c**
Board of Pension Advocates:
Veterans Affairs, Department of **2255b**
Board of Public Works (Province of Canada):
Canals and Inland Waterways **353a**;
Crown Corporation **545c**;
Keefer, Samuel **1130a**;
Killaly, Hamilton Hartley **1135b**
Board of Railway Commissioners:
Canadian Manufacturers' Association **344b**;
Crow's Nest Pass Agreement **547a**;
Norris, Tobias Crawford **1507c**;
Sise, Charles Fleetford **2007c**;
Telegraph **2123b**;
Telephones **2124b**;
Transportation Regulation **2189b**
Board of Stock and Bond Brokers:
Stock and Bond Markets **2080c**
Board of Trade Building (Toronto):
Architecture, Development of **102b**
Board of Transport Commissioners:
Canadian Transport Commission **351a**;
Transportation Regulation **2189b**; **2189c**
boards of trade:
Chamber of Commerce **392a**
Boards of Trade Act:
Associations **137c**

C

Canadian Society of Environmental
　Biologists:
　Botany **255c**;
　Zoology **2361c**
Canadian Society of Equity:
　United Farmers of Alberta **2216a**
Canadian Society of Exploration
　Geophysicists:
　Geology **891a**
Canadian Society of Graphic Art:
　Artists' Organiza-
　　tions **131a**; **131c**;
　Printmaking **1758b**; **1759a**;
　Wood, William John **2331b**
Canadian Society of Immunology:
　Immunology **1049a**;
　Microbiology **1349b**
Canadian Society of Landscape
　Architects:
　Botany **255c**;
　Landscape Architec-
　　ture **1172b**; **1172c**
Canadian Society of Microbiolo-
　gists:
　Botany **255c**;
　Microbiology **1349b**
Canadian Society of Painters in
　Watercolour:
　Artists' Organizations **131b**;
　Bush, John Hamilton **302b**;
　Carmichael, Franklin **365a**
Canadian Society of Petroleum
　Geologists:
　Geology **891b**
Canadian Society of Plant Physiol-
　ogists:
　Botany **255c**
Canadian Society of Soil Science:
　Geology **891b**;
　Soil Conservation **2040b**;
　Soil Science **2042a**; **2042c**
Canadian Society of Technical
　Agriculturists:
　Soil Science **2042c**
Canadian Society of Tropical
　Medicine and International
　Health:
　Parasitology **1613b**
Canadian Society of Wildlife and
　Fishery Biologists:
　Zoology **2361c**
Canadian Society of Zoologists:
　Entomology **711a**;
　Parasitology **1613b**;
　Zoology **2361c**
Canadian Society of Zoologists Fry
　Medal:
　Dunbar, Maxwell John **634c**;
　Fry, Frederick Ernest
　　Joseph **851c**
Canadian Sociology and Anthro-
　pology Association:
　Sociology **2036c**
Canadian Soft Drink Association:
　Soft-Drink Industry **2037b**
Canadian Solar Industries Associa-
　tion:
　Solar Energy **2043c**
Canadian Song Book, A:
　MacMillan, Sir Ernest Alexander
　　Campbell **1279b**
Canadian Songs and Poems:
　*Songs of the Great Domin-
　　ion* **2047a**
Canadian South African Memorial
　Association:
　South African War **2048b**
Canadian Southern Railway:
　Murray, John Wilson **1407a**
Canadian Space Agency:
　Space Technology **2054c**
*Canadian Specialist Plant Soci-
　eties*:
　Flowers, Cultivated **793b**
Canadian Spectator:
　Duvernay, Ludger **638c**
Canadian Sport Parachuting
　Association:
　Parachuting, Sport **1612c**
Canadian Sports Advisory Council:
　Sports Organization, Ama-
　　teur **2063b**
Canadian Sports Pool Corporation:
　Lottery **1244b**
Canadian Squash Racquets Associ-
　ation:
　Squash Racquets **2065b**
Canadian Standardbred Horse
　Society:
　Harness Racing **962b**

Canadian Standards Association:
　Building Codes and Regula-
　　tions **296c**;
　Cement Industry **384b**;
　Industrial Quality Con-
　　trol **1060b**;
　Metric Conversion **1346c**;
　Safety Standards **1907c**
Canadian Standards Association
　John Jenkins Award:
　Convey, John **512b**
Canadian Statistical Review:
　Mathematics **1315b**;
　Statistics Canada **2072c**
Canadian Stock Exchange:
　Stock and Bond Markets **2080c**
Canadian Student Film Festival:
　Film Festivals, Prizes **772a**
Canadian Studies **350a**:
　Association for Canadian
　　Studies **136c**;
　Canada Studies Founda-
　　tion **327c**;
　International Council for Can-
　　adian Studies **1079b**;
　Klinck, Carl Frederick **1143c**
Canadian Studies in Population:
　Demography **585a**;
　Sociology **2037a**
Canadian Suffrage Association:
　Denison, Flora MacDonald **585b**
Canadian Sugar Institute:
　Sugar Industry **2092a**
"Canadian Summer":
　Liberation of Holland **1208c**
Canadian Superstore:
　Retail Trade **1865a**
Canadian Table Tennis Associa-
　tion:
　Table Tennis **2108a**
Canadian Talent Library:
　McConnell, Robert Murray
　　Gordon **1257c**;
　Music Broadcasting **1412a**
Canadian Tax Foundation **350c**:
　Pressure Group **1744b**
Canadian Tax Journal:
　Canadian Tax Foundation **350c**
Canadian Teachers' Federation:
　Lloyd, Woodrow Stanley **1234a**;
　Teaching Profession **2115c**
Canadian Team Handball Federa-
　tion:
　Team Handball **2116c**
Canadian Television Network
　(CTV):
　Television Program-
　　ming **2127c**; **2128a**;
　Templeton, Charles
　　Bradley **2130a**
Canadian Textile and Chemical
　Union:
　Parent, Madeleine **1613c**
Canadian Theatre Centre:
　Hendry, Thomas Best **978b**;
　Theatre, English-
　　Language **2139a**
Canadian Theatre Critics Associa-
　tion:
　Theatre, English-
　　Language **2144a**
"Canadian Theatre of the Air":
　Canadian Broadcasting Corpo-
　　ration **334b**
Canadian Theatre Review:
　Drama in English **621c**; **622a**;
　Simons, Beverly **2005c**;
　Theatre, English-
　　Language **2142b**
Canadian Theological College:
　University of Regina **2223a**
Canadian Theological Society:
　Religion **1850c**
Canadian Theosophist, The:
　Theosophy **2149b**
*Canadian Theses/Thèses canadi-
　ennes*:
　Literary Bibliography in
　　French **1219a**
Canadian Thoracic Society:
　Canadian Lung Association **344a**
Canadian Tidal Survey:
　Oceanography **1557a**;
　Tide **2159b**
Canadian Tire Corporation,
　Limited **350c**
Canadian Toys Ltd:
　Toys and Games **2178a**
Canadian Track and Field Associa-
　tion:
　Track and Field **2178b**; **2179b**

Canadian Trade Commissioner
　Service:
　Ambassadors and Em-
　　bassies **68a**;
　Canadian Manufacturers'
　　Association **344b**
Canadian Transport Commis-
　sion **351a**:
　Air Canada **41c**;
　Air Law and Space Law **42a**;
　Canadian Radio-television and
　　Telecommunications Commis-
　　sion **349b**;
　Economic Regulation **648a**;
　Marchand, Jean **1304c**;
　Nielsen, Erik Hersholt **1499c**;
　Pickersgill, John Whit-
　　ney **1675c**;
　Railway Safety **1823a**;
　Telecommunications **2123a**;
　Transport Canada **2184a**
Canadian Transport Commission
　Air Transport Committee:
　Aviation **155a**
Canadian Transport Commission
　Water Transport Committee:
　Shipping Industry **1994c**
Canadian Travellers Abroad **351a**
Canadian Treaty Making:
　Gotlieb, Allan Ezra **913c**
Canadian Trio:
　Hétu, Pierre **984b**
Canadian Trotting Association:
　Harness Racing **962b**
Canadian Tuberculosis Associa-
　tion:
　Canadian Lung Association **344a**
Canadian Turkey Marketing
　Agency:
　Agriculture and Food Policy **36b**
Canadian-UK-US Atomic Energy
　Project:
　Pryce, Maurice Henry Lecor-
　　ney **1776c**
Canadian Ukrainian Opera Associ-
　ation:
　Theatre, Multicultural **2147a**
Canadian Union College:
　Lacombe, Alta **1162b**
Canadian Union of Postal Workers:
　Davidson, Joe **571a**;
　Parrot, Jean-Claude **1623b**;
　Postal Strikes, CUPW **1728c**;
　Public-Service Unions **1787c**;
　Union Centrals, Québec **2214a**
Canadian Union of Public Employ-
　ees **351c**:
　Carr, Shirley **366c**;
　Hartman, Grace **965c**
Canadian Union of Students:
　Housing Co-operatives **1017b**;
　New Left **1479b**
Canadian Unitarian Council:
　Unitarians **2215a**
Canadian Unity, Task Force
　on **351c**:
　Atlantic Provinces **142a**;
　Cashin, Richard **377c**;
　Chaput-Rolland, Solange **395c**;
　Community **475b**
Canadian University Music Society:
　Music Education **1415c**;
　Music History **1418b**;
　Musicology **1420c**
Canadian University Services
　Overseas:
　CUSO **558a**
Canadian Upper Mantle Project:
　Van Steenburgh, William
　　Elgin **2239c**
Canadian Uranium Research
　Foundation:
　Forward, Frank Arthur **826b**
Canadian Urban Transit Associa-
　tion:
　Urban Transportation **2235a**
Canadian Utilities Ltd:
　Reid, Richard Gavin **1849a**
Canadian Veterinary Council:
　Veterinary Medicine, His-
　　tory **2257c**
Canadian Veterinary Medical
　Association:
　Savage, Alfred **1944c**;
　Smith, David Laurence Thom-
　　son **2015b**;
　Veterinary Medicine **2255c**
Canadian Veterinary Medical
　Association Act (1948):
　Veterinary Medicine, His-
　　tory **2258a**

Canadian Vickers Ltd:
　Canadair Ltd **328c**;
　Richardson, James Arm-
　　strong, Sr **1868c**;
　Shipbuilding and Ship Re-
　　pair **1992c**
Canadian Videotex Consultative
　Committee:
　Telidon **2129a**
Canadian Views and Studies ...:
　Photography **1664b**
Canadian Volleyball Association:
　Volleyball **2268b**
Canadian Volunteer Service Medal:
　Medal **1320a**
Canadian War Art Program:
　War Artists **2273c**
Canadian War Memorial, the:
　Sculpture **1964c**
Canadian War Memorials Exhibi-
　tion:
　Printmaking **1758b**
Canadian War Memorials Fund:
　Johnston, Francis Hans **1114b**;
　War Artists **2273c**
Canadian War Museum:
　Canadian Museum of Civiliza-
　　tion **344c**;
　Medal **1320a**;
　National Museum of Science and
　　Technology **1432a**
Canadian War News, The:
　Graphic Art and Design **928b**
Canadian War Records Office:
　Jackson, Alexander
　　Young **1101c**;
　Lismer, Arthur **1217c**;
　Photography **1665a**;
　Varley, Frederick Hors-
　　man **2245c**;
　War Artists **2273c**
Canadian Warbler, The:
　Hymns **1035b**
Canadian Water Polo Association:
　Water Polo **2281b**
Canadian Water Resources Associ-
　ation:
　Hydrology **1035b**
*Canadian Water Resources
　Journal*:
　Hydrology **1035b**
Canadian Water Ski Association:
　Water Skiing **2281c**
Canadian Weightlifting Federation:
　Weightlifting **2289c**
Canadian Welding Code:
　Safety Standards **1907c**
Canadian Welfare Council Com-
　mittee on Aging:
　Gerontology **897c**
Canadian Well Logging Society:
　Geology **891b**
Canadian West in Fiction, The:
　Regionalism in Literature **1847b**
Canadian Wheat Board **351c**:
　Agriculture and Food Pol-
　　icy **35c**; **36a**;
　McIvor, George Harold **1268b**;
　Mazankowski, Donald
　　Frank **1318b**;
　Remote Sensing **1856a**
Canadian Wheelmen's Association:
　Bicycling **213b**;
　Cycling **559b**;
　Rubenstein, Louis **1899a**
Canadian White Ribbon Tidings:
　Prohibition **1765a**
Canadian White Water Affiliation:
　Canoeing **356a**
Canadian Who's Who:
　Biography in English **220b**;
　Popular Literature in Eng-
　　lish **1716c**
Canadian Wild Flowers:
　Illustration, Art **1042b**;
　Traill, Catharine Parr **2181a**
Canadian Wildlife Federation **352a**
Canadian Wildlife Service **352a**:
　Bison **233a**;
　Fuller, William Albert **852c**;
　Heritage Trail **982b**;
　Whooping Crane **2303b**
Canadian Wildlife Service National
　Wildlife Area:
　Bird Sanctuaries and Re-
　　serves **230a**;
　Canadian Wildlife Service **352a**;
　Tantramar Marsh **2111a**

corn dolly:
Folk Art **795b**
corn earworm:
Moth **1394c**
Corn Laws **517c**:
Canada Corn Act **325b**
corn oil:
Cereal Crops **390a**
corn syrup:
Cereal Crops **390a**;
John Labatt Corporation **1112c**;
Sugar Industry **2092a**
Corne de brume, La:
Caron, Louis **366a**;
Novel in French **1542a**
corneal graft:
Transplantation **2183b**
Cornelius, Julius:
Silver, Domestic **2003b**
Corner, John:
Pictographs and Petroglyphs **1676b**
Corner Brook, Nfld **518a**:
Royal Newfoundland Constabulary **1896b**;
Theatre, English-Language **2140a**
Corner Brook East, Nfld:
Corner Brook, Nfld **518a**
Corner Brook West, Nfld:
Corner Brook, Nfld **518a**
Corner of Old Québec:
Pellan, Alfred **1638a**
Cornerstone Architects:
Shopping Centre **1996a**
Cornfield:
Watson, Homer Ransford **2284a**
Cornish chicken:
Poultry Farming **1732a**
Cornish Hug, The:
Starnes, John Kennett **2070c**
Cornish language:
Celtic Languages **383c**;
Celtic Music **384a**
Cornplanter Medal:
Trigger, Bruce Graham **2193c**
cornstarch:
Cereal Crops **390a**
Cornut, Jacques Philippe:
Botany History **255c**; **256a**;
Floras and Botanical Journals **792b**;
Illustration, Art **1041c**
Cornwall, Clement Francis:
Ashcroft, BC **134c**
Cornwall, Henry Pennant:
Ashcroft, BC **134c**
Cornwall, James Kennedy **518b**:
Soldiers of Fortune **2044a**
Cornwall, Ont **518b**:
Air Traffic Control **44a**;
Earthquake **640c**;
Electric-Power Development **679b**;
Freemasonry **845a**;
Strachan, John **2082b**;
Technology **2119a**; **2120b**;
Theatre, French-Language **2146b**
Cornwall, PEI:
Charlottetown, PEI **397a**
Cornwall and York, Duke and Duchess of (King George V and Queen Mary):
Notman, William McFarlane **1526a**;
Royal Tours **1898a**
Cornwall Canal:
Canals and Inland Waterways **353a**
Cornwall Island **518b**
Cornwallis, Canadian Forces Base **518c**
Cornwallis, Edward **518c**
Cornwallis, Sir William:
Cornwallis Island **518c**
Cornwallis Baptist Church:
Manning, Edward **1300c**;
Oliver, William Pearly **1565a**
Cornwallis Belt:
Mineral Resources **1358c**
Cornwallis Island **518c**:
Arctic Sovereignty **113b**
Cornwallis River:
Annapolis Lowlands **79b**;
Nova Scotia **1526c**
Coronation:
Robertson, Sarah Margaret Armour **1879b**

Coronation Futurity:
Northern Dancer **1514b**
Coronation Games:
Kerr, Robert **1133b**
Coronation Gulf **519a**
Coronation Mass, A:
Choral Music **420a**
Coronelli, Vincenzo:
Cartography, History of **370c**
Coroner **519a**
corporal punishment:
Student Rights **2088a**
Corporate Concentration, Royal Commission on **519a**:
Pressure Group **1744c**
corporate crime:
White-Collar Crime **2300b**
corporate elite:
Business Elites **304c**;
Elites **686c**;
Journalism **1117c**
corporate name:
Corporation Law **521a**
"corporate welfare bums":
Lewis, David **1205b**
corporation:
Consumer and Corporate Affairs, Department of **508c**;
Corporation Law **519a**;
Farm Law **750b**
Corporation de la vieille pulperie:
Chicoutimi, Qué **408b**
Corporation des éditions fides:
Anciens canadiens, Les **72c**;
Book Publishing, French-Language **249c**; **250a**;
Children's Literature in French **414c**;
Encyclopedia of Music in Canada **694c**;
Popular Literature in French **1718a**
Corporation des enseignants du Québec:
Teaching Profession **2116a**
Corporation des urbanistes du Québec:
Urban and Regional Planning **2230c**
Corporation du salon des métiers d'art du Québec:
Crafts **530c**
Corporation générale des instituteurs et des institutrices catholiques de la province du Québec:
Gaudreault, Laure **876c**;
Teaching Profession **2116a**
Corporation Image M&M:
Decline of the American Empire, The **578c**
Corporation Law **519a**
Corporation professionnelle des psychologues du Québec:
Psychology **1779a**
Corporations and Labour Unions Returns Act:
Confederation of Canadian Unions **489c**
Corporatism **521b**
Corps célestes, Les:
Carle, Gilles **363c**
Corps de l'instant:
Lapointe, Gatien **1178a**
Corps et graphies:
Lapointe, Gatien **1178a**
corpse plant:
Indian Pipe **1055c**
Corpus Almanac & Canadian Sourcebook:
Almanacs **66b**;
Popular Literature in English **1716c**
Corpus Chemical Report:
Petrochemical Industry **1649c**
Corral:
Daly, Thomas Cullen **564a**;
Film, Documentary **769c**
correctional investigator's office:
Ombudsman **1566a**
Correctional Services of Canada:
Prison **1760b**;
Solicitor General **2044c**;
Solicitor General, Department of **2044c**
Corrections, Department of (BC):
Barrett, David **180c**
Corrections, Department of (Man):
Manitoba **1296c**

Corrections Exemplary Service Medal:
Medal **1320b**
Correspondence:
Smith, Goldwin **2016b**
correspondence art:
Art, Contemporary Trends **124b**
correspondence schools:
Athabasca University **141a**;
British Columbia **278b**;
Distance Learning **605a**;
Simon Fraser University **2005b**;
University of Regina **2223a**
Correspondent and Advocate:
O'Grady, William John **1561a**
Corridart:
Art, Contemporary Trends **124b**;
Charney, Melvin **398b**;
Public Art **1780b**
Corriere Canadese, Il:
Italians **1100b**
Corriere Italiano, Il:
Italians **1100b**
Corriveau, Hugues:
Barre du jour, La **180c**
Corriveau, Jean:
Skiing, Freestyle **2010a**
Corriveau, Joseph:
Corriveau, La **522a**
Corriveau, La **522a**
Corriveau, Marie-Josephte:
Corriveau, La **522a**
Corriveau, Monique:
Children's Literature in French **414b**
Corruption **522a**:
Baie des Chaleurs Scandal **163a**;
Organized Crime **1587b**
Corry, J.A.:
Political Science **1711b**
Cort, John:
Newcastle, NB **1482b**
Corte-Real, Gaspar **523b**:
Slavery **2010c**
Corte-Real, João Vaz:
Portuguese **1727c**
Corte-Real, Miguel:
Corte-Real, Gaspar **523b**
Cortes Island:
Northern Georgia Strait Coast Salish **1514b**
Cortinarii:
Mushroom and Puffball **1410b**
cortisone:
Endangered Plants **697c**
Cortland apple:
Apple **86b**
corundum:
Mineral **1355a**; **1355b**;
Mineral Resources **1360c**
Corunna, Ont:
Place-names **1683c**
Corvée **523b**
Corvée, La:
Theatre, French-Language **2146b**
Cosa Nostra:
Organized Crime **1586b**
Cosentino, Frank **523b**
Cosgrave, Dick:
Chuckwagon Races **425b**
Cosgrove, Stanley Morel **523b**
Cosgrove and Co:
Toys and Games **2177c**
Cosmic Chef, The:
Poetry in English **1698c**
Cosmic Consciousness:
Bucke, Richard Maurice **292a**
Cosmographie:
Montmorency Falls **1379a**
Cosmology **523c**
cosmonaut:
Astronaut **138b**
COSPAS system:
Space Technology **2054a**
Cost and Management:
Accounting **11b**
cost-price squeeze:
Agriculture and Food Policy **36b**
cost sharing:
Economic and Regional Development Agreements **643b**;
Health Policy **971c**;
Legal Aid **1197c**
Costain, C.C.:
Physics **1668c**
Costain, Thomas Bertram **524a**
Coste, Donat:
Acadia **9c**

Costello Mine:
Coal **447b**
Côté, Cyrille:
Rebellions of 1837 **1832b**
Côté, Gérard **524a**
Côté, Jean-Baptiste:
Folk Art **796a**;
Sculpture **1964a**
Côté, Jean-Léon **524a**
Côté, Jean-Pierre **524a**
Côté, L.:
Cartoons, Political **376a**
Côté, Maryse:
Children's Literature in French **415b**
Côté, Mount:
Côté, Jean-Léon **524a**
Côté, P.M.:
Architectural Styles **99b**
"Côte de sable, La":
Television Drama, French-Language **2127a**
Côte-des-Neiges cemetery:
Houde, Camillien **1011c**;
Medicine, History of **1329c**
Côte Ste Catherine lock:
St Lawrence Seaway **1921b**
Côte-St-Paul, Qué:
Evans, William **730c**;
Verville, Alphonse **2255a**
Coteau Creek generating station:
Reservoir **1859b**
Côteau-du-Lac site:
Indian Art **1053a**
Cotnam, Jacques:
Essay in French **721c**
Cotnoir, Louise:
Barre du jour, La **180c**;
Literature in English – Theory and Criticism **1228a**
Cotroni, Frank and Vincenzo:
Organized Crime **1587a**
cottage cheese:
Cheese and Cheesemaking **400a**
cottage hospitals:
Newfoundland **1488c**;
Victorian Order of Nurses **2262a**
Cottnam, Deborah **524b**
Cottnam, Samuel:
Cottnam, Deborah **524b**
cotton:
Pulp and Paper Industry **1789b**;
Quilt **1814b**;
Textile Industry **2134c**
Cotton, John:
Printmaking **1758a**
cottonberry:
Berries, Cultivated **207c**
Cotton's Patch:
Burke, Johnny **299c**
cottonwood:
Autumn Colours **152a**;
Poplar **1716b**;
Vegetation Regions **2250c**
cottony maple scale:
Scale Insect **1946a**
Coty Award:
Fashion Design **752c**
Couchiching, Lake:
Couchiching Conference **524b**;
Orillia, Ont **1587c**;
Simcoe, Lake **2005a**
Couchiching Conference **524b**:
NATO (North Atlantic Treaty Organization) **1462c**
Coudari, Camille:
Chess **406b**; **406c**
Coudres, Île aux **524c**:
Aide-Créquy, Jean-Antoine **41a**;
Astronomy **139b**;
Painting **1603b**
Cougar **524c**:
Fur Trapping **860b**
Cougar footwear:
Footwear Industry **805a**
Coughlan, Laurence **524c**
Coughlin, Angela:
Swimming, Speed **2103c**
Coughtry, Graham **525a**:
Art Dealers **125b**;
Beatty, Patricia **190b**
coulee:
Aeolian Landform **19a**
Coulicou:
Children's Literature in French **414c**
coulomb:
Weights and Measures **2290b**
Coulter, John William **525a**:
Drama in English **621b**

Good Friday:
Christianity 424b;
National Holidays 1430a
Good Neighbour Peak:
Vancouver, Mount 2243a
Good News, Toronto:
Peel, Paul 1636c
Good Place to Come From, A:
Torgov, Morley 2167c
Goodbye Harold Good Luck:
Thomas, Audrey Grace 2151a
Goodchild, Frederick:
McClelland and Stewart Limited 1256c
Goode, Arthur C.:
Illustration, Art 1043a
Gooderham, Sir Albert Edward:
Gooderham, William 911c
Gooderham, George:
Gooderham, William 911c
Gooderham, Kent:
Ethnic Literature 726a
Gooderham, William 911c
Gooderham, William, Jr:
Gooderham, William 911c
Gooderham and Worts, Ltd:
Gooderham, William 911c
Gooderham Mansion:
Sproatt and Rolph 2064b
Goodman, Aaron:
Bridge 269b
Goodman, Edwin:
Committee for an Independent Canada 465c
Goodread Biographies:
Biography in English 220c
Goodridge, Augustus Frederick 911c
Goodstoney, Jacob:
Stoney 2081c
Goodwin, Albert, "Ginger" 912a:
Revolutionary Industrial Unionism 1866b
Goodwin, Helen:
Dance, Modern 567c
Goodwin, Henry:
Physical Education 1666a
Goodwin, Michael and John:
Bicycling 213b
Goodyear, Scott:
Automobile Racing 150b
Goodyear Tire and Rubber Co of Canada:
Berkinshaw, Richard Coulton 206c;
Medicine Hat, Alta 1331a;
Rubber Products Industry 1898c
gooeyduck (geoduck) clam:
Chinook Jargon 417c
Gool, Reshard:
Ethnic Literature 727c
Goold Cycle Co:
Bicycling 213c
Goose 912a:
Attawapiskat River 142c;
Gander River 872c;
Hunting 1030a;
Miner, John Thomas 1354c
goose, domestic:
Poultry Farming 1732a
Goose, William:
Nanogak, Agnes 1425b
goose barnacle:
Barnacle 179a
Goose Bay:
Ice 1037c;
Melville, Lake 1333c;
Newfoundland 1485c
Goose Bay, Nfld:
Happy Valley-Goose Bay, Nfld 960c
Goose Lake, Man:
Roblin, Man 1880b
Goose Lake (Man):
Roblin, Man 1880b
Goose River:
Hamilton Inlet 958b
gooseberry:
Berries, Wild 208c
Gooseberry Lake Provincial Park:
Parks, Provincial 1619a
gopher:
Literature in English 1224a
Gopher Creek:
Virden, Man 2265c
gopher snake:
Snake 2019a
Gordon, Andrew Robertson 912b:
Chemistry Subdisciplines 405c

Gordon, Sir Arthur Hamilton:
Tilley, Sir Samuel Leonard 2160a
Gordon, Bryan H.:
Archaeology 93c
Gordon, Sir Charles Blair 912b
Gordon, Charles William 912b:
Canmore, Alta 354c;
Ethnic Literature 725c;
Gordon, John King 913a;
McClelland and Stewart Limited 1256c
Gordon, Crawford 912c
Gordon, Dianna:
Bridge 269b
Gordon, Donald 912c:
Canadian National Railways 346a
Gordon, Hortense:
Painters Eleven 1602b
Gordon, J.P.:
Laser 1179b
Gordon, Jean:
Bowling, Indoor 263a
Gordon, John King 913a
Gordon, Lamont:
Bobsledding 245c
Gordon, Sydney:
Biography in English 221a
Gordon, Thomas:
Clocks and Watches 441c
Gordon, Walter Lockhart 913a:
Autobiographies, Political 148c;
Canada Studies Foundation 327c;
Canadian Institute for Economic Policy 343a;
Liberal Party 1207a;
Nationalism 1434a
Gordon Commission:
Canada's Economic Prospects, Royal Commission on 329b;
Economic Nationalism 646b
Gordon Howe Park:
Saskatoon, Sask 1941a
Gordon-Howell Report:
Business Education 304b
Gordon Island:
Thousand Islands 2155c
Gordon M. Shrum Generating Station:
BC Hydro 188b;
Electric-Power Generation 680a;
Peace River 1633b
Gordon press:
Print Industry 1756b
Gordon R. Arnott and Associates:
Shopping Centre 1996a
Gordon Shrum: An Autobiography:
Shrum, Gordon Merritt 1999a
Gordon Southam Observatory:
Kitsilano 1142b
Gordon V. Thompson Ltd:
Music Publishing 1419b;
Religious Music 1855a
Gore, Arabella Wentworth:
Belleville, Ont 202c
Gore, Charles S.:
Cartier, Sir George-Étienne 368a;
Rebellions of 1837 1832a
Gore, Francis 913a:
Alien Question 63a;
St-Denis, Battle of 1912a;
Upper Canada 2226a
Gore, Samuel:
Cobourg and Peterborough Railway 453a
Gore Bank:
Canadian Imperial Bank of Commerce 343a
Gore Bay, Ont:
Manitowaning, Ont 1300a
Gore Park:
Hamilton, Ont 956c
Goreham, Joseph:
Fort Beauséjour 819b
Gorge Waters:
Victoria, BC 2261b
Gorman, Charles 913a
Gorman, Donald G.:
Mineral Resources 1358b
Gorman, Harry:
Baseball 182c
Gorman, Peter:
Vanier Cup 2245b
Gorman, Richard:
Painting 1607a;
Printmaking 1758c

gormanite:
Mineral Resources 1358b
Gosford, Archibald Acheson, 2nd Earl of 913b
Gosling, William Gilbert 913b
Gospel Band:
Evangelism 729c
Gospel music:
Religious Music 1855a
Gospel Witness:
Shields, Thomas Todhunter 1991c
Gospel Workers Church:
Holiness Churches 1001c
Goss, Sandy:
Swimming, Speed 2103c
Goss, William Arthur Scott 913b
Goss Metroliners:
Edmonton Journal 660b
Gosse, Clarence L.:
Nova Scotia 1531b
Gosse, Philip Henry 913b
Gosse, Richard:
Canadian Security Intelligence Service 350a
Gosselin, Auguste:
Biography in French 221c
Gosselin, B.:
Film 768a; 768b
Gossip, William:
Archaeology 92b
Gossipcuses, Les:
Acadia 9a
Gothic revival style:
Architectural Styles 98a
Gotlieb, Allan Ezra 913c
Gotlieb, Calvin Carl 913c
Gotlieb, Phyllis Fay 913c
Gotlieb, Sondra 913c
Gotta, Jack:
Ottawa Rough Riders 1597b
Gottlieb, Robert:
Poussière sur la ville 1732b
Gottlieb, Selma:
Helicopter 976c
Gottschalk, Fritz:
Graphic Art and Design 929a; 929b
Gottschalk and Ash International:
Graphic Art and Design 929b;
Logo 1239b
Gouda cheese:
Cheese and Cheesemaking 400b
Goudge, Thomas Anderson 914a
Goudie, Elizabeth 914a
Goudie, Jim:
Goudie, Elizabeth 914a
Goudsmit, S.A.:
Spectroscopy 2056c
Gouffre a toujours soif, Le:
Novel in French 1540b
gouge:
Tools, Carpentry 2167a
Gouin, Alice Amos:
Amos, Qué 71a
Gouin, Sir Jean-Lomer 914a:
Amos, Qué 71a;
Gouin, Paul 914a;
Gouin Réservoir 914b
Gouin, Judy:
Printmaking 1759c
Gouin, Paul 914a
Gouin Réservoir 914b
Gouinlock, George W.:
Architecture, Development of 102c
Gould, Glenn Herbert 914b:
Louie, Alexina Diane 1245c;
Vancouver International Festival 2243b
Gould, Joseph:
Uxbridge, Ont 2237c
Goulden, Cyril Harold 915a
Goulding, George Henry 915a
Goulds, Nfld 915a
Goulet, Charles:
Conductors and Conducting 487c
Goulet, Joseph-Jean:
Conductors and Conducting 487b;
Orchestre symphonique de Montréal 1584a
Goulet, Michel:
Québec Nordiques 1807b
Goulet, Robert Gerard 915a
Goupil, Laval:
Theatre, French-Language 2146b

Goupil, René:
Saints 1925a
gourd:
Vegetable 2246c
Gourlay, Robert Fleming 915a:
Hagerman, Christopher Alexander 949c;
Powell, William Dummer 1734b;
Robinson, Sir John Beverley 1880a;
Upper Canada 2226c
Gourmet's Canada, The:
Gotlieb, Sondra 914a
gout:
Arthritis 129a
Goût de la farine, Le:
Perrault, Pierre 1645b
Gouttelettes, Les:
Poetry in French 1699b
Gouverneur 915b
Gouzenko, Igor Sergeievich 915b:
"Front Page Challenge" 850a;
Official Secrets Act 1560a
Government 915c:
Administrative Law 14c;
Budgetary Process 294a;
Cabinet 310a;
Federal Government 753c;
Local Government 1236a;
Minority Government 1364b;
Political History 1708c;
Provincial Government 1774b;
Representative Government 1857a;
Responsible Government 1864a
government (American and Canadian systems contrasted):
Constitutional Law 506a
Government Building 916c:
Fuller, Thomas 852b;
Kingston City Hall 1139b;
Parliament Buildings 1621a;
Saskatchewan Legislative Building 1938c
government debt:
Public Debt 1780c
Government House (Alberta):
Edmonton, Alta 657c;
Lieutenant-Governor 1212c
Government House (NB):
Tilley, Sir Samuel Leonard 2160a
Government House (North-West Territories):
Battleford, Sask 187a
Government House (Nova Scotia):
Halifax, NS 952a
Government House (PEI):
Prince Edward Island 1753b
Government/Industry Seabed Project:
Sonar 2046a
government information:
Access to Information Act 10c;
Freedom of Information 844b
Government Insurance Act (1944) (Sask):
Saskatchewan 1935b
government intervention:
Air Transport Industry 44a;
Economic Regulation 647b;
Economics, Radical 651b;
Food Legislation 801c;
Foreign Ownership and the Structure of Canadian Investment, Task Force on 808c;
Labour Organization 1157b;
Labour Policy 1157c;
Labour Relations 1159c;
Petroleum 1651a;
Pipeline 1680a;
Regulatory Process 1847c;
Soil Conservation 2042a;
Telecommunications 2122c;
Transportation Regulation 2189b;
Trucking Industry 2196c;
Utilities 2236c;
Wage and Price Controls 2270c;
Welfare State 2292b
Government of Canada, The:
Dawson, Robert McGregor 574b
Government of Man, The:
Brett, George Sidney 268b;
Philosophy 1659b
Government of Newfoundland and Labrador Arts and Letters Competition:
Literary Prizes in English 1222a

Government of Yukon Territorial Libraries and Archives Branch: Yukon Territory **2358c**

Government Organization, Royal Commission on **918c**:
Hodgetts, John Edwin **1000a**;
Science Policy **1957a**;
Sellar, Robert Watson **1977a**;
Social Insurance Number **2029a**

Government Organization Act:
Energy, Mines and Resources, Department of **698c**;
Government Organization, Royal Commission on **918c**

Government Organization (Scientific Activities) Act (1976):
Social Sciences and Humanities Research Council of Canada **2032a**

government policy:
Public Policy **1785c**

Government Policy Consultants Inc:
Pressure Group **1744b**

Government Printing Bureau:
Draper, Patrick Martin **625a**

Government Purchasing Standards Committee:
Canadian General Standards Board **342b**

government spending:
Public Expenditure **1781b**

Governor General **918c**:
Ambassadors and Embassies **67c**;
Constitutional Law **505c**;
Gouverneur **915b**;
Monarchism **1373c**;
Order-in-council **1584b**;
Order of St John **1585b**;
Prerogative Powers **1743c**;
Rideau Hall **1870b**;
Scouts Canada **1962c**

Governor General's Award for Science:
Hiebert, Paul **985b**

Governor General's Body Guard:
Denison, George Taylor **585b**

Governor General's Foot Guards:
Lisgar, Sir John Young, Baron **1217b**;
Regiment **1841a**

Governor General's Horse Guards:
Regiment **1840c**; **1841a**

Governor General's Literary Awards **919c**

Governor General's Medals:
Architectural Competitions **97a**;
Colville, Alexander **463b**;
Medal **1320c**;
Moriyama, Raymond **1390b**;
Whiten, Colette **2302a**

Governor General's Persons Award:
Bird, Florence Bayard **227c**;
MacInnis, Grace Winona **1268a**;
Persons Case **1645c**

Governor General's Prize:
Curling **556a**

governor-in-council:
Cabinet **310a**;
Canadian Radio-television and Telecommunications Commission **349b**;
Citizenship **427c**;
Disallowance **601a**;
Order-in-council **1584c**

Governor's Bridge:
Technology **2120b**

Governor's Bridge is Closed, The:
Essay in English **720b**

Governor's Lady, The:
Raddall, Thomas Head **1817c**

Gowan, Alan:
Art Writing and Criticism **128a**

Gowan, Sir James Robert **920a**

Gowan, Ogle Robert:
Orange Order **1583a**

Gowans, Kent and Company:
Glass **905b**

Gowe, Robert:
Animal Breeding **77c**

Gowen sites:
Saskatoon, Sask **1940a**

Gower, John Arthur:
Mineral Resources **1358b**

Gowsell, Paul:
Curling **556b**

GPA Group Ltd:
Air Canada **41c**

GPSS (General Purpose Systems Simulation):
Computer Science **482b**

Graafiko:
Graphic Art and Design **929b**

Grâce, Île de:
Grosse Île **941b**

Grace, Nathaniel Hew **920b**

Grace, W.G.:
Cricket **534c**

Grace Hospital (Halifax):
Fairn, Leslie Raymond **743c**

Grace Hospital (Winnipeg):
Salvation Army **1928a**

Grace Presbyterian Church (Calgary):
Aberhart, William **3b**

grackle:
Blackbird **236c**

grading:
Agricultural Economics **26a**;
Commodity Inspection and Grading **466b**;
Crops **544b**;
Fruit and Vegetable Industry **851a**;
Grain Handling and Marketing **922a**

Graduate Centre for the Study of Drama:
Theatre Education **2148b**

Graduated Payment Mortgage Plan:
Housing and Housing Policy **1016c**

Graduel (Processional Vespéral) romain, Le:
Music History **1416c**;
Music Publishing **1419a**

Gradus, Lawrence **920b**:
Theatre Ballet of Canada **2147c**

GRAFF:
Printmaking **1759b**

Graff, Oscar:
Guitar **945c**

graft:
Corruption **522b**

Grafton, Ont:
Architecture, Development of **102b**

Graham, Andrew **920c**:
Henday, Anthony **978a**

Graham, Billy:
Evangelism **730a**

Graham, Gwethalyn:
Best-Sellers in English **210b**;
Chaput-Rolland, Solange **395b**;
Jewish Writing **1109c**

Graham, Harvey:
Trenton, NS **2193b**

Graham, Howard Douglas **920c**

Graham, Hugh, Baron Atholstan **920c**:
McConnell, John Wilson **1257c**

Graham, Laurie **920c**

Graham, Roger:
Biography in English **220c**

Graham, Stuart **920c**

Graham, W.A.G.:
Chemistry Subdisciplines **404c**

Graham, Wallace:
Arthritis Society **129b**

Graham Brothers (Canada):
Chrysler Canada Ltd **425a**

Graham City, BC:
Masset, BC **1312a**

Graham Island:
Masset, BC **1312a**;
Queen Charlotte Islands **1811b**

Graham Towers and his Times:
Fullerton, Douglas H. **852c**

Grahame:
Fort Chipewyan **819c**

grain:
Barley **179a**;
Buckwheat **292b**;
Commodity Trading **466b**;
Corn, Field **517b**;
Flax **789c**;
Flour Milling **792c**;
General Agreement on Tariffs and Trade **879c**;
Oats **1550a**;
Rye **1904c**;
Triticale **2194c**;
Wheat **2298c**

Grain:
Novel in English **1536c**

grain:
Weights and Measures **2290c**

Grain:
Royal Winnipeg Ballet **1898b**

Grain:
Stead, Robert James Campbell **2075b**

grain alcohol:
Biomass Energy **224c**

Grain Elevators **921a**:
Grain Handling and Marketing **922a**;
Howe, Clarence Decatur **1018a**;
Manitoba **1294b**;
Montréal, Qué **1382b**;
Saskatchewan Wheat Pool **1939b**;
Trois-Rivières, Qué **2195c**

Grain Exchange Building (Calgary):
Architecture, Development of **103b**

Grain Growers' Associations **921b**:
Alberta Wheat Pool **57c**;
Saskatchewan Wheat Pool **1939b**

Grain Growers' Grain Co:
Agriculture History **39b**;
Crerar, Thomas Alexander **534b**;
Grain Growers' Associations **921b**;
Partridge, Edward Alexander **1625b**;
United Farmers of Alberta **2216a**

Grain Growers' Guide **921c**:
Beynon, Francis Marion **211c**;
Bland, Salem Goldworth **241b**;
Cartoons, Humorous **374c**

Grain Handling and Marketing **921c**:
Alberta Wheat Pool **57c**;
Canadian Wheat Board **351c**;
Crow's Nest Pass Agreement **547a**;
Saskatchewan Wheat Pool **1939b**

Grain Research Laboratory:
Grain Handling and Marketing **922a**

Grainger, Martin Allerdale:
Literature in English **1225a**;
Novel in English **1536a**

Gramineae:
Vegetable **2246b**

Grammar of the Cree Language:
Howse, Joseph **1019a**

grammar school:
Secondary School **1971c**

Grammont, Joseph-Éloi-Augustin dit de Grandmont **922b**:
Poetry in French **1700b**

Grammy Award:
McConnell, Robert Murray Gordon **1257c**;
Mitchell, Joni **1367c**;
Murray, Anne **1406a**;
Peterson, Oscar Emmanuel **1648b**

gramophone:
Recording Industry **1834a**

Gramsci x 3:
Drama in English **622b**;
Watson, Wilfred **2284c**

granary weevil:
Beetle **198b**

Granby, Qué **922c**

Granby Bay:
Anyox, BC **86a**

Granby College:
Granby, Qué **922c**

Granby Consolidated Mining, Smelting and Power Co Ltd:
Anyox, BC **86a**;
Grand Forks, BC **923c**

Granby River:
Grand Forks, BC **923b**

Granby Zoo:
Granby, Qué **923a**

Grand Association:
Working-Class History **2339b**

Grand Attentif, le:
Legault, Émile **1199c**

Grand Bank, Nfld **923a**

Grand Banks **923a**:
Great Auk **933a**;
Newfoundland **1485c**

Grand Bay:
Grand Bay, NB **923a**

Grand Bay, NB **923a**

Grand Bay East, Nfld:
Channel-Port aux Basques **394c**

Grand Bay West, Nfld:
Channel-Port aux Basques **394c**

Grand Brûlé, North-West Territories:
Morinville, Alta **1390a**

Grand Canyon:
Stikine River **2080a**

Grand-Cascapédia, Qué:
Pidgeon, George Campbell **1676c**

Grand Cirque ordinaire:
Drama in French **623c**;
Theatre, French-Language **2145c**

Grand Company, The:
Grand Theatre **924c**

Grand Council of the Cree of Québec:
Diamond, Billy **592b**

Grand Duke of Moscow's Favourite Solo, The:
Finch, Robert Duer Claydon **773a**

Grand Falls:
Exploits River **732b**;
Waterfall **2282c**

Grand Falls:
Saint John River **1915c**

Grand Falls, NB **923b**:
Heritage Trail **982b**

Grand Falls, Nfld **923b**:
Heraldry **980b**;
Peat **1636a**

Grand Falls Central Railway:
Newfoundland **1488b**

Grand Falls Station, Nfld:
Windsor, Nfld **2313b**

grand fir:
Fir **773c**

Grand Forchee, NB:
Kedgwick, NB **1130a**

Grand Forks, BC **923b**:
Kettle Valley **1133c**;
Monashee Mountains **1374a**

Grand General Indian Council of Ontario:
Native People, Political Organization and Activism **1457a**

Grand Harbour, NB:
Grand Manan Island **923c**

Grand Junction Railroad:
Grand Trunk Railway of Canada **925a**

grand jury:
Jury **1123a**

Grand Khan, Le:
Basile, Jean **183c**

Grand-Lac-Victoria:
Ottawa River **1596c**;
Victoria, Queen of England **2259c**

Grand Lake (Lab):
Melville, Lake **1333c**

Grand Lake (NB):
Coal **447a**;
New Brunswick **1469b**; **1469c**; **1473a**

Grand Lake (Nfld) **923c**

Grand Lodge of Ancient and Accepted Masons Canada in the Province of Ontario, The:
Freemasonry **845b**

Grand Lodge of BC Fishermen's Unions:
Fraser River Fishermen's Strikes **841c**

Grand Lodge of British North America:
Bowell, Sir Mackenzie **262b**;
Irish **1092a**;
Orange Order **1582c**

Grand Lodge of Canada:
Freemasonry **845b**

Grand Lodge of Upper Canada of the Ancient Free and Accepted Masons:
Associations **137a**

Grand-Louis L'innocent:
Foreign Writers on Canada in French **810a**

Grand Manan Island **923c**:
Dark Harbour **569c**

Grand Manan Museum:
Grand Manan Island **924a**

Grand Medicine Society:
Midewiwin **1350b**

Grand Memory for Forgetting, A:
Scobie, Stephen **1959b**

Grand-Mère, Qué **924a**:
Graham, Stuart **921a**

Great Victorian Collection, The:
Moore, Brian **1386b**;
Popular Literature in English **1717b**
Great Wall of 1984:
Art, Contemporary Trends **124c**
Great War Veterans Association:
Royal Canadian Legion **1893a**
Great-West Life Assurance Building (Winnipeg) (1911):
Atchison, John D. **140a**
Great-West Life Assurance Building (Winnipeg) (post-war):
Rounthwaite, Dick & Hadley Architects & Engineers **1889b**
Great-West Life Assurance Co:
Richardson, James Armstrong, Sr **1868b**
Great-West Lifeco Inc:
Power Corporation of Canada **1734c**
Great West Magazine:
Literary Magazines in English **1219c**
Great Western Rail Road Co:
Great Western Railway **935c**
Great Western Railway **935c**:
Birge, Cyrus Albert **231a**;
Blacks **238a**;
Disasters **603b**;
Guarantee Act **944a**;
Hamilton, Ont **956a**;
Hobson, Joseph **998b**;
Railway History **1821c**;
St Catharines, Ont **1910c**;
Sarnia, Ont **1930b**;
Wilcox, Charles Seward **2305a**;
Zimmerman, Samuel **2359c**
Great Whale River. *See* Grande rivière de la Baleine
great white shark:
Shark **1987c**
greater prairie chicken:
Endangered Animals **695a**;
Grouse **943b**
greater sandhill crane:
Whooping Crane **2303b**
greater shearwater:
Shearwater **1989a**
greater snow goose:
St Lawrence River **1920c**
Greater Vancouver Regional District:
Metropolitan Government **1347a**;
Regional Government **1845c**;
Surrey, BC **2098c**;
Vancouver, BC **2242c**
Greater Victoria:
Saanich Peninsula **1906a**
Greater Victoria Water District:
Victoria, BC **2261c**
greater white-fronted goose:
Goose **912a**
Greater Winnipeg Floodway:
Barber, Clarence Lyle **178a**;
Manitoba **1293b**;
Red River **1836b**;
Roblin, Dufferin **1880c**
Greatest Show on Earth, The:
Music Composition **1413b**
Greaves, Sandra:
Judo **1121c**
Greb Industries:
Footwear Industry **804c**
Grebe **935c**:
Bird Classification and Evolution **228b**
Grèber, Jacques:
National Capital Commission **1428a**
Greek Canadian Weekly:
Greeks **936b**
Greek Church:
Orthodox Church **1589b**
Greek Courier:
Greeks **936b**
Greek Independence Day:
Greeks **936b**
Greek language:
Algae **61a**; **61c**;
Amphibian **71a**;
Annelida **80a**;
Arthritis **128c**;
Astronaut **138b**;
Bacteria **159a**;
Bearberry **189b**;
Beetle **198a**;
Biology **223a**;
Butterfly **307c**;

Caddisfly **313b**;
Catholicism **379a**;
Cemeteries **384c**;
Chiropractic **418c**;
Christianity **422c**;
Classics **434b**;
Cryptozoology **549b**;
Damselfly **564a**;
Dietetics **595b**;
Dinosaur **595c**;
Echinodermata **642c**;
English Language **710b**;
Evangelical and Fundamentalist Movements **728c**;
Geography **882c**;
Greeks **936b**;
Insect Classification **1071a**;
Ku Klux Klan **1149a**;
Language **1175a**;
Languages in Use **1177a**;
Logo **1239a**;
Mayfly **1318a**;
Metamorphic Rock **1340b**;
Mineral **1355a**;
Mineral Naming **1357c**;
Optometry **1580b**;
Orthodox Church **1590a**;
Physics **1669c**;
Plankton **1686a**;
Pondweed **1715b**;
Pornography **1723b**;
Psychology **1778b**;
Rhododendron **1867b**;
Sedge **1973b**;
Stonefly **2081b**;
Swift **2103a**;
Telephones **2123c**;
Telidon **2128c**;
Wind **2312b**
Greek Orthodox Cathedral (Montréal):
Religious Building **1853a**
Greek Orthodox Church:
Canadian Council of Churches **336c**;
Greeks **936b**;
New Brunswick **1471a**;
Orthodox Church **1590a**
Greek Orthodox Youth of America:
Greeks **936b**
Greeks **936a**:
Fort William Freight Handlers Strike **824a**;
Fur Industry **856a**;
Immigration **1046b**;
Macedonians **1264b**
Greely, Adolphus Washington:
Arctic Sovereignty **113a**;
Ellesmere Island **687c**;
Fosheim Peninsula **826b**
Greely Fiord:
Fosheim Peninsula **826b**
Green, Bartholomew, Jr:
Magazines **1284b**;
Print Industry **1756a**
Green, Blankstein, Russell **936c**
Green, Daniel:
Furniture, English, Scottish and American **863b**
Green, Daniel:
Summerside, PEI **2094b**
Green, George Mason:
Soldiers of Fortune **2043c**
Green, H. Gordon:
Essay in English **720c**
Green, Howard Charles **936c**:
Cuban Missile Crisis **549c**;
Robertson, Norman Alexander **1879b**
Green, L.J.:
Green, Blankstein, Russell **936c**
Green, Mark:
Furniture, Country **861c**
Green, Terence M.:
Popular Literature in English **1717b**;
Science Fiction **1956c**
green alder:
Alder **60a**
green algae:
Algae **61c**;
Biology **223b**;
Fossil Plants **828b**;
Lichen **1211c**;
Seaweeds **1970b**;
Vegetation Regions **2252b**
green ash:
Biomass Energy **225a**;
Vegetation Regions **2250c**

green-backed heron:
Heron **982c**
Green Bank:
Grand Banks **923a**
green bean:
Bean, Green **188c**
Green Cloister, The:
Scott, Duncan Campbell **1960c**
Green Corn Ceremonial:
Handsome Lake Religion **959a**;
Native People, Religion **1458b**
green feed:
Forage Crops **805a**
Green Fishery **936c**
green foxtail:
Weeds **2289b**
green frog:
Frog **849b**
Green Gables:
Prince Edward Island National Park **1754b**
Green Gardens Trail:
Heritage Trail **982b**
Green Gold:
Community **475c**
green lacewing:
Lacewing **1161c**
Green Lawn Rest Home:
Simons, Beverly **2005c**
green manure:
Beet **198a**;
Buckwheat **292b**;
Grape **927c**;
Legume **1200c**;
Lupine **1252b**
green mint:
Mint **1364c**
Green North, The:
Rohmer, Richard **1884c**
Green Paper **936c**
green peach aphid:
Pepper **1641c**
Green Pitcher:
Livesay, Dorothy **1233b**
Green Plain, The:
Newlove, John **1492a**
Green Point (BC):
Ucluelet **2206b**
green sturgeon:
Endangered Animals **695b**;
Sturgeon **2089c**
Green Thumb Theatre for Young People:
Theatre, English-Language **2139c**;
Theatre for Young Audiences **2149a**
green violet:
Violet **2265c**
Green Water, Green Sky:
Gallant, Mavis Leslie **868c**
Green World:
Waddington, Miriam **2270a**
Greenaway, K.R.:
Dunbar, Isobel Moira **634b**
Greenberg, Clement:
Kiyooka, Roy Kenzie **1142c**;
Painting **1607b**;
Perehudoff, William **1643a**
Greencourt, Alta:
Whitecourt, Alta **2301a**
Greene, Daniel Joseph **936c**
Greene, Henry:
Hudson, Henry **1019c**
Greene, Hugh:
Printmaking **1757c**
Greene, J.J.:
Roman, Stephen Boleslav **1885a**
Greene, Lorne Hyman **937a**:
Canadian Broadcasting Corporation **334b**;
Jews **1111b**
Greene, Nancy **937a**
Greene, Thomas G.:
Graphic Art and Design **928c**;
Illustration, Art **1043a**;
Printmaking **1758b**
Greenfield, Herbert **937b**
Greenhills Mine:
Coal **447b**
greenhouse centipede:
Centipede **386c**
Greenhouse Crops **937b**:
Cucumber **550a**;
Endive **697c**;
Flowers, Cultivated **793b**;
Groundsel **942b**;
Lettuce **1203c**;
Melon **1333c**;
Ornamentals **1588c**;
Tomato **2165c**

greenhouse effect:
Hare, Frederick Kenneth **962a**;
Ozone Layer **1599c**
Greenland **937c**
Greenland Current:
Ocean Current **1554c**
"*Greenland* Disaster, The":
Songs and Songwriting **2040b**
Greenland shark:
Arctic Animals **109a**;
Fishing, Ice **786b**
Greenleaf, Elizabeth:
Folk Music, Anglo-Canadian **798a**
greenockite:
Cadmium **313c**;
Cathcart, Charles Murray, 2nd Earl **378c**
Greenough, Gail **937c**
Greenpeace **937c**
Greenpeace and Her Enemies:
Eayrs, James George **642b**
Green's Shore, NS:
Summerside, PEI **2094b**
Greenspond Island:
Newfoundland **1488a**
Greenstone **938a**:
Geological History **884b**;
Geological Regions **885b**
Greenville, BC:
Nass River **1426b**
Greenway, S.A.:
Country Life Movement **526a**
Greenway, Thomas **938a**
Greenwich, Sonny **938a**
Greenwich Gallery:
Art Dealers **125b**;
Coughtry, Graham **525a**;
Snow, Michael James Aleck **2019c**
Greenwich Mean Time:
Time **2162b**
Greenwood, BC **938b**:
Monashee Mountains **1374a**
Greenwood, Canadian Forces Base:
Canadair CL-28 Argus **328c**
Gregg, Allan:
Public Opinion **1785a**
Gregg, Milton Fowler **938b**
Gregg River Mine:
Coal **447b**
Grégoire, Ernest:
Action libérale nationale **13b**
Grégoire, Gilles:
Parti Québécois **1624c**
Gregoire Lake:
Bitumen **234c**
Gregorian calendar:
Orthodox Church **1589c**; **1590c**;
Religious Festivals **1854a**
Gregorian chant:
Religious Music **1854c**;
St-Benoît-du-Lac, Qué **1910a**
Gregory XIII, Pope:
Religious Festivals **1854a**
Gregory, McLeod and Co:
Mackenzie, Sir Alexander **1269c**;
North West Company **1511a**
Gregory, William T. and Francis:
Tobacco-Products Industry **2165a**
Grenadians:
West Indians **2294c**
Grenfell, Anne MacClanahan:
Grenfell, Sir Wilfred Thomason **938c**
Grenfell, Sask:
Patterson, William John **1630a**
Grenfell, Sir Wilfred Thomason **938b**:
Autobiographical Writing in English **147a**;
Crafts **530b**;
Macpherson, Cluny **1281c**
Grenfell Association of Newfoundland:
Cartwright, Nfld **376c**;
Macpherson, Cluny **1281c**
Grenfell Mission:
Forteau, Nfld **824b**
Grenfell rugs:
Rugs and Rug Making **1899c**
Grenville, William Windham:
Constitutional Act, 1791 **502b**
Grenville Canal:
Canals and Inland Waterways **353a**; **353b**;
Construction Industry, History of **508b**;
Hawkesbury, Ont **968a**

Heintzman, Theodore August:
Heintzman & Co Ltd **976b**;
Musical Instruments **1419c**
Heintzman & Co Ltd **976b**
Heinz-Lehmann Award:
Sourkes, Theodore Lionel **2047c**
Heinz Unger Award:
Conductors and Conducting **488a**;
Music Awards and Competitions **1411b**
Heinze, F. Augustus:
Trail, BC **2180c**
"Heirs of the Living Body":
Munro, Alice **1404c**
Heisenberg, Werner Karl:
Science and Society **1954a**;
Spectroscopy **2056c**
Heisler, Alta:
Kroetsch, Robert **1148b**
Hejira:
Mitchell, Joni **1367c**
Hélal, Georges:
Philosophy **1661c**
Helava, Uno Vilho **976b**
Helders, Johan (John) Anton Joseph **976b**
Helena, Qué:
Dairy Industry **562c**
Helenic Tribune:
Greeks **936b**
Helicopter **976c**:
Agar, Carlyle Clare **22b**;
Armaments **115b**
helium:
Balloon **168c**;
Laser **1179b**;
Mineral Resources **1360c**;
Nuclear Fusion **1544a**; **1544b**;
Ocean Industry **1556a**;
Physics **1668b**;
Star **2069a**;
University of Toronto **2223c**;
Wood Mountain **2331c**
Hell Gate:
Arctic Archipelago **110a**
Hellaby, Charles:
Cosmology **523c**
Hellenic Canadian Congress:
Greeks **936b**
Hellenic Canadian Federation of Ontario:
Greeks **936b**
Hellenic Canadian Federation of Québec:
Greeks **936b**
Heller, Irving:
Vivier, Claude **2266c**
hellgrammite:
Dobsonfly **607c**
Hell's Angels:
Organized Crime **1587a**
Hell's Gate **976c**
Hell's Gate:
South Nahanni River **2050c**
"Helluland":
Baffin Island **161a**;
Bjarni Herjolfsson **235b**;
Leif Ericsson **1200c**;
Norse Voyages **1508a**
Hellyer, Paul Theodore **977a**:
Armed Forces **118a**
Helm, Levon:
Band, The **169b**
Helmcken, John Sebastian **977a**:
Helmcken Falls **977b**
Helmcken Falls **977b**
Helmer, Terence:
Orford String Quartet **1586a**
Helmuth, Izaak:
Poles **1704a**
Helmuth, J.F.:
Tennis **2130c**
Héloise:
Hébert, Anne **974c**
Heloise and Abelard:
Opera **1579b**
"Help for Poland" program:
Poles **1704c**
Helwig, David Gordon **977b**:
Short Fiction in English **1997c**
hematite:
Bell Island **201b**;
Beothuk **205a**;
Iron Ore **1094a**;
Mineral **1355a**; **1355b**; **1356a**
hemimorphite:
Mineral **1356a**

Hemingway, Ernest:
Memoirs of Montparnasse **1334c**;
Star Weekly **2070b**;
Toronto Star **2173c**
Hemingway in Toronto:
Donnell, David **613a**
Hemiptera:
Insect Classification **1071b**
Hemlo, Ont:
Gold **908b**;
Mining **1362b**;
Ontario **1569c**;
Superior, Lake **2097a**
Hemlock **977b**:
Kejimkujik National Park **1130c**;
Koerner, Leon Joseph **1145b**;
Leatherworking **1194c**;
Vegetation Regions **2250c**
hemlock looper:
Insect Pests **1071c**
Hemmingford, Qué:
Zoos **2363b**
Hémon, Louis **977c**:
Chapleau, Ont **395b**
hemophilia:
AIDS **41b**;
Biological Product **223a**;
Genetic Diseases **880c**;
Genetics **882a**
Hénault, Gilles **977c**:
Liberté **1208c**;
Poetry in French **1700b**; **1700c**
Henday, Anthony **977c**
Henders, R.C.:
Social Gospel **2026b**
Henderson, Alexander **978a**:
Photography **1664b**
Henderson, Alexander **978a**
Henderson, Bill:
Chilliwack **415c**
Henderson, Elen:
Fashion Design **752b**
Henderson, G.H.:
Physics **1667c**
Henderson, James:
Kenderdine, Augustus Frederick **1131c**
Henderson, John Tasker **978a**
Henderson, Paul:
Canada-Soviet Hockey Series, 1972 **327a**
Henderson, Robert:
Klondike Gold Rush **1143c**
Henderson, Stuart:
Gunanoot, Simon Peter **946c**
Henderson House:
Brantford, Ont **266c**
Henderson Lake:
Weather Forecasting **2286a**
Henderson Lake Park:
Lethbridge, Alta **1203c**
Hendery, Robert:
Jewellery and Silverware Industry **1109b**;
Silver, Church **2002c**;
Silver, Domestic **2003b**
Hendery and Leslie:
Silver, Domestic **2003b**
Hendin, Judith:
Danny Grossman Dance Company **569a**
Hendrie, John Strathearn:
Ontario **1571a**
Hendry, Thomas Best **978b**
Hendry, William:
Exploration **735c**
Heneker, R.W.:
British American Land Company **271a**
Henley House:
Hudson's Bay Company **1022b**
Hennepin, Louis **978b**:
Niagara Falls **1497a**;
Sarnia, Ont **1930b**
Hennessey, Michael:
Theatre, English-Language **2141c**
Henning, Cam:
Swimming, Speed **2103c**
Henning, Douglas James:
Canadian Expatriates in Show Business **339a**;
Magic **1285c**
Henri II, King of France:
Sovereign **2052a**
Henri III, King of France:
Sovereign **2052a**

Henri IV, King of France:
Biencourt de Poutrincourt, Jean de, Baron de Saint-Just **214c**;
Gemstone **878b**;
Sovereign **2052a**
Henri, Laurie:
Acadia **8c**
Henri Bourassa:
Biography in French **222a**
Henripin, Jacques:
Status of Women in Canada, Royal Commission on the **2074b**
Henriquez, Richard:
Architectural Styles **99b**;
Architecture, Development of **106a**
henry:
Weights and Measures **2290b**
Henry VII, King of England:
Cabot, John **312b**;
Newfoundland **1483a**;
Sovereign **2052a**
Henry VIII, King of England:
Sovereign **2052a**
Henry, Alexander, the Elder **978b**
Henry, Alexander, the Younger **978b**
Henry, Ann:
Festival Lennoxville **761a**
Henry, Anthony (Anton Heinrich):
Almanacs **66a**;
Printmaking **1757a**
Henry, George **978c**
Henry, George Stewart **978c**
Henry, Jeff:
Theatre, Multicultural **2147b**
Henry, Martha **978c**
Henry, Robert Alexander Cecil, "Red" **978c**
Henry, William Alexander **979a**
Henry Birks and Sons Ltd:
Birks, Henry **231a**;
Grey Cup **939a**;
Maxwell, Edward **1317c**;
Silver, Domestic **2003c**
Henry Birks Collection:
Jewellery and Silverware Industry **1109b**
Henry Brougham:
New, Chester William **1467c**
Henry Hudson and Other Plays:
Denison, Merrill **585c**
Henry James: A Life:
Edel, Leon **656c**
Henry James: Selected Letters:
Edel, Leon **656c**
Henry Marshall Tory Medal:
Laidler, Keith James **1165a**
Henry Morgan & Co:
Morgan, Henry **1389a**
Henry White Kinnear Foundation:
Foundations **831c**
Henshaw, Don:
Radio Drama, English-Language **1817c**
Hensley, Almon:
Hensley, Sophia Margaretta **979a**
Hensley, Sophia Margaretta **979a**
Henslow's sparrow:
Endangered Animals **695b**;
Sparrow **2056a**
Henson, Josiah **979a**
Henson, Matthew:
North Pole **1510a**
Henty, G.A.:
Children's Literature in English **412a**
Heparin:
Murray, Gordon **1406b**
hepatitis:
Funeral Practices **853c**;
Water-Borne Disease **2280b**
hepatitis A:
Water-Borne Disease **2280a**
hepatitis B:
Virus **2266a**
Hepburn, Douglas **979a**
Hepburn, Mitchell Frederick **979b**:
Lieutenant-Governor **1212c**;
Ontario **1576b**;
Oshawa Strike **1592a**
"Hepburn's Hussars":
Hepburn, Mitchell Frederick **979b**;
Oshawa Strike **1592a**
Hepner, Lee:
Edmonton Symphony Orchestra **660c**

heptathlon:
Track and Field **2178b**
Her Majesty's Theatre:
Theatre, English-Language **2139a**;
Theatre, Multicultural **2147b**
Herald (Hamilton):
Newspapers **1493b**
Herald (Montréal):
Edmonton Journal **660b**;
Macdonald, Brian **1259a**;
Mitchell, Peter **1368a**;
Newspapers **1492c**; **1493b**
Herald (Prince Albert):
Prince Albert, Sask **1747a**
Heraldry **979c**:
Emblems, Provincial and Territorial **691b**;
Emblems of Canada **689c**;
Motto **1395b**
Heraldry in Canada:
Heraldry Society of Canada **980b**
Heraldry Society of Canada **980b**
Héraly, François:
Pelletier, Wilfrid **1638c**
Hérauts:
Popular Literature in French **1718a**
Herbarium **980b**
Herbert, Ivor:
Armed Forces **116b**
Herbert, John:
Brundage, John Herbert **290c**
Herbert, Neil:
Guitar **945c**
Herbert Inlet:
Ahousaht **40c**;
Strathcona Provincial Park **2083c**
Herbert of Lea, Sidney Herbert, 1st Baron:
Pembroke, Ont **1638c**
Herbes rouges, Les:
Brossard, Nicole **287a**;
Literary Periodicals in French **1221b**;
Poetry in French **1701a**
herbicides:
Agricultural Soil Practices **32a**;
Pesticide **1646a**;
Weeds **2289b**
Herbier Louis-Marie:
Cinq-Mars, Lionel **427a**;
Louis-Marie **1245c**
Herbier Marie-Victorin:
Herbarium **980b**
Herbison, Brian:
Equestrian Sports **716c**
Herbs **980c**:
Mint **1364c**;
Phlox **1663b**
Herchmer, Lawrence William **981a**
Hercule et Omphale:
Champagne, Claude **392c**
Hercules:
Albion Mines Railway **57c**
Hercules:
Shipbuilding and Ship Repair **1992c**
Hercules transport:
Bush Flying **303b**
Here and Now:
Layton, Irving Peter **1191a**;
Literary Magazines in English **1220a**;
Literature in English **1225c**
Here and Now Art Gallery:
Art Dealers **125c**
Here and There in the Homeland:
Canadian Travellers Abroad **351a**
Here at the Eye of the Hurricane:
Anna Wyman Dance Theatre **79a**
Here Stays Good Yorkshire:
Bird, William Richard **227c**
heredity:
Genetics **881b**
Hereford cattle:
Beef Cattle Farming **196a**;
Boyd, Mossom **264a**
Here's to Canada:
Exploration and Travel Literature in English **736c**
heresy:
Crime **535b**;
Macdonnell, Daniel James **1263a**
Heriot, George **981a**:
Printmaking **1757a**;

I

J

McNeill, K.G.:
Physics **1668a**
MacNeish, Richard S.:
Archaeology **92a**; **93a**
McNutt, Alexander:
Nova Scotia, 1714-84 **1535a**
MacNutt, W.S.:
New Brunswick **1474b**
Macoah Reserve:
Toquaht **2167c**
Macoun, John **1280c**:
Floras and Botanical Journals **792c**
Macoun, William Tyrrell:
Macoun, John **1281a**;
Preston, Isabella **1745a**
McPeek, Ben:
Delamont, Gordon **581c**;
Opera **1579a**
Macphail, Agnes Campbell **1281a**:
Ginger Group **900b**;
Pacifism **1601c**;
Ryan, Norman, "Red" **1904c**
McPhail, Alexander James **1281b**
MacPhail, Sir Andrew **1281b**:
Essay in English **719c**;
University Magazine, The **2220b**
McPhail, Lloyd:
Prince Edward Island **1751b**
McPhee, Colin:
Music History **1418a**;
Orchestral Music **1583c**
McPhee, Joseph:
Courtenay, BC **526c**
McPherson, Aimee Semple **1281c**
Macpherson, Annie, Rachel and Louisa:
Immigrant Children **1044b**
Macpherson, Campbell L.:
Newfoundland **1486a**
Macpherson, Cluny **1281c**
Macpherson, Crawford Brough **1281c**:
Liberalism **1208b**
MacPherson, Daniel:
LeMoine, Sir James MacPherson **1201c**
Macpherson, Sir David Lewis **1282a**
McPherson, Donald **1282a**
Macpherson, Duncan Ian **1282a**:
Cartoons, Political **376b**;
Clark, Gregory **433a**
MacPherson, Fraser:
Jazz **1106c**
McPherson, Hugh:
Cod Liver Oil **454b**
Macpherson, Jean Jay **1282a**:
Tamarack Review **2110b**
Macpherson, John:
Edmonton Journal **660b**
MacPherson, M.:
Transportation, Royal Commission on **2188b**
MacPherson, Michelle:
Swimming, Speed **2103c**
MacPherson, Susan:
Dance, Modern **567b**
MacPherson Commission:
Railways, Contemporary **1824a**; **1824b**;
Transportation, Royal Commission on **2188b**;
Transportation Regulation **2189c**
Macquarie, Lachlan:
Canada and Australia **322c**
"McQueen":
Television Drama, English-Language **2126b**
McQuesten, LeRoy Napoleon, "Jack":
Forty Mile, YT **826a**
McRae, Robert:
Philosophy **1659c**; **1660a**; **1661b**
MacRae, Warren:
Messer, Don, and the Islanders **1338c**
McRobbie, Kenneth:
Mosaic **1393b**
McRoberts, Hugh:
Richmond, BC **1869b**
macroeconomics:
Economics **648c**; **649b**;
Keynesian Economics **1133c**
Macrorie, Sask.:
Fredeen, Howard **842b**

Mactaggart, John:
Exploration and Travel Literature in English **736c**
McTaggart-Cowan, Ian **1282b**:
McTaggart-Cowan, Patrick Duncan **1282b**
McTaggart-Cowan, Patrick Duncan **1282b**
McTague, C.P.:
National War Labour Board **1433b**
Mactaquac hydroelectric station:
New Brunswick **1473a**;
Woodstock, NB **2333b**
Mactaquac Lake:
Reservoir **1859a**
Mactaquac Provincial Park:
Heritage Trail **982b**
McTavish, Frobisher and Co:
Frobisher, Joseph **848c**;
Mackenzie, Sir Alexander **1270a**;
McTavish, Simon **1282b**;
North West Company **1511a**
McTavish, John George:
Isaac Todd **1096c**;
Racoon **1816c**
MacTavish, Newton:
Art Writing and Criticism **128a**;
Essay in English **720a**
McTavish, Simon **1282b**:
McGillivray, Duncan **1266a**;
North West Company **1511a**
McTavish Arm:
Great Bear Lake **933b**
McTeer, Maureen:
Clark, Charles Joseph **432b**
McVicar Arm:
Great Bear Lake **933b**
McWilliams, Ronald F.:
Manitoba **1296c**
Mad Carews, The:
Ostenso, Martha **1593a**
MAD (Mutual Assured Destruction):
Defence Policy **581a**;
Science and Society **1955a**
Mad-Ren Press:
Private Presses **1762a**
Mad Shadows:
Blais, Marie-Claire **240a**
Mad Shadows:
Dance on Television and Film **568b**
"Mad Trapper":
Johnson, Albert **1112c**
Mad Trapper, The:
Wiebe, Rudy Henry **2304b**
Madame Benoît's Microwave Cook Book:
Benoît, Jehane **204c**
"Madame Pouliche":
Laberge, Albert **1154a**
Madame Z:
Brother Twelve **287b**
Madawaska, Ont:
Hôtel-Dieu **1011c**
Madawaska River (NB):
Aroostook War **121c**;
Saint John River **1915b**
Madawaska River (Ont):
Arnprior, Ont **121a**;
Cemeteries **385c**;
McNab, Archibald **1280a**;
Ottawa River **1596c**;
St Lawrence Lowland **1919a**
Madawaska Weavers:
Saint-Léonard, NB **1922a**
Maddened by Mystery:
Popular Literature in English **1717a**
Made Beaver **1282c**
Made in Italy:
Italian Writing **1099a**
Madeleine, Îles de la **1282c**:
Bayfield, Henry Wolsey **188a**;
Cap aux Meules, Île du **357b**;
Ceramics **388b**;
French Language **847b**;
Grande Entrée, Île de **925b**;
Lighthouses **1213c**;
Wind Energy **2313b**
Madeleine de Verchères:
Sculpture **1964c**
Madeleine is . . .:
Film **767a**
Madhyamaka philosophy:
Buddhism **293b**
Madill Church:
Huntsville, Ont **1030b**

Madoc, Ont:
Dafoe, Allan Roy **561a**;
Mineral Naming **1357b**;
Soapstone **2021a**
madocite:
Mineral Naming **1357b**
Madones canadiennes:
Lasnier, Rina **1179c**
madonna lily:
Lily **1215c**
Madott, Darlene:
Italian Writing **1099a**
Madran, NB:
New Brunswick **1469c**
Madrigalls III:
Rideout, Patricia Irene **1870c**
Madsen, Soren:
Private Presses **1762a**
Madsen Red Lake Gold Mines:
Brown, Eldon Leslie **288b**
madtom:
Catfish **378c**
Mae Pass:
Whitehorse, YT **2301c**
Mafia:
Organized Crime **1586b**; **1586c**
Magadan:
Jewish Writing **1110a**
Magasin du Bas-Canada, La:
Magazines **1284c**
Magazine Digest:
Campbell, Marjorie Wilkins **320c**
Magazine Maclean, Le:
Actualité, L' **13c**;
Langevin, André **1173b**;
Lapointe, Paul-Marie **1178b**;
Popular Literature in French **1718a**
Magazines **1282c**:
Action française, L' **13b**;
Action nationale, L' **13b**;
Actualité, L' **13c**;
Advertising **18a**;
Art Writing and Criticism **127c**;
Beaver, The **193a**;
Books in Canada **250c**;
Canadian Business **335c**;
Canadian Business Review **335c**;
Canadian Forum **342a**;
Canadian Geographic **342b**;
Capilano Review **359c**;
Châtelaine **399b**;
Chatelaine **399a**;
Cité libre **427b**;
Contact **510b**;
Contemporary Verse **511a**;
Financial Post **772b**;
Grain Growers' Guide **921c**;
Graphic Art and Design **928b**;
Illustration, Art **1043c**;
Journalism **1117a**;
Literary Magazines in English **1219b**;
Maclean's **1276a**;
Media Ownership **1321c**;
Montreal Standard **1384a**;
Quill & Quire **1814a**;
Saturday Night **1943a**;
Soirées canadiennes, Les **2043a**;
Star Weekly **2070b**;
Weekend Magazine **2289b**
Magdalen Island Co:
Grande Entrée, Île de **925b**
Magdalen Islands:
Madeleine, Îles de la **1282c**
Magdalen Shallows:
St Lawrence, Gulf of **1918c**
Magellan radar system:
Radar **1817b**
Maggie and Pierre:
Drama in English **622c**;
Humorous Writing in English **1027a**;
Royal Alexandra Theatre **1892b**;
Theatre, English-Language **2141a**;
Thompson, Paul **2152b**
Maggie Bassett Studio:
Tarragon Theatre **2111b**
"Maggie Muggins":
Radio Programming **1819c**
Maggie Muggins and Mr. McGarrity:
Children's Literature in English **412b**

maggot:
Fly **793c**;
Grasshopper **930c**;
Plum **1694c**
Magic **1285b**:
Folklore **799b**;
Religion **1850c**
"Magic Carpet Ride":
Steppenwolf **2078b**
Magic House: Labor and the Angel, The:
Scott, Duncan Campbell **1960c**
Magic House and Other Poems, The:
Scott, Duncan Campbell **1960c**
Magic Realism:
Canadian Fiction Magazine **341c**
Magicien, Le:
Vallerand, Jean **2238c**
Magill, Dennis William:
Community **475c**
Magistrate **1285c**:
Courts of Law **527c**;
Justice of the Peace **1123b**;
Murphy, Emily **1405c**
magma:
Igneous Rock **1041b**;
Mineral **1355a**;
Volcano **2267a**
Magna Carta (1215) (British):
Constitution **496c**
Magna International Ltd:
North Sydney, NS **1510b**
Magnan, Charles-Joseph:
Exploration and Travel Literature in French **737c**
Magnan, François:
Orchestre symphonique de Québec **1584b**
magnesium:
Metallurgy **1338c**; **1340a**;
Mineral Resources **1360c**;
Nuclear Power Plants **1545b**;
Pidgeon, Lloyd Montgomery **1677a**
Magnetawan, Ont:
Rayner, Gordon **1830a**
Magnetawan River:
Georgian Bay **893c**
Magnetic Hill:
Moncton, NB **1374c**
magnetite:
Iron and Steel Industry **1093b**;
Iron Ore **1094a**;
Mineral **1355a**; **1355c**;
Plate Tectonics **1691c**;
Prospecting **1768a**
magnetometer:
Petroleum Exploration and Production **1651b**;
Prospecting **1768a**
magnetosphere:
Northern Lights **1514c**
magnolia:
Endangered Plants **697b**;
Forest **811a**
Magnox Reactor:
Nuclear Power Plants **1545b**
Magnus Theatre Company North-West:
Theatre, English-Language **2139b**
Magnussen, Karen Diane **1285c**
Magog, Lake (BC):
Mount Assiniboine Provincial Park **1395c**
Magog, Qué **1285c**
Magog, Rivière:
Magog, Qué **1285c**;
St-François, Rivière **1912c**;
Sherbrooke, Qué **1990a**
Magog and Waterloo Railroad:
Magog, Qué **1285c**
Magog Cotton and Print Co:
Magog, Qué **1285c**
Magoon, H.A.:
Architecture, Development of **103b**
Magpie **1285c**
Magpie, The:
Durkin, Douglas Leader **638a**
magpie goose:
Waterfowl **2283c**
Magpie River:
Waterfall **2282c**
Magrath, Alta:
Grain Elevators **921b**
Maguire, Thomas **1286a**

Magyar Élet (Hungarian Life):
Hungarians **1028c**
Magyars:
Hungarians **1028b**
mahaleb cherry:
Cherry **406a**
Mahayanist Buddhism:
Buddhism **292c; 293b**;
Tibetans **2158b**
Maher, Peter:
Long-Distance Running **1241b**
Maher, Thomas:
Canadian Broadcasting Corporation **333c**
Maher v The Town of Portland:
New Brunswick School Question **1476b**
Maheu, Pierre:
Parti pris **1624b**
Maheu, Rivière:
Orléans, Île d' **1588b**
Maheux-Forcier, Louise **1286a**
Mahktosis, BC:
Ahousaht **40c**
Mahlstick Club:
Artists' Organizations **131a**;
Illustration, Art **1043a**;
Printmaking **1758b**
mahogany:
Furniture, English, Scottish and American **863b; 863c**
Mahogany Rush:
Popular Music **1719a**
Mahon Hall:
Ganges, BC **872c**
Mahone Bay:
Chester, NS **407a**;
Island **1098c**;
Oak Island **1549c**
Mahone Bay, NS **1286a**
Mahovlich, Francis William **1286a**
Maid of the Mist:
Niagara Falls **1497a**
Maidstone, Sask:
Wesson, John Henry **2294b**
Mail, The (Halifax):
Newspapers **1493c**
Mail, The (Toronto):
Armstrong, John **120b**;
Davin, Nicholas Flood **572a**;
Farrer, Edward **752a**;
Globe and Mail **906b**;
Journalism **1117c**;
Maclean, John Bayne **1275c**;
Newspapers **1493a; 1493c**
Mail and Empire (Toronto):
Canadian Travellers Abroad **351b**;
Canadian Women's Press Club **352b**;
Deacon, William Arthur **577a**;
Edmonton Journal **660b**;
Globe and Mail **906b**;
Hopkins, John Castell **1007a**;
Journalism **1117c**;
Newspapers **1493c**
mail-order catalogue:
Advertising **17b; 18a**;
Architecture, Development of **103b**;
Ceramics **388b**;
Clothing **443a**;
Eaton, Timothy **641c**;
Furniture, Country **862a**;
Furniture, English, Scottish and American **864a**;
Games **871c**;
Rugs and Rug Making **1900a**;
School Facilities **1948a**;
Sears Canada Inc **1969b**;
Simpsons, Limited **2006b**
mail service, continental:
Air Canada **41c**;
Postal System **1729a; 1729b**
mail service, trans-ocean:
Allan, Sir Hugh **63c**;
Canadian Pacific Railway **347c**;
Cunard, Sir Samuel **555a**;
Postal System **1729a; 1729c**;
Van Horne, Sir William Cornelius **2239c**
mail service in Canada:
Aviation **154b**;
Dickins, Clennell Haggerston, "Punch" **592c**;
Postal System **1728c**;
Turnbull Walter James **2202c**
Mail-Star, The:
Halifax, NS **953b**;
Newspapers **1495a**;
Nova Scotia **1533a**

mail steam boats:
Postal System **1729b**
Mailhot, Laurent:
Essay in French **721c**;
Humorous Writing in French **1027b**;
Literature in French – Scholarship and Teaching **1231b**
Mailing, Phyllis:
Singing **2007a**
Maillard, Charles:
Cosgrove, Stanley Morel **523b**;
Grammont, Joseph-Éloi-Augustin *dit* de Grandmont **922b**;
Pellan, Alfred **1638a**
Maillard, Keith:
Novel in English **1538a**
Maillard, Pierre **1286b**
Maillardville, BC:
Coquitlam, BC **516b**
Maillet, Andrée:
Amérique française **70a**;
Children's Literature in French **414a**;
Poetry in French **1700c**
Maillet, Antonine **1286b**:
Acadia **8c; 9a; 9c**;
Novel in French **1541b**;
Theatre, French-Language **2146a**
Maillet, Marguerite:
Literature in French – Scholarship and Teaching **1231c**
Maillou, *dit* Desmoulins, Jean-Baptiste **1286c**
Maillou, Joseph:
Maillou, *dit* Desmoulins, Jean-Baptiste **1286c**
Mailloux, N.:
Psychology **1778c**
Main, O.W.:
Business History **306a**
Main au feu, La:
Giguère, Roland **899b**
Main Channel:
Georgian Bay **893c**
"Main Street Jamboree":
Hunter, Thomas James **1029b**
Maine, Gulf of:
Fundy, Bay of **853a**;
Scotian Shelf **1959c**
Maine d'Anjou cattle:
Beef Cattle Farming **196b**
mainframe:
Computer Science **482c**
Mainguy, Edmond Rollo **1286c**
Mainguy Report:
Mainguy, Edmond Rollo **1286c**
Mainitoba Theatre Workshop:
Theatre, English-Language **2139b**
Mainland Comox:
Northern Georgia Strait Coast Salish **1514b**
Mainmise:
Basile, Jean **183c**;
Beausoleil, Claude **192a**;
Chamberland, Paul **392b**;
Literary Periodicals in French **1221c**;
Popular Literature in French **1718a**
Mainse, David:
Evangelism **730b**
Maintenant:
Literary Periodicals in French **1221c**
Maintiens le Droit **1286c**
Mainwaring, Sir Henry **1287a**
Mair, Charles **1287a**:
Poetry in English **1696b**
Maire of St Brieux, The:
Dixon, Frederick Augustus **607c**
Maison Alcan:
Affleck, Raymond Tait **21b**
Maison Déom:
Small Presses in French **2013b; 2013c**
Maison des Coopérant:
Webb Zerafa Menkès Housden Partnership **2288b**
Maison du Québec (London):
Quiet Revolution **1813c**
Maison du Québec (New York):
Quiet Revolution **1813c**
Maison du Québec (Paris):
Québec **1802b**;
Quiet Revolution **1813c**

Maison Girardin:
Architecture, Development of **101c**
Maison Montmorency:
Lévesque, Georges-Henri **1204b**
Maisonneuve:
Hébert, Louis-Philippe **975b**;
Sculpture **1964c**
Maisonneuve, Paul de Chomedey de **1287a**:
Art **121b**;
Montréal, Qué **1379b; 1380b**
Maitland, Ont **1287a**:
W.D. Lawrence **2270a**
Maitland, Sir Peregrine **1287b**:
Maitland, Ont **1287a**;
Matthews, John **1316c**;
Orillia, Ont **1587c**
Maitland River:
Goderich, Ont **907c**
"Maître chez nous":
Lesage, Jean **1202c**
maize:
Corn, Field **517b**;
Palynology **1610c**;
Prehistory **1739a**
Major, André **1287b**:
Novel in French **1541a; 1542a**
Major, Ascanio J.:
Stornoway **2082a**
Major, Jean-Louis:
Literature in French – Scholarship and Teaching **1231c**
Major, Kevin:
Children's Literature in English **412b**
Major, Leon:
Neptune Theatre **1466a**
Makah:
Clayoquot **435b**;
Nootka **1503b**
Makara:
Literary Magazines in English **1220b**
Makaryk, Iryna:
Ukrainian Writing **2206c**
"Make and Break Harbour":
Rogers, Stan **1884a**
Make This Your Canada:
Lewis, David **1205b**
Makedonija:
Macedonians **1264b**
Makers of Canada, The **1287b**:
Historiography **993c**;
Scott, Duncan Campbell **1961a**
Makers of Canadian Literature series:
Book Publishing, English-Language **248c**;
Pierce, Lorne Albert **1677a**
Making a Start in Canada:
Exploration and Travel Literature in English **736c**
Making Arrangements:
Harlow, Robert **962b**
Making It Again:
Hawkins, Ronald **968b**
Making of a Peacemonger, The:
Ignatieff, George **1041b**
Making of a Socialist, The:
Autobiographies, Political **148c**
Making of Modern Poetry in Canada, The:
Dudek, Louis **632a**
Making of Nicholas Montour:
Novel in French **1539c**
Making of Personality, The:
Carman, Bliss **365a**
Makinson, T.C.:
Arctic Sovereignty **113b**
Makinson Inlet:
Arctic Sovereignty **113b**
Makivik Corporation:
Inuit Tapirisat of Canada **1089b**;
Watt, Charlie **2285a**
Makkovik, Nfld:
Labrador **1159c**;
Labrador Inuit **1161a**
mako shark:
Shark **1987c**
Mal du jour de l'an ou scènes de la vie écolière, Le:
Theatre, French-Language **2144b**
Malachan, BC:
Ditidaht **606c**
malachite:
Copper **514c**
malacology:
Mollusc **1371a**

Malacostraca:
Crustacean **548c**
Malahat Review:
Literary Magazines in English **1220b**;
Literary Periodicals in English **1221a**
Malahat Review Awards for Book Design:
Literary Prizes in English **1222c**
Malahat Ridge:
Victoria, BC **2261a**
Malaria **1287c**:
Baldoon **166a**;
Parasitology **1613a**;
Veterinary Medicine **2256c**
Malartic, Anne-Joseph-Hippolyte de Maurès, Comte de:
Malartic, Qué **1287c**
Malartic, Qué **1287c**
Malartic goldfields:
Malartic, Qué **1287c**
Malaspina, Alejandro **1287c**:
Sutil and *Mexicana* **2100a**
Malaspina College Theatre:
Theatre, English-Language **2142c**
Malayalam language:
South Asians **2050a**
Malays:
Malaysians **1288a**
Malaysian prawn:
Shrimp **1999a**
Malaysians **1288a**
Malbaie, Rivière:
La Malbaie, Qué **1151b**
Malbête, La:
Paradis, Suzanne **1612c**
Malcolm Island:
Sointula, BC **2043a**
"Malcolm's Katie":
Poetry in English **1696b**
Maldonado, Lorenzo Ferrer:
Northwest Coast **1516a**
Malecite:
Maliseet **1288a**
malemute:
English Language **710b**
Malenfant, Anna:
Acadia **8a**
Malépart, Germaine:
Gagnon, André **867b**;
Hétu, Pierre **984b**;
Tremblay, Gilles **2192b**
Mâles, Les:
Carle, Gilles **363c**
Maley, S.R.:
Music Criticism **1414a**
Malgré tout la joie:
Novel in French **1540b**
Malice in Blunderland:
Essay in English **720c**;
Fotheringham, Allan **831a**
malicious arrest:
Jury **1122c**
Maligne Lake:
Harris, Lawren Stewart **963c**
Maligne River:
Karst Landform **1129a**
Maliseet **1288a**:
Fredericton, NB **842c**;
Métis **1343c**;
New Brunswick **1470c**
Maliseet language:
Oromocto, NB **1588c**;
Saint John River **1915c**
Maliseet wampum:
Emblems, Provincial and Territorial **691c**
Malksope Inlet:
Chickliset **408a**
Mallabar:
Stage and Costume Design **2066b**
Mallabec:
Walker, David Harry **2271c**
mallard:
Bird Sanctuaries and Reserves **230a**;
Duck **631b**
Mallard's Long Room:
Concert Halls and Opera Houses **486a**
Malle, Louis:
Héroux, Denis **983a**
Mallery, Garrick:
Pictographs and Petroglyphs **1676a**

Militia Act (1868):
Militia Acts **1352a**;
Regiment **1840c**
Militia Act (1883):
Militia Acts **1352a**
Militia Act (1904):
Militia Acts **1352a**
Militia Acts **1352a**
Militia and Defence, Department of:
Armed Forces **117a**;
Cartography, History of **373b**;
Internment **1084a**;
National Defence, Department of **1428b**
Militia Council:
Militia Acts **1352a**;
Veterinary Medicine, History **2258b**
milk, pasteurized:
Dairy Industry **562c**;
Disease, Animal **605a**;
Ontario **1576b**;
Public Health **1783b**
milk and milk products:
Agricultural Marketing Board **30c**;
Animal Agriculture **76b**; **77b**;
Beef Cattle Farming **196b**;
Canada's Food Guide **329c**;
Cheese and Cheesemaking **400a**;
Dairy Farming **561c**;
Dairy Industry **562b**;
Goat Farming **907b**;
Newfoundland **1487a**;
Sheep Farming **1989c**;
Veterinary Medicine **2256c**
milk-marketing boards:
Agricultural Economics **26a**;
Dairy Farming **561c**
milk powder:
Dairy Industry **562c**
Milk River **1352b**:
Fossil Plants **829c**;
Hoodoo Rock **1006b**;
Pictographs and Petroglyphs **1675c**
milk snake:
Snake **2019a**
Milk Stone:
Lowther, Patricia Louise **1249c**
milk vetch:
Legume **1200c**;
Locoweed **1238a**;
Vegetation Regions **2249c**
Milkweed **1352b**:
Biomass Energy **225a**;
Monarch Butterfly **1373c**;
Poisonous Plants **1702b**
Milky Way Galaxy:
Native People, Religion **1458c**;
Pearce, Joseph Algernon **1634c**;
Plaskett, John Stanley **1690a**
Mill, John Stuart:
Economics, Radical **651a**;
Philosophy **1660a**
Mill, Richard:
Painting **1607c**
Mill Brook, NS:
Swan, Anna Haining **2102a**
Mill Falls Trail:
Heritage Trail **982c**
Mill of Kintail:
Hudson Strait **1021c**
Mill of Kintail:
Almonte, Ont **66b**
Millan, Gonzalo:
Ethnic Literature **728a**
Millar, Charles Vance **1352b**
Millar, Ian:
Equestrian Sports **717a**
Millar, James F.V.:
Archaeology **93c**
Millar, Margaret:
Popular Literature in English **1717a**
Millar, Terrance:
Equestrian Sports **717a**
Millar Channel:
Ahousaht **40c**
Millard, Charles Hibbert **1352b**
Mille-Îles, Rivière des:
Ottawa River **1596c**;
St-Eustache, Qué **1912b**;
St Lawrence River **1920a**
Millen, Edgar:
Johnson, Albert **1113a**
Millenarianism **1352c**:
Jehovah's Witnesses **1107b**;
Shaker Religion **1987a**

miller:
Moth **1394c**
Miller I Map:
Cartography, History of **370a**
Miller, Buzz:
Ballets Jazz de Montréal, Les **168c**
Miller, Charles:
O'Keefe, Eugene **1563b**
Miller, Clarence Horatio, "Big" **1352c**
Miller, David:
Photography **1665c**
Miller, E.:
Physical Geography **1667a**
Miller, Elizabeth Russell:
Russell, Edward **1902c**
Miller, Frank **1353a**
Miller, Frank Robert **1353a**
Miller, Fritz:
Atlin, BC **142b**
Miller, George Martell **1353a**
Miller, Henry C.:
Graphic Publishers Limited **930a**
Miller, J.H.:
Miller and Cockriell Case **1353b**
Miller, J.J.:
Canadian Travellers Abroad **351b**
Miller, Joey:
Musical Theatre **1420b**
Miller, John Henry **1353a**
Miller, Kate:
Nursing Sisters **1548b**
Miller, Lewis:
Lewisporte, Nfld **1206a**
Miller, Mark:
Music Criticism **1414a**
Miller, Michael:
Choral Music **420a**
Miller, Orlo:
Donnellys, The **613b**
Miller, Owen:
Literature in English – Theory and Criticism **1228a**
Miller, Riel:
Economics, Radical **652a**
Miller, Thomas:
Saskatchewan **1936b**
Miller, William Lash **1353b**
Miller and Cockriell Case **1353b**
Miller Pickering village:
Archaeology **93a**
Miller Site, The:
Kenyon, Walter Andrew **1133a**
Millerite Adventists:
Seventh-Day Adventists **1984c**
Millertown, Nfld:
Lewisporte, Nfld **1206a**
Millet **1353b**
Millgate, Michael:
Biography in English **221b**
Millidge, Thomas Edward **1353b**
Milligan, Henry:
Hart House String Quartet **965b**
Milligan, James:
Opera **1579a**;
Singing **2007a**
milling:
Asbestos **133c**;
Metallurgy **1339a**
Millipede **1353b**
Millman, Peter MacKenzie **1353c**
mills:
Sawmill **1945b**;
Technology **2117b**
Mills, Alan:
Music History **1418c**
Mills, Anthony J.:
Archaeology, Mediterranean **95b**
Mills, Frank:
Popular Music **1719a**
Mills, Fred:
Canadian Brass **333b**
Mills, Frederick W.:
Dixon, Frederick Augustus **607c**
Mills, Robert:
Rowing **1891a**
Mills of the Gods, The:
"This Hour Has Seven Days" **2150b**
millstones:
Cap aux Meules, Île du **357b**;
Flour Milling **793a**
Milltown, NB:
St Stephen, NB **1924b**
Milne, David, Jr:
Milne, David Brown **1354a**

Milne, David Brown **1353c**:
Art Writing and Criticism **128b**;
Painting **1605b**
Milne, Kathleen Pavey:
Milne, David Brown **1354a**
Milne, Patsy:
Milne, David Brown **1354a**
Milne, W.S.:
Drama in English **621a**
Milner, B.:
Neuroscience **1467a**
Milner, P.M.:
Neuroscience **1467a**
Milnes, H.:
German Writing **895c**
Milton, Nfld:
Newfoundland **1487b**
Milton, NS:
Saunders, Margaret Marshall **1944a**
Milton, Ont **1354b**:
Glass **905a**;
Niagara Escarpment **1496a**;
Thoroughbred Racing **2154c**
Milton, William F., Viscount:
Exploration and Travel Literature in English **737a**
Milton-Est, Qué:
Fessenden, Reginald Aubrey **761a**
Milton's Royalism and Dogma:
Ross, Malcolm **1888a**
Mimas satellite:
Planet and Satellite **1685c**
Mime omnibus, le:
Drama in French **623c**
Mimico, Ont:
MacMillan, Sir Ernest Alexander Campbell **1279a**
Mimosa and Other Poems:
di Michele, Mary **592a**;
Italian Writing **1099a**
Mimran, Saul and Joseph:
Sung, Alfred **2096b**
Minamata disease:
Grassy Narrows Reserve **931a**
Minas Basin **1354b**:
Annapolis Lowlands **79a**;
Cape Blomidon **357c**;
Cottnam, Deborah **524b**
Minas Channel:
Minas Basin **1354b**
Mind That Found Itself, A:
Mental Health **1336c**
Mindemoya, Ont:
Ense, Donald Orion Henry **710c**
Minden, Robert:
Marlatt, Daphne **1307a**;
Photography **1665c**
Mind's I:
Shadbolt, Jack Leonard **1986c**
Mindscapes:
Jiles, Paulette **1111c**
mine-assisted *in situ* production:
Bitumen **234c**
Mine de Rien:
Acadia **9a**
Mine for Keeps:
Children's Literature in English **412b**
Mine Inheritance:
Niven, Frederick John **1501b**
mine rescue:
Disasters **602b**
Mine Workers' Union of Canada:
All-Canadian Congress of Labour **63c**;
Crowsnest Pass Strike, 1932 **547b**;
Drumheller Strike **628c**;
Estevan Coal Miners' Strike **722b**;
Murphy, Harvey **1406a**
Miner, Horace:
Anthropology **82c**
Miner, John Thomas **1354c**
Miner, William **1354c**
Mineral **1354c**:
Antimony **85a**;
Asbestos **133b**;
Cadmium **313c**;
Chromium **425a**;
Clay **435a**;
Columbium **463a**;
Gemstone **878b**;
Gold **908a**;
Gypsum **948b**;
Iron Ore **1094a**;
Lead **1192c**;
Molybdenum **1373b**;

Ocean Mining **1556b**;
Silica **2001c**;
Titanium **2164a**;
Zinc **2359c**
Mineral and Mining Engineering **1356c**
mineral dressing:
Metallurgy **1339a**
Mineral King Mine:
Invermere, BC **1090b**
Mineral Naming **1357b**
Mineral Resources **1358a**:
Gravity **931c**;
Prospecting **1767b**
Mineral Resources of Ontario, Royal Commission on the:
Bell, Robert **201a**
mineral rights:
Offshore Mineral Rights Reference **1560b**;
Petroleum **1651a**;
Real Estate **1831a**;
Resource Rights **1860b**
mineral springs:
Soft-Drink Industry **2037a**;
Spring **2063c**;
Volcano **2267b**
Mineralogical Association of Canada:
Geology **891b**
Mineralogical Society of America:
Mineral Resources **1358a**; **1358c**
Mineralogy of Nova Scotia, The:
Mineral Resources **1358b**
mineraloids:
Mineral **1354c**
Minerals and Mining, Nova Scotia:
Drummond, Robert **629b**
Miners' Festival:
Cobalt, Ont **452c**
miner's lettuce:
Wildflowers **2306a**
Miners' Memorial Day:
Cape Breton Strikes, 1920s **358c**
Miners' Mutual Protective Society:
Union Centrals, District and Regional **2213a**
Minerva Films:
Colville, Alexander **463b**
Minerve, La:
Book Publishing, French-Language **249c**;
Couture, Guillaume **528a**;
Duvernay, Ludger **638c**;
Gérin-Lajoie, Antoine **895a**;
Intellectual History **1073c**;
Morin, Augustin-Norbert **1389c**;
Music Criticism **1414a**;
Newspapers **1492a**;
Tardivel, Jules-Paul **2111a**
Mines, Department of:
Anthropology, Linguistic **83c**;
Energy, Mines and Resources, Department of **698c**;
Geological Survey of Canada **889b**;
Petroleum Research and Development **1653c**;
Science **1951a**
Mines, Department of (Ont):
Kirkland Lake, Ont **1140a**;
Mineral Resources **1358c**
Mines, Ministry of (Qué):
Malartic, Qué **1287c**
Mines and Energy, Department of (NS):
Nova Scotia **1531b**
Mines and Resources, Department of:
Energy, Mines and Resources, Department of **698c**;
Geological Survey of Canada **889b**
Mines and Technical Surveys, Department of:
Cameron, William Maxwell **319c**;
Energy, Mines and Resources, Department of **698c**;
Fisheries Research Board **786a**;
Geological Survey of Canada **889b**;
National Atlas of Canada **1427b**
Minesing Swamp:
Swamp, Marsh and Bog **2101b**
minesweeper:
Armed Forces **117a**
Minetown, Milltown, Railtown:
Sociology **2036c**

N

P

Pump Drill **1790b**
pump jack:
Petroleum Exploration and
Production **1652a**
Pumpkin **1790b**
Punch in Canada:
Cartoons, Political **375c**
pundit:
Hinduism **989b**
punishment and penalties:
Abortion **4c**;
Capital Punishment **360c**;
Crime **535c**; **536b**;
Criminal Procedure **539c**;
Food Legislation **801c**;
Impaired Driving **1049a**;
Law and Society **1188a**;
Prison **1760b**;
Student Rights **2087c**;
Treason **2190c**
Punjabi language:
Ethnic Literature **727c**;
Hinduism **989c**;
Sikhism **2000b**; **2001b**;
South Asians **2050a**
Punjabis:
Sikhism **2000b**
Punkeydoodles Corners, Ont:
Place-names **1683c**
Puntous, Sylviane and Patricia:
Triathlon **2193c**
puppets:
Theatre, English-
Language **2139b**; **2140c**
"Puppy Love":
Anka, Paul Albert **79a**
Purbrook, Canada West:
Steele, Sir Samuel Ben-
field **2076a**
Purcell, Gillis Philip **1790b**
Purcell, Jack **1790b**
Purcell, James **1790c**
Purcell Mountains **1790c**:
Columbia Mountains **461c**;
Glacier National Park **904a**;
Invermere, BC **1090b**;
Jumbo Pass **1122a**
Purcell String Quartet **1790c**
Purcell Wilderness Conservancy:
Purcell Mountains **1790c**
purdah:
Sikhism **2000c**
Purdie, J.E.:
Evangelism **730a**
Purdy, Alfred Wellington **1790c**:
Acorn, Milton **12c**;
Humorous Writing in Eng-
lish **1027a**;
League of Canadian Po-
ets, The **1194a**;
Poetry in English **1697c**;
Queen's Quarterly **1812c**
Purdy, William:
Chemistry Subdisciplines **404b**
Purdy, William:
Lindsay, Ont **1216b**
Purdy's Mills, Upper Canada:
Lindsay, Ont **1216b**
Pure Land Buddhism:
Buddhism **293c**
Purim:
Religious Festivals **1853c**
Puritanism:
Calvinism **319b**;
Congregational Churches **490b**;
Quakers **1792a**
Puritanism and Liberty:
Woodhouse, Arthur Sutherland
Piggott **2332c**
Purolator Courier Ltd:
Transportation **2186b**
purple blotch:
Onion **1567b**
purple finch:
Biogeography **219c**
purple gallinule:
Gallinule **869b**
purple laver:
Seaweeds **1970b**
Purple Martin **1791b**
Purple Partridge Press:
Private Presses **1762b**
purple pitcher plant:
Pitcher Plant **1681b**
purple saxifrage:
Auyuittuq National Park **152c**;
Biogeography **219c**;
Saxifrage **1945c**;
Wildflowers **2306b**

purple violet:
Emblems, Provincial and
Territorial **692a**;
Violet **2265c**
purse seine:
Fisheries History **782a**; **782c**;
783c;
Shark **1987c**
Pursh, Frederick **1791b**
purslane:
Weeds **2289a**
Purtex Knitting Co:
Parent, Madeleine **1613c**
Purvis, Arthur Blaikie **1791b**
puschkinia:
Flowers, Cultivated **793b**
Pushkin:
Jonas, George **1115c**
puss-in-the-corner:
Games **871a**
Put-In-Bay **1791c**
Putnam, Donald Fulton **1791c**
Puttee, Arthur **1791c**
PW100 engines:
Aerospace Industry **20b**
pygmy goose:
Waterfowl **2283a**
pygmy nuthatch:
Nuthatch **1548c**
pygmy smelt:
Smelt **2015a**
pygmy water lily:
Water Lily **2280c**
pygmy whitefish:
Whitefish **2301b**
pyloric stenosis:
Genetic Diseases **880c**
Pylyshyn, Zenon:
Philosophy **1661b**
Pyper, C.B.:
Essay in English **720a**
Pypypiw, Ivan:
Ukrainians **2207a**
pyragyrite:
Mineral **1356a**
pyramid schemes:
Competition Policy **479a**
pyrite:
Gold **908a**;
Iron and Steel Indus-
try **1092c**; **1093b**;
Sulphur **2093b**
pyrochlore:
Columbium **463a**;
Mineral Resources **1360c**
pyroclastic rocks:
Sedimentary Rock **1974b**
pyrophyllite:
Mineral Resources **1360c**;
Newfoundland **1485c**; **1487b**;
Soapstone **2021a**
pyroxene:
Mineral **1356c**;
Soapstone **2021a**
pyrrhotite:
Iron and Steel Indus-
try **1092c**; **1093b**;
Mineral **1355c**
pyx:
Silver, Church **2002b**
Pyx, The:
Novel in English **1538b**

Q

"Q for Quest":
Television Drama, English-
Language **2126a**
Qadyanis:
Islam **1097c**
Qajartalik:
Pictographs and Petro-
glyphs **1676a**
Qaqaq Ashoona **1792a**:
Kiugak Ashoona **1142b**
Qataris:
Arabs **90a**
Qikaaluktut:
Illustration, Art **1044a**
QIT-Fer et Titane Inc:
Romaine, Rivière **1885a**;
Titanium **2164a**
Qitdlarssuaq **1792a**
Quadra:
Station PAPA **2072a**
Quadra:
Walbran, John Thomas **2271b**

Quadra Island **1792a**
Quadra Rocks:
Spanish **2055a**
Quadragesimo Anno:
Social Doctrine of the Roman
Catholic Church **2025c**
Quaestiones Entomologicae:
Zoology **2361c**
Quail **1792a**:
Bird Classification and Evolu-
tion **228b**;
Game Bird **870c**
Quaker Oats Co of Canada Ltd:
Bicycling **214a**;
Peterborough, Ont **1646c**
Quakers **1792a**:
Canadian Council of
Churches **336c**;
Mental Health **1336b**;
Newmarket, Ont **1492b**;
Pacifism **1601b**;
Prison **1760b**
Qualen, John:
Canadian Expatriates in Show
Business **340a**
Qualicum Beach, BC **1792b**
Quality Assurance Education
Association of Canada:
Industrial Quality Control **1060c**
quality control:
Industrial Quality Con-
trol **1060b**
"quality of life":
Boys and Girls Clubs of
Canada **264c**;
Franklin, Ursula Martius **839a**;
Medical Ethics **1324c**
"quality of working life":
Corporatism **522a**;
Work **2335c**
Quality Records Ltd:
Buck, Gary **292a**
Quand j'aurai payé ton visage:
Martin, Claire **1310a**
Quand j'parl'tout seul:
Poetry in French **1700a**
Quand le peuple fait la loi:
Cliche, Robert C.R. **436b**
"Quand les hommes vivront
d'amour":
Popular Music **1719b**
Quand même:
Theatre, French-Language
2146c
Quand nous serons Leureux:
Brault, Jacques **267a**
"Quand on aime on a toujours
vingt ans":
Ferland, Jean-Pierre **758b**
quantum mechanics:
Black Hole **236b**;
Philosophy **1661b**;
Physics **1667c**;
Spectroscopy **2056c**
quantum statistical mechanics:
Gordon, Andrew Robert-
son **912b**
quantum theory:
Physics **1669a**;
Spectroscopy **2056c**
Qu'Appelle Dam:
Elbow, Sask **673c**
Qu'Appelle River **1792b**:
Dakota **563a**;
Fort Ellice **819c**;
Reservoir **1859b**
Quarantaine, La:
Poirier, Anne-Claire **1701c**
quarantine:
Brockville, Ont **285b**;
Epidemic **715b**;
Immigration Policy **1047b**;
Influenza **1067b**;
MacEachran, Duncan **1264a**;
Medicine, History of **1330a**;
Partridge Island **1625c**;
Plant Disease **1688c**;
Potato Wart Disease **1731b**;
Public Health **1783b**;
Royal William **1898a**
Quarantine Island:
Grosse Île **941b**
quarks:
Physics **1670c**
Quarry:
Fox, Gail **833a**;
Literary Magazines in Eng-
lish **1220a**; **1220b**
Quarry Press:
Small Presses **2013b**

Quarrying Industry **1792c**:
Stonewall, Man **2081b**
quart (qt):
Weights and Measures **2290c**
quarter:
Coinage **457a**
Quarter Horse:
Horse **1008b**;
Longden, Johnny **1242a**
Quartet:
Music Composition **1412c**
Quartet for Three Actors:
Deverell, Rex **590b**
Quartier latin:
Beaulieu, Michel **191c**
quartz:
Diamonds of Canada **592b**;
Geological Regions **887a**;
Metamorphic Rock **1340b**;
Mineral **1355a**; **1355b**; **1356c**;
Mineral Naming **1357c**;
Sedimentary Rock **1973c**;
Silica **2001c**;
Soapstone **2021a**;
Trilobite **2194a**
quartz clock:
Time **2161c**
quartzite:
Banks Island **175b**;
Casson, Alfred Joseph **378a**;
Silica **2001c**
Quasar **1792c**
Quasars:
Pépin, Clermont **1641b**
Quastel, Judah Hirsch **1793a**:
Biochemistry **218a**;
Neuroscience **1467a**
Quaternary period:
Cypress Hills **560b**;
Drumlin **628c**;
Nunatak **1546b**;
River Landform **1875c**
"Quatorze, rue de Galais":
Television Drama, French-
Language **2127a**
Quatre montréalais en l'an 3000:
Children's Literature in
French **414a**
Quatre Saisons de Piquot, Les:
Children's Literature in
French **415a**
Quatre Saisons network:
Communications in
Québec **471c**;
Jasmin, Claude **1106a**
85 Ans de Théâtre à Hull:
Theatre, French-Language
2146b
Quatsino Reserve:
Kwakiutl **1150b**
"Quatuor":
Choquette, Robert **419b**
Quatuor à cordes no 2:
Prévost, André **1745b**
Quatuor no. 1:
Chamber Music **391c**
Québec **1793a**:
Aid to (or of) the Civil
Power **40c**;
Anthropology **82c**;
Arpent **121a**;
Botanical Garden **254c**;
Bridges **269c**;
Canadian Charter of Rights and
Freedoms **336a**;
Churchill Falls **426a**;
Civil Procedure **431c**;
Conscription **492a**; **492b**;
Constitution, Patriation of **497c**;
Constitutional History **503c**;
Constitutional Problems, Royal
Commission of Inquiry on
(Qué) **507a**;
County **526b**;
Crown Land **547a**;
Délégations du Québec **581c**;
Distribution of Powers **606b**;
Earthquake **640c**;
Energy Policy **701c**;
Equalization Payments **716b**;
Foundations **831b**;
Housing and Housing Pol-
icy **1017a**;
Human Rights **1025b**;
Immigration **1046b**;
Immigration Policy **1047c**;
Jesuits' Estates Act **1109a**;
Labrador Boundary Dis-
pute **1160b**;
Lapointe, Ernest **1178a**;

R

S

Schofield, Francis William **1947a**:
Veterinary Medicine **2256c**
Schofield Reference Bible:
Aberhart, William **3a**
scholarly publishing:
University Presses **2224c**
Scholarly Publishing:
Halpenny, Frances
Georgina **955a**
Scholastic-TAB Publications Ltd:
Book Clubs **248a**;
Children's Literature in English **413b**
Scholes, Lou:
Rowing **1891a**
Scholfield, John:
Railway Station **1823c**
Schoodic River:
Boundaries **258b**
School Act (1841) (Province of Canada):
Education, History of **665b**
School Act (1864) (NS):
Nova Scotia **1533c**
School Act (1865) (NS):
Nova Scotia **1532b**; **1533c**
School Act (1871) (Man):
Manitoba **1297a**
School Act (1871) (Ont):
Ryerson, Adolphus
Egerton **1905a**
School Act (Sask):
Anderson, James Thomas
Milton **73a**
School Attendance Act (1916) (Man):
Manitoba **1297b**
School Boards **1947a**
school bus:
Bus Transportation **301c**
school cars:
Canadian National Railways **345c**
School Facilities **1947c**
School-Marm Tree, The:
O'Hagan, Howard **1561b**
School of Agriculture:
Nova Scotia Agricultural College **1534c**
School of Agriculture of Oka:
Agricultural Education **26b**
School of Agriculture of Sainte-Anne-de-la-Pocatière:
Agricultural Education **26b**
School of Comparative Medicine and Veterinary Science:
Veterinary Medicine, History **2257b**
School of Dental Technology:
Côté, Jean-Pierre **524a**
School of Dramatic Arts (Hull):
Theatre, French-Language **2146b**
School of Fisheries:
New Brunswick **1474a**
School of Horticulture:
Nova Scotia Agricultural College **1534c**
School of Practical Science:
Architecture, Development of **103c**;
Chemical Engineering **400c**;
Civil Engineering **430b**;
Engineering **704a**;
Loudon, James **1245a**;
Mineral and Mining Engineering **1356c**;
University of Toronto **2223b**
School of Technology:
Loudon, James **1245a**
School Systems **1949a**:
Private School **1762b**;
Public School **1786c**;
Separate School **1979a**
School Trustee **1950a**
Schoolcraft, Henry Rowe:
Pictographs and Petroglyphs **1676a**;
Shinguacöuse **1992a**
Schott, Carl:
Historical Geography **991b**
schrank:
Furniture, German **866a**
Schreiber, Charlotte Mount
Brock **1950b**
Schreiber, Sir Collingwood:
Architecture, Development of **102b**
Schreiber, Ont:
Bennett, William John **204b**

Schreiber, Weymouth:
Schreiber, Charlotte Mount
Brock **1950b**
Schreibman, Phil:
Musical Theatre **1420b**
Schreiner, Michael:
Musical Instruments **1419c**
Schreyer, Edward Richard **1950b**:
Shilling, Arthur **1991c**
Schrödinger, Erwin:
Spectroscopy **2056c**
Schroeder, Andreas:
German Writing **895c**;
Short Fiction in English **1997b**
Schubert, Catherine O'Hare:
Armstrong, BC **120b**;
Overlanders of 1862 **1598b**
Schubert Choir:
Music History **1417c**
Schull, Joseph **1950b**
Schulte, Paul:
Arctic Bay, NWT **110a**
Schultz, Sir John Christian **1950c**:
Riel, Louis **1871a**
Schultz, Marvin:
Archaeology **92b**
Schultz Lake:
Thelon River **2149b**
Schwartz, H.T.:
Illustration, Art **1044a**
Schwarz/Sewell Productions:
Theatre, English-Language **2143c**
Schwarzschild radius:
Black Hole **236b**
Schwatka, Frederick:
Franklin Search **839a**;
Tookoolito **2166c**
Schwengers, B.P.:
Tennis **2131a**
Science **1950c**:
Acoustics **12c**;
Astronomy **138c**;
Biochemistry **217c**;
Biology **223a**;
Chemistry **402b**;
Mathematics **1313c**;
Meteorology **1341b**;
Oceanography **1556c**;
Philosophy **1661b**;
Physics **1667b**;
Psychology **1778b**;
Soil Science **2042a**;
Statistics **2072a**
Science, Technology and Innovation:
Patents, Copyright and Industrial Designs, Royal
Commission on **1628b**
Science and Health, with Key to the Scriptures:
Christian Science **422c**
Science and Madness:
Drama in English **622b**
science and religion:
Intellectual History **1074c**;
Philosophy **1662a**;
Science and Society **1953c**
Science and Society **1953b**:
Mathematics and Society **1315b**
Science and Technology Branch:
National Museum of Science and
Technology **1431c**
Science and Technology Canada:
Astronaut **138b**;
Biotechnology **226b**;
Natural Sciences and Engineering Research Council **1463a**;
Regional Development Planning **1843a**;
Science Policy **1957a**; **1958a**
Science Centre **1955c**:
Ontario Science Centre **1578b**
"Science Circus":
Ontario Science Centre **1578b**
Science Council of Canada **1956b**:
Chemistry Subdisciplines **404b**;
Conserver Society **496a**;
Economy **655c**;
Franklin, Ursula Martius **839a**;
Gauvin, William Henry **877a**;
Gray, Jessie Catherine **932a**;
Inventors and Innovations **1089c**;
Le Roy, Donald James **1192a**;
McTaggart-Cowan, Patrick
Duncan **1282b**;
Microchips and Transistors **1349c**;
Pollution **1714a**;

Science and Society **1955b**;
Science Policy **1957a**;
Solandt, Ormond McKillop **2043b**;
Suzuki, David Takayoshi **2100c**;
Wilson, John Tuzo **2311b**;
Women and Education **2323c**
science education:
Science and Society **1955b**
Science et esprit:
Religion **1851b**
Science Fiction **1956c**:
Children's Literature in English **412c**;
Children's Literature in
French **414b**;
Popular Literature in English **1717b**;
Popular Literature in
French **1717c**
Science Fiction Writers of America:
Science Fiction **1956c**
Science for Peace:
Franklin, Ursula Martius **839a**
Science Forum:
Science **1952c**;
Siminovitch, Louis **2005b**
Science North:
Science Centre **1956a**;
Sudbury, Ont **2090c**
Science Policy **1956c**:
Science Council of
Canada **1956b**
Science Réalité:
Seguin, Fernand **1975b**
Science Secretariat of Canada:
Forward, Frank Arthur **826b**;
Science Policy **1957a**; **1957c**
Science World:
Expo 86 **739a**;
Science Centre **1956a**
Sciences pastorales:
Religion **1851b**
Sciences religieuses:
Religion **1851b**
Scientific and Industrial Research
Council of Alberta:
Alberta Research Council **57b**
Scientific Image, The:
Philosophy **1661b**
Scientific Realism and the Plasticity of Mind:
Philosophy **1661b**
Scientific Research and Development **1958a**
Scientists for Peace:
Peace Movement **1632c**
Scientology:
New Religious Movements **1479c**; **1480b**;
Religion **1850b**
Sciff-Zamaro, Roberta:
Italian Writing **1099a**
scilla:
Flowers, Cultivated **793b**
scintillometer:
Mineral **1355c**;
Prospecting **1768b**
Sciuridae:
Mammals **1290a**
Scobie, Hugh:
Almanacs **66b**;
Drama in English **620c**;
Graphic Art and Design **928a**;
Printmaking **1757c**
Scobie, Stephen **1959b**:
Humorous Writing in English **1026c**;
Literature in English – Theory
and Criticism **1228c**;
Nichol, Barrie Phillip,
"bp" **1498b**
Scoggan, H.J.:
Botany History **256b**
Scorched-Wood People, The:
Wiebe, Rudy Henry **2304b**
Scorpion **1959b**
Scorpionfish **1959b**
scorpionfly:
Fly **793c**;
Insect Classification **1071b**
Scotch, The:
Galbraith, John Kenneth **868b**
Scotch Cup:
Brier **270b**;
Curling **556a**;
Richardson, Ernie **1868a**
Scotch Lake:
Passenger Pigeon **1628b**

Scotch Settlement, NB:
Mitchell, James **1367c**
Scotchfort, PEI:
Prince Edward Island **1750a**
Scotchman's Return:
Essay in English **720b**
Scotia Square:
Halifax, NS **952b**;
Shopping Centre **1996a**
Scotia-Toronto Dominion Leasing
Limited:
Toronto-Dominion Bank **2173a**
Scotiabank:
Bank of Nova Scotia **172a**
Scotian Shelf **1959c**:
Coastal Waters **450c**
Scots **1959c**:
Baldoon **166a**;
Catholicism **380a**;
Curling **555c**;
Fur Industry **856a**;
Galt, Ont **869c**;
Glengarry School Days **906b**;
Highland Games **986c**;
Inverness, NS **1090b**;
McNab, Archibald **1280a**;
Maxville, Ont **1317b**;
Métis **1344c**;
North West Company **1510c**;
Orkneymen **1588a**;
Philosophy **1659b**;
Pictou, NS **1676c**;
Red Deer, Alta **1835c**;
Red River Colony **1836c**;
St Anns, NS **1910a**;
Textiles, Woven **2135c**
Scots Bay:
Cape Blomidon **357c**
Scots in Canada:
Gibbon, John Murray **898c**
Scots pine:
Forestry **816a**
Scott, Adrian G.:
Religious Building **1853a**
Scott, Amy:
Scott, Francis Reginald **1961b**
Scott, Anthony Dalton **1960b**:
Canadian Public Policy/Analyse de politique **349b**
Scott, Barbara Ann **1960b**
Scott, David:
Cape Scott Provincial Park **359b**
Scott, Duncan Campbell **1960c**:
Brown, Edward Killoran **288b**;
Lampman, Archibald **1169b**;
Literature in English **1225a**;
McClelland and Stewart Limited **1256c**;
Poetry in English **1696c**
Scott, Edward Walter **1961a**
Scott, F.H.:
Neuroscience **1466c**
Scott, Francis Reginald **1961b**:
Canadian Literature **344a**;
Contact Press **510c**;
Edel, Leon **656c**;
Humorous Writing in English **1026c**;
League of Canadian Poets, The **1194a**;
Lewis, David **1205b**;
New Provinces **1479c**;
Queen's Quarterly **1812c**;
Scott, Marian Mildred
Dale **1962a**
Scott, Frederick George:
Scott, Francis Reginald **1961b**
Scott, Gail:
Literature in English – Theory
and Criticism **1228a**
Scott, George Gilbert:
Architecture, Development
of **102b**;
St John's, Nfld **1917b**
Scott, Jack:
Essay in English **720a**;
Journalism **1118a**
Scott, James:
Film **765c**
Scott, John:
Drawing **626b**;
Painting **1608a**
Scott, M.:
National Library of
Canada **1431b**
Scott, Marian Mildred Dale **1961c**
Scott, Michael:
Film, Documentary **770a**
Scott, Richard:
Province House (NS) **1771b**
Scott, Robert Austin **1962a**

Society of Canadian Painter-
Etchers and Engravers:
Artists' Organizations **131a**;
Printmaking **1758b**; **1759a**;
Wood, William John **2331b**
Society of Chemical Industry:
Chemistry **403c**
Society of Contemporary Music of
Québec **2035c**
Society of Cooperative Artists:
Artists' Organizations **131c**
Society of Equity:
Wood, Henry Wise **2330c**
Society of Foreign Missions:
Missions and Missionaries **1366b**
Society of Friends:
Quakers **1792b**
Society of Graphic Designers of
Canada:
Graphic Art and Design **929c**
Society of International Missionar-
ies:
Missions and Missionaries **1366c**
Society of Jesus:
Jesuits **1108b**
Society of Limners:
Pavelic, Myfanwy Spencer **1630c**
Society of Management Accoun-
tants:
Accounting **11a**
Society of Merchants:
MacBraire, James **1255c**
Society of Neurological Surgeons:
McKenzie, Kenneth
George **1270c**
Society of Neuroscience:
Neuroscience **1467a**
Society of Our Lady of Montréal:
Sulpicians **2093c**
Society of Plastics Engineers:
Plastics-Processing Indus-
try **1690b**
Society of Plastics Industry:
Plastics-Processing Indus-
try **1690b**
Society of St John the Evangelist:
Christian Religious Communi-
ties **422b**
Society of St Margaret:
Christian Religious Communi-
ties **422b**
Society of Typographic Designers
of Canada:
Graphic Art and Design **929c**
Society of United Irishmen:
Secret Societies **1973a**
Sociologie et sociétés:
Sociology **2037a**
Sociology **2035c**:
Clark, Samuel Delbert **433b**;
Community **475b**
sockeye salmon:
Fish **778b**;
Hell's Gate **976c**;
Pacific Salmon **1600c**;
Parsons, Timothy
Richard **1624a**;
Salish, Interior **1926b**
Socrates:
Sinclair, Lister Shedden **2006c**
Sod Houses **2037a**
Soda Creek, BC:
Bus Transportation **301b**
sodalite:
Gemstone **878c**
Sodarcan Ltée:
Parizeau, Gérard **1614c**
Soddy, Frederick:
Chemistry **403a**;
Chemistry Subdisciplines **405c**;
Nuclear Energy **1542c**;
Rutherford, Ernest, Baron
Rutherford of Nelson **1904a**;
Science **1952a**
sodium chloride:
Salt **1927c**
Soeur Bourgeoys:
Biography in French **221c**
Soeur Saint-Alphonse:
Plamondon, Antoine **1685a**
Soeurs de miséricorde:
Christian Religious Communi-
ties **422a**
sofa:
Furniture, English, Scottish and
American **863c**; **864a**
Soft-Drink Industry **2037a**
soft-shell clam:
Clam **432a**

softball:
Baseball **183c**
softwood:
Conifers **491b**;
Fir **774a**;
Forestry **815b**;
Furniture, German **866a**;
Lumber and Wood Indus-
tries **1251a**;
New Brunswick **1469c**;
Pulp and Paper Industry **1789c**;
Trees **2191c**;
Woodenware **2332b**
Softwood Lumber Dispute **2037c**
Softwords:
Godfrey, Dave **907c**
Sohier, G.H.:
Sculpture **1964a**
Soil **2037c**:
Crops **544a**;
Earthworm **640c**
Soil at Risk:
Soil Conservation **2040b**
Soil Classification **2038a**
Soil Conservation **2040b**:
Agricultural Soil Practices **32a**;
Animal Agriculture **76c**;
Crop Research **543a**;
Farm Drainage **749b**;
Prairie Farm Rehabilitation
Administration **1735a**
Soil Conservation Act (Alta):
Soil Conservation **2042a**
soil mechanics:
Civil Engineering **430c**
soil pollution:
Pollution **1714b**
Soil Science **2042a**:
Hydrology **1035a**
Soils Group:
Soil Science **2042c**
Sointula, BC **2043a**
"Soirée à Québec":
Radio Programming **1819b**
"Soirée du hockey, La":
Lecavalier, René **1196a**
Soirées canadiennes, Les **2043a**:
Anciens canadiens, Les **72c**;
Forestiers et voyageurs **815a**
*Soirées de l'école littéraire de
Montréal*:
Poetry in French **1699c**
*Soirées du Château de
Ramezay, Les*:
Poetry in French **1699c**
Soirs rouges, Les:
Poetry in French **1700a**
Soka Gakkai:
Buddhism **293c**
Soka Kyoiku Gakkai:
Buddhism **293c**
Sokoki:
Abenaki **2b**
Sokol (Falcon) Movement:
Czechs **560c**
"Sol et Bouton":
Favreau, Marc **753b**
"Sol et Gobelet":
Favreau, Marc **753b**
Solanaceae:
Vegetable **2246b**
Solandt, Ormond McKillop **2043a**:
Science and Society **1954a**
solar eclipse:
Astronomy **139a**;
Chant, Clarence Augustus **395a**;
Covington, Arthur Edwin **528c**;
Sun **2094c**
Solar Energy **2043b**
Solar Energy Society of Canada:
Solar Energy **2043c**;
Wind Energy **2313b**
solar flares:
Northern Lights **1515a**;
Observatory **1552a**;
Sun **2094c**
solar radiation:
Climatology **440b**;
Desert **588b**;
Lake **1166c**;
Meteorology **1341b**
solar radio emission:
Covington, Arthur Edwin **528b**
Solar Stage:
Theatre, English-
Language **2140c**
solar system:
Planet and Satellite **1685b**
solar time:
Religious Festivals **1853b**;
Time **2161c**

solar wind:
Comet **464a**;
Northern Lights **1514c**
Solaris:
Popular Literature in
French **1717c**;
Science Fiction **1956c**
Sold Out:
Novel in French **1541c**
Soldier Settlement Act (1919):
Veterans' Land Act
(1942) **2255b**
Soldier Settlement Board:
Gregg, Milton Fowler **938b**
Soldiers:
Colicos, John **458b**;
Theatre, English-
Language **2139a**
Soldiers and Politicians:
Pope, Maurice Arthur **1716a**
Soldiers' Civil Re-establishment,
Department of:
National Health and Welfare,
Department of **1430a**
Soldiers of Fortune **2043c**
Soldier's Story, A:
Jewison, Norman Freder-
ick **1110b**
Soldier's Tale, A:
Alberta Ballet Company **57a**
Soldier's Town memorial:
Hart House **965b**
"Soldier's Wife":
Radio Programming **1819b**
Soldier's Wives League:
South African War **2048b**
sole:
Flatfish **789a**; **789b**
sole proprietorship:
Corporation Law **519b**
Soleil, Le **2044b**:
Black, Conrad Moffat **235b**;
Harvey, Jean-Charles **966a**;
Journalism **1118b**;
Lapointe, Louise-Marguerite-
Renaude **1178b**;
Literary Prizes in French **1223a**;
Newspapers **1493c**; **1494b**;
1495a;
Potvin, Damase **1731c**
Soleil pas comme ailleurs, Un:
Acadia **9b**
Soleil sous la mort, Le:
Ouellette, Fernand **1597c**
Solicitor **2044b**
Solicitor General **2044b**:
Attorney General **143a**;
Royal Prerogative of
Mercy **1897a**
Solicitor General, Department
of **2044c**:
Canadian Security Intelligence
Service **349c**;
Criminology **540c**
Solicitor General Act (1945):
Solicitor General, Department
of **2044c**
solid angle:
Weights and Measures **2291a**
Solid Waste **2044c**:
Waste Disposal **2278c**
Solidarity **2045b**
Solifugae:
Arachnida **90c**
Solitaire **2045b**
Solitary City, The:
Ford, Robert Arthur Dou-
glas **805c**
*Solitary Rambles and Adventures
of a Hunter in the Prairies*:
Palliser, John **1610a**
solitary sandpiper:
Sandpiper **1928c**
solitary vireo:
Vireo **2266a**
Solitude of the Passion, The:
Choral Music **420a**
Solomon, Michel:
Jewish Writing **1110a**
Solomon's Seal **2045b**
Solonetzic soils:
Soil Classification **2038c**;
Soil Conservation **2041a**
sols:
Coinage **455c**
Solstices:
Music Composition **1413c**
Somali language:
Laurence, Margaret **1181b**

Somalians.
Arabs **90a**
Somass River:
Opetchesaht **1579c**;
Sheshaht **1991a**
Some Questions of Balance:
Symons, Thomas Henry
Bull **2106c**;
Women and Education **2323b**
Someone Cares:
Archer, Violet **96a**
Someone With Me:
Kurelek, William **1150a**
Somers, Harry Stewart **2045b**:
Chamber Music **392a**;
Forrester, Maureen **818c**;
Guitar **945c**;
Music Composition **1413a**;
1413b;
Rubeš, Jan **1899a**;
Strate, Grant **2083b**
Somerset, Dorothy:
Theatre, English-
Language **2142c**
Somerset Island **2045c**:
Periglacial Landform **1643c**
Somerville, C. Ross, "Sandy":
Golf **910c**
Something Hidden:
Film, Documentary **770a**
*Something I've Been Meaning to
Tell You*:
Munro, Alice **1405a**
Something Red:
Drama in English **622c**;
Walmsley, Thomas **2272c**
Sometimes I Think of Moving:
Brewster, Elizabeth
Winifred **269a**
"Sometimes When We Touch":
Popular Music **1719a**
Somme, Battle of the **2045c**
Sommer, Richard:
Poetry in English **1699a**
Sommers, Frank:
Canadian Physicians for the Pre-
vention of Nuclear War **348c**
Sommets de Concertation:
Parti Québécois **1624c**
Son des français d'Amérique, Le
(series):
Brault, Michel **267b**;
Film, Documentary **770a**
Son of a Hundred Kings:
Costain, Thomas Bertram **524a**
Son of a Smaller Hero:
Richler, Mordecai **1869a**
Son of Raven, Son of Deer:
Clutesi, George Charles **445c**;
Illustration, Art **1044a**
Son of the Forests:
Autobiographical Writing in
English **147c**
Son of the Morning:
Science Fiction **1956c**
Sonar **2045c**
Sonata for Solo Guitar:
Guitar **945c**
Sonata Tragica:
Morawetz, Oskar **1388c**
Sonate:
Prévost, André **1745b**
Sonate no 1:
Prévost, André **1745b**
Sondages:
Sylvestre, Joseph Jean
Guy **2105b**
Song, Bang-Song:
Musicology **1421b**
"Song My Paddle Sings, The":
Johnson, Emily Pauline **1113c**
Song of the Pearl:
Nichols, Joanna Ruth **1498c**
Song of the Prairie Land:
MacDonald, Wilson Pugs-
ley **1262b**
song sparrow:
Sparrow **2055c**
Songbook:
Barbour, Douglas **178a**
Songes en équilibre, Les:
Hébert, Anne **974b**;
Poetry in French **1700b**
Songhees Peninsula:
Victoria, BC **2261b**

V

R
a71.003
M365

1988
v.4

2736 Youville, François d'

LINCOLN CHRISTIAN COLLEGE

77148

Artist's rendition of Canada as seen from far
above the Arctic Archipelago. Courtesy
Northern Transportation Company Limited.